THE OXFORD HANDBOOK OF
GREEK DRAMA IN THE AMERICAS

THE OXFORD HANDBOOK OF
GREEK DRAMA IN THE AMERICAS

Edited by
KATHRYN BOSHER, FIONA MACINTOSH,
JUSTINE McCONNELL,
AND
PATRICE RANKINE

Great Clarendon Street, Oxford, OX2 6DP,
United Kingdom

Oxford University Press is a department of the University of Oxford.
It furthers the University's objective of excellence in research, scholarship,
and education by publishing worldwide. Oxford is a registered trade mark of
Oxford University Press in the UK and in certain other countries

© Oxford University Press 2015

The moral rights of the authors have been asserted

First Edition published in 2015

Impression: 1

All rights reserved. No part of this publication may be reproduced, stored in
a retrieval system, or transmitted, in any form or by any means, without the
prior permission in writing of Oxford University Press, or as expressly permitted
by law, by licence or under terms agreed with the appropriate reprographics
rights organization. Enquiries concerning reproduction outside the scope of the
above should be sent to the Rights Department, Oxford University Press, at the
address above

You must not circulate this work in any other form
and you must impose this same condition on any acquirer

Published in the United States of America by Oxford University Press
198 Madison Avenue, New York, NY 10016, United States of America

British Library Cataloguing in Publication Data
Data available

Library of Congress Control Number: 2014950700

ISBN 978-0-19-966130-5

Printed and bound by
CPI Group (UK) Ltd, Croydon, CR0 4YY

Links to third party websites are provided by Oxford in good faith and
for information only. Oxford disclaims any responsibility for the materials
contained in any third party website referenced in this work.

In memory of Kathryn Grace Bosher
1974–2013

Kate Bosher (right) and Justine McConnell. Wisconsin, 2009.

Preface

KARELISA HARTIGAN

For many centuries of the post-classical world, Greek drama was frequently read but seldom heard and rarely seen. From the 1880s onward a few scattered performances of the *Antigone* and *Oedipus Tyrannus* were staged in France, Britain, Australia, Canada, and America, but these productions, especially in England and America, rarely won critical or popular acclaim.[1] Critics recognized that the plays were to be appreciated as works from a glorious past but they rarely consider them to be stage-worthy productions, both because of the dramas' static style and their apparently immoral content.

The first performance in America of a Greek tragedy recognized as suitable and relevant to its times occurred in 1915, when Granville Barker brought Euripides' *Trojan Women* to outdoor theaters in New York and other venues in the northeast.[2] Throughout the twentieth and into the twenty-first century, this script has remained continuously popular, brought to theaters every time the United States has entered into a military conflict. *Trojan Women*, most frequently staged during the Vietnam War, was also the anti-war play for the 1900s during the years that American soldiers and innocent civilians have died in Iraq and Afghanistan.

Since that early production, the number of Greek tragedies staged in the Americas has steadily increased, while interest in the history of performances of ancient dramas has also continued to grow in Europe and expanded into Latin America, with the number of performances reaching new heights within the last several decades of the last century and the initial years of the present. One might wonder why these most ancient scripts were performed in a culture that prefers the new to the old, action to words, happy to tragic endings. As the many chapters in this volume show, the reasons for the more frequent staging of Greek plays are various but, in many cases, the choice to offer a Greek tragedy has been tied to contemporary events: using the old to illustrate the new. Directors, producers, and actors have come to understand that the ideas from the classic texts ring true for any age. Throughout the decades of the twentieth century, the people who do theater have come to realize that it is important for an audience to see characters on stage take responsibility for their actions, to seek the truth at whatever cost, and to stand up to tyranny. Especially popular have been plays that show the results of war, the ruin it brings both upon the innocent who suffer its consequences, as evidenced in *Trojan Women*, but also upon those who fight the battles; in this context Sophocles' *Ajax* takes pride of place in recent years as illustrative of the post-traumatic stress from which so many returning veterans suffer (see further Lodewyck and Monoson, Shannon, this volume).[3]

As Greek dramas gained further popularity in the 1900s, it was often the female characters created by Sophocles and Euripides that earned their plays a place in theater repertoires; Aeschylus' Clytemnestra had to wait to gain recognition, perhaps because she is not the titular character in her play (Hall 2005: 53–76). Well-known actresses opted for Euripides' Medea as their character of choice, followed closely by a preference for Sophocles' Electra. It must be the famous monologues of these tragic women which attracted attention, as neither character is particularly appealing. Nevertheless, the production history of Greek drama on the post-classical stage includes numerous performances of *Medea* and Sophocles' *Electra*. From the 1920s to the 1990s, actresses

FIG. 0.1 Margaret Anglin as Medea, by courtesy of the APGRD.

FIG. 0.2 Judith Anderson as Medea (1951). Van Vechten Collection, Library of Congress.

who brought Medea, Electra, and Clytemnestra to life include Margaret Anglin, Judith Anderson (Figs. 0.1, 0.2), and Isabell Monk.

That other great female protagonist of the ancient stage, Antigone, seems to have been less popular as a character herself. Sophocles' play has been more frequently produced in a political context (see further Macintosh, Dixon, Fradinger, Marshall, this volume). In more recent times the idea that Creon is the drama's main character has probably pushed *Antigone* from the American boards, although (as several essays in this volume show) the play has wide popularity in countries where the politics closely reflect those of Sophocles' Thebes.

In the middle of the twentieth century, productions of Greek tragedy, again especially the Electra plays, began to feature touring companies from Greece, whose performances were widely acclaimed. At the same time, the ancient plays began to be performed in more popular venues and with a more varied cast. Joseph Papp offered the *Electra* at the Delacorte Theatre in Central Park and in 1969 the Mobile Theatre produced the play in Washington Square Park with an African-American cast, the first Greek play so staged. In all of these productions, it was Sophocles' drama that was selected; Euripides—and Aeschylus—had to wait until the later years of the century to be seen in American theaters. The growing popularity of the Athenian dramatists was not limited to the United States or Canada; as readers of this volume will see, the ancient texts were brought to audiences in the Caribbean and Latin American countries, while performances became ever more frequent in Europe as well. Directors in Japan also turned to Greek drama, using the plays as comments upon their nation's experiences during World War II, and Japanese productions of *Medea* attracted audiences totaling in the thousands (Macintosh 1997: 312–14).

Greek drama came into its own on the American stage with the dawn of the Vietnam War era and all of its challenges to society and authority, its sexual and verbal freedom. The years 1960–70 might well be termed the Decade of Euripides, with a touch of Aristophanes. To anti-war productions of *Trojan Women* and the ever more popular *Iphigenia in Aulis* was added Euripides' psychologically interesting *Orestes*, as producers recognized the play as a testament to how suffering can destroy a man's sanity. The tear-producing anti-war plays were, however, frequently lightened with productions of Aristophanes' *Lysistrata*.

In the 1960s Euripides' *Bacchae* was finally, to use the ancient expression, "granted a chorus"; indeed, it became the play of the decade. Not once during the first 60 years of the twentieth century had this play appeared on the American commercial stage. The story of Dionysus, who demands recognition, and Pentheus, King of Thebes, who refuses to do him honor, and whom the god brings to a violent death, was not selected for production. The *Bacchae* was apparently too foreign, too frightening, and too disturbing to be offered to an American public that preferred musicals to mysterious tragedies. The events of the 1960s changed such preferences. While many interpretations of Euripides' play were probably too extreme even for an ancient Greek audience who understood a god's anger—the Greeks preferred to hear about, not see, sex or violence on stage—one can say that the true message of the *Bacchae* was evident in several productions. The more reasoned versions recognized that it was good to live at one with nature, to celebrate the god who gave wine to mortals, to acknowledge new cults and accept new ideas. Most productions, however, neglected the final message of the play, namely that excess is, in the end, dangerous and that it is impossible for a government to triumph against its people's beliefs.

In the final decades of the twentieth century Aeschylus finally garnered a recurring place on the American stage. Staging his complete *Oresteia* trilogy is a major undertaking but, as soon became clear, doing the *Agamemnon* without the remainder of the plays left audiences thinking that they had seen but one act of a drama and their feelings were correct. When for the 1967–8 season Douglas Campbell and Sir Tyrone Guthrie staged

John Lewin's version, a trilogy he titled *Atreus* to make it clear it was not Aeschylus' drama, the show, first offered at the Guthrie Theatre in Minneapolis and then toured to New York, attracted attention on many fronts: theme, costumes, and stage grandeur. It did not, however, initiate a general interest in the great 458 BCE trilogy; it was finally in the 1990s that Aeschylus' drama came to the boards most frequently, often with various Euripidean tragedies added to round out the theme. Beginning in the 1980s the John Barton–Kenneth Cavander ten-play epic, *The Greeks*, which had premièred in London in 1980, offered as a multi-day production, was attempted at various theaters. The most widely acclaimed, however, was the version created by Ariane Mnouchkine, who brought her Théâtre du Soleil from Paris to America in 1992 to present the House of Atreus story, opening Aeschylus' trilogy with Euripides' *Iphigenia at Aulis* and titling her play *Les Atrides*.

In the opening decades of the twenty-first century, Greek dramas have appeared as almost regular offerings in theaters of the United States, Canada, and Latin America. The staging of these ancient texts, however, has been various and varied. Seldom does an audience see characters in what is generally considered to be ancient garb, although masks are, perhaps, more frequently used as a part of a character's costume than in earlier generations. The African-American theater companies have also embraced the ancient texts, recognizing how they feature characters often caught in situations over which they have no control.

Theater audiences around the Americas also see not only updated versions of the plays but rewrites of the scripts to make their ideas and concepts better known, lifting the stories beyond their classical contexts. A leader among those using ancient themes for his contemporary plays is Charles Mee, whose Greek-based plays are considered to be a part of his (re)making dramas (see Erin Mee's interview with her father, this volume).

In whatever venue, however, and in whatever ancient or updated form, the texts of the Athenian playwrights are brought to the contemporary theater for their relevance to the world today. In ancient Athens, the playwrights' texts broadly reflected current political and social concerns; on stages in the Americas these plays are also staged in response to these concerns. The interpretations of the myths told in these plays have varied over the years, of course, and each decade has added its own understanding of the ancient plays. Only *Trojan Women* has remained constant in its message: from 415 BCE to the present time, the suffering of war's innocent victims has consistently spoken to audiences in nearly every decade of the past century—and, alas, it is still relevant in the early years of the current one.

Although the concepts set out in the ancient dramas have been variously interpreted over the years, the unchanging texts of the ancient Greek playwrights have offered producers, directors, and actors a message that has had validity for their own society. During the years covered within this volume the plays from ancient Athens have been recognized as important not only because they were "classics" but because they set out ideas of morality, political protest, and responsibility, a quest for self-identity, and the nature of sacrifice and the need for it. These are concepts important to any society at any time.

Notes

1. Macintosh 1997: 286–8 for an overview of *Antigone*'s early production history.
2. For this and other production histories in the States, see Hartigan 1995 and for the 1915 *Trojan Women*, in particular, see 15–17.
3. Brian Doerries's *Theater of War* project brought the *Ajax* to modern attention, with productions beginning in 2008.

References

Foley, H. P. (2012), *Reimagining Greek Tragedy on the American Stage*. Berkeley, Los Angeles, and London.

Hall, E. (2005), "Aeschylus' Clytemnestra versus her Senecan Tradition," in F. Macintosh, P. Michelakis, E. Hall, and O. Taplin eds., *Agamemenon in Performance* 458 BC to AD 2004. Oxford.

Hartigan, K. V. (1995), *Greek Tragedy on the American Stage: Ancient Drama in the Commercial Theater, 1882–1994*. Westport, CT, and London.

Macintosh, F. (1997), "Tragedy in Performance: Nineteenth and Twentieth Century Productions," in P. E. Easterling ed., *The Cambridge Companion to Greek Tragedy*. Cambridge, 284–323.

Acknowledgments

This book has had a long and intensely emotionally painful gestation. It is the brainchild of our dear friend and fellow editor, Kate Bosher, who tirelessly worked on the text right until the end of her tragically short life in March 2013. It was Kate's inspiration and perspicacity that led to her obtaining a Mellon-Sawyer grant at Northwestern University in 2008 to work on the reception of ancient drama in America and the "Classicizing Chicago" project, in particular. Kate organized a seminar series and three international conferences during 2008–10, from which the present volume ultimately stemmed. On account of her own Canadian perspective, and with the increasing scholarly focus on Greek drama in Latin America, it became apparent to all the editors that a volume encompassing the Americas as a whole was most timely. We are very grateful to Hilary O'Shea at Oxford University Press for her encouragement and support of our decision to widen the volume's focus. As the project has grown we are fully aware that the material has become richer and the further perspectives afforded during the course of the process have become more incisive and pertinent to the new debates within classical reception and theater and performance studies.

On Kate's behalf, we warmly thank all of those who attended the seminars and conferences at Northwestern and especially the speakers, many of whose papers appear in this volume. Those from whom we commissioned new pieces have shown enormous good will and unfailing good humor. We are most grateful to the Jowett Trustees at the University of Oxford for financial assistance toward the picture costs. To our copyeditor at Oxford University Press, Jackie Pritchard, and to our indexer, Jane Horton, we remain indebted for their insightful comments and unfailing precision. We wish to thank the following in particular for their help and support in various ways: Sara Monoson, Edith Hall, Naomi Setchell, Tom Wrobel, and Claire Kenward. Finally, the volume is dedicated to the memory of Kate, but it is her husband, Dale, and her son, Ernest, who will receive the first copy and who have remained very prominently in our thoughts throughout the final stages of the editorial process. This book is for them.

Contents

List of Illustrations	xxi
List of Contributors	xxxi
Note on Nomenclature, Spelling, and Texts	xliii

PART I THEORIES AND METHODS

1. Introduction — FIONA MACINTOSH, JUSTINE MCCONNELL, AND PATRICE RANKINE — 3
2. An Archival Interrogation — SUSAN CURTIS — 17
3. New Worlds, Old Dreams? Postcolonial Theory and Reception of Greek Drama — BARBARA GOFF AND MICHAEL SIMPSON — 30

PART II SHAPING AMERICAN THEATER (1800–1900)

4. Grecian Theater in Philadelphia, 1800–1870 — LEE T. PEARCY — 53
5. Thebes in the New World: Revisiting the New York *Antigone* of 1845 — FIONA MACINTOSH — 70
6. Julia Ward Howe's *Hippolytus* — HELENE P. FOLEY — 85
7. Professional Tragedy: The Case of *Medea* in Chicago, 1867 — KATHRYN BOSHER AND JORDANA COX — 97
8. Barbarian Queens: Race, Violence, and Antiquity on the Nineteenth-Century United States Stage — ROBERT DAVIS — 112

9. When Greeks Stand you up, Invite Romans: The Ancient World
   on the Nineteenth-Century American Stage   133
   DAVID MAYER

PART III MODERNISMS IN THE AMERICAS (1900–1930)

10. The Migrant Muse: Greek Drama as Feminist Window on American
    Identity, 1900–1925   149
    EDITH HALL

11. Iphigenia amongst the Ivies, 1915   166
    NIALL W. SLATER

12. Treading the Arduous Road to Eleusis, Nationalism, and Feminism
    in Early Post-World War I Canada: Roy Mitchell's 1920 *The Trojan
    Women*   184
    MOIRA DAY

13. Greek Tragedy and Modern Dance: An Alternative Archaeology?   204
    ARTEMIS LEONTIS

14. Eugene O'Neill's Quest for Greek Tragedy   221
    VASSILIS LAMBROPOULOS

PART IV THE LIVING PASTS (1925–1970)

15. Choreographing the Classics, Performing Sexual Dissidence   233
    SUSAN MANNING

16. Greek Tragedy in Mexico   252
    FRANCISCO BARRENECHEA

17. Moving and Dramatic Athenian Citizenship: Edith Hamilton's
    Americanization of Greek Tragedy   271
    JUDITH P. HALLETT

18. A New Stage of Laughter for Zora Neale Hurston and Theodore
    Browne: *Lysistrata* and the Negro Units of the Federal
    Theatre Project   286
    LENA M. HILL

19. Aristophanic Comedy in American Musical Theater, 1925–1969   301
    JOHN GIVEN

20. Cubanizing Greek Drama: José Triana's *Medea in the Mirror* (1960)   333
    KONSTANTINOS P. NIKOLOUTSOS

PART V CREATIVE COLLISIONS (1948–1968)

21. Revolutionizing Greek Tragedy in Cuba: Virgilio Piñera's *Electra Garrigó*   361
    ROSA ANDÚJAR

22. A Brazilian Echo of *Antigone*'s "Collision": Tragedy, Clean and Filthy   380
    PAUL B. DIXON

23. The Darkening of Medea: Geographies of Race, (Dis)Placement, and Identity in Agostinho Olavo's *Além do Rio (Medea)*   400
    JOSÉ DE PAIVA DOS SANTOS

24. The Frontiers of David Cureses' *La frontera*   417
    ANÍBAL A. BIGLIERI

25. Brothers at War: Aeschylus in Cuba, 1968 and 2007   434
    ISABELLE TORRANCE

PART VI THE SEARCH FOR THE OMNI-AMERICANS (1970s–2013)

26. Metaphor and Modernity: American Themes in *Herakles* and *Dionysus in 69*   457
    THOMAS E. JENKINS

27. Lee Breuer's New American Classicism: *The Gospel at Colonus*' "Integration Statement"   474
    JUSTINE McCONNELL

28. Greek Tragedy, Enslaving or Liberating? The Example of Rita Dove's *The Darker Face of the Earth*   495
    NANCY SORKIN RABINOWITZ

29. The Power of Medea's Sisterhood: Democracy on the Margins in Cherríe Moraga's *The Hungry Woman: A Mexican Medea*   514
    KATIE BILLOTTE

30. August Wilson and Greek Drama: Blackface Minstrelsy, "Spectacle" from Aristotle's *Poetics*, and *Radio Golf*   525
    PATRICE RANKINE

31. "Aeschylus Got Flow!": Afrosporic Greek Tragedy and Will Power's *The Seven*   543
    KEVIN J. WETMORE, JR.

32. Making Women Visible: Multiple Antigones on the Colombian Twenty-First-Century Stage   556
    MOIRA FRADINGER

33. Democratic Appropriations: *Lysistrata* and Political Activism   575
    DOROTA DUTSCH

34. Reclaiming Euripides in Harlem   595
    MELINDA POWERS

35. *Oedipus Tyrannus* in South America   611
    MARÍA FLORENCIA NELLI

36. Greek Drama on the U.S. West Coast, 1970–2013   628
    MARY-KAY GAMEL

37. Performing for Soldiers: Twenty-First-Century Experiments in Greek Theater in the U.S.A.   651
    LAURA LODEWYCK AND S. SARA MONOSON

38. Greek Drama in Canada: Women's Voices and Minority Views   671
    HALLIE REBECCA MARSHALL

PART VII PRACTITIONER PERSPECTIVES

39. On Remixing the Classics and Directing Countee Cullen's *Medea* and Law Chavez's *Señora de la pinta*: An Interview with Theater Director Daniel Banks   683
    PATRICE RANKINE AND DANIEL BANKS

40. This Bird That Never Settles: A Virtual Conversation with Anne Carson about Greek Tragedy   699
    YOPIE PRINS

41. Medea in Brazil: Interview with Director Heron Coelho   708
    CESAR GEMELLI

42. An Interview with Héctor Levy-Daniel   726
  María Florencia Nelli

43. Charles Mee's "(Re)Making" of Greek Drama   731
  Erin B. Mee

44. An Interview with Carey Perloff   736
  Margaret Williamson

45. Eclectic Encounters: Staging Greek Tragedy in America, 1973–2009   746
  Rush Rehm

46. The Shock of Recognition: Nicholas Rudall's Translation of Greek Drama for the Chicago Stage at Court Theatre   764
  Justine McConnell and Patrice Rankine

47. In Conversation with Peter Sellars: What Does Greek Tragedy Mean to You?   773
  Avery Willis Hoffman

48. The Women and War Project   790
  Peggy Shannon

49. *Dionysus in 69* in 2009   798
  Shawn Sides

50. Talking Greeks with Derek Walcott   807
  Helen Eastman

AFTERWORD

51. Audiences across the Pond: Oceans Apart or Shared Experiences?   819
  Lorna Hardwick

Index   841

List of Illustrations

Preface

0.1   Margaret Anglin as Medea, by courtesy of the APGRD.   viii
0.2   Judith Anderson as Medea (1951). Van Vechten Collection, Library of Congress.   ix

Fiona Macintosh, Justine McConnell, and Patrice Rankine

1.1   Douglas Campbell in the Stratford Ontario Festival's production of *Oedipus Rex*, directed by Tyrone Guthrie (Photo: McKague, Toronto).   4
1.2   Charlotte Cushman as Ion (1846). Reproduced from *ILN* 8.199 (1846), by courtesy of the Bodleian Library.   5

Lee T. Pearcy

4.1   *The Modern Medea*, wood engraving after Thomas Satterwhite Noble's painting *Margaret Garner*, reproduced from *Harper's Weekly* (May 18, 1867).   64

Fiona Macintosh

5.1   Palmo's Opera-House, Afterward Burton's Theatre. (After a watercolor drawing in the collection of Thomas J. McKee, Esq.) W. L. Keese, *William E. Burton, Actor, Author and Manager, A Sketch of his Career with Recollections of his Performances* (New York and London 1885).   71
5.2   Engraving of the interior of Palmo's Opera House (*c*.1845). The Granger Collection.   76

Helene P. Foley

6.1 Margaret Anglin as Phaedra and Maude Granger as Oenone in Julia Ward Howe's *Hippolytus*, Tremont Theatre, March 24, 1911, *Theatre Magazine*, Volume 13, June 1911, p. 201.   86

Robert Davis

8.1 *Types of Mankind* (458). Source: The University of Michigan Library.   114

8.2 Detail from William Wetmore Story's *Medea*, 1865, executed 1868. The Metropolitan Museum of Art, Gift of Henry Chauncey, 1894 (94.8a–d). Photograph by Jerry L. Thompson.   117

8.3 Death of Cleopatra, Edmonia Lewis, 1876. Smithsonian American Art Museum.   118

David Mayer

9.1 Pain's Fireworks Company's *The Last Days of Pompeii*.   138

Niall W. Slater

11.1 Iphigenia offering libations (Fitts 1915, opp. p. 11) Research Library, The Getty Research Institute, Los Angeles (91-B13114).   169

11.2 Close-up of executioners—*Philadelphia Public Ledger* June 9, 1915, 11.   170

11.3 Two soldiers from Thoas's guard (unattributed newspaper photo, University of Pennsylvania scrapbooks).   173

11.4 Messenger and Thoas (unattributed newspaper photo, University of Pennsylvania scrapbooks).   174

11.5 Rains and Dorizas (center) as herdsmen (unattributed newspaper photo, University of Pennsylvania scrapbooks).   175

11.6 McCarthy as Iphigenia (Fitts 1915, opp. p. 3) Research Library, The Getty Research Institute, Los Angeles (91-B13114).   177

Moira Day

12.1 Professor Maurice Hutton as Antigone in 1882 University of
Toronto production of Sophocles' *Antigone*—(A73-0003/001) University
of Toronto Archives. 187

12.2 1894 University of Toronto production of Sophocles' *Antigone*.
Antigone (Charlotte Hunter) is condemned by Creon (K. D. MacMillan).
Borrowed American set in background. Academy of Music, Toronto.—
(A73-0003/009) University of Toronto Archives. 189

12.3 Image of Hart House 1920 rehearsal for the *Trojan Women*: Elizabeth
Sterling standing: left background, Roy Mitchell. Charity Mitchell.
Set pieces (grate) from *The Queen's Enemies* in background. James & Son
Photographers, 1920. York University Libraries, Clara Thomas Archives
and Special Collections, Roy Matthews Mitchell fonds, ASC05341. 197

Artemis Leontis

13.1 Ted Shawn posing as Hermes in a costume woven by Eva Palmer Sikelianos
in the full-scale replica of the Parthenon in Nashville, Tennessee, July 11, 1939.
ESP-BMHA No. 557, courtesy of the Benaki Museum Historical Archives. 206

13.2 One of Bella Raftopoulou's drawings, and Eva Palmer Sikelianos
in the same pose in an undated photograph. ESP-BMHA No. 323,
courtesy of the Benaki Museum Historical Archives. 211

13.3 Ted Shawn's students and dancers performing the first chorus of Aeschylus'
Persians in a collaborative composition by choreographer Shawn, and
composer Eva Palmer Sikelianos. ESP-BMHA No. 535 or 541,
courtesy of the Benaki Museum Historical Archives. 215

Susan Manning

15.1 Isadora Duncan, watercolor by Abraham Walkowitz, Jerome Robbins
Dance Division, The New York Public Library for the Performing
Arts, Astor, Lenox, and Tilden Foundations. 238

15.2 Vaslav Nijinsky in *Afternoon of a Faun*, Jerome Robbins Dance
Division, The New York Public Library for the Performing Arts,
Astor, Lenox, and Tilden Foundations. 241

15.3 Jacques D'Amboise with Allegra Kent in Balanchine's *Apollo*,
New York City Ballet, photograph by Martha Swope/© The
New York Public Library. 243

15.4 Helen McGehee (in Graham's role) and Clive Thompson in Graham's *Errand into the Maze*, photograph by Umaña, Helen McGehee Archive, Music Division, Library of Congress. 246

15.5 Guillermo Resto and Mark Morris in Morris's *Dido and Aeneas*, photograph by Cylla von Tiedemann courtesy of the Mark Morris Dance Group. 248

Judith P. Hallett

17.1 A close-up of a few members of the chorus in Eva Palmer Sikelianos's *Prometheus* at Delphi, 1927. © APGRD. 275

Lena M. Hill

18.1 A scene from *Lysistrata*. Courtesy of the University of Washington Library, Special Collections Division, UW Theatres Photograph Collection (PH Collection #236), box 4, folder 13. 293

John Given

19.1 Moscow Art Theatre's *Lysistrata* (1925), with set design by Isaak Rabinovich. Billy Rose Theatre Division, The New York Public Library for the Performing Arts, Astor, Lenox, and Tilden Foundations. 306

19.2 Al Carmines and Tim Reynolds's *Peace*. Kenn Duncan/© Billy Rose Theatre Division, The New York Public Library for the Performing Arts. 317

Konstantinos P. Nikoloutsos

20.1 Asenneh Rodríguez (1934–2013) as María in José Triana's *Medea in the Mirror* (dir. Francisco Morín, Sala Teatro Prometeo, Havana, 1960). Courtesy of the Cuban Digital Theater Archive and Enrique Río Prado. 334

20.2 Cover page of the program of Sophocles' *Antigone* (dir. Ludwig Schajowicz, Plaza Rector Cadenas, Havana, May 20, 1941). Courtesy of the Cuban Digital Theater Archive and Enrique Río Prado. 337

20.3 Cover page of the program of Euripides' *Medea* (dir. Antonio Vázquez Gallo, Plaza Rector Cadenas, Havana, August 9–10, 1948). Courtesy of the Cuban Digital Theater Archive and Enrique Río Prado. 338

Paul B. Dixon

22.1 The plaque from Escadaria do Passo, the staircase leading up to the Church of Santa Barbara in Pelourinho, Salvador da Bahia, Brazil, where Anselmo Duarte's movie adaptation of *O pagador de promessas* is set. Photo: Patrice Rankine. — 381

22.2 The Church of Santa Barbara in Salvador, Brazil, in the Pelourinho neighborhood. Photo: Patrice Rankine. — 383

22.3 A view from Santa Barbara onto the streets of Pelourinho and the tenements reaching up to the sky. This is the public sphere, and not the interior of the church, where the modern Brazilian tragedy has its resolution. Photo: Patrice Rankine. — 394

José de Paiva dos Santos

23.1 The Bay of Barra, Salvador da Bahia, Brazil. Salvador was one of the main slave ports into the Americas during the transatlantic slave trade. Photo: Patrice Rankine. — 409

23.2 The iconic "Baiana" or black woman of Salvador da Bahia, remnant of the slaves who cooked, cleaned, and washed for their masters. Photo: Patrice Rankine. — 413

Justine McConnell

27.1 Morgan Freeman as Preacher Oedipus in the 1985 production of *The Gospel at Colonus* at the American Musical Festival in Philadelphia. ©PBS. — 478

27.2 Clarence Fountain as Oedipus arising from his grave, in the 1985 production of *The Gospel at Colonus* at the American Musical Festival in Philadelphia. ©PBS. — 488

20.4 Georgios Doussis as Julián in José Triana's *Medea in the Mirror* (dir. Ioannis Petsopoulos, Akis Dhavis Theater, Athens, November 7, 2008–January 4, 2009). Courtesy of Georgios Doussis and Ioannis Petsopoulos. — 348

xxvi LIST OF ILLUSTRATIONS

Nancy Sorkin Rabinowitz

28.1 Playbill (cover), from Take Wing And Soar Productions presents Poet Laureate Rita Dove's New American Classic, *The Darker Face of the Earth*, directed by Trezana Beverley. 504

28.2 Scene of the slaves on the Southern plantation, in prayer. Take Wing And Soar Productions presents Poet Laureate Rita Dove's New American Classic, *The Darker Face of the Earth*, directed by Trezana Beverley. ©2006 Hubert Williams. 507

28.3 Augustus (Oedipus) and Amalia (Jocasta), Take Wing And Soar Productions presents Poet Laureate Rita Dove's New American Classic, *The Darker Face of the Earth*, directed by Trezana Beverley. ©2006 Hubert Williams. 510

Moira Fradinger

32.1 Carlos Satizábal's *Antígona y actriz*. ©Tramaluna Teatro. Reproduced with permission. 563

32.2 The three Antigones and two Ismenes of Patricia Ariza's *Antígona*. Photograph by Carlos Mario Lema. Reproduced with the kind permission of Patricia Ariza. 564

32.3 The two Ismenes of Patricia Ariza's *Antígona*. Photograph by Carlos Mario Lema. Reproduced with the kind permission of Patricia Ariza. 567

Dorota Dutsch

33.1 Promotional poster for the Lysistrata Project. Design by Mark Greene. © Lysistrata Project. Reproduced with permission. 578

33.2 Publicity photo for (Mostly) Harmless Theatre's staged reading of The Lysistrata Project in St. Louis, MO, March 2003. (Photo Credit: John Lamb.) Reproduced with permission. 584

Melinda Powers

34.1 Creon, in Take Wing And Soar Productions' *MEDEA*, directed by Petronia Paley, starring Trezana Beverley. Photo ©2008 Renaldo Davidson. 599

34.2	Medea, in Take Wing And Soar Productions' *MEDEA*, directed by Petronia Paley, starring Trezana Beverley. Photo ©2008 Renaldo Davidson.	600

Mary-Kay Gamel

36.1	The Chorus and Prometheus. *Prometheus Bound* at the Getty Villa 2013. Photo by Craig Schwartz, used by kind permission of The J. Paul Getty Trust.	631
36.2	Telemachus (Daniel Petzold) and Odysseus (Daniel Bruno) confront the Scylla monster. *The Salt Plays 2: Of the Earth* at Ashby Stage 2010. Photo by Pak Han, used by kind permission of Shotgun Players.	639
36.3	Cole Smith as Achilles in *Achilles and Patroklos* 2005. Photo by Daniel David, used by kind permission of Central Works.	640
36.4	Actors and audience at Aiolia in *The Odyssey on Angel Island* 2010. Photo by Mark Kitaoka, used by kind permission of We Players.	641
36.5	Sabina Zuniga Varela as Medea in *Bruja* 2012. Photo by Jennifer Reiley, used by kind permission of Magic Theatre.	644
36.6	Annie Ritschel as Elektra and Keith Burgelin as Orestes. *Orestes Terrorist* 2011. Photo by Steve DiBartolomeo, used by kind permission of the University of California, Santa Cruz.	647

Patrice Rankine and Daniel Banks

39.1	Medea and Jason, from *Medea*, which Daniel Banks directed at Williams College, in 2002. Photo by Miguel Romero.	687
39.2	From Banks's staging of Countee Cullen's *Medea* at Williams College. Photo by Miguel Romero.	689
39.3	Gringo and Josefina mourn the death of Yvonne, "Bon," at the crossroads, with the *lechuzas*, the folkloric owl figures from Chicano stories, in the background. From Law Chavez's *Señora de la pinta*, which Daniel Banks directed at the Words Afire Festival, University of New Mexico, in 2012. Photo by Pat Berrett.	692

Cesar Gemelli

41.1	Joana (Georgette Fadel) preparing the poisoned bread. © Heron Coelho.	715
41.2	Joana (Georgette Fadel) lying dead next to the poisoned bread. © Heron Coelho.	715

Rush Rehm

45.1	Electra (Roxanne Hart) with the head of Aegisthus, Euripides' *Electra* (1973). Photograph by John Coventry.	749
45.2	Chorus (Andre Braugher standing), Sophocles' *Oedipus Tyrannus* (1981). Photograph by James Carmody.	751
45.3	Satyrs (Frank Murray, Michael Ramsey-Perez, Graham Winton, Sam Barker) with Odysseus (Marc Accornero), *Cyclops—Nobody's Musical* (1983), adapted from Euripides' *Cyclops*. Photograph by Connie Strayer.	752
45.4	Chorus (with Adrastos in background), Euripides' *Suppliant Women* (1993). Photograph by John B. Wilson.	755
45.5	Chorus leader (Kay Kostopoulos) with Chorus, Sophocles' *Electra* (2009). Photograph by Sefanie Okuda.	759
45.6	Clytemnestra (Courtney Walsh) and Aegisthus (Donnell Hill) over the corpse of Agamemnon (James Kierstead), with the young Electra (Davia Schendel) watching, Sophocles' *Electra* (2009). Photograph by Sefanie Okuda.	761

Justine McConnell and Patrice Rankine

46.1	Anne Dudek as Iphigenia in Court Theatre's 1997 production of Nicholas Rudall's *Iphigenia Cycle*, directed by JoAnne Akalaitis. Photograph by Dan Rest.	771

Avery Willis Hoffman

47.1	Program for *Ajax*, Cover image, La Jolla Playhouse (1986).	775
47.2	Peter Sellars in rehearsal, *Children of Herakles* by Euripides (directed by Peter Sellars, Ruhr Triennale, Bottrop, Germany, 2002). Courtesy of Ruth Walz.	776
47.3	Julie Baldauff (attendant), Julyana Soelysto (Macaria), Albert S. (attendant), Brenda Wehle (Demophon). *Children of Herakles* by Euripides (directed by Peter Sellars, Ruhr Triennale, Bottrop, Germany, 2002). Courtesy of Ruth Walz.	777
47.4	Peter Sellars in rehearsal with Martinus Miroto (Chorus/dancer), *The Persians* by Aeschylus (directed by Peter Sellars, Salzburg, 1993). Courtesy of Ruth Walz.	785

47.5	Hyunah Yu (Zaide), Norman Shankle (Gomatz), Terry Cook (Osmin), Russell Thomas (Sultan Soliman). *Zaide* by Wolfgang Amadeus Mozart (directed by Peter Sellars, Vienna, 2006). Courtesy of Ruth Walz.	786
47.6	Hyunah Yu (Zaide), Norman Shankle (Gomatz), Alfred Walker (Allazim), Russell Thomas (Sultan Soliman). *Zaide* by Wolfgang Amadeus Mozart (directed by Peter Sellars, Vienna, 2006). Courtesy of Ruth Walz.	786

Peggy Shannon

48.1	Animals in the Forest. From left to right: Kaleigh Gorka, Sierra Chin Sawdy, Rhanda Jones. Photographer: Richard Burdett. Reproduced with kind permission.	793
48.2	Cassandra and Agamemnon in a brothel. Kaleigh Gorka and Stathis Grapsas. Photographer: Richard Burdett. Reproduced with kind permission.	794
48.3	Agamemnon and his men restless for war. From left to right: Felix Beauchamp, Andrew Pimento, Andrew Lawrie, Jordan Campbell, Tal Shulman. Photographer: Richard Burdett. Reproduced with kind permission.	795

Shawn Sides

49.1	Preparing for the birth of Dionysus. Photograph by Bret Brookshire. Reproduced with kind permission of Rude Mechs.	799
49.2	The death of Pentheus. Photograph by Bret Brookshire. Reproduced with kind permission of Rude Mechs.	801
49.3	From Rude Mechs' *Dionysus in 69*. Photograph by Bret Brookshire. Reproduced with kind permission of Rude Mechs.	805

Helen Eastman

50.1	A Derek Walcott illustration in the rehearsal notebook of his 2008 production of *Burial at Thebes*. Held at the APGRD, and reproduced with kind permission of Derek Walcott.	813
50.2	A Derek Walcott illustration in the rehearsal notebook of his 2008 production of *Burial at Thebes*. Held at the APGRD, and reproduced with kind permission of Derek Walcott.	814

Lorna Hardwick

51.1 The RSC's *Hecuba* at the Albery Theatre, London (2005). Written by Tony Harrison, directed by Laurence Boswell, with stage design by Es Devlin. Photograph reproduced with kind permission of Es Devlin. 820

51.2 *Hecuba* at Brooklyn Academy of Music, New York (2005). As the stage designer, Es Devlin, remarked, "We had a design that suddenly found new resonance in the light of the events of 2003. I sourced the tents from the army surplus shops around Washington DC—some of them had sand in them—presumably from the gulf states." Photograph reproduced with kind permission of Es Devlin. 822

51.3 Vanessa Redgrave as Hecuba in Tony Harrison's *Hecuba* at BAM, New York (2005), with stage design by Es Devlin. Photograph reproduced with kind permission of Es Devlin. 835

List of Contributors

Rosa Andújar is the A. G. Leventis Research Fellow in the Department of Greek & Latin, University College London. Her research interests range broadly across the spectrum of Greek literature and its afterlife: from fifth-century tragedy, to the Greek literature of the Roman Empire, to the reception of classical drama in postcolonial contexts. Rosa is currently working on two book projects: one which provides an account of the varied and experimental ways in which actors and chorus interact in Greek tragedy, and another on twentieth-century reimaginings of Greek drama in the Spanish-speaking Caribbean.

Daniel Banks, Ph.D., is a theater director, choreographer, educator, and dialogue facilitator. He has served on the faculties of the Tisch School of the Arts, New York University, and the M.F.A. in Contemporary Performance at Naropa University, and currently at the M.A. in Applied Theatre at City University of New York and the Institute of American Indian Arts, Santa Fe, NM. Daniel is co-director of DNAWORKS, an arts and service organization dedicated to using the arts as a catalyst for dialogue and healing. His writing appears in *American Theatre*, *Classical World*, and *Theatre Topics*, and in the collections *A Boal Companion* and *Acting Together: Performance and the Creative Transformation of Conflict* (vol. ii). He is editor of the critical anthology *Say Word! Voices from Hip Hop Theater*.

Francisco Barrenechea is Assistant Professor in the Department of Classics at the University of Maryland, College Park. His research interests include Greek drama, Latin epic, and the performance and reception of ancient theater. He has written articles on Euripides, Lucan, and Alfonso Reyes, and is currently at work on a book on the Mexican reception of ancient Greek drama.

Aníbal A. Biglieri received his Masters in Literature from the National University of La Plata and his Ph.D. in Hispanic Studies from the University of Syracuse. After teaching at several American institutions, he moved to the University of Kentucky, where he teaches Medieval Spanish literature. He has published articles on several topics, including pilgrimage literature, Medieval Spanish historiography, and the city in Medieval Spanish texts. He is the author of *Hacia una poética del relato didáctico: ocho estudios sobre El conde Lucanor* (1989), *Medea en la literatura española medieval* (2005), and *Las ideas geográficas y la imagen del mundo en la literatura española medieval* (2012). He is interested in the reception of classical authors in Argentine literature, especially in the works of Leopoldo Marechal, David Cureses, and Alberto de Zavalía.

Katie Billotte is a freelance writer based in the United States, who specializes in the reception of Greek and Roman tragedy in contemporary Latin America. She has worked at the University of London and the Freie Universität in Berlin, and is currently writing a book on Horace and U.S. politics.

Kathryn Bosher was Assistant Professor of Classics at Northwestern University. She co-edited *Theater Outside Athens: Drama in Greek Sicily and South Italy* (2012), and her monograph *Greek Theatre in Ancient Sicily* will be published by Cambridge University Press in 2015. Kate won an Andrew W. Mellon Foundation grant for the Sawyer Seminar series, "Theatre After Athens: Reception and Revision of Ancient Greek Drama," which she led in 2008–10, and she founded the digital humanities project "Classicizing Chicago" at Northwestern. She also wrote on the staging of Greek drama, the development of theater in the Greek West, and on western Greek comic vases.

Jordana Cox is a doctoral candidate in the Interdisciplinary Ph.D. in Theatre and Drama at Northwestern University. Her dissertation investigates the U.S. Federal Theatre Project's Living Newspapers, focusing on how they developed and revised popular understandings of democratic participation.

Susan Curtis has been teaching History and American Studies at Purdue University since 1989. She is the author of four books, *A Consuming Faith: The Social Gospel and Modern American Culture* (1991); *Dancing to a Black Man's Tune: A Life of Scott Joplin* (1994); *The First Black Actors on the Great White Way* (1998); and *Colored Memories: A Biographer's Quest for the Elusive Lester A. Walton* (2008). She served as Director of the American Studies Program at Purdue, 1999–2003 and 2010–12. She was the 2013 Maxwell C. Weiner Visiting Distinguished Professor of the Humanities at the Missouri University of Science and Technology.

Robert Davis recently completed his dissertation, "Performance and Spectatorship in United States International Expositions, 1876–1893," which looked at audience experience in three world's fairs. He has published articles on public engagement with the Classics in *New Voices in Classical Reception Studies*, *Comparative Drama*, and *The Journal of American Drama and Theatre* (co-authored with Amanda Wrigley). His essay "Is Mr. Euripides a Communist?" won the 2012 Philadelphia Constantinidis Critical Theory Award.

Moira Day is a Professor of Drama at the University of Saskatchewan, Canada. She is also an adjunct professor of the Women's and Gender Studies program, and member of the Classical, Medieval, and Renaissance Studies unit. A former co-editor of *Theatre Research in Canada*, she has edited two play anthologies and the essay collection *West-Words: Celebrating Western Canadian Theatre and Playwriting*. She has published extensively on Canadian theater, women in Western Canadian theater, and the classical tradition in Canadian theater, as well as speaking at conferences within Canada and internationally in the U.S.A., Ireland, China, the Czech Republic, and Greece.

Paul B. Dixon has taught Portuguese, Spanish, and Latin American Literature at Purdue University. His specialty is Brazilian Literature, an area in which he has published four books and numerous articles. Most of his work has been devoted to Brazil's most studied author, Machado de Assis, who loved and constantly referred to classical texts. A recent essay explored "Sabina," a short story by that author, in its connections to the legend of the abduction of the Sabine women.

Dorota Dutsch is Associate Professor of Classics at the University of California, Santa Barbara. Her research has touched on various aspects of social performance, from funeral rites to scripted drama, focusing especially on gender, and, most recently, on classical reception. She has published articles and book chapters on Plautine jokes, Roman lament, pharmacology of seduction, and the language of gesture. She is the author of *Feminine Discourse in Roman Comedy: On Echoes and Voices* (OUP, 2008), and co-editor, with Ann Suter, of *Ancient Obscenities* (UMP, forthcoming). Her current research project examines the pseudonymous writings attributed to female Pythagoreans.

Helen Eastman is a director and writer of theater and opera working in the U.K. and internationally. She trained at the London Academy of Music and Dramatic Art (LAMDA) after graduating from Oxford. She is Artistic Associate of the Archive of Performances of Greek and Roman Drama (APGRD) at the University of Oxford and Director of the Cambridge Greek Play 2010, 2013, and 2016. She was Producer of the Onassis Programme at the University of Oxford 2005–10 commissioning contemporary theater, dance, and opera inspired by ancient drama. She is Artistic Director of the Live Canon ensemble. She writes and lectures on classical reception, ancient drama, and contemporary poetry.

Helene P. Foley is Professor of Classics, Barnard College, Columbia University. She is the author of books and articles on Greek epic and drama, on women and gender in antiquity, and on modern performance and adaptation of Greek drama. Author of *Ritual Irony: Poetry and Sacrifice in Euripides, The Homeric Hymn to Demeter, Female Acts in Greek Tragedy*, and *Reimagining Greek Tragedy on the American Stage*, and co-author of *Women in the Classical World: Image and Text*. She edited *Reflections of Women in Antiquity* and co-edited *Visualizing the Tragic: Drama, Myth and Ritual in Greek Art and Literature* and *Antigone on the Contemporary World Stage*.

Moira Fradinger is an Associate Professor of Comparative Literature at Yale University. She is the author of *Binding Violence: Literary Visions of Political Origins* (Stanford, CA, 2010) and is currently finishing two book-length projects. One is tentatively entitled *Antigonas: A Latin American Itinerary*, and the other is a translation anthology of five Antigone-plays into English, from languages such as Spanish, Portuguese, and Haitian Creole. She teaches European and Latin American literature and film, critical theory, gender studies, psychoanalysis, and intellectual history.

Mary-Kay Gamel teaches Greek, Latin, and theater at the University of California, Santa Cruz. She has been involved (as translator/adaptor, director, dramaturge, and/or producer) in more than twenty-eight productions of ancient drama in Santa Cruz, across the U.S.A. and abroad. She has written widely on ancient drama in performance. She is at work on a volume on authenticity in staging Greek and Roman drama and hopes to publish her adaptations with notes and video.

Cesar Gemelli is a graduate student in the Ph.D. in Literature program at the University of Notre Dame. He has a M.A. in Comparative Literature from Universidade Federal do Rio Grande do Sul. His main research interests are Greek drama and its reception in Brazilian literature.

John Given is an Associate Professor and Program Director of Classical Studies at East Carolina University. His research interests include identity performance in Greek tragedy and comedy and American reception of Greek drama. He serves on the editorial board of the journal *Didaskalia* and has been a member of the American Philological Association's Committee on Ancient and Modern Performance. As a theater practitioner, he has directed productions of *Lysistrata, Menaechmi, Rudens*, and *Oedipus Tyrannus*. Also an avid musical theater aficionado, he has published on the musicals of Stephen Sondheim, Stephen Schwartz, and Marvin Hamlisch.

Barbara Goff is Professor of Classics at the University of Reading. She has published extensively in the fields of Greek tragedy and classical reception. Her most recent monograph is *Your Secret Language: Classics in the British Colonies of West Africa* (Bloomsbury, 2013). With Michael Simpson, she is currently working on a study of Classics within the British Left; she will publish a related article in *Greek and Roman Classics in the British Struggle for Social Change*, edited by Henry Stead and Edith Hall (Bloomsbury, 2015).

Edith Hall is Professor in the Department of Classics and Centre for Hellenic Studies at King's College London. She co-founded the Archive of Performances of Greek and Roman Drama in 1996 and is now a Consultant Director of the project. Her latest books are *Adventures with Iphigenia in Tauris: A Cultural History of Euripides' Black Sea Tragedy* (2013) and *Introducing the Ancient Greeks: From Bronze Age Seafarers to Navigators of the Western Mind* (2014).

Judith P. Hallett, Professor of Classics and Distinguished Scholar-Teacher at the University of Maryland, College Park, has published widely in the areas of Latin language and literature; gender, sexuality, and the family in ancient Greece and Rome; classical reception and the history of classical learning in the anglophone world.

Lorna Hardwick is Emeritus Professor of Classical Studies at the Open University, U.K., and Director of the Reception of Classical Texts Research Project (<www2.open.ac.uk/ClassicalStudies/GreekPlays>). Publications include *Translating Words, Translating Cultures* (2000), *Reception Studies* (2003), *Classics in Postcolonial Worlds* (edited with Carol Gillespie, 2007), *Companion to Classical Receptions* (edited with Christopher Stray, 2008), and *Classics in the Modern World: A "Democratic Turn?"* (edited with Stephen

Harrison, 2013). She is co-editor with Professor James Porter of the Oxford University Press series *Classical Presences* and is founding editor of the Oxford journal *Classical Receptions Journal*.

Karelisa Hartigan (Ph.D. University of Chicago) is Professor Emerita of Classics at the University of Florida, where she taught Greek language, literature, and history for 35 years. She has published extensively on Greek drama and the reception of the classical world in contemporary culture. Hartigan is the founder and long time director of the Comparative Drama Conference. She did improv acting with the Arts-in-Medicine program at the UF hospital for a decade and currently directs a program of Applied Improv for the rehabilitation of formerly homeless veterans. She also acts on the legitimate stage in a local community theater.

Lena M. Hill is Associate Professor of English and African-American Studies at the University of Iowa. She is the author of *Visualizing Blackness and the Creation of the African American Literary Tradition* (2014) and co-author of *Ralph Ellison's Invisible Man: A Reference Guide* (2008). Among her current projects is a co-edited collection that explores Ralph and Fanny Ellison's relationship to Iowa and the rich history of African-American students who studied the arts at UI between 1930 and 1960. She is also working on a monograph that analyzes the conservative politics of important African-American writers.

Avery Willis Hoffman earned her Classics B.A. with honors from Stanford University and a M.St. and D.Phil. from University of Oxford; her doctoral thesis examined twentieth-century interpretations of Euripides' *Trojan Women* on the international stage. As a Marshall Scholar at Oxford, Avery was President of the Oxford University Classical Drama Society, created the Oxford Greek Festival 2004, and directed her own translation of *Trojan Women* at The Oxford Playhouse. Recently, Avery has worked with Peter Sellars as an Assistant Director, in Communications for the William J. Clinton Foundation, and as an Exhibit Content Developer for the Smithsonian's National Museum of African-American History and Culture. She is currently working on a modern adaptation of Aeschylus' *Prometheus Bound*.

Thomas E. Jenkins is Associate Professor and Chair of Classical Studies at Trinity University, and is the author of *Intercepted Letters: Epistolarity and Narrative in Greek and Roman Literature* as well as numerous essays on the reception of the classical world. His current project, *Antiquity Now: Classical World in the Contemporary American Imagination* (2015), focuses on strongly ideological appropriations of the ancient world in modern film, performance, and art.

Vassilis Lambropoulos is the C. P. Cavafy Professor of Modern Greek at the University of Michigan, teaching in the Departments of Classical Studies and Comparative Literature and serving on the steering committee of the interdepartmental faculty consortium Contexts for Classics. His books are *Literature as National Institution: Studies in the Politics of Modern Greek Criticism* (1988), *The Rise of Eurocentrism: Anatomy of*

Interpretation (1993), and *The Tragic Idea* (2006). He has co-edited the volumes *The Text and its Margins: Post-Structuralist Approaches to Twentieth-Century Greek Literature* (1985) and *Twentieth-Century Literary Theory: An Introductory Anthology* (1987), and special issues of the journal *October*, "The Humanities as Social Technology" (1990), and *South Atlantic Quarterly*, "Ethical Politics" (1996). He is currently writing a book on the idea of revolution as hubris in modern tragedy.

Artemis Leontis is Professor and Coordinator of Modern Greek in the Department of Classical Studies at the University of Michigan. Her books include *Topographies of Hellenism: Mapping the Homeland* (1995, Greek translation in 1998); *Greece; A Travelers' Literary Companion* (1997), an anthology introducing readers to the landscapes of Greece through 24 stories by Greek authors; *"What these Ithakas mean . . .": Readings in Cavafy* (2002), co-edited with Lauren Talalay and Keith Taylor and a companion to the exhibit "Cavafy's World" at the Kelsey Museum of Archaeology; and *Culture and Customs of Greece* (2009), an overview of contemporary Greece for a general readership. She is currently writing a cultural biography of Eva Palmer Sikelianos. She is Humanities Editor of the *Journal of Modern Greek Studies*.

Laura Lodewyck is a Ph.D. candidate in Northwestern University's Interdisciplinary Theatre and Drama program. Her dissertation investigates contemporary American theater organizations that create performances with and for military veterans in order to examine the transformative potential of theater during times of war. Laura also holds an M.F.A. in Acting Performance from Roosevelt University's Chicago College of the Performing Arts.

Fiona Macintosh is Professor of Classical Reception, Director of the Archive of Performances of Greek and Roman Drama (APGRD), and Fellow of St Hilda's College, University of Oxford. She is the author of *Dying Acts* (Cork University Press, 1994; St Martin's Press, 1995), *Greek Tragedy and the British Theatre 1660–1914* (Oxford University Press, 2005—with Edith Hall), and *Sophocles' Oedipus Tyrannus* (Plays in Production Series, Cambridge University Press, 2009). She has edited a number of APGRD volumes, most recently *The Ancient Dancer in the Modern World: Responses to Greek and Roman Dance* (Oxford University Press, 2010, paperback 2012) and *Choruses, Ancient and Modern* (Oxford University Press, 2012, with Joshua Billings and Felix Budelmann).

Justine McConnell is a Leverhulme Early Career Fellow at the University of Oxford, where she works on contemporary African, Caribbean, and ancient Greek poetics. Prior to this, she was a Leverhulme Postdoctoral Research Associate at the Archive of Performances of Greek and Roman Drama (APGRD), and a Mellon Postdoctoral Fellow at Northwestern University. She is author of *Black Odysseys: The Homeric Odyssey in the African Diaspora since 1939* (2013), and co-editor of *Ancient Slavery and Abolition: From Hobbes to Hollywood* (2011).

Susan Manning is an internationally recognized historian of modern dance who has presented her research in Germany, Great Britain, France, Japan, and Argentina as well as in the United States and Canada. She is the author of *Ecstasy and the Demon: The Dances of Mary Wigman* (1993; 2nd edn. 2006) and *Modern Dance, Negro Dance: Race in Motion*; curator of *Danses Noires/Blanche Amérique* (2008); and co-editor of *New German Dance Studies* (2012). She is a Professor of English, Theatre, and Performance Studies at Northwestern University and Principal Investigator for the Mellon-funded initiative Dance Studies in/and the Humanities.

Hallie Rebecca Marshall is an Assistant Professor in the Department of Theatre and Film at the University of British Columbia. She has published a number of articles on classical reception in twentieth-century British theater. She is currently completing a book on the classical plays of Tony Harrison.

David Mayer, Emeritus Professor of Drama and Research Professor, University of Manchester, studies British and American popular entertainment of the nineteenth and early twentieth century. Recent writings explore links between the Victorian stage and early motion pictures. He is co-founder of The Victorian and Edwardian Stage on Film Project, a contributing member to The [D. W.] Griffith Project developed between Le Giornate del Cinema Muto, Pordenone, the British Film Institute, and the U.S. Library of Congress. His books include *Harlequin in his Element: English Pantomime, 1806–1836* (1968), *Henry Irving and "The Bells"* (1984), *Playing Out the Empire: Ben-Hur and Other Toga-Plays and Films* (1994), and *Stagestruck Filmmaker: D. W. Griffith and the American Theatre* (2009). In 2012 he received the Distinguished Scholar Award from the American Society for Theatre Research.

Erin B. Mee's book *The Theatre of Roots: Redirecting the Modern Indian Stage* was published in 2009 by Seagull Books and Palgrave-McMillan. She co-edited *Antigone on the Contemporary World Stage* with Helene P. Foley (OUP, 2011), and *The Methuen Anthology of Modern Asian Drama* with Kevin Wetmore (Methuen, 2014), She is the editor of *Drama Contemporary: India*, a collection of modern Indian plays published in the United States by Johns Hopkins University Press and in India by Oxford University Press. Her articles have appeared in *TDR, Theater Journal, Performing Arts Journal, Seagull Theatre Quarterly, American Theatre Magazine*, and in numerous books.

S. Sara Monoson is Professor of Political Science and Classics at Northwestern University. She works on Greek political theory and the reception of ancient sources in American political discourse. She is the author of *Plato's Democratic Entanglements* (2000) and is now completing a book, *Socrates in the Vernacular*, on twentieth-century uses of this character in popular media. Her recent work in edited volumes includes "Socrates in Combat: Trauma and Resilience in Plato's Political Thought" (in *Combat Trauma and the Ancient Greeks*) and "Dionysius I and Sicilian Theatrical Traditions in Plato's *Republic*" (in *Theatre Outside Athens*).

María Florencia Nelli graduated from Universidad Nacional de La Plata (UNLP), Argentina, with a degree in Spanish Language and Literature in 1998 and a second degree in Classics in 2002. She holds a Master of Philosophy in Ancient Greek Language and Literature from Oxford University and a D.Phil. in Greek Language and Literature from the same institution on the subject of Demonstrative Pronouns of Early Greek Dialects. She has taught Ancient Greek Language and Literature at Universidad Nacional de La Plata and Universidad Católica de La Plata, and Greek Syntax at Oxford University. Her interest in ancient Greek drama and Reception Studies in Latin America stems from her many years working as an actress, assistant property master, and assistant stage manager at Experimental Theatre Company "Taller de Teatro de la U.N.L.P." in Argentina. She has several publications on Reception Studies in Latin America, Sophocles, Homer, and ancient lyric.

Konstantinos P. Nikoloutsos is Assistant Professor of Latin and Director of Ancient Studies at Saint Joseph's University in Philadelphia. He has published numerous journal articles and book chapters in the fields of Roman elegy, ancient history on film, and the classical tradition in Latin America and the Caribbean. He is the editor of *Ancient Greek Women in Film* (OUP, 2013) and guest-editor of a special issue of *Romance Quarterly* (59.1: 2012) entitled *Reception of Greek and Roman Drama in Latin America*. His honors include the 2008 Paul Rehak Prize from the Lambda Classical Caucus and the 2012–13 Loeb Classical Library Foundation Fellowship from Harvard University.

Lee T. Pearcy spent nearly 30 years as teacher and administrator at the Episcopal Academy in Newtown Square, Pennsylvania, before retiring in 2013. He is Research Associate in the Department of Classics at Bryn Mawr College, where he directs a digital humanities project, Classicizing Philadelphia, and he serves as co-editor of *Classical World*. His research focuses on classical receptions, ancient medicine, and Latin poetry, and his most recent book is *The Grammar of our Civility: Classical Education in America* (2005).

Melinda Powers is an Associate Professor in the Department of English at John Jay College of Criminal Justice, CUNY. She is the author of *Athenian Tragedy in Performance: A Guide to Contemporary Studies and Historical Debates* (University of Iowa Press, 2014) and of various articles on the adaptation and production of ancient Greek drama on the U.S. stage.

Yopie Prins is Professor of English and Comparative Literature at the University of Michigan, Ann Arbor. She is the author of *Victorian Sappho* (1999) and *Ladies' Greek: Victorian Translations of Tragedy* (2015), and co-editor of *The Lyric Theory Reader: A Critical Anthology* (2014), *Dwelling in Possibility: Women Poets and Critics on Poetry* (1997), and a special issue of *Cultural Critique* on "Classical Reception and the Political" (2010). Additional publications include articles on Victorian poetry and prosody, classical Greek literature and its reception, and the history and theory of translation.

Nancy Sorkin Rabinowitz is Professor of Comparative Literature at Hamilton College. Author of *Anxiety Veiled: Euripides and the Traffic in Women* (1993) and *Greek Tragedy* (2008), she co-edited *From Abortion to Pederasty: Addressing Difficult Topics in the Classics Classroom* (with Fiona McHardy) (2014); *Vision and Viewing in Ancient Greece*, with Sue Blundell and Douglas Cairns (Helios 40 [2013]); *Among Women: From the Homosocial to the Homoerotic in the Ancient World*, with Lisa Auanger (2002); *Women on the Edge: Four Plays by Euripides* with Ruby Blondell, Mary-Kay Gamel, and Bella Vivante (1999); and *Feminist Theory and the Classics*, with Amy Richlin (1993). In progress at the present is *Sex in Antiquity: Sexuality and Gender in the Ancient World* (with Mark Masterson and James Robson) (2015).

Patrice Rankine is Professor of Classics and Dean for the Arts and Humanities at Hope College, in Holland, Michigan. He is author of *Ulysses in Black: Ralph Ellison, Classicism, and African American Literature*, published in 2006 with the University of Wisconsin Press, which was named one of *Choice* magazine's outstanding academic books in 2007 and is currently in its second printing. His second book is *Aristotle and Black Drama: A Theater of Civil Disobedience*, which Baylor University Press published in 2013. He is a member of the Archive of Performances of Greek and Roman Drama's Advisory Board at the University of Oxford, and his publications also include numerous articles, book chapters, and book reviews.

Rush Rehm is Professor of Classics and Theater and Performance Studies at Stanford University. He has written extensively on Greek tragedy, including *Greek Tragic Theatre*, *Marriage to Death: The Conflation of Wedding and Funeral Rituals in Greek Tragedy*, *The Play of Space: Spatial Transformation in Greek Tragedy* and *Radical Theatre: Greek Tragedy and the Modern World* (Duckworth, 2003). As Artistic Director of Stanford Repertory Theater, Rush has directed many Greek tragedies and adaptations of Homer, including *The Wanderings of Odysseus*, with productions at the Getty Museum in Malibu and the Cacoyannis Foundation in Athens. His bilingual production of Beckett's *Happy Days* recently played in Paris and Montpellier, France.

José de Paiva dos Santos holds a Ph.D. in Comparative Literature from Purdue University and has recently completed post-doctoral research at State University of Rio de Janeiro in Afro-Brazilian and African-American Literature. He is currently an associate professor of American Literature at the Federal University of Minas Gerais, Brazil, where he teaches courses in American and African-American Literature, Literary Theory, and Comparative Studies. His current research involves African-American Literature and Religion, Critical Race theory, and Literature and Cultural Memory. He has published articles on nineteenth- and twentieth-century American, African-American, and Brazilian Literature.

Peggy Shannon is Chair of the Ryerson Theatre School in Toronto. She has directed in professional theaters including Atlanta's Alliance Theatre, Seattle Repertory Theatre, A Contemporary Theatre, San Jose Repertory Theatre, Los Angeles Theatre Center, LA Theatre Works, Mixed Blood Theatre, as well as at New Jersey, Colorado, Utah, Idaho,

California, and Oregon Shakespearian Festivals, Portland Repertory Theatre, Long Beach Civic Light Opera, International City Theatre, and Sacramento Theatre Company. She has also worked at Hydrama Theatre in Greece. She has served as Artistic Director of A Contemporary Theatre (Seattle), Sacramento Theatre Company in California, and as Associate Producing Director of LA Theatre Works.

Shawn Sides is a theater artist who lives and works in Austin, Texas, with her partner, composer Graham Reynolds. She holds an M.A. in Theatre and Performance Studies from New York University. Shawn is a founder and Co-Producing Artistic Director of Rude Mechs with whom she has co-conceived, -devised, and/or directed a new work every year, give or take, since 1996, as well as staging several adaptations and "re-enactments" of germinal works from the American avant-garde of the 1960s–1980s. With Rudes, she has toured her work throughout the U.S.A., Europe, and Australia.

Michael Simpson is Senior Lecturer in English Literature at Goldsmiths, University of London. His research interests span Romanticism, classical reception, and postcolonialism. He is the author of *Closet Performances: Political Exhibition and Prohibition in the Dramas of Byron and Shelley* (1998). His interest in the Graeco-Roman Classics lies particularly in how they have been adapted within postcolonial and especially African and African-Caribbean literatures and theaters. With Barbara Goff, he is co-author of *Crossroads in the Black Aegean: Oedipus, Antigone, and Dramas of the African Diaspora* (2007) and co-editor of *Thinking the Olympics: The Classical Tradition and the Modern Games* (2011), as well as currently co-writing a study of Classics and the British Labour Movement.

Niall W. Slater (Samuel Candler Dobbs Professor of Latin and Greek, Emory University) focuses on the ancient theater and its production conditions, prose fiction, and popular reception of classical literature. His books include *Spectator Politics: Metatheatre and Performance in Aristophanes* (Penn, 2002); *Reading Petronius* (JHUP, 1990); and *Plautus in Performance: The Theatre of the Mind* (Princeton, 1985; 2nd revised edn. 2000), as well as translations for *The Birth of Comedy* (ed. J. R. Rusten, JHUP, 2011) and the Bloomsbury Companion to Euripides' *Alcestis* (2013). Current work includes studies of Harley Granville Barker and classical memories in C. S. Lewis's children's books.

Isabelle Torrance is Associate Professor of Classics at the University of Notre Dame. Her publications include *Aeschylus: Seven Against Thebes* (London, 2007), *Metapoetry in Euripides* (Oxford, 2013), *Oaths and Swearing in Ancient Greece* (Berlin, 2014, co-authored with A. H. Sommerstein), as well as articles and book chapters on Greek tragedy and its reception.

Kevin J. Wetmore, Jr. is Professor and Chair of Theatre Arts at Loyola Marymount University. He is the author and/or editor of over twenty books, including *Athenian Sun in an African Sky: Modern African Adaptation of Classical Greek Tragedy* (McFarland, 2001), *Black Dionysus: Greek Tragedy and African-American Theatre* (McFarland, 2003), and *Black Medea: Adaptations for Modern Plays* (Cambria, 2013). He has published articles in such journals as *Revue de littérature comparée, International Journal of the Classical Tradition, Text and Presentation*, and *The Classical Review*. He is also a Los Angeles-based actor, director, and stage combat choreographer.

Margaret Williamson teaches Classics and Comparative Literature at Dartmouth College. She has worked with the playwright Timberlake Wertenbaker for over twenty years on the Greek texts of plays by Sophocles and Euripides, leading to versions by Wertenbaker that have been staged in the U.K., U.S.A., Canada, and Greece. She is the author of *Sappho's Immortal Daughters* (Harvard, 1995). Her present interests include translation studies, the reception of lyric poetry, and the uses of Classics in colonial contexts. She is currently working on a book entitled *Creole Classics*, on classical names given to Caribbean slaves in the eighteenth and nineteenth centuries.

Note on Nomenclature, Spelling, and Texts

Our policy has been to use the names as they appear in the text/program/publicity for modern adaptations/versions of the ancient plays. But with the names and characters of the ancient plays and their abbreviations, we have adopted the Latinized versions of Greek proper names where those are well established, broadly in line with the practice of the fourth edition of the *Oxford Classical Dictionary*. American spellings (with apologies to our Canadian readers!) are adopted throughout the text, except with the word "theater," where names of a particular theater adopt standard English spelling (e.g., The Chicago Theatre).

Abbreviated references to ancient works and editions of ancient works are those of the *Oxford Classical Dictionary* where possible.

When referring to the ancient authors in the original language, we have used the most recent edition published in the Oxford Classical Texts series.

PART I

THEORIES AND METHODS

CHAPTER 1

INTRODUCTION

FIONA MACINTOSH, JUSTINE MᶜCONNELL, AND PATRICE RANKINE

THE 1954 *Oedipus Rex* in Stratford, Ontario was in many respects a watershed production in the history of modern performances of ancient plays. Tyrone Guthrie's direction marked the end of the star system that had dominated the professional theater and productions of Greek drama, in particular, since the nineteenth century. Although the part of Oedipus was played by James Mason in 1954 and by Douglas Campbell from 1955 onward, the vast expressionist masks by Tanya Moiseiwitsch guaranteed that the stars here were completely eclipsed (Fig. 1.1).[1] This highly ritualistic production sought archetypes rather than psychological realism; and when it was filmed in April 1956, the producer, Leonid Kipnis (a.k.a. Lola) succeeded in liberating Greek tragedy from the exclusive preserve of the western world. As the first commercially available film version of an ancient play, the Canadian production could be said with hindsight to have played a key role in the globalization of Greek tragedy that has become its hallmark since the 1960s (Hall, Macintosh, and Wrigley 2004).

This landmark Canadian production, with its migrant director, is representative of many of the productions discussed in this volume. Irish by birth, educated at Oxford, Guthrie had worked uncomfortably alongside the quintessentially English star actor Laurence Olivier at the Old Vic in London in the early 1940s. It was this experience that led him ultimately to North America, and which shaped in important ways the 1954 *Oedipus Rex*. Like many other productions of ancient plays in the Americas, it wasn't simply informed by a monocultural lens. Although it was cast very much in contradistinction to Olivier's own seminal Oedipus of 1945, it was Guthrie's staging of *Oedipus Rex* in Hebrew with the Habimah Theatre Company in Tel Aviv that year and his direction of the play in Swedish in 1947 with the Swedish Theatre in Helsinki that were equally formative (Macintosh 2009: 163–8). Indeed, the experience of working with Sophocles' play in languages not his own convinced him of the need to find the non-naturalistic performance vocabulary, which eventually led to the production's ready translation onto screens around the world (Guthrie 1960: 233–46).

FIG. 1.1 Douglas Campbell in the Stratford, Ontario Festival's production of *Oedipus Rex*, directed by Tyrone Guthrie (Photo: McKague, Toronto).

Thanks to Guthrie's role as first Artistic Director of the Stratford Shakespearian Festival and his inclusion of this ancient play within its second year in Ontario, Greek drama went on to enjoy a prominent position within the repertoire of North American theater. Furthermore, it was Guthrie who lent his name in 1963 to the theater in Minneapolis, which was an attempt to take the Classics beyond metropolitan New York; and the Guthrie Theatre has continued, under the artistic direction of Garland Wright in the early 1990s and from 1995 under Joe Dowling's leadership, to include pioneering productions of Greek plays within its repertoire (Foley 2012: 162–70, 183, 190, 234).

The mapping of Greek drama in the Americas involves tracking networks of communication across continents and across oceans. With the expansion of the railroad from the mid-nineteenth century onward, entire companies were transported across the continent rather than simply the star, who had hitherto performed with a different stock company in each city (Engle and Miller 2003). Theater has always afforded an important window on a culture and the early attempts to stage Greek plays in the United States in the nineteenth century testify to the agonistic relations between America and Europe at this time, with high-class patronage and overly respectful imitation of European productions leading to occasional bafflement and often explicit hostility (see Macintosh, Bosher and Cox, and Davis, this volume). Yet it could be equally argued that these nineteenth-century appropriations of the classical material, albeit mediated via European touring companies, benefited hugely from the New World context and input. When the American actress Charlotte Cushman accompanied Charles Macready to Europe in the part of Talfourd's *Ion* in 1845–6, she brought to the role a renewed vigor and authority that mesmerized London audiences (Fig. 1.2) (Hall and Macintosh 2005: 311–12).

Theater histories have generally focused on the "newness," the "rawness" of the performance culture of the "New" Worlds of the Americas. Any native engagements with the ancient dramatic corpus have consequently been given short shrift on the grounds that they betray, at best, conservative, Eurocentric leanings, or, at worst, evidence of colonial cultural hegemony. However, as theater practitioners have routinely discovered from at least the Modernist period onward, the most innovative work very often comes from a serious engagement with the works of the past, especially the theater of ancient Greece. Indeed while the Italian actress Adelaide Ristori failed to attract the crowds in 1874 on her visit to Mexico as Medea in Legouvé's famous version, the celebrated Spanish actor José Valero had won huge acclaim and prompted serious discussion about the future of Mexican theater some six years earlier, when he visited with

FIG. 1.2 Charlotte Cushman as Ion (1846). Reproduced from *ILN* 8.199 (1846), by courtesy of the Bodleian Library.

Francisco Martinez de la Rosa's *Edipo* (see Barrenechea, this volume). This volume seeks to define the complex and often surprising contours of the reception of ancient Greek drama in the Americas, and to articulate how these different engagements—at local, national, or trans-continental levels as well as across borders—have been distinct from each other and from those of Europe and Asia. A comparative perspective is helpful, and in the nineteenth century essential (see Macintosh, this volume), so that both the distinctions and the interconnections across time and place can be charted.

This volume does not attempt to be anything other than a "handbook" to what is in many ways *terra nova*. Taking its cues from Theater and Performance Studies, and especially from Shakespearian performance histories, classical performance reception began to take root in British Classics in the 1990s and with a few notable, earlier exceptions within the United States, in North America in the new millennium.[2] Now the spotlight has shifted very sharply upon Latin America and its engagement with Greek drama at a time when Classical Studies in that region is undergoing a substantial renewal of resources and demonstrating an attendant intellectual energy. Classical Reception can never be tied by geographical nor linguistic boundaries and in the case of the Americas long colonial histories have often imposed these boundaries arbitrarily. Much like the Hemispheric Institute of Performance and Politics at New York University, which seeks to uncover the ways in which the performance arts in the Americas have been inextricably linked to histories of colonialism, this volume seeks in many ways to look at the shared histories and practices in the Americas that defy national boundaries.[3]

If Guthrie's production was the first commercial film of a Greek play with worldwide circulation, it is now possible with the existence of numerous research archives—such as the Hemispheric Institute Digital Video Library (HIDVL) and the international Archive of Performances of Greek and Roman Drama (APGRD) in Oxford—as well as through YouTube, to watch video recordings of many recent productions of ancient plays in the Americas. Of course, there are both pitfalls and challenges to using video recordings of live performances as scholarly records (Bratton and Peterson 2013). However, when this material is used with some circumspection and together with other contextual evidence, it enables the hitherto inaccessible material to be made available (and hopefully to be preserved) and for interconnections to be forged and gleaned from the messy records that constitute the raw material of theater history (Postlewait 2009).

The chaos of the interwar period in Europe intensified the collecting impulse and led to the realization that records, not least those relating to theater history that had often only resided in private hands and/or within the bodily memory of individual performers, needed to be held centrally in order to be protected for posterity (Macintosh 2013). Similar archiving impulses amongst African Americans were fueled in the wake of the Civil War, when the ravages and displacements attendant on the war prompted new searches for identity through the collation of material relating to living performance traditions (see both Curtis and Manning, this volume). The most recent archival turn, resulting from the new digital technologies, has meant that it is not just the performance that is important but the recording of it as well; and with relatively low cost, both professional and amateur productions can now for the first time enjoy online presence. Although the proliferation of data has not come without its own set of anxieties—especially surrounding the reality of censorship at the touch of a key—it has brought with it the possibility of viewing theater history differently, enabling "new relational patterns and genealogies" (Bratton and Peterson 2013: 304) that are specially illuminating for any study of performance history of ancient Greek drama in the Americas.

The contributors to this volume come from a number of academic disciplines—Classics, Latin American Studies, Theatre and Performance Studies, Comparative Literature—and many are poets/playwrights or theater practitioners. The language they employ often reflects the range of their professional experiences and not surprisingly we find that certain words and phrases bear slightly different semantic resonances for different authors. The term "classical," for example, is often applied to theater "classics" such as Shakespeare, Calderón, Racine, Goethe, and Schiller as readily as it is to Greek "classical" theater of fifth-century BCE Athens. We have deliberately allowed the individual authors their own "vocabularies" since "classical" in both these cases draws its essential meaning from the word "classic," which, in Calvino's terms, is a text (ancient or modern) which merits reading and/or rewriting in each generation (Calvino 1999). That is not to say that there is no need for rigor in respect to matters of terminology: indeed, in a volume covering the Americas as a whole, there are areas that are in especial need of lexical precision and finessing. And it is the language of postcoloniality, above all, that demands such exactitude.

THE POSTCOLONIAL NATURE OF THE AMERICAS

If the Americas are to be considered "postcolonial" (and it seems undeniable that this is an apt label in at least a number of respects), then it is nonetheless important not to allow the term to sweep over the many differences that exist across the continent, even in terms of their colonial and neo-colonial experiences. Amitav Ghosh's salutary warning that "'Postcolonial' is essentially a term that describes you as negative" should not be neglected either. Ghosh goes on to elaborate, explaining that the chronological sense of "postcolonialism" is undeniable but should not be made to define whole nations that were previously colonized, as if that past comprises their whole identity. Furthermore, he remarks that the postcolony of each nation is different and distinct, and must not be elided into one state of "the postcolony" (on the importance of thinking in terms of specificities rather than generalities in postcolonial discourse, see Goff and Simpson, this volume; Kumar 2007: 105; cf. Mbembe 2001).

The United States' central role in the transatlantic slave trade ensured that it has never been overlooked in discourses of colonialism; as such, its place in the discourse of postcolonial theory has never been under threat, even while it has not been unchanging. The positions of Canada, Central America, and South America in these discourses have, on the other hand, tended to be neglected or erroneously assumed to partake of the same experiences as the United States.[4] As Moraña, Dussel, and Jáuregui make clear in their introduction to *Coloniality at Large: Latin America and the Postcolonial Debate* (2008), there has been a systematic exclusion of the region (i.e., Latin America) from the vast repertoire of historical experiences and philosophical and political discourses often examined in connection with the topic of colonialism (Moraña, Dussel, and Jáuregui 2008: 5). The Caribbean, too, has a different postcolonial history and identity from the U.S.A., but its centrality in the colonial processes of the eighteenth and nineteenth centuries, in particular, has ensured that it figures prominently and decisively in most discussions of postcolonialism and postcolonial theory.[5]

The same has not been true of continental Latin America, however; indeed, Iberian colonialism has often been overlooked, especially by anglophone scholars. The fact that the Spanish and Portuguese began colonizing South America more than 100 years prior to the first successful colonizing missions of the French, Dutch, and British is often neglected. A tendency to sweep all nations into the category of the postmodern has, at times, led to a blind-spot which fails to take account of the different situations which pertain across the Americas as a whole, and which demand that only specificities can accurately illuminate the diversity of histories and cultures found across North and South America, which includes Canada, Central America, and the Caribbean. This fact may be cause to reassess not only the widely accepted history of colonialism, but also our sense of modernity as a whole. Gilroy's influential model of the Black Atlantic tied in colonialism to modernity, but if his vision of colonialism (pertinent, powerful, and important as it is) fails to take account of the Iberian empires, the different circumstances of the latter may mean that the model does not fit Latin America so aptly (and Gilroy never claimed that it would) and that this view of modernity should be adjusted. Moraña, Dussel, and Jáuregui's important 2008 edited volume makes this point most clearly.[6]

For a handbook of Greek drama in the Americas, it is also fitting to note that the first use of the term "post-colonial" (hyphenated and in a mostly temporal sense) comes in an essay by T. W. Allen in the *Journal of Hellenic Studies* in 1910.[7] Yet it is not until the 1990s that the primarily temporal use of the term begins to be predominantly replaced by the more theoretical use in published works (Quayson 2012: 5). When it does, and when the classification "postcolonial literature" becomes common, classical literature took a place in the discourse as a body of work that contributed to the foundation of the "western canon" with which many modern writers were engaging. A number of scholars over the last decade have explored these literary engagements, and theorized about postcolonial engagements with Classics (Goff 2005; Ronnick 2005; Rankine 2006; Goff and Simpson 2007; Hardwick and Gillespie 2007; Bradley 2010; Cook and Tatum 2010; Greenwood 2010; Stephens and Vasunia 2010; Hall and Vasunia 2010; Goff 2013; McConnell 2013; Rankine 2013). Indeed, in this volume, Classics and postcolonialism loom large not only in Goff and Simpson's chapter, but also in discussions by Rabinowitz, McConnell, Fradinger,

Powers, Eastman and Walcott, and Hardwick. Some of the reasons behind this prevalent connection between Classics and colonialism have been lucidly delineated by Goff in the introduction to her 2005 edited volume, *Classics and Colonialism*: in particular, the fact that Classics frequently played a part in the ideology of European imperialists—and had nearly always featured in their education—and that it likewise had a role in the opposing movements of anti-colonialism and resistance (Goff 2005: 1–24).

In addition to nations that were part of the eighteenth- and nineteenth-century European empires, the United States should be considered as a postcolonial nation, although not unilaterally. For more than 150 years the Thirteen Colonies that went on to form the United States were ruled by Britain;[8] after the American Revolution therefore, the United States was a postcolonial nation. However, the story does not end there because, as Sangeeta Ray and Henry Schwarz have remarked:

> It is in the US, of all the "postcolonial" societies around the world, in which we find perhaps the most dramatic example of turning the colonial relationship on its head. Post-colonies are obviously capable of becoming oppressor states, but none has been quite so "successful" as the US. (Ray and Schwarz 1995: 165 n. 3)

In addition to the neo-colonialism referred to here, the United States also very soon became implicated in the European colonization of Africa and the Caribbean by its prominent role in the transatlantic slave trade. The United States' colonial past is complex and its engagement with Classics can often be seen to reflect and illuminate this; so too can be the response of Canada to both the United States and classical literature (see Day, this volume).

OMNI-AMERICANS

Postcolonial or otherwise, the U.S.A., like all other nations covered in this volume, has a past, and that past is often mythologized and then mixed into deeper, older—and often classical—layers. In her discussion of the play *Topdog/Underdog*, in which she names two black street hustlers as [Abraham] Lincoln and [John Wilkes] Booth, associated allusions intended, Suzan-Lori Parks accounts for her persistent return to the character of Lincoln in terms of an American mythology. For Parks, Lincoln's role in the grand story of the United States of America is a "subterranean thing," to which she keeps returning (quoted in Shenk 2002). Lincoln is to the U.S.A. what an Antigone, Medea, or Oedipus was to the Greeks. (Parks makes this association (Rankine 2013).) We might extend Parks and say that all of these figures (the Greek ones as well as Lincoln and Booth) are, for Americans, "subterranean things." Parks's reference to the "subterranean thing" is consonant with the approach that Hall and Macintosh take in speaking of the "subterranean" presence of the Classics in modern life, a reality always there to be dug up from under our feet, at once primarily unnoticed and permeable, solidly tangible yet easily disregarded (Hall and Macintosh 2005).

If the classical past is in the modern world a "subterranean thing," then the idea of an archaeological dig—a botched one, like that of Heinrich Schliemann, where the expert muddles layers of cultural artifacts, to the extent that onlookers no longer know which remnant relates to which society—might be an apt metaphor for the processes whereby Greek drama has come to the Americas. The promiscuous mix of the Greek and the contemporary, like a black street hustler named Abraham Lincoln, is true not only in the U.S.A.; the imagery obtains throughout the Americas. As with the archaeological dig, an investigation of classical presences in the new worlds of the Americas reveals the past as under our feet, though hidden from plain sight. In fact, the reality of the Classics as a discipline in the New World is not that deeply buried (see Goff and Simpson, this volume). Colonizers to the New World as early as the sixteenth century brought with them their education, however incomplete, steeped in knowledge of Greece and Rome. This was true whether they were Dutch, Spanish, Portuguese, French, or English. These colonizers and explorers often saw themselves in the imperial light of Rome, or in the civilizing vein of Greek colonization from the eighth century BCE, but many posited that they were in certain respects better than their forebears (Lupher 2006). In other words, it is not necessary to go as far back as the ancient world for an archaeology of the "subterranean thing": classical artifacts, the metaphors and contexts out of which nineteenth-, twentieth-, and twenty-first-century Americans have crafted the world around them, are within three, four, and five centuries respectively. We might argue, as do Goff and Simpson, that the colonists quickly became *post*-colonial in their relationship to the empires that they left behind, whether Greece, Rome, in the distant past, or Spain, Britain, and France, more recently. At the same time, the presence of the "New," the promiscuous contact with local populations and black slaves, would forever impact how the "New World" came to know the past, and what it came to be. These presences, too, would leave their imprint on the postcolonial states.

Once we account for the recentness of the Americas as a phenomenon in the world, we are less surprised by the fact that the subterranean presence of the past is closer to the surface than it is generally conceived in everyday life, or by the extent to which it keeps emerging. The Greek dramatic presence in the New World is evident in the archival approach to what Americans remembered—and chose to forget, or bury (see Manning, this volume). Just like the attempt of women writers such as Margaret Fuller to deploy the Greeks for their sense of place within the United States, the Frogs Society of African-American artists in the early twentieth century remind the reader of a penetration (though not easily achieved) beneath the cultural overlay in North America of gender inequity and segregation. The overlay is a façade, a cover that belies the real: namely that, whatever the apparent social order, black people, brown people, and women of any color engaged with the Classics and crafted their sense of self out of this material, at least in part. As black women engaging with the Classics in public spaces, Phillis Wheatley and Harriet Jacobs might be anomalies, but their existence gives the lie to the real and uncovers the façade of a certain social order.

The realities of gender and racial inequity are as true across South, Central, and North America as they are within the United States. Notwithstanding a social framework that denied their essential humanity—their "inalienable" rights—women and racial minorities realized their own potentialities. For much of the nineteenth and twentieth centuries, the artifacts that could reify freedom and equality were, for blacks as well as women, just beneath the surface and very often ancient Greek in their provenance. Harriet Jacobs's confinement to a closet as she likely read and absorbed everything from *Robinson Crusoe* to contemporary poetry is an example of the closeted reality of suppressed groups in the Americas. Blacks and women read and engaged in the subterranean Classics to craft their values in the New World, those of freedom, equality, literacy, art, and so on. As Curtis shows, the Frogs of Aristophanes were present as a reality for African-American artists in the U.S.A. at the beginning of the twentieth century, even if the significance of the reference to classical drama was lost on the judge who rejected their plea for legitimacy. The juxtaposition of the knowledgeable black artists, a phrase that for many at the time would have been an oxymoron, and the ignorant judge is emblematic of the American joke that so tickled Ralph Ellison. In his reference to Constance Rourke, Ellison affirmed that in America, the absence of class and the easy, trickster-like play on identity mean that anyone can be anything at any time, no matter what others think, and this is the joke. As it pertains to race, lighter complexioned blacks might "pass" out of the racial hierarchy and segregation; and the mutability of social status is to some extent true even for those who might not be able to pass with regard to appearance. In this case, there is always the closet.

For Ellison, the reality of the American joke called for individuals to be cultures unto themselves, to "always be your best," because one never knows whether the person with whom you are interacting might be a connoisseur of music, fine art, or the Classics. This is Ellison's "Little Man at Chehaw Station," the seemingly homeless, seemingly ignorant man who sits in the stove at the train station but is conversant with the Classics. The American joke, the knowing, comedic wink of the Little Man at Chehaw Station, or even of the serious writer, is not only a reality in the U.S.A.: the joke is equally at home in Brazil, as Alfredo Dias Gomes's *O pagador de promessas* (*Payment as Pledged*) demonstrates (see Dixon, this volume). Here the character Joe wants to fulfill a promise to St Barbara because an African religious figure told him to do so. In contrast to this seemingly illegitimate authority, the priest at the Catholic (Portuguese) church refuses to hear Joe's pleas. Little does this priest, the legitimate embodiment of God on earth, know that Joe's source also has power. The Catholic priest neither knows nor understands the influence of knowledge other than his own. Here is Antigone's dilemma, the choice between state-sanctioned authority and *physis*, natural or divine law, which Gomes presents with characteristic Brazilian social satire and irony. Gomes accomplishes his joke with the subterranean material of Sophocles' *Antigone*. The ostensibly illegitimate power of African knowledge is, to Joe, as the natural law to Antigone, which says that her renegade brother Polyneices is to be buried. The priest is no more in a position to acknowledge a power other than his own knowledge than Creon is in Sophocles' play. Ellison's joke is alive and well in Brazil.

Given the ubiquity of the Classics as a "subterranean thing"—their presence under the ground, as it were, as material as the black soil, whose "enduring value" need not be argued—the archaeological metaphor of Greek drama in the Americas is apt. As with the archaeological dig, attempts to dig up these realities often further disturb the setting. Social constructions of race, class, and gender confront the Americas as if permanent realities, and yet right beneath the surface is the truth of more permanent artifacts, such as the primitivism concomitant with proclaimed modernities. Thus performances of Greek drama in Philadelphia were staged alongside the burlesque renditions of blackface Medeas and lowbrow versions of the high classical forms. To be in an American theater in the nineteenth century was to know Euripides alongside Joe Coon. Rather than an edifice of race (black, white, brown), class (high-culture and low-culture, the classic and the new), and gender, the muddled mess of identity in the Americas disturbs all of these categories. These juxtapositions occurred in the old worlds as well. Blackface farces were staged in London alongside classical theater. But in the Americas, the closeted and those who pass—women, blacks, Latinos, Asians, and so on—take up the Classics as their own at an unprecedented rate.

Within the seemingly surreal context of these experiences in America, we see the struggle for the real in primitivism. In answer to the question, "What is Greek Drama?" at the dawn of Modernism in the United States, we find primitivism, ritual, and a critique of the military and capital, all in the name of gender equity and the search for an American idiom (see Hall, this volume). In this sense, Greek drama frames the material realities of what Toni Morrison might allude to in *Playing in the Dark*, namely the way that dark bodies and non-European genealogies served to reify identities in the Americas. The juxtaposition of the burlesque with the classical within the American context takes on specific form, with particular bodies in distinct spaces. Lost American cultures (Aztec, Inca, and so on) were onstage alongside the Greek textual artifact of a Euripidean tragedy, in the form of sets built from the visual realities of these local spaces and characters. The Taurians of 1915, in this sense, illuminated the parallel encounters in the New World (see Slater, this volume). Blackface comedy in the U.S.A. drew from the presence of black slaves on Southern plantations; and in the mid-nineteenth century, white performers mimicked the African slaves' folklore, gestures, and rhythms, right alongside imported, European theatrical troupes performing Euripides' *Medea*. Here again, black artists take up the form as their own by the late nineteenth century.

American identities were formed in the shadows, beneath the surface, as it were, of genteel, civil society. And shadows, unlike realities, are soon forgotten, or at least sublimated while the haunting presence remains. That Susan Glaspell is a chief influence for Eugene O'Neill and yet forgotten is resonant with so many claims within this volume (see Hall, Lambropoulos, Leontis, this volume). The "migrant muse," in Hall's designation, provides an alternative narrative and continues to inspire from the shadows, routinely undetected. The imprint of Greek drama may be readily detectable in anglophone North American modern drama (from O'Neill through Miller and down to La Bute), but there is equally importantly a primitive, subterranean presence consonant with the discovery of indigenous ruins in the American West, or Machu Picchu in Peru. These primitivisms continue to inspire, along with the African presences, and are simultaneously set against conceptions of the modern, and of the slave body in North, Central, and South Americas. These "primitivisms" reveal that there is in fact no modern, only a thin veneer over the realities that form the Americas. Civilized Europe is a fiction, as is the falsehood of the "primitive" that Hegel, Nietzsche, and others perpetuated. Behind the masks of the Taurians in the 1915 production of *Iphigenia* menacingly lurked the hoods of the Ku Klux Klan (see Slater, this volume). Should there be any surprise, when beneath the surface of modernity is a nascent world where black bodies are mixed up with Greek artifacts daily, where native "civilizations" find parallel archaeologies in the discoveries of Argos and Crete?

Modernity is thus a normativity that belies these subterranean realities. In her article on Greek dance on the American dramatic stage, Susan Manning refers to normativity as a cloak, which overlays the gender trouble of Martha Graham and Nijinsky's Greek dances. The cloak, the myth of normativity, might also metaphorically apply to receptions of Greek drama in Aristotelian terms (see Lodewyck and Monoson, this volume). We can queer Aristotle's *Poetics* because it was never the straight truth in the first place. The overprioritization of Aristotle's *Poetics* as an avenue back to Greek drama led the Brazilian critic and theater director Augusto Boal and August Wilson to different places. In the latter case, we find a Greek drama devoid of Aeschylus, Euripides, or Sophocles, as Rankine shows in his chapter. August Wilson's *Radio Golf* features no Oedipus, Clytemnestra, or Jason, and yet it is Greek drama, given Wilson's deep reading—and perhaps misreading—of the *Poetics*. Wilson wanted to craft an expressly American drama out of the artifact of Aristotle, which he knows to be tantamount to "European drama." At the same time, the renditions of Greek drama were countenanced in the Theater of War before and beyond Aristotle's *Poetics*. Here we see the Greek playwrights not as experts in Aristotelian approaches to drama, but rather as war veterans. As Monoson and Lodewyck reveal, the disturbance of Aristotelian narrative priorities in these twenty-first-century community theater events unearths some truths in Greek drama to which Augusto Boal points us (Boal 1979). There is nothing "white" or anesthetized about Greek drama, as Ancient Greek/Modern Lives, and the Theater of War project demonstrate. The crude realities of war were onstage in ancient Greece, as they are in the U.S.A. in (post)modern times.

When we dig beneath the surface, we disturb the sense of normativity and linearity that the "modern," with its Hegelian direction, brings. Beyond black and white, old and new, is the reality that the artifact was always present; it was never deeply buried. The artifact of Greek drama is present in the Americas because of the seafaring journey across the Atlantic Ocean. The sea journey is the unifying factor for all of *Greek Drama in the Americas*. The sea journey is the reality of black bodies transported across the Atlantic Ocean between the fifteenth and the nineteenth centuries, evident in the Brazilian receptions of Greek drama, whether that of Alfredo Dias Gomes, or Agostinho Olavo (see Dixon, Santos, this volume); and it is there too in Lee Breuer's *The Gospel at Colonus* (see McConnell, this volume). Equally, the sea journey is the reality of instantiations of Greek drama in the nineteenth and early twentieth centuries, when Americans within the United States imported much of their Greek drama through

European theatrical companies (see Pearcy, Macintosh, Bosher and Cox, Davis, Hall, Slater, Day, this volume). The sea journey is central to the "alternative archaeology" which Artemis Leontis charts in the work of Isadora Duncan and Eva Palmer Sikelianos. That is, the transatlantic journey is not only true of the black Atlantic of Paul Gilroy; it is *the* unifying reality of any New World archaeology, equally applicable to Greek drama in the Americas or the reification of "the Americas" for any discursive practice.

In the end, what we have in *Greek Drama in the Americas* is an archaeology that reveals what the Omni-American might look like. *The Omni-Americans* of course refers to the work of the late Albert Murray (d. 2013), who argued that the Negro was the quintessential American because of the way that she or he embodied the struggles for freedom, equality, and democracy which best encapsulate the Americas. We would expand the Omni-Americans to include all of the strivers represented in this volume because, in the end, these strivings incorporate what it might look like to be "American" or to practise Greek drama in the Americas. The Omni-American embodies an archaeology of disturbed layers, Parks's "subterranean thing"; and it includes the atemporality that comes when we disrupt artifacts from their layers of meaning. Murray was referring to the Negro American as the Omni-American, but the appellation can obtain beyond the U.S.A. The Brazilian Medea is no more American than she is Greek, no more black than she is European, in her embodiment of the various practices and relics that make her whole (see Santos, Gemelli, this volume). The sea journey across the Atlantic broke bodies as much as it made the American experience whole, embodied in black, white, brown, and everything in between. Here there is no black, white, brown, high or low culture; there is only meaning newly generated and regenerated.

Notes

1. Douglas Campbell does appear, however, unmasked in the prologue to the film version of April 1956 before metatheatrically masking himself in front of the camera to signal that the play proper is about to begin.
2. The Archive of Performances of Greek and Roman Drama (APGRD) was set up in Oxford in 1996 (see Macintosh (2013) for an overview of the scholarship in the 1980s and 1990s that led to this). Hartigan 1995 was the first systematic study of Greek drama in the American commercial theater, although there was Pluggé 1938 on university drama in America and Colakis 1993 on the 1960s and early 1970s, and the unpublished doctorate of Rogers (1986) on the New York theater. On classical performance reception, see Hall and Harrop 2010.
3. <http://hemisphericinstitute.org/hemi/en/hidvl>. The Institute was set up in 1998 as a collaboration between NYU and the Andrew Mellon Foundation.
4. Majid 2001, quoted in Moraña, Dussel, and Jáuregui 2008: 18 n. 9: "As established and practiced in the Anglo-American academy, postcolonial theory has been largely oblivious to nonwestern articulations of self and identity, and has thus tended to interpellate the non-western cultures it seeks to foreground and defend into a solidly Eurocentric frame of consciousness."

5. Carole Boyce Davies would disagree; her *Caribbean Spaces: Escapes from Twilight Zones* (2013) is, in part, an effort to reinscribe the centrality of the Caribbean in discourses of postcolonialism and the transatlantic.
6. Moraña, Dussel, and Jáuregui 2008: 5–9. However, see also Salvatore 2010.
7. Quayson 2012: 5. The essay is on the Homeric Catalogue and appeared in *JHS* 30: 292–322.
8. The first of the Thirteen Colonies was founded by the British in Virginia in 1607, the last in Georgia in 1733. The American Declaration of Independence was issued by these Thirteen Colonies on July 4, 1776, but the United States was only officially "recognized" in 1783 after seven years of war.

References

Boal, A. (1979), *The Theatre of the Oppressed*. Trans. C. A. and M.-O. L. McBride. New York.
Bradley, M. (ed. 2010), *Classics and Imperialism in the British Empire*. Oxford.
Bratton, J. and G. T. Peterson (2013), "The Internet: History 2.0?," in D. Wiles and C. Dymkowski eds., *The Cambridge Companion to Theatre History*. Oxford, 299–313.
Calvino, I. (1999), *Why Read the Classics?* Trans. M. McLaughlin. New York.
Colakis, M. (1993), *The Classics in the American Theater of the 1960s and Early 1970s*. Lanham, MD.
Cook, W. W. and J. Tatum (2010), *African American Writers and Classical Tradition*. Chicago and London.
Davies, C. B. (2013), *Caribbean Spaces: Escapes from Twilight Zones*. Champaign, IL.
Engle, R. and T. L Miller (eds. 2003), *The American Stage: Social and Economic Issues from the Colonial Period to the Present*. Cambridge.
Foley, H. P. (2012), *Reimagining Greek Tragedy on the American Stage*. Berkeley, Los Angeles, and London.
Goff, B. (ed. 2005), *Classics and Colonialism*. London.
Goff, B. (2013), *"Your Secret Language": Classics in the British Colonies of West Africa*. London.
Goff, B. and M. Simpson (2007), *Crossroads in the Black Aegean: Oedipus, Antigone, and Dramas of the African Diaspora*. Oxford.
Greenwood, E. (2010), *Afro-Greeks: Dialogues between Classics and Anglophone Caribbean Literature in the Twentieth Century*. Oxford.
Guthrie, T. (1960), *A Life in the Theatre*. London.
Hall, E. and S. Harrop (eds. 2010), *Theorising Performance: Greek Drama, Cultural History and Critical Practice*. London.
Hall, E. and F. Macintosh (2005), *Greek Tragedy and the British Theatre 1660–1914*. Oxford.
Hall, E. and P. Vasunia (eds. 2010), *India, Greece, and Rome, 1757–2007*. London.
Hall, E., F. Macintosh, and A. Wrigley (eds. 2004), *Dionysus Since 69: Greek Tragedy at the Dawn of the Third Millennium*. Oxford.
Hardwick, L. and C. Gillespie (eds. 2007), *Classics in Post-Colonial Worlds*. Oxford.
Hartigan, K. (1995), *Greek Tragedy on the American Stage: Ancient Drama in the Commercial Theater, 1882–1994*. Westport, CT, and London.
Kumar, T. V. (2007), ""Postcolonial" Describes You as a Negative': An Interview with Amitav Ghosh," *Interventions: International Journal of Postcolonial Studies* 9.1, 99–105.
Lupher, D. A. (2006), *Romans in a New World: Classical Models in Sixteenth-Century Spanish America*. Ann Arbor.

Macintosh, F. (2009), *Oedipus tyrannus*. Cambridge.

Macintosh, F. (2013), "Museums, Archives and Collecting," in P. E. Easterling ed., *The Cambridge Companion to Greek Tragedy*. Cambridge, 284–323.

McConnell, J. (2013), *Black Odysseys: The Homeric Odyssey in the African Diaspora since 1939*. Oxford.

Majid, A. (2001), "Provincial Acts: The Limits of Postcolonial Theory." Paper presented at the international congress "Postcolonial/Political Correctnesses," Casablanca (April 12–14).

Mbembe, A. (2001), *On the Postcolony*. Berkeley and Los Angeles.

Moraña, M., E. Dussel, and C. A. Jáuregui (eds. 2008), *Coloniality at Large: Latin America and the Postcolonial Debate*. Durham and London.

Parks, S.-L. (2001), *Topdog/Underdog*. New York.

Pluggé, D. E. (1938), *The History of Greek Play Production in American Colleges and Universities 1881–1936*. New York.

Postlewait, T. (2009), *The Cambridge Introduction to Theatre Historiography*. Cambridge.

Quayson, A. (2012), "Introduction: Postcolonial Literature in a Changing Historical Frame," in Quayson ed., *The Cambridge History of Postcolonial Literature*. Cambridge, 1–29.

Rankine, P. D. (2006), *Ulysses in Black: Ralph Ellison, Classicism, and African American Literature*. Madison.

Rankine, P. D. (2013), *Aristotle and Black Drama: A Theater of Civil Disobedience*. Waco, TX.

Ray, S. and H. Schwarz (1995), "Postcolonial Discourse: The Raw and the Cooked," *Ariel: A Review of International English Literature* 26.1, 147–66.

Rogers, S. M. (1986), *Greek Tragedy in the New York Theatre* (unpublished Ph.D. thesis, University of Michigan).

Ronnick, M. V. (ed. 2005), *The Autobiography of William Sanders Scarborough: An American Journey from Slavery to Scholarship*. Detroit.

Salvatore, R. D. (2010), "The Postcolonial in Latin America and the Concept of Coloniality: A Historian's Point of View," *A Contracorriente* 8.1 (Fall), 332–48.

Shenk, J. W. (2002), "Beyond a Black-and-White Lincoln," *New York Times* (April 7).

Stephens, S. A. and P. Vasunia (eds. 2010), *Classics and National Cultures*. Oxford.

Wiles, D. and C. Dymkowski (eds. 2012), *The Cambridge Companion to Theatre History*. Cambridge.

CHAPTER 2

AN ARCHIVAL INTERROGATION

SUSAN CURTIS

It was a Sunday evening in 1908 that a group of prominent African-American artists, writers, and performers in New York City gathered at the home of George W. Walker to found a new social organization. The purpose of this organization was to promote "social intercourse between the representative members of the Negro theatrical profession and to those connected directly or indirectly with art, literature, music, scientific and liberal professions and the patrons of the arts." They determined to build a library for the study of the history of the Negro and "all the worthy achievements and the collection and preservation of all folk-lore, whether that of song or terpsichorean originality, of pictures and bills of the plays in which the Negro has participated."

Theirs was something of a declaration of independence that came at a time when African-American performers, artists, and intellectuals routinely faced discrimination and doubts about their capacity for greatness. Appropriately, in the tradition of Frederick Douglass a little over a half-century earlier, they met on July 5 to found an organization committed to promoting and preserving African-American culture. They called themselves the "Frogs."[1]

George W. Walker, Bert Williams, Lester A. Walton, Bob Cole, and Rosamond Johnson, officers in the new organization, selected the name "Frogs" in honor of Aristophanes' comedy by the same name. It was a name that underscored the significance of the group's aims by allying it to a classical work of unquestioned significance. These men had undoubtedly encountered this famous comedy in high school or college, where in the late nineteenth century, when they were students, the Classics were part of the curriculum.[2] Probably the most memorable dimension of *The Frogs* as a play is the chorus of frogs that accompanies Dionysus' trip to Hades, but a good deal of the humor derives from the relationship between, and the repeated exchanging of identities of, the god and his slave, Xanthias. The two have traveled to Hades in search of Euripides and Aeschylus, long-dead great dramatists, because Dionysus believes that Athens sorely needs an inspiring tragedian. He proposes a contest between Euripides and Aeschylus to determine who shall be returned to the land of the living. The first half of the play shows the slave as the superior of the god, an aspect of *The Frogs* that undoubtedly resonated with the early twentieth-century African-American performers. That Xanthias could successfully "pass" for the god Dionysus no doubt deepened the appeal.

I open this discussion on archives and Greek drama with the story of the "Frogs" in the early twentieth century, because it represents but one small archival trace of Greek drama in the Americas. The organization founded in 1908 lasted for about a quarter of a century, but its most active years were behind it by the time the Great War in Europe erupted in 1914. In other words, aside from a handful of academics who study early twentieth-century African-American theater, few Americans are aware of this organization and its gesture toward the ancient Greek drama. As an example of the influence of classical Greek drama on American theater and culture, the story of the "Frogs" in New York represents the tip of an iceberg of similar archival traces in the Americas—moments when a reference to or an identification with a classical Greek character or drama reflected awareness of the ancients even as it spoke to the later period. The incident reminds us that a full accounting of the impact of Greek drama on the Americas would require endless sifting through private and public documents, including newspapers like the *New York Age*, for evidence. The assembling of these myriad traces would constitute a formidable—though always incomplete—archive.

The entire project—this *Oxford Handbook of Greek Drama in the Americas*—is also something of an archive. It brings together, in the most comprehensive manner to date, what is known of the influence of Greek drama on the theater and culture of the Americas. All chapters here seek to preserve some memory of the presence of Greek drama in the western hemisphere. The handbook is not the first such archive to have been produced. It builds upon a foundation constructed over the past two decades: Karelisa Hartigan's *Greek Tragedy on the American Stage, 1882–1994* (1995), Marianthe Colakis's *The Classics in the American Theater of the 1960s and Early 1970s* (1993), and E. Teresa Choate's *Electra USA* (2009) take up particular moments in the history of the U.S. stage or focus on particular Greek works adapted for American audiences. Each carefully delimits the focus of her work, noting the monumental challenge of the subject. Similarly, Kevin Wetmore, Jr. narrows his focus to the African-American stage in *Black Dionysus* (2003), and Patrice Rankine more recently has explored the resonances of the Classics in African-American literature in *Ulysses in Black* (2006). Helene Foley, in *Reimagining Greek Tragedy on the American Stage* (2012), notes of all this work, including her own important contributions to the field, that "these efforts, supplemented by a growing number of articles and another book in progress that has emerged from a project at Northwestern, have barely scratched the surface on the American side" (Foley 2012: xii).[3]

What interests me as a U.S. cultural historian (and not a Classicist) is not the extent of each of these "archives" of Greek drama in the Americas. Every archival collection, after all, is incomplete—a construction that has come about because someone chose to preserve the thing itself or the memory of a text, a performance, or an adaptation. Rather, what intrigues me is the timing of the creation of these archives. Starting with Colakis, the effort to begin to account for the effect of Greek drama in America is, in scholarly terms, recent—a mere 20 years. Yet the raw materials have been available to be collected, gathered, for centuries.[4] The cultural archons, to use Jacques Derrida's term, it would seem, determined that there was nothing to preserve—or better said, what existed failed the basic test that every archivist must apply to potential collections; it lacked "enduring value."

As these archives were beginning to take shape a scholar of early American literature, John C. Shields, was revisiting the materials that constitute the archive for early American thought and letters. He discovered that alongside the familiar tropes of Judaeo-Christianity—the mythos in which received wisdom believed "true Americanness resides"—a second, equally potent source for the American self could be found in the Graeco-Roman Classics. Writing in 2001, Shields observed, "When the tenets of the Aeneas myth are allowed to come into play along with those of the Adamic myth while reading the works of Early American writers, their writings ... do not display a dependence upon British authors. Rather, they demonstrate an originality and independence whose temper predicts the struggle for political and economic independence. Contrary to conventional wisdom, Early American writers were original thinkers, discovering for themselves an original identity" (Shields 2001: ix, x–xi). Shields, of course, could draw upon the groundbreaking work by Meyer Reinhold that had established a "Greek and Roman heritage in the United States," as well as on Carl J. Richard's exploration of the impact of the Classics on the founding fathers (Reinhold 1984; Richard 1994). All three scholars can be seen as participating in the renewal of consciousness about America's dependence on Classics for a distinctive identity long thought to have sprung primarily from an exceptional Christian/Puritan character.

My aim in this discussion is to interrogate this flurry of archival work (Shields actually calls it "extensive archaeology") that has led to the production of this handbook. I will conduct the inquiry from the vantage of an archival theorist and exclusively from the vantage of the United States. Beginning with Derrida's *Archive Fever: A Freudian Impression* in 1995, a body of scholarship has emerged that calls for a more theoretical consideration of archives. Rather than lifeless storehouses of materials generated by our ancestors—the record, as it were, of the "known world"—archives contain insight in their gaps as well as in their holdings. Carolyn Steedman insists that Derrida has helped us to understand that "if we find nothing, we will find nothing in a place; and then that an absence is not *nothing*, but is rather the space left by what has now gone: how the emptiness indicates how once it was filled and animated."[5] She also contends that the "grammatical tense" of the archive is not the past, but rather the "future perfect," when we will know what it will have meant (Steedman 2002: 7). Like Steedman, Derrida insists that the collectors of materials—the "archons"—"have the power to interpret the archives" (Derrida 1995: 2). The meaning of these assembled traces is not stable and unchanging, but alive with signification for each succeeding generation. Likewise the archives being considered here do not represent the end of the process; they are the beginning of a continuing inquiry into what Greek drama in the United States will have meant for each generation who seeks to know.[6]

When users and keepers of archives speak to one another, they find common ground on the terrain of meaning. That is, each, in turn, imposes meaning upon the detritus that remains from the past. The archivist's first responsibility—after establishing the provenance of a collection and maintaining, as far as feasible, its original order—is to determine what to keep and what to discard. The final assemblage of materials consists of that which the archivist has decided has value for now and into the future. The scholar assigns a different kind of value by seeing the items or the collections as part of a pattern of experience.

In the case of these monographic and encyclopedic archives of Greek drama in the Americas, the question that presses for an answer is: Why have they come into being at the turn of the twenty-first century? Given the long history of classical consciousness in general and of the Greek dramas in particular, why did "archivists" resist the need for a collection earlier? What planted doubts about the enduring significance of Greek culture to American identity?

What I offer in the remaining pages of this chapter is not a definitive answer but a possibility that arises from the kinds of archival traces I introduced at the outset. My analysis begins with Derrida's definition of the archive: "the meaning of 'archive', its only meaning, comes to it from the Greek *arkheion*: initially a house, a domicile, an address, the residence of the superior magistrates, the *archons*, those who commanded. The citizens who thus held and signified political power were considered to possess the right to make or to represent the law . . . The archons are first of all the documents' guardians. . . . Entrusted to such archons, these documents in effect speak the law: they recall the law and call on or impose the law" (Derrida 1995: 2). This definition invites us to think about the relationship between the thing to be preserved and the structure of power within the society in which its merits are determined. As we shall see, some of these dramas and classical tropes were too unruly to be admitted to an arkheion.

Let us return to the story of the "Frogs." Most of what is known about this organization appeared in the *New York Age*, a prominent African-American weekly newspaper published in Harlem. Because of the generally hostile attitude toward African-Americans, white Americans were typically not regular readers of this or any other black paper. Even in the decades after the historic civil rights legislation passed in the 1960s, scholars are not likely to consult it for insight into "American culture," unless theirs is a project that explores some aspect of the African-American experience. As I discovered more than a decade ago, "American theater" has rarely encompassed "African-American theater" in the United States (Curtis 1998: 28–30; 2008: 29–30). Race, then, must be considered as a crucial factor in evaluating what is worth saving.

As it turns out, this particular issue—the effort to found a social and cultural organization by African-American artists, intellectuals, and performers—reached a wider audience because of racism itself. When the would-be Frogs submitted their petition to incorporate to the State Supreme Court of New York, the judge assigned to consider it refused to approve it. As Lester A. Walton put it in the *Age*, "It is doubtful if ever an organization composed of colored citizens attracted such widespread attention as has the Frogs in the past week. Less than seven days ago only a small portion of the New Yorkers and a few outside of the Empire State knew of the existence of such a club, but to-day it is known far and wide, due to the refusal of Justice Goff to approve of the organization's incorporation and the zeal displayed in the daily papers in making known just what they thought of the Judge for adopting such a course." John W. Goff failed to see any connection between "Frogs" and the noble artistic aims of the group. Along with the *Age*, the *New York Tribune*, *New York World*, *New York Evening Sun*, *Brooklyn Eagle*, and *New Haven Register* skewered him for the gap in his cultural awareness. Goff is quoted as having dismissed the petition with these words: "The corporate name is so incongruous that I hesitate to cement the connection between the sublime and the grotesque." As one of the founders of the organization, Walton noted that "it can not be denied that Frogs had something to do with Grecian history, and that is one of the reasons the organization was given the name of Frogs." Obviously, Goff either had missed the reference or chose not to acknowledge it.[7]

One by one, Walton quoted excerpts from the leading New York dailies as they scoffed at Justice Goff's ignorance of the Classics. The *New York World*, for example, recited an "Aesopian fable" about frogs overthrowing "King Log" in favor of "King Stork," a story that "reveals them in a well-organized union which knew how to demand its rights."[8] The writer for the *New Haven Register*, perhaps not surprisingly, lectured readers on Aristophanes and his play, *The Frogs*. But it was Walton's observation in the end that struck at the heart of the matter. "It could be possible that it was not the combination of art and frogs that appeared so incongruous to the learned Judge as it was the combination of the Negro and art."[9]

To have ascended to the New York Supreme Court in 1907, Goff surely was familiar with the Classics, which were foundational to elite education in the nineteenth century.[10] But even after being humiliated in the New York press for his failure to connect frogs to art, Goff did not back down from his original decision. Indeed, Goff ordered his secretary to send the editor of the *Age* a note to express his "surprise" at being called out by "a writer in your paper" for basing his decision on race prejudice. The judge neither apologized nor acknowledged the writer by name.[11] His only concession was to allow the Frogs to submit their petition for a charter to Henry Bischoff, one of his colleagues on the Supreme Court. Justice Bischoff duly approved the petition after a brief hearing.[12]

In this case, Justice Goff represented the law in the State of New York—not merely metaphorically as one of the "archons" of the state. His refusal to approve the formation of an African-American cultural organization that took its name from an ancient Greek play sheds some light on the matter of an archive of Greek drama in America. African-Americans invoking Aristophanes to legitimize their art created an unwelcome association between classical Greek drama and black performance. The early twentieth century apparently was not an auspicious moment for considering the influence of Greek Classics on America's stage and culture, for at least in this instance, the Greeks had inspired African-American pride and agency at a time when many white Americans were working diligently to keep them in a subordinate position.[13] It was at about this time that the great African-American Classicist William S. Scarborough quit attending the annual meetings of the Modern Language Association. As Michele V. Ronnick recently has shown, Scarborough, although a respected Classicist and published author, was often denied admission to the hotels where the MLA meetings were held. Much as Goff questioned the legitimacy of the "Frogs," Scarborough's credentials as a Classicist were also considered suspect.[14]

In this fleeting episode—a drama played out in a courtroom in the summer of 1908 over the right to name an organization after a play by Aristophanes and recorded in an African-American weekly newspaper—one can see at least one possible reason for repressing America's relationship with classic Greek drama. But even this possibility is shrouded in mystery, as are many questions of the archive. Perhaps it was simply the audacity of African-American performers to form a group to promote their artistic and intellectual endeavors that put off Judge Goff—in other words, the connection with Aristophanes had nothing to do with his decision. But perhaps it was, in fact, the dramatist's comedy itself, which exposed both the foibles of the god and the capacity of the slave, that raised a red flag for a turn-of-the-century keeper of the law and social order. Regardless of the specific reasons—reasons that are not fully articulated in the extant sources—this archival trace alerts us to the relationship between the prevailing assumptions of an era and what is sanctioned to be known and preserved as valuable knowledge.

Race relations did not provide the only reasons for suppressing awareness of the influence of Greek drama on America. As many Classicists and theater scholars have noted, the worldview and general outlook of the Greeks diverged considerably from the American. Some have characterized the divergence in terms of pessimism (Greek) versus optimism (American). And others have argued that the reception of Greek plays depended upon the socio-political moment at which they were staged (Foley 2012: 1; Hartigan 1995: 147). I have no grounds for disputing these interpretations. I would, however, return to my suggestion that the uses to which Greek dramas were put might account for the resistance to preserving their memory.

Another earlier episode—outside of the stage—indicates another kind of unruliness sparked by the Classics. In 1845, Margaret Fuller published *Woman in the Nineteenth Century* as a "broader protest . . . made in behalf of woman." In the midst of increasing clangor for the abolition of slavery and the extension of equal rights and citizenship for bondsmen, Fuller penned an extraordinary and erudite treatise exposing the faulty logic of inequality between the sexes. In the opening pages, she invokes the ancients to build a foundation for her case: "[T]he time is come when Eurydice is to call for an Orpheus, rather than Orpheus for Eurydice: that the idea of Man, however imperfectly brought out, has been far more than that of Woman, that she, the other half of the same thought, the other chamber of the heart of life, needs now to take her turn in the full pulsation and that improvement in the daughters will best aid in the reformation of the sons of this age."[15]

Margaret Fuller was in a position to make this argument on behalf of her sisters in America because of her own extraordinary education. Her father, Timothy Fuller, oversaw his first child's education as if she had been a son. He introduced her to the

Classics, to Latin, and several modern languages at a very young age. His instruction far surpassed what was available to most girls in the early nineteenth century. Margaret's teen years at the School for Young Ladies at Groton, Massachusetts, were marked by frustration and unhappiness at the uninteresting and uninspiring lessons; when Fuller returned to the family home at the age of 16, she immersed herself once again in the Classics and in contemporary French, German, and Italian literature. In the mid-1830s, she became part of the lively conversations in Concord with Ralph Waldo Emerson presiding and thus became associated with the intellectuals of the Transcendentalist's circle. Emerson appointed her editor of *The Dial*, an outlet for their work, and in that position, Fuller engaged with some of the most challenging and learned writing produced in the early nineteenth century.[16]

Fuller's reading of the Classics fueled her dissatisfaction with the lot of women in the nineteenth-century United States. She drew female friends into conversation about their status as women, helping to mobilize at least some in the middle class to push for greater autonomy. In 1843, she published an essay entitled "The Great Lawsuit: Man versus Men, Woman versus Women," in *The Dial*. Two years later she published a much expanded version of the essay as *Woman in the Nineteenth Century*.

Woman in the Nineteenth Century is a remarkable achievement in many respects, not the least of which is that Fuller was so fully versed in the Classics. She recognized that she had been "fortunate" to have been educated by her father, and it was a conscious decision to put this learning on display. Early in the volume, she insists that her education had helped her to "depend on myself," noting that "This self-dependence, which was honored in me, is deprecated as a fault in most women. They are taught to learn their rule from without, not to unfold it from within." Fuller also identified role models she had derived from the ancient Greeks and Romans: Ceres, Proserpine, Diana, Minerva, and Vesta—"each," she insisted, "was self-sufficing" (Fuller 1999: 17, 24).

Woman in the Nineteenth Century is an intellectual tour-de-force. Fuller enlists the modern European Romantics as well as the ancient Greeks in the defense of her demand for full equality for women. She moves effortlessly from Ovid's *Metamorphoses* to a line from Schiller's *Jungfrau von Orleans* to Manzoni on the law—in just the first ten pages. She displays immediately her extraordinarily broad exposure to the Classics and to the literary *avant garde* of the eighteenth and nineteenth centuries. It is clear that Fuller found inspiration in George Sand, Mary Wollstonecraft, Lord Byron, and Wolfgang von Goethe, of the last of whose poems Fuller was an early English translator. Her eager identification with their ideas undoubtedly drew fire from their critics in the United States. But on the whole, the strongest examples came from ancient Greece. Fuller distinguishes Greek from Roman culture, arguing that the former was "deep-eyed" and "deep-discerning" compared to "ruder Rome," and she indicates that America's founders had followed Rome. Fuller credits Xenophon with catching "glimpses of the ideal woman," and she gestures throughout to female figures from classical mythology, drama, poetry, and history to build her argument. Near the end of a lengthy passage addressed directly to the women of America, Fuller concludes with a "wish to see men and women capable of such relations as are depicted by Landor in his Pericles and Aspasia, where grace is the natural garb of strength, and the affections are calm, because deep" (Fuller 1999: 30, 96).

Following the formal text, Fuller added a series of appendices, the longest of which is entitled "Euripides. Sophocles." In it, she cries out: "Iphigenia! Antigone! You were worthy to live! *We* are fallen on evil times my sisters! Our feelings have been checked; our thoughts questioned; our forms dwarfed and defaced by a bad nurture. Yet hearts, like yours, are in our breasts, living, if unawakened; and our minds are capable of the same resolves" (Fuller 1999: 113). Near the end of the appendix, Fuller explains why she has catalogued the inspiring women from Greek drama and mythology. "Certainly the Greeks knew more of real home intercourse, and more of woman than the Americans. It is in vain to tell me of outward observances. The poets, the sculptors always tell the truth. In proportion as a nation is refined, women must have an ascendancy, it is the law of nature" (Fuller 1999: 124). Although not the final passage of the work, this reference to Greeks struck a nerve with at least some reviewers.

Woman in the Nineteenth Century beckons us back to a moment when American social values were in flux and as a consequence when the ancient Greek works were refracted through various competing critical lenses. Not surprisingly, Lydia Maria Child, a writer and advocate for women's rights, found Fuller's book a positive and inspiring contribution and Fuller herself "a woman of more powerful intellect, comprehensive thought, and thorough education than any other American authoress, with whose productions I am acquainted."[17] Child was at the center of the woman's rights movement of the 1840s and supported the Seneca Falls Convention in 1848, where the *Declaration of Sentiments* articulated women's claim for equality and independence in the terms of the American Declaration of Independence of 1776. Some scholars claim that Fuller's book was the most important inspiration for the gathering in Seneca Falls, even though at the time of that meeting, Fuller was in Italy as a foreign correspondent for the *New York Tribune*.

Horace Greeley, Fuller's editor at the *Tribune*, not surprisingly also supported her work with a positive review of *Woman in the Nineteenth Century*. Greeley had hired Fuller in 1844 to serve as the literary editor of the paper, when *The Dial* ceased publication (Capper 2007: 13). But after Fuller's untimely death in 1850, he criticized her for her independence and refusal to conform to womanly ideals of the day: "If I had attempted to say that," he wrote, "I should have somehow blundered out that noble and great as she was, a good husband and two or three bouncing babies would have emancipated her from a deal of cant and nonsense" (Greeley 1896: 176). Presumably some of the "cant and nonsense" to which he refers was articulated in *Woman in the Nineteenth Century*, and in point of fact Greeley was expressing a more honest response to Fuller and her ideas later than at the time of publication.

Another friendly reviewer, Edgar Allan Poe, also recognized that Fuller's magisterial work challenged conventions: "Woman in the Nineteenth Century," he writes in his review for *Godey's Ladies Book*, "is a book which few women in the country could have written, and no woman in the country would have published, with the exception of Miss Fuller. In the way of independence, of unmitigated radicalism, it is one of the 'Curiosities of American Literature.'" Though he defended Fuller's ideas as not being "too bold ... too novel, too startling, or too dangerous in their consequences," Poe nevertheless asserted that the chief flaw of *Woman in the Nineteenth Century* is that most women were *not* like Fuller (Poe 1846: 72–8).

For the purpose of this chapter, it is essential to note the critiques offered by those who utterly dismissed the work, for in these writings we find most clearly the resistance to classical influence on American culture. More than one critic rejected Fuller's adoration of Minerva as suitable feminine ideal for American women. The chief complaint was that Minerva was a virgin. Charles Briggs was both acerbic and direct: "Woman is nothing but as a wife. How, then, can she truly represent the female character who has never filled it? No woman can be a true woman, who has not been a wife and a mother." In Part Two of his review he noted acidly that Fuller's book lacked distinctiveness: "We have too much of the Scandinavian mythology and the Greek tragedy" (Briggs 1845: 131, 145). Frederic Dan Huntington in a fairly supportive review in the *Christian Examiner* nevertheless identified one of the key flaws to be Fuller's over-reliance on classical references. He writes: "Classical characters, and references to mythological fables, are introduced with a frequency which the best taste would hardly sanction."[18]

No critic, however, struck more directly at the unwholesome influence of the ancients than Orestes Brownson (despite his own first name derived from Greek mythology). He opens his review by taking a swipe at Fuller's affiliation with Transcendentalism, an intellectual movement that Brownson had renounced two years before. He called Fuller the "chieftainess" of the "sect," and comparing her to Theodore Parker, Brownson saw Parker as having "more of the German in his taste, she (Fuller) more of the Grecian." Reading more like a screed than a literary review, Brownson's essay on *Woman in the Nineteenth Century* sounded a cranky refrain uttered by many opponents of women's rights: "What is the lady driving at? What does she want?" Fuller's demand for full equality for women, he equated with the "ravings" of a delirious woman.

Two passages from Brownson's review stand out. About halfway through the essay Brownson huffs, "No doubt, there are evils enough to redress, but we do not think the insane clamor for 'woman's rights,' for 'woman's equality,' 'woman's liberation,' and all this, will do much to redress them. Woman is no more deprived of her rights than a man is of his, and no more enslaved." In one sentence, Brownson dismisses Fuller's work as a form of insanity and raises an issue that rocked the United States in 1845—enslavement. As the nation wrestled with its collective conscience over the institution of chattel slavery, the last thing Brownson wanted was more social turmoil between men and women. The language of liberation apparently was infectious.

Here was the fundamental problem for Brownson: recently converted to Catholicism, God, he believed, had bestowed on men dominion over women, and the call for equality simply ignored Christian truth:

> Miss Fuller would have all offices, professions, callings, pursuits thrown open to woman as to man; and seems to think that the lost eden (sic) will not be recovered till the petticoat carries it over the breeches. She is quite sure the ancient heathens understood the matter better than we do. They had a juster appreciation of the

dignity of woman. Their principal deities were goddesses, and women ministered in the fane, and gave the responses of the oracles. She is greatly taken with Isis, Sita, Egyptian Sphinx, Ceres, Proserpine. (Brownson 1845: 245)

Brownson goes on to dismiss the lot by linking "the ancient heathen deities" with "obscene rites and frightful orgies," "filthy rites and shameful practices" (Brownson 1845: 57). Although a Catholic in a militantly Protestant America, Brownson and his Christian recoiling from classical ("heathen") culture helps us see why Americans in the nineteenth century would have denied the significance of this archive. As Caroline Winterer recently has demonstrated, classical Greek works were part of the curriculum in elite academies and schools in the antebellum United States. As Shields, Reinhold, Richard, Ronnick, and Winterer have demonstrated, the Classics were an indispensable part of the learning of the United States' Founding Fathers, intellectuals, statesmen, and educated elite—all ideally white and male. It would not be surprising to discover student performances of Greek plays in those years, although they do not appear to have become regularly part of the curriculum until after 1880 (Pluggé 1938). The response to *Woman in the Nineteenth Century* helps to explain why there was no will to stage, let alone assemble and preserve, any such traces of ancient Greece in American culture. The chain of connections from classical Greece to women's rights and equality ended, as men like Briggs, Greeley, and Brownson saw it, in a fundamental challenge to the authority of the archon and a need to revise the law.

Attending to these two episodes—the fight over the "Frogs" and the reception of Fuller's feminist tract *Woman in the Nineteenth Century*—shines a light on the problems posed by creating an archive of the Classics in American culture. Archivists preserve that which holds the promise of "enduring value," but in these two moments in American history, the caretakers of the law and of the status quo fervently hoped that the demands for racial and gender equality would *not* endure. By diminishing or marginalizing or seeking to quash these two expressions of egalitarianism derived from a reading of Greek drama, the "archons" elected to ignore the record that could be preserved.

From an archivist's perspective the final question to be addressed is this: Why was the end of the twentieth century and beginning of the twenty-first the right moment to preserve the memory of Greek drama in the Americas? From the perspective of Europe, one answer would be the rise of Classical Reception Studies within the discipline of Classics (Macintosh 2013: 273–7). Another broader answer might be that this moment coincided with the "archival turn" itself—the moment in the mid-1990s when scholars began to think critically and theoretically about the nature and construction of the archives.[19] But beneath that archival impulse lies another powerful drive that, I would argue, called the "archival turn" into being—the quest for a multicultural heritage. Critics, of course, dubbed this a time of "culture wars" or an era marked by "political correctness." But for others, the desire to tell a richer and different story about America required strategies for reading conventional archives, the construction of new archives, and new theoretical tools for documenting that experience which had been marginalized for centuries.

Coincidental, then, with works theorizing the archives and the collecting of materials related to ancient Greek drama in the Americas came the emergence of a body of work seeking to create a new narrative for multicultural America. This spate of scholarship beginning in the early 1990s rejected the idea that focusing on racial or ethnic minorities only fragmented a clear picture of America.[20] These works sought to break with the long-established narrative arc of American progress. John Demos, for example, followed the archival trail of Eunice Williams, who was taken captive by Native Americans during an early eighteenth-century raid on Deerfield, Massachusetts, and who chose to remain with her captors. He subtitled his work, "A Family Story from Early America," and it was a story that refused to focus only on Euro-American ties and timelines. Priscilla Wald read between the lines of canonical American works—laws, Supreme Court decisions, presidential addresses, and the like—to expose the ways that people were marginalized by racial, gender, and ethnic difference. She also reintroduced American readers to the non-canonical authors who had sought to write themselves into existence. Like Demos, Wald used her subtitle, "Cultural Anxiety and Narrative Form," to advance a new understanding of America. Ronald Takaki brought out *A Different Mirror* at this time in the hope of writing "A History of Multicultural America." In short, recognizing that a diverse, multiracial and multicultural society existed in the 1990s, these authors and many others also saw the need for a history that made sense of the society the United States had always been (Demos 1995; Takaki 1993; Wald 1995).

New narratives require new archives. Through the archivist's lens, one can see the *Oxford Handbook of Greek Drama in the Americas* as yet another archive that permits the exploration of a shaping influence that up to this point has been less than fully explored. The chapters in this volume promise to continue the work of national and hemispheric self-discovery. As Benedict Anderson noted three decades ago, in the new world of the Americas, nationalism as a project developed through print culture in "creole societies." Shared ideals and destiny, articulated in print media, called forth a willingness to imagine oneself as part of a single community—belonging to the nation in spite of the differences that potentially divided individuals from one another. The archival turn promises to restore the experiences and expressions that had to be suppressed in the name of the "Imagined Community" (Anderson 1983). The Americas' relationship with ancient Greece is part of that recovery.

Notes

1. "Well Known Performers Organize the 'Frogs,'" *New York Age* (July 9, 1908), 6, col. 2; see also Frederick Douglass's speech entitled "What to the Slave is the Fourth of July," delivered on July 5, 1852; and Colaiaco (2007). It may well be significant that the first serious attempt at establishing "national" theater history with Max Hermann's series of lectures in Berlin (which laid the foundations for the Theaterwissenschaft Institut in Berlin in 1923) had only recently taken place in 1900. See Macintosh 2013: 270–1.
2. I base this assumption on the curriculum available to Lester A. Walton in St. Louis in the 1890s. Sumner High School, the first high school opened for African-Americans west of the Mississippi River, featured classes in Latin and Greek, taught by highly educated African-American instructors. For the basic curriculum from the 1890s, see *Course of Study, St. Louis Normal and High School, July 1895* (n.p., 1895) at St. Louis Public Schools

Record Center/Archives, St. Louis, MO; for students' memories of the Classicists at Sumner, see *Down Memory Lane* (St. Louis: St. Louis Public Library, 1976), 30.
3. The book in progress referred to here is, of course, this very volume, *The Oxford Handbook of Greek Drama in the Americas*.
4. Macintosh (2013: 274–5) similarly observes that the founding of the international Archive of Performances of Greek and Roman Drama (APGRD) at the University of Oxford in 1996 was "belated." She notes as well that even though many theater professionals had been keeping their own archives of these performances, there was "no one obvious centre for such a collection" until late in the twentieth century.
5. Steedman 2002: 11. See also Derrida 1995.
6. This intervention from a U.S. perspective stands as an invitation to other scholars of nations and regions in the Americas to interrogate this archive from their particular vantages.
7. Lester A. Walton, "The Frogs," *New York Age*, August 6, 1908, 6, col. 1.
8. Walton, "The Frogs," col. 1.
9. Walton, "The Frogs," col. 2.
10. According to *The Medico-Legal Journal* 25 (1907), 26, John W. Goff's appointment to the New York State Supreme Court took effect on January 1, 1907.
11. Lester A. Walton, "Judge Goff Heard From," *New York Age*, August 13, 1908, 6, col. 1.
12. "Frogs Are Incorporated," *New York Age*, August 20, 1908, 6, col. 3.
13. African Americans were not alone in finding psychological sustenance from the ancient Greeks. Goff and Simpson (2008) argue that Greek dramas historically have resonated with African-descended people in postcolonial settings.
14. Ronnick 2000: 1791. For additional insight into Scarborough and the politicization of the Classics, see Ronnick 2006.
15. Fuller 1999: 8. This edition is an unabridged, slightly corrected republication of the original work published in 1845 by Greeley and McElrath, New York.
16. For this brief summary of Fuller's youth, I rely on Capper 1992.
17. Quoted in Wayne 2007: 177.
18. The review originally appeared in the *Christian Examiner* 38 (May 1845), 416–17, and can be found in Fuller 1999: 221–2.
19. Works that contributed significantly to the emergence of a focus on archives include Derrida 1995, Stoler 2010, Baker 2002, and Cox 2003.
20. For one important statement of the critical position, see Bender 1986.

References

Anderson, B. (1983), *Imagined Communities: Reflections on the Origins and Spread of Nationalism*. London.
Baker, N. (2002), *Double Fold: Libraries and the Assault on Paper*. New York.
Bender, T. (1986), "Wholes and Parts: The Need for Synthesis in American History," *Journal of American History* 73 (June), 120–36.
Burton, A. (ed. 2006), *Archive Stories: Facts, Fictions and the Writing of History*. Durham.
Briggs, C. F. (1845), "Review of *Woman in the Nineteenth Century*," *Broadway Journal* 1 (March), 131–45.
Brownson, O. (1845), "Miss Fuller and Reformers," *Brownson's Quarterly Review* (April), 245–57.
Capper, C. (1992), *Margaret Fuller: An American Romantic Life, The Private Years*. New York and Oxford.

Capper, C. (2007), "Getting from Here to There," in C. Capper and C. Giorcelli eds., *Margaret Fuller: Transatlantic Crossings in a Revolutionary Age*. Madison, NJ.
Choate, E. T. (2009), *Electra USA*. Madison, NJ.
Colaiaco, J. A. (2007), *Frederick Douglass and the Fourth of July*. New York.
Colakis, M. (1993), *The Classics in the American Theater of the 1960s and Early 1970s*. Lanham, MD.
Cox, R. (2003), *No Innocent Deposits: Forming Archives by Rethinking Appraisal*. Lanham, MD.
Curtis, S. (1998), *The First Black Actors on the Great White Way*. Columbia, MO.
Curtis, S. (2008), *Colored Memories: A Biographer's Quest for the Elusive Lester A. Walton*. Columbia, MO.
Demos, J. (1995), *The Unredeemed Captive: A Family Story from Early America*. New York.
Derrida, J. (1995), *Archive Fever: A Freudian Impression*. Chicago.
Foley, H. P. (2012), *Reimagining Greek Tragedy on the American Stage*. Berkeley, Los Angeles, and London.
Fuller, M. (1999), *Woman in the Nineteenth Century*. Mineola, NY.
Goff, B. and M. Simpson (2008), *Crossroads in the Black Aegean: Oedipus, Antigone, and Dramas of the African Diaspora*. Oxford and New York.
Greeley, H. (1896), *Recollections of a Busy Life*. New York.
Hartigan, K. V. (1995), *Greek Tragedy on the American Stage: Ancient Drama in the Commercial Theater, 1882-1994*. Westport, CT, and London.
Macintosh, F. (2013), "Museums, Archives, Collecting," in D. Wiles and C. Dymkowski eds., *The Cambridge Companion to Theatre History*. Cambridge, 267-80.
Pluggé, D. E. (1938), *A History of Greek Play Production in American Colleges, 1881-1936*. New York.
Poe, E. A. (1846), "The Literati of New York—No. IV," *Godey's Lady's Book* (August), 72-8.
Rankine, P. (2006), *Ulysses in Black: Ralph Ellison, Classicism, and African American Literature*. Madison, NJ.
Reinhold, M. (1984), *Classica Americana: The Greek and Roman Heritage in the United States*. Detroit.
Richard, C. J. (1994), *The Founders and the Classics: Greece, Rome, and the American Enlightenment*. Cambridge, MA.
Ronnick, M. V. (2000), "William Sanders Scarborough: The First African American Member of the Modern Language Association," *PMLA* 115.7, 1791.
Ronnick, M. V. (2006), "William Sanders Scarborough and the Politics of Classical Education," in M. Meckler ed., *Classical Antiquity and the Politics of America: From George Washington to George W. Bush*. Waco, TX.
Shields, J. C. (2001), *The American Aeneas: Classical Origins of the American Self*. Knoxville, TN.
Steedman, C. (2002), *Dust: The Archive and Cultural History*. New Brunswick, NJ.
Stoler, A. L. (2010), *Along the Archival Grain: Epistemic Anxieties and Colonial Common Sense*. Princeton.
Takaki, R. (1993), *A Different Mirror: A History of Multicultural America*. Boston.
Wald, P. (1995), *Constituting Americans: Cultural Anxiety and Narrative Form*. Durham, NC.
Wayne, T. K. (2007), *Women's Roles in Nineteenth-Century America*. Westport, CT.
Wetmore, K. Jr. (2003), *Black Dionysus: Greek Tragedy and the African American Theater*. Jefferson, NC.
Winterer, C. (2002), *The Culture of Classicism: Ancient Greece and Rome in American Intellectual Life, 1780-1910*. Baltimore.

CHAPTER 3

NEW WORLDS, OLD DREAMS?

Postcolonial Theory and Reception of Greek Drama

BARBARA GOFF AND MICHAEL SIMPSON

Varieties of the Postcolonial

Classical reception in the contemporary world is almost necessarily reception within a "postcolonial" context. Since the conditions of the nineteenth century, and most of the twentieth, were largely determined by the activities of the European empires as they made unprecedented inroads into other societies, most modern cultures bear the imprints of the postcolonial condition. This is the case whether we understand the "post" as largely chronological or as with the more ideological force of resistance and critique. Similarly, societies are subject to the postcolonial condition whether they were originally colonizing or colonized; in either situation, the experience of empire is one of the major determinants of their culture and consequently, in the field of classical reception, of the ways in which they approach Greek drama.[1]

In the case of the Americas, however, the analysis is complicated by at least two factors. The first stems from the fact that "the Americas" does not designate just one society; several different societies share the continents, with histories that are "postcolonial" in notably different ways. The recourse to Greek drama and its receptions is correspondingly varied. While the present volume ranges impressively among different American cultures, it showcases, for instance, few engagements with ancient drama by indigenous peoples of the Americas.[2] We say this not in a spirit of exhausting inclusivity but to underline the fact that the devastating experiences suffered by many indigenous peoples in their encounters with European colonizers may have rendered engagements with Greek drama by these writers less frequent—or, as yet, less examined by classical reception scholars—than those by writers in other American communities. There are a range of situations which may be classed as "postcolonial," in the Americas as elsewhere, and classical drama will play very different roles within them. The societies which do feature in the present volume as engaging with Greek drama range from the early white settler cultures of the U.S.A. to the cultures of Latin America and the Caribbean, all of which are arguably marked with the signs of different European empires.

This complication, of the significances of the term "postcolonial," which we shall shortly explore at greater length, is accompanied by a second one, which is that the Americas, particularly perhaps the U.S.A., have long been discussed under the heading of "American exceptionalism." This position, recognizable as a strand of "American studies," holds that the history of the American continents is not comparable to other histories, except in very minor ways, because it is marked by unparalleled events like the "first contact" and the institution of African slavery. The notion that America (which in this context often implicitly stands for the U.S.A. alone) is an exception helped to make American studies "remarkably insular" and resistant to theories of western imperialism and colonialism (Schueller 2004: 162). Even when the impulse was not "insular," some commentators questioned whether theories of postcoloniality, developed first to take account of cultures in, for instance, the Indian sub-continent, were properly equipped to address the very different contours of the Americas. Jorge Klor de Alva (1995) questions whether three centuries of Latin American experience, from 1492 onward, could usefully be summed up in this way, and Bauer and Mazzotti argue that since postcolonial theory "emerged from the specific historical and ideological context of the Second British Empire in Asia and Africa" it has only limited usefulness for scholarship on early America (Bauer and Mazzotti 2009: 10). These positions suggest a desire to discriminate carefully among different varieties of imperial subjection, and as we shall see, much recent postcolonial analysis has focused on the need to avoid totalizing gestures and to respect specificities. But we should also bear in mind the strong connection that Robert Stam and Ella Shohat make between postcolonial analysis and the Americas: "If postcolonial theory did not come from America (that is, the United States), it did partially come from the Americas (that is, from the resistant thought of indigenous peoples and Afro-diasporic 'minorities' in the Americas)" (Stam and Shohat 2012: 380). Here, the reflection on their subjugated condition by both indigenous peoples and imported African-Americans is seen as instrumental in forging the tools of postcolonial analysis.

In the contemporary context, however, "postcolonial," when used of the U.S.A., often has the extra connotation of "neo-colonial." The U.S.A. is criticized for behaving in ways similar to the European empires of the colonial period, using military force to acquire territory and resources, and to impose culture, with regards to neighboring states in the past but also more recently in overseas locations like the Middle East. The contemporary context also troubles, and extends, the significance of "postcolonialism" with an emphasis on "globalization," which implicitly offers to flatten the potential political charge of the postcolonial by embracing all cultures in an unavoidable commercial and financial nexus. In what follows we shall try to explore both the various possibilities and liabilities of postcolonial analysis insofar as they are germane to the projects of the current volume. The topic is potentially huge and our treatment of it necessarily introductory, but we hope to point to the salient features of the contemporary critical context.

One of the liabilities is that it is not always clear what exactly is designated by "the postcolonial" and related terms. Within academic discourse on postcolonialism, which is what chiefly concerns us here, there has been a widely recognized shift, over the last few decades, from a focus on economic and political structures to the analysis of cultural and discursive modes. This shift has been accompanied by a critique which holds that postcolonialism, as an academic enterprise, has lost polemic edge or bite and has subsided into an abstractly theoretical discipline which is ineffective in countering the actual consequences of European activity in areas such as Africa (Olaniyan 2005). A related critique claims that "postcolonial" cannot usefully name anything, because it necessarily slips among several different categories of history and culture (Parry 1997). This is the weakness of the overall observation with which we began this chapter, that the postcolonial describes the experience of most of the globe. Despite these critiques, which deserve much more attention than we can afford in this context, we shall suggest that "postcolonial" can still be a productive way in which to view the Americas' engagement with Greek drama, precisely because it brings with it attention to history, politics, and culture. Only such a ramified category could attempt to approach such an extensive topic. In the context of receptions of Greek drama, postcolonial analysis can combine an attention to the strict binaries of hierarchical power, dominance, and exploitation, which typically structure the colonial society and have lasting repercussions for the social formations that succeed it, with the issues of cultural transmission, hybridity, multiple and migratory identity, and voice, which tend to undermine binaries and question oversimplified divisions. Under both these aspects Greek drama has often proved a sensitive instrument with which to probe the experience of the Americas.

VARIETIES OF THE AMERICAS

If we think of the early settler societies in the Americas, we can see that they can be described as "postcolonial" in at least two different ways. Britain, France, Holland, and Spain colonized the continents with settlers of European descent, who immediately laid waste to the indigenous populations; subsequent inhabitants may thus be considered "postcolonial" in that both sides emerge from a situation of colonial violence and oppression. The postcolonial on this model implicitly extends back far beyond the independence movements of the mid-twentieth century. Peter Hulme notes that early settler society was "postcolonial" in that "the United States continued to colonize North America, completing the genocide of the Native population begun by the Spanish and British" (Hulme 1995: 122). Concerned with South rather than North America, Fernando Coronil called for "a view of colonialism as starting from the fifteenth century [which] would offer a different understanding of modern colonialism and colonial modernity" while Stam and Shohat insist that "the colonial debates go back to the Reconquista and the Conquista" (Coronil in Yaeger 2007: 637; Stam and Shohat 2012: 379). Having said that, some of the crucial works that emerge in the 1990s, such as King 2000 and Singh and Schmidt 2000, do not address the early period extensively, and so do not investigate the postcolonial identity of the early settler communities.

Such communities have also been understood as "postcolonial" in that they experienced a form of "cultural cringe" *vis-à-vis* the European cultures. People of European descent in the Americas might variously celebrate their European identities, or resist them in favor of a newly developing "American" identity, but in either case their identity was defined by relation to the European colonizers. In this vein, in the particular case of the U.S.A., Ashcroft, Griffiths, and Tiffin account it the first postcolonial society, insofar as it tries to develop a "national" literature against considerable pressure from Europe: "In many ways the American experience and its attempts to produce a new kind of literature can be seen to be the model for all later post-colonial writing" (Ashcroft, Griffiths, and Tiffin 1989: 16). Many commentators were quick to question this identification on a variety of grounds, and many would suggest further that the multiple forms of power wielded by the U.S.A. require more nuanced description. Jenny Sharpe writes that "the term *postcolonial* does not fully capture the history of a white settler colony that appropriated land from Native Americans, incorporated parts of Mexico, and imported slaves and indentured labor from Africa and Asia" (Sharpe 2000: 106). White citizens of the early U.S.A. may have been "postcolonial" with respect to Europe, but it was hardly their only defining power relation; as Schueller emphasizes: "Postcolonial readings of settler American literature . . . cannot ignore the simultaneous brutality of US colonization" (Schueller 2004: 164).

Early settler societies throughout the Americas may thus be considered as "postcolonial" in divergent ways. If we examine these cultures, we cannot necessarily identify extensive reception of Greek drama, but we can see that colonizers were assisted in assuming superiority to the indigenous populations whom they encountered by the long European tradition of written literature and history. Whether British, Dutch, French, or Spanish, the colonizers saw themselves as going into virgin nature and making it over into culture, entitled to ride roughshod over indigenous societies which were not recognizably literate. Within this cultural struggle, to be able to claim some kind of descent from classical Europe was to claim participation in the highest activities of humanity—a useful move when the colonizers were both fighting among themselves, as representatives of different nations, and unleashing epochal violence against indigenous people. As an acknowledged high point of European culture, Greek drama also became valuable over time to those non-European colonized who needed to transform the European inheritance to their own ends (see, for example, Barrenechea, this volume). This centrality of the classical inheritance is recognized by one of the first studies of postcolonial drama, which features a chapter on ancient Greek sources as well as on Shakespeare (Gilbert and Tompkins 1996).

Recent work on neo-Latin in Mexico shows other ways in which early settlers drew on the classical tradition to underpin claims of European superiority, and suggests the complications that ensued (Laird 2003, 2006). Struggles over the command of Latin could be part of the hostile traffic between Spanish colonizers and indigenes, especially when the aptitude of Native Americans for learning Latin caused consternation.[3] But the tradition culminates in the eighteenth-century Latin epic *Rusticatio Mexicana*, which makes a claim for the equality of the New World with the ancient, and sometimes its superiority (Laird 2006). Although this material does not include Greek drama, it demonstrates the range of possible significances wielded by the classical tradition in the Americas.

We cannot readily trace a history of Greek drama in the Americas until the nineteenth century. Much of the earlier, eighteenth-century engagement with classical antiquity, which we can reconstruct most easily for the U.S.A., seems to have been driven by political rather than literary needs. Scholars like Ward Briggs (2007) and Margaret Malamud (2010, 2011), following Meyer Reinhold, have shown how the classical tradition was invoked to signify civic virtue, but might also be rejected because of its connections with monarchical Europe. The elite of the new republic drew on classical tropes to help them in their nation-building, assisted by the notion of classical antiquity as a possession of the Enlightenment and thus available for deployment in different contexts where reason and order were at stake. Classical languages and texts held an important place in education, although they also came under question as being impractical and suited to neither of the republic's characteristic pursuits of agriculture and commerce (Briggs 2007).

In the nineteenth century, neoclassical architecture transformed the American built environment, again in the service of a political agenda: "The utilization of the architectural language of Rome ... created a deeply satisfying illusion of imperial grandeur, civic order, prosperity, and authority" (Malamud 2010: 259). Drama also began to gain a foothold. The first performance of a Greek drama in the United States is generally considered to be the *Oedipus Tyrannus* produced at Harvard in 1881. The run lasted a week and an estimated 6,000 people saw the play (Norman 1882); there were other performances in schools and at Randolph Macon Women's College (Pluggé 1938). As the essays in this volume show, there were probably more nineteenth-century performances and productions of Greek drama than scholars previously realized. In these contexts, there is only very occasional anxiety that the symbols of classical antiquity signify the superiority of European culture over American. The reception of classical antiquity appears to have been largely untroubled by the kinds of cultural struggle for identity and voice that are so often characteristic of the postcolonial predicament, and the tradition was welcomed as helping rather than hindering the production of an American identity.

But these engagements with classical antiquity, on the part of a culture which is now among the supreme global powers, are hardly the kinds of things that are routinely named postcolonial. It is when the subaltern populations of the Americas—women, the poor and working class, but especially those of non-European descent—get hold of Greek drama that it becomes more relevant to invoke postcolonial analysis.[4] As Schueller observes: "Once we begin to think of Native Americans, Mexican Americans, African-Americans, and Asian Americans as part of the subjects of America, the questions raised by a postcolonial American studies rapidly change" (Schueller 2004: 164). An important strand of the debate about the postcolonial status of the Americas is thus the notion of "internal colonization," naming the relation of white settlers, in the

U.S.A., to both Native Americans and African-American slaves, and often also to Latin American populations. In this connection Sharpe writes: "when used to describe the United States, *postcolonial* does not name its past as a white settler colony or its emergence as a neo-colonial power; rather, it designates the presence of racial minorities and Third World immigrants" (Sharpe 2000: 104). Other critics, such as Blauner, concur:

> The third world perspective returns us to the origins of the American experience, reminding us that this nation owes its very existence to colonialism, and that along with settlers and immigrants there have always been conquered Indians and black slaves, and later defeated Mexicans—that is, colonial subjects—on national soil. (Blauner 2001: 46)

For many commentators, then, the U.S.A. is a postcolonial society with respect to its minority populations, which struggle, so these commentators hold, with the same kinds of issues as face people in other societies that have emerged from colonialism. Populations in Latin America and the Caribbean can also be considered by this approach; even though they have mostly emerged from Dutch, Spanish, Portuguese, British, or French colonialism, and are not "internal" to the U.S.A., they are often understood as more or less subject to U.S. political and cultural intervention. This is not the only way to describe the internal divisions of American societies, but it is productive, especially if we accept that what postcolonial analysis primarily addresses are the social and cultural corollaries of organizing legal and economic powers to discriminate among populations along lines of conquest. Postcolonial analysis will then be closely bound up with issues of inequality, its maintenance and demolition, identity, voice, migration, and the ownership and transmission of culture and tradition. Resistance to imperial domination will be seen to link different "colonized" populations on the American continents as it has done populations elsewhere, for instance in Africa. All of these concerns may be read in the American reception of Greek drama, as the chapters in this volume eloquently show.

To describe relations among different cultures in the U.S.A. as "postcolonial" in the sense of "internal colonization" has proved fruitful for many critics. But analyses of internal colonization in the Americas immediately imply issues of race, because the largest single subjugated population in the U.S.A. has historically been the African-American.[5] It is not always clear exactly how we should theorize the mutual implication of postcolonialism and race. A recent argument insists that "Race is the key prism through which all postcolonial analysis is refracted" (Nayar 2010: 1), but other coordinations are possible. Many would agree that historically, empire and race have been mutually defining—the justifications of empire being built on the notion of inferior races, which were then confirmed in their inferiority by conquest and exploitation. In the case of the U.S.A., Stam and Shohat suggest that "the settler colonialism that dispossessed the 'Red' and the racial slavery that exploited the 'Black' were the twin engines of racial supremacy" working together to entrench the power of the new republic (Stam and Shohat 2012: 376). Many would also stress that it is important not to collapse the categories together so that race is subsumed. Thus Schueller criticizes both King (2000) and Singh and Schmidt (2000) for not confronting race consistently within their postcolonial frameworks, and notes that "minority groups risk being homogenized if race is simply kept out of the picture." Postcolonial analysis that dispenses with the idea of race is, she suggests, "shorn of power dynamics and systemic oppression" (Schueller 2004: 168–9).

Others are eager to show how the divisions of racial politics on the American continents have participated in what Stuart Hall calls "structures of dominance" that are shared by other postcolonial societies (Hall 1980). Ann Stoler notes the many scholars who compare the plantation societies of the Old South to institutions in "British, French and Dutch colonies of Asia, Africa, and the Caribbean" (Stoler 2001: 841–2). Such work implicitly undermines American exceptionalism by a focus on how related patterns of exploitation and discrimination emerge repeatedly across the globe. Conversely, the debates on race that have so often informed the public discourse of the Americas can be understood in a global perspective. Thus Howard Winant writes:

> The social movements and revolutionary upsurges that succeeded the [second world] war and brought the colonial era to an end also raised the problematic of race to a new level of prominence. The civil rights movement in the United States and the anti-apartheid mobilization in South Africa are but the most prominent examples of this. As it gained its independence, the postcolonial world was quickly embroiled in the competition of the Cold War, a situation that placed not only the legacy of imperial rule but also the racial policies of the superpowers (especially those of the United States) under additional scrutiny. (Winant 2000: 170)

Understanding of race is here shown to be entwined with the history of colonial and anti-colonial struggle. But Winant also shows that the two are distinct from each other when he goes on to question how racial injustice persists in an era without empire: "Empires have been ended and Jim Crow and apartheid abolished (at least officially). How then is continuing racial inequality and bias to be explained?" (Winant 2000: 171). Neither "race" nor "the postcolonial" can be analyzed without each other, but they are not the same thing.

African-American Classical Tradition

The African-American population of the U.S.A. is the most closely defined by the term "internal colonization," and most extensively oppressed by the discourse of "race." When we turn to the reception of Greek drama within this population, there is a substantial critical discourse already in place. As the discipline of Classics has become more open and demotic, in line with many other twentieth-century developments, so it has elaborated an understanding of itself that modifies its traditional Eurocentrism, and it now pays sustained attention to reception in many global contexts. To an extent, the African-American reception of Greek drama can stand as a case study for "postcolonial" reception in the Americas generally, although as we shall go on to show, there are other dimensions in other parts of the continents. What is especially "postcolonial" about

African-American reception is that the classical texts are acknowledged as part of the cultural equipment of the white Europeans who brought Africans to the American continent as slaves, so that the texts themselves cannot help but operate to some extent as a sign of subjugation. To take on this tradition within African-American writing, then, risks internalizing subjection; this is the problem "inherent in every black humanism that inherits the legacy of Western canonicity and knowledge" (Orrells, Bhambra, and Roynon 2011: 13).

Indeed, we could argue that the very gesture of focusing on African-American deployment of the Classics risks reinscribing the Classics as necessarily white, and "humanist" or "universal" only under the white aegis. African-American culture has defied these proliferating hazards by claiming the classical tradition as its own. In the context of slavery, for instance, the classical past was invoked by slavers and abolitionists alike, so that a potentially pernicious resource was forced to yield some dividend (Hall, Alston, and McConnell 2011). The famous ex-slave and abolitionist Frederick Douglass represents himself as learning how to organize discourse and sway audiences from the Ciceronian repertoire of *The Columbian Orator*, one of the premier school texts of the period (Cook and Tatum 2010; Goings and O'Connor 2011). Phillis Wheatley mobilizes the classical repertoire in her poetry, deploying the highly recognizable symbols to construct a persona that might well have struck contemporary readers as "American" in the religious affiliations and sense of community, even as the poetry also draws attention to the writer's identity as black, African, and enslaved. As Cook and Tatum show, Wheatley's multiple revisions of poetry and consciousness regarding the classical tradition stand as significant refutation of Thomas Jefferson's claim that her writing was mere mimicry (Cook and Tatum 2010).

This dialectical situation, where the classical texts are simultaneously means of oppression and tools for liberation, is recognizable in other colonial contexts such as India (Vasunia 2013). After emancipation, the persistent authority of the classical languages could offer cultural capital, even to the extent that the white establishment wished to prevent African-Americans from learning the languages (Walters 2007: 51). Michele Ronnick (2006) has unearthed the difficult histories of early black Classicists, and Kenneth Goings and Eugene O'Connor have documented the struggles among black students to continue classical education in the face of various kinds of opposition. Malamud sums up thus: "Knowledge of the classics offered intellectual enrichment, a usable past, civic guidance, and cultural virtue to African Americans" (Malamud 2011: 73). The Classics here enable participation rather than forbidding it.

What particular aspects of classical antiquity helped to serve African-Americans in this way? One feature was a tradition in which Africa predated the classical world, and helped to form it, via the power of Egypt over ancient Greece. This was very relevant to critics and writers in Africa, who mobilized this version of classical antiquity in their anti-colonial writings from the mid-nineteenth century, but it was also important to African-Americans in their struggles against slavery and discrimination (Goff 2013; Selden 1998). Although Bernal's *Black Athena* (1987), which first brought this version of Africa into widespread scholarly acknowledgment, did not investigate African-American writings, recent work, such as Keita (2011), has reconstructed this tradition, in which knowledge of classical antiquity is used to construct defences against racial terror and hatred.

As well as offering this resource for polemic, the cultural authority of Graeco-Roman antiquity is such that its metaphors of continuity can be useful to a population who were early deprived of much of their own traditions. Due to its many mythic ramifications, moreover, the classical tradition can meld with other mythic traditions, and with folklore, to produce resonant narratives. We see syncretism in the present volume in the chapters on classical drama in Brazil, in particular. Classical images and metaphors have thus been found independently useful to African-American (or Afro-descendent, as the Brazilians put it) creative expression, as well as helping to signify African-American (Afro-descendent) participation in the making of America and in the making of antiquity itself. But while the classical tradition can thus be made inclusive and even salvific, it is important not to lose sight of the subversive and rebellious politics of African-American reception.

To rewrite classical texts or artifacts from within African-American discourse is always potentially a gesture of protest and defiance, turning European supremacy's weapons against itself. As Orrells et al. note, the very movement of Africans into the Americas, under the compulsion of Europeans, produced the cultural intersections which meant that "European constructions of the past, present and future would not go uncontested." Instead, "the deployment of classical texts and images by African Americans enabled profound revisions of white hegemonic historical narratives" (Orrells, Bhambra, and Roynon 2011: 8, 10). In a plural movement, then, African-American creative writers have contributed to the African-American literary tradition, the classical tradition, and the American tradition; in the same way, the American tradition includes work that is classically descended and work that is descended from Africa. Within this plurality, the African-American classical voice can acknowledge subjection and exclusion, but also refuse to be confined by these, and instead find symbols and metaphors with which to construct a viable future, as well as a usable past.

African-American reception of Greek drama has become an important genre, even if the plays are not very many, with some like *The Darker Face of the Earth* moving straight from theatrical performance to university syllabi. Recent scholarly works have both drawn new attention to such dramas and offered theoretical models with which to address them. Initially, Gilbert and Tompkins (1996) promulgated the model of "canonical counter-discourse," in which the colonized "write back" to the imperial center using the center's own texts, the canon, against it; in the African-American context the "center" would be the European tradition of classical culture, which would be the object of critique and protest. The notion of canonical counter-discourse was criticized, however, for reinscribing the center–margins dichotomy which helped to fuel imperial fantasies of European domination in the first place. A few years after Gilbert and Tompkins, Kevin Wetmore (2003) describes African-American adaptations of Greek drama in a tripartite scheme. "Black Orpheus" names a Eurocentric tradition whereby the "African," here the African-American, is explained by the Greek; "Black Athena" names those few Afrocentric works which explicitly derive Greek drama from African traditions; and Wetmore seeks to type many of his chosen dramas as "Black Dionysus" because they work in a "counter-hegemonic, subversive manner" (Wetmore 2003: 11). Subsequent critics acknowledge the importance of Wetmore's contributions while sometimes querying his terminology (Rankine 2013; Van Weyenberg 2011: 335).

Several writers on African-American reception of Greek drama have also been concerned with analyzing African receptions; among these, Hardwick (2004, 2005, 2006) and Budelmann (2005) have been inclined to posit the possibilities of "decolonization" made available by the receptions, while Goff and Simpson (2007) have stressed the continuing need to struggle with Oedipal models of colonial violence. More focused on the works of African-American writers are Rankine (2006) and Walters (2007), which together offer further reflections on the use of writerly "craft," rhetoric, and myth in "black classicism." Rankine urges that "Black writers have always been interested in the classics and have at times used them to master their own American experience... [and] to engage immediate concerns of racism and oppression" (Rankine 2006: 3). Walters further suggests that the Classics can offer "a liberating space to engage readers in a feminist critique of the misrepresentation, silencing, and subjugation of Black women both in literature and society" (Walters 2007: 51). This version of the classical voice is implicitly counter to more prevalent types of postcolonial critique.

While Greenwood (2009) provides a helpful overview of several of these works of criticism, her own book (2010) focuses on the Caribbean, and shows how writers and intellectuals trade representations of ancient Greece, as well as other cultural goods, not in neat hierarchical models but in a plurality of "fragmented" and even "chaotic" relationships, which include African and African-American cultures. Greenwood foregrounds the "frail connections" by which such representations circulate, and suggests that Caribbean writers use the classical in the spirit of "antagonistic cooperation" (Greenwood 2010: 1, 15). Her discussions of Classics in Caribbean educational and political discourses suggest ways in which the different postcolonial sites of the Americas may be linked in their engagements with classical antiquity. Similar perspectives are offered by Orrells et al.'s *African Athena: New Agendas*. Although there is no specific discussion of African-American reception of Greek drama, there are several inquiries into other African-descended uses of classical material in the Americas, such as historiography; and the editors, in the wake of Bernal, suggest that we consider distinctions between ancient and modern, classical and postcolonial, as artificially imposed on a global culture "always and already hybrid" (Orrells, Bhambra, and Roynon 2011: 13). While this critical stance is productive, the subversive, combative politics of African-American adaptations of Greek drama, in their historical specificity, may be at risk of dissolution in this gesture.

The most recent study of "black classicism" is Cook and Tatum's *African American Writers and Classical Tradition* (2010). This comprehensive celebration embraces the plurality of African-American responses to the Classics, and thus implicitly rejects any postcolonial framework. Not only is there no one model for African-American response, there is also no "single notion of Greco-Roman classics informing African American writers" (Cook and Tatum 2010: 3). Each chapter adopts a different perspective on its chosen writer/s, and while no theoretical synthesis is offered, the book is lavish with close readings and stylistic analyses that pay full respect to the "craft" of the writers. What is perhaps likely to be controversial about this volume, along with the absence of wider claims, is that the "craft" may sometimes seem to outweigh the politics, implicitly undervaluing the cultural struggles outlined above (Cook and Tatum 2010: 4).

Taken together, these scholarly works celebrate the creativity of African-Americans in the face of a classical tradition that has often been interpreted as hostile to their interests, but they also implicitly question the usefulness of "postcolonial" as a term of analysis, by repeatedly focusing on creative freedom rather than its constraints. They also implicitly question the category of "African-American" by making links to Africa, the Caribbean, and other societies that have emerged from colonial occupation. While the debate about identities and differences between "African" and "African-American" has a long history of its own, it is rendered newly interesting by the latest contribution to reception of Greek drama in the Americas, *Black Odysseys* by Justine McConnell (2013). This takes an explicitly postcolonial stance on its subjects, embracing not only American writers of African descent but also writers in the Caribbean and South Africa. Crucial for this book is the fact that the "postcolonial responses" to the *Odyssey*, including the dramatic, are found to be plural, and to "differ radically from each other" (McConnell 2013: 3). The increasing sophistication of analysis of postcolonial reception of Greek drama in the Americas has also offered increasingly fine-grained descriptions which value differences as much as they do an emphasis on the shared experience of empire and subjugation.

OTHER AMERICAN CLASSICAL TRADITIONS

We suggested above that African-American reception of Greek drama raises issues that are relevant to the rest of the Americas in their different experiences of colonization, internal colonization, and postcoloniality. This initial position must now be somewhat modified, because the African-American case shows so many internal differences that it cannot immediately stand for all the other cases, and indeed is itself susceptible of several kinds of examination. In this context we may recall that "neither the term postcolonial nor words such as diaspora, migrant, or transnational . . . [should be] used in such a broad way as to erase the many constituencies and communities of people" (Singh and Schmidt 2000: 39). While the expansive, comprehensive terms of analysis are useful, they must almost always be modified in the encounter with a particular text. For our purposes, the reception of Greek drama in the Caribbean, or in Latin America, may sometimes be seen to overlap with African-American reception, but must sometimes be examined in its specificities.

A wide range of "postcolonial" interpretations of the Latin American tradition of Greek drama reception is possible. Edith Hall has recently suggested an emphatically postcolonial understanding of Alfonso Reyes's *Ifigenia cruel*; she reads the play as part of Mexican nation-building in the wake of Spain's loss of her last colonies.[6] Orestes is criticized for travelling across the sea to make incursions into the peaceful, pastoral society of Tauris, and the whole play is interpreted as a meditation on the nature of "home," "exile," and "return" in a world disfigured by empire and colonialism (Hall 2013: 278). Yet Moira Fradinger, in her recent work on Latin American receptions of Antigone, implicitly queries the usefulness of the "postcolonial" identification. She points out that the history of Antigone in South America cannot be confined to reflexes about European colonization, because the plays pit European-descended settlers variously against Indians and against each other, along lines of class and gender: "The large web of intertextual relations and literary communities associated with the Greek myth in the region goes back to the nineteenth century and is embedded in two centuries of national debates over the meaning of modernity." Fradinger suggests instead that the Argentine Antigones develop into a "national tradition" of reflection on political foundations (Fradinger 2011: 67–8).

Between the two American hemispheres, and slightly off center from Central America, lies, of course, the Caribbean, where different and competing waves of imperial occupation have moved, serially, symmetrically or asymmetrically, island by island. In this geographically disparate and historically dynamic region, the postcolonial has some purchase. Of all the plays that might be treated as representing the reception of Greek drama within the Americas, especially with a postcolonial slant, one of the most compelling is Derek Walcott's *The Odyssey: A Stage Version*. There is some irony here, since this work was commissioned by the Royal Shakespeare Company and premièred in Stratford-upon-Avon in July 1992. A play by a Caribbean artist produced in the heart of England thus exemplifies the American reception of Greek drama. More significant than this diasporic irony is the fact that the canvas of Walcott's *Odyssey* does not appear as evidently postcolonial. We want to focus, for an interval, on Walcott's creative theorization of a globalized Caribbean that can take the postcolonial in its stride.

Like Homer's Odysseus, Walcott's version is a "sacker of cities," motivated by prospects of plunder, but he is also characterized as much more impelled to return "home," as this term recurs throughout the text. To Thersites, the mercenary, he not only expresses this priority but he also tries to convert Thersites to it, unavailingly. His dalliance with Circe is likewise presented as "for the crew's sake" (78). In the oppressive state where the Cyclops, as "the Eye," dominates indigenous human subjects, his intervention appears clearly as a liberation for the human community, as well as an escape for himself and his surviving crew.

As in Homer's *Odyssey*, Walcott's protagonist brings with him standards of community that do not apply in the societies that he visits, and which he cannot impose, even as he finds devious, even dubious means to defend these standards for the sake of his crew and himself. These standards are, of course, tested in the process, as when the Homeric Odysseus performs the calculation that results in six of his crewmen being sacrificed to Scylla; this results from a rational calculation of risk that itself risks contradicting the principles of community that require the calculation to be made in the first place.

For all the ruthless resourcefulness of Homer and Walcott's versions of Odysseus, he is not able, or even inclined, to operate as a colonizer in any of the communities or anti-communities that he encounters. The standards that he brings with him are not embedded there after he has made his grateful, and often hasty exits from these places. Only in the Cyclops's state is there the implication of a lasting change brought by Odysseus, but this state seems a special case because it is identified with the historical Greece of the Colonels' military rule. Of this oppressive state Odysseus asks, incredulously: "Is this the Greece that I loved? Is this my city?," whereupon the Philosopher replies, "Philosophy's cradle, where Thought is forbidden" (61). Odysseus' decimation of the Cyclops's power can be understood not as the act of a colonizer, but rather as an exceptional, initially philhellenic gesture, which ultimately liberates the ideals of Greece from "the era of the grey Colonels" (62), so that they may once again inspire other, "unknown archipelagoes" (59). If anything, Walcott's Odysseus, in particular, as he struggles to return from Troy, is quite systematically purged of any colonialist impulses. His mind is effectively decolonized by the various failures and costs of colonization, at Troy, on Calypso's island, and in the Underworld. In the event, any such intrinsic colonialist motivation on his part is reckoned as marginal, since the play recalls (151), in an intervention by Eumaeus absent from Homer, the test set by Palamedes to determine whether Odysseus was feigning madness in order to escape recruitment for the mission to Troy. Odysseus duly fails the test and must unwillingly go.

Notwithstanding the various signs of Odysseus as a reluctant and then lapsing colonialist, there are several related aspects of Walcott's Odysseus that bespeak an imperial will to power and which place him, as protagonist, at some variance with the poets Phemius and Demodocus, within the play.[7] Nestor characterizes him as one who "reduced to reason every omen" (26), and later Athena amplifies this observation when she responds to Odysseus' question, "What sins, dazzling Athena, marked me from men?," thus: "You mocked the immortal ones . . . You are the first to question the constant shining" (119). He gamely rejoins, "With good reason" (119), and she echoes Nestor more closely: "The first to discount each omen!" (119). Well beyond the world of Homeric epic, Walcott's Odysseus here represents the Greek Enlightenment, centered on Athens. Meanwhile, the responses to him on the part of Nestor, and especially of Athena, may plot the limitations of that Enlightenment, as the ancient authorities are questioned and "reduced." Just as the Enlightenment questioned itself in Athens, via such critical reflections on reason as Sophocles' *Oedipus Tyrannus*, so Odysseus' definitive characteristic of reason is remarked as conspicuous by mortals and immortals alike.

Where Odysseus' reason is most imperial, in the event, is back in Ithaca, which, like Troy, invites conquest and colonization, but, like all the other communities that he has encountered, cannot be so treated. Ithaca is different from both, as it is from Odysseus' memory of it, so that none of his experiences prepares him for what must be done, and not done. For Walcott's Odysseus in particular, reason seems the one asset that he possesses for himself, beyond the possible loyalty of others to him. Only this faculty might allow him to abstract from his alien experiences in order to draw out resources to address a home that is itself become alien. The conclusions that this faculty draws, however, are wanting, as becomes clear in Walcott's reunion of Penelope and Odysseus.

Having insinuated himself into his old household, appraised the field of forces, tested the potential loyalty of allies, revealed himself or been recognized, and having led the extermination of the suitors, Odysseus is now confronted by Penelope, still unacknowledged in his identity. Penelope enters as Odysseus is compulsively refiguring the scene of carnage in terms of his previous experiences, at Troy, on the high seas, in the Underworld; in this context, he glosses the dead Antinous, leader of the suitors, as a log from the sea and as Ajax from both Troy and Hades. Eumaeus glosses Odysseus' words, in turn: "This is a madness that I've seen on him before" (151). Eumaeus equates Odysseus' behavior now with his conduct when Palamedes first came calling to enlist Odysseus for Troy. But there is an incongruity, even contradiction here: the insanity with which he equates it was, in fact, feigned. Penelope's response to Odysseus' current "madness," when she enters just after Eumaeus' intervention, is consistent with this fact: "This cunning beggar is the smartest of suitors" (153). Unlike Eumaeus and Telemachus, Penelope grasps Odysseus' orgy of refiguration as his latest ruse, motivated by his reason. There is also a lurking implication: the reason of the colonizer may look like insanity to the colonized, and vice versa. Whether Penelope or Eumaeus is correct, Odysseus' comportment suddenly changes, at Penelope's challenge, and rationality returns. It is a rationality, however, for which Penelope rapidly weaves some parameters by precluding certain permutations: "This is not Troy. I'm not Menelaus' whore" (154). As Odysseus extrapolates from his past experiences to try and control the present, he begins to impose a grid on Ithaca which Penelope fears would "make this a second Troy!" (154). Much more than Homer's character, Walcott's Penelope asserts herself against the ready recycling of a colonialist past.

This danger is highlighted by a self-conscious strain throughout Walcott's *Odyssey*, whereby characters sense such repetitions. As readers or spectators, we are incited, even challenged, to identify internal echoes and equations. These two perspectives, from outside the play and from within, correspond respectively with the narrative perspective of Walcott's text, standing above the action, in a postcolonial scene occupied by Billy Blue, and with the dramatic perspective embedded within the action, where a violent colonial past and a decolonization of the mind are experienced. One of the effects of recasting Odysseus as a dramatic character is that his narrative to the Phaeacians does not figure as qualitatively different from the rest of the action; it unfolds in the present like the rest, save for the slender narrative frame inhabited by Billy Blue. A crucial implication of this effect is that Odysseus' narrative to Alcinous' court is not set off as poetry, as it is in Homer's epic, and Odysseus himself is not ranked with the singers Phemius, Demodocus, or Billy Blue. Walcott's Odysseus is figured more singularly as a creature of reason, rather than poetry, devising his way to survival and homecoming. It is there that Penelope forces some reflexivity into his reason, so that it becomes more than an instrument for calculating means toward unexamined, historically repetitive ends. He is thus forced to confront who he is and how he has become so: "Monsters . . . We make them ourselves" (160).

More vividly than his earlier *Omeros*, Walcott's *Odyssey* admits colonial history and decolonization into the frame, not only as preludes to a properly postcolonial cultural scene where European literary traditions are potentially as available to Caribbean subjects as any other traditions, but also as historical experiences that can still be felt. Perhaps only the katabasis in *Omeros*, where Achille undergoes a reversed Middle Passage to Africa, either equals or exceeds this poignant characteristic of the play. Yet this *Odyssey* is aligned with *Omeros* in a more crucial respect. Even as Walcott's *Odyssey* may accord a more immediate profile to colonial history and decolonization, behind an achieved postcolonial present, it seems to repeat the emphasis of *Omeros* on the permeability of subject positions under imperialism, whereby all are closely touched by past injustices and present justifications, as well as by some imaginative liberty within and from them. In Walcott's Odysseus, we may trace the figure of Achille the fisherman, in *Omeros*, as he washes his boat: recalling, from the night before, Bob Marley's song "Buffalo Soldier," and the line "Heart of America," he imagines himself not as such a soldier in the American Civil War, fighting for his own interest, against racial slavery, but rather as a cowboy shooting "Indians," as depicted by Hollywood. The following historical simile is applied to the victims of Achille's fantasized adventure: "like Aruacs before the muskets of the Conquistadors" (161). The Aruacs were the indigenous people of the Caribbean, and, crucially, *Omeros* begins with a scene in which Achille and other African-Caribbean fisherman cut down the ancient trees of the Aruacs to build their boats. A powerful implication of Walcott's epic is that the European imperial project recruits everyone to its violence, just as Odysseus, as a reluctant colonialist, is dragged to Troy in Walcott's play. Even those who are later victims of colonialism become instrumental in the ultimate displacement and forgetting of the earlier victims.

Such unwilling, unwitting complicity may be a further extreme of Rankine's notion of Ulysses in black. Walcott's Odysseus can certainly range beyond a Caribbean ambit into the Americas, as well as into the European culture that was exported to both. In doing so, however, he also brings with him an African heritage, in the form of the stories that Eurycleia, the "black" Egyptian "slave and nurse" (9), has formatively told both to him and to Telemachus. It is, furthermore, no coincidence that Eurycleia helps Penelope to reintegrate Odysseus into the community, as she protects Melantho from him. Such a late effort sustains Eurycleia's mission, as declared: "Is Egypt who cradle Greece till Greece mature" (9). The reception of Greek dramas into the Americas may be understood as a further nourishing stage in this long maturation. In Walcott's *Odyssey* in 1992, that postcolonial maturation manifests itself, in Stratford, England, as a Caribbean version of a global, or world, culture that archly recognizes, but is historically deeper than, the cultural globalization that is regularly identified with the proliferation of American popular culture.

Beyond the Postcolonial?

Postcolonial analysis has been crucial to the humanities in recent decades, but with its dominance have come criticisms. In addition to the challenges we have already discussed, many commentators have expressed unease about the ways in which the categories of postcolonial analysis can be made to obscure other important types of difference, notably those of class and gender, which we have seen registered in the plays treated above. Thus even Homi Bhabha, a critic often identified with postcolonial theory in its more abstract versions, worries that the debate has been "focused perhaps too exclusively on the culture wars, the politics of identity, and the politics of recognition" instead of on "social equity" (Bhabha 2004: xviii). Without a plurality of large identifications such as race, gender, or class, it is hard to mount any effective politics, to account for lived experience, or to render the complexity of significant postcolonial texts. Yet Schueller notes that as late as 2000, the essays collected in King 2000 hardly discuss gender (Schueller 2004: 168). In the same volume, however, Sharpe is very clear on the necessity to theorize class together with race and postcoloniality, and goes so far as to state that "internal colonization is only an analogy for describing the economic marginalization of racial minorities" (Sharpe 2000: 106). The "postcolonial" terms have thus to be modified, or rather expanded, in order to account properly for the dynamics of American cultures, and crucially to ameliorate them.

Another strand of criticism is that which suggests that postcolonialism "throws limited light on the world we now face" because it does not readily encompass the relatively new phenomenon of globalization (Coronil in Yaeger 2007: 636). Globalization, within academic discourse, appears under several different headings. As Brennan writes: "On the one hand, it holds out hope for the creation of new communities and unforeseen solidarities; on the other hand, it appears merely to euphemize corporatization and imperial expansion."[8] Both these versions invite further scrutiny. While postcolonialism offered insights into a variety of links between the metropolis and the colonies, globalization can suggest that the entire world is becoming "a single social space" constructed by the free circulation of money and information as well as by unprecedented movements of populations (Brennan 2004: 123). If there is indeed such a transformation under way, it is appropriate that commentators seek to render it properly via new models which move beyond postcolonial polarities of colonizer and colonized, center and periphery, in order to draw on more mobile terms like transnationalism and border theory.

Since the Americas already constitute a continental space comprised of plural nations, and several borders, it has proved central to such theorizing. Katherine Sugg suggests that in a period when "an emerging 'cultural politics' of hybridity and post-national identities supersedes the nation-state-based identities and oppositional politics of immigrant paradigms," commentators need to account for the newly globalized context, and "the move to the transnational vantage of the Americas offers that accounting, as does the popularity of transnational paradigms such as latinidad and 'the border-lands'" (Sugg 2004: 229–31). She goes on to show how the Americas have contributed to the new paradigms: "Border theory, the enterprise that began in scholarship and writing focused on the US–Mexico border . . . has expanded its critical reach across the Americas and into theories of contemporary world cultures, postcoloniality, and globalization" (Sugg 2004: 231). The plurality of approaches to Greek drama throughout this volume is representative of the kind of porosity that constitutes the postcolonial.

The Americas are also relevant because the plurality of peoples who share the continents gives rise to flexible models which allow for complex relations among different communities, many of whom might be termed "postcolonial" in one way or another: "Román de la Campa offered the model of the 'split state' as a means of conceptualizing those Latino communities in the US who maintain economic, familial, and cultural ties to the various homeland nations in Latin America and the Caribbean from which (and to which) they migrate" (Sugg 2004: 228). The Americas appear here under the sign of transnational globalization insofar as the communities within them forge various ties that cannot be comprehended by a model of center and periphery, or even of imperial exploitation. Globalized transnationalism offers to render the nation-state, as a term of analysis, redundant, thus decreasing the purchase of "postcolonialism" as an apt description for the contemporary world. As it pertains to Greek drama, a play such as *The Angry Woman* exemplifies such challenges to the postcolonial, in its language and its theme of resistance against corporate—and imperial—authority (see further Billotte, this volume).

Some commentators also suggest that globalization, understood in these ways, will put an end to race. Winant outlines the position: "Some would argue that since racial injustice is at least tendentially [sic] diminishing, the race concept is finally being obviated: In the globalized twenty-first century, world society and transnational culture will finally attain a state of colorblindness and racial (or better, ethnic) pluralism" (Winant 2000: 171). But he appends a more skeptical caveat: "Others note that this new situation . . . provides a much prettier fig leaf for policies of laissez-faire vis-a-vis continuing racial exclusion and inequality than any intransigent white supremacy could ever have offered" (Winant 2000: 171). What if "globalization" is merely a new name for the atavistic drive of capital to find ever more markets, exploit ever more workers, drain resources from ever more territory? "Globalization" would then figure as a new form of untrammeled imperial exploitation as multinational corporations, usually enriching people who live in the white west and north, extract rich resources, and poorly paid labor, from people who live in the non-white south and east. Thus Schueller stresses the dimensions of globalization which see "gross economic inequities unleashed by multinational corporations as well as the one-way movement of American pop culture to Third World countries" (Schueller 2004: 170). She links the economic to the cultural as parallel means of domination, suggesting that goods and information do not circulate the globe so much as move in restricted directions determined by familiar neo-colonial hierarchies.

Germane to our inquiry here is that "globalization" is often understood bluntly as the "Americanization" of the world, as we noted above in our discussion of Walcott.

The inquiry into globalization shares concerns with yet another way to critique postcolonialism. Some scholars argue that postcolonialism is an empty term because we are *not* yet out of the age of empire. Even for Edward Said, the founder of the academic discipline, postcolonialism became a "misnomer" that did not sufficiently recognize the persistence of neo-colonialism, imperialism, and "structures of dependency" (Said 2002: 2). Such critics often claim that the U.S.A. in particular is a neo-colonial power: after World War II, the argument goes, the U.S.A. compromised its anti-imperial credentials in favor of becoming "successor to the European empires," wielding both "hard" and "soft" power with respect to neighboring territories like the Caribbean and the Philippines in the twentieth century, and, more recently, with respect to nations in the Middle East (Gilroy 2004: 3). These questions have been posed with renewed vigor in the wake of the attacks of 9/11, which have led the U.S.A. both to invade other countries and to institute the highly colonial practices of torture and detention without trial. These "novel geopolitical rules," as Paul Gilroy scorchingly terms them, in an analysis that makes clear the colonial antecedents of such practices, are supported in the ideological sphere by the construction of the "war against terror" as a "clash of civilizations" which brooks no compromise because it is fundamentally a clash of civilization with barbarism (Gilroy 2004: 3, 20–1). This construction in turn results in the various calls for the U.S.A. to take on the mantle of empire explicitly; hence the "repeated invocations of differences between our civilization and their barbarity, entreaties for a 'new imperialism' and calls for reinstating a nineteenth-century type of colonialism, now with the US replacing Britain and France" (Schueller 2004: 162). Not only is the condition of the world postcolonial, but it is sufficiently consciously postcolonial to desire the return of empire.

This chapter has canvassed some ways in which postcolonial analysis might be fruitful for assessing the reception of Greek drama in the Americas, but has also drawn attention to limitations in "postcolonialism" and to the ways in which the critical conversation is moving beyond it. We can conclude that it is appropriate to consider reception of Greek drama in the Americas under the heading of "postcolonial," because the Americas are home to an incredibly diverse population which has been marked by a series of empires in a variety of ways, and because the Americas is a site in which colonial, postcolonial, and neo-colonial tensions have been worked out in a plurality of forms since the inception of modernity. Yet how might the last two points raised, on globalization and neo-colonialism, be relevant for understanding Greek drama in the Americas? This chapter cannot, of course, anticipate the findings of the rest of this volume, but we can say that the volume itself is driven by a comprehensively global notion of the Americas, paying attention to reception in numerous locations and offering a number of ways to read strategic similarities and differences. We can also see that many of the later receptions are produced by people of non-European descent, so that the issues of unequal political power, of hemispheric dominance by white U.S. culture, will be in play, even as many other issues, including those of class and gender, may clamor for attention. Conversely, the volume makes clear that Greek drama, with its relentless attention to political power and rhetoric, and its scrutiny of corruption of all kinds, can prove a sharp critical instrument for examining the Americas.

Notes

1. The distinctions that can be made between the terms "colonial" and "imperial" are not germane to our purposes here.
2. Marshall and Biglieri are exceptions, as are Billotte and Rankine and Banks.
3. Zapién 2000: 13–14; see also Laird 2003.
4. On the subaltern see Nayar 2010: 93–6. See Manning on the "archival" turn in this respect.
5. We use race here not as a scientific category, which of course it is not, but in the way suggested by Winant 2000: 170: "World history has, arguably, been racialized at least since the rise of the modern world system; racial hierarchy remains global even in the postcolonial present; and popular concepts of race, however variegated, remain in general everyday use almost everywhere."
6. Hall 2013: 275. See also Barrenechea, this volume.
7. Hamner 2001: 383 reads "an imperialist mind-set" in Walcott's Odysseus and identifies him with Robinson Crusoe (385–6). Martyniuk (2005) follows suit, but also reads the play's role reversals within colonial relations. Hardwick's (1996) reading of the Cyclops episode is sensitive to the play's exposure of easy polarities.
8. Brennan 2004: 122. Brennan goes on to suggest five different models of "globalization," but they can be understood largely as occupying points on a spectrum between these two possibilities.

References

Ashcroft, B., G. Griffiths, and H. Tiffin (1989), *The Empire Writes Back: Theory and Practice in Post-colonial Literatures.* London and New York.
Bauer, R. and J. A. Mazzotti (2009), *Creole Subjects in the Colonial Americas: Empires, Texts, Identities.* Chapel Hill, NC.
Bernal, M. (1987), *Black Athena: The Afroasiatic Roots of Classical Civilization, i: The Fabrication of Ancient Greece 1785–1985.* New Brunswick, NJ.
Bhabha, H. (2004), *The Location of Culture.* Abingdon.
Blauner, R. (2001; 1972), *Still the Big News: Racial Oppression in America.* New York and London.
Brennan, T. (2004), "From Development to Globalization: Postcolonial Studies and Globalization Theory," in N. Lazarus ed., *The Cambridge Companion to Postcolonial Literary Studies.* Cambridge, 120–38.
Briggs, W. (2007), "United States," in C. W. Kallendorf ed., *A Companion to the Classical Tradition.* Malden, MA, and Oxford, 279–94.
Budelmann, F. (2005), "Greek Tragedies in West African Adaptations," in B. Goff ed., *Classics and Colonialism.* London, 118–46.
Cook, W. and J. Tatum (2010), *African American Writers and Classical Tradition.* Chicago.
Fradinger, M. (2011), "An Argentine Tradition," in E. Mee and H. P. Foley eds., *Antigone on the Contemporary World Stage.* Oxford, 67–90.
Gilbert, H, and J. Tompkins (1996), *Post-Colonial Drama: Theory, Practice, Politics.* London.

Gilroy, P. (2004), *Postcolonial Melancholia*. New York.
Goff, B. (ed. 2005), *Classics and Colonialism*. London.
Goff, B. (2013), *Your Secret Language: Classics in the British Colonies of West Africa*. London.
Goff, B. and M. Simpson (2007), *Crossroads in the Black Aegean: Oedipus, Antigone, and Dramas of the African Diaspora*. Oxford.
Goings, K. and E. O'Connor (2011), "Black Athena before *Black Athena*: The Teaching of Greek and Latin at Black Colleges and Universities during the Nineteenth Century," in D. Orrells, G. K. Bhambra, and T. Roynon eds., *African Athena: New Agendas*. Oxford, 90–105.
Greenwood, E. (2009), "Re-Rooting the Classical Tradition: New Directions in Black Classicism," *Classical Receptions Journal* 1.1, 87–103.
Greenwood, E. (2010), *Afro-Greeks: Dialogues between Anglophone Caribbean Literature and Classics in the Twentieth Century*. Oxford.
Hall, E. (2013), *Adventures with Iphigenia in Tauris*. Oxford.
Hall, E., R. Alston, and J. McConnell (eds. 2011), *Ancient Slavery and Abolition: From Hobbes to Hollywood*. Oxford.
Hall, S. (1980), "Race, Articulation, and Societies Structured in Dominance," in Hall, ed., *Sociological Theories: Race and Colonialism*. Paris.
Hamner, R. D. (2001), "Creolizing Homer for the Stage: Walcott's *The Odyssey*," *Twentieth Century Literature* 7.43, 374–90.
Hardwick, L. (1996), "A Daidalos in the Late Modern Age? Transplanting Homer into Derek Walcott's *The Odyssey: A Stage Version*." <http://www2.open.ac.uk/ClassicalStudies/GreekPlays/conf96/hardwick.htm> accessed July 3, 2013.
Hardwick, L. (2004), "Greek Drama and Anti-Colonialism: Decolonizing Classics," in E. Hall, F. Macintosh, and A. Wrigley eds., *Dionysus Since 69: Greek Tragedy at the Dawn of the Third Millennium*. Oxford, 219–42.
Hardwick, L. (2005), "Refiguring Classical Texts: Aspects of the Postcolonial Condition," in B. Goff ed., *Classics and Colonialism*. London, 107–17.
Hardwick, L. (2006), "Remodeling Receptions: Greek Drama as Diaspora in Performance," in C. Martindale and R. F. Thomas eds., *Classics and the Uses of Reception*. Malden, MA, 204–15.
Hulme, P. (1995), "Including America," *Ariel: A Review of International English Literature* 26, 117–23.
Keita, M. (2011), "Believing in Ethiopians," in D. Orrells, G. K. Bhambra, and T. Roynon eds., *African Athena*. Oxford, 19–39.
King, R. C. (ed. 2000), *Postcolonial America*. Champaign, IL.
Klor de Alva, J. J. (1995), "The Postcolonization of the (Latin) American Experience: A Reconsideration of 'Colonialism,' 'Postcolonialism,' and 'Mestizaje,'" in G. Prakash ed., *After Colonialism: Imperial Histories and Postcolonial Displacements*. Princeton, 241–75.
Laird, A. (2003), "Review of T. Herrera Zapién, *Historia del Humanismo Mexicano*," *Journal of Roman Studies* 93, 45–7.
Laird, A. (2006), *The Epic of America: An Introduction to Rafael Landívar and the Rusticatio Mexicana*. London.
McConnell, J. (2013), *Black Odysseys: 'The Homeric Odyssey in the African Diaspora since 1939'*. Oxford.
Malamud, M. (2010), "Translatio imperii: America as the New Rome c.1900," in M. Bradley ed., *Classics and Imperialism in the British Empire*. Oxford, 249–82.
Malamud, M. (2011), "Black Minerva: Antiquity in Antebellum African American History," in D. Orrells, G. K. Bhambra, and T. Roynon eds., *Black Athena*. Oxford, 71–89.
Martyniuk, I. (2005), "Playing with Europe: Derek Walcott's Retelling of Homer's Odyssey," *Callaloo* 238.1, 188–200.

Moster, K. (2000), "Postcolonialism after W. E. B. Du Bois," in A. Singh and P. Schmidt eds., *Postcolonial Theory and the United States: Race, Ethnicity, and Literature.* Jackson, MS, 258–78.

Muthyala, J. (2001), "Reworlding America: The Globalization of American Studies," *Cultural Critique* 47, 91–119.

Nayar, P. K. (2010), *Postcolonialism: A Guide for the Perplexed.* London and New York.

Norman, H. (1882), *An Account of the Harvard Greek Play.* Boston.

Olaniyan, T. (2005), "Postmodernity, Postcoloniality, and African Studies," in Z. Mugabane ed., *Postmodernism, Postcoloniality, and African Studies.* Trenton, NJ, 39–60.

Orrells, D. L, G. K. Bhambra, and T. Roynon (eds. 2011), *African Athena: New Agendas.* Oxford.

Parry, B. (1997), "The Postcolonial: Conceptual Category or Chimera?" *The Yearbook of English Studies* 27, 3–21.

Pluggé, D. E. (1938), *The History of Greek Play Production in American Colleges and Universities 1881–1936.* New York.

Rankine, P. D. (2006), *Ulysses in Black: Ralph Ellison, Classicism, and African American Literature.* Madison.

Rankine, P. D. (2013), *Aristotle and Black Drama: A Theater of Civil Disobedience.* Waco.

Ronnick, M. (2006), *The Works of William Scarborough, Black Classicist and Race Leader.* Oxford.

Said, E. (2002), "A Conversation with Neeldari Bhattacharya, Suvir Kaul, and Ania Loomba," in D. T. Goldberg and A. Quayson eds., *Relocating Postcolonialism.* Oxford, 1–14.

Schueller, M. J. (2004), "Postcolonial American Studies," *American Literary History* 16.1, 162–75.

Selden, D. (1998), "Aithiopika and Ethiopianism," in R. Hunter ed., *Studies in Heliodorus.* Cambridge, 182–218.

Sharpe, J. (2000), "Is the United States Postcolonial? Transnationalism, Immigration, and Race," in R. King ed., *Postcolonial America.* Champaign, IL, 103–21.

Singh, A. and P. Schmidt (eds. 2000), *Postcolonial Theory and the United States: Race, Ethnicity, and Literature.* Jackson, MS.

Stam, R. and E. Shohat (2012), "Whence and Whither Postcolonial Theory?" *New Literary History* 43.2, 371–90.

Stoler, A. L. (2001), "Tense and Tender Ties: The Politics of Comparison in North American History and (Post) Colonial Studies," *The Journal of American History* 88.3, 829–65.

Sugg, K. (2004), "Literatures of the Americas, Latinidad, and the Re-Formation of Multi-Ethnic Literatures," *MELUS* 29.3/4, 227–42.

van der Woude, J. (2013), "Comparative Work on the Colonial Americas," *The William and Mary Quarterly* 70.3, 618–34.

Van Weyenberg, A. (2011), "Wole Soyinka's Yoruba Tragedy: Performing Politics," in D. Orrells, G. Bhambra, and T. Roynon eds., *Black Athena.* Oxford, 326–42.

Vasunia, P. (2013), *The Classics and Colonial India.* Oxford.

Walcott, D. (1993), *The Odyssey: A Stage Version.* London.

Walters, T. (2007), *African American Literature and the Classicist Tradition: Black Women Writers from Wheatley to Morrison.* New York.

Wetmore, K. J. Jr. (2002), *The Athenian Sun in an African Sky.* Jefferson, NC.

Wetmore, K. J. Jr. (2003), *Black Dionysus.* Jefferson, NC.

Winant, H. (2000), "Race and Race Theory," *Annual Review of Sociology* 26, 169–85.

Yeager, P. (2007), "Editor's Column: The End of Postcolonial Theory?" *PMLA* 122.3, 633–51.

Zapién, T. H. (2000), *Historia del humanismo mexicano.* Universidad Nacional Autónoma de México.

PART II
SHAPING AMERICAN THEATER (1800–1900)

CHAPTER 4

GRECIAN THEATER IN PHILADELPHIA, 1800–1870

LEE T. PEARCY

PRESIDENT George Washington died on December 14, 1799.[1] Ten days later, on December 23, the curtain at the Chestnut Street Theatre in Philadelphia rose on "an affecting scene of a tomb, in the center of which was a portrait of the sage and hero, encircled by oak leaves. On the pyramidal top of the 'catafalque' perched an eagle weeping tears of blood" (Davis 1957: 15). The producers of the tribute had prepared a carefully chosen mélange of classical symbols and civilizations. The eagle of Rome and the *corona civica*, a garland of oak leaves awarded to a Roman who had saved the life of a fellow citizen in battle, connected the Father of his Country to the founder of the Roman Empire, who had been given the title Augustus and awarded the civic crown in 27 BCE and in 2 BCE had received the title *pater patriae*.[2] The pyramid evoked the Great Seal of the United States, adopted seventeen years earlier, and caught the crest of a rising wave of interest in Egyptian symbols and building styles (Carrott 1978). The company of actors next assembled on stage and sang a composition by Alexander Reinagle (1756–1809), one of Washington's favorite composers. Thomas Wignell (1753–1803), co-founder with Reinagle of the Chestnut Street Theatre, eulogized the late president. The show must go on, though, and it did. The Chestnut Street company had chosen one of Washington's favorite plays, William Whitehead's (1712–85) *The Roman Father*, based on Corneille's *Horace*. At an emotionally charged time of national mourning and political anxiety, Wignell and Reinagle reached for the stability and clarity of neoclassical iconography and drama. Even though their Roman drama was an English playwright's reworking of a French playwright's adaptation of a narrative from Livy, Wignell and Reinagle's introductory tableau invited viewers to look beyond the mediators and find consolation in the evening's evocation of resonances between Rome and the new Republic. In this chapter I hope to explore what neoclassical drama meant to the citizens of Philadelphia in the first three-quarters of the nineteenth century. Many of the features of the Chestnut Street Theatre's commemoration of Washington's death will recur: an assumption that the audience would understand and respond to classical iconography and actions, mediation through English or French playwrights, and use of the classical world as a lens through which to view contemporary American social and political concerns.

In a volume devoted to Greek drama throughout the Americas, some explanation is needed for its focus on a single city. Histories of theater in America often amount to a history of theater in New York, where generous documentation allows due attention to important themes and events: class distinctions between audiences at the Park and Bowery, the Astor Place riot, the place of imported plays and actors, and so on. Yet Philadelphia was the capital of the country until 1800 and remained the second largest city in the country until the 1830 census, when Baltimore nudged it into third place.[3] Philadelphia also had a thriving theatrical culture, and like New York to the north and Charleston to the south, it formed a focus of regional activity. Companies from the Chestnut Street and Walnut Street Theatres regularly toured south to Baltimore and west to Pittsburgh and Ohio.

Classical reception, also, is not a uniform phenomenon, and even within a single country regional differences can be observed. This is especially true for the United States in the first three-quarters of the nineteenth century, as geographical expansion led to increased pluralism and regional diversity. After the Civil War, on the other hand, the rise of touring "combination companies," facilitated by the increased ease and range of railroad travel, and from 1896 the domination of the New York-based Theatrical Syndicate, led to a decline in the variety of local and regional theatrical cultures (Frick 1999). Exploring classical reception in a single city may lead to a richer, more nuanced picture of America's long conversation with the ancient world.

The Theaters

For theater-goers in early nineteenth-century Philadelphia, engagement with the classical world began before the curtain went up, and even before they entered the theater itself. The three leading houses for serious drama were named after their locations on the city's grid: the Arch Street, Chestnut Street, and Walnut Street Theatres. Prior to the Revolutionary War, Philadelphia's playhouses had either been adapted from existing, utilitarian buildings, like the waterfront warehouse converted by Walter Murray and Thomas Kean in 1749, or if built as theaters, were as plain and unadorned as the spaces that they replaced. A contemporary witness described the Southwark Theatre at South and Apollo, built for the Hallam–Douglass company in 1766, as "an ugly ill-conceived affair outside and inside."[4] The Arch Street, Chestnut Street, and Walnut Street houses, however, declared their allegiance to classical and European models, and perhaps the status of their hoped-for audiences, in the neoclassical balances of their elegant façades, built from the designs of some of the young country's leading architects.

When the earliest of these theaters, the Chestnut Street,[5] opened in 1794, its red brick Colonial architecture harmonized with the State House (Independence Hall) a few steps away, but a remodeling in 1805 under the direction of its original architect, Benjamin Latrobe, gave it a Corinthian portico between projecting wings and an interior program with neoclassical and patriotic themes (Glazer 1986: 83–4). The Walnut Street Theatre underwent several bouts of remodeling, changing from an equestran circus to a theater and back to a circus before becoming a theater finally in 1827. Like its rival on Chestnut Street, it invited audiences to pass through a Doric colonnade under six arched windows before they entered the auditorium. John Haviland (1792–1852), the architect of its 1809 structure, was along with Latrobe one of the pioneers of Greek Revival architecture in the United States. The Arch Street, built in 1828, boasted a Doric porch reached by a six-step stylobate in front of the two story main house, which was crowned by a pediment with a "standing heroic statue grasping a classic scene" (Glazer 1986: 61). In their architecture all three of these houses proclaimed to the outside world their participation in America's reception of classical models and their affiliation with the Greek and Roman origins of theater (Hamlin 1944: 63–89). From the 1840s onward, also, "the commercial theatre became increasingly divided between 'respectable' fare for pacified bourgeois spectators and unrespectable entertainments for rowdy workers" (McConachie 1999: 147). It is tempting to suggest that the neoclassical façades of the Arch Street, Chestnut Street, and Walnut Street houses were intended to serve as gateways to admit the genteel and filters to exclude the vulgar.

The Plays

Once inside, Philadelphia audiences could expect to see tragedies, comedies, farces, operas both serious and comic, and a variety of other entertainments. On Wednesday March 2, 1859, for example, playgoers at the Arch Street Theatre were treated to Talfourd's *Ion, or, The Foundling of Argos*, followed by a ballet (a pas de deux by "Miss Wood and M'lle Therese"), musical selections, and finally a one-act comedy, Richard Butler Glengall's *The Irish Tutor*.[6] The leap from neoclassical tragedy to dance to comedy was typical of theatrical evenings throughout the period covered by this chapter; on Tuesday, November 12, 1867, the Walnut Street Theatre presented John Banim's *Damon and Pythias* introduced by an overture (see further Mayer, this volume). Instrumental and vocal interludes, including Schubert's setting of Goethe's "Erl König" and selections from Bellini's *Norma*, punctuated the acts of the drama.[7]

Plays drawn from ancient Greece or Rome formed only one part of Philadelphia's thriving dramatic culture in the nineteenth century. How large a part? A. H. Wilson's catalogue of mid-nineteenth-century Philadelphia dramatic life lists well over 3,300 titles produced between 1835 and 1855.[8] Only about 36 of the 3,000-plus plays in Wilson's catalogue have titles that suggest a Greek or Roman setting or theme, and so it may seem that classical drama was not very popular among Philadelphia audiences in the decades before the Civil War. Sheer number of titles, however, may not be the most reliable indicator of either popular taste or cultural influence. Dramas that draw audiences to performances year after year could shape nineteenth-century taste in a way that repeated iterations of Mose the Fireman or comical Yankees could not.

Ancient Greek Drama in Nineteenth-Century Philadelphia: *Medea* and Others

Despite the reverence that devotees of high culture had for the origins of drama in ancient Athens, Greek tragedy on the American stage before the 1880s was represented by adaptations, and often adaptations of adaptations, like Matilda Heron's version of Ernest Legouvé's *Médée*. These adaptations use ancient Greek drama as a point of departure, and their course often takes them far from anything that a twenty-first-century audience would accept as Aeschylus, Sophocles, Euripides, or Aristophanes; Legouvé's *Médée,* for example, adds Orpheus as a character, and his Medea, unlike Euripides' heroine, can be seen as driven to infanticide—the last scene makes it clear that she loves her children, and in the final moments of the play, as she is pursued by a mob of Corinthians calling for her death, she stabs her children to prevent them being taken from her. The final words of Legouvé's play transfer the blame for their deaths to Jason:

> JASON: Ah! Mes fils! . . . morts, aussi! Tous deux! tous deux!
> Ah, l'horreur! . . . Mes enfants! . . . morts! . . . Qui les a tués?
> MÉDÉE: Toi!

In Heron's rendering: "Great gods, what is't I see? my children dead! who hath killed them? MEDEA: Thou!"[9]

In fact, if we define "ancient Greek drama" as the scripts of the four Athenian dramatists, no ancient Greek play appeared on any North American public stage until students at Harvard produced an *Oedipus Tyrannus* in 1881 (cf. Mayer, this volume; Norman 1882; Pluggé 1938). Philadelphians had no opportunity to see ancient Greek drama in anything like its original form until the University of Pennsylvania's *Acharnians* of 1886 (Pearcy 2003). This performance formed part of a wave of academic productions of ancient drama in the United States, in Europe, Australia, and New Zealand, often in the original languages, in the 1880s and 1890s.[10] Between 1881 and 1903, 18 different colleges and universities put on 12 different Greek plays in 48 productions (Pluggé 1938: 14–16). At least 16 of these productions were performed in Greek (Pluggé 1938: table XI, 149). Until the 1880s, however, Aeschylus, Sophocles, Euripides, and Aristophanes existed in American life as authors, not playwrights, and their scripts were known, when they were known at all, either as objects of academic study or as curiosities read in translation.

Most college-educated American men encountered Greek drama through the pages of Andrew Dalzell's (1784–1812) *Graeca Majora* (1789), a hefty anthology that included Sophocles' *Oedipus Tyrannus* and Euripides' *Medea*. The first American edition appeared in 1809, and it was quickly adopted by Harvard, Yale, Columbia, Hamilton, and many other colleges and universities (Winterer 2002: 32–4). The Laws of the University of Pennsylvania for 1826 specify *Graeca Majora* among the required readings for the freshman, sophomore, and junior years (Snow 1907: 140–1). The second volume, containing *Oedipus* and *Medea*, appears along with Persius and Juvenal among the readings for the junior year, and so there is a good possibility that some elite Philadelphian young men first experienced Greek drama through the daily grind of college recitations. Others may have met Greek drama in a less formal way, through private reading or amateur productions.[11] Philadelphia, like other American cities in the earnestly self-improving early nineteenth century, had amateur dramatic societies like the Boothenian Dramatic Society, which met and gave performances on the fourth floor of an abandoned warehouse (Winter 1913: 243). Perhaps one of these clubs attempted a *Medea* or *Oedipus*; if so, it has left no trace.

In nineteenth-century Philadelphia until the 1880s, classical Athenian drama was too alien, too academic, and too completely textual and literary to imagine on the stage. To find *Medea*, or any other ancient drama, on Philadelphia stages before 1881 we must look to what Edith Hall calls "the rich parallel life that ancient texts have enjoyed in post-Renaissance theatres."[12] In many cases, especially early in the period under consideration here, an ancient myth in general rather than a specific Greek tragedy seems to be the inspiration for Greece on stage; for example, a pantomime, *Medea and Jason*, performed in New York in 1798 and again in 1800, 1801, and 1805, may not owe much to Euripides, especially if it is an American revival of either Gaetano Vestris's *Medea and Jason* or George Colman the Elder's burlesque of it, "*Medea and Jason*, A Ballet Tragi-Comique by Signior Novestris." Both were first produced a few months apart in 1780.[13] If it was the latter, then American audiences saw the ancient story re-enacted by characters from British panto: Jason as Pierrot, Medea as Mother Shipton, and Creon as Mr. Punch (McDonagh 2003: 50). Likewise a melodrama, *Theseus and Ariadna*, which appeared at the Chestnut Street Theatre sometime before 1810 and so antedates John Vanderlyn's controversial painting of 1812, probably reflects general interest in myth, and not a desire to represent any specific text on stage.[14]

Even a play explicitly based on Athenian drama could draw from several different tragedies rather than attempting to present a single ancient drama on stage. Talfourd's *Ion, or, The Foundling of Argos*, which had at least 31 separate, multi-evening runs in Philadelphia between 1836 and 1867, is not, despite its title, much like Euripides' *Ion* or any other Greek tragedy. Talfourd himself wrote of his play that Euripides' *Ion* "gave the first hint of the situation in which its hero is introduced . . . but otherwise there is no resemblance between this imperfect sketch and that exquisite picture" (Talfourd 1846: 17). Audiences inclined to look for sources must have thought of Sophocles more than Euripides, and especially of *Oedipus Tyrannus* when they saw the play's opening scene, with elders lamenting the plague that afflicts their city, or the first encounter between Ion and Adrastus, which evokes the exchange between Oedipus and Teiresias. *Antigone* may have contributed Ion's deliberate disobedience of the tyrant's edict and his insistence that "the eternal law, that where guilt is | Sorrow shall answer it" trumps Adrastus' human law. Edith Hall suggests that "the motif of the patriotic youth's suicide owes something to Euripides' *Phoenician Women*" and that "the reconciliation of the dying king Adrastus with his long-lost son Ion powerfully recalls the endings of both *Hippolytus* and *Trachiniae*" (Hall 1997: 291). To these I am tempted to add two plays in which Euripides presents kings of Argos opposed by young monarchs with democratic leanings: *Suppliant Women*, which turns on the contrast between Adrastus, King of Argos, and Theseus, and *The Children of Heracles*, in which the young King of Athens, Demophon, is really a democrat in disguise, and another King of Argos, Eurystheus, becomes a more sympathetic character as his life ends, just as Adrastus does in Talfourd's play.

Even so, Philadelphia audiences in the mid-nineteenth century could have received some impression of at least one play of Euripides, *Medea*, from a string of visiting productions between 1858 and 1886.[15] These productions originated in European theater and came to Philadelphia on tour; they exemplify the growing power of touring star actors and companies made possible by the revolution in travel and communication that railroads and telegraph brought about. The earliest of this group saw the English-born actress Jean Margaret Davenport (1829–1903) brought in for three weeks in December, 1858, to give star power to the Walnut Street Theatre's then struggling company.[16] The recently widowed Mrs. David P. Bowers (born Elizabeth Crocker), a well-known Philadelphia actress, had assumed management of the Walnut Street in 1857 and attempted to revive the already obsolescent stock company system. The need to import a star like Davenport, like John Drew's appearance a few weeks before, confirmed the imminent failure of Bowers's experiment, and she gave up control of the Walnut on January 20 (Davis 2010: 115). Davenport appeared in two standards of the repertoire, *Camille* and Legouvé's *Medea* in the English adaptation by Oliver C. Wyman, and she returned to the Walnut Street house for another turn as Medea in October 1859.[17] M. Augusta Garrettson, a shrewd businesswoman who recognized the inevitablilty of the star system, took over the management of the Walnut Street in January 1859. Only a few weeks after Davenport's second appearance, she brought in Matilda Heron (1830–77) for another *Medea*, this time in Heron's own translation of Legouvé's version.[18] Although Heron, who had been born in Ireland, made her home in Philadelphia, she was part of the new system of touring star actors, as familiar to audiences in New York and San Francisco as she was in her home town. In her January 1860 appearance, Heron alternated her Medea with another signature role, Camille, and also brought her own new play, *Lesbia*, to Philadelphia audiences (see further Davis, this volume).[19] Another visiting actress known for her portrayal of Medea, Avonia Jones (1839–67), appeared in Heron's translation of Legouvé's version at the Chestnut Street Theatre for a two-week run in November 1863.[20]

Two European actresses, however, Adelaide Ristori and Francesca Janauschek, performing in Italian and German respectively, defined Philadelphia's experience of Medea in the 1860s (see further Davis, this volume). Ristori appeared at the Academy of Music on December 10, 1866, in an Italian translation of Legouvé's *Medée*. The *Evening*

Telegraph's anonymous critic confessed disappointment with the "tameness" of her conception of the role: "At times she reached to the stern, inborn dignity and lofty command of the Colchian princess; but more frequently fell beneath it and became almost trivial."[21] A few days later he was happier with her Phaedra and praised the same qualities of naturalness and reality that he had condemned in her Medea.[22] This reviewer's response to Ristori's Medea may have been influenced by awareness of Euripides' text, or at least by a feeling that he ought to be aware of it: nineteenth-century elite theater-goers encountered Greek tragedy, and Euripides' *Medea* in particular, in the first place as a text on the page, and that experience colored their perception of Medea when they saw her on stage. Even a reviewer who, whether from lack of a classical education or fading memory of one, betrays his ignorance of the Greek original feels obliged to pretend to familiarity with it. In reviewing Ristori's *Medea*, the *Evening Telegraph*'s critic remarks that "the 'Medea' of Legouve [*sic*], and the 'Medea' of Sophocles [*sic*], are two different creations," and he reinforces the literary orientation of his review by peppering it with what seem to be quotations from the play: "Yet enough remains of the original to recognize the dark enchantress of Colchis; she who, for the love of the 'yellow-haired Jason', stained her white hands with the blood of her young brother, and forsaking the barbaric splendor of the 'marble walls and roofs of gold' of Aeetes' palace, dared the perils of the 'unknown sea' with the bold Argonauts of Hellas." Ristori toured the Unitied States in Legouvé's *Médée* for nearly 20 years and returned to Philadelphia at least twice. The part was so identified with her that in 1870 Duprez and Benedict's Minstrels could hope to draw a crowd to their theater at 47–9 North Seventh Street for an evening including skits titled "Man Life Boat," "Medea, or Ristori Restored," and "Sports of the Arena."[23]

The Medea most often seen in Philadelphia in the years after the Civil War, however, was not Ristori but another European actress, Francesca Janauschek (1830–1904), who appeared in Franz Grillparzer's *Medea*.[24] Janauschek appeared as Medea at the Chestnut Street Theatre in 1867, and the Academy of Music in 1868, at the Walnut Street in 1873, 1874, 1877, 1878, and 1881, and at the Chestnut Street Opera House in 1886 (Foley 2012: 279). Her performances in German attracted enthusiastic crowds from Philadelphia's large German-speaking population.[25] Attention seems to have focused, though, on her performances in other roles, on her celebrity, and, as she became more proficient in English, on her skill in portraying roles like Lady Macbeth. Both Ristori and Janauschek, in fact, represent a new kind of actress who emerged in the second half of the nineteenth century: the international star, known often by a single name—Rachel, Ristori—and famous as much for who she was as for the parts that she played. These actresses, as Shannyn Fiske suggests, concentrated on portraying intense emotions in a way that would move their audience to an analogous response (see further Davis, this volume; Fiske 2008: 30–5).

But what made Medea in particular a vehicle for stardom? What were Philadelphia audiences watching for when they saw Ristori or Janauschek as Medea (see further Bosher and Cox, this volume, for the very different audience responses to Ristori in Chicago)? Two intersecting cultural movements, I suggest, gave *Medea* special relevance for American theater audiences from about 1850 on. First, actual and potential changes in the social, legal, and existential status of women, subsumed under the heading "the woman question," became matters of cultural urgency. The various Medeas of the nineteenth century join in this dialogue by posing the question of what a woman can be.[26] Is Medea monstrous, barbarous, an "other" beyond comprehension, or is she recognizably the same as the women who, with their husbands, brothers, fathers, and lovers, filled theaters to watch Ristori or Janauschek? Contemporary responses suggest that Philadelphia audiences brought these questions to the theater or found them there when they arrived. Reporting on Janauschek's first appearance in Philadelphia, an anonymous reviewer in the *Daily Evening Telegraph* in 1867 noted Grillparzer's omission of Legouvé's character Orpheus and thought that this created a difference between his Medea and Legouvé's heroine:

> If anything, this omission is an improvement, for it gives more decision and greater strength to the prominent *role* of the play, and demands an increased versatility in the personator of that *role*. Helpless, forsaken by "Jason," pursued with unrelenting hate by gods and men alike, the character of "Medea" is deprived of much of its usual barbarity, is made more human and less ferocious; and the strong love of country and earnest devotion to the welfare of her children which pervade it appeal irresistibly to the sympathies of every auditor. M'lle Janauschek's conception of this difficult and imposing character is wonderfully faithful. She does not storm and rave, but, despite the harshness of her fate, is still human, and womanly withal.[27]

On December 11 of the previous year the same or another reviewer for the *Evening Telegraph* confessed disappointment with Ristori's Medea at the Academy of Music, which he found tame and lacking in the "subtle effect" and "irresistible impulse of intense feeling" that he felt the character required.[28] Both responses reveal a concern to demarcate the appropriate range of Medea's passion. Medea had to remain recognizable as a woman, but to portray her as an ordinary woman risked suggesting that any woman, even those in the audience, might become a Medea (see further Davis, this volume).[29]

By mid-century, American theater audiences included increasing numbers of women, and by the third quarter of the century women may have made up a majority, as they do now, in theaters catering to upper- and middle-class audiences (Butsch 1994). The audience for Ristori's Medea, announced the *Evening Telegraph* on December 10, 1866, would be "large, elite, and *distingue* [sic]." A decade earlier, renovations of the Walnut Street Theatre had included removing partitions between boxes so as to accommodate the newly fashionable hoop skirts (Davis 2010: 114). That change coincided with an expansion in the audience for classical, and specifically Greek, culture. Caroline Winterer has documented the ways in which a new turn from elite "Grecian" taste to middle-class moral edification in mid-nineteenth-century American classicism opened a door for women into the previously masculine world of classical learning (Winterer 2007: 142–64). Excluded from universities and the delights of *Graeca Majora*, middle-class and elite women could nevertheless find a way to the classical world through translations, mythological compendia like Thomas Bulfinch's *Age of Fable* (1855), and neoclassical drama. Greece especially was thought to offer examples of the kind of spiritual, moral, and emotional truths and experiences that were as available to women as to men. Women's involvement in popular Hellenism, expansion of classical learning beyond universities and their male graduates, and destabilization of gender roles created an audience for the Philadelphia Medeas of the second half of the nineteenth century.

THE OTHER GREEKS: SPECTACLE, BURLESQUE, BLACKFACE

Neoclassical tragedies like Payne's *Brutus* and Talfourd's *Ion* or adaptations like Legouvé's *Medea* may have provoked thought and given the audiences who stepped under the classical porticoes of the Walnut Street, Chestnut Street, and Arch Street Theatres a sense that their concerns about authority in the family, social status, and gender roles had antecedents in the culturally approved world of ancient Greece and Rome. The ancient world, however, served other functions as well. Greece more than Rome provided matter for farce, parody, burlesque, spectacle, and other modes of dramatic representation that extended beyond the grave, political, and paternal subjects of plays like *Brutus, or, The Fall of Tarquin* and *Virginius, or, The Roman Father*. Yet in these less elevated genres as well, Philadelphia audiences could find cultural sanction for their beliefs about society.

Especially in the early part of the nineteenth century, Philadelphia audiences appreciated a good spectacle, and such pieces often stood by themselves as part of an evening's bill, without any dramatic structure or context. *The Siege of Oxydrache*, at the Chestnut Street Theatre on January 12, 1800, offered a pageant of pure action and called upon the city's military resources:

> The antique battering rams were in full operation. The scaling of the walls by Alexander and his officers was exciting. The warriors were poised on the large Grecian shields of the soldiery, who formed bridges, one rising above the other like turrets or platforms of scaffolding, forming a tortoise, as it was called in the bills. Over this shield work Alexander, Hephestian, etc., sword in hand, with their scaling ladders, mounted and threw the rope-ladders over the coping of the turrets. They climbed up, fighting at every step. They severally gained the top of the battlements and precipitated themselves, apparently into the city. On the bridge at the back [were] overwhelming numbers in hand to hand contention—receiving the darts of enemies in a shield, plucking them out and hurling them back to the enemy.... They employed real horses in this piece, clad in full armorial housings, or coverings, a kind of scale armor... The march into Babylon was a most imposing processional exhibition. The properties, banners and trophies, with eagles, elephants, lions, etc., were composed of papier-mache [*sic*], in the most artistical style. The marching of the troops in sections, hollow squares and phalanx, were most admirably performed by eighty marines from the Navy Yard, drilled by night rehearsals for this purpose.[30]

The Siege of Oxydrache claimed to be derived from Nathaniel Lee's popular drama *The Rival Queens, or, The Death of Alexander the Great* (1677), but its military excitements remain offstage in that play. Another classically themed spectacle, the pantomime *Hercules and Omphale* of 1801, featured a "shower of fire" (Davis 1957: 45).

The 1830s and 1840s saw a vogue for classical burlesques with titles like *Hercules, King of Clubs* (Chestnut Street, 1839); first at the Walnut Street in 1843, it returned to the New Theatre in 1844, to the Arch Street house in 1847, and to both the Arch Street and Walnut Street in 1849. The most popular of these classical burlesques were the "extravaganzas" of James Robinson Planché (1796–1880). Planché's playlets, with titles like *Olympic Revels, or, Prometheus and Pandora*; *Olympic Devils, or, Orpheus and Eurydice* (both 1831); *The Paphian Bower, or, Venus and Adonis* (1832); and *Telemachus, or, The Island of Calypso* (1834), can still entertain because they depend on the humor inherent in transplanting contemporary sentiments, songs, and character types into the world of Greek mythology.[31] They occupy a place between John Gay and Gilbert and Sullivan, "recalling the burlettas and pantomimes of the eighteenth century and pointing the way toward the comic operas of the late nineteenth."[32] *Olympic Devils* had a brief run at the Chestnut Street in 1839, but in Philadelphia the most popular by far of Planché's sketches was the exuberantly titled *The Deep, Deep Sea or Perseus and Andromeda or the American Sea Serpent*.[33] It played at the Walnut and Arch Street Theatres in 1835, returned to the Arch Street in 1836 and to the Arch and Chestnut Street in 1837, and was revived at Barnum's Circus in 1848. More than Planché's other extravaganzas it appealed to American audiences. Planché presents the sea serpent in pursuit of Andromeda as yet another variation on the comical Yankee, described as "a Yankee-Doodle *come* to Town—'half man', with a *Sea*-gar in his mouth—'half horse', with an azure *mane*—and 'half alligator', with an endless *tale*" (Croker and Tucker n.d.: 1. 145). The phrase "half horse, half alligator" alludes to "The Hunters of Kentucky," President Jackson's popular campaign song of 1828, according to which Kentucky frontiersmen at the Battle of New Orleans made up a force in which "ev'ry man was half a horse, and half an alligator." A rash of reported sightings of sea serpents off the coast of New England from 1817 on may also have given *The Deep, Deep Sea* topical interest.

A Medea of a Different Color

Philadelphia audiences who laughed at the Yankee sea serpent in Planché's entertainment also found humor in another stereotypical character. The list of *dramatis personae* describes him as the "Black Cook of the Ocean, a white-livered runagate." Played by a white actor in blackface and speaking in exaggerated Negro dialect,[34] he appears only to announce the sea serpent with the words "Help! murder! massa captain; only look! . . . Nebber see him any such man. Him sarpent!—dan a tousand cable bigger." Discomfiting though Planché's Cook may be to readers in the twenty-first century, he is not the only corked up comic character in the history of Philadelphia's reception of Greek drama. As we have heard, in 1870 Duprez and Benedict's Minstrels included "Medea, or Ristori

Restored" in the program for their appearance in Philadelphia.³⁵ That blackface skit itself has left no trace.

The negative racial stereotyping of extravaganza and minstrel show finds its positive counterpoise in the use of classical paradigms to ennoble African-American resistance to slavery. Margaret Garner, the fugitive who killed her own children rather than see them returned to slavery, was compared to several figures from Greek and Roman antiquity; in these comparisons we can see black and white abolitionists and other anti-slavery advocates drawing on their experience of neoclassical drama to understand Garner's tragic action in significantly different ways. To James Bell, writing in the Canadian *Provincial Freeman*, Garner evoked the hero of James Sheridan Knowles's play *Virginius, or, The Roman Father*, who murdered his daughter rather than see her become a slave:

Thus, did a Roman Father slay, The idol of his soul, To screen her from a tyrant's lust, A tyrant's foul control. Though this was done, in days of yore, The act was truly brave; What value, pray, is life to man, If that man be a slave. Go and ask of Margaret Garner, Who's now in prison bound, (No braver woman e'er hath trod, Columbia's slave-cursed ground:) Why did she with a mother's hand, Deprive her child of breath! She'll tell you, with a Roman's smile, That slavery's worse than death. (Bell 1856)

Frances Ellen Watkins Harper's poem "The Slave Mother: A Tale of the Ohio" also compares Garner to Roman heroes (Winterer 2007: 187). The *Provincial Freeman* was written, edited, and published between 1854 and 1857 by ex-slaves and freeborn blacks living in Toronto.³⁶ F. E. W. Harper was a black American poet. For them, the appropriate classical analogues for Garner were to be found in Rome; it was there that they sought patterns of self-sacrifice and heroic moral acts animated by a sense of public duty. In mid-nineteenth-century Philadelphia, African-Americans were forced to pay more for seats at the elite theaters.³⁷ This differential pricing reinforced exclusion of African-Americans from an important medium of popular bourgeois Hellenism, but groups like the Colored Reading Society of Philadelphia and the Philadelphia Female Literary Association provided a space within which African-Americans could appropriate and refashion the literary taste and moral consciousness that classicism and classical education had given their white counterparts (Bacon and McClish 2000; Malamud 2011).

Elite, largely white audiences needed to see Garner through a different classical lens. In a striking parallel to the multiply mediated Medeas on stage as audiences experienced Ristori's realization of an Italian translation of Legouvés reworking of Euripides' play, Garner became known as Medea primarily through the caption to the *Harper's Weekly* engraving of Matthew Brady's photograph of Thomas Satterwhite Noble's 1867 painting, *Margaret Garner* (Fig. 4.1). Noble's painting itself sets the confrontation between Garner and her pursuers in a stage-like setting framed by an open window. Downstage left, Garner gestures dramatically toward the bodies of her children center; facing her stand four slave-catchers, who appear to have just made their entrance, carefully blocked from upstage center to downstage right so that their various emotions and responses can each be seen and appreciated. Even whites sympathetic to the abolitionist cause, Caroline

FIG. 4.1 *The Modern Medea*, wood engraving after Thomas Satterwhite Noble's painting *Margaret Garner*, reproduced from *Harper's Weekly* (May 18, 1867).

Winterer has suggested, were reluctant to draw parallels between acts of resistance by enslaved women and the heroism of ancient Romans. As Charles Darwin put it, an act that if done by a Roman matron would have counted as noble love of freedom was "in a poor negress . . . mere brutal obstinacy" (Winterer 2007: 186). It may have been easier for the readers of *Harper's Weekly* and other elite whites to see Garner through the lens of Medea, the barbarian sorceress who, rightly interpreted and enacted by a Ristori or Janauschek, could be seen as animated by maternal love and feminine passion, than for them to understand her deed as an act of political agency. Resistance to tyranny, like other political virtues, remained the province of whites, men, and Romans.

Conclusion

Measuring the psychological distance between the Medea of Ristori at the Chestnut Street Theatre or Academy of Music and the blackface Medea of Duprez and Benedict's Minstrels only a few blocks away serves to remind us of the diversity of classical receptions within a single American city. Yet Duprez and Benedict's "Ristori Restored" could not have made sense without Adelaide Ristori's portrayal of Legouvé's heroine. Drama with Greek or Roman settings, based on myth, legend, history, or actual Greek drama, and always mediated through adaptation, translation, and imagination of the ancient world, allowed Philadelphia audiences in the first two-thirds of the nineteenth century to affirm and subvert simultaneously their ideas about gender, race, and society. Hellenism, then as now, was a contested arena.

Notes

1. Some material in this chapter appears in slightly different form in Pearcy 2003 and Pearcy 2013. An early version was delivered at Northwestern University on December 5, 2009 as part of a Sawyer Seminar series on "Theatre after Athens" (<http://www.sawyerseminar.northwestern.edu>), organized by Kathryn Bosher. Her memory continues to inspire my work on ancient drama and its modern receptions. This chapter draws heavily on the collections of the Free Library of Philadelphia, the Library Company of Philadelphia, and the Historical Society of Pennsylvania. I am grateful to Karin Suri at the Free Library, Cornelia King at the Library Company, and the other librarians and staff of those institutions. APGRD = The Archive of Performances of Greek and Roman Drama, Oxford (<http://www.apgrd.ox.ac.uk/>). Numbers following the abbreviation APGRD point to performances in the database of the Archive. References to *The Evening Telegraph* (Philadelphia) refer to issues found in the Library of Congress digital archive *Chronicling America: Historic American Newspapers* (<http://chroniclingamerica.loc.gov/>).
2. Rembrandt Peale's 1824 painting "George Washington, Patriae Pater," now in the collection of the Pennsylvania Academy of the Fine Arts, combines the motto "Patriae Pater" with the *corona civica* in an illusionistic "porthole" style portrait of Washington; see <http://www.pafa.org/museum/The-Collection-Greenfield-American-Art-Resource/

Tour-the-Collection/Category/Collection-Detail/985/let--P/mkey--1627/nameid--527/> accessed March 28, 2013.

3. In the 1830 census Baltimore counted 80,620 citizens to Philadelphia's 80,462. Philadelphia would drop to fourth place in the 1840 census, behind New York, New Orleans (which grew from 27,176 citizens in the 1830 census to 102,913 in 1840), and Baltimore. See Gibson 1998.
4. John F. Watson, *Annals of Philadelphia and Pennsylvania*, quoted in Rankin 1965: 112.
5. "Chesnut" appears to have been the regular spelling in the nineteenth century.
6. Playbill, Wheatley and Clarke's Arch Street Theatre, March 2, 1859; in Scrapbook 12, 19th Century Playbills, 1803–1939, The Free Library of Philadelphia, Rare Book Department—Theatre Collection.
7. Playbill, Walnut Street Theatre, November 12, 1867; in Scrapbook 62, 19th Century Playbills, 1803–1939, The Free Library of Philadelphia, Rare Book Department—Theatre Collection.
8. My rough count gives 3,346, including alternative titles; see Wilson 1935.
9. Legouvé 1854: 85 = Heron 1857: 56. On Legouvé's *Médée* in Paris and London, see Macintosh 2000a: 14–17; and Hall and Macintosh 2005: 201–5. For the New York reception, see Davis, this volume.
10. For productions from 1880 in Europe, Australia, and New Zealand, see Macintosh 1997.
11. As early as 1676, at least one Harvard freshman was interested enough to purchase an edition of Sophocles; Morrison 1936: i. 197.
12. Hall 2004: 51–89; quotation from p. 58.
13. On Noverre's ballet d'action *Médée et Jason* (1776), upon which Vestris' Medea and Jason is based, see Lada-Richards 2010: 24–9.
14. Vanderlyn's painting is now part of the collection of the Pennsylvania Academy of the Fine Arts; see <http://www.pafa.org/Museum/The-Collection-Greenfield-American-Art-Resource/Tour-the-Collection/Category/Collection-Detail/985/mkey--2514/> accessed November 26, 2012.
15. And even earlier from Giudetta Pasta's 1828 tour in Johann Mayr's opera, *Medea in Corinto*, which was at least known in Philadelphia; see *Philadelphia Album and Ladies Literary Portfolio*, September 24, 1831, 310, cited Foley 2012: 277–93.
16. APGRD 7087, December 10–24, 1858; for this and later productions, see also Foley 2012: 277.
17. APGRD 7088, October 17–25, 1859.
18. APGRD 7089, January 10–21, 1860.
19. Heron's non-classical *Lesbia*, which is set in Venice, is not to be confused with Richard Davey's one-act curtain raiser based on Catullus, which had its first performance in 1888; see Brown 1903: 442.
20. APGRD 7090, November 9–21, 1863. For Heron's and Jones's appearances as Medea in London in 1861, see Hall and Macintosh 2005: 423.
21. *The Evening Telegraph* (Philadelphia), December 11, 1866, fifth edition, 4.
22. "But if in *Phaedra* Ristori did not rise to the classic grandeur of Rachel, she gathered the character to her heart, humanized it, and made it natural," *The Evening Telegraph* (Philadelphia), December 15, 1866, fourth edition, 8.
23. Advertisement in *The Evening Telegraph* (Philadelphia), January 22, 1870, fifth edition, 3. For the numerous burlesques of Ristori's *Medea* in London, see Macintosh 2000b: 75–99; Hall and Macintosh 2005: 401–22.
24. For Grillparzer's 1821 version, see Macintosh 2000a: 12–14; and for the negative impact of Janauschek's appearances in London in 1876, compared to her popularity in Germany, Austria, and Russia, see Hall and Macintosh 2005: 424.

25. "Our German residents are greatly exercised about the appearance of M'lle Fanny Janauschek at the New Chestnut Street Theatre next week, and they will vie with their American-born friends in giving the great tragedienne an immense reception;" *The Evening Telegraph* (Philadelphia), December 11, 1867, fifth edition, 3.
26. Cf. Hall and Macintosh 2005: 391–429 on Medea in Britain.
27. *Daily Evening Telegraph*, December 17, 1867.
28. *The Evening Telegraph* (Philadelphia), December 11, 1866, fifth edition, 4.
29. On similar concerns about gender integrity in the title role in Talfourd's *Ion*, which was usually a breeches role in America, see Pearcy 2013.
30. Durang, quoted in Davis 1957: 31.
31. On classical burlesques and Greek tragic burlesques in particular, see Hall and Macintosh 2005: 350–90.
32. MacMillan 1928: 340. See also Diercks 1976.
33. Planché's original title was simply *The Deep, Deep Sea, or, Perseus and Andromeda*. For American audiences the sea serpent got top billing.
34. Black actors did not appear on American stages until after the Civil War; see Austin 1966.
35. Advertisement in *The Evening Telegraph* (Philadelphia), January 22, 1870, fifth edition, 3.
36. <http://www.accessible-archives.com/collections/african-american-newspapers/provincial-freeman/> accessed March 22, 2013.
37. At least through the 1850s, as playbills show, a gallery seat at the Arch Street Theatre cost 13 cents for white patrons but 25 cents for "colored persons."

References

Austin, G. E. (1966), "The Advent of the Negro Actor on the Legitimate Stage in America," *Journal of Negro Education* 35, 237–45.
Bacon, J. and G. McClish (2000), "Reinventing the Master's Tools: Nineteenth-Century African-American Literary Societies of Philadelphia and Rhetorical Education," *Rhetoric Society Quarterly* 30.4, 19–47.
Bell, J. (1856), "Liberty or Death," *The Provincial Freeman*, March 8. Toronto.
Brown, T. A. (1903), *A History of the New York Stage from the First Performance in 1732 to 1901*. New York.
Butsch, R. (1994), "Bowery B'hoys and Matinee Ladies: The Re-Gendering of Nineteenth-Century Theater Audiences," *American Quarterly* 46, 374–405.
Carrott, R. G. (1978), *The Egyptian Revival: Its Sources, Monuments, and Meaning, 1808–1858*. Berkeley.
Croker, T. F. and S. Tucker (eds. n.d.) *The Extravaganzas of J. R. Planché, Esq. (Somerset Herald) 1825–1871*. London.
Davis, A. (2010), *America's Longest Run: A History of the Walnut Street Theatre*. University Park, PA.
Davis, R. J. (1957), *Cradle of Culture: The Philadelphia Stage 1800–1810*. Philadelphia.
Diercks, P. T. (1976), "James Robinson Planché and the English Burletta Tradition," *Theatre Survey* 17, 68–81.
Fiske, S. (2008), *Heretical Hellenism: Women Writers, Ancient Greece, and the Victorian Popular Imagination*. Athens, OH.
Foley, H. P. (2012), *Reimagining Greek Tragedy on the American Stage*, Berkeley, Los Angeles, and London.

Frick, J. (1999), "A Changing Theatre: New York and Beyond," in D. B. Wilmeth and C. Bigsby eds., *The Cambridge History of American Theatre, ii: 1870–1945*. Cambridge, 196–232.

Gibson, C. (1998), "Population of the 100 Largest Cities and Other Urban Places in the United States: 1790 to 1900," Population Division Working Paper No. 27, U.S. Bureau of the Census, <http://www.census.gov/population/www/documentation/twps0027/twps0027.html> accessed March 27, 2013. Washington, DC.

Glazer, I. R. (1986), *Philadelphia Theatres, A–Z: A Comprehensive, Descriptive Record of 813 Theatres Constructed Since 1724*. New York, Westport, CT, and London.

Hall, E. (1997), "Talfourd's Ancient Greeks in the Theatre of Reform," *International Journal of the Classical Tradition* 3.3, 283–307.

Hall, E. (2004), "Towards a Theory of Performance Reception," *Arion* Third Series 12.1, 51–89.

Hall, E. and F. Macintosh (2005), *Greek Tragedy and the British Theatre 1660–1914*. Oxford.

Hamlin, T. (1944), *Greek Revival Architecture in America: Being an Account of Important Trends in American Architecture and American Life prior to The War Between the States*. London, New York, and Toronto.

Heron, M. (trans. 1857), *Medea*. New York.

Lada-Richards, I. (2010), "Dead but not Extinct: On Reinventing Pantomime Dancing in Eighteenth-Century England," in F. Macintosh ed., *The Ancient Dancer in the Modern World*. Oxford, 19–39.

Macintosh, F. (1997), "Tragedy in Performance: Nineteenth and Twentieth-Century Productions," in P. Easterling ed., *The Cambridge Companion to Greek Tragedy*. Cambridge, 284–323.

Macintosh, F. (2000a), "Introduction: The Performer in Performance," in E. Hall, F. Macintosh, and O. Taplin eds., *Medea in Performance*. Oxford, 1–31.

Macintosh, F. (2000b), "Medea Transposed: Burlesque and Gender on the Mid-Victorian Stage," in E. Hall, F. Macintosh, and O. Taplin eds., *Medea in Performance*. Oxford, 75–99.

Macintosh, F. (ed. 2010), *The Ancient Dancer in the Modern World: Responses to Greek and Roman Dance*. Oxford.

McConachie, B. (1999), "American Theatre in Context, from the Beginnings to 1870," in D. B. Wilmeth and C. Bigsby eds., *The Cambridge History of American Theatre, i: Beginnings to 1870*. Cambridge, 111–81.

McDonagh, J. (2003), *Child Murder & British Culture, 1720–1900*. Cambridge.

Macmillan, D. (1928), "Planché's Early Classical Burlesques," *Studies in Philology* 25, 340–5.

Malamud, M. (2011), "The *Auctoritas* of Antiquity: Debating Slavery through Classical Exempla in the Antebellum USA," in E. Hall, R. Alston, and J. McConnell eds., *Ancient Slavery and Abolition: From Hobbes to Hollywood*, Classical Presences. Oxford, 279–318.

Morrison, S. E. (1936), *Harvard College in the Seventeenth Century*, 2 vols. Cambridge, MA.

Norman, H. (1882), *An Account of the Harvard Greek Play*. Boston.

Pearcy, L. T. (2003), "Aristophanes in Philadelphia: The *Acharnians* of 1886," *Classical World* 96.3, 299–313.

Pearcy, L. T. (2013), "Talfourd's *Ion*: Classical Reception and Gender in Nineteenth-Century Philadelphia," in B. Gold, D. Lateiner, and J. Perkins eds., *Domina Illustris: Essays for Judith P. Hallett*. London, 241–51.

Pluggé, D. E. (1938), *History of Greek Play Production in American Colleges and Universities from 1881 to 1936*. New York.

Rankin, H. F. (1965, 2nd edn.), *The Theatre in Colonial America*. Chapel Hill, NC.

Snow, L. F. (1907), *The College Curriculum in the United States*. New York. Also available at <http://archive.org/details/collegecurriculo4snowgoog> accessed March 25, 2013.

Talfourd, T. N. (1846), *Tragedies: To Which are Added A Few Sonnets and Verses*. New York.

Wilson, A. H. (1935), *A History of the Philadelphia Theatre, 1835–1885*. Philadelphia.

Winter, W. (1913), *The Wallet of Time, Containing Personal, Biographical, and Critical Reminiscence of the American Theatre*, 2 vols. New York.

Winterer, C. (2002), *The Culture of Classicism: Ancient Greece and Rome in American Intellectual Life*. Baltimore.

Winterer, C. (2007), *The Mirror of Antiquity: American Women and the Classical Tradition, 1750–1900*. Ithaca, NY, and London.

CHAPTER 5

THEBES IN THE NEW WORLD

Revisiting the New York Antigone *of 1845*

FIONA MACINTOSH

In Dublin, on February 22, 1845 Sophocles' *Antigone*, with an orchestral introduction and settings for the *parodos* and six choral odes by Felix Mendelssohn Bartholdy, opened to huge acclaim and went on to play well into April of that year to packed houses. It overlapped with another less successful *Antigone* in New York, which opened on April 7, 1845 and played for eleven nights to indifferent houses. Both productions used the same English version by William Bartholomew (which had been commissioned for the London production a couple of months earlier in January 1845). This was a translation not of Sophocles' text directly but of the close German translation by Johann Jakob Christian Donner, which in turn had been commissioned for the founding production of this run of *Antigones*, the so-called Mendelssohn *Antigone* in the Neues Palais in Potsdam, which opened on October 28, 1841. From 1841 to 1845, the Mendelssohn *Antigone* had enjoyed numerous incarnations in different languages with different casts across the stages of Europe—Potsdam, Berlin, Hamburg, Leipzig, Munich, Paris, London—and was now playing concurrently in Dublin and New York.[1]

In many ways referring to these productions loosely and collectively as the Mendelssohn *Antigone* is misleading for the label hides as much as it reveals. The label gained currency during the second part of the nineteenth century when Mendelssohn's pre-eminence was sealed (especially within Britain) and regular concert performances of the musical settings were given. By 1888 Richard Jebb can state, in the Preface to his commentary on the play, that everyone knows the Mendelssohn *Antigone* (Jebb 1900: xliii). But in the 1840s, the music was always considered but one (integrated and often complicated and abstruse) aspect of a whole, despite Mendelssohn's rising popularity within the concert repertoire of Europe. In fact in New York, the 1845 *Antigone* is never referred to as the Mendelssohn *Antigone* at all, but the Dinneford *Antigone* after its producer, the financier turned actor-manager William Dinneford, who bankrolled the production as his inaugurating show at Palmo's Opera House, on Chamber's Street, whose lease he had just acquired (Fig. 5.1). In Dublin it is referred to as Faucit's *Antigone*,

FIG. 5.1 Palmo's Opera-House, Afterward Burton's Theatre. (After a watercolor drawing in the collection of Thomas J. McKee, Esq.) W. L. Keese, *William E. Burton, Actor, Author and Manager, A Sketch of his Career with Recollections of his Performances* (New York and London 1885).

after the actress Helen Faucit who made herself inseparable from the eponymous heroine. Faucit had taken over the role from Charlotte Vandenhoff, who had appeared in the part at London's Covent Garden in January. Faucit's performance took not only Dublin but subsequently Edinburgh, Glasgow, and eventually London, the following year, by storm; and she became *the* definitive Antigone for the Victorians causing not only de Quincey and Matthew Arnold, but also both male and female audience members, to fall victim to her charms. As de Quincey said, "we . . . all . . . fell in love with Antigone . . ." (Quincey 1863: 225).

What, then, can we learn from revisiting this notorious New York staging? First, it is necessary to debunk the numerous myths that have been spawned in its wake, notably that it was the first professional staging of an ancient play in the United States (Hartigan 1995: 11; Lawrence 1988: 433; Rogers 1986: 10). As other chapters in this volume amply demonstrate, there were numerous other London imports of adapted ancient plays from the 1830s onward, some of which went on successfully to take root in an American context. The earliest of these was *Oedipus; or, the Riddle of the Sphinx* staged at the Bowery Theatre in New York in 1834, based on John Savill Faucit's (the father of Helen Faucit, the star of the Dublin *Antigone*) domestic tragedy *Oedipus: A Musical Drama in Three*

Acts (1821).² While this *Oedipus* did not enjoy any afterlife following the first production, this was not the case for Talfourd's *Ion*, which remained prominent in the repertoire from its American première in 1836 (see further Pearcy, Bosher and Cox, Davis, this volume).

Secondly and most importantly, re-examining the New York *Antigone* demonstrates unequivocally that the imposition of geographical boundaries in nineteenth-century American reception must be resisted and a comparative rather than isolationist approach adopted. The New York and Dublin productions were widely divergent both in terms of how they were constituted and in their impact; and in order to understand what happened in New York, it is important to consider not only what happened in Dublin, but equally to take into account the other European stagings of the Mendelssohn *Antigone* from 1841 onward. As in London and earlier in Berlin, a burlesque of *Antigone* played in New York to popular acclaim. This is not (as is often maintained, e.g., by Rogers 1986) an indicator of a production's failure: on the contrary, it marks its status within contemporary cultural discourse. New York audiences may well have voted with their feet after the first few nights in opting for the burlesque at the Olympic rather than sampling the fare at Palmo's Theatre. But so too did London audiences (including George Henry Lewes), who flocked to the Olympic Theatre to see Frederick Robson's interpretation of Medea in Robert Brough burlesque rather than go to watch the great Italian tragedian Adelaide Ristori in Legouvé's *Medée* at the Lyceum.³ The burlesque, moreover, as in the case of other European burlesques, does not simply signal the production's cultural status; it can also illuminate its reception and, in this instance, it demonstrates how centrally perceived was the role played by the German-speaking, singing chorus. The New York *Antigone* was no ephemeral, damp squib for, despite its short run, it is still being discussed in the press some seven months after the production had closed.⁴

To speak of the Mendelssohn *Antigone* might imply that it was only the audience members who changed—in this case from Londoners to Dubliners or to the people of New York. This has led to some absurd stereotyping that has been commonplace in accounts of the nineteenth-century reception of ancient drama: so the failure of the production in New York, for example, has been put down to the audience's unpreparedness for "high" cultural acts. Some have alleged that the provinces may well have been more "prepared" than New York for drama that ranged beyond the staple fare of melodrama and burlesque.⁵ But a closer look at the evidence does not indicate any kind of cultural limitation on the part of New York audiences, for whom both English and Italian opera, at the very least, had been widely available at varied venues since the 1820s onward (Alquist 1997: 40).

However, mounting opera was always a risky business in New York; and German opera was something new to a city that was only very recently receiving significant numbers of German immigrants (Alquist 1997: 130; McConachie 1998: 157). Indeed, the experimental nature of the Mendelssohn *Antigone* needs to be seen in conjunction with the short season of German opera later in the year and the largely German repertoire of the newly formed New York Philharmonic and the New York Choral Society (both founded in 1842).⁶ In this sense, New York, like London under the influence of Prince

Albert, was being encouraged to widen its experience of German culture through the Mendelssohn *Antigone*; and German culture, in turn, was significantly shaping the cultural landscape of New York (McConachie 1998: 157; Pochmann 1957: 357–8). The New York production was not only hastily conceived, as we shall see, it was poorly executed as well. Furthermore, it opened against a background of economic depression, which had particularly hit the theaters. In 1842 Charles Dickens noted that the Park and Bowery Theatres were "generally deserted" (Dickens 1913: 80); and in the wake of the recent wave of German immigration, significant numbers of Italian and English actors were losing their foothold in the theaters (Alquist 1997: 40; Pochmann 1957: 358).

Finally, and more generally, revisiting the production raises important questions about the political potential of the play itself. Studies by Winterer and Richard on the Classics in America would lead us to expect that audiences in 1845 would readily relish an ancient play that had been routinely invoked in discussions of "Natural" law (Richard 2009; Winterer 2001, 2002, 2007). Indeed, advance notices of the production in the *Albion* both anticipate and seek to generate considerable interest in and enthusiasm for the forthcoming *Antigone*.[7] Sophocles' tragedy was understood as a highly "political" text in American scholarship from 1830 to 1850. However, Winterer has argued that by the second half of the nineteenth century, *Antigone* in America is no longer deemed a political play but is read as a thoroughly domesticated text, in which Creon is patriarch and Antigone the womanly ideal who reluctantly transgresses the patriarchy only to perform her religious and familial duties (Winterer 2007: 205). Does the 1845 *Antigone* mark the turning away from political readings and augur the apolitical ones to come? Although with Bartholomew's Schlegelian translation—according to which Creon is tyrant to Antigone's noble young woman—the production had a perfect vehicle for a tragedy of political resistance, this does not seem to have been the reading on offer. With Miss Clarendon in the role (rather than, say, her rival Charlotte Cushman),[8] *Antigone* does not appear to grab the headlines; and instead of the dynamic between protagonist and deuteragonist, the focus of attention falls on a controversial German, singing chorus. While Margaret Fuller reported that she found some solace in the New York *Antigone* because the protagonist afforded her a kindred spirit, it was generally felt that Miss Clarendon had failed to inspire the kind of confidence that Antigones, and especially Helen Faucit, were able to command elsewhere (Fuller 1903: 22). Indeed, a close look at the details surrounding the production will demonstrate that New York ended up with the B-team to Dublin's class-act, which resulted in a production that prompted local rather than broader political concerns.

Antigone in Europe

When Friedrich Wilhelm IV came to the throne of Prussia in June 1840, he embarked upon a series of liberal reforms (that included abolition of press censorship, amnesty for many prisoners) as well as a plan to institute a cultural programme that would make

Prussia the envy of Europe. He invited intellectuals to come to court—the Brothers Grimm, Schelling, Alexander von Humboldt (as a minister)—and appointed Ludwig Tieck, the poet, as his Vorleser. After Tieck gave a reading to the Court of *Antigone* in Donner's recently published close translation of 1839, the King decided that a performance of Sophocles' tragedy should take place in Potsdam.

In its collaborative nature (under the direction of Tieck himself, with the music of Mendelssohn and the academic advice of the famous philologist August Boeckh, for whom *Antigone* had been a subject of detailed research), the production was to reflect the ideal "bourgeois society" (*bürgerliche Gesellschaft*), which in turn was to reflect Hegel's "moral community" (*sittliche Gemeinschaft*) of fifth-century Athens. Even though in Boeckh's reading Creon was "harsh and tyrannical," there have been attempts to impose a Hegelian reading upon this production (Flashar 1991: 76–8; Steiner 1984). More likely, the liberal audience would have identified with Antigone (Boeckh's "great and noble" (*gross und edel*) young woman who is unskilled in moderation (*des Masses unkundig*)). The set in accordance with the Vitruvian study of Genelli of 1818 had a raised stage for actors (and aided by the amphitheater-stage of the Neues Palais), a sizeable *orchestra* for the chorus (fifteen plus one leader from the Berlin Continental Opera) and the instrumentalists. If the passing of the eighteenth century could be said to mark the turning away from the idea of appropriation of and improvement upon the ancients, this production heralded the new era in which imitation and revival were to become the norm.

From Potsdam, the production went to the Hoftheater in Berlin, where it was promptly burlesqued and where it remained in the repertoire until 1842. It toured to Hamburg, Vienna, Leipzig, and Munich and very soon it came to be recognized as a cultural phenomenon across the whole of Europe, prompting a conference of philologists in Kassel as well as a commemorative medal with the heads of the composer and the producer stamped upon it.

The Paris production of 1844 (March 21 at the Odéon) is worthy of note because it showed how the Mendelssohn *Antigone* need not remain a "foreign" import, but could be domesticated to enormous effect. The Romantic poet Gérard de Nerval pronounced in advance of the opening of the production: "Greece has risen from the grave."[9] The French translation was by two ardent Romantic poets, Paul Meurice and Auguste Vacquerie, which guaranteed that this Prussian-Greek revival was hailed by many as an illuminating contribution to the vibrant French Romantic theater. Greek tragedy—like Shakespearian tragedy—was now enlisted on the side of French Romanticism. In the preface to their translation (that appeared fifteen days after the performance), Meurice and Vacquerie eloquently outline the reasons for their appropriation of a Greek tragedy: the greatest mistake, in their estimation, is to take Greek tragedy as tragedy; with its ability to evoke both laughter and tears in the audience, and with its inclusion of music, it is best understood not in relation to neoclassical tragedy, but to Romantic melodrama instead. This highly contentious claim inevitably led to opposition toward the translation per se, and we find many traditionalists playing down the content of the play in their reviews and emphasizing instead (as in London the following year) the impressive set and the arresting (but not necessarily immediately pleasing) Mendelssohn score.

What these traditionalists found hardest to cope with was that tragic drama was now being expected to encompass a new, less restrained emotional range ("une violence de sentiment"). At the Odéon, Antigone's passage to her death was said to have been characterized by deliriously convulsive movements as she clung onto the Theban elders in the chorus in despair and desperation. These divided responses apart, the overall impact of the Mendelssohn *Antigone* was inspirational. It showed French audiences that Greek drama could resist the neoclassical strictures in terms of its linguistic and emotional range and its flexibility; and it also showed that when tragedy was played out in a theatrical space that included two separate performance levels—one for the actors and one for a singing chorus—the play's meaning and emotional amplitude were considerably enhanced.

When London's *Antigone* opened on January 2, 1845, the set again was noted with great interest. Historical accuracy in sets had become an important goal in the wake of Stuart and Revett's multivolume *The Antiquities of Athens and Other Monuments of Greece* (1762); and with Louis Daguerre and William Fox Talbot's recent early photographic experiments very much in the public eye in the early 1840s, antiquarian accuracy was of considerable academic and popular interest. The set designed by John Macfarren met with widespread approval and in many ways proved a greater talking point than other aspects of the production. When the *Antigone* opened in New York, it was the limited budget, rather than any lack of archaeological knowledge that led to the glaring anachronisms in the set that prompted Edgar Allan Poe's ridicule and contempt.[10] With a chorus in London nearly four times the size of the original one in Potsdam (now consisting of 60 male singers), and a ballet chorus for the Ode to Bacchus, the music (under the direction of George Macfarren) proved somewhat controversial, especially in respect to the delivery of the choral odes, for which the chorus were famously satirized in *Punch* magazine. In this respect, as we will see, the chorus in New York fared no better.[11]

Certain other features of the London production become significant for the New York *Antigone* in hindsight, notably the principal actors—John and Charlotte Vandenhoff, father and sister respectively of George Vandenhoff who played Creon in New York and who was responsible in many ways for the production. John Vandenhoff was widely acknowledged as William Macready's rival and was greatly admired in Britain and America for his tragic roles, notably for his Adrastus in Thomas Talfourd's *Ion* 1836, which enjoyed much success in America.[12] Charlotte Vandenhoff was widely praised in the role of Antigone in London; and the translator, William Bartholomew, after extolling the "united exertions of all concerned in its representation," dedicated his translation to Charlotte, "[w]hose classic impersonation of its heroine so greatly aided the favourable reception it obtained on the British stage" (Bartholomew 1845: i)

Antigone in New York

Why didn't the London production transfer to New York? For many, the New York *Antigone*, as we have heard, is Dinneford's production pure and simple: the financier and theater manager, who took over the running of Palmo's Opera House from the Italian restaurateur Ferdinand Palmo. In many ways, it was Palmo who can be said with hindsight to have democratized opera in New York, when he arranged musical soirées in Palmo's Garden that was attached to his restaurant (Dizikes 1993: 158–9; Horowitz 2005: 125; Krehbiel 1909: 44; McConachie 1988: 181–92). Following the success of the garden concerts, in February in 1844 Palmo had converted the adjacent public baths into an opera house and encouraged his regular clientele to attend the opera and have a meal after the show. The Opera House was not funded by subscriptions—there were no stakeholders—but depended on admissions charges (there were of course "free lists" for the press). Seats for the first season, at least, were benches—there were no private boxes—and were all priced at one dollar. During the second season he was forced to reduce the second tier of seats to 50 cents after sales proved disappointing and to build some private boxes to satisfy the demands of the elite (see Fig. 5.2). Palmo may well have only survived a couple of seasons as opera impresario but he had clearly put the Opera House on the map, not least by attracting members of the elite, for whom he also provided transport to return uptown after their night at the opera and meal in his restaurant (Towse 1913).

FIG. 5.2 Engraving of the interior of Palmo's Opera House (c.1845). The Granger Collection.

When Dinneford took over the lease from Palmo, he did not plan to run Palmo's as an opera house pure and simple but as a venue for legitimate theater and as a rival to the Park Theatre. In this sense, Mendelssohn's opera-tragedy was a perfect choice and, as with London's patent theaters, the repertoire he had in mind was a broad one. Immediately before the *Antigone*, Palmo's hosted a successful run from a blackface minstrel company called the Ethiopian Burlesques Opera Company (Lawrence 1988: 25); and during the *Antigone*'s short run, the opera-tragedy played alongside popular, light comedies (as indeed had been the case in London at Covent Garden in January).[13] As we have heard, the early 1840s were difficult times in the New York theater and Dinneford fared even less well than his predecessor because by May 1845, just after the eleven nights of *Antigone*, he announced his plans to relinquish the lease.[14]

However significant the financial role played by Dinneford, in many ways it was George Vandenhoff who was the catalyst for the New York *Antigone*. Dinneford's desire to make Palmo's into a serious rival to the Park Theatre no doubt determined his collaboration with Vandenhoff, who had made his New York debut as Hamlet at the Park.[15] But the Vandenhoff connection seems to have been overlooked, despite the fact that George was the obvious mediator in the transaction to mount the opera-tragedy, in which his father and sister had starred in London. Indeed, it seems highly likely that he was the instigator and talked Dinneford into the production because he was actively laying the ground for the arrival of the *Antigone* on March 4 by giving a lecture on Greek drama at the Society Library with readings from both Sophocles' *Antigone* and *King Lear* as illustrations (Odell 1931: 144). George Vandenhoff (like his father John) had received a good classical education at Stonyhurst, the Jesuit public school in Lancashire, England, and a public lecture on tragedy was well within his reach. Moreover, in 1845 the young Vandenhoff was clearly in need of work—he had a wife and family on the way (Vandenhoff 1860)—and there was no better prospect of easy success than bringing Europe's cultural phenomenon to New York.

The avowedly republican George Vandenhoff had arrived in America in September 1842, where he found a political climate that suited him well and work in the theater on the strength of his father's connections. But his choice of profession had not been endorsed by his father: it appears that his decision to leave the Bar and to join the family profession was not much welcomed by the acting dynasty. A revival of Talfourd's *Ion* in Liverpool in 1842, with John Vandenhoff in his usual role as Adrastus and both siblings, Charlotte and George, in the cast, may well have determined the personnel behind the New York *Antigone*. Here in Liverpool, according George Vandenhoff, the tensions within this famous acting dynasty became so awkward that George decided to go to America to find work. What these tensions consisted of is hard to ascertain, but they were certainly fueled by George's very recent decision to leave the Bar and join the family profession (Vandenhoff 1860: 119).

It is important to stress that George Vandenhoff had only been acting professionally for three years when he arrived in America (indeed he was still only 20 years old); and after finding himself a wife, he decided to stay in what he called enthusiastically the "land of the free" (Vandenhoff 1860: 77). In 1845 he took on the part of Creon at Palmo's

Opera House—inheriting the role from his father—when he was only 25. His youth and inexperience, and no doubt the opportunism of the young George, combined with no inconsiderable insouciance, account in many ways for some of the shortcomings of the New York *Antigone*. According to Edgar Allan Poe, George was to be commended for being "a capital elocutionist"—that year he was to publish the first edition of his book called *The Plain System of Elocution* (Poe 1965: 133). And it is, perhaps, significant that between 1843 and 1852 he gave more lecture hall recitals than he made appearances in plays; and his preliminary training at the English Bar—and later training in 1856–8 in order to practice at the American Bar—may well account for Poe's compliment.

It is, perhaps, too bold to suggest that George was a mere elocutionist, but it is important to note that he has gone down in the annals of theater history as a good rather than a great actor. Joseph Ireland in *Records of the New York Stage* (1867) comments:

> Though lacking the passion and intensity requisite for the loftiest assumptions of drama, Mr Vandenhoff possessed all the accomplishments and elegancies of mind and persons demanded for the higher grades of genteel comedy, and a wide range of serious parts somewhat subordinate to the standard of Shakespeare's subtlest creations.[16]

Was George Vandenhoff not quite up to his New York debut role as Hamlet, one of Shakespeare's "subtlest creations"? And can we infer that he was not, at 25, quite up to the role of Creon? He lacked gravitas; and perhaps some of the tensions between the family members on the stage in Liverpool were due to this perceived shortcoming on George's part. And George may well have been fully aware that his strengths lay elsewhere and the light-hearted farces that accompanied the *Antigone*, including Bulwer Lytton's *The Lady of Lyons* in which both he and Miss Clarendon starred, may well have been much better suited to his talents.

If George was perhaps too young and inexperienced in the part of Creon, Miss Clarendon receives no mention at all from Poe (an extraordinary putdown for any Antigone) and elsewhere she is dismissed as mediocre.[17] She had previously and notoriously suffered poor notices, and no inconsiderable spite from the now well-established star, Charlotte Cushman, when she had appeared in the American première of Boucicault's *London Assurance* (Dudden 1994: 83; Merrill 2000: 50). With ever-diminishing houses in spite of massively reduced seat prices, the New York *Antigone* continued but Miss Clarendon appears (perhaps under the strain) to have fallen ill and been unable to continue in the role.[18] Even if Margaret Fuller was impressed with Antigone, it seems more likely that the would-be star collapsed under the pressure of an over-demanding role and some hostile reviews.

However, the real problem with the production was not confined to the actors: the chorus, whose role is central in the Mendelssohn *Antigone* and who interact constantly with the actors, was the major weakness. In London, the chorus had been badly rehearsed; in New York they were perceived to be even less prepared for the demanding role. The chorus's plaid trousers poked out under their togas and prompted a famous *Punch* cartoon in London; George Vandenhoff comments on the New York chorus's comical dress with goat's-hair beards and wigs.[19] Now, instead of over-confidently singing across the footlights, as they had comically done in London, the New York (predominantly German) 40 all-male chorus under-confidently sing with their backs to the audience with copies of the score stuck to their noses (Lawrence 1988: 346; Vandenhoff 1860: 226). While the clearly respected Musical Director of the Opera House, George Loder, had been retained by Dinneford after he had taken over the lease from Palmo, the chorus members had been sacked and the new members were clearly not yet up to the task. Loder had conducted the American première of Mendelssohn's "The Hebrides; or Fingal's Cave" the previous November and he was now conducting an orchestra of 36, led by John St Luke whom Loder taught in return for performances at his behest (Lawrence 1988: 346n.). As Poe commented, Loder should have protested about the lack of rehearsal time and threatened to withdraw his services (Poe 1965: 135). Clearly neither Mendelssohn, nor Sophocles, was done justice in this hasty, unprofessional commercial venture.

However, the production didn't sink without trace: as we have already heard, it was still being discussed in November in the *Albion* as an example of the problems involved in attempts at copious reconstruction of antiquity.[20] It may well also have inspired another *Antigone* on June 16 and 17 in Philadelphia at Burton's Theatre, Arch Street (Wilson 1935). Furthermore, as in Berlin and London, it provided the inspiration for a burlesque; and William Mitchell's parodic *Antigone* at the Olympic was a success because it had something important to say, notably about the circumstances surrounding the production at Palmo's. The chorus in the burlesque at the Olympic was cast as the out-of-work "Artistes of the Italian opera," who had recently been made redundant following Dinneford's takeover of Palmo's Opera House. As we have heard, Dinneford hadn't kept on the chorus; and even more galling, the burlesque implies, he had taken on German-speaking singers in their stead. And if New Yorkers had begun to get used to opera being sung in Italian by Italians, here were German singers singing in (rather poor) English, presumably making their dependence on the score all the heavier. In the burlesque the Italian chorus protests in front of the façade of Palmo's Opera House (substituting for the Theban palace) about the introduction of English drama (read German versions of Greek tragedy), which on linguistic grounds alone has literally put them out of work. The burlesque is clearly picking up on the broader tensions that were coalescing here at Palmo's: German immigration brought new cultural models and new personnel that were displacing the old; and it is no doubt significant that by August of 1845, Palmo's Opera House had become one of New York's new German-speaking theaters (McConachie 1998: 157).

Over and beyond the problem of under rehearsal and the ethnic tensions, the perception that the New York *Antigone* had nothing particular to say appears to have been a major problem. If London had something to say about authenticity with its copiously reconstructed set, as we have heard, in New York the resources (however considerable) did not stretch far enough to achieve this end (Poe 1965: 133). In marked contrast to London's audience at Covent Garden, the audiences at Palmo's were considerably more diverse. While Margaret Fuller and her circle of intellectuals would have appreciated, at the very least, the spirit behind the attempts at historical accuracy in the creation of the set, the audience also included those (now paying 50 cents in the upper tier) who were equally at home in the popular playhouse of The Bowery. It was one such audience member who launched a piece of chewing tobacco at the guard's shield during the second episode.[21] This has regularly been construed as an act of contempt at the spectacle because it is said that it provoked great hilarity in the house. But could it not also be read as an act of political intervention, since those in the upper tier, in marked contrast to those in the lower tier and in the newly built private boxes, were regularly accustomed to express their (political or dismissive) feelings thus? Or are we forced to conclude, as Bosher and Cox do concerning the 1867 Chicago *Medea*, that any political message—beyond the local one inferred from Mitchell's burlesque—was unintended or remained indecipherable to the New York audience?

It is important to turn briefly to the contemporaneous Dublin production, which succeeded because it spoke to a more homogeneous, socially, even if religiously diverse, audience (Morash 2003: 79). *The Dublin Monitor* remarked how the Irish actress Helen Faucit stood "before the tyrant" like a "statue fresh from the chisel of Phidias."[22] If Miss Clarendon in New York was deemed to have a classical profile (Vandenhoff 1860: 225), she was unable to bring that profile to life as Faucit was felt to have done. Faucit's sculptural gestures, especially her upward hands, led her to create "forms of outline ever varying, yet always graceful, which have never before been witnessed."[23]

It was the *kommos*, above all, that marked out Faucit's performance:

> ... her address to her native citizens so feelingly pronounced, and aided by the effect of slow and solemn music, quite identifies the audience with the scene. We see before us the victim, pale, sinking, broken ... and finally she sinks exhausted, quivering with anguish—her hair, not by any art or stage trick, naturally falling over her face and neck—yet, Niobe-like, in every attitude, the same flexibility, the same grace is preserved. We see the noble girl sinking, not beneath the fear of death, as death—that, it is evident, she had from the first anticipated—no, it is the dying of such a death, and in such a cause. We learn this from her remembrance of her family wrongs even in her last moments—for the disgrace heaped on her beloved Polynices—*for the sorrows of her country* and the gloomy dungeon being made her "dreary bridal bed". For these it is she prostrated. These past—she arises still the noble Athenian maid, and rushes to her death with courage, if not with welcome.[24]

Against the background of British rule in Ireland, Antigone here clearly becomes Ireland, oppressed by the tyrant yet a hopeful resistance figure of Irish romantic nationalism. Indeed Bartholomew's Schlegelian (rather than Hegelian) translation invites this reading: Antigone is "rebel" in Bartholomew's text, as indeed is her beloved Haemon (Macintosh 2015).

While Faucit's Antigone spoke to audiences in ways that perhaps even the Theatre Royal, Dublin's actor-manager John Calcraft had not intended, it is striking how absent any political reading is from accounts of the New York production. We have heard already of George Vandenhoff's professed political republican and liberal sympathies; and in the same playhouse in New York, only six months before the production, there was a lecture entitled "American Liberty Vindicated and the Right of Adopted Citizens to Share its Blessings Defended" delivered by E. D. Connery, which was followed by the singing of Irish songs (Odell 1931: 143). There was clearly a burgeoning Irish nationalist community that frequented Palmo's, and who would have relished the Faucit *Antigone*, even if they shunned the Dinneford/Vandenhoff one.

It might be tempting, but I think ultimately implausible, to argue that the New York production was pivotal and representative of the mid-nineteenth-century shift in the American reception of tragedy generally and the *Antigone* in particular that Winterer identifies, in which tragedy ceases to be political and is understood to address domestic matters instead (Winterer 2007: 205). Political readings of the text were commonplace at this time; and given New York's various and swelling immigrant communities strongly identifying with nationalist movements in their mother countries (Italian as much as Irish, not to mention those German singers who were dragooned into joining the chorus), republican discourse still had a place in the city in 1845 as much as "Natural" law featured in discussions amongst the intelligentsia. Yet, none of these topical concerns featured in this *Antigone* because it was so very far from the Potsdam synthesis of the arts: it lacked a genuine star and it lacked an experienced actor-manager to pull it all together; and, above all, given such a socially and ethnically diverse audience, any message of "colonial" struggle was clearly belated and too diffuse to be effective. The "political" reading, relating to the very recent changes within the ethnic composition of New York and affecting Palmo's in particular, seems to have been the only "political" message that resonated widely.

In this sense, Thebes didn't quite make it to the New World in 1845. In 1894, Jean Mounet-Sully toured America as Creon with the same French version of Sophocles' translation that had been used in the 1844 Paris *Antigone* and with a new score by Saint-Saens. He performed on March 16 on board *La Bretagne* in the part of Oedipus and Creon in both Sophoclean tragedies before disembarkng in New York on March 18 (Penesco 2000). The North American tour lasted a month, beginning in New York's Abbey Theatre and going to Washington, Baltimore, Philadelphia, Boston, and Montreal. The *Antigone* had opened the previous year in France to great acclaim and what was particularly notable about the American tour was the twinning with the *Oedipus* (in which Mounet-Sully had performed since 1880). His Oedipus was renowned for his humanity—his irascibility but ultimately the plangency afforded by his utter vulnerability (Macintosh 2009). As Creon, he brought a new ferocity to the king's anger that made him the tyrant *par excellence*. But ultimately Mounet-Sully offered a much more Hegelian rather than Schegelian reading for beyond the earlier violence, there was a tragic pathos in the final scene that only a great tragic actor can pull off. According to *The New York Times*:

> It was by the adjustments of traits, mental and physical, to the making up of a living and consistent man that Mounet-Sully proved the accuracy of his conception, won his triumph, and made his Creon, as an artistic realization worthy to take place in memory beside the nobler form of Oedipus.[25]

Finally, albeit in French, Thebes became real in the New World.

Notes

1. For the Dublin production, see Macintosh 2015; for the London production, see Hall and Macintosh 2005; for the European productions, see Fischer-Lichte 2010.
2. Davis 2008. For the London 1821 première, see Hall and Macintosh 2005: 240–2.
3. Hall and Macintosh 2005: 401–19. For the American reception of Ristori, see Pearcy, Bosher and Cox, Davis, this volume.
4. November 1845, *The Albion*.
5. Hartigan 1995; and generally Nolan 1961: 410–13.
6. For the opera season, see Margaret Fuller in *Tribune* December 11, 1845; *Broadway Journal* December 22, 1845, 375, January 3, 1846; for German musical impact generally, see Horowitz 2005: 151.
7. *Albion* April 5, 1845, 164–8. For an excellent list of reviews, see Foley 2012: 249.
8. On the rivalry between Cushman and Miss Clarendon, see Merrill 2000: 50.
9. "La Grèce est sortie du tombeau," *L'Artiste* May 26, 1844, 61–2. Cited in Nostrand 1934: 42.
10. *Broadway Journal* April 12, 1845 in Poe 1965: 133; cf. *Albion* April 5, 1845, 164: "No expense had been spared in getting up the piece."
11. For further details of the London production, see Hall and Macintosh 2005.
12. See further Pearcy, Bosher and Cox, Davis, Mayer, this volume.
13. At Covent Garden, *Antigone* played together with *Crotchet and Quaver*, a "Grand Comic Pantomime." See playbill for January 2, 1845 (APGRD collection).
14. *Albion* May 3, 1845, 212.
15. Henry Seymour's Preface to Vandenhoff 1860.
16. Cited in Bordman 2004: s.v. Vandenhoff, George.
17. A. D. Paterson in *Anglo-American* April 12, 1845, 594–5.
18. *Spirit of the Times* April 12, 1845, 92 cited in Rogers 1986: 14.
19. *Punch* 8, January 18, 1845, 42; Vandenhoff 1860: 225–6.
20. *Albion* November 8, 1845, 540, November 15, 551–2.
21. *New York Evening Post* April 8, 1845, 2; *Albion* April 12. For comment, see Davis 2008.
22. As reported in *The Scotsman* March 15, 1845.
23. *The Scotsman* March 15, 1845.
24. *Dublin Monitor*, cited in *The Scotsman* March 15, 1845.
25. *New York Times* April 4, 1894. Cf. the earlier less enthusiastic review of March 28, 1894, which found the second part of the play overly long.

References

Alquist, K. (1997), *Democracy at the Opera: Music, Theatre, and Culture in New York City 1815–60*. Urbana, IL, and Chicago.

Bartholomew, W. (1845), *An Imitative Version of Sophocles' Tragedy Antigone, with its Melo-Dramatic Dialogue and Choruses, as Written and Adapted to the Music of Dr. Felix Mendelssohn Bartholdy by W. Bartholomew*. London.

Bordman, G. (2004), *The Oxford Companion to the American Theatre*. Oxford.

Davis, R. (2008), "The Riddle of the *Oedipus*: Practicing Reception and Antebellum American Theatre," *New Voices in Classical Reception Studies* 3, 1–13.

Dickens, C. (1913), *American Notes for General Circulation and Pictures from Italy*. London.

Dizikes, J. (1993), *Opera in America*. New Haven.
Dudden, F. E. (1994), *Women in the American Theatre: Actresses and Audiences, 1790–1870*. New Haven.
Fischer-Lichte, E. (2010), "Politicising Antigone," in S. E. Wilmer and A. Zukauskaite eds, *Interrogating Antigone in Postmodern Philosophy and Criticism*. Oxford, 329–52.
Flashar, H. (1991), *Inszenierung der Antike: das griechische Drama auf der Bühne der Neuzeit*. Munich.
Foley, H. P. (2012), *Reimagining Greek Tragedy on the American Stage*. Berkeley, Los Angeles, and London.
Fuller, M. (1903), *Love Letters of Margaret Fuller 1845*. Introduction by Julia Ward Howe. London.
Hall, E. and F. Macintosh (2005), *Greek Tragedy and the British Theatre 1660–1914*. Oxford.
Hartigan, K. V. (1995), *Greek Tragedy on the American Stage: Ancient Drama in the Commercial Theater, 1882–1994*. Westport, CT, and London.
Horowitz, J. (2005), *Classical Music in America*. New York.
Jebb, R. C (1900 edn.), Sophocles, *Antigone*, 3rd edn. Cambridge.
Krehbiel, H. E. (1909), *Chapters of Opera*, rev. edn. New York.
Lawrence, V. B. (1988), *Strong on Music: The New York Music Scene in the Days of George Templeton Strong 1836–75*, i: *Resonances*. New York and Oxford.
Macintosh, F. (2009), *Sophocles' Oedipus tyrannus*. Cambridge.
Macintosh, F. (2015), "Shakespearean Sophocles: (Re)-discovering and Performing Greek Tragedy in the Nineteenth Century," in N. Vance and J. Wallace eds., *The Oxford History of Classical Reception in English Literature*, iv: *1780–1880*. Oxford.
McConachie, B. (1988), "New York Opera-going, 1825–50: Creating an Elite Social Ritual," *American Music* 6 no. 2 (Summer), 181–92.
McConachie, B. (1998), "American Theatre in Context from the Beginnings to 1870," in D. B. Wimeth and C. Bigsby eds., *The Cambridge History of American Theatre*, i: *Beginnings to 1870*. Cambridge.
Merrill, L. (2000), *When Romeo was a Woman: Charlotte Cushman and her Circle of Female Spectators*. Ann Arbor.
Morash, C. (2003), *A History of Irish Theatre 1601–2000*. Cambridge.
Nolan, P. T. (1961), "Classical Tragedy in the Provincial Theater," *American Quarterly* 13.3 (Autumn), 410–13.
Nostrand, H. L. (1934), *Le Théâtre antique et à la antique en France de 1840 à 1900*. Paris.
Odell, G. C. (1931), *Annals of the New York Stage*, v: *1843–50*. New York.
Penesco, A. (2000). *Mounet-Sully et la partition intérieure*. Lyon.
Pochmann, H. A. (1957, repr. 1978), *German Culture in America: Philosophical and Literary Influences 1600–1900*. Madison.
Poe, E. A. (1965), *The Complete Works*. Ed. J. A. Harrison, vol. xii. New York.
Quincey, Thomas de (1863), "The Antigone of Sophocles as Represented on the Edinburgh Stage," in *The Art of Conversation and Other Papers*. Edinburgh, xiii. 199–233.
Richard, C. J. (2009), *The Golden Age of the Classics in America*. Cambridge, MA.
Rogers, S. M. (1986), *Greek Tragedy in the New York Theatre* (unpublished Ph.D. thesis, University of Michigan).
Steiner, G. (1984), *Antigones*. Oxford.
Towse, J. R. (1913), *Sixty Years of the Theatre*. New York.
Vandenhoff, G. (1860), *Dramatic Reminiscences*. London.

Wilson, A. H. (1935), *A History of the Philadelphia Theatre 1835–1855*. New York.
Winterer, C. (2001), "Victorian Antigone: Classicism and Women's Education in America, 1840–1900," *American Quarterly* 53.1 (March), 70–93.
Winterer, C. (2002), *The Culture of Classicism: Ancient Greece and Rome in American Intellectual Life 1780–1910*. Baltimore and London.
Winterer, C. (2007), *The Mirror of Antiquity: American Women and the Classical Tradition 1750–1900*. Ithaca, NY, and London.

CHAPTER 6

JULIA WARD HOWE'S *HIPPOLYTUS*

HELENE P. FOLEY

In 1857, shortly after she had seen the young and soon to be famous Edwin Booth play both Richelieu and Hamlet in Boston, Julia Ward Howe was asked by Booth's manager, and then by Booth himself, to write a play for him (Hall 1918: 92; Howe 1899: 237; Richards and Elliott 1916: i. 203–5). Howe, a member of the American east coast elite and initially a wealthy New York heiress, author of the 1861 "The Battle Hymn to the Republic" along with other fiction, essays, and poetry, and later a noted social activist, above all in abolitionist, women's rights, and global peace causes, was inspired by Booth's youthful beauty, reserve, shyness, and intelligence, to oblige with a new blank verse version of *Hippolytus* in 1858.[1] The noted actress Charlotte Cushman was slated to play Phaedra, and corresponded with Howe during the writing of the play. E. L. Davenport, the actor/manager of the Howard Athenaeum in Boston, agreed to produce the play in 1864, but reneged after rehearsals had begun. Reasons for this change of heart remain obscure: the play would have appeared late in the season and required new scenery; his actress wife did not like the secondary part she would have played.[2] Yet, as Cushman remarked, "My dear, if Edwin Booth and I had done nothing more than to stand upon the stage and say 'good evening' to each other, the house would have been filled" (Howe in Richards and Elliott 1916: 240–1).

Although she gave up playwriting after this disappointment, the highly educated Howe remained fascinated with Greek literature and began to add ancient Greek to her six other languages in the late 1860s.[3] Long afterward, Howe persuaded the noted actress Margaret Anglin to undertake the role of Phaedra with the British actor Walter Hampden as Hippolytus (Fig. 6.1),[4] although the well-received one-day performance took place at the Tremont Theatre in Boston on March 24, 1911 shortly after Howe's death in 1910. The play itself was not published until 1941.

Howe's *Hippolytus*, on which Euripides and Racine were the major influences, was one of two new American versions of Greek tragedy written in the nineteenth century.[5]

FIG. 6.1 Margaret Anglin as Phaedra and Maude Granger as Oenone in Julia Ward Howe's *Hippolytus*, Tremont Theatre, March 24, 1911, *Theatre Magazine*, Volume 13, June 1911, p. 201.

In Euripides' play, Phaedra, the wife of the Athenian hero Theseus, is made to fall in love with her stepson Hippolytus by the goddess of love Aphrodite, who wishes to punish him for exclusively worshipping the virgin goddess Artemis. In order to save her suicidal mistress's life, Phaedra's nurse solicits Hippolytus, who violently rejects her. To preserve the reputation of herself and her sons, Phaedra kills herself leaving a note accusing Hippolytus of raping her. Theseus returns from a disappearance into the underworld, reads the note, questions Hippolytus, and curses his son with a curse promised him by the god of the sea Poseidon. A monster from the sea destroys Hippolytus, who is dragged to death by his own maddened horses. Artemis reveals his error to Theseus, who then embraces his dying son. Racine's version follows Euripides' lost first version of the play along with the Roman poet Seneca's in having Phaedra solicit Hippolytus in person. Racine also provides a love interest for the otherwise chaste Hippolytus, and politicizes further issues relating to the inheritance of Theseus' kingdom. In echoing but modifying Euripides, Howe, as we shall see in more detail shortly, creates an attractively chaste Hippolytus whose inspired relation with the goddess Artemis frames her play. As one critic remarked: "In Mrs. Howe's play, Hippolytus is a more considerable and vivid figure, vowed and set apart. It is the tragedy of the youth as well as the woman" (*New York Times*, March 24, 1911).

In Howe's play, Hippolytus' chastity is motivated more elaborately than in earlier versions, and the hyperpassionate Phaedra is more deliberately seductive and vengeful. Hippolytus' inspired relation to Artemis, pointedly linked to his love for his Amazon mother, is emphasized by the goddess's direct encounters and engagement with him and the presence of Amazons in the woodland where Hippolytus hunts: "My mother was the lofty Amazon— | Wedded by Theseus—as she bequeathed to me | Her worship, dearer than my father's fame" (80). In an era where passionate primitive heroines (a specialty for Cushman and other actresses of this period) and a new spiritual, idealized, even feminized male acting style (above all, that of Booth) were reaching the height of their popularity in American theater, Howe's play also seems, as we shall see, to respond in a new way to the gender role reversals that appear in Euripides' version, where the virginal Hippolytus becomes the object of a cult worship after death for young women before marriage, and the love-sick Phaedra longs to break out of domestic confinement and become a huntress in the wilds.

This chapter will not only examine Howe's play as a novel interpretation of the Hippolytus/Phaedra story, but as a partial reflection of issues central to Howe's other fiction written shortly before it. Howe's earlier poetry books *Passion Flowers* and *Words for the Hour*, her controversial first play, *The World's Own,* and her unpublished and unfinished novel (begun before *Hippolytus*), *The Hermaphrodite*, offer representations of sexuality and gender relations unusually frank for the period and remarkable for a married woman of her status. Her own tensions with her much older husband, Samuel Gridley Howe, who tried to repress her intellectual and public life in favor of having her bear and devote herself to six children and to his own career, may also have played a role in her remaking of the play. The chapter will conclude with a discussion of what we know of Anglin's production.

Hippolytus

In a gesture that affirms Artemis' superiority to the vindictive Aphrodite, Howe's play opens with an enslaved Priestess, accompanied by virgin huntresses, including those of Hippolytus, entering to make dedications to the goddess in hope of gaining protection from her master's will. (Howe's already active commitment to abolitionist causes emerges here.) Artemis responds by rejecting "the man, who | With unholy purpose dares o'erstep | The sad defenses of captivity" (79), then vows to protect Hippolytus from inevitable doom as long as possible. Aphrodite immediately confronts her with a promise to mobilize the love-sick Phaedra against the hated Hippolytus. Aphrodite opens and frames Euripides' play; the delay in her entrance in Howe's version deprives the audience of sympathy for Phaedra as an innocent victim of the goddess and of the immediate demonstration of Hippolytus' pointed refusal to worship Aphrodite that followed.[6] Neither deity appears on stage in Seneca or Racine, and Artemis appears only at the conclusion of Euripides' version. By contrast, Howe develops a complex divine–human bond between Artemis and Hippolytus. Hippolytus, who has long pursued a flitting image of Artemis in his hunts, finally meets her, is tested by her as she enumerates the dangers (familiar in myth) faced by mortals who wished to see the goddess, and resolves on eternal fidelity to Artemis in order "to grow to be a hero thus." Hippolytus' spiritual passion meets with a response verging on reciprocal love. As the goddess says in the final scene: "I live in holy cherished maidenhood, | But thou are dearer than the world to me" (126). The empowering sight of the long sought divinity (an experience denied to Euripides' Hippolytus, who only hears her) makes Howe's Hippolytus feel "invincible" to mortal distractions (94).

Phaedra, as in Racine, then enters seeking Hippolytus, with whom she fell in love immediately after being "coldly wed" (83) to Theseus in Athens and whom she has attempted to avoid through exiling her stepson until events brought her near him in Troezen. In this version Phaedra's obsession began with an opening gaze on Hippolytus during athletic games (again as in Racine); her only wish now is one hour of love with him before her death. Too timid to address Hippolytus after observing him, she decides, encouraged by her nurse, to approach Aphrodite's shrine for help with rich offerings. There a soothsayer Leton takes over the role of active conspirator from Racine's nurse Oenone and devises a banquet plot at which Phaedra will seduce Hippolytus with wine drugged with a love potion. Hippolytus, on the verge of leaving to seek his father, is warned by his companion Creon, a figure partially based on the tutor Theramenes in Racine, against the invitation of the dangerous Phaedra, but agrees to go out of piety. His arrival at the banquet is once again framed by a conflict between Artemis and Aphrodite. Greeted with intense gazes from Phaedra, who pretends to see Theseus in him (a version of a speech also central in both Seneca and Racine), and a song about Theseus' exploits in Crete that include his betrayal of Phaedra's sister Ariadne, Hippolytus, increasingly disturbed by the music, wine, and song, is rescued as he pulls back the curtains and sees Artemis beckoning in the moon's light as well as a ghostly image (another gaze) of his revered father. He dashes the drugged wine cup to the ground and leaves.

In Howe's novel version, Hippolytus is summoned to power as his legitimate heir by the people after Theseus' false death is announced.[7] The play uniquely eliminates Phaedra's concern with her sons' political future until she briefly wants to use their claim against Hippolytus after he rejects her. Here Hippolytus is reluctant to assume the crown through pious grief, not through a devotion to his apolitical earlier life. Indeed, unlike Euripides' Hippolytus, he is repeatedly ready to move on to mature manly roles including war or quest. As in Euripides' first but not his second extant *Hippolytus*, as well as in Seneca's and Racine's versions, Phaedra, in this case made hopeful by Leton that grief will soften Hippolytus, then kneels, unveils, and solicits his love herself. Hippolytus rejects as blasphemy her argument about universal human and divine vulnerability to passion voiced in other versions by the nurse; with a brief misogynist outburst in which he calls Phaedra a monster whom Theseus himself should have slain, he leaves. The scorned Phaedra, now bent on revenge, is temporarily diverted by Theseus' return from Hades, but soon she not only accuses Hippolytus of rape, but is willing to affirm her accusation with a silent nod as she looks directly at the shocked Hippolytus himself. Hippolytus departs urging Phaedra to spare Theseus the truth up to the grave.

The final scenes expand the focus on Hippolytus. After the maddened Phaedra, still longing to pursue Hippolytus, commits suicide in response to his plea for silence despite the efforts of Leton and Oenone to calm her, a chorus of nymphs and satyrs celebrate and lament the departing Hippolytus, then withdraw before the melancholy hero, who insists against his devoted friend Creon's urging that he must go into exile alone. Artemis arrives as a chorus of winds prepares to carry out Theseus' curse for Poseidon, and promises to punish Aphrodite's beloved Adonis in recompense for Hippolytus' death. She tries to persuade Hippolytus to avoid departing for exile along the seashore or to accept an offer to conceal him until danger passes. Hippolytus insists on preserving silence and adhering to his father's commands and heroically refuses Artemis' suggestions. In the face of Hippolytus' insistence on silence until Theseus can understand events as part of an ordained pattern, Artemis affirms, "thou art perfect still" (126). Artemis and an Amazon watch Hippolytus meet his death, but the scene is far briefer than the usual lengthy messenger speech central to all other versions.[8] Theseus, who was alerted to the truth by the triple silence of Phaedra, Leton, and Oenone, enters too late to save Hippolytus. The goddess, with others, carries Hippolytus to his father; he gasps out a forgiveness to Theseus, but saves his final gaze for Artemis, who, in contrast to Euripides, where she leaves father and son to restore their human bond at some length, remains on stage to receive it. This final gaze, among the many stressed in the play, echoes Hippolytus' first gaze at Artemis as a source of more than human inspiration that transfigured his life.

In 1923, the theater historian Arthur Hobson Quinn viewed Howe, especially for her *Hippolytus*, as one of the few important American representatives of a brief mid-nineteenth-century enthusiasm for native romantic tragedies in verse that had "merit as literature as well as possibilities of stage success ... The talent of Mrs. Howe was perhaps more truly lyric than dramatic, as the exquisite songs of the nymphs presaging the death of Hippolytus indicate. But with any real encouragement she would have contributed plays to our stage that would have enriched our literature as well as our theatre" (Quinn 1923: 366–7). In contrast to Quinn's views of Howe's choruses, Charlotte Cushman herself had urged Howe in a letter (October 23, 1860) to imitate the choral odes in George Vandenhoff's 1845 *Antigone* with their elaborately composed music by Felix Mendelssohn (see further Macintosh, this volume). "The Classic plays of Rachel [acting in Racine] could do us no good," she insisted, due to their lack of choral music.[9] Howe's choice to underline only Hippolytus' departure and death with choral song and music instead lyrically emphasizes the separate world of nature that Hippolytus shared with Artemis. The Nymphs echo Euripides' emphasis on Hippolytus as a chaste figure to be celebrated by future maidens, but decline to mention Phaedra's own story:

Maids unborn shall shear their tresses
For the hero we bewail,
He shall live in our distresses
Till the voice of song shall fail. (117–18)

Contextualizing *Hippolytus*

Howe's outrageously impassioned and vengeful Phaedra is easier to locate in the literature and performance of this period than her Hippolytus. This kind of role was beginning to make the careers of actresses like Matilda Heron, who starred (with E. A. Sothern) in Julia Ward Howe's first play, *The World's Own*, at New York's Wallack's Lyceum Theatre for a week starting March 16, 1857 in New York and later for one day at the Boston Theatre in 1858.[10] In this romantic verse tragedy set in a small Italian principality, the heroine, a talented village beauty ambitious to immerse herself in high culture (reading music, plays, and novels), is led astray by Lothair, a traveling nobleman in disguise. Lothair leaves hurriedly after the return of Leonora's childhood love, Edward. The maddened Leonora pursues her beloved, followed by Edward, only to meet and be cruelly rejected by Lothair, who is accompanied by his wife and child. The beautiful Leonora devotes the rest of her life to diabolical revenge. She becomes the consort of a Prince to whom Lothair owes allegiance and manages to accuse Lothair of treason and destroy his entire family. In the final scene, Edward, whose best friend died to defend Leonora's honor, confronts her with her infamous past; she seizes his dagger and commits suicide, while forgiving Lothair.

The play received strong notices for the performance and the play's literary qualities, but audiences were shocked by the heroine's total and villainous obsession with revenge.[11] In a sense, *Hippolytus* represents a reworking of an impassioned heroine's shockingly active and in this case unrepentant revenge against a now innocent beloved that could rely on the authority of Greek tragedy. Cushman, a long-established stage figure (the first American actress to achieve star status), would presumably have brought gravitas to the role without undercutting the contemporary attraction to uncontrollable, suffering, and divided women. Indeed, after the controversial reception of *The World's Own*, Cushman urged Howe in a letter to "do battle with the asses who have pronounced their dictum with regard to *The World's Own* . . . [and] destroy their power with a new weapon whose force they cannot comprehend."[12]

Howe's reimagined *Hippolytus* was of course designed to serve the talents of the newly popular Booth. While Racine had made Hippolytus himself vulnerable to love and passion in the person of the Athenian princess Aricie, a rival with Phaedra's son and Hippolytus for Theseus' throne, Howe pointedly chose to develop new implications for his sublimated passion. Booth's large haunting eyes, dark wavy hair, and more subdued, spiritual, and sensitive acting style contrasted sharply with that of "manly" American actors of the previous generation, including his father Junius Booth and the famous Edwin Forrest. His androgynous aura would have underlined Howe's own emphasis on Hippolytus' combination of "feminine" purity and impassioned asexuality with a masculine nobility and sense of duty. By contrast, the powerful, taller, and older Cushman, who was as successful in breeches roles as in roles such as Lady Macbeth, the gypsy Meg Merrilies in *Guy Mannering*, or Nancy in *Oliver Twist*, and known in private life for her female companions, could have brought an ambiguous range of implications to her own part.[13]

Howe's earlier poetry, moreover, makes clear that the play's conflicts were central to her own work and life. In a strictly personal sense, Hippolytus' resistance to Phaedra's passion resonated with the refusal of her husband, Samuel Gridley Howe, to respond emotionally to herself, and with her distress over his lifelong, intense intellectual and spiritual relation to his friend Charles Sumner. As Samuel Howe noted in a letter to Sumner: "When my heart is full of sorrow it turns to you & yearns for your sympathy; in fact as Julia often says—Sumner ought to have been a woman & you to have married her: but I should not agree to this in any monogamic land, for Julia is my love as a wife."[14] At the same time, Howe's effort to devote herself to philosophical and Christian ideals remained in constant tension with her own passions, aesthetic sensibility, and search for independence and understanding. As a play that pitted spiritual intensity against unregulated passion and frustration at a loveless marriage, Hippolytus and Phaedra could also be interpreted as exploring sides of herself that she was unable to unite in her own life.[15]

Passion Flowers, Howe's first moderately successful book of poetry (Williams 1999: 172), published in 1854 without her husband's full awareness and consent, was in fact interpreted at the time, as well as by later critics, as unmistakably autobiographical.[16] Contemporary critics viewed her poetry as spontaneous, unconventional for a woman (Williams 1999: 137), "the product of a spiritual history too passionate and intense for concealment,"[17] "powerful, pungent, and unripe," or marked by a "personalism" that was "terrible."[18] Although other critics praised the book's impersonal, even "masculine" intellectual authority (Williams 1999: 137). Howe's concern in these poems with Christ's own as well as human suffering barely concealed in other poems her female resistance to the yoke of domesticity and hints of an intimacy with another man during an 1850 sojourn without her husband in Rome (her relation with Horace Binney Wallace is addressed more openly in her second book of poetry) (Williams 1999: 180–3). "Mind versus Mill-Stream," for example, clearly addresses her own marriage (and prefigures aspects of Phaedra's):

> If you would marry happily
> On the shady side of life
> Choose out some quietly-disposed
> And placid tempered wife,
> . . .
> For men will woo the tempest,
> And wed it, to their cost,

> Then swear they took it for summer dew,
> And ah! Their peace is lost![19]

"Fervent hearts must borrow the disguise of art, if they would win the right to express, in any outward form, the internal fire that consumes them," as Howe put it in her unpublished novel *The Hermaphrodite* (121). Nathaniel Hawthorne, writing to William Ticknor, remarked of *Passion Flowers* that "the devil must be in the woman to publish them" since they "let out a whole history of domestic unhappiness."[20] Henry Wadsworth Longfellow's diary reported: "Here is revolt enough, between these blue covers."[21]

Hippolytus' merging of ideal female purity and spirituality with a masculine rationality and sense of duty also emerged in the hermaphroditic hero, Laurence, of her unpublished novel. Modeled on the statue of "The Sleeping Hermaphrodite" whom Howe saw in the Villa Borghese in Rome, but inspired by Ovid's *Metamorphoses*, the novels of Georges Sand, and Alphonse de Lamartine's long narrative poem *Jocelyn*, the hermaphrodite Laurence combines the best of both sexes, but can satisfy no one due to his "monstrous" body.[22] When Laurence is finally forced to reveal this body to Emma von P., a beautiful and devoted older widow, she collapses and dies. Roland, the youth to whom then he becomes a devoted tutor, also forces Laurence to escape from his passionate attentions. In a final argument about his gender between a Roman brother and sister with whom Laurence (called Laurent in this fragment) has lived both as a man and disguised as a woman to escape his angry father, Berto argues:

> I recognize nothing distinctly feminine in the intellectual nature of Laurent . . . he is sometimes poetical and rhapsodical, but he reasons severely and logically, even as a man—he has moreover stern notions of duty which blend and fashion his life, instead of living fashioned by it, as is the case with women.
>
> Unjust Berto! Said Briseida.

Briseida then counters with:

> I recognize in Laurent much that is strictly feminine . . . and in the name of the female sex, I claim her as one of us. Her modesty, her purity, her tenderness of heart belong only to woman. The blood of a man does not rush so instantaneously to his cheek at the bold glance of another—the eye of a man does not flash so quickly and proudly at the slightest breath of aught worthy or impure—the tears of no man flow as hers before the sublimity of nature, or the unhappiness of man. It is true that she can reason better than most women, yet she is most herself when she feels, when she follows that instinctive, undoubting sense of inner truths which is given only to women and to angels. (194)

When the doctor who has examined the dying Laurent remarks that he is neither a man nor a woman, Briseida responds:

> 'Ah!' said Briseida, who had read something of Swedenborg, 'a heavenly superhuman mystery, one undivided, integral soul, needing not to seek on earth its other moiety, needing only to adore the God above it, and to labour for its brethren around it.' (195–6)

Howe, who also interpreted the eighteenth-century Swedish philosopher and theologian Swedenborg as proposing an afterlife that transcended gender divisions,[23] seemed equally taken at this period of her life with a desire expressed by Laurent to overcome gender boundaries by being "lost in the impersonality of art" (149).

ANGLIN IN *HIPPOLYTUS*

Margaret Anglin's one-day 1911 production of *Hippolytus* at Boston's Tremont Theatre in support of the Julia Ward Howe Memorial Fund took place five months after Howe's death on November 17, 1910 (see Fig. 6.1),[24] shortly after Anglin's successful 1910 performance of Sophocles' *Antigone* at the Hearst Greek Theatre in Berkeley, California.[25] Anglin, who had longed to follow in the wake of the French actresses Rachel and Sarah Bernhardt's successes as Racine's Phèdre, found the play poetic, speakable, and sufficiently modern to appeal (see also Philip Hale, *Boston Herald*, March 25, 1911). Her managers Liebler and Company provided new scenery and costumes despite the one-day run; Wallace Goodrich of the Boston Opera House prepared string and reed music to punctuate lyric moments. The appreciative house was packed with Boston dignitaries.[26]

Reviews generally found the last act, especially Phaedra's suicide and the final Hippolytus scene, weaker than the rest and not all critics were enthusiastic about "classic tragedy—especially declamatory tragedy—" which "is not often played nowadays and does not appeal to modern theatre goers" (*New York Times*, March 25, 1911). Others, rather surprisingly given the active presence of deities in the play, praised the effort to motivate events on the human level rather than relying on fate.[27] Most reviews, responding to both her own star power and that of Phaedra in famous performances by Rachel and Sarah Bernhardt, focused on Anglin: "As far as Miss Anglin was concerned, her acting was true to the spirit of tragedy, powerful, dignified and deeply impressive."[28] The *Globe* review raved over her eloquent facial display, as she expressed ecstasy, deceit, revenge, and terror; Philip Hale of the *Herald* found her intelligent and "feverishly erotic," while at times her "reserve was eloquent and thrilling." Mrs. S. C. Williams of the *Boston Advertiser*, however, thought Anglin "insufficiently frenzied" in comparison to Sarah Bernhardt. The well-known Ruth Holt Boucicault as Artemis and Charles Garry as Leton received better notices for their delivery and fluency in the *Globe* and *Herald* reviews than the sonorous Hampden, who "became stiff in being cold" (*Advertiser*). The performance was successful enough that Anglin planned a longer run in New York the next season, but was unable to do so because of her production schedule.[29]

Both Howe and Harriette Fanning Read, the author of a new nineteenth-century American version of *Medea*, turned to Greek tragedy in part because of its complex exploration of gender issues and gender conflict. Hippolytus' link with ideals often associated with women and the passionate Phaedra's resistance to confinement in a female role offered Howe a chance to explore what she clearly viewed as a tragic confinement in limiting gender roles during her youth and child-bearing and -rearing years. Under the cover of Greek tragedy, she was able to explore ambiguities that emerged not only in her life, but in the changing acting conventions of her own day.

Howe's first diary entry after her husband's death was, "Began my new life today. Pray God that it might have a greatly added use and earnestness" (Richards and Elliott 1916: ii. 356). It did. Howe's later career was a public one that left impassioned fiction writing and the gendered self-division that marked her earlier life behind. Speaking, writing, and working, especially for women's causes, were no longer anomalous for an elite woman in Howe's position. But she never forgot *Hippolytus*, whose failure to be performed she described as "the greatest 'let down' that I ever experienced."[30] Although she died with a dream about to be fulfilled, she might have regretted the production's shift of focus from Hippolytus to Phaedra. By 1911, however, famous actresses had made this shift inevitable.

NOTES

1. Howe 1899: 203, 237, 238–9. "I found him modest, intelligent, and above all, genuine,—the man as worthy of admiration as the artist. Although I had seen Mr. Booth in a variety of characters, I could only think of representing him as Hippolytus, a beautiful youth, of heroic type, enamored of a high ideal" (238). Booth's letter on receiving the play was enthusiastic (August 26, 1858, quoted in Hall 1918: 96 and *Christian Science Monitor* March 18, 1911). The Howe family were enthusiastic theater-goers. See further Hall 1918: 102 on Booth's intelligent and poetic acting; on Cushman, see 105–6. For further discussion of the relation of Howe and Booth, see also Ruggles 1953: 88–9, 94–6, 131–3, and 141.
2. Hall 1918: 96; she describes Mrs. E. L. Davenport as "middle-aged, thin and not beautiful" (94).
3. Richards and Elliott 1916: i. 287–8 and ii. 130 on Howe's lecture on "Women in Greek Drama."
4. Charles Waldron, who was originally to play the role, was replaced by Hampden due to another engagement.
5. The other American new version was Harriette Fanning Read's *Medea* (1848). For further discussion, see Foley 2012: 197–200.
6. His companion Creon, fearful of Aphrodite's jealousy of Artemis' favor to Hippolytus, does suggest making offerings to all the gods. Hippolytus declines, having made his offer to Artemis, but the play calls no attention to his refusal (83).
7. In Euripides' version, Hippolytus, as a bastard, does not have first claim on the throne. In Racine the Athenian princess Aricie, Hippolytus, and Phaedra's son have rival claims.
8. Euripides' messenger speech symbolically forces Hippolytus to experience violence equivalent to Phaedra's own female suffering. Howe perhaps wished to reduce a symbolic connection between her innocent Hippolytus and his punishment.
9. Quoted in the *Christian Science Monitor* March 23, 1911.
10. For Heron's performances in the role of Medea, see especially Davis, this volume.
11. Howe 1899: 230 mentions that a critic pronounced it "full of literary merits and of dramatic defects." For further critical responses to the play, which also disapproved of the original seduction of the innocent Lenore, see Williams 1999: 200 and 203–4.

12. Charlotte Cushman to J. W. H., n.d. (1857), Howe papers, Houghton Library, Cambridge, MA.
13. On Cushman's status in this period, see McConachie 1998: 165–8.
14. S. G. H. to Sumner, September 11, 1844, # 920.
15. Williams 1999 and the introduction to Howe 2004 interpret her poetry and novel from this perspective.
16. See generally Williams 1999, who cites earlier views, including Grant 1994.
17. Ralph Waldo Emerson quoted in Richards and Elliott 1916: i. 139–40, December 30, 1853.
18. Calhoun 1868: 621–8 from a biographical sketch, quoted in Williams 1999: 138.
19. For the whole poem, see Howe 1854: 80–5.
20. Hawthorne, *Works*, xvii. 177, quoted in Williams 1999: 135 with n. 5, which includes other similar contemporary views.
21. Quoted in Williams 1999: 136 n. 10.
22. Williams 1999 and Howe 2004 also refer to other French treatments of androgynous figures by Théophile Gautier, *Mademoiselle de Maupin* (1835) and Balzac, *Séraphita* (1834–5).
23. Williams introduction to Howe 2004: xxxiv–xxxv.
24. Anglin reported on her interview with Howe after agreeing to the production in the *Boston Herald* March 19, 1911. On pre-play notices, see also *New York Review* April 22, 1911, *Christian Science Monitor* March 23, 1911.
25. T. A. Wise, *New York Times* March 14, 1911.
26. *Boston Globe* March 25, 1911, *New York Times* March 25, 1911, *Christian Science Monitor* March 18, 1911.
27. Philip Hale, *Boston Herald* March 25, 1911.
28. William E. Sage, *Cleveland Leader* March 28, 1911.
29. Introduction to Howe 1941: 74.
30. Howe 1899: 240; for a later regretful recollection of the play by Howe, see also Richards and Elliott 1916: ii. 345.

References

Calhoun, L. G. (1868), *Eminent Women of the Age*. Hartford, CT.
Foley, H. P. (2012), *Reimagining Greek Tragedy on the American Stage*. Berkeley, Los Angeles, and London.
Grant, M. H. (1994), *Private Woman, Public Person: An Account of the Life of Julia Ward Howe from 1819–1868*. Brooklyn, NY.
Hall, F. H. (1918), *Memories Grave and Gay*. New York and London.
Howe, J. W. (1854), *Passion Flowers*. Boston.
Howe, J. W. (1857a), *Words for the Hour*. Boston.
Howe, J. W. (1857b), *The World's Own*. Boston.
Howe, J. W. (1899), *Reminiscences 1819–1899*. Boston and New York.
Howe, J. W. (1941), "Hippolytus," in *Monte Cristo and Other Plays*. Princeton. [See also an electronic edition by Alexander Street Press, 2010.]
Howe, J. W. (2004), *The Hermaphrodite*. Edited with an introduction by G. Williams. Lincoln and London.

McConachie, B. (1998), "American Theatre in Context, from the Beginnings to 1870," in D. B. Wilmeth and C. Bigsby eds., *The Cambridge History of American Theatre*, vol. i. Cambridge, 111–82.

Quinn, A. H. (1923), *A History of American Drama From the Beginning to the Civil War*. New York.

Richards, L. E. (1909), *Letters and Journals of Samuel Gridley Howe*, 2 vols. Boston.

Richards, L. E. and M. H. Elliott (1916), *Julia Ward Howe, 1819–1910*, 2 vols. Boston.

Ruggles, E. (1953), *Prince of Players: Edwin Booth*. New York.

Williams, G. (1999), *Hungry Heart: The Literary Emergence of Julia Ward Howe*. Amherst, MA.

CHAPTER 7

PROFESSIONAL TRAGEDY

The Case of Medea *in Chicago, 1867*

KATHRYN BOSHER AND JORDANA COX

IN the late nineteenth and early twentieth centuries, Chicago was home to some of the first theaters in America to introduce the independent theater movement, an alternative to the large-scale, commercial theater of the day. At the turn of the twentieth century, two Chicagoans, Jane Addams and Maurice Browne, were pioneers of the movement in Chicago and they both chose to produce Greek drama. Addams's Hull-House, a social settlement in Chicago, and Browne's Chicago Little Theatre were hubs of community activism that used Greek tragedy in community building efforts to bring about social change. At Hull-House, stagings of Greek tragedy offered venues of participation for marginalized immigrant communities. The Chicago Little Theatre offered challenging productions of Greek tragedy, which the company, in keeping with the values of the Little Theatre movement, went to some pains to make widely affordable.[1] For these institutions, driven as they were by progressive social agendas, Greek tragedy became a tool for social change and eventually, a voice for political critique: in 1915 Browne toured a production of *Trojan Women*, funded by Addams's Woman's Peace Party, to protest World War I.[2] "No one," Tingley notes, "missed the antiwar message" (Tingley 1987: 143). In fact, a reporter at the *San Francisco Chronicle* called the play "the most potent argument against war that the art of man has ever produced."[3] The genre of Greek tragedy, as *Trojan Women* demonstrated, could offer powerful arguments in contemporary public discourse, and American artists could use it to sway popular opinion—albeit on a limited scale—about contemporary political issues. Indeed, across the United States, politically charged stagings of Greek tragedy have proliferated in the twentieth and twenty-first centuries (Foley 2012; Hall, Macintosh, and Wrigley 2004).

This chapter examines a possible nineteenth-century precedent to productions like Browne's *Trojan Women*. Although Browne and Addams both disparaged the popular, commercial plays that dominated nineteenth-century Chicago theater, their interest in Greek tragedy offers us at least one common link with the mainstream theater they rejected.[4] Addams and Browne chose Greek tragedy partly as a rejection of popular theater, but Greek tragedy was also present in the popular theater they rejected. In the century before *Trojan Women* was staged, Chicago's entertaining array of toga dramas and burlesques on classical themes introduced Chicago audiences to ancient Graeco-Roman history, figures, and ideas. Although ancient tragedies themselves were infrequently produced, a few translations and adaptations do appear on the commercial stage in the mid-nineteenth century (see Pearcy, Macintosh, Davis, this volume). After a brief survey of the toga dramas and burlesques that drew on the stories and characters from classical antiquity, we examine in detail an explicitly political and popular production of Euripides' *Medea* that came to Chicago as part of a tour in 1867, the month after her appearance in Philadelphia (see Pearcy, this volume). This was Ernest Legouvé's translation and adaptation of the play, written to raise interest in the struggle for legal rights for women in France.[5]

Nineteenth-century Chicago, a young and intensely industrial city, nevertheless saw dozens of modern plays on classical themes.[6] Incorporated in 1837, a scant generation before the Civil War, it boasted one theater by 1838, a room 30 feet by 80 feet on the upper floor of a former auction house (Christiansen 2004: 3). It was a rough city, and early visitors regularly complained about the streets, which often had them ankle deep in mud. From very early, however, there is a record of performances of classically inspired plays. *Damon and Pythias* by John Banin, for example, seems to have been staged several times, starting in 1839; and we have a record of *The Gladiator* by Robert Montgomery Bird, and *Virginius* by Sheridan Knowles in 1848 (see Pearcy, Mayer, this volume; Sherman 1947: 45–6, 131, 134). By the 1850s the city was growing rapidly for it was at a useful nexus of lake, river, and then, most importantly, became the hub of the new rail system. With the advent of rail, suddenly a three-week trip from New York could be accomplished in three days. Chicago audiences saw increasing numbers of productions of plays on classical themes, primarily those of traveling companies.[7]

The majority of these classicizing productions were melodramas based on Greek or Roman history. These dramas were immensely popular throughout the U.S.A., and had been for generations.[8] American-authored plays were particularly well received in the nineteenth century, most famously Robert Montgomery Bird's *The Gladiator* written for the American actor Edwin Forrest.[9] Such dramas on ancient themes, written in modern times, often resonated with political or social issues of the day, but were seldom overtly critical of accepted social and domestic practices; indeed, their melodramatic form relied on the gendered social arrangements that, as we argue below, Legouvé's *Medea* tried to destabilize.

Burlesques on stories from classical antiquity played alongside the mainstream culture-affirming melodramas. For instance, in 1869 Lydia Thompson and her troupe of Blondes, as they were popularly known, brought an enormously popular classical burlesque to Chicago called *Ixion, or, The Man at the Wheel*.[10] In 1880, *The New York Ixion Burlesque and Novelty Combination* came to Chicago, and in 1888 Lydia Thompson returned with *Penelope*, a burlesque about Odysseus. Most burlesques on classical antiquity that toured through Chicago were imported from England. Although some satirized or parodied modern events and people familiar to British audiences, it is likely that, by the time they reached Chicago, specific political resonances were either displaced or lost. The jokes created by the juxtaposition of antiquity and modernity, however, were not tied to the British context, and may have appealed to the same broad cross-section of society in Chicago as they had in England. Classical burlesques had reached a wide audience in England for they did not cater exclusively to those educated in Classics. Rather, as Hall and Macintosh have shown, such burlesques served to introduce those unfamiliar with antiquity to classical stories, even as they engaged those literate in classical antiquity with more subtle jokes (Hall and Macintosh 2005: 350–90).

Both classical and non-classical burlesques frequently pushed the limits of gender decorum. *Ixion*, in particular, which, as was common, featured a woman dressed as a man in the main role, sparked vehement criticism from the local Democratic newspaper, *The Chicago Times*.[11] The editor attacked the production as immoral and indecent, in large part because of the exposure of so many female legs, and the argument became so inflamed that the lead actress Lydia Thompson eventually tracked down the editor of the paper, Wilbur Storey, and bullwhipped him.[12] Neither the *ad hominem* attacks on Thompson nor her physically violent rebuttal were as shocking or remarkable as they appear to us now. As Si Sheppard puts it: "Vicious polemics were a standard trope of editorial dialogue throughout the era" (Sheppard 2008: 146). Indeed, whippings of editors, burning of printing presses, and fighting with newsmen seem to have become so frequent during the Civil War that many Southern presses actually employed "fighting editors" to whom the regular editor could send angry visitors.[13] So, Lydia Thompson's bullwhipping of the editor who had been slandering her in the press, though she was brought to trial on account of it, may have been something of a recognizable political statement. Such lively and, as on this occasion, heated public debate about female behavior in burlesque suggests that we might also have expected a public response to politically charged adaptations of Greek drama, particularly a tragedy like Legouvé's *Medea*, which was adapted precisely to raise awareness about gender imbalances in modern society.

Next to melodramas and burlesques, plays adapted from Greek tragedy constituted the smallest category of classical theater. It is in this category that we place Legouvé's *Medea*, which came to Chicago in 1867 as part of a larger tour of the United States. The city was not unacquainted with the play, for two pre-Civil War productions of *Medea* had come through Chicago, one in 1857 starring Miss Jean Davenport and another in 1859 with the American actress Matilda Heron performing her own translation (see Pearcy, this volume, for her performances in Philadelphia in the role; and further Davis, this volume, for her performances in New York). These productions received vague approbation and almost no comment in the Chicago papers, but the third production in 1867, starring the famous Italian actress Adelaide Ristori, was announced with great fanfare and continued to be widely discussed in the press. The play quickly sold out as Chicago's wealthier classes clamored to see Ristori at work. In 1947, theater historian Robert Sherman wrote: "The social climbers made this an event that has seldom been surpassed in the entertainment history of this city" (Sherman 1947: 670–1). In terms of the scale of its audiences, the production of *Medea* of 1867 was undeniably popular.

It was also overtly political. Ernest Legouvé's 1856 adaptation had been written with the goal of alerting audiences to the difficulties many mothers faced under the laws and social mores of the day in France (Macintosh 2000: 15–18; Offen 1986: 452–84). Legouvé was a member of the Académie Française and a public supporter of women's rights, within limits, and best known for his 450-page volume on the Moral History of Women. He set out to use the Medea story to bring the social and economic problems women faced vividly to the minds of the audience. In his introduction to the play, he lays out his aims:

> In truth, if it were necessary to define in one word the legend of Medea, I would say: it is the most terrible chapter in *the history of seduction* in the world! What, in effect, is this Jason, this Greek, this civilized man, going in pursuit of a treasure amongst the savage peoples, seducing a girl from the sticks, using her to accomplish his plans, tearing her, already pregnant, from her country and from her family, and then abandoning her as soon as he has set foot in his own country. What is he, if not the faraway and poetic symbol of these vile corruptors of our own day who drag to Paris, from the depths of our provinces, the sad victims of their promises. They dishonor our society with their cynicism and their unpunished ingratitude![14]

In ancient play versions of the myth of Euripides and Seneca, for all the pathos and heartbreak of Medea's situation, her physical destitution as a result of Jason's abandonment is not the key element in the story. Euripides, for example, adds a scene in which Medea assures her own future with King Aegeus of Athens. In both plays, Medea exits at the end of the story in a magical chariot, clearly capable of taking care of herself.[15]

In Legouvé's version, however, the bitter physical deprivation that Medea and her children suffer as a result of Jason's abandonment is paramount. When Medea first appears on stage she relates that she was abandoned in some other country and has traveled far and wide searching for her husband. She doesn't know if he is alive or dead. Her two children are constantly hungry, cold, and without shelter:

> MEDEA: . . . Oh, Jason! . . . dear Jason! Are you dead? Have you fled? Does some dark prison hold you far away? Where are you, my master? Where are you?
> MELANTHE (MEDEA'S SON): I am right here.
> MEDEA: Dear little one! . . . You break my heart! No shelter! No support! . . . This bare rock, here is your bed for tonight! . . .
> LYCAON (MEDEA'S SON): Hunger weakens us more than the journey.[16]

We understand that this desperate search for Jason has gone on for a long time: months if not years. This is a marked addition to ancient versions of the tale in Euripides and Seneca where Medea is accompanied by a nurse, and seems to enjoy at the very least basic physical comforts, even though these are threatened by Jason's new marriage. Certainly, we understand in both ancient plays that Medea accompanied Jason to Corinth, where he met his new bride, and she has not spent any time wandering on her own or with her children, physically destitute and penniless, looking for him.

An even more significant innovation in Legouvé's play, however, is the addition of the character Orpheus. Orpheus is introduced in the first scene as the counterpart to Jason. When he learns of Jason's abandonment of Medea and his plan to re-marry, he is horrified. He then serves as Medea's greatest defender and as Jason's critic for the first few scenes of the play: "You," he says to Jason, "you love as the mountain bear loves the honeycomb, as the leopard loves the well fed flocks of sheep, or as the torrent loves the flowering bank—loves to dirty their treasures in its muddy wave."[17] It is not until scene 4 that Medea appears on stage, lonely and starving, holding the hands of her two cold and hungry children, and by that point Jason has already been established as a muscle-bound, self-interested brute by another Greek man, Orpheus. Legouvé writes in his introduction that it was to point out Jason's failings that he introduced Orpheus to the play: "Orpheus . . . *offered himself as poetic interpreter of the moral point of view which I* [Legouvé] *wanted to make clear*; Orpheus, in fact, who, like all great poets, represented at once his own time and the future, had the right, in my work, to go beyond Greek ideas while remaining Greek himself, he had the right to become like a modern thinker without ceasing to be an ancient personage."[18]

Legouvé's introduction suggests that he thinks the classical legend and characters will make his political message accessible to his audiences. As a Greek, Jason is marked as "civilized" and aligned with the audience of the play and the injustice of his behavior toward the unsophisticated Medea becomes apparent. Moreover, Legouvé includes the famous poet Orpheus as a mouthpiece for his harshest critiques of Jason.

How was this social criticism received in Chicago? Did classical references help make Legouvé's social and political message more legible to audiences in the American Midwest, as it seems to have done to those in Britain (Hall and Macintosh 2005: 391–429)? Despite our lack of information about production choices in the Chicago performance, we know that Legouvé intended his adaptation to convey a strong social message. Further, three elements seem to have been in place for the Chicago production to press this social message to a wide audience. First, the play, advocating women's rights, played to a large Chicago audience with a high proportion of women. The mid-nineteenth century in America had seen a dramatic change in audience composition. Women had been successfully courted by theater producers in an effort to expand the audience base, and became regular attendees. Indeed, Chicago's first opera house, or major theater, meant to cater to this new audience, had been built only two years before in 1865 (Cropsey 1999: 20). It was to this theater that the producer E. J. Rau brought Legouvé's *Medea* in 1867, with Adelaide Ristori as star.

When the play opened, performances were sold out and filled with Chicago's wealthier classes fascinated by the fame of Ristori, and eager to see her at work.[19] That Ristori and her production successfully appealed to women in particular is apparent from newspaper descriptions of the audience in attendance. The *Chicago Republican*, for example, printed an article by "A Woman in the Balcony" who described the audience: "There were hosts of ladies, fair haired, flaxen, and dark and bright: the air was like a conservatory and the seats were banks of human flowers."[20] Indeed, according to a review of Ristori in *Mary Stuart* the following evening, men came to the performance largely to please their wives. An anonymous "Gentleman in the Saloon" summarizes the position of some of the men in the saloon as: "Were I not engaged, I should frown on Ristori: as it is I adore her. If I didn't, my love would scorn me."[21]

Not only was the audience made up in large part of women, and thus perhaps a particularly receptive group for commentary on women's rights, but (and this is the second element which suggests that the political issues of the play might have resonated) the very issue that Legouvé foregrounded (the real suffering of mothers who had no legal recourse, and frequently no economic support, when they had been abandoned by lovers and husbands) was a hot button topic in the Chicago press of the day.

In Chicago in the 1860s, gender relations were strained and in flux as they were throughout the country. The burgeoning women's movement seeking reform to marriage laws, access to education and employment, as well as suffrage, was met with sensational and melodramatic reporting of women's suffering in the press.[22] The sufferings of American women after failed marriages and love affairs were widely reported in the 1860s. One danger, in particular, excited the sympathy of all the Chicago papers of the time. This was the danger of seduction and abandonment. In the first week that *Medea* played in Chicago in 1867, two such cases were reported in the *Chicago Times*. In one report, a young girl who had been seduced and abandoned went away to have her baby and give it up for adoption. When she returned to Chicago and, as the *Times* reported it, her arrogant seducer mocked her in public, she shot him.[23] A few days later, a headline read "One More Unfortunate" and the story told the sad tale of an adopted girl, who, as the paper reports it, "in an unguarded moment . . . was tempted with many fair promises of a young man, and yielding, she fell."[24] When her pregnancy became apparent, her adoptive parents threw her out of the house. As it was January and she could find no one to take her in, she died of exposure. Her adoptive parents refused to own their relationship to her or to bury her body. The melodrama of these tales of single women matched that of sensational stories of wives abandoned and left destitute by husbands. For example, two days before the opening of *Ixion* on May 17, 1869, a headline in the *Times* declared: "The History of a Long and Weary Search: How a Deceived Wife was Treated by her Faithless Husband." He had, apparently, suggested she go to England to visit relatives, and, when she returned to their home in New York, he had disappeared. She tracked him to Chicago, where she found him living with another woman, whereupon he left for Indiana, where in that "Land of easy divorces," wrote the *Times*, "he was at rest from further persecution by a true and loving wife."[25] Many other such stories fill the papers, with the pitiful aspect of the abandoned and penniless wife and hungry children presented in stark contrast to the feckless selfishness of the husband.

In 1868, the year after Ristori's performance, the first women's group in Chicago explicitly to raise the issue of women's suffrage was formed. The *Chicago Tribune* cited its mission as follows: "to increase the social relations of woman and mankind, and to advocate anything that will, in any way, tend to promote the welfare of both sexes—the female sex especially" (Buechler 1986: 67). A convention on women's rights was held in 1869. It is clear that the plight of mothers and their children without sufficient legal recourse to aid or sufficient access to support, perhaps particularly in their relations with men, was one of the hot topics of the moment, both in the popular press and in some political circles.

Thus, Legouvé's adaptation, the Chicago audience, the controversial issues of the times, and examples from other receptions of the play all suggest that Legouvé's *Medea* should have been a recognizably politicized production—a precursor in the nineteenth-century mainstream to Addams's and Browne's political deployment of another Euripidean tragedy, *The Trojan Women*. It seems well placed to have spurred the citizens of Chicago to think about the plight of mothers and their few legal, economic, and social recourses when abandoned by their husbands or lovers. Whereas the historical melodramas we briefly discussed at the beginning of this chapter idealized stable domestic relationships, Legouvé's critical emphasis on an abandoned mother's plight politicized them.

However, a closer look at the evidence in the newspapers that survive from these few years just before the great fire of Chicago devastated the city suggests that this play seems not to have catalyzed the public response one would expect. Unlike the lively British reception of this play during their parliamentary battles about divorce law (Hall and Macintosh 2005: 391–429), Chicagoans seem not to have interpreted the production in the local context of women's rights.

First, Legouvé's artful adaptations of the ancient text do not seem to have overcome the physical constraints of the performance. The reviewers and the majority of the audience faced two problems as spectators of this production. One problem was that Ristori and her troupe performed in Italian and the audience followed along with an English translation provided for them in booklet form. Our friend, "A Gentleman in the Saloon" commented sarcastically on the difficulty of understanding the action in *Mary Stuart*: "As a matter of course, I adore Ristori. If I didn't I should betray my ignorance of Italian, which between you and I, I don't understand in the least. If I say her acting is superb, I show at once that I am a fine Italian scholar . . ."

A related performance problem was that it appears that the troupe that supported Ristori was, by the judgement of the press at least, made up of mediocre actors. The producer E. J. Rau was universally excoriated in all Chicago presses of the day, for his penny-pinching methods of producing plays in which, apart from the star, he employed, apparently, the very cheapest supporting actors he could. The *Chicago Republican* for example writes: "With one or two exceptions, every member of the troupe is utterly incompetent, and devoid of the slightest vestige of acting talent."[26] Eight years later, the *Daily Inter-Ocean* was still complaining about a subsequent tour, ". . . a company of actors most of whom would be denominated sticks, were they not Italian . . . The general public, as far as my observation has extended, yawns over them" (Grumley 1875). Of the 1867 tour, the *Chicago Tribune* wrote: "The opening scene between Jason and Orpheus . . . was regarded with little interest. All were waiting for the appearance of Ristori . . ."[27] The *Times* described the audience chattering until Ristori appeared and indeed recommended that the audience "follow the example of the members of the orchestra, and take a newspaper or some other readable literature to peruse during those passages in which Ristori does not make her appearance."[28] The audience was uninterested in, or had difficulty understanding, the play, and they seem to have given up and made no attempt to pay attention to the first few scenes in which Orpheus and Jason lay out the moral groundwork of the play. Thus, the framing narrative of social commentary that Legouvé had introduced to the plot of the ancient Greek drama was effectively erased in the Chicago production.

Secondly, the connection between the topical issues that the play raised about women's hardships and the same issues omnipresent in newspapers of the day seems never to have been explicitly made in reviews. Whether the play did resonate with the immediate audience is a question we have not been able to answer satisfactorily. But the received and public reviews of the play in local newspapers did not make this association.

Indeed, the press seems to have steered its readership to dissociate the story from contemporary life and to view Medea herself as an exotic barbarian. Three days before the play opened, the *Chicago Times* published an article with strong misgivings about the play: "[. . . *Medea*] is too classical for the engagement of an American audience. There is nothing in common with the taste or sympathy of the country and times."[29] In the following days, offhand comments about Medea as a barbarian, recorded in the same paper, give some hint of this paper's view of the main subject of the play. At one point, for example, the paper, noting the poor heating in the theater, writes: "Medea . . . will be able to keep warm only from the burning passion of her barbarian nature."[30] The papers seem to anticipate that Medea would be too monstrous for audiences to relate to (see further Davis, this volume).

After the performance, however, newspapers' descriptions of Medea changed—she was no longer judged the passionate barbarian, but a womanly and noble character. Indeed, the womanly nobility Adelaide Ristori brought to the character of Medea dominated the reports in all newspapers that survive from the period. There is no commentary, however, on the innovative opening scenes of the play in which Legouvé had Orpheus not only plead Medea's case, but also establish the callousness and dishonorable conduct of Jason (indeed if the newspaper reports are to be believed, the audience used this time to chatter with those sitting next to them). Jason, in fact, fades into the background. This diminution of the cad of the story blunts the social point that Legouvé proposes in his introduction and expresses in his adaptation. The newspaper reviews did not contemplate this reprobate Jason at all. Instead, the reviews gave a picture of a noble woman struggling against a series of difficult, but vague and disconnected, setbacks. She was celebrated for her strength and courage in the face of disaster, but the cause of that disaster was not emphasized. A reviewer in the *Chicago Tribune* wrote:

> In her [Ristori's] hands, Medea is one who might have been the loveliest and happiest of her sex—a devoted wife, a tender mother, and a sweet friend to all the world. Because she was a devoted wife she braved all things for her husband, and faltered at no crime to serve him. She gave everything for his love, and so intertwined herself with him thus to be separated from him was death, and to be thrust away by him to make room for a rival was hell.[31]

In a sense, then, this Chicago *Medea* of 1867 was, at least in the press of the day, stripped of its problematic gender relations, and of its pressing socio-political commentary on the fate of seduced, abandoned women. This may be attributable, in part, to the classical melodramas, more familiar to most Chicago spectators than tragedy, which often bound their moral commentaries to more conservative gender norms. The plots of classical melodramas, and, from what we can glean from reviews, the acting choices made particular use of stereotypical gender roles to reinforce a moral or political point. In *The Gladiator*, for instance, the heroic masculinity of the doomed slave reinforced his noble battle for freedom against all odds. In *Ingomar the Barbarian*, the gentle, loving Greek girl Parthenia is able to win the heart of the barbarian chieftain, who releases her father from captivity and agrees to become civilized for Parthenia's sake. These portrayals of feminine women and masculine men were warmly received in the Chicago press. Of the heroine in *Ingomar the Barbarian*, for example, the *Chicago Daily Tribune* writes: "Her embodiment of the gentle, self-sacrificing, loving yet impetuous Greek girl was all that we could have wished for, and the audience frequently testified their delight by hearty outbursts of applause."[32] Of the actor Edwin Forrest, for whom Montgomery Bird wrote *The Gladiator*, the paper's obituary writes: "His symmetrical development of muscle, his broad chest, and especially his neck and the superb poise of his head, gave him the statuesqueness of an antique. The statue of the Gladiator was not a more perfect embodiment of Spartacus than Mr. Forrest, with his magnificent and colossal physique. There has never been on the American stage such a powerfully, and at the same time symmetrically, developed man. His presence in whatever role he appeared, was imposing and majestic."[33] Many other reviews of this kind suggest that Chicago audiences often drew on gender norms to come to the moral conclusions that the plays invited.

The reviews of *Medea* in Chicago suggest that these melodramas set the tone for the way some spectators responded to Medea. As the womanly courage of Medea was brought forward, and her enemies blurred into unidentifiable villainy and bad acting, the play was, perhaps, brought into agreement with the essential moral structure of the popular plays based on Roman history of the time. Legouvé's political message seems to have been lost altogether here.

Finally, another reason for the reviewers' neglect of Legouvé's political critique may be the commercial structure of touring plays in the U.S.A., combined with the very real financial difficulties of maintaining a theater. In fact, the grand new Opera House in which Medea played faced such dire financial difficulties that in the very week that Ristori appeared its owner raffled off the theater![34] In order to stay afloat he had been accepting all manner of productions from acrobats to burlesque to recitations. Heavily influenced by economic considerations, Chicago theaters presented a medley of foreign and domestic plays, the majority of which were touring productions. Relying heavily on the drawing power of star actors and actresses, most of Chicago's theater producers did not concertedly engage in pointed, contemporary social critique.

Of course, newspaper reviews do not tell the whole story of the play's reception, especially in the midst of profound changes in the nature of audience engagement. As Richard Butsch has noted, the behavior of American audiences changed dramatically over the second half of the nineteenth century: the immersion of audiences in darkness to focus attention on lit stages, the introduction of women to theater audiences, and the gentrification especially in highbrow venues like Crosby's Opera House, all institutionalized a mode of theater-going that was decorous and subdued, with audiences paying more attention to their immediate group than to the larger audience. As a result, while spontaneous and rowdy political discourse was quite at home in early nineteenth-century American theaters, the latter half of the century saw its retreat "to private clubs, fraternal associations, union halls and political party halls" (Butsch 2000: 16). In this context, newspaper reports are the best evidence we have for tracing the circulation of Medea's politics in public discourse. However, there is, of course, an untold story about the play's political impact not in the media, but in discussions at home or in small groups.

All the same, it seems clear from the evidence we have that *Medea* in Chicago did not *widely circulate* the social and political messages that Legouvé intended. The reasons for this owe much to the economic and commercial forces that drove late nineteenth-century traveling productions, a press uninterested in drawing social and political points from the production, and viewing practices associated with melodrama and burlesque. Despite the playtext's call for reform, then, *Medea*'s receptions in Chicago, do not suggest a precursor to the politically engaged deployments of tragedy that would proliferate in the next century.

Thus, in the case of Chicago, Hull-House and the Chicago Little Theatre still seem to offer the first instances in which artistic intentions and public receptions aligned to politicize Greek tragedy. The social and political purposes of both of these institutions were never in doubt, and this is, in part, because those in control of the production made the socio-political agenda paramount. Moreover, both of these productions were firmly rooted in a larger context that foregrounded their social and political aims: the Hull-House productions were clearly part of the larger social effort of the settlement house, and the Little Theatre production not only aligned itself with the Little Theatre movement across the country and in Europe, but also with political sponsors like the women's anti-war league. To the extent that we can recover the reception of *Medea* in Chicago, it seems that the popular theater could not fully convey the politics of Legouvé's adaptation.[35]

APPENDIX

A Sample of Plays on Classical Themes and Classical Plays Performed in Chicago between 1832 and 1900

1832 *Damon and Pythias* by John Banin[36]
1848 *The Gladiator* by Robert Montgomery Bird
    Virginius by Sheridan Knowles
1850 *The Greek Slave* by Edward Fitzball

1852 *Ingomar the Barbarian* by Friedrick Halm trans. Maria Lovell
Brutus, or, The Fall of Tarquin by John Howard Payne
Ion
1853 *Ingomar the Barbarian* by Friedrick Halm trans. Maria Lovell
1854 *Virginius* by Sheridan Knowles
Ingomar the Barbarian by Friedrick Halm trans. Maria Lovell
1856 *Ingomar the Barbarian* by Friedrick Halm trans. Maria Lovell
Damon and Pythias by John Banin
1857 *Ingomar the Barbarian* by Friedrick Halm trans. Maria Lovell
Damon and Pythias by John Banin
The Last Days of Pompeii (twice)
Ion
Medea in the adaptation by Ernest Legouvé (in English translation)
Julius Caesar by Shakespeare
1858 *Virginius* by Sheridan Knowles
Damon and Pythias by John Banin
Brutus, or, The Fall of Tarquin by John Howard Payne
1859 *Virginius* by Sheridan Knowles
Damon and Pythias by John Banin
Medea in the adaptation by Ernest Legouvé trans. Matilda Heron
1864 *Ingomar the Barbarian* by Friedrick Halm trans. Maria Lovell
1866 *The Gladiator* by Robert Montgomery Bird
Ingomar the Barbarian by Friedrick Halm trans. Maria Lovell
Virginius by Sheridan Knowles
1867 *Ingomar the Barbarian* by Friedrick Halm trans. Maria Lovell
Virginius by Sheridan Knowles
Medea in the adaptation by Ernest Legouvé (in Italian translation)
1869 *Ixion, or, The Man at the Wheel* by F. C. Burnand
1870 *Ingomar the Barbarian* by Friedrick Halm trans. Maria Lovell
1872 *Damon and Pythias* by John Banin
1874 *Ingomar the Barbarian* by Friedrick Halm trans. Maria Lovell
1875 *The Gladiator* by Robert Montgomery Bird
Virginius by Sheridan Knowles
1876 *Ingomar the Barbarian* by Friedrick Halm trans. Maria Lovell
1877 *Ingomar the Barbarian* by Friedrick Halm trans. Maria Lovell
1878 *The Gladiator* by Robert Montgomery Bird
1880 *The Gladiator* by Robert Montgomery Bird
Virginius by Sheridan Knowles

    Damon and Pythias by John Banin
1881 *Gladiator* by M. Soumet
    The Gladiator by Robert Montgomery Bird
    Ingomar the Barbarian by Friedrick Halm trans. Maria Lovell
    Virginius by Sheridan Knowles
1882 *Pygmalion and Galatea* by W. S. Gilbert
    Virginius by Sheridan Knowles
1884 *Der Fechter von Ravenna (The Gladiator of Ravenna)* by Ralm
1886 *Claudian*
1887 *Clito*
    Galba, The Gladiator by A. Saumet
    Pygmalion and Galatea by W. S. Gilbert
    Virginius by Sheridan Knowles
1888 *The Gladiator* by Robert Montgomery Bird
    Penelope (burlesque) by H. P. Stevens and Edward Solomon
1890 *Claudian* by Henry Herman and W. G. Wills
    Menaechmi (Plautus) performed in Latin
    The Gladiator by A. Saumet
    Nero, or, The Destruction of Rome by Imre Kiralfy
1891 *The Gladiator* by Robert Montgomery Bird
    Claudian (date uncertain)
    Cleopatra by Sardou trans. Fanny Davenport

Notes

1. Christiansen 2004: 59. Tingley (1987: 131) writes that the Chicago Little Theatre was the first of its kind.
2. Jane Addams also gave a speech before the second production of the play in Chicago, see Tingley 1987: 142.
3. Tingley 1987: 141–3, who gives a full discussion of the political motivation of the touring production of *Trojan Women* and of the response in many local papers around the country.
4. Addams (1914: 43–5, 153–4, 194–5) draws close links between cheap commercial theaters and prostitution. Browne (1956) discusses his dissatisfaction with commercial theater and interest in Greek drama throughout his autobiography. For a detailed treatment of theater and performance at Hull-House, see Jackson 2000. For more on the Little Theatre Movement's relationship with commercial, touring productions, see Chansky 2004.
5. For Legouvé's text, see Macintosh 2000: 14–19.
6. See appendix.
7. See appendix.

8. Malamud 2009: 86. Plays on classical themes were popular in America at least from the eighteenth century: we know, for example, of Washington's delight in the play *Cato*, and his famous staging of the play at Valley Forge to rally his troops in 1778. See also Winterer 2002: 25.
9. While most classicizing melodramas met positive receptions in Chicago, Forrest's performance in *The Gladiator* in 1848 did not. Offended, Forrest did not return to the city for some 20 years. *Chicago Daily Tribune* December 13, 1872.
10. This is presumably based more or less on the burlesque by Francis Burnand, *Ixion, or, The Man at the Wheel*, which premièred in London at the Royalty Theatre, 1863. See Hall and Macintosh 2005: 364.
11. Hall and Macintosh 2005: 367–71 on the female breeches role in classical burlesque.
12. The story is covered repeatedly in both the *Chicago Tribune* and the *Chicago Times* of February and March 1870. See, for example: "The whole city is ringing from end to end with the Terrific battle of the Blondes [a popular term for Lydia Thompson's troupe] . . . we are living, moving and breathing in an atmosphere of Blondism." *Chicago Tribune* February 27, 1870.
13. Sheppard 2008: 146: "Vicious polemics were a standard trope of editorial dialogue throughout the era. Mark Twain campaigning for Jane Garfield in 1880 made a wry observation on the prevailing tendency in the nation's press to counter policy with personal abuse when he told an audience at the Hartford, Connecticut, opera house 'I have never made but one political speech before this. That was years ago. I made a logical, closely reasoned, compact powerful argument against a discriminating opposition. I may say I made a most thoughtful, symmetrical, and admirable argument, but a Michigan newspaper editor answered it, refuted it, utterly demolished it, by saying I was in the constant habit of horse whipping my great grandmother.'"
14. Legouvé 1873: 7–8, "En réalité, s'il fallait définir d'un mot la légende de Médée, je dirais: c'est le plus terrible chapitre de *l'histoire de la séduction* dans le monde! Qu'est-ce, en effet, que Jason, ce Grec, ce civilisé, s'en allant à la poursuite d'un trésor chez les peuplades sauvages, séduisant une fille de ces rudes contrées, se servant d'elle pour l'accomplissement de ses desseins, l'arrachant, déjà mère, à son pays comme à sa famille, et l'abandonnant ensuite, dès qu'il a mis le pied sur sa terre natale; qu'est-ce? Sinon le symbole lointain et poétique de ces vils corrupteurs de nos jours qui, entraînant à Paris, du fond de nos provinces, les tristes victimes de leurs promesses, déshonorent notre société par leur cynisme et leur ingratitude impunie!" All translations are ours, unless otherwise noted.
15. Cf. Macintosh 2000: 2, for a discussion of the importance of the chariot exit scene: "It is this finale that makes Medea the performer *par excellence*; and it is by no means fortuitous that it is this 'theatrical' version (as opposed to earlier versions) of the myth of Medea that predominates in the modern world."
16. (Act 1, scene 4)

> MÉDÉE: . . . ô Jason! . . . cher Jason!
> Es-tu mort? As-tu fui? Quelque somber prison
> Te retient-elle au loin? Où donc es-tu, mon maître?
> Où donc es-tu?
> MÉLANTHE [MEDEA'S SON]: Je suis bien là.
> MÉDÉE: Cher petit être! . . .
> Tu me brises le Cœur! Pas d'abri! Pas d'appui! . . .
> Ce rocher nu, voilà votre couche aujourd'hui! . . .
> LYCAON [MEDEA'S SON]: La faim nous affaiblit plus encore que la route.

17. (Act I, scene 3). (p. 20)

    ORPHÉE: . . . vous aimez, vous, les vièrges vermeilles,
    Comme l'ours montagnard les ruches des abeilles,
    Comme le léopard les troupeauz bien nourris,
    Ou comme le torrent aime les bords fleuris,
    Pour suiller leurs trésors en sa course orageuse . . .

18. "Orphée, par le caractère des chants si purs qui nous restent de lui, s'offrait de lui-même comme l'interprète poétique de la pensée morale que je voulais mettre en lumière; Orphée enfin représentant à la fois, comme tous les grands poëtes, son temps et l'avenir, avait le droit, dans mon ouvrage, d'aller au delà des idées grecques en restant Grec, de ressembler à un penseur moderne sans cesser d'être un personage antique . . ." (p. 9).

19. On the history of *Medea* as a vehicle for star performers, see Macintosh 2000: 3: "It has often been speculated that Euripides' *Medea* of 431 BC, like that other atypical central-figure Greek tragedy from a similar date, Sophocles' *Oedipus Tyrannus*, was written with a particular actor in mind. And the performance history of the play from AD 1500 to 2000 may well lend credence to such speculation, with the roll-call of those associated with the part of Medea reading like an account of the leading actresses and opera singers in European theatre history . . ."

20. *Chicago Republican* January 23, 1867.

21. *Chicago Republican* January 24, 1867.

22. In her analysis of women's municipal politics in Chicago, Maureen A. Flanagan notes, "between 1871 and 1933, a large number of Chicago activist women made common cause in politics" (2002: 6). For detailed discussions of the women's movement at the time, see Parker and Cole 2000.

23. *Chicago Times* January 23, 1867.

24. *Chicago Times* January 23, 1867.

25. *Chicago Times* May 15, 1869.

26. *Chicago Republican* January 25, 1867.

27. *Chicago Tribune* January 23, 1867. Cf. Pearcy, this volume, on the Philadelphian reviewer's bemusement at the figure of Orpheus.

28. *Chicago Times* January 23, 1867.

29. *Chicago Times* January 20, 1867.

30. *Chicago Times* January 22, 1867.

31. *Chicago Tribune* January 23, 1867.

32. *Chicago Daily Tribune* April 9, 1856.

33. *Chicago Daily Tribune*, "The Death of Edwin Forrest," December 13, 1872.

34. Harry Hansen (1946), "How to Give Away an Opera House," *Journal of the Illinois State Historical Society (1908–1984)* 39.4: 419–24; *Chicago Tribune* January 22, 1867.

35. We are very grateful to LaDonna Forsgren, Louise Edwards, Dawn Tracey Brandes, and Eric Johnson for many hours spent combing through Chicago archives and newspapers to help ferret out the theatrical context of these productions. The fruits of their archival work will be made publicly available on the Classicizing Chicago website (<http://www.classicizingchicago.northwestern.edu/>).

36. Fuller details of each of these productions will be made available on the Classicizing Chicago website and database (<http://www.classicizingchicago.northwestern.edu/>).

References

Addams, J. (1914), *A New Conscience and an Ancient Evil*. New York.
Browne, M. (1956), *Too Late to Lament: An Autobiography*. Bloomington, IN.
Buechler, S. M. (1986), *The Transformation of the Woman Suffrage Movement: The Case of Illinois, 1850–1920*. New Brunswick, NJ.
Butsch, R. (2000), *The Making of American Audiences: From Stage to Television, 1750–1990*. Cambridge Studies in the History of Mass Communication. Cambridge and New York.
Chansky, D. (2004), *Composing Ourselves: The Little Theatre Movement and the American Audience*. Carbondale, IL.
Christiansen, R. (2004), *A Theater of our Own: A History and a Memoir of 1,001 Nights in Chicago*. Evanston, IL.
Cropsey, E. H. (1999), *Crosby's Opera House: A Symbol of Chicago's Cultural Awakening*. Madison, NJ.
Flanagan, M. A. (2002), *Seeing with their Hearts: Chicago Women and the Vision of the Good City, 1871–1933*. Princeton.
Foley, H. P. (2012), *Reimagining Greek Tragedy on the American Stage*. Berkeley, Los Angeles, and London.
Grumley, J. (1875), "The Last Week of Mme. Adelaide Ristori in Chicago," *Daily Inter-Ocean*, May 15, 2.
Hall, E. and F. Macintosh (2005), *Greek Tragedy and the British Theatre 1660–1914*. Oxford.
Hall, E., F. Macintosh, and O. Taplin (eds. 2000), *Medea in Performance 1500–2000*. Oxford.
Hall, E., F. Macintosh, and A. Wrigley (eds. 2004), *Dionysus Since 69: Greek Tragedy at the Dawn of the Third Millenium*. Oxford.
Hirsch, F. (1998), *The Boys from Syracuse: The Shuberts' Theatrical Empire*. Carbondale, IL.
Jackson, S. (2000), *Lines of Activity: Performance, Historiography, and Hull-House Domesticity*. Ann Arbor.
Legouvé, E. (1873), *Théâtre complet: pièces en vers*. Paris.
Legouvé, E. (1874), *Histoire morale des femmes*. Paris.
Macintosh, F. (2000), "Introduction: The Performer in Performance," in E. Hall, F. Macintosh, and O. Taplin eds., *Medea in Performance 1500–2000*. Oxford, 1–31.
Malamud, M. (2009), *Ancient Rome and Modern America*. Malden, MA.
Offen, K. (1986), "Ernest Legouvé and the Doctrine of 'Equality in Difference' for Women: A Case Study of Male Feminism in Nineteenth-Century French Thought," *Journal of Modern History* 58.2: 452–84.
Parker, A. M. and S. Cole (2000), *Women and the Unstable State in Nineteenth-Century America*. Walter Prescott Webb Memorial Lectures 33. Arlington, TX.
Sheppard, S. (2008), *The Partisan Press: A History of Media Bias in the United States*. Jefferson, NC.
Sherman, R. (1947), *Chicago Stage: Its Records and Achievements*. Chicago.
Stagg, J. (1968, 1969), *The Brothers Shubert*. New York.
Tingley, D. (1987), "Ellen Van Volkenburg, Maurice Browne and the Chicago Little Theatre," *Illinois Historical Journal* 80.3, 130–46.
Winterer, C. (2002), *The Culture of Classicism: Ancient Greece and Rome in American Intellectual Life, 1780–1910*. Baltimore.
Wrigley, A. and R. Davis (2011), "Greek Immigrants Playing Ancient Greeks at Chicago's Hull-House: Whose Antiquity?," *Journal of American Drama and Theatre* 23.2 (Spring), 7–29.

CHAPTER 8

BARBARIAN QUEENS

Race, Violence, and Antiquity on the Nineteenth-Century United States Stage

ROBERT DAVIS

From the Revolutionary period through the nineteenth century, Americans looked to ancient Greece and Rome for exemplary models of democratic ideals. Scholars such as Caroline Winterer and Carl J. Richard have documented classical ideals at work shaping the political rhetoric, philosophy, and activism of the period (Richard 1995; Winterer 2002). Whether it was the early Republic's "imagined affinities" with Rome or a late century equivalence between Greece and high art, Americans were encouraged to think of themselves as heirs to classical civilization.[1] A typical example of this intellectual perspective is Elias Magoon's 1856 *Westward Empire, or, The Great Drama of Human Progress*, which charts a direct historical path through five ages: Periclean Athens, Augustan Rome, Renaissance Italy, and, finally, the Age of Washington. In Magoon's teleological model, Egypt and Judea were the "exalted cradle of the human race," Greece was "the prepared field of their first grand development," and the United States the "manifest goal" of civilization (Magoon 1856: x. 28).

However, American classicism was not so simple. One cannot speak of "antiquity" in this period as much as "antiquities." While Greece and Rome were often invoked as positive models of civilized values, representations of Egypt and other regions could prove more problematic. Taken as a whole, antiquity generated a constellation of referents that destabilized the typical laudatory associations that writers like Magoon had with the ancient past. What follows is a cultural history of representations and refigurations of two figures, Medea and Cleopatra, that plots tensions between American Philhellenism and Egyptomania.

I am going to read late nineteenth-century official, respectable classical cultures against what was perceived to be the exciting world of barbarian women. The tension between the two gets at the heart of how American experiences of antiquities in the theater conversed with the culture at large. As female, barbarian, and royal, these two women represented stark Others against the backdrop of a culture that was largely masculine, nativist, and populist. Both women acted outside of conventional boundaries, offering audiences glimpses of dark—and popular—fantasies. Two major strategies that artists employed to represent ancient subjects were either to domesticate the unruly barbarian or to revel in her so-called uncivilized qualities. Critical opinion may have heaped scorned on the barbarian, but barbarian women, in particular, remained popular with audiences and artists alike.

In the period that I am surveying, roughly 1855–95, depictions of Greeks and barbarians were shaped by discourses of social evolution. Scientists and philosophers theorized that as species developed unevenly in nature, so did societies progress unevenly through history. In this formulation, so-called primitive cultures were less sophisticated because they had lagged in evolutionary development, while technologically advanced societies had naturally progressed in a contest of the fittest. By this argument, white, United States civilization was proven superior to African or Asian cultures.

Ideas about social and cultural evolution had a rich history before Darwin's *Origin of Species* in 1859.[2] In contrast to Darwin's later thought, Josiah Nott and George Gliddon believed that different races were fixed. In other words, peoples and their cultures existed on an immovable hierarchy of superiority (white, European) to inferiority (African). Although similar theories attracted wide audiences throughout the century, ancient Egypt and Carthage occupied a fiercely contested place in nineteenth-century American culture.[3] Figure 8.1, from the 1854 *Types of Mankind* by Nott and Gliddon, is an example of how classicism and racial science were intertwined. Drawing on examples from ancient art and history, *Types of Mankind*, subtitled *Ethnographical Researches, Based on Ancient Monuments, Paintings, Sculptures and Crania of Races, and Upon their Natural, Geographical, Philological, and Biblical History*, "proved" an uneven development across race based on pseudoscientific principles such as cranial capacity and facial type (Gould 1981). The image is meant to be read spatially. The *Apollo Belvedere*, the much-copied sculpture that had been rediscovered in the fifteenth century, represents the white, classical ideal, which is deemed to occupy the highest point of the evolutionary scale. Then, within this clear hierarchy, there is the African, who is placed one step up in development from the chimpanzee.

Evolutionary theory was often invoked to justify, *inter alia*, slavery, colonialism, or industrialization.[4] In *Primitive Culture* (1871), British anthropologist Edward Tylor (as well as his American counterpart Lewis Henry Morgan) confirmed the reigning discourse of the era when his work divided human progress into three distinct, evolutionary stages: savage, barbarian, and, at the top, civilized. The savage might be applied to describe African tribal villages, the barbarian to, for example, China, while civilization was the exclusive property of western cultures. Here, Greek culture represents the West's earliest departure from barbarism. To many, western society had been evolving since classical Athens, edging closer to what Magoon called the "supreme sway of perfect civilization."[5] Far from being contained in academic lecture halls, this paradigm was the subject of popular books, lecture tours, and public policy (Bender

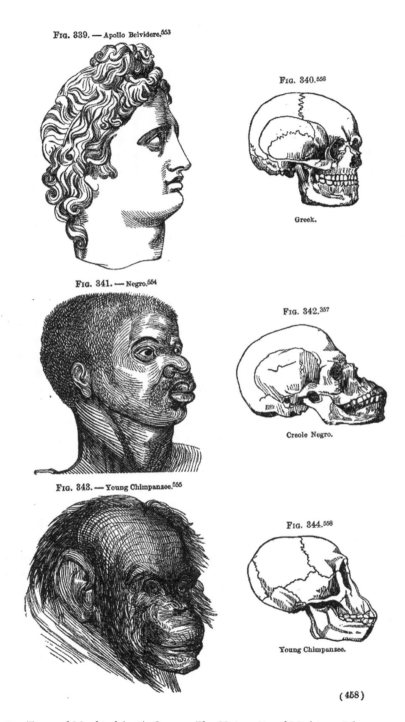

FIG. 8.1 *Types of Mankind* (458). Source: The University of Michigan Library.

2009). It shaped what audiences expected from barbarians like Medea and Cleopatra, as well as how they responded.

Preface: The 1876 Centennial Exhibition in Philadelphia

The 1876 Centennial International Exhibition in Philadelphia, which commemorated the 100-year anniversary of the signing of the Declaration of Independence, was a defining moment in American intellectual and cultural history. Often built on classical designs, international expositions provided highly popular *fora* for displaying American civilization. Industrial machinery, horticulture, art, history, and ethnographic objects were gathered and exhibited in a legible picture of national progress. Exposition visitors could expect to be both educated and entertained while viewing fine art, Native American artifacts, exotic plants, as well as marvels of technology like the first telephone or the tremendous Corliss engine. To make for a pleasurable experience, there were also restaurants, cigar pavilions, beer gardens, a photograph gallery, a Turkish coffee house, a Bible Pavilion, a Fair Bank, a Woman's School House, and a working dairy.

The sheer numbers were designed to impress: divided among more than 200 buildings, stretching over three miles, the Exhibition showed off western agriculture, craft, art, and industry. The intended audience was officially universal. "All the nations of the civilized world will join in a grand celebration," the official guidebook says, but the main audience was North Americans, who were expected to make "a pilgrimage to the Mecca of American Nationality," which they did, in droves.[6] The Exposition opening day alone attracted 186,672 visitors, and the total attendance from May to November 1876 was over 10 million, roughly 20 percent of the population of the United States.[7]

The Official Guidebook states that the purpose of the Centennial was to "celebrate" and "illustrate the unparalleled advancement in science and art, and all the various appliances of human ingenuity for the refinement and comfort of man."[8] While the Exhibition presented a symbolic picture of national progress, it also performed America. Visitors could literally move through representations of entire worlds and encounter set pieces that articulated the majesty of the country. An example was a nine foot tall automated model of George Washington's tomb, where Washington emerged at regular intervals, guarded by marching toy soldiers (Rydell 1984: 35). The national past was resurrected by contemporary technology.

The Centennial is a particularly valuable frame for this discussion because while it celebrated so-called civilized values, it was haunted by contrary subjects and positions. While Exhibition visitors took part in a glorified—and neatly ordered—picture of achievement inside the fair walls, a thriving shantytown of wood, canvas, and occasionally brick buildings known as "Centennial City" sprung up just outside the gates. Here, in this unplanned, crowded community of often-makeshift restaurants, saloons, hotels, beer gardens, and sideshows, visitors were offered the opportunity to see "primitive" wild men, cannibals, and a familiar assortment of traveling acts, such as the fat lady and Learned Pig. Contrary to the values inherent in the Civilized/Savage model, Exhibition visitors apparently wanted to see both sides of society. Eventually, the appeal of variety entertainment would prove so popular that it would be incorporated into subsequent world's fairs, most famously at the Columbian Exposition in 1893, where there was a classical "White City" separate from a jumbled Midway Plaisance of more dubious entertainments. When the Philadelphia shantytown finally burned down on September 9, newspapers and tastemakers greeted the news with glee, even if the flames got close enough to the Exhibition, getting to scorch the turnstiles.[9] By being critically rejected as "uncivilized" but attracting broad crowds, the "Centennial City" is emblematic of the sculptural and theatrical performances that I discuss in this chapter.

Memorial Hall, a sumptuous art gallery, was a featured building in the Exhibition's spectacle of congratulatory self-presentation. Raised temple-like on a terrace six feet above the rest of the fair, the beaux-arts style building included 3,256 paintings and 627 sculptures from around the world. Here, among a fair that attempted to define America, were two key sculptures of barbarian women: William Wetmore Story's *Medea* (1868) (Fig. 8.2) and Mary Edmonia Lewis's the *Death of Cleopatra* (1876) (Fig. 8.3). At first glance, these two pieces appear to be cast from the same mold. Indeed, they both conform to neoclassical principles, yet, they elicited contradictory responses consistent with how different constituencies viewed respectable Greeks versus inferior barbarians.

The backgrounds of the two sculptors were as different as one could find. Story, the son of a Supreme Court justice and co-founder of the Harvard Law School, took up sculpture later in life, almost as a hobby. He maintained a genteel studio in Rome where notable visitors often stopped on the Grand Tour. Edmonia Lewis was the mixed-race daughter of an African-American father and Chippewa mother. Raised largely by her mother's tribe after being orphaned at 10, Lewis studied at Oberlin College, but did not graduate, eventually making her way to Boston and Rome to work. Story and his circle of literati stayed aloof of Lewis and her fellow artists and actresses, which included the celebrated Charlotte Cushman.

According to one contemporary critic, Story's *Medea* was "the embodiment of jealousy and feminine revenge" (Strahan 1880: 216). Nevertheless, the artist ennobled his subject by dressing her in simple, classical robes and concentrating on the moment before Medea kills her children rather than the sensational murder itself. The viewer's focus is drawn to the face; the dagger is held away. In a poem he wrote on the subject (Story was also an amateur poet, actor, and playwright), Story dwells on "Her brow shut down, her mouth irresolute, | Her thin arm twitching at her robes the while" (Story 1868: 158). This contemplative Medea is frozen in the moment before engaging in a barbaric act, the spectacle of a noble woman weighing family and revenge. The result was a resounding critical success that attracted buyers for decades. While a critic praised Medea as "indicat[ing] the work of a rich and highly cultivated mind," the public response was somewhat cold (Benjamin 1879: 668). In fact, the author of an exposition souvenir book criticized its "bookish culture ... overgrown with this creeping feeling of

FIG. 8.2 Detail from William Wetmore Story's *Medea*, 1865, executed 1868. The Metropolitan Museum of Art, Gift of Henry Chauncey, 1894 (94.8a–d). Photograph by Jerry L. Thompson.

legend and tradition," claiming that it felt like Story had approached the work through literature, not life (Strahan 1880: 215–16). Regardless of her Colchian identity, Story's Medea was synonymous with American neoclassical admiration of supposed Greek ideals of harmony, rationality, and beauty. The barbarian had become a naturalized Greek.

Edmonia Lewis was an outsider to Story's gilded world, existing beyond conventional norms for women of her time. Story espoused a common view that Lewis and her circle were unnatural: women doing men's work. Furthermore, African-Americans were widely believed to only be able to imitate, not create. Lewis's *Death of Cleopatra* was placed at a tangle of contradictions. Both classical and Egyptian, it was neoclassical in style, even while violating representational norms.

FIG. 8.3 Death of Cleopatra, Edmonia Lewis, 1876. Smithsonian American Art Museum.

While Lewis's *Death of Cleopatra* stays within the bounds of accepted form, it is a major departure from the cultural tradition that Story had mastered. In 1860, Story himself had created a celebrated *Cleopatra*. Like Medea, his Cleopatra was silent, lost in thought before taking action (Gardner 1943). By contrast, Lewis depicted Cleopatra after her suicide. Her reclining body, displayed in Memorial Hall under an "oriental" canopy that colored her body a crimson hue, was offered so the viewer could gaze upon the features of death. In the post-reconstruction period, artists representing deceased female bodies largely erased the overt signs of death by emphasizing domesticity and the features of sleep; Lewis, by contrast, shows Cleopatra with her arms aside, revealing a body in pain and lacking physical control (Nelson 2007). Such a strategy, while controversial, would not have been appropriate in a depiction of a "civilized" woman, but barbarian women, who were at lower stages of development, provided natural opportunities to reveal "lower" emotions, a trend that would remain popular throughout the century.

A typical response to *Death of Cleopatra* is that of William J. Clark, who mixes praise for Lewis's skill with a fascinated horror at her representation: "the effects of death are represented with such skill as to be absolutely repellent—and it is a question whether a statue of the ghastly characteristics of this one does not overstep the bounds of legitimate art" (Clark 1878: 141–2). While guidebook author J. S. Ingram wrote that Lewis's

Cleopatra was "the most remarkable piece of sculpture in the American section . . .", he also judged that "the classic standard had been departed from . . . and detracted from the dignity" of the figure (Ingram 1876: 294).

Story and Lewis's sculptures mark the parameters of admiration and repulsion that guided public interaction with ancient subjects. While people responded with admiration to Story's intellectual Medea, they were fascinated by Lewis's sensual Cleopatra.[10] In fact, Lewis's queen was by no means the only Cleopatra present in Memorial Hall. In sculpture, there was a Cleopatra by James Haseltine as well as one by expatriate Margaret Foley, Valentine Prinsep's *Death of Cleopatra*, and Enrico Braga's seductive bronze of Cleopatra emerging from the rug she had used to gain an audience with Caesar. Among the numerous other mythic, historical, and biblical subjects, there was also a moving wax sculpture that showed Cleopatra on her barge being attended by a cupid and slave that made seductive gestures at spectators. Writing on the piece's state of undress, William Dean Howells comments that it "advertises a museum of anatomy in Philadelphia" (Howells 1876: 93). It is telling that an exposition symbolizing the best of American civilization should also be so full of barbarians. This tension between the noble, if tragic, Greece and the dangerous, sensual Egypt would dominate the last third of the century, but to understand its popular roots, we must go back to 1856.

Matilda Heron's Medea

Antebellum American theater audiences of all classes took part in a widespread culture of classicism. Whether based on myth, history, or fantasy, plays with ancient subject matter pervaded the stage from the colonial period (Malamud 2011). The majority of these plays, whether *The Last Days of Pompeii* (1835) or *Caius Gracchus* (1815), grafted antebellum values of masculine vigor and feminine sentimentality onto the source material. In other words, the men were men and the women were women, with no ambiguity. Male characters tended to fume with injustice and revel in righteous bloodshed. Most visible here was Edwin Forrest's Brutus, Virginius, and, especially, Spartacus. Forrest's strong, defiant, Spartacus in Robert Montgomery Bird's *The Gladiator* (1831), for example, possesses an American manliness that is interchangeable with his Thracianness as he pledges to fight aristocratic Romans relentlessly for his liberty. By contrast, the women are almost entirely passive, following a strict code of decorum (see further Bosher and Cox, this volume). In Jacksonian America, respectable women were expected to stay at home and exert a moral influence over the men.[11] The most a woman does in *The Gladiator* is inspire Spartacus to spare a helpless captive. Embedded in this prevailing culture of meek heroines, the first American production of Ernest Legouvé's *Médée*, in a translation by actress Matilda Heron, would change the American landscape of classical dramatic roles (see further Pearcy, Bosher and Cox, this volume).

Matilda Heron, at times lauded as "America's Tragedienne," "The American Rachel," or simply "the best tragic actress in America," worked in relative obscurity until her version of Alexandre Dumas's *La Dame aux camélias* earned her lasting fame. An early pioneer of what was called the "emotional school," Heron was known for her spectacular displays of feeling. To one prominent critic, she was a force of nature: "an exponent of the elemental passions, in their universal flow and ebb; she was the whirlwind" (Winter 1915: 71). Heron's two chief roles were Camille, a noble courtesan, and the violent Medea, both of which she played throughout her celebrated, if short, career.

Heron provided the translation for *La Dame aux camélias*, and in her interpretation of the role she broke new ground. Unlike her predecessors, Heron daringly retained the fact that her heroine was a courtesan.[12] Despite a small house on opening night in January 1857 at Wallack's Theatre in New York, Heron's *Camille* (as it was known) was soon the sold-out sensation of the year. Hardly complacent about her success, Heron introduced her *Medea* a month later. Professors and popular crowds alike flocked to see the brazen Heron as the infamous Greek character, making it the most anticipated production of the season. While *Camille* was charged with being an immoral production, it remained predominantly sentimental. Contemporary *cartes de visite* barely hint at Camille's sordid life. Instead, Heron is demurely dressed in white, almost like a bride or girl getting her first communion. Medea, by contrast, was an exotic, fearful figure, hardly recognizable in mainstream contemporary society.

The play adapts the texts of both Legouvé and Euripides to suit an audience accustomed to melodrama. For example, it is written in three acts in prose and there is no chorus. A major change in both Legouvé and Heron's versions is an added recognition scene. In Heron's production, Medea leaves her children in a grove while she supplicates a statue of Diana. The children are discovered by none other than Creon's daughter, Creusa, who pledges to help them. When Medea enters, the two women strike a fast, deep bond. Creusa, drawn to help Medea, pledges, "I will be thy sister." Medea unburdens her pain and hatred of the man—as yet unnamed—who has abandoned her. Frightened but sympathetic, Creusa asks what Medea would do to this man, and Medea, in what critics referred to as "the leopard scene," provides the audience with their first glimpse of the figure who exceeds customary womanhood: "Do? What does the leopard do, when, from the forest depths, seized with a terrible and bloody joy, it bounds, like the thunder, and falls upon its prey?" (Heron 1857: 13–14). Moments later, the poet Orpheus reveals Medea's identity and Creusa flees from the din of Medea's bloodthirsty cries for vengeance to a falling curtain.

Medea spends the remaining two acts working herself up again and again to higher pitches of emotional volcanism. The play revels in Medea's violent temper, but it seeks an explanation, if not a justification, in her treatment at the hands of Jason. In particular, Jason's villainy is suggested by his threat to take her away from her children. Unwomanned, Medea turns to revenge by destroying Creusa. When the citizens of Corinth discover the crime, they storm the palace to kill Medea and her children; however, Medea kills her own children to spare them death at the mob's hands. After she murders the children, momentarily hidden by an encroaching mob, Jason enters, asking "Who hath killed them?" Medea roars, "Thou!" and holds an accusatory tableau as music brings down a slow curtain.

The driving force behind Heron's *Medea* was not the dramatic text, but the thrilling acting. Even the critics who didn't care for the play admired, and were moved by, Heron's performance. William Winter, the chief critic of his day, said: "Her *Medea* was half a prowling maniac and half a slattern gypsy, the only merit of it consisting in the occasional gleams of fateful fury, like intermittent flickering of fire from a slumbering volcano" (Winter 1915: 71).

Heron's version premièred in St. Louis in 1856. A year later, she took New York by storm with a bold repertoire that kept Medea alive as a dominant figure in American tragedy into the mid-1880s. *Medea* played 16 times over its first month and a half in New York, second in her repertoire that season only to *Camille*. Although *Medea* had its detractors, it was also a recognized success. One popular weekly concluded that there was "little difference of opinion as to the high excellence of Miss Heron's delineation." To counter any naysayers, of whom there were a few, the reviewer retorted, "the sun has spots, say they."[13]

The list of actresses who made Legouvé's role their own is a run-down of postbellum powerhouses: Matilda Heron, the Australian Avonia Jones, the Italian Adelaide Ristori, and the Central European Fanny Janauschek, to name a few (see Pearcy, Bosher and Cox, this volume). I focus on Heron and Ristori, because they were the most popular Medeas and because their performances embody respectable and transgressive classicisms at one and the same time. Heron's Medea, in particular, became a critical site for the challenge of dominant notions of female propriety and agency.

As we have heard, *Camille* broke ground but it was still a sentimental melodrama: Camille suffered with pathos. Medea acted with violence; and with *Medea*, Heron erased the binary of the passive woman and heroic, manly man, as exemplified by Forrest, and replaced it with the vengeful woman, "the leopard." While the public reception was at turns laudatory and hostile, it was always spellbound.

Narratives of audience responses to Heron follow a familiar pattern of individuals being mentally overcome by her display. *Camille* generated sentimental emotions but *Medea* evoked something dangerous. It was, in the words of one critic, "far more terribly powerful."[14] By putting so much naked emotion on stage, Heron's role violated key gender boundaries, placing her Medea definitively lower on the chain of civilized to savage, but thrilling audiences with her aggression.

Heron's affective power cut across lines of class and taste. The composition of the opening night New York audience for *Medea* included "all the well-known representatives and exponents of art, science, and literature ... the ensemble being an audience of the most ... highly critical."[15] The response of this sophisticated, distant audience was wild applause. Heron was called out at the end of each act for multiple encores, and twice at the final curtain. She stirred people up. A reviewer for *Ballou's Pictorial Drawing-Room Companion* tells the story of a sailor in the crowd to suggest that *Medea*'s story was a rousing tale typical of any revenge melodrama. The reviewer found the sailor in question alternating between weeping and giving a "forecastle cheer" for Medea.[16] On a similar note, when the play had premièred in St. Louis, a reviewer reported:

> The more intellectual of Medea's audience were entirely carried away, and seemed afraid to breathe, lest they should break the spell which had introduced them to her tearful history as if by enchantment.[17]

This word "enchantment" is a key. Again and again, Heron (like Medea herself) is spoken of as working a spell over her audience.

In a more thorough example, Adam Badeau, critic, soldier, and future secretary to General Ulysses S. Grant, recorded a typical young man's view of the performance one evening: "I was prepared to judge severely, and by comparison with the highest standard" but he "experienced such a wrenching and tightening of emotions, such a whirlwind of feeling, as made criticism impossible." Ultimately, Badeau felt an "overpowering influence" that he charged the reader: "Admire her or not, I defy you to remain calm" (Badeau 1859: 42).

At times, critics and audience members equated the enchantment of Heron's acting style with moral danger. William Winter, a staunch moral conservative, offers an oft-quoted description of praise for Heron's ability that betrays a fear of her danger to women: "She [Heron] could, and did, so deeply affect the feelings and so entirely beguile the sympathies as to confuse, if not destroy, perception of the difference between right and wrong" (Winter 1915: 68).

A few years after Heron's successful debut, bohemian poet, playwright, and writer Fitz-James O'Brien penned a short story for *Harper's Magazine* entitled "Mother of Pearl" that shows how Heron's affective power could sway women in her spell. In the story, set in Heron's first major New York season, the hero and his mysterious wife travel to New York to witness Heron's *Camille*. Immediately "electrified," the couple returns the next night to see her *Medea*. During the performance, the narrator is preoccupied with his wife's reaction:

> I never saw a human being so rocked by emotion as was my wife during the progress of this tragedy. Her countenance was a mirror of every incident and passion. She swayed to and fro under those gusts of indignant love that the actress sent forth from time to time, and which swept the house like a storm. When the curtain fell she sat trembling,—vibrating still with those thunders of passion that the swift lightnings of genius had awakened. She seemed almost in a dream... (O'Brien 1860: 396)

Here we see, some three years after Heron's New York debut, how responses continue to be captured by the language of enchantment, natural imagery, and moral anxiety. In the story, the narrator wakes in the night to find his mild-mannered wife perched above him, brandishing a knife. She strikes, but he escapes with minor injuries. Later, she attempts to kill their child. When she is caught and restrained, she admits that she is addicted to hashish, which has rendered her unable to resist the force of Heron's performance. No other response gets as close to expressing how Americans feared and loved this new woman on the stage than by showing how easily Medea can drive a woman to unspeakable crime. O'Brien's story works only if there is a general consensus that Heron's *Medea* can in some way enchant one's being, albeit for a temporary period.

After enjoying success in New York and across the country, Heron's career declined sharply after the Civil War. Although she had worked hard to expand her repertoire by adding plays, including her own version of Racine's *Phèdre*, Heron continued only to be known for the roles she had developed in 1857. By the late 1860s, critical and public opinion found her emotional style out of step with popular taste.

Frequently infirm, Heron went through two failed (simultaneous) marriages, financial ruin, and continued poor health. Her last performance of *Medea* was for her daughter's benefit on June 1, 1876, the year of the Centennial. Shortly after, she took to bed and died early the next year. *Medea* remained popular, but a growing culture of middle-class respectability demanded a new *Medea*. While many actresses continued to play Legouvé and Grillparzer's Medea (see Pearcy, this volume), Italian star Adelaide Ristori reigned over them all.

Adelaide Ristori

Italian star Adelaide Ristori, who would become famous for playing Medea, Lady Macbeth, and Mary Stuart, created a sensation in her 1855 Parisian debut, quickly followed by wider European engagements,[18] but she did not tour the United States until the end of the Civil War. A rival to the great French tragedienne Rachel, Ristori offered strong, tragic female characters. Both were courted by Legouvé to star in his *Médée*. Rachel scandalously declined at the last minute because she did not want to be associated with infanticide. Legouvé then courted Ristori. In her autobiography, Ristori recounts the feelings that she had upon first reading the play during the hours it took one morning to dress her hair. Although she had been skeptical, she claims, she was "possessed by enthusiastic admiration" for the piece (Ristori 1907: 178). To entice Ristori further, Legouvé toned down the ending to make the murders less bloodthirsty. Contrary to Heron, this was a Medea who would be known for her maternal affections.

Comparing Ristori to Rachel, a *Harper's* correspondent in Italy in 1857 lauds Rachel's moments of genius, so similar to Heron's, but concludes that Ristori "as a whole, woman and actress, . . . is superior." When Ristori reached America in 1866, she earned instant stardom. Her tour was unlike anything Americans had seen before. Her manager, Jacob Grau, launched an unprecedented publicity campaign, flooding the press with notices, reviews, announcements of his star's social engagements, as well as saturating the marketplace with preview photographs that created an irresistible flurry of interest. Press photos repeatedly show her in poses of maternal affection, tenderly cradling her young children.[19] It barely mattered that audiences would have to read a translation as Ristori acted in Italian.[20] Theater-goers came to see the celebrated international star in person. Ristori was, without a doubt, the most successful Medea of the century, even if her performances in both Philadelphia and Chicago met with mixed reviews (see further Pearcy, Bosher and Cox, this volume). Not only did she possess a sophisticated infrastructure for touring and publicity, her Medea also conformed to neoclassical ideals and the culture of respectability that were dominant in the post-bellum period.[21] Rather than dwell on her violent tendencies, Ristori, a consummate actress with broad range, highlighted Medea's maternal nature.

From Ristori's account of the play, we infer that the production was more discreet than Heron's in its handling of the murders. Ristori relates how they were the only way to save her children from the raging mob:

> I tried to escape, hurrying precipitately to the right side of the stage, but the noise of the infuriated mob drove me back in terrified haste to the other. In vain I sought safety in every direction. The cries of "Death! Death!" which resounded throughout the palace, forced me to try some other way. At the moment the mob broke in on every side, like an overwhelming torrent, seeking to tear my children from me ... —
>
> "seize them! To death with her!"
> I exclaimed desperately—
> "Never! You shall not have them!"

And so, she dragged them behind the altar. Afterward: "the people fell back from such a sight, and let the audience see Medea with her murdered sons lying behind her at Saturn's feet; her eyes sternly set, her face stony, her whole attitude befitting that of a statue of remorse."[22]

Ristori inspired unprecedented devotion from highly discerning admirers. Leading Parisian critic Jules Janin wrote of her debut: "*Ristori, Ristori!* She is the rage of the day! She is tragedy itself. She is comedy itself. She is the drame. She reigns—she governs—she commands, and the crowd obeys."[23] Men and women of taste paid court to her as if to royalty. Following a performance, Alexandre Dumas père reportedly knelt to kiss her skirt. American actress and expatriate Charlotte Cushman wrote, after seeing Ristori: "Rachel is a great artist and is almost faultless, but Rachel is a machine; Ristori is a woman."[24] Ristori was someone you could feel good about adoring, sanctioned by the elite; Heron, on the other hand, immersed in a circle of bohemians, was sketchy. As in O'Brien's short story, Heron-worship was the realm of drug addicts and immoral women. Her Medea was a wild figure of violence and revenge; Ristori's a familiar woman and mother.

One other person who responded particularly strongly to Ristori was William Story, who began his "Medea" sculpture shortly after seeing her in the role. Reportedly, Story developed an obsession with Ristori, following her "like a shadow."[25] In his book *Roba di Roma*, Story writes that "her Medea is as affecting as it is terrible," yet in comparing her to Rachel (who "seemed to joy in the doing of horrible acts") Ristori was "driven to them by violent impulses beyond her power to control" (Story 1864: 228). She "excels in the representation of the more womanly and gentle qualities" befitting a proper woman, who, driven to violence by extreme circumstances rather than her barbarian nature, is more deserving of sympathy. Ristori conjured idealized associations with classical referents, and the highest literary and artistic circles opened to her as a result.[26] *Frank Leslie's Popular Monthly* notes that "Society opened its arms to her—she became its central attraction; the *élite* of the native as well as the foreign citizenship crowded around her."²⁷ In contrast to Rachel or Heron's violent women, who invoked a dangerous barbarism, Ristori was civilized and safe.

Story's *Medea* deliberately references Ristori's performance. In *Marble Queens and Captives*, Joy Kasson notes that the image of Story's Medea with dagger in hand was one regularly associated with Ristori. Engravings in this pose accompanied many reviews, and Ristori references the scene as one of her most powerful in the play: "I drew myself up in such a manner as to appear of gigantic size, holding my dagger clasped aloft, so that men might well have been thunderstruck at my aspect" (Ristori 1888: 212). Undoubtedly, they were. This moment must have been iconic; it echoes throughout the iterations of Ristori's image. A popular London burlesque, for example, climaxes with Medea holding her dagger high to deliver a final blow to Jason, as Orpheus turns it into a jester's staff.²⁸ As Ristori was still touring in 1876, we can read the critical adulation heaped on Story's sculpture in Philadelphia as endorsing this new, domesticated Medea that audiences had been witnessing on stage for the better part of a decade.

CLEOPATRA: BETWEEN GREECE AND EGYPT

As elite Americans were invoking classical examples to provide a foundation for their historical destiny, many feared that too much civilization, too much culture, would weaken Americans by divorcing them from nature. Influential neurologist and mental health reformer George Miller Beard popularized the malady "Neurasthenia" to describe a condition that his peers saw as besieging the civilized world. In *American Nervousness: Its Causes and Consequences* (1881), Beard noted that the stresses of civilization could directly cause symptoms such as fatigue, headache, anxiety, and even impotence.²⁹ This "lack of nerve-force" was thought to be endemic to the nineteenth-century United States, thriving in urban centers.³⁰ To Beard, "the chief and primary cause of this development and very rapid increase of nervousness is *modern civilization*."³¹ Later in the century, Theodore Roosevelt expressed in a letter what many thought when he said: "Over-sentimentality, over softness, in fact washiness and mushiness are the great dangers of the age and of this people. Unless we keep the *barbarian virtues*, gaining the civilized ones will be of little avail" (Roosevelt 1899). As the nation grew into a world power, Americans were heavily invested in showing off their progress and civilization, yet at the same time, they remained fascinated by the imagined vitality of the barbarian.

Few figures intrigued Americans like Cleopatra. Throughout the century, she was one of the most talked about women in popular fiction and history. She brought together conflicting signs of the civilized/savage divide. From her Macedonian heritage, she was an inheritor of Hellenism; yet, she was supposedly tainted by African barbarity. Cleopatra's identity as either civilized or barbarian woman was a high-stakes mystery. Artists, writers, and scholars invoking Cleopatra were preoccupied with untangling her roots in both classical and African civilizations.

A theater-goer wrote in to *The Nation* complaining that "Cleopatra was, as you know, a Greek by blood . . . hence, although an Egyptian Queen, she was not of the Egyptian race . . . she herself . . . must have possessed all the characteristics of the Aryan—at least a white skin."[32] In *The Girls' Book of Famous Queens*, Lydia Hoyt Farmer asks simply, "Why is Cleopatra so fair of skin, though an Egyptian by birth?" She concludes, like many, "Though Egypt was her birthplace, Grecian blood flows through her veins, and whitens her skin . . . Grecian culture gives her voice its oft-narrated magic charm of melting sweetness and a spark of Grecian genius quickens her powers of mind." In other words, her best qualities are claimed by white authors as their own, while her dangerous sensuality must be due to her Egyptian upbringing, or as Farmer puts it, "the oriental voluptuous indolence of the Egyptian" (Farmer 1887: 36).

In imagining Cleopatra's life, Farmer paints a picture of placid Nile cruises and Roman pageants, but she also warns: in her life "there are dark and bloody deeds and savage barbarities and revolting vices" that make for an "unpleasant recital of vice and crime" (Farmer 1887: 35). Strong words for a girl's book! It was the presence of this mixture of unabashed sensuality and high culture that attracted unflagging audiences in the 1890s.

The late nineteenth century saw a revival of Shakespeare's *Antony and Cleopatra*, but it is Victorien Sardou's blockbuster *Cleopatra* that will be my focus here. The eponymous heroine of Sardou's play was played by Fanny Davenport, who owned the American rights and was in the American première in 1890. But it was her rival, Sarah Bernhardt, who would significantly go on to play Medea in Catulle Mendès's version in Paris in 1898, created the role of Cleopatra, and toured America with it in 1891. Both versions were very popular, if not consistently critical, hits.[33]

Sardou's play roughly follows Shakespeare, but is hardly as expansive. The plot reads like a mobius strip showing a strong, Roman man dominated by a foreign woman's sexuality. Act I, for example, begins with Antony arriving in Egypt to punish Cleopatra. Once she is magnificently revealed scantily clad on a barge, reclining under a decorous canopy—much like Lewis's statue at the Centennial—it is but the work of a moment before Antony is kneeling at her feet.

Act II is a scene of revelry, with the lovers enjoying every manner of sensual delight. There is food, wine, and plenty of dancing. This would prove the most contentious scene in moral terms. One *Times* reviewer at the Paris première hastily reports that "the dancing girls . . . abandoned the traditions of the European ballet for the strange Nubian style of dancing, which came into vogue at the time of the recent exposition."[34] By "strange Nubian style," the reviewer is referencing what was known as the *danse du ventre*, or, more colloquially "belly dance" or "cooch dance," which would become infamous in Chicago when reformers attempted to have it banned at the 1893 World's Columbian Exposition. By displacing ballet with exotic dance, *Cleopatra* staged its own subversion of European tradition. Repeatedly, we watch Antony fall prey to Cleopatra, who is at turns noble or wanton, and always seductive.

Almost unanimously, critics left Sardou's *Cleopatra* complaining about the overlong and dull plot; almost unanimously, too, they were enthralled by its excessive spectacle of exotic locations, a tremendous panorama of Giza, bare bodies, pleasure barges, and Cleopatra being unrolled from a carpet to meet Antony. Perhaps not unsurprisingly, most attention was focused on the body of Cleopatra.

Watching the first production at the Théâtre Porte St. Martin in Paris, an American critic offers a typical response by likening the role to a state of undress: "The part is cut like a robe—or, better, like the winding softness, the clinging transparency, of Sarah's jeweled gowns." Later, he talks of Cleopatra hiding a letter "under the scant folds of her white gauze robe."[35] Comparing Sardou and Shakespeare, one journalist wrote that "Shakespeare's play was noble, Marmorean, Occidental; Sardou's is ignoble, chryselephantine, Oriental," which, he later distills to mean that the Sardou version "gives me more poignant emotion than Shakespeare."[36] Barbaric characters did not have the tragic dignity of high art, but they were ready vehicles for expressing intense emotion.

According to Nott and Gliddon, ancient Egypt was a hotbed of miscegenation. Over time, in their study, Egyptian royalty bred with Greeks, Jews, and Asians. Performing Sardou in a period of intense debate over immigration policy that produced a burgeoning eugenics movement, Cleopatra activated fears of racial pollution, even as she titillated. The racial dynamic was not lost on the play. Bernhardt thrilled audiences when she painted her body a ruddy "African hue."[37] Yet, Cleopatra remained racially ambivalent. The staging offered many opportunities to contrast her light body with the darker, identifiably "Nubian" bodies of her slaves.

While theatrical representations of Medea transgressed mid-nineteenth-century norms of respectability by inviting the audience to share the protagonist's extreme emotions and justify her violent acts, Sardou's Cleopatra was intertwined with questions of race and sexuality. Here was an exalted queen of ambiguous racial identity who openly used her sexuality to control strong-willed men. Barbarian women, it was widely believed, were more libidinous that their civilized counterparts. To see this onstage both concerned and excited audiences. A young aspiring actress reportedly approached Fanny Davenport, known as the "American Cleopatra," looking for a part. To win over the star, the actress claimed she could provide her own extravagant dresses, to which Davenport supposedly quipped, "My dear young lady, in *Cleopatra*, it is not so much a matter of dress as of undress."[38] The contrasting reviews for Bernhardt's New York première lets us glimpse the contradictions that Cleopatra performed for her audience.

First, the *New York Daily Tribune* jumps right in with the language of evolution: Bernhardt, he says, must have "a better use of her powers than the paltry and ignominious employment of presenting an ideal of womanhood that degrades it to the level of the tiger and the ape."[39] Also, we have, like the Paris première, a focus on metaphors of undress: "The part has not one shred of decency to cover it, and, worse still, it has not one fibre of nobility to exalt it." Here "the bog of sensuality is opened before you" and you "see womanhood at its worst. On every side of the picture the limit is the carnal limit," all so you can watch the "vulgar subjugation" of a man by a woman. The *New York Times*, on the other hand, finds her "queenlike and womanly, a vision of loveliness and grace . . . A creature of pure romance."

During Davenport's initial run in New York in 1890, disaster struck as the Fifth Avenue Theatre burnt down, taking most of *Cleopatra*'s expensive sets and costumes with it. Undaunted, Davenport quickly rebuilt the production and took it on tour. Problematically, when she returned to New York, Bernhardt was already present, performing the role to acclaim. What ensued was a volatile period of comparisons and heated exchanges, no doubt stoked by both actresses' publicity agents. Bernhardt and Davenport exchanged a series of letters in the *New York Tribune*, each claiming that their Cleopatra was superior. With titles like "Which is the Real Sardou's Cleopatra?" the letters show a stark contrast: Bernhardt criticized Davenport for her lack of sensuality and Davenport attacked Bernhardt for her lack of queenliness.[40] There is no doubt that Bernhardt's queen excited audiences more, but it is worth noting that if a good deal of this may have been in the acting of the role, a starker, undiscussed contrast between the two was Bernhardt's racial coloring and Davenport's portrayal of Cleopatra as a purely white queen. Bored by the dramatic text, Bernhardt's reviewers spoke at length of her personal seductiveness, while Davenport's of her nobility. The more domesticated the Cleopatra, the more intellectual and respected; however, the exotic "other" Cleopatra was far more alluring to audiences.

Writing of an opulent *Antony and Cleopatra*, William Winter—who had reviewed Heron sternly—complained that although "the critical tribunals of the town" had largely agreed "with considerable virulence that the play was dull, yet this performance draws crowded houses, and, no doubt, it will continue to draw them, here and all over the country" (Winter 1889: 36). Winter is not simply leveling criticism at sensuality on stage. Cleopatra's sexuality was different from, say, the attraction of a flimsily clad chorus girl. She was a queen. She had power. She had to be reckoned with.

Conclusion

Since Americans regularly adopted antiquity to define their place in the world, barbarians should be moved from the margins of the discussion of American identity to the center. The means by which classical subjects were defined relied on their spectral other. In the theater, ancient barbarian subjects proliferated. The number of roles, African, Egyptian, Gaul, or Persian, suggest an ongoing contest at the heart of the practice of embodying civilization. Whether it was the violent Medea or seductive Cleopatra, audiences hungered for figures who were antithetical to idealized American values. Audiences denounced these barbarian women with the forceful rhetoric of evolution, but they also wanted to experience the emotions and sensuality that were, they believed, the exclusive domain of barbarians. In the nineteenth century, the theater enabled Americans to enjoy their civilization, but have their barbarian virtues too.

Notes

1. Winterer 2002: 17–18. American culture eagerly claimed descent from anything considered proto-democratic in the past. James Fenimore Cooper, author of *The Last of the Mohicans* (1826), said, without a touch of irony, "Shakespeare is, of course, the great author of America."
2. See Hawkins 1997 for a discussion of the range of theories that we now file under the term "evolution."
3. On Nott and Gliddon, see Fabian 2010. For a discussion of the fraught battles over ancient Africa, see, in particular, Trafton 2004 and Malamud 2011.
4. The theory is more familiar from its twentieth-century designation, "Social Darwinism," but that term, which would not be used until the 1880s, is misleading. It did not catch on in the United States for decades more and different aspects of evolutionary theory appealed to widely different audiences, making a consensus impossible.
5. Magoon 1856: iv. Not every historian was as utopian.
6. *Visitor's Guide* (1876), 3.
7. Such a figure should be met with some skepticism. There is no way to know how many individuals attended the fair, as official gate receipts make no allowance for repeat visitors.
8. *Visitor's Guide* (1876), 4.
9. For example, the *Philadelphia Inquirer* (1876), 2: "The universal opinion seemed to be that, with a few exceptions, the shambles that were being wiped out were meeting a fate that they very decidedly merited."
10. Story's *Medea* won many accolades, including a rare Medal of Excellence from the exhibition (only one of five American statues).
11. See Welter 1966 for a classic work on respectable, sentimental culture in the nineteenth-century United States.
12. *La Dame aux camélias* was popular at the time, but the other stars who assumed the role avoided acknowledging that the protagonist was a courtesan. Manager and star Laura Keene opened her version of the play in 1856 and framed the play as a serving girl's sordid dream to avoid acknowledging the subject matter of the original.
13. *Frank Leslie's Illustrated Newspaper* March 14, 1857, 223.
14. *Spirit of the Times* (1857), 408.
15. *Spirit of the Times* (1857), 408.
16. "Honest Feeling" (1857), *Ballou's Pictorial Drawing-Room Companion* June 20, 397.
17. *Daily Missourian* September 15, 1856.
18. For Ristori's European successes with *Médée*, see Macintosh 2000a: 14–19; and Hall and Macintosh 2005: 401–23.
19. The first modern-style publicity blitz in nineteenth-century America was P. T. Barnum's publicity for Jenny Lind's lucrative 1850 American tour. Grau, however, utilized the full range of current technologies and press availability. See Carlson 1985: 27, which also provides an excellent overview of Ristori's career.
20. A typical American audience member would be reading an English translation of an Italian translation of a French adaptation of Euripides. This is the source of much mirth and derision in the English burlesques, see Macintosh 2000b: 93–5.
21. For an in-depth look at the culture of respectability and how it shaped theater audiences, see Butsch 2000.

22. Ristori 1907: 219–20. This is very different from her use of a large cloak to conceal the murders that was the normal staging in European productions. See Macintosh 2000a: 17.
23. Quoted in "Adelaide Ristori," *Harper's Weekly* 10, September 29, 1886, 609. Emphasis in the original.
24. Quoted in Leach 1972: 270.
25. "American Studies in Rome and Florence," *Harper's New Monthly Magazine* 33 (1886), 101.
26. For example, *Frank Leslie's Popular Monthly* (1885) describes her acting as inherently noble, as "she seemed to lose hold upon herself in the taking on of the ideal" (Lester 1885: 260).
27. *Frank Leslie's Popular Monthly* (1885), 262.
28. For a fuller discussion of this production and trends in burlesque versions of *Medea*, see Macintosh 2000b.
29. In fact, the pressure of living in an industrial, advanced civilization could also lead to tooth decay, hay-fever, baldness, drug use, and, at its worse, insanity. Interestingly, Beard cited overcivilization also as a cause for the "unprecedented beauty of American women" (Beard 1881: 65–73).
30. He notes that "All this is modern, and originally American; and no age, no country, and no form of civilization, not Greece, nor Rome, nor Spain, nor the Netherlands, in the days of their glory, possessed such maladies" (Beard 1881: vii–viii).
31. Beard 1881: vi, emphasis in the original.
32. *The Nation* (1890), 1441.
33. It is worth noting that theatrical representations were so popular in the period that the real and staged Cleopatra are often interchangeable. In works of the period, Bernhardt or Davenport's photos appear as illustrations of Shakespeare's play and historical articles.
34. "The Latest 'Cleopatra': Sardou's Play Produced in Paris Last Night," *New York Times* October 24, 1890, 1.
35. "Bernhardt's New Role: The Triumph She Had in Sardou's 'Cleopatra,'" *New York Times* November 9, 1890.
36. Walkely 1892: 125 for quote.
37. "Sarah Bernhardt's Complexion," *Chicago Daily Tribune* January 17, 1891, 16. According to the article, the cosmetic was a mixture of saffron, coffee, musk, and chicory, all diluted with rose water. See too, "C.", "Cleopatra's Complexion," *The Nation* 51 (1890), 1441.
38. "The Stage," *Munsey's Magazine* 11 (1894), 521.
39. "The Drama: Sarah Bernhardt as Cleopatra," *New York Tribune* February 27, 1891, 6.
40. "Which is the Real Sardou's Cleopatra?," *New York Tribune* February 22, 1891, 11.

References

Badeau, A. (1859), *The Vagabond*. New York.

Beard, G. M. (1881), *American Nervousness: Its Causes and Consequences*. New York.

Bender, D. (2009), *American Abyss: Savagery and Civilization in the Age of Industry*. Ithaca, NY.

Benjamin, S. G. W. (1879), "Sculpture in America," *Harper's New Monthly Magazine* 58, 657–72.

Butsch, R. (2000), *The Making of American Audiences: From Stage to Television, 1750–1990*. Cambridge.

Carlson, M. (1985), *The Italian Shakespearians: Performances by Ristori, Salvini and Rossi in England and America*. Cranbury, NJ.

Centennial Board of Finance (1876), *Visitor's Guide to the Centennial Exhibition*. Philadelphia.
Clark, W. J. (1878), *Great American Sculptures*. Philadelphia.
Fabian, A. (2010), *The Skull Collectors: Race, Science, and America's Unburied Dead*. Chicago.
Farmer, L. H. (1887), *The Girls' Book of Famous Queens*. New York.
Gardner, A. T. (1943), "William Story and Cleopatra," *The Metropolitan Museum of Art Bulletin* 2, 147–52.
Gould, S. J. (1981), *The Mismeasure of Man*. New York.
Hall, E. and F. Macintosh (2005), *Greek Tragedy and the British Theatre 1660–1914*. Oxford.
Hawkins, M. (1997), *Social Darwinism in European and American Thought, 1860–1945: Nature as Model and Nature as Threat*. Cambridge.
Heron, M. (tr. 1857), *Medea*. New York.
Howells, W. D. (1876), "A Sennight of the Centennial," *Atlantic Monthly* 38, 92–107.
Ingram, J. S. (1876), *The Centennial Exposition, Described and Illustrated*. Philadelphia.
Kasson, J. (1990), *Marble Queens and Captives: Women in Nineteenth-Century American Sculpture*. New Haven.
Leach, J. (1972), *Bright Particular Star*. New Haven.
Lester, L. (1885), "Adelaide Capranica Marchesa Del Grillo Nata Ristori," *Frank Leslie's Popular Monthly* 14, 257–62.
Macintosh, F. (2000a), "Introduction: The Performer in Performance," in E. Hall, F. Macintosh, and O. Taplin eds., *Medea in Performance 1500–2000*. Oxford, 1–31.
Macintosh, F. (2000b), "Medea Transposed: Burlesque and Gender on the Mid Victorian Stage," in E. Hall, F. Macintosh, and O. Taplin eds., *Medea in Performance 1500–2000*. Oxford, 75–99.
Magoon, E. L. (1856), *Westward Empire, or, The Great Drama of Human Progress*. New York.
Malamud, M. (2011), "Black Minerva: Antiquity in Antebellum African American History," in D. Orrells, G. Bhambra, and T. Roynon eds., *African Athena: New Agendas*. Oxford, 71–89.
Nelson, C. A. (2007), *The Color of Stone: Sculpting the Black Female Subject in Nineteenth-Century America*. Minneapolis.
Nott, J. and G. Gliddon (1854), *Types of Mankind: Ethnographical Researches, Based on Ancient Monuments, Paintings, Sculptures and Crania of Races, And Upon Their Natural, Geographical, Philological, and Biblical History*. Philadelphia.
O'Brien, F. (1860), "Mother of Pearl," *Harper's New Monthly Magazine* 20, 392–9.
Richard, C. J. (1995), *The Founders and the Classics: Greece, Rome, and the American Enlightenment*. Cambridge, MA.
Ristori, A. (1888), *Studies and Memoirs: An Autobiography*. Boston.
Ristori, A. (1907), *Memoirs and Artistic Studies of Adelaide Ristori*. Trans. G. Mantellini. New York.
Roosevelt, T. (1899), "Letter to G. Stanley Hall."
Rydell, R. (1984), *All the World's a Fair: Visions of Empire at American International Expositions, 1876–1916*. Chicago.
Story, W. W. (1864), *Roba di Roma*. New York.
Story, W. W. (1868), *Graffiti d'Italia*. New York.
Strahan, E. (1880), *The World's Art from the International Exhibition*. New York.
Trafton, S. (2004), *Egypt Land: Race and Nineteenth-Century Egyptomania*. Durham, NC.
Tylor, E. B. (1871), *Primitive Culture: Researches into the Development of Mythology, Art, Religion, and Custom*. London.
Walkely, A. B. (1892), "The Drama," *New Review* 7, 123–8.

Welter, B. (1966), "The Cult of True Womanhood, 1820–1860," *American Quarterly* 18, 151–74.
Winter, W. (1889), *The Press and the Stage: An Oration*. New York.
Winter, W. (1915), *Vagrant Memories*. New York.
Winterer, C. (2002), *The Culture of Classicism: Ancient Greece and Rome in American Intellectual Life, 1780–1910*. Baltimore.

CHAPTER 9

WHEN GREEKS STAND YOU UP, INVITE ROMANS

The Ancient World on the Nineteenth-Century American Stage

DAVID MAYER

IF you expect to read about dramas from fifth-century BCE Athens enacted on the nineteenth-century American commercial stage, you are doomed to disappointment. I answer the plenitude of seven (or eight plays, if one includes *Prometheus Bound*) by Aeschylus, seven by Sophocles, 19 by Euripides, and 11 by Aristophanes with a genuine dearth—a vacuum. The presence of these plays is met in nineteenth-century America by almost total absence. Barring a few adaptations of a few tragedies performed in a foreign language—French, German, or Italian—or often spoken in heavily accented English by visiting stars from Europe, there are no performances of Athenian dramas on American commercial stages for the entire century. Nineteenth-century American theater-goers did not take to Greek plays; or rather, were not given the opportunity to do so.

But that does not mean that the ancient Mediterranean, Near East, and the biblical world escaped theatrical notice. Far from it. What I argue is that actions, subjects, and characters which nineteenth-century Americans found repugnant in Greek plays re-emerged and found expression in numerous dramas about Republican and Imperial Rome and the Roman-occupied provinces of Asia Minor. I will argue that it was not until the first decades of the twentieth century—an era when the conditions and repertoire of the Victorian stage still dominated stage performance—that the first glimmers of Modernism were seen as North Americans, Isadora Duncan and Maud Allan, began performing what they hoped were Dionysiac and Apollonian dances and the Artemis dances of the Brauronia. I will also look at dramas which drew from the deutero-canonical books, those late additions to the *Old Testament* and apocryphal additions to the Christian Gospels, as well as dramatized fierce, but partly imagined, clashes of civilizations between the Babylonian and Persian empires. The ancient world is there on the nineteenth-century American stage and in live outdoor spectacles, but not the ancient world of Greece.

I am aware of Robert Davis's account of the two-performance run of an Oedipus play at the Bowery Theatre in 1830 and his reports of a handful of classical burlesques imported about that same time from the London stage (Davis 2008). The former constituted an attempt at melodrama at some considerable distance from Sophocles' play, the latter musical playlets performed *en travesté*, the male roles taken by shapely females, the female roles performed by large comic men. Medea was such a comic actor's role. Yes, there were rare sightings of a character from the Athenian canon, there were rewritings of the ancient plays (see Pearcy, Macintosh, Bosher and Cox, Davis, Foley, this volume), but there were no dramas by Aeschylus, Sophocles, Euripides, Aristophanes, or Menander *au naturel* on American commercial stages.

I realize that this apparent dearth is unexpected and appears inconsistent with other manifestations of Greek culture in American life. Why do Americans celebrate "Greek revival" architecture? Why are the porticoes of nineteenth-century plantation houses in Georgia (Scarlet O'Hara's "Tara"), Louisiana, and South Carolina built to resemble Greek temples? Why are there cities named Athens in Georgia and Ohio, and a Sparta in Tennessee and New Jersey? And why is there, in Nashville, the self-styled "The Athens of the South," a full-size replica of the Parthenon (now the city's art museum) built for the 1897 Exposition? Why was Hiram Powers's statue of a nude woman, entitled *The Greek Slave*, accepted as art viewable by wives and daughters, the hit of the 1851 Great Exhibition, and copied in numerous sizes for public and private consumption, yet more modest Greek heroines made no appearances on our stages? Why do Yale cheerleaders still call for "a long cheer for the team" and by that "long cheer" Yalies—like my uncles Levi and Isaac in the 1880s, my Dad in the early 1910s, and myself in the 1940s—kneel to respond with the Frogs' chorus: "Brek, kek, kek, kex, coax, coax, Brek, kek, kek, kex, coax, coax," from Aristophanes' comedy, yet no Aristophanic comedy was performed anywhere near New Haven until Monty Woolley staged *The Frogs* in the Yale swimming pool in 1941? What kept translated Greek drama and Greek subject matter from our commercial stages two centuries ago?

There are several plausible explanations: the first is nineteenth-century America itself. It was a century of expansion, urban growth, and industrialization and, also, a century in which a system of popular free education was established in most communities. But that education, while in some few instances fostering the study of classical languages, placed Latin and Hebrew on a par with, or superior to, Greek. Moreover, those students who actually studied these "dead" languages read from texts other than the plays. The great majority of educated or semi-educated people, if they knew anything of Greek literature and mythologies, knew these subjects through translations of Homer or from Bulfinch's *Fables* rather than at first hand through the texts (Winterer 2007).

Further, the structure of the Victorian theater company on both sides of the Atlantic—and, consequently, the structure of Victorian plays—was based on a group of from a dozen to 15 actors undertaking stock roles: the male lead, the villain, the "walking gentleman," the heroine, the soubrette, the adventuress, the comic couple, the old man, the comic spinster, the "low" comic, and so forth. Play after Victorian play, although varied in subject matter, setting, and social classes depicted, is predicated on the certain presence of experienced actors to assume these standard roles. It would have been a considerable wrench and a dangerous financial step to reshape a company to accommodate three agonists, a coryphaeus, and a chorus.

But more important than either of these explanations was the fact that the moral fabric and purposes of the Athenian plays—infrequently translated, published, and certainly not widely read—jarred sharply with the pervading American social ethos. The theater historian Jeffrey Richards suggests a significant reason why the dramas of fifth-century Athens failed to be staged. Writing about the "Olympian" painters of Victorian England, Richards states: ". . . classical painters turned again and again to the heroes of ancient Greece for their archetypes of male behavior (active, energetic, fearless, self reliant) and to the myth of rescue as the paradigm of the male–female relationship." And here Richards states the clincher: "The female role models they chose from mythology conformed to two overarching stereotypes: the submissive woman, (passive, loving, self-effacing, companiable, compliant) and the destructive woman (fatal, dangerous, cruel, perverse, aggressive, demonic, deceptive, unfaithful, treacherous)" (Richards 2009: 23). Richards goes on to quote Adrienne Munich: "The Victorian myth portrays the helplessness of women and their need for protection . . . It presents the helpless maiden as a permanent truth against a changing, evolving reality. By counselling men against rape and women against ambition, it promises an eternity as a heavenly constellation" (Munich 1989: 185).

Now Richards is speaking of painters, their choices of subjects, and, by implication, their private clients and the public spaces in which their works were displayed. The theater, especially the American theater, in contrast to the painter's studio, was far more prudish and circumspect in its renditions of outrageous domestic, especially female, behavior. Even had actor-managers been presented with translations adapted to the configurations of standard theater companies and had taken the trouble to cast and mount a production, shocked American audiences were unlikely to have tolerated performances. An adulterous Agamemnon, his new bed-partner, Cassandra, on stage, a vengeful murderous Clytemnestra or Electra, a homicidally treacherous Medea moving on to infanticide, a Deianeira committing involuntary manslaughter, an obstreperously defiant Antigone, a sexually aroused and potentially incestuous Phaedra, a blood-smeared Agave with scraps of her son's body—these roles just weren't possible on the commercial stage without radical rewritings (see further, the other chapters in this section). These heroine-agonists were females who grossly overstepped nineteenth-century American moral sensibilities.

There *are* roles in the nineteenth-century theatrical repertoire for angry and vengeful and seductive women who'll stop at nothing, however low: women who poison and murder and betray, and embezzle and lie and scheme, and who often commit their outrageous acts with an ironic humor invariably lacking in stage heroines, but these interesting roles are more likely to be cast from actresses skilled at enacting the wicked "adventuress" than from leading ingénues. So, for a moment, try imagining who might have appealed to the Victorian preference for heroes and heroines. Chaste Hippolytus might have made a good subject for a play if he weren't dogged by such a sexy stepmother and punished by a vengeful Aphrodite resentful of his celibacy (see Foley, this volume). Alcestis, a super-self-sacrificing wife, just might have succeeded with American audiences (as she did in London) (Hall and Macintosh 2005: 438–42). But imagine for a moment a play entitled *Chrysothemis* or another called *Ismene*, and we are closer to the acceptable and allowable: we would have witnessed the shining goodness, passivity, and admirable *sophrosyne* of the leading character, but we'd be starved for characters of interest and action. The closest nineteenth-century Americans got to seeing the world of the Greek Classics on a commercial stage was a 1712 play by Ambrose Phillips called *The Distress'd Mother* (Hall and Macintosh 2005: 66–70). But this drama, which lingered long in the professional repertoire until about the 1820s and in the amateur repertoire for a few decades longer, is actually Phillips's adaptation of Racine's, not Euripides', *Andromache*.

So it fell to the imagined Roman and biblical worlds to supply the heroic characters, the virtuous heroines, the patriotic and morally centered action in the void left by unperformed Greek plays. The Roman dramas—dramas of American and British origin—which appealed to American audiences before the 1880s fall into two categories: those which celebrate the alleged democracy and resistance to tyrannical oppression characteristic of a corrupted, degenerate Roman Republic and those which have been labeled by the theater historian Bruce McConachie as "apocalyptic melodramas" (McConachie 1992: 119–55). The former plays and their adaptations, described as screenplays by Classicist-historians such as Margaret Malamud, Maria Wyke, and Jon Solomon, reflect the acute social tension in Britain surrounding agitation for the First Reform Bill and, in America, the cultural dynamics of Jacksonian democracy and the rise of a political underclass. Performed by the stentorian demotic actor Edwin Forrest, these plays oppose republican virtues—austerity and rectitude—to the growing threats of imperial corruption. The chief dramas in the group are the British dramatist James Sheridan Knowles's *Caius Gracchus*, 1815, and, more popularly, *Virginius*, 1820, in which the Roman patrician Virginius, defying the Roman Emperor Appius Claudius, slays his own daughter, Virginia, rather than permit her to be enslaved and sexually abused by this ruling tyrant. Forrest similarly chose Robert Montgomery Bird's *The Gladiator*, 1831, which offered the role of Spartacus, leading the slave revolt of 73–71 BCE against the Emperor Crassus' rule.

In this group there is a third play, also dramatizing opposition to tyranny, which initially had a much lower profile but which had a more profound effect and a more prolonged life on American public stages. This drama is one of the many theatrical imports from England: John Banim and John Sheil's 1821 verse play *Damon and Pythias* (see further Pearcy, this volume). The attraction of this melodrama as a political parable is understandable. Formerly a vehicle for Edwin Forrest, *Damon and Pythias* is crammed with sententious verse, easily turned into bombast, on themes of loyalty, friendship, patriotism, and, above all, legitimate opposition to arbitrary tyranny. Both the rhetoric and opportunities for declamatory acting repeatedly proved irresistible to Southern audiences and to Southern collegiate amateur actors in the first three decades following the Civil War because *Damon and Pythias* offered a covert text of defiance to what was perceived as an illegal abusive tyranny. The rhetoric of Northern abuse and mistreatment of the defeated South still permeated Southern thought.

Damon and Pythias, set in Grecian Syracuse, begins as war veterans, led by Dionysius, plot to seize the city. When Damon, a senator, protests this successful and distasteful military coup, he is arrested and sentenced to death by Dionysius, now tyrant head of state. Damon's friend Pythias, however, offers himself as a temporary substitute so that Damon might say farewell to his wife and child who, on Damon's instructions, fled Syracuse before the coup. Damon's long absence jeopardizes Pythias' life, but Damon's timely return impresses Dionysus who grants reprieves to both Damon and Pythias. *Damon and Pythias* holds interest for me (as a theater historian interested in the stage's links with early film) because the American film-maker D. W. Griffith, then at the very beginning of his career, undertook one of his first professional roles as the tyrannical Dionysius in May, 1896. Discovering in a popular play the subtext of subversion and resistance to an abusive occupying tyranny may have contributed to Griffith's subsequent filmic treatments of a beleaguered *post*-bellum South. It foreshadows *The Birth of a Nation*. Or so I believe.

America's foremost apocalyptic melodrama, Louisa Medina's 1835 *The Last Days of Pompeii*, was derived from Edward Bulwer-Lytton's novel published in Britain a year earlier, two years after the passage of the First Reform Bill and in the immediate shadow of the Catholic Emancipation Bill of 1829. Both novel and play express contempt for the greed and tastelessness of a rising merchant class and similarly reject hereditary authority and an encroaching subversive ecclesiastical power. In both novel and play the Egyptian cult of Isis is covertly the Roman Catholic Church. In America the fearsome Egyptian was more locally read as Irish immigration. The hero of *The Last Days of Pompeii* is a Greek poet indifferently aware of the dangers posed by Egyptians; its two heroines a blind flower-girl and a passively agreeable young woman; its villains a rapacious, lubricious priest of Isis and a crass merchant. Translated from the stage into massive outdoor pyrodramas in 1882—plays staged before audiences in the thousands with vast casts reaching 300 performers—the drama's climactic moments came as Vesuvius erupted, an effect achieved with massive fireworks and a scenic city which appeared to burn and collapse.[1] In this chaos of blinding smoke and flames, the blind girl, in love with the hero and, unlike sighted Pompeiians, able to navigate the dark streets of Pompeii, eventually leads the hero and heroine to safety aboard a skiff before sacrificing herself by quietly, in the darkness, slipping into the sea.

As a pyrodrama, seen first at Coney Island's Manhattan Beach and thereafter reproduced in numerous American cities including Chicago's midway *plaisance* for the World's Columbian Exposition of 1893, *The Last Days of Pompeii* was staged by Pain's Fireworks Company in a special outdoor theater (Fig. 9.1). There, before the eruption and final conflagration, audiences, separated from the gigantic stage by a reflecting lagoon, found Bulwer's narrative supplemented with gladiatorial combats and

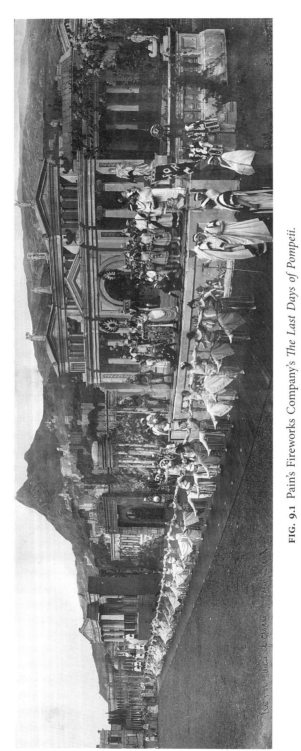

FIG. 9.1 Pain's Fireworks Company's *The Last Days of Pompeii*.

purported Roman games—including Roman bicycle races—and choruses of dancing Roman maidens performing a very un-Roman can-can.

This spectacle, inevitably, brings us to toga plays (Mayer 1994). If the stage in the first 60 years of the nineteenth century expressed democratic resistance to the capriciously wielded power of a new mercantile class, sovereigns, and the papacy, American theater, passing the centenary of the War of Independence in 1876, thereafter explored cultural and political division through the toga play. The term "toga play" emerged in the 1880s or 1890s as a derisive label enabling critics to describe a species of drama which brought into sharp focus and placed on the stage the century's second pair of melodramatic binary antagonists: in one corner evangelical Christianity and, opposite, the wealth and luxury of the West's new empires, the latter supported by industrial power and by military conquest.

Toga plays can be described as dramas depicting Romans, especially those occupying positions of trust and power in the reigns of such Julio-Claudians as Nero and Domitian, in moral, spiritual, and political conflict with new Christian converts. These numerous toga plays were all Christian but deliberately of a non-sectarian Protestant character, so non-sectarian, in fact, that they did not advocate temperance or attack the consumption of alcohol—one of the chief complaints against Catholics. Others—fewer—were specifically Roman Catholic or Anglican and celebrate the martyrdom of saints at the hands of Roman oppressors. All toga plays offer a continually mutating platform where issues ranging from support for and dissent from empire and imperial conquest, nineteenth-century radicalism, feminism and female suffrage, class, and nationalism might be played out before theater audiences. Although some of the focus of toga drama was undeniably European, America was not in the least exempted, and some of the toga plays which went on to entertain European audiences had their origins on American theatrical circuits, most notably Wilson Barrett's *The Sign of the Cross*, premièring in St. Louis in 1894. Several American adaptations of Henryk Sienkiewicz's novel *Quo Vadis?* followed two and three years later.

Toga plays are "sensation melodramas" set somewhere in the post-republican Roman Empire, periods remembered by the early Christian writers as times of persecution and martyrdom. These dramas describe an empire at or past the summit of its power and influence. It is a multicultural empire enriched by the Asian, African, and European nations it has subdued, dominated, pillaged, and colonized: an empire rich in possessions, in the arts, in luxury, in philosophy, and in remnants of the austere morality so visible in the plays of Sheridan Knowles and Louisa Medina. Thus the Rome of toga drama is already poisoned and corrupted by its own conquests and by a world of available pleasure, immediate sensual gratification, and almost omni-present vice. There is, however, a new voice—Christianity in its evangelical form—raised against vice, luxury, decadence, and the arbitrary and cruel abuse of power, its spokesperson almost invariably a female Christian convert. Toga Christianity is characterized by a rejection of worldliness and, equally, by its insistence on deferring pleasure to another realm or to another life. Conflict between pagan Rome and subversive Christianity becomes inevitable.

Christians are outlaws; Romans must collude and participate in their persecution. But these plays typically offer a troubled romance between a Christian, usually a female, and a Roman, normally a male who is powerful, noble, and wealthy. It is a mixture of lust and compassion that turns the Roman by stages from rapist to seducer to lover to husband, while the Christian steadfastly clings to her faith. This unshakeable faith and her moral stance has given her the right to challenge her captors. The male, however, previously successful in his conquest of women and ready to act in the name of the Roman state, is reduced to bemused impotence. The couple are threatened with death in the arena—to be crushed by a maddened wild bull, devoured by lions, or slain by gladiators. However, a choice is offered: all can be reconciled if both parties sacrifice to the Roman gods. But the Roman hero has discovered an ethical core to his character and is gravitating toward Christianity. Neither the heroine nor hero will weaken. He and his Christian fiancée-bride now willingly accept martyrdom by lions or, conveniently, are rescued and therefore escape by a timely proletarian revolt which overthrows the emperor.

Toga plays offer only a partial counterpart to the Athenian repertoire. In the toga heroine there is the palest reflection of Antigone, a heroine who, offered escape, refuses to back down. In the toga hero of *The Sign of the Cross* there is a similar echo of Haemon who joins his fiancée in facing the lions. In the sexually predatory and bloodthirsty females, the adventuresses, of the imperial courts there are the merest shadows of Phaedra and Clytemnestra and Medea. Indeed, I blanch at the comparisons.

The most American toga play is William Young's 1899 *Ben-Hur* (Mayer 1994: 189–290), a spectacularly theatrical adaptation of the Union Civil War General Lew Wallace's 1880 novel (Wallace 1998). It is a religious play, in the sense that its hero Judah Ben-Hur experiences several encounters with Jesus (performed—because an actual portrayal of Jesus might be seen as blasphemous—by a blue light). If the reader believes that Athenian dramas were thymelic—that is, an act of worship at a theatrical altar—then *Ben-Hur* invites a kind of direct comparison with the Greek repertoire. Otherwise not. I tend to view both the novel and the play as a quest narrative: a quest for estate and lost patrimony, for freedom, for vengeance and justice against the Roman villain whose accusation put him into the galleys—a living death sentence—and who immured his mother and sister in a prison where they contracted leprosy, a quest to find a virtuous Jewish girl, Esther, who can be a wife, not mistress, but ultimately a quest for a father, at first temporal, but ultimately spiritual. Judah achieves all his objectives but, having been succored by Jesus and by witnessing Jesus's healing of his mother and sister and—moments later—the crucifixion, converts to Christianity. Apart from these incidents, *Ben-Hur* takes its audience and hero on a quest through the outposts of the empire, which is depicted as a variegated society offering diverse perils, pleasures, riches, and secular temptations. One of these temptations is the "adventuress" Iras—unscrupulous in bestowing her favors (while pretending to love Judah, she is secretly the mistress of his tormentor and rival Messala). Perhaps, because it is a quest narrative, *Ben-Hur* is akin to Telemachus' search for Odysseus—except that Judah must be both Telemachus, the searcher, and Odysseus, who returns to wreck terrible vengeance upon the despoilers—as Judah does, both hideously crippling and bankrupting Messala.

With this episodic structure, *Ben-Hur* anticipates something we begin to see in early narrative film: the entire narrative abridged to brief set-piece scenes because these episodes are previously known to audiences who have read the novel and remember its highlights. An entire film narrative plays out in 10—or at the most 20 minutes. *Ben-Hur* was dramatized for the stage in six acts and in 1907 filmed in six brief tableaux.

This episodic structure—a new location and an encounter, then on to the next—in some respects also resembles the great Protestant narrative of 1678, *Pilgrim's Progress*—except that *Ben-Hur* describes the material, the very physical, ancient world and is not intended as an allegory. If there is allegory, it is in its almost accidental referencing of Lew Wallace's appointment as President Rutherford Hayes's first Governor of the Territory of New Mexico. Arriving in Santa Fe, New Mexico's capital abandoned by the Spanish, Wallace found in progress a bloody feud, the so-called Lincoln County range-war of 1878–81, which pitted immigrant white ranchers against the native Mexican-Spanish. One of the ranchers' hired gunmen, who was said to have personally threatened Wallace, was the outlaw William "Billy the Kid" Bonney. Adding to the danger, both rancher and Spanish factions were subject to attacks from Apache Indians descending from the Guadalupe Mountains. Wallace set about ending the feuds, reconciling the disputing parties, and arranging amnesties for those whose crimes excluded murder. His respect and unfeigned admiration for all cultures and his desire to prevent another rebellion characterized his governorship, and these qualities and wishes find expression in *Ben-Hur*, imparting to the novel an intentional ambiguity. The New Mexican landscape fuses with the deserts, mountains, and valleys of the Holy Land; the ethnic mixture of arriving Anglo-whites, Mexicans, Spaniards, and Native Americans is translated into the plural cultures of the East and Mediterranean world: Romans, Jews, Syrian Arabs, Egyptians, and Greeks. The Judaean desert landscape of *Ben-Hur* is alternately and both the Holy Land and New Mexico, Roman-occupied Jerusalem and Santa Fe. Rome is at once Rome and its expanding empire and the United States with faraway Washington indifferently responding to Governor Lew Wallace's pleas for troops, obliging him to be resourceful in seeking solutions and ending conflict. Wallace occupies Gratus' and Pontius Pilate's Proconsul's throne, judging, sentencing, making and maintaining peace between volatile factions.

Now from Rome to *The Bible*. In marked contrast to Britain, where biblical subjects were proscribed on stage, scripture in the United States sanctioned and enabled stage dramatizations of depravity proscribed—or perhaps now forgotten—in the plays of the fifth-century Athenians. I cite but two examples, both strangely alike: plays about Judith, the Jewish patriot, and Holofernes, Nebuchadnezzar's Assyrian general, their narrative taken from the deutero-canonical Book of Judith and Salomé and John the Baptist, this narrative drawn from the Jewish historian Josephus and somehow conflated with the Salomés of Mark and Matthew. The Judith narratives reached American audiences through three consecutive stage plays, the first, Paolo Giacometti's *Giudetta,* which the Italian actress Adelaide Ristori had introduced to American audiences on her farewell tour in 1866. A subsequent version, taking its English-language text from the interlinear translation found in the Ristori tour program, was subsequently performed by

Nance O'Neil's company between 1903 and 1904. Judith plays dramatize the rescue of the Hebrew city of Bethulia from the armies of the Assyrian king, Nebuchadnezzar, the siege lifted and the invaders routed when the recently widowed Jewish patriot Judith dons her most seductive garments, goes to the tent of the Assyrian general Holofernes, and, using her charms, gets him drunk and decapitates him, bringing the severed head back to Bethulia. Sometime in 1904 Nance O'Neil jettisoned the inferior Giacometti translation and commissioned a reworking from the Boston poet Thomas Bailey Aldrich (Aldrich 1904). Where have we seen this action before? The three Judiths placate, lull, and kill a conquering general. True, Judith is more overtly sexual than Clytemnestra and less bloodthirsty and far less vengeful, but my point is that this narrative, sanctioned by biblical text, caused only limited offense to American audiences.

Oscar Wilde's 1892–3 *Salomé*, banned from the British stage by the censor who described it as "half-Biblical, half pornographic," was not performed on the American stage until decades later. However, Salomé dances, performed first by Isadora Duncan in 1905 and Maud Allan from 1907, appeared in European and American variety theaters (Macintosh 2010; Webb 2010). Allan was then followed by other American Salomés. Such dances depicted neither Salomé's seduction of Herod Antipas nor the decollation of John the Baptist, but all featured an erotic dance with the Baptist's severed head. The illusion of near nudity again challenged audiences' sensibilities, but again the veil of biblical association allowed the dances to continue. Among the American *Salomé*s was Gertrude Hoffman. Her 1909 *The Vision of Salomé*, a deliberate imitation of Maud Allan's Salomé dance, and her "high temperature costume" were described by a New York observer:

> Miss Hoffman's Salomé costume consists specifically of one pair of flesh colored silk trunks, reaching from the waist halfway to the knee; one skirt of black gauze, gold embroidered at the bottom and reaching to the ankles; a girdle of pearls and brilliants, breastplate and décolletage of pearls and emeralds, with ropes of pearls looped to the girdle, and necklace and armlets of brilliants and jade. A diadem and a red wig complete the costume. Neither tights nor sandals are worn, the arms, limbs, and torso being entirely bare.
>
> After the first gasp, when the heavy velvet curtains were drawn back to disclose Miss Hoffman, the audience of first nighters refused to credit their senses. The dim blue light of the really magnificent setting of the courtyard of Herod's palace half disclosed the semi-nude figure of Salomé. From the first sinuous movement of the dancer's arms the guessing contest began, and it left the theatre only with the audience. Miss Hoffman does not give all her pack of tricks at the first glance. The black skirt acts as a delusion and a snare to the eye. The audience is so spellbound with the stage picture, with the gliding gesture dancing of Salomé, they forget even the exotic costume.[2]

Meanwhile, as Allan and Hoffman continued with their Salomé performances, Isadora Duncan turned to the ancient Greeks, stepping out of confining corsets, out of legitimate playhouses, and onto the vaudeville and music hall stages. Duncan was one of the dancers, largely self-taught, who broke with the rigid formalities of ballet and who, following the dicta of the French musicologist François Delsarte, sought to link intimate feelings with movements, attitudes, and gestures which immediately—and silently—expressed those emotions. Around 1905, her interests began to coincide with the so-called "Cambridge Ritualists" and anthropologists—Gilbert Murray, Jane Harrison, James Frazer—who spurred investigation into the archaic Greek world and Near Eastern dance-as-ritual, and whose writings encouraged experimentation in achieving the non-codified movements of dancers depicted on vases, statuary, and murals. In simpler terms, Duncan saw herself re-creating ancient Greek dance and herself an exponent of Hellenic civilization (see further Leontis, this volume). She haunted classical sites, seeking inspiration and publicity and attempting to perform in these venues.

As she performed her imagined ancient dances, there was a strong, unspoken, element of racism and Nietzschean philosophy (Macintosh 2010: 205–8). In espousing Dionysiac dance and Greek civilization, she consciously positioned herself in opposition to the "primitive" savagery she deplored in the dances of African-Americans, in particular to the dances of Aida Overton Walker, the "Queen of the cakewalk," choreographer for the Black Patti Troubadours, and, in 1907, the first African-American dancer, costumed as Salomé, to perform "the dance of the seven veils." Subsequently and parenthetically, these white versus black/civilization versus primitivism dichotomies—arising from Duncan's stance—long affected the Hollywood films of white America, as endless troupes of so-called "native" dancing girls were cast exclusively from white females, and "browned-up" with body makeup and black wigs if the occasion required.

I want to close with one more American theatrical excursion into the imagined—and only vaguely historic—ancient world, here the decline of Babylon and the rise of the Assyrian Empire. While there is a notional correspondence to *The Persians* of Aeschylus, any resemblance, particularly in the depiction of a defeated army, is in the eye of the beholder. I have in mind one particular spectacle: *The Fall of Babylon*, a drama of rival civilizations launched in 1886 by the Anglo-Hungarian dancer and impresario Imre Kiralfy and elaborated thereafter through the 1890s by P. T. Barnum and John Rettig. In 1886, Kiralfy accepted a commission from Cincinnati to stage *The Fall of Babylon* which he and Rettig mounted on a 400-foot stage erected in a baseball park. A year later, on a plot on New York's Staten Island, Kiralfy staged a further version of *The Fall of Babylon*, in 1890 transporting his Babylon to Boston and thereafter, under Barnum's management, to other American cities. *Babylon*'s plot was derived from two sources, the Old Testament Book of Daniel and Herodotus' account of the Persian conquests. The Book of Daniel tells of the Jews' "Babylonian captivity," the cruelty of King Nebuchadnezzar compelling the captives to worship a gigantic golden image or face death in a fiery furnace, and the succession to the Chaldean throne of Belshazzar. Daniel, in Kiralfy's version, is a captive prophet who counsels both kings and who—interpreting Belshazzar's dreams and the meaning of God's handwriting upon a palace wall—warns of Babylon's fate. Herodotus continues the narrative of Babylon's fall to the armies of Cyrus and the strategies of the Persians in taking and sacking the city. Neither of these accounts stands up to archaeological evidence, but both describe an empire in its decline. Nor does either account describe processions, competitive games, and spectacular dances, but

Kiralfy made up for that deficiency by dramatically drawing back the city walls to reveal a monumental plaza for dancing and display, described in *Babylon's* programme as

> ... a scene, whose prodigality of splendor and picturesqueness of grouping was a marvel in those days of unparalleled oriental luxury. Preceded by richly-robed priests, armor-clad horsemen, and dancing maidens with melodious timbrels, comes the king, garbed in all the jewelled richness of regal trappings, seated in a lofty chariot throne, drawn by milk-white steeds. In his rear follow prisoners of war, heavily manacled, soldiers, diviners, astrologers, priest, satraps, rulers of provinces and the royal banners of Babylon ...[3]

The ancient world held its spectacular attractions, even if these attractions were infrequently Greek.

I feel reasonably confident that I have, perhaps, overstayed my welcome by talking about absence, not presence, about substitution and evasion rather than what Classicists recognize as the genuine article. However, I've attempted to fill this gaping hole in the performance record by suggesting the determination and energy with which Victorian Americans overlaid Christian morality and melodramatic dichotomies onto the historic past—colonizing, bowdlerizing, and evangelizing history in what they saw as a time of primitive pagans. Americans rewrote and dramatized history to suit their own moral squeamishness and social concerns, discarding the Greeks but handily finding and substituting others to take their place.

Notes

1. In addition to numerous fireworks and burning flares, many of the scenic houses were constructed of light canvas thinly painted and translucent, so that fires from behind gave the illusion of burning interiors. Other buildings were constructed from hinged frameworks so that, as props were removed, the structures appeared to collapse in flames.
2. *Cass City* [Michigan] *Chronicle* February 26, 1909, 7.
3. Souvenir programme, *The Fall of Babylon*, Boston, 1890.

References

Aldrich, T. B. (1904), *Judith of Bethulia*. Boston and New York.
Davis, R. (2008), "The Riddle of the *Oedipus*: Practicing Reception and Antebellum American Theatre," *New Voices in Classical Reception Studies* 3, 1–13.
Hall, E. and F. Macintosh (2005), *Greek Tragedy and the British Theatre 1660–1914*. Oxford.
Macintosh, F. (2010), "Dancing Maenads in Early Twentieth-Century Britain," in Fiona Macintosh ed., *The Ancient Dancer in the Modern World*. Oxford.
McConachie, B. (1992), *Melodramatic Formations: American Theatre and Society, 1820–1870*. Iowa City.
Mayer, D. (1994), *Playing Out the Empire: Ben Hur and Other Toga Plays and Films, 1883–1908. A Critical Anthology*. Oxford.

Munich, A. (1989), *Andromeda's Chains: Gender and Interpretation in Victorian Literature and Art*. New York.

Richards, J. (2009), "John Ruskin, the Olympian Painters and the Amateur Stage," in A. Heinrich, K. Newey, and J. Richards eds., *Ruskin, the Theatre, and Victorian Visual Culture*. Basingstoke.

Wallace, L. (1998), *Ben-Hur*. Ed. D. Mayer. Oxford World's Classics. Oxford.

Webb, R. (2010), "'Where there is Dance there is the Devil': Ancient and Modern Representations of Salome," in F. Macintosh ed., *The Ancient Dancer in the Modern World*. Oxford, 123–44.

Winterer, C. (2007), *The Mirror of Antiquity: American Women and the Classical Tradition, 1750–1900*. Ithaca, NY, and London.

PART III

MODERNISMS IN THE AMERICAS (1900–1930)

CHAPTER 10

THE MIGRANT MUSE

Greek Drama as Feminist Window on American Identity, 1900–1925

EDITH HALL

THE QUEST FOR A NEW MUSE

JUST before the academic rediscovery of ancient Greek drama in performance in the 1880s, Walt Whitman appealed for a new form of poetry to replace worn-out classicism, in "Song of the exposition" (1871):

> Come, Muse, migrate from Greece and Ionia;
> Cross out, please, those immensely overpaid accounts.
> That matter of Troy, and Achilles' wrath, and Eneas', Odysseus' wanderings;
> Place 'Removed' and 'To Let' on the rocks of your snowy Parnassus...
> For know a better, fresher, busier sphere—a wide, untried domain, awaits, demands you.

But what, precisely, would be the nature of the Muse's fresher, busier, untried North American domain? If she was to migrate from Greece and Ionia, how was she to adapt herself to a new destination far from her original home? This chapter looks at some ways in which American Modernist feminists used the Muse of Greek drama in the reconfiguration of American identity.

Fifty years later, on July 7, 1921, Calvin Coolidge, Vice-President of the U.S.A., addressed the American Classical League at UPenn in Philadelphia. Despite the tumultuous history of the intervening decades, he still defended the American tradition of classical education, even while confessing his desire for a distinctively American identity:

> We do not wish to be Greek. We do not wish to be Roman. We have a great desire to be supremely American. That purpose we know we can accomplish by continuing the process which has made us Americans. (Coolidge 1924: 66)

The process that had made Americans "American," according to Coolidge, was the same study of ancient Greece and Rome, which had made Europe European. The question, then, to which Coolidge had no answer, was how American identity could be forged without the new, fresh American input—however conceived—for which Whitman had already been calling half a century before.

By the time Coolidge delivered that address, several women had discovered that appreciation of ancient Greek drama could help them analyze alternative constituents of "America" with little bearing on classical culture. These included the feminist perspective of the liberated western and Midwestern woman; the evanescent pre-Christian world of the Native American; the contestation of capitalism by an increasingly organized labor movement; and the technological revolution, especially the invention of aviation—even Isadora Duncan said that she could not perform her upwardly directed dance, rooted in muscles from deep in the solar plexus, without placing a motor in her soul (Duncan 1927: 168). Besides Duncan, three other Hellenophile women were particularly influential: Hilda Doolittle, Willa Cather, and Susan Glaspell, who sometimes worked in inextricable collaboration with her husband, George Cram Cook. In their work—dance, lyric poetry, fiction, drama—Greek theater contributed to the creation of a new Modernist cultural identity for the twentieth-century American citizen.

The ancient texts whose dead weight Whitman had identified as preventing American innovation were epic poems—the *Iliad*, *Odyssey*, and *Aeneid*. Classical epic had indeed long been associated with the project of European imperialism, as Quint demonstrated in *Epic and Empire* (1993). But the significant Greeks from the 1880s onward are less the epic poets than the dramatists. Greek drama was instrumental in creating in the U.S.A. "the explosive energy that made the early twentieth-century world modern" (Staley 2004: 6). Greek drama tinges the light refracted through several surfaces of the prism of American Modernist identity—primitivism, ritual, technology, and the critique of militarism and capitalism. It helps to think about Modernism in America less as a set of phenomena—the typewriter, the aeroplane, the Great War—but as a holistic culture—"a constellation of related ideas, beliefs, values and modes of perception" (Singal 1987: 9). This constellation was itself a response to "American Victorianism," which had been based on its own modes of perception, including the adulation of traditional classical education, represented by the masculine "sign" of Epic, as Whitman was aware. The Victorians yearned to keep the concepts of "the human" and "civilization" distinct from "the animal" and "barbarism." They used religion and culture to maintain this distinction, as well as those separating male from female, white from black, or genteel from laboring class. Modernism contested all these dichotomies, proposing that religion could be a sign of atavistic reaction and could lead to bloody terror, that the symbol systems of primitive art might be superior to realism, and that women could do almost everything of which they had long been assumed incapable.[1]

The ancient plays which were performed or informed new works in this era were mostly those with female protagonists or women in the title—*Iphigenia in Tauris, Trojan Women, Medea, Antigone*, and *Lysistrata, Assemblywomen, Women at the Thesmophoria*. This is partly because the significant Americans *responding* to the Greeks in this period are often women. Women's response to Greek theater made possible the emergence of a distinctive "indigenous" reading of the ancient plays which threatened to sever the aesthetic umbilical cord which had tied American dramatic Hellenism to Europe. But the presence of Greek drama in this crucible of social and cultural change is often disguised or inexplicit, since it is as connected with aesthetic form as with plot content.

The epic genre from which Whitman wanted liberation had also always been seen as masculine, attracting few female translators (Hall 2008: 115–29). This generic gendering contrasted with the perceived femininity of classical tragedy, for example in the eighteenth-century tradition of adapting Euripidean plays into sentimental neoclassical "She-Tragedies" featuring traumatized heroines (Hall and Macintosh 2005: 64–98). But as women gradually began to assert independence in the first two decades of the twentieth century, they sustained a consistent dialogue with Greek drama, demonstrating the seismic transformation of social and cultural life that had been ushered in by late nineteenth-century feminism. This had been presaged by the election of Susanna Salter as the first female mayor in the Unites States in Argonia, Kansas in 1887, and by the award of the right to vote to the women of Colorado in 1893, even though women in most states could neither vote nor sit on juries for years to come.

Transformations of Greek Tragedy

The most famous figure in making Greek tragedy relevant to avant-garde American women was the Californian Isadora Duncan, born in 1877. She used her growing fame to advocate "her own version of feminism" (Morgenroth 1998: 93). In her project, the figure of Iphigenia, as musically presented in Gluck's two *Iphigénie* operas, derived from Euripides' *Iphigenia in Aulis* and *Iphigenia in Tauris*, proved inspirational. Between 1903 and 1916 Duncan worked on selected sections of both pieces, developing the choreography of a total of 20 dances, into a composite dance-drama—the only one of its kind that she attempted (Layson 1983: 43; Zanobi 2010: 236). It was a huge success everywhere. In 1915 she even commissioned from the poet Witter Bynner a new translation of the play as a personal star vehicle. Although the production was not a success, Bynner's lackluster translation was performed subsequently on college campuses, for example in 1921 at Hunter College in New York.[2] It has had an important afterlife since a revised version was included in the famous Grene and Lattimore Chicago translations of Greek tragedy.

Duncan's Iphigenia choreography took from Nietzsche's *The Birth of Tragedy* (1872) her idea that her dance, in affirming the selfhood of the dancer and the spirit of music itself, was the modern equivalent of the chorus of Attic tragedy (Duncan 1927: 96). The story of Iphigenia also offered Duncan hardcore religious ritual. Sacrificial ritual, as socially orchestrated violence, was felt by Modernists to reflect the explosive energy which "made the early twentieth-century world modern" (Staley 2004: 6). In line with the contemporary interest in ritual, Duncan's interpretation gave a powerful role to an additional Priestess of Tauris. Duncan wanted to recreate the primitive ritual dance for Dionysus for which the classical scholar Jane Ellen Harrison had called in her denunciation of contemporary theater and her work on ancient myth and religion (Stone Peters 2008).

In 1903, the young Pennsylvanian Hilda Doolittle, born nine years later than Duncan in 1886, went to watch the same sacrifice-based Greek play, *Iphigenia in Tauris*, performed at UPenn in Philadelphia. But the cultural impact of this production was out of proportion to its small scale and amateur quality. H.D. was 16 years old, and had met Ezra Pound, then a UPenn student, two years previously. Pound was in the chorus, and made an impression his friend William Williams called comical, "in a togalike ensemble topped by a great blond wig at which he tore as he waved his arms about and heaved his massive breasts in ecstasies of emotion."[3] Perhaps Pound's own seminal experiments in Modernist poetry were affected by his intimate knowledge of the choruses of that Greek tragedy, especially its non-iambic metres. Looking back on his early development as a poet, later, in Canto 81, he remembers that "To break the pentameter, that was the first heave." As the postmodern writer Brooke-Rose has put it, "The first free verse of the moderns, usually attributed to Eliot, is stilted compared to Pound's, whose gift this has been to all successors, even those who have never read him" (Brooke-Rose 2004: 11). Of course Pound was affected by poetry in many traditions, including Japanese, but his experience of the lyric stanzas in Euripides, contrasting so starkly with the iambic dialogues, must not be underestimated.

The play inspired H.D. She wrote much later in her unpublished novel of the 1940s, *The Sword Went Out to Sea*, about her early flirtation with Pound, who appears under the pseudonym of Allen Flint. But the narrator's attention is fixed on another boy, who reads William Morris to her, brings her books, and appears amongst the maidens in a chorus in a Greek play. H.D. has here split her Pound into two different individuals, and she clearly did not react to his performance as a Greek maiden in the same way that the cynical Williams had done. Yet the one performer whom even the caustic Williams said was "superb" was the Messenger. It was this actor who rekindled H.D.'s childhood interest in the ancient Greeks, and "awakened" her to the riches of Greek drama and the ancient language: she felt she "had heard Greek at last." Euripides was to remain central to her work for the remainder of her life. In the 1920s alone she published *Hippolytus Temporizes* (1927, a verse drama responding to Euripides' *Hippolytus*), and four essays about Euripides, as well as translating parts of *Helen*, *Ion*, and *Bacchae*.

The production prompted H.D. to conceive her lifelong fascination with Euripidean choruses. They were subsequently an element in her romance with Richard Aldington, who chose Euripides to read on their honeymoon. Many critics have noted that in her translations of Euripides she presents him as an imagist in the sense meant by Ezra Pound in his *ABC of Reading* (Pound 1934: 37). H.D.'s 1916 collection *Sea Garden* reveals the unmistakable influence of Euripidean choruses, and indeed specifically of the *Iphigenia in Tauris*, especially in the delicate lyrics, with their short lines, sharply etched imagery, and strong sense of color, of "The Cliff Temple" and "Sea Gods."

"Sea gods," however, suggests another important way in which the Euripidean tragedy is informing H.D.'s poetic method, and that is through the identification of the poetic voice with the primitive barbarians of Euripides' play, some of whom, according to the messenger, did indeed think that Orestes and Pylades were gods (*IT* 268–74). H.D. is using the multiple viewpoints expressed in the messenger speech to think about the arrival of the Greeks from a primitive, pastoral perspective.

The impact of the performance of *Iphigenia in Tauris* on H.D. raises two important questions. The first is how we are to talk about the relationship between the ancient Greek text and the Modernist poems: "influence" is too banal and imprecise a term when a new creative artist is defining their own avant-garde agenda through an intense interactive and creative dialogue with an earlier cultural tradition. Secondly, H.D.'s idiosyncratic response to the Euripidean messenger actually revolves around the conundrum of what exactly should be made of pastoral barbarians and their relationship to the white European North American self, traditionally defined as the cultural descendant of ancient Greece and Rome. It is a sign of the tendency of certain ancient plays to become simultaneously attractive across wide constituencies at key moments in cultural history that *Iphigenia in Tauris* also underlay the most important early Mexican adaptation of a Greek tragedy, which used the barbarians of the Euripidean Crimea to think about the interaction between the European colonizers of Central America and its indigenous cultures: *Ifigenia cruel* by Alfonso Reyes (1924).[4] For the first time in the reception of Euripides' tragedy, Iphigenia—Reyes's Ifigenia—refuses to return to Greece at all, preferring to remain with the community that has adopted her. Perhaps this radical revision could only have come about in the work of a poet whose country was itself the result of a colonial invasion of an indigenous culture by Europeans—the formerly Aztec territory incorporated into the Spanish Empire in the sixteenth century under the name "New Spain."

Reyes's *Ifigenia cruel* has become one of the founding texts of Mexican literature, Mexican Modernism, and of appropriations of ancient Greek literature in the Spanish language. It is still performed today in Latin America (Aponte 1972: 26; Hall 2013: 276–7). By the time he wrote *Ifigenia cruel*, Reyes had conceived his plan to give voice to the "Aztec muse," by according Mexican literature autochthonous roots to merge with those that had grown in Spain (Conn 2002: 121–3). This project had already been articulated in his *Visión de Anáhuac* (1917), where Aztecs and conquistadors encounter one another for the first time. Ifigenia's religion therefore has reverberations of ancient Mesoamerican culture before it was destroyed by the conquistadors' Christian imperialism. Reyes's Ifigenia asks the Greek visitors why they are surprised to find themselves condemned after invading a civilization more ancient than they can imagine:

> You are strong men for the Virgin.
> Civilization was established long before your infancy.
> History began long ago. (Reyes 1924: 41)

The pre-Columbus Indian and the ancient Greek are similarly brought into dialogue in *The Professor's House*, an important novel—some critics say her masterpiece—by Willa Cather, published the year after *Ifigenia cruel*, in 1925. Born in Virginia in 1873, raised in Nebraska, and spending her young adulthood in Pittsburgh, Cather used the geographical size and diversity of the United States in *The Professor's House* to examine the problems involved in creating a new collective identity adequate to the history and hybridity of the emergent superpower. Hermione Lee has shown how Cather in other novels uses Latin epic and pastoral to configure stories of the North American frontier (Lee 2008: 84–99), for she loved Classics from childhood. She read Latin and Greek at school in the small town of Red Cloud from the age of 9 and claimed that she had read Caesar and Homer by the age of 15. Before she left high school, she presented herself in ways declaring her membership of a new generation of emancipated women—she wore her hair short, chose "rationalized" fashion, and ostentatiously studied the "boys' subjects" of Latin and Greek (Stout 2000: 29). Acutely aware that women's study of Classics threatened traditional gender roles, she included in her *Shadows on the Rock* (1931) a discussion about the propriety of girls in colonial French Canada being taught Latin at all (Stout 2000: 14). On arrival at the University of Nebraska in 1890, Cather turned her enrolment for Greek classes into a theatrical statement of her identity as a New Woman (Stout 2000: 31). Like the heroine of her story *Tommy the Unsentimental* (1896), she began reading both sciences and Classics, but swiftly concentrated on literature in Greek, Latin, French, and English. She was inspired by the teaching of her Classics Professor, Herbert Bates, who made all his students learn Greek verse off by heart to recite in class (Downs 1999: 46–7). Before she finished college, Cather had herself assumed the role of Electra in a flowing gown, in a tableau given in conjunction with a student production. She had read and annotated Aristotle's *Poetics*, as well as Browning's longer poems, which engage with ancient Greek theatrical poetry. She had also spent many hours watching plays, new and old, in the theater at Lincoln (Stout 2000: 41, 44). Her experience of Greek theater affected her approach to creating environments in her fiction. In her manifesto in the *New Republic* of 1922, she had said she wanted to throw the crowded furniture of literary realism "out of the window . . . and leave the room as bare as the stage of a Greek theatre" (Swift 2005).

In *The Professor's House*, Cather involves Euripides and the lost civilization of the Pueblo Indians in analyzing the nascent sense of American selfhood. The history of the European colonization of America is presented as a collision between two perspectives. On the one hand, Cather illuminates eastern-facing and conservative cultural values nostalgically looking back across the Atlantic to a classical past. The character who represents these is the titular Professor, Godfrey St. Peter, a classically handsome man of late middle age, whose head seemed "more like a statue's head than a man's" (Cather 1981: 13). His professorship is in European History at Hamilton College. With no interest in money, he is appalled by politics, retreating from the world to sip illicit old wines imported from Europe in defiance of Prohibition. He is psychologically alienated from his snobbish, coquettish, and worldly wife. Beneath this characterization lurks Euripides as he is presented in the ancient biographical tradition—a misogynist loner with a vast personal library. When hurt by his daughter, the Professor says that he is thinking "about Euripides; how, when he was an old man, he went and lived in a cave by the sea . . . it seems that houses had become insupportable to him" (Cather 1981: 156). Born on Lake Michigan, a true North American with both French Canadian and British

Methodist ancestry, he also represents Spanish conquerors of the "New" World: for 15 years he has been writing his *Spanish Adventurers in North America*.

Cather creates a memorable character, Tom Outland, to balance St. Peter by holding out the hope of a brighter new American morning. In a trope typical also of male American Modernists drawn to the Greeks—Faulkner, Eliot, Fitzgerald—she paradoxically symbolizes this hope *both* by technological and scientific advance *and* by a return to the past (Orvell 1995: 7), in her case the evocation of the indigenous people of the continent before the Europeans came. Outland is filled with the spirit of the Indigenous Muse as opposed to St. Peter's Migrant Melpomene. The hope is still only that—a hope—and its fragility is underlined by the death of Outland at the age of 30, fighting at Flanders. Outland does not enter the story as a living character until a long "flashback" half-way through the novel, by which time Cather has established the staleness overwhelming the subjectivity of the Professor.

Outland was a brilliant scientist who discovered a principle relating to vacuums, patented as the Outland Engine. At the time of the novel it has already revolutionized aviation. Like St. Peter, he had no time for American capitalism and was in pursuit of more cerebral ideals than the other, business-oriented characters. But in other respects he differs from the Professor. He is a working-class orphan with little idea of his biological family's historical roots, thus symbolizing the entire uprooted, transplanted population of modern America. Outland was born on an unknown date to an unknown mother crossing Kansas in a "prairie schooner"—one of the iconic covered waggons symbolic of the white winning of the west—but she had died and he was raised as a foundling by an Irish locomotive engineer in the liminal geospatial zone of New Mexico. Outland never attended high school, but had a passion for books and persuaded a priest to teach him classical Latin. At the age of 20 he turned up at Hamilton College with a few hundred dollars and persuaded St. Peter to support his enrolment.

In a Hellenism carefully distinguished from the Professor's Periclean hauteur, Outland is identified with the pre-classical, Minoan-Mycenaean world. The novel establishes parallels between its culture and that of the indigenous Americans. Outland has associated with Indians, and speaks in their defence. But he is also an expert on the pre-Columbus Pueblo "Cliff-Dwellers"; indeed, he possesses samples of their pottery. One is described as "shaped like those common in Greek sculpture, and ornamented with a geometrical pattern" (Cather 1981: 118). The lack of value accorded to these ancient creations of indigenous Americans is emphasized when he dismisses the idea that museums might be interested, saying, "they don't care about our things. They want something that came from Crete or Egypt" (Cather 1981: 119).

Outland is thus a spokesman for the possibility of an "indigenous Muse," as for the possibility of a more egalitarian America. In adopting Outland as his protégé, the Professor discovers a love of an entirely non-sexual kind for another human which transforms the musty tedium of his life and opens up thrilling horizons. One is Outland's intuitive socialism: St. Peter admires the way he will not let financial considerations contaminate friendship, "a result of Tom's strange bringing-up and early associations," of a "dream of self-sacrificing friendship and disinterested love down among the day-labourers, the men who run the railroad trains and boats and reapers and thrashers and mine-drills of the world" (Cather 1981: 173).

Outland's sustained voice is only heard in the long first-person account constituting much of the second half of the novel. His life had been spent with the working classes of the south-west, allowing Cather to remind her reader of the industrial conflicts which had blighted recent history, including the hanging of the Chicago anarchists in 1887. But most of the story consists of Outland's exquisite account of his exploration, when working as a cowboy, of the "Cliff Palace" at Mesa Verde. This fictionalized narrative is based on the historical discovery, in 1885, of the ruins of the Anasazi people, near the remote crossroads where Colorado, New Mexico, Arizona, and Utah meet.[5] The discovery had resulted in the foundation of the Mesa Verde National Park according to the terms of the Antiquities Act 1906.

The Mesa Verde ruins were important in the late nineteenth-century attempt to reconcile pre-Columbus strands in the nation's identity with the narrative of heroic immigrant pioneers who "won the west." They were instrumental in the foundation of Anthropology and Ethnology as respectable American intellectual pursuits (Horwitz 1995: 353–4). But in Cather's hands, they bring to life the whole lost story of the real, original Americans, with whom the disadvantaged young man becomes obsessed, and whom he adopts as "true" cultural ancestors. The ruins dated from the twelfth and thirteenth centuries CE, and created a stir because they had the potential to bestow on the new United States "a prehistory distinct from, and rival to, that of ancient Greece or Egypt" (Horwitz 1995: 362). Outland notes the resemblance between pottery designs he discovered and those of early Cretan pottery, which in the early twentieth century were being dug up apace by Sir Arthur Evans, amongst others. Suddenly, America might not just be a migrant offspring of old Europe, but an equal and a sibling. Although few dared consider the possibility that the Anasazis' ancestors had not arrived from Europe, the sophistication of the Pueblo culture surprised visitors. They were settled, lived in built dwellings, fired pots, and decorated them with geometric designs: the logical inference was that America had been home to a people so ancient that they could be considered autochthonous (however they had originally arrived there), at a level of development equivalent to the Minoans and Mycenaeans. They were on the verge of creating a civilization as advanced as that of classical, "Periclean" Athens.

Cather herself had tried to visit Cliff Palace in 1915, with her lifetime companion Edith Lewis. The experience impressed her. In *The Professor's House*, by reinvigorating the cynical Euripides-figure in the recollection of Outland's account of the discovery of a "true" American ancestry, Cather offers a partial solution to the problem of the identity of contemporary Americans—they must acknowledge both the imported European Muse and the silenced indigenous Muse, who could be accessed, if only remotely, through her pottery. Curiously absent from the novel is any female figure of intellectual stature: the Professor's wife and discontented daughters seem to be expressions of Cather's contempt for the narrowness of most middle-class women's horizons and aspirations. Yet in the Cliff City, we are given one powerful female figure, "Mother Eve," a mummified Indian who comes to symbolize, for Tom, the real human civilization which had existed on those dusty cliff-tops. Cather may not in this novel offer her reader adventurous feminists, but she does create an inspirational, mummified indigenous Muse in this elemental Mother figure.

The Feminist Theater of Susan Glaspell

In the theater itself, the female figure whose immersion in ancient Greek drama had most impact was Susan Glaspell, pillar of the Provincetown Players, playwright, novelist, and incalculable influence on Eugene O'Neill. Born in 1876, just three years after Cather, she was raised on an Iowa farm, fascinated by the native Sauk people, and throughout her life remained deeply identified with the Midwest and the people who had inhabited it before the Europeans came, an identification most explicit in her *The Inheritors* (1921), which, as we shall see, is partly inspired by Sophocles' *Antigone*.

Glaspell was from a down-at-heel Iowa farming family who could not afford to educate her. But she became a local journalist and saved up to enter Drake University at Des Moines in 1897, where she studied philosophy, Greek, French, history, and biblical studies. In 1902 she also took courses in literature at Chicago University, before hurling herself into a bohemian lifestyle and circle of friends in Paris and New York. Her own immersion in Greek literature is a neglected aspect of her work; Greek tragedy informed many of her novels, especially *Fugitive's Return* (1929), a bestseller. It tells the story of a Midwestern woman who travels to Greece in a plot which reverberates with motifs and scenery from Euripides' *Ion* (as well as partly modeling the heroine on Eva Sikelianos).

Glaspell is difficult to write about, because her major contributions to the Provincetown Players have been obscured by those of two men, her husband George ("Jig") Cram Cook and the playwright she mentored, Eugene O'Neill. She systematically presented Cook as the intellectual guiding force in their relationship, even though she was equally well read and by far the better dramatist. Their passionate affair, which began in about 1908, did later turn into a marriage, but Cook was often unfaithful to Glaspell as well. A flavor of her feelings about her limited emotional choices emerges from her short story "From A to Z," published in a collection suggestively entitled *Lifted Masks* in 1912, concerning a young female student at Chicago University, studying Greek and philosophy. She fantasizes about securing a real paid job in a publishing house, enhanced by "books and pictures and cultivated gentlemen who spoke often of Greek tragedies and the Renaissance." She has a passionate relationship with a free-thinking publisher with whom she works on a revolutionary dictionary. But in the end she relinquishes her freedom, with foreboding in her heart, for a life with a conventional suitor.

Glaspell cannot be fully understood without recognizing how impressed she was by Cook's Ivy League education and accomplishments. He came from an old English colonial family, and was born in 1873 at Davenport in Iowa. He had studied Classics and English literature at both Harvard and Heidelberg. He worked as a literary critic, taught literature at Iowa and Stanford Universities, and published a novel about the relationship between Nietzsche and Marx (*Chasm*, 1911). Much of our information derives from Glaspell's 1926 biography, *The Road to the Temple*, which tells Cook's life story leading up to foundation of the Provincetown Players, their move to Greece in 1922, and his death at Delphi two years later. It is hagiographical in tone, undoubtedly misrepresents the history of his troubled relationships both with her and the Provincetown Players, and underestimates the threat to his creativity and efficiency caused by his lifelong alcoholism. Yet there is no doubt that their mutual obsession with ancient Greek culture, and especially theater, proved a strong bond and that they must have discussed individual plays in detail.

This is clear in the case of Aristophanes' *Lysistrata*. Cook had seen the Greek play in New York City in 1914, and wrote to Glaspell lamenting the lack of political theater in contemporary society (Glaspell 1926: 191). With an uncertain amount of help from Glaspell, who helped shape the dialogue and some scenes (Ozieblo 2000: 119–20), he then wrote his most substantial drama, *The Athenian Women*, inspired by *Lysistrata* and the Russian revolution and set in Periclean Athens. Premiering on March 1, 1918, it was given seven performances. The U.S.A. had been at war with Germany for a year, which had included the bloody Battle of Passchendaele. The Russian government had fallen on November 7 to the Bolsheviks, whose revolutionary government had agreed an armistice with the Central Powers. On March 3, just after the opening of *The Athenian Women*, they signed the treaty of Brest Litovsk which made that armistice official. President Woodrow Wilson wanted to persuade the world to respect the Russians' right to self-determination. This specific moment in the political history of the United States is mirrored at every stage in *The Athenian Women*.

Cram was convinced of parallels between the Peloponnesian War and World War I. He believed there had been communists in Periclean Athens comparable to those who were making strides in Russia (in 1922 to become the U.S.S.R.) and the socialists in America, amongst whom he and Glaspell counted themselves. In the "Preface" to the text of *The Athenian Women* (published posthumously, in 1926, under Glaspell's supervision, with a facing Modern Greek translation), he claims that the *Assemblywomen* of Aristophanes proves that there was "a communist movement" in Athens, and that "there is nothing to show" that Lysicles, Aspasia's lover, "was not a communist" (Cook 1926: 2). Lysicles, claims Cook, was responsible after Pericles' death for introducing the first tax on property ever levied in Athens (Thucydides 3.19.1 mentions this measure). But the most important figure in the play is Aspasia, the Asiatic courtesan whom Pericles loved and eventually married. The Provincetown Aspasia is a feminist and a passionate proponent of peace, with attributes both of Aristophanes' Lysistrata and of Praxagora in *Assemblywomen*.

Act I of the play is set in Aspasia's house in 445 BCE. Pericles is married to Kallia, and pursuing an imperialist policy against other Greek states. The visionary pacifist Aspasia is attached to the politician Lysicles, and they discuss how to stop Pericles' militarism. But she also persuades Kallia to pressurize Pericles to cease from warmongering and to help her make an alliance with the women of Sparta. Act II includes an Assembly of Women taking place during the women-only festival of the Thesmophoria in the temple of Demeter (Cook here borrows from the third Aristophanic "women" play, *Thesmophoriazusae*). Pericles is persuaded by Aspasia to make Athens a city of artistic rather than imperialist enterprise. He transfers his affections from Kallia to Aspasia, and the passion is mutual. Between Acts II and III, set in 431 BCE, the audience are to imagine a 14-year peace blessing Athens. The Parthenon has been erected, and endless artistic and philosophical dialogues conducted in the salon of Pericles and Aspasia, where the action is now set. But when a vengeful Kallia joins forces with a politician to bring Pericles and Aspasia down, events spiral out of control, and the Peloponnesian War breaks out. The dream of the peace-loving democratic "City Beautiful" is over.

The socialist politics of the play are emphatically stated. Lysicles fails to stop Pericles from receiving endorsement for annexing Euboea because the Assembly is blighted by class snobbery. Lysicles is a livestock-merchant. When he tries to speak, Pericles' claque makes sheep noises (Cook 1926: 60). Aspasia announces that inherited wealth stops people thinking independently and turns women into "merchants of love" (Cook 1926: 36–8). But the play also shows a commitment to feminism which I suspect is the result of Glaspell's steady input. Although colluding in stereotypes of women as irationally swayable by physical desire, it voices trenchant opinions: Aspasia says, "the Athenian woman who marries accepts the life of a cow" (Cook 1926: 40).

Glaspell's contribution to the birth of indigenous American theater is obscured by her relationship with Eugene O'Neill as well as her marriage to Cook. She learned from O'Neill, but he certainly learned from her and benefited from her encouragement. Glaspell herself, although published as a journalist and novelist, did not attempt to write drama until her husband demanded it in 1915, needing new plays for the company. She later admitted that she had then abandoned her successful career as a novelist to throw herself full-time into the establishment of the Players and producing material for them (Ozieblo 2000: 139). Glaspell co-wrote (some said "wrote") their Freudian satire *Suppressed Desires*. But just as she started her one-act *Trifles*, O'Neill joined them with his *Bound East for Cardiff*. During the next two years the dialogue between all three was intense and incessant. Fifteen of O'Neill's plays and eleven of Glaspell's were produced by the Provincetown Players before the original company disintegrated in 1922. Her influence upon O'Neill has never been systematically evaluated, although their contemporaries were in little doubt about it, and Linda Ben-Zvi has begun to analyze the complexities of their intertextual relationship (Ben-Zvi 2005; Ozieblo 2000: 150–1).

Trifles is an outstanding play, which still finds performances. Glaspell subsequently rewrote it as a story entitled *A Jury of her Peers*, and this version is guaranteed a wide feminist audience in the twenty-first century because Elaine Showalter borrowed the title for her classic study of American women writers (2009). *Trifles* was first performed on August 8, 1916 at the Wharf Theatre. It was inspired by Glaspell's experience in 1900–1 of the trial of a woman named Margaret Hossack. She was charged with murdering her husband, an Iowa farmer, Clytemnestra-like with an axe. Glaspell had covered the trial for the *Des Moines Daily News*. Hossack was convicted, but was released in 1903 after a retrial ended in a hung jury. There was only circumstantial evidence against her—the relationship with her husband was unhappy and involved quarrels over his treatment of at least one of their children. No other suspect was ever in the frame.

Glaspell turns this mysterious "unsolved" murder case into a one-act play. She stages a visit to a farmhouse where a man has been murdered and his wife Minnie Foster is under arrest. The County Attorney, the Sheriff, and a neighbor are accompanied by the wives of the Sheriff and the neighbor. The group assessing the evidence—the "jury of her peers"—thus includes peers of the alleged murderess's own sex (women were not allowed to serve on juries in Iowa until 1921) (Angel 1996: 238–9). The word "trifles" is used disparagingly by the men in the play to refer to domestic objects belonging to the world of women. But the women realize that such "trifles" are clues to the distressing psychological history which underlies the murder: the dead man had been controlling and joyless, while Minnie had long since stopped being the happy girl they remember, who loved clothes and singing. One "trifle" is a quilt which Minnie had been sewing for years. The earlier stitches are careful, but the more recent ones deteriorate as if she was undergoing psychological disturbance. The women find an empty birdcage, and Minnie's canary, with a broken neck, in a pretty box ready for burial (the implication is that her husband had killed it). In the end, the two women rebel and secretly hide the deranged sewing and the dead canary, to prevent them being used in evidence.

My prosaic summary does not convey the taut brilliance of the dialogue and its intellectual clout. Glaspell's achievement, besides producing a play of exceptional feminist insight, is that she has made "the slightest of dramatic forms carry such a burden of meaning."[6] It is in this *formal* sense that Glaspell's *Trifles* reveals the scale of her debt to Greek tragedy. With a tiny cast, a single location, and a short episode exploring a violent household crime, she yet reveals all its antecedents and consequences and wider social significance. The hermetic atmosphere and onstage experience of the memory of offstage suffering are like no other tradition of tragic theater except Greek. No particular ancient Greek play is specifically referenced, and yet Glaspell's immersion in Greek dramatic culture is palpable. It is not just the husband-murdering theme (*Agamemnon*), nor the detective trail on which the women embark (*Oedipus*), nor the loneliness and resentment of insensitivity which might lead a woman to kill (*Medea*). Even more significant are the speaking testimony of the needlework and silenced songbird, which must have been inspired by the several references in Greek tragedy to the story of Procne and Philomela, Sophocles' own famous version of which is mentioned in both Thucydides and Aristotle's *Poetics*. As Marina Angel has observed, the decision to take collective action on behalf of Minnie against the men, and the thematic importance of the theme of "unravelling" both of the stitches and Minnie's true story, both also show Glaspell responding to Aristophanes' *Lysistrata* (Angel 2002: 89–90).

Glaspell's *The Outside* (which premièred at the Playwrights' Theatre on December 28, 1917) is shorter and lacks the feminist clarity of *Trifles*. Here the presence of Greek tragedy in the cocktail of ingredients is felt mostly through the setting. Once again, Glaspell chooses just five characters and an episode that lasts less than an hour. The setting is Cape Cod. The play opens, in a scenario reminiscent of Euripides' *Hecuba*, with the corpse of a young man who has just drowned in the sea.[7] The beach can be seen through the doorway constituting the set. The two women are associated with the inside of the house and the three men with the outside. The corpse is the visual center of the play, brought on at the beginning and picked up at the end. One woman has been mute for 20 years, but the events inspire her to break her silence; the other has been abandoned by her man, and is able through dialogue with the unmuted woman (faintly reminiscent of the encounter between Cassandra and Clytemnestra in *Agamemnon*) to recover her will to live. As in *Trifles*, Glaspell's fascination with Greek tragedy is expressed not in adaptation but in experiment with particular aspects of dramaturgy, especially the relationship between the living and the dead and the disciplined "unities" of time and place.

Glaspell's most respected play besides *Trifles* is *The Verge* (premièred November 14, 1921 and also staged by Edith Craig's Pioneer Players at the Regent Theatre). It is admired for the originality of its central scenographic conception—an enormous flowering plant which reflects the psychological experiences of the central character, Claire, an intellectual who reads books in Latin. The only time she has ever been happy is while soaring above the earth in an aeroplane. She seeks self-fulfillment, unable to find happiness through her marriage, motherhood, or an affair. On the verge of madness, she kills the man with whom she shares a passionate but intellectual bond. *The Verge* shows Glaspell, again, framing the drastic psychological journey of a woman held captive by societal expectations of her sex, but exploring her interiority more deeply, in a way reminiscent of Ibsen's heroines and of the "interior" monologues of Euripides' Medea, Phaedra, and Creusa in *Ion*; with Creusa and Medea, Claire also shares a trauma related to the birth of a boy-child; her son Harry died young. The action compresses Claire's breakdown into less than 24 hours, while exploring her life history, and culminates in tragic violence, although bearing a far less strongly marked relationship to an individual Greek tragedy than the four-act *Inheritors*, her other, more conventional play of 1921.

Inheritors was first performed by the Provincetown Players on April 27, 1921. Like *The Verge* it was performed, to acclaim, in Europe—at the Liverpool Repertory under the management of William Armstrong on January 18, 1926. *Inheritors* owes a debt to Sophocles' *Antigone*, but relocating the heroine's protest to a Midwestern prairie. The first act is set 40 years earlier than the others, in a farmhouse on the same prairie in about 1880, where Grandmother Morton reminisces about the Blackhawk War with the Indians fought back in 1832. She herself had received nothing but kindness from the Indians when she had arrived. Blackhawk was the chief, and it was in this valley that the Indians used to come to hold their games and funerals, like Iliadic warlords. She remembers her husband and Blackhawk climbing the local hill together and talking "about how the red and the white man might live together" (Glaspell 1987: 105). Her son Silas Morton, an autodidact, has never recovered from what white people did to the local Indians. He conceives a mission to found a college on that hill, to honor the land's original inhabitants, as a form of restitution. He is desperate to be able to "lie under same sod with the red boys and not be ashamed" (Glaspell 1987: 138).

The subsequent three acts are set in 1920. Silas Morton did found his college. The Antigone figure is Madeline, his granddaughter, now a student there. The political question is her support of two Hindu students from British India, who are threatened with deportation as campaigners for Indian independence. This was a pressing issue in 1920, after the Imperial Legislative Council in London had passed the Rowlatt Act, granting the Indian Viceroy powers to detain suspected activists without warrant or trial. The crisis produced the Amritsar massacre of April 13, 1919, when the British army fired into an unarmed assembly, killing over a thousand people. At Morton College, Madeline attempts to prevent a policeman from arresting an Indian student. She strikes the officer with her tennis racket. The climax of the drama is the confrontation of Madeline with her powerful Hungarian-American uncle, Felix Fejevary, which replays in Glaspell's modern idiom the confrontation of Antigone and Creon.

Since the death of her mother, and her father's decline into insanity (a suitably tragic nuclear family for an avatar of Sophocles' heroine), Fejevary has assumed a parental role in Madeline's life. Now that her brother has been killed in the war (like Antigone's brothers), Fejevary is all the family she has left. But as a banker with old-fashioned views on feminine decorum he repudiates her values and valor. He demands to know why she is not "ashamed" to be "a girl who rushes in and assaults an officer" (Glaspell 1987: 137). Madeline insists that she was acting in defense of the principle of freedom of speech on which the college and America were founded, and that she intends to fight for the release of her Indian comrades. Her defiance infuriates her uncle: "You could get twenty years in prison for things you'll say if you rush there now (*she laughs*) You laugh because you're ignorant. Do you know that in America today there are women in our prisons for saying no more you've said here to me!" (Glaspell 1987: 141).

At the conclusion, Madeline is due to go before the United States Commissioner, but refuses to apologize to her uncle and let him intervene on her behalf. She has been writing to a political prisoner, and knows the size of the dark cell which awaits her: she draws its outline in chalk to prepare herself, as Antigone imagines going to be buried in her sunless cave. But Glaspell wants her audience to understand that more is at stake than one young woman's liberty: it is a battle for the heart, soul, and identity of America. When a friend protests that Madeline is powerless to change things, she replies that she is "an American. And for that reason I think I have something to say about America" (Glaspell 1987: 145). At the end she breaks down in despair, but resolutely departs for her appointment with destiny.

The neglect this play has suffered is inexplicable, both because it is such a radical response to the famous Sophoclean tragedy and because it was written by a woman. If Eugene O'Neill were the author, it would have been read as much as *Mourning becomes Electra* or *Desire under the Elms*. The connections Glaspell draws between the pioneers' expropriation of Indian land on the Mississippi prairies and the struggles of Hindus under the British Raj is ambitious; by adopting from the Greek play the theme of the distinctive family character which Madeline inherits down the paternal line, the transhistorical story is handled deftly and with concision. Madeline herself sees no connection between her gender and her activism—she defines herself simply as an American. On the other hand, the men who would control her—not only her uncle, but her cousin, her disturbed father, the police, and the judiciary—find her behavior more deplorable in a woman. This feminist undertext is paralleled in Glaspell's own *oeuvre* by her novel *The Visioning* (1911), which examines sexual double standards in a Midwestern military community.

In the first quarter of the twentieth century, the classical Muse successfully migrated westward in that Greek drama played a role in the creation by women of a new American cultural identity. All four discussed in this chapter used Greek plays to meditate on their identity as feminists and as creators of artworks which could challenge the complacent, patriarchal, Ivy League monopoly on the Greek Classics and their legacy. Greek tragedy helped them make innovatory strides in aesthetic form—whether the liberated, emotionally expressive dance of Duncan, the imagism and cut-crystal diction of H.D., the dialogue between Cather's Professor and young scientist, or the tightly coiled theater of violence and female subjectivity which Glaspell pioneered. Duncan, H.D., and Glaspell all responded to individual ancient Greek dramas, the most neglected example being the use of *Antigone* in Glaspell's *Inheritors*. Cather and Glaspell both found imagining a relationship between ancient Greek culture and the forgotten indigenous Americans fruitful in the exploration of identity politics.

Cather and Glaspell also both used the Greeks to face the challenge that disparities in income and class status posed to "official" American ideals of equality and freedom. Glaspell, however, did this from a startlingly committed and explicitly revolutionary (her own word was "revolutionist") political position. She certainly at least contributed to Cook's delineation of Aspasia in *The Athenian Women* as a feminist Bolshevik; she was the sole creator of the Madeline/Antigone who in *Inheritors* speaks as a sincere American supporter of the poor as well as treasonable dissidence against the British Raj. History has shown how later in the twentieth century, gender and race are no longer regarded as acceptable grounds for disqualification from possession of a full "American identity," yet the problem of disparities in wealth and opportunity has never been fully acknowledged. Perhaps that is the reason why, of these four women Modernist pioneers inspired by Greek drama, it is only Glaspell—in some ways the most original of all—who has long become almost inaudible.

Notes

1. Singal 1987: 9–10; see also the discussion of Millington 2005: 52–3.
2. According to the *New York Times* for November 23, 1921, the production, in the college's chapel, was directed by Elizabeth Vera Loeb, and Bynner himself assisted with the staging. See also Kraft 1981: 19.
3. Williams 1951: 57; see Carpenter 1988: 42, but note that he is incorrect in his statement that the production was in English.
4. On Reyes's *Ifigenia cruel*, also see Barrenechea 2012 and Barrenechea, this volume.
5. For details, see Horwitz 1995: 358–9.
6. Bigsby in Glaspell 1987: 12.
7. It also recalls Synge's *Riders to the Sea* (1908), which also draws on Euripides' *Hecuba*. See Macintosh 1994: 165–70.

REFERENCES

Angel, M. (1996), "Criminal Law and Women: Giving the Abused Woman who Kills A *Jury of her Peers* who Appreciate *Trifles*," *American Criminal Law Review* 33, 229–348.
Angel, M. (2002), "A Classical Greek Influences an American Feminist: Susan Glaspell's Debt to Aristophanes," *Syracuse Law Review* 52, 81–103.
Aponte, B. B. (1972), *Alfonso Reyes and Spain*. Austin, TX, and London.
Barrenechea, F. (2012), "At the Feet of the Gods: Myth, Tragedy, and Redemption in Alfonso Reyes's *Ifigenia cruel*," *Romance Quarterly* 59, 6–18.
Ben-Zvi, L. (2005), *Susan Glaspell: Her Life and Times*. New York.
Brooke-Rose, C. (2004), "Gifts Above Price: The Legacy of Ezra Pound," in K. Heinzelman ed., *Make It New: The Rise of Modernism*. Austin.
Carpenter, H. (1988), *A Serious Character: The Life of Ezra Pound*. London.
Cather, W. (1981 [1925]), *The Professor's House*. London.
Conn, R. T. (2002), *The Politics of Philology: Alfonso Reyes and the Invention of the Latin American Literary Tradition*. Lewisburg, PA, and London.
Cook, G. C. (1926), *The Athenian Women*. With a Modern Greek translation revised by C. Carthaio. Athens.
Coolidge, C. (1924), *The Price of Freedom: Speeches and Addresses*. New York and London.
Downs, M. C. (1999), *Becoming Modern: Willa Cather's Journalism*. Selinsgrove, PA, and London.
Duncan, I. (1927), *My Life*. New York.
Glaspell, S. (1926), *The Road to the Temple*. London.
Glaspell, S. (1929), *Fugitive's Return*. London.
Glaspell, S. (1987), *Plays*. Ed. C. W. E. Rigsby with additional material by C. Dymkowski. Cambridge.
Hall, E. (2008), *The Return of Ulysses*. London and Baltimore.
Hall, E. (2013), *Adventures with* Iphigenia in Tauris: *Euripides' Black Sea Tragedy*. New York.
Hall, E. and F. Macintosh (2005), *Greek Tragedy and the British Theatre 1660–1914*. Oxford.
Horwitz, H. (1995), "Selling Relics, Preserving Antiquities: *The Professor's House* and the Narrative of American Anthropology," *Configurations* 3, 353–89.
Kraft, J. (ed. 1981), *The Works of Witter Bynner: Selected Letters*. New York.
Layson, J. (1983), "Isadora Duncan: A Preliminary Analysis of her Work," *Dance Research* 1, 39–49.
Lee, H. (2008), *Willa Cather: A Life Saved Up*. 2nd edn. London.
Lindemann, M. (ed. 2005), *The Cambridge Companion to Willa Cather*. Cambridge.
Macintosh, F. (1994), *Dying Acts: Death in Ancient Greek and Modern Irish Tragic Drama*. Cork.
Macintosh, F. (ed. 2010), *The Ancient Dancer in the Modern World: Responses to Greek and Roman Dance*. Oxford.
Millington, R. H. (2005), "Willa Cather's American Modernism," in M. Lindemann ed., *The Cambridge Companion to Willa Cather*. Cambridge, 51–65.
Morgenroth, J. (1998), "Dressing for the Dance," *Wilson Quarterly* 22, 88–95.
Orvell, M. (1995), *After the Machine: Visual Arts and the Erasing of Cultural Boundaries*. Jackson, MS.
Ozieblo, B. (2000), *Susan Glaspell: A Critical Biography*. Chapel Hill, NC, and London.
Pound, E. (1934), *ABC of Reading*. New York.
Reyes, A. (1924), *Ifigenia cruel*. Madrid.

Singal, D. J. (1987), "Towards a Definition of American Modernism," *American Quarterly* 39, 7–26.
Staley, T. (2004), "Foreword" to Kurt Heinzelman ed., *Make it New: The Rise of Modernism.* Austin, TX, 6–7.
Stone Peters, J. (2008), "Jane Harrison and the Savage Dionysus: Archaeological Voyages, Ritual Origins, Anthropology, and the Modern Theatre," *Modern Drama* 51, 1–41.
Stout, J. P. (2000), *Willa Cather: The Writer and her World.* Charlottesville, VA, and London.
Swift, J. P. (2005), "Fictions of Possession in *The Professor's House*," in M. Lindemann ed., *The Cambridge Companion to Willa Cather.* Cambridge, 175–90.
Williams, W. C. (1951), *Autobiography.* New York.
Zanobi, A. (2010), "From Duncan to Bausch with Iphigenia," in F. Macintosh ed., *The Ancient Dancer in the Modern World: Responses to Greek and Roman Dance.* Oxford, 236–54.

CHAPTER 11

IPHIGENIA AMONGST THE IVIES, 1915

NIALL W. SLATER

When Harley Granville Barker and his wife, Lillah McCarthy, sailed for America to open a season in New York in 1915, they had no specific plans to offer American audiences Euripides.[1] Yet as Barker later told the story, American experiences were key to his decision to mount a tour of the northeast with two of Euripides' tragedies in the largest outdoor productions of Greek drama ever done in America.[2] Barker came to America at the invitation of the New York Stage Society (Kennedy 1985: 179; Purdom 1955: 170). War conditions were already making production of serious drama in London difficult, and the trip would help build goodwill for Britain in the officially neutral United States.[3] The planned repertory included Shaw and Shakespeare, with both of whom Barker and McCarthy were very much associated in the public mind. Barker had previously directed landmark performances of Gilbert Murray's translations of Euripides, beginning with *Hippolytus* in 1904. *Trojan Women, Medea*, and *Iphigenia in Tauris* with McCarthy in the title role followed, the last in 1912. Barker speculated to Murray before leaving England about producing *Trojan Women* in America in the context of the war, but only in February 1915 did he wire Murray with a concrete proposal.[4]

As Barker told the story to journalists, the aetiology of this tour was a visit to Yale during which he was shown the 70,000-seat Yale Bowl (Smith 1915: 409). The sight inspired him with the possibility of producing Greek tragedy outdoors by daylight, in spaces and conditions similar to that of the ancient theaters.[5] In an interview with a Yale student journalist he also mentions a visit that he and McCarthy made to the ancient theater of Syracuse as another inspiration.[6] Although he talked of producing more scripts,[7] in the end he organized a tour of the northeast with just two of Murray's translations: the *Trojan Women* and the *Iphigenia*. With the help of several fundraising committees at the universities, he put together a tour to Yale, Harvard, Princeton, the City College of New York, and the University of Pennsylvania, primarily utilizing university stadia for productions with a running time of about two hours (Foley 2012: 40–2; Kennedy 1985: 182).

The choice of plays offers an intriguing pairing. In light of the Great War in Europe, the selection of *Trojan Women* seemed obvious then as now. The reaction of the *Philadelphia Inquirer*'s correspondent is representative:

> There is something timely in the great open-air performance of "The Trojan Women" before an American audience of many thousand persons at a moment when the eyes of the world are centred on Europe, when the sympathies of neutral nations are concentrated in alleviating the sufferings of war. "The Trojan Women" has been said to be the greatest war play ever written, since it contains a message for peace and plea for consideration for women and children in times of international strife.[8]

Another reviewer aimed for an even more pointed historical analysis, comparing the original Athenian audience, witnessing the play in the aftermath of the Melian massacre, to that in New York watching:

> . . . a-thrill with recent memories of Louvain and Malines, of Rheims and Ypres,— and of the *Lusitania*. This fact afforded a double meaning to the lines, which was analogous to that other double meaning which must have swept through the minds of the twenty thousand citizens of Athens who first listened to this tragic drama two thousand three hundred and thirty years before.[9]

Barker himself said Lillah McCarthy, playing Hecuba, looked "like the Queen of the Belgians."[10] The play's reception might fairly be called reverent.

Reviews of its companion piece, the *Iphigenia in Tauris*, varied much more widely and may show how Barker's attempts to connect with traditions of American spectacle and perhaps American views of the barbarian "Other" disturbed rather than conformed to audience expectations of the classical past. The catalyst for public discussion was usually the production design, although some reviewers were more critical of McCarthy's performance in the title role than they were of her Hecuba.[11] Some debate fell along familiar lines of archaeological "authenticity," but others questioned the production's affiliation with the work of Max Reinhardt. Criticism of the production's "primitivism" framed itself in aesthetic terms, resisting Barker's attempts to construct the primitive in other than familiarly classical terms.

The selection of *Iphigenia*, largely absent from current performance, may seem more surprising today than it did in 1915, though it could hardly be deemed an obvious choice. *Iphigenia in Tauris* was the third most often produced play on American college campuses in the decades preceding Barker's tour,[12] and Aristotle's praise of the play's recognition scene cannot be irrelevant here.[13] It was certainly a very deliberate choice. In interviews with both commercial and college newspapers, Barker regularly made the case that the play was entertainment. He told the *Yale Daily News*:

> I hope that people will not get the idea that this drama is a very serious affair, because that is just what it is not. The Greek drama is very closely related to modern drama, and if the people only go in the spirit that they go to see "Kick In," for instance, I am sure that they will find it fully as entertaining.[14]

Another motivation must have been star power: Lillah McCarthy had had great success with the role in England in 1912, and she clearly loved the play (Hall and Macintosh 2005: 542–4). In her memoirs, charmingly entitled *Myself and My Friends*, she calls it a "lovely play, the greatest I think that was ever written," and continued playing it until 1932.[15] The American public was impressed too. The memoir of an anonymous Princeton undergraduate, published in 1915 by one of his teachers, tells how he put himself through college, including this vignette at the end of his undergraduate career:

> I have just now come back from a trip as advertising agent for the Granville Barker Greek plays at Princeton, and I have earned nearly as much in a week as I did in a term as a freshman. I'm strong for Lillah McCarthy and Iphigenia. (Gauss 1915: 156)

Barker's decision to put *Iphigenia* regularly first on the schedule for each tour stop testifies to his belief that it was the more likely to draw spectators to the second as well.

Barker sent for Norman Wilkinson, who had designed his earlier production of *Iphigenia* at the Kingsway Theatre in Britain. I have been able to find little documentation of that earlier design, although one photograph of McCarthy as Iphigenia in 1912 does show a strong resemblance to her 1915 costume.[16] It is nonetheless clear that Barker charged Wilkinson with designing both set and costumes on a scale capable of being "read" in the huge outdoor space of the Yale Bowl and other stadia.

Some photographs of the 1915 production, particularly of McCarthy, are reasonably well known, at least to researchers. One source, however, does not seem to have been exploited or even much noted in almost a century since its production. The American branch of Oxford University Press issued Murray's translation of *Iphigenia* in both 1910 and 1915. Some copies of the 1915 printing were used for a limited edition, illustrated by photographs of the Yale production taken by Donald Cummings Fitts of the Class of 1916.[17] One of these copies, now in the library of the Getty Research Institute, allows us a more detailed glimpse of that memorable staging,[18] and these will help us examine the impact of the performance.

A quick précis of the play's background is in order: becalmed in the harbor, King Agamemnon lured his daughter Iphigenia to Aulis with the promise of marriage to Achilles, but in fact, yielding to a prophecy, the king planned to sacrifice her to Artemis in order to change the winds and allow the Greek fleet to sail to Troy. In Euripides' version of the myth, however, Artemis rescued her at the last minute, substituting a deer, but made her a priestess in the barbaric land of the Taurians—presiding over a cult of human sacrifice, from which she yearns to escape.

The play itself opens with a speech from Iphigenia "in the dress of a Priestess," according to Murray's published stage directions, after a dream she thinks foretells the death of her brother Orestes. Wilkinson's costumes liberally mixed ancient inspiration with contemporary design, while using color in an ever bolder fashion. At the Yale production:

> Iphigenia was disclosed, costumed in light tints, as one of the pre-Persian statues of the Acropolis, against a wall of red—a charming figure as she came forward

and spoke the prologue, a figure hardly improved later by the fantastic headdress assumed when she brought out the figure.[19]

The *New York Times* reviewer, markedly less sympathetic to Wilkinson's design concept, gives this picture:

> Iphigenia in the earlier scenes before she donned an astonishing headdress, wore a costume exasperatingly suggestive of highly contemporary dishabille...[20]

Iphigenia's robe and hair were "copied from one of the Acropolis maidens, even to the wig with its long, straight locks," while the drapery was "spotted as if with great drops of blood, and the tunic... striped with waves of red."[21] Despite the unity of time in Euripides' script, Wilkinson sought to illustrate a development in time within the play. He told the *New York Times*:

> Miss McCarthy's first costume is semi-barbaric, and later, when she has been longer under the influence of the Taurians, her dress is almost wholly barbaric.[22]

The first impression of Iphigenia would have been as a predominantly white and vulnerable figure, first alone on stage, then returning to meet the chorus and offer libations to her brother's memory because a dream has led her to fear he has died. One of the earliest photographs in Fitts's volume shows us this moment and her early costume (Fig. 11.1).[23]

FIG. 11.1 Iphigenia offering libations (Fitts 1915, opp. p. 11) Research Library, The Getty Research Institute, Los Angeles (91-B13114).

Between her first appearance on stage and the arrival of the chorus, however, two Greek travelers appear on the vacant stage: Iphigenia's brother Orestes and his comrade Pylades, revealing their mission to capture the cult statue of the goddess Artemis from the Taurian shrine and bring it back to Greece. Fearing capture, they retreat to hide until nightfall. Iphigenia returns and meets the chorus. A messenger then interrupts Iphigenia's lament to report the seizure of two strangers in the land, whom it is her duty to sacrifice to Artemis. When the captive Greeks are brought in, Iphigenia re-appears from the temple, surrounded by much taller and more menacing figures of Taurians, the executioners who carry out the work.[24] The soaring blood-red caps and costumes of those surrounding Iphigenia clearly demonstrate that she is as much their prisoner and victim as are the luckless travelers who happen to be captured and sacrificed by the cult. A contemporary news photograph,[25] though not taken during the production, shows how (as other sources indicate) these executioners later pull down masks from their headdresses over their faces (Fig. 11.2).

A visual allusion to a current image of terror seems very likely. On the same page of advertisements in the *Boston Globe* that announced the Harvard Stadium performances of Barker's Greek tour appeared a larger ad for a film, "now in its second month": D. W. Griffiths's *Birth of a Nation*. Did Wilkinson (and Barker) conceive the Taurian executioners as Klansmen?[26]

Questioned by Iphigenia, the captured Orestes and Pylades refuse to identify themselves by name but acknowledge they are Greeks. This gives Iphigenia the idea to free

FIG. 11.2 Close-up of executioners—*Philadelphia Public Ledger* June 9, 1915, 11.

one of the captives so that he might carry a letter back to Greece to her brother appealing for rescue. Having dismissed her attendants, she goes to fetch the letter. In her absence Orestes and Pylades debate who will sacrifice himself by remaining while the other carries the letter. Orestes of course prevails. Pylades, however, insists on Iphigenia revealing the contents of the letter, lest he should lose it on the way—and when he learns the letter is to her brother Orestes, he delivers the letter on the spot, bringing about the recognition of brother and long-lost sister. This is the moment that Aristotle loved,[27] and it was clearly no less effective in this rendition designed to reach the back rows of the Yale Bowl. A Philadelphia reviewer waxed lyrical over this moment:

> Miss Lillah McCarthy made a noble figure of the . . . exiled and hopelessly homesick priestess. In her red robe, set off by two close braids of hair, she dominated the stage, yet in all of her tragic pose there was an underlying warmth of feeling that made her a very human figure and heightened the poignancy of her situation. It was in the recognition scene with Orestes, however, that her power to convey the richness of the character rose to its fullest expression.[28]

Had the performance ended here, it might have been as much lauded and perhaps more loved than the accompanying *Trojan Women*. Reunited, brother and sister then win over the chorus, who are themselves captive women, to their cause and formulate a plan for all to escape by sea.[29] Euripides engineers the suspense well: when Iphigenia, Orestes, and Pylades retreat into the temple, we in the audience have no idea how they will flee this land. The intervening chorus fantasizes about escape, but gives no details.

Up until this point, despite a much brighter and bolder color palette, the production had not differed so radically from the contemporary expectations for Greek tragedy. With the sudden arrival of Thoas, King of the Taurians, the atmosphere and the visual impression changed sharply. Thoas was played by Lionel Braham, a 6 foot 4 actor, not from a subtle school.[30] Reviewers and spectators alike were astounded by

> the brawny King of the Tauri, with arms like sawed-off logs, a blood red beard . . . and a gilded scepter, shaped roughly like a sapling; and in the curled branches of the scepter-tree roosted green and scarlet birds, cut flat out of wood, like nursery toys.
> The King wore a tunic of yellow and bluish green and figured green leggings . . .[31]
>
> a cloak as big as a Baghdad mosque carpet[32]

At the first performance at Yale, Braham apparently forgot his lines on entrance and could not hear the prompter from behind the massive set.[33] He tried to cover by roaring, but his suit of many colors and his retinue of bodyguards also contributed heavily to a comic reception (for Thoas's costume, but at a later moment in the production, see Fig. 11.4). The *New York Times* reviewer of this première performance said:

> . . . when he came to trick out King Thoas and the warriors who attended him . . . Mr. Wilkinson seemed resolved to outdo anything he had achieved [earlier] . . . There is simply no describing those soldiers with their union suits of black and white adorned with whisk-brooms of the hue of tomato bisque. There is no describing

Thoas himself with his ornithological scepter, his checkered robe and his scarlet beard. It was a great reception accorded to this apparition. However Mr. Wilkinson's art may be received in the more precious circles of the metropolis, it was received by the unregenerate undergraduates of New Haven with loud roars of laughter.[34]

The *New York Sun* blamed the Yale freshmen.[35] The *Christian Science Monitor* was more impressed, finding Braham "magnificent in the childlike-ness of his animalism" and "a thing of wonder and terror."[36] Thoas has come to find out if the sacrifice has been carried out—and is shocked to discover Iphigenia with the image of Artemis in her hands.[37]

Another reviewer observed that the soldiers' costumes "too nearly resemble the latest mode of the Dahomey chieftains to be other than farcical."[38] This brief comment suggests an American context Barker may have been trying to tap into, giving the production a disturbing contemporaneity. The allusion is almost certainly not to the first African-American musical to reach Broadway, *In Dahomey* (Cook, Shipp, and Dunbar, 1903). Far more likely seems a connection to a tradition of open-air exhibitions of "authentic" African life in the form of a "Dahomey Village," first seen at the 1893 Columbian Exposition, but repeated or imitated at later large international expositions as well.[39] It is worth noting that, unlike the well-trained singers of the chorus who traveled with the production throughout its tour, Barker recruited supernumerary players for the roles of Thoas's soldiers and extra herdsmen from men at the host universities. A photograph from another Philadelphia paper names two of the Penn undergraduates who took on these roles (Fig. 11.3).

Barker himself seems to have been taken aback by the audience response to Thoas and company. Although he never seems to have addressed the portrayal of the soldiers in particular, in later interviews he worked to defend the "primitivist" portrayal of Thoas and the Taurians. He told the *Daily Princetonian*:

> But when, for example, Euripides furnishes me with such characters as the Tauri, people whom every line describes as fierce savages, offering human sacrifice in a grim and austere temple, I see no reason why the doors of that temple should not open upon a blood-red interior. The King of that land must obviously have been the apotheosis of everything they stood for. Why should not I make him so, primitive and rudely gorgeous in dress and weapons?[40]

"Primitive and rudely gorgeous" but also somewhat expressionist: a close-up of King Thoas receiving news of the Greeks' escape shows those green and scarlet cut-out wooden birds that perched in his tree-like sceptre as well as the enormous crown that added more than a foot to his already impressive height (Fig. 11.4).

At this remove we cannot definitely separate audience response to the costume design from mirth over Braham's failure to remember his lines on entrance. The power of a line miscue to destroy a tragic mood should not be underestimated.[41] Whether Barker's defense of the production concept influenced subsequent audience response or not is also hard to say. Certainly by later in the run, a review of the New York performances in the stadium of the City College shows that the audience reaction was under somewhat better control:

FIG. 11.3 Two soldiers from Thoas's guard (unattributed newspaper photo, University of Pennsylvania scrapbooks).

> Norman Wilkinson's super-fantastic costuming for the luckless Taurian monarch and his attendants were [sic] received with hearty laughter at New Haven. The audience at the Stadium yesterday just grinned.[42]

The production of *Trojan Women* in New York officially inaugurated the new stadium, and Barker scheduled three more performances (one of *Trojan Women*, two of *Iphigenia*). McCarthy thought they drew 30,000 spectators in New York altogether, implying capacity audiences.[43] While students from the public schools as well as city colleges were admitted at a subsidized rate, it is unclear whether a plan to require all the graduating students from the city's high schools to attend was put into effect.[44] Conscript audiences might not have been very attentive.

FIG. 11.4 Messenger and Thoas (unattributed newspaper photo, University of Pennsylvania scrapbooks).

Earlier audiences seem to have been much more interested in the text. Barker saw to it that copies of the plays were available to patrons of the productions on the day, in paperback copies. Some 1,500 copies of the *Trojan Women* were sold for the Harvard Stadium performance, and combined sales of the two plays in New York reached 5,000 copies before they opened.[45]

Whether attendance dropped during the tour is an open question. Certainly no subsequent performance was as large as the opening at Yale, which may have drawn 10,000 spectators, doubtless more than saw all the performances of *Iphigenia* in two previous productions in England.[46] Inclement weather at Harvard certainly limited attendance, and the one performance given at a country club on Long Island had been twice postponed by rain (Elberson 1968: 177–8). Undoubtedly Barker lost money on the tour, despite calling on his financial backers for their guarantees, and it affected his finances for years thereafter.[47]

Was there a gendered reception of *Iphigenia*? One reviewer of the Harvard production noted that in the audience of 3,000 to 4,000 "more than three-fourths . . . were women."[48] If that is anywhere near the truth, it means that the large majority of the audience were not students but from the town. The reviewer's comments about the "unregenerate undergraduates" who greeted Braham's appearance as King Thoas with laughter suggest more men in the audience—as do reports of men posted at the top of the Bowl to signal to the audience how Yale fared in the track meet taking place simultaneously on an adjacent field!⁴⁹ Another anecdote relates that when the sun dipped below the edge of the Bowl and hundreds of men got up to put on their overcoats, there was more joking in the audience about a seventh inning stretch.⁵⁰

As already noted, Barker recruited undergraduates at his all-male host institutions to swell the scene on that 140-foot-long stage. Undoubtedly he understood the promotional power of local interest, as the local newspaper called attention to the "scores of Yale men" in the minor parts at the première.⁵¹ One feature of the later performance at the University of Pennsylvania (held in the Botanical Gardens) may suggest that Barker looked for more than generic local appeal. The production recruited Mike Dorizas, who, though a graduate student at the time, played football for Penn and could be billed as "the famous Greek student of the University, who is the strongest man in the collegiate world."⁵² Casting did pay attention to body type. While taller students were soldiers in the retinue of the enormous King Thoas, Dorizas, a much stockier type, played an additional shepherd next to the actor with the speaking part of the Herdsman: a young Claude Rains! (Fig. 11.5).⁵³ Dorizas, a medalist at the 1908 Olympics for his native Greece,

FIG. 11.5 Rains and Dorizas (center) as herdsmen (unattributed newspaper photo, University of Pennsylvania scrapbooks).

had a presence not only as an athlete but also as a public speaker on such topics as "The European War."[54] Whether deliberately or not, Barker's casting of this "Greek Wrestler and Athlete" would certainly have bolstered the "masculine" appeal of the *Iphigenia* production.

At the end of the tour, Lillah McCarthy returned to Europe alone. Barker had met someone else in New York, Helen Huntington. Although he tried returning to England and even took up a commission in the army, he eventually asked McCarthy for a divorce and married Huntington. He never again directed a major West End production, and he was primarily active as a lecturer and writer. McCarthy continued to act until her marriage to an Oxford professor, whereupon she retired from the stage.[55] Although she did perform as Iphigenia thereafter,[56] the American tour marked the end of her partnership with Barker and the end of a remarkable experiment with Greek tragedy on the scale of ancient performances.

Iphigenia's tour of the Ivies was a sensation in its day. It remained alive in the academic memory for some time, though not as long in the public mind, if we are to trust the judgement of Thornton Wilder. Surveying the theater scene in America and the prospects for new productions and directions in a letter to H.D. in 1935, Wilder asserted, "The public must now have forgotten Granville Barker's immense stadium productions . . ."[57] The spaces that seem to have inspired Barker to such scale did not or could not tempt subsequent directors. Changing economics certainly play one part here, and competition from motion pictures another. That advertisement for *Birth of a Nation* in the *Boston Globe* promised "18,000 PEOPLE . . . 3,000 HORSES."[58] After the war theater could no longer compete on such a scale of spectacle. Star culture moved toward motion pictures as well. Lillah McCarthy was clearly a powerful draw for the productions, but once sound came to motion pictures few stage actresses (or actors) could command the attention their competitors in film did. It is not even clear how successful Donald Cummings Fitts was in capitalizing on the tour with the volume from which some of our illustrations have come. Fitts undoubtedly hoped to make a profit from his illustrated edition, built around Miss McCarthy's iconic image (Fig. 11.6). But its appeal apparently proved rather ephemeral,[59] and Fitts does not seem to have enjoyed a professional career in photography thereafter.

In many ways the Barker productions of Greek drama in 1915 represent a road not taken. Although his influence on the staging of Shakespeare continued long after he himself ceased to act and direct, his attempt to restore Greek tragedy to its original scale and something like original production conditions did not have a similar effect. Changing public taste, economics, competition from spectacle in movies, and the vagaries of star culture all played a role, as did a very different spirit in the commercial theater both in Britain and America after the Great War. Lillah McCarthy's post-war performances as Iphigenia must already have seemed echoes from another age. Yet they had proven the ability of Euripides' two-millenia-old texts to move a broad public and generate a spirited debate in both press and academic circles which boded well for American writers' engagement with tragedy in the next generation.

FIG. 11.6 McCarthy as Iphigenia (Fitts 1915, opp. p. 3) Research Library, The Getty Research Institute, Los Angeles (91-B13114).

Notes

1. I thank the Getty Research Institute, both for their support of my work as a Villa Visiting Scholar through which I began the research for this article and for their gracious permission to reproduce photographs from the key volume in their collection (Murray, *Iphigenia in Tauris*, OUP, 1915, limited edition; see n. 18, below). I am also most grateful to Nancy Miller of the University of Pennsylvania Archives for generous help with materials there. My student research assistant, Julia Victor, has done wonders in finding obscure materials for me. Some material in this article has appeared previously in Slater 2011.
2. Despite Barker's claim to the *Yale Daily News* (May 14, 1915), his was not the first *Iphigenia* in America, nor were these strictly the first outdoor performances of Greek drama in America. The advance notice in the *Boston Daily Globe* May 16, 1915, mentions an *Iphigenia* performance in Harvard's Sanders Theater in 1900 (a mistake for 1902), although this cannot have been Murray's translation. The Coburn Players had mounted Euripides' *Electra* in New York City in 1910, using Murray, and added *Iphigenia in Tauris* to their repertoire in 1913 (Hartigan 1995: 21–2; cf. Durham 1987: 86–90), with at least one outdoor performance

at Columbia University (so Foley 2012: 39–40). The British actor-manager Ben Greet (in whose company both Barker and Lillah McCarthy performed in the 1890s: McCarthy 1933: 39–42; Purdom 1955: 191) proposed "a Greek play" for his 1910 tour in New York (Isaac 1964: 115–16), but Durham (1987: 197–203) has no record of a production. Greet did direct the student company that opened Berkeley's outdoor Hearst Greek Theatre in 1903 with a production of Aristophanes' *Birds* (199). The Harvard Stadium was the location for a student production of *Agamemnon* in 1906, given in Greek, and at least one college production played outdoors (Randolph-Macon Women's College, 1914: Pluggé 1938: 82).

3. Prime Minister Asquith reportedly encouraged McCarthy to go, saying, "Go to America. We don't want Barker as a soldier" (Purdom 1955: 170). McCarthy's own account is slightly different: "I went to Mr. Asquith hoping that he would bid me stay. He bade me go: 'You can do nothing by staying. Go and produce plays there and come back with enough money to begin in management again when the war is over'" (McCarthy 1933: 185).

4. Letter to Murray November 6, 1914: "I do wish we could do the Trojan Women, but perhaps it is an end of the War play, not a middle War" (Salmon 1986: 287); cf. Kennedy 1985: 180.

5. The *New Haven Evening Register* (May 9, 1915, 2) notes that local promoters, who had earlier persuaded the famous Irish tenor John McCormack to test the Bowl acoustics, "urged" Barker to consider a "spectacular production" in the Bowl.

6. *Yale Daily News* May 14, 1915.

7. Kennedy (1985: 181) cites a March letter to Murray, suggesting he hoped to revive *Hippolytus* and add *Alcestis* as well.

8. *Philadelphia Inquirer* May 30, 1915; cf. *Christian Science Monitor* May 18, 1915: "the greatest anti-war poem imaginable." Barker planned to give receipts above expenses to war relief (Elberson 1968: 175), but since he made a considerable loss, it is unclear if any donations were actually made. Maurice Browne's Chicago Little Theatre had premièred Murray's translation of *Trojan Women* in America in 1913. Their production toured the Midwest under the sponsorship of the Women's Peace Party at the same time as Barker's tour—on which, see Kennedy 1985: 181 and Hartigan 1995: 17–19.

9. Clayton Hamilton in *Vogue* (1915), 82 [= (1939), 412]. A few were less reverent even at the time: see Moses 1915. The influential and acerbic drama critic George Jean Nathan, who terrorized players and playwrights alike for more than 40 years, responded to "Mr. Granville Barker's dramatic Fresh Air Fund" by suggesting that "it seems as logical and 'educational' to play Euripides out-of-doors (merely because Euripides was originally played thus) as it would be to compel students to glimpse the Homeric epics off goat-skin merely because they were originally transcribed upon goat-skin" (Nathan 1915: 16).

10. Letter to Murray quoted in Kennedy 1985: 181. The effect is clear from a much-reproduced photograph of McCarthy in the role, most easily accessible in Stratton 1916: 260 (Fitts's version is Fig. 11.6). The sufferings of the Belgians were much in the public mind: the *Philadelphia Public Ledger*'s review of the *Trojan Women* suggested the play was "so modern in its intent that it might be called 'The Belgian Women'" (June 9, 1915, 11).

11. Moses 1915: 396: "We cannot say that Mrs. Barker infused into Iphigenia the warmth or mystery that is in the part; there was a tendency to be dead level. She was decorative, but Euripides requires something more than pose."

12. Absolute numbers are small, but the four productions of *IT* in the period 1893–1903 were outpaced only by 11 of *Antigone* and five of *Oedipus Tyrannus*, while for 1904–14, the numbers were *Antigone* (14), *Alcestis* (12), and *IT* (10): Pluggé 1938: 15–20. See also Hains 1910 and Hall 2013: esp. 233–4 on the interest of women's colleges in *IT*. For

professional productions of *IT* since 1913, see the listing in appendix F of Foley 2012: 300–2.
13. *Poetics* 55a: "... of all recognitions, the best is that which arises from the incidents themselves, where the startling discovery is made by natural means. Such is that in the Oedipus of Sophocles, and in the Iphigenia; for it was natural that Iphigenia should wish to dispatch a letter." (Translation S. H. Butcher.)
14. *Yale Daily News* April 22, 1915.
15. McCarthy 1933: 314. Her memoir contains wonderful vignettes of rehearsing for the original production, and she was still playing the role for charity productions in 1932.
16. See now the very important discussion of the 1912 production in Hall 2013: 241–9. Her fig. XI.5, originally from McCarthy (1933), shows the 1912 costume.
17. The Yale Library Special Collections preserves a copy "interleaved with photographs of production in New Haven, 1915, in the Yale Bowl, given under the auspices of the Yale Dramatic Association." It is bound in blue cloth, unlike the Getty copy (see next note), but otherwise seems to be the same edition. Biographical information on Fitts comes from *Catalogue of the Officers and Graduates of Yale University* (Yale, 1924), 748.
18. Apparently the limited edition simply used the sheets of the regular 1915 OUP edition of Murray's *Iphigenia in Tauris* with some blank leaves bound in on which the photographs were tipped in. The National Union Catalogue has no record of this limited edition. All the information comes from the Getty's copy, which bears this handwritten annotation: "Limited Edition | Illustrated | by | Donald Cummings Fitts | Copy #4 | 1915." Stamped in gold on the leather binding is the name, "Rhea Ruth Fuller."
19. Undated and unsourced newspaper clipping entitled "Iphigenia in Tauris," preserved on page 6 of a scrapbook on the Barker productions, Box 13, Archives of the University of Pennsylvania. The best-known image of McCarthy as Iphigenia, reproduced in Stratton 1916: 252, shows this much-discussed headdress and an elaborately geometric over-garment. Though no source identifies the precise origin of the photograph in Stratton, the grass and melting snow in the background suggest to me that this is a "backstage" photo taken at the Harvard performance, which was cold and wet. Fitts's version of McCarthy in this costume and with the same gesture is the first production photograph bound into the text of the play itself (after a head shot of Barker). See Fig. 11.6.
20. *New York Times* May 16, 1915.
21. Smith 1915: 412. The reviewer for the *Philadelphia Bulletin*, "Iphigenia in Tauris: Ancient Glories of Greek Drama's Golden Age" (scrapbook on the Barker productions, Box 13, Archives of the University of Pennsylvania), objected to her "painfully brick red gown" as "an offense to the eye."
22. *New York Times* May 23, 1915.
23. Iphigenia holds a good imitation of a Geometric krater, preparing to pour a libation in front of the chorus.
24. For Fitts's photograph of this moment, see Slater 2011: 445 fig. 1.
25. *Philadelphia Public Ledger* June 9, 1915, 11.
26. One reviewer did see an allusion. Elberson 1968: 189–90 and n. 78 cites an unidentified news clipping (which I have not seen), saying the executioners "looked like some weird Ku Klux Klan, 'born out of their time.'" A Philadelphia reviewer suggested more frivolously: "Her attendants were gorgeous creatures suggestive of vermilion octopi minus the tentacles..." (*Telegraph*, "War, of Old, as Now, Made Innocent Suffer," perhaps June 9 (scrapbook on the Barker productions, Box 13, Archives of the University of Pennsylvania).

27. Aristotle, *Poetics* 55a. For Fitts's photograph of this moment, see Slater 2011: 446 fig. 2.
28. *Philadelphia Inquirer* June 9, 1915.
29. For Fitts's photograph of this moment, see Slater 2011: 447 fig. 3.
30. Barker himself said that Braham had a method "like an overgrown good-natured bull"—quoted in Kennedy 1985: 185.
31. *Boston Journal* May 19, 1915.
32. *Philadelphia Bulletin*, "Iphigenia in Tauris: Ancient Glories of Greek Drama's Golden Age," (scrapbook on the Barker productions, Box 13, Archives of the University of Pennsylvania, perhaps June 9, 1915).
33. *New York Times* May 30, 1915: "... when the massive barbaric monarch ... forgot his lines in the flutter caused by the first sight of his amazing costume ... [h]e could only roar, which he did repeatedly and with great virtuosity." A Philadelphia reviewer thought "Thoas had not learned his lines..."—"Iphigenia in Tauris" (scrapbook on the Barker productions, Box 13, Archives of the University of Pennsylvania, page 6).
34. *New York Times* May 16, 1915.
35. *New York Sun* May 17, 1915, "Irreverent Yale Freshmen Laugh." With false sympathy, the article noted that "the Yale freshmen had never seen the famous Ballet Russe or the productions of Reinhardt and Gordon Craig."
36. *Christian Science Monitor* May 18, 1915, 4.
37. For Fitts's photograph of this moment, see Slater 2011: 448 fig. 4. Smith (1915: 412) shows the same scene from a more direct view and is reproduced by Hall 2013: 21 fig. I.7.
38. *Philadelphia Bulletin*, "Iphigenia in Tauris: Ancient Glories of Greek Drama's Golden Age" (scrapbook on the Barker productions, Box 13, Archives of the University of Pennsylvania, perhaps June 9, 1915).
39. Such as the 1895 Cotton States Exposition in Atlanta and the 1909 Imperial International Exhibition in London. Wollaeger (2001: 49 and fig. 2) illustrates a postcard of grass-skirted "*Fetish Priests at the Dahomey Village Imperial International Exhibition*," an example of ephemera in circulation that helped form a public visual repertoire. See also Hall 2013: 246–7.
40. Granville Barker interviewed in *Daily Princetonian* June 5, 1915.
41. All Classicists will recall the story of the actor Hegelochus in the original Athenian production of Euripides' *Orestes* who, by breathing at the wrong moment, turned the Greek word for "calm" into the word "weasel." The audience did not forgive him for saying "After the storm, I see the weasel appear."
42. *New York Times* June 1, 1915.
43. McCarthy 1933: 310. The New York stadium was the smallest they played, with an official capacity of 6,000, but more seats were added and standing room sold for the Greek plays—*Philadelphia Inquirer* May 30, 1915, 10; Elberson 1968: 157.
44. Smith (1915: 415) reports the plan.
45. *New York Times* May 30, 1915. Cf. Elberson 1968: 154. Hawkers sold copies at the Yale opening as well, while total sales for the two plays during the tour reached 25,000 (Leiter 1991: 38–9). The *Princeton Press* June 5, 1915, 3 announced that copies of Murray's translations were on reserve at the University Library and encouraged potential spectators to "familiarize themselves beforehand." They were on sale in Princeton for 25 cents (ad in *Princeton Press* June 5, 1915, 5) and in Philadelphia in both hardback and paperback (25 cents and 75 cents respectively, *Philadelphia Press*, Wanamaker ad, June 4, 1915).

46. *New Haven Evening Register* May 15, 1915, 2, gives the figure of 10,000. The later estimate of 16,000 at the Yale performance, given in the *Philadelphia Inquirer* May 23, 1915, is surely exaggerated. For the performances in England, see Kennedy 1985: 116–22, 207–11.
47. Elberson 1968: 179–80. Local venues bore significant costs: the University of Pennsylvania spent 10,000 dollars readying its venue—*Pennsylvanian* April 6, 1915, "Plan Greek Play Spectacle Here."
48. *Boston Daily Globe* May 19, 1915, 8. This means that necessarily less than a quarter of the audience were Harvard students.
49. *New York Times* May 16, 1915: "small messengers perched at the topmost rim waved the news that Yale was winning there." Elberson (1968: 164) quotes an eyewitness recollection that the laughter came primarily from the students.
50. *New York Times* May 30, 1915; Elberson 1968: 164. Foley (2012: 314 n. 78) cites a study of the Yale production and reception by Richard C. Beacham, "Tragedy in the Bowl!," in the Archive of Performances of Greek and Roman Drama at Oxford, which I have not been able to see.
51. *New Haven Evening Register* May 9, 1915, 2. Presumably these include the Herdsmen, Executioners, and Soldiers to Thoas listed with the cast in the *Yale Daily News* May 15, 1915 (altogether totaling less than a score!).
52. *Philadelphia Record*, probably June 9, 1915. Cf. *Philadelphia Inquirer* June 9, 1915.
53. Rains was also billed as Barker's "chief stage director" in the *Philadelphia Public Ledger* June 8, 1915. The future Invisible Man originally "was perhaps a shade too forceful in his gestures" in the view of J. R. Crawford (*Yale Daily News* May 17, 1915), while the *Christian Science Monitor* May 19, 1915, thought at the Harvard performance he delivered his speech "with a headlong rush that carried his audience with him." Cf. Meeker 1915: 128. While the *New York Times* reviewer (June 1, 1915) thought Rains had "modified somewhat the sheer physical vigor of his performance" by the time they played the stadium in New York, in Philadelphia still "Claude Rains shook the very planks of the marble temple with the dynamic emphasis of his single scene as the herdsman" (*Philadelphia Bulletin*, "Iphigenia in Tauris: Ancient Glories of Greek Drama's Golden Age," scrapbook on the Barker productions, Box 13, Archives of the University of Pennsylvania).
54. Dorizas later became a faculty member at the University of Pennsylvania and eventually donated his papers to the university archives, including a placard for the named talk at Lehigh University in March 1915.
55. McCarthy (1933) does not mention Barker's name once—because he would not allow it.
56. See Trewin 1967 for a reminiscence of McCarthy in recital as Iphigenia, a reference I owe to Hall 2013.
57. Wilder and Bryer 2008: 301. I am indebted to Judith Hallett for this reference.
58. *Boston Daily Globe* May 2, 1915, 59. The best seats for *Birth* were $2, the same as the Greek plays, while most other motion pictures topped out at 50 cents. Another ad on the same page announced Wagner's *Siegfried* for the Harvard Stadium on June 4.
59. An ad for some of Fitts's photographs, on sale at the Brick Row Print and Book Shop, appeared in the *Yale Daily News* June 14, 1915, but it is interesting to find no explicit mention of the *Iphigenia* volume or photographs, just one month after the performance.

References

Boston Daily Globe, "Greek Plays in the Stadium," May 16, 1915, 53.
Boston Daily Globe, "Greek Play in the Harvard Stadium," May 19, 1915, 8.
Boston Journal, "Wonders of Tauri Shown in Stadium," May 19, 1915, 5.
Christian Science Monitor, "Euripides at Cambridge," May 18, 1915, 4.
Christian Science Monitor, "The 'Iphigenia in Tauris' at the Harvard Stadium," May 19, 1915, 8.
Cook, W. M., J. A. Shipp, and P. L. Dunbar (1903), *In Dahomey: A Negro Musical Comedy*. London.
The Daily Princetonian, "Granville Barker in Talk on Greek Plays," June 5, 1915, 1.
The Daily Princetonian, "Scenes from the Greek Plays," June 5, 1915, 3.
Durham, W. B. (1987), *American Theatre Companies, 1888–1930*. New York and Westport, CT.
Elberson, S. D. (1968), *The Nature of Harley Granville Barker's Productions in America in 1915*. Diss. University of Oregon.
Foley, H. P. (2012), *Reimagining Greek Tragedy on the American Stage*. Berkeley, Los Angeles, and London.
Gauss, C. (1915), *Through College on Nothing a Year: Literally Recorded from a Student's Story*. New York.
Hains, D. D. (1910), "Greek Plays in America," *Classical Journal* 6, 24–39.
Hall, E. (2013), *Adventures with* Iphigenia in Tauris: *A Cultural History of Euripides' Black Sea Tragedy*. Oxford.
Hall, E. and F. Macintosh (2005), *Greek Tragedy and the British Theatre 1660–1914*. Oxford.
Hamilton, C. (1915), "Seen on the Stage," *Vogue*, July 1, 52–3, 82, 84 [text substantially reprinted 1939 in C. Hamilton, *The Theory of the Theatre* (New York), 408–13, without photographs].
Hartigan, K. V. (1995), *Greek Tragedy on the American Stage: Ancient Drama in the Commercial Theater, 1882–1994*. Westport, CT, and London.
Isaac, W. F. E. C. (1964), *Ben Greet and the Old Vic*. London.
Kennedy, D. (1985), *Granville Barker and the Dream of Theatre*. Cambridge.
Leiter, S. (1991), *From Belasco to Brook: Representative Directors of the English-Speaking Stage*. New York.
McCarthy, L. (1933), *Myself and My Friends*. New York.
Meeker, W. L. (1915), "Granville Barker's Greek Revivals," *Harvard Advocate* June 2, 128–9.
Moses, M. J. (1915), "The Stadium and the Greek Play," *The Independent Weekly Magazine* June 7, 394–8.
Nathan, G. J. (1915), "When Greek Meets Granville," in *Another Book on the Theater*. New York, 16–22.
New Haven Evening Register, "Greek Play in Bowl Most Novel Production Ever Attempted," May 9, 1915, 2.
New Haven Evening Register, "Greek Play in Yale Bowl Novel Event," May 15, 1915, 2.
New York Sun, "Irreverent Yale Freshmen Laugh on Seeing King Thoas in Greek Play," May 17, 1915.
New York Times, "Euripides Played in the Yale Bowl," May 16, 1915, sec. 2, 19.
New York Times, "Decorating Iphigenia," May 23, 1915.
New York Times, "Second Thoughts on First Nights," May 30, 1915, sec. 7, 8.
New York Times, "*Iphigenia in Tauris*," June 1, 1915, 15.
Pennsylvanian, "Plan Greek Play Spectacle Here," April 6, 1915.
Philadelphia Inquirer, "Theatre News of New York," May 23, 1915, 15.

Philadelphia Inquirer, "Gotham Theatre Gossip," May 30, 1915, 10.
Philadelphia Inquirer, "Euripides' Play Presented Here," June 9, 1915, 13.
Philadelphia Inquirer, "Ancient Greece, in Drama's Golden Age Made to Live Again," June 9, 1915, 13.
Philadelphia Public Ledger, "Ancient Greece, in Drama, to Live Again Here Today," June 8, 1915, 16.
Philadelphia Public Ledger, "Visual and Poetic Charm of Ancient Greek Drama Presented by Barker's Company before 8000 Persons in Botanic Gardens," June 9, 1915, 11.
Philadelphia Record, "Play by Euripides Seen at University," probably June 9, 1915.
Pluggé, D. E. (1938), *History of Greek Play Production in American Colleges and Universities from 1881 to 1936*. New York.
The Princeton Press, "Greek Play Translations," June 5, 1915, 3.
Purdom, C. B. (1955), *Harley Granville Barker, Man of the Theatre, Dramatist and Scholar*. London.
Salmon, E. (1986), *Granville Barker and his Correspondents: A Selection of Letters by Him and to Him*, edited and annotated. Detroit.
Slater, N. W. (2011), "Touring the Ivies with Iphigenia, 1915," *Comparative Drama* 44.5 and 45.1, Winter 2010/ Spring 2011, 441–55.
Smith, H. (1915), "The Revival of Greek Tragedy in America," *The Bookman: A Review of Books and Life* 41.4 (June), 409–16.
Stratton, C. (1916), "Greek Influence Upon the Stage," *Art and Archaeology* 3.5, 250–63.
Trewin, J. (1967), "Euripides in Modern Dress," *Illustrated London News*, No. 6669 (May 27), 39.
Wilder, R. and J. Bryer (eds. 2008), *Selected Letters of Thornton Wilder*. New York.
Wollaeger, M. A. (2001), "Woolf, Postcards, and the Elision of Race: Colonizing Women in *The Voyage Out*," *Modernism/modernity* 8, 43–75.
Yale Daily News, "Greek Drama on Modern Stage," May 14, 1915.
Yale Daily News, "Greek Play in Bowl," April 22, 1915.
Yale Daily News, "Iphigenia at 4:30," May 15, 1915.
Yale Daily News, "Iphigenia a Success," May 17, 1915.

CHAPTER 12

TREADING THE ARDUOUS ROAD TO ELEUSIS, NATIONALISM, AND FEMINISM IN EARLY POST-WORLD WAR I CANADA

Roy Mitchell's 1920 The Trojan Women

MOIRA DAY

THE year 1915 saw two significant productions of Euripides' *The Trojan Women* tour America. Slater has suggested that Granville Barker, who first produced *Trojan Women* in 1905, represented his American tour as an official part of the Allied war effort sanctioned by the British government because "war conditions were already making production of serious drama in London difficult, and the trip would help build good will for Britain in the officially neutral United States" (Slater, this volume, 166). Maurice Browne, who had first produced the play at the Chicago Little Theatre in 1913, took his own *Trojan Women* on an extensive thirty-one city tour westward, with the opposite hope: that his production of "The World's Greatest Peace Play" would "play its part" in reinforcing America's "pacifist and isolationist" stance as the fastest route to peace (Browne 1955: 178; Hartigan 1995: 17–19). Both productions reflected an upsurge of interest in Greek drama amidst an American theatrical scene that was both enriched by an enormous migration of British and European artists fleeing the war, and better able to adopt a chorus-like position of observation, reflection, and debate on the sidelines of the European conflict.

Significantly, Canada saw neither production. Unlike America, Canada declared war immediately in 1914 as a welcome chance, in the words of one young soldier, for our young nation to relearn, as Canadians and British subjects, the double lesson of "the old Greek legend [of the Greek states against the Persians] and the new colonial relationship with

Britain" which demanded a new egalitarian relationship in the face of a common enemy (Oliver 1917: 72). As with Britain, the seconding of transportation routes and modes of travel for the war effort and high male recruitment disrupted commercial touring circuits and local theater activity alike. By 1915, the year of the Granville Barker and Browne tours, there was little taste for Greek tragedy in Canada in any event. Young men expecting to fight their fathers' war—total Canadian casualties from the Boer War amounted to less than 300[1]—encountered chlorine gas in the Second Battle of Ypres in April, 1915, leaving Canadian casualties of 6,035 with 2,000 dead.[2] Worse was to follow in 1916 with 24,713 Canadians perishing in the ultimately futile Battle of the Somme (Roy 2012: n.p.).

Canadians seeking classical inspiration in response to the horrors of war were inclined to construct themselves less as spectators of tragedy than as heroic Greeks active in an epic theater of martial destiny. In 1916, Saskatchewan's E. H. Oliver proclaimed, "Once again Athens goes forth to Marathon. The Muses march with Mars ... We are students of the Western Universities and heirs to Athens" (Oliver 1917: 70–3). In coupling these two seemingly incongruous concepts, Oliver was expanding on a common trope in the student newspapers of the time: that the Canadian soldier marching to war in 1916 against the Germans had similar historic and mythic dimensions to the ancient Greek soldier marching to the Battle of Marathon in 490 BCE against the Persians. More than that, having "awoke—in the wilderness" from the dream that the dawning century would usher in "a millennium of peace," it was university students, wrote Alberta's A. L. Burt, confronted with the chaos of "old forms of religion dissolving and government discredited by incompetence and corruption," who best understood, as the "leaders of tomorrow," the need to fight for and preserve the best of the classical heritage—with all that meant of living and interpreting life as "a work of art" (Burt 1917: 17–19).

Both men, in turn, were drawing on a tradition going back to the seventeenth century, of using classical imagery and drama to evoke emerging concepts of Canadian nationhood and cultural aspiration in the face of hostile outward forces and an overwhelming experience of "wilderness." *The Theatre of Neptune in the New World*, a short masque written by French colonist Marc Lescarbot, and performed on the waves of Port Royal (now Nova Scotia) in 1606, did more than mark the beginnings of European playwriting in North America. With its representation of Neptune and his tritons appearing to bless the endeavors of Sieur de Poutrincourt, the French governor, "[i]n this new world" (Lescarbot 1982: 39), it also marked the advent of a distinctively Canadian tradition of neoclassicism as well.

Created to celebrate the delayed return of a failed expedition down the Atlantic seaboard to find a warmer home, the play was even more profoundly an inspired attempt, on the eve of a third horrendous Canadian winter, to strike a vision of soaring transcendent destiny, ardent cultural identity, and inspiring Nature out of a profound experience of fear, uncertainty, and loss. The masque, like the naming of the new region "Acadia," was to be only one of many dramatic manifestations of a deeply felt European need to impose some degree of classical order, form, structure, and familiarity on what was perceived as the chaotic darkness of a land and climate that were terrifyingly un-Grecian.

That such enterprises could prove fragile, quixotic, and absurd is indicated by the fact that less than a year after Neptune had bid de Poutrincourt,

> go forth joyously and follow the path
> Where destiny guides you, because I see Fate
> Preparing a flourishing Empire for France
> In this new world, (Lescarbot 1982: 39)

the colony dissolved and returned to France. Similarly, the occasional productions of Jean Racine's *Mithridate* and Pierre Corneille's *Le Cid* and *Nicomède* in the new colony of Québec between 1608 and 1694 did little to ward off the Fall of Québec in 1760 that finished any hope of the pan-American "Empire for France" Neptune had promised. That classical production could also paradoxically be a powerful tool in sustaining visions of national and cultural destiny in the face of threatened extinction is argued by the fact that 1760 only marked the beginning of an effective long-term campaign of classical education, including the study and presentation of Molière, Racine, and Corneille within the school and college system of Québec, to preserve a distinct cultural, linguistic, and national identity in the midst of an overwhelming anglophone hegemony.[3]

English Canadian neoclassicism, especially in the post-Confederation years between 1867 and 1900, was surprisingly similar in its use of the Classics to create a distinct cultural and national identity defined by a perceived heroic winnowing of the national character through its ecstatic though terrifying encounters with the vast, frozen wilderness and an enduring, voluntary kinship with a physically and temporally distant continental "homeland." It was also marked by a fierce determination to resist assimilation by an overwhelming anglophone hegemony—in this case the United States—seen as foreign and antithetical to national aspirations. As Confederation poet Wilfred Campbell eloquently expressed it, the sublime spirit that had lit the drama of Periclean Greece and had been reborn in Shakespeare and the great age of Elizabethan drama would most truly manifest itself next not in the "clever or sensational" but spiritually bankrupt commercial theater of America, but in British North America, where the true cultural, racial, and historical heirs of Shakespeare were still potentially capable of "such drama . . . which opens eternally doors of hope into that future morning of the universe toward which our best ideals are trending" (Campbell 1907: 17).

By the late nineteenth century, the University of Toronto (1827) actually *was* aspiring to assume the laurel as the "Athens of Canada" by mounting its own ancient-language productions of Greek tragedy. In 1881, Maurice Hutton, a newly appointed Professor of Classics, late of Oxford, proposed partnering with the newly founded University College Glee Club (1879) to perform a joint faculty/student production of Sophocles' *Antigone* in the original Greek, with translations provided by Hutton, and music for the Glee Club chorus adapted from Mendelssohn and rehearsed by Professor Ramsay Wright. The production was successfully launched on the small Convocation Hall stage in April 1882, with an all-male cast (women not being admitted to the university until 1884) led by the 26-year-old Hutton himself in the role of Antigone (Fig. 12.1) (Averill 1986: 1–2, 14, 17–18).

FIG. 12.1 Professor Maurice Hutton as Antigone in 1882 University of Toronto production of Sophocles' *Antigone*—(A73-0003/001) University of Toronto Archives.

The production illustrated the ideals of Canadian neoclassicism on almost every significant point. By connecting Canada into the string of nations—including Germany, France, England, and the United States—that had done significant productions of *Antigone* in the second half of the nineteenth century, it also brought Toronto into mystical communion with the play's perceived universal plea for the creation of moral community (Macintosh 1997: 284–323). More immediately, Toronto's *Antigone* further established and reinforced Canada's bonds of cross-Atlantic kinship not only with the larger international art movement abroad, but quite consciously, with the "rush of philhellenism particularly marked in Britain at the end of the nineteenth century" (Macintosh 1997: 292), which led to university-based productions of *Agamemnon* (in translation) at Edinburgh and (in ancient Greek) at Oxford in spring 1880.

At the same time, the Toronto *Antigone* was also consciously represented as a manifestation of the tough, northern Canadian spirit's ability to strike the sublime out of the most austere, difficult material circumstances in a way unprecedented by older (British) or better-monied (American) productions. Even the [London] *Spectator* rhapsodized,

> It is necessary to use the strongest terms consistent with the truth to impress on our readers the paradox that the best Greek play ever acted in the Empire should have been produced in Upper Canada, in a mushroom university.[4]

Of the *Oedipus Tyrannus* produced at Harvard in spring 1881, he could only comment that he could not really compare the two North American productions not having seen the *Oedipus*, but was sure that since the latter had more than four times the budget of the Canadian production, "we imagine that whatever money could do was better done in Boston."[5]

Having preceded by many months the 1882 Cambridge and Notre Dame original-Greek-language productions of *Ajax* and *Oedipus* respectively, as well as the transfer of the Harvard *Oedipus* to Broadway,[6] Toronto signalled its intention to consolidate its reputation as the Athens of the North, by producing its own *Oedipus* in 1883 (Averill 1986: 2, 14). Sadly, Toronto also proved true to the Canadian classical tradition in striking an exultant, ambitious vision that soon stumbled over a lack of human and physical resources to sustain it. Not until 1894, with the help of the recently formed Classical Association of University College, was Hutton able to surpass his 1882 *Antigone* with a far more lavish original-Greek-language production of the same play (Averill 1986: 2, 14, 18–19). In addition to providing audiences with a more elaborate program and translation of the libretto (also printed for wider distribution), the university moved the production, featuring both a larger and much more experienced Glee Club as the chorus and a splendid set of scenery that had been used previously in a production of *Antigone* in the States, into the far more spacious and well-equipped Academy of Music.[7] Despite the American set, the metonymic relationship between Periclean Athens, British Empire, and Canada was powerfully reinforced in the theater by the attendance of Governor-General and Lady Aberdeen, the vice-regal representatives of the Queen in Canada, transforming the 1894 production into a social and political as well as artistic triumph (Fig. 12.2).[8]

Little wonder, then, that at least one Canadian university president, almost 25 years later, could confidently draw on that same metonymy to assert that in a time of deepening global crisis, when the social and political order that Britain and Canada represented was threatened, it was more important than ever that the universities at home serve as "Athens." Their critical role was to preserve not just the letter but the spirit of that gentler, more ordered world of the humanities, languages, and arts that was key "to the British reverence for individual liberty . . . and humanity," that had so far saved Canadians "as a people" from the tragic Teutonic tendency toward totalitarianism (Murray 1918: 8). If it was the duty of the men to fight to defend that heritage abroad through martial action,

FIG. 12.2 1894 University of Toronto production of Sophocles' *Antigone*. Antigone (Charlotte Hunter) is condemned by Creon (K. D. MacMillan). Borrowed American set in background. Academy of Music, Toronto.—(A73-0003/009) University of Toronto Archives.

it was the equally important responsibility of those remaining, and of women in particular, to preserve within the halls of higher learning that vital humanistic tradition of culture, art, and learning going back to the Greeks.

Following in the footsteps of the first woman B.A. in the British Empire (Grace Annie Lockhart, Mount Allison, 1875), Canadian co-eds were very much aware, in the words of a 1912 Alberta student, that while their British sisters had had to battle "nine hundred and fifty years of masculine tradition" to gain entrance at Oxford and Cambridge and even now could only attend lectures, Canadian women, by contrast, had the progressiveness of "this new country where we ourselves are forming the traditions" to thank for not only being able to attend classes alongside the male students, but graduate beside them with the same degrees.[9] In that sense, the five female University of Toronto students in the 1894 *Antigone*—Charlotte Hunter (Antigone), Evelyn Durand (Ismene), Christine Steen (Eurydice), Florence Neelands and Agnes Burnham (Maids of Honor)—were very much conspicuous by their presence, and part of an accelerating trend after 1884 toward women exerting an influence on campus disproportionate to their numbers (Ford 1985: 19). Despite some early stirrings of co-ed drama in the 1894 *Antigone*, the alumni associations, and Modern Languages Club, dramatic societies at Toronto (unlike their prairie counterparts which were co-ed from the start) still tended to be divided along gender lines, with the women's groups emerging as the most successful. Out of their activities, and particularly those of the University Women's Dramatic Club (1905) under Mrs. Emma Scott Raff, notes Robert Scott, "developed those qualities which were to make the University a major drama centre" (Scott 1966: i. 146).

Between 1914 and 1918 that influence exploded, not only in Toronto but right across the country as university men—often the quickest to enlist by reason of their age, health, education, idealism, and relative lack of family and essential industry commitments—streamed overseas, leaving behind highly feminized campuses dominated by female leadership, a pattern that was also very much apparent at the University of Toronto and its affiliated religious colleges. In comparison to 1914 when women had constituted less than a quarter of the Methodist Victoria College population, by 1918, almost two-thirds—191 of the 331—of the Victoria students were women (Semple 1996: 414). The only serious masculine challenge to the domination of the older women's groups, the Players' Club, organized in 1913 to accommodate male students, graduates, and staff of the University of Toronto with a similar interest in "specialising exclusively upon plays whose nature makes them unsuited to performance in the down-town theatres,"[10] dissolved for the durance. So great was the demand on the University Women's Dramatic Club resources, that yet another all-women's dramatic society, the Victoria College Women's Dramatic Club, was formed in 1917 and was soon offering a full program of one-acts and a large spring play each year. Between fall 1914 and spring 1919, 36 of the 56 recorded productions on the Toronto campus featured all-women casts.[11]

On October 17, 1919, the Victoria College Women's Dramatic Club produced *Twelfth Night*, their first full-length Shakespearian production, to celebrate the return of the veterans. As portrayed by an all-women cast, including the Club president, Elizabeth Sterling, as Orsino, the play's lyrical, romantic pastoral spirit, and faith in the powers of life, love, and order to prevail over those of confusion and death may have strongly captured the mood of the moment; at least one veteran found the production and the tea that followed inexpressibly poignant and moving for precisely that reason (J.C.M. 1919: 92–3). By the time the war ended in 1918, almost a third of the 611,711 Canadians (out of a small population of 7,879,000) who had enlisted had either been killed (56,638) or wounded (141,148).[12] The only way to justify such unprecedented sacrifice, it was argued, was if it finally did usher in that "millennium of peace" (Burt 1917: 17–19) in which "the soul of mankind energized by the sense of achievement and purified in its ideals" (Sullivan 1918: 165–7) would reinherit the earth. Again, the ancient Greeks at Marathon, argued a Saskatchewan student, indicated the path for post-war Canada to follow with the universities leading the way:

> Greek history perhaps gives us an instance of national inspiration after the successful termination of a war. If the Greeks had failed in the momentous years of the struggle against Persia the history of the Western world and the character of its civilization would have been completely changed. Their achievement in the field of war was a great one, and it was followed by a correspondingly great achievement in art and literature. The noble architecture of the succeeding Periclean Age and its perfection in literature and art may have been another expression of the same spirit that won victory against countless odds. (Sullivan 1918: 165–7)

Canadian women, having swept in women's suffrage in six of the nation's then-nine provinces and federally in just two years (1916–18), were left to envision their own role in this "succeeding Periclean Age." Knowing they had gained their unique "opportunity to come forward and show themselves to be of equal value to their country economically as well as intellectually" only at a fearful cost to their male colleagues, some co-eds argued that the only way to repay the debt was to "take this advantage and use it to the utmost, so that in the coming days we may be capable and efficient co-workers in the great business of life."[13] The question of what roles women and men were to play in the new "drama" about to unfold was already in a state of considerable flux as the final curtain dropped on *Twelfth Night* in October of 1919.

It was out of a desire to both honor that sacrifice and celebrate the rising hope that post-war Canada, having passed through the valley of the shadow of death, was now treading the ardent road to Eleusis, feminism, and nationalism on the way to its own Periclean Age, that Roy Mitchell's landmark production of *The Trojan Women* seized the stage at Hart House Theatre at the University of Toronto in March, 1920.

Mitchell's chief justification for "the choice of *The Trojan Women* of Euripides as the first Greek play of the Player's Club"—that it "was in many regards the most modern of Euripides' tragedies, and lends itself best to modern methods of staging"[14]—was deceptively simple. If Hutton had connected Canada to the larger Zeitgeist and international art movement of the nineteenth century through Sophocles, then the brilliant, charismatic Mitchell was eminently the man to accomplish the same feat for twentieth-century Canada through Euripides. Born to Canadian parents in Michigan in 1884, he attended the University of Toronto (1903–6) before doing a 13-year stint of newspaper work in the States and Canada, which involved his being "constantly in or around the theatres as press agent, dramatic critic and dramatic editor" (Mitchell 1929: viii). It was a background that left Mitchell enormously knowledgeable not only of "popular theatrical and entertainment fare," but the "latest innovations from continental Europe and England and New York" (Stoesser 2007: 40) as he began to conduct his first experiments with art theater production under the aegis of the Arts and Letters Club (1909–15) and associated Players' Club (1913–15).

With the closing of the Players' Club in 1915, Mitchell gravitated to New York. While he worked briefly as a stage manager on Broadway, he spent most of the war in Greenwich Village at a time when three of New York's most famous art theaters, the Neighborhood Playhouse and the Washington Square and Provincetown Players, were producing their most influential work, including the early plays of Eugene O'Neill and Susan Glaspell. Mitchell was also there when influential British and European artists such as Granville Barker, Jacques Copeau, Max Reinhardt, Joseph Urban, and the Irish Players were resident in New York. Consequently, Stoesser concludes, Mitchell's tenure in New York as a practicing director and designer coincided not only with the rise of the American art theater, but "with the introduction of Europe's New Stagecraft" via some of the Continent's most influential designers, directors, and actors (Stoesser 2007: 68). While it is unlikely that Mitchell saw Browne's *Trojan Women*, he did see Granville Barker's, and given his enthusiasm for the British director's entire New York season, was almost certainly influenced by the 1915 production in his own choice of the play (Stoesser 2007: 75–8; Stoesser 2013a: n.p.).

Mitchell's own career in the American art theater movement culminated in his appointment as founding technical director for the new Greenwich Village Theatre over 1917–18. Unfortunately, the company faltered financially, but Mitchell returned to a post-war Canada that now held an exciting opportunity for him to apply in Toronto everything he had learnt abroad. In 1917, he was commissioned by Vincent Massey to design a state-of-the-art theater for the new Hart House building being endowed by the Masseys as a gift to the Toronto campus, and Mitchell devoted much of 1918–19, when he wasn't working as Director of Motion Pictures for the Department of Public Information, to overseeing its completion in anticipation of becoming its first artistic director (Stoesser 2007: 98–157).

Mitchell's choice of *Trojan Women* as Euripides at his most modern in spirit and staging may be relatively clear. However, in drawing attention to the fact that this was the first Greek play done by the Players' Club, he subtly reminded audiences that it was also the first major Greek tragedy to be performed at Toronto in 26 years, and the first full-length classical play in 18. In addressing the question of *why*, Mitchell's *Trojan Women* ended up becoming, no less than Hutton's *Antigones*, an extraordinary assertion of Canadian nationalism, cultural aspiration, and what was perceived as its uniquely luminescent Nordic spirit.

The hiatus in production even before the war may seem strange at a time when American productions of Greek plays were proliferating on both the academic and commercial stage, and at least one other University of Toronto production had not hesitated to draw on American expertise and resources to improve their production quality. Instead, *The Return of Odysseus* in 1900, a fundraising event sponsored by the Classical Association of University College and the Woman's Residence Association, and directed by Mabel Hay Barrows of Boston, and a lively outdoor production of Aristophanes' *The Frogs* performed by Trinity College students in the grounds of the College to celebrate its Jubilee in 1902, were the only Greek plays or adaptations staged beyond 1894.[15]

One factor, entering the twentieth century, was a strengthening of the longstanding identification of English-Canadians as British North Americans fed by a nostalgic desire to hold on to the familiar in a rapidly changing age, and events like the Boer War (1899–1902) which saw 7,000 Canadians, including 12 women nurses, voluntarily join the British forces.[16] Between 1900 and 1914, much of University of Toronto "high culture" tended to center around productions of Shakespeare—by Campbell's reasoning, Canada's best classical *and* national playwright by reason of a shared British heritage, descended in turn from the Greeks—with occasional ventures into later British playwrights, such as Hannah Cowley, Sheridan, and Barrie (Averill 1986: 3–5). Later touring artists took their cue from the Ben Greet Players, who gave Toronto "its first open-air performances of Shakespearean plays" on campus in 1903 using student players in bit parts, and who were warmly welcomed back in 1905, 1906, and 1908 (Averill 1986: 3). Sir John Martin-Harvey, John Kellard, Harley Granville Barker, and even Canadian-born Margaret Anglin, may all have made their reputations on notable productions of Greek plays in the States, but they toured Shakespeare when they came to Canada.

Another factor was material. Greek tragedy production, especially if it aimed at approximating original performance conditions and spaces, was not only time-consuming, but labor-intensive, expensive, and technically demanding. Even the nearby Margaret Eaton School of Literature and Expression, again founded by Mrs. Scott Raff, in 1901 to give female students a sound classical training that exposed them to Delsarte movement, and Greek theater in study and production in their own neo-Grecian temple, did not venture into full-scale public production of Greek plays.[17] Similarly, the Arts and Letters Club, even at its most innovative, tended to gravitate toward the production of one-act plays as much for pragmatic as for aesthetic reasons. Scott suggests that "the leadership of theatre in the community" may have passed into the hands of the university dramatic clubs by the end of the war years. However, while the University of Toronto boasted the highest concentration of dramatic societies adhering to the Little Theatre principles of experimentation, "it was impossible under war-time conditions and amid the crowded, inadequate facilities at the University to operate efficiently" (Scott 1966: i. 251).

The third is that for a complex of reasons, Greek theater production became implicitly associated with the American cultural imperialism. The absurdity of "Athens" trying to function without a theater was further exacerbated by a deepening isolation of the university art theater from the human and technical resources of the professional theater in the city that was not wholly born of artistic idealism. Even by 1882, the collapse in the 1870s of the last Toronto-based resident stock company run by a Canadian manager, Clara Morrison (Shortt 1989: 349), would have made it difficult for the Toronto *Antigone* to follow the same route as the Harvard *Oedipus* to a second life on the professional stage of its own country. According to Gardiner, even the more flexible arrangements that had allowed local managers to book productions like the 1894 *Antigone* or 1900 *Return of Odysseus* between the dominant stream of touring productions from Britain and the United States began to disappear with the arrival of the New York theatrical syndicate in 1896, which was much more aggressive about protecting its monopoly against potential competition (Gardiner 2009: 202–32).

Noted Montréal theater critic Bernard K. Sandwell was only one of many who railed against a foreign, commercial touring theater, manifested at its worst in the Shuberts, that had prevented Canadians from developing a national theater commensurate with the vision, resources, and socio-political ambitions of their young nation. He took the protest of "an intelligent young Toronto girl" as embodying "the protest of a young nation against the state of its stage." To embrace a successful professional career in the theater, she complained,

> I must go to a foreign country in order even to get an engagement . . . to make New York my headquarters, go the rounds of the New York managers, rehearse in New York, act the plays that New York wants, and by the time I get anywhere in the profession everybody, myself included, will have forgotten that I was ever a Canadian. It isn't fair! (Sandwell 1996: 17)

Sandwell might well have been thinking of Canada-born and -raised Margaret Anglin when he further commented, "as painter, as writer, as musician, as sculptor, as poet she could have held an honoured place in the community and help build up the culture of the nation to which she belonged. Only as actress was she obliged to expatriate herself" (Sandwell 1996: 17). In other words, how could a Canadian rejoice in Anglin's remarkable 1910 *Antigone* at Berkeley without simultaneously being aware of all the reasons that she had had to leave Canada to *become* Margaret Anglin, and why, even 30 years after its own *Antigone*, Toronto was still not capable of being her Athens? It was not a stance calculated to encourage further cooperation between American and Canadian universities on classical productions, especially since it could be argued that American cultural aggression was one of the reasons Toronto still lacked the resources to easily follow Cambridge or Oxford's lead in regularly producing its own Greek plays.

Mitchell's production of Euripides at Hart House Theatre addressed every single factor in some respect. The new theater, boasting a stage capacious enough for a cast of 70, as well as its own workshop, scenic studio, and one of the most complete light boards in North America, not only housed the returning Arts and Letters, and Players' Club members now synthesized into the reorganized Players' Club, but placed the vanguard of Canada's reawakening Little Theatre movement squarely in the middle of the University of Toronto campus. At last, the "Athens of Canada" had a "noble architecture" commensurate with its Periclean ambitions to achieve the kind of "perfection in literature and art" represented by Euripides. While the building of Hart House had gone too far to provide the new theater with a fly gallery, in every other way, noted the *Toronto Star* it had "no superior among the little theatres of the continent":

> Its stage equipment is particularly complete, and those who have charge of it believe that in this regard it surpasses any other art theatre in America, most of which are private enterprises, backed by amateurs with artistic theatrical ideals. Some of the devices in the Toronto theatre have been modelled upon the apparatus of the famous little theatres of Europe and they are being installed for the first time on this side of the Atlantic.[18]

The other two points were addressed by Mitchell's unique fusion of an equally fervent passion for theosophy, theater, and nationalism incorporated in various ways into the production. Foley, in discussing the 1898–1927 Greek productions of American theosophist Katharine Tingley, suggests that the theosophical movement, founded in 1875 "to discover universal, esoteric truths from the religious and occult traditions from many world cultures," also helped inspire avant-garde approaches to Greek tragedy in Europe (Foley 2012: 42–3). She might well have added Canada to the list as well. While Stoesser suggests that there is nothing to indicate that Mitchell saw or was directly influenced by Tingley's productions (Stoesser 2013b: n.p.), Moore, Usmiani, and Duchesne have strongly documented the impact of the Toronto Theosophical Society (1891) on his work after 1909, and of the lively circle of theosophical thinkers, artists, musicians, and theater practitioners active in both the Arts and Letters and Players' Club (Duchesne 2006: 227–44; Moore 1974: 689–71; Usmiani 1987: 147–68).

There is little doubt that Mitchell's theosophical philosophy, especially as reflected in his masterpiece *Creative Theatre* (1929), reverberated strongly with post-war imagery calling for the rebirth of the world spirit and a new millennium of peace and brotherhood. But while he may have accepted Campbell's assessment of Shakespeare as one of those prophets capable of opening the door, in communion with others, to "the living soul of man" (Mitchell 1929: 189), he strongly disagreed with the evolutionary view that that revelation had culminated in and found its highest expression to date in Elizabethan England. Acknowledging "that drama has always been first of the methods of revelation" also meant learning "to see Shakespeare and Kalidasa as prophets no less than John and Isaiah, and to say that Aeschylus, no less than Enoch, walked with God" (Mitchell 1929: 124). Mitchell's choice of a Greek tragedy as the fourth bill of a seven-play season that included Dunsany, Jonson, Hastings, medieval farce, and mystery plays as well as Shakespeare was a way of affirming that Euripides no less than Shakespeare or Aeschylus walked toward Eleusis.

While disappointed in his intent to also present "a bill of three original plays" (Anon. 1920: 30–1), his vision of a season that also included Canadian plays acknowledged the truth that one of the purposes of a "Periclean Age" was "to build with native stone, to carve in native woods" (Mitchell 1929: 143), a truly Canadian theater in the image of the spiritually ecstatic theater of the ancient Greeks "free from the prejudices and trammells (sic) of the commercial stage."[19] From where he stood, he could see two different roads leading to two completely different theaters:

> One is the theatre of the barrel-organ and a monkey whose master knows only enough to yank the rope when he sees a penny somewhere else. The other is older. It is a dim, distant theatre in a village at the end of the Sacred Road outside Athens. It was called the Theatre of the Earth Mother. One did not say of that theatre, "I think I'll run out to Eleusis to-night and see what they are doing". One said "if I am patient and worthy, please God, I shall one day be admitted to that theatre". Emperors, kings, poets, philosophers came to it from all over the world. . . . Its theme was the vicissitudes and triumph of the soul of man. It called its director a Hierophant, a revealer of sacred elements in life. When I think of that theatre all things seem possible. (Mitchell 1929: 256)

By explicitly identifying the first theater with the American commercial stage as the spiritual descendant of the expensive and cynical bread-and-circuses entertainment of the Roman Empire, Mitchell left Canadians free to position themselves as the Greeks in the narrative. Mitchell himself might not have ruled out the possibility of the second road *eventually* leading to a professional art theater, but interwar Canadian idealists—including Massey—committed to the ideal of an amateur art theater operating at professional standards that would function nationally as the Dominion Drama Festival (1933–70), were willing to press the Greek analogy even further. Was it not true that the greatest of western tragedies had been *originally* composed with minimum design requirements, for dedicated and exceptionally well-trained *non-professional* performers drawn largely from the general populace who appeared largely at great civic festivals (Haynes n.d.: n.p.)?

If the Canadian Euripides had yet to emerge in 1920, Mitchell was more fortunate in drawing together a circle of Canadian musicians and artists willing to work with him to create *mise-en-scène* that hinted at the spiritual dimensions beneath "native stone" and "native woods." Significantly, many of his sets were designed by key members—A. Y. Jackson, Lawren Harris (a fellow theosophist), J. E. H. MacDonald, and Arthur Lismer—of the Group of Seven, a well-known school of Canadian art that captured the essence of the Canadian wilderness in luminescent, mystical, expressionistic painting (Stoesser 2007: 221–2).

While Mitchell's choice of *Trojan Women* as the first all-student, co-ed production of the first Hart House season may have been intended to honour the "voice" of women in war as well as the female "Muses" who had upheld the torch of the humanities at home in the absence of "Mars,"[20] it may also have been predicated by practicality: the greatest body of experienced student actors were still women. Unfortunately, the technical progressiveness of the new theater overlaid a deeply entrenched gender division that likely owed more to Oxford than to Greenwich Village. Constructed by the Masseys as "an experimental theater for the use of the University of Toronto and the wider community which it serves,"[21] Hart House Theatre tried to balance between being a home for the various student groups on campus, and a center for the broader, more community-based Players' Club. While the latter, as the "senior dramatic club of the University," had certain privileges including the care of the immensely costly lighting system, which would be handled by a carefully trained staff "of undergraduate technicians," it was stressed that every student "should realise that this theatre has been built for him or her" and that Mitchell, the director of the Players' Club, would "at all times be ready to consult and assist in any way desired in the production of any play."[22] In practice, there was little room for female undergraduates in the formal training and production structure of Hart House Theatre. While it was the stated aim of the Players' Club "to act its own plays (with assistance of ladies from other organizations),"[23] it was also made clear that actual membership remained limited to "men, graduates, undergraduates, and staff of the University of Toronto."[24] Even the "carefully trained" undergraduate technical crew were drawn completely from male students. It was also stated that consistent with Hart House Theatre's status as a high quality experimental art theater, Mitchell would be working mostly with "more experienced men and women from downtown" in his productions (Montagnes 1969: 106).

Nonetheless, there are indications that Mitchell had started to work informally with the Toronto women, and the Victoria Club in particular, as early as 1917–18. It seems hardly coincidental that both the Gerstenberg (*Overtones*) and Moeller (*Helena's Husband*) one-acts produced by the Victoria in 1918 were originally staged in New York art theaters that Mitchell frequented at that time, and that the Club's choice of Dunsany's *The Gods of the Mountains* followed Mitchell's own major New York production of Dunsany's *The Tents of the Arabs* in 1917. Quite possibly, speculates Stoesser, "Mitchell advised on all three of these plays" as well as the club's all-women production of *The Tents of the Arabs* in 1919–20 (Stoesser 2007: 256). Mitchell's estimation of the talent of the Victoria Club is demonstrated in the fact that while two-thirds of the chorus were recruited from University College ranks, the three female leads, Hecuba, Cassandra, and Andromache (the scene between Helen and Menelaus was cut), were all recruited from Victoria College, Elizabeth Sterling assuming the pivotal role of Hecuba. It was the first time in her four university years that the tall, big-boned, baritone-voiced young woman had been cast in a female role. Perhaps sharing Granville Barker's concern about "performance technicalities of verse handling in the relatively static dramatic situation," Mitchell also appears to have engaged in an unusually lengthy rehearsal period; Stoesser has suggested that the presence of *The Queen's Enemy* set in the background of the *Trojan Women* rehearsal photo (Fig. 12.3), indicates that the cast was already deeply into work on the play by November 1919 (Stoesser 2013a: n.p.).

The production opened on March 4, 1920 to glowing reviews that acknowledged that for an audience to whom the horrors of the recent war—and the memories of "many such Hecubas, Cassandras and Andromaches" (Charlesworth 1920: 6)—were still vivid, the ancient play in the Gilbert Murray translation presented a timeless human tragedy with an acutely felt poignancy and power that was only enhanced by the sublimity of Mitchell's carefully orchestrated *mise-en-scène*. Arthur Lismer of the Group of Seven designed "massive settings" set in "half light" to suggest the size and somber atmosphere

FIG. 12.3 Image of Hart House 1920 rehearsal for the *Trojan Women*: Elizabeth Sterling standing; left background, Roy Mitchell. Charity Mitchell. Set pieces (grate) from *The Queen's Enemies* in background. James & Son Photographers, 1920. York University Libraries, Clara Thomas Archives and Special Collections, Roy Matthews Mitchell fonds, ASC05341.

of "the walls of an ancient town."²⁵ Healey Willan, later the Dean of Canadian composers, was called on to compose and direct music for the choral interludes "based on the rhythmic principle of plain song as the first step in a new effort to reconstruct the Greek method of delivering the lines." To both, Mitchell added his mastery of color and lighting to complete his conception of the play as "a dramatic poem with colour and tone backgrounds."²⁶

By all accounts, it was a compelling practical demonstration of Mitchell's concept of theater as an art "filling the senses with form and sound" in motion, thus "stirring the emotions to sympathy, and shaping ideas to one intense accord" (Mitchell 1929: 6). Mitchell was also warmly congratulated by both Charlesworth and *Globe* critic E. R. Parkhurst, for getting performances of remarkable "emotional intensity" and sustained "dramatic values" from inexperienced actresses confronted with dense scenes of poetic text "calculated to afright—or intrigue—the most experienced tragedienne" (Parkhurst 1920: 8). Even when "their readings lacked music and tonal volume," Charlesworth noted, Mitchell "managed to make his women give a feeling of intense emotion to their utterances" (Charlesworth 1920: 6). Amidst Mitchell's dark somber Troy of looming walls, choral chant interludes, deep shadow, crimson splashes, and striking shafts of light illuminating tableaux and high points of action, Elizabeth Sterling's deeply moving portrayal of the play's central figure was perceived as shining with particular brilliance:

> The effectiveness of the presentation was largely due to the excellence of Miss Elizabeth Sterling, who played Hecuba, Queen of Troy. Miss Sterling made a striking figure of the wife of Priam, and she has a voice that is a wonderful asset. It is not often one hears an inexperienced actress speak her part with dignity and a fine sweep of emotional feeling. It was such an outstanding piece of acting that one almost hesitates to suggest that if Miss Sterling had secured a crescendo, instead of keying the whole performance so high, she would have reached a more gripping climax. She made the scene of the body of the murdered child of Hector the great moment of the play, and there was less emphasis upon the scene of utter desolation when the city is destroyed, However, no one dreamt that Toronto contained an actress who could do the role of Hecuba half so well.²⁷

More than that, commented the same critic, the production to a remarkable degree had caught in an extraordinary moment of magic and power, a vision of what the Canadian theater in such a Periclean Age could and should be:

> Hart House Theatre has brought more than arts to Toronto. It cannot but indirectly help in establishing a Canadian drama free from the mastery of New York. . . . an Art Theatre free from the prejudices and trammels of the commercial stage has also come into being. It will fill the void left by the regular theatre and will make an appeal for which the intelligent public have been long waiting.²⁸

No less than Hutton's 1882 and 1894 *Antigone*, Mitchell's 1920 *Trojan Women* attempted to stake Canada's claim as the "Athens" of the north through a strategic production of Greek tragedy that also became a site of national aspirations and dreams. But regardless of its power, Mitchell's effort was also ultimately as fleeting in its realization as the performance itself. The impact on the 18 young women drawn from across the university to directly and communally express, within the full resources of the theater, a female voice of rage, despair, grief, and mourning over the devastating human cost of war, can be judged from Elizabeth Sterling (Haynes)'s frequent crediting of *Trojan Women* as the road to Damascus experience that set her on the path to becoming a seminal force in the emerging Western Canadian theater. Yet, if it was the greatest moment of triumph for the all-women dramatic societies, it was also their swan song; virtually all of them, and the era of female theatrical dominance and early aspiring feminism on campus that they represented, were gone by the early 1920s (Averill 1986: 7).

As for the hope that *Trojan Women* presaged the advent of a "Canadian drama free from the mastery of New York," an ominous note was sounded by the *Acta Victoriana* reviewer: the production itself may have been "excellent and the acting far above the average of the amateur play"—but that did not alter the fact that "the character of the play itself" made it less than "suitable for production by University students." First, he regarded the emotional intensity required by such roles as Hecuba as being potentially dangerous to inexperienced young actors. Euripides didn't seem to "recognize the need of relief from an emotional strain" and introduced "neither humor nor comedy . . . although these are not foreign to war" or to the great Shakespearean tragedies. Secondly, in an educational context, he felt that "dramatic performances valuable as they are, should be nevertheless secondary to the discipline of study" and that "shorter plays . . . train more students and do not exact from any one an abnormal period of preparation."[29] The reviewer's call for a return to Shakespeare and short plays is less alarming than his astute intuiting that Hart House's success, while impressive, was building on conflicting and possibly irreconcilable goals. It was an art theater housed in a university without any adequate mechanism for safely and consistently training students to meet its high standards. Yet Hart House's commitment to functioning as a combination community and educational theater prevented it from developing into the kind of professional art theater that Mitchell had encountered in the States. Mitchell left the theater after only two years; returning to America in 1927, he served on the faculty of New York University from 1930 until his death in 1944. In 1954, over 30 years after *Trojan Women* and another war later, Canadian critic Nathan Cohen sardonically commented that in terms of a professional theater created out of native wood and stone, Canada was obviously still awaiting "the coming of this Periclean Age" (Edmonstone 1977: 218).

The road to "Eleusis"—the hope for life after death—remained something more elusive. Like the 1606 masque, Mitchell's 1920 *Trojan Women* also struck a vision of soaring transcendent destiny, ardent cultural identity, and inspiring Nature out of a profound experience of fear, uncertainty, and loss. However, as Burt had suggested, in the absence of the exalted belief in "moral community" that had sustained the nineteenth-century *Antigones*, the wilderness was now a spiritual rather than a geographical one. Emerging from that darkness into the first Armistice Day was to experience an incredible ecstasy, that in the remembering, noted an Alberta student, "even now is to make a draft upon feelings and imagination that exhausts them and still fails to satisfy"—an intensity of joy, relief, and exhilarating lightness rendered all the more poignant by the utter disillusionment of only three years later:

We are living in times when the very name of war is overshadowed by the aftermath of economic disturbance, national beggary and unemployment.

Beyond the heights of ecstasy and idealism, and the depths of depression and disillusionment, lay the arduous road to the profound wisdom and redemption of shared pain:

> It appears as if the common suffering of the war and also after the war has been a factor in banishing that legacy of hatred with which we were threatened.[30]

In catching the extraordinary vision of an aspiring Eleusis, feminism, and nationalism at a high moment of joy, relief, and exhilaration, that hinted at their inevitable dissolution into something lesser, and the shared pain of that loss even in the moment of fulfillment, Mitchell's *Trojan Women* proved to be *the* Greek tragedy for early post-war Canada.[31]

Notes

1. "Canada and the South African War" (2009), n.p.
2. "Canada at War" (2007), n.p.
3. Most of this chapter's information on French-language theater in Canada from 1606 to 1914 is derived from Doucette 1984 and Wagner 1982.
4. *Spectator* (1882), 12.
5. *Spectator* (1882), 12.
6. Information taken from Hartigan 1995, Macintosh 1997, and Foley 2012.
7. The source of the set was not identified, but it might very well have been borrowed from the Vassar College production of *Antigone* staged in May 1893. See "The *Antigone* of Sophocles" (1984), n.p.
8. "*Antigone* Acted" (1894), 8.
9. "Women's Share in the Government of Old England" (1912), 14.
10. "Reorganization" (1919), 1.
11. Statistics assembled from Scott 1966, and *Varsity* (1914–20).
12. "Number" (2009), n.p.
13. "Women Students" (1917), 6.
14. "The *Trojan Women* of Euripides" (1920 program), 2.
15. Averill 1986: 3, 19–21. Outside of a small satirical burlesque, *Télémaque* presented by the Modern languages Club in December, 1916, Averill suggests the next classical play, a Latin-language production of *Andromeda*, by the all-women Loretto College Dramatic Society, did not appear until later in 1920 (10).
16. "Canada and the South African War" (2009), n.p.
17. Murray 1991: 39–57. A graduate of Margaret Eaton, Elizabeth Pitt, remembers the Isadora Duncan dancers visiting the school in the 1920s. See Lathrop 1997: 109.
18. *Toronto Star Weekly* (1920), 24.
19. *Daily Mail and Empire* (1920), 4.
20. Only the roles of Poseidon, Astyanax (Sonia Darovan), Talthybius, and the Leader of the Chorus were assumed by faculty or community players. The cohort of six male students attending Talthybius as soldiers included Gordon Sparling, a pioneering Canadian film-maker.

21. *Hart House Theatre, Toronto* (1928), 4.
22. *Varsity* (October 17, 1919), 2.
23. *Varsity* (October 15, 1919), 1, 4.
24. *Varsity* (October 15, 1919), 1.
25. *Daily Mail and Empire* (1920), 4.
26. "*Trojan*" (1920 program), 2.
27. "*Daily Mail and Empire*" (1920), 4.
28. "*Daily Mail and Empire*" (1920), 4.
29. "The *Trojan Women*" (1920), 395.
30. *Gateway* (1921), 4.
31. I would like to thank Paul Stoesser for answering additional questions on Mitchell's work in New York and Toronto. His generosity and knowledgeability have contributed much to this chapter. I would also like to thank Loryl MacDonald and Emily Sommers of the University of Toronto Archives for their help in locating photos and additional information on the 1882 and 1894 *Antigone*, and the Clara Thomas Archives and Special Collections at York University in Toronto for the photo of the 1920 *Trojan Women*.

References

"*Antigone* Acted, Sophocles' Great Play Set Forth in Toronto" (February 16, 1894), *Globe* (Toronto), 8.
"The *Antigone* at Toronto" (May 13, 1882), *Spectator* (London), 12.
"The *Antigone* of Sophocles to be given by the Greek Department, May 26" (1893), *Vassar Miscellany* XXII.7, n.p.
Anon. (1920), "The Work of Hart House," *Canadian Bookman* 2 (December), 30–1.
Averill, H. (1986), *Dramatis Personae: An Exhibition of Amateur Theatre at the University of Toronto 1879–1939*. October 6, 1986–January 5, 1987, 1–30.
Browne, M. (1955), *Too Late To Lament: An Autobiography*. London.
Burt, A. L. (1917), "Is Life Worth Living?" *Gateway* (Graduation Number), 17–19.
Campbell, W. (1907), "Shakespeare and the Latter-Day Drama," *Canadian Magazine* 30.1, 14–18.
"Canada and the South African War" (2009), Canadian War Museum <http://www.warmuseum.ca/cwm/exhibitions/boer/boerwarhistory_e.shtml>.
"Canada at War: Second Battle of Ypres, 1915" (2007), Canada at War <http://www.canadaatwar.ca/content-19/wwi-second-battle-of-ypres/>.
Charlesworth, H. (1920), "Music and Drama," *Saturday Night* 34, 6.
Doucette, L. E. (1984), *Theatre in French Canada: Laying the Foundations 1606–1867*. Toronto.
Duchesne, S. (2006), "The Impossible Theatre: Roy Mitchell and The Chester Mysteries: Experience, Initiation and Brotherhood," *Theatre Research in Canada* 27:2, 227–44.
Edmonstone, W. E. (1977), *Nathan Cohen: The Making of a Critic*. Toronto.
Foley, H. P. (2012), *Reimagining Greek Tragedy on the American Stage*. Berkeley, Los Angeles, and London.
Ford, A. R. (1985), *A Path Not Strewn With Roses: One Hundred Years of Women at the University of Toronto 1884–1984*. Toronto.
Gardiner, J. (2009), *"The Amusement World": Theatre as Social Practice in Eighteen-Nineties Toronto*. Ph.D. diss. University of Toronto. Toronto.

"Greek Tragedy Well Presented" (March 8, 1920), *Daily Mail and Empire* (Toronto), 4.
"The Hart House Theatre" (October 17, 1919), Editorial, *Varsity* (University of Toronto), 2.
"Hart House Theatre Opens Next Month" (October 25, 1920), *Toronto Star Weekly*, 24.
Hart House Theatre, Toronto: A Description of the Theatre and the Record of its First Nine Seasons 1919–1928 (c.1928). Toronto.
Hartigan, K. V. (1995), *Greek Tragedy on the American Stage: Ancient Drama in the Commercial Theater, 1882–1994*. Westport, CT, and London.
Haynes, E. S. (n.d.), Unpublished lecture notes, n.p. Private collection in the possession of Walter Kaasa (Edmonton, Alberta).
J. C. M. (1919), "*Twelfth Night*," *Acta Victoriana* (University of Toronto) XLVI.2, 92–3.
Lathrop, A. H. (1997), *Elegance and Expression, Sweat and Strength: Body Training, Physical Culture and Female Embodiment in Women's Education at the Margaret Eaton Schools (1901–1941)*. Ph.D. diss. University of Toronto. Toronto.
Lescarbot, M. (1982), "The Theatre of Neptune in the New World." Trans. Eugene Benson and Renate Usmiani in Anton Wagner ed., *Canada's Lost Plays*, iv: *Colonial Quebec: French-Canadian Drama, 1606 to 1966*. Toronto, 35–43.
Macintosh, F. (1997), "Tragedy in Performance: Nineteenth and Twentieth-Century Productions," in P. E. Easterling ed., *The Cambridge Companion to Greek Tragedy*. Cambridge, 284–323.
Mitchell, R. (1929), *Creative Theatre With Seventeen Geometrical Projections in Woodblock by Jocelyn Taylor*. New York.
Montagnes, I. (1969), *An Uncommon Fellowship: The Story of Hart House*. Toronto.
Moore, M. (1974), "Canada's Great Theatre Prophet: Roy Who?" *Canadian Theatre Review* 1, 68–71.
Murray, H. (1991), "Making the Modern: Twenty Five Years of the Margaret Eaton School of Literature and Expression," *Essays in Theatre/Études théâtrales* 10.1, 39–57.
Murray, W. (1918), Annual Report of the President of the University to the Board of Directors 1918. University of Saskatchewan Archives and Special Collections. Saskatoon, Saskatchewan.
"Number of Casualties in the First World War, 1914 to 1918, and the Second World War, 1939 to 1945" (2009) Statistics Canada <http://www65.statcan.gc.ca/acyb02/1947/acyb02_19471126002-eng.htm>.
Oliver, E. H. (1917), "A Preachment by Padre," first published in Western Universities Battalion October 1916, *Sheaf* (University of Saskatchewan) 5.2, 72.
Parkhurst, E. R. (1920), "Music and Drama: Hart House Theatre," *Globe* (Toronto) March 8, 8.
"Reorganization of Players Club" (October 15, 1919) *Varsity* (University of Toronto), 1.
Roy, R. H. (2012), "Battle of the Somme," *The Canadian Encyclopedia* <http://www.canadaatwar.ca/content-19/wwi-second-battle-of-ypres/>.
Sandwell, B. K. (1996 [1911]), "The Annexation of our Stage," in Don Rubin ed., *Canadian Theatre History: Selected Readings*. Toronto, 16–20.
Scott, R. B. (1966), *A Study of Amateur Theatre in Toronto 1990–1930*, M.A. thesis, University of New Brunswick. Fredericton. Volumes i and ii.
Semple, N. (1996), *The Lord's Dominion: The History of Canadian Methodism*. Montreal.
Shortt, M. (1989), "Morrison, Charlotte," in E. Benson and L. W. Conolly eds., *Oxford Companion to Canadian Theatre*. Toronto, Oxford, and New York.
Stoesser, P. J. M. (2007), *Hart House and the International Art Theatre*. Ph.D. diss. University of Toronto. Toronto.
Stoesser, P. J. M. (2013a), "Roy Mitchell Question." Letter to Moira Day. E-mail, August 13.

Stoesser, P. J. M. (2013b), "Roy Mitchell Question." Letter to Moira Day. E-mail, August 22.
Sullivan, W. G. (1918), "After the War," *Sheaf* (March) (University of Saskatchewan), 165–7.
"The Trojan Women" (1920), *Acta Victoriana* (University of Toronto) XLIV.7, 395.
"The *Trojan Women* of Euripides" (Play program notes) (March 1920), The Players' Club of the University of Toronto. Fourth Production of the Third Season. Hart House Theatre.
Usmiani, R. (1987), "Roy Mitchell: Prophet in our Past," *Theatre Research in Canada* 8.2, 147–68.
Wagner, A. (ed. 1982), *Canada's Lost Plays*, iv: *Colonial Quebec: French-Canadian Drama, 1606 to 1966*. Toronto.
"What Shall Armistice Day Mean to Us" (1921), Editorial. *Gateway* (University of Alberta) XII.4, 4.
"Women's Share in the Government of Old England" (1912), *Gateway* (University of Alberta) III.2, 12–14.
"Women Students and War" (1917), *Gateway* (University of Alberta) VII.12, 6.

CHAPTER 13

GREEK TRAGEDY AND MODERN DANCE

An Alternative Archaeology?

ARTEMIS LEONTIS

On May 7, 1927 at Delphi, following a performance of *Prometheus Bound*, the first modern revival of an ancient Greek play in the archaeological site's recently excavated theater, Ernst Buschor, Head of the Deutsches Archäologisches Institut in Athens who acquired fame for his study of archaic Greece, approached Eva Palmer Sikelianos (1874–1952), the American director of the play, with unexpected words of approval.[1] "'You have solved', he said, 'archaeological problems which we have been working on fruitlessly for years'" (Palmer-Sikelianos 1993: 113). He was referring to questions about the elusive elements of movement and sound in the archaic Greek chorus, about which the hard evidence of stone and fired clay is so reticent. Buschor's admission was especially welcome to Palmer because he had frankly discouraged her when she sought his prior approval for her production of the play at Delphi. "He considered it a sacrilege to defile any ancient movement with a miserable modern attempt to perform ancient dramas. 'Leave them in peace'"—Palmer recalled his warnings in her autobiography. "'You cannot possibly do them right, so why do them at all'" (Palmer-Sikelianos 1993: 113). As happily as Palmer may have received Buschor's belated approval, she disclaimed archaeological expertise. She responded:

> I have read archaeological books only to forget them, and I have never thought of your problems. And besides . . . the performance was bristling with archaeological mistakes, but even you did not detect them, and you are not even conscious of them now. And that is because the place was moving around its own pivot; it was emotionally true, or almost true—and that was sufficient to make you feel that it was correct archaeologically. (Palmer-Sikelianos 1993: 113)

Palmer punctuated her disclaimer with this hard rejection of the very foundations of Mr. Buschor's mode of inquiry:

> There is no such thing as archaeological correctness. There is nothing in Greek drama except the emotional truth and consistency of the performers, and the immense responding emotion of those who are present. (Palmer-Sikelianos 1993: 113–14)

This scene, with an expert in Greek antiquity "hailing" an artist's archaeological achievement and the artist countering his criteria of judgement, frames my study. The subject is modern dance's exploration of the relics of ancient movement and sound as part of an effort to renew dance and give dancers legitimacy, credibility, and a tradition to build on apart from ballet. I trace three moments in the story of these explorations with three American agents. At one chronological end is Isadora Duncan (1877–1927), the self-styled mother of modern dance. Her famous bare feet on ancient sites in Athens are said to have set a dance revolution in motion. While Duncan's steps on Greek soil, made famous by Edward Steichen's photogravure, "Isadora Duncan at the Portal of the Parthenon, Athens,"[2] taken in 1921 in the most famous of Athenian ruins, have been frequently retraced, the lines connecting Duncan to Ted Shawn (1891–1972), the "papa" of modern dance,[3] need to be revisited. In an unpublished photograph of 1939 (Fig. 13.1), we see Ted Shawn posing inside the replica of the Parthenon in Nashville, Tennessee, on July 10, 1939,[4] perhaps as a response to Isadora Duncan's claim on Greece. The pivotal figure linking Duncan to Shawn is Eva Palmer Sikelianos. For Shawn's Nashville Parthenon photo shoot, she supplied one of the costumes she designed and wove for the performances of *Prometheus Bound* at Delphi. More important, Palmer's efforts to solve the problems of how to dress and give voice and motion to the tragic chorus gave a new layer of archaeological depth to Duncan's experiments and carried a well-developed approach and method across the Atlantic to Shawn. By rereading some of the better-known sources on modern dance alongside unpublished material from Eva Palmer Sikelianos's papers in the Benaki Museum Historical Archives in Athens and Ted Shawn's Papers in the Library of the Performing Arts in New York, I piece together an important episode in Modernism's encounter with the memory-rich site of Greece. I use this episode to reflect on how archaeological problems raised by experts made their way from academic to non-academic work, and there generated their own set of investigations to become creative, contested ground.

Isadora Duncan in Greece

Isadora Duncan's encounter with Greece, the first moment in this story, took shape in the museums of Europe, especially the Louvre from 1900 to 1902, where she and her brother Raymond combed through the Greek collections, copying gestures from ancient statuary and vase painting and reproducing them with their bodies. Certainly Isadora and Raymond Duncan were not the first to concentrate on Greek gestures as a source for modern taste. Codifying and adapting for physical culture in the United States the

FIG. 13.1 Ted Shawn posing as Hermes in a costume woven by Eva Palmer Sikelianos in the full-scale replica of the Parthenon in Nashville, Tennessee, July 11, 1939. ESP-BMHA No. 557, courtesy of the Benaki Museum Historical Archives.

gestural vocabulary developed for the theater by François Delsarte, Steele Mackaye, Genevieve Stebbins, Henrietta Russell, and others used classical Greek sculpture "to illustrate principles of expression and to teach by example" (Ruyter 1996: 69–70). From these practices, a Delsartean form of entertainment developed, in which "a series of statue-poses modeled after classic works of art" told a story (Wilbor 1905: 462). The Delsartean system reformed not only physical education but also women's dress (Cunningham 2003: 144), and even women's education. Women studying Greek on both sides of the Atlantic were called upon to perform the exercise of animating statue poses, as if their bodies were the tools for writing Greek letters and their accurate recovery of a pose proved their level of competence in reading Greek prose.[5] The question of how gestures frozen in material relics might have moved, like the question of how Greek texts might have sounded, mobilized women to stage amateur performances of ancient plays. And so it was not in a cultural vacuum that Duncan the dancer aspired to embody and animate the Greek chorus.

Duncan did not learn Greek, but she studied books steeped in Greek learning. Among the influential books of the era was *La Danse grecque antique d'après les monuments figurés*, a massive compendium of poses and a reconstruction of dances based on those poses, published in French by composer Maurice Emmanuel in 1896 and translated into English in 1916. Emmanuel's motto, "sculptures by ancient artists are the relics of old dance" [ἐστὶ δὲ καὶ τὰ τῶν ἀρχαίων δημιουργῶν ἀγάλματα τῆς παλαιᾶς ὀρχήσεως λείψανα (Athenaeus 629 b)] (Emmanuel 1896: title page) succinctly articulated an archaeological assumption: that material remains are signs of an old, lost, but somehow restorable life. For archaeologists, restoration goes as far as recovering and then endlessly rereading an archaeological record. But an artist such as Isadora Duncan could take "the relics of old dance" in another direction by transforming lost traces of life into potential and then kinetic energy. Isadora and Raymond Duncan thus pored over Maurice Emmanuel's and other books in the Paris Opera Library in 1901 (Naerebout 2010).

What was the reason for this revolutionary dancer's attraction to Greek relics? For Duncan and other artistic rebels such as Loie Fuller,[6] the desired ends were both women's liberation from Victorian constrictions and their triumph over associations with crude forms of exploitation in dance halls.[7] Duncan adored Greek art's depictions of women's uncorseted torsos, unbound breasts, flowing tunics, and loosened hair captured in the midst of motion, with bare or sandaled feet in parallel—not ballet's turned out—position. She wanted to set those images free. She used her own body as the medium of exploration, her own movements to develop *this* argument: that Greek poses "evolved . . . from the movements of nature." "Dancing naked upon the earth," she wrote of her experiments, "I naturally fall into Greek positions, for Greek positions are only earth positions" (Duncan 1996: 173). Here we see the suturing of nature and culture in the idea of an ever youthful Greece, a common interwar figure of thought present also in archaeologist Ernst Buschor's belief that archaic Greek culture represented the "youth of the world" (Dyson 2006: 191) and the hope for a present-day rejuvenation.[8] What is important here is that women artists such as Isadora Duncan, whose taste-shaping weapons were their bodies, used the trope of Greece's "earth positions"—with its assumption that relics from the Greek earth gave evidence of a culture both closer to nature and more highly cultivated than modern civilization—to blaze a path for women's physical, sexual, and social liberation.

Because she was a dancer with a powerful kinesthetic sensibility, Duncan found inspiration especially in the lacunae of Greek art: the traces of motion lost to the living successors. She wanted her dance to supply the lost movements that would unite still poses. Her journey to Greece in 1903 served the purpose of animating what existed in her imagination as a still, silent world. Her physical presence in Greece, her body's relationship to Greece's imposing temple architecture, became a source of inspiration, as an essay she wrote entitled "The Parthenon" suggests, and the later Steichen photograph of her from 1921 illustrates. During the four months of her stay in Athens, Isadora studied the Parthenon, "lifting my eyes to the rhythmical succession of Doric columns," she later wrote, while trying to "express the feeling of the human body in relation to the Doric column." Movement at first eluded her because she sensed that all she "had danced was forbidden in this Temple—neither love nor hate nor fear, nor joy nor sorrow—only a rhythmic cadence, those Doric columns—only in perfect harmony this glorious Temple, calm through all the ages." Her close attention to the architectural refinements—the columns' gentle curves "from the base to the height, each one . . . in flowing movement, never resting . . . in harmony with the others" then gave the spiritual lift we see in the Steichen photograph: "my arms rose slowly toward the Temple, and I leaned forward—and then I knew I had found my dance, and it was a Prayer" (Duncan 1903/1904: 64–5).

At the Theatre of Dionysus on the south slope of the Acropolis, Duncan, barelegged in her signature white tunic and sandaled feet, gave physical expression to Dionysian ecstasy—another Greek conundrum for classical philologists as well as artists. A series of photographs taken by Isadora's brother Raymond show Isadora creating the impression that her body has freed itself from the limits of the ego to become the site of rapture. Isadora produced this effect by dancing with curvilinear movements emanating from the solar plexus. In one beautiful movement, she contracted the muscles of the solar plexus to produce a graceful C Curve.[9] In another, she extended those muscles, arched her back, and tossed her head to produce the backward bend, also known as the "Bacchic shiver," a gesture of lost inhibitions found in Maurice Emmanuel's compendium of ancient images.[10]

For Duncan the Dionysian dance was a step toward something greater than a powerfully expressive solo of liberation. It was a move to recover the artistic origins of the tragic chorus, a notion she conceived through her encounter with Nietzsche's *Birth of Tragedy* as that work circulated beyond philology at the turn of the century. Duncan embraced Nietzsche's appreciation of the body and called him "the first dancing philosopher" (Duncan 1927 (reissue 1995): 341). She was especially inspired by Nietzsche's ideas about the tragic chorus, namely that "tragedy emerged from the tragic chorus and was nothing but the chorus" (Nietzsche 1967: 42) and that "the chorus . . . produces the vision from itself and speaks of it with the whole symbolism of dance, music, and word" (Nietzsche 1967: 51). As she translated these ideas into dance, she "conceived the dance as a chorus or community expression" (Duncan 1927 (reissue 1995): 103). She wanted to reinvent the choral entity in her own solo dance. She wrote: "I don't mean to copy it, to imitate it, but to be inspired by it, to recreate it in myself with personal inspiration; to take its beauty with me toward the future" (Franko 1995: 18).

Duncan's experiments in Greek dance included a revival of an ancient tragedy. With help from Raymond's Greek wife, Penelope Sikelianos, Duncan staged the *Suppliant Women* by Aeschylus in 1903. She selected this play, with its chorus as the protagonist, because she considered it to be the earliest extant Aeschylean tragedy. For the musical chorus, Duncan assembled a group of boys she and Raymond had heard singing folk songs in the vicinity of Athens, and gave the role of *koryphaios*, the chorus's leader, to a seminarian trained in Byzantine-style, Greek Orthodox church music. Influenced by Penelope, a student of Greek music, she was convinced that surviving Greek religious and folk music traditions most closely approximated the lost music of ancient Greece. Penelope worked with the seminarian to fit the ancient Greek words of the chorus to the tunes of existing folk songs and Byzantine hymns. He then taught the boys to chant the words in a Byzantine style. In performances at the Royal Theatre in Athens first, then, with less critical success, in Vienna, Munich, and Berlin, the Greek boys chanted while Isadora danced the part of the chorus of fifty maidens. According to Duncan's recollection of the performance, "I found it very difficult to express in my slight figure the emotions of fifty maidens all at once, but I had the feeling of multiple oneness" (Duncan 1927 (reissue 1995): 100).

EVA PALMER AFTER DUNCAN

The usual telling of modern dance's "Greek story" begins with Isadora Duncan's journey to Greece. From there the story crosses the Atlantic to describe Ruth St. Denis's independent development of ethnic and Asian dance styles in works she created with her husband, Ted Shawn, for their company, Denishawn. Numerous Greek-inspired dances were part of the group's repertoire, which aimed to make dance a vehicle for expressing transhistorical, global, emotional, and spiritual truths. A piece called the *Bacchanale*, for example, was part of their *Dance Pageant of Egypt, Greece, and India*, performed at the Berkeley Open Air Theatre in 1916 with their student Martha Graham as one of their dancers.[11] In contrast to Isadora Duncan, who performed only in the theaters of high art, Denishawn took its Greek-style pageants, for example, Ruth St. Denis performing in *From a Grecian Vase*, on vaudeville tours, where they reached a broad audience.[12] From the Denishawn pageants, modern dance's "Greek story" is likely to jump to Martha Graham's post-World War II *Hellenic Journey*, a series of dances Graham based on Greek tragedy, including her evening-length dance drama *Clytemnestra* performed in 1958, while skipping over "Ted Shawn and his Men Dancers," the breakaway group Ted Shawn led after he and Ruth St. Denis divorced. In this version of dance history, the desire to remake and animate the "Greek" seems to arise independently in intermittent spurts from the individual genius of unrelated creators searching for new sources of inspiration.

A closer view of Duncan's residual influence in Greece, however, provides a much fuller understanding of modern dance's lingering, systematic study of the tragic chorus. The second moment in the story of dance's engagement with Greek tragedy takes place when Eva Palmer Sikelianos directs performances of Greek tragedy in the theater at Delphi for two festivals she and her husband produced at Delphi in 1927 and 1930. As noted earlier, Palmer's staging of *Prometheus Bound* in 1927 received Classicist Ernst Buschor's nod of professional assent for its solution of "archaeological problems" that had troubled scholars "fruitlessly for years." Yet Palmer disavowed archaeological correctness, preferring to embrace "emotional truth . . . and the immense responding emotion of those who are present" (Palmer-Sikelianos 1993: 113–14).

In many ways, Palmer was following Duncan's path, with the difference that she formally studied Greek at Bryn Mawr from 1896 to 1899 and read scholarly and popular works on Greece all her life. Like Duncan, Palmer was bisexual, and she found in Greek antiquity a source of liberation from the physical constraints of Victorian dress and its sexual and social conventions. In Paris in the early 1900s, Palmer moved in the same bohemian circles as Duncan and even traveled to Bayreuth to attend Duncan's performance there in 1904 (Palmer-Sikelianos 1993: 187). She examined some of the same vase paintings and statuary in the Louvre and books in Paris's libraries. In 1906 she followed Isadora Duncan's footsteps to Greece, traveling with Raymond and Penelope Duncan and staying in the Duncans' unfinished house, the "Palace of Agamemnon," as they called it, on the southwest slope of Mt. Hymettos.[13] She married Penelope Duncan's brother, Angelos Sikelianos, and entered the school of Byzantine chanting attended by Penelope. Throughout her 27-year sojourn in Greece, Palmer made prolonged studies of the Greek language, music, movements, and dead and living artistic forms, in order to build on experiments Isadora Duncan began and correct her methods of reviving ancient movement and song which Palmer considered superficial or misguided.

Palmer's staging of *Prometheus Bound* in 1927 and 1930 and the *Suppliants* in 1930 reveals her artistic dialogue with Duncan's earlier Greek experiments. Palmer was developing elements Duncan had concentrated on decades before: the materials and shape of tunics, physical poses and movements, and composition of the musical line to render the presumed integrity of music, dance, words, and meaning of the Greek tragic chorus. Palmer could imagine the political potential of a chorus singing and dancing for a large, elite audience in an ancient amphitheater. She staged her choral formations with an eye to the circular orchestra and surrounding amphitheater and landscape (Van Steen 2002). Surely the desire to create Greek movement reviving a mythic story of high emotional impact follows a traceable line from Isadora Duncan's brilliant chorus of one to Eva Palmer Sikelianos's circular configuration of a choral group in the magically located theater at Delphi.

Yet the relationship of Palmer's work in theater and Duncan's dances is not one of direct continuation; instead it involves influence, contestation, and revision of Duncan's methods. Palmer followed certain elements of Duncan's approach to excavating the past and swerved from others. Like Duncan, Palmer gathered material evidence from visual representations of human gestures in ancient Greek art, and then concentrated on lacunae where material evidence suffered immediate decay, for example, human movements and sounds, where she developed her own art. She did preparatory work replicating the ancient gestures and exploring their expressive possibilities. Only after she had studied a wide range of gestures did she create the movement vocabulary linked with the words and sounds of the chorus.

I have already mentioned Duncan's revolutionary shift of the dancing body's center from the line connecting the head, sternum, pubic bone, and heels to the solar plexus, the complex of abdominal muscles that meet below the breast. In her autobiography, *Upward Panic*, Palmer recalled that she had often

> seen Isadora stand[ing] quite motionless before large audiences for quite a long spell, with her hands over her solar plexus . . . Then, when she gave the sign for starting,

she really had "placed a motor in her soul," and from then on her dancing gave the impression of being involuntary on her part. It was purely Dionysian.

Photographs show Palmer herself using a less exaggerated contraction of the same core muscles as a starting point for movement.[14]

Palmer distinguished her work from Duncan's through the material evidence she selected and the ways she turned gestures into movement and sound. She commissioned sculptor Bella Raftopoulou to copy poses from archaic vases in the Greek National Archaeological Museum, from which Palmer would choreograph the movements of the chorus of Oceanids. She selected pre-classical vase painting because it was contemporaneous with tragedy's emergence in archaic Greece. As Raftopoulou copied the poses, she also wrote notes on the meaning of each pose. Initially Palmer planned that each Oceanid would choreograph her own part based on the poses and their meanings and her own interpretation of her lines, so that there would be individual differentiation within the unity of the chorus as it sang in unison and moved as a group on the stage. In the end, however, Palmer choreographed all the movements herself. She identified poses with strong, sharp angles, in contrast to Duncan's "soft undulations," her perpetual "flow," and the "frank," "straight-ahead" gaze that placed her head and chest in direct alignment. In all there were 285 changes of pose which were correlated with lines of the play recited by the Oceanids. To set her archaic sources in motion, Palmer "isolat[ed the] effect of keeping the head in profile and the chest 'en face'" (Fig. 13.2).[15] And she developed a special exercise program to keep this effect as the body moved.

FIG. 13.2 One of Bella Raftopoulou's drawings (left), and Eva Palmer Sikelianos in the same pose in an undated photograph (right). ESP-BMHA No. 323, courtesy of the Benaki Museum Historical Archives.

Palmer also worked to revise Duncan's approach to recovering the melody and rhythm of the Greek chorus. She criticized both Duncan's brief experiments with a chorus of Greeks singing folk and Byzantine church melodies and her abandonment of those experiments and return to music by the giants of the western classical canon—Gluck, Beethoven, Mendelssohn, Chopin, and Wagner. For Palmer, the genius of Greek art lay in the primacy it gave to words and their meaning. Accordingly, she surveyed traditions of music making in Greece to identify a method for enhancing words with melodies and rhythms that supported their meaning. When she settled on Byzantine chant, it was not because she believed that Byzantine church hymns represented ancient survivals, as Duncan had thought. Instead she learned a very difficult tradition of improvised chanting as it was used in the present day to make the ancient words of the Greek Orthodox services "the basis for new melodies" (Palmer-Sikelianos 1993: 186), and then sought to deploy the tradition to make the ancient words of Greek dramatic poetry the basis of new music.

Palmer's artistic differences with Duncan turned on the greater value she gave to the pre-classical sources she studied in the National Archaeological Museum in Athens, in contrast to the post-classical visual sources upon which Duncan relied. Palmer observed: "The strong invocation of Isadora's art brought to life a period which was not archaic Greece, not classic Greece, but Greece in a later decadent period. In fact, what we were seeing and raving over was Hellenistic bas-relief, or a Southern Italian vase come to life" (Palmer-Sikelianos 1993: 182). Emphasis in this passage falls on the contrast between the "archaic," on the one hand, a historians' term naming an era prior to 480 BCE, and the "decadent," on the other hand, an evaluative term very much in fashion in Palmer's day, denoting decline. During the interwar years, "archaic" had become a code word used by experts and non-experts of different ideological convictions to distinguish true, pure Greeks from later Greeks, who were seen to have softened the essence of Greece. In Palmer's choreography the opposition of the archaic to the later, Hellenistic, southern Italian, "decadent" Greek finds its correlative in the angular lines of her dancers' movements, in contrast to the soft undulations of Duncan's dancing, and in the melodic, rhythmic, unison singing Palmer directed, as opposed to the complex harmonic structures of Duncan's musical obsessions.

Eva Palmer and Ted Shawn

Even this cursory look at Palmer's revivals of Greek tragedy at Delphi shows that Palmer was revisiting Duncan's ideas but broadening the reserve of Greek visual and musical sources and using this to revise her approach. As news, photographs, and a film Palmer made of the Delphic festival traveled across the Atlantic through an American publicity machine that recognized Palmer, the wealthy New York heiress, as one of its own, they reached the American dancer and choreographer Ted Shawn. Shawn's exploration of Greek drama in the 1930s is the third moment in the story I am telling. Before he became acquainted with Palmer's work, Shawn performed hero-prophet roles in Denishawn productions that were more like tableaux with vaudeville-inspired acts than tragic drama with a singing and dancing chorus. Shawn then became increasingly interested in Isadora Duncan's work. In his sculptural Plastique, *Death of Adonis*,[16] a controlled dance dealing with the pictorial and sculptural elements of the body and testing the audience's tolerance for Greek-style nudity, Shawn acknowledged the influence of Duncan, who, Shawn remarked in a lecture entitled "Dancing and Nudity," "had so absolutely an idea about the art of dance and about the rightness of the naked human body that [she] dared to discard . . . clumsy, awkward, and ugly clothes . . . and appeared in the simple tunic of Greece."[17]

After 1927, Shawn's work began to show awareness of Palmer's Greek productions. In 1929 he performed his own *Prometheus Bound* dance mime choreographed to Alexander Scriabin's experimental composition "Prometheus: The Poem of Fire." Pantelis Michelakis's comparison of film versions of Shawn's and Eva Palmer Sikelianos's Prometheus story finds shared "aesthetic and artistic preoccupations" in the 1920s, a decade before the two artists collaborated in 1939.[18] Like Duncan and Palmer, Shawn turned to Greece as an origin for modern dance, in this case because he "wanted to restore *male* dancing to the dignity he believed it possessed in ancient Greece."[19] Accordingly he grappled with the origins of the dancing, singing chorus in ancient Greek poetic practice in a piece he choreographed for himself as koryphaios (chorus leader) and his Men Dancers, entitled, *Kinetic Molpai*, with music by Jess Meeker. The piece premiered on October 5, 1935 at Goshen, New York, and was performed widely in the United States. The program notes for *Kinetic Molpai* reveal Shawn's thinking about the encounter of modernity with antiquity, as mediated by Classicist and translator of Greek drama Gilbert Murray:[20]

> According to Gilbert Murray, the Molpe was the ancient art form which includes rhythmic movement, instrumental music, singing, poetry, and drama. Strife, Death, and the Thing Beyond Death constituted the subject matter of the ancient Molpai. *But in its essence it was only the yearning of the whole dumb body to express that emotion for which words and harps and singing were not enough.* Out of the old Molpai have come the separate arts of Drama, Vocal and Instrumental Music, Poetry, and the Dance.[21]

While Palmer emphasized the primacy of poetry, music, and costumes in her stagings of Greek drama at Delphi, Shawn's Greek-inspired, popular, American work subordinated everything to masculine, athletic movement.[22] Dance was for him "the outgrowth of the ancient Molpai in kinetic forms," and, in his mind at least, America's "greatest art expression."[23] Thus, as compellingly as his "molpai" may have moved, they did not sing. Shawn may have had the missing singing in mind when Eva Sikelianos was introduced to him backstage after a performance of *Dance of the Ages* at Washington Irving High School in New York in January 1939. In any case, his words expressed a long-held yearning to meet this artist, who could teach him that thing which he did not know: "But I have been looking for you for years; where have you been?" (Palmer-Sikelianos 1993: 201).

It is tempting to think that Palmer's contribution to Shawn's artistry in their collaboration from the summer of 1939 through 1940 involved music, words, drama, and the textiles she wove for the group,[24] but had little to do with dance. Palmer was "widely known as a musician, producer, and weaver of fine textiles [who] . . . brought an unusual range of knowledge and experience to her revivals of Greek drama" (M.E.M. 1936: 134–5). While choreography was within her "range of knowledge," the folk-inspired steps that animated her large tragic choruses had little to do with the longer, faster, more complex movement phrases that Shawn interwove in his work. In May 1939 at Jacob's Pillow, the school Shawn established in the Berkshires in Lee, Massachusetts, Palmer taught Shawn's group to sing in unison while dancing using the "Greek" method she developed through years of studying Byzantine music in Greece. The Men Dancers worked on several of her original compositions. There was one based on Isaiah, ch. 52, verse 1 ("Awake, awake, put on thy strength, O Zion"), two more based on short poems by Walt Whitman, and two Pyrrhic dances from Aristophanes. In the middle of the Pyrrhic dances Shawn, according to Palmer-Sikelianos:

> Got up with an exclamation . . . and . . . taught the choreography of this dance which had sprung from his mind, fully armed, as it were by merely hearing the music. So there were men singing and dancing in an hour's time as if they had done it all their lives. (Palmer-Sikelianos 1993: 203)

It seems that even when Palmer had already choreographed her musical compositions, she deferred to Shawn in the art of dance. She had complete confidence in his choreography, and felt for the first time that she had met the perfect match for producing an integrated singing and dancing chorus. A group of almost 30 men from Shawn's students at Jacob's Pillow and his Men Dancers featured some of Shawn's and Palmer's collaboratively produced creations—including new pieces composed to psalms, *By the Waters of Babylon*, Percy Shelley's *Prometheus Unbound*, and Whitman's *Song of the Open Road* from his *Leaves of Grass*—in performances during "Friday Teas" at Jacob's Pillow in the summer of 1939, in St. Augustine, Florida, and in Shawn's Carnegie Hall debut in February 1940.

The two artists also began work on the first chorus of the *Persians*, with some notion that they might take Aeschylus' play "first to American Universities and other centers in America" and eventually to a festival at Delphi that Palmer had in mind to "resume" in 1942.[25] Shawn's Men Dancers disbanded before he and Palmer completed work on the chorus. Yet their experiments left a visual record from a rehearsal or a performance at Jacob's Pillow's "last Friday Tea in the beginning of September 1939" (Palmer-Sikelianos 1993: 204). Photographs from a rehearsal indicate that Shawn was absorbing lessons from Palmer's work on the circular stage in the open-air amphitheater at Delphi. For most of his career, Shawn had been producing work on a raised stage against a curtained background. He "believed that dance should be performed on the proscenium stage so that the audience could see the dancer's relationships within the space, much like the visual artist creates composition in a painting" (Kassing 2007: 187). Palmer's work in the open-air amphitheater of Delphi assumed the audience's three-dimensional sense of space, where the stage was a circle and the audience viewed the performance from above. The circular architectural arrangement gave Palmer a distinct sense of both movement and the performers' line of vision. Performers did not have to adjust

FIG. 13.3 Ted Shawn's students and dancers performing the first chorus of Aeschylus' *Persians* in a collaborative composition by choreographer Shawn, and composer Eva Palmer Sikelianos. ESP-BMHA No. 535 or 541, courtesy of the Benaki Museum Historical Archives.

their heads or bodies to face the audience but instead kept the integrity of their poses as they moved on the stage. Shawn's choreography for the *Persians* suggests that he and his dancers were imagining themselves on a circular, amphitheatric stage. Shawn was also trying to reproduce the angularity of archaic poses and to harness the potential of what Palmer called the "Apollonian movement," in which "the head and feet are in profile, and the chest or back in full view" (Palmer-Sikelianos 1993: 223; Fig. 13.3). A comparison with Shawn's *pas de basque* earlier in the same decade suggests that Shawn's collaboration with Palmer in 1939 and 1940 extended his movement vocabulary. Palmer's cross-lateral rotations, drawn from archaic visual sources, and Maurice Emmanuel's *Art of Antique Dance*—which Shawn nearly replicated in the promotional photo he took in the Parthenon in Nashville, Tennessee, dressed in Palmer's hand-woven costume for Hermes in *Prometheus Bound*—gave Shawn new expressive tools to embody the liberating male roles he was seeking to make acceptable to American audiences.

MODERN DANCE'S ALTERNATIVE ARCHAEOLOGY

A comparison of Eva Palmer Sikelianos posing as one of the Oceanids in 1927, Ted Shawn dressed as Hermes in 1939, and Martha Graham fiercely dancing the story of

Clytemnestra in 1958 with movements "etch[ing] patterns on the space as clear as those that travel around ancient vases"[26] can be used to make a very strong claim about lineage in modern dance. Isadora Duncan's bare feet on the Acropolis may have set a dance revolution in motion. But the lesser-known Eva Palmer Sikelianos, with her longstanding engagement with Greek culture of all eras and her attachment to an archaic Greek sensibility, did a great deal to shape the outlines of dance's movement vocabulary while also keeping an interest in the Greek tragic chorus alive.

Yet I do not want the weight of my conclusion to fall exclusively on the overlooked importance of Palmer. Instead I would like to tread gingerly on the question of archaeology and its limits. There is nothing to suggest that the choreographers I have been discussing made a direct contribution to conventional archaeology, as the German scholar Buschor thought Palmer had in 1927. Their work did not consist in the systematic, scientific recovery of buried material remains or aim to contribute to historical knowledge. Yet it treated artifacts of the Greek past as the contested ground of inquiry, and fastened its attention on these materials as sources for those things in life that are the first to decay: lost movements, fleeting gestures—the sounds, rhythms, and emotions that might have filled ancient social space. It may be useful to think of their approach to ancient drama as an "alternative archaeology," following Bruce Trigger's reminder, in a much-quoted article of 1984, that "archaeology always operates within a social context" (Trigger 1984: 357), which in turn bears weight on the kind of record archaeologists produce and the kinds of questions they ask. Calling modern dance's extensive engagement with relics of Greece's past an "alternative archaeology" brings into view the role artists play in speculating on the lost performing arts using their peculiar talents, experience, and knowledge, and asking interesting questions about ancient space and the human activities that distributed themselves within it from an alternative perspective (Macintosh 2013). "Alternative archaeology" also draws into the story of classical scholarship invisible or forgotten women such as Eva Palmer Sikelianos, who studied ancient sources carefully yet disclaimed scholarly expertise in order to claim an alternative way of knowing Greek[27]—what Bonnie Smith has identified as "expanded cognition . . . beyond the horizon of the professional" (Smith 1998: 171–2). The distinct language Palmer, Isadora Duncan, and Ted Shawn, Martha Graham, and others developed, with its aesthetic, kinetic, and emotional registers, not only expanded the horizons of archaeology. As Palmer's dismissive response to the eminent Ernst Buschor suggests, it challenged the very notion of archaeological correctness.

NOTES

1. The present chapter is based on research I conducted in the Ted Shawn Papers (1913–82) in The New York Public Library for the Performing Arts Jerome Robbins Dance Division, with assistance from Charles Perrier, and in the Eva Sikelianos Papers at the Benaki Museum Historical Archives, with assistance from the archive's staff, who also gave me permission to reproduce materials, including photographs, from the archive. The University of

Michigan Institute for Research on Women and Gender at the University of Michigan supported my research with a generous research grant, and the College of Literature, Science, and Art gave me semester's research leave from teaching and service. I benefited immensely from discussion with colleagues who attended the workshop on "Archaeology and Imagination—Archaeological Objects in Modern Fine Arts, Literature, and Science" at the Collegium Budapest Institute for Advanced Study. I am grateful to Eva Kocziszky, the organizer and intellectual center of that workshop, and to Tünde Szabolcs and Farkas Edit, Editorial Production Coordinator, for their assistance. I also thank Kathryn Bosher, Danny Herwitz, and Gregory Jusdanis for their invitations to present versions of this work at the Northwestern University Sawyer Seminar, "Greek Drama in America: 1900–1970," University of Michigan Humanities Institute, and Ohio State University Department of Classics respectively, and Julian Anderson, Ruth Caston, Jessica Fogel, Beth Genné, Michelle Hanoosh, Eugene Holland, Angela Kane, Amy Shuman, Peter Sparling, Susan Van Pelt, Judith Hallett, and many others for their helpful feedback. Special thanks go to my colleagues Peggy McKracken, Yopie Prins, and Liz Wingrove for nurturing this project.

2. Digital copies of Edward Steichen, *Isadora Duncan at the Portal of the Parthenon, Athens*, are ubiquitous. See, for example, the website *Art of the Photogravure*, <http://www.photogravure.com/>.

3. Sources concur that Ted Shawn encouraged his students to call him "papa." For example, the website of Jacob's Pillow states: "For most of his career he encouraged his students to call him 'Papa' and his legacy as the artistic father for generations of dancers and teachers suggests that 'Papa' was a very apt name indeed" (<http://www.jacobspillow.org/exhibits-archives/ted-shawn.php>).

4. In Ted Shawn, Letter to Eva Sikelianou dated July 10, 1939, found in the *Eva Sikelianou Papers*, Benaki Museum Historical Archive, Kifissia, Greece, 1939 correspondence, Shawn informs Palmer Sikelianos: "tomorrow afternoon I am going to have a session of photographs at the Nashville Parthenon—the head of the Park Board having given orders the building is to remain closed while I am using it! And I will either bring or send the results."

5. Prins (2015) makes this argument.

6. Albright (2007: 173) argues that Loie Fuller's work, like Duncan's, "incorporated the contemporary cultural evocations of 'nature' and 'Greek' in her stagings of what were essentially modernist theatrical landscapes" and established connections "to the ancient Greeks, who 'danced with their whole bodies—with their head and arms and trunk and feet.'" Fuller contested Duncan's claim on Greece, however, by arguing that whereas Duncan was "imitating movements of dancers as represented on Greek vases," her dancing achieved "the original natural expression and movements which inspired the Greeks when they made their vases."

7. Holst-Warhaft (1998: 8) states that canonization, nostalgic references to art of the past, and the equation of moral rectitude with aesthetics are aims or effects of the "classicizing process" in modern art forms.

8. Marchand (1996: 336) points out that Ernst Buschor, like other Weimar archaeologists, wanted to use "the revival of Greece to regenerate mankind" and archaeology to conquer history. Marchand quotes from Buschor (1932: 336): "classical archaeology is not only a historical discipline, it can participate in a still greater task: the conquest of history itself."

9. See the photograph, *Duncan in a Dionysian Mode*, in Franko 1995: 19, taken from the Isadora Duncan Collection, San Francisco Performing Arts Library and Museum.

10. See Raymond Duncan's photograph of Isadora Duncan's dancing in the Theatre of Dionysus in 1903, Image ID ps_dan_cd3_38, on the *New York Public Library* website, <http://digitalgallery.nypl.org/nypldigital/id?isadora_0058va>.
11. See the photograph, *Ruth St. Denis, Ted Shawn and company in Bacchanale from the Greek section of the Greek pageant, San Diego performance* (1916), Image ID DEN_0387V in the *New York Public Library Digital Gallery*, <http://digitalgallery.nypl.org/>.
12. See the photographs, *Ruth St Denis in From a Grecian Vase, Orpheum*, Image ID DEN_0444V through DEN_0448V, from the Orpheum vaudeville act based on the Greek Theatre pageant of 1916 in the *New York Public Library Digital Gallery*, <http://digitalgallery.nypl.org/>.
13. Katie Rask: *Success*, in her blog: *Antiquated Vagaries*, Sunday, May 3, 2009, <http://antiquatedvagaries.blogspot.com/2009_05_01_archive.html>, chronicles the author's "quest for the long-ago home of dancer, feminist, hippy-before-there-were-hippies, Isadora Duncan." The blog (now open only to invited readers) includes a map of the neighborhood and photographs of the house, which currently stands at 34 Chrisafis & Dikearchou in the municipality of Vyronas in Athens and houses the "Isadora et Raymond Duncan Centre de Recherche sur la Danse." See also the *Isadora et Raymond Duncan Centre de Recherche sur la Danse* website, <http://isadoraduncancenter.free.fr/accueil.htm>.
14. Palmer-Sikelianos 1993: 183. See, for example, Nelly Sougioutzoglou-Seraidare: *Eva Sikelianou in Delphi*, on the *Art Topos* website, <http://www.artopos.org/main-en.html?artists/nellys/eva-en.html&3>.
15. Palmer-Sikelianos 1993: 182. A series of photographs appearing in Eleni Sikelianos, "The Lefevre–Sikelianos–Waldman Tree and the Imaginative Utopian Attempt," in *Jacket Magazine* 27 (April 2005), <http://jacketmagazine.com/27/w-sike.html>, illustrates the angularity of movements in Palmer's choreography of *Prometheus Bound*.
16. See the photographs, *Ted Shawn in Death of Adonis*, Image ID: DEN_1522V through DEN_1526V, in the *New York Public Library Digital Gallery*, <http://digitalgallery.nypl.org/>.
17. Ted Shawn, "Dancing and Nudity." In the *Ted Shawn Papers 1913–1982*, The New York Public Library for the Performing Arts Jerome Robbins Dance Division, The New York Public Library, Box 65, Folder 27.
18. Pantelis Michelakis, "Dancing with Prometheus: Performance and Spectacle in the 1920s." Paper presented at 139th Annual Meeting of the American Philological Association (APA), panel on Classical Reception, Chicago, 2008, p. 2, <http://www.apaclassics.org/AnnualMeeting/08mtg/abstracts/Michelakis.pdf>. See too Michelakis 2010. On Shawn's approach to filming his work and the archive of those films, see Owen 2002: 61–7.
19. Hanna 1987: 36, my emphasis.
20. Murray (1930: ch. 2) treats the subject of "Molpê." The book appeared just a few years before Shawn choreographed *Kinetic Molpai*.
21. Program notes for Ted Shawn's Men Dancers: *O! Libertad: An American Saga in Three Acts*, performed February 22, 1939 at State Teachers College Millersville, Pennsylvania. In the *Ted Shawn Papers 1913–1982*, The New York Public Library for the Performing Arts Jerome Robbins Dance Division, Box 89 Folder 2: "Programs 1930–1939."
22. See Foulkes 2002: 99–101 for a detailed description of the *Kinetic Molpai*.
23. Program notes for Ted Shawn's Men Dancers' *O! Libertad* (*Ted Shawn Papers 1913-1982*, The New York Public Library for the Performing Arts Jerome Robbins Dance Division Box 89 Folder 2: "Programs 1930–1939.")

24. Palmer-Sikelianos 1993, ch. 25, *Ted Shawn*, 199–214, and Shawn's correspondence with Palmer found in the *Eva Sikelianou Papers*, in the Benaki Museum Historical Archive, and the *Ted Shawn Papers* in The New York Public Library for the Performing Arts Jerome Robbins Dance Division contain references to costumes from the 1927 *Prometheus Bound* Palmer loaned to Shawn and new costumes Palmer designed and wove for *Kinetic Molpai* and for *Isaiah 52: 1*.
25. Eva Palmer Sikelianos, "Letter to Katherine Dreier" dated May 17, [1939], in the *Eva Sikelianou Papers*, Benaki Museum Historical Archive, Correspondence 1939.
26. Jowitt (May 19, 2009), <http://www.villagevoice.com/2009-05-20/dance/martha-graham-s-clytemnestra-lives-to-kill-again/>.
27. Prins (2015) repeatedly calls attention to women's claims of not knowing Greek, which function to reclaim alternative ways of knowing, for example, through the sometimes loose translation of Greek tragedy into other media.

References

Buschor, E. (1932, republished 1969), "Begriff und Methode der Archäologie," in U. Haussmann, *Algemeine Grundlagen der Archäologie. Begriff und Methode, Geschichte, Problem der Form, Schrifzeugnisse. Handbuch der Archäeologie*. Munich, 3–10.

Cooper Albright, A. (2007), *Traces of Light: Absence and Presence in the Work of Loïe Fuller*. Middletown, CT.

Cunningham, P. A. (2003), *Reforming Women's Fashion, 1850–1920: Politics, Health, and Art*. Kent, OH.

Duncan, I. (1903 and 1904, republished 1969), "The Parthenon," in S. Cheney ed., *The Art of Dance*. New York, 64–5.

Duncan, I. (1927, reissued 1995), *My Life*. New York.

Duncan, I. (1996), "The Dancer of the Future," in M. Huxley and N. Witts eds., *The Twentieth-Century Performance Reader*. London and New York, 171–7.

Dyson, S. (2006), *In Pursuit of Ancient Pasts: A History of Classical Archaeology in the Nineteenth and Twentieth Centuries*. New Haven.

Emmanuel, M. (1896), *La Danse grecque antique d'après les monuments figurés*. Paris.

Foulkes, J. (2002), *Modern Bodies: Dance and American Modernism from Martha Graham to Alvin Ailey*. Chapel Hill, NC.

Franko, M. (1995), *Dancing Modernism/Performing Politics*. Bloomington, IN.

Hanna, J. (1987), "Patterns of Dominance: Men, Women, and Homosexuality in Dance," *Drama Review* 31, 22–47.

Holst-Warhaft, G. (1998), "In the Wake of the Greek Classical Moment," in G. Holst-Warhaft and D. R. McCann eds., *The Classical Moment: Views from Seven Literatures*. Lanham, MD, 1–21.

Jowitt, D. (2009), "Martha Graham's Clytemnestra Lives to Kill Again," *The Village Voice* (May 20), <http://www.villagevoice.com/2009-05-20/dance/martha-graham-s-clytemnestra-lives-to-kill-again/>.

Kassing, G. (2007), *History of Dance: An Interactive Arts Approach*. Champaign, IL.

Macintosh, F. (ed. 2010), *The Ancient Dancer in the Modern World: Responses to Greek and Roman Dance*. Oxford.

Macintosh, F. (2013), "From Sculpture to Vase-Painting: Archaeological Models for the Actor," in G. W. M. Harrison and V. Liapis eds., *Performance in Greek and Roman Theatre*. Leiden and Boston, 517–34.

Marchand, S. (1996), *Down from Olympus: Archaeology and Philhellenism in Germany, 1750–1950*. Princeton.

Michelakis, P. (2010), "Dancing with Prometheus: Performance and Spectacle in the 1920s," in F. Macintosh ed., *The Ancient Dancer in the Modern World: Responses to Greek and Roman Dance*. Oxford, 224–35.

Murray, G. (1930), *The Classical Tradition in Poetry: The Charles Eliot Norton Lectures*. Cambridge.

M.E.M. (1936), "Costume in Revivals of Greek Drama," *The Metropolitan Museum of Art Bulletin* 31, 134–5.

Naerebout, F. (2010), "'In Search of a Dead Rat': The Reception of Ancient Greek Dance in Late Nineteenth-Century Europe and America," in F. Macintosh ed., *The Ancient Dancer in the Modern World: Responses to Greek and Roman Dance*. Oxford, 39–56.

Nietzsche, F. (1967), *The Birth of Tragedy, and the Case of Wagner*. Trans. W. Kaufmann. New York.

Owen, N. (2002), "Ted Shawn's Moving Images," in J. Mitoma, E. Zimmer, and D. A. Stieber eds., *Envisioning Dance on Film and Video*. New York, 61–5.

Palmer-Sikelianos, E. (1993), *Upward Panic*. Trans. and ed. J. P. Anton, *Choreography and Dance Studies*. Chur, vol. iv.

Prins, Y. (2015), *Ladies' Greek: Victorian Translations of Tragedy*. Princeton.

Ruyter, N. (1996), "The Delsarte Heritage," *Dance Research: The Journal of the Society for Dance Research* 14.1, 62–74.

Sikelianos, Eleni (2005), "The Lefevre–Sikelianos–Waldman Tree and the Imaginative Utopian Attempt," *Jacket* 27 (April) <http://jacketmagazine.com/27/w-sike.html>.

Smith, B. (1998), *The Gender of History: Men, Women, and Historical Practice*. Cambridge.

Trigger, B. (1984), "Alternative Archaeologies: Nationalist, Colonialist, Imperialist," *Man, New Series* 19, 355–70.

Van Steen, G. (2002), "'The World's a Circular Stage': Aeschylean Tragedy through the Eyes of Eva Palmer-Sikelianou," *International Journal of the Classical Tradition* 8, 375–93.

Wilbor, E. (1905), *Delsarte Recitation Book*. New York.

CHAPTER 14

EUGENE O'NEILL'S QUEST FOR GREEK TRAGEDY

VASSILIS LAMBROPOULOS

During the decade of the 1920s, the most productive period of his long career, Eugene O'Neill (1888–1953) systematically explored several aspects of tragedy—formal, religious, psychological, and other. Between *The Emperor Jones* (1920) and *Mourning Becomes Electra* (1931), he experimented with ancient and modern tragic themes, techniques, and ideas. In the productions of his plays he collaborated with major theater people who shared his interests, such as George Cram "Jig" Cook (1873–1924), who founded the Provincetown Players in 1915 (see Hall, this volume), and Kenneth Macgowan (1888–1963) and Robert Edmond Jones (1887–1954), who transformed the Players into The Experimental Theatre. He also discussed his plays and ideas with emerging theater critics with a strong interest in tragedy, such as George Jean Nathan (1882–1958) and Joseph Wood Krutch (1893–1970). In short, in the 1920s O'Neill found himself at the center of a broad artistic and intellectual milieu that, like its contemporary European one, explored the function of tragedy on the post-Wagnerian stage.

The imaginative combination of Hippolytus, Oedipus, and Medea and their transposition to nineteenth-century New England in *Desire under the Elms* (1924) established O'Neill internationally as the leading American artistic playwright. Following this success, he turned his attention to Greek tragedy itself in an attempt to recuperate its fundamentals. The result was *The Great God Brown* (1926), one of his most experimental and little-known works. It is a play that grapples with several issues central to the question of modern tragedy, and does that in a radically *theatrical* way. Specifically, through an elaborate use of masks, O'Neill presents agonistic doubling (friends as brothers and rivals) as the basic structure of contemporary tragedy. In it, the suffering of Dionysus is not the individuation of the will, as Nietzsche had argued, but the duality of identity. But without individuation is rebellion possible?

Dionysus, the god of theater, presides over *The Great God Brown*. There are many possible reasons for his appeal to O'Neill. One is the playwright's intense reading of

Nietzsche's *The Birth of Tragedy* (1872) at the time. Another is the distinct theatricality of the Dionysian cult, the fact that from the earliest times Greeks worshipped Dionysus through theatrical means such as masks, costumes, music, and dance. A third reason is that ancient drama was closely linked to Dionysus: it originated in his cult; in its earliest manifestations it dramatized his myth; it was performed in Athens at his theater and during his festival; and throughout antiquity retained strong associations with the god. (For example, we know that both Thespis and Aeschylus wrote plays called *Pentheus* while later playwrights also drew on themes related to the *Bacchae*). In *The Birth of Tragedy*, Nietzsche writes:

> The tradition is undisputed that Greek tragedy in its earliest form had for its sole theme the sufferings of Dionysus and that for a long time the only stage hero was Dionysus himself. But it may be claimed with equal confidence that until Euripides, Dionysus never ceased to be the tragic hero; that all the celebrated figures of the Greek stage—Prometheus, Oedipus, etc.—are mere masks of this original hero, Dionysus. (Nietzsche 1967: 73)

Drawing on the *Bacchae*, the most self-reflexive tragedy among those that have survived, O'Neill's *The Great God Brown* is another tragedy with Dionysus as its hero. Yet it is not modeled on Euripides. Instead O'Neill wrote a play that presupposes the *Bacchae*. If the *Bacchae*, as a reflection on tragedy, is metatheatrical, *The Great God Brown*, as a tragedy about the *Bacchae*'s reflection on tragedy, is metabacchic.

The play tells the story of two childhood friends, the sons of business partners whom they were supposed to succeed: Dion Anthony is an unsuccessful painter and William Brown a successful architect and businessman. The former, always torn between paganism and asceticism, retires from the business partnership, fails to become an artist, returns to the firm as Brown's draftsman, and dies an alcoholic at the end of Act II. After his death, Brown takes his mask and his wife but is torn between his identity and his friend's identity and is killed accidentally (dismembered) by the police at the end of Act IV. They are rivals for the love of Margaret, who marries first Dion and later William, and of Cybel, a Mother Earth who has been "corrupted" to become a prostitute. O'Neill expressed the wish that Dion in the first half and Brown in the second half of the play should be played by the same actor. (See Jenkins, this volume.)

In the same passage from *The Birth of Tragedy*, Nietzsche proposes that in all tragedy Dionysus suffers individuation:

> The one truly real Dionysus appears in a variety of forms, in the mask of a fighting hero, and entangled, as it were, in the net of the individual will. The god who appears, talks and acts so as to resemble an erring, striving, suffering individual.... In truth, however, the hero is the suffering Dionysus of the Mysteries, the god experiencing in himself the agonies of individuation ... [W]e are therefore to regard the state of individuation as the origin and primal cause of all suffering, as something objectionable in itself.... In this existence as a dismembered god, Dionysus possesses the dual nature of a cruel, barbarized demon and a mild, gentle ruler. (Nietzsche 1967: 72)

O'Neill writes a tragedy not of individuation but of the god's dual nature, of dismemberment as irreconcilable duality. The entire play is fraught with agonistic doubling. The two friends are brothers and rivals, and they compete for both wife and prostitute. There is constant doubling in their views, actions, and careers. There is also much thematic doubling that refers to paganism and Christianity, the public and the private, male and female, and innocence and guilt. All this material is duplicated in the structural plan of the play. As the agonism intensifies, roles and relations become increasingly interchangeable.

In many respects the same fatal doubling connects the two protagonists of the *Bacchae*. Recall that Harmonia was the daughter of Ares and Aphrodite. Cadmus, the founder of Thebes, married Harmonia, and they had six children. One of them, Semele, had Dionysus with Zeus while another, Agave, had Pentheus with Echion. (Later, Cadmus abdicated in favor of Pentheus.) Thus Dionysus and Pentheus, the two grandchildren of Harmonia, are first cousins. The two antagonists competing for power over Thebes are doubles. (Furthermore, the god and his sacrificial victim are ritual doubles.) O'Neill makes this relation the central issue in his play.

Classicists have noted that there is a lot of elaborate doubling throughout the *Bacchae*. This can be seen in the doubling of images (Pentheus sees two suns, two cities of Thebes, and two sets of gates—*Bacchae* 918–19) and in the chiasmus of characters (Dionysus starts as actor and ends as spectator, Pentheus starts as spectator and ends as actor). It is also there in the structural homologies: Foley has included among the doubles of the play itself the festival on the mountain (which we only hear about), as well as the opening day of the Great Dionysia, the three stages of the festival, and the genre of Old Comedy (Foley 1980). The doubling also extends to the theatrical devices: Segal proposes that, when Agave arrives with Pentheus' head, she is holding the mask that the actor of Pentheus had worn earlier (Segal 1982: 260–1). It is also more than likely that the same actor played Pentheus and Agave. O'Neill organizes his tragedy on the principle of "difference-in-identity" that Segal sees as structuring the *Bacchae* (Segal 1986: 65). However, between identity and difference O'Neill interpolates a third dimension, a strictly theatrical one, the mask: his four major characters don an array of full-face masks in a variety of masked, as it were, settings, all of them with backgrounds consisting of deliberately over-detailed painted backdrops.

Despite early uses like Goethe's in 1801–2, the modern mask is post-Nietzschean: it presupposes *The Birth of Tragedy* and the philosopher's subsequent reflections on its idea. Writing about ancient life, Nietzsche exclaimed: "What can we understand of that as long as we do not understand the delight in masks and the good conscience in using any kind of mask! Here is the bath and the recreation of ancient spirit" (Nietzsche 1974: 132). The immediate use of the mask is to question the conventions of naturalism, such as the identification of actor and character. It is also experimental as it operates at the limits of theatricality: the modern mask is neither representational nor anti-representational—it is masked representation. Furthermore, as a device, it is often integrated in the total artwork that collectives of creators pursue. For the moderns, the mask is idololatrous:

> Masks are almost ubiquitous in non-western cultures. The western and Islamic worlds are unusual in regarding the mask as a mode of concealment, not a mode of revelation and transformation. It seems to be a correlative of monotheistic religions that they want human nature to be single, not multiple. The one god who sees and knows everything is naturally hostile to the idea of disguises. (Wiles 2004: 245–6)

It has the capacity to open up Greek drama to any culture in the world and any historical period: it becomes a dramatic universal that retains its cultural specificity. Last, it functions as the internal other of performance, encouraging self-reflexivity. In his "Memoranda on Masks" (1932) O'Neill says:

> Looked at from even the most practical standpoint of the practicing playwright, the mask *is* dramatic in itself, *has always* been dramatic in itself, *is* a proven weapon of attack. (Krasner 2008: 186)

The mask returned to western theater with Symbolism and flourished with Modernism. Its earliest advocates included Maurice Maeterlinck (1890), Alfred Jarry (1896), Vyacheslav Ivanov (1904), Edward Gordon Craig (1910), Vsevolod Meyerhold (1912), Yeats (1916), and Ivan Goll (1920). It was of intense interest to playwrights, directors, designers, costume makers, actors, dancers, choreographers, philosophers, and many others.

> In every significant and influential experimental artistic movement in the early decades of the century—futurism, Dadaism, surrealism, symbolism, and expressionism—the mask figured as a seminal device. (Smith 1984: 6)

To O'Neill and other Modernists the mask offered contradictory possibilities: a symbolist one whereby it hides and protects the inner person, and a ritualist one whereby it depersonalizes acting. Ultimately, however, the mask works against both (realist or symbolist) interiority and (ritualist or nudist) exteriority. The mask is by definition performative: it cannot but involve performance. O'Neill, who had already experimented with masks, drew heavily on this Modernist tradition for *The Great God Brown*. This time, however, he developed a far more direct connection with the Greek mask.

Recall the opening of the *Bacchae*, where Dionysus returns to his native Thebes to assert his true identity and appears first disguised as a priest. Here we see on the stage an actor who is wearing a mask of Dionysus (a god) who is wearing a mask of his priest (a man). This scene is the epiphany of the masked god, a god who was worshipped in cult as a mask; that is, a mask worked as an idol of Dionysus. At the same time, it is the epiphany of the frontally facing god with whom humans can make contact only face to face. Writing on ancient drama, Claude Calame has argued that, when it comes to the public's confrontation with theater, the mask has a function central to tragic representation because

> It is only the mask that allows direct confrontation simultaneously with dissimulation. This double function can be traced to the etymology of the Greek term for mask: *prosopon* can be understood both as "that which is close to the eyes" and "that

which faces the eyes" (of another). On its own terms, the word for mask appears to imply the ideas both of appearance and of confrontation through the gaze. Analyzing the actual use of these tragic and comic masks during dramatic representations for the Great Dionysia, we find that the function of the classical Athenian mask is first to dissimulate, and only secondly to identify. Thus the individual and social identity of the real face of the actor is hidden, without, on the other hand, precisely representing the identity of the character on stage.... The mask creates a confrontation between the dramatic action and the public, while, by the same token, mediating this confrontation. (Calame 1996: 27–8)

The mask is not confrontation with otherness but what Derrida would call "*différance*," the tension between two dialectical terms. It captures the tension between audience and stage, identity and dissimulation. The Greek word *prosopon* means both face and person, both mask and character in a play. Therefore the face is a mask (operating between identity and dissimulation), and the person a dramatic part (like that of a chorus member acting between audience and stage). *The Great God Brown* is a four-act elaboration of this theatrical insight, using it to explore the fundamentals of tragedy.

The play opens with a scene that is chiasmatic to the opening of the *Bacchae*: an actor is playing a modern-day Dionysus (a man) who is wearing a mask of Pan (a god). What follows is a complex study of agonistic doubling mediated by the mask. As the circulation of masks shows, agonism doubles and dramatic parts become interchangeable:

Dion wears four masks in the play, each marking a stage in his external transformation from Pan to demon.... The mask grows increasingly cruel, from Pan to Mephistopheles, to a "diabolical Mephistopheles," until, in its last manifestation, it is so cruelly malignant that it has the appearance of a real "demon". As Dion's mask undergoes transformations, so does his face, changing finally into the ascetic, pure, radiant visage of a Christian martyr. As Dion's suffering and isolation increase, the gap between the mask and the face widens. (Smith 1984: 132–3)

One night, sensing that his end is near and "in a wild state," a disheveled Dion visits Brown at home. He tells him that throughout his life he has rebelled against God, injustice, and society. He has turned into the Bad Boy Pan and Bacchus, the Prince of Darkness and the devil, embracing blasphemy and defiance until his last moments. At this point, the actor playing Dion, who has the "appearance" of a demon, takes off the mask of Pan and is left with the face of a "martyr" which is still not his real face. He then dies, leaving himself to his friend and antagonist. Brown is ready to free himself from his fear of the Pan's mask by putting it on. It is going to be his first mask. Margaret arrives, looking for Dion, her husband, and wearing her mask. When Brown appears wearing Dion's mask, that is, the mask of Pan, she takes hers off, freeing herself from it. End of Act II.

Masks remain equally important in the second half of the play, as Susan Smith has discussed:

Billy Brown's masks and faces are no less complex than Dion's and even more difficult for an audience to understand because O'Neill does not follow the pattern he established with Dion.

The mask, which on Dion was the opposite of his face, on Brown possesses him, transforming his face.... At Dion's death Brown dons the Mephistophelean mask. Lacking Dion's divine inner strength, Brown submits to the evil mask; his face becomes "ravaged and haggard ... tortured and distorted" by the demon. When he needs to be Brown, he must now wear a mask that duplicates his old features.

Through the masking Brown relives Dion's martyrdom and emotional life with two women, Cybel and Margaret. Cybel is to Dion as Margaret is to Brown. (Smith 1984: 133)

What Foley says about the end of Pentheus applies to both Dion and Brown:

> The conventional identification between the tragic figure and his mask formally corresponds to his dramatic situation. He cannot completely step outside of or internally withdraw from and control his character or his fate; he is strictly human. As Euripides' staging brilliantly demonstrates, the tragic character *is* his mask, and is ultimately limited in the action to what his mask represents. (Foley 1980: 131)

Scholars have discussed the so-called play-within-the-play effects in the *Bacchae*. Dionysus reveals his divinity to the Thebans by staging a play, the destruction of Pentheus. Set, costume, design, sound, even a chorus (of his followers) is deployed to create a spectacle. "That is, theatrical illusion demonstrates the reality of the god and illusion and symbol are our only mode of access to a god who can take whatever form he wishes" (Foley 1980: 110). Dionysus introduces his worship by directing a play, and expects that worship to take a similar form. His divinity and his disguise are the same thing. He may be apprehended only through theatrical means, such as a mask or the *deus ex machina* of the play's conclusion. Cadmus and Teiresias show that responding properly to Dionysus' revelation and honoring the god entails theatrical self-transformation. In the end of the play, Pentheus, who resisted the god's challenge, survives only as a mask impaled on his mother's maenadic thyrsus.

The *Bacchae* shows why Dionysian ritual and theater had always been closely connected:

> The invention of theatre ... could only make its impact within the framework of the cult of Dionysus, the god of illusions, confusion, and the constant muddling of reality and appearances, truth and fiction. (Vernant and Vidal-Naquet 1990: 205)

This god turns the world into an elaborate play:

> Wherever he appears on the stage of the world, the god sets up a theater of fantasies to take the place of the familiar everyday setting. Not only is he the great hunter but also the great illusionist, the master conjuror, the author and chorus leader of a sophisticated performance in which nothing and no one ever remain what they seem. (Vernant and Vidal-Naquet 1990: 398)

While in the *Bacchae* Dionysus entraps Pentheus in a series of scenes that he directs, in *The Great God Brown* both heroes get entrapped in several scenes of their own making, scenes they attempt to direct. We might say that *The Great God Brown* consists of a series of plays within a play where Dionysus stages confrontations between him and Pentheus. O'Neill's god is obsessed with staging his own dual nature. Here agonism is trapped in an inescapable doubling. If, as Vernant proposed, a central theme of the *Bacchae* is to become other than oneself, in *The Great God Brown* the theme is being double. While Nietzsche claims that the hero of all tragedy is Dionysus experiencing the agonies of individuation, O'Neill proposes that the god's true suffering is his doubling, that is, his constitutive agonism with Pentheus. Nietzsche hoped for an "end of individuation," "rebirth of Dionysus," and a restoration of "the oneness of everything existent" (Nietzsche 1967: 74). O'Neill sees no such escape from the play of masks. In his "Memoranda on Masks" (1932) he says that theater needs "a new form of drama . . . a drama of souls, and the adventures of 'free wills,' with the masks that govern them and constitute their fates" (Krasner 2008: 186). In *The Great God Brown* masks govern free wills by doubling them. At the end the play affirms the eternal recurrence of birth and dismemberment, the eternal doubling of the cycle.

The Great God Brown is a tragedy of rebellion written as a study of agonistic doubling, and based on the device of the mask. The two sides of Dionysus are constantly rehearsing their individuation, their liberation from one another, family ties, moral norms, profession, artistic conventions, and the divine. They want to be autonomous but remain caught between multiple doubles like Dionysus and Anthony (Dion) or Dionysus and Apollo (Brown) and of course between themselves. Dion is "tortured into torturing others" (O'Neill 1988b: 506) while Brown is Dion's "murderer" and "murdered" (O'Neill 1988b: 530). Through the use of masks they discover that individuation doubles, duality is agonistic, and rebellion cancels itself. Dionysus cannot design "the Temple of Man's Soul" (O'Neill 1988b: 510). When asked to design a capitol or a cathedral, all he can do is to question the authority of such edifices by including images of Silenus, his companion. His nature is similar to that of the rebel Prometheus, one of Dionysus' masks, as defined by Nietzsche: "All that exists is just and unjust and equally justified in both" (Nietzsche 1967: 72).

O'Neill did not write a treatise on drama. He experimented with a *theatrical* study of tragedy to explore the future of this genre. Like so many of his contemporaries, he had taken Nietzsche's challenge to heart. In Section 11 of *The Birth of Tragedy*, the philosopher alludes to Pan's death to describe the death of tragedy and also to issue a warning to epigones about their life in the shadow of past masters. He writes:

> When Greek tragedy died, there rose everywhere the deep sense of an immense void. Just as Greek sailors in the time of Tiberius once heard on a lonesome island the soul-shaking cry, "Great Pan is dead", so the Hellenic world was now pierced by the grievous lament: "Tragedy is dead! Poetry itself has perished with her! Away with you, pale, meager epigones! Away to Hades, that you may for once eat your fill of the crumbs of our former masters!" (Nietzsche 1967: 76)

Was Pan, the goat god, really dead? Was tragedy exhausted? The question was important to O'Neill. For example, referring to "Aristotle's purging," he noted in 1931:

> It is about time we purged his purging out of modern criticism, candidly speaking! What modern audience was ever purged by pity and terror by witnessing a Greek tragedy or what modern mind by reading one? It can't be done! We are too far away,

we are in a world of different values! . . . What we need is a definition of Modern and not Classical Tragedy by which to guide our judgments. If we had Gods or a God, if we had a Faith, if we had some healing subterfuge by which to conquer Death, then the Aristotelian criterion might apply in part to our Tragedy. But our tragedy is just that we have only ourselves, that there is nothing to be purged into except a belief in the guts of man, good or evil, who faces unflinchingly the black mystery of his own soul. (O'Neill 1988a: 390–1)

In *The Great God Brown* O'Neill brings Pan back to the stage to see how he might function in a tragedy without the consolation of catharsis.

Pan was important to the Modernists for two major reasons. First, because of his dual nature: as a hybrid creature (with human torso and arms but legs, ears, and horns of a goat), he defies unity and harmony. Part human, part animal; part benevolent, part sinister; part inspiring, part alarming—the Arcadian divinity personifies in one and the same powerful creature several contrasting qualities that haunted the fin-de-siècle: Dionysus vs. Christ, Paganism vs. Christianity, profane vs. sacred, sensual vs. spiritual, hedonism vs. morality, Arcadia vs. modernity, nature vs. society, primitive vs. civilized. In contrast to the opposition between Apollo and Dionysus, which is seeking a fusion of the two forces, in the case of Pan we have a dialectical tension beyond transcendence, a coexistence of two irreconcilable forces. The second reason for Pan's importance during the period concerns the question of Hellenism in modern times. If Pan was a deity who died, did that mean that the Greek gods are not immortal? Over the centuries, various writers (most recently, Romantic poets) had suspected that the gods of Greece had departed or withdrawn. But now, in the wake of Nietzsche's call for a rebirth of tragedy, from which divinities might the new drama draw inspiration? Thus the enigmatic, self-contradictory figure of this half-man, half-goat became a paradigmatic cipher for Modernists as artists and intellectuals appealed to his powers to find out whether the oracles are silent (a concern that was of importance to the Greek historian Plutarch at the dawn of another millennium 19 centuries earlier).

Not coincidentally, the widespread interest in Pan overlaps with a tremendous exploration of the idea of the tragic across the western world, from Russia to the U.S.A. While artists like Mallarmé, Debussy, Diaghilev, and Nijinsky were putting the faun on the stage in order to bring back the archetypal goat of theater, thinkers were taking the goat's song (i.e., tragedy) away from the stage and placing it in metaphysics (Lukács, Unamuno, Scheler, Heidegger), society (Simmel, Benjamin, Spengler), prehistory (Harrison, Cornford), or the individual (Freud, Sologub, Berdyaev). Both artists and thinkers were raising questions about the place of oracles in a world where, while the gods seemed long gone, panic could strike again.

O'Neill's dual Dionysus wears Pan's mask both at the opening and the closing scene. Is the "Great God Brown," the title of the play, affirmative or sarcastic? A question or a lament? What is certain is that it operates like a mask and renews the philosophical issue of tragedy in radical theatrical terms. Olga Taxidou has rightly expressed reservations about a view of tragedy as speculative philosophy. Her approach to the *Bacchae* refuses to reduce theater to theory:

> The speculation that Dionysus represents is enacted through tragic form itself... The Euripidean Dionysus is both ritualistic and critical, both spectacular and speculative. This approach changes both tragic form and philosophy in the process. (Taxidou 2004: 109)

O'Neill achieves something similar by writing a post-Nietzschean tragedy, the metabacchic *The Great God Brown*, where tragic form becomes philosophical and philosophy spectacularized. Gradually his contemporaries recognized this achievement. Joseph Wood Krutch, O'Neill's admirer and friend, first denied the possibility of modern tragedy. In the famous chapter "The Tragic Fallacy" of his book *The Modern Temper: A Study and a Confession* (1929), he argued that the faiths and convictions that sustained it are extinct. Ten years later, in *The American Drama since 1918* (1939), he acknowledged that American tragedy was possible in a chapter simply called "Tragedy: Eugene O'Neill." Since O'Neill's plays from the 1920s, the claim remains valid. Suffice to note Edward Albee's 2002 take on the *Bacchae*: the title of the play is *The Goat, or Who is Sylvia?* and its subtitle, *Notes towards a Definition of Tragedy*.

REFERENCES

Calame, C. (1996), "Vision, Blindness, and Mask: The Radicalization of the Emotions in Sophocles' *Oedipus rex*," in M. Silk ed., *Tragedy and the Tragic: Greek Theatre and Beyond*. Oxford, 17–37.
Clark, B. H. (1947), *Eugene O'Neill: The Man and his Plays* [1926?]. New York.
Foley, H. P. (1980), "The Masque of Dionysus," *Transactions of the American Philological Association* 110, 107–33.
Krasner, D. (ed. 2008), *Theatre in Theory 1900–2000: An Anthology*. Oxford.
Nietzsche, F. (1967), *The Birth of Tragedy* [1872]. Trans. W. Kaufmann New York.
Nietzsche, F. (1974), *The Gay Science* [1887]. Trans. W. Kaufmann. New York.
O'Neill, E. (1988a), *Selected Letters*. Ed. T. Bogard and J. R. Bryer. New Haven.
O'Neill, E. (1988b), *Complete Plays 1920–1931*. New York.
Segal, C. (1982), *Dionysiac Poetics and Euripides' Bacchae*. Princeton.
Segal, C. (1986), "Greek Tragedy and Society: A Structuralist Perspective," in J. P. Euben ed., *Greek Tragedy and Political Theory*. Berkeley, 43–75.
Silk, M. S. (ed. 1996), *Tragedy and the Tragic: Greek Theatre and Beyond*. Oxford.
Smith, S. V. H. (1984), *Masks in Modern Drama*. Berkeley.
Taplin, O. (1996), "Comedy and the Tragic," in M. Silk ed., *Tragedy and the Tragic: Greek Theatre and Beyond*. Oxford, 188–202.
Taxidou, O. (2004), *Tragedy, Modernity and Mourning*. Edinburgh.
Vernant, J.-P. and P. Vidal-Naquet (1990), *Myth and Tragedy in Ancient Greece* [1972, 1986]. Trans. J. Lloyd. New York.
Wiles, D. (2004), "The Use of Masks in Modern Performances of Greek Drama," in E. Hall, F. Macintosh, and A. Wrigley eds., *Dionysus since 69: Greek Tragedy at the Dawn of the Third Millennium*. Oxford, 245–63.

PART IV
THE LIVING PASTS (1925–1970)

CHAPTER 15

CHOREOGRAPHING THE CLASSICS, PERFORMING SEXUAL DISSIDENCE

SUSAN MANNING

WITH the 2010 publication of *The Ancient Dancer in the Modern World*, editor Fiona Macintosh initiated a rich dialogue between classical reception studies and dance studies. Bringing together more than twenty essays by Classicists, dance scholars, and dance practitioners, Macintosh demonstrates the significance of theatrical dance in Europe, Britain, and the United States for "classical performance reception" from the seventeenth through the early twentieth-first centuries. Noting that "it is often the dancers who get there first" (Macintosh 2010b: 6), Macintosh points out that French dancer Marie Sallé performed a *tableau vivant* of Pygmalion at Covent Garden "some five decades before the much better known 'Attitudes' of Emma Hamilton" and that the American choreographer Martha Graham's 1947 work *Night Journey* "anticipated just about every shift that has become emblematic in the reception of Sophocles' [*Oedipus Rex*] in the last four decades" (Macintosh 2010b: 6, 9).

The collected essays—and the invaluable list of première dates for the 90 dances discussed in the volume—organize the classical reception of theatrical dance into two periods: first the transition from court entertainment to the public stage in Europe and Britain, a move that culminates with the *ballet d'action* of Jean-Georges Noverre in the late eighteenth century, "by which time," Macintosh writes, "ballet had acquired sufficient status to become a high cultural art form *sui generis*: and it had done so with the ancient example as both guide and legitimizing authority" (Macintosh 2010b: 2). After a hiatus of nearly a century in the list of works—from Salvatore Viganò's 1801 *The Creatures of Prometheus* (set to Beethoven's ballet score of the same title) to Loie Fuller's 1897 *La Danse du feu* (set to Scriabin's *Prometheus: Poem of Fire*)—the twentieth century inaugurates a second period of "fascination with ancient dance... especially as a means of liberating the body and soul from the repressive forces of nature and society and in turn from the strictures of balletic tradition itself" (Macintosh 2010b: 2).

Although Macintosh's introduction to *The Ancient Dancer in the Modern World* masterfully balances the two periods, the collected essays devote far more attention to the twentieth century. Given the predominance of the last century as a research focus in dance studies, this is not surprising. Taken together, the essays demonstrate the explosive convergence of ideas espoused by Friedrich Nietzsche, Maurice Emmanuel, Jane Harrison, and Lillian Lawler with the performance practices of Isadora Duncan, Maud Allan, Eva Palmer, and Ted Shawn in the early twentieth century. Later in the century these ideas and practices continue to reverberate through the work of Martha Graham, George Balanchine, Pina Bausch, Mark Morris, Michael Clark, and William Forsythe. As Macintosh cautions her fellow Classicists, "we ignore dance history at our peril" (Macintosh 2010b: 9).

In this chapter, I would like to complement the pioneering research of *The Ancient Dancer in the Modern World* by drawing attention to the way that twentieth-century choreographers deploy Graeco-Roman antiquity as source material, subject matter, reference, and allusion to perform dissident stagings of gender and sexuality for both male and female dancers. My use of the term "dissidence" derives from Alan Sinfield and expands his usage, for while Sinfield typically refers to "sexual dissidence," I use the term also to refer to practices and representations of gender, in addition to sexuality, that depart from dominant norms as these norms are defined culturally and historically. When the departures from dominant norms are visible only to some but not to all viewers, I use the term "cloak" rather than "closet," in order to underscore that unconventional images of gender at times hide in plain sight, along with non-normative images of sexuality.[1]

Looking closely at dances across the century, I will suggest that choreographers significantly shifted the ways they used the Classics to articulate gender and sexual dissidence from the years before World War I to the decades surrounding World War II to the closing decades of the century. In this way, my account further periodizes the larger narrative of *The Ancient Dancer in the Modern World*. During the early years of the twentieth century, Isadora Duncan staged a radically new image of the female dancer while Vaslav Nijinsky staged a radically new image of the male dancer, and both relied on classical imagery to legitimize their dissident performances of gender and sexuality. At mid-century George Balanchine and Martha Graham narrated classical myths in ways that cloaked the performance of gender and sexual dissidence. At century's end Mark Morris, among other postmodernists, revisited classical myths in order to stage gender and sexual dissidence more openly than was possible at mid-century. Thus choreographing the Classics embodies and enacts changing conceptions of gender and sexuality across the twentieth century.

These changing conceptions shape and are shaped by broad socio-cultural changes. The late nineteenth and early twentieth centuries witnessed the entry of middle-class women into the university and the professions, the suffrage movement, the emergence of sexology and sex reform, and the formation of social worlds where sexual dissidence flourished. Mid-century occasioned backlash: in response to economic depression, the rise of authoritarianism, and world war, many states criminalized and medicalized sexual dissidence and traditional gender roles reasserted their dominance. The 1960s and 1970s initiated pushback, as second-wave feminism, womanism, and gay rights challenged social norms, medical policy, and state oppression and discrimination. These broad socio-cultural changes played out differently in the United States, in Great Britain, and across Europe, but some variation of early twentieth-century progress, mid-century backlash, and late twentieth-century reform held across Europe and America and informed the choreography of the Classics.

I

Perhaps no dancer has received more discussion in classical reception studies than Isadora Duncan. From essays by Frederick Naerebout, Ann Cooper Albright, Tyler Jo Smith, Ruth Webb, Alessandra Zanobi, and Susan Jones in *The Ancient Dancer in the Modern World* (2010) to Carrie Preston's *Modernism's Mythic Pose* (2011) and Helene Foley's *Reimagining Greek Tragedy on the American Stage* (2012), scholars have probed Duncan's reading of Nietzsche, familiarity with Maurice Emmanuel, engagement with Delsarte, and acquaintance with Jane Harrison, as well as her study of Greek vases in museums across Europe and her own writings on Greek dance. In an essay on "The Greek Theatre" (1915) Duncan wrote:

> Greek tragedy sprang from the dancing and singing of the first Greek Chorus. Dancing has gone a long way astray. She must return to her original place—hand in hand with the Muses encircling Apollo. She must become again the primitive Chorus, and the drama will be reborn from her inspiration. (Duncan 1928/1969: 87)

Although Duncan surely influenced the staging of Greek tragedy by her brother Raymond and his wife Penelope Sikelanios and even attempted her own production, she made her name as a soloist.[2]

Yet she did not see herself as a soloist exhibiting her dance for the audience. Rather, as she wrote in an essay titled "The Dance of the Greeks" (undated):

> When I have danced I have tried always to be the Chorus: I have been the Chorus of young girls hailing the return of the fleet, I have been the Chorus dancing the Pyrrhic Dance, or the Bacchic; I have never once danced a solo. The dance, again joined with poetry and with music, must become once more the tragic Chorus ... That is the only way for it to become again an art. (Duncan 1928/1969: 96)

Rejecting the term "solo," Duncan reacted against what she perceived as the limitations of late nineteenth-century ballet—the "unnatural" demands of the technique, its reliance on the corseted figure and the toe shoe, and its emphasis on virtuosity. Along with other late nineteenth-century reformers, she abandoned the corset in favor of free-flowing silk tunics, a silhouette adapted from the images on Greek vases. She had studied Delsarte as a young woman, and her movement vocabulary adopted many of its precepts, along with basic steps such as runs, walks, skips, hops, simple leaps, and turns—all performed in bare feet, a radical gesture at the turn of the century, barely a generation away from the Victorian bustle. Duncan resisted codifying her technique, and instead believed that each dancer should develop her own signature style. This became the founding move of what later generations would call "modern dance"—each dancer her own choreographer.

The female pronoun is significant here, because Duncan appealed especially to female spectators in her reconfiguring of the female body onstage. At once spiritual *and* sensual, Duncan emphasized the kinesthetic dimension of movement, its flow, and in so doing symbolized the heightened possibilities for female mobility in an era when white middle-class women first entered university and the professions and organized for suffrage. As Eva Palmer later recalled her first encounters with Duncan's dancing: "[We] all felt that the shackles of the world were loosened, that liberation was ahead of us."[3]

Many of Duncan's female spectators took up forms of corporeal practice that resembled her dancing. As Macintosh demonstrates, legions of women studied and performed Greek dance during the years before and after World War I (Macintosh 2010c). Yet this phenomenon was not limited to Britain, but also widespread across the British Empire, continental Europe, and the United States (Carter and Fensham 2011; Tomko 1999). Embodying a range of forms in addition to Greek dancing—Delsarte theatricals, Dalcroze eurhythmics, aesthetic gymnastics, *Körperkultur* ("body culture")—Duncan's female followers experienced new forms of physical and imaginative mobility.

Although Duncan looked to Greek dance as her inspiration, she did not attempt to recreate Greek dance, as Eva Palmer did in her staging of *Prometheus Bound* at the Delphic Festival in 1927 and 1930. Rather, as early as her 1903 manifesto, "The Dancer of the Future," Duncan articulated her vision of dance regaining the central place it had occupied in ancient Greece and linked that vision to new possibilities for women's lives and expressive practices:

> To return to the dances of the Greeks would be as impossible as it is unnecessary. But the dance of the future will have to become again a high religious art as it was with the Greeks . . . The dancer of the future will be one whose body and soul have grown so harmoniously together that the natural language of that soul will have become the movement of the body . . . [The dancer] will dance not in the form of nymph, nor fairy, nor coquette, but in the form of woman in her greatest and purest expression . . . She will dance the freedom of woman. (Duncan 1928/1969: 62–3)

In one sense, Duncan's allusions to "the dances of the Greeks" legitimized her radical reconfiguration of the female dancer, a reconfiguration that defined modern dance as a high art at precisely the moment when the distinction between high and low took shape in American culture. Not uncoincidentally, as a high art modern dance also became a "white art," for Duncan defined her new art of the dance not only in opposition to ballet but also in opposition to jazz dance, in particular the ragtime craze of the 1910s and 1920s.[4]

Although Duncan never codified her technique, her followers did. Over the course of her career, she founded several schools for young girls. Her students in turn became professional dancers in their own right and further disseminated her technique and repertory. That's how her works survive into the present, through oral and kinesthetic transmission from student to student, and there are videos available for educational distribution that demonstrate the performance of second- and third-generation students.[5] However, like many dance scholars, I find contemporary visual images of Duncan as illuminating as the reverential recreations of her dancing. Consider the watercolor of Duncan by Abraham Walkowitz (see Fig. 15.1). The viewer's gaze encounters her body as a single mass, her forearms tucked behind her back, her breasts and pubis visible behind the diaphanous folds of her sleeveless tunic, her neck exposed, her face upturned. The expressiveness of the pose resides in the body's fulsome stance and dynamic balance. As Cooper Albright writes: "Walkowitz's sketches . . . help us to comprehend how Duncan was able to transform her ideas . . . into a fleshy, weighty corporeality."[6]

Responses to Duncan dancing emphasized her dissident images of gender, and most feminist analyses of her work have advanced this argument, supported by Duncan's decisions to bear children out of wedlock.[7] Yet for some viewers, the images of gender dissidence also connoted sexual dissidence. As Samuel Dorf has demonstrated, Duncan participated in Natalie Barney's social circle, known for its open expression of same-sex desire. Duncan may well have had an affair with Mercedes de Acosta late in her life, but even if scholars' suspicions of this affair prove unfounded, Acosta was a passionate fan. As Acosta later recalled:

> Many nights Isadora danced for me. She danced for me three and four hours at a time. She would completely lose herself as she moved about, and became utterly unconscious of anything but the rhythm of her own body and the exaltation of her own spirit. She accompanied herself by singing or humming in a curiously low tone that often gave me the illusion that the sound was coming from somewhere far away and not from her at all . . . Often she danced until the first light of morning began to creep in, then suddenly she would stop and look about bewildered, like someone returning from a long journey. (Acosta 1960: 178–9)

Other women-loving women of Acosta's generation were also drawn to Duncan's dancing, including Margaret Anderson, Janet Flanner, Charlotte Perkins Gilman, Emma Goldman, Eva Le Gallienne, Mabel Dodge Luhan, Harriet Monroe, and Gertrude Stein. Some of these women focused their erotic and domestic lives exclusively around other women; others found passion and romance with men as well as women. In both cases, the question remains of how their spectatorship of Duncan differed from the many women who, like Eva Palmer, saw the choreographer anticipating the "liberation . . . ahead of us." It seems there was a continuum of response among lesbian, bisexual, and straight female spectators, for whom Duncan's dancing resonated with their own diverse explorations of female subjectivity and agency.[8]

FIG. 15.1 Isadora Duncan, watercolor by Abraham Walkowitz, Jerome Robbins Dance Division, The New York Public Library for the Performing Arts, Astor, Lenox, and Tilden Foundations.

II

Whereas Isadora Duncan is widely considered the founder of modern dance, Vaslav Nijinsky is widely considered the founder of modern ballet. Duncan and Nijinsky both spent most of their adult lives in Paris, she in exile from Victorian America, he in exile from tsarist Russia. Both did tour the U.S.A., although as many Americans knew them by reputation as actually saw them perform onstage. Like Duncan, Nijinsky grounded his artistic rebellion in an imagined classical world.

Nijinsky's choreographic innovations—and his reconfiguration of the image of the male dancer—cannot be separated from Diaghilev's Ballets Russes, a legendary company of St. Petersburg-trained dancers based in Paris from 1909 to 1929. Serge Diaghilev was an impresario who had a knack for discovering young talent; he brought together composers such as Claude Debussy, Maurice Ravel, and Erik Satie with painters such as Henri Matisse, Georges Rouault, and Pablo Picasso. He nurtured young dancers as choreographers, among them Nijinsky, who was also his lover for a time.

It is rare in historical research to be able to point to a single event that changed broader cultural conceptions, but in this case it is not an exaggeration to state that Nijinsky's performances with Diaghilev's Ballets Russes before World War I introduced an association between the male concert dance and homosexuality that has persisted into the present.[9] After the Romantic ballerina went up on pointe during the 1830s and 1840s, the male dancer had mostly disappeared from the ballet stages of western Europe and the United States, surviving only in the court-supported theaters of Denmark and Russia. So when Nijinsky reappeared on the feminized stage of ballet in Paris and London, he introduced a new set of meanings for the male dancer.

As Ramsay Burt has demonstrated, the bourgeois norms of masculinity established during the Industrial Revolution resulted in the near disappearance of the male dancer during the Victorian era.[10] During the seventeenth and early eighteenth centuries the male dancer had embodied the aristocratic ideal of masculinity, projecting the power of the aristocratic subject as object of the gaze, his authority announced through fashionable dress and leisure pursuits, including dancing. This ideal reached its apotheosis in the dancing of Louis XIV as Apollo, the Sun King. During the Victorian era the bourgeois man rejected the aristocratic ideal, redefining male authority as the bearer, not the object, of the gaze. This accompanied a sharpened division between the public and the private sphere brought about by the Industrial Revolution. Adopting the standardized dress of frock coat, waistcoat, and trousers—the precursor of today's suit—the Victorian bourgeois man focused on the public sphere of work and politics rather than the newly privatized sphere of domesticity and the emotions. Maintaining an ideology of separate spheres, men socialized with one another outside the home, often attending the theater together, where the Victorian actress and dancer occupied a cultural space associated with "public women" and where prostitutes inhabited the "third tier" of the auditorium.[11] Within the gendered ideology of separate spheres, male artists became an exception, as the Romantic genius defied the division between masculine and feminine pursuits, bringing emotion into the public sphere.

Thus, when Nijinsky became a star dancer in the years before World War I, he fulfilled the expectations for an artistic genius whose virtuosic performance and charisma rendered him an exception to bourgeois norms for masculinity. For many spectators, Nijinsky's otherness was part and parcel of the innovative spectacle of the Ballets Russes as a whole. But for some spectators, Njinsky's dancing connoted the otherness of non-normative sexuality, during an era when homosexuality was taking shape as a social identity in western culture. In fact, Lynn Garafola demonstrates that by the late 1920s performances of the Ballets Russes drew a visibly gay circle of viewers (Garafola 1989: 373). By this time Nijinsky had not performed in public for a decade, but the subcultural meanings of his performance continued to mark the reception of ballet.

Diaghilev first presented Nijinsky in the reform ballets of Michel Fokine, who had rejected the strict Classicism of the Maryinsky's artistic director Marius Petipa and, entranced by Duncan, brought a heightened expressiveness and fluidity to ballet. In Fokine's ballets, Nijinsky took on androgynous personae as the Spirit of the Rose in the work of the same title, the Blue God in *Le Dieu bleu,* the melancholy puppet in *Petrouchka,* the Golden Slave in *Scheherezade.* Fokine choreographed two works on classical themes for Nijinsky—*Narcisse* (1911) to music by Nicholas Tcherepnin with libretto, set, and costumes by Léon Bakst; and *Daphnis and Chloë* (1912) to music by Maurice Ravel with set and costumes by Bakst. A photograph of Nijinsky in *Narcisse* shows him dressed in a Duncan-style tunic and posed on half-pointe with arms angled overhead, his Duncanesque silhouette confounded by his defined musculature.[12]

By the time *Daphnis and Chloë* premièred, Fokine had lost favor as the Ballets Russes house choreographer, and Diaghilev had turned his attention to developing Nijinsky as a choreographer. Thus in 1912 Diaghilev commissioned costumes and décor from Bakst and selected Claude Debussy's lush score inspired by Mallarmé's poem *L'Après-midi d'un faune (Afternoon of a Faun)* for his protégé's choreographic debut. Known for his astonishing jumps in Fokine's works, Nijinsky eschewed virtuosic technique in creating *L'Après-midi d'un faune.* Rather, he experimented with two-dimensional movement, angular lines, awkward poses, slow tempos, and long pauses. As Nijinsky told an interviewer in London at the time of the work's première, he had studied "the ancient marbles, the bas reliefs, the vases" in museums in Paris and London, seeking inspiration for "dance gestures, physical balance, and purity of movement." He continued, "It has no story really: it is simply a fragment drawn from a classic bas-relief."[13] A photograph (Fig. 15.2) shows Nijinsky in a characteristic pose, arms held stiffly in front of his body, torso angled, legs in parallel, balanced on half-toe, his stance weighted with stillness—so contrary to the fulsome curves of Isadora Duncan or the virtuosic display of Petipa's ballets.[14]

Onstage, Nijinsky's planar movement—created at exactly the moment Cubism was taking shape in Paris—contrasted the sustained breath of Debussy's score and the rich colors of Bakst's palette. Taking the role of the Faun, Nijinsky devised a simple plot for the ballet. The work begins and ends with the Faun alone onstage, lying outstretched

FIG. 15.2 Vaslav Nijinsky in *Afternoon of a Faun*, Jerome Robbins Dance Division, The New York Public Library for the Performing Arts, Astor, Lenox, and Tilden Foundations.

on a concealed platform, difficult to distinguish from the impressionist backdrop. He slowly arches back, like a cat waking from a nap, then returns to his repose. A group of nymphs enters, and the Faun is roused from his perch; he descends and encounters one of the nymphs. When she departs, she leaves a scarf behind; the Faun picks up the scarf, takes it back to his perch, and lies on top of it, ending the dance with an orgasmic gesture like a wet dream.

To paraphrase Nijinsky, no story really? At the time of the première some critics were appalled by the ending gesture, while others saw the gesture in keeping with the archaic Greek world depicted onstage. The morning after the première, the reviewer for *Le Figaro* protested:

> We are shown a lecherous faun, whose movements are filthy and bestial in their eroticism, and whose gestures are as crude as they are indecent . . . Decent people will never accept such animal realism.[15]

But when reprised in London later that season, many critics saw the ending gesture as part of the larger stylization of the work. The reviewer for the *Times* noted:

> M. Nijinsky as the faun is . . . another creature from the [dancer] we have known [in other works]. Yet his crouching movements, his stiff poses, and particularly his last action when he lies down to dream beside the scarf, are extraordinarily expressive.[16]

Subsequent scholars have recast this critical debate. For some (e.g., Garafola 1989), the work depicts the Faun's awakening sexuality, his awkward adolescent longing for the nymph realized only in fantasy. For others, the Faun exudes a queer sexuality, turning away from male–female coupling and evoking non-normative desires (Farfan 2008; Kopelson 1997). In my teaching, it is hard for students to see levels of meaning beyond the queer reading, and it is difficult to convince them that in the early twentieth century many spectators saw Modernist experimentation, while only some saw same-sex desire. Yet the historical record demonstrates exactly such double-coded reception.

After *L'Après-midi d'un faune*, Nijinsky created three more works for Diaghilev's Ballets Russes, including the choreography for the riotous 1913 première of Stravinsky's *The Rite of Spring*. While on tour of North and South America during the years of World War I, Nijinsky married another member of the company and Diaghilev, infuriated, dismissed him. Within a few years, Nijinsky was diagnosed as schizophrenic and confined to an asylum, although his reputation as an artistic genius and gay icon outlived him.

III

After Nijinsky left the company, Diaghilev turned his attention to other dancers who became his lovers and whom he groomed as choreographers—first Leonide Massine and then Serge Lifar. He also engaged Nijinsky's sister, Bronislava Nijinska, and another recent Russian émigré, George Balanchine, to choreograph new works for the company. In 1928 Diaghilev commissioned Balanchine to choreograph a work to a new score by Igor Stravinsky, *Apollon Musagète*, with scenery designed by André Bauchant and costumes by Bauchant and Chanel. The dance featured Serge Lifar as the protagonist and three female dancers who represented Calliope (goddess of poetry), Polyhymnia (goddess of mime), and Terpsichore (goddess of dance). After choosing Terpsichore as his favored Muse and performing a duet with her, Apollo dances with all three Muses at the end.

In both plot and movement style, *Apollon Musagète* was the inverse of Nijinsky's *Faune*. Whereas in *Faune* the nymphs barely touch the Faun before leaving the stage, in *Apollon Musagète* the Muses engage Apollo physically throughout the work. Near the end, as Balanchine describes the image, "the three Muses pose in arabesque behind Apollo's profiled figure to form a tableau in which the goddesses are as one with him" (see Fig. 15.3) (Balanchine and Mason 1975: 16). Here the female dancers' lifted and curved torsos, extended legs, and pointed toes contrast with the stiff and angular stance Nijinsky adopted in *Faune*. Here Balanchine returns to Petipa's Classicism, revitalizing its precepts with novel partnering—one man supporting three women "as one with him."

At the same time as Balanchine returns to Classicism, his choreography also reasserts a hetero-normative understanding of gender. Here it seems significant that Apollo remains onstage through all the solos of the Muses, so we watch him watching the women: the male dancer is the bearer of the gaze. In this way Apollo serves as a projection of the choreographer himself, who once famously declared, "Ballet is Woman," and typically pursued romantic relationships with his leading ballerinas. Like Apollo at the

FIG. 15.3 Jacques D'Amboise with Allegra Kent in Balanchine's *Apollo*, New York City Ballet, photograph by Martha Swope/© The New York Public Library.

end of the dance, Balanchine was entangled with many women over the course of his career. Yet the work originally starred Serge Lifar, Diaghilev's lover at the time, and the male protagonist remains at the center of the spectacle, the object of the audience's gaze. Thus the reassertion of hetero-normative gender roles does not displace the centering of Diaghilev's repertoire around his favorite male dancer.

The year after the première of *Apollon Musagète*, Diaghilev died and the Ballets Russes collapsed. Its dancers scattered across the globe, seeding dance Modernism from Argentina to Australia. At the invitation of Lincoln Kirstein, George Balanchine came to the United States, established the School of American Ballet in 1934, and after working on Broadway and starting several short-lived companies, founded New York City Ballet in 1948. In an essay published the following year, Balanchine wrote:

> *Apollon* I look back on as the turning point of my life. In its discipline and restraint, in its sustained oneness of tone and feeling the score was a revelation. It seemed to tell me that I could dare not to use everything, that I, too, could eliminate ... I could clarify, by limiting, by reducing what seemed to be multiple possibilities to the one that is inevitable. (Balanchine 1949/1975: 81)

In retrospect, critics have hailed the work as a significant moment of transition in Balanchine's career and in the history of modern ballet—the advent of neoclassicism, a term that applies as well as Stravinsky's musical allusions to earlier forms.

In 1937 and then in 1979 Balanchine revised the work, stripping the earlier décor and costuming and cutting the prologue to the original, in which Leto gives birth to Apollo. The revised work took the shortened title by which it has continued to be known in the repertoire of New York City Ballet—*Apollo*.[17] Stanger interprets the revision of the work as a shift from "the exotic, erotic, and Dionysiac world of Diaghilev's Ballets Russes" to "a choreographic realization of . . . the Apolline ideal" (Stanger 2010: 351). Jones calls the ending "a Socratic, perfected picture of beauty" (Jones 2010: 327).

How do the gender and sexual politics of the work change from its 1928 première to the later repertoire version? As Jones and Stanger note, the revisions crystallized the neoclassicism of Balanchine's aesthetic. In *A Queer History of the Ballet* Peter Stoneley argues that the consolidation of Balanchine's neoclassicism after 1948 "meant the foreclosing of other, more obviously queer possibilities" (Stoneley 2007: 115). By this, Stoneley meant the ascent of Balanchine's women-centered ballets after 1948 and his turn away from Diaghilev's focus on star male dancers. Yet Stoneley also notes the many queer men (some married, some not) who supported Balanchine's neoclassical aesthetic, beginning with Lincoln Kirstein and including Edwin Denby, Frank O'Hara, and George Platt Lynes, among many others. During the early years of the New York City Ballet, simply to visit a gay bar was warrant for arrest, and thousands of men during these years were jailed on this pretext in New York City alone. Perhaps attending the ballet was a safer way to assert a gay identity.

IV

Martha Graham's Greek dance dramas took shape during this same complicated moment in American sexual and gender politics during the years surrounding World War II. While the U.S. military for the first time criminalized homosexuality, legions of gay men and women experienced what historian Alan Bérubé narrated in this book of the same title as "coming out under fire." Women on the homefront experienced an unprecedented degree of financial, emotional, and sexual independence, yet were also expected to conform to the "return to normalcy" promised and promulgated at war's end.

These broader social tensions resonated with changes in Graham's career. Over the course of the 1930s she had developed her technique and repertory in collaboration with her all-female company and with Louis Horst, her accompanist, composer, artistic mentor, and lover 12 years her senior. In 1938 she met Erick Hawkins, a Harvard graduate in Classics and a young dancer and aspiring choreographer 15 years her junior. Hawkins became her lover and later, briefly, her husband. He joined her company, and his presence accompanied a significant shift in her artistic career: with a mixed-sex company, her style became more narrative and more theatrical, and her company appeared for the first time on Broadway; she turned away from the American themes and social concerns that had predominated in her work from the 1930s and embraced more universal and more psychological subject matter, above all in her Greek dance dramas.

Many of her dances from the 1940s can be read in Jungian terms. Graham typically took the role of the female protagonist who is torn between her needs for intimacy and for independence. She confronts a masculine antagonist and in so doing confronts her own fears and her own desires for freedom. The psychodrama resolves as Graham integrates the masculine principle within herself, a drama played out in movement terms as Graham's characteristically inward style integrates the more expansive style of her male characters.

This arc clearly structures *Errand in the Maze*, a 1947 work set to music by Gian-Carlo Menotti and designed by Isamu Noguchi.[18] Graham based the dance loosely on the myth of Ariadne and Theseus, casting herself as the unnamed protagonist and a male dancer as her antagonist, the Creature of Fear. As the dance opens, Graham follows the wavy line of a rope placed on the floor to a sculptured object, resembling a door or perhaps a vulva. Her steps cross over one another, echoing the zigzag of the rope and echoed in turn by the decoration on her dress. The Creature of Fear enters, his arms bound at shoulder height by a shaft he carries. He walks stiffly, lifting his knees and flexing his feet at strong angles, commanding the space and threatening the female protagonist. She retreats behind the sculpted object, using the rope to construct a makeshift barrier (see Fig. 15.4). His crouched stance recalls Nijinsky's weighted angular pose, and the stand-off between the two magnifies the lack of interaction and touch between Nijinsky and the nymphs in *Faune*.

The work draws to a close once the female protagonist determines to vanquish the Creature of Fear, confronting him face to face for the first time. He falls backward, his threat extinguished, and at last her movements gesture beyond herself, "as if swimming through a substance suddenly become light," in the words of one critic (Siegel 1979: 201). By the end, she has incorporated the space-filling movements of her masculine antagonist into her own more interior movement quality, and stands her ground calmly. The ending image could not be more different from *Apollo*, where the work concludes with one man supporting three women "as one with him."

In her solos and dances for her all-female group before 1938, Graham presented the female dancer as a representative subject. But after 1938 she and her female dancers took on more gendered identities in relation to the presence of male dancers in the company. Nonetheless, as *Errand into the Maze* demonstrates, female subjectivity and agency remained center stage in her oeuvre. In one sense, the presence of male dancers in her work after 1938 served to cloak Graham's dissident staging of gender, her protagonists' desires for independence as well as for intimacy. The men's stiff and strong movement style also served to cloak the sexual dissidence of the male dancers, foregrounding their hypermasculine presentation. Graham's challenge to the status quo was hiding in plain sight.

FIG. 15.4 Helen McGehee (in Graham's role) and Clive Thompson in Graham's *Errand into the Maze*, photograph by Umaña, Helen McGehee Archive, Music Division, Library of Congress.

V

Not only Balanchine and Graham, arguably the most influential choreographers of their generation, created works on classical themes on the American stage at mid-century. Indeed, it would be hard to name a major American choreographer from the 1930s through the 1960s who did *not* create one or more works on classical themes. Here is a partial catalogue: Doris Humphrey's *Lysistrata* (1930) and *Iphigenia in Aulis* (1935); Hanya Holm's *The Golden Fleece* (1941) and *Orestes and the Furies* (1943); Lester

Horton's *Medea* (1951); Erick Hawkins's *The Minotaur Discovered* (1952) and *Meditation on Orpheus* (1974); Jose Limon's *Antigona* (1951), *I, Odysseus* (1962), and *Orfeo* (1972); Jerome Robbins's *Afternoon of a Faun* (1953); Alvin Ailey's *Labyrinth* (1963), *Ariadne* (1965), *Myth* (1971), *Hidden Rites* (1973), and *Satyriade* (1982); Merce Cunningham's *The Ruse of Medusa* (1948), *Orestes* (1948), *Labyrinthian Dances* (1957), and *Rune* (1960).

What conclusions might we draw from this profusion of works? Strikingly, classical reception among dance artists follows a different pattern than reception among theater artists. In the introduction to *Dionysus Since 69*, Edith Hall notes an explosion in productions of Greek tragedies since the late 1960s, an explosion she relates to the myriad social and intellectual movements of the time—from feminism and sexual liberation to anti-war activism, multiculturalism, and poststructuralism (Hall 2004). In contrast, choreographers appear more preoccupied by the Classics before 1969 than after. Although the list of premières in *The Ancient Dancer in the Modern World* consists only of those discussed in the volume, it does document more than three times as many twentieth-century works before 1969 as after.[19] Perhaps it was the ability of works to cloak dissident performances of gender and sexuality that made choreographing the Classics so popular before 1969.

After all, 1969 also marks the date of the Stonewall Rebellion, and the gay rights movement of the 1970s occurred alongside second-wave feminism, and both social movements rendered the choreographic strategies of double-coding and subtexting evident earlier in the century no longer necessary among artists and audiences for modern and postmodern dance and contemporary ballet. If my supposition is right, then the same social and intellectual trends that led theater artists to the Classics led dance artists away from the Classics, for they no longer needed the high-cultural legitimization to stage gender and sexual dissidence.

This is not to say that dance artists after 1969 did not continue to choreograph the classical texts. Alessandra Zanobi and Nadine Meisner have explored Pina Bausch's engagement with classical subject matter, while Arabella Stanger has demonstrated how Michael Clark's *Stravinsky Project* (1994) and William Forsythe's *Eidos: Telos* (1995) revisit "Balanchine's Modernist Apolline classicism" (Meisner 2010; Stanger 2010: 366; Zanobi 2010). That both Clark and Forsythe make reference to *Apollo* is telling, for given the ubiquity of classical motifs in early and mid-century choreography, it is hard for contemporary dance works on classical themes not to refer to previous works. And so, in closing, I will turn to a dance that stages a particularly self-conscious revision of its predecessors, Mark Morris's *Dido and Aeneas* (1989) set to Purcell's score.[20]

Morris himself took the doubled role of Dido and the Sorceress, and as critic Joan Acocella has noted, created a "profoundly sexual dance" to the "notably chaste" libretto (Acocella 1993: 98). Figure 15.5 shows Morris as Dido—not in drag, but clearly a man playing a woman—with Guillermo Resto as Aeneas. The two mirror one another, lunging forward, interlocking arms and touching hands, their mutual gaze and mirrored positions suggesting full and equal partnership in same-sex desire. Their angled and weighted pose recalls both Nijinsky in *Faune* and the Creature of Fear in *Errand into the Maze*. Indeed, the entire work is shot through with references to Graham (back falls, deep

FIG. 15.5 Guillermo Resto and Mark Morris in Morris's *Dido and Aeneas*, photograph by Cylla von Tiedemann courtesy of the Mark Morris Dance Group.

second-position pliés, hands covering the eyes) and Nijinsky (two-dimensional, planar movement). The costuming for all the characters, male and female, evokes Graham's characteristic torso-hugging, broad-skirted silhouette. As the Sorceress Morris wears his long hair loose; as Dido he pulls his hair back with the sort of oversized hairpin that Graham often favored. The most unexpected allusion comes near the end, when Morris-as-the-Sorceress lounges downstage and mimes female masturbation to the point of orgasm, recalling the final gesture of Nijinsky's *Faune*. The filmed version of the dance does not fully show this moment. In our time, it seems, showing a man impersonating a woman masturbating is far more dangerous than showing two men desiring one another.

Morris's iteration and revision of Nijinsky's ending gesture in *Faune* underscores how clearly the choreography of the Classics has performed dissident images of gender and sexuality. The dialogue between classical reception studies and dance studies has only just started.

Notes

1. For a fuller explication of how Sinfield's cultural materialism may be adapted as a method for dance studies, see Manning 2004: xviii–xx.
2. Raymond and Penelope produced and starred in Sophocles' *Elektra*, a production in Greek that emphasized music and dance. The production toured Hellenic societies in the U.S.A. in

1910 and was presented in Paris in 1912. In 1915 Isadora collaborated with her other brother Augustin to stage *Oedipus Rex* in New York. Duncan, Pratl, and Splatt 1993: 112–13, 134.
3. Quoted in Macintosh 2010a: 67.
4. See Daly (1995: 215–20) on the construction of whiteness in Duncan's choreography. See Manning (2004) on the construction of whiteness in subsequent practices of modern dance.
5. The most comprehensive video is *Isadora Duncan Dance: Technique and Repertory* (1995), directed by second-generation Duncan dancer Julia Levien. *Isadora Duncan: Movement from the Soul* (1988) features third-generation dancer Lori Belilove. My favorite video documentary is *On Dancing Isadora's Dances* (1988), where Annabelle Gamson describes the resources for her reconstruction, including the myriad of visual images of Duncan made by contemporary artists.
6. Albright 2010a: 63. See further Albright 2010b, a compilation of Walkowitz's images of Duncan, which further explores the relation of dancer and artist.
7. For earlier analyses of Duncan that emphasize the gender dissidence of her dancing, see Manning 1993/2006: 33–40 and Manning 1997.
8. This paragraph summarizes Manning 1999, at this point available only in German.
9. See Hall 2010 for the prehistory to this association in antiquity.
10. Smith 2007 qualifies Burt 1995/2007 but the predominance of female dancers on the ballet stage in western Europe is incontrovertible. However, male dancing remained popular on the minstrel stage, and this history inflects the cultural associations carried by male dancers of color.
11. Davis (1991) is particularly astute on the eroticization of the actress and dancer in the Victorian theater.
12. This photograph is reproduced in Kirstein 1975: 122. Neither *Narcisse* nor *Daphnis and Chloë* has survived in repertoire.
13. Cited in MacDonald 1975: 79.
14. *Faune*, as the work is known in the dance world, has survived in repertoire, handed down from one dancer to another. Nijinsky also recorded the work in a notation system of his own devising, and scholars Anne Hutchinson Guest and Claudia Jeschke have decoded his system and staged their version of his work, available on video, which differs in subtle ways from the versions handed down from dancer to dancer. Nonetheless, the plot and movement style of *Faune* described here characterize all versions in contemporary repertoire attributed to Nijinsky.
15. Cited in Farfan 2008: 76–7.
16. Cited in MacDonald 1975: 80.
17. Excerpts of *Apollo* are available on video from the George Balanchine Foundation (*Music Dances: Balanchine Choreographs Stravinsky*) and from PBS (*Balanchine Celebration*).
18. *Errand into the Maze* has survived in the repertoire of the Martha Graham Dance Company. A video recording is available on *Martha Graham, Three Contemporary Classics* (Video Arts International, 1984).
19. To be exact, *The Ancient Dancer in the Modern World* lists 48 works from Loie Fuller's *La Danse du feu* (1897) to Martha Graham's *Phaedra* (1962) and only 15 works from Frederick Ashton's *The Creature of Prometheus* (1970) to Lucinda Childs's *Daphnis and Chloe* (2003). Many of the mid-century titles mentioned here are not discussed in the volume.

20. Morris's performance in *Dido and Aeneas* is documented on a 1995 video by Image Entertainment. The work continues in the repertoire of the Mark Morris Dance Group, although Morris no longer performs the title role.

REFERENCES

Acocella, J. (1993), *Mark Morris*. New York.
Acosta, M. de (1960), *Here Lies the Heart: A Tale of my Life*. New York.
Albright, A. C. (2010a), "The Tanagra Effect: Wrapping the Modern Body in the Folds of Ancient Greece," in F. Macintosh ed., *The Ancient Dancer in the Modern World: Responses to Greek and Roman Dance*. Oxford, 57–76.
Albright, A. C. (2010b), *Modern Gestures: Abraham Walkowitz Draws Isadora Duncan Dancing*. Middletown, CT.
Balanchine, G. (1949; repr. 1975), "The Dance Element in Stravinsky's Music," in M. Lederman ed., *Stravinsky in the Theatre*. New York, 75–84.
Balanchine, G. and F. Mason (1975), *101 Stories of the Great Ballets*. Garden City, NY.
Bérubé, A. (1990), *Coming Out Under Fire: The History of Gay Men and Women in World War Two*. New York.
Burt, R. (1995; 2nd edn. 2007), *The Male Dancer: Bodies, Spectacle, Sexualities*. London and New York.
Carter, A. and R. Fensham (eds. 2011), *Dancing Naturally: Nature, Neo-Classicism and Modernity in Early Twentieth-Century Dance*. Houndmills and New York.
Daly, A. (1995), *Done into Dance: Isadora Duncan in America*. Bloomington and Indianapolis.
Davis, T. C. (1991), *Actresses as Working Women: Their Social Identity in Victorian Culture*. London and New York.
Dorf, S. (2012), "Dancing Greek Antiquity in Private and Public: Isadora Duncan's Early Patronage in Paris," *Dance Research Journal* 44.1, 3–27.
Duncan, D., C. Pratl, and C. Splatt (1993), *Life into Art: Isadora Duncan and her World*. New York and London.
Duncan, I. (1928/1969), *The Art of the Dance*. New York.
Farfan, P. (2008), "Man as Beast: Nijinsky's Faun," *South Central Review* 25.1, 74–92.
Foley, H. P. (2012), *Reimagining Greek Tragedy on the American Stage*. Berkeley, Los Angeles, and London.
Garafola, L. (1989), *Diaghilev's Ballets Russes*. New York and Oxford.
Guest, A. H. and C. Jeschke (2010), *Nijinksy's Faune Restored*. Binsted.
Hall, E. (2004), "Introduction," in E. Hall, F. Macintosh, and A. Wrigley eds., *Dionysus Since 69*. Oxford, 1–46.
Hall, E. (2010), "'Heroes of the Dance Floor': The Missing Exemplary Male Dancer in Ancient Sources," in F. Macintosh ed., *The Ancient Dancer in the Modern World: Responses to Greek and Roman Dance*. Oxford, 145–68.
Hall, E., F. Macintosh, and A. Wrigley (eds. 2004), *Dionysus Since 69*. Oxford.
Jones, S. (2010), "Modernism and Dance: Apolline or Dionysiac?" in F. Macintosh ed., *The Ancient Dancer in the Modern World: Responses to Greek and Roman Dance*. Oxford, 313–29.
Kirstein, L. (1975), *Nijinsky Dancing*. New York.
Kopelson, K. (1997), *The Queer Afterlife of Vaslav Nijinsky*. Stanford, CA.

MacDonald, N. (1975), *Diaghilev Observed by Critics in England and the United States 1911–1929*. New York and London.

Macintosh, F. (ed. 2010a), *The Ancient Dancer in the Modern World: Responses to Greek and Roman Dance*. Oxford.

Macintosh, F. (2010b), "Introduction," in F. Macintosh ed., *The Ancient Dancer in the Modern World: Responses to Greek and Roman Dance*. Oxford, 1–18.

Macintosh, F. (2010c), "Dancing Maenads in Twentieth-Century Britain," in F. Macintosh ed., *The Ancient Dancer in the Modern World: Responses to Greek and Roman Dance*. Oxford, 188–210.

Manning, S. (1993; 2nd edn. 2006), *Ecstasy and the Demon: The Dances of Mary Wigman*. Minneapolis and London.

Manning, S. (1997), "The Female Dancer and the Male Gaze: Feminist Critiques of Early Modern Dance," in J. Desmond ed., *Meaning in Motion: New Cultural Studies of Dance*. Durham and London.

Manning, S. (1999), "Isadora Duncan, Martha Graham und die lesbische Rezeption," *Tanzdrama* 44–5, 18–25.

Manning, S. (2004), *Modern Dance, Negro Dance: Race in Motion*. Minneapolis.

Meisner, N. (2010), "Iphigenia, Orpheus and Eurydice in the Human Narrative of Pina Bausch," in F. Macintosh ed., *The Ancient Dancer in the Modern World: Responses to Greek and Roman Dance*. Oxford, 277–97.

Naerebout, F. (2010), "'In Search of a Dead Rat': The Reception of Ancient Greek Dance in Late Nineteenth-Century Europe and America," in F. Macintosh ed., *The Ancient Dancer in the Modern World: Responses to Greek and Roman Dance*. Oxford, 39–56.

Preston, C. (2011), *Modernism's Mythic Pose: Gender, Genre, Solo Performance*. Oxford and New York.

Siegel, M. (1979), *The Shapes of Change: Images of American Dance*. Boston.

Sinfield, A. (1994), *Cultural Politics—Queer Reading*. Philadelphia.

Smith, M. (2007), "The Disappearing Danseur," *Cambridge Opera Journal* 19.1, 33–57.

Smith, T. J. (2010), "Reception or Deception? Approaching Greek Dance through Vase-Painting," in F. Macintosh ed., *The Ancient Dancer in the Modern World: Responses to Greek and Roman Dance*. Oxford, 77–98.

Stanger, A. (2010), "Striking a Balance: The Apolline and Dionysiac in Contemporary Classical Choreography," in F. Macintosh ed., *The Ancient Dancer in the Modern World: Responses to Greek and Roman Dance*. Oxford, 347–67.

Stoneley, P. (2007), *A Queer History of the Ballet*. London and New York.

Tomko, L. (1999), *Dancing Class: Gender, Ethnicity, and Social Divides in American Dance, 1890–1920*. Bloomington and Indianapolis.

Webb, R. (2010), "'Where there is Dance there is the Devil': Ancient and Modern Representations of Salome," in F. Macintosh ed., *The Ancient Dancer in the Modern World: Responses to Greek and Roman Dance*. Oxford, 123–44.

Zanobi, A. (2010), "From Duncan to Bausch with Iphigenia," in F. Macintosh ed., *The Ancient Dancer in the Modern World: Responses to Greek and Roman Dance*. Oxford, 236–54.

CHAPTER 16

GREEK TRAGEDY IN MEXICO

FRANCISCO BARRENECHEA

GREEK tragedy has had a small but significant presence on the Mexican stage. Although productions only became frequent from the 1930s, the ancient genre has often been a point of departure for discussions of the state of the Mexican theater.[1] Greek tragedy has repeatedly been linked to innovation and progress in the theater, in a recurrent association with questions of aesthetic reform and the maturity of the Mexican theater. My study will span the period from the second half of the eighteenth century, when neoclassical intellectuals began to discuss plays inspired by Greek tragedy as vehicles for theater reform, to 1961, when Rodolfo Usigli attempted—and failed—to create a modern national tragedy that would rival the ancient genre. I shall examine a selection of adaptations and stagings inspired by Greek tragedy, but I also consider debates and critical studies that have been significant in the reception of tragedy in Mexico. I focus on productions staged in Mexico City, the administrative and cultural center of the Viceroyalty of New Spain and, from 1821, of the independent nation of Mexico. This choice should *not* be taken to mean that the reception outside the capital has been insignificant. One of the earliest adaptations of a story from Greek tragedy written in Mexico, Fernando Calderón's *Ifigenia*, never played in Mexico City—that honor went to Guadalajara or Zacatecas, where it was staged sometime between 1826 and 1837.[2] However, the major milestones of this reception have been in the capital, the center of what has traditionally been a quite centralized society.

AN INITIAL SENSE OF ABSENCE: GREEK TRAGEDY AND THE NATIONAL THEATER

The noted Spanish actor José Valero visited Mexico with his theater company in 1868, a pivotal moment in Mexican history. President Benito Juarez had restored the Republic after the defeat of the Mexican Empire of Maximilian, a triumph that would lead to the pacification and growth of the country under liberal policies in the next decades. The repertoire of classical and modern plays that Valero brought to Mexican audiences included *Edipo*, an adaptation of Sophocles written in 1829 by the Spanish playwright Francisco Martínez de la Rosa.[3] The tragedy played to a full house at the Gran Teatro Nacional and was a popular and critical success.[4] The production made a lasting impression on Ignacio Manuel Altamirano (1834–93), one of the leading literary figures of the age.

Altamirano used his review of Valero's performance to reflect on the state and prospects of Mexican theater after years of disruption by foreign invasion and civil conflict. He lamented that there was no tradition of staging classical plays in Mexico, even though these plays were known and appreciated by Mexican audiences, as the packed house for *Edipo* demonstrated. For Altamirano, the absence of tragedy in Mexico needed to be remedied, for the lack of this important genre, present in other national theaters, was a mark of Mexican theater's underdeveloped state. "For now," he wrote, "let us content ourselves with having middling actors who present us with comedies and weepy dramas, just as we content ourselves with our short rail tracks that until now have served to take us in a snap to eat pears in [country towns close by] . . ., all to give us the illusion of believing that we have a railroad" (Altamirano 2011: i. 307).

Despite Altamirano's complaint, adaptations of Greek tragedy were no strangers to the Mexican stage. In the early nineteenth century, in the first decades of independence, audiences in Mexico City enjoyed translations of French and Italian eighteenth-century tragedies based on stories from Greek plays, such as Némopucène Lemercier's *Agamemnon* (1797) and Vittorio Alfieri's *Oreste* (1783);[5] these two plays were even presented back to back in 1833 as a sort of improvised *Oresteia*.[6] However, these commercial ventures, despite their relative success, were isolated occurrences. They did not foster the theatrical tradition of staging tragic plays that Altamirano felt the country needed. Where Greek tragedy does have a long tradition in Mexico, however, is in its association to complaints about the sorry state of the theater. As we shall see, long before Altamirano—and long after him—the ancient genre was being linked to questions of theatrical reform and national development.

Enlightened Entertainment: Pedro de Silva's Andromache in New Spain

At the end of the viceregal period, a century before Altamirano wrote, Greek tragedy had already been invoked in an earlier call for reform and modernity, which had appealed against the extravagances of the baroque dramas that were still popular at the time. In the second half of the eighteenth century, the entire Spanish Empire saw a series of ambitious reforms that sought to modernize the state along Enlightenment principles, and to improve the moral character of the subjects of the crown. Reformers agreed that the immense popularity of the theater made it a powerful tool to educate, as well as entertain, the masses, so intellectual and political elites dedicated much energy to regulating the theatrical experience in their communities, and to discussing the ideal composition and content of the plays to be performed.[7]

Greek tragedy began to have a presence on the Mexican stage during this period through adaptations and translations of French and Italian works based on the ancient plays. One of these, the tragedy *Al amor de madre no hay afecto que le iguale* (*There's no love like a mother's love*) (1764), had a long theatrical life in New Spain and may be one of the most successful Greek plays ever produced in the country. It was a loose adaptation of the Andromaches of Jean Racine (1667) and Apostolo Zeno (1724), written by the Spanish academic and self-styled reformer Pedro de Silva y Sarmiento (1742–1808).[8] The play was "in vogue" in Mexico City around 1778, and it remained in repertoire as late as 1824, after independence.[9]

Reformers like Silva subscribed to new dramatic ideals inspired by modern interpretations of Aristotelian and Horatian poetics, which were informally called "good taste" but are better known today as neoclassicism. Reason and verisimilitude in plot and character were seen as essential to a successful dramatic illusion, which would facilitate the audience's assimilation of models of virtuous and patriotic behavior. The "bad taste" they reacted against was the baroque theater of Pedro Calderón de la Barca (1600–81) and his epigones: their complex plots, filled with extravagant incidents and jumps in time and place, their penchant for spectacle, and their mixture of the tragic and the comic, were all found to strain reason. The audience was to be weaned off this "corrupt" taste, which was not conducive to the new didactic ideal.

Tragedy was deemed a suitable vehicle for the new didactic theater. Silvestre Díaz de la Vega, who in 1786 drew up the regulations for the Coliseo Nuevo, the principal theater of Mexico City, defined tragedy as "a school for virtue, and the art of making men humane and good" (Díaz de la Vega 1990: 196). Reformers noted that this "school" had largely been absent from the Spanish stage, and took this as a sign that the theater of the Spanish Empire had not reached the maturity of other European theaters. Silva himself had translated Racine's *Phèdre* with the explicit intention to "correct our national theater" by providing Spanish playwrights with the best models of tragedy other nations could offer.[10] The fact that his *Al amor de madre* is identified as a "new tragedy" in all printed editions signals that he saw his own play in the same light (Ríos 1997: 206–7, A.6–10 and A.13).

Silva had his own approach to modernizing the stage. While a firm believer in the new rules of dramatic art and the didactic potential of tragedy, he nevertheless did not lose sight of the practical consideration of creating a *successful* play. He sought to "reconcile" the "vulgar" and the "erudite," by giving the former what they enjoyed, but keeping infractions of "good taste" to a level tolerable for the latter.[11] For instance, he does not shy away from spectacular stage actions: whereas Racine has an unnamed contingent of Greeks kill Pyrrhus offstage for breaking his oath to marry Hermione, Silva shockingly has Orestes himself attempt the crime on stage. This sets the scene for an elaborate escape plot reminiscent of Euripides' *Orestes*: Hermione and Pylades kidnap and threaten to kill the child Astyanax to achieve Orestes' release; the ploy works and the criminals escape scot-free. Needless to say, the erudite were not amused by these inventions. The Spanish poet Margarita Hickey, who had also translated Racine's *Andromache*, excoriated Silva's "monstrosity" and asked, with respect to the staged regicide, how this example could produce more virtuous and patriotic citizens (Hickey 1789: i. viii–x).

Silva departed from the new ideals in another significant respect. Surprisingly, Greek myths were not prized by reformers as material for tragedies. As Sala Valldaura explains, the pagan heroes of Greek tragedy were seen as too foreign to be appropriate models for the Catholic subjects of the Spanish crown: measured against the many examples of patriotic behavior in the history of the Spanish Empire, the myths were found wanting (Sala Valldaura 2005: 99–123). In Mexico, even pre-Columbian history was felt to have a greater didactic significance: in 1808, for instance, a contest for a "national tragedy" based on the "antiquities" of the land was announced in Mexico City newspapers (Hernández Reyes 2008: 407–8)—the first manifestation of a nationalist trend that would pervade later discussions of Greek tragedy in the country.

In choosing the Andromache myth for his *Al amor de madre*, Silva was drawing on baroque tradition (Silva y Sarmiento 1764: 8), which had often used Greek myth, culled from a variety of sources and spun into freewheeling, imaginative plots. For instance, *Troya abrasada* [*Troy ablaze*] (1639?), by Calderón de la Barca and Juan Zabaleta, which was still popular in Mexico City at the end of the eighteenth century, packs the entire Trojan war into three acts, transforming Cassandra into the spurned, *Greek* wife of Paris, whose jealousy brings about the destruction of the city. "Whatever may have been the playwrights' sources," writes an editor of this play, "the greater part of the plot seems to be *de su cosecha* [of their own invention]" (Northup 1913: 27). As we have seen, Silva, too, was unafraid of radically altering his models.

Al amor de madre was so popular in Mexico that it fostered a sequel.[12] The Spanish actor Fernando Gavila, who worked at the Coliseo Nuevo, wrote a play called *Eleno* [*Helenus*]—now lost—which he billed as "the second part" of *Al amor de madre*.[13] The two plays were scheduled back to back in December 1794, a few days after *Troya abrasada*, apparently in an attempt to program a cycle of Troy-related plays. Gavila was certainly a champion of the new poetic ideals, which are evident in his play *La lealtad americana* [*American loyalty*] (1796) and its preface; however, his position as house dramatist and main actor for the company, and the fact that the success of his play may have depended on the popularity of a "monstrosity," meant that he must also have kept an eye on the box office. It would not be surprising if he, too, sought to reconcile the two "tastes."

This confrontation of neoclassical and baroque taste forms the initial stage in the reception of Greek drama in Mexico. From proponents of "good taste," like the actor Gavila and the academic Silva, came the identification of the ancient tragic genre, as defined by Aristotelian poetics, as a modern way of doing theater, and, more significantly, as a sign of a *mature* national theater. From the baroque tradition, shared by audiences, actors, and playwrights alike—including Gavila and Silva—came an enthusiasm for Greek myths, which at times ran counter to the reformers' desire for plays on national topics, but which nevertheless proved very popular. By a compromise that drew on both traditions, plays were introduced to the Mexican stage that were closer to the ancient Greek models than the more heterogeneous baroque dramas that had come before.

Eventually, "good taste" would entirely prevail, as testified by the productions of Lemercier and Alfieri of the 1830s, mentioned above. However, these productions were soon forgotten. By the 1860s, as we have seen, Altamirano would again invoke the need for a tradition of tragic theater in Mexico.

Heroines of Progress: Altamirano and Ristori's Medea

The Italian actress Adelaide Ristori arrived in Mexico City in the final days of 1874, on the recently completed railroad line that connected the capital to the port city of Veracruz and the world beyond. Progress had taken a major stride, and tragedy came along with it. The famous actress, then in the middle of a world tour, introduced herself to the audience of Mexico City with Ernest Legouvé's *Médée* (1855), performed in Italian, as was her usual practice.[14] Her performance did not attract the throngs which, as we saw above, had attended Valero's *Edipo* in 1868—Altamirano ruefully notes that she played to an almost empty house at the Gran Teatro Nacional—but it was a critical success (Altamirano 2011: ii. 158–9). Like Valero's play, Ristori's visit was a catalyst for discussion of ancient Greek tragedy in Mexico.[15] As we have seen, Altamirano had used the success of Valero's *Edipo* to reflect on the undeveloped state of the Mexican theater, and now in 1875 he published a substantial essay dedicated to the myth of Medea, Legouvé's play, and Ristori's performance in the title role (Altamirano 2011: ii. 160–187).

Altamirano gives a remarkably positive interpretation of the legendary figure of Medea. For him, she is a Promethean figure who betrays her own civilized people to foster the growth of a young, eager nation. This is a far cry from Legouvé's all-too-human Medea, who is portrayed as a destitute, abandoned wife and mother, rejected even by her children, and revealed as barbaric in her desperate ploy to sacrifice them to her primitive gods to assure their help.[16] Part of the success of Euripides' *Medea*, according to Altamirano, is that the ancient playwright preserves the legendary aspects of the character with surprising naturalism (Altamirano 2011: ii. 171). Seeking the "natural and simple origin" behind the mythical tales surrounding Medea, Altamirano sees in the legend of the Argonauts a historical expedition of the Greeks, "poor, valiant, enterprising" people, who set out "to reap the secret of prosperity, predominance at sea, and the throne of civilization from older cultures" (Altamirano 2011: ii. 161). Medea, "one of those extraordinary women who know how to associate their destinies to those of the great men of her era," was instrumental to their success, and so to the future prosperity and culture of the Hellenic world (Altamirano 2011: ii. 161). This is why, according to Altamirano, her name, in an act of gratitude, became "entwined with the names of gods and heroes, and consecrated by religion and national pride in the spirit of the Greek people" (Altamirano 2011: ii. 164). In this way, historical figures pass into legendary fame.

How could Altamirano turn the destitute character of Legouvé into this heroine of progress? The answer, I believe, lies in the *tour de force* of Ristori's performance. Altamirano treats it as an interpretation of the myth in its own right: the negative aspects of Legouvé's characterization vanish in the actress's impersonation, which conveyed to the audience the full force of the legendary figure. This was, in fact, how Ristori herself understood the role: as Legouvé records, she wished to convey in performance that Medea was not merely "a mother, a woman, an exile," but also "an epic and legendary creature."[17] Altamirano had prepared himself for this: he chose not to form part of the welcoming committee for the actress at the railway station, because meeting her out of character would have spoiled that initial encounter with the performer's creation. When Ristori first entered the stage, Altamirano reports, "a nervous shiver took hold of us. The figure, the mere figure began to impose itself on us. It was the Medea of the poems and traditional tales, grand, pale, severe and sad, powerful and proud."[18]

For Altamirano, Ristori's role as Medea was also the embodiment of theatrical progress. Her performance was that of a thaumaturge, who not only conjured up a mythical figure, but also resurrected "the beautiful age of Greece, to produce, not only admiration, but the religious introspection of those of us who profess the poetic cult of the artistic ideal" (Altamirano 2011: ii. 185). Through her art, the actress managed to link "two sister civilizations [Greece and Mexico] in their aspiration for perfection" (Altamirano 2011: ii. 158). This reflection needs to be understood in light of his previous lament over the absence of tragedy in Mexico: admiration of the artistic peaks of Greece and other civilizations was a precondition for progress. This was to begin by establishing a school of staging classical dramas, which would appreciate, study, and emulate the examples of Valero and Ristori.

Despite his admiration for Greece and its myths, Altamirano held that the "stimulus and taste" acquired by playwrights through this study should be applied to the rich subject matter offered by Mexican history and be adapted "to the necessities and character of our country."[19] He even dismissed earlier Mexican attempts at tragedy, such as those of Fernando Calderón (who, as we have seen, had written an *Ifigenia*), specifically for having eschewed national topics.[20] In this respect, Altamirano came close to the neoclassical reformers, not in their concern for the proper education of citizens, but rather in the quest to create a corpus of plays—by Mexicans and about Mexico—that would form a national theater to rival those of other nations, including Spain.

The playwrights of Altamirano's age heeded his call for tragedies on national topics, but his call to establish a tradition of *staging* Greek tragedy and other examples of classical drama fell on deaf ears. During the long liberal regime of Porfirio Diaz, which began a year after Ristori's departure and lasted until 1910, and during the turbulent years of the Mexican Revolution that followed, the few fleeting opportunities to see a Greek-style tragedy on stage would continue to be those provided by foreign theater companies touring the country.[21] Moreover, in the post-revolutionary period, the nationalist trend embraced by Altamirano would prove a hurdle for those who wished to write on the plight of foreign princesses on alien shores.

Shadows of a Tragic Universe: Alfonso Reyes's *Ifigenia cruel*

On Christmas Day 1908, a coterie of intellectuals met in Mexico City to celebrate the birth of Dionysus by reading literary works inspired by Greek tragedy.[22] The young Alfonso Reyes (1889–1959), who would go on to become one of the leading literary figures of his generation, read a choral poem called "Coro de sátiros en el bosque" ["Chorus of satyrs in the forest"], which evoked the rhythmic, regenerative power of nature and its affinities with ritual song (Reyes 1959: 481–4). This minor work already manifests Reyes's conception of Greek tragedy, which he would develop in his essays on the ancient genre and in his own tragedy, *Ifigenia cruel* [*Cruel Ifigenia*] (1923): for him, it is a communion with forces that transcend the human, a mystical experience intimately tied to the creative process itself.

This conception originated not in the theater but in the classroom. At its root lay a reaction by students against the curriculum of their alma mater, the Escuela Nacional Preparatoria, Mexico's premier institution of secondary education during the Liberal regime of Díaz, from which Reyes graduated in 1907. The curriculum was heavily influenced by positivism and it privileged empiricism and scientific research as arbiters of truth. Latin and Greek were reduced to the study of etymologies, and the few courses on literature that remained became, in Reyes's words, a space for "sentimental vagaries." For Reyes, "[t]hose who wanted to learn any Humanities had to conquer them on their own, with no effective help from the school."[23] He and other students began to organize outside the classroom, recommending books to each other and discussing in coteries those authors and traditions for which positivism had no use. Among these, as Pedro Henríquez Ureña recalls, "we read the Greeks, who were our passion."[24]

A few teachers did bring some salutary air into the rarified positivist atmosphere of Reyes's school years: Jesús Urueta, for instance, began to challenge this educational system in 1903 by making room for the aesthetic ideals of *modernismo*, a contemporary literary movement, in a series of lectures on literature that became very popular with the students and the general public. Amado Nervo, a famous *modernista* poet at the time, lent a hand by joining him in a reading of Aeschylus' *Agamemnon* in 1904.[25] In a talk on Greek tragedy that Urueta gave at the school that same year, he argued that what the Athenians derived from watching the ancient genre was an "exclusively aesthetic pleasure," the same pleasure they experienced by contemplating a statue or a temple (Urueta 1904: 95–6). These "aesthetic influences of the poets" formed the basis of Greek education "which oriented the sensibilities of Athenian citizens towards beauty, and correspondingly harmony and sociability" (Urueta 1904: 101–2).

The generation of Reyes went beyond the idealistic education Urueta proposed. José Vasconcelos, for instance, states that they were

> inspired by a *different* aesthetic than that of its immediate predecessors, by an *ideal creed*... that is not romantic or *modernista* and much less positivist or realist, but a type of *mysticism founded upon beauty*, a tendency to seek ineffable clarities and eternal significances. It is not Platonic faith in the immortality of ideas, but something very different, a notion of the affinities and rhythm of an eternal and divine substance.[26]

Reyes's satyr chorus, with its attention to the rhythms of nature evoked by song, exemplifies this assessment of his generation, but it is his work on Greek tragedy that best embodies it.

In an essay entitled "Las tres *Electras* del teatro ateniense" ["The Three *Electras* of the Athenian Theater"] (1908) and in later commentaries and notes on his *Ifigenia cruel*, Reyes expounds his conception of the ancient genre:[27] in Greek tragedy, nature has a sympathetic connection to man's individual sufferings—thus the Theban plague follows Oedipus' crime, as Reyes observes—but the purpose of the genre is not merely to express this connection, but above all to portray those cosmic, metaphysical forces that encompass human suffering (Reyes 1955: 42). These forces are identified with "destiny, divine influence, [and the] compensation of natural forces (or necessity of equilibrium)," abstractions which take part in a "universal tragedy" or "cosmic dialogue," which the poet, attuned to this "suffering consciousness of the universe," transcribes into elements that can be understood at a human level.[28] In this respect, the characters of Greek tragedy are mere "shadows" or "outlines" that give form to these superhuman forces; the image Reyes uses is that of a screen which, when held up in the dark, suddenly reveals images projected by a magic lantern (Reyes 1955: 47–8). The structural forms of Greek tragedy are also projections of this "cosmic dialogue," since the (according to Reyes) fixed progression of prologues, parodoi, episodes, stasima, and exodoi that give tragedy its rhythm "suggest[s] . . . a universe ruled by harmonious, musical laws, much more than an individual drama."[29] Consequently, the poetic dimension of Greek tragedy reflects a similar, aesthetic dimension of the universe.

Reyes would eventually put his theory into practice by writing his own tragedy, *Ifigenia cruel*. He based the play on Euripides' *Iphigenia in Tauris*, but introduced radical innovations to the myth: in his adaptation, Iphigenia has forgotten her identity and knows only her role as priestess of Artemis; Reyes has her kill the human victims herself, whereas in Euripides she handed them over for others to kill. Orestes arrives from Greece at the express command of Apollo to seek Iphigenia; after he recognizes his sister, he forces her to remember who she is, and in the process makes her recall the crimes of their family. Horrified, Iphigenia refuses to return with her brother to Mycene and repudiates her family with the following curt remark: "Take in your hands, grasped with your mind, | these hollow shells of words: *I do not want to!*" (Reyes 1955: 348). She chooses to remain in Tauris and continue her bloody service to the goddess. By this act of free will, the individual has rebelled and liberated herself from her own destiny.

Ifigenia cruel is much more than an academic exercise in composing Greek tragedy. Reyes repeatedly hints at the connection between his play and a traumatic experience in his life—the death of his father. In 1913, during one of the bloodiest periods of the Mexican Revolution, General Bernardo Reyes ill-advisedly took part in an attempted military coup against President Francisco Madero, and lost his life. As Arenas Monreal has nicely put it, Reyes "chose the path of freedom," and abandoned, in Reyes's own words, every "impulse of rancor and vengeance" at those responsible for this death, so as not to enslave himself "to low vendettas."[30] His Iphigenia, who also "chose the path of freedom," and thus redeemed herself from a cycle of violence and rancor, can be understood as the dramatization of this choice.

Most scholars have echoed Reyes's redemptive optimism in their interpretations of the play, but there is an unsettling side to Iphigenia's decision: her rejection of her former identity leaves her only her duty as human sacrificer—an imposed identity (Reyes 1959: 313, 318). As Iphigenia declares, the price that she pays for her liberation is to be "reborn a slave" of the goddess Artemis (Reyes 1959: 348). Although he is aware of the harshness of this "last extreme," Reyes does not explain why this should be preferred to the violence of her family's society and culture, or how this identity, though freely chosen, contributes to her redemption from violence.[31] A few interpreters have perceived these difficulties. Carlos Montemayor, in particular, has argued that Iphigenia channels the murderous instinct of the Atreids into the human sacrifices she performs; in this way, she sublimates the curse into an action that is religiously sanctioned and transcends vendettas; consequently, what redeems Iphigenia is her acceptance and elevation of her family's criminal instinct to the level of "a sacrality" (Montemayor 2009: 4).

Reyes's understanding of Greek tragedy itself complicates his character's redemption. Both in his essays and in *Ifigenia cruel*, there is an uneasy tension between the individual and the universal. In "Las tres *Electras*," for instance, he claims that Greek tragedy is "more universal than human," but in his "Commentary" to *Ifigenia cruel*, he concedes that Greek tragedy is nonetheless attentive to the human element (Reyes 1955: 44; Reyes 1959: 353). Iphigenia's retreat into the ritual of human sacrifice, as Montemayor has observed, takes violence out of the human order, but does so by transferring this violence to the agency of a universal force, the goddess Artemis, whose colossal statue in the play is the axis around which "dance the stars" (Reyes 1959: 325). Iphigenia's acceptance of this ritual act carries her beyond her limits as an individual, transmuting her into the embodiment of that divine force that imposed itself on her and "articulated [her] broken hinges, fashioning from the puppet" the ritual killer (Reyes 1959: 318). In this light, Iphigenia achieves her redemption by "submerging" herself "in the frame of the energies that overflow [her] being," and so, by her choice, losing her humanity (Reyes 1959: 353).

Arenas Monreal has argued that Reyes "tried to heal the wounds of his spirit by inserting it in the cosmogonic frame of universal human suffering that Greek tragedy offered him" (Arenas Monreal 2004: 113); this interpretation reads the genre as inherently therapeutic and consolatory. However, this overlooks the tension outlined above, of which Reyes himself was aware. He described his father's death as "a natural cataclysm, alien to the will of men and superior to it."[32] His only consolation would be to match the nature of the event by retreating into an activity that goes beyond the individual, "projecting" his suffering upward onto "the artistic sky," as he put it, and "unloading it" as a "dialogue of shadows." This consolatory activity was the act of adapting a Greek tragedy; the imitation of its dramatic structure, given its ritual connection to cosmic forces, yields a powerful experience of an almost mystic nature (Reyes 1959: 354). The liberation of both character and playwright becomes, by this ritual, a creative act that transfers their suffering to a superhuman level: to Artemis, in the case of Iphigenia's choice, and to a tragic universe, in the case of Reyes writing his tragedy. In doing so, both have taken refuge in what transcends and obliterates them, the aesthetic and the universal.

Tragedy for Aesthetes: The Teatro de Orientación

After the demise of positivism, another hurdle blocked the establishment of a tradition of Greek tragedy in Mexico: the rise of a strident form of nationalism in the post-revolutionary period. The revolutionary regimes that followed the end of the armed conflict in 1921 inaugurated important changes in Mexican society, such as land expropriation, progressive education, and labor reform, and the theater, along with the rest of the arts, was not left untouched. Discussions raged about what role the stage should take in the cultural program of the Revolution. In the early 1930s, Alfonso Reyes and the Teatro de Orientación, which staged the first adaptations of Greek tragedy in the post-revolutionary period, were drawn into bitter debates about the appropriateness of Greek and other foreign theatrical traditions to Mexican culture and society.[33]

There were two distinct views of what "the national" meant. The nationalist critics, fierce advocates of the Revolution, in general maintained that the arts had to reflect the country's history and problems *exclusively*; those who chose to write or stage plays based on any other topic were reviled as reactionaries. Reyes, with his interest in Greek tragedy and culture, was in 1932 accused of being a "spinner of strange routes that do not even add a guiding principle to what is [Mexican]" (Sheridan 1999: 214). In his response to these critics, Reyes neatly summed up the opposing view, stating that "the only way to be advantageously national consists in being generously universal, since the part has never been understood without the whole"; in his view, only the healthy embrace of "the common patrimony of the [human] spirit"—that is, other literary traditions and cultures, such as that of ancient Greece—would "strengthen and enrich the Mexican soul" (Sheridan 1999: 290–1).

The Teatro de Orientación, which became one of the most influential avant-garde theater companies in Mexico, shared Reyes's view. It attracted even more nationalist ire than he, since it had been organized under the auspices of the Secretary of Public Education, in 1931. Orientación, however, was so successful in both defending and achieving its vision for a more universal Mexican theater that it became part of the cultural program of the new regime.[34]

Orientación's staging of Jean Cocteau's *Antigone* in 1932 became one of its signature productions.[35] Faced with what its director, Celestino Gorostiza, judged a "stagnant" theater scene, the company sought to instill a taste for a more cosmopolitan theater among playwrights, actors, theater critics, and the public.[36] They sought a repertory theater that combined classical plays with works by contemporary foreign playwrights, much as the traveling companies of Valero and Ristori had done in the previous century. Their performances were renowned for their aesthetic simplicity, their experimental nature, and a controlled, cerebral tone—all features present in their *Antigone* (Schneider 1995: 101, 105). Their choice of Cocteau sprang from their interest in staging modern adaptations of classical texts—in this case, a streamlined version of the myth of Antigone, "as if viewed from an airplane," as the playwright explained.[37] Nevertheless, the fact that they billed the play as "Sophocles' *Antigone*, according to Cocteau," also makes clear their interest in claiming the Greek tradition.

One nationalist theater critic did not see the point: why, he asked, was the Secretary of Public Education funding a theater for a small and select group of aesthetes, whose repertoire was completely disengaged from the socially progressive ideas of the Revolution (Schneider 1995: 213–15)? The company responded to these accusations by claiming that their program had in fact succeeded in its goal of creating a more cosmopolitan national theater. Gorostiza himself, in an open letter dated to 1934, noted that Orientación's repertoire now included plays by Mexican writers who shared the company's agenda, among them Reyes's *Ifigenia cruel*, which was premièred by Orientación that year (Schneider 1995: 267–68). The aesthetic and superhuman cosmos of Reyes's deeply personal tragedy now became a prime example of a modern Mexican theater.

Orientación's success was responsible for "the establishment of a cultural policy regarding the theater that continues in Mexico up to this day: the promotion of an art theater in the hands of an intellectual and artistic elite," as Ortiz Bullé Goyri has stated (Ortiz Bullé Goyri 2005: 210). It managed to stake a place in the state-funded theater of the revolutionary regime, and so both validated its aestheticizing and apolitical approach, and fostered a welcoming environment for future productions of Greek tragedy and other "foreign" plays that chose not to engage with national issues.

Artists associated with Orientación would go on to stage the first productions of Greek drama in translation, and all on the government's dime. The playwright and critic Rodolfo Usigli (1905–79), who was familiar with the artistic program of Orientación, supervised a production of Cocteau's *Antigone* in Monterrey in 1933, using the costumes and scenery created by the artist Agustín Lazo for Orientación. That same year and the next, as director of the Teatro Radiofónico of the Secretary of Public Education, he transmitted the first productions of translations of Greek drama in Mexico.[38] The director Julio Bracho, who had adapted Cocteau's *Antigone* for Orientación, staged translations of Euripides' *Trojan Women* and Aristophanes' *Knights* with the Teatro de la Universidad in 1936, under the auspices of the National University of Mexico.[39]

The Fall of a National Tragedy: Rodolfo Usigli's *Corona de Fuego*

The political triumph of the apolitical avant-garde had not ended the call for a national Mexican tragedy that would rival the Greek models. Usigli, whose interest in addressing the country's social and political reality had distanced him from Orientación, mulled the issue for 30 years, and then took up the challenge with his *Corona de fuego* [*Crown of Fire*] (1960). This play on the execution of the Aztec emperor Cuauhtémoc was subtitled "a first scheme towards a Mexican tragedy." Usigli believed that he could foster a theatrical tradition analogous to that of Greek tragedy from within Mexican culture, by taking his plots from the early myths and history of the country, which, he argued, represented what the Greek myths had meant for their original audiences. His goal was "to open the way for tragedy in Mexican theater . . . and to incorporate the grand figures of tragic Mexican history to the universal gallery" of heroes such as Prometheus and Oedipus (Usigli 1979: 808). Ultimately, his aim was to create a truly universal Mexican tragedy that would take its place alongside those of other nations. However, his topic—the creation of a Mexican nation through the sacrifice of Cuauhtémoc—proved fatal to his goal, by bringing its message close, albeit unintentionally, to the nationalist propaganda of the revolutionary regime.

Usigli was far from the first playwright to attempt a tragedy on the Greek model based on Mexican antiquities. This tradition predates even Altamirano's call for a national tragedy: the 1808 contest (Hernández Reyes 2008: 407–8), mentioned above, gave rise to the first known example, a tragedy called *Xóchitl*, now lost. Again, in Altamirano's time, the historian and playwright Alfredo Chavero had written *Quetzalcóatl* (1877), subtitled "an attempt at tragedy"; Chavero states, in a note to the play, that the pre-Hispanic mythology of the country "was called to form the true Mexican theater."[40] Finally, a few years before Usigli wrote his *Corona de fuego*, the playwright Sergio Magaña staged a tragedy on another Aztec emperor, *Moctezuma II* (1953), which he claimed followed the model of the ancient genre, and is classed by some critics as among the best Mexican tragedies.[41]

Nevertheless, Usigli's *Corona de fuego* deserves a special place in a study of the reception of Greek tragedy in Mexico, because it is based on a level of critical engagement with Greek tragedy that is paralleled only by Reyes with his *Ifigenia*. Unlike the nationalist critics, Usigli was convinced that careful study and emulation of Greek tragedy and other foreign dramatic traditions was essential for the formation of a mature national theater, and before he attempted his *Corona de fuego* he wrote important essays on Greek drama.[42] *Corona de fuego* was structured by formal elements associated with Greek tragedy, such as a double chorus, but these structural elements are merely vehicles for Usigli's deeper interest in the ancient genre, namely the question of whether tragedy could arise from Mexican culture, as it had done from the culture of ancient Greece.

Tragedy, according to Usigli, springs from those ancient stories that carry the "blood and temperament" of a nation: these include the Greek myths that Aeschylus employed, and the English chronicles on which Shakespeare based his plays (Usigli 1979: 794–5; Usigli 2005: 261, 275–7). To create a Mexican tragedy, a playwright needs to employ those accounts that function as repositories of the people's past. The most relevant, for him, were the legends and historical accounts of the Aztecs. The fate of Cuauhtémoc, in particular, embodied that of a "tragic hero unique in his purity" (Usigli 2005: 198). According to Usigli, this last Aztec emperor, who was executed by Cortés, is a tragic character along the lines of *Oedipus at Colonus*: an innocent man whose suffering and final fate has a deeply transcendental dimension—in this case, one that is connected to the future Mexican nation. Cuauhtémoc also has a Promethean dimension, as he is aware that, despite his own destruction, he will become the founder of a nation (Usigli 1979: 801–2; Usigli 2005: 277–8).

In *Corona de fuego*, Cuauhtémoc, a prisoner of Cortés, is tempted by his Indian allies to rebel against his Spanish captors. Observing the mutual mistrust among the allies, he realizes that successful rebellion against Spanish rule would end in strife between the indigenous nations and in the break-up of the "Mexican nation" that he had previously ruled. Caught between his allies and the Spanish enemies, Cuauhtémoc chooses not to rebel and sacrifices himself to found a new nation: "Today's battle has already been fought. | Fought and lost," he says. "But there's still | tomorrow's battle, whose leader | I must be" (Usigli 1966: 814). Cuauhtémoc's execution, a deeply unjust act based on petty suspicions, would, Usigli hoped, "show to the audiences of the world the crime of the conquistadors and Mexico's hope for greatness" (Usigli 1979: 815). Cuauhtémoc's triumph will come in the rise of a united Mexican nation formed by the children of both conquerors and conquered, but one that favors its native origin and banishes Cortés to be "only a shadow over the map of Mexico" (Usigli 1966: 835).

Corona de fuego, which premièred in 1961, was not well received by critics and audiences. Rankled by the accusation that his tragedy was a fraud, Usigli published his "Notas a *Corona de fuego*" ["Notes on *Crown of Fire*"], a detailed, scholarly defense of his work that aimed to prove that it truly fit the parameters of the genre (Usigli 1979). However, he failed to address what I believe is the play's weakest point: namely, his belief that tragedy arises from the myths of the Mexican nation, and thus, that the genre is the expression of a particular national character. This belief ultimately undermined his tragedy. As Flavio González Mello points out, the playwright who, in his best-known play, *El gesticulador* [*The impostor*], had exposed the hypocrisy behind the regime's careful manipulation of historical characters and events of the Revolution in order to legitimize itself, now seems strangely unaware that the same political manipulation may be present behind the myth of the character and event that he dramatized in *Corona de fuego*.[43]

The pre-Columbian history of Mexico had not escaped manipulation by the regime. After the purported bones of Cuauhtémoc were discovered in 1949 in Ichcateopan, Guerrero, representatives of the state and national legislatures had met there on October 12—the "Day of the Race" in Mexico—in order to "honor the memory of the greatest, purest, and most venerated national hero," as a state-sponsored newspaper excitedly reported.⁴⁴ When further analyses of the remains conclusively disproved this identification, the results were cavalierly ignored by the politicians who had capitalized on this discovery for their nationalistic discourse. Usigli's gesture, however sincere, could not but be assimilated to this juggernaut ready to pounce on anything that could be linked to "our blood." The playwright Jorge Ibargüengoitia perceived this and wrote a devastating little parody of *Corona de fuego* that reduced its entire message to a handful of kitschy, patriotic platitudes (Ibargüengoitia 1961).

Thus collapsed Usigli's "scheme" of a tragedy on Mexican history, weighed down by the same unifying nationalism it had sought to promote. After Usigli's failure, the reception of Greek tragedy would for the most part keep to the path of the "universally national" blazed by Reyes and Orientación. Attempts to unite Mexican antiquities and Greek tragedy did continue, however: Salvador Novo, for instance, shared Usigli's belief that the legends and historical accounts of the Aztecs represented what the Greek myths had meant to their original audiences, and wrote plays on Aztec topics that emulated Greek drama, though in a farcical vein: his comic opera *In ticitezcatl o El espejo encantado* [*In Ticitezcatl or The Magic Mirror*], based on the myth of Quetzalcóatl, mocks the nationalism behind this blend of pre-Hispanic and Greek elements.⁴⁵

A Universal Presence: Greek Tragedy in Contemporary Mexico

By 1961, the year when *Corona de fuego* failed, Greek tragedy staged by Mexican artists had become a small but continuous presence on the Mexican stage. In the same state-sponsored program in which Usigli's tragedy was staged, the director Ignacio Retes staged Sophocles' *Edipo rey*, another example of the long life of the policy inaugurated by Orientación. Greek drama also gained ground in the commercial theater, again thanks to former members of Orientación: the poet and dramatist Xavier Villaurrutia wrote *La hiedra* [*Ivy*], a contemporary version of the Hippolytus myth, at the request of the Mexican actress María Tereza Montoya; her theater company premièred the play in 1941 and took it to Spain on one of its tours.

The restoration of the humanities in post-revolutionary public education programs, as well as the wider availability of translations, may have had a part in this increased interest in the Greek theatrical tradition. In 1921, José Vasconcelos, as head of the Secretaría de Educación, ordered copies of the "great books" to be printed and handed out to all elementary schools in the country; among them were selected plays of Aeschylus and Euripides. Likewise, Ángel María Garibay K., a Hellenist and Nahuatl scholar, published idiomatic translations of the three Greek tragedians for the modern Mexican reader in 1962 and 1963, remarking that "a society has the right . . . to be spoken to in their own way of speaking."⁴⁶ These inexpensive translations became widely available and were used in schools and in many theater productions.

The generations that came after Orientación and Usigli have been thoroughly conversant with Greek drama and have done much to secure its presence on the Mexican stage. Special mention should go to the director José Solé, who has had a long career directing Greek dramas that continues to this day. His first production, Euripides' *Las troyanas* [*Trojan Women*] (1963), translated by Garibay and sponsored by the Mexican Institute of Social Security, was a major commercial success and was even turned into a film that same year.[47] Among Solé's generation, the playwright Héctor Mendoza, a student of Usigli, stands out for his continuous engagement with Greek drama in adaptations such as *Reso* (1973), *Fedra* (1988), and *Secretos de familia* (1991), his version of the Electra myth;[48] others, like Emilio Carballido and Hugo Hiriart, have gone back to the baroque tradition of inventive plots derived from Greek myth with their *Medusa* (1966) and *Minotastasio y su familia* (1980), respectively (Carballido 1976; Hiriart 1999). Younger generations of playwrights have continued this engagement: Ximena Escalante, for instance, has written plays based on Greek tragedy, such as *Fedra y otras griegas* (2002), as has Flavio González Mello, with his *Edip en Colofón* (2009) (Escalante 2004; González Mello 2009).

This regular and widely appreciated tradition of staging and adapting Greek tragedy would surely have satisfied Altamirano. It has signaled the arrival of that brand of Mexican theater that Reyes, Orientación, and even Usigli had clamored for: a universal theater that is confident in its engagement and conversation with older traditions.

Notes

1. This chapter is dedicated to Kate Bosher, whose kindness and generosity will always be remembered. Thanks also to Eduardo Contreras Soto, whose critical eye has done much to improve this chapter, and to Ramón Layera and Maya Ramos Smith, for their help navigating the works of Rodolfo Usigli and archives related to eighteenth-century Mexican theater, respectively.
2. Manuel Payno, foreword to Calderón 1844: xiv. I infer the Greek subject matter from the title *Ifigenia*; the play itself is lost. It may have been a translation of a French or Italian version of the myth, but an adaptation seems more likely, given Calderón's free treatment of the story of Appius and Virginia in his play *Muerte de Virginia por la libertad de Roma* and his dramatization of Voltaire's short story *Zadig*, both written in the same period as *Ifigenia*.
3. The play, which premièred in Seville in 1830, was extremely popular throughout Spain and Latin America: see Ojeda Escudero 1997: 141–2.
4. For an eyewitness account of Valero's visit, see Olavarría y Ferrari 1961: ii. 762–70.
5. *Agamenón* was first staged in Madrid—see Andioc and Coulon 2008: 480, 617. The tragedy also went under the title *La muerte de Agamenón* (Coe 1935: 6). *Orestes* was premièred in 1807 (Andioc and Coulon 2008: 539, 747); it was also known as *El hijo de Agamenón* (Coe 1935: 113).
6. The Mexico City newspaper *El Demócrata* (November 23), 4, mentions the staging of both tragedies "in succession" in 1833.

7. An excellent overview of the theater reforms in Mexico City, together with their social and cultural impact, can be found in Viqueira Albán 1999: 27–95.
8. The première was in Madrid in 1764—see Andioc and Couldon 2008: 257, 618. Silva, writing under the pen name "Joseph Cumplido," mentions Racine and Zeno as models; see his preface in Silva y Sarmiento 1764: 8–10. Since the main title of the play varies a lot (*Andrómaca, Astianacte, Andrómaca y Pirro,* or *Andrómaca y Astianacte*: see Coe 1935: 21), for ease of reference I shall use its distinctive alternative title.
9. Olavarría y Ferrari 1961: i. 28. The late performance is announced in 1824 in *El Águila Mexicana* (June 19), 4.
10. Biblioteca Nacional de España, MS 14861, fos. 3–3^v.
11. Silva y Sarmiento 1764: 8; he also mentions a prior version for the stage that made even more concession to popular taste, such as the addition of a *gracioso*, or clown character, to the play (3–4).
12. The success of *Al amor de madre* may have also moved a Mexican university student, Ignacio Fernández de Córdova, to compose a play called *Hermione* (now lost), which he tried to sell to the Coliseo Nuevo in 1793. See Olavarría y Ferrari 1961: i. 150–2. The title suggests a play based on the Andromache myth; its meter, the hendecasyllable, suggests a neoclassical drama. *Hermione* may very well be the earliest example of a Mexican play based on Greek tragedy, though it was surely filtered through a French or Italian adaptation.
13. See Archivo General de la Nación (Mexico), Historia, vol. 478, file 6, for the program.
14. Ristori premièred the play in Paris in 1856. For Ristori's performances in the United States, see Pearcy, Bosher and Cox, and Davis, this volume.
15. Besides Altamirano's work, Manuel Peredo's critical essay on Valero's *Edipo* deserves special mention; it was first published in 1868 in *El semanario ilustrado* (September 11), 309–12, and later, in 1874, in *El artista* 1, 145–55.
16. For Legouvé's humanized Medea, see Macintosh 2000: 17.
17. Ernest Legouvé, quoted by Viziano 2000: 138.
18. Altamirano 2011: ii. 186. Olavarría y Ferrari (1961) also remarks upon the striking stage presence of Ristori in *Medea* (ii. 898).
19. Altamirano 2011: ii. 149–50; see also Altamirano 1988: 33–9.
20. Altamirano 1988: 196. For Calderón's *Ifigenia*, see n. 2.
21. To name a few examples: the Italian opera singer Adelaide Cortesi staged Giovanni Pacini's *Medea* (1843) in 1858—see Olavarría y Ferrari 1961: i. 656. Legouvé's *Medée* was again performed in 1878 by the Italian actress Giacinta Pezzana (Gutiérrez Nájera 1974: 78 n. 3). Another Italian, the actor Ermete Novelli, brought an *Oedipus* to Mexico in 1907 (Olavarría y Ferrari 1961: iv. 2890, 2893), which he staged "with archaeological love," according to a reviewer in a Mexican paper (Maza 1968: 346). The Catalan actress Margarita Xirgu did an open-air production of Hugo von Hoffmansthal's *Elektra* (1903) in 1922 (Olavarría y Ferrari 1961: v. 3445).
22. The Dominican Pedro Henriquez Ureña, for instance, on that occasion read *El nacimiento de Dionisos* (Henríquez Ureña 2003), a thumbnail prose tragedy on the birth of the god.
23. Reyes 1960: 191; this work, "Pasado inmediato," provides an excellent overview of the period. See also Vasconcelos 2010: 63.
24. Henríquez Ureña 1960: 612. See also Vasconcelos 2010: 64 and Reyes 1960: 211.
25. For an account of this event, see Díaz y de Ovando and García Barragán 1972: 461–2.
26. Vasconcelos 2010: 70. Italics are his.
27. What follows is a condensed version of Barrenechea 2012.

28. Reyes 1959: 353. The mention of "universal tragedy" appears in Reyes 1955: 48.
29. Reyes 1955: 45. The "cosmic dialogue" is mentioned in Reyes 1959: 353.
30. Arenas Monreal 2004: 273, quoting Reyes 1963: 29.
31. For the "last extreme," see Reyes 1959: 313.
32. Quoted by Arenas Monreal 2004: 106.
33. For a detailed study of this debate, see Sheridan 1999.
34. See Ortiz Bullé Goyri 2005: 205–12, and Versényi 2006: 145–67 for a recent overview of the history of the Teatro de Orientación. For the company's defense of their vision, see the combative speech of Gorostiza in Schneider 1995: 145–52, which was delivered in 1933 and published in a national newspaper.
35. Orientación first produced *Antigone* in 1932; see Schneider 1995: 99. The company staged it again in 1933 (Schneider 1995: 188), and apparently planned to restage it in 1938 (Schneider 1995: 312). Cocteau's *Antigone* was first staged in Paris in 1922.
36. Ortiz Bullé Goyri 2005: 210. Gorostiza is quoted in Schneider 1995: 218.
37. Cocteau 2003: 305, quoted in the 1932 and 1933 playbills of Orientación's *Antígona*.
38. The first production was Aeschylus' *Seven against Thebes*, transmitted in July 1933; see Secretaría de Educación Pública 1933: 911. The entire month of February 1934 was dedicated to Greek drama, with transmissions of Sophocles' *Oedipus at Colonus*, Euripides' *Medea*, and Aristophanes' *Clouds*, the latter adapted by Usigli himself; see Secretaría de Educación Pública 1934: 566.
39. For Bracho's adaptation of Cocteau, see Schneider 1995: 99. For his staging of the two Greek dramas, see Usigli 1937.
40. Chavero 1877: v. The tragedy was first staged in Mexico City in 1878 (Contreras Soto 2006: 576).
41. Magaña 1985: 8. *Moctezuma II* premièred in Xalapa, Veracruz, in 1953.
42. For instance, see his "Confrontación del teatro griego o la investigación inútil" (Usigli 1937), his "Primer ensayo hacia una tragedia mexicana" (Usigli 2005), and finally, his "Notas a *Corona de fuego*" (Usigli 1979). For studies of Usigli's concept of the tragic, see Beardsell 1980 and 1992: 181–92, and Luzuriaga 1990: 21–61.
43. Gonzáles Mello 2001: 83–5. *El gesticulador*, written in 1938, was first brought to the stage in 1947.
44. See "Aquí está el Señor Cuauhtémoc" in Pipsa 1989: 1946–52, 7.
45. Novo 1966; the play premièred in Hermosillo, México, in 1970.
46. See Garibay K. 1962: xiv. For a critical account of Garibay's translations, in particular his translation of Aristophanes (Garibay K. 1967), see Díaz Cíntora 1987.
47. See, for instance, the testimony in Garibay K. 1963: ix. The film, also called *Las troyanas*, was directed by Sergio Véjar.
48. All his adaptations are collected in Mendoza 1996.

References

Altamirano, I. M. (1988), *Obras completas*, xii: *Escritos de literatura y arte 1*. Ed. José Luis Martínez. Mexico City.

Altamirano, I. M. (2011), *Obras completas*, x–xi: *Crónicas teatrales*, 1–2. Ed. Héctor Azar. Mexico City.

Andioc, R. and M. Coulon (2008), *Cartelera teatral madrileña del siglo XVIII (1708–1808)*. Madrid.

Arenas Monreal, R. (2004), *Alfonso Reyes y los hados de febrero*. Mexicali.
Barrenechea, F. (2012), "At the Feet of the Gods: Myth, Tragedy, and Redemption in Alfonso Reyes's *Ifigenia cruel*," *Romance Quarterly* 59, 6–18.
Beardsell, P. (1980), "Usigli and the Search for Tragedy," in J. England ed., *Hispanic Studies in Honour of Frank Pierce*. Sheffield, 1–15.
Beardsell, P. (1992), *A Theatre for Cannibals: Rodolfo Usigli and the Mexican Stage*. Rutherford, NJ.
Calderón, F. (1844), *Obras completas*. Mexico City.
Carballido, E. (1976), *Teatro*. Mexico City.
Chavero, A. (1877), *Quetzalcóatl: ensayo trágico en tres actos y en verso*. Mexico City.
Cocteau, J. (2003), *Théâtre complet*. Ed. Michel Décaudin. Paris.
Coe, Ada May (1935), *Catálogo bibliográfico y crítico de las comedias anunciadas en los periódicos de Madrid desde 1661 hasta 1819*. Baltimore.
Contreras Soto, E. (2006), *Teatro mexicano decimonónico*. Mexico City.
Díaz Cíntora, S. (1987), "Garibay helenista," *Nova tellus* 5, 203–38.
Díaz de la Vega, S. (1990), "Discurso sobre los dramas," in G. Viveros ed., *Teatro dieciochesco de Nueva España*. Mexico City, 189–209.
Díaz y de Ovando, C. and E. García Barragán (1972), *La Escuela Nacional Preparatoria: los afanes y los días 1867–1910*. Mexico City.
Escalante, X. (2004), *Fedra y otras griegas*. Mexico City.
Garibay K., A. M. (trans. 1962), *Sófocles: las siete tragedias*. Mexico City.
Garibay K., A. M. (trans. 1963), *Eurípides: las diecinueve tragedias*. Mexico City.
Garibay K., A. M. (trans. 1967), *Aristófanes: las once comedias*. Mexico City.
González Mello, F. (2001), "Un teatro para caníbales: Rodolfo Usigli," in D. Olguín ed., *Un siglo de teatro en México*. Mexico City, 71–93.
González Mello, F. (2009), *Edip en Colofón: tragedia de enredos*. Mexico City.
Gutiérrez Nájera, M. (1974), *Obras, iii: Crónica y artículos sobre teatro 1 (1876–1880)*. Mexico City.
Henríquez Ureña, P. (1960), "La revolución y la vida intelectual en México," in E. S. S. Piñero ed., *Obra crítica*. Mexico City, 610–17.
Henríquez Ureña, P. (2003), "El nacimiento de Dionisos," in T. Raful et al. eds., *Obras completas*, i: *Ficción*. Santo Domingo, 49–66.
Hernández Reyes, D. (2008), "La renovación teatral en las postrimerías del virreinato novohispano: los concursos del *Diario de México*," in I. Arellano and J. A. Rodríguez Garrido eds., *El teatro en la Hispanoamérica colonial*. Madrid.
Hickey, M. (1789), *Poesías varias sagradas, morales, y profanas o amorosas*. Madrid.
Hiriart, H. (1999), *Minotastasio y su familia*. Mexico City.
Ibargüengoitia, J. (1961), "Sublime alarido del exalumno herido," *México en la Cultura: novedades* [Mexico City] September 17, 7.
Luzuriaga, G. (1990), *Introducción a las teorías latinoamericanas del teatro: de 1930 al presente*. Puebla.
Macintosh, F. (2000), "Introduction: The Performer in Performance," in E. Hall, F. Macintosh, and O. Taplin eds., *Medea in Performance 1500–2000*. Oxford.
Magaña, S. (1985), *Moctezuma II: Cortés y la Malinche (Los Argonautas)*. Mexico City.
Maza, L. R. de la (1968), *El teatro en México durante el Porfirismo III (1900–1910)*. Mexico City.
Mendoza, H. (1996), *Secretos de familia*. Mexico City.
Montemayor, C. (2009), "Nota introductoria," in *Alfonso Reyes: Ifigenia cruel*. Mexico City, 3–4.

Northup, G. T. (ed. 1913), *Pedro Calderón de la Barca and Juan de Zabaleta: Troya abrasada*. New York and Paris.
Novo, S. (1966), *In ticitezcatl o El espejo encantado, Cuauhtémoc, El sofá, Diálogo de ilustres en la rotonda*. Xalapa.
Ojeda Escudero, P. (1997), *El justo medio: neoclasicismo y romanticismo en la obra dramática de Martínez de la Rosa*. Burgos.
Olavarría y Ferrari, E. (1961), *Reseña histórica del teatro en México, 1538–1911*. Mexico City.
Ortiz Bullé Goyri, A. (2005), *Teatro y vanguardia en el México posrevolucionario (1920–1940)*. Mexico City.
Pipsa (1989), *El Papel: diario de Pipsa*. Mexico City.
Reyes, A. (1955), "Las tres *Electras* del teatro ateniense," *Obras completas*, i. Mexico City, 15–48.
Reyes, A. (1959), *Obras completas*, x: *Constancia poética*. Mexico City.
Reyes, A. (1960), "Pasado inmediato," *Obras completas*, xii. Mexico City, 182–216.
Reyes, A. (1963), *Oración del 9 de febrero*. Mexico City.
Reyes, A. (2009), *Ifigenia cruel*. Mexico City.
Ríos, J. A. (1997), "Traducciones de tragedias francesas," in F. Lafarga ed., *El teatro europeo en la España del siglo XVIII*. Lleida.
Sala Valldaura, J. M. (2005), *De amor y política: la tragedia neoclásica española*. Madrid.
Schneider, L. M. (1995), *Fragua y gesta del teatro experimental en México*. Mexico City.
Secretaría de Educación Pública (1933), *Memoria relativa al estado que guarda el Ramo de Educación Pública el 31 de agosto de 1933*, ii: *Documentos*. Mexico City.
Secretaría de Educación Pública (1934), *Memoria relativa al estado que guarda el ramo de educacion publica el 31 de Agosto de 1934*, ii: *Documentos*. Mexico City.
Sheridan, G. (1999), *México en 1932: la polémica nacionalista*. Mexico City.
Silva y Sarmiento, P. de (1764), *El Astianacte: tragedia nueva, por otro título: Al amor de madre no hay afecto que le iguale*. Madrid.
Urueta, J. (1904), "Ensayo sobre la tragedia ática," *Alma poesía*. Mexico City, 77–138.
Usigli, R. (1937), "Confrontación del teatro griego o la investigación inútil," *Letras de México* 3, 2 and 8.
Usigli, R. (1966), "Corona de fuego," *Teatro completo*, ii. Mexico City, 774–840.
Usigli, R. (1979), "Notas a *Corona de fuego*," *Teatro completo*, iii. Mexico City, 791–819.
Usigli, R. (2005), "Primer ensayo hacia una tragedia mexicana," in L. de Tavira and A. Usigli eds., *Teatro completo*, v. Mexico City, 253–80.
Vasconcelos, J. (2010), "El movimiento intelectual contemporáneo de México," in C. D. Michael ed., *Los retornos de Ulises: una antología de José Vasconcelos*. Mexico City, 58–73.
Versényi, A. (2006), "Made in Mexico: The Theatrical Avant-Garde and the Formation of a Nation," in J. M. Harding and J. Rouse eds., *Not the Other Avant-Garde: The Transnational Foundations of Avant-Garde Performance*. Ann Arbor.
Viqueira Albán, J. P. (1999), *Propriety and Permissiveness in Bourbon Mexico*. Wilmington, DE.
Viziano, T. (2000), *Il Palcoscenico di Adelaide Ristori: repertorio, scenario e costumi di una Compagnia Drammatica dell'Ottocento*. Rome.

CHAPTER 17

MOVING AND DRAMATIC ATHENIAN CITIZENSHIP

Edith Hamilton's Americanization of Greek Tragedy

JUDITH P. HALLETT

My title derives from the U.S. news media coverage of words spoken, in English, albeit in an Athenian dramatic setting, by the American educator and best-selling author Edith Hamilton. The date was 1957, the year that Hamilton celebrated her 90th birthday. The locale was the ancient theater of Herodes Atticus, where her translation of Aeschylus' *Prometheus Bound*, published decades earlier, was performed.[1] The occasion was a ceremony preceding the performance, at which the city's mayor proclaimed her an honorary Athenian citizen (Reid 1967: 104–18). The press emphasized the majesty, monumentality, and emotional impact of the *mise-en-scène*. Hamilton's life partner and biographer Doris Fielding Reid quotes the observations of *Publisher's Weekly*: "floodlights in [Hamilton's] honor were thrown on the Parthenon, the Temple of Zeus and, for the first time in history, the Stoa . . . We can think of no other of the year's literary events that could be more moving and dramatic than this" (Reid 1967: 115).

In her speech, Reid reports, Hamilton called this moving and dramatic citizenship ceremony "the proudest moment of my life," terming Athens "the city I have for so long loved as much as I love my own country . . . the mother of beauty and of thought, and also the mother of freedom." To underscore the contemporary, American relevance of the play to be performed, Hamilton then asserted, "The Greeks were the first free nation in the world. In the *Prometheus* they have sent a ringing call down through the centuries to all who would be free" (Reid 1967: 113–14). According to Reid, however, the performance itself "was disappointing." "Mr. Bourlos, [the actor] who took the part of Prometheus spoke in modern Greek. The rest of the cast, all American, did their parts in English." *Time* magazine concluded, "Though the performance was a bit too complicated to arouse noisy enthusiasm, Miss Hamilton's appearance more than made the evening" (Reid 1967: 115–16).

By such accounts, therefore, Hamilton's own performance in that theater—her moving and dramatic delivery of her own message about the meaning of Greece, and its drama, for her own society and time—rendered the actual dramatic performance of an "Americanized" Greek tragedy in Athens incidental on that occasion. My discussion of Hamilton's role in the American reception of classical Greek theater during the first seven decades of the twentieth century makes a similar claim about her writing and thinking on the topic. Elucidating Athenian drama lay at the heart of Hamilton's influential efforts at interpreting ancient Greece for a broadly constituted, mid-twentieth-century American audience. Yet performance as a concern of her work, like performances of her work itself, proved largely incidental to her success. Rather, she exercised her influence through her books and essays, first and foremost *The Greek Way*, in which she "Americanized" the idea of Greek tragic drama, and thereby captured the devotion of a middlebrow U.S. readership that included Senator Robert F. Kennedy.[2]

I will be contrasting Hamilton with her contemporary Eva Palmer Sikelianos: an American feminist as well as an "amateur historian" of culture who also reinterpreted the classical past for a non-specialist audience, by staging performances of Greek dramas and writing about her artistic goals and achievements.[3] (See Leontis, in this volume.) Thus my chapter calls attention to the negligible role played by gender in Hamilton's writings on Greek tragedy. Finally, I will briefly situate Hamilton's vision of Greek tragedy, first formulated in the late 1920s, in its own cultural context by comparing it with Theodore Dreiser's literary re-envisioning of tragedy for the American reading public, a product of the same decade.

Edith Hamilton's Engagement and Re-engagement with the Graeco-Roman Past

Some details about Hamilton's academic and intellectual engagements with classical Greek and Latin languages and literatures help illuminate her unusual relationship with ancient Athenian dramatic texts. As we will see, Reid's 1967 memoir testifies that Edith Hamilton's specific interest in Greek drama spurred her to embark upon her second career as a popular writer about classical antiquity in the late 1920s, when she was in her early sixties. To be sure, Hamilton had devoted much time and energy to studying Classics before then, at least until she assumed the position of headmistress at the Bryn Mawr School in Baltimore, in 1896, at the age of 29 (Reid 1967: 38–41, 66–9). Still, Greek drama does not appear to have occupied much of her attention until 1922. Rather, Latin loomed much larger than Greek in her educational background.

Reid asseverates that Edith's father—who refused to send his four daughters to the Fort Wayne, Indiana public schools, because their curriculum overemphasized American history and arithmetic—launched Edith on Latin at the age of 8. By way of contrast, Reid merely quotes a cousin's later recollection as testimony that Edith was reading ancient Greek by the age of 13 (Reid 1967: 23, 30). Records from Miss Porter's School in Farmington, Connecticut document that Edith enrolled in several Latin classes, taught by retired Yale Classics professor Thomas Day Seymour, when she was a student there, from 1884 through 1886.[4] Yet Edith's younger sister Alice, later to pioneer the field of industrial medicine and become the first female professor at Harvard, reports in her autobiography that she also availed herself of the opportunity to study Greek, specifically plays by Aeschylus and Sophocles, as well as several Latin authors with Seymour at Miss Porter's two years later. Evidently Edith did not (Hamilton 1943: 24–38).

In 1894, four years after entering Bryn Mawr College, Edith received B.A. and M.A. degrees in both Latin and Greek. But she concentrated her efforts almost exclusively on Latin thereafter: first as a Bryn Mawr graduate fellow in Latin, then while studying, on a Bryn Mawr European fellowship, at the German universities of Leipzig and Munich. Between 1896 and 1922 Hamilton's heavy administrative responsibilities at the Bryn Mawr School, the first all-female college preparatory institution in the U.S.A., barely allowed her time to sustain any serious involvement with classical learning other than teaching an advanced Latin class on Virgil's *Aeneid* to the senior girls each year (Bacon 1980: 307; Hallett 1996–7: 109–10, 128–9; Hallett 2009a: 162; Hamilton 1943: 43–51; Reid 1967: 34–7, 65).

Hamilton's circumstances after 1922, however, afforded her far more opportunity to immerse herself in Greek as well as Latin texts, although it is not clear how or why she developed her enthusiasm for the Greek dramatists. Before retiring in June of 1922, Hamilton adopted 4-year-old Dorian Fielding Reid, grandson of Edith Gittings Reid and Harry Fielding Reid, her contemporaries and close Baltimore friends. She then departed from Baltimore with Dorian and the Reids' daughter Doris, a former Bryn Mawr School student twenty-eight years her junior. After spending much of the next year at the senior Reids' home in Mount Desert Island, Maine, Edith, Doris, and Dorian relocated to Manhattan, returning to Maine each summer. In the spring of 1929 the three of them sailed off on a trip to Egypt and Greece, Edith's first. Upon their return, Doris, who had been teaching music, took a job at a Wall Street investment firm (Bacon 1980: 307; Hallett 1996–7: 111; Hallett 2009b: 109–10; Reid 1967: 56–64, 77–9).

During these years immediately following her retirement, Edith kept house, reading and rereading classical authors (along with a few secondary works about classical antiquity), and home-schooling Dorian as she herself had been home-schooled back home in Indiana. From her experiences of relating classical and biblical lore to Dorian she also appears to have honed the valuable skill of making this challenging material accessible to those who were not necessarily steeped in classical languages or learning. This talent was to serve her, and her interest in Greek drama, admirably (Hallett 2009b: 109–10, 114–18; Reid 1967: 65–6, 77–8, 80).

Hamilton and Reid frequently socialized with friends from the New York theatrical and literary worlds, the drama critics John Mason Brown and Rosamond Gilder among them. According to Reid, questions to Edith about "the difference between Aeschylus, Sophocles and Euripides" at a tea party of intimate friends prompted her to get down "her volume of the Greek plays, and [translate] bits from each of the poets. She then started talking about, and explaining, Aeschylus, the tragedian for whom she cared most." As she spoke of Aeschylus "exactly as though he were her eldest son," and made one of her friends feel as if "she had just had lunch with [Aeschylus]," her rapt audience kept prodding her for more information of this kind. Finally, after a discussion on the idea of tragedy, Gilder, an editor of *Theatre Arts Monthly*, insisted that Edith write it all down and send it in to the magazine. Although Reid says that Edith initially protested against "urging and beseeching" by Gilder and others, she reports that "the article was written and Edith's important and unique talent was instantly recognized. Mrs. Edith J. R. Isaacs [the journal's founder and editor-in-chief] . . . published with enthusiasm [her] article on tragedy" (Reid 1967: 66–7, 79).

Reid relates that what Hamilton wrote for Isaacs, a series of articles on the Greek theater as well as her *Prometheus* translation, then caught the eye of Elling Aannestad, an editor at W. W. Norton and Company. "[Spotting] a real writer," he asked her "to do a book for them on Greece." Edith, according to Reid, tried to dissuade him "but he persisted" and the result was *The Greek Way*, published in 1930, to (again in Reid's words) "instant acclaim." Edith immediately followed up on this success with *The Roman Way* two years later (Reid 1967: 68–9, 81).

But in 1937, she published *Three Greek Plays: Prometheus Bound, Agamemnon, Trojan Women*, translations of tragedies by Aeschylus and Euripides that she had begun a decade earlier, and from which she quotes in *The Greek Way*. With the exception of three works on biblical antiquity and Christianity, the rest of her books, and indeed most of her other writings, focused almost exclusively on the Greeks: *Mythology* and an expanded version of *The Greek Way* entitled *The Great Age of Greek Literature* in 1942; *The Echo of Greece* in 1957; *The Collected Dialogues of Plato* in 1961; and *The Ever-Present Past* in 1964 (Hallett 2009a: 152–3; Reid 1967: 81–2). Hamilton's passion for and inspired teatime performances about the Greek tragedians deserve credit, a veritable round of applause, owing to the appeal that these publications have continued to possess for innumerable American readers.

Performing Edith Hamilton's Translations

I am contending that performance itself was largely incidental to Edith Hamilton's success as a thinker and writer about ancient Greek drama, and that she was not greatly concerned with performances of ancient Greek drama, whether in the remote Greek past or in her own American present. Both performance and performances, however, do play some role in Hamilton's engagements with classical Greek dramatic texts. As we will see, she was hailed as a kindred soul and dramatic inspiration by Palmer Sikelianos, an expatriate who for decades sought to stage, in modern Greek, what she viewed as authentic performances of classical Greek tragedies in the original theaters of Greece.⁵

Reid's memoir also rehearses at some length contentions advanced in a 1933 essay by Hamilton about a key matter of Greek dramatic stagecraft: namely, the number of actors and chorus members who performed in each play. Here, Hamilton marshaled evidence of various kinds to argue against the "rules" she had learned at [Bryn Mawr] College: that there were only three actors, and only 15 members of the chorus, in every tragedy. This evidence, to which we will return later, included her own observations, from examining photographs of the *Prometheus* when Sikelianos staged it at Delphi in 1927, and on her visit to the theater at Epidaurus in 1929 (Fig. 17.1).⁶ (See Leontis, this volume.)

Most important, the three Greek tragedies that she translated, and published in 1937, were performed, primarily although not only, in the United States. Admittedly, Hamilton published these translations of Aeschylus and Euripides seven years after *The Greek Way*, under separate cover and ostensibly as an afterthought. Still, she gives the tragedians and their plays much attention in *The Greek Way* itself. In fact, Hamilton expanded *The Greek Way* so as to incorporate more discussion of Greek prose writers, and thereby remedy an original imbalance in her selection of authors and texts that allowed the Athenian tragic dramatists to monopolize the limelight. Aeschylus, Sophocles, and Euripides each get a chapter of *The Greek Way* to themselves; she prefaces this entire section on the tragic playwrights with an additional chapter on the idea of tragedy.⁷

FIG. 17.1 A close-up of a few members of the chorus in Eva Palmer Sikelianos's *Prometheus* at Delphi, 1927. © APGRD.

Among the productions of these translations are some major, commercial, theatrical, and cinematic undertakings, in the U.S.A. and abroad. In her study of Greek tragedy on the American stage, Karelisa Hartigan provides details on the 1938 Broadway production of Hamilton's *The Trojan Women*, the second time the play was produced on the New York stage that year. Mildred Dunnock, a Baltimore native, starred as Hecuba. Hartigan also quotes from a *New York Post* review by Edith's friend John Mason Brown, terming the play "propaganda" but "art with beauty, brutality and majesty" (Hartigan 1995: 44). Curiously, in his autobiography, the playwright and screenwriter Horton Foote, who played a soldier in that production, characterizes it as "dismal," and as panned, eliciting the comment "if Helen of Troy had resembled our Helen there would have been no Trojan War" (Foote 2002: 185).

Twenty-five years later, a few months after Hamilton's death in 1963, the Greek director Michael Cacoyannis again used Hamilton's translation, and again cast Dunnock as Hecuba, when staging *The Trojan Women* at Broadway's Circle in the Square. Hartigan quotes the favorable reviews that this production received from, *inter alios*, the celebrated critic Walter Kerr. Cacoyannis also relied on Hamilton's translation when filming *The Trojan Women* eight years later, this time with Katharine Hepburn —like Hamilton a Bryn Mawr College graduate—rather than Dunnock as Hecuba (Hartigan 1995: 45; Hallett 2009a: 160). According to Reid, moreover, a production of Aeschylus' *Oresteia* staged in London not long after Edith's 92nd birthday featured her translation of the *Agamemnon* too, although Reid does not furnish further details (Reid 1967: 135–6).

Most significantly, the Athenian production of the *Prometheus Bound* in the summer of 1957 may have evolved from a Broadway production mounted earlier that year. At least Hartigan refers to such a production, remarking that "James Elliott, a Broadway producer of Greek descent, directed" and that Blanche Yurka was among the cast members (Hartigan 1995: 132). Reid's memoir includes the press release "sent to the newspapers from the United States Delphic Festival Committee," with the punning headline "'Prometheus Bound' for Greece." It states: "the President's Special International Program for cultural presentations (administered by ANTA as the professional agency of the State Department) in cooperation with the Greek Ministry for Education, will sponsor James S. Elliott's production." It then lists the members of the honorary committee, among them Clarence Derwent, Elsa Maxwell, and Tennessee Williams. Reid also relates an incident about Blanche Yurka, a cast member who sailed over to Greece with them on the S.S. *Queen Frederika*. Though Yurka, born in 1887, was only 20 years younger than the nonagenarian Edith, she played the young nymph Io. The other actors chose her to approach Edith and request that the script be shortened (Hallett 2008: 79–82; Meserve 1980; Reid 1967: 104–8).

Hartigan also claims that "the 1957 [New York] *Prometheus* production was a revival" of the earlier "text" from a production 27 years earlier, in the spring of 1930. According to Hartigan, several performances had been staged in New York by Eva Palmer Sikelianos as benefits for its opening in Greece, at the Second Delphic Festival in May

1930. Hartigan contrasts the 1930 with the 1957 production by noting that the latter was "performed only in English, not modern Greek."[8] She remarks that, in 1957, "Blanche Yurka... and Clarence Derwent played the same roles they had created for Delphi, and the costumes were those designed by Eva Sikelianos."[9]

It is striking that Reid's memoir says nothing about any 1957 Broadway production of the *Prometheus*, since the performance in Athens would have involved the same director, Elliott. Furthermore, one member of the United States Delphic Festival Honorary Committee, Clarence Derwent, had, according to Hartigan, just played the male lead on Broadway, to be replaced in Athens by Bourlos, who had also performed Prometheus at Delphi in 1930.[10] Or, more importantly, that Reid does not mention the 1930 New York production, since the 1957 U.S. Delphic Festival presumably had some connection with the Delphic festivals organized by Eva Sikelianos back in 1927 and 1930.

Indeed, a *New York Times* article of August 3, 1957 announces that "The bilingual production of 'Prometheus Bound' scheduled for an Aug. 8 performance in the theatre of Herodes Atticus in Athens, has stirred enough interest to be invited by Greek government officials to perform in the ancient theatre in Delphi on August 11. The latter performance will be given in honor and memory of Eva and Angelo Sikelianos, who established the first Delphic Festival in May 1927" (Calta 1957). No less important, Reid does not contextualize the combination of English and modern Greek spoken by the actors in the 1957 Athens performance. While she gives the impression that this bilingualism was some bizarre innovation, it was apparently a feature of the 1930 production in New York. By the same token, Reid's 1967 memoir does not mention anything about the Broadway productions of *The Trojan Women* in 1938 and 1963 either.

Yet Reid's memoir is also highly selective in what she shares about the entire event in Athens during the summer of 1957. While she drops the names of all the celebrities who served on the honorary committee, and quotes lavishly from encomiastic reviews of the ceremony, she obscures the fact that the trip was sponsored by the U.S. State Department, as a Cold War propaganda initiative (Hallett 2008: 80–1). She thereby also omits important contextual information about the choice of this play, with its focus on freedom, and Edith's speech. Small wonder, then, that the U.S. press regarded Hamilton's remarks preceding the performance as more newsworthy than the performance itself. Hamilton was sent onto that ancient Greek stage to promote the American way of freedom and democracy—and she delivered.

It warrants emphasis, too, that Reid's memoir does not mention Eva Palmer Sikelianos by name. She does, however, quote the following statement from Hamilton's 1933 article on the Greek chorus:

> But so far the rule of fifteen for the chorus has not been called into serious question. The theatrical difficulty involved in it presented it first to my mind when I was shown pictures of the performances of the *Prometheus* at Delphi. The tiny band of fifteen appeared ludicrously inadequate on that great orchestra surrounded by the immense auditorium with the mighty cliffs of the mountain towering above.

As Reid remarks, Hamilton regarded these photos as a strong argument against what she had imbibed about the size of Greek choruses from her teachers at Bryn Mawr College (Reid 1967: 146–8).

Yet, as noted above, these pictures to which Hamilton refers are evidently photos that *Theatre Arts Monthly* used to illustrate Hamilton's *Prometheus* translation: of a production at the First Delphic Festival in 1927 that was directed, choreographed, and orchestrated by Palmer Sikelianos. Reid's willingness to quote Hamilton's argument based on these photos renders her failure to mention Palmer Sikelianos herself especially significant. Hamilton and Palmer Sikelianos had other close connections as well. Seven years Hamilton's junior, Palmer Sikelianos also attended both Miss Porter's School and Bryn Mawr College not long after Hamilton. While matriculating at the latter, she even studied along with Lucy Donnelly, an English professor who was Hamilton's significant other before Reid; she even salutes Donnelly for continuing to embody "the virtues that she and her fellow students so ardently cultivated" (Anton 1993: 24–7, 105; Hallett 2009a: 151). The Benaki Museum archives in Athens contain correspondence between Hamilton and Palmer Sikelianos; one of the more memorable letters associates both Palmer Sikelianos and Hamilton with "the lunatic fringe" in their thinking about Greek antiquity.

What is more, Palmer Sikelianos awards Hamilton a prominent place in her autobiography: calling her "my deeply admired friend"; quoting her "very noble words" about Greek drama from *The Greek Way* and "wise" remarks about translation from the introduction to *Three Greek Plays*. She cites Hamilton's translation of a passage from the *Agamemnon* as immortal, great English poetry. "Drop, drop—in our sleep, upon the heart, | sorrow falls, memory's pain, | and to us, though against our very will, | even in our despite, comes wisdom by the awful grace of God" (Anton 1993: 199–200). Yopi Prins maintains that, in their re-presentations of the *Prometheus*, neither Hamilton nor Sikelianos "claim[ed] the authority of professional philology," working instead on the border between amateur and professional.[11] Reid's memoir supports this view, even asserting that Hamilton proudly denigrated scholarly authority (Reid 1967: 153). And, as has been observed, Hamilton's "statements frequently lack documentation from ancient texts, rarely if ever cite modern scholarly authorities, and rely on highly arbitrary selections of evidence" (Hallett 2009a: 156).

Prins, however, would also locate Palmer Sikelianos among a group of early twentieth-century female historical writers whom she characterizes as "articulat[ing] liminality that worked to mark the boundaries, spaces and locations of femininity" and "expand[ing] cognition to include aesthetic, emotional and kinetic registers" within "a historical knowledge . . . beyond the horizon of the professional."[12] Like these women, and unlike Hamilton, Palmer Sikelianos positioned issues of gender "front and center" in her stagecraft and writing: energetically recruiting and training women to act in her productions; analyzing the strengths and limitations of such female star performers as Isadora Duncan and Duncan's Greek sister-in-law Penelope. Palmer Sikelianos even spends an entire chapter of her autobiography on "Men as Creators," expressing the hope that males, because they possess a greater latent capacity for synthesis than females, might restore the tragic chorus to the world.[13]

Ultimately, Palmer Sikelianos's work proved marginal as well as liminal. Hamilton, of course, had well-connected champions in the power-centers of the American press and book trade, allies and supporters like Brown, Gilder, and Aannestad (Hallett 2009a: 155–62). Shrewdly, their endeavors to promote Hamilton as authority and personality de-emphasized her gender much as she herself erased gender (and downplayed social class) when generalizing about the ancient Greeks. Yet Palmer Sikelianos, who died in 1952, had powerful connections, too; Artemis Leontis has suggested that her single-mindedness and inflexibility, and support of the communist-led Greek resistance movement, denied her a sympathetic following in the American cultural mainstream.[14]

Edith Hamilton's Writings About Tragedy

The selective account of Edith Hamilton's life and labors by her lover and longtime companion Doris Fielding Reid presumably reflected Hamilton's own perspective and priorities on what and how to communicate about ancient Greece to a twentieth-century American audience. It suggests, therefore, that performances of Greek tragedy, even in her own translations, did not greatly concern Hamilton. But Hamilton's own writing and thinking also proved incidental to the theatrical reception of Greek tragedy in the first seven decades of that century, because her books and essays, her vehicles for expounding her vision, rarely address issues related to performance, other than the technical question of cast and chorus size.

To be sure, Robert F. Kennedy performed, and truly immortalized, Hamilton's rendition of the choral passage from the *Agamemnon* hailed by Sikelianos as immortal English poetry on April 4, 1968. It was on that evening that he quoted her words from memory to console a crowd of African-Americans in Indianapolis grieving over Martin Luther King's assassination (Hallett 2009a: 155–6). Kennedy, however, had not become acquainted with this passage from viewing a stage production of Aeschylus' tragedy, but from reading Hamilton's writings (Kennedy 1998: xxvii, 90–1, 180). It is worth observing, too, that Hamilton quotes the passage, *Agamemnon* 179–81, in *The Greek Way* out of context, as proof that the "lonely" Aeschylus himself found "truth to reconcile truths in the experience of men" (Hamilton 1930/1963: 186). Similarly, the playwright Mary Zimmerman credits her childhood exposure to Hamilton's work for her decision to explore classical myths in two of her plays, *Metamorphoses* and *Argonautica*. Zimmerman, however, draws exclusively on Hamilton's *Mythology*, not her translations or explications of classical Greek dramas (Nouryeh 2009: 61–5).

To my mind, one of Edith Hamilton's major contributions as what Brown called "an ambassador of an ancient civilization" to the United States in the twentieth century, and as what I am calling a moving, dramatic citizen of Athens, was the universalizing, emotionalizing vision of tragedy that she ascribed to the ancient Athenians, memorably articulated in *The Greek Way* (Brown 1963). Evan Thomas succinctly summarizes how this vision resonated for Robert F. Kennedy after his brother's assassination:

> Reading Hamilton's description of Aeschylus' *Oresteia*, Kennedy may have found at least a measure of solace in learning that the fall of great houses is fated—and felt kinship with Agamemnon and the House of Atreus, doomed to repeat the sins of their fathers, generation upon generation ... The saving grace for Kennedy was the exultation Greeks found in suffering ... By reading the great tragedies, Kennedy could find meaning (and relief) because "tragedy is nothing less than pain transmuted into exaltation by the alchemy of poetry." Hamilton writes, "Tragedy's one essential is a soul that can feel greatly." Few souls ever felt more than Robert Kennedy's. (Thomas 2000: 287)

So, too, Hamilton reconstructs Greek tragedy as a distinctively American phenomenon, focused intensely on individual suffering, democratic to the extent that it equalizes, and minimizes differences among, individuals who suffer and exult in their suffering. But at the same time her vision of tragedy as poetically transmuted pain simplifies the complexities of lived human existence. This vision acknowledges that the Athenian dramatists privileged their characters through portraying "the fall of great houses," but only to emphasize that even the most privileged may suffer; it thereby conveys the message that in tragic scenarios economic and social advantages are no guarantee or protection against suffering, and indeed render individuals more vulnerable to human pain.

In *The Greek Way*, when illustrating how the tragedians "felt," and how tragedy "makes us feel," Hamilton supplies several specific illustrations from the three Greek plays she translated. She states the obvious about *The Trojan Women*: that it looks at "war as it appears to a handful of captive women waiting for the victors to carry them away to all that slavery means for women" (Hamilton 1930/1963: 200–1). But other than that, her discussion erases gender and downplays class as important elements of human social and personal identity that affect how, when, and why different individuals may suffer.

Although the passages from Aeschylus that she quotes are mostly words assigned to women—Clytemnestra, Cassandra, and the female chorus of the *Prometheus*—Hamilton judges him the "most tragic of the tragedians" for showing "man's misery at its blackest and man's grandeur at its greatest" (Hamilton 1930/1963: 176). She never discusses how these Aeschylean female characters differ from their male counterparts, in their suffering or otherwise. Similarly, she acknowledges that the Trojan women are captives facing slavery, but not that the play's female protagonists come from immensely privileged families. In her chapter on Euripides she admits that "in the antique scale of human values," slaves were "not persons any more but goods and chattel." But she refuses to recognize, much less critique, the Greeks' whole-hearted embrace of slavery as a social institution: by crediting Plato with viewing slaves as "men among men," and by praising Euripides himself for denying that slavery oppresses, asserting "a man without fear cannot be a slave" (Hamilton 1930/1963: 200–1).

Hamilton's "Tragedy" in its American Literary Context

Finally, what Hamilton identifies as the significance of Athenian tragedy for her American readership merits comparison with the re-envisioning of this Greek literary genre by Theodore Dreiser in *An American Tragedy*. Dreiser published his novel in 1925, at the very time Hamilton began to write on the topic of tragedy for the readers of *Theatre Arts Monthly*.[15] Nevertheless, Hamilton seems oblivious to the role of social class and gender in the Greek tragedies she analyzes, in tragedy generally, and in Dreiser's work as well.

In Dreiser's *An American Tragedy*, ambition for social and economic advancement in fulfillment of the American dream, coupled with strong sexual desires, drive his male protagonist, Clyde Griffith, to wrong a female worker in his uncle's factory, with painful human consequences. As critics have remarked, Dreiser foregrounds both social class and gender in these fictional efforts to define what is both American and tragic. Jackson Lears regards Dreiser as "trivializing" tragedy, saying, "this is what happens to tragedy in a country that exalts the pursuit of material happiness while denying to most people the power of attaining it"; indeed, he views Clyde as "pathetic rather than tragic." But Lears also discerns "something like classical Nemesis" in the swift way that Clyde is brought down, and brought to justice. Clare Eby likens Dreiser's novel to Fitzgerald's *The Great Gatsby*, published the same year, because both "explore the constraining force of social class on individual freedom, while investing in women the combined power of sexual appeal and social position" (Eby 2004: 154; Lears 2004: 73).

It is surprising that neither Hamilton nor Reid mentions Dreiser's work on tragedy. A fellow Hoosier four years her junior, he and Hamilton, though from different social strata, shared a germanophone background. His years as a reporter in Chicago overlapped with those spent at Jane Addams's Hull House in that city by Alice Hamilton; of similar political outlook, he and Alice both chronicled, and tried to ameliorate, the conditions of Chicago's working poor. During the two decades that Edith and Doris resided in New York City, frequently interacting with cogs in its literary industry, Dreiser was living there too. As Shawn St. Jean documents, Dreiser concentrated on Classics (indeed Latin philology) before dropping out of Indiana University in 1890. Classical allusions and themes abound in his novels (Cassuto and Eby 2004: xi–xx; Hamilton 1943: 53–219; St. Jean 2001: 17–18).

Curiously, in a 1932 letter to the *Saturday Review*, Hamilton savages a book by Burton Rascoe, author of an earlier biography of Dreiser. Even though she sought to differentiate her own writing from conventional classical scholarship, she takes strong umbrage at its dismissive stereotyping of scholars, particularly those specializing in Greek and Roman antiquity. But she evidently felt no need to take Dreiser's work and ideas into account, and was validated by her middlebrow, reading public all the same (Hamilton 1932).

The award of Athenian citizenship, in an ancient Greek theater, and on her 90th birthday, to Edith Hamilton also validated what Hamilton sought to and did accomplish through her writings on Greek tragedy. As she performed movingly and dramatically on that occasion, so she performed her own, idiosyncratic, version of Athenian citizenship in twentieth-century America, to which the actual performance of Greek plays proved tangential. Yet hers was a narrow if influential concept of how ancient Greek drama reflected, and informed, the lives of its original spectators.

Notes

1. In Hamilton, *Three Greek Plays*, published by W. W. Norton in 1937, although Hamilton's translation of this particular play had appeared in the periodical *Theatre Arts Monthly* ten years before that. See Prins 2010: 174–7.
2. For Robert Kennedy's devotion to, and frequent quotations from, Edith Hamilton's work, see Hallett 2008: 84–7 and 2009a: 154–5 and 162–5, Kennedy 1998, and Thomas 2000, as well as the discussion below.
3. For Palmer Sikelianos, see Anton 1993, who posthumously edited her autobiography, and Michelakis 2010: 155–6, as well as Leontis, this volume. For the term "amateur historian," used to characterize women who wrote for a popular audience about different periods of the past, see Smith 1998: 6ff.
4. I would like to thank Susan Tracy, the archivist of Miss Porter's School, for providing me with information about the courses taken by Edith Hamilton at Miss Porter's, in an email of January 21, 2008. On page 18, Davis and Donahue provide a photograph of Edith (in a jaunty neck scarf) and her Latin class on Catullus and Terence's *Adelphoe*, with Thomas Day Seymour, taken in 1886.
5. *New York Times* 1927; Anton 1993: 103–51; Leontis, this volume.
6. *New York Times* 1927; Reid 1967: 146–50. The essay, "The Greek Chorus: Fifteen or Fifty?," was originally published by *Theatre Arts Monthly* in 1933, four years after Hamilton's 1929 trip to Greece and four years before the appearance of *Three Greek Plays*. It was reprinted in *The Ever-Present Past*, a collection of Hamilton's writings which came out in 1964, the year after her death.
7. Hamilton 1930/1963; Reid 1967: 81, 156–7. Although Reid acknowledges that Hamilton published an expanded version of *The Greek Way* in 1942, and quotes Bowra's praise of the book in 1964, she does not indicate that his encomiastic words in fact come from the introduction that he was commissioned to write for the 1963 edition.
8. Hartigan (1995: 145 n. 3) states: "The performance at Delphi was to be part of a festival inaugurating the 'Delphic Dream' of Angelos and Eva Palmer Sikelianos. There, in costumes designed by Eva Sikelianos and to Byzantine music performed by the Athens Symphony Orchestra, the actors read their lines in both English and modern Greek. Nether reviewers nor audience were pleased with the dual languages or that the lines were read, not spoken." By "there," Hartigan may be referring to the 1930 New York performance, since she notes, a propos of the 1957 New York production, that "it was a revival of the earlier text, but performed only in English, not modern Greek." These performances presumably featured a somewhat altered production of the Delphic 1927 *Prometheus* described in the May 10, 1927 *New York Times* article headlined "Kahn At Delphi Festival [With Other New Yorkers,

Sees an Aeschylus Play in Greek Theatre]." The *Times* reports that the play was presented on May 9, "in the modern Greek version [by Ioannis Psycharis] in an ancient Greek theatre," at "a Delphic festival organized by the poet Angelos Sikelianos and Mme. Sikelianos of New York." It notes in addition "many Americans, including [the banker and philanthropist] Otto Kahn, B. H. Hill, Director of the American School of Archaeology [in Athens], and Professor Carl Blegen, Acting Director, were among the spectators." Although the article states that M. Sikelianos explained "the object of the festival" in an address, it does not indicate in what language he spoke. Photos of this, 1927, production of the *Prometheus* at the Delphi Festival illustrated Hamilton's translation of the play in *Theatre Arts Monthly*. I am grateful to Artemis Leontis for calling my attention to this article.

9. Hartigan 1995: 132. By "at Delphi," Hartigan must mean at the benefit performance for the Delphi Festival in New York. I have found it impossible to reconcile Hartigan's assertions with Yurka's own autobiography, which describes the difficulties she experienced when playing Io in the 1957 production of the *Prometheus* in Athens (280–3), but says nothing about having performed the role prior to that time. Yurka's account of that production mentions that Clarence Derwent was in the cast, includes many complimentary words about "dear Edith Hamilton," and even quotes some of Hamilton's speech in the Theater of Herodes Atticus (without providing a source). In this context, moreover, Yurka mentions that Bourlos had played the role of Prometheus in "Eve [*sic*] Sikelianos' famous production several years previously."

   Earlier in the volume (165–6) Yurka describes her own relationship with Palmer Sikelianos, mentioning how Palmer Sikelianos had trained Bourlos—who "had no theatre experience"—at the Delphi Festival, and how in the 1930s she had tried to help the impoverished Palmer Sikelianos obtain U.S. government support for her theatrical projects. Yet, here too she does not mention performing in one of Palmer Sikelianos's own productions, as Io or in any other role.

10. Hartigan 1995: 132. In Anton 1993: 148, Palmer Sikelianos also relates that in the late 1930s Yurka had supported her efforts to obtain a chorus of men when staging Aeschylus' *Persians* for a production under the auspices of the WPA Federal Theatre Project.

11. Prins shared these observations in an abstract submitted for a seminar on "Classical Reception and the Education of Women" that she and Christopher Stray organized at the American Philological Association meeting in January 2009, and at which I presented a paper on Edith Hamilton's classical education.

12. Prins 2009 APA seminar abstract, quoting Smith 171–2. See also Leontis, this volume.

13. Anton 1993: 109, 43–51, 181–90, 191–8. For further details on the plays staged by Palmer Sikelianos at the Delphi Festival, see Michelakis 2010: 155–9, and Leontis, this volume.

14. Leontis, email correspondence, January 18, 2010.

15. Cassuto and Eby 2004: xi–xx. Cassuto and Eby also note that in 1926 Horace Liveright produced a Broadway play of *An American Tragedy*. The novel was adapted into a critically and commercially successful Hollywood film, *A Place in the Sun*, in 1951, 12 years before Hamilton's death.

References

Anton, J. (ed. 1993), *Upward Panic: The Autobiography of Eva Palmer-Sikelianos*. Philadelphia.
Bacon, H. (1980), "Edith Hamilton," in B. Sicherman and C. H. Greene eds., *Notable American Women: The Modern Period*. Cambridge, MA, 306–8.

Brown, J. M. (1963), "The Heritage of Edith Hamilton 1867–1963," *Saturday Review of Literature* (June 2), 16–17.
Calta, L. (1957), "Prometheus Stirs Interest," *New York Times* (August 3), 9.
Cassuto, L. and C. V. Eby (eds. 2004), *The Cambridge Companion to Theodore Dreiser*. Cambridge.
Davis, N. and B. Donahue (1992), *Miss Porter's School: A History*. Farmington, CT.
Eby, C. V. (2004), "Dreiser and Women," in L. Cassuto and C. V. Eby, The Cambridge Companion to Theodore Dreiser. Cambridge, 142–70.
Foote, H. (2002), *Beginnings: A Memoir*. New York.
Hallett, J. P. (1996–7), "Edith Hamilton (1867–1963)," *Classical World* 90, 107–47.
Hallett, J. P. (2008), "The Kennedy Family and Edith Hamilton's Greece," in "Classics in the Kennedy Era," special section of *Classical Bulletin* 84.2, 77–90.
Hallett, J. P. (2009a), "'The Anglicizing Way': Edith Hamilton (1867–1963) and the Twentieth-Century Transformation of Classics in the U.S.A.," in J. P. Hallett and C. Stray eds., *British Classics Outside England: The Academy and Beyond*. Waco, TX, 149–65.
Hallett, J. P. (2009b), "Edith Hamilton and Greco-Roman Mythology," in G. Staley ed., *American Women and Classical Myths*. Waco, TX, 105–30.
Hamilton, A. (1943), *Exploring the Dangerous Trades: The Autobiography of Alice Hamilton, MD*. Boston, reprinted with new introduction by B. Sicherman, 1985.
Hamilton, E. (1930), *The Greek Way*. New York, expanded 1942, reprinted with new introduction by C. M. Bowra, 1963.
Hamilton, E. (1932), "This Will Never Do," letter to the *Saturday Review of Literature*, December 31, on Burton Rascoe's *Titans of Literature*. Reprinted in E. Hamilton, *The Ever-Present Past*. New York, 120–6.
Hamilton, E. (1933), "The Greek Chorus: Fifteen or Fifty?," in *Theatre Arts Monthly*, June 31, 1932. Reprinted in E. Hamilton, *The Ever-Present Past*. New York, 48–59.
Hamilton, E. (1937), *Three Greek Plays: Prometheus Bound, Agamemnon, Trojan Women*. New York.
Hamilton, E. (1942), *Mythology*. Boston.
Hartigan, K. V. (1995), *Greek Tragedy on the American Stage: Ancient Drama in the Commercial Theater, 1882–1994*. Westport, CT, and London.
Kennedy, M. T. (ed. 1998), *Make Gentle the Life of This World: The Vision of Robert F. Kennedy*. New York.
Lears, J. (2004), "Dreiser and the History of American Longing," in L. Cassuto and C. V. Eby, The Cambridge Companion to Theodore Dreiser. Cambridge, 63–70.
Meserve, W. (1980), "Blanche Yurka," in B. Sicherman and C. H. Greene eds., *Notable American Women: The Modern Period*. Cambridge, MA, 754–56.
Michelakis, P. (2010), "Theater Festivals, Total Works of Art, the Revival of Greek Tragedy, and the Modern Stage," *Cultural Critique* 74, 149–63.
New York Times (1927), "Kahn at Delphic Festival" (May 10), 24.
Nouryeh, A. (2009), "Mary Zimmerman's *Metamorphoses*: Storytelling Theater as Feminist Process," in S. Friedman ed., *Feminist Theatrical Revisions of Classic Works: Critical Essays*. Jefferson, NC, 61–78.
Prins, Y. (2010), "The Sexual Politics of Translating *Prometheus Bound*," *Cultural Critique* 74, 164–80.

Reid, D. F. (1967), *Edith Hamilton: An Intimate Portrait*. New York.
St. Jean, S. (2001), *Pagan Dreiser: Songs from American Mythology*. Cranbury, NJ.
Sicherman, B. (1991), "Edith Hamilton," in E. Foner and J. S. Garraty eds., *The Reader's Companion to American History*. Boston, 483–4.
Smith, B. G. (1998), *The Gender of History. Men, Women and Historical Practice*. Cambridge, MA.
Thomas, E. (2000), *Robert Kennedy: His Life*. New York.
Yurka, B. (1970), *Bohemian Girl: Blanche Yurka's Theatrical Life*. Athens, OH.

CHAPTER 18

A NEW STAGE OF LAUGHTER FOR ZORA NEALE HURSTON AND THEODORE BROWNE

Lysistrata *and the Negro Units of the Federal Theatre Project*

LENA M. HILL

The history of portraying African-Americans on the U.S. dramatic stage often left black audiences with little to laugh about. The earliest American plays featuring black characters routinely included white actors in blackface. And while a few theaters spotlighted black actors like Ira Aldridge in Shakespearian dramas as early as the 1820s, U.S. audiences remained wary of African-Americans taking to the stage in roles that departed from the stereotypes they associated with authentic blackness.[1] As a result of such expectations, the years before the Harlem Renaissance allowed very few black playwrights the opportunity to craft serious, realistic works for venues that catered to white or even diverse audiences. Instead, most Americans before the first decade of the twentieth century saw blacks featured as comedic characters consigned to a few predictable roles. Even as more sensitive parts by directors like Paul Green and Eugene O'Neill paved the way for stars from Paul Robeson to Charles Gilpin to show the range and depth of their talent, the minstrel tradition continued to loom large and set expectations for white audiences. For instance, from 1910 through 1917, the comedian Bert Williams was the lone black performer to appear on Broadway (Fraden 1994: 58), and by the 1920s, the radio show "Amos 'n' Andy" took the nation by storm. Hollywood produced the first movies with predominantly black casts in 1929, but they continued to focus on song and dance to portray what mainstream audiences understood as black culture.

In fact, racial stereotypes formed in the theater saturated almost every aspect of U.S. popular culture. When Richard Wright reviewed Zora Neale Hurston's *Their Eyes Were Watching God* in a piece he titled "Between Laughter and Tears" (1937), he lamented, "Miss Hurston *voluntarily* continues in her novel the tradition which was *forced* upon the Negro in the theatre, that is, the minstrel technique that makes the 'white folks' laugh."[2] Yet, from her earliest years, Hurston purposefully worked against the minstrel tradition in her novels and plays. Writing to Langston Hughes in 1928 from one of her first anthropological research trips, she gushed about the material she collected: "Did I tell you before I left about the new, the *real* Negro art theatre I plan? Well, I shall, or rather *we* shall act out the folk tales, however short, with the abrupt angularity and naivete of the primitive 'bama nigger."[3] In a different letter she assures Hughes, "I *know* it is going to be *Glorious*! A really new departure in the drama."[4] Hurston was determined to transform the folklore she collected into new, authentic material for the theater.

An easy way to explain the gulf between Wright's assessment of Hurston's creative work and Hurston's own goals is their attitude toward the role of comedy in black art.[5] Mel Watkins's superb study of black humor traces the complicated history of African-American comedy in mainstream literature and U.S. popular culture (Watkins 1999: parts One and Two). On the stage, the black image suffered enormously from the gross distortions fostered in the minstrel tradition of the nineteenth century and vaudeville, silent films, and Hollywood movies in the twentieth century. During the years following the Harlem Renaissance, one of the first periods that witnessed African-American writers experimenting daringly with comedy, black writers retreated from promoting comic images of black citizens that might provide fodder for racist detractors. Adding to the uncertain position of humor in black art, Wright ushered in the protest-realist genre of African-American literature and advocated publishing material so raw that white audiences would not dream of laughing or have the consolation of crying. Hurston, however, continued to find value in humor.[6] She explains the complexity of black laughter in *Mules and Men* (1935) as indicative of African-American resistance to invasive research tactics: "the Negro, in spite of his open-faced laughter, his seeming acquiescence . . . offers a feather-bed resistance. That is, we let the probe enter, but it never comes out. It gets smothered under a lot of laughter and pleasantries" (Hurston 1995: 10). With this reality in mind, Hurston strove to write drama, fiction, and ethnographic collections that elicited laughter even as the material forced audiences to acknowledge the complexity of African-American culture.

A close look at the comic episodes Hurston positioned at the center of her plots reveals the cultural, political, and ideological issues she engages under the gauzy cover of laughter. Her work on the stage offers a particularly intriguing example of the varied and sophisticated ways she, and other black writers of the 1930s, craft plays that challenge traditional ideas about black humor on the U.S. stage. Greek comedy, for instance, offered Hurston a valuable source for reassessing comic African-American drama. Together with contemporary dramatists like Theodore Browne, she sought to remind audiences of the theatrical roots of comedy that proved laughter could serve as a vehicle for serious socio-political and cultural discussions. An analysis of Hurston's and Browne's separate versions of *Lysistrata* reveals the complicated nature of black playwrights' turn to Greek humor on the 1930s stage.

The Negro Units of the FTP and Hurston's *Lysistrata*

The Harlem Renaissance, the term scholars use to describe the outburst of artistic productivity in Harlem and other metropolitan areas after World War I, waned when the Great Depression took hold of the nation and the wealthy patrons who supported individual black artists found their fortunes severely diminished. But aspects of this artistic flowering continued late into the 1930s with one of the clearest areas of success emerging under the auspices of the Federal Theatre Project (FTP). The FTP was born after President Roosevelt's New Deal created the Works Progress Administration (WPA) and identified four Arts Projects that the government agency would support. Hallie Flanagan, a drama professor at Vassar College, was appointed to direct the FTP, and she committed herself to making the federal arts program a theater organization that was both popular and thought provoking. A major part of her strategy focused on including ethnic plays and actors that would challenge U.S. audiences' worldview.

As a result of the rich productivity fostered during the height of the New Negro movement, when the FTP decided to establish black units in cities across the country, its directors found a firm foundation upon which to build in the shape of experimental theater groups. Flanagan forged ahead to found units in four geographical regions of the country. In her autobiography, she recalls forming inaugural units in "Seattle, Hartford, Philadelphia, Newark, Los Angeles, Boston, Raleigh, Birmingham, San Francisco, and Chicago." She further acknowledged that this work was all "undertaken with the advice of Rose McClendon" (Davis 1940: 62–3). McClendon, one of the most prominent black women in U.S. theater during the Harlem Renaissance, had gained national fame through her roles in hits like *In Abraham's Bosom* (1926) and *Porgy* (1927). She had also advised the Harlem Experimental Theatre since 1927.[7]

Flanagan admits asking McClendon "whether it would not be advisable to have the direction and designing of their project by a member of their own race"; however, she explains that McClendon insisted that the Negro units begin under "more experienced direction" from whites (Davis 1940: 63). Flanagan accepted her advice, but McClendon continued to work closely with John Houseman, who was appointed to head the Harlem Unit. Jay Plum credits McClendon's willingness to share the directing responsibilities with Housemen as a major factor in the early success of not only the Harlem Unit but the FTP as a whole. Reflecting on the volatile politics of the moment, Plum notes that a short five months prior to the Negro Unit's conception, Harlem had erupted in riots and desperately needed to see racially balanced leadership of the federally funded project which at its height came to employ "over 500 artists and technicians, becoming the largest employer of African-Americans in Harlem" (Plum 1992: 152). By the end of the FTP's four-year run, 22 cities across the U.S.A. had served as the headquarters for a black theater unit.

A major goal of the FTP focused upon training future black playwrights as well as locating and supporting new black plays to be produced by the newly formed Negro Units. Ronald Ross explains that Flanagan worked hard to find job opportunities for "approximately forty jobless young black playwrights who had only recently graduated from Negro colleges around the nation" (Ross 1974: 46). Although the relations between the white administrators and black workers were not always ideal, there was much to applaud in the endeavor. The partnership represented a real opportunity for African-Americans striving to improve their acting, writing, or technical skills as they gained access to greater resources and larger audiences. The stated goals of the FTP also aided their attempts to present innovative material, and the adaptation of Greek work fitted nicely into their project.[8] Both Hurston and actor-turned-playwright Theodore Browne emerged as two members of the Negro Units who took advantage of these resources and introduced a new subject for laughter onto the American stage: Aristophanes' *Lysistrata*.

Lysistrata tells the story of one Athenian woman determined to bring the Peloponnesian War to an end. (See Dutsch, this volume.) To accomplish her goal, Lysistrata brings all the women of Greece together and convinces them to refuse to indulge in sexual relations with their husbands until they agree to stop fighting wars. In addition to forming this pact, Lysistrata enlists the help of the older women of Athens who take hold of the Acropolis. Although the core story provides a comic epicenter for the play, Aristophanes clearly used it to offer political commentary. Michael Ewans notes that Greek "comic and tragic playwrights enjoyed an almost unparalleled license to use their dramas to critique any aspect they wished of the city's policies and values," and *Lysistrata* in particular represented "a new kind of comedy" reflecting the sensitive nature of "the political situation" (Ewans 2010: 3–4, 11). In fact, Ewans declares it "a mistake to regard" the play "as less politically engaged" simply because it avoided the "overt vitriol" of early works like *Knights* (Ewans 2010: 3–4, 11). Examining Hurston's and Browne's adaptations suggests that they, too, sought to comment upon their contemporary socio-political reality.

Scholars have discounted the role of black initiative in the choice of this classical comedy. Instead, they account for African-American interest in Aristophanes as the result of heavy-handed white administrators projecting their political ideology onto less savvy black playwrights. Considering Browne's Seattle experience with *Lysistrata*, Ron West declares that the Negro Repertory Company's "white sponsors projected their academic and political agendas onto the black unit" and felt no compunction about displacing "their Marxist political agenda onto the black company."[9] But the fact that both Hurston and Browne wrote versions of this Greek comedy that reflect the concerns of their broader corpus suggests their genuine interest in the play. Hurston's version has apparently been lost, but what we know of her adaptation makes it appear a natural choice. John Houseman recalls the challenge of finding quality scripts devoted to African-American subjects, a problem exacerbated by what he describes as "a widening split between the 'social-conscious' members" of the Negro Theatre and other participants. His discovery of Hurston's version of *Lysistrata* left him feeling certain that he had solved the problem since her adaptation updated the classic tale by setting the action in "a Florida fishing community, where the men's wives refused them intercourse until they won their fight with the canning company for a living wage." Houseman's description leaves no doubt that Hurston's adaptation not only addressed contemporary issues but depended upon the theater to probe a politically explosive topic. Unfortunately, Houseman notes that her script "scandalized both Left and Right by its saltiness," and her work was apparently never staged.[10]

Houseman's description of Hurston's *Lysistrata* positions it comfortably within her oeuvre, which includes numerous considerations of working-class issues. Although she became a fixture of the Harlem Renaissance after she arrived to New York in 1925, Hurston grew up in the rural black town of Eatonville, Florida, and her creative work bears the stamp of this background. Even after attending Howard University and Barnard College, she remained deeply invested in sharing the black folklore of her youth with the wider world. Hurston's anthropological work with Franz Boas gave her the formal training she needed to collect the vernacular arts of the black South and Caribbean, and these tales, songs, and lies became a mainstay in her short stories, plays, revues, ethnographies, and novels. Her best-known novel, *Their Eyes Were Watching God* (1937), captures the beauty of black Southern speech as it threads folktales and rural Southern culture around the story of a woman's evolving sense of self through the experience of three marriages.

Hurston's abiding interest in black oral culture likely led her to see parallels between the basic plot of Aristophanes' play and a well-known African-American folktale. In her first published collection of black folklore, Hurston records the story of how women gained control over the bedroom while men secured greater physical strength. According to the woman who shares the tale, man initially petitioned God, "[P]*lease* to give me mo' strength than dat woman . . . so Ah kin make her mind" (Hurston 1995: 35). When God granted his desire, man used his superior strength to keep woman under his control while woman was left to implore God for equal strength. When God refused her request, the devil advised woman to ask God for the "bunch of keys hangin' by de mantel-piece," and he explains their power and how to use them: "Now dis first big key is to de do' of de kitchen, and you know a man always favors his stomach. Dis second one is de key to de bedroom and he don't like to be shut out from dat neither and dis last key is de key to de cradle and he don't want to be cut off from his generations at all. So now you take dese keys and go lock up everything and wait till he come to you" (Hurston 1995: 37). Woman's control over these areas of the domestic space ultimately gives her power in male–female relationships even as men retain physical strength, power in the law, and economic dominance.

The similarities between *Lysistrata* and the folktale—both plots revolve around women's dependence on feminine appeal to gain power over men—no doubt resonated with Hurston. Yet her decision to place a labor dispute at the center of her adaptation testifies to her familiarity with the Greek comedy form. Classicist Eric Hairston notes that "Hurston . . . imbibed the classics" early in life as well as in college, a point evidenced by Hurston's recollection of the first major gift of books she received as a child (Hairston 2013: 197). She recalls a fifth grade experience of confidently reciting the "story of Pluto and Persephone" for visiting white women since "this Greco-Roman myth was one of [her] favorites." As a reward for her efforts, the women sent her a box of books that included numerous "Greek and Roman Myths" (Boyd 2003: 36, 37). As a student at Howard many years later, she was required to complete "four years of Latin and two years of Greek" (Boyd 2003: 79). Indeed, Hurston received a traditional, classical education at Howard University.

Adapting classical forms for black audiences, however, could be tricky. Houseman notes that black drama of the period walked a fine line in selecting subjects that appealed to competing interests in the black community. For instance, focusing specifically on the Negro People's Theatre in Chicago, Melissa Barton examines the struggle to negotiate the contradictory aesthetic and political desires motivating radical leftist theater-goers compared to those inspiring the black bourgeoisie. Barton, considering Fannie McConnell's role in mediating these differences, quotes a member of the Young Communist League who avowed that that while many in the audience looked to the stage to help them escape their immediate struggles, others yearned to see "the social problems of the Negro" take center stage so it might be a space "of educational value to workers" (Barton 2010: 55). McConnell, who would later marry novelist Ralph Ellison, wrote to Howard Cordery in 1939 reflecting on the difficulty of achieving this balancing act: "We are constantly trying to explain that since the time of the Greek theatre it has been the function of the stage to point out what was wrong with the world and that in periods when the stage ceased to do this it fell to rock-bottom" (Barton 2010: 55).

Hurston, it seems, found a way to combine these competing interests. She had long nursed a belief that the stage offered the best venue to explore fiery issues related to contemporary society even as she interwove such stories with the comedy of rural culture. For instance, the frame for *Mules and Men* highlights the labor reality of black men in the rural South. As she documents her search for new material, Hurston records her interactions with the men in the "swamp-gang" who share tale upon tale as they wait to be assigned their work for the day (Hurston 1995: 68). Their interactions with an overbearing foreman are braided throughout their lies, and they depend on their creativity to negotiate an exploitative labor environment. Many of their tales focus upon "Ole Massa"—a convenient stand-in for the contemporary boss—and elicit laughter as they portray "John" repeatedly outsmarting his mean master. Hurston placed the realities of life around the rural "job" at the center of her work, and her version of *Lysistrata* was no exception. Aristophanes' comedy offered an innovative approach to probing abusive rural labor practices even as the story invited laughter. She was not alone in her belief that *Lysistrata* presented an important new opportunity for the black stage.

Theodore Browne and the Politics of Staging Greek Comedy

When Theodore Browne began working on his adaptation of *Lysistrata*, he had just completed a leading performance in *Stevedore* and had also acted in *Noah*, the first pieces produced by the Seattle Negro Unit of the FTP. Both plays included a good deal of music and dance in an effort to participate in the popular musical forms inspired by 1920s Broadway trends. The Seattle unit of the FTP was one of the most exciting in the country, but its fascination with such performance elements reveals its white directors' comfort with promulgating black stereotypes. Tina Redd's excellent work on *Stevedore* unearths the challenges African-American theater practitioners faced as they strove to move beyond the caricatures fostered on the U.S. stage. In some cases, blacks faced the difficulty of the predilections of African-American audiences who raved over minstrel inspired productions like *Swing Mikado* and *Little Black Sambo* staged by the Chicago Negro Unit while they reacted tepidly to more serious works like Theodore Ward's *Big White Fog*. Shirley Graham, the African-American writer and activist enlisted to promote Ward's play in the black community, expressed "disappointment with Chicago blacks whom she believed lacked interest in culture" (Jamison-Hall 2011: 421). This resistance to serious dramatic fare in black theater-going circles was exacerbated by the FTP's refusal to reject black stereotypes. Redd explains that when the Seattle Negro Unit began making plans to open at the Playhouse theater, "Work Project No. 818-(1)'s Negro Minstrels were already performing in the area" to great demand (Redd 1995: 78). Their continued popularity together with the persistent emphasis on song and dance in plays like *Stevedore* presented a hurdle to black playwrights committed to producing more progressive work.

Browne was well aware of the tension between the black community's desire to dramatize respectable images of black life and the established theater community's support for plays promoting derogatory notions of African-American culture. Indeed, when the black members of the newly formed Seattle Negro Unit learned of plans to stage *Porgy* in the upcoming season, they passionately spoke out against a work "too degrading to be on" (Redd 1995: 67). On the other hand, even as Browne starred in *Stevedore*, the chorus members of the play regularly made public appearances that one audience member applauded for maintaining expected stereotypes: "The Negro Minstrels are . . . offering standard song and dance and comedy which is bringing in constant letters of appreciation" (Redd 1995: 82). Browne himself was often celebrated in racially heightened terms that exaggerated his blackness and alternately placed him squarely into the legacy of "a very believable Negro singer, Paul Robeson or Roland Hayes" (Redd 1995: 73–4). One newspaper crafted an article around Browne's front-page photograph that assured readers of the authenticity of the "All-Negro" shows performed at the Playhouse (Redd 1995: 82).

This reality underscores Browne's goals in adapting *Lysistrata*. He sought to progress beyond the stilted stereotypes prescribed for black characters on the U.S. stage. In an interview, Browne recalled:

> We were going to do [*Macbeth*], and I'll tell you what happened there . . . We had a lot of trouble in getting the people to learn those lines. The lines were unfamiliar to them. This is Shakespeare, you see, and we had that trouble . . . You had to have material that they could handle. (West 1996: 95)

Browne's words acknowledge the success of Orson Welles's 1936 version of Shakespeare's *Macbeth*, a New York production by the FTP that boasted an all-black cast and set the action in a fictional Caribbean island. Commonly called *Voodoo Macbeth*, the production left other Negro Units anxious to follow Welles's achievement. Browne, however, turns to Aristophanes rather than Shakespeare, a decision that speaks to his independent investment in choosing *Lysistrata* (Fig. 18.1).

Born in Suffolk, Virginia, and educated in New York, Browne was a creature of the stage. As an actor, playwright, and future founder of the Negro Playwrights company, he was deeply steeped in dramatic history. Like Hurston, Browne maintained a great interest in black folk culture as well as labor issues in Southern rural communities. His best-known work, *Natural Man* (1937), focuses upon the folk hero John Henry but places him in a context that questions the exploitative reality facing the rural black working man. Browne's other productions in Seattle included *A Black Woman Called Moses* (1937), a two-act drama about Harriet Tubman. His plays display an abiding interest in illuminating the power, beauty, and unique contributions of black folk

FIG. 18.1 A scene from *Lysistrata*. Courtesy of the University of Washington Library, Special Collections Division, UW Theatres Photograph Collection (PH Collection #236), box 4, folder 13.

culture while unearthing the social and economic hurdles stacked against African-American progress.

Although we cannot be sure of the exact Greek translation of *Lysistrata* that Browne worked from as he completed his script, his changes to the standard plot reveal clear objectives that inform his adaptation and support my contention that he uses the play to address the 1930s African-American socio-political reality. By focusing on women in the fictional African nation of Ebonia, he slyly presents a politicized play that argues for the necessity of a strong black community under the auspices of a comical gender dispute. From the opening lines, Browne emphasizes Lysistrata's hyperpoliticized nature and disappointment with her fellow women in contrast to the playful acceptance of pejorative feminine characteristics displayed by her neighbor, Calonice. While the Greek version portrays a similar dynamic, Calonice traditionally emerges as a cynical jokester who carelessly voices agreement with the disparaging stereotypes of women.[11] Browne retains Calonice's wistful focus upon the physical pleasure her husband's return will bring, but he omits her comic tendencies. His Lysistrata leaves little room for joking as she launches into the seriousness of the matter at hand, politicizing the situation by stressing the importance of feminine solidarity to the future of the country. Rather than emphasizing her allegiance to Ebonia, Lysistrata repeatedly substitutes a reference to the fictional country with general comments about national loyalty. This lack of specificity allows Browne to elide the fictional setting of Ebonia with the U.S.A. For example, without referring directly to Ebonia, Lysistrata alternately refuses to make light of a lack of "patriotism," "the fate of one's country," and the possibility of making the "country a better place to live" (1.3).[12] Listening to her, the audience might easily slip into believing that she refers to the U.S.A.

By foregrounding patriotism and feminine will from the outset—and quickly bringing in the regional clash—Browne complicates the core dispute beyond the contours of a male–female conflict. He highlights his distinct approach to presenting the discord by removing Aristophanes' lesbian undertones that mark the entrance of women from outside of Athens and replacing this narrative line with an urban–rural quarrel. Where the Greek version accentuates the Athenian women's appreciation for the attractive physique their neighbors flaunt, Browne introduces intraracial strife rooted in regional stereotypes. When Lysistrata announces her intention to include the women of Boeotia and Sparta in their plan, Myrrhina exclaims, "I resent having to hobnob with those tribal hussies who live in the bush. They're heathens, all of them, uncivilized and they still practice voodoo" (1.6). The Athenian woman's words reflect her sense of superiority stemming from living in the city. Browne, however, undermines the legitimacy of her attitude by implicitly connecting the women from rural areas to the sophistication of Welles's *Voodoo Macbeth*, a performance most audiences would have in mind as representing the pinnacle of cultural complexity.

Lysistrata's compliment of Lampito's physical form prompts Myrrhina to joke that the Spartan leader looks like a "cow" as a result of being forced to work in the fields "behind a plow" (1.7). Although the reference to a cow is directly derived from the Greek version, Browne adds the insult that the Boeotian men force their women to work in the fields, a clear dig at their agrarian lifestyle. His detail nods to the shifting demographics of the 1930s black population. More than half of the African-American population resided in rural areas even as huge numbers poured into urban spaces. The conflicts ensuing from the Great Migration intensified as the Great Depression made jobs difficult to find, and this new economic landscape left cosmopolitan black Americans resenting the influx of Southern blacks into their carefully stratified communities. For her part, Lampito accuses the Athenian women of the haughty laziness agrarian blacks often associated with city living. A Corinthian woman complains, "These Athenians think they're the cream of Ebonia just because they happen to live in the capital," and Lampito agrees, declaring, "I may be from the bush country, but I'm not as dumb as you think"! (1.12).

Browne's portrayal of the urban–rural tension is obvious. Although Lysistrata briefly refers to the ladies as "comrades" in her first speech, the potential emphasis on a Marxist narrative is quickly removed as the other women shout down Lysistrata's attempt to introduce what they interpret as unnecessary pomp and circumstance (1.8). This narrative strain only returns in the final moments of the play as the Athenian men attempt to make a desperate argument to explain the women's actions. The Committeeman, who appears as the fool of the play, flails about ridiculously as Lysistrata and the other men work out a formal agreement. Enraged by his impotence, the Committeeman exclaims, "This is an outrage! Scandalous! I'll call out the national guard to put down this mutiny!" As he is booed and hissed away, he continues to shout, "Communists! Treason! Anarchists! Revolution!" (2.24). His hysterical shrieks appear more like the absurd outburst of an irrelevant clown than ideas worthy of serious consideration. Browne seems disinclined to promote this narrative line.

Instead, the central conflict mirrors the reality of 1930s African-American politics in which blacks living in urban centers looked down upon the large numbers of migrating African-Americans fleeing the countryside and an agrarian lifestyle. Historians estimate that the decades immediately preceding the Great Depression saw roughly 1.6 million black Americans from Southern and rural areas relocate to northern and Midwestern industrial cities. Although white theater audiences were trained to think of African-Americans as a monolithic group, Browne refused to give credence to this naive assumption. His decision to set *Lysistrata* in Africa denied the growing desire to see black gospel choirs on stage no matter the plot and effectively demanded that the audience acknowledge black Americans' rich history and complicated contemporary cultural reality. (See McConnell, this volume.)

His diversification of the women participating in Lysistrata's resistance extends his contemplation of the heterogeneous experiences of black citizens. While Aristophanes focuses upon married women alone, Browne adds single ladies to the discussion, signaling his concern with capturing a realistic picture of the black community. Marriage rates fell dramatically amongst African-Americans during the 1930s, a trend common across racial groups due to the general challenges posed by the Great Depression as well as specific policies, such as "marriage bars," regulations that empowered firms to dismiss single women who became married or prohibited hiring married women (Margo 1993: 56). Yet in black communities, this trend was intensified by more extreme rates of unemployment.

Reflecting on this dilemma, Browne adds a striking scene to Aristophanes' examples of the women's refusal to be intimate with their husbands. When Leonidas begs Melistice to "be nice," she protests, "No!—In the first place, we are not married" (2.20). As he continues to entreat her, she reminds him that he has not yet completed her "dowry":

MELISTICE: There [is] still the balance due before I'm lawfully yours!
LEONIDAS: I'll pay the balance in cash from my army bonus.
MELISTICE: I hate being married on the installment plan! (2.20–2.21)

Browne's audience would have been familiar with such conversations and the widespread practice of young couples waiting to get married because of financial difficulties. Clifford Odets emphasized this issue in *Waiting for Lefty* (1935) by including a vignette of a young couple, Sid and Florence, who face the reality that their love alone is not enough to gain their families' support for their marriage. Odets's work was widely criticized for its socialist sympathies, but many audiences applauded his willingness to tackle unspoken hardships of the Depression era. Browne clearly sought to underscore analogous issues, but the comedic foundation he built upon diminished the radical implications of his work.

One of the most tendentious aspects of Browne's decision to adapt *Lysistrata* springs from the very heart of the play. By adapting a comedy centered on women who initiate a political disturbance, Browne subtly engages the sociological discussion of black Americans in the 1930s. Robert E. Park's description of African-Americans as the "lady of the races" in the *Introduction to the Science of Sociology* (1919), a text he co-edited with Ernest W. Burgess, intensified the argument that black citizens were physiologically unfit for a range of activities and positions. Although science had long been deployed to declare African-Americans intellectually inferior to their white counterparts, Park's research distinguished itself in its generally positive approach to black culture. His work with black leaders like Booker T. Washington gave his research credence in the African-American community and made it more difficult to challenge his pronouncements. In truth, Park did not intend to provide fodder for racist leaders. Nevertheless, the growing field of sociology—and specifically the Chicago school that Park led—inadvertently updated time-worn arguments that declared blacks perpetual adolescents even as it sought to defend African-Americans by highlighting societal structures that disproportionately impacted urban blacks. In *Lysistrata*, the clown-like Committeeman depends upon sociological language and inflammatory tactics to denounce Lysistrata and the women participating in her resistance. He authoritatively claims, "I have my own methods of dealing with mob-violence and civil disobedience. I *have* studied the psychology of the mob" (1.32).

Browne's understated engagement of sociological rhetoric departs from the more expected subjects explored in plays written by or focused upon black women. During the Harlem Renaissance in particular, African-American female playwrights frequently looked to the stage to celebrate folklore and cultural legends or to examine the painful reality of lynching.[13] Browne, however, plainly diverges from these established themes.

Early in the play, he emphasizes Lysistrata's argument that women—here, easily read as code for "African-Americans" whom Parks declared the "lady" of the races—are worthy of fulfilling political roles:

> CALONICE: Just what do women know about running a country? They can't even run the men!
> LYSISTRATA: If the women assemble, those from the Boetian and Spartan tribes, and we women of Athens—in one united front—we can save our country from war. I'll bet you, and you can take all the odds you want.
> CALONICE: War is a man's business. Not ours. I don't want to get mixed up in some silly war!
> LYSISTRATA: (rises to her feet, argumentative) War concerns us just as much as it does men. Our family life and marriage relationships are broken up. We bring children into the world—for what? to be used for cannon-fodder. And you say war is man's business?
> CALONICE: Well, don't our statesmen take care of all that for us?
> LYSISTRATA: They sure do! And what a hell of a mess the country's in right now! (1.4)

The women's exchange recalls a debate common at the turn of the century and leading up to World War I. Black leaders like W. E. B. Du Bois and Frances E. W. Harper declared the necessity that African-Americans remain actively involved in politics so that the entire county might benefit from their moral views and retention of core attributes of American character. Browne deepens the allusion during the confrontation between the Chorus of Old Men and the Chorus of Old Women by having an old man appeal to rhetoric used by white racists and male chauvinists alike. The leader of the old men exclaims, "Sluts! If we let them get away with this, this republic won't be fit to live in. Pretty soon, they'll be wanting to run for President or Governor!" The women reply to his verbal assault by mocking them as "dotards" and "specie[s] of monkey" (1.25). With this retort, they turn the men's argument on its head as they recall the least savory aspects of racist political attacks. During the Reconstruction era, vicious cartoons depicted black legislators in simian terms that visually pronounced them unfit for public service. To support these claims, the science of the day focused upon brain sizes and other anatomical measurements to declare blacks in public office a danger to the nation. Blacks and women were considered kindred in their mental inferiority to white men.

Browne continues his allusion to the danger of rehearsing the worst elements of racist assaults against African-Americans' intellectualism in his revision of the dispute between Cinisias and Myrrhina. He reminds his audience that throughout U.S. history, white Americans discouraged black education. Cinisias, frustrated by his wife's obstinate refusal to succumb to his advances, complains about Lysistrata: "I hate these females with brains! . . . You listen to me, Myrrhina. Stay away from that woman. She's not your kind. She's touched in the head from reading too many books" (2.15). Piling on to the historical practice of discouraging African-Americans from intellectual pursuits, Browne revises a well-known line from Frederick Douglass's *The Narrative of the Life of Frederick Douglass, An American Slave* (1845). Upon hearing about the disturbance the old women cause at the Acropolis, the Committeeman blames the leniency of men for the women's misbehavior: "I have always said that i[f] you give a woman an inch, she'll take an el" (1.29). In Douglass's canonical slave narrative, his master uses the same language to reprimand his wife for teaching the young Douglass to read. As a result of hearing his master connect reading to making blacks unfit for slavery, Douglass commits himself to attaining literacy. Browne intimates that Lysistrata's political activism represents a similar act of racial agency and self-determination, and he links her actions to such heroism as that of Douglass and the necessity for black independent action to make cultural progress a reality. Notwithstanding the humor at the center of the play, Browne's heroine hails from a long line of serious black activists.

For Browne and Hurston, *Lysistrata* is both comical and serious, evoking laughter and rigorous thinking about the nation's problems. Although Hurston's adaptation fell victim to the censorship of the 1930s social context, and Browne's version was closed down after one performance to a sold-out crowd, both playwrights continued to experiment with the political subjects they explored through the lens of Aristophanes' comedy. Browne, who enjoyed the opening night success of performing *Lysistrata* before an audience of 1,100 with tickets sold for six months in advance, noted that he had avoided "indecency" in his adaptation (Hill and Hatch 2003: 328). He recognized the racism that undermined his success. In West's careful review of the accounts that led to the abrupt closure of a play that promised to be extremely profitable, he concludes that instead "of transgressing a generalized moral standard, *Lysistrata* violated Seattle's socially and ethnically coded local definition of 'decency' that was tantamount to a structure for cultural and racial control"; in other words, "black performers of *Lysistrata* acquired 'indecency' ... through the understanding of spectators" (Hill and Hatch 2003: 328). But rather than leave the theater in disgust, his work with the saucy Greek comedy led to Browne's more adventurous experimentation in future plays. Indeed, Hurston's and Browne's turn to Aristophanes was rooted in a desire for bold innovation that remained at the center of their artistic agendas. Under the cover of laughter, Hurston and Browne explored the true reasons for many of the tears shed by African-Americans of the 1930s.

Notes

1. Rena Fraden discusses this history in Fraden 1994: 58.
2. In *New Masses* (October 5, 1937), reprinted in Gates and Appiah 1993: 17.
3. Zora Neale Hurston, letter April 12, 1928, in Hurston 2002: 116.
4. Hurston 2002: 117 (original letter May 1, 1928).
5. Jennifer Cayer also discusses Hurston's attitude toward laughter in her work, and she notes the stark contrast to Wright's sensibility. Focusing particularly on Hurston's play *Cold Keener* and the complexity around laughter in black works of the Harlem Renaissance, Cayer notes that "black laughter is transgressive and threatening"—Cayer 2008: 57.
6. Wall (1994: 288) concludes that Richard Wright's review tied "Hurston to a politics he deemed reactionary and to a quest for the beautiful which, to him, served no 'serious' purpose."

7. Plum (1992: 148) notes that McClendon's role with the Harlem Experimental Theatre "laid the foundation upon which future companies such as the Negro People's Theatre (1935), the Harlem Suitcase Theatre (1937), the Rose McClendon Players (1938), and the American Negro Theatre (1940) could build."
8. Wetmore (2003: 67) reviews the origins of African-American adaptations of Greek drama. He notes that although "African Americans were performing Greek tragedies in the universities before the turn of the century," it "was not until the Great Depression ... that Greek tragedy began to be performed by all-black companies in earnest. The Federal Theatre Project's Negro Theatre Units were the first major professional producing organization to present African American Greek tragedy in adaptation."
9. See West 1996: 93, 95. West is one of the few critics who considers Browne's *Lysistrata*, but he focuses almost exclusively on the politics surrounding its premature closing.
10. Quoted in Houseman 1972: 205.
11. For my reference, I refer to the Athenian Society, London, 1912 edition of *Lysistrata*. See Aristophanes 1936.
12. Throughout my analysis, I refer to Browne's original typescript, which is held at George Mason University Libraries.
13. For a comprehensive discussion of lynching on stage during the early twentieth century, see Mitchell 2011.

References

Aristophanes (1936), *Aristophanes: The Eleven Comedies*. New York.
Barton, M. (2010), "'Speaking a Mutual Language': The Negro People's Theatre in Chicago," *Drama Review* 54, 54–70.
Boyd, V. (2003), *Wrapped in Rainbows: The Life of Zora Neale Hurston*. New York.
Browne, T. *"Lysistrata" of Aristophanes: An "African Version."* Federal Theatre Project Collection. Special Collections & Archives, George Mason University Libraries, Fairfax, VA.
Cayer, J. (2008), "'Roll yo' hips don't roll yo' eyes': Angularity and Embodied Spectatorship in Zora Neale Hurston's Play, Cold Keener," *Theatre Journal* 60, 37–69.
Davis, H. F. (1940), *Arena*. New York.
Ewans, M. (trans. 2010), *Aristophanes: Lysistrata, The Women's Festival, and Frogs*. Norman, OK.
Fraden, R. (1994), *Blueprints for a Black Federal Theatre, 1935–1939*. Cambridge.
Gates, H. L. Jr. and K. A. Appiah (1993), *Zora Neale Hurston: Critical Perspectives Past and Present*. New York.
Hairston, E. (2013), *The Ebony Column: Classics, Civilization, and the African American Reclamation of the West*. Knoxville, TN.
Hill, E. G. and J. V. Hatch (2003), *A History of African American Theatre*. Cambridge.
Houseman, J. (1972), *Run-Through: A Memoir*. New York.
Hurston, Z. N. (1995), *Zora Neale Hurston: Folklore, Memoirs, and Other Writings*. New York.
Hurston, Z. N. (2002), *Zora Neale Hurston: A Life in Letters*. Ed. Carla Kaplan. New York.
Jamison-Hall, A. (2011), "Black Writers and the Federal Theatre Project: August 1935–June 1939," in S. Tracy ed., *Writers of the Black Chicago Renaissance*. Urbana, IL.
Margo, R. A. (1993), "Employment and Unemployment in the 1930s," *Journal of Economic Perspectives* 7, 41–59.

Mitchell, K. (2011), *Living with Lynching: African American Lynching Plays, Performance and Citizenship, 1890–1930*. Urbana, IL.

Plum, J. (1992), "Rose McClendon and the Black Units of the Federal Theatre Project: A Lost Contribution," *Theatre Survey* 33, 144–53.

Redd, T. (1995), "Stevedore in Seattle: A Case Study in The Politics of Presenting Race on Stage," *Journal of American Drama and Theatre* 7, 66–87.

Ross, R. (1974), "The Role of Blacks in the Federal Theatre, 1935–1938," *Journal of Negro History* 59, 38–50.

Wall, C. (1994), "On Freedom and the Will to Adorn: Debating Aesthetics and/as Ideology in African American Literature," in G. Levine ed., *Aesthetics and Ideology*. New Brunswick, NJ.

Watkins, M. (1999), *On the Real Side: A History of African American Comedy*. Chicago.

West, R. (1996), "Others, Adults, Censored: The Federal Theatre Project's Black *Lysistrata* Cancellation," *Theatre Survey* 37, 93–113.

Wetmore, K. Jr. (2003), *Black Dionysus: Greek Tragedy and African American Theatre*. Jefferson, NC.

CHAPTER 19

ARISTOPHANIC COMEDY IN AMERICAN MUSICAL THEATER, 1925–1969

JOHN GIVEN

Musicals feature song, dance, and spoken dialogue that, on the one hand, are strongly enough integrated to present a coherent narrative or coherently themed revue but, on the other hand, are loosely enough integrated to allow diverse musical and theatrical materials. Different types of integration have come in and out of fashion in the musical's nearly 150-year history. For example, structural integration requires that song, dance, and dialogue equally support the musical's storytelling; removing an element results in the collapse of the whole. Or, integration with regard to characterization demands that characters possess a unique voice that remains consistent across speech and song; lyrics and music need to arise naturalistically out of a character's spoken dialogue. Integration, however, is not always a primary goal. Musicals by their nature are composed of diverse elements that always create a certain tension within a show, and creators may exploit such tensions. An orchestra, for example, belongs to the real world of the audience but makes possible the fictional characters' singing.[1] Some stagings of musicals such as *Cabaret* exploit the orchestra's existence by bringing it into the show. *Cabaret* has some songs in which the orchestra is the band at the Kit Kat Club and thus is a character in the play, but other songs that arise naturalistically out of a character's dialogue and so make the orchestra an extra-dramatic element. As we will see, playwrights, composers, lyricists, critics, and scholars frequently distinguish musicals according to how they handle the question of integration.

This chapter studies musical adaptations of Aristophanes with special attention to the question of integration. Aristophanes has been frequently tapped as source material for musicals. All 11 of his extant comedies have been adapted. His comedies seem a ripe source for adaptation not only because they combine song, dance, and dialogue but also because they strike a balance between integration and disintegration. Plots tell a story but with a loose, episodic structure. Songs, whether solos or choral odes, rarely advance plot or characterization. Characters—like the plays in general—possess what one scholar has called "discontinuity": character change seems to happen by aleatoric sequence rather than rational consequence.[2] Adaptations have often embraced Aristophanes' discontinuities but have also imposed integration according to fashionable musical theater trends. This chapter examines the structural and characterological qualities of three Aristophanic musicals produced in the U.S.A. In 1925–6, the Moscow Art Theatre (MAT) Musical Studio toured the U.S.A. with a production of *Lysistrata*. In 1961, lyricist E. Y. "Yip" Harburg adapted *Lysistrata* under the title *The Happiest Girl in the World*. In 1968–9, Al Carmines and Tim Reynolds's version of *Peace* ran for over 200 performances in New York. These three productions have been selected because of their significantly diverse cultural origins and aesthetic features, not necessarily their artistic or commercial success. They are an avant-garde foreign import, a traditional scene-and-song Broadway musical comedy, and a musically eclectic anti-war celebration. Each approaches the question of integration in significantly different ways; each thus also approaches Aristophanes differently. They represent the spectrum of twentieth-century American reception of Aristophanes as well as the range of twentieth-century American musicals.

From *Acharnians* to *Lysistrata Jones*

Our three productions form a small part of a long history of Greek comedy productions in anglophone North America.[3] We have space here for only the briefest sketch of this history, done for contextualization. Although Aristophanes once appeared, reading one of his comedies, on a drop curtain before an 1859 musical adaptation of Dickens's *The Cricket on the Hearth* (*New York Times* 1859), the first production of one of his comedies occurred in Philadelphia in 1886. *Acharnians* was staged in Greek, with original music, by the faculty and students of the University of Pennsylvania.[4] Thereafter, Aristophanes has never been long absent from American stages. University productions have been a mainstay: *Frogs* at University of the South, 1892 (Day 2001: 198). *Birds* at Harvard, 1901 (*New York Times* 1901); *Birds* at Vassar College, 1902 (*New York Times* 1902); *Birds*, the inaugural production at the Hearst amphitheater in Berkeley, 1903 (Birdsall 1904; Day 2001: 148–9); *Frogs* at Temple University, 1916 (*Philadelphia Inquirer* 1916); *Birds* at Randolph-Macon Woman's College (Lynchburg, Virginia), 1937;[5] *Birds* and *Peace* at Harvard, 1939 and 1941, with music by undergraduate Leonard Bernstein (*Christian Science Monitor* 1939; *Christian Science Monitor* 1941); *Birds* at Catholic University, 1948, translated and directed by the future theater critic Walter Kerr (Coe 1948); *Lysistrata* at Brock University (St. Catharines, Ontario), 1969 (*Toronto Star* 1969); *Birds* at Cleveland State University and *Clouds* at University of Massachusetts, 1970, both of which participated in the American College Theater Festival in Washington (Coe 1971a; Coe 1971b); *Lysistrata* at University of Toronto, 1980

(Pashley 1981); *Lysistrata* at East Carolina University (Greenville, NC), 2010, directed by this chapter's author;[5] and many, many more.

Professional productions began in the early twentieth century. Several productions of *Lysistrata, Thesmophoriazusae*, and *Ecclesiazusae* were staged in support of the women's suffrage movement (Day 2001: 159–76; *New York Times* 1913). The Moscow Art Theatre tour seems to have been the first large-scale professional production in North America. In 1930, the MAT's co-translator, Gilbert Seldes, produced a new *Lysistrata*. Its initial Philadelphia run was so popular that it toured New York, Chicago, Pittsburgh, Detroit, and Los Angeles; in the last city, it was shut down by an overzealous police censor.[7] Other notable productions have included a 1946 Broadway *Lysistrata* with an all-black cast;[8] a 1955 Off-Broadway *Thesmophoriazusae* under influential director Arthur Lithgow;[9] an odd 1964 Off-Broadway musical called *The Athenian Touch*, in which Aristophanes, while writing *Lysistrata*, competes with Cleon for the affections of a courtesan;[10] a 1966 *Birds* in an Ypsilanti, Michigan baseball stadium, starring comedian Bert Lahr;[11] a 1969 French-language musical *Lysistrata* entitled *Faites l'amour, pas la guerre*, one of the inaugural productions of the Canadian National Arts Centre in Ottawa;[12] the unsuccessful 1972 Broadway *Lysistrata* starring Melina Mercouri and directed by Michael Cacoyannis;[13] the 1974 musical *Frogs* by Burt Shevelove and Stephen Sondheim in the Yale swimming pool, later revised by Nathan Lane for a Broadway bow in 2004 (the only American adaptation to receive significant scholarly attention);[14] a curious 1985 musical *Lysistrata*, "set in 2085 on Alpha Centauri, a 'blue-collar planet'" and performed at the Cleveland Zoo;[15] competing 2002 musical versions of *Lysistrata* by theater bigwigs Robert Brustein and Galt MacDermot, on the one hand, and Alan Menken, David Zippel, and Larry Gelbart, on the other hand;[16] and most recently, *Lysistrata Jones*, a 2011 Broadway musical that transposed Aristophanes' story onto a university basketball court.[17]

In this brief survey, we should not neglect Menander. In 1954, an enterprising teacher mounted a professional production of three fragmentary Menandrian works under the title of *The Girl from Samos*.[18] More recently, a musical production of *Samia* was staged in New York and Washington (1990) and a *Dyskolos* was seen at the New Jersey Shakespeare Festival (2002).[19] Finally, a musical adaptation of *Dyskolos* under the titles *Wild Goat* and *The Girl, the Grouch and the Goat* has played in Chicago (twice); Lawrence, Kansas; Anaheim, California; and Orem, Utah (2004–10).[20]

This is not an exhaustive list of Menander productions, but its scale in comparison to the previous two paragraphs is an accurate representation of the difference in popularity between Menander and Aristophanes. One major reason for the difference must be the quality of scripts available. Even apart from the paucity of stageable Menander translations, no complete Greek script was even available until the 1959 publication of *Dyskolos*, discovered on an Egyptian papyrus. The 1954 production mentioned above had to be constructed out of fragments culled from other, smaller papyri. More importantly, Aristophanes has political and aesthetic advantages for American audiences. While Aristophanes is notoriously difficult to adapt because of chronologically specific political references, it is easier to construct parallel political satire than to adapt Menandrian social mores. It is no coincidence that *Lysistrata* has been the most popular Aristophanic play on modern American stages. Its protofeminist and anti-war themes have found easy homes during years that saw advances in women's rights and nearly constant warfare. Even when the setting remains ancient Athens, as it does in both *Lysistrata* adaptations studied here, the political themes resonate strongly in the modern theater. Aesthetically, ancient New Comedy like Menander's can be successful on the American stage.[21] Fifty years after it first opened, the Plautine concoction *A Funny Thing Happened on the Way to the Forum* remains one of the most produced American plays of the twentieth century. Like Plautus' plays—and Menander's—it is a tightly plotted comic romp, so well constructed that it cannot fail to please audiences. Therein, however, lies the challenge for any potential adapter of Menander. If almost any scene or character is altered, the entire play needs to be rewritten.[22] In contrast, Aristophanes' comedies possess great plasticity. If Kinesias becomes Lysistrata's husband instead of Myrrhine's, as happens in both the MAT *Lysistrata* and *Happiest Girl*, the dynamic of Aristophanes' play will be altered but the core plot will remain intact. The present study focuses on such structural and characterological issues. Since the three shows considered here approach integration in significantly different ways, they will serve as useful signposts along the road from *Acharnians* to *Lysistrata Jones*.

The Moscow Art Theatre Musical Studio *Lysistrata*

First staged in Moscow in 1923 under the direction of Vladimir Nemirovich-Danchenko, *Lysistrata* was part of an attempt to find a middle ground between the realism on which the MAT's reputation had been built and the newest avant-garde trends in Russian theater. In the U.S.A., the production opened at Jolson's 59th Street Theatre in New York on December 14, 1925, the first offering in the MAT Musical Studio's repertoire. It was performed entirely in Russian, but English translations (from the Russian, not the Greek) were available to audiences.[23] American critics praised many of the production's uniquely Russian artistic pretensions, but they also described it in terms appropriate to mid-1920s New York musical theater.

The Moscow Art Theatre was founded by Nemirovich-Danchenko and Konstantin Stanislavsky in 1897.[24] Their purpose was to build on artistic trends in realism and create an ensemble-based repertory company dedicated to meticulous training in acting skills, in a search for authenticity on the stage.[25] Authenticity included careful attention to historical accuracy in set construction and stage properties as well as an acting style grounded in the actors' psychological exploration of their characters' motives. Although they began their collaboration with a common vision, the co-founders had always had their different approaches. Nemirovich-Danchenko, himself a playwright, brought strong literary knowledge to the director's chair, while Stanislavsky approached productions with an actor's eye. By the time of the October Revolution in 1917, with significant artistic differences having existed for over a decade, they were largely pursuing their artistic goals independently.[26] Stanislavsky had begun experimenting with new Symbolist ideas, but when he took the MAT on an international tour, visiting Germany, France, and the United States in 1921–4, the repertoire was decidedly conservative, with productions dating back to 1904 and earlier (Benedetti 1999: 273). Our concern, though, is with Nemirovich-Danchenko. Theater historians pay him less attention than his more famous partner,[27] but it is clear that Nemirovich-Danchenko was imbibing the avant-garde trends of Moscow and Petrograd while maintaining his interest in psychological realism. Many experiments were undertaken in his newly founded Musical Studio. The aim of the Studio, as Nemirovich-Danchenko specified, was to present a "new, simplified and intensified art." He explained, "The Russian revolution has necessitated a revolution of the stage, new plays, new productions, a new realism. . . . The old conception of realism has been abandoned and everything now is concentrated to bring out the realism of the soul."[28] The new stage required realism, but no longer bourgeois authenticity. And so when Nemirovoich-Danchenko took the Studio on an international tour in 1925, he unlike Stanislavsky took new works. The repertoire included Lecocq's *The Daughter of Madame Angot*; Offenbach's *La Périchole*; a new version of Bizet's *Carmen*, under the title *Carmencita and the Soldier*; and a ribald musical production of *Lysistrata*.[29]

The theatrical revolution involved Nemirovich-Danchenko in trends known as Constructivism and synthetic theater. Constructivism was an artistic movement that entered the theater primarily in the realm of scenic design, though it also influenced costuming. Arising out of Cubism and Futurism in the 1910s, Constructivism highlighted the study of the artistic object as an object, particularly a three-dimensional object, with its lines, shapes, colors, and interstitial space. Especially after the Revolution, the movement's artists found themselves in strong sympathy with Bolshevist ideology. They depicted themselves as workers, or experimenters and producers of artistic objects. Their art rejected traditional, bourgeois painterly or sculpted representation. Instead, it took on a decidedly utilitarian and even technological character.[30] Constructivists came to work in concert with non-representational trends in theater, such as director Vsevolod Meyerhold's "emphasis on the movement of the actor and not on the historical, emotional or thematic value of the spectacle" (Bowlt 1977: 64). As a result, Russian theater saw a decline in the naturalism and historical authenticity that had been particularly associated with the MAT.

Nemirovich-Danchenko was not left behind. *Lysistrata*'s set design, by Isaak Rabinovich, adhered to the principles of Constructivism (Fig. 19.1).[31] There was no historically authentic backdrop depicting the Acropolis or Parthenon. There were no reconstructions of stoas or temples. Instead, against a simple blue background, there arose five sets of white columns, each set a different height, some stretching high over the actors' heads, and each set placed in an arc with an unadorned cornice delineating its curvature. The columns were placed upon a rotating stage so that the audience could view scenes from multiple perspectives, as if in a Cubist painting.[32] Such manipulation

FIG. 19.1 Moscow Art Theatre's *Lysistrata* (1925), with set design by Isaak Rabinovich. Billy Rose Theatre Division, The New York Public Library for the Performing Arts, Astor, Lenox, and Tilden Foundations.

of space is the aim of the Constructivist set. The curved sets of columns disrupt the audience's expectation of rigid, classical right angles. The columns' immense height brings the playhouse's upper reaches into the performance space. The play is no longer performed *on* the stage, on its two-dimensional floor; it is played in a three-dimensional space.[33] Its tridimensionality is emphasized by the stairs and platforms placed among the columns. One photograph shows the women's chorus pouring their water jars on their male counterparts. Some of the women confront the men face to face, but others stand on platforms above them. The attack comes from multiple directions and multiple heights. Another photo shows a moment in the confrontation between Lysistrata and the Probulos [*sic*]. Here, Lysistrata stares down at the Probulos, who can only peer up at his vanquisher.[34] Nothing in the text necessitates the vertical distances. It seems that Nemirovich-Danchenko has used his Constructivist set to create gendered spaces on his stage. In a play that depends on the women's entrance into male public space,[35] Nemirovich-Danchenko uses his non-representational set to reconceive how the women control space.

The second avant-garde trend, synthetic theater, was a movement associated principally with the director Alexander Tairov, the head of Moscow's Kamerny Theatre. The term incorporated several meanings. First, Tairov's actors were required to excel in all dramatic modes: acting, singing, dancing, and even circus performing and pantomime. Beyond this, Tairov sought to integrate all the design aspects of drama, including lights, costumes, sound, and scene, into a unified representation of the dramatic world. Finally, Tairov's dramaturgy occupied a middle ground between Stanislavsky's representational theater, in which dramatic illusion was meant to be complete, and Meyerhold's presentational theater, in which theatrical artifice was dominant. Tairov aimed at a more dynamic interaction between stage and audience, an interaction by which "neither aesthetically pleasing empty forms nor moving but formless emotionalizing was fully competent."[36]

Although Nemirovich-Danchenko frequently mentioned its importance in interviews, it is difficult to understand from available sources precisely what role synthetic theater played in *Lysistrata*. The production incorporated multiple artistic disciplines, including original music by Reinhold Glière. The published translation gives occasional indications of song and dance via the stage directions (Seldes and Seldes 1925: 17, 64, 67, 68), but does not detail what is sung. Reviews praise the music, but it is not clear what role the music played in the show (e.g., Gabriel 1925; Gordon 1925). Reviews also briefly mention acrobatics and clowning, but without detailed description.[37] Probably more indicative of Nemirovich-Danchenko's synthetic approach—and indicative of his continued belief in MAT traditions—are script revisions designed to make characters psychologically realistic. We know that actors had to perform in numerous artistic disciplines. Careful psychological motivation, the trademark of the MAT, would allow the actors to integrate all aspects of their performances.

In the MAT production, Kinesias is Lysistrata's husband, not Myrrhine's. The change has two significant effects. First, from the character's perspective, Lysistrata is given a stronger reason to desire peace—bringing her own husband home—a motivation lacking in Aristophanes' text, which does not define Lysistrata's marital status.[38] Now, the MAT production does not emphasize Lysistrata's marriage. In Act I, Lysistrata only speaks in the ambiguous first person plural, as in Aristophanes (e.g., 120–2: "we must abstain," 507–8: "we endured what you men did"). It is only with Kinesias' mid-Act II entrance (p. 49) that we learn Lysistrata is married. The payoff is significant. Act II opens with Lysistrata's women trying to escape, plans which Lysistrata quickly foils (pp. 43–7 = ll. 718–61). She then exercises her authority over the women by producing an oracle promising their victory (pp. 47–8 = ll. 762–80). A few moments later, in Aristophanes, Lysistrata spots Kinesias approaching, summons Myrrhine, and instructs her to give him everything except what her oath requires (839–41). In the MAT version, those instructions are now Kalonike's to Lysistrata. Lysistrata proves worthy of her own oath by never surrendering to her husband's sexual temptations, temptations that Aristophanes' Lysistrata never had to face. The scene thus becomes a complement to the oracle scene. There, Lysistrata demonstrated control over the women; now she demonstrates control over herself. With the revision, the actor playing Lysistrata (Olga Baklanova) also has greater psychological motivation for her performance. In Aristophanes, because Lysistrata is not identified as a wife, the modern actor is left to search for extra-textual motivations for Lysistrata's desire for peace. The MAT revision gives Lysistrata a realistic motivation. The actor in true Stanislavskian fashion can think of herself standing in solidarity with the other women when she laments, "We have long been deprived of love's caresses" (p. 8). The oath becomes more personal when she recites, "I'll grant no joys of my own free will" (p. 14). Because of the revisions, the actor is able to give a richer psychological performance. We can only assume that this extended to whatever other performance disciplines she had to use, including singing. Her performance can achieve a greater dynamic resonance with the audience, one of the goals of Tairov's synthetic theater.[39]

American critics recognized the innovative nature of the MAT's Constructivist set design and synthetic theater, though perhaps not their nuances.[40] They gave high praise to the set design and how the actors utilized the unusual space. The set, says the *Christian Science Monitor*, is "a veritable theorem in solid geometry" that in its non-representationality is "the Athens that Pericles built" and yet "nothing but a windlass" (Tryon 1925). Another critic says it bears the mark of the "Greek ideal of simplicity," for "every square foot of the scenery contributes something essential to the projection of the play," enabling groups of actors to create "the single impression of rhythmic motion against the blue sky" (*New York Times* 1925e). Others find that the set and costumes "proclaim the strong pulse, the almost savage originality" of the play, and praise the "fairly majestic" set as "simplicity itself" (Gabriel 1925; Gordon 1925). Although they betray no knowledge of the artistic movement or political implications behind Rabinovich's design, they at least recognize its innovation and its integration into the overall production.

The critics also paid keen attention to Nemirovich-Danchenko's claim that he employed "singing actors." Throughout 1925, in anticipation of the December visit, notices described the Russians as a "remarkable young company of actors who can sing" or "an acting company which can sing as well as act."[41] While the critics thus paid tribute to the concept of synthetic theater, several of the articles suggest a further, specifically American level of understanding. American musicals, as we have said, are often defined and judged by their level of integration. This criterion was fundamental in the mid-1920s, as creators of the newly popular operettas sought to distinguish their plays from the more loosely organized revues and musical comedies.[42] Oscar Hammerstein II, co-author of the operetta *Rose-Marie*, which had opened in 1924, championed the integration of song and story. In a published essay, Hammerstein wrote,

> Here was a musical show [*Rose-Marie*] with a melodramatic plot and a cast of players who were called upon to actually sing the music—*sing*, mind you—not just talk through the lyrics and then go into their dance.

Hammerstein placed *Rose-Marie* within the broader context of musical theater history, from John Gay's *The Beggar's Opera* through Gilbert and Sullivan operettas to his own work:

> The history of musical comedy has passed through a variety of phases, but the type that persists, that shows the signs of ultimate victory, is the operetta—the musical play with music and plot welded together in skillful cohesion. (Hammerstein 1925: 14, 70)

Hammerstein's language is reminiscent of Nemirovich-Danchenko's interviews published the same year. Both men emphasize that their actors sing well and that the singing actor is a necessary component of their artistic vision. The *raisons d'être* of the singing actor, however, differ. For Hammerstein, the actor must sing in order that music and plot may be "welded together in skillful cohesion." For Nemirovich-Danchenko, the actor must sing (and dance and mime, etc.) in order that all theatrical disciplines (acting, music, lighting, etc.) may be fused together into a coherent whole. There are thus two complementary and easily confused types of "integration" at work. On the one hand, there was a Russian *artistic* synthesis of the various theatrical disciplines; on the other hand, American writers were formulating a *structural* synthesis of music, lyrics, and book.

A *New York Times* essay shows how a critic could combine these two understandings of "synthesis." The author, H. I. Brock, begins by drawing a parallel between the MAT repertoire (including Lecocq and Offenbach as well as *Lysistrata*) and older operetta. He writes that "in a way [Nemirovich-Danchenko] undertook to do to the lyric stage of this time what Gilbert and Sullivan did to the lyric stage of their time—to put life and *sense* into it" (emphasis added) (Brock 1925). Like Hammerstein, Brock places 1925 theater into the history of operetta. His evaluations of the Lecocq and Offenbach productions are instructive. Of Lecocq, he writes that Nemirovich-Danchenko's revisions make the operetta "both lyric and dramatic," as if the integration of the actors' disciplines causes the structural improvement of both "lyric" song and "dramatic" story. (Cf. Hammerstein's "melodramatic plot" above.) The changes to Offenbach, he says, "improve the composite effect" so that "the thing held together," as if, again, artistic and structural synthesis go hand in hand. In short, they make "sense." Brock speaks of synthetic theater in the same way that critics—and in fact Rodgers and Hammerstein themselves[43]—would speak of the innovative *Oklahoma!* 18 years later: as an organic whole. The seed that theater historians would find in operettas and that they would see blossoming in *Oklahoma!*, Brock sees already growing in the MAT's work. And he sees it flourishing in *Lysistrata*, not just because Nemirovich-Danchenko turned it into an operetta but also because Aristophanes left a "libretto belonging to the original synthetic theater.... Undoubtedly 'Lysistrata', like all the other satiric works of Aristophanes, was originally a lyric drama—an operetta—even a musical comedy, if you choose to look at it that way."[44] He hesitates about which musical theater genre Aristophanes' *Lysistrata* belongs to, but he cannot help reading the MAT production in contemporary Broadway vocabulary.

THE HAPPIEST GIRL IN THE WORLD, 1961

Stephen Sondheim has described lyricist E. Y. "Yip" Harburg as a "maverick, pointedly socio-political and heavily whimsical" (Sondheim 2010: 99). Harburg, the moving force behind the 1961 adaptation of *Lysistrata* called *The Happiest Girl in the World*,[45] proved his socio-political concerns and his whimsy repeatedly throughout his career. From his iconic anthem "Brother, Can You Spare a Dime?" to musicals like *Bloomer Girl, Finian's Rainbow*, and *Flahooley*, Harburg frequently employed his art for social critique.[46] At the same time, lyrics from "Follow the Yellow Brick Road" and "Somewhere over the Rainbow" (*The Wizard of Oz*) to "Look to the Rainbow" and "Something Sort of Grandish" (*Finian's Rainbow*) show Harburg's masterful use of rhyme, wit, and wordplay to create characters who long for an idealistic life without lapsing into simple sentimentality. In the late 1950s, this political and whimsical craftsman undertook an adaptation of *Lysistrata*.[47] He collaborated with living book writers Henry Myers and Fred Saidy,[48] but set his lyrics to the nineteenth-century music of Jacques Offenbach.[49] The combination could have produced a musical both entertaining and politically astute. It didn't. It ran from April 3 to June 24, 1961 for a total of 97 performances.[50] Although critics appreciated the talents of lead actors Janice Rule and "the one and only Cyril Ritchard,"[51] they found the story uninteresting and the jokes flat. Walter Kerr complained that Harburg's adaptation only went halfway; it is "a slightly apologetic bit of 1961, a not too confident bit of old shoe" (Kerr 1961). Howard Taubman found the book "tame and heavy-handed," while Richard P. Cooke joined Kerr in complaining about the superficial politics but at least found some redeeming qualities: the musical may have "had some intention of being a serious lampoon upon the follies of 1961. But this aspect is no more than the poppy seed upon the cake, which is filled with other goodies" (Taubman 1961; Cooke 1961).

The critics were appropriately judging *Happiest Girl* according to the standards of the fully integrated musical, then in its heyday after the triumph of the Rodgers-and-Hammerstein model in musicals such as *Oklahoma!* (1943) and *Carousel* (1945). The techniques of integrated musicals had always come naturally to Harburg. *The Wizard of Oz*, for example, shows expert use of extended musical scenes.[52] *Happiest Girl* too is well integrated. Its songs arise naturally from the dialogue.[53] Songs and dance advance the action. It is admittedly strange to recycle Offenbach operetta for a new musical comedy, but the music is not poorly suited to the show.[54] The melodies are well chosen to suit their dramatic scenes and through good orchestrations they were made to sound like mid-twentieth-century show tunes.[55] The lyrics, though perhaps not Harburg's finest, are first rate.[56] In short, the musical possesses excellent structural integration. But if songs are going to arise coherently from dialogue, the story containing the dialogue must create coherent characters and action. Here the play fails. The story devised by Harburg, Saidy, and Myers crams Aristophanes' plot into a standard Broadway tale of romance and intrigue by subordinating Lysistrata and her troubles to a dispute among the gods. It thus treats her as the gods' pawn instead of a comic hero. It obscures its source's central character and central plot element to the point of incomprehensibility.

In brief: Pluto is on earth causing perpetual war between Athens and Sparta. The situation is intolerable to the Athenian General Kinesias, who announces a truce with Sparta so that he may return to his wife, Lysistrata. Before they can consummate their reunion, Pluto stirs up war again and Kinesias departs. Lysistrata prays to the gods and threatens that mortals will destroy them unless peace arrives soon. The scene switches to Mt. Olympus, where Jupiter confirms that the gods will die if mortals stop believing in them. After a fruitless meeting with Pluto, Jupiter agrees to listen to a proposal from Diana: war will end if women deny themselves to their husbands. The gods rejoice in the plan, and Jupiter dispatches Diana to earth, warning that she will be subject to human emotions there. Dancing around a sleeping Lysistrata, Diana puts the idea in Lysistrata's mind and the sex strike is enacted. Diana stays on earth in the guise of her own priestess. Pluto develops two lines of attack against Diana's plan: first, he tries to convince the women that they will miss sex too much and, second, he works to make Diana fall in love. His first plot fails, but the second succeeds, creating a strange love triangle among Diana, Lysistrata, and Kinesias. Eventually, Diana renews her virtue and ends her claim to Kinesias. Lysistrata appears in disguise as a Persian courtesan and effects reconciliation with her husband along with an end to war.

Pluto and Diana are the play's main characters. The setup fits *Happiest Girl* into the mold of many contemporary musicals that featured two couples, one that carried the main action and one that provided comedy or romance. Thus, *Oklahoma!* has its main lovers in Curly and Laurey and its secondary couple in the comic Will Parker and Ado Annie. The lead couple need not be lovers. *The King and I* features the King of Siam and Anna Leonowens who are not romantically involved; the romance is left to Lun Tha and Tuptim. The title character need not even be part of the main couple. In *Bye Bye Birdie*, the main couple is Albert, the manager to rock 'n' roll star Conrad Birdie, and his secretary Rosie. It seems Birdie himself will be a member of the secondary couple, paired with high school student Kim, but in the end she chooses her schoolmate Hugo. *The Happiest Girl in the World* follows this same pattern, with Pluto and Diana (Ritchard and Rule, who received top billing) as the primary couple, and Lysistrata and Kinesias (Dran Seitz and Bruce Yarnell) as the secondary couple.

The arrangement destroys the fabric of Aristophanes' story by reducing Lysistrata to secondary status.[57] Like Lun Tha and Tuptim in *The King and I*, she and Kinesias fill the slot of the romantic subplot while Pluto and Diana provide the main conflict. The play defines Pluto as the protagonist immediately. Act I opens with messengers carrying a message from Kinesias. Before we discover its contents, Pluto interrupts the action by entering as a narrator. He is dressed in disguise as the Athenian Chief of State—for he will step into the scene to receive Kinesias' message—except for a plumed hat that he will otherwise wear as Pluto (1.1.2). The disjunction, together with his direct address to the audience, mark him as controlling the play's action, a metatheatrical director—doubly appropriate since Ritchard was the musical's real director. In the scenes that follow, Pluto controls not only the war but also its general when Kinesias is pulled away from his wife by a threatening message "intercepted" from the Spartans but in fact written by Pluto. After Kinesias leaves, we get some sense that Lysistrata might take over as a leading character, but that impression is quickly dispelled. She threatens the gods with annihilation, an act of control straight out of Aristophanes' *Birds*, but instead of following the bold example of Peisetaerus, she falls asleep. We then meet Pluto's complement, Diana, who introduces the idea for the sex strike and inspires Lysistrata to pursue it. Within the first four scenes, then, we see both Pluto and Diana assuming their authoritative places and manipulating their human counterparts. What appeared to be Lysistrata's claim to agency proves to be only the opportunity Diana needs to assert her own initiative.

As a result, the secondary plot takes on several strange and self-defeating characteristics. In order for Pluto's power to be demonstrated, the musical begins with Kinesias concluding a truce with Sparta. He wants to be with his wife, not at war. In other words, the final goal of Aristophanes' plot is reached in the first three minutes. But only in this way can Pluto send Kinesias back to war. Moreover, before he reaches home, Lysistrata tells her maid that Kinesias hasn't come home for a medal; she knows "his real objective is this boudoir" (1.3.11). Yet in an immediate reversal, she proclaims her frustration that he is taking too long, and so when he finally does arrive she greets him coolly (1.3.12–13). Since Lysistrata and Kinesias have been reduced to a sweet romantic couple, we need tension between them in order to have a reunion at the end. More importantly, we need to see her frustration so that she will be willing to put Diana's sex strike into action. After she does so, the playwrights give us the famous striptease scene, played (as in the MAT *Lysistrata*) between Kinesias and Lysistrata. Again, Kinesias arrives for the purpose of being home with his wife. They reminisce about their honeymoon and sing the most beautiful song in the score, "Adrift on a Star," which ends "wherever you are | In this star-sprinkled dome | If there's love in your star | You're home | You're home" (1.6.48–9).[58] It is the perfect reunion. They kiss deeply and Kinesias carries Lysistrata toward the bedroom. Only then does Lysistrata deploy her delaying tactics. Kinesias outwits her by serving wine supplied earlier in the scene by a surreptitious Pluto. When an inebriated Lysistrata is on the verge of giving in, Diana appears and shoots her with an arrow. Lysistrata screams, comes back to her senses, hands Kinesias his sword, and orders him out of the house. The MAT rewrote this scene to prove Lysistrata's total control over the plot and herself. *Happiest Girl* rewrites it so that Pluto and Diana can continue manipulating the secondary characters. Lysistrata has lost all claim to control over anything. And so, in the finale, it may be less shocking to hear Lysistrata ask a hesitant Kinesias, "Let me be yours! I don't want to sit on a conquered throne and be a Queen—but to rest here at home in your arms, and *feel* like a Queen" (2.3.30). She wins by being possessed, initially by Diana and now by Kinesias. By introducing the gods as primary characters, the authors constructed an integrated musical, but they also turned Lysistrata into a manipulated possession. Such was the fate of "the happiest girl in the world."

Peace, 1968–1969

The third musical on our program differs radically from *Lysistrata* and *Happiest Girl* by embracing and celebrating a lack of integration. *Peace*, with music by Al Carmines and book and lyrics by Tim Reynolds, played November 1–5 and 8–12, 1968 at the Off-Off-Broadway Judson Poets' Theatre. A revised production opened January 27, 1969 at the Off-Broadway Astor Place Theatre, where it ran for 192 performances. The musical follows Aristophanes' highly episodic plot in broad outline: Trygaeus flies to heaven on a dung beetle, rescues the goddess Peace, brings her back to earth, and celebrates peace. Multiple reviewers refer to the production as camp, which Susan Sontag famously described as "the sensibility of failed seriousness, of the theatricalization of experience" (Sontag 1991: 106). It is an aesthetic that prizes artifice and style, and usually possesses an air of frivolity. *Peace* is undoubtedly campy, but it is much more. It is a dramatic and musical collage whose artifice enables seriousness and whose theatricality closes the gap between theater and experience. As Bolshevik theater rebelled against its bourgeois past by rejecting MAT-style naturalism, Carmines and Reynolds work by jettisoning the integration exemplified in *Happiest Girl*. But like Nemirovich-Danchenko using synthetic theater and revised operettas to retain a certain MAT sensibility, Carmines and Reynolds retain enough of the form and even mine the form's history to recreate the musical as an unintegrated, discontinuous romp that is undeniably an American musical. Its lack of integration can be seen in three aspects: first, its transience, which is reflected in the conflicting evidence we now possess; second, the mismatching of story and song; and third, its use of three different temporal and geographical settings, which has particular implications for its reflections upon American race politics thanks to minstrel scenes set in the pre-Civil War U.S.A. that featured actors in blackface makeup.

Peace originated at the Judson Poets' Theatre, one of the most influential of the 1960s Off-Off-Broadway movement. It was located at the Judson Memorial Church on Greenwich Village's Washington Square, a Christian church with a racially and socioeconomically diverse congregation devoted to social activism.[59] In 1961, the church hired a new clergyman named Reverend Al Carmines, 24 years old and freshly graduated from Union Theological Seminary. One of Carmines's first actions was to found the Poets' Theatre, a place "where experimentation and process would be more important than results" (Crespy 2003: 101). Through the next 20 years, Carmines was celebrated as an original and magnificently talented composer. During his career, he composed about 80 musicals, operas, and oratorios. His work was marked by a deft ability to combine musical styles into an eclectic mélange that lifted sometimes pedestrian plays into realms of artistic excellence.[60] *Peace* was called, in several reviews, his best work to date (e.g., Gottfried 1969). Yet the play and the composer are largely forgotten today.

The oblivion is partially due to the transience of 1960s Village theaters. The movement featured nontraditional performance spaces. Plays, which often focused on issues of class, gender, drugs, sexuality, and race, often promoted values anathema to the mainstream middle-class patrons of uptown theaters. Because the practitioners rejected not only the aesthetic but also the commercialism associated with Broadway and even Off-Broadway theaters, the movement became known as Off-Off-Broadway.[61] The rejection of commercialism went hand in hand with a lack of concern for posterity. Off-Off-Broadway was a theater for the present. It typically presented plays as performance-centered events, not as text-centered dramas. Theater historians have thus had a difficult time describing and assessing the movement, having to rely on participants' ageing memories where written and audiovisual records are few. For Judson, we are fortunate to have an archive located at New York University's Fales Library,[62] which includes photographs, programs, clippings, and an incomplete rehearsal script from *Peace*.[63] The New York Public Library for the Performing Arts archive holds more *Peace* materials, including photographs, programs, and clippings. Outside these archives, our knowledge of *Peace* comes from newspaper reviews, a cast recording from the Off-Broadway production,[64] and a rare though extant published script from the Off-Broadway production.[65] Problems for the scholar arise because neither the cast recording nor either script corresponds precisely to the performances described in the reviews.[66]

While reasonable guesses about what took place onstage are possible and will be hazarded below, we should first note how Off-Off-Broadway's transient nature impacts our understanding of *Peace*. The contradictions in the evidence are not a historical accident. They are an inevitable result of practitioners' aesthetic, (anti-)commercial, and political choices. The script and cast recording were not published until the more commercial Off-Broadway production. Both were whitewashed with the result that potentially offensive elements of the production, most notably the use of blackface in the minstrel scenes, do not appear in the published materials. The published script retains the play's obscene language but apologizes for it and asks potential producers to keep an open mind. It even grants permission to alter language to make it less offensive, if necessary. The sanitized published materials efface not just the musical's blackface and obscenity, but the reasons for them: the disconcerting clash of obscenity with the cultural cachet of a "Greek play," the clash of the Aristophanic setting with the American settings, the clash of blackfaced actors with a mid-twentieth-century stage—in short, the liberating lack of integration in the theatrical event. The further uptown *Peace* went, the closer it approached middle-class values. The contradictions of the historical record reflect both this uptown movement and the original disconcerting lack of integration that made mainstreaming revisions necessary.

The second noteworthy aspect of *Peace*'s lack of integration is its structure. It can best be summarized in its composer's description of the "sort of communal way" his shows were put together:

> We got together as a group of actors and dancers and for two weeks simply sat and read the play through. Somebody would say, "I want to do *that* line the next time," and he would. A dancer would say, "I want to choreograph *that* part." And when I felt some lines should be sung, I wrote music. The result was that everybody chose moments in the script that had to do with their own personalities, and created characters, dances or songs that were very personal to them. It's a wonderful way of eliminating the traditional approach in which you press the part on the person, as if you are stamping him with a cookie cutter. It allows for a very strong evocation of the person beneath the performer.[67]

The Judson's practice is opposite to the MAT or Rodgers-and-Hammerstein conception of character. Traditional psychological realism required actors to suppress their own identities. To be sure, the actors could be asked to find events in their own past to infuse the characters' emotions. The emotions, however, were to be transferred wholly to the character. Carmines expects the actors' personalities to be mixed with the character.[68] The construction of the musical is dictated as much by the actors' choices as by the characters' choices.

Without better knowledge of the actors themselves, it is difficult to see the creativity in action. We can, though, see what Carmines did when he "felt some lines should be sung." Carmines crafts his lyrics directly from Reynolds's dialogue and so there is a close relationship between book and lyrics. The accompanying music, however, keeps the songs from being fully integrated into the book. The song "Plumbing" is a fine example. This Act I scene is an adaptation of Aristophanes' episode in which War seeks a mortar and pestle to grind the Greek *poleis*. In Carmines's *Peace*, War comes on with a giant toilet bowl and pours the "essence" of various cities in (apparently some sort of liquid from a vial). The toilet malfunctions and War sends his sidekick Disorder to search for a plunger. When he cannot find one, they sing a hilarious song about the glories of modern plumbing. The lyrics, repeated endlessly, state, "Plumbing has been raised to such an art that they don't need plungers any more" (Carmines and Reynolds (1969?), track 5). The music is an impeccable pastiche of a Handel fugue.[69] The combination of Handel and a clogged commode is absurd; more to the point, it is incoherent with the dramatic situation. Any composer writing a song meant to arise naturally from this situation would have struck an angry tone, even in a comic mode. (Think of "Just You Wait" from *My Fair Lady*.) With Carmines's adoption of a jaunty Handel fugue, the actors cannot move seamlessly from book into song.

Not all the songs are as dramatically disconcerting as "Plumbing," but Carmines's eclectic score keeps the show from having what one theorist calls a single musical "voice" (McMillan 2006: 68–9). Thus, in a show like *Happiest Girl*, it is no surprise that songs as temperamentally different as "Vive la Virtue!" and "Adrift on a Star" come from the same musical. There is a musical consistency to them so that they form a coherent score. (What is surprising is that Harburg and his orchestrators were able to create a single voice from different Offenbach operettas.) In *Peace*, the next song is always a musical surprise. Mother explains her "Excessive Concern" about her "Baby Trygaeus" in a torch song, as she sits on the piano. The Chorus pleads, "Don't Do It, Mr. Hermes," in a Charleston-like frenzy. The cast celebrates peace by singing "Just Sit Around," a minstrel song worthy of Stephen Foster. The musical ends with a beautiful resetting of "America the Beautiful," sung by the entire cast (as one critic put it) "not wholly ironically."[70] The songs all sound like Carmines compositions, but only in the sense that songs from *Company* and *Sweeney Todd* sound like Sondheim compositions. Sondheim's songs possess the composer's trademark qualities, but are evidently from different scores. In Carmines's case, though, they are disconcertingly from the same score.

The third level of incoherence in *Peace* is its intermingled settings. The play moves among ancient Greece (including the trip to the gods), the nineteenth-cenutry American South, and the contemporary (1960s) U.S.A. When the play opens (in the Off-Off-Broadway production), the audience is immediately plunged into a world of contradiction. As in Aristophanes, Greek gods are mentioned by name, and Trygaeus cites Aesop as his inspiration.[71] Yet Aristophanes' slaves have become American black slaves named Rastus and Liza. We are also in the pre-Civil War South. The slaves use plantation dialect when they refer to Trygaeus as "Massa" (2, 6) and compare the dung beetle's frenetic arms to 'a whole fiel' of cottonpickers" (3). To make matters more complex, the slaves are white actors in blackface, straight out of the nineteenth-century minstrel show. The creators did not use blackface without understanding its offensiveness.[72] Some critics did complain, but most understood it as part of a larger project. The blackface, then, takes this strange mixture of settings and heightens the strangeness so that the audience cannot but consider it a campy, stylized artifice. The musical's joy is a celebration of *Peace*, not peace.

In the revised Off-Broadway script, the slaves are gone, replaced with Trygaeus' Mother and Father, although the Southern setting has been kept.[73] Nevertheless, a campy atmosphere is achieved by the absurd juxtaposition of the elderly, genteel Mother and Father with their task of preparing the "shitcake" for the beetle. Most startlingly, when Mother turns to address the audience directly, as one of Aristophanes' slaves does, she leaves the stage and lounges across the grand piano in the pit, which was played by Carmines himself. She sings a number ("My Baby Trygaeus | Through Excessive Concern") that starts as a torch song but morphs into a chaotic, neurotic patter, culminating in a plea to God to prevent "these cretins" from pushing "the buttons" (Reynolds and Carmines 1969: 3).

The point is reinforced when the beetle and his owner are finally seen. In Reynolds's original script, Trygaeus is said to be dressed in "a cowboy suit, chaps, sombrero, etc." (5). By the time of the Off-Broadway production, for which we have photographic evidence (Fig. 19.2), Trygaeus (Reathal Bean) wears a white, threadbare sweater and a fur-lined, aviator-style hat with earflaps and an attached chinstrap. The beetle itself is an enormous conglomeration of found objects, with clear plastic hemispheres as eyes, a jug as a nose, and football helmet face guards as pincers. If the audience has any expectation of a gentlemanly plantation owner, those expectations are quickly destroyed by Trygaeus' entrance. In contrast to the stereotypes of Liza and Rastus, his character defies stereotype. He engages in slapstick when the beetle's flatulence knocks him over, but he also claims that his actions are "heroic . . . for the sake of all the Greeks" (7). At once, his appearance and behavior point to a campy absurdity, but his singularity and even earnestness make him fit uncomfortably in the campy world.

The musical runs up against the limits of camp. The tension between artificiality and Trygaeus' earnestness persists into the next section of the play, when Trygaeus rides the beetle to heaven. The musical becomes dominated by references to the Vietnam War era and its real toll, spoken primarily by a chorus of 1960s Americans who have no particular business being in heaven. It seems strange to produce *Peace* and have important contemporary references be potentially undermined by artificiality.[74] In fact, Carmines and director Lawrence Kornfeld said they think of their musicals not as camp, but as grotesque. They did not want to be associated with camp's unseriousness. Carmines said, "we took the grotesque very seriously."[75] There are, to be sure, campy elements in the play's central section. When Trygaeus flies to heaven, he meets a flamboyantly homosexual Hermes, whose own exaggerated stereotype mirrors Liza's and Rastus's.[76] Overall, however, the play abandons its self-referentiality and creates a realistic sensibility. The realism is not tragic. It remains always comic, as in the aforementioned "Plumbing" scene. The scene strikes a different tone than in the absurd plantation scene. Instead of

FIG. 19.2 Al Carmines and Tim Reynolds's *Peace*. Kenn Duncan/© Billy Rose Theatre Division, The New York Public Library for the Performing Arts.

camp or even grotesquerie, it seems comic relief. It mocks the pretentiousness of War and his delight in destruction. Foiled from flushing, all he can do is turn his energy into musical melismata. His failure enables the play to celebrate peace, not *Peace*.

After the more earnest central scenes, in which Peace is rescued, it is surprising to return to the world of minstrelsy in order to celebrate the effects of peace. The reviews attest that, in both productions, the second act was staged as a full-fledged minstrel show, with numerous actors in blackface, portraying traditional minstrel characters, including an interlocutor.[77] The performance recalls the traditional minstrel show's final act, which was usually set on a plantation and featured a skit about the happy lives of the estate's slaves, in no way (it was implied) in need of emancipation. It is not clear what the content of *Peace*'s second act was. One Off-Off-Broadway review describes that production's act as "a kind of minstrel show, in which nothing happens and the actors merely comment at large" (Barnes 1968). An Off-Broadway review says that the act is "never adequately worked into the evening's context";[78] another says that it was about "civil rights" (Oliver 1969), but there is no indication of specific content. There was music. The slave chorus (in the early script, at least) sings Stephen Foster's minstrel standard "Swanee River," with new lyrics in which the slaves, "his faithful darkies," wish Trygaeus good luck (83). The act had at least two Carmines songs, "Just Sit Around" and "Summer's Nice."[79] The singers celebrate their rest after a long day's work, and they do so in a manner characteristic of the stereotypical lazy slave of the minstrel tradition.

It seems clear that we have returned to the artificiality of the opening scene. The extreme stereotypes and the clear allusions to a discredited theatrical tradition may lead the audience to interpret the events as theater artifice and nothing more. It may be, again, a celebration of *Peace*, not peace, even as the personified Peace is on the stage. Yet the theme of civil rights, mentioned by one reviewer, and the final, not wholly ironic "America the Beautiful" point to a privileging of peace over *Peace*. Neither reading is wholly satisfactory. Rather, both readings are likely justifiable. It is a fitting conclusion about a musical whose success depended on its ludic rejection of mainstream Broadway theater and Broadway's neatly integrated structures.

Conclusions

For all that we cannot say about Carmines and Reynolds's *Peace*, we can say with certainty that it bears a significant dissimilarity to the MAT *Lysistrata* and *The Happiest Girl in the World*. Those two shows sought integration in their productions. *Lysistrata* found it in the synthesis of artistic fields, although American critics saw a structural integration. *Happiest Girl* found it in the integration of book and songs. Although neither show can be called simply realistic, for both realism is an important component. *Lysistrata*'s Constructivist set prevents the audience from seeing the action as taking place in historical Athens, but the psychological motivation of the characters is consistent with real human experience. No one—the classic complaint about musicals—breaks into song in real life, as the *Happiest Girl* characters do, but Harburg, Saidy, and Myers's words blend seamlessly from book to lyric and back again so that the songs become not realistic expression but expression of realistic thoughts and feelings. *Peace*, in contrast, rejects realism and integration. Although it contains acting, singing, dancing, and so forth, synthesis is not an artistic priority. *Peace*'s rejection of integration and realism links its aesthetic world closely to Aristophanes'. Although Aristophanes' comedies are not campy, their discontinuities inhibit movement toward realism. One of the reasons we have trouble pinning down the second act of the musical *Peace* is probably because the second half of Aristophanes' *Peace* is so unnaturalistic. Reynolds's early script started with a faithful translation of all the intruder scenes, but the scenes' logically loose relationship surely enabled the adaptors to experiment more freely. *Peace* exploits Aristophanic discontinuity and lays bare the seams in its construction. The MAT *Lysistrata* and *Happiest Girl* work hard to hide the seams.

Peace's aesthetic proximity to Aristophanes cannot be straightforwardly attributed to authors who wished to remain faithful to Aristophanes' spirit. Like the other musicals studied here, *Peace* began with Aristophanes but was a creature of its own time. This survey of musicals from three different periods in theatrical history has demonstrated how Aristophanes' comedies fit into multiple theatrical traditions. They have given birth to a campy romp like *Peace*, but also realistically motivated heroes like MAT's Lysistrata. They have spawned integration and its lack, realism and absurdity, camp and political activism, feminism and Bolshevism, Constructivism and *Oklahoma!*ism. Although these musicals have not been the most prominent or successful productions of their day, each is a significant window into how Aristophanes has been adapted into the various influential strains of American musical theater.

Notes

1. Discussed on a theoretical level by McMillan (2006: 126–48). McMillan's book is a fine theoretical reflection on the limitations of studying musicals from the perspective of coherence and integration.
2. On Aristophanes' discontinuity, see Silk 2000: 136–52, 207–55. On similar methods of characterization in musicals, see McMillan 2006: 54–77. Given 2005 is a comparative study of characterization in Aristophanes and musicals. Silk (2000: 268–70) also compares Athenian comedy to American musicals. Cf. Silk 2007: 293–303, where he describes his own involvement in a production of *Frogs* that used Tin Pan Alley tunes for setting Aristophanes' lyrics.
3. Only one attempt has been made to write a history of Aristophanic (or Menandrian) reception in the Americas. Day (2001) offers a good starting point for a history of Aristophanic reception in North America. Her Ph.D. research included significant archival work, and she lists 185 productions up to 1999 (pp. 198–214). The main discussions, though, while uniformly excellent, are limited to a small handful of the many significant productions. See too Kotzamani (1997), on the MAT *Lysistrata*. Scholarship on European reception of Aristophanes has fared better: e.g., Hall and Wrigley 2007; Van Steen 2000.
4. Day 2001: 13–50; Pearcy 2003. Contemporary notices: Dale 1886; *New York Times* 1886; *Philadelphia Inquirer* 1886.
5. *New York Times* 1937, an article which includes a fine photograph of the costumed actors in the outdoor amphitheater. *Birds* had already been staged at RMWC in 1926. The Greek Play tradition is still alive today, under the direction of Amy R. Cohen. See "The Randolph College Greek Play": <http://web.randolphcollege.edu/greekplay/about_us/rplays.asp> accessed June 19, 2012.
6. I have written about this production in Given 2011a.
7. Review of Philadelphia performance: Atkinson 1930a. Atkinson's preview of the New York production (Atkinson 1930b) compares it to the musical political satire *Strike Up the Band* by Morrie Ryskind, Ira Gershwin, and George Gershwin. New York reviews: Atkinson 1930c, Bowen 1930, Fergusson 1930, Hammond 1930, Leonard 1930. The *Los Angeles Times* covered the censorship and trial of the *Lysistrata* cast extensively in 1932. A good retrospective of the events, based on *Times* archives: Smith 1980.

8. Reviews: Atkinson 1946; Cooke 1946.
9. Atkinson (1955) complained that the play was not successfully adapted for a modern audience. Ads for the production urged theater-goers, "See it! Don't say it!," since the title was nearly unpronounceable. In the same vein, 56 years later, ads for *Lysistrata Jones* provided a phonetic guide for pronouncing its title.
10. Reviews: Bernheimer 1964; Cooke 1964; Funke 1964. It closed after one performance. Despite its short run, the show produced a cast recording, which is available on CD: Straight and Eddy 1994.
11. According to the reviews (Kauffmann 1966; Smith 1966), the production highlighted Lahr's expert clowning rather than political satire. The play was staged at the Eastern Michigan University baseball stadium in repertory with the *Oresteia*, in the hopes of establishing a Greek theater festival, but the effort did not pan out. One article (Esterow 1966) mentions that a Classics professor from the University of Michigan in neighboring Ann Arbor walked the streets with her students to collect donations for the festival.
12. Review: Cohen 1969.
13. In the *New York Times*, Clive Barnes (1972) called it a "gloomy comedy … purporting to be by Aristophanes."
14. Scholarship: Beye 2004; English 2005; Gamel 2007; Given 2011b; Mendelsohn 2004; Stein 2004.
15. Review: Evett 1985. Quote from *Wall Street Journal* 1985.
16. A review of the controversy at Taylor 2002.
17. Reviews: Brantley 2011; Given 2012.
18. Review: Atkinson 1954. Atkinson's words are worth quoting not only for their pathos but also as a representation of the uphill climb faced by those who would stage ancient dramas: "Infatuated with certain obscure dramas, [Ida Ehrlich] saves as much money as she can from her income as a teacher, and when she has enough she puts on a production. She hires Equity actors and pays them herself. She provides the script, makes the costumes by hand, attends to the direction, sends out the publicity and waits patiently in the miniature box office, hoping that someone will come. At the Monday evening performance the audience outnumbered the actors by two. Mrs. Ehrlich is a bright, cultivated woman with mild manners and a shy obsession with a few unusual plays that she knows and likes. So far the public has taken no interest in what she is doing. She is alone."
19. *Samia*: advertisements in *New York Times* (March 11, 1990, p. H6) and *Washington Post* (March 11, 1990, p. G4). *Dyskolos*: see Beckerman 2002 and Klein 2002.
20. The various iterations of this show are described at: *Chicago Sun-Times* 2004; States News Service 2008; Morgan 2009; Hansen 2010.
21. On the characteristics of New Comedy (Menander, Plautus, and the tradition that followed) as opposed to Old Comedy (Aristophanes, and the lost comic poets of the classical period) see, e.g., Ireland 2010.
22. *Forum* provides a good test case. Most of its songs do not advance plot or character and could be removed without being missed. Similarly, the choral songs of Menander and Plautus have been lost, but their absence from the plot is not missed. Change a single scene of *Forum*, though, and the entire farce would be destroyed.
23. The English translation is published in Seldes and Seldes 1925: 1–78. Contemporary reports state that the Russian text was unexpurgated (Fineman 1925a—a review with a Moscow dateline). The English translation lacks all but the mildest obscenities, but it is significantly more faithful to the Aristophanic spirit than the bowdlerized translation Benjamin Bickley

Rogers produced for the Loeb Classical Library, also in 1925. Unfortunately, I have been unable to find a copy of the Russian text, nor is Russian among my languages.

24. On the early history of the Moscow Art Theatre, see Benedetti 1999: 254–66; Nemirovitch-Dantchenko [sic] 1968: 79–222; Stanislavsky 2008: 158–201; Worrall 1996.
25. On the MAT and contemporary artistic trends, see Marsh 1999.
26. Benedetti (1991) collects and translates important correspondence between the MAT co-founders. On their artistic differences, see especially letters #265–7, from June 1905.
27. Unfortunately for our purposes, Nemirovich-Danchenko's own memoir (Nemirovitch-Dantchenko [sic] 1968) trails off during the 1920s. He does not discuss the Musical Studio.
28. Quoted in Brown 1923.
29. Sayler (1925a) provides a contemporary account of each production as they were seen in Moscow.
30. I have found the following overviews of Russian Constructivism most helpful: Gough 2005; Henry Art Gallery 1990; Lodder 1983.
31. Besides Fig. 19.1, good photographs, drawings, and descriptions can be found in Sayler 1925a.
32. Sayler (1925a: 98–9) attests the rotating stage in Moscow. A rotating stage was announced for the New York production (*New York Times* 1924), but a review of the New York production (*New York Times* 1925e) mentions that the actors turn the set about, implying that the stage was not mechanical.
33. The designer, Isaak Rabinovich, seems to have been influenced by the set designs of Lyubov Popova, especially her work on Meyerhold's 1922 production of *The Magnanimous Cuckold* in Moscow. See Lodder 1983: 170–2. For more on Rabinovich and his background in the Moscow Jewish Theatre, see Zivanovic 1975.
34. Both photos appear between pp. 100 and 101 of Sayler 1925a.
35. With the proviso articulated by Foley in her now classic article (1982) that private and public space are not mutually exclusive in the play.
36. Kuhlke in Tairov 1969: 29.
37. One review from the pre-U.S. production in Berlin mentions "acrobatic tricks": *New York Times* 1925c. A review of the New York production describes "rowdy humors, clowneries, buffonnade, even burlesque" (*New York Times* 1925e).
38. In my 2010 production, using an unpublished translation by Peter Green, we gave Lysistrata motivation by dressing her in black to denote her as a widow. Cf. Henderson (1987: xxxvii–xxxviii) on the implications of Lysistrata not being identified as a housewife or an elderly woman.
39. Worrall (1989: 40) helpfully distinguishes the differences between Nemirovich-Danchenko's and Tairov's approaches to synthetic theater: "Both directors were up in arms against cliched tradition, although Tairov defended his emphasis on 'convention', where Nemirovich sought to approximate the comic opera to real life, discovering subtle psychological approaches for the actors. Tairov was not interested in the logic of character but in the logic of the genre."
40. Journalists who did understand the MAT's nuances include the anonymous Moscow correspondent for the *Christian Science Monitor* (1925), who describes the Musical Studio as judiciously influenced by experimenters such as Meyerhold and Tairov, and Frances Fineman (1925b), who in a letter to the *New York Times* editor offers insightful praise for the innovations of set designer Isaak Rabinovich and stresses (without using the term

"constructivism") his conservative streak in the face of the more daring designs championed by Meyerhold.

41. Daly 1925; *New York Times* 1925a. Cf. "singers who can act" (Sayler 1925b); "singing actors" (*New York Times* 1925c).
42. The New York theater listings from December 1925 show how popular all three genres were. By way of revues, one could see the long running series *George White's Scandals* (*Ziegfeld's Follies* being on temporary hiatus) as well as Frank X. Silk in the *Silk Stocking Revue*. December 1925 musical comedies included Al Jolson in *Big Boy*, the Marx Brothers in *The Cocoanuts* (music and lyrics by Irving Berlin, book by George S. Kaufman), George M. Cohan in his own *American Born*, and the international hit *No, No, Nanette*. *Lysistrata*'s operetta contemporaries included Rudolf Friml's *The Vagabond King*; *Rose-Marie* by Friml, Herbert Stothart, Otto Harbach, and Oscar Hammerstein II; and Sigmund Romberg's *The Student Prince*, the longest running Broadway show of the 1920s, which moved from Jolson's Theatre to the Ambassador so that the MAT could use Jolson's.
43. To quote Hammerstein again: "The songs we were to write [for *Oklahoma!*] had a different function. They must help tell our story and delineate characters, supplementing the dialogue and seeming to be, as much as possible, a continuation of the dialogue. This is, of course, true of the songs by any well-made musical play. . . . What we aimed to do was to write in our own style and yet seem 'in character' with the background and substance of the story" (Hammerstein 1943: 2).
44. The anonymous reviewer at *New York Times* (1925e) also notes how the ancient Greek chorus was essential to a synthetic theater.
45. Incredibly, *Happiest Girl* was one of five different musical adaptations of *Lysistrata* that were being written in the late 1950s and early 1960s, but the only one that seems to have reached production. Besides *Happiest Girl*, the other four projects were: (1) Composer Georges Auric and lyricist Ogden Nash were employed by producer Norman Bel Geddes to write an adaptation. Geddes had directed the Gilbert Seldes *Lysistrata* in 1930. The show seems to have been abandoned after Geddes's sudden death in May 1958. See Zolotow 1958a. (2) A long-gestating show called *All's Fair*, with book, music, and lyrics by Hans Holzer, who would later become famous as the parapsychologist associated with the Amityville Horror. See Gelb 1958a; Zolotow 1960. A website, <http://www.lysistrata.com>, has recently appeared, claiming the Holzer piece will finally see the stage in spring 2013 under the title *Lysistrata the Musical*. (3) *Listen to Liz* by composer Bernie Wayne. See Calta 1958. (4) *Lizzie Strotter*, music and lyrics by Martin Kalmanoff. See Gelb 1958b.
46. Meyerson and (Ernie) Harburg 1993 is a fine biography of Yip Harburg. Details of his contributions to *Bloomer Girl*, *Finian's Rainbow*, and *Flahooley* are summarized on p. 221.
47. Keating (1961: 3) reports that Harburg was inspired to write *Happiest Girl* when he read about the MAT *Lysistrata*.
48. Harburg had collaborated with Saidy on *Bloomer Girl*, *Finian's Rainbow*, *Flahooley*, and *Jamaica*.
49. The script of *Happiest Girl* remains unpublished. I quote from a bound typescript preserved at the New York Public Library for the Performing Arts archives (Saidy, Myers, and Harburg 1961?). The script is undated, but it corresponds to the character list and song list in the Broadway opening night program (also preserved at the NYPL-PA). The page numbers, as typed in the script, denote act number, scene number, and page number. Curiously, the typescript's cover is imprinted with the title *The Ladies and the Devil*, a title I know from no other source. (It is attested that, during the show's gestation, Harburg was calling it *Five*

Minutes of Spring, the title of another of the show's songs: Zolotow 1958b.) A cast recording was made and has been released on CD: Offenbach and Harburg 2002.

50. Norton 2002: iii. 108. Its competition did not help its business. *Happiest Girl* ran concurrently with some of the most celebrated musicals and stars in Broadway history: *Bye Bye Birdie*, *Camelot* (with Richard Burton and Julie Andrews), *Do Re Mi* (with Phil Silvers), *Fiorello!*, *My Fair Lady*, *The Music Man*, *The Sound of Music*, *The Unsinkable Molly Brown*, and *Wildcat* (with Lucille Ball).
51. Coleman 1961. Ritchard, who also directed *Happiest Girl*, had established his persona on Broadway as "the overripe, foppish pirate chief" Captain Hook in *Peter Pan* (1954). Quote from Haun (2012: 4) in a description of Christian Borle's portrayal of Captain Hook (known here as Black Stache) in *Peter and the Starcatcher* in 2012.
52. The sequence after the Wicked Witch of the East's death (from Glinda's 'Come Out, Come Out' through 'Ding Dong! The Witch Is Dead' to 'Follow the Yellow Brick Road') and the sequence upon entering the Emerald City are two of the earliest examples of the type of musical scenes that would become popular with Sondheim and his epigones.
53. e.g., Kinesias—again Lysistrata's husband—assures her that he only wins medals as "part of my campaign to make you the most famous woman in the world. And the happiest" (p. 1.3.14), a line which leads directly into their title duet, "The Happiest Girl in the World."
54. Mandelbaum (1991: 217) blames the show's failure on the use of Offenbach's "old" music, but contemporary reviews generally praised the music as one of the show's redeeming qualities. Research into Offenbach's music was performed by Harburg's former collaborator Jay Gorney, the composer of "Brother, Can You Spare a Dime?" Selections came from across Offenbach's oeuvre. For example, "Adrift on a Star" is the barcarolle ("Belle nuit, ô nuit d'amour") from *Les Contes d'Hoffmann* and "How Soon, O Moon" is "La Mort m'apparaît" from *Orphée aux enfers*.
55. The two orchestrators, Hershy Kay and particularly Robert Russell Bennett, were among a small group of orchestrators who created the orchestral sound that we still associate with classic show tunes. See Suskin 2009: 24–32 and 48–54, on their techniques and influence. (Suskin 2009: 416–17 catalogues which orchestrator worked on which songs.)
56. e.g., his usual wit shines through when Diana coyly convinces the Olympians that the sex strike will work because "Each new tot | That is begat | Cannot be got | Without that 'that' | Whatever that may be" (1.4.28).
57. I have written about the importance of divine absence in Aristophanes for promoting extraordinary human agency in Given 2009.
58. In an interview, Harburg explains that this lyric is a love song for a post-Einsteinian and post-Freudian age (Keating 1961). That may be, but it's not a love song for this dramatic situation.
59. Cf. Moody 1969, an archived document from the church detailing its progressive social and political agenda. The church still operates a theater today in its gymnasium. It is the site, coincidentally, where the 2011 adaptation *Lysistrata Jones* made its New York debut before moving to the Walter Kerr Theater on Broadway. The church also remains politically active today. When I visited recently (June 2012), it was displaying a prominent running tally of casualties in the American wars in Iraq and Afghanistan.
60. Carmines's music was widely praised by critics, and often named as the best aspect of the Judson productions. He was noted for his ability to write in multiple musical voices, not as pastiche, or not simply as pastiche, but in disparate fragments that betrayed "a fresh and beguiling original art" (Rich 1972). Cf. Barnes 1968; Barnes 1971; DeMaio 1969; Hering

1969; Van Gelder 1969. By the end of his career, Carmines had written about 80 musicals, operas, and oratorios (Martin 2005: Carmines's obituary).

61. The term is said to have been coined by *Village Voice* critic Jeffrey Talmer (Crespy 2003: 17). Bottoms (2004), Crespy (2003), and Stone (2005) provide good histories of the early Off-Off-Broadway movement.

62. Let me take this opportunity to thank Marvin J. Taylor and the entire staff of the NYU Fales Library. Their efficient professionalism made my visit not just productive but pleasurable.

63. Reynolds 1968. The archive in fact possesses two undated typescripts, but they are two copies of the same script, one of which is bound. They are identical except for handwriting in the bound copy (including a missing page 25 in both copies). The bound copy was the rehearsal script of cast member Jeffrey Apter, whose name is handwritten on the cover sheet. The scripts lack most of the musical's lyrics. Apter's copy is marked throughout with revisions, cuts, cues, and stage directions, all in the same hand. The folder in which they are kept is labeled "November 1968," the date of the Judson run, but the missing lyrics and handwritten revisions indicate that the scripts do not represent the show as performed at Judson.

64. Carmines and Reynolds 1969? The recording lacks a date but the liner notes name the 1969 Off-Broadway production and the cast list matches the *dramatis personae* in the Astor Place program. The recording exists only on vinyl LP; it has never been released on compact disc.

65. Reynolds and Carmines 1969. The script, published by Metromedia Onstage, is undated, but its title page references the 1969 Off-Broadway production and its lyrics match those heard on the cast recording. The script also contains vocal selections for several of the musical's songs.

66. Some source criticism may be included here. The greatest differences between the two scripts are: the new lyrics that appear in the published script, the elimination of most second act material, and the elimination of blackface conventions. Many of the new lyrics are Carmines's adaptation of Reynolds's original words. On Carmines's compositional methods, see Burke 1969. The earlier script contains all of Aristophanes' intruder scenes (the priest Hierocles, the military industry representatives, etc.), but to judge from reviews these were cut entirely before the Off-Off-Broadway première and are absent from the published script. Causing particular confusion is *Peace*'s usage of conventions from the minstrel tradition, including blackface makeup. Blackfaced characters, including two stereotypical Southern slaves named Rastus and Liza, mainstays of nineteenth-century minstrel shows, appear in both acts of the earlier script, which is explicitly set in the antebellum South. Their language and movement clearly mark them as minstrel stereotypes. The stage directions describe Liza as "a greatly exaggerated Aunt Jemima" and Rastus as "a greatly exaggerated blackface fieldhand, wooly poll, much given to footshuffling and head-scratching" (p. 1). Their words are close translations of Aristophanes' text into the stereotypical black dialect of the minstrel tradition. Lines 1 and 2 are translated in this way: Liza: "ANUDDER SHITCAKE FO'DE BEETLE!," Rastus: "Hyar she am. An' I sho' hopes dat ugly mutha never git no *better'n* dat too" (1). In the published script, the Astor Place program and the cast recording, the slaves disappear altogether. They are replaced by Trygaeus' Father and Mother, but played by the same actors who had played Rastus and Liza (George McGrath and Julie Kurnitz). Yet it is clear from the reviews (e.g., Bunce 1969) that the blackface and the Southern setting were not eliminated. Most reviews state that the second act followed minstrel show conventions, including blackface, and a few

even mention Rastus and Liza by name. I proceed with the following not completely justified working assumptions: The Judson production was explicitly set in the South throughout the play although the script used was probably revised—and indeed truncated— from the extant typescript. I shall nevertheless use the extant script as a tentative guide. For the Astor Place production, I again use the published script and cast recording as tentative guides, keeping in mind that, even though they avoid describing it, the second act was staged in blackface as a minstrel show. According to the script, the characters of Father and Mother still exist in Act II—they are addressed as such, and call Trygaeus "son"—but their blackface also transforms them into Rastus and Liza.

67. Carmines quoted in Burke 1969: 7.
68. Here is another reason for the disjunction between what the reviews report and what the rehearsal and published scripts print.
69. To me, it sounds more like Mozart than Handel, but Carmines says it's Handel: Burke 1969.
70. Oliver 1969. In the extant script, the song comes earlier in the play (p. 52 out of 115), but it is in last position on the cast recording and the review here cited states that it occurs in the finale.
71. Reynolds 1968: 4, 10. All subsequent references appear in brackets within the text.
72. Carmines makes clear in an interview that he was not naive about racism: "I'm from the South, and when I was a kid, I played the piano for a lot of minstrel shows. I saw that by adding the minstrel form to 'Peace,' we could make those odes entertaining, and comment on racial tension at the same time. Let's face it: the minstrel show Negro is the Negro that still walks around in the heads of most white people. And rather than repress this, I thought, why not be absolutely open about it? Why not say, 'Look, this is the stereotype that inhibits your unconsciousness, and it's high time you did something about it'" (Burke 1969).
73. The published script's stage directions describe Father as having "the exaggerated manner of a southern gentleman" (Reynolds and Carmines 1969?: 1). A newspaper profile puts the show in "the archaic American south" (Burke 1969).
74. Gottfried (1969) makes this point forcefully. He recognizes the usual goodness of the Judson's typical "refreshing scorn for serious points," but argues that such scorn is not welcome in such a politically relevant play. He also recognizes that Carmines's musicals are deliberately derivative. "The irony is that this outlook is so very close to Aristophanes', far more so than the sobriety of a classical production. It was a real chance for easy-going, legitimate Greek comedy. Instead, it is just another Judson's musical—the best I've seen, but still the same business."
75. Quoted in Bottoms 2004: 159.
76. The reviews fervently praise David Vaughan's performance as Hermes. One writer even notes that he plays the god "with overtones of [*Happiest Girl* star] Cyril Ritchard" (Novick 1969).
77. In the early script, Reynolds translates Aristophanes' episodic plot directly, including the scenes with the intruders Hierocles and the Arms-Dealer. The chorus of black slaves divides the episodes with song. The handwritten comments, though, suggest that much of this material was later cut. The published script gives no indication of minstrelsy conventions. Unfortunately, neither the cast recording nor the reviews nor the liner notes make clear what replaced these episodes, if they were in fact cut. Reviews of both productions (Barnes 1968, Jeffreys 1969, Oliver 1969, Seligsohn 1969) attest that the second act was staged as a minstrel show, but give no information about content. For a good overview of the history and conventions of the minstrel show, see Stempel 2010: 57–60.

78. Bunce 1969. Brennan (1969) reports that Aristophanes was abandoned altogether in the minstrel show; Novick (1969) more specifically says that the arms-dealers and the children of warmongers have been eliminated.
79. The cast recording's liner notes state that they were sung by Mother and Father. This is almost certainly wrong. "Just Sit Around" sounds like a pastiche of a minstrel song that morphs into a blues number. It is a song whose music and content demand black or blackface singers. It is highly unlikely that Mother and Father sing it. The voices on the recording do not help because, according to the programs, the same actors played Mother and Liza, on the one hand, and Father and Rastus, on the other hand.

References

Atkinson, B. (1946), "The Play," *New York Times* October 18, 27e.
A[tkinson], B. (1954), "Teacher Produces Play of Menander," *New York Times* November 24, 17a.
Atkinson, B. (1955), "Theatre: Aristophanes: 'Thesmophoriazusae' at Rooftop Theatre," *New York Times* December 14, 52d.
Atkinson, J. B. (1930a), "Aristophanes Play Is Sprightly Acted: 'Lysistrata's' Humor Laid on Thick by the Philadelphia Theatre Association," *New York Times* April 29, 30e.
Atkinson, J. B. (1930b), "Direct from Athens," *New York Times* June 1, section 8, p. 1a.
Atkinson, J. B. (1930c), "'Lysistrata' Here with Broad Humor: Aristophanes' Comedy Revived with Horse Play and Slapstick at 44th St. Theatre," *New York Times* June 6, 20a.
Barnes, C. (1968), "Theater: Camping It Up: Judson Poets' Theater Offers a Musical Version of Aristophanes' 'Peace,'" *New York Times* November 10, 87a.
Barnes, C. (1971), "Theater: 'Snow White' in New Guise: Al Carmines Creates an Innocent Hit," *New York Times* March 22, 39a.
Barnes, C. (1972), "The Theater: Melina Mercouri Stars in 'Lysistrata': Aristophanes Variation at Brooks Atkinson," *New York Times* November 14, 54a.
Beckerman, J. (2002), "Ancient Comedy in Classic Venue: 'Grouch' at Outdoor Amphitheater," *The Record* (Hackensack, NJ) July 21, section E, p. 5.
Benedetti, J. (ed. 1991), *The Moscow Art Theatre Letters*. New York.
Benedetti, J. (1999), "Stanislavsky and the Moscow Art Theatre, 1898–1938," in R. Leach and V. Borovsky eds., *A History of Russian Theatre*. Cambridge, 254–77.
Bernheimer, M. (1964), "Athenian Touch at the Jan Hus," *Christian Science Monitor* January 17, Arts and Entertainment Section, 2a.
Beye, C. R. (2004), "A Funny Thing Happened on the Way to the Agora," blog post, August 23 <http://www.greekworks.com/content/index.php/weblog/extended/a_funny_thing_happened_on_the_way_to_the_agora>.
Birdsall, O. (1904), "In Lighter Vein at the University," *Overland Monthly* 44.3 (September), 207–12.
Bottoms, S. J. (2004), *Playing Underground: A Critical History of the 1960s Off-Off-Broadway Movement*. Ann Arbor.
Bowen, S. (1930), "Theatre: Aristophanes," *Wall Street Journal* June 7, 4a.
Bowlt, J. E. (1977), "Constructivism and Russian Stage Design," *Performing Arts Journal* 3: 62–84.
Brantley, B. (2011), "Theater Review: 'Lysistrata Jones': Yes, Even Sexting Is Off Limits," *New York Times* December 14, <http://theater.nytimes.com/2011/12/15/theater/reviews/lysistrata-jones-at-walter-kerr-theater-review.html>.

Brennan, T. (1969), "Peace," *The Villager* January 30, 8–9. Folder 1, Judson Poets' Theatre *Peace* Scrapbooks and Clippings File, Billy Rose Theatre Division, New York Public Library for the Performing Arts.

Brock, H. I. (1925), "Out of Russia Comes the Singing Actor: Voice, Acting and Music Are Combined in a New Form for the Stage by the Moscow Art Theatre Musical Studio—and Now Insurgency Charges the Lines of Conservative Opera," *New York Times Magazine* December 6, 6–7.

Brown, C. (1923), "Russians to Revive Opera of 'Carmen': Music To Be Kept Intact 'As Much As Possible', but Libretto To Be Made 'Realistic,'" *New York Times* July 12, 20a.

Bunce, A. N. (1969), "Aristophanes with Music," *Christian Science Monitor* February 3, 10. Folder 1, Judson Poets' Theatre *Peace* Scrapbooks and Clippings File, Billy Rose Theatre Division, New York Public Library for the Performing Arts.

Burke, T. (1969), "'And I Call *That* God'" (interview with Al Carmines), *New York Times* February 23, section 2, 1e, 7.

Calta, L. (1958), "New Nash Drama Slated for Fall: David Susskind and Roger Stevens Buy Untitled Play—Third 'Lysistrata,'" *New York Times* April 10, 33a.

Carmines, A. and T. Reynolds (1969?), *Peace*, Original Cast Recording, vinyl LP. Metromedia Records MP 33001.

Chicago Sun-Times (2004), "10 Really Cool Things To Do," January 16, 3.

Christian Science Monitor (1925), "Theatrical News of the World—Musical Events: The Musical Studio of the Moscow Art Theater," April 28, 8a.

Christian Science Monitor (1939), "Aristophanes at Harvard," April 24, 11b.

Christian Science Monitor (1941), "Stage News," May 22, 12d.

Coe, R. L. (1948), "Aristophanes Comedy at C.U. Afflicted by Rare Disease," *Washington Post* December 11, 11c.

Coe, R. L. (1971a), "College Theater's 'Birds,'" *Washington Post* March 22, section B, p. 10a.

Coe, R. L. (1971b), "College Theater Finale," *Washington Post* April 5, section B, p. 6e.

Cohen, N. (1969), "Arts Centre Theatre Off to Lively Start with Lysistrata," *Toronto Daily Star* June 4, 32a.

Coleman, R. (1961), "'Happiest Girl' Happy Musical," *New York Mirror* April 4, 26a, 29a. *The Happiest Girl in the World* Clippings File, Billy Rose Theatre Division, New York Public Library for the Performing Arts.

Cooke, R. P. (1946), "The Theatre: Aristophanes in Sepia," *Wall Street Journal* October 19, 3a.

Cooke, R. P. (1961), "The Theatre: Big Package," *Wall Street Journal* April 5, 16f.

Cooke, R. P. (1964), "The Theatre: Unauthentic Athens," *Wall Street Journal* January 16, 8c.

Crespy, D. A. (2003), *Off-Off-Broadway Explosion: How Provocative Playwrights of the 1960s Ignited a New American Theater*. New York.

Dale, A. (1886), "Drama" (Review of *Acharnians*), *Life Magazine* December 2, 342.

Daly, J. J. (1925), "Footlights and Shadows," *Washington Post* March 1, 14a.

Day, S. C. (2001), "Aristophanes' Plays in the United States: A Production History in the Context of Sociopolitical Revelations," Ph.D. diss., Tufts University.

DeMaio, R. (1969), "In Praise of Peace," *Greenwich Time* March 26, 15. Folder 1, Judson Poets' Theatre *Peace* Scrapbooks and Clippings File, Billy Rose Theatre Division, New York Public Library for the Performing Arts.

Dietz, D. (2010), *Off-Broadway Musicals, 1910–2007: Casts, Credits, Songs, Critical Reception and Performance Data of More Than 1,800 Shows*. Jefferson, NC, and London.

English, M. (2005), "Aristophanes' Frogs: Brek-kek-kek-kek! on Broadway," *American Journal of Philology* 126, 127–33.

Esterow, M. (1966), "Ypsilanti Greek Theater Casts Judith Anderson in 'Oresteia': New Repertory Company to Play Classics in English in Baseball Park," *New York Times* April 28, 50b.

Evett, M. (1985), "Theater: 'Lysistrata': Greek Play Transported to the Future,"*Cleveland Plain Dealer* August 11, section A, p. 36a.

Fergusson, F. (1930), "The Theatre," *The Bookman: A Review of Books and Life* 72.3 (November), 295.

Fineman, F. (1925a), "The Moscow Theatre," *New York Times* January 11, 2g.

Fineman, F. (1925b), "Hailing a New Designer," *New York Times* September 27, 2h.

Foley, H. P. (1982), "The 'Female Intruder' Reconsidered: Women in Aristophanes' Lysistrata and *Ecclesiazusae*," *Classical Philology* 77, 1–21.

Funke, L. (1964), "'The Athenian Touch,'" *New York Times* January 15, 25d.

Gabriel, G. W. (1925), "Moscow Art's Musical Studio: A Stunning Start of the Russians' Visit with the Ancient Merriment of 'Lysistrata,'" *New York Sun* December 15. Moscow Art Theatre Musical Studio *Lysistrata* Clippings File, Billy Rose Theatre Division, New York Public Library for the Performing Arts.

Gamel, M.-K. (2007), "Sondheim Floats *Frogs*," in E. Hall and A. Wrigley eds., *Aristophanes in Performance 421 BC–AD 2007: Peace, Birds and Frogs*. London, 209–30.

Gelb, A. (1958a), "Playhouse Here Ready to Reopen: Court-Named Receiver May Book Shows for National—Lots of 'Lysistratas,'" *New York Times* March 10, 18d.

Gelb, A. (1958b), "Robert Anderson Completes Drama: Playwrights Company Gets 'Silent Night, Holy Night'—5 Previews for 'The Visit,'" *New York Times* April 14, 22a.

Given, J. (2005), "Narrative Discontinuity and Identity in Greek Old Comedy and the American Concept Musical," in S. E. Constantinidis ed., *Text & Presentation, 2004*. Jefferson, NC, and London, 119–33.

Given, J. (2009), "When Gods Don't Appear: Divine Absence and Human Agency in Aristophanes," *Classical World* 102, 107–28.

Given, J. (2011a), "Staging the Reconciliation Scene of Aristophanes' *Lysistrata*," *Didaskalia* 8.29, 189–97 <http://www.didaskalia.net/issues/8/29/>.

Given, J. (2011b), "Creating the Outsider's Political Identity: Nathan Lane's Dionysus," *Helios* 38, 221–36.

Given, J. (2012), "Review: *Lysistrata Jones*," *Didaskalia* 9.2 <http://www.didaskalia.net/issues/9/2/>.

Goode, M. (1969?), Liner notes to the cast recording of *Peace* by Al Carmines and Tim Reynolds. Metromedia Records MP 33001.

Gordon, [no first name given] (1925), "'Lysistrata,' Interpretation a Noteworthy Achievement," *Wall Street News* December 17. Moscow Art Theatre Musical Studio *Lysistrata* Clippings File, Billy Rose Theatre Division, New York Public Library for the Performing Arts.

Gottfried, M. (1969), "Theatre: 'Peace,'" *Women's Wear Daily* January 28. Folder 1, Judson Poets' Theatre *Peace* Scrapbooks and Clippings File, Billy Rose Theatre Division, New York Public Library for the Performing Arts.

Gough, M. (2005), *The Artist as Producer: Russian Constructivism in Revolution*. Berkeley, Los Angeles, and London.

Hall, E. and A. Wrigley (eds. 2007), *Aristophanes in Performance 421 BC–AD 2007: Peace, Birds and Frogs*. London.

Hammerstein, O. II (1925), "Voices Versus Feet," *Theatre Magazine* 41 (May), 14, 70.

Hammerstein, O. II (1943), "In Re 'Oklahoma!': The Adapter-Lyricist Describes How the Musical Hit Came Into Being," *New York Times* May 23, section 2, p. 1d, 2a.

Hammond, P. (1930), "'Lysistrata' Dares: Aristophanes Invades Broadway, and Is Hailed as Artistic and Sanctified Guest from Past," *Los Angeles Times* June 15, section 3, p. 11e.

Hansen, E. (2010), "Hale Center Theater Boasts New Musical," *Deseret Morning News* (Salt Lake City, Utah) August 14. Accessed via LexisNexis Academic.

Haun, H. (2012), "Starstuff 'n' Stache," *Playbill* (*Peter and the Starcatcher*, Brooks Atkinson Theatre edition) June, 4–6.

Henderson, J. (ed. 1987), *Aristophanes: Lysistrata*. Oxford.

Henry Art Gallery of the University of Washington (1990), *Art into Life: Russian Constructivism 1914–1932*. New York.

Hering, D. (1969), "Theatre: Dear World, Peace," *Dance Magazine* 43 (4, April), 20, 23, 71. Folder 1, Judson Poets' Theatre *Peace* Scrapbooks and Clippings File, Billy Rose Theatre Division, New York Public Library for the Performing Arts.

Ireland, S. (2010), "New Comedy," in G. W. Dobrov ed., *Brill's Companion to the Study of Greek Comedy*. Leiden and Boston, 333–96.

Jeffreys, A. (1969), Review of *Peace* by Al Carmines and Tim Reynolds, television transcript, WABC-TV, January 27. Folder 1, Judson Poets' Theatre *Peace* Scrapbooks and Clippings File, Billy Rose Theatre Division, New York Public Library for the Performing Arts.

Kauffmann, S. (1966), "Theater: Ypsilanti Tries 'The Birds': Aristophanes Comedy Staged in Michigan," *New York Times* July 1, 40a.

Keating, J. (1961), "Yip's Labor of Love," *New York Times* April 2, section 2, pp. 1b, 3a.

Kerr, W. (1961), "First Night Report: 'Happiest Girl in the World,'" *New York Herald Tribune* April 4. *The Happiest Girl in the World* Clippings File, Billy Rose Theatre Division, New York Public Library for the Performing Arts.

Klein, A. (2002), "Staying Grumpy for 2,300 Years," *New York Times* August 4, New Jersey section, p. 7.

Kotzamani, M. A. (1997), "*Lysistrata*, Playgirl of the Western World: Aristophanes on the Early Modern Stage" (Ph.D. thesis, The City University of New York).

Leonard, B. (1930), "Theatre," *Life Magazine* June 27, 16.

Lodder, C. (1983), *Russian Constructivism*. New Haven and London.

McMillan, S. (2006), *The Musical as Drama: A Study of the Principles and Conventions behind Musical Shows from Kern to Sondheim*. Princeton and Oxford.

Mandelbaum, K. (1991), *Not Since Carrie: 40 Years of Broadway Musical Flops*. New York.

Marsh, C. (1999), "Realism in the Russian Theatre, 1850–1882," in Robert Leach and Victor Borovsky eds., *A History of Russian Theatre*. Cambridge, 146–65.

Martin, D. (2005), "Al Carmines, Experimental Theater Force, Is Dead at 69," *New York Times* August 13, section B, p. 7c.

Mendelsohn, D. (2004), "For the Birds," *New York Review of Books* December 2, 51–4.

Meyerson, H. and E. Harburg (1993), *Who Put the Rainbow in The Wizard of Oz? Yip Harburg, Lyricist*. Ann Arbor.

Moody, H., Revd. (1969), "Proposal for Community Issues and Action Emphasis at Judson," typescript memorandum, August. Folder 3, Judson Poets' Theatre *Peace* Scrapbooks and Clippings File, Billy Rose Theatre Division, New York Public Library for the Performing Arts.

Morgan, S. C. (2009), "It's All Go for 'Wild Goat,'" *Chicago Daily Herald* May 15, 31.

Nemirovitch-Dantchenko, V. (1968), *My Life in the Russian Theatre*. Trans. J. Cournos, introd. J. Logan, foreword by O. M. Sayler. New York.

New York Times (1859), "Amusements" (Classified Advertisements), September 26, 7e.

New York Times (1886), "Reviving Aristophanes: A Greek Comedy to Be Acted in Philadelphia," May 14, 5c.

New York Times (1901), "Greek Play at Harvard: Scenes from the 'Birds' of Aristophanes Presented," May 7, 1c.

New York Times (1902), "Greek Comedy at Vassar: 'The Birds' of Aristophanes Given Out of Doors with Spectators Seated on Ground," May 18, 2f.

New York Times (1913), "First Suffragettes Seen in Greek Play: Aristophanes's Famous Comedy, 'Lysistrata,' Presented at Maxine Elliott's Theatre", February 18, 5c.

New York Times (1924), "Gest to Bring Here More Novelties: Moscow Art Theatre Operatic Studio, Also Fritzi Massary, Light Opera Prima Donna," September 4, 12a.

New York Times (1925a), "Moscow Musical Studio Plans Visit: Dr. Leonid D. Leonidoff Arrives to Start Negotiations with Morris Gest," March 28, 18a.

New York Times (1925b), "More Russian Theatre," October 5, 20d.

New York Times (1925c), "Moscow Studio Does Acrobatics in Opera: Dantchenko's Singing Actors Make Berlin Debut in Aristophanes's 'Lysistrata,'" October 17, 18c.

New York Times (1925d), "Moscow Opera Ideals Won Through Audience: How Art Theatre Studio, Soon to Be Seen Here, Revolutionized Old Stage Conventions," November 22, X8a.

New York Times (1925e), "The Play: The Synthetic Russians," December 15, 28b.

New York Times (1937), "Women of Randolph-Macon College in Annual Greek Play: Art, Music and Dance Directors Cooperate with Greek Department in the Production of the 'Birds,' Comedy by Aristophanes, the Twenty-Second in the Series Given by Students," May 23, 85b.

New York Times (1968), "Aristophanes at the Judson," October 22, 37c.

Norton, R. C. (2002), *A Chronology of American Musical Theater*, 3 vols. Oxford and New York.

Novick, J. (1969), "Greekless As We Are," *The Village Voice* February 6, 40, 45. Folder 3, Judson Poets' Theatre *Peace* Scrapbooks and Clippings File, Billy Rose Theatre Division, New York Public Library for the Performing Arts.

Offenbach, J. and E. Y. Harburg (2002), *The Happiest Girl in the World*, Original Broadway Cast Recording, compact disc, DRG Records 19032.

Oliver, E. (1969), "Off Broadway: Peace in our Time," *New Yorker* 44 (no. 51, February 8), 98–100. Folder 3, Judson Poets' Theatre *Peace* Scrapbooks and Clippings File, Billy Rose Theatre Division, New York Public Library for the Performing Arts.

Pashley, N. (1981), "Heady Days for a U of T Actor," *Globe and Mail* (Canada) April 15.

Pearcy, L. T. (2003), "Aristophanes in Philadelphia: The *Acharnians* of 1886," *Classical World* 96, 299–313.

Philadelphia Inquirer (1886), "B.C. 425: 'The Acharnians' of Aristophanes at the Academy of Music," May 15, 1f–2a.

Philadelphia Inquirer (1916), "Announcements of the Musical Season," April 23, 4a.

Reynolds, T. (1968), *Peace*, typescript. The Judson Memorial Church Archive, MSS 094, Box 11, Folder 19. Fales Library and Special Collections, New York University Libraries.

Reynolds, T. and A. Carmines (1969), *Peace*. Script and Vocal Selections. New York.

Rich, A. (1972), "The Lively Arts: Life Is Like a Basketball Game, Isn't It?" *New York* (magazine) May 8, 74a.

Saidy, F., H. Myers, and E. Y. Harburg (1961?), *The Happiest Girl in the World*, undated typescript. Script #5542, Billy Rose Theatre Division, New York Public Library for the Performing Arts.

Sayler, O. M. (1925a), *Inside the Moscow Art Theatre*. New York.

Sayler, O. M. (1925b), "Moscow Sends Us Singers Who Can Act: Musical Studio Players Likely to Upset Old Stage Ideas," *New York Times Magazine* August 16, 17a, 22c.

Seldes, G. S. and G. Seldes (trans. 1925), *Plays of the Moscow Art Theatre Musical Studio*. New York.
Seligsohn, L. (1969), "Old Greek Would Laugh at his Updated 'Peace,'" *Newsday* January 28. Folder 1, Judson Poets' Theatre *Peace* Scrapbooks and Clippings File, Billy Rose Theatre Division, New York Public Library for the Performing Arts.
Silk, M. S. (2000), *Aristophanes and the Definition of Comedy*. Oxford.
Silk, M. S. (2007), "Translating/Transposing Aristophanes," in E. Hall and A. Wrigley eds., *Aristophanes in Performance 421 BC–AD 2007: Peace, Birds and Frogs*. London, 287–308.
Smith, C. (1966), "Lahr Hams Up 'The Birds,'" *Los Angeles Times* July 1, section 4, p. 9a.
Smith, J. (1980), "Raiding on their Parade," *Los Angeles Times* February 28, section 5, p. 1a.
Sondheim, S. (2010), *Finishing the Hat: Collected Lyrics (1954–1981) with Attendant Comments, Principles, Heresies, Grudges, Whines and Anecdotes*. New York.
Sontag, S. (1991), "Notes on 'Camp,'" in Sally Everett ed., *Art Theory and Criticism: An Anthology of Formalist, Avant-Garde, Contextualist and Post-Modernist Thought*. Jefferson, NC, 96–109.
Stanislavsky, K. (2008), *My Life in Art*. Trans. and ed. Jean Benedetti. London and New York.
States News Service (2008), "Kansas Summer Theatre Stages World Premiere of New Musical," July 2. Accessed online via LexisNexis Academic.
Stein, H. (2004), "The Unhappy Journey of The *Frogs* from Athens to New York City," *Arion* 12, 199–206.
Stempel, L. (2010), *Showtime: A History of the Broadway Musical Theater*. New York and London.
Stone, W. C. (2005), *Caffe Cino: The Birthplace of Off-Off-Broadway*. Carbondale, IL.
Straight, W. and D. Eddy (1994), *The Athenian Touch: A New Musical Comedy*, compact disc, AEI Records/The Council for Musical Theatre AEI-CD 010.
Suskin, S. (2009), *The Sound of Broadway Music: A Book of Orchestrators and Orchestrations*. Oxford and New York.
Tairov, A. (1969), *Notes of a Director*. Trans. and introd. W. Kuhlke. Coral Gables, FL.
Taubman, H. (1961), "Theatre: Song-and-Dance 'Lysistrata': 'Happiest Girl in the World' Stars Ritchard," *New York Times* April 4, 42a.
Taylor, M. (2002), "'Lysistrata' Makes Waves: Brustein Preps Script After Gelbart's Is Nixed," *Variety* March 18, 38.
Toronto Star (1969), "Students to Update Greek Comedy," July 22, 28f.
Tryon, W. P. (1925), "Moscow Art Theater Musical Studio Opens New York Season," *Christian Science Monitor* December 16, 10d.
Van Gelder, L. (1969), "Stage: Minstrel Musical: Aristophanes Basis for 'Peace' at Astor Pl.," *New York Times* January 28, 49a.
Van Steen, G. A. H. (2000), *Venom in Verse: Aristophanes in Modern Greece*. Princeton.
Wall Street Journal (1935), "Time Off: Diversions and Excursions Aug. 1–14: Theater," August 1, 15c.
Wetzsteon, R. (1968), "Theatre Journal," *The Village Voice* November 7, 39, 41. Folder 3, Judson Poets' Theatre *Peace* Scrapbooks and Clippings File, Billy Rose Theatre Division, New York Public Library for the Performing Arts.
Worrall, N. (1989), *Modernism to Realism on the Soviet Stage: Tairov—Vakhtangov—Okhlopov*. Cambridge.
Worrall, N. (1996), *The Moscow Art Theatre*. London and New York.
Zivanovic, J. (1975), "GOSET: Little-Known Theatre of Widely Known Influence," *Educational Theatre Journal* 27, 236–44.

Zolotow, S. (1958a), "Play by Cocteau Here Next Month: Auden's Version of 'Knights of Round Table' Planned—Whyte to Produce Revue," *New York Times* April 4, 17c.

Zolotow, S. (1958b), "Play to Try Out in Atlantic City: Resort to Regain Status as Test Center with Comedy—'Wong' Role Cast," *New York Times* June 13, 28a.

Zolotow, S. (1960), "Lee Guber Plans Musical For Fall: His First Broadway Show to Be '*The Happiest Girl*'—Spewack Comedy Due," *New York Times* March 7, 24a.

CHAPTER 20

CUBANIZING GREEK DRAMA

José Triana's Medea in the Mirror *(1960)*

KONSTANTINOS P. NIKOLOUTSOS

UNTIL recently, the reception of Medea in Latin American theater and cinema had been almost entirely unexplored in anglophone scholarship.[1] The versions of James Maxwell Anderson, Jean Anouilh, Jules Dassin, Robinson Jeffers, Pier Paolo Pasolini, Lars von Trier, and Christa Wolf—just to mention a few authors and directors from Europe and the United States—occupy a prominent position in the canon of twentieth-century retellings of the myth. As such, they have often received attention from Classicists in the northern hemisphere who investigate the afterlife of ancient drama. By contrast, Latin American reworkings, such as Juan Esteban Ríos Rey's *Medea* (Peru, 1950), Agostinho Olavo's *Além do rio (Medea)* [*Beyond the River (Medea)*] (Brazil, 1957), Jesús Sotelo Inclán's *Malintzin, Medea americana* [*Malintzin, An American Medea*] (Mexico, 1957), Sergio Magaña's *Los argonautas* [*The Argonauts*], later renamed *Cortés y la Malinche* (Mexico, 1967), Chico Buarque de Hollanda and Paulo Pontes's *Gota d'água* [variously translated as *Drop of Water* or *The Last Straw*] (Brazil, 1975), Pedro Santaliz's *El castillo interior de Medea Camuñas* [*The Inner Castle of Medea Camuñas*] (Puerto Rico, 1984), Luis María Salvaneschi's *Medea de Moquehua* [*Medea of Moquehua*] (Argentina, 1992), Reinaldo Montenero's *Medea* (Cuba, 1997), Juan Radrigán's *Medea Mapuche* (Chile, 2000), and Arturo Ripstein's *Así es la vida* [*Thus is Life*] (Mexico, 2000),[2] have all been neglected.

These are some of the several works produced in Latin America in the second half of the twentieth century, which illustrate the wide geographical spread of Medea's appeal and the frequency with which her image has been resurrected and exploited in the artistic production of the region. Yet most of these works are completely unknown, some even as titles, to the majority of Classicists in Europe and the United States.

Part of the reason for this unawareness must be sought in the educational system of Europe and the United States, which perpetuates the centrality of western literature and has confined Latin American theater to the role of the peripheral other—a marginal activity, that is—denying it a place in the production of counter-discourse vis-à-vis the hegemonic literary models of the so-called First World. Another reason for this critical elitism is linguistic. Composed in Spanish or Portuguese, Latin American adaptations of [ancient] drama fall outside the primary focus zone of Anglophone classical scholarship. By contrast, West African playwrights, who usually write in English, have received adequate attention in modern criticism. (Nikoloutsos 2012a: 1)

This essay aims to fill a lacuna in contemporary scholarship by examining *Medea in the Mirror* (*Medea en el espejo*), a three-act reworking of Euripides' tragedy by Cuban poet and playwright José Triana. Directed by Francisco Morín, the play premiered at the Sala Teatro Prometeo in Havana on December 17, 1960,[3] and was staged at several other venues in the Cuban capital before it was brought on national television (Edwards 2004: xxi). It narrates the story of María—played by Afro-Cuban actress Asenneh Rodríguez (Fig. 20.1)—a mulatta who has two children with Julián, a low-rank member of Havana's underworld. Seeking to advance his position in the crime hierarchy, Julián, who is blonde and handsome, marries Esperancita, the daughter of Perico Piedra Fina, a corrupt slumlord who owns María's tenement building. When María hears the news,

FIG. 20.1 Asenneh Rodríguez (1934–2013) as María in José Triana's *Medea in the Mirror* (dir. Francisco Morín, Sala Teatro Prometeo, Havana, 1960). Courtesy of the Cuban Digital Theater Archive and Enrique Río Prado.

she initially refuses to accept the fact that Julián has left her for another woman, but soon she comes to terms with the reality of her abandonment and carefully orchestrates her revenge. First, she kills her erotic opponent and her father Perico with a bottle of poisoned red wine that she offers them as a wedding gift, feigning subservience. Having exterminated those who blocked her path to Julián's heart, María decides to eradicate what has kept her bound to her white oppressor all this time: their two sons. At first, she contemplates their murder and declares herself unable to perform such a terrible crime. Her maternal love, however, is quickly transformed into uncontrolled rage at their self-serving father, giving María the courage to commit filicide and thus break free from the state of submission, abuse, inferiority, and exploitation she has lived in for so long. As much as it is painful and heartbreaking, taking the life of her own children is, to the scorned and betrayed heroine of Triana's play, an empowering and highly liberating act—so uplifting that it causes her to exclaim at the end of the play: "Soy Dios" ("I am God") (62).[4]

Ancient Tragedy and the Modernization of the Cuban Stage

José Triana was born to a low-income family in Hatuey, a small town in the province of Camagüey in central Cuba, in 1931. He started to write poetry at the age of 10, when his family moved to Bayamo, the capital city of the Granma province in southeastern Cuba, where his father was employed at a telephone company. In 1950, he decided to pursue a degree in Philosophy and Letters at the newly founded University of Oriente in Santiago de Cuba, the island's second largest city. Four years later, while in Havana, he saw *The Maids* [*Les Bonnes*] of French playwright Jean Genet, performed by the collective Teatro Prometeo under the direction of Francisco Morín, who had already gained a reputation as an innovative artist after the notorious première of Virgilio Piñera's *Electra Garrigó* on October 23, 1948 (on which see below). The play made such a strong impression upon the young Triana that, as he confessed in a recent interview, that very year the dramatist was born in him: "El espectáculo fue tan impactante que decidí, en adelante, escribir teatro" ("The spectacle was so overwhelming that I decided, in the future, to write theater").[5]

Medea in the Mirror is the first play that Triana wrote upon return to Cuba from exile in 1959, after the Revolution succeeded in overthrowing the regime of General Fulgencio Batista. Like many Cuban intellectuals who lived abroad in the 1950s during the dictatorship, Triana left his native island in 1955. After a short stay in Miami and then New York, he finally settled in Madrid, where he worked as an actor with the group Dido and as an assistant director for Teatro Ensayo (Rehearsal Theater). In 1956, Triana wrote his first play titled *El mayor general hablará de teogonía* (*The Major General Will Speak of Theogony*), which draws on Hesiod's poem—in particular the hierarchical organization of the divine world operating, since its creation, under the autocratic rule of a despot—to criticize the patriarchal structures of Cuban families and allegorize the abuse of political power throughout the island's modern history, from the colonial days, when the Spanish conquistadors set foot on it, until the military coup of 1952, when Batista seized control of the country and became de facto president. This preoccupation with power dynamics and asymmetries in the private and by extension in the public sphere is also evident in the next play that Triana wrote in 1957–8,[6] while he was still living in Spain: *La noche de los asesinos* (*The Night of the Assassins*). Borrowing plot elements from classical myth—specifically the parricide cases of Cronus, Zeus, Orestes and Electra—Triana produced a two-act drama in which three adult children (named Cuca, Beba, and Lalo) re-enact, in a sealed space, the murder of their parents, a story intended by the author to be understood as a metaphor for the uprising of the Cuban people against the oppression and corruption of the pre-revolutionary past.[7]

Medea in the Mirror, thus, is not Triana's first attempt to transplant classical material into a Cuban setting and rework it to discuss, albeit in an allegorical manner, concerns and social practices of his time. This turn to European antiquity as a source of inspiration and a means for commenting on the present is also symptomatic of an artistic effort to modernize Cuban theater in the period 1939–58.[8] After the collapse of Batista's regime, an era characterized by cultural stagnation, Triana returned to his native island with an enthusiasm about the Revolution shared by the majority of Cuba's intellectual community and sought to participate in the revival of Havana's theatrical scene, ardently advocated by Virgilio Piñera and other prominent literary figures. Urging young writers to seize the unique opportunity presented by the Revolution and contribute to the nation's rebirth, Piñera wrote in one of his essays published in 1959:

> Estamos en ese punto crítico en que una oclusión, por leve que sea de nuestra vida cultural, nos pondría en peligro de muerte ... Si desaprovechamos la ocasión o si nos la malogran, retrasaremos nuestro reloj cultural en cincuenta años.
>
> [We are at this critical juncture in which an occlusion of our cultural life, however minor it may be, would put us at the risk of death ... If we do not take advantage of the occasion, or if they ruin it for us, we will turn our cultural clock back fifty years.][9]

To set an example for the kind of artistic innovation Piñera believed the regeneration of Cuban theater needed after a prolonged period of producing plays adhering to Spanish colonial aesthetics, he staged *Electra Garrigó*, a provocative adaptation of Sophocles' tragedy he wrote in 1941. The play was first performed in 1948 amidst severe criticism[10] that caused it to remain unpublished until 1960.[11] That year *Electra Garrigó* was put on stage again, and on account of Piñera's growing reputation,[12] its reception was totally different. It received rave reviews from critics, the shows were frequently sold out, and the play soon became a classic in Cuban theater. *Electra Garrigó* was such as a big success that Jean-Paul Sartre (who visited Cuba with his life partner Simone de Beauvoir to interview Ernesto "Che" Guevara) reportedly expressed his eagerness to bring the play to Paris after he attended the performance of March 19, 1960.[13]

CUBANIZING GREEK DRAMA 337

Critics nowadays consider Piñera's *Electra Garrigó* as the play that marks the beginning of Modernism in Cuban theater after a long period during which the theatrical production of the island was bound, thematically and stylistically, to the Spanish dramatic tradition. Most plays written in Havana during the first decades of the Republic (1902–38) were melodramas inspired by the genre of *zarzuela* (on which see the section "María and Lacan's Mirror Stage"), and their plots were usually placed in colonial times. *Electra Garrigó* signals a rupture with the colonial canon, achieved paradoxically through recourse to the foundations of European theater. Greek drama occupied a prominent position in Cuba's theatrical landscape. The first play that Havana's University Theater produced upon its formation was *Antigone* on May 20, 1941—for

FIG. 20.2 Cover page of the program of Sophocles' *Antigone* (dir. Ludwig Schajowicz, Plaza Rector Cadenas, Havana, May 20, 1941). Courtesy of the Cuban Digital Theater Archive and Enrique Río Prado.

the first time in Latin America, as advertised on the promotion poster (Fig. 20.2)—on the occasion of the celebration of the thirty-ninth anniversary of the Republic of Cuba (20 May 1902). Sophocles' tragedy was put on stage for the purpose of raising funds for the construction of the University Martyrs Monument and inaugurated a series of performances of Greek drama by the University Theater, such as Aeschylus' *Libation Bearers* and Johann Wolfgang von Goethe's *Iphigenia among the Taurians* (both on December 4, 1941 under the direction of Ludwig Schajowicz).[14] More Greek tragedies were produced in subsequent years. On August 9–10, 1948, two months before the notorious première of *Electra Garrigó*, *Medea* was put on stage, for the first time in Cuba, under the direction of Antonio Vázquez Gallo (Fig. 20.3).[15] Other performances

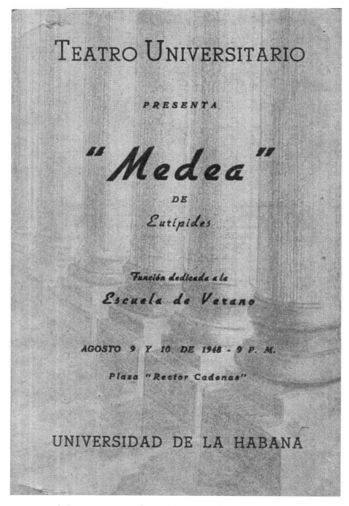

FIG. 20.3 Cover page of the program of Euripides' *Medea* (dir. Antonio Vázquez Gallo, Plaza Rector Cadenas, Havana, August 9–10, 1948). Courtesy of the Cuban Digital Theater Archive and Enrique Río Prado.

of ancient Greek drama included *Electra* (dir. Rafael Ugarte) on August 6–7, 1951 and *Agamemnon* (dir. Luis Alejandro Baralt) on December 9, 1952.

Situated in this artistic climate, Piñera resorted to Athenian drama, itself a product of a time of social and political change, to legitimize his call for innovation and the need to build a new national theater, and inserted the ancient characters in a modern context, producing an absurdist, completely Cubanized version of the story of Electra.[16] Instead of treating Sophocles' play as a "taboo" or "sacred" text of the western canon that cannot be transgressed and violated, Piñera "cannibalized" it. The schism with the colonial past that Piñera advocated did not entail, as *Electra Garrigó* illustrates, a reactive rejection of it as a whole. In his hands, the Greek model undergoes a quasi-postcolonial experience. The ancient heroes are liberated from the ideological imperatives and confines of the colonial period, and assume new identities appropriate for the time of their theatrical revival.[17] As Cuban critic Rine Leal notes in the introduction to the 2002 edition of Piñera's *Teatro completo*:

> Pero lo que irritaba en 1948 y que hoy encanta a los espectadores es esa parodia de la tragedia ateniense, esa caricatura de la "alta" cultura, que en el fondo no era más que una burla a la subcultura oficializada y anquilosada que transformaba los modelos antiguos en un patrón sagrado e inviolable. El asesinato de los padres por los hijos como única forma de liberación real, es en la década del 40 una inteligente manera de afirmar la necesidad de cambiar la vida, destruir el pasado, desmitificar la estructura familiar como reflejo caduco y sentimental de una falsa realidad social. (Leal 2002 vii)

> [But what was annoying in 1948 and nowadays the spectators love is this parody of Athenian tragedy, this caricature of "high" culture, which was in essence nothing more than a mockery of the formalized and stagnant subculture that transformed the old models into a sacred and inviolable pattern. The murder of the parents by the children as the only form of true liberation is, in the 40s, a clever way to affirm the need to change the life, to destroy the past, to demythicize the family structure as an outdated and sentimental reflection of a false social reality.]

Triana, who was 29 years old when he returned to Cuba in early 1959, sought to establish himself as a dramaturge and took part in the theatrical reform of the island with a play that, following the example of his mentor, revisited a seminal story from European antiquity—a story with a long tradition in the literature of the Spanish conquistadors[18]—and adapted it to contemporary Cuban reality. Influenced by Piñera, Triana believed that the new can be born from the old and that something that is perceived as dead, like Greek drama, can give life. As noted on the program of the March 10–19, 1961 performances of *Medea in the Mirror*:

> Señoras y señores: sírvanse dejar la lógica en el vestíbulo, que van ustedes a penetrar en el mundo dionysíaco de la Tragedia.
>   Para nosotros la tragedia clásica es algo así como un formidable cadáver. Cuando llegamos a tocarla, a fuerza de estirones intelectuales en lugar de estremecimiento, percibimos la distancia, una distancia abrumadora y fría. Y es que no logramos reconocernos en ese Mito que nos llega descarnado y el gesto magnífico de la tragedia queda suspendido en el vacío como el puñetazo en la mesa dado por un cobarde; como algo terriblemente falso, algo que no responde a una realidad....

En la obra que está a punto de comenzar el espectador hallará algo muy próximo a lo que el griego encontraba en sus tragedias: en lugar del mito descarnado, el mito hecho carne de su carne, el mito en carne viva. Y de inmediato empezará a reconocer—y quizá a reconocerse en ellos—el tono de los mitos autóctonos: un pregón aquí, un patriarca político allá, un matrimonio acá, concertado sobre la base de que a un tránsfuga solo puede heredarlo con éxito otro tránsfuga.[19]

MEDEA EN EL ESPEJO es el intento deliberado y audaz de darle voz y dimensión trágicas a lo cubano, de universalizarlo a través del mito griego. Este, que cautivó a Eurípides, a Séneca, a Corneille, es de sobra conocido.

[Ladies and gentlemen: Please leave the logic in the lobby; you are going to infiltrate the Dionysian world of tragedy.

For us classical tragedy is something like a formidable corpse. When we bring ourselves to touch it, by force of intellectual attraction rather than shudder, we perceive the distance, an overwhelming and cold distance. And it is that we fail to recognize ourselves in this myth that comes to us in its bare bones, and the magnificent gesture of tragedy remains suspended in the void like the fist of a coward slamming a table; like something terribly false, something that does not respond to a reality . . .

In the play that is about to begin, the spectator will find something very close to what the Greeks found in their tragedies: instead of a bare skeleton of myth, a myth made flesh out of its own flesh, a myth in raw flesh. And immediately he will begin to recognize—and perhaps to recognize himself in them—the tone of the autochthonous myths: a proclamation here, a political patriarch there, a marriage over there, agreeing on the premise that only a scoundrel can successfully succeed another scoundrel.

Medea in the Mirror is the deliberate and bold attempt to give voice and tragic dimension to the Cuban spirit, to universalize it through the Greek myth. This, which captivated Euripides, Seneca, Corneille, is well known.] (A synopsis of the Medea myth follows in the program.)

The above excerpt highlights two important aspects of the reception of classical drama in Latin America and the Caribbean. First, at liminal moments in national history that sit at the boundaries between the old and the new socio-political order,[20] such as the passage from Batista's dictatorship to democracy that the Revolution promised to restore, authors resort to Greek drama to discuss issues of the present through the lens of the past. The political patriarch that Triana invites his viewers to see behind Perico Piedra Fina is none other than Batista himself. The succession of one scoundrel (Perico Piedra Fina) by another (Julián) is a hint at the string of corrupt puppet presidents through whom Batista exerted his influence on Cuban politics from 1933, when he led a military uprising known as the "Revolt of the Sergeants" that overthrew the government of general Gerardo Machado, until 1940, when he was first elected president. As he rose to popularity, Batista, seeking acceptance by Cuba's high society, divorced his first wife Elisa,[21] who was of humble origins like himself, to marry Marta Fernández Miranda, a 20-year-old, fair-skinned, green-eyed beauty of Spanish ancestry, with whom he had an affair for about seven years before his divorce in 1946.[22] Triana rewrites the story of Medea to comment, albeit allegorically, on contemporary events like these. This process of reinscribing the ancient myth into a modern setting is beneficial for both the source text and its adaptation. The former renews its relevance to the present and is registered as a seminal text in the artistic consciousness of a region outside its original sphere of influence; the latter is legitimized through association with a globally accepted tradition and seeks entrance in a canon from which works produced outside the borders of the Old World have been traditionally excluded. The local is thus universalized and the universal is localized.

Second, the excerpt above points to the very fact that Latin American reworkings of classical drama do not draw exclusively on the Greek source text.[23] Triana's play is not a direct derivative of Euripides' *Medea*, but rather a synthesis of different versions of the story of the tragic heroine presented on the European stage, from antiquity to modernity. While the skeleton of the plot is appropriated from Euripides, Triana's rewriting, as the author hints above and has clearly stated elsewhere (Vasserot 1995: 126–7), is also informed by adaptations of *Medea* in Roman, Spanish, and French theater, such as those written by Lucius Annaeus Seneca, Pierre Corneille, Miguel de Unamuno, and Jean Anouilh. An attempt, therefore, to trace a linear, unidirectional flow of influences in *Medea in the Mirror* is, for historical reasons, invalid and fails to do justice to Triana's play. When it comes to the reception of Greek drama in Latin America, it is necessary to take into account the mediating cultures in the transmission of ancient texts, images, and ideas across the Atlantic. In other words, we must bear in mind, at all times, the existence of a "triangle"[24] formed between ancient Athens, Europe (predominantly Spain and Portugal, but also other cultures, such as Rome and France, that have been registered as "superior" and "hegemonic" in the consciousness of formerly colonized nations), and Latin America. Paying close attention to this triangular model of cultural traffic will help us identify the diverse ways in which the heroes and heroines of Greek drama have been extracted from their original context and have been refigured and (re) used in different time periods and countries before they embark on their transatlantic voyage to the New World. Simply put, *Medea in the Mirror* is another link in the "chain of receptions"[25] of Euripides' tragedy. As such, it cannot be fully appreciated, if it is read disconnected from the reception history of Medea—the play as well as the figure—in the Old World. Ancient texts and images are not static and monosemantic, but have taken up various meanings transnationally and transhistorically. As Charles Martindale points out: "Antiquity is constantly changing as ever-changing modernities engage in a dialogue with it ... Interpretations demonstrably change over the course of history ... and they continue to bear the traces of earlier meanings" (Martindale 2013: 171, 172).

Tracing all the influences in Triana's play is a project that exceeds the confines of the present study.[26] In what follows, I shall explore the commonalities between the Cuban play and its core influence, Euripides' text, aiming to show how Triana renews a seminal story from European antiquity by constructing a heroine constantly oscillating between antithetical positions: man and woman, subject and object, white master and black slave, Cuban self and African other. I shall argue that María's indeterminacy is symptomatic of Cuba's own liminal position and the collapse of hierarchical distinctions with the advent of the Revolution in 1959, a temporal border that marked the beginning of a new era on the island and caused the blurring of social boundaries. Building upon Lorna

Hardwick's thesis that classical texts are reinscribed in postcolonial contexts as interrogators, whether explicit or implicit, of contemporary socio-political issues (Hardwick 2003: 110–11; 2005: 110; 2007: 320), I shall propose, in a departure from previous interpretations of *Medea in the Mirror*,[27] that Triana revisits the ancient myth and uses it as a vehicle through which to raise questions about the abuse of power and the continuous suppression of black agency under Castro.

María and Lacan's Mirror Stage

Euripides' heroine is the ultimate other: she is a "barbarian" witch from the distant land of Colchis, located at the far end of the then known world. Pindar (*Pythian* 4.212) describes the Colchians as "black-faced" (κελαινώπεσσι). Herodotus (2.103–4), in turn, reports that they are "black-skinned and curly-haired" (μελάγχροες εἰσὶ καὶ οὐλότριχες) and resembled the Egyptians, from whom he believed they descended as a result of the conquests of King Sesostris, most likely a composite name for Seti I (1313–1301) and Ramses II (1301–1234 BCE).[28] In Euripides' tragedy, there is no indication that Medea wore a black mask,[29] and her children are characterized as "light-haired" (ξανθὸν κάρα παίδων, 1142–3). But Medea probably appeared in exotic "barbarian" costume in the ἔξοδος (final scene) of the play as a visual reminder of her alienness and transgressiveness before she left Corinth (Allan 2002: 123–4 n. 37; Sourvinou-Inwood 1997: 288–94).

Following Euripides, Triana portrays his heroine as an outsider, a woman who is marginalized in her own society. María is a mulatta. She lives in a *solar* and is a devotee of *brujería* ("witchcraft"). The *solar* (also known as *ciudadela*, *cuartería*, *pasaje*, and *casa de vecindad*) is a large inner-city building divided into several small units, of one or two rooms each, with shared cooking and bathing facilities. All units face a central courtyard, from which the residents have access to their dwellings. In the colonial period, such big buildings were the property of rich white families who moved to the countryside after the island became independent in 1902 to become owners of large estates and profit from the boom of the sugar, coffee, and tobacco industries.[30] The rise of latifundism, combined with the import of cheap black labor from other Caribbean islands, led Afro-Cubans and white peasants to migrate, especially during the Great Depression, to big urban centers in pursuit of employment opportunities. This mass influx of people from rural areas into the cities caused an acute housing problem, especially in Havana, which was solved, since the early Republican period, through the conversion of former single-family houses into multi-family dwellings. The large number of tenants—the *solares* could be shared by as many as sometimes 60 families—resulted in the rapid deterioration of these previously expensive buildings and the creation of slums, where an entire colored underclass lived in conditions of extreme poverty and segregation. As Alejandro de la Fuente explains:

> Both the slums and the urban *solares* were frequently inhabited by individuals of all colors, but blacks and mulattoes seem to have been greatly overrepresented in this population. . . . [T]he identification of *solares* as black spaces was a construct aimed at excluding the poorest from the city's geography and society, a cultural validation of social hierarchies. In the mainstream press, the slums were linked to marginality, crime, and promiscuity—attributes frequently used to characterize blackness. (de la Fuente 2001: 114)

Triana's play is set in the courtyard of a *solar*.[31] The action takes place a few years before *Medea in the Mirror* was staged. Contrary to what we anticipate from the title, there is no character named Medea in the play. Its heroine is called María.[32] This is a rather common name in the Spanish-speaking world, chosen to emphasize the ordinariness of its bearer, a low-class woman who commits an extraordinary crime.[33] Replacing Medea with María is an innovation that seeks to Cubanize a seminal story from the western theatrical repertoire and thus break away from the current practice of naming the central character(s) in Latin American adaptations of classical drama after their ancient Greek counterparts.[34] Triana writes himself out of this tradition, but at the same time subscribes to a different one, the *zarzuela*, a genre that combined spoken and sung scenes, as well as dance. It originated in Spain, but flourished in the Cuban capital in the early twentieth century.[35] Triana's María recalls the eponymous heroine of Ernesto Lecuona's *María la O*, a popular *zarzuela* that premièred in 1930. Set in the nineteenth-century Cuban countryside, this operetta narrates the story of a mulatto freedwoman of exceptional beauty who is in love with Fernando, a white man and heir of a prosperous plantation. Fernando's heart belongs to María, but for socio-economic reasons he marries Tula, the granddaughter of a wealthy aristocrat from Havana. Seeking revenge, María plots to kill him. Her love, however, is so deep that she uses the knife intended for his murder to commit suicide, revealing, as she dies, that she is pregnant with his son.[36] The title song of Lecuona's *zarzuela*, originally performed by Afro-Cuban soprano Rita Montaner, became a smash hit in Cuba, was frequently played at the bars of Havana, and was translated into French, Italian, and Portuguese. In 1948, *María la O* became a film (a co-production with Mexico), written and directed by Adolfo Fernández Bustamante.

On an island where Catholicism was, and still is, the dominant religion until 1959 when Castro rose to power and tried, unsuccessfully, to impose atheism on its population, the name "María" also brings to mind the image of the Virgin Mary.[37] Cuba's patron saint is Our Lady of Charity of El Cobre, a mulatto-looking Madonna. She is syncretized with Oshún, the goddess of maternity in Yorùbá religion, and is venerated as the mother of the Cuban nation and as a figure of harmonious racial and cultural symbiosis (Díaz 2000).

Triana's heroine disrupts this Marian imagery. The Virgin Mary is the symbol for the woman as a life-giver. María, by contrast, is a life-taker. She detests the sight of her children (16)[38] and verbally abuses Erundina, her old black servant, when the latter tries to make her realize, albeit in vain, that Julián lies to her (16–18). Blinded by her passion for her white lover, María refuses to face the truth and constantly asserts her superiority over other people of color around her, including the mestiza nanny of her boys,

Señorita Amparo (19–20). María's problem, which leads her to treat members of her own race with contempt, is not love per se. Like Medea in Euripides' play, what María suffers from is possessive aggression and excessive desire, an inability to "tame" herself (15, 24).[39] These qualities have gained her a reputation of being a vengeful person, a Vampire woman (24) who will eradicate those who will seek to harm her. María mimics the manners of a white Señora, and thus crosses racial and social thresholds. While she asks others to obey her, she fails to exercise mastery over herself. Her uncontrolled passion for Julián, inflamed by his departure with a white, rich, and younger woman, clouds her reason. It transforms María into a cruel murderer who will resort to magic to exterminate her malefactors and thus earn the title "queen of the witches" ("la reina bruja," 46) from the father of her rival, Perico Piedra Fina, before he falls dead, poisoned by her wine, close to her door.[40]

One of the key aspects of Medea's post-Euripidean reception is her possession of extraordinary magical powers.[41] She and her paternal aunt, Circe, are classical antiquity's most dreadful witches. Triana exploits this feature and establishes his heroine's reliance on the powers of Afro-Cuban *brujería* right at the beginning of his play. In Act 1, Julián has disappeared from home for over a month. María has not closed her eyes for nights. Erundina feels sorry for her mistress and brings her a mirror, an object used in Yorùbá-based religions "to locate the whereabouts of a missing person,"[42] as the famous Cuban anthropologist Fernando Ortiz notes in his 1906 monumental study entitled *Hampa afro-cubana: los negros brujos* (*The Afro-Cuban Underworld: Black Sorcerers*). María, who ignores the reasons of Julián's vanishing and believes that he is under a spell, summons Madame Pitonisa, a black practitioner of magic, who arrives in Act 3 escorted by another *negro brujo*, Doctor Mandinga.[43] The old couple perform an incantation on stage. First, they sprinkle some herbal powders to consecrate the space. Then, they call upon satanic powers, while they move their bodies in a ritualistic trance, until María arrives on stage, weeping and obsessively recalling the humiliation and physical abuse she (un)willingly received from Julián in the past. Taking advantage of her emotional condition, Madame Pitonisa and Doctor Mandinga hand over to her a small voodoo doll that represents Julián and urge her to stab it. María begins to chant a prayer, but then drops the knife and faints on stage unable to terminate the life of her lover-tyrant.

José Triana transculturates—to use a term coined by Ortiz in 1942 to describe the process of amalgamating diverse cultures to produce a new one—the myth of Medea. He reinterprets it through the lens of West African religious beliefs and traditions that had a profound impact upon the formation of Cuban national identity in the Republican period (1902–59), when *Afrocubanidad* evolved as the antidote to, and a vehicle for resistance against, the island's submission to the cultural hegemony of the United States.[44] Although *Medea in the Mirror* embraces Afro-Cuban rituals and puts them center stage, at the same time it problematizes the use of witchcraft and exposes its inefficacy. While the recourse to *brujería* is cast in the play as a means of revolt of the marginalized black other against white oppression, it fails to give María the power she needs to break free from the racist ideology legitimized in her own society. Scene 3 of Act 3 closes with María aiming at the voodoo doll with the knife and chanting a demonic prayer, following Doctor Mandinga's instructions: "Espíritu dañino e infernal, te conjuro a que pongas tus diversas cualidades al servicio mío para atormentar y hacer desaparecer a . . . ." (56) ("Harmful spirit from hell, I beg you to place your several powers at my service, in order to torment and make him vanish"). Physically and emotionally drained, María drops the knife and faints on stage, thereby demonstrating that this ritual is a utopian fantasy, a substitute for reality in which women of color cannot escape victimization by means of magic. *Santería* is meant to be liberating, but here it has the opposite effect. It shows that female agency and autonomy are limited and subject to gender (as well as racial and class) constraints.

Gender is a central concern in the Greek source text. In her famous monologue in which Medea contemplates the murder of her children (1021–80), she oscillates between her heroic/masculine self and her maternal/feminine side.[45] One minute, she speaks like a mother and tries to negate her avenging impulses and spare the life of her sons. The next minute, she speaks like a warrior whose pride has been dishonored and seeks revenge to avoid mockery from her enemies.[46] In the end, the male inside Medea prevails, leading her to grab a sword, the manly weapon par excellence,[47] and take the life of her own children. Triana's heroine displays analogous emotional vacillations. One minute, she declares her complete submission to Julián to the extent that her own personality is erased, stating that she could kiss the dust and stones where he steps and even give her blood to know if he feels something for her, however small (52). The next minute, María looks at herself in the mirror and experiences a spiritual transformation. Her catoptric image changes into that of the indomitable Medea, leading her to find the courage to break the manacles of oppression and restore her honor. María realizes that Julián is no longer her destiny; she no longer needs a man in her life, but she can take charge of her fate; she is no longer a victim, but a victimizer. In her last monologue, before she murders her children, María converses with her specular reflection[48] and says:

> Tú eres mi enemiga. Yo soy la otra, la que está en el espejo, la que estaba esperando y tenía miedo y no quería salir y se escapaba y no veía que estaba sola. . . . Ahora comprendo. Ahora empiezo a descubrir lo que me rodea, lo que era mío y rechazaba . . . Ahora no tengo miedo. . . . Ahora sé qué soy. . . . Yo soy yo. . . .
>
> [You are my enemy. I am the other, the one who stands in the mirror, who was hoping, who was afraid, who did not want to come out and escape and did not see that I was alone. . . . Now I understand. Now I begin to discover what surrounds me, what was mine and I turned down. . . . Now I am not afraid. . . . Now I know what I am. . . . I am myself. . . .] (57–8)

Like an infant standing in front of a mirror, María recognizes her image and gains a sense of wholeness and self-reliance. Describing this mirror stage, Jacques Lacan notes:

> It suffices to understand the mirror stage . . . *as an identification*, in the full sense analysis gives to the term: namely, the transformation that takes place in the subject when he assumes [*assume*] an image. . . . [T]he specular image seems to be the threshold of the visible world, if we take into account the mirrored disposition of the

imago of one's own body in hallucinations and dreams, whether it involves one's individual features, or even one's infirmities or object projections....[49]

While the infant begins to understand that his/her body is made up by different parts—in other words, it is a fragmented whole—it is the image in the mirror that provides him/her with the feeling of unity and mastery over himself/herself. The ego is formed at that very moment of specular reflection—a moment of illusionary self-cohesion. Thus, instead of serving as a magical portal to the whereabouts of her missing lover, the mirror, ironically, becomes an object through which María discovers her inner self and indulges in a dream of salvation from her sufferings. The mirror is a portal to María's soul, or, to borrow queer terminology, a door through which she "comes out" of her racial closet and embraces her mulatto self.

Medea and Cuba's New Age

Jason's union with Medea is described as γάμος ("marriage") twice in Euripides (1336–41, 1388),[50] but, as opposed to his wedding with Creon's daughter, there is no mention in the play of an official ceremony, in Iolcus or elsewhere, through which he took Medea as his lawful wife. As Ruby Blondell notes:

> Despite [Medea's] implicit claim to marital status in her opening speech, her position is more like that of a παλλακή in Athens, a concubine or common-law wife, who might be a foreigner cohabitating with an Athenian citizen and had little or no legal protection for herself or her children. (Blondell 1999: 159)

In his dialogue with Medea in the second episode where he responds to her accusations, Jason does not argue that the two of them were not married, although his decision to take a royal bride behind Medea's back suggests that he did not feel he was legally bound to her. Jason does acknowledge, albeit deceitfully, that he has an ethical obligation, as a φίλος ("friend," 549) rather than as a husband and father, to Medea and the children he has begotten with her, and defends his choice to remarry by explaining that his original plan was to run two parallel families and then join them into a big one under the same roof (564).

Triana situates the relationship between María and Julián in the same context of parallel families. María calls Julián husband twice in the play (31, 32). Their partnership, however, is a marriage only in her imagination; it has no legal standing in real life. The term that could best describe their household arrangement is intermittent cohabitation or faithful concubinage. In Act 1, Julián is said to have often been absent for long periods of time, during which María was responsible for the upbringing of their children, thus acting as both mother and father. María's household is basically a female-headed family, which helps explain her dominant personality. Such matrifocal unions are a phenomenon rooted in the racial protocols of Cuban society. Until 1902, interracial marriages were subject to legal restrictions that aimed to control mobility across classes and safeguard the island's white complexion. Post-Independence Cuba inherited these discriminatory attitudes. As Verena Martinez-Alier explains:

> [C]olored women were the prey of white men in sexual liaisons that were very rarely legitimized through marriage. Legal marriage was the appropriate form of union among social-racial equals, while interracial unions, that is, unions among partners who were regarded as social-racial unequals, usually resulted in more or less stable concubinage and/or matrifocal domestic units. (Martinez-Alier 1989: xiv)

This social script is echoed when Antonio's wife, a neighbor and member of the chorus, wonders if María would tolerate the idea of having an extramarital affair with Julián (30). This scenario would reduce her to the status of Julián's mistress, a childless mistress, that is, for, unlike Creon in Euripides' tragedy, Perico Piedra Fina threatens to take the boys away from their mother (44).[51] This racist ideology is reverberated throughout the play. Commenting on the abusive manners of Julián's father-in-law, Antonio's wife states: "En este país tener el pellejo prieto es una desgracia" ("In this country, to be dark-skinned is a misfortune," 29). The barber, another member of the chorus, advises the rest of them to be silent. Perico Piedra Fina, he stresses, owns the *solar* and will try to penalize them, if he hears their noise: "He never leaves us alone. He is a kind of inquisitor. In colonial times, when people were treated like oxen, the situation was never so frightening" (28). Perico is a proponent of this treatment of people of color—especially women—as lesser humans. When he orders María to evacuate her room by the next morning, he tells her: "te vas con tus matules a cuestas" ("you are leaving with your stuff piggy-back," 45).[52] This command encapsulates the discriminatory attitudes legitimized in pre-revolutionary Cuba. As the product of slavery and exploitation, the body of the mulatta (a derivative of *mula*, "mule") was easily stripped of its dignity and was equated with that of an animal. In her ritualistic trance, María cries out: "Mi cuerpo es el espejo" ("My body is the mirror," 56). Indeed, the body of María is a mirror of the entire Cuban society and reflects a deep-rooted colonial legacy of slavery, miscegenation, and racial inequalities. As Vera Kutzinski points out: "what the mulata . . . represents is not the stable synthesis but a precarious and tenuous multiplicity, a 'concentration of differences,' of 'insoluble differential equations'" (Kutzinski 1993: 172).

To argue, however, as scholars have done thus far, that Triana revisits the story of Medea to offer a critique of racial politics in pre-revolutionary Cuba is reductive, given the time in which the play was written. As the product of a liminal period marked by the collapse of Batista's regime and the arrival of the Revolution, *Medea in the Mirror* looks both backward and forward. The revival of the myth of Medea at a time of national reconstitution should not strike us as odd.[53] Although known primarily for infanticide and revenge, Medea's story is also about rebirth. In other versions, Medea rejuvenates Jason and his father Aeson, and makes false promises to do the same with Jason's uncle Pelias. In Triana, Medea's phantom stands for personal regeneration, thus echoing the political climate of the play's production. María looks at herself in the mirror and is born as a new person, just as Cuba emerges—at least in theory—as a new nation after the Revolution. In December 1960, however, when *Medea in the Mirror* was produced, the Cuban society that Castro's July 26 Movement envisioned was still at an embryonic, liminal stage, poised between a past social system and a new political ethos.⁵⁴ Triana's play reflects this in-betweenness in terms of setting and character construction. The courtyard of the *solar* where the action takes place is the epitome of liminality—a term that is derived from the Latin word *limen* (threshold). It is the middle space that connects the inside with the outside, the private with the public, the home with the world. The courtyard symbolizes an ambivalence and fluctuation between antithetical states, which are typical of the play's central characters. María, Julián, and Perico attempt to exercise dominion over others and each other, but at the same time they are slaves to their passions. María is infatuated with Julián who is her polar opposite, white and blonde (Fig. 20.4).⁵⁵ Julián and Perico are obsessed with money and power. All three impose limits on others, but they fail to limit themselves.

These contradictions are not without relation to the play's socio-political ambience and the goals of Castro's regime. Since its first months in power, the new administration sought to eliminate the boundaries between the classes and races, and create a color-blind society. Castro exploited the appeal of the "new"—i.e., a Cuban citizen liberated from the hierarchical constraints of the colonial era—to gain the support of the marginalized Afro-Cuban community. In his 1953 "History Will Absolve Me" manifesto delivered after he was

FIG. 20.4 Georgios Doussis as Julián in José Triana's *Medea in the Mirror* (dir. Ioannis Petsopoulos, Akis Dhavis Theater, Athens, November 7, 2008–January 4, 2009). Courtesy of Georgios Doussis and Ioannis Petsopoulos.

captured by the forces of Batista, following the failed attack on the military barracks at Moncada, Castro declared his intention to implement "adequate measures in education and legislation to put an end to every vestige of discrimination for reasons of race [and] sex, which regrettably still exists in our social and economic life."[56] In spite of this bold pronouncement, Castro and his associates adopted a rather contradictory policy toward issues of race when they assumed power in January 1959. As Mark Sawyer notes:

> They attempted to treat blacks as clients of the revolution and to contain their growing power and influence, maintaining the regime's image as a champion of blacks without causing fear and alienation among whites. (Kutzinski 1993: 172)

Although Castro fervently propagated the myth of racial democracy, especially when he traveled outside Cuba, Afro-Cubans did not reach parity with whites in the first two years of his rule.

By contrast, his own power increased. Castro gradually became an authoritarian figure, and people had many indications to fear he would try to establish a dictatorship, such as the arbitrary trials and executions of dissidents in 1959, the gradual confiscation of private property, the complete elimination of free press, and the increased placement of communists and their sympathizers in government positions. In August 1960, Cardinal Arteaga and eight Cuban archbishops signed a collective pastoral letter condemning the growing advance of communism on the island. The letter infuriated Castro and allegedly made him shout that "whoever 'condemns the revolution betrays Christ' and is 'capable of crucifying Christ again.'"[57] Castro identified himself and the Revolution with God, especially after the ill-fated Bay of Pigs invasion that resulted in religious restrictions.[58] In a similar manner, at the end of the play María shouts, "I am God" and then collapses on stage. Her apotheosis is celebrated by the chorus who lifts her up in the air like a trophy, just as Castro and Che Guevara were often carried on the shoulders of their rebel recruits and the local people who welcomed them as saviors and liberators of the oppressed, when their army marched victoriously in small towns and villages after ousting Batista's forces.

Euripides' tragedy ends with Medea's triumphant exit from the city of Corinth on a dragon-driven chariot supplied by her paternal grandfather, the god Helios. Despite this victorious image of Medea, the play is all about loss and shows that vengeance is painful for avenger and avenged alike. Like Medea herself, the Peloponnesian War that broke out in 431 BCE, when the play was produced, caused the death of thousands of soldiers over the next 27 years. Its appropriation by Triana is pertinent to Cuban society in 1960, at the end of a six-year period of civil strife and war between the armies of Batista and Castro. Medea's story is also about exile. She first flees Colchis, her fatherland, then Iolcus, Jason's birthplace, and now Creon is banishing her from Corinth. Triana returned to Cuba from exile at the same time as thousands of his co-patriots from all social classes were fleeing the island to escape the advent of communism and imminent sovietization of Cuban society. His return to Cuba, however, was short-lived. In 1965, Triana received the prestigious *Casa de las Américas* prize for *La noche de los asesinos*. At the time, the play was seen as a condemnation of practices associated with Batista's regime. In the 1970s, however, the paranoia of Castro and his associates led to a reinterpretation of it as a critique of the Revolution. As a result, Triana's work was repeatedly denied performance. In 1980, during the massive emigration of Cubans, Triana, taking advantage of the fact that his wife is French, took the road to exile again and went to Paris, where he currently lives.

Conclusion

My purpose in this chapter was to use *Medea in the Mirror* as a case study through which to illustrate the conditioned character and embeddedness of Latin American rewritings of Greek drama. I argued that Triana's play is the product of a particular historical juncture; as such, it has to be examined within its original context. An investigation of the artistic and socio-political climate in which Triana's play was written and produced can cast light on the ways in which a story that is considered to be "classic" precisely because it has been unaffected by historical forces and is intrinsically transcendent[59] has been altered and embedded in a new cultural space. Exploring the conditions that inspired and shaped *Medea in the Mirror* provides a more nuanced framework for understanding the affinities of the Cuban play with the Greek source text, and its departures from it. With Triana, a seminal story from the western canon, used in the past to sustain the colonial project and propagate the values and supposed cultural superiority of the white elites,[60] changes to give voice to, and make visible on the national stage, the Afro-Cuban community, which until then had received representation in lead roles only in light genres, such as the *bufo* and the *zarzuela*, and whose only recognized contribution to Cuban culture had been the production of popular music, such as mambo, cha-cha, and rumba.[61] The story of Medea is revisited at a liminal moment in Cuban history and is retold from a black perspective to enable a marginalized social group to break the confines of low culture and inscribe itself in the realm of high art—in other words, to make the transition from subculture to serious theater. By embracing African-based religious traditions and putting them center stage, *Medea in the Mirror* inaugurates (along with Ramiro Guerra's *Suite Yoruba* performed in 1961) a new trend on the post-Revolutionary Cuban stage called "ritual theater."[62] One of the best examples of this trend of staging Afro-Cuban drumming-singing-dancing rituals as fully integrated dramatic elements, instead of using them as a form of exotic audience entertainment alien to the plot, is Eugenio Hernández Espinosa's *María Antonia*, written in 1965 and produced two years later. Its story echoes Triana's play,[63] thus adding a new link (albeit a remote one) to the chain of *Medea*'s Cuban receptions.

Plays like *Medea in the Mirror* and its literary descendants attest to the powerful hold that Medea has in contemporary artistic imagination. No matter how disturbing we find her actions, we are still attracted to her. No matter how many authors will attempt to appropriate her story and recast it to suit their own ideological goals, Medea will always transcend spatial and temporal boundaries.[64]

Notes

1. Of the four anthologies available in English at the time this piece was first published (Clauss and Iles Johnston 1997; Corti 1998; Hall, Macintosh, and Taplin 2000; Bartel and Simon 2010), only the last includes a chapter about a play by an author of Latin American origins that is based on the myth of Medea (Straile-Costa). For further work on the reception of *Medea* in Latin America, see Croce 2006; Biglieri, Billotte, Gemelli, Santos (all this volume); Lauriola 2015.
2. For these and other titles, see Miranda Cancela 1999a, 1999b, 2002a, 2002b, 2005; Pociña 2006: 519. For a complete list of performances of *Medea* in Cuba from 1941 until 2010, see <http://cubantheater.org/search/?q=medea> accessed August 5, 2013.
3. The 1950s is known as the era of the *salitas* because of the many small halls (usually of less than 200 seats) that opened in Havana. The explosion in the number of *salitas* is, to a large degree, the result of the advent of the television on the island in 1950. Because television's purported goal was to promote high culture and the ideology of Cubanness, stage productions (including *Medea in the Mirror* and Piñera's *Electra Garrigó*) were shown on the small screen on a regular basis. See Martin 1994: 149–50; González 2003: 189; Rivero 2007.
4. All quotations from the play are from Triana 1991. All translations are my own.
5. <http://www.cervantesvirtual.com/portales/jose_triana/autor_apunte/> accessed August 5, 2013.
6. Taylor (2008: 197) discusses how, after 1965 when *The Night of the Assassins* was published, Triana actively promoted the idea that the play was first written during the years of his exile, in an effort to avert criticism of it as anti-revolutionary and convince the new regime that his goal was to expose and condemn practices and policies during Batista's dictatorship.
7. *The Night of the Assassins* is the play to which Triana owes his international acclaim. It was awarded the prestigious *Casa de las Américas* prize in 1965 and has since then been translated into more than 20 languages. In 1967, the play was performed at the Theater of Nations Festival in Paris, and also staged at Stratford-upon-Avon by the Royal Shakespeare Company under the title *The Criminals*. See Salvat 2007: 97.
8. Here I follow periodization in Montes Huidobro 2004.
9. Quoted in Anderson 2006: 91.
10. *Electra Garrigó* was first performed by actors of Teatro Prometeo, named by Francisco Morín after the Titan of Greek mythology to denote the group's rebellious stance toward Cuban theatrical tradition. The name proved suitable as Miranda Cancela (1990: 40) and Townsend (2008: 174) point out: during the performance of *Electra Garrigó*, one renowned director walked out of the theater, allegedly denouncing the play as "a spitball thrown at Olympus." Leal (2002: vii) and Townsend (2008: 174) discuss how the polemic about *Electra Garrigó*'s première was compared to the Battle of Hernani in 1830, when the debut of Victor Hugo's famous play resulted in a fist fight between Romantics and defenders of the classical tradition. *Electra Garrigó* received such harsh criticism after its opening night that the Association of Theater and Cinematographic Redactors ordered its removal from its index of works presented that year—see Townsend 2008: 178 n. 4.
11. *Electra Garrigó* was first published in *Teatro completo*, a collection of eight plays that Piñera wrote in 1941–60. On the history of this publication, see Anderson 2006: 97. The play was translated into English by Margaret Carson, and is included in Taylor and Townsend 2008: 180–95.

12. When Piñera returned to Cuba from exile in 1958, he wrote three plays through which he was established as a towering figure in Cuban theater: *Aire frío* (*Cold Air*), *El flaco y el gordo* (*The Skinny Man and the Fat Man*), and *El filántropo* (*The Philanthropist*).
13. On the reception of the play in 1960, see Anderson 2006: 97–9.
14. For performances of Greek drama before the notorious première of *Electra Garrigó*, see Miranda Cancela 1990: 45 and Andújar (this volume). For individual titles, see also <http://cubantheater.org/>.
15. The role of Medea was played by Violeta Casals; two months later, she played Electra in Piñera's rewriting of the myth. In the mid-1950s, Casals joined Fidel Castro's July 26 Movement and became known as "the voice of the Rebel Radio of Sierra Maestra." See <http://www.encaribe.org/Article/violeta-casals> accessed November 14, 2013.
16. On the reasons why Piñera was drawn to Greek drama and the ways in which he sought to Cubanize Sophocles' characters, see the prologue of *Teatro completo* (1960), 7–17. On *Electra Garrigó*, see Piñera 1967 and Andújar (this volume) with further bibliography.
17. On the postcolonial experience that ancient works undergo in countries that were once colonized, see Hardwick 2005: 109. Piñera's approach to the Greek model undermines and simultaneously reproduces the views of Cuban national hero and major literary figure José Martí (2002: 291): "The European University must yield to the American University. The history of America from the Incas to the present must be taught, even if the Greek Archons go untaught. Our own Greece is preferable to the Greece that is not ours. . . ."
18. On Medea in medieval and Golden Age Spanish literature, see Biglieri 2005; Julio 2002; Pociña 2002. On Seneca's *Medea* (lines 375–9) as an inspiration for Columbus and the navigators in the age of discovery, see Clay 1992; Laird 2007: 227.
19. <http://cubantheater.org/production/3000> accessed September 1, 2013. I wish to thank my colleague Heather Hennes for discussing aspects of the English translation of the text with me.
20. Here I depart from terminology proposed by other scholars. Taylor (1991) talks about "moments of crisis" in the history of Latin American countries, whereas Fradinger (2011: 68) uses the term "foundational moments."
21. Argote-Freyre 2006: 284 n. 30: her first name was María, like that of Triana's heroine, but everyone addressed her by her middle name.
22. Perico Piedra Fina is a caricature of the *gallego* (Salvat 2007: 96 n. 2), the white Spaniard who arrived in Cuba penniless and made money by exploiting the island's gold and vast plantations. Batista's second wife was the daughter of a Spanish immigrant. On his two marriages, see Argote-Freyre 2006: 29–30, 125, 274, 361 n. 94. Batista fathered at least one child out of wedlock, a theme also discussed in *Medea in the Mirror*.
23. See further Nikoloutsos 2012a: 3.
24. I borrow the idea from Greenwood (2004), who works herself with Gilroy's seminal notion of "the Black Atlantic" (1993) and adapts it to the reception of classical literature in particular. See further Hardwick 2007: 324–5, and Goff and Simpson 2007 on the "black Aegean."
25. On the term, see Jauss 1982: 20; Martindale 2007: 300.
26. Other readings of *Medea in the Mirror*, in addition to Nikoloutsos (2012b), include Dauster 1969: 3–4, 1976: 170–2; de la Campa 1979: 45–60; García 1996; Lima 2004: 561–5; Pérez Asensio 2009: esp. 232–51.
27. Edwards (2004: xxii) suggests a similar reading, but does not pursue the idea.
28. For a discussion of these sources, see Allan 2002: 69; Blondell 1999: 152–3; O'Higgins 1997: 118.

29. Sourvinou-Inwood (1997: 262–6) demonstrates that in her iconography before 431 BCE, the year in which Euripides' play was first staged, Medea does not differ from Greek women. Euripides casts Medea as the granddaughter of Helios, and sun exposure causes the skin to become darker. In a fifth- or fourth-century Kabeiric vase, now at the Ashmolean Museum, Circe, Medea's paternal aunt, is depicted as a black woman—see O'Higgins 1997: 118 n. 48.
30. For a detailed account of these socio-economic changes, see Kutzinski 1993: 134–62.
31. The setting is similar to Euripides' tragedy. The stage building represents the façade of the house of Medea and Jason in Corinth. The action takes place outside of it.
32. From 1953 until 1961, *Medea* became internationally identified with the name "Maria" through Maria Callas's critically acclaimed rendition of the title role in Luigi Cherubini's revived opera performed at various venues worldwide and released on record in 1957. In popular imagination, this identification became more prominent when the Greek tycoon Aristotle Onassis left Callas—who allegedly aborted their child—to marry the American "princess" Jackie Kennedy. See Kerrigan 1996: 102–3 with further bibliography.
33. During a talkback at Akis Dhavis Theater in Athens, where the play was performed (November 7, 2008–January 4, 2009), when Triana was asked why he chose the name María for his heroine, he replied: "there is a María in almost every Cuban family" (quoted from a telephone conversation I had with director Ioannis Petsopoulos on August 11, 2011).
34. Cf., e.g., *Electra Garrigó*; José Bergamín Gutiérrez's *Medea, la encantadora* ([*Medea, the Sorceress*], Uruguay, 1954); Leopoldo Marechal's *Antígona Vélez* (Argentina, 1950). The Puerto Rican author Luis Rafael Sánchez continues the tradition in *La Pasión según Antígona Pérez* (*The Passion of Antígona Pérez*, 1968). See further Nikoloutsos 2012a: 4.
35. Thomas (2008) traces the birth of the genre in Cuba back to 1927.
36. Another *zarzuela* that premièred in Havana in 1932 is *Cecilia Valdés* based on Cirilo Villaverde's novel of the same title, which is regarded as the best Cuban work of fiction from the nineteenth century. Set in colonial Cuba in about 1830, its eponymous heroine is a mulatta who falls in love with a white man named Leonardo de Gamboa, son of a land magnate and slave trader. Cecilia is the product of an affair that Leonardo's father had in secret with a woman of color, but the two young people do not know that they are half-brother and -sister. Leonardo promises to marry Cecilia, but when he abandons her for a white upper-class woman, Cecilia takes revenge by arranging his assassination on the day of his wedding.
37. This religious association is also suggested by María's cry at the end of the play: "I am God." Of course, as I discuss later, given the political context of the play's performance, this is not the only reading of the exclamation.
38. All numbers in parentheses in my text refer to the pages in Triana 1991.
39. I deliberately use the verb "tame." Perico compares María's uncontrollable character to that of a "wild beast" and "lioness" (44). María, in turn, describes herself as a "cat" that cannot be caged (15). Medea is also likened to a λέαινα ("lioness") in Euripides (187, 1342, 1407). This animal imagery is intended as a stereotyped reminder of the African origins of Triana's mulatto heroine, emphasizing her purported savage nature and lack of human feelings that will lead her to take the life of her own children.
40. Another epithet attached by Perico Piedra Fina to María is "Snow White's stepmother" (46). As well as their vindictiveness and use of witchcraft, Triana's heroine and Snow White's stepmother also share an obsession with a magic mirror, which they use as an object of self-gratification and self-assurance.

41. Pre-431 BCE art emphasizes the connection between Jason's Colchian wife and magic, on which see, e.g., Sourvinou-Inwood 1997: 262–6. There is also literary evidence that Euripides' play draws on an earlier tragedy by an otherwise unknown dramatist named Neophron, on which see Manuwald 1983; Michelini 1989; Séchan 1927; Thompson 1944. Although Medea's portrayal as a sorceress is emphasized less in Euripides than in the other traditions, which are extensively developed by Seneca, nevertheless Euripides' text gives Medea her canonical identity as a terrible witch, and it is this image of her that has become the point of reference for all later versions.
42. Salvat 2007: 96. On catoptromancy, i.e., the practice of divination by means of a mirror, and the reception of Medea in seventeenth-century France, see Wygant 2007: 127–51. On the mirror as a symbol for the psychological vicissitudes and inner conflicts of Triana's heroine, see Nikoloutsos 2012b: 27.
43. Doctor Mandinga bears the generic name of one of the African ethnic groups that were brought as slaves to Cuba after the sugar boom in 1760–1870. The Mandingas introduced the cult of Ozain, the Yorùbá spirit of medicinal and magical herbs. As Brandon (1997: 137, citing Robert Farris Thompson) points out: "Ozain priests in Nigeria are not simply skilled herbalists; there is also a theatrical aspect to their role in that they allow the deity Ozain to speak to human beings by means of their training as ventriloquists."
44. See, for example, Ayorinde 2004: 40–82; Brandon 1997: 79–103; Kutzinski 1993: 134–62.
45. On Medea's self-division, see, for example, Foley 2001: 243–71; Gill 1987: 25–30.
46. Scholars have likened Medea to Homer's Achilles and Sophocles' Ajax. See Blondell 1999: 162–6, 414 n. 40 with further bibliography.
47. On swords in antiquity, see Loraux 1987: 7–30.
48. The dialectic between characters and their image is a motif attested in *Electra Garrigó* and other plays of Piñera, on which see Leal 2002: xiii–xvi.
49. Lacan 2006: 76; 77. Emphasis in the original.
50. As Blondell (1999: 413 n. 32) notes, γάμος can be simply a reference to sexual union.
51. In this detail Triana follows Seneca's *Medea*. See Nikoloutsos 2012b: 28.
52. Literally, *matules* means the "bundles" of tobacco piled one over another in the barns.
53. On the ways in which twentieth-century European rewritings of *Medea* are associated with new beginnings in modern history, see Nikoloutsos 2012b: 29–30. Of course, 431 BCE, when *Medea* was first staged, saw the start of the Peloponnesian War that marked the end of Athens's golden age and the beginning of an era of decline over the next quarter-century. Democracy was suspended and a new regime of Thirty Tyrants was installed by the victorious city of Sparta.
54. See Franqui 1985: 65: "Nineteen fifty-nine had been a year of experiments, discoveries, and conflicts, a strange mixture of the old and the new, of collective justice mixed with individual injustice. Nineteen sixty would be the final test." The invasion at the Bay of Pigs will follow in April 1961 and the Missile Crisis in October 1962.
55. By being blonde, Julián recalls Jason and the Golden Fleece called χρυσόμαλλον ("with golden hair/wool") δέρας in ancient Greek. Julián also wears a gaudy golden chain around his neck and golden rings (39). I owe this observation to director Ioannis Petsopoulos.
56. Quoted in Sawyer 2006: 52.
57. <http://www.time.com/time/magazine/article/0,9171,869811,00.html> accessed December 7, 2013.
58. These restrictions were Castro's response to the suspected involvement of the Church in the unsuccessful attempt of paramilitary forces supported by the CIA to overthrow him in 1961.

59. This, of course, is not the only definition of "classic." See further Calvino 2001.
60. In his 1931 adaptation called *Asie*, Lenormand used the myth of Medea to challenge the French colonial policy in Indochina, on which see Macintosh 2005.
61. Afrocubanismo rose as a movement in the period 1920–40, and classical Greece played an important role in its early years. Club Atenas, founded in Havana in 1917, provided a congregation and recreation space for educated Cubans of African descent and served as the chief advocacy group for the rights of the politically oppressed community. The name of the club, which became the island's most prestigious black society, reflects the popular misconception about ancient Athens as the birthplace of democracy and social equality. See Pappademos 2011: 148–222.
62. Edwards (2004: xxi) mentions that Triana did not include Madame Pitonisa and Doctor Mandinga in the original version of the play. He added these two characters four years later, as a response to criticism he received when *Medea in the Mirror* was first performed.
63. The play narrates the story of a black woman of astounding beauty who is in love with a black boxer named Julián. Motivated by jealousy, María Antonia resorts to Afro-Cuban religious ceremonies to kill her lover. On Cuban ritual theater, see Martiatu Terry 1998.
64. This chapter appeared in an earlier form in *Romance Quarterly* 59.1 (2012), 19–35 and is published here by kind permission of Routledge, Taylor and Francis Group. It has been substantially revised and expanded to include illustrations and archival material to which I did not have access previously. I am grateful to Lillian Manzor, founding director of the Cuban Theater Digital Archive at the University of Miami, for granting me permission to use three of the images included here. Many thanks are also due to Professor Elina Miranda Cancela at the University of Havana for supplying me with bibliography unavailable in the U.S.A. Finally, I wish to thank the editors of the volume for their patience and helpful suggestions for revision.

References

Allan, W. (2002), *Euripides: Medea*. London.
Anderson, T. F. (2006), *Everything in its Place: The Life and Works of Virgilio Piñera*. Lewisburg, PA.
Argote-Freyre, F. (2006), *Fulgencio Batista: From Revolutionary to Strongman*. Piscataway, NJ.
Ayorinde, C. (2004), *Afro-Cuban Religiosity, Revolution, and National Identity*. Gainesville, FL.
Bartel, H. and A. Simon (eds. 2010), *Unbinding Medea: Interdisciplinary Approaches to a Classical Myth from Antiquity to the 21st Century*. Oxford.
Biglieri, A. A. (2005), *Medea en la literatura española medieval*. La Plata.
Blondell, R. (1999), "Introduction," in R. Blondell, M.-K. Gamel, N. S. Rabinowitz, and B. Zweig, *Women on the Edge: Four Plays by Euripides*. New York, 149–69.
Brandon, G. (1997), *Santeria from Africa to the New World: The Dead Sell Memories*. Bloomington and Indianapolis.
Calvino, I. (2001), *Why Read the Classics?* Trans. Martin McLaughlin. New York.
Clauss, J. J. and S. Iles Johnston (eds. 1997), *Medea: Essays on Medea in Myth, Literature, Philosophy, and Art*. Princeton.
Clay, D. (1992), "Columbus' Senecan Prophecy," *American Journal of Philology* 113.4, 617–20.
Corti, L. (1998), *The Myth of Medea and the Murder of Children*. Westport, CT.

Croce, C. (2006), "Medea from Brazil: Canonical 'Counter-Discourse' in Post-Colonial Latin America," *New Voices in Classical Reception Studies* 1, 10–18.

Dauster, F. N. (1969), "The Game of Chance: The Theater of José Triana," *Latin American Theater Review* 3.1, 3–8.

Dauster, F. N. (1976), "The Game of Chance: The Theater of José Triana," in L. F. Lyday and G. W. Woodyard eds., *Dramatists in Revolt: The New Latin American Theater*. Austin, TX, 167–89.

De la Campa, R. V. (1979), *José Triana: Ritualización de la sociedad cubana*. Minneapolis.

De la Fuente, A. (2001), *A Nation for All: Race, Inequality, and Politics in Twentieth-Century Cuba*. Chapel Hill, NC.

Díaz, M. E. (2000), "Rethinking Tradition and Identity: The Virgin of Charity of El Cobre," in D. J. Fernández and M. C. Betancourt eds., *Cuba, The Elusive Nation: Interpretations of National Identity*. Gainesville, FL, 43–59.

Edwards, G. (2004), *The Methuen Book of Contemporary Latin American Plays: La Chunga by Mario Vargas Llosa, Paper Flowers by Egon Wolff, Medea in the Mirror by José Triana*. London.

Foley, H. P. (2001), *Female Acts in Greek Tragedy*. Princeton.

Fradinger, M. (2011), "An Argentine Tradition," in E. B. Mee and H. P. Foley eds., *Antigone on the Contemporary World Stage*. Oxford, 67–89.

Franqui, C. (1985), *Family Portrait with Fidel: A Memoir*. New York.

García, W. (1996), "Tragedy and Marginality in José Triana's *Medea en el espejo*," in F. Dauster ed., *Perspectives on Contemporary Spanish American Theatre*. Lewisburg, PA, 145–57.

Gill, C. (1987), "Two Monologues of Self-Division: Euripides, *Medea* 1021–180 and Seneca, *Medea* 893–977," in M. Whitby, P. Hardie, and M. Whitby eds., *Homo Viator: Classical Essays for John Bramble*. Bristol, 25–37.

Gilroy, P. (1993), *The Black Atlantic: Modernity and Double Consciousness*. London.

Goff, B. and M. Simpson (eds. 2007), *Crossroads in the Black Aegean: Oedipus, Antigone, and Dramas of the African Diaspora*. Oxford.

González, M. A. (2003), "Cuba," in E. Cortés and M. Barrea-Marlys eds., *Encyclopedia of Latin American Theater*. Westport, CT, 188–200.

Greenwood, E. (2004), "Classics and the Atlantic Triangle: Caribbean Readings of Greece and Rome via Africa," *Forum of Modern Language Studies* 11.4, 365–76.

Hall, E., F. Macintosh, and O. Taplin (eds. 2000), *Medea in Performance 1500–2000*. Oxford.

Hardwick, L. (2003), *Reception Studies: Greece and Rome New Surveys in the Classics 33*. Oxford.

Hardwick, L. (2005), "Refiguring Classical Contexts: Aspects of the Postcolonial Condition," in B. Goff ed., *Classics and Colonialism*. London, 107–17.

Hardwick, L. (2007), "Postcolonial Studies," in C. W. Kallendorf ed., *A Companion to the Classical Tradition*. Malden, MA, 312–27.

Jauss, H. R. (1982). *Toward an Aesthetic of Reception*. Trans. Timothy Bahti. Brighton.

Julio, T. M. (2002), "Tradición y creación en *Los encantos de Medea* de Francisco de Rojas Zorrilla," in A. López and A. Pociña eds., *Medeas: Versiones de un mito desde Grecia hasta hoy*. Granada, 779–95.

Kerrigan, J. (1996), *Revenge Tragedy: Aeschylus to Armageddon*. New York.

Kutzinski, V. M. (1993), *Sugar's Secrets: Race and the Erotics of Cuban Nationalism*. Charlottesville, VA.

Lacan, J. (2006), *Écrits: The First Complete Edition in English*. Translated by B. Fink in collaboration with H. Fink and R. Grigg. New York.

Laird, A. (2007), "Latin America," in C. W. Kallendorf ed., *A Companion to the Classical Tradition*. Malden, MA, 222–36.

Lauriola, R. (2015), "Medea," in R. Lauriola and K. Demetriou eds., *Brill Companion to the Reception of Euripides*. Leiden.

Leal, R. (2002), "Piñera todo teatral," in *Virgilio Piñera: teatro completo*. Compilación, ordenamiento y prólogo de Rine Leal. Havana, v–xxxiii.

Lima, R. (2004), "José Triana and the Tragic Mode: Three Plays," *Neophilologus* 88, 559–68.

Loraux, N. (1987). *Tragic Ways of Killing a Woman*. Trans. Anthony Forster. Cambridge, MA.

Macintosh, F. (2005), "Medea between the Wars: The Politics of Race and Empire," in J. M. Dillon and S. E. Wilmer eds., *Rebel Women: Staging Ancient Greek Drama Today*. London, 65–77.

Manuwald, B. (1983), "Der Mord an den Kindern. Bemerkungen zu den *Medea*-Tragödien des Euripides und des Neophron," *Wiener Studien N.F.* 17, 27–61.

Martí, J. (2002), *Selected Writings*. Ed. and trans. E. Allen, introduction by R. G. Echevarría. New York.

Martiatu Terry, I. M. (1998), "Mythological and Ritual Theatre in Cuba," *Performance Research* 3.3, 43–9.

Martin, R. (1994), *Socialist Ensembles: Theater and State in Cuba and Nicaragua*. Minneapolis.

Martindale, C. (2007). "Reception," in C. W. Kallendorf ed., *A Companion to the Classical Tradition*. Malden, MA, 297–311.

Martindale, C. (2013), "Reception—A New Humanism? Receptivity, Pedagogy, the Transhistorical," *Classical Receptions Journal* 5.2, 169–83.

Martinez-Alier, V. (1989), *Marriage, Class and Colour in Nineteenth-Century Cuba: A Study of Racial Attitudes and Sexual Values in a Slave Society*. 2nd edn. Ann Arbor.

Michelini, A. N. (1989), "Neophron and Euripides' *Medea* 1056–80," *Transactions of the American Philological Association* 119, 115–35.

Miranda Cancela, E. (1990), "Electra en Piñera," *Revista de literatura cubana* 14, 40–53.

Miranda Cancela, E. (1999a), "Palinodia de Medea en el teatro cubano actual," in M. C. Á. Morán and R. M. I. Montiel eds., *Contemporaneidad de los clásicos en el umbral del tercer milenio: actas del congreso internacional "Contemporaneidad de los clásicos: la tradición greco-latina ante el siglo XXI (La Habana, 1 a 5 de diciembre de 1998)."* Murcia, 289–96.

Miranda Cancela, E. (1999b), "Un espejo para Medea en el teatro cubano," in K. Andresen, J. V. Bañuls, and F. De Martino eds., *El teatre clàssic al marc de la cultura grega i la seua pervivència dins la cultura occidental*, ii: *El teatre, eina política*. Bari, 207–25.

Miranda Cancela, E. (2002a), "Medea y su palinodia cubana en el teatro de Reinaldo Montero (1997)," in A. López and A. Pociña eds., *Medeas: versiones de un mito desde Grecia hasta hoy*. Granada, 1105–24.

Miranda Cancela, E. (2002b), "Medea: otredad y subversión en el teatro latinoamericano," in F. De Martino and C. Morenilla eds., *El teatre clàssic al marc de la cultura grega i la seua pervivència dins la cultura occidental*, v: *El perfil de les ombres*. Bari, 317–32.

Miranda Cancela, E. (2005), "Medea y la voz del otro en el teatro latinoamericano contemporáneo," *La Ventana* 22, 69–90.

Montes Huidobro, M. (2004), *El teatro cubano durante la República: Cuba detrás del telón*. Boulder, CO.

Nikoloutsos, K. P. (2012a), "Introduction," in K. P. Nikoloutsos ed., *Reception of Greek and Roman Drama in Latin America*. Special Issue of *Romance Quarterly* 59.1, 1–5.

Nikoloutsos, K. P. (2012b), "Seneca in Cuba: Gender, Race, and the Revolution in José Triana's *Medea en el espejo*," in K. P. Nikoloutsos ed., *Reception of Greek and Roman Drama in Latin America*. Special issue of *Romance Quarterly* 59.1, 19–35.

O'Higgins, D. M. (1997), "Medea as Muse: Pindar's *Pythian 4*," in J. J. Clauss and S. Iles Johnston eds., *Medea: Essays on Medea in Myth, Literature, Philosophy, and Art*. Princeton, 103–26.

Pappademos, M. (2011), *Black Political Activism and the Cuban Republic*. Chapel Hill, NC.

Pérez Asensio, M. (2009), *El mito en el teatro cubano contemporáneo*. Diss. University of Málaga <http://interclassica.um.es/investigacion/tesis/el_mito_en_el_teatro_cubano_contemporaneo/(ver)/1> accessed July 15, 2010.

Piñera, V. (1960), *Teatro completo*. Havana.

Piñera, V. (1967), "Notas sobre el teatro cubano," *Unión* 6.2, 130–43.

Pociña, A. (2002), "Tres dramatizaciones del tema de Medea en siglo de oro español: Lope de Vega, Calderón de la Barca y Rojas Zorrilla," in A. López and A. Pociña eds., *Medeas: versiones de un mito desde Grecia hasta hoy*. Granada, 751–77.

Pociña, A. (2006), "Motivos del éxito de un mito clásico en el siglo XX: el ejemplo de Medea," in J. V. Bañuls, F. De Martino, and C. Morenilla eds., *El teatro greco-latino y su recepción en la tradición occidental*. Bari, 515–32.

Rivero, Y. M. (2007), "Broadcasting Modernity: Cuban Television, 1950–1953," *Cinema Journal* 46.3, 3–25.

Salvat, R. (2007), "José Triana: An Interview by Ricard Salvat. Introduction and Translation by Joanne Pottlitzer," *TDR: The Drama Review* 51.2, 94–118.

Sawyer, M. Q. (2006), *Racial Politics in Post-Revolutionary Cuba*. Cambridge.

Séchan, L. (1927), "La Légende de Médée," *Revue des études grecques* 40, 234–310.

Sourvinou-Inwood, C. (1997), "Medea at a Shifting Distance: Images and Euripidean Tragedy," in J. J. Clauss and S. Iles Johnston eds., *Medea: Essays on Medea in Myth, Literature, Philosophy, and Art*. Princeton, 253–96.

Straile-Costa, P. (2010), "Myth and Ritual in *The Hungry Woman: A Mexican Medea*: Cherríe Moraga's Xicana-Indígena Interpretation of Euripides' *Medea*," in H. Bartel and A. Simon eds., *Unbinding Medea: Interdisciplinary Approaches to a Classical Myth from Antiquity to the 21st Century*. Oxford, 209–23.

Taylor, D. (1991), *Theatre of Crisis: Drama and Politics in Latin America*. Lexington, KY.

Taylor, D. (2008), "*Night of the Assassins* (José Triana)," in D. Taylor and S. J. Townsend eds., *Stages of Conflict: A Critical Anthology of Latin American Theater and Performance*. Ann Arbor, 196–9.

Taylor, D. and S. J. Townsend (eds. 2008), *Stages of Conflict: A Critical Anthology of Latin American Theater and Performance*. Ann Arbor.

Thomas, S. (2008), *Cuban Zarzuela: Performing Race and Gender on Havana's Lyric Stage*. Urbana and Chicago.

Thompson, E. A. (1944), "Neophron and Euripides' *Medea*," *Classical Quarterly* 38.1–2, 10–14.

Townsend, S. J. (2008), "Cuba: *Electra Garrigó* (Virgilio Piñera)," in D. Taylor and S. J. Townsend eds., *Stages of Conflict: A Critical Anthology of Latin American Theater and Performance*. Ann Arbor, 173–9.

Triana, J. (1991), *Medea en el espejo, La noche de los asesinos, Palabras comunes*. Madrid.

Vasserot, C. (1995), "Entrevista con José Triana," *Latin American Theater Review* 29.1, 119–29.

Wygant, A. (2007), *Medea, Magic, and Modernity in France: Stages and Histories, 1553–1797*. Burlington, VT.

PART V

CREATIVE COLLISIONS (1948–1968)

CHAPTER 21

REVOLUTIONIZING GREEK TRAGEDY IN CUBA
Virgilio Piñera's Electra Garrigó

ROSA ANDÚJAR

From its first performance in 1948, *Electra Garrigó* fundamentally altered both the course and the face of modern Cuban theater. Though inspired by Sophocles' *Electra*, Virgilio Piñera (1912–79) experiments with the myth of Electra and Orestes' return with an almost Euripidean flair: his version uniquely features an Agamemnon who is still alive and living with his family years after his return from Troy. Unlike other modern adaptations that expand and elaborate upon various aspects of the *Electra* plays (along with the *Oresteia*) as they are transplanted to a different location and context, Piñera's *Electra Garrigó* is the only version, ancient or modern, that not only depicts the entire nuclear family interacting in the same dramatic space but also stages the deaths of both Agamemnon and Clytemnestra in the course of its action.[1]

Despite featuring a classical cast of characters in a new configuration, the play nevertheless displays a distinctive Cuban stamp: Aegisthus kills Agamemnon in a ritual that mimics a cockfight, Orestes poisons Clytemnestra with a papaya, and a lone peasant acts as chorus while singing to the tune of the popular "Guantanamera." Throughout all characters are referred to by both their first name and Cuban surname, e.g., Orestes Garrigó and Clytemnestra Pla. At its debut, this act of "Cubanizing" and reconfiguring Sophocles' *Electra* (as well as Aeschylus' *Oresteia*) scandalized the viewing audience which consisted of important Cuban theater critics and directors, many of whom walked out of the performance, one supposedly shouting that the play was "a gob of spit aimed at Olympus" ("un escupitajo al Olimpo").[2] This animosity could be partly explained by the fact that prior to the debut of *Electra Garrigó*, Cuban theater aspired to be a "learned" stage, featuring—and fashioning itself after—predominantly European models.[3] This "serious" theater was kept entirely separate from other more popular forms, typically humorous and melodramatic types descending from *bufo* theater, a native comic genre populated by stock figures.[4] By uniting these two strands, previously seen as irreconcilable, in a play that appropriated and visibly reconfigured ancient Greek tragedy, Piñera modernized Cuban theater.[5]

This chapter examines this provocative play, in which Piñera went beyond transplanting (or "Cubanizing") the myth and inserting local elements into a "classical" play.[6] Instead, Piñera fuses the Cuban and classical in a play that simultaneously adopts (and adapts) the choral structure of Greek tragedy while parodying—and arguably desacralizing—Greek mythical figures through *choteo*, a distinct form of Cuban humor. This crossing of popular and classical creates an original mix of genres that ultimately works to unsettle the tragic original: *Electra Garrigó* blends tragedy, comedy, farce, and melodrama, as well as strands of the absurd nearly a decade before Beckett's *Waiting for Godot* and Ionesco's *The Bald Soprano*.[7] Furthermore, in a play that unsettles the myth of Orestes' return by featuring a living Agamemnon and an Orestes who never left Argos, Piñera contests the function and the purpose of one of Greek drama's most depicted families. With *Electra Garrigó* Piñera thus revolutionized Cuban theater by challenging the notion and relevance of a "classic" through the very structures and characters that defined the ancient Greek tragic form. Moreover, his engagement with the House of Atreus stands out in Latin American theater, which has tended to find mythical figures of resistance such as Antigone more palatable and more relevant to its stage.[8]

In this chapter I first outline the ways in which Piñera unsettled a "classic": the innovations that he made to the myth of the House of Atreus which set his play apart from other Electra adaptations. As I argue, *Electra Garrigó* self-consciously performs its difference from the Greek original through a series of provocative scenes that deconstruct ancient characters and conventions. Given that Piñera's version famously features Greek heroes in short sleeves (specifically, in the distinctive *Guayabera*) and wielding poisonous tropical fruit, I then examine the local Cuban elements that Piñera inserted into this classical play in order to interrogate the repeated claim that he "Cubanized" Greek drama (e.g., Aguilú de Murphy 1989: 25; Carrió Mendía 1990: 876; Cervera Salinas 1995: 152; Espinosa Domínguez 1989: 80; Pérez León 2002: 118). Finally, I discuss the play's crucial significance for Cuban theatrical and political history. Though reviled in its initial performance, this play, which depicts a young generation that engineers the death of its parents, was upheld as a powerful symbol of the Revolution led by Fidel Castro and consciously re-performed in the Revolution's aftermath as being emblematic of the transformed nation. Given *Electra Garrigó*'s success as a "revolutionary" play, Piñera also inspired other young Cuban writers to use Greek tragedy as a vehicle for dramatizing contemporary Cuban life: José Triana (*Medea en el espejo*, 1960) and Antón Arrufat (*Los siete contra Tebas*, 1968) are two prominent examples (see Nikoloutsos and Torrance, both this volume, on Triana and Arrufat respectively). Despite these multiple and varied acts of "revolution," *Electra Garrigó* has long been excluded from accounts of the influence of classical writings in the modern world, and specifically those dealing with the vibrant and diverse afterlife of Greek drama. In this chapter I also aim to correct this unfortunate omission by illustrating that *Electra Garrigó* is one of the most innovative modern engagements with ancient Greek literature. As one scholar writes, had

Piñera been based in Paris in the 1940s, his play might have been "a staple of the college literary reading lists" (West 1997: 55).

Unsettling a Classic

At the outset *Electra Garrigó* gives the impression of being just another Electra adaptation: the first act opens with a young woman dressed in black who steps forward out of her palatial home ostensibly in order to narrate her misfortunes. The opening choral song preceding her entrance had also announced that this would be the case: "Electra, now in mournful tones, tells this house's tale of woe."[9] However, these expectations are immediately subverted as a robust 60-year-old Agamemnon enters the stage, interrupting the complaints of his daughter. The presence of the Greek leader, which reveals that the nuclear family is still intact, demonstrates that Piñera's play is not a mere recapitulation of the mythological stories first dramatized by Aeschylus, but rather a radical departure which creates new roles for Agamemnon and his family and demands new responses from the audience. *Electra Garrigó* thus opens with an act of defiance: in one fell swoop Piñera up-ends the myth of Orestes, which is no longer a story of revenge and homecoming, and robs the family of their tragic stature. Piñera's Electra, for example, is fundamentally denied her characteristic role as a mourning daughter. Since Orestes never left, there is no longer a need for the recognition scene that underpins all Electra plays. Piñera's innovations therefore deny the three salient elements that, according to Froma Zeitlin, constitute "the irreducible minimum that characterizes the Orestes–Electra plot": return (*nostos*), recognition (*anagnorisis*), and intrigue (*mechanêma*) (Zeitlin 2012: 361). This act of dislocation is a self-conscious one, as I show, as Piñera forces his audience to witness what happens when familiar characters are removed from their tragic element. *Electra Garrigó* can be thus described as an elaborate experiment with Greek tragedy, in which Piñera tests the possibilities of classical characters and tragic conventions.

Whereas the spectre of Agamemnon's catastrophic death dominates and steers the action of many "Electra" plays from *Choephoroi* to *Mourning Becomes Electra*, his living presence in Piñera's tragedy serves to unsettle. The play's second act uniquely features a drunken Agamemnon who, for the first time in dramatic history, faces and openly accuses his wife. The stage directions set a very specific scene implying Agamemnon's loss of purpose and heroism: "Agamemnon enters, wearing bed sheets and a washbasin to imitate the garments and helmet of a Greek leader. He's drunk, but behaves with dignity" (186). Throughout, Piñera oscillates between the absurd and the dignified:

AGAMEMNON: You've cuckolded me, Clytemnestra Pla.
AEGISTHUS: (*Terrified, but pretending not to be*) And who has Clytemnestra left you for, brave Agamemnon?

> AGAMEMNON: (*Poking his forefinger into AEGISTHUS's chest*) You, Aegisthus! I know you're sleeping with Clytemnestra, my wife, daughter of Tyndareos and Leda, wife of Agamemnon, mother of Electra and Orestes, Iphigenia and Chrysothemis.
> CLYTEMNESTRA: Don't offend us, Agamemnon Garrigó. But we forgive you because you're drunk. I am the forever chaste Clytemnestra Pla.
> AGAMEMNON: You have a terrible sense of humor, Clytemnestra Pla. Will you never see me as Agamemnon, King of Mycenae and Argos, from the House of Atreus, brother of Menelaus, leader of the Greeks, who sacrificed Iphigenia? (*Long pause. He looks upwards*). I wanted to lead a vaguely heroic life, but I'm only well fed and middle class. (*Pleading*) Tell me, I beg you, tell me. What is my tragedy? Because I must have a tragedy like all human beings, a tragedy to fulfill, but it escapes me!
> AEGISTHUS: (*Sarcastic*) Beer has given him epic dimensions. (*To AGAMEMNON*) You don't have any tragedy to fulfill. You're a happy father who amuses himself by improvising pleasant comedies, a father who is so merry that he dresses up in sheets and washbasins... (*Slapping him on the back*) Go on, Agamemnon of Cuba! Go on, have some more beer! Maybe that will help you decipher the secret of your life.
> AGAMEMNON: (*Backing away majestically*) A tragedy! I'm living through a tragedy and I don't know what it is... I'm living through a tragedy; would anyone care to tell me what it is? (187)

In this scene, Piñera insists on a contradictory image of Agamemnon, one that is at the same time both majestic and ridiculous. His epic utterances, which are coupled with his "dignified" and "majestic" behavior (as outlined by the stage directions), stand in stark contrast to his ludicrous appearance. In presenting Agamemnon as a silly drunk who dresses up as a hero while talking and behaving like one, Piñera effectively marries silliness and nobility and treads the fine line between them. By pushing Agamemnon's death into the dramatic time of Electra and Orestes, Piñera furthermore casts the interesting conundrum of "tragic overliving" over the *Oresteia*, which, as Emily Wilson points out, is of central concern to plays such as Sophocles' *Oedipus Rex* and Euripides' *Heracles* (Wilson 2004). Like Oedipus in Euripides' *Phoenician Women* and Sophocles' *Oedipus at Colonus*, Piñera's Agamemnon is now imagined interacting with his adult children. By not dying, the now well-fed and middle-class Greek leader has moreover missed the chance to have a neat structure and purpose to his life. Rudderless, he is instead forced to carry out mundane activities like confronting his cheating wife and her lover. Throughout *Electra Garrigó* Piñera unsettles his viewers by exposing them to multiple paradoxes. This is certainly the case in this scene, which encapsulates the brilliance and complexity of Piñera's theater in its depiction of a ridiculous but still noble Agamemnon who plays at being a hero with the most mundane of objects. Is a drunk, still living, and continually cuckolded Agamemnon a figure of pity or mockery? The viewer is as clueless as Piñera's Agamemnon.

Piñera's Orestes is similarly denied his tragic role. Orestes Garrigó continually dreams of the day he can leave his family's home. The verb *partir* (to leave), which is explicitly associated with Orestes throughout the play (Montes Huidobro 2004: 448). takes on a particular urgency in the play's latter half:

> ORESTES: So the idea is to leave. But how? (190)
> CLYTEMNESTRA: You will not leave.

ORESTES: *(pretending)* No one's talking about leaving, Clytemnestra Pla. (190)
ORESTES: Here's what it boils down to: me, Clytemnestra, the columns, my departure... I have to destroy that part of myself that resists, and once I've done that, have to achieve the other goal, that is eliminate Clytemnestra Pla. And then immediately tear down the columns, and then, and then only, leave. (192)

At the end of the play, Electra will furthermore point out the direction of freedom to Orestes by saying: "Leave! (*She points to the door that is closed.*) Here is the door of your departure. (*Takes ORESTES to the door*). It's always good to leave... (*Opens the door and a bright light enters*) Go ahead! (*With tragic joy*) Leave, Orestes, leave! (195)." Though some critics have argued that Orestes' desire to leave Cuba expresses a common feeling among young people at the time (Montes Huidobro 1973: 141), the explicit association of Orestes with parting is, in dramatic terms, an announcement of his now superfluous role in Piñera's reconceived tragedy. Piñera denies Orestes' fundamental role in the myth, as a young man who returns and accomplishes a great deed worthy of praise. No longer can he be upheld as a victorious model to be emulated by other young men, as he had in the *Odyssey* or in Pindar's eleventh *Pythian*. Lacking any purpose, Orestes flounders in the play and can only dream of his exit.

With Electra, however, Piñera demonstrates the full extent to which he can unsettle an established tragic character. His Electra Garrigó is robbed of her characteristic grief which has served as her primary distinguishing mark since antiquity.[10] Electra, no longer allowed the mourning role that typically defines her, has now become the ultimate symbol of self-awareness and theatricality. Above all, Piñera's Electra is a performer. In the beginning of the second act, after Electra delivers a long monologue, Piñera stages the reactions of Aegisthus and Clytemnestra who praise her for her impressive theatrical skills:

AEGISTHUS: Have you finished yet, Electra?... Next time it'll sound better. (*To CLYTEMNESTRA*) She'd be a great actress.
CLYTEMNESTRA: (*Taking ELECTRA's chin in her hand*) She's already a great actress. She lives to act. I'm sure she feels nothing. What she shows us is a plaster mask. (186)

Contrary to all other Electras who are defined in terms of her relationship to her brother or father, this Electra is indeed devoid of her characteristic sisterly and filial duty, and indeed of all passion, described as being "hardened as a diamond" (180) and "cold" (189). Instead, Piñera's Electra is a mask, the mistress of ceremonies who controls and guides what will happen. It is she who persuades Clytemnestra and Aegisthus to kill her father, goads Orestes to kill their mother, and convinces Orestes to leave, without suffering any consequence. At the end of the play we see her alone, bragging of her success: "and the Furies? I don't see them, they haven't come... No, there are no Furies, there's no remorse" (195). Instead as Clytemnestra had feared ("Here everything is Electra. The color is Electra, the sound, Electra, hate, Electra, the day, Electra, the night, Electra, revenge, Electra... Electra, Electra, Electra, Electra!," 193) everything that remains is indeed "Electra": the play's final words equate the murmur, noise, and thunder to her ("El rumor Electra, el ruido Electra, el trueno Electra, el trueno Electra,"

195).[11] Twentieth-century Electras usually seethe with violence, rage, and aggression.[12] Like Euripides, who denies Electra her chief traditional attribute of being unmarried (ἄλεκτρος), Piñera thus fundamentally diverges from tradition by creating a "cold" and emotionless Electra.

Electra's purely theatrical role and lack of emotion also reveal a fundamental difference between *Electra Garrigó* and other twentieth-century adaptations staged in the aftermath of psychoanalysis. Strauss's *Elektra* and O'Neill's *Mourning Becomes Electra*, which engage with Freudian ideas, are dominated by "three central and recurring tropes: hysteria, death, and mourning" (Scott 2005: 2). In many of these adaptations Electra exhibits various psychological disorders as she wavers between hysteria and melancholia. Instead, the hysteria typically associated with Electra is now transferred to her parents, whose incestuous love for the child of the opposite sex borders on the ludicrous. Clytemnestra describes Orestes as her possession:

> My beloved Orestes will have whatever he wants, he need only ask. Except for one thing: he's to be eternally celibate! He belongs to me. I don't want him to leave, I don't want any woman to enjoy him. I'll be the one he adores, the one to whom he offers sacrifices—bloody or not! (188)

Similarly, Agamemnon openly expresses his passion for his daughter whenever confronted with the idea of her fiancé: "I love you too much to lose you, Electra Garrigó" (181). Both Clytemnestra and Agamemnon see the other child as a threat, and each plots for his daughter or son to be removed: Clytemnestra actively arranges for Electra's marriage while Agamemnon pushes Orestes to pursue a journey to distant lands. Clytemnestra's extreme love for Orestes transforms her into a hysteric, who actively and continually imagines the death of her son, at which prospect she promptly dissolves into tears.[13] Throughout the play Piñera inverts both the "Electra" and "Oedipal" complexes, which are now projected onto the parents.

Despite these innovations that advertise the play's difference from the original, *Electra Garrigó* could also be seen an attempt to revitalize the traditional structures of Greek tragedy, particularly the chorus. Piñera's adaptation features a singing chorus, which sings décimas, a ballad form of ten-line octosyllabic stanzas. With its songs, the chorus opens each of the three acts of the play, and closes the first and second acts. Like its Athenian predecessor, the chorus introduces the action and theme of the tragedy and comments on the play's happenings, serving as a crucial link between audience and stage. Piñera's chorus also intervenes during critical junctures in the plot, such as the middle of the second and third acts, immediately preceding the deaths of Agamemnon and Clytemnestra. Thus although Piñera's play is divided into three formal acts that are more typical of comedies, the eight choral interventions divide the play's action into six episodes, making Piñera's tragedy appear in its structure more like its ancient Athenian precursor.

While acutely aware of the structures and conventions that govern ancient plays, Piñera is also sensitive to the disruptions that his alterations now present to the myth and tragedy. The first act, which stages an extended interaction between the now reunited family, ends with a self-conscious discussion of the place of destiny that had motivated other Electra plays:

> AGAMEMNON: Destiny, oh destiny!
> ORESTES: Perhaps I'm destiny?
> CLYTEMNESTRA: No, no, no, you're not!
> ELECTRA: Yes, yes, yes, you are!
> AGAMEMNON: Destiny, oh destiny!
> ORESTES: Who will make me leave?
> CLYTEMNESTRA: No one! Destiny doesn't want it.
> ELECTRA: Then you will die, Clytemnestra Pla.
> AGAMEMNON: Destiny, oh destiny!
> ORESTES: Will Clytemnestra Pla die?
> CLYTEMNESTRA: Will Agamemnon Garrigó die?
> ELECTRA: Will Agamemnon Garrigó die?
> AGAMEMNON: Destiny, oh destiny!
> ORESTES: Will Agamemnon Garrigó die?
> CLYTEMNESTRA: Will Agamemnon Garrigó die?
> ELECTRA: Agamemnon Garrigó will die.
> AGAMEMNON: Destiny, oh destiny! (185)

This scene, which closes the first act, raises fundamental questions about the place of fate and destiny in a play that is no longer a tale of retribution and revenge: what is tragic destiny? Is it fulfilled by the close of this innovative play, which also ends with Agamemnon and Clytemnestra both dead? And is their murder now devoid of meaning and purpose? These questions are meant to challenge—and perhaps even needle—the audience, especially those claiming to possess an intimate knowledge of the source text.

"Cubanizing" Greek Tragedy?

By presenting a new conception of ancient characters and chorus, *Electra Garrigó* revolutionizes the Greek myth in fundamental ways. *Electra Garrigó* is also revolutionary in another sense: this is a play that is closely intertwined with Cuba's recent and tumultuous history. At the dawn of the twentieth century Cuba emerged as a new nation, recently freed from Spanish rule, but one that came increasingly under the direct influence of the United States. In the 1930s Cuban students and intellectuals, Piñera included, attempted to fight the rising authoritarianism of the first Cuban "presidents" who were visibly in the pocket of American business interests.[14] Despite their efforts, the end of their failed uprising saw another dictatorial figure in power, Fulgencio Batista. At the same time as Piñera dared to caricature one of the greatest ancient Greek tragic families by depicting them as bourgeois Cubans (*Electra Garrigó* was written in 1941, though performed for the first time seven years later), the political system in Cuba, fraught with corruption and nepotism, could be described as "a parody of Athenian democracy" (Townsend 2008: 175). The 1940s were a time of social and political unrest, generating a general sense of disillusionment. Piñera's theatrical depiction of a younger generation that engineers the death of its oppressive and corrupt parents is thus rooted in a particular fraught time and place.

The sights and sounds of 1940s Cuba permeate the play. The chorus which structures Piñera's tragedy (in the same manner as its ancient predecessor) is very much a Cuban one: the décimas it employs were the same ones that filled Cuban radio at the time with passionate stories of crime and romance.[15] Thus though it structures and comments on various scenes, Piñera's chorus is also crucially broadcasting in the sung vernacular mode most readily available to the Cuban masses.[16] The costumes were furthermore bright and suited to the typically hot weather of the island: the men are in short sleeves, with Aegisthus wearing the fashionable white *Guayabera*, and the actor who sings the choral parts wears the white robe of peasants (*guajiros*) (Espinosa Domínguez 2003: 153–4). Moreover, some characters embody Cuban stereotypes: Aegisthus and Orestes, for example, stand at the two extremes of conceptions of Cuban masculinity, one a swaggering aggressive male and the other a cowardly momma's boy.[17] Similarly, Piñera's Clytemnestra proudly advertises her distinct Cuban sensuality: "while that Clytemnestra doesn't move, look at this one who moves and circulates like a menacing draft of air" (184).[18] Even the stage is "Cubanized": it calls for a façade of neoclassical colonial architecture much like that found in the old colonial homes in Havana. From its outset, *Electra Garrigó* is audibly and visibly a Cuban play.

Focusing on these elements, critics have emphasized that with *Electra Garrigó* Piñera "Cubanizes" Greek drama: one of the foremost critics of Cuban theater, for example, writes that "Piñera offers us . . . a beautiful, fascinating and colourful Cuban spectacle."[19] The play, however, is not a simple act of transference, despite the fact that Agamemnon and his clan are now imagined as a bourgeois Cuban family in the 1940s. In his various writings about Cuban theater and the significance of *Electra Garrigó*, Piñera himself is conscious of this interpretative possibility. This we can see most prominently in the program notes to the first performance of the play:

> *Electra Garrigó* springs, naturally, from Sophocles' drama. Now, it is not, by any means, another version of said drama, as, for example, occurs in the trilogy of O'Neill *Mourning Becomes Electra*. What has been used in *Electra Garrigo* from the [Sophoclean] tragedy are "characters" and "atmosphere": the former caricatured and the latter parodied. That is to say that *Electra Garrigó* is not yet another attempt to produce neoclassicism or to update the conflicts of a Greek family from the 5th century BC . . . rather it exposes and develops a typical drama [that is pertinent to] yesterday's and today's Cuban family. I am referring to the conflict produced by the sentimental dictatorship of parents over their children. (Espinosa Domínguez 2003: 150)

In defending his choice of working with a canonical Greek tragedy and its characters, he notes that his aim is to stage the problems of modern family life in Cuba. In the rest of these program notes, Piñera continues to discuss his characters in terms of their familial roles: Agamemnon, for example, is a "father of honourable honour" who "loves his daughter with excessive force," whereas Electra must be reassured that Orestes is "worthy of being her brother, and not simply the spoiled and effeminate child of Clytemnestra" (Espinosa Domínguez 2003: 150, 152). By stripping his play of the revenge and retribution that lies at the heart of the *Oresteia* and all Electra plays, Piñera has reduced the play to the familial and domestic relationships that exist between the characters. *Electra Garrigó* thus places an intense spotlight on the family, an institution which lies at the heart of Cuban society and culture. In other words, instead of simply "Cubanizing" Greek drama, Piñera chooses to dramatize Cuban life through a reconstruction of Greek myth and tragedy.

To dramatize Cuban life while using the markers of a serious and established theatrical tradition was then an unprecedented and extraordinary move. The early 1940s were a critical time for Cuban theater, a time when the most important theatrical organizations were established in the country, such as the Academy of Dramatic Arts (Academia de Artes Dramáticas) in 1940, the University Theater (Teatro Universitario) in 1941, and the Theater Council (Patronato del Teatro) and Popular Theater (Teatro Popular) in 1942.[20] All of these featured an international repertoire, mostly European and North American plays,[21] except for the University Theater which focused on theater "classics," mostly Greek tragedies.[22] The works of Cuban playwrights were hardly ever staged and were generally kept separate from the foreign models which were considered emblems of "high culture."[23]

Initially Piñera wanted the Academy of the Dramatic Arts to produce *Electra Garrigó*, but according to Francisco Morín, who eventually directed the play in 1948, 1958, and 1960, they did not like it because it "was too strange," citing the fact that the play featured a pedagogue with a horse's tail.[24] Piñera himself recalls that he had also approached one of the founders of the University Theater, Austrian émigré Ludwig Schajowicz:

> He read the play, told me that he had liked it, but would not put it on. I sincerely don't believe that he was scared by the papaya, the roosters and the Guantanamera... but perhaps he thought of the objections which might be raised by the university authorities, who were, incidentally, happily content to see his productions of Sophocles, Aeschylus and Euripides, but not so happy if they were to see Agamemnon in disguise wearing a sheet and a washbasin.[25]

To insist that the Garrigó family deserved to share the same theatrical space as many European and North American "greats" was in itself a revolutionary act that challenged the concept of "serious theater" for literary-minded Cubans at the time.

The specific examples recalled here as objections to the play, such as Agamemnon disguised with a sheet and a washbasin, also reveal another problem posed by Piñera's adaptation, that of parody. Piñera had openly admitted his intent to caricature in the program notes when he commented on his use of ancient tragedy's characters and atmosphere (Espinosa Domínguez 2003: 150). This parodic element can be seen at various points in the play, most notably in the scene above when Aegisthus points out that "beer has given Agamemnon epic dimensions" (187) or when Clytemnestra imagines Orestes' death in what could be seen as specifically Cuban ways: "Orestes exposed to the wind, Orestes at the mercy of the waves, Orestes lashed by a hurricane, Orestes bitten by mosquitoes" (182). With *Electra Garrigó* Piñera presents what is at times a comic version of one of the most represented Greek families in western theatrical history. Yet Piñera's intent is neither to mock nor to present these characters as objects of scorn. Rather, he exposes the play and its characters to a deep-seated part of Cuban culture: el *choteo*, the act of caricaturing or parodying what is sacred or authoritative.[26] To insert *choteo* into the Electra myth was not only a crucial part of creating a convincing portrayal of Agamemnon and his family as Cubans, but it also aided in the creation of a modern Cuban theater. Decades later, when director Francisco Morín was asked to define "Cuban" tragedy in an interview, he immediately declares, "a Cuban tragedy is a great *choteo*!" ("una tragedia cubana es un gran choteo!") (Montes Huidobro 2004: 432). By incorporating the native *choteo* into serious theater, Piñera initiates a revolutionary theatrical movement in Cuba, resulting in plays in which humor and parody appear alongside the somber.[27]

This fusion generates a vibrant dramatic hybrid that integrates both vernacular and "classical" theatrical traditions, which had been until then kept separate. Throughout *Electra Garrigó* Piñera's language has epic, formal, and Cuban elements coexisting with one another: the play features the Cuban counting rhyme "tin marín de dos pingüe, cúcara mácara titirí fué" (rendered in translation as "eeny meeny miney mo," 184) alongside Greek epithets and the formal "vosotros," which is virtually nonexistent in Latin American Spanish. As he transforms the play into a new mixture, Piñera once again retains and emphasizes aspects of the original: the death of Agamemnon (repeatedly referred to as "this old rooster") continues to be portrayed as a corrupt sacrifice as in Aeschylus' eponymous play (Zeitlin 1965), but this time crucially in the context of a ritual recreation of sacrifice of a rooster, which evokes the rites of Santería and other Afro-Cuban religions that were marginalized at the time. Rather than restating that Piñera "Cubanized" Greek drama, we should instead address *Electra Garrigó*'s unique combinations and refigurations of the Hellenic and Cuban.

In the preface to the 1960 edition of his then *Complete Theater*, Piñera discusses the pitfalls that a modern author who attempts to work with Greek tragedy potentially faces. He not only demonstrates a nuanced understanding of the issues relating to the adaptation of classical works, but he also directly addresses the notion of "Cubanizing" Greek tragedy:

> When I was attacked by the "Greek bug" (this Greek bug continues to carry out its function as the required violin in the grand orchestra of Western dramaturgy: Hofmannsthal, O'Neill, Racine, Shakespeare and the rest), that is to say, when I felt tempted by the heroes of Greek tragedy, it seemed to me that the end result would be soporific if I limited myself to presenting them on stage more or less masked with the clothing and the thoughts of our era . . . To me it made no sense at all to repeat Sophocles or Euripides from beginning to end. And I say from beginning to end because the modern author who attempts to handle the tragic Greeks, even if he does not wish it, is inevitably forced to repeat them to a certain degree. Well, I told myself, Electra, Agamemnon and Clytemnestra will have to continue to

be themselves. It was two thousand years ago that they were created by authors who knew their people very well. But I also told myself: speaking of the people, that is to say, of my people, would it not be possible to Cubanize them? But, to Cubanize them externally, that is, in terms of clothing, symbols, and language? Such a contribution would not be a negative one; however, it would not resolve the legitimacy and the justification of my tragedy. So that Electra would not fall into absolute repetition, so that the public would not fall asleep, I had to find the element, the imponderable, that, as it is said in theater speak, "would knock the viewer out of his glasses". And what is that said imponderable? Here we touch on precisely the nature of the Cuban. In my understanding the Cuban defines itself through a systematic rupture with seriousness. (Piñera 1960: 9)

In Piñera's view, adapting a Greek tragedy in the modern age involves varying degrees of repetition. "Absolute repetition," besides boring the modern public, is a form of imitation that erases the agency of the adapter, who merely reproduces the ancient for the modern. Even a simple exercise of changing the externals, such as "the clothing, symbols, and language," also condemns the new work to repetition, as it merely updates the original. Piñera rejects both these models, which to some degree rely on the belief that the original text is automatically relevant to a modern audience, and instead advocates a more radical mode of reception, that of "systematic rupture." He eschews this model of absolute repetition in favor of an alternative form of repetition, rupturing the seriousness of the original without compromising its tragic ambitions. This is what allows him to achieve the unstable combination of dignity and parody that we encountered in the spectacle of Agamemnon with a washbasin on his head. This notion of repetition through rupture enables him to incorporate the more intimate rhythms of Cuban life and personality into the Electra source text, creating a hybrid mix of genres that seeks not so much to abandon tragic seriousness as to change its audience's sense of what this seriousness might be. What Piñera accomplishes in *Electra Garrigó* is not just an exercise in cultural assimilation but rather a more sophisticated attempt to think through the multiple possibilities of tragic seriousness in the modern world.

From "Tasty Little Scandal" to Emblem of a New Nation

In January 1948 Ernesto Ardura of the Havana newspaper *El mundo* interviewed Piñera, who had recently returned from two years in Argentina. The article, entitled "The Tone of Cuban Life Today is Foolishness, Affirms Virgilio Piñera" ("El tono de la vida cubana de hoy es el disparate, afirma Virgilio Piñera"), outlines Piñera's broad disenchantment with Cuban economic, political, and social life (Anderson 2006: 61; Espinosa Domínguez 2003: 142–3). Many were aggravated by the sweeping claims of a man who had only been physically present in Cuba for a short time before openly denouncing his nation in a public interview (Anderson 2006: 61). Months before *Electra Garrigó* debuted on the Havana stage, Piñera had thus already broadcast himself as a polemicist and provocateur.

As we saw in the last section, the initial hostile reception to *Electra Garrigó* could in part be explained by the fact that Piñera radically broke with theatrical tradition, inserting comic and popular strands into serious classical theater in order to dramatize the problems of contemporary Cuban life. But it was also crucially affected by Piñera's antagonistic persona. The play premièred only a few months after his controversial comments on Cuban life, on October 23, 1948 in the Sala Valdés Rodríguez.[28] The play had all the ingredients of success: it was directed by Francisco Morín, who was then a prominent young director recently returned from studying in New York with the German director Erwin Piscator.[29] The cast was made up of young actors from the newly formed Prometheus collective;[30] the famous singer Radeúnda Lima acted as chorus, singing the décimas of the Guantanamera (Espinosa Domínguez 2003: 149, 154). Despite these attractions, the play was overwhelmed by the critics' strong and negative reaction to what was perceived to be an irreverent play by a dramaturge with malicious intent (Espinosa Domínguez 2003: 156). In a letter to friend and collaborator José Rodriguez Feo who was then living in the U.S.A., writer José Lezama Lima described the play's reception among critics: "the critics, bourgeois idiots, have been tremendously hostile towards him, which surely pleased him and made him dream of protests, hissing and carrots being thrown."[31] His comments crucially suggest that Piñera's aim was precisely this, to stir up "a tasty little scandal" ("un pequeño y sabroso escandalito") (Rodríguez Feo 1991: 130). Lezama's suppositions turned out to be eerily prophetic: incensed by all the criticism, Piñera wrote a biting response entitled "Beware of the Critic" ("Ojo con el crítico") that was published in the November issue of the theater journal *Prometeo*, in which he denounced *Electra Garrigó*'s critics as frustrated dramatists.[32] His scathing remarks in turn prompted an immediate and public response by the director of the country's most important group of theater and film-makers (Agrupación de Redactores Teatrales y Cinematográficos, or ARTYC), Luis Amado Blanco. Published widely in multiple Havana newspapers and journals on December 15, 1948, Blanco's article sealed the fate of Piñera, who now became like "a man infected with the plague" (Anderson 2006: 62–3). *Electra Garrigó* was as a result not staged again in Cuba for nearly ten years, during which time Piñera lived mostly in Argentina (Espinosa Domínguez 1989).

Though Piñera's provocations led to *Electra Garrigó*'s ban from the Cuban stage for a decade, the play gained new impetus and significance after the removal of Batista, as Cuba underwent major social and political changes with the rise of Fidel Castro. In the wake of the new Cuban Revolution, *Electra Garrigó* was performed several times as an example of the best Cuban theater had to offer: it was restaged at various theaters in Havana in 1958 and in 1960, broadcast on Cuban television in 1961 when the play was entered for the international *Casa de las Américas* literary prize (featuring Joseíto Fernández, the composer of the Guantanamera, as chorus) (Montes Huidobro 2002: 148), and staged again in 1964 as the official selection of the Union of Writers and Artists to commemorate the "World Theater Day" in Cuba.[33] The play seems to have been resurrected in February 1958 because it was seen as a "metaphorical call to end with the tyrant

Batista," and various reports mention the public's approving whistles and shouts when Clytemnestra tells Aegisthus to end with the "old rooster" (Matas 1989: 73). Though Piñera had flown back for the February performance, he did not return definitively from Argentina until November 1958, just a month before the rebel army headed by Fidel Castro made its victorious entrance to Havana.

Piñera's earlier transgressions were immediately forgotten in the aftermath of the Revolution's new social and cultural program. As a writer whose work had already prominently featured Cuban culture, he was especially valued. He was appointed as the editor of the weekly cultural magazine *Lunes de revolución*, Cuba's most important source for its intellectual life (Montes Huidobro 2002: 19–130). In addition to his role as editor of *Lunes*, in 1960 Piñera was also put in charge of Ediciones R, a publishing firm created by the new government, a post which he held until 1964.[34] These appointments not only further confirmed Piñera's worth to the young revolution but they also revealed the weight and importance that the state was now placing on cultural matters. On the first anniversary issue of *Lunes*, Fidel Castro commented on the crucial role that writers would play in the rebirth of their new nation:

> Culture in our country was until the triumph of the Revolution a privilege of the minority, a form of slavery and colonialism that twisted thinking, and kept the nation from the truth and a knowledge of itself . . . The Revolution initiates a double contract: the nation begins to discover culture and culture begins to discover the nation. By submerging themselves intensely in the problems, history, and life of our country, now transformed by the extraordinary impulse of its Revolution, young writers and artists will find new media for expression for the national culture. (Castro 1960: 196)

In an essay published in 1959, Piñera had similarly urged fellow writers to take advantage of the Revolution, as the cultural life of the nation was at stake:

> We are at this critical juncture in which an occlusion of our cultural life, however minor it may be, would put us at the risk of death. . . . If we do not take advantage of the occasion, or if we throw it away, we will turn our cultural clock back fifty years. (Anderson 2006: 91)

When Jean-Paul Sartre and Simone de Beauvoir visited Cuba in 1960 at the invitation of Carlos Franqui (the editor of Havana's most important newspaper who had previously directed "Rebel Radio" from the Sierra Maestra), Piñera and his *Electra* were part of their itinerary (Ammar 2011: 104–21). As soon as their Cubana Airlines plane landed, Piñera was there to welcome them, along with other Cuban luminaries such as Franqui, José Alvarez Baragaño, and Walterio Carbonell (Ammar 2011: 130). Piñera was present during Sartre's famous interview with Cuban writers and intellectuals, and asked him a few questions (Sartre 1960: 44). Sartre and de Beauvoir were also taken to see a production of *Electra Garrigó*. In a letter dated March 1, 1960 and addressed to his Argentine friend Humberto Rodríguez Tomeu, Piñera comments that Sartre was among the first to arrive, that he "clapped and shouted enthusiastically," and that he hoped to bring the play to Paris (Rodríguez Tomeu 1960). Though unfortunately this was not to be, the episode nevertheless illustrates Piñera's importance as a major figure of Cuban theater at the time, and in particular *Electra Garrigó*'s significance for a revolution that was still in progress. Its many re-performances in the early 1960s were a fundamental part of the narrative of a nation that was rebuilding itself and its canon. The play, which was formerly a call to arms for the new generation, now became a de facto symbol of Castro's new revolutionary era, one that had prophesied the changes to come with the new regime.

Despite this early recognition of Piñera's importance as a dramatist of the Revolution, he soon fell out of favor and *Electra Garrigó* ceased to be performed. On the night of October 11, 1961, Piñera was jailed in a government crackdown on prostitution and homosexuality (West 1997: 56). Though he was not sent to the notorious camps in which the new government imprisoned homosexuals, Piñera was soon ostracized (Quiroga 1995: 169–70). In 1964, when Ernesto "Ché" Guevara saw a volume of Virgilio Piñera's 1960 *Complete Theater* on a visit to a Cuban embassy in Algiers, he immediately threw the book against a wall, yelling, "how dare you have in our embassy a book by this foul faggot" (Morín 1998: 295; Quiroga 1995: 168). When Piñera died in 1979, it was in obscurity as an "ideologically suspect" writer that younger writers had to avoid (West 1997: 56).

Despite Piñera's marginalization in the final years of his life, *Electra Garrigó* once again jolted a languishing Cuban theater in the 1980s, when Piñera was reinstated as one of the country's most important literary figures. Multiple performances and adaptations suddenly proliferated: the dramatist Flora Lauten created a loose version in 1984 in which the Garrigó family were depicted as a troupe of circus performers; in 1987 Gustavo Herrera created a classical ballet adaptation of the play for the National Ballet of Cuba; a production of *Electra Garrigó* directed by Carlos Piñeiro was shown on television in 1989 (Machado Vento 2012; Townsend 2008: 178). The play's frequent ability to revolutionize the Cuban theatrical scene is remarkable, particularly given the fact that it is not an overtly political play like *City of Paradise*, a South African Electra adaptation which interrogated issues relating to revenge and retribution in the post-apartheid democracy (Steinmeyer 2007). The play's continued ability to assume new relevance in different contexts is partly a product of Piñera's own dramatic ambitions, which went beyond updating a Greek tragedy to a particular time and place. Instead, his *Electra Garrigó* is both a renewal of the Sophoclean version, and a probing experiment in what it means to renew.

Notes

1. See Brunel 1971 for a list of Electra adaptations from Voltaire's *Oreste* to László Gyurkó's *Szerelmem, Elektra*, which includes the twentieth-century adaptations that were known to Piñera, such as Hofmannsthal's *Elektra*, O'Neill's *Mourning Becomes Electra*, and Sartre's *Les Mouches*. On the potential influence of Sartre's play on Piñera, see Espinosa Domínguez 1989 and Piñera 1960: 15, where he claims that he wrote *Electra Garrigó* before Sartre's play

became available. For other important modern engagements with Electra see also Hall 1999 and Bakogianni 2011.
2. Leal 1988: 24. According to Morín (1998: 89) the play was considered disastrous by all critics, except for two: Matilde Muñoz of *El siglo* newspaper and Manolo Casal writing for the *Prometeo* magazine issue of November 1948. See Leal 2002: viii and Montes Huidobro 2004: 431 for Casal's favorable yet lukewarm review.
3. As Leal (1988: 17) summarizes, "the 'serious' and 'learned' authors plunged themselves into the history of others, foreign themes, to bourgeois sentimentalism and to the hypocritical superficiality, developing an artificial creation that had no resonances." All translations are my own, unless otherwise indicated.
4. See Moisés Pérez Coterillo's preface in Espinosa Domínguez 1992: 9. On *bufo* theater and its influence, see Leal 1982 and Versényi 1993: 67–9.
5. As Espinosa Domínguez (1992: 20) dramatically puts it, "Virgilio Piñera burst in on the Havana scene with the speed of a meteorite and the shaking force of an earthquake. His *Electra Garrigó* is in our theater a seminal and liberating piece, one that breaks with [the tradition of] salon comedies and lightweight dialogue." Some critics, such as Antón Arrufat (who later went on to write one of the other most famous Cuban adaptations of a Greek tragedy, a version of the *Seven Against Thebes* which evokes the American Bay of Pigs attack) and Rine Leal, go as far as calling *Electra Garrigó* the Cuban "battle of Hernani," referring to Victor Hugo's famous play whose debut was just as controversial and divisive; see Espinosa Domínguez 2003: 154–5 and Leal 2002: vii.
6. That Piñera "Cubanized" Greek tragedy with his *Electra* is a pervasive notion in scholarship on Cuban theater, and is a term continually invoked by Piñera scholars. This is partly due to the fact that Piñera himself employs the term in the preface to his 1960 *Complete Theater* when discussing *Electra Garrigó*; see Piñera 1960: 9. However, as I demonstrate in the section "Unsettling a Classic," he speaks of "Cubanizing" as a general tactic available to artists interested in adapting ancient plays for a modern audience.
7. On the play's absurd strands, see Aguilú de Murphy 1989 and Lobato Morchón 2002.
8. There are few Electra adaptations in Latin America, besides *Electra Garrigó*. In Brazil, Nelson Rodrigues's *Senhora dos afogados* (1947) deals with the myth, but the work was originally inspired by O'Neill's *Mourning Becomes Electra*. In Ecuador, Electra as a Freudian concept appears on stage in Ricardo Descalzi del Castillo's *Clamor de sombras* (1951), a psychological drama about the Oedipus and Electra complexes. A series of Electra plays were staged in Argentina, but unfortunately the texts of many of these are difficult to find: these include Omar del Carlo's *Electra al amanecer* (1948), David Cureses's *Una cruz para Electra* (1957), Julio Imbert's *Electra* (1961), Sergio De Cecco's *El reñidero* (1962), Ricardo Monti's *La oscuridad de la razón* (1993), and Roberto González's *La declaración de Electra* (1994). In contrast, there are countless Latin American Antígonas, most famously among them Leopoldo Marechal's *Antígona Vélez* (Argentina, 1950), Jorge Andrade's *Pedreira das Almas* (Brazil, 1958), Luis Rafael Sánchez's *La Pasión según Antígona Pérez* (Puerto Rico, 1968) Griselda Gambaro's *Antígona furiosa* (Argentina, 1986), José Watanabe's *Antígona* (Peru, 2000). On Antigone as a unique Argentine tradition, see Fradinger 2011.
9. Piñera 2008: 180. All quotations from *Electra Garrigó* are from Margaret Carson's translation, which is reprinted in Taylor and Townsend 2008 and listed in the References as Piñera 2008.
10. This is a grief which has crucially also served as a model for inspiration for ancient and modern actors, such as Polus, who according to Aulus Gellius 6.5 channeled the authentic

grief that he felt for the death of his son into his performance of Electra for a production of Sophocles' play.
11. As Montes Huidobro (2004: 454) writes, she is a "monster who swallows everything up."
12. Scott 2005: 7: "The twentieth century embraced [Electra's] capacity for cruelty and her naked pain, perhaps in an effort to come to terms with the appalling violence in the world around us."
13. For example: "(*Wrings her hands hysterically*) Ah, Orestes, don't cross the street!" (182); "I would die of sadness, dear Orestes... My frenzy would be so strong, that I'd search desperately in the neighborhood for movies about a mother who dies because her child has left!" (183); and "Anything is possible to a mother who faces the threat of losing her only son. (*Crying and ridiculous*) Yes, who faces the threat of losing you, Orestes, oh, Orestes!" (183).
14. As a young man Piñera had been detained several times for taking part in the uprisings opposing the corruption of President Gerardo Machado; see Anderson 2006: 20–1.
15. The form had been made popular by Joseíto Fernández in the radio program *The Happening of the Day* (*El suceso del día*) which recounted a bloody or scandalous deed. Pérez-Galdós Ortiz (2000: 40–3) reports that it was widely referred to as "the Guantanamera show."
16. Montes Huidobro (1973: 144) argues that the décima was especially suited for ancient tragedy: "Just like the dramatic function of the Greek chorus, the native décima anticipates and comments."
17. Barreda 1985: 123. Aegisthus is first described as "forty years old, very handsome and strong, he's dressed in white, like a Cuban pimp" (181). See above on Orestes' lack of purpose.
18. On the sexual dynamics of the play, see Montes Huidobro 2004.
19. Montes Huidobro 1973: 140, who quotes his own review of a 1960 performance of the play which was published in Havana's *Revolution* newspaper on March 8, 1960. See further pp. 146–7, where he outlines the Cuban elements present in the play.
20. Vasserot 2008: 166. See also Piñera 1967: 132–3, who also highlights the foundation of experimental theater company *La Cueva* in 1936 as the first time when Cuban theatrical activity began to organize itself.
21. Vasserot 2008: 166. Morín (1998: 23–6) recalls the early productions staged by the Academy of Dramatic Arts, which include Eugene O'Neill's *Before Breakfast*, *Becky Sharp* (a play based on Thackeray's *Vanity Fair*), Clay L. Shaw's *Submerged*, and Anton Chekhov's *The Anniversary*. Further on pp. 26–7 Morín muses on the first University Theater plays, specifically how in the spring of 1941 the "University precinct—in the glorious Plaza Cadenas—resounded with the voices of the female chorus, who transformed into song the writings of Sophocles in order to calm and advise the desperate Antigone"; on this production of *Antigone*, see also Miranda Cancela 2006: 34–6. The Theater Council had as its first play *Liliom* by the Hungarian Ferenç Molnar, according to Morín (1998: 39); whereas the Popular Theater featured O'Neill's *All God's Chillun Got Wings*, and two plays by Russian dramatists: Maxim Gorky's *The Lower Depths* and Leonid Leonov's *Invasion*; see Morín 1998: 61.
22. Lobato Morchón (2002: 118 n. 27) mentions that between 1941 and 1946 the University Theater showed productions of *Antigone, Oedipus King, Hecuba*, and *Choephoroi* (directed by Ludwig Schajowicz), and *Agamemnon* and *Prometheus Bound* (by Alejandro Baralt).
23. Muguercia 1988: 11: "This type of pseudo-artistic theater satisfied the demands of determined sectors of the petit bourgeoisie which, being in contact with a scene that was in reality poor and banal, fed the illusion of participating in an aesthetic experience that was particularly refined, and not comparable with that which the habitual vehicles of mass culture placed within its reach."

24. Morín 1998: 81–2. On the function of the pedagogue, whom I do not discuss in this chapter, see Cervera Salinas 1995: 153–4.
25. Piñera 1967: 133. On Schajowicz's influence on the Cuban theatrical scene, see Miranda Cancela 2006: 33–47.
26. Mañach (1969: 21) defines it as "an attitude, a form of not taking anything seriously. Through it, a Cuban makes fun of authority. Anything that inherently entails a sense of authority is transformed in the eyes of a Cuban into a motive for *choteo*." See also Piñera 1960: 10: "it is said that when a Cuban jokes, he makes fun of what is most sacred."
27. Piñera 1960: 8–9: "I am he who makes seriousness more serious through humor, the absurd and the grotesque." Montes Huidobro (1961: 88) sees this as characteristic of Piñera's entire oeuvre.
28. Espinosa Domínguez 2003: 155 contains Antón Arrufat's recollections on the theatrical space, which was a hall in the José M. Valdés Rodríguez Municipal School; see also Morín 1998: 58.
29. This was the New York Dramatic Workshop (under Erwin Piscator), where Morín was taught directly by Reiken Ben-Ari, who was a student of Constantin Stanislavski; see Morín 1998: 77.
30. Espinosa Domínguez (2003: 149) gives a list of actors. On the Prometheus (Prometeo) theater collective, see González Freire 1958: 130–2; Morín 1998: 82; and Vasserot 2008: 16.
31. Rodríguez Feo 1991: 130. Morín (1998: 85) states that "the work received an extremely severe criticism by the members of the ARTYC simply because they did not understand a play that was far more advanced than they were." See also Espinosa Domínguez 2003: 149.
32. Anderson 2006: 62 and Pérez León 2002: 120–1. Morín (1998: 85) says that Piñera was alluding to Luis Amado Blanco's own failed play *Suicide*, which had premièred in the Theater Council five years before *Electra*.
33. On the reception of the play see Anderson 2006: 97–9.
34. This editorial also published his 1960 *Complete Theater*, which then only consisted of seven plays: *Electra Garrigó*, *Jesús*, *Falsa Alarma*, *La boda*, *El flaco y el gordo*, *Aire frío*, and *El filántropo*; see Barreto 1996: 150.

References

Aguilú de Murphy, R. (1989), *Los textos dramáticos de Virgilio Piñera y el teatro del absurdo*. Madrid.
Ammar, A. (2011), *Sartre, passions cubaines*. Paris.
Anderson, T. F. (2006), *Everything in its Place: The Life and Works of Virgilio Piñera*. Lewisburg, PA.
Bakogianni, A. (2011), *Electra Ancient & Modern: Aspects of the Reception of the Tragic Heroine*. London.
Barreda, P. (1985), "La tragedia griega y su historización en Cuba: *Electra Garrigó* de Virgilio Piñera," *Escritura: revista de teoría y crítica literarias* 10, 117–26.
Barreto, T. C. (1996), *A Libélula, a Pitonisa: revolução, homossexualismo e literatura em Virgilio Piñera*. São Paulo.
Brunel, P. (1971), *Le Mythe d'Électre*. Paris.
Carrió Mendía, R. (1990), "Estudio en blanco y negro: teatro de Virgilio Piñera," *Revista Iberoamericana* 56.152–3 (July–December), 871–900.

Carrió Mendía, R. (1992), "Una brillante entrada en la modernidad," in Espinosa Domínguez 1992: 131–7.
Castro, F. (1960), "¿Por qué me gusta y no me gusta Lunes?," *Lunes de revolución número del primer aniversario* (special issue dated March 28), 2.
Cervera Salinas, V. (1995), "Electra Garrigó de Virgilio Piñera: años y leguas de un mito teatral," *Cuadernos hispanoamericanos* 545, 149–56.
Civil, F. M. (ed. 2008), *Cuba 1959–2006: révolution dans la culture, culture dans la Révolution*. Paris.
Espinosa Domínguez, C. (1989), "El poder mágico de los bifes: la estancia en Buenos Aires de Virgilio Piñera," *Cuadernos hispanoamericanos* 471, 73–88.
Espinosa Domínguez, C. (ed. 1992), *Teatro cubano contemporáneo: antología*. Madrid.
Espinosa Domínguez, C. (2003), *Virgilio Piñera en persona*. La Habana.
Fradinger, M. (2011), "An Argentine Tradition," in E. Mee and H. P. Foley eds., *Antigone on the Contemporary World Stage*. Oxford, 67–89.
González Freire, N. (1958), *Teatro cubano contemporáneo (1928–1957)*. La Habana.
Hall, E. (1999), "Sophocles' *Electra* in Britain," in J. Griffin ed., *Sophocles Revisited: Essays Presented to Sir Hugh Lloyd-Jones*. Oxford, 261–306.
Leal, R. (1982), *La selva oscura: de los bufos a la neocolonia (Historia del teatro cubano de 1868 a 1902)*. La Habana.
Leal, R. (1988), "1902–1958: la República," in *Escenarios de dos mundos: inventario teatral de Iberoamérica*. Madrid, 17–26.
Leal, R. (2002), "Piñera todo teatral," in Piñera 2002: v–xxxiii.
Lobato Morchón, R. (2002), *El teatro del absurdo en Cuba (1948–1968)*. Madrid.
Machado Vento, D. (2012), "El regreso de Virgilio Piñera," *Mar desnudo* 32 (April) <http://mardesnudo.atenas.cult.cu/?q=el_regreso_de_virgilio>.
Mañach, J. (1969), *Indagación del choteo*. Miami.
Matas, J. (1989), "Vuelta a Electra Garrigó de Virgilio Piñera," *Latin American Theatre Review* 22, 73–9.
Miranda Cancela, E. (2006), *Calzar el coturno americano: mito, tragedia griega y teatro cubano*. La Habana.
Montes Huidobro, M. (1961), Review of Virgilio Piñera: *Teatro completo* (La Habana, 1960), *Casa de las Américas* 1.5 (March–April), 88–90.
Montes Huidobro, M. (1973), *Persona, vida y máscara en el teatro cubano*. Miami.
Montes Huidobro, M. (2002), *El teatro cubano en el vórtice del compromiso: 1959–1961*. Miami.
Montes Huidobro, M. (2004), *El teatro cubano durante la república: Cuba detrás del telón*. Boulder, CO.
Morín, F. (1998), *Por amor al arte: memorias de un teatrista cubano 1940–1970*. Miami.
Muguercia, M. (1988), *El teatro cubano en vísperas de la revolución*. La Habana.
Pérez León, R. (2002), *Virgilio Piñera: vitalidad de una paradoja*. Caracas.
Pérez-Galdós Ortiz, V. (2000), *Joseíto Fernández e la sua Guajira Guantanamera*. Verona.
Piñera, V. (1960), "Piñera Teatral," in *Teatro completo*. La Habana, 7–30.
Piñera, V. (1967), "Notas sobre el teatro cubano," *Unión* 6 (issue 2, Abril–Junio), 130–43.
Piñera, V. (2002), *Teatro completo*. La Habana.
Piñera, V. (2008), *Electra Garrigó*. Trans. M. Carson, in D. Taylor and S. J. Townsend eds, *Stages of Conflict: A Critical Anthology of Latin American Theater and Performance*. Ann Arbor, 180–95.
Quiroga, J. (1995), "Fleshing out Virgilio Piñera from the Cuban Closet," in E. L. Bergmann and P. J. Smith eds., *¿Entiendes? Queer Readings, Hispanic Writings*. Durham, NC, 168–80.

Rodríguez Feo, J. (1991), *Mi correspondencia con Lezama Lima*. México D.F.
Rodríguez Tomeu, H. (1959–76), *Letters received from Virgilio Piñera; 1959–1976*; Virgilio Piñera Collection, Box 1, Folder 11; Manuscripts Division, Department of Rare Books and Special Collections, Princeton University Library.
Sartre, J.-P. (1960), "Una entrevista con los escritores cubanos," in *Sartre visita a Cuba*. La Habana, 19–54.
Scott, J. (2005), *Electra after Freud: Myth and Culture*. Ithaca, NY.
Steinmeyer, E. (2007), "Post-Apartheid Electra: *In the City of Paradise*," in L. Hardwick and C. Gillespie eds., *Classics in Post-Colonial World*. Oxford, 102–18.
Taylor, D. and S. J. Townsend (2008), *Stages of Conflict: A Critical Anthology of Latin American Theater and Performance*. Ann Arbor.
Townsend, S. J. (2008), "Cuba: Electra Garrigó (Virgilio Piñera)," in D. Taylor and S. J. Townsend eds., *Stages of Conflict: A Critical Anthology of Latin American Theater and Performance*. Ann Arbor, 173–9.
Vasserot, C. (2008), "Théâtre et revolution à Cuba," in F. M. Civil ed., *Cuba 1959–2006: révolution dans la culture, culture dans la Révolution*. Paris, 165–76.
Versényi, A. (1993), *Theatre in Latin America: Religion, Politics, and Culture from Cortés to the 1980s*. Cambridge.
West, A. (1997), *Tropics of History: Cuba Imagined*. Westport, CT.
Wilson, E. (2004), *Mocked with Death: Tragic Overliving from Sophocles to Milton*. Baltimore, MD.
Zeitlin, F. I. (1965), "The Motif of the Corrupted Sacrifice in Aeschylus' *Oresteia*," *Transactions of the American Philological Association* 96, 463–505.
Zeitlin, F. I. (2012), "A Study in Form: Three Recognition Scenes in the Three Electra Plays," *Lexis* 30, 361–78.

CHAPTER 22

A BRAZILIAN ECHO OF *ANTIGONE*'S "COLLISION"

Tragedy, Clean and Filthy

PAUL B. DIXON

When it comes to the migration of the traditions of ancient drama to the Americas, or the adaptation of classical paradigms to the realities of the African Diaspora, it would be hard to find a better example than the Brazilian play *O pagador de promessas* (*Payment as Pledged*) by Dias Gomes.

First presented in São Paulo in 1960, the play has strong echoes of classical tragedy, particularly of the tradition involving the collision of conflicting ethical positions, most often associated with Sophocles' *Antigone* and with particular ideas about tragedy, which have become "classical" in their own right, ideas associated with the theories of Georg Wilhelm Friedrich Hegel. While as a Brazilianist, rather than a Classicist, I am not prepared to provide a serious account of the huge body of commentary on Sophocles' play (for which we might begin with Bonnie Honig's *Antigone Interrupted*) (Honig 2013), I do find it interesting that the confrontation of opposing positions seen in *Antigone* itself also seems to be replicated, in similar terms, in the work's critical reception. On the one hand, students of the drama have provided what George Steiner calls a "high," or philosophical reading (Steiner 1984: 104), stressing universal existential challenges, matters of individual integrity, and ethical questions that rise above the immediate political or social circumstances of the author's historical moment. On the other hand, analysts, especially more recently, have countered with what might be called a "lower" reading of the play, a mode of reception more closely attentive to the interests and values of subaltern classes. Recent lines of inquiry, for example, have looked at the play's feminist implications (Butler 2000; duBois 1986; Irigaray 1985a; Mader 2005), as well as its treatment of codes of exclusion, especially concerning slavery (Chanter 2011; Segal 1999).

When we think of the diffusion of a classical paradigm such as tragedy, of its implantation across the world, it seems unavoidable that there be a certain gravitation from "high" to "low." Tragic essences or universals must necessarily descend to the telluric particulars of their new environments (a phenomenon that the present volume is well poised to address).[1] Otherwise, they would seem irrelevant or even ungrounded in these diasporic contexts. This lowering of tragic focus is surely a feature of the Brazilian play.[2] While *O pagador de promessas* has the normal generic gravity, it also has many humorous elements, satirizing several versions of a recognizable Brazilian type—the opportunistic rogue or *malandro*. Further, the drama is profoundly rooted in significant aspects of Brazilian culture—most notably, folk Catholicism on the one hand, and Afro-Brazilian religious syncretism on the other. This particular combination of elements gives us a text that is universal or classical, in the sense of having the timeless appeal of lasting human values, and at the same time richly imbued with local color and customs. Given that happy coincidence, it is perhaps not surprising that the 1962 film of the same name, directed by Anselmo Duarte and closely based on the text of the play, was the first Brazilian work to win the Golden Palm award at the Cannes Film Festival (Fig. 22.1).

FIG. 22.1 The plaque from Escadaria do Passo, the staircase leading up to the Church of Santa Barbara in Pelourinho, Salvador da Bahia, Brazil, where Anselmo Duarte's movie adaptation of *O pagador de promessas* is set. Photo: Patrice Rankine.

Alfredo de Freitas Dias Gomes was born in the most African of Brazilian cities, Salvador, Bahia, in 1922. Salvador was a center of Brazil's slave trade during its colonial period, when sugar cane plantations dominated the national economy. The author moved with his family to Rio de Janeiro, and by the time of his death in 1999 he had practiced fruitful careers as a writer in the theater, in radio, and in television. He is considered one of the founding fathers of Brazil's renowned *telenovela* ("soap opera") industry, which dominates domestic television and exports its products all over the world. A notable aspect of his radio career is that during 20 years he wrote radio adaptations of nearly 500 different plays, a process that provided him with an excellent knowledge of world drama. His career in theater involved interruptions while he worked in those other areas but nevertheless displayed a constant trajectory. Dias Gomes consistently engaged in social and political criticism. In his more light-hearted vein, he satirized the colorful characters tied to Brazil's patriarchal traditions, types belonging to various levels of society. In a more serious mode, he denounced several forms of corruption and repression. During Brazil's military dictatorship (1964–85) Dias Gomes's dramatic texts were frequently the target of official censorship.

The central premise of *O pagador de promessas* (translated by Oscar Fernández with the title *Payment as Pledged*) involves an element of what is called popular Catholicism or folk Catholicism, which is a manner of religiosity that emphasizes concrete practices over abstract theological understanding. Lighting candles. decorating altars, counting prayers on a rosary, holding novenas, cherishing images or statues, engaging in the cult of the Virgin or of saints, participating in pilgrimages—these are all examples of such folk practices. Students of Brazil are quick to identify such popular manifestations with an underlying national culture. The promise made to God—a kind of bargain by which the supplicant shows an especially strong faith or commitment (the pledge), and by which commensurately strong blessings are to be obtained from heaven, is a noteworthy practice of Brazilian folk Catholicism. Such a promise is at the heart of Dias Gomes's play.

Of Faith, Folk, and Friendship

Joe Burro (Zé do Burro), the main character, has gone to great lengths to save the life of his "very best friend" (64), Nicholas. After being injured by a fallen tree branch, Nicholas has bled profusely, fallen ill, and come dangerously close to death. To save his beloved friend, Joe makes a promise to St. Barbara. If she will intervene with God to save his comrade, Joe will carry a cross on her feast day, as heavy as that borne by Jesus, 25 miles, from his village in the interior of Bahia to inside the Church of Santa Barbara in Salvador (64–7) (Fig. 22.2).

Joe sees his persuasion of St. Barbara in terms of the pledge, practically a commercial exchange:

> JOE: ... A promise is a promise. It's like a business deal. If you set a price, and get the goods, you have to pay. I know a lot of welshing goes on. But not with me. It's give and take. (64)

FIG. 22.2 The Church of Santa Barbara in Salvador, Brazil, in the Pelourinho neighborhood. Photo: Patrice Rankine.

The choice of St. Barbara as an intercessor before God reveals Joe's desire for a more-neighborly source of divine power, who might be more immediately sensitive to his concrete human needs. St. Barbara as an intermediary reveals an interesting logic on the part of Joe Burro. Nicholas has been injured by a tree limb that fell when it was struck by lightning. Joe consults a counselor, who suggests that it makes sense to appeal to a supernatural figure associated with thunder and lightning, since that being may have been responsible for the accident in the first place. According to legend, Barbara was a beautiful young Syrian woman killed by her own pagan father, who was enraged at her steadfast conversion to Christianity. After he executed her, he himself was killed by a bolt of lightning (Jones 1994: 39). St. Barbara involves a kind of primal logic that is especially sensitive to the power of natural forces, such as those of the weather, and that tends to associate holy personages with those same forces, in an almost animistic way.

In reality, this association between St. Barbara and lightning is even richer and more complicated because it also involves specific circumstances relating to Afro-Brazilian culture. *Candomblé* is one of the syncretic religious influences of African slaves in Bahia and many of their descendants to this day. (See Santos, this volume.) The slaves came from Africa with a pluralistic system of divinities. Although there may have been one supreme being, Ôlorún (Carneiro 1967: 18), there were also numerous secondary deities, called *orixás*, who tended to be associated with earthly elements such as iron, wells, and oceans, or with powerful phenomena such as the rain, thunder, war, or pestilence (Carneiro 1967: 57–73). When the symbols and practices of Christianity were imposed upon the slaves, they unconsciously or consciously found a way of resisting (and at the same time accepting) this alien ideology, by associating members of the godhead, the Virgin, Satan, and the saints with the various *orixás* they had brought from Africa. For example, they paired Óxoce, god of the hunt, with St. George, and celebrated both deities on the same day, Corpus Christi. The domination of George over the dragon related to the power of the hunter over his prey, and the iconic representation of the weapon carrier could be connected to both entities (Carneiro 1967: 59). To the eyes of their masters, the slaves might seem to be celebrating a Catholic saint; this might have been the case, but they were certainly also continuing to pay honor to the *orixá* worshipped in their days of freedom.

The syncretic situation of St. Barbara is especially crucial to Dias Gomes's play. When Joe Burro's spiritual counselor suggests that he seek aid from a deity associated with lightning, she does not actually mention St. Barbara, but rather the *orixá* Yansan: "She said that indeed it had to do with Yansan, goddess of lightning and thunder. It was Yansan who had injured Nicholas . . . It was to her that I should make reparation" (67). Joe leans more toward Catholicism than *candomblé*, stating, "I . . . was never one to attend voodoo ceremonies.[3] But poor Nicholas was dying. It wouldn't cost anything to try" (67). Joe is willing to try anything to save Nicholas, and goes to the *candomblé* ceremony. But in his own mind, he does not appeal to the African deity: "And then I remembered that Yansan is St. Barbara and I promised that if Nicholas got well I would carry a wooden cross from my farm to her church, on her feast day, a cross as heavy as Christ's" (67). So Joe's promise is to St. Barbara, but it is solemnized at a service for a corresponding African goddess. This displacement is made possible by syncretic logic by which, as Joe says, "Yansan is St. Barbara."

One of the big jokes of the play (and one to which I now admit a degree of complicity) is that Nicholas is not the sort of friend many people would expect. This comes out through a delightfully confusing exchange with the priest in charge of the Church of

St. Barbara, Father Olavo. Joe explains that everyone perceived that Nicholas was ill, because he was no longer by his side:

> JOE: ...Everybody noticed it, because if anyone wanted to know where I was, all he had to do was to look for Nicholas. If I went to Mass, he waited for me at the church door...
>
> PRIEST: At the door? Why didn't he go in? Isn't he a Catholic?
>
> JOE: Having such a good heart, Nicholas can't help being a Catholic. But that's not the reason he doesn't go into the Church. It's because the priest doesn't allow it. (*Very sadly.*) Nicholas had the luck to be born a burro...a four-legged one.
>
> PRIEST: A burro? Then that...that one you call Nicholas is a burro? An animal?!
>
> JOE: My burro...yes, sir.
>
> PRIEST: And it was for him, for a burro, that you made this promise? (65)

The fact that Joe has gone to such lengths for an animal, and that he considers this creature to be his "best friend," sheds further light upon the system of values belonging to the protagonist's worldview. He clearly has an egalitarian perception of social relationships, which extends all the way into the non-human sphere. He greatly appreciates his donkey's "good heart" and is sincerely disappointed that his friend is excluded from accompanying him into the church when he goes to Mass.

The surprise identification of Nicholas's animal status now sheds light on the humorous discussion of certain attempted cures for his injury. While Father Olavo still thinks that Nicholas is a human being, Joe explains that the bleeding of his head wound was quite difficult to stop:

> JOE: ...He came home, bleeding all over the place! My wife and I took care of him, but no matter what we did, we couldn't stop the bleeding.
>
> PRIEST: A hemorrhage.
>
> JOE: And it didn't stop until I went to the stable, took a bit of cow dung and applied it to the wound.
>
> PRIEST (*nauseated*): But my son, what a backward thing to do! Filthy!
>
> JOE: That's what the doctor said when he arrived. He ordered me to take that filth from the wound or else Nicholas would die. (64–5)

The folk remedies described here reveal a decidedly earthy orientation. All notions of sterility or freedom from contamination seem irrelevant in a perspective where bloody wounds are part of a natural sphere of organic ripeness, and where elements from that same gamy heap may be used as tools for natural remediation.

The non-hierarchical nature of Joe's ideology is made evident by another feature of his promise to St. Barbara. In addition to the pilgrimage he has made another pledge:

> JOE: I also promised to divide my land among the poor farmers, poorer than me.
>
> PRIEST: To divide? Equally?
>
> JOE: Yes, Father, equally. (67)

Joe has already shown that he finds an animal to be an equal, his "best friend." He now reveals that he also has no use for hierarchies in the strictly human realm. In a world where Joe's only thought is the survival of his beloved companion, to prove the intensity of his appeal to St. Barbara, he makes a decision that takes Christian charity to an impressive extent. He will share not the income from his means, as is the custom, but rather the means for his income. The equal division of his land ensures that he will be no different from his poorer acquaintances, when it comes to the capacity for productivity and wealth.

We might summarize the faith of Joe Burro, then, by stating that it is strong and spontaneous, devoid of any egotism, and that it is remarkably inclusive. It is open to influences from others, even when they appear inconsistent with narrower inclinations. It is based on material interactions, the kind of exchanges that are carried out in everyday social negotiations. And it belongs to a world where all earthly elements—dirt, blood, plants, living creatures, and all their excretions—interact at the most concrete and practical way. The whole matter is perhaps summed up by Joe's approach to saving his esteemed burro, when he declares, "I tried everything" (66).

Conserving the Creed

The play's opposing worldview, represented primarily by Father Olavo, is decidedly exclusive in its orientation. The principal manifestation of this position is obvious, and functions as the dominant source of conflict throughout the play: the priest refuses to let Joe Burro carry his cross into the church. This exclusionary attitude is by no means out of harmony with the general tenor of Christian theology, whereby eternal rewards are reserved only for certain individuals: "Because strait is the gate, and narrow is the way, which leadeth unto life, and few there be that find it" (Matthew 7: 14). In fact, the spatial situation suggested by this well-known verse is in complete consonance with that of the play. The narrow gate guarding the path to paradise has its counterpart in the imposing door of the church, which occupies the center of the scenic space throughout the play. (The second image is the iconic view of the Church of St. Barbara's steep ascent and narrow gate.) Implicitly the door represents not just the entry to a chapel, but also the threshold of one's arrival at a state of benediction or salvation. Joe's wife Rosa accompanies him on his pilgrimage with the cross. When they arrive at the church at four-thirty in the morning, before it is open, she suggests that having carried the cross to the churchyard, they are done with their obligations to St. Barbara. But Joe is adamant in his insistence that they will only have arrived when they have gone inside: "But St. Barbara's church is not here. The church is beyond that door" (49).

Father Olavo, as the parochial authority assigned to the church, clearly sees himself as the guardian of that door. And when he learns that the promise was made at a *candomblé* gathering, he puts his foot down: "... you are not going into this church with that cross! ... A pagan ritual, which began in a voodoo session, cannot end in the nave of the church" (69). The conflict between Joe's inclusive faith and Father Olavo's exclusive faith could not be more clear than at this moment: "You cannot serve two masters, God and the Devil! . . . The church is the House of God. Voodoo is the cult of the Devil!" (69). There is a tendency in Brazil for the Catholic Church and many other Christian denominations to disparage *candomblé* as the religion of the Devil, probably because possession by spirits is such a prominent part in the practice of the Afro-Brazilian cult (Carneiro 1967: 52–3), and because in the New Testament such possession is always associated with the Evil One. At the same time, it is hard to avoid the perception of at least some degree of racism in this negative outlook. In using the language of "serving one or the other," Father Olavo is paraphrasing the words of Jesus in the New Testament: "No man can serve two masters: for either he will hate the one, and love the other; or else he will hold to the one, and despise the other. Ye cannot serve God and mammon" (Matthew 6: 24). The disjunctive nature of the priest's declaration, like that of Jesus in the Bible, is absolute. Serving God prohibits serving mammon (or "Voodoo"), and vice versa. The crux of the play's conflict thus resides in the fact that in Father Olavo's system of values, Christianity and *candomblé* exclude each other in no uncertain terms, while in the mind of Joe (and many other of his compatriots), the relationship between the two religions is actually much more compatible.

The need for rigid distinctions extends to other aspects of the priest's worldview. First, he is bothered by the fact that Joe has so much devotion to a mere animal, and that to revive him he has re-enacted Christ's *via dolorosa*:

> Why then do you repeat the Divine Passion?! To save humanity? No, to save a burro! . . . A burro with a Christian name! A quadruped, an animal! (69)

When Joe protests that burros were also created by God, the priest answers: "But not in his likeness. And it wasn't to save them that he sent his son. It was for us, for you, for me, for humanity!" (69). The priest apparently feels that Christianity, with its entire system of appeals and blessings, was intended only for humans, and that other creatures are better off not being included either on the side of the supplicants or on that of the blessed. Like the priest in Joe's hometown, he would prevent Nicholas from following his master in to Mass.

There is a suggestion that Father Olavo's exclusivity extends to other aspects of nature as well as the animals. Joe tells of once asking a special prayer from Black Zeferino because of a persistent headache, and of being told that he was ill because he had the sun inside his head. Joe recites the prayer offered by Zeferino:

> God made the Sun, God made the light, God made all the illumination of the grandiose universe. With his Grace I bless you, I cure you. Sun, leave the head of this creature and go to the waves of the Sacred Sea, through the holy powers of the Father, of the Son, and of the Holy Ghost. (66)

In spite of the fact that Zeferino invokes the Holy Trinity in his prayer, Father Olavo has no trouble identifying it as a prayer of a "witch doctor" (66). It irritates him that Joe, who is a Catholic and who regularly attends Mass, would seek out such a person for spiritual support. But beyond that, he may well be bristling at the way Zeferino speaks directly to the sun, and how both the sun and the "sacred sea" have been brought into the language of a prayer. The discourse has become too pantheistic, or perhaps animistic, for his liking.

Also consistent with the Priest's categorical and exclusionary mindset is his reaction to Joe's discussion of folk remedies such as cow dung or spider webs to stop bleeding. In disgust, the Priest calls these applications "filthy" (64). This attitude is of course consistent with modern medical understanding, where infection occurs when a wound is contaminated by too many bacteria. Healing is promoted when the wound is sterilized and allowed to heal in isolation from unclean substances. Father Olavo's resistance to "filthy" cures resonates perfectly with his desire to protect the Catholic Church from alien influences. The Church, like a vulnerable body, needs to be kept in a sterile environment, clear of unclean outside contacts, which like germs might try to invade and contaminate its tender tissue.

Another aspect of the Priest's set of values is his respect for hierarchies. We have already seen that he objects to Joe's egalitarian attitudes about burros and other animals; even more important, apparently, are those hierarchies involving the difference between humanity and deity. Father Olavo is taken aback by Joe's decision to carry a cross "as heavy as Christ's" (67), suspecting that he is "going to try to be taken for a new Christ" (68):

> PRIEST: ... You ... have just repeated the Way of the Cross, suffering the martyrdom of Jesus. You who, presumptuously, try to imitate the Son of God ...
> JOE: Father ... I did not try to imitate Jesus ...
> PRIEST (*cutting him off sharply*): You lie! I marked your words! You yourself said that you promised to carry a cross *as heavy as Christ's*.
> JOE: Yes, but that ...
> PRIEST: That proves that you are being submitted to an even greater temptation.
> JOE: What's that, Father?
> PRIEST: To make yourself equal to the Son of God. (68–9)

The re-enactment of the *via crucis*, which in Joe's mind seems to have been a form of homage, is taken by Father Olavo as a kind of presumptuous thinking, by which a person casts doubt on the superior status of the Messiah.

Finally, I should note the Priest's firm regard for institutional authority. We see this in the following exchange, where Joe has become frustrated at the cleric's refusal to allow him to carry his cross into the church:

> JOE: I didn't walk twenty-five miles to turn back here. You can't keep me from entering. The church is not yours, it's God's!
> PRIEST: You are going to disregard my authority? (69–70)

Like Joe, Father Olavo displays an impressive piety and a sincere commitment to religious values as he sees them. His is clearly a more institutionalized religiosity, less spontaneous than Joe's and more governed by a sense of necessary rules and formalities. He takes seriously all injunctions to shield the Church from unrighteous influences, and feels that he is called to guarantee that only the worthy and duly authorized should enjoy official ecclesiastical sanctions. He has a keen sense of authority, and will not countenance any questioning of the Lord's superior status.

A "Tragic Collision"

Here it is important to stress that both the main characters of Dias Gomes's play, Joe Burro and Padre Olavo, are positive and even admirable characters in that they are devoid of hypocrisy, and committed to principles rather than to circumstantial exigencies—a commitment that causes them to undergo considerable tribulation. That is not to say that both are equally sympathetic characters. In his earnest, ingenuous, and humble faith (not to mention his devotion to a pet) Joe must be the more likeable character for practically any modern observer. Padre Olavo seems austere and dogmatic, and is not the kind of character who warms the cockles of one's heart. But the standards of classical tragedy have little to do with sympathetic characterization. To follow the famous reasoning of Georg Wilhelm Friedric Hegel, tragedy involves not so much a single tragic hero as a conflict of commitments:

> The collision between the two highest moral powers is enacted in plastic fashion in that absolute *exemplum* of tragedy, Antigone. Here, familial love, the holy, the inward, belonging to inner feeling, and therefore known also as the law of the nether gods, collides with the right of the state. Creon is not a tyrant, but actually an ethical power. Creon is not in the wrong. He maintains that the law of the state, the authority of government, must be held in respect, and that infraction of the law must be followed by punishment. Each of these two sides actualizes only one of the ethical powers, and has only one as its content. This is their one-sidedness. The meaning of eternal justice is made manifest thus: both attain injustice just because they are one-sided, but both also attain justice. Both are recognized as valid in the "unclouded" course and process of morality. Here both possess their validity, but an equalized validity. Justice only comes forward to oppose one-sidedness. (Hegel: 1895, vol. 2, 264–5)

The appreciation of Father Olavo as a tragic hero seems to involve some degree of acceptance of the "higher" tragic vision that I have mentioned in connection with the reception of *Antigone*. It requires adherence to certain rather universal, pristine, or disembodied concepts, to a notion of the hero that is perhaps sanitized from more natural concerns, "cleaner" or "less contaminated" by easy sympathies. The appreciation of Joe Burro is more spontaneous, certainly more natural, more grounded in the immediate environment, and more sympathetic to the plight of the underdog. It belongs to the "lower" tendency in tragic reception, and might be called "dirty" or even "filthy" (to borrow from the vocabulary of Father Olavo) by those with more purist leanings.

I have shown how the respective positions of the main characters are exposed in the opening scenes of the play. In Act 2, after Joe has had to wait for several hours with his cross, the Priest comes out of the church and again speaks to him. The ensuing dialogue summarizes the values the two characters have chosen to champion:

PRIEST: What are you trying to do with all that shouting? To show a lack of respect for this house, the house of God?
JOE: No, Father, just to remind you that I am still here with my cross.
PRIEST: So I see. And that insistence on heresy shows how much you have strayed from the Church.
JOE: Very well, Father. If that's so, God will punish me and you'll not be to blame.
PRIEST: Yes, I will. I am a priest. I must concern myself with the glory of the Lord and the happiness of men.
JOE: But you are making me so unhappy, Father.
PRIEST (*sincerely convinced*):   No! I am defending your happiness, keeping you from losing yourself in the darkness of witchcraft. (93–4)

At this point the dialogue makes it clear that Joe's conception of faith is personal, while the Priest's is institutional. Joe perceives his promise as a matter between him and God; if he has erred, it will be up to God to correct him, and the Priest should have nothing to do with it. The priest denies such individualistic commitments, and maintains that the Church is the necessary vehicle for individuals to work out their salvation. If Joe has promised to carry his cross into the chapel, then the Church is necessarily involved. And as the duly appointed representative of the Church, he is responsible for guarding against heresy, against anything that might pervert the Church's true doctrines and practices. The two characters have opposing views of what constitutes happiness. For Joe, happiness seems to consist of freedom to follow his personal sense of righteousness, while for Father Olavo it is a matter of conforming to established institutional norms, of following the "straight and narrow" path.

The incompatibility of the two positions is emphasized even further when the Monsignor hears of the disturbance at the Church of St. Barbara, and comes to consult with Father Olavo. The two men of the Church devise a proposal by which they hope to resolve the conflict:

MONSIGNOR: Very well. We are going to give you an opportunity. If you are a Catholic, renounce all the acts you practiced through the Devil's inspiration and return to the fold of Holy Mother Church.
JOE (*not understanding*):   How, Father?
MONSIGNOR: Renounce the promise you made, recognize that it was made to the Devil, cast that cross aside and come alone, to ask God's pardon.
JOE (*seized by a terrible conflict of conscience*):   Do you really think I should do that?!
MONSIGNOR: It is the only way in which you can save yourself. The Catholic Church grants us, the priests, the right to exchange one promise for another.
ROSA (*urging him to yield*):   Joe . . . perhaps it would be better . . .
JOE (in anguish):   But Rosa . . . if I do this, I'm failing to keep my promise . . . be it to Yansan, or St. Barbara . . . I'm failing to keep it . . .
MONSIGNOR: Under the authority with which I am invested, I free you from that promise, as I said. Come make another . . .

PRIEST: Monsignor is giving a proof of Christian tolerance. It now remains for you to choose between the Church's tolerance and your own stubbornness.

JOE (*pausing*): You free me ... but it was not to you I made the promise. It was to St. Barbara. (96)

Of course, rather than resolving anything, the exchange reveals how the Fathers, in their self-assuredness, have only misunderstood the true nature of Joe Burro's commitment. They continue to insist that the Church holds the keys to the soul's salvation, and therefore offer a plan that rests on their own authority. Within their own frame of reference, the idea of releasing Joe from his promise is logical and would certainly bring an end to the impasse. But they have failed to understand Joe's perspective, which he makes clear when he states, "but it was not to you I made the promise. It was to St Barbara." From his point of view, the Fathers are only interfering with personal contract between him and the saint.

Pagador and *Antigone*: Continuities and Contrasts

The clash of two firmly committed characters, each representing positive values, a conflict that creates an unsustainable standoff, is the main tragic thread connecting the Brazilian play with its Greek ancestor. Like *Antigone*, *O pagador de promessas* also presents a situation where one side has superior authority, while the other side is in a position of rebellion against that more potent force. Dias Gomes's adherence to the tradition of classical tragedy was not accidental. Perhaps the clearest marker of this intention to establish kinship with the classical lineage is the inclusion of a chorus in the third and final act. Like the conflict itself, this feature is firmly grounded in aspects of Brazilian culture. The chorus is sung by a *capoeira* group. *Capoeira* is a unique blend of dance and martial arts, originating in the slave culture of Bahia and now popular in almost all regions of Brazil. The practice is said to have its origins in the resistance of captives to the rules imposed by their masters (Merrell 2005). The slaves were strictly forbidden from fighting amongst themselves, or from engaging in training exercises for any sort of combat. By disguising their kicks, lunges, and parries as dance moves, and by performing these exercises to the accompaniment of singing and musical instruments, the slaves were able to "do battle," at least symbolically, while claiming only to be involved in an innocent choreographic diversion. To the extent that the tragic chorus establishes a kind of collective moral backdrop for the play, it is interesting to note the clear tie between *capoeira* and slavery.

The specified musical instruments are the ones typically used to accompany the dances—the *berimbau*, a wire strung on a bow with a gourd attached to amplify its vibrations, and struck with a stick;[4] the *pandeiro*, a kind of tambourine, and the *reco-reco*, which is a notched gourd scraped with a stick. All have African origins (Murphy 2006: 7–11, 59). The words sung by the chorus are evocative of the call-and-response chants sung by the slaves as they worked in the sugar fields. The vocabulary is easily connected with that of the slaves, with words such as "missy" and her "black boy, Joe," "boss" in the English version (98.10) and many more in the original Portuguese. Thematically, the words combine references to slavery (from being given commands by the boss, to the possibility of a forced separation from one's lover), to *capoeira* (sly moves learned from an esteemed teacher), and to the content of the play (appealing to St. Barbara, with her lightning, for help). One motif, that of a "Knife to kill" (99), seems to have a mixed reference; on the one hand it appears to be a vague expression of the possibility of slaves taking up arms in rebellion, and on the other it has a prophetic tone, referring to Joe Burro's desperate measure of drawing a knife just before he dies. The general tone of the play's chorus, it would seem, is to acknowledge the oppression that exists in the world, the need for subversive resistance or even open rebellion, and the possibility of supernatural aid. This general frame of reference is relevant both to the situation of Joe Burro and his trials before the church, and also to the conditions of the slaves.

The contribution of *Pagador*'s chorus is compelling in light of recent commentary on *Antigone*, which claims that Greek play also involves an undercurrent of slavery, which has largely been suppressed or ignored in the receptive tradition (Chanter 2011). The line to which Tina Chanter devotes most attention is from a moment when Antigone is brought before Creon to answer to him for defying his orders to leave the body of her brother, Polyneices, unburied because of his subversion against the state. She says, "It was a brother, not a slave, who died" (176). According to Chanter, the statement almost surreptitiously reveals the problematic of exclusionary citizenship that underlies not only *Antigone* but all the plays of the Oedipus cycle (133–40). Who will be allowed to belong? What is the extent of one's tolerance of difference? Males born of Greek parents merit citizenship, which includes the right to have their bodies respected, even in the form of burial after they have died. Others, including slaves and Antigone herself, as a woman, do not qualify for such guarantees. Thus, Antigone's heroic defense of her brother's burial allies itself with his privileges as a member of an inner circle, and falls short of condemning the discriminatory views and practices that make females and non-citizens lesser human beings. The tension at the heart of Hellenic society, where exclusive tribalism contended against democratic principles, is present in the background, but is not a battle in which Antigone chooses to become involved. In fact, according to Chanter, "Antigone colludes with a system of chattel slavery" (132).

Agents of Satire, Agents of Catastrophe

One of the main differences between *Antigone* and *O pagador de promessas*, in terms of a tragic trajectory, is that the former has a more direct and simple line leading to its catastrophe. Antigone openly defies the decree of Creon that her rebellious brother

Polyneicês, felled in battle, shall not be buried. He declares: "Leave him unburied, leave his corpse disgraced, a dinner for the birds and for the dogs" (165). Antigone steals in to give him a burial, knowing full well her act will lead to punishment by death:

> If I die before my time, I say it is a gain. Who lives in sorrows many as are mine how shall he not be glad to gain his death? And so, for me to meet this fate, no grief. But if I left that corpse, my mother's son, dead and unburied then I'd have cause to grieve as now I grieve not. (174)

The path to the ultimate disaster is the direct result of the positions taken by Antigone and Creon. Antigone insists on providing burial for her brother, in spite of its resulting in her own death, while Creon insists on punishing her for disobeying his orders, in spite of protestations from some of his most beloved associates. Creon has the authority to take life; Antigone, by defying that authority, agrees to lose her life and in fact kills herself before Creon can perform the execution.

The conflict of *O pagador de promessas* is not quite so clean. Were it set in an earlier time, perhaps in the sixteenth, seventeenth, or eighteenth century when the Inquisition was at the height of its power, the Church would have been empowered to impose capital punishment for certain infractions. Dias Gomes in fact wrote a tragedy in which a female protagonist enters into conflict with the Inquisition, and is eventually executed. In other words, Gomes wrestled with Antigone's dilemma elsewhere in his body of work. His *O santo inquérito* (*The Holy Inquisition*) was first produced in 1966. The protagonist, Blanca, saves Father Bernardo from drowning but in the process reveals certain eccentricities in her religious faith. The priest is compelled to denounce her before the Inquisition. She can save herself by denying some of her positions, but she refuses to do so. The allegorical associations with Brazil's authoritative political situation are quite evident. Its basic conflict is similar to that of *Pagador* in that it represents the clash of opposing values; however, a certain predatory complex in the psychology of Father Bernardo in my opinion weakens its tragic aspect.

Pagador is set in modern times, however, when the Church's power to punish only extends to excommunication. This circumstance, in conjunction with the rigid positions of Joe Burro and Father Olavo, creates an impasse. The priest can only go so far as to prohibit Joe's entrance, while Joe can only go so far as to refuse to go away from the public space in front of the church. Without the interference of some force external to the basic conflict, the play would have nowhere to go.

It is here that Dias Gomes introduces some interesting characters and situations, which might "contaminate" the purity of the play as a tragedy, but which make it quite relevant to the realities of everyday Brazil, as well as to the Brazil at the historical moment of the play's writing. Joe Burro is forced to wait in an open public space, which means that he is immediately visible to every type of passing citizen (Fig. 22.3).

He draws a crowd. The playwright chooses to enlist the participation of a few recognizable stereotypical characters, all of whom are in one way or another opportunistic, and who try to turn the situation to their own advantage. Dias Gomes ties into the consecrated figure of the "malandro," which is Brazil's version of a picaresque anti-hero,

FIG. 22.3 A view from Santa Barbara onto the streets of Pelourinho and the tenements reaching up to the sky. This is the public sphere, and not the interior of the church, where the modern Brazilian tragedy has its resolution. Photo: Patrice Rankine.

driven by hunger of one kind or another, and relying on artful manipulation to satisfy his desires (DaMatta 2000: 93–105).

A Spanish immigrant, called the Galician, owns a bar across the street and discovers that Joe's problem is increasing his business. He provides snacks to the waiting pilgrim, and would be happy if he never went away. Ray-the-Rimer, who is recognizable as a purveyor of "literatura de cordel" (cheap booklets written in verse about fantastic and popular topics, sold in the open markets), also finds that the increased traffic is promising for his business. Furthermore, he is interested in writing, printing, and selling a versified account of Joe's adventure. A reporter from the local newspaper seizes upon Joe's predicament as an opportunity for dramatic headlines and increased circulation. The reporter, however, distorts the true interests of Joe for sensationalistic effect. Besides exaggerating the defiance of Joe Burro, the reporter twists the facts concerning his decision to divide up his land among the poor. "Agrarian reform" and "exploitation of man by man" are phrases automatically associated with leftist social activism; the reporter suggests that Joe is an "agitator."

As we see, the Police are present along with the other social types in the crowd observing Joe's standoff. I will observe that while the Police are not in themselves "malandros" or opportunistic tricksters, they are subject to manipulation from others because they are especially wary of "agitators" or anything suggestive of a socialist program. In this, they are consistent with the values that will lead to the military dictatorship, which removed the left-leaning president, João Goulart, in 1964 (with the support of the United States)[5] and which controlled Brazil until 1985. (See Gemelli, this volume.) The presence of a Secret Agent in the play, who is intent on collecting sinister information about Joe, reinforces this representation of governmental authority (which is not far removed from the authority of the Church).

The most important "malandro" in the play is Pretty Boy, the sharp-dressing, fast-talking pimp who claims he wants to "help" Joe and Rosa to resolve their problems. He is the first person to appear when Joe and his wife trudge into the city before sunrise. Rosa is exhausted and says she would like nothing better than to lie down; however, her husband cannot leave his cross, for fear that someone might steal it while he is away. Pretty Boy comes to their aid, offering to take Rosa to a hotel where she may rest. The ingenuous Joe thanks him for the favor and encourages her to go, not realizing until later that he is sending his wife off to become one of Pretty Boy's sexual conquests. Indeed, this rivalry between Pretty Boy and Joe, prompted by the former's desire to have control over Rosa, is what precipitates the catastrophe of the play. Pretty Boy has a chummy relationship with several policemen, because he was once a member of the force. He plants seeds of suspicion in the Police Agent:

> PRETTY BOY (*laughing*):   . . . You people don't even know what's going on. Look over there. . .(*He nods in the direction of Joe Burro.*) In my day, that guy would already be in the "cooler." (*In another tone.*) And you fellows drove me out . . .
> POLICE AGENT: Who is he?
> PRETTY BOY (*pointing to the newspaper*):   Take it, read it . . . You don't even read the newspaper and you want to be up-to-date.

POLICE AGENT: Have you already talked to him?
PRETTY BOY: Yeah. The man's dangerous. He'd have us believe he's a saint, but that priest fellow there knew what he was doing when he closed the church and swore he wouldn't let him in.
POLICE AGENT: But that's kind of strange.
PRETTY BOY: If I were you, I'd "put him away" for a few days ... (91)

Pretty Boy's insinuations to the Police lead to the appearance of the Police Commissioner at the end of the play, to arrest Joe Burro. We note that the bystanders, with their own interests, are quick to become involved:

JOE (*having decided to resist*): No! Nobody is going to arrest me! I didn't do anything to be arrested for!
COMMISIONER: If you didn't do anything, you have nothing to fear. You will be released later. Let's go to the police station.
ROSA: No, Joe, don't go!
POLICEMAN: It's better ... at the police station you can explain everything.
RIMER: Don't fall for that, my friend.
JOE: I've just decided: only dead will they take me away from here. I swear it by St Barbara, only dead.
AGENT (*sees the knife in Joe Burro's hand*): Watch out, chief, he's armed! (*He notices the hostile attitude of the* capoeira *group.*) And those people are on his side!
COCA [the capoeira leader]: That's right! And you ain't going to arrest nobody here.
COMMISIONER: And why aren't we?
MANNY: Because it ain't right!
COMMISIONER: Are you trying to start trouble?
COCA: That's up to you ...
COMMISIONER: Stay out of it, or you'll be sorry!
ROSA: Joe!
JOE: Go away, Rosa! Don't come over here!
Joe Burro, a knife in his hand, recedes in the direction of the church. He goes up one or two steps backwards. The Priest comes behind him, strikes him on the arm, and the knife falls in the middle of the square. Joe Burro runs and bends down to pick it up. The police take advantage of the situation to fall on him, to subjugate him. And the capoeira *group falls on the police to defend him. Joe Burro disappears in this human mass. A shot is heard. The crowd disperses as if before a stampede of cattle. Just Joe Burro remains in the middle of the square, his hands on his stomach. He takes one more step in the direction of the church and falls dead.* (115–16)

The engagement of the characters in the play's central conflict, I believe, has three main degrees. On the level of principle, which is traditionally seen as the properly tragic level, the persons involved are Joe Burro and Father Olavo. On a more social level, a whole cross-section of Brazilian street characters is involved. While some, such as the *capoeiras*, are engaged because of sympathy with Joe and his predicament, the most important of these more marginal characters participate because of raw self-interest. And then on a more political level, tied to the particular tensions in Brazilian society during the 1960s, we have characters who are involved in an atmosphere of hypersensitivity about socialistic ideologies and movements, who have entered into the orbit of the United States in its Cold War with the Soviet Union, who see Joe's generous partition of his land as evidence of a communistic impulse, and who interpret his pilgrimage as a kind of political campaign, rather along the lines of the famous march conducted through the countryside by the leftist leader, Luís Carlos Prestes, during the 1920s or the circulation of Francisco Julião among the poor of the sugar cane plantations in the 1940s and 1950s. Were there only the ideal, tragic conflict, the trajectory of the drama would seem to be left in an impasse; it is the play's "messier" characters, its lower and less principled participants, who are able to bring an end to the standoff.

The Dénouement: A Gesture of Engagement

The unfolding of events after Joe's death is rapid, and takes place in a kind of ritual silence:

> *The Priest lowers his head and returns to the top of the steps. Pretty Boy appears on the hill. Master Coca looks at his friends inquisitively. They all understand his intention and respond affirmatively by nodding their heads. Master Coca bends over in front of Joe Burro, takes him by the arms; the other men also come over and help him carry the body. They put it on the cross, facing upward, with the arms extended, like a person crucified. They carry him in this way, as if on a stretcher, and advance toward the church. Pretty Boy grasps Rosa by the arm, trying to take her away. But Rosa repels him with a jerk and follows the group. Pretty Boy shrugs his shoulders and goes up the hill. Afraid, the Priest and the Sexton draw back, the Religious Woman flees, and the capoeira group goes into the church with the cross with Joe Burro's body on it. The Galician, Ray-the-Rimer, and Rosa bring up the rear of the procession. Only Auntie remains on the scene. A tremendous roar of thunder breaks out over the square.*
>
> AUNTIE [a black street vendor] (*cringing in fear, with the tips of her fingers she touches and ground and then her forehead*): Mercy on us, Saintly Mother! (116–17)

How similar is *Pagador*'s conclusion to the classical moment of recognition and concession in *Antigone*, and yet how different! The ancient play's *anagnorisis* is a verbal gesture, consisting in Creon's acknowledgment that he is responsible for the death of his son and his wife: "This is my guilt, all mine. I killed you, I say it clear. Servants, take me away, out of the sight of men. I who am nothing more than nothing now" (87). Creon's last words are an expression, at last, of humility, even of abjection, completed by the words of the Chorus about the punishment of pride (88).

In the Brazilian play, a similar effect is accomplished through wordless actions. The Priest's bowing his head, and drawing back as the cross is taken into the church, seems to signify a kind of recognition on his part. The lowering of the head is associated with an acknowledgment of culpability, while stepping back to allow passage seems to signify the recognition of the rights or validity of another party. It seems important to remember that the *capoeiristas*, those who place Joe's body upon the cross and carry the cross into the church, are the same actors who have assumed the function of the chorus in the third act. Their gesture, wherein they assert the validity of Joe's promise and his claim to enter the church with his cross, carries the authority of this ancient tragic voice, which affirms collective insights and values. Placing this final act in the hands of the "chorus" of capoeirists amounts to giving the people the last word, in contrast to the contentions of individuals who have been so insistent until this moment. And while as an individual Joe Burro has lost his campaign, the action reverses that loss and causes him to prevail. The obvious comparison to Christ carries all of the associations of martyrdom, followed by triumphal resurrection. Joe's cause, the popular values he espouses, are affirmed as righteous and unstoppable.

And a full appreciation of this gesture requires us to recognize the specific associations with African ethnicity, and, in particular, with slavery. Capoeira, like the *candomblé* that conflates Yansan and St. Barbara, stand as form of Afrocentric resistance to the masters' impositions. The play's final procession is a reaffirmation of that resistance.

The demographic implications of the gesture are also undeniable. The entrance of African-tainted Joe into the church, which has strived to maintain its European purity, carries suggestions of racial population dynamics in the new world. The people eventually triumph by populating. The act's sexual suggestiveness, its penetrative sense, cannot be ignored. And the final gesture suggests an ultimate inversion of historical power relations. The long history of miscegenation, in general, has been the history of white males imposing themselves, through various degrees of coercion or consent, upon darker females. Here, the play suggests a reversal of this traditional paradigm.

In its ending, *O pagador de promessas* clearly gives weight to its socially engaged aspect. It emphatically favors the interests of the underdogs. In this sense, I think it would qualify as an example of what Augusto Boal calls the "theater of the oppressed." (See Lodewyck and Monoson, this volume.) Implicitly, it also weighs in on the debate regarding the authentic meaning of tragedy, particularly of tragedies such as *Antigone*, by silently giving the last word to the people who are products of abuse.

Notes

1. See Chanter 2011: 22–3 for her enumeration of decidedly political performances of Antigone.
2. While critics of *Pagador* have surely acknowledged its classical echoes and essential tragedy (see Clark 1978: 92, Rosenfeld 1972: xii–xiv), the more general reception has been along social and political lines—for example, Clark 1978: 93–103, Magaldi 1972: 6–8, and Rosenfeld 1972: xvi–xvii. Dias Gomes himself refers to his play as a parable about the difficulty of surviving in the mechanism of modern capitalist society (1972: 9–11).
3. The translation of "candomblé" as "voodoo" is questionable, because it might suggest images of pin-filled dolls and zombies to some readers. *Candomblé* does not really have

such a sinister or predatory connotation for most Brazilians. Another English version of the play, by Stanley Richards, leaves "candomblé" untranslated, in quotation marks.

4. Fernández translates "berimbau" as "Jew's harp," an instrument that sounds vaguely similar to the Brazilian one but carries none of its cultural connotations. Richards wisely refrains from trying to translate the term in his version of the play.

5. See Bell 1972: 85–92 on the prevailing opinion that the United States did not directly sponsor the military takeover, but that its agents were deeply concerned about Goulart, in favor of the takeover, and were well informed about its progress.

References

Bell, P. D. (1972), "Brazilian–American Relations," in R. Roett ed., *Brazil in the Sixties*. Nashville, TN, 77–102.
Boal, A. (1985), *Theatre of the Oppressed*. New York.
Butler, J. (2000), *Antigone's Claim: Kinship Between Life and Death*. New York.
Carneiro, E. (1967), *Candomblés da Bahia*. Rio de Janeiro.
Chanter, T. (2011), *Whose Antigone? The Tragic Marginalization of Slavery*. Albany, NY.
Clark, F. M. (1978), *Twentieth-Century Brazilian Theatre: Essays*. Chapel Hill, NC.
DaMatta, R. (2000), *O que faz o brasil, Brasil?* Rio de Janeiro.
DuBois, P. (1986), "*Antigone* and the Feminist Critic," *Genre* 19, 371–83.
Gomes, A. D. (1962), *O pagador de promessas*. Rio de Janeiro.
Gomes, A. D. (1964), *Journey to Bahia: Dias Gomes' Prize Play, "O Pagador de Promessas."* Trans. S. Richards. Washington, DC.
Gomes, A. D. (1971), *Payment as Pledged*. Trans. O. Fernández, in G. Woodyard ed., *The Modern Stage in Latin America: Six Plays*. New York, 46–117.
Gomes, A. D. (1972), "Nota do autor," in *Teatro*. Vol. i. Rio de Janeiro, 9–11.
Gomes, A. D. (1972), *O santo inquérito*. *Teatro*. Vol. ii. Rio de Janeiro, 585–666.
Hegel, G. W. F. (1895), *Lectures on the Philosophy of Religion*. 3 vols. Trans. E. B. Speirs. London.
Honig, B. (2013), *Antigone Interrupted*. Cambridge.
Irigaray, L. (1985a), *Speculum of the Other Woman*. Trans. G. C. Gill. Ithaca, NY.
Irigaray, L. (1985b), *This Sex Which Is Not One*. Trans. C. Porter. Ithaca, NY.
Jones, A. (1994), *The Wordsworth Dictionary of Saints*. Ware.
Mader, M. B. (2005), "Antigone's Line," *Bulletin de la Société Américaine de Philosophie de Langue Française* 14.2, 18–40.
Magaldi, S. (1972), "Crítica a *O pagador de promessas*," in Dias Gomes, *Teatro*. Vol. i. Rio de Janeiro, 3–8.
Merrell, F. (2005), *Capoeira and Candomblé: Conformity and Resistance in Brazil*. Princeton.
Murphy, J. P. (2006), *Music in Brazil*. New York.
O pagador de promessas (The Payer of Promises) (1964), dir. A. Duarte. Per. Leonardo Villar, Glória Menezes, Dionísio Azevedo. DVD. Cinedistri.
Rosenfeld, A. (1972), "A obra de Dias Gomes," in Dias Gomes, *Teatro*. Vol. i. Rio de Janeiro, ix–xliii.
Segal, C. (1999), *Tragedy and Civilization: An Interpretation of Sophocles*. Norman, OK.
Sophocles (1954), *Antigone*. Trans. E. Wyckoff, in D. Grene and R. Lattimore, eds., *Sophocles I*. Chicago, 157–205.
Steiner, G. (1984), *Antigones*. New York.

CHAPTER 23

THE DARKENING OF MEDEA

Geographies of Race, (Dis)Placement, and Identity in Agostinho Olavo's Além do Rio (Medea)

JOSÉ DE PAIVA DOS SANTOS

SPACE is a social construct, a concept that impacts the reception of Greek drama in the Americas. As Greek drama migrates to each new space, the cultures within the New World that receive it alter its meaning while at the same time generating meaning in its new space. Geography as fate is true of Agostinho Olavo's *Além do Rio*, as it is of many plays in the Latin American contexts (see Barrenechea, this volume). Before turning to this chapter's chief concern, which is Olavo's play in its new environment, I offer a brief survey of other Latin American examples.

Instances of rewritings or adaptations of Greek myths abound in the history of western literature. In Latin America, due to the economic and political instability of various nation-states in the twentieth century, looking back to the classical past has allowed writers to work with a tradition and a body of motifs, tropes, and themes their audiences can relate to, as well as make adaptations without perhaps drawing too much attention from military governments and censorship agencies (see Barrenechea and Gemelli, both this volume). Carlinda Fragale Pate Nuñes remarks that the second half of the twentieth century bore witness to a migration, for example, of the Antigone myth from Europe to the stages of Latin America, this time to represent not world conflicts but the more local, domestic struggles of societies attempting to gain political freedom and cultural autonomy (Nuñes 2003: 34). Argentinian Griselda Gambaro's reworking of the Greek Antigone in *Antígona furiosa* (1986) illustrates well Nuñes's comments on the nature of these adaptations in Latin America. Here, Gambaro resorts to Greek myth to bring to the fore the atrocities carried out during the so-called "Dirty War" (1976–83) in Argentina, a period in which approximately 10,000 to 30,000 people, comprising political dissidents, armed rebels, and left-wing civilians, were killed or simply disappeared under the military dictatorship of Lieutenant Jorge Rafaél Videla. Videla took over the country after a military coup deposed the president Isabel Perón in 1976. It is against the backdrop of this political landscape that Gambaro's *Antígona furiosa* stages the story of courageous women, similar to the Antigone of old, daring enough to come forward and claim the right to bury the men and women murdered by the government forces. Another Argentinian example comes from Leopoldo Marechal's *Antígona Vélez* (1951), which follows the myth closely, but this time against the backdrop of Argentina's struggle for territorial and national autonomy in the nineteenth century. A similar political agenda also constitutes the background of *Antígona* (2000), by the Peruvian José Watanabe and the theatrical group Yuyachkani. In this adaption, the poet and playwright depicts, in the form of dramatic monologue, the horrors of the civil war waged from 1980 through 2000 between the Marxist-Maoist group called *Sendero Luminoso* (Shining Path) and Peru's dictatorial forces led by President Alberto Fujimori. Here, the ancient Thebes is represented in the mountains and plains of central Peru, territory where the Peruvian Antigone searches for and buries many of those killed during the confrontation so as "to return them to Pachamama, the Inca mother earth," as well as "ask the blessings of countless Catholic *virgenes*, like the Virgen de Chiquinquirá or the Virgen del Carmen" (Lane 2007: 18).

Similar to the Antigone myth, the story of Medea has also been adapted by numerous playwrights in Latin America, with the same purpose of using the ancient to address contemporary issues such as gender and racial alterity, marginalization, and economic exploitation of impoverished subjects. *Medea en el espejo* (1960) by the Cuban José Triana illustrates well this insertion of the Greek myth in a completely different context, so as to explore its various semantic layers (see Nikoloutsos, this volume). Using Euripides' version of the *Medea*, in Triana's rendition, the heroine becomes María, a poor mulatto living on the margins of society and struggling for survival in an urban space highly hierarchized along racial and gender lines. Unlike the Greek Medea, María is not a foreigner per se, but her social condition casts her as an outsider in a society divided between haves and have-nots. In this modern scenario, she is the mistress of a white man, Julián, who eventually abandons her to marry a white woman, the daughter of a local politician, out of ambition for upward mobility. The craving for revenge leads María to poison Julián's wife to-be, Esperancita, and his father-in-law, Perico Piedra Fina. Later, she also kills their children, for they represent not only a connection to Julián and the dominating culture, but also a mirror of what she is not—a member of the white class, with all the privileges it confers. Conceived against the backdrop of the Cuban Revolution in the 1960s, Triana's María represents a call for black identity and return to her Afro-Caribbean roots suffocated by the hegemonic culture (Anjos 2010: 31).

In the 1980s and 1990s, several other important productions appear: *El castillo interior de Medea Camuñas* (1984) by the Puerto Rican Pedro Santaliz; *Medea de Moquehua* (1992) by the Argentinian L. Salvaneschi; *The Hungry Woman: A Mexican Medea* (1995) by the Mexican-American Cherríe Moraga; and *Medea* (1997) by the Cuban R. Montenero (see Billotte, this volume). Worthy of note is Moraga's use of Medea to interrogate the position of Chicanos and Chicanas in the United States as well as address issues of cultural and sexual identity. To achieve these aims, Moraga "balance[s] elements of the Greek story with the Mexican La Llorona and the Aztec goddess Coatlicue," so as to examine "the intersections between aspects of identity, particularly as a Chicana lesbian, but also in relationship to indigenous cultures and motherhood" (Eschen 2006: 103). This play has gone much further than most rewritings of the Greek Medea, for it places the story in the context of contemporary concerns about global terrorism, displacement of indigenous peoples, and marginalization of the other.

In Brazil, adaptations and rewritings of the Antigone and Medea myths have also resulted in a variety of stage productions engaging various moments of Brazil's cultural and political landscape. Jorge Andrade, for instance, resorts to Antigone to stage *Pedreira das Almas* (1958) a critical analysis of Brazil's nineteenth-century imperial regime as well that of the 1960s and 1970s, the period in which the play was published and staged. Similar to other productions in Latin America, the revolutionary, sociopolitical overtones prevail. In the play, the action takes place in the context of the 1842 Liberal Revolution, a period of intense conflict in Brazil between conservatives and liberals in the struggle for political control. The action focuses on a small town in the state of Minas Gerais, southeastern Brazil, called Pedreira das Almas, torn between tradition and change, past and present, natural laws versus the laws of the state. The town knew better days when gold mining brought in wealth and prosperity but now faces economic and social problems (the region of Minas Gerais means "General Mines"), as the new generation desires to leave in search of better opportunities. Besides, some of its residents have become involved in the widespread uprising against the imperial government, which has exploited the natural resources of the country and towns such as Pedreira das Almas, with no assistance to its residents after the exhaustion of wealth. The dramatic tension reaches a climax when Mariana decides not to depart with her boyfriend Gabriel like the rest of the village residents. In the meantime, her brother Martiniano is killed by the police for supporting the subversive liberal revolution and for not reporting his friend Gabriel, also Mariana's boyfriend. To make things worse, the local cemetery is full, and Mariana cannot leave and search for another place to bury her brother and the others killed during the skirmishes. Here is where the tension between natural laws and the laws of the state begins. She confronts the police by exposing all the unburied bodies in the church building. Mariana wins the battle, for after this episode the police give up on the persecution of Gabriel and leave town. Free to search for better horizons, Gabriel and others depart, but Mariana chooses to remain behind. She has to take care of the dead, she explains (Arantes 2009: 86). More recently, the folklorist and writer Gisa Gonsioroski produced *Antígona: o nordeste quer falar* ("Antigone: The Northwest Wants to Speak") (2002), a text in which Gonsioroski mixes elements from the Greek myth with Brazil's northeastern popular culture and religiosity. Here, to make the classic text accessible to popular audiences, Gonsioroski employs the language of street theater, puppetry, and circus language (Motta 2006: 114).

Similar to the Antigone story, Medea's drama has received various stage versions in the last decades. Maria Cecília de Miranda Nogueira Coelho points out that in the last 50 years, four major productions involving rewritings or adaptations of Medea deserve attention: *Além do Rio (Medea)* (1961), by Agostinho Olavo; *Gota d'água* (1975), by Chico

Buarque de Hollanda and Paulo Pontes (see Gemelli, this volume); *Des-Medeia* (1995), by Denise Stoklos; and the opera *Kseni—A Estrangeira* (2006), by Joci de Oliveira. In all of them, Coelho observes, the authors re-enact, from different perspectives, Medea's drama and tragic ending in the context of the socio-economic conditions of marginalized groups in Brazil (Coelho 2005: 157). Of these four productions, Oliveira's *Kseni* goes furthest in her efforts to adapt the myth to a modern context. A multi-media pioneer in Brazil, she writes, produces, and records the opera version of the drama and releases it on DVD. In the production, Oliveira highlights the subversive, barbarian, foreigner side of Medea: "It's a barbarian Opera about a foreign woman who is in truth able to be anyone, depending on the setting—a periphery that depends on where the center is, where inclusion and exclusion are certainly related concepts" (Coelho 2005: 172).

What these Latin American works attest is the power of Greek drama in the imaginary of the Americas. Above all, they reflect, as Helene P. Foley has observed, twentieth-century theatrical trends in which Greek dramas have served "as a façade for staging political protest or a response to a particular political climate" (Foley 1999: 4). A quick look at these plays demonstrates that all of them stage out diverse forms of political repression, persecution, or (mis)representation of marginalized groups.

Além do Rio (Medea)

Além do Rio (Medea), by Agostinho Olavo, has received little critical attention over the years from the academic community in Brazil and elsewhere, when compared, for example, to *Gota d'água*, by Chico Buarque de Hollanda and Paulo Pontes. More important, though, is the manner in which Olavo successfully adapts Euripides' rendering of the myth of Medea, in an attempt to explore broader issues of race, diaspora, and cultural identity in Brazil. With this view in mind, this chapter looks into the play's representation of space, race, and identity, as well as the way these discourses interconnect to foreground a critique of the politics of race and maintenance of racialized spaces in Brazil's purportedly racial democracy.

Além do Rio (Medea) belongs to a group of plays produced in the aftermath of the creation of the Black Experimental Theater (TEN), in 1944, by the activist, artist, poet, and playwright Abdias do Nascimento. A tireless defender of the political rights of Afro-descendants in Brazil, Nascimento, since his college years, became involved in movements against all forms of racial discrimination. The decision to create the "Teatro Experimental Negro" came after he watched in Lima, Peru, a white actor, painted black, playing the role of a character of African ancestry in a performance of Eugene O'Neill's *The Emperor Jones*. This episode triggered the desire to use dramaturgy as the vehicle to render more evident the artistic talents and social aspirations of Afro-descendants in Brazil. In regard to the Black Experimental Theater, Nascimento remarks: "We propose to restore, in Brazil, the human values of black Africans, who have been disgraced and negated by the dominant culture, since colonial times, and who now carry the mental baggage of their European urban formation, founded on the pseudo-scientific pretense of the inferiority of the black race" (Nascimento 2004: 210). Even though Agostinho Olavo did not claim to be an Afro-descendant himself, he sympathized with the group's cause, as did many intellectuals of the time.

Published in 1961, the play adapts Euripides' *Medea* to the context of African slave traffic in seventeenth-century Brazil as well as the strategies of enslaved blacks to confront the regime. In Olavo's adaptation, Jason is a trader who travels to Africa not in search of an amulet (the Golden Fleece), but of slaves to feed a growing market eager for free labor in the Americas. In Africa, he meets Jinga, an African queen and sorcerer, whose love he gains and who then becomes his aid in the capture of blacks to be enslaved. Her father Aetes, the local chief, tries to stop her, but she murders him as well as her brother Suana Mulopo before she leaves for Brazil with a throng of captive people. Once in Brazil she betrays her cultural traditions by getting baptized into the Catholic Church, a common practice during the slave trade period, and receiving a new name—Medea—and thereby leaving behind her African name Jinga. In the process, she also abandons her religious beliefs, mother tongue, and divination practices when she (unofficially) marries Jason, with whom she has two children who show no physical traits of African lineage. In her new land, she lives on an isolated island, separated from the white community and rejected by her own compatriots, who see her as a traitor and assimilationist. Similar to Euripides' Medea, she is never fully integrated in the community.

The play's denouement follows closely Euripides' tragedy as well. The tragic reversal begins when Jason, out of ambition for social mobility, decides to marry the daughter of a rich landowner—Creon—and abandons Medea to her fate. To make matters worse, she cannot even remain on the island, the place she has been living since she arrived and believes it is her home. Creon makes it clear she is no longer wanted around; she is actually a menace because of her knowledge of African magic. She is commanded to quit the land and leave her children to Jason's care, for they are white and were born free. Jason's and later Creon's act serve thus as the trigger for Medea's vengeance. Having pleaded with Creon to remain in the city one more day, she orchestrates her revenge: first, she sends Creusa, Jason's fiancée, a bewitched necklace, which kills her during the wedding celebration at the village. She then slays their two children by making them cross the river and drown in the torrents. The play ends with Jason cursing her for the death of his children, his future wife, and commanding her to leave the island. Unlike Euripides' *Medea*, which ends with an affirmation of the protagonist's otherness, or her divinity, Olavo's Medea is bound to the land. The play, then, follows Euripides' structure very closely, though the particulars of place have changed.

In the end, Medea jettisons her Christian name and assumes her former title, Jinga the queen and sorcerer, and joins a band of runaway slaves hiding in the woods (this is the apotheosis of Euripides' play). Instead of quitting the foreign space and finding security somewhere else, Olavo's Medea has nowhere to turn but her fellow countrymen. Thus she appropriates her foreign space—or perhaps the Brazilian city is what was foreign—(re)joining her people hiding in the "quilombo" (autonomous communities of runaway slaves that in fact warred with the Portuguese historically, which I discuss more fully below). This reintegration and affirmation of her roots, negritude, and religion is emphasized through the different rhythms and beats calling for Medea from the jungle. In the end, instead of flying away, Medea remains, on the margins, but affirming: "I am still a queen. I am still black and a Yoruba deity!" (231)

Além do Rio stands out, as we can see, for the careful adaptation and insertion of the tragedy in the context of colonization and traffic of black slaves in Brazil. Olavo's play serves the author's purpose very well, since it stages the theme of the strong versus the weak, dominator versus dominated, local versus the strange, and center versus margin. Yet, the play goes further in its appropriation of the tragedy. For one thing, in the attempt to highlight the different environments and conflicts of the displaced black subject in a foreign space, the playwright combines elements from Portuguese folklore and African traditions, thereby creating a spectacle in which "Songs and ritual dances—maracatu (Afro-Brazilian performance of the Northeast) and candomblé"—are combined with "street vendors selling flowers, fruit, and parrots" (Nascimento 2004: 161) (see Dixon, this volume). This theatrical strategy enables Olavo to depict Jinga, later baptized as Medea, as an individual torn between two different worlds, not knowing exactly where to place her loyalty. The sounds of the drums stir up the desire to return to her origins, but her Catholic vows prevent her from doing it. It is only when she realizes that her love and loyalty have been betrayed that she re-evaluates her decision. By killing her two sons, she ruptures all biological ties with Jason and his culture; leaving the island she conceived as a sign of protection, maybe even privilege, becomes an act of redemption and reclaiming of her former allegiances. Thus, it is against the backdrop of this tragedy about displacement, otherness, loyalty, and betrayal that Olavo sets out to examine, as this chapter will further argue, the dynamics and formation of racialized spaces, as well as issues of social marginalization and cultural identification of Afro-descendants in Brazil.

SPACES AND PLACES

The notion that spaces are more than physical locations with distinct boundaries has been at the center of anthropological and geographical studies since at least the 1970s, when scholars in these fields began to regard space more as a social rather than simply a geographical category of human experience. In other words, differently from previous periods, which saw spaces as mere sites of or for human activities, toward the late twentieth century geographers started to look at spaces as the product of social practices. More than passive recipients of human actions and behaviors, spaces began to be perceived as active elements in the configuration of individuals both at the personal and collective level. Yu-Fu Tuan is among a number of social geographers whose theorizations about spaces and places in the 1970s and 1980s set the tone for much of the critical thinking on the subject later in the century. An important contribution is Tuan's distinction between space and place, the former consisting of the domain of the immeasurable, infinite, and indistinguishable, and the latter belonging to the realm of the personal, experiential, and relational. In his conception, spaces turn into places when they become meaningful to individuals: "What begins as undifferentiated space becomes place as we get to know it better and endow it with value" (Tuan 1977: 6). For Tuan, places are collective constructions, the product of emotional, sensual, and aesthetic experiences. Along these lines, Tuan coins the term *topophilia* and *topophobia* to describe the manner in which people interact with and develop feelings of either attachment or antipathy to particular places. Geography becomes, in this conception, "the study of the earth as the *home* of people."[1]

Toward the end of the past century, other geographers elaborated on this notion of place as the product of social relationships, mostly by blurring or problematizing the space–place dichotomy. For scholars such as Edward Casey, for instance, whose work is heavily influenced by phenomenology, conceiving a realm free from the constraints of human interactions, such as space, is problematic, for it presumes the existence of an a priori state of human affairs apart from experience. This dichotomy is false, he affirms, for "our lives are so place-oriented and place-saturated that we cannot begin to comprehend . . . what sheer placelessness would be like" (Casey 1993: ix). For him, place precedes space, since individuals are always inserted in or belong to a spatial domain; as with time, one cannot exist outside the constraints of a particular locality. As he remarks: "We come to the world—we come into it and keep returning to it—as already placed there. Places are not added to sensations any more than they are imposed on spaces" (Casey 1996: 18). The philosopher Michel de Certeau further elaborates on this space–place distinction by arguing that place stands for the stable, the setting in "which elements are distributed in relationships of coexistence" (de Certeau 2002: 117). Besides, place is the realm in which the law of the "proper" operates, that is, places are governed by definite positionalities of things and individuals. Space comes into existence, according to de Certeau, when the ensemble of elements within a certain place is set into movement, thereby destabilizing that which had been fixed and established. In this sense, de Certeau remarks, "space consists of intersections of mobile elements" (de Certeau 2002: 117). To illustrate this distinction, he talks about how urban places become spaces when taken over by pedestrians, or how readers transform a book—a place governed by a system of linguistic signs—into a space—a site ruled by movement and destabilization—during the act of reading. Both readers and city-dwellers are agents as well as receptors in this whole process. In this context, space is synonymous with lived experience, or in de Certeau's words, "*space is a practiced place*."[2]

Along with debates about the nature of space and place, the rise of gender and race studies in the last decades has brought new insights into discussions about spatiality. If space, as de Certeau argues, is the realm of the intersectional, the mobile, and the unstable, then elements such as race and gender, and the power struggles they generate, should be examined as potential agents of instability and positionality. It is with this conception of gendered space in mind that Doreen Massey highlights the role sexual hierarchy has played, since the nineteenth century, in the manner spaces have been divided, for example, between the private and the public, the homelike and the streetlike, the former being naturally women's domain and the latter men's. In this setting, the woman is expected to be the guardian of moral values, modesty, and religious piety, while the man pursues more mundane affairs outside the confines of the house. In her view, then, "space and place are not only in themselves gendered but . . . reflect and affect the ways in which gender is constructed and understood" (Massey 1994: 179). Even when women challenge spatial conventions and venture themselves in the so-called male's world, they still have to confront a system encoded with "predominant forms of representation, such as monuments, commemorative buildings, and historic sites," which stand as emblems of patriarchal values (Urry 2004: 13). Therefore, what these critics argue is that spaces often contribute to create and maintain gendered practices that place men in positions of power and authority while relegating women to subaltern roles.

If gender as a category of human experience influences significantly the way spaces are formed as well as how they "are used strategically to inform identity and produce asymmetrical gendered relations" (Low and Lawrence-Zúñiga 2003: 7), the category of race, cultural geographers affirm, plays an even more crucial role in the dynamics of space formation and its accompanying cultural practices. It is widely known that race as a biological concept has been debunked by the scientific community. Yet, this knowledge has not prevented race from becoming a social category informing most aspects of human experience, especially in places and cultures with a history of racial segregation. In these settings, scholars observe, "race inscribes and circumscribes the experiences of space and time, of geography and history, just as race itself acquires its specificity in terms of space–time correlates" (Goldberg 1993: 206). In other words, there is a symbiotic relationship between space and race, which means that spatiality as a topological category cannot be divorced from practices Kevin Durrheim and John Dixon denominate "the social construction of the foreign" (434). Yet, this Other, in turn, actively acts upon processes of space formation in a constant exchange of discourses and practices. But how does the Other become racially constructed and what role do spaces play in this symbiotic process?

Geographers and cultural scholars point to structural as well as cultural elements as key determinants connecting space and race. In terms of structure, Ronald R. Sundstrom uses the United States as the typical example of a setting in which, due to a long history of Jim Crow segregation, race still persists as a structural category in the way cities, towns, and neighborhoods are mapped. He remarks that to maintain racial and social differences, residential patterns in the United States normally follow "a vertical axis of status, with whites on top, blacks on the bottom, and Asian Americans, Latin Americans, and Native Americans at points in between" (Sundstrom 2003: 90). The consequence is the formation of enclaves such as Chinatowns, barrios, and Indian reservations, which testify to the endemic presence of race as a spatial determinant in the construction of the "foreign" as the Other. Be it the beaches of South Africa during apartheid or the slums in Brazil's large cities, the presence of race as a political construct is perceived as significant in the structural and cultural formation of spaces. In this scenario, Sundstrom reiterates, race "is not just expressed spatially, but is experienced and produced spatially." In other words, "[r]ace is placed . . ." (Sundstrom 2003: 90).

In sum, for social geographers, spaces and places do not originate in a cultural vacuum and are then randomly configured as history moves forward. Spaces are the products, rather, of complex social, economic, and cultural forces, which determine the way they are shaped and interrelate to people and institutions. As researchers have demonstrated, in the dynamics of space formation, gender, and especially for the purpose of this chapter, race, constitute important agents in the arrangement and maintenance of particular cultural geographies.

MAKING SPACE AND PLACE IN *ALÉM DO RIO*

Olavo's drama thematizes these interrelations in the Brazilian context by representing, among other elements, the structural and cultural mechanisms whereby spaces and places are formed and the role of race in these sites of struggle, resistance, and cultural identification. In Euripides' *Medea*, space and race are important, since, for one thing, Medea, from the beginning, is constructed as the other. She comes from Colchis, an island in the middle of the Black Sea considered by the Greeks the edge of the earth, a place inhabited by barbarians. Medea's love and marriage to the adventurous Jason places her in an awkward situation. They move to Greece and settle first in Iolchus and then in Corinth, places completely foreign to her. Medea's origin and cultural background soon stand out and turn her into an outsider in a strange land. Her remarks to the chorus that humans have the tendency to quickly judge others without honestly knowing them testify to her sentiment of being seen as an outsider.

In *Além do Rio*, as we have seen, Medea—formerly called Jinga—also comes from a place considered uncivilized—Africa, and, after marrying the adventurous Jason, settles down in Brazil. Despite her efforts to assimilate the new culture, she remains isolated on an island, unable to expunge the stereotypes associated with her skin color, customs, and, especially, religious practices. In both cases, spatial negotiation and race are significant in that they unveil the role cultural marks, stereotypes, and fear of the foreign play in maintaining racial hierarchies in power. In both Euripides' rendition and Olavo's adaptation of the tragedy, then, spaces serve, in Caroline Knowles's words, not only as motifs of past and present "racial orders," but also as one of the "possibilities in which race is fabricated" (Knowles 2003: 80). Spaces and places constitute, in other words, the set where race as a category is constructed, performed, and reified as well as contested, confronted, and resisted; these spatial domains, in turn, become racialized as discourses about race and space get so intertwined their presence can hardly be detected.

Olavo employs several strategies to dramatize the issue of racialized spaces, the most important one being the way he creates, from the very beginning, an ambience in which the characters transit through spaces divided not along traditional geographical lines. What one sees throughout the play is the manifestation of deeply embedded notions of race configuring and determining how particular spaces are delimited, appropriated, and inhabited. The description of the set in the opening scene is revealing in this regard: "An island formed on the shoulder of the river. At the base, along the waters, virgin woods. On the first plane, a dangerous and narrow pass, where the women go to wash clothes. On the island, to the left, Medea's mud hut and, to the right, a hurried little wooden bridge, connected to the island at the bank of the first plane" (200) (Fig. 23.1).

Three places are juxtaposed in this description: an island, a jungle, and a third space not clearly defined, but connected to the island by a wooden bridge. It is the dialogue among the washerwomen at the river that first hints at the configuration of these three spaces. They explain first what the sounds of drums coming from the jungle are about: "They are runaway slaves who have escaped their overseer. They live in a group, endure hunger, sleep in the woods, in peace, they shake of fever—from malaria" (200). They are singing, beating the drums, and invoking spirits, they further explain. The audience perceives straightway the existence of a subversive space over which the institutionalized power seems to have no jurisdiction. The ones dwelling in this space have fled from oppression, claiming a territory that has now become politically and culturally distinct from the rest of the landscape.

The fact that this community remains invisible throughout the play is significant. Nobody sees them, not even the audience, who only hears the sounds of their music. (Thus the comparison to Emperor Jones is even more apt.) Later, the conversation

FIG. 23.1 The Bay of Barra, Salvador da Bahia, Brazil. Salvador was one of the main slave ports into the Americas during the transatlantic slave trade. Photo: Patrice Rankine.

switches to the person inhabiting the island, a place that has also acquired a different formation since Medea, whom they characterize as dirty, dangerous, black, and a sorceress, moved there: "They say she's the queen of the island. Lazy, she does nothing. She lives like white *donas* of the house, with a female slave at her side" (202). They gossip about Medea's betrayal of her people back in Africa and her marriage to Jason, the slave trader, who is about to abandon her. They mostly criticize her attempt to assimilate to white culture and pretension to be like the other women in the village. They, like the rest of the people, avoid that space, for fear of being bewitched. Some people, though, have crossed the bridge leading to the island, but in this case it is to request Medea's services as a conjuror. As of late, she has apparently abandoned these practices due to her commitment to Catholicism, which forbids veneration of pagan idols and use of divination art. Contrary to the runaways' drumming in the jungle, Medea's presence is very much visible to everyone due to her demeanor, attire, and her geographical position. She can see and be seen by everyone walking by.

The third space is not clearly delineated, but it is evident it encompasses the village and the surrounding farms owned by the wealthy landowners. It is the place where Jason, the slave trader who brought Medea and her fellow countrymen, lives. Despite Medea's claim that Jason is her husband and has fathered her two children, it is evident they do not share the same space. In fact, he has not been to the island for quite some time. This third space is also conveyed as less confined and more interactive. At the moment, for instance, the whole community is gathered for a very important event: Jason's marriage to Creusa, the daughter of a rich landowner. Everyone is invited including the slaves. The festive atmosphere is best described by Egeu, the one who breaks the news to Medea about Jason's wedding: "The blacks of the plantation dance, the mulattos dance the *lundu* (a dance from Africa). Black and white dance there at the marketplace. The old man rolls tobacco because Jason, our bravest warrior, dances a wedding dance among the whites for the beautiful Creusa" (214). In this space beyond the river the audience sees movement, interaction, an apparent mixing of people and cultures. There is even a moment when Creusa steps down the scaffold where she is gathered with her family to dance with the slaves: "Don't you want to dance with me? But, why not? Don't be afraid. My father is permitting it, and no one will be punished. Come on, dance" (222). This third space is presented thus as less rigid in terms of social conventions. The slave owners are depicted as receptive and willing to include everyone in the celebrations taking place; the slaves are portrayed as content to serve their masters and participate in their festivities. A revealing moment in this respect is when Creusa's household slave tells the washerwomen: "What are you doing? Today, no one ought to work. The dance is it! Everyone's partying in the marketplace. Aren't you going to party? God! It's not possible! Jaia prepared a present, made a garment of silk and a *mantilha* (headscarf) and gold. Just come see how beautiful it is! Come see the golden crown" (213). She flaunts the skirt she got from her mistress and behaves as a member of the family. The mixture of different rhythms and songs adds to the place an atmosphere of mutual friendship and communal living, as black slaves come from all the surrounding farms to participate in the major event in the village.

Yet, the play does more than simply map the different social contours of these territories in preparation for Medea's tragic act of vengeance against Jason. By probing the social and cultural dynamics of these spaces, Olavo delineates a poetics of space in which he shows how race and geography are so intertwined they can pass for givens, thereby masking the socio-cultural discourses from which they originated in the first place. Just as important is the suggestion that the racialization of particular spaces naturalizes social inequalities at the same time it fosters segregation and cultural marginalization.

In *Além do Rio*, Olavo's metaphorical use of the island (along with the river which surrounds it) to examine questions of race and space formation is illuminating. An island, by definition, is a tract of land surrounded by water, isolated, with no contact or direct communication with others. In the play, the island gains racial contours the moment Medea is placed on it and begins to be constructed as the different other. Despite the opulence of her garments, Medea is depicted as barbarian and evil-looking, thereby standing in contrast to the washerwomen who observe her from a distance. The description emphasizes mainly the hairstyle and jewelry around the arms and legs, which is painted as unsophisticated and outlandish. The dialogue by the washerwomen does suggest that she is considered a pariah in the community: "Be careful! She is a dangerous woman. Dirty nigger! Sorceress!" (202). It is true that Jason has given her some social privileges, such as having a household slave, but this has not made any difference in the way she is perceived by the community. For them, she is a witch and should be kept at a distance. The warning by one of the washerwomen confirms it. The community outside the island associates Medea with conjuring, spirit worshipping, and other pagan practices. In fact, they sound out common stereotypes in which black culture and religious beliefs are demonized by mainstream Christianity, in an effort to maintain the hegemony of the Catholic Church. Medea, just for being black and different, is associated with these and other supposedly demonic practices which further place her in the category of the Other. Even Christian baptism and abandonment of her traditional religious beliefs do not place her within the white community as a free woman.

The river surrounding the island further distances Medea from the rest of the village. Her only connection to the community outside is a wooden bridge. The bridge here also gains metaphorical significance in that it sets, along with the river, a boundary between a world hegemonically ruled by whites—the village, the site of institutionalized racism—and the island, a space grounded on racial difference. It implies communication, but the gap remains regardless. Her marginalization becomes even more evident when Creon, Creusa's father, demands that she leave the island. He does not see any reason for Medea to remain there now that Jason is about to marry his daughter. Her mention of the fact that she has been married to Jason and has children with him does not dissuade Creon, who quickly replies that their union has no legal significance under the country's legislation due to her race. The children also belong to Jason, for phenotypically they all took after him. When Creon tells she must cross the river and depart, she replies: "The whites are along the river (*além do rio*). There's no place for me" (217). Here, she recognizes the dimension of her dilemma, for now she realizes she cannot go back to her former country, neither does she belong to Brazil, despite her union to Jason. Her predicament is that she has been displaced twice: first, after leaving her motherland; secondly, by being expelled from the island. Either way, race has been the determinant factor.

Drawing on Edward Said's insights, Brooke Neely and Michelle Samura explain that space and race are interconnected in the sense that both "involve 'other-ing' processes that establish and maintain particular racial and spatial positionings." They maintain also that racialized spaces have much to do with how whiteness, in western culture, has acquired the status of property in that it carries "a privileged sense of belonging and entitlement to space [that] is fundamentally defined by exclusion and subjugation" (Neely and Samura 2011: 1944). Olavo's treatment of the island and surrounding river as metaphors for (dis)placement and exclusion puts into relief these socio-political ideologies at work in the racialization of spaces. Despite her status as queen back in Africa, her marriage to Jason, and even her Christian baptism, she has been constructed as member of an ethnic group doomed to be slaves and servants. The washerwomen laugh at one point during conversation at the mention that Medea is a "monjola" (priestess), among the bravest and freest blacks from Costa d'Ouro. Since Medea is framed from the beginning as the bonded other, for her to have some measure of movement, she had to be placed somewhere else, on the fringe of the free world, under the protection of the white colonizer. But even on the island she remains captive of an ideology that does not allow her to cross racial and cultural boundaries. Creusa's father Creon makes it clear that were it not for Jason, her situation would be quite different: "You are a nigger brought by a powerful slavetrader, [a man] who protected you against the entire population" (217). For her, what little freedom she has is a privilege, not a human right. Her expulsion from the island further illustrates Neely and Samura's view of whiteness as synonymous with entitlement. Due to her color and heritage, Medea belongs neither to the island, the place she took for home, nor the village, owned by whites, and the place she can only live as a slave. Creon's claim of ownership based on white supremacy is incisive. Whiteness and prerogative to space are viewed as givens, thereby reiterating Neely and Samura's remarks that "the maintenance of white property and the sense of entitlement that accompanies white identity" is strongly connected to "systemic exclusion of people of color" (Neely and Samura 2011: 1944). Medea's permanence on the island disrupts a seemingly natural order in which whiteness and space are like two sides of a coin. (The influence of black slave women on Brazilian culture extends into the contemporary iconography, such as that of the "Baiana," the women who cook, dance, and sell goods, even today, as this last image conveys (Fig. 23.2). Gilberto Freyre discusses the influence of such women in his Brazilian sociologies of the early twentieth century).

If Medea's placement, estrangement, and eventual removal from the island make visible race and space-making ideologies, the forest as the hideout of runaway slaves functions in a similar manner, but in this case, Olavo resorts to the trope of invisibility, which, along with the music and singing, highlights strategies of appropriation and subversion of particular spaces by oppressed groups. Unlike the island, the forest, a quilombo, does not reveal its occupants, although the audience is able to hear their music and singing. Nobody knows either what the forest looks like after being taken over by its new residents except that, as put by one of the washerwomen, "They are free,

FIG. 23.2 The iconic "Baiana" or black woman of Salvador da Bahia, remnant of the slaves who cooked, cleaned, and washed for their masters. Photo: Patrice Rankine.

they are content . . . but woe to the whites that try to approach them" (202). Despite this invisibility, the sounds coming from the forest and their power hint at the social configuration of this particular space as well as the subversive potential of its dwellers.

Edvanda Bonavina da Rosa remarks that by joining the group of runaway slaves after her eviction, Medea chooses to live "in a peripheral group, in the *habitus* of a cultural milieu, which is the *quilombo*" (Rosa 1993: 85). Rosa points here at Olavo's representation of an important aspect of the racial geographies of slavery: the formation of enclaves by blacks of the African diaspora who would confront the system, many times at the cost of their own lives. Scott Joseph Allen explains that slaves used all sorts of stratagems to challenge a system that insisted on treating them as subhuman, working in plantations under violent and inhumane circumstances. Forming communities in areas of difficult access such as swamps, mountains, and jungles constituted one among the many strategies they employed to evade slave hunters and fight the brutal regime (Allen 1998: 142). In seventeenth-century Brazil, the establishment of the quilombo of Palmares exemplifies a significant moment in the struggle of enslaved blacks to gain back their lost physical and cultural autonomy. Located in northeastern Brazil, this maroon society achieved unprecedented political sovereignty, resisting numerous incursions by the Portuguese crown and colonial authorities. Archaeological and historical records inform us that they possessed "a highly organized social and political structure," consisting of "irrigated fields, villages containing from 220–2000 houses, churches, iron forges, and a training village" (Allen 1998: 145). Just as important as political resistance to colonial power was the role these maroon societies played in forging new forms of cultural and religious expressions, needless to say, perceived as heretic by the Catholic Church. In the case of Palmares, as in most *mocambos* throughout the Atlantic, for a variety of reasons, black fugitives could not go back to their native forms of cultural and religious expression. Thus, in terms of spirituality, syncretic forms of spiritual manifestation prevailed, which allowed for the mingling of indigenous and Christian rituals. Journal entries by the expedition leader Fernão Carrillo, sent out to find and destroy mocambos, record interesting observations regarding the syncretic religiosity at Palmares, which took shape by mixing Catholic prayers with the residents' indigenous beliefs: "And although these barbarians have all but forgotten their subjugation, they have not completely lost allegiance to the Church. There is a *capela*, to which they flock whenever time allows, and *imagens* to which they direct their worship. . . . One of the most crafty, whom they venerate as *paroco*, baptizes and marries them" (quoted in Kent 1965: 168). The presence of the dominator's faith still prevailed, but grew transformed in the process. In addition, resistance came by means of "cultural symbols such as place-names, clothing, and in the creation of a material world, the manifestation of which was clearly distinct from that of the Dutch and Portuguese colonists and native Brazilian groups" (Allen 1998: 173). Therefore, these *mocambos* displayed not only political but also cultural autonomy, in an attempt to maintain social cohesion amidst the disintegration of their native language and traditions.

The forest in *Além do Rio* constitutes a site in which race and identity are performed through appropriation and transformation by means of place-meaning practices. Sociologists remark that although ethnic groups, due to structural forces, end up concentrating in particular areas on the fringe of society, these places gain a particular identity in that their residents deliberately endow them with meaning through music, dance, food, and syncretic spirituality (Pattillo-McCoy 1999: 202). In the play, the quilombo is distinct from the village in that music and instruments of African origin are employed to emphasize elements of African spirituality and cultural identity, in contrast to the Catholic religious ceremony—Jason's wedding—taking place at the village. But more important, however, is Olavo's setting up the quilombo as the place where Medea can finally perform an identity based on her racial and cultural background. Throughout the play, the audience is exposed to Medea's constant struggle between the culture of the dominator and the call from her compatriots. The quilombo functions, thus, as a space where Medea's negritude can be affirmed and sustained by means of rituals of African origin. As Leda M. Martins puts it, in Medea's choice to live in the periphery, Olavo thematizes, on the one hand, "the process of the reconstruction of the identity of the black subject, who was assimilated, in a forced manner, into the emblems and values of European culture," and, on the other, the protagonist's reinsertion "into an order and patrimony of Afro-Brazilian cultures" (Martins 1995: 104).

Conclusion

Olavo's adaptation or 'brazilianization' of Euripides' Medea serves, therefore, as a powerful tool to probe the ideologies and mechanisms which have contributed to legitimate the formation and maintenance of racialized spaces in Brazil. In this new setting, Olavo explores the role racial constructs play in shaping, establishing, and preserving particular social spaces and hierarchies. He also sets into relief the strategies individuals devise to challenge spatial boundaries and thus fashion new spaces out of oppression and disenfranchisement. As an adaptation, then, Além do Rio (Medea) is significant in that Olavo takes something distant and foreign–the world of Greek myths and tragedies–and sets it in a familiar terrain, thereby defamiliarizing or deconstructing the local so as to unmask the discourses and ideologies that have–and still do in different ways–categorized, marginalized, and relegated Afro-Brazilians to the margins of Brazilian society.

Notes

1. Tuan 1977: 91 (italics added).
2. De Certeau 2002: 117 (italics in original).

References

Allen, S. J. (1998), "A 'Cultural Mosaic' at Palmares? Grappling with the Historical Archaeology of a Seventeenth-Century Brazilian Quilombo," in Pedro Paulo A. Funari org., *Cultura material e arqueologia histórica*. Campinas.

Anjos, S. A. Dos (2010), "Medeia em seus espelhos," in A. López, A. Pociña, and M. de Fátima Silva, eds., *De ayer a hoy: influencias clásicas en la literatura*. Coimbra.

Arantes, L. H. M. (2009), "*Pedreira das Almas* de Jorge Andrade e Alberto D'Aversa: cinquenta anos de criação dramatúrgica e transposição cênica," *Opsis*, Catalão 9, 82–93.

Casey, E. (1991), "A View of Geography," *Geographical Review* 81, 99–107.

Casey, E. (1993), *Getting Back into Place: Toward a Renewed Understanding of Place-World*. Bloomington, IN.

Casey, E. (1996), "How to Get from Space to Place in a Fairly Short Stretch of Time: Phenomenological Prolegomena," in S. Feld and K. H. Blasso, eds., *Senses of Place*. Santa Fe, NM.

Coelho, M. C. de M. N. (2005), "Medéias: metamorfoses do gênero," *Letras clássicas* 9, 157–78.

De Certeau, M. (2002), *The Practice of Everyday Life*. Trans. S. Rendall. Berkeley.

Durrheim, K. and J. Dixon (2001), "The Role of Place and Metaphor in Racial Exclusion: South Africa's Beaches as Sites of Shifting Racialization," *Ethnic and Racial Studies* 24, 433–50.

Eschen, N. (2006), "The Hungry Woman: A Mexican Medea by Cherríe Moraga; Adelina Anthony," Review of *The Hungry Woman: A Mexican Medea*, by Cherríe Moraga. Directed by Cherríe Moraga and Adelina Anthony. *Theatre Journal* 58, 103–6.

Foley, H. P. (1999), "Modern Performance and Adaptation of Greek Tragedy," *Transactions of the American Philological Association* 129, 1–12.

Goldberg, D. T. (1993), *Racist Culture*. Oxford.

Kent, R. K. (1965), "Palmares: An African State in Brazil," *Journal of African History* 6.2, 161–75.

Knowles, C. (2003), *Race and Social Analysis*. London.

Lane, J. (2007), "Antígona and the Modernity of the Dead," *Modern Drama* 50.4, 517–31.

Low, S. M. and D. Lawrence-Zúñiga (2003), "Locating Culture," in S. M. Low and D. Lawrence-Zúñiga eds., *The Anthropology of Space and Place: Locating Culture*. Oxford.

Martins, L. M. (1995), *A cena em sombras*. São Paulo.

Massey, D. (1994), *Space, Place and Gender*. Minneapolis.

Motta, G. (2006), "A encenação da tragédia grega e do trágico na cena brasileira contemporânea," *Artefilosofia* 1, 105–19.

Nascimento, A. do. (2004), "Teatro Experimental Negro: trajetórias e reflexões," *Estudos avançados* 18 (50).

Neely, B. and M. Samura (2011), *Ethnic and Racial Studies* 34, 1933–52.

Nuñes, C. F. P. (2003), "Máscaras gregas no teatro latino-americano," in L. Fachin and M. C. C. Dezotti eds., *Teatro em debate*. Série Estudos Literários 2. Araraquara, 33–44.

Olavo, A. (1961), "Além do rio," in A. D. Nascimento ed., *Drama para negros e prólogo para brancos: antologia de teatro negro-brasileiro*. Rio de Janeiro.

Pattillo-McCoy, M. (1999), *Black Picket Fences: Privilege and Peril Among the Black Middle Class*. Chicago.

Rosa, E. B. da (1993), "De Eurípedes a Agostinho Olavo: Medéia e Medea," *Itinerários* 6, 77–86.

Sundstrom, R. R. (2003), "Race and Place: Social Space in the Production of Human Kinds," *Philosophy & Geography* 6, 83–95.

Tuan, Y.-F. (1977), *Space and Place: The Perspective of Experience*. 8th Printing. Minneapolis.

Urry, J. (2004), "The Sociology of Space and Place," in J. R. Blau ed., *Blackwell Companion to Sociology*. Oxford.

CHAPTER 24

THE FRONTIERS OF DAVID CURESES' *LA FRONTERA*

ANÍBAL A. BIGLIERI

La frontera, a play in two acts by David Cureses (1935–2006), premièred in Buenos Aires, Argentina, on December 2, 1960.[1] The play reworks the myth of Medea in the *pampas* during the "Conquista del desierto" (*Conquest of the Desert*), a military campaign led in the 1870s by the future president of Argentina, General Julio A. Roca (1880–6, 1898–1904), to gain new lands for the state in the south of the Province of Buenos Aires and in Patagonia.

The Quechua word *pampa* means "plain" and designates the South American lowlands that include, in Argentina, the provinces of Buenos Aires, Santa Fé, Entre Ríos, Córdoba, and La Pampa. They are vast prairies with mild climate and fertile soils appropriate for agriculture, and cattle breeding. Although they were nominally under the Spanish administration during colonial times, and later claimed as territories for the new Argentine nation after the independence in 1810, practically all the lands south of the Salado River in the Province of Buenos Aires were under Indian rule. Some advances beyond the south of that frontier were made by several governments between 1810 and 1828, and 1852 and 1876, but the fact remained that those campaigns never achieved the effective and permanent control of the *pampas* by the Argentine state. This situation drove General Roca, at the time Secretary of War in the Nicolás Avellaneda administration (1874–80), to lead the "final push" toward the south of the Buenos Aires province and into the Patagonia region as part of a wider program of nation-building promoted by the ruling elites of the country. The military campaigns reached the Negro River in 1879, resulting in the definitive appropriation by the state of some 15,000 leagues (*leguas*) of rich lands that, for the most part, became the property of landowners settled in the city of Buenos Aires. In these geographical and historical contexts the action of *La frontera* takes place.

Thus far, Cureses' *La frontera* has attracted some but not sufficient critical attention.[2] Several aspects of the play have been already discussed and elucidated, but we still miss a closer examination of how the protagonists of this drama construct the concept of *frontier* itself. As will be seen in the following pages, this is an all-encompassing concept: it starts, to be sure, "down," at the "ground level" so to speak, but it is not reduced to a purely geographic and territorial dimension; on the contrary, this is a multidimensional frontier that goes all the way "up" to that old dichotomy between *civilization* and *barbarism* first articulated in Argentine literature by Sarmiento in his *Facundo: civilización o barbarie*. Briefly put, what starts as a spatial opposition ends up as a conflict between two civilizations.

The frontier between "Christian" (as the white, non-Indian inhabitants of Argentina are called in the play) and Indian lands is a never clearly demarcated boundary in Cureses' play (nor, for that matter, in Marechal's *Antígona Vélez*). Moreover, it is not just an administrative and military line that fluctuates all the time, but rather an undefined and open area without fixed borders in a continuous process of *bordering, debordering*, and *rebordering*. In order, then, to clarify this idea of *frontier* around which the whole play revolves, it is necessary to elaborate a conceptual framework capable of encompassing Cureses' frontiers in their several levels of analysis and dimensions (geographical, ethnographic, economic, political, religious, cultural, symbolic, etc.), all of them viewed not in isolation but in their multiple connections and interrelationships. This is one of the best ways (if not the best) to apprehend the ultimate meaning of the play, if it has one.

The most adequate theoretical framework for analyzing the concept of *frontier* in Cureses' play comes from the burgeoning field of so-called Border Studies. To be sure, most of the contributions in this area deal with historical contexts that have nothing to do with the reworking of a Greek myth in the Argentine plains of the nineteenth century by a playwright of the twentieth century. The bibliography accumulated is already vast, research agendas proliferate, and the problems are so many that Paasi (2011) wonders whether a border theory is an "unattainable dream" or a "realistic aim" for border scholars. He states that theory and practice are interdependent (19) and that there is an obvious need to theorize, despite the fact that for many researchers it may seem an unrealistic and even an undesirable task. It is difficult, if not impossible, to elaborate a theory valid everywhere (27–8), since each case is unique. Jones and Newman agree (Jones 1943: 101, 116; Newman 2011: 33): every case is different, and so is Cureses' *La frontera*, as were also Esteban Echeverría's *La cautiva* (1837), Domingo Faustino Sarmiento's *Facundo* (1845), Lucio V. Mansilla's *Una excursión a los indios ranqueles* (1870), and José Hernández's *Martín Fierro* (1872, 1879), to name just a few other works that deal with the same problems in nineteenth-century Argentine literature, to which one can add Leopoldo Marechal's *Antígona Vélez* (1951), a reworking of the Sophoclean tragedy also placed in the Buenos Aires *pampas* in the 1820s. Moreover, most of the contributions to the field of Border Studies deal with international frontiers and conflicts between states rather than with internal borders (Minghi 1963: 424–7), which is the case of *La frontera*, where the opposition is between two societies that, different identities notwithstanding, belong to the same state and, arguably, share the same nationality.

Despite all these risks, the reading of several contributions within the field of Border Studies (especially those that present a review of the bibliography) offers a very attractive research framework for the study not only of *La frontera* but of all the other works mentioned above that deal with these issues in Argentine literature. Obviously, all of them, from Echeverría to Hernández, were written long before what today we call Border Studies, and it is certain that Cureses (and Marechal) were also unfamiliar with these theoretical developments. But in many of them we find useful definitions, conceptual distinctions, and levels of analysis that can be applied to *La frontera* in fruitful ways. The purpose of this chapter, then, is to lay the foundation for a new analysis of Cureses' play. A whole range of issues coalesce around the field of Border Studies, and most of them are reflected in *La frontera*. Definitions and conceptual distinctions, border typologies and the nature of the social processes involved, ethnic conflicts and cultural oppositions, national identities and borderless societies, are among the several problems raised by Cureses' characters. Space limitations, however, force us to focus on very few problems, but even this contribution might lead to further analyses and open up new avenues of research.

Before proceeding to the analysis of Cureses' play, here is a brief summary of its plot: Bárbara (Medea) receives into her tribe, protects, and marries Captain Jasón Ahumada (Jason), who had been wounded and abandoned by his men after a battle between Christians and Indians. In addition to betraying her people, by marrying a "foreigner," Bárbara raised, as adoptive mother, Botijo and his sister Huinca, children of Colonel Ordóñez, the new commanding officer of the small fort in the frontier between Indians and Christians. With Bárbara lives also in her *rancho* an Old Indian woman (*la Vieja*) and the two sons she had with Captain Ahumada. Colonel Ordóñez (Creon) goes to the *rancho* to retrieve Botijo and Huinca, giving Bárbara two days to leave the frontier and return to her camp. His daughter Huinca (Creusa) and Jasón are planning to get married according to the Christian rites, but the Indian Anambá, a character introduced to the plot by Cureses, kills her at Bárbara's instigation. Two friars also show up to retrieve Bárbara and Jasón's sons and take them to his father, but Bárbara kills them with herbs.

Borders and Frontiers

The English terminology is certainly prolific: *frontier, frontier region, zone, border, boundary, boundary zone, borderland* are some of the terms most commonly used in the bibliography.[3] None of them offers a clear and unambiguous conceptual demarcation, nor can they always be translated satisfactorily in Spanish. And there is no researcher who, sooner rather than later, has not faced these problems, nor is there any need to insist now on the difficulty of summarizing their findings in a clear and concise way. But soon one notices a certain consensus among the proponents of Border Studies around a very basic distinction between *frontier* (*frontera*) and *boundary* (*límite*). According to

Kristof, *frontier* is an area, region, zone, or extension of separation, contact, and transition between political units, whereas a *boundary* is the line of demarcation establishing the borders and territorial sovereignties of the states (269–71).[4] For Weber and Rausch, the frontiers are also geographical zones of interaction among two or more different cultures (Weber and Rausch 1994: xiv). "Borders are lines," says Newman, that is to say, lines of delimitation between *borderlands* (or areas situated on both sides of those boundaries), which constitute "transition zones" (Newman 2011: 37). In another article, Newman describes the frontier as an indefinite area on both sides of the boundary line (Newman 2003: 142), and in collaboration with Paasi, notes that *boundaries* and *borders* were first conceived as lines of separation between sovereign states, while *frontiers* referred to zones in the proximities of those borders whose internal developments were dictated by the existence of that line (Newman and Paasi 1998: 189). To summarize: *boundary* (*límite*) will designate here that line between two or more zones, and *frontier* (*frontera*) will refer to the regions on both sides of the line of ill-defined extension, or hybrid spaces made of transitions and *continua*. In Cureses' play we have, then, three overlapping spaces of a rather complex nature, namely the Indian territories, the Argentine state proper, and the *frontera* in which the action of the drama takes place: they are geographical and morphological, ethnic and cultural, political and economic units, and it is the multidimensionality of this frontier that will be the main focus of this chapter. That this division runs along a zone and not a boundary marking a clear separation between both worlds is clearly stated by Huinca in her dialogue with her father, Colonel Ordóñez: "Tuito esto lo esperaba como espero lo que hay más allá d'esa lonja e tierra que me separa e lo mío" (22) ["I was expecting all of this, as I expect what there is beyond that strip (= *lonja*) of land that separates me from what is mine"]. It will be in that *lonja* that the drama between Bárbara-Medea and Jasón Ahumada-Jason will take place.

The first problem presented by the frontier conceived as a geomorphological unit is its territorial imprecision: the borders between Indian and Christian countries were never clearly established and, in the case of the Argentine plains, *La frontera* mentions only one, probably two rivers, but without naming them or indicating their location, thereby making it impossible to draw a map of the region. However, in successive readings one discovers how, starting with a first and very vague distinction between two zones, others are added, going from "below" (*here/there*) all the way "up" to a confrontation between *civilization* and *barbarism*.

In several passages the topic of the frontier comes to the fore. For example, the dialogue between Botijo and Huinca articulates these oppositions on different scales and levels, from the geographic to the cultural. For the moment, one should note a first elemental configuration of the space based on the opposition between "here," "this side" (*acá, este lado*) versus "there," "the other side" (*allá, el otro lado*). Huinca affirms without any doubt not only the existence of that boundary but the impossibility of its crossing as well. Her brother, on the other hand, believes in the possibility of overcoming all the differences that divide the Indian and the Christian societies, defending the equality of all human beings without any distinctions whatsoever. Huinca replies:

¡Tuitos iguales! . . . Sí . . . pero ellos siguen siendo loj de allá y nosotros loj de acá . . . El límite está en el medio . . . nadie lo ve pero está . . . ancho, grande, tanto que no se puede cruzar . . . y nosotros Botijo . . . vos y io . . . somos del otro lao . . . aunque estemos d'este. D'este están la Bárbara . . . y la Vieja . . . (15)

[We all are equal! Yes . . . but they are still those from there and we are those from here. The boundary is in the middle . . . nobody sees it but it exists . . . wide, so big that nobody can cross it . . . and we, Botijo, you and I belong to the other side, although we live on this side. On this side live Bárbara . . . and the Old Woman . . .]

By birth and culture, Huinca and Botijo belong to the "over there," "us" versus "them," as Bárbara will say later on to Colonel Ordóñez: "Io soy una pobre mujer . . . io estoy aquí y ellos allá y la frontera está en el medio" (25) ["I am a poor woman . . . I am here and they are over there and the frontier is in the middle"]. The frontier is indeed a very complex and multidimensional reality. In fact, Newman reaffirms the necessity of understanding this "multidimensionality" in order to explain the current conflicts between Israelis and Palestinians (Newman 2001: 148), noting also, with Paasi, that a frontier is also a multi-layered reality. And the same happens, *mutatis mutandis*, with Cureses' frontiers: they are spatial, to be sure, but also ethnographic and cultural. Starting with Huinca's words a first dichotomy obtains dividing the country in two zones:

this side ← ‖ → *the other side*[5]

This very basic and rudimentary opposition is expanded with the introduction of new terms between the *here* in which the Indians live and a *far away* (*lejos*) or *further away* (*más lejos*) that invariably alludes to the *North* and the Christian civilization to which belong, among others, Colonel Ordóñez and Captain Jasón Ahumada (69, 71). This geographical and cultural space is now divided according to this more refined configuration:

here ← ‖ → *there* → *away* → *(far) away* → *further away*[6]

But there is also another *there*, toward the South and the lands still inhabited by the Indians: *allá en la tierra nuestra* . . . (10) ["there in our lands"] where, according to the Old Woman (*la Vieja*), Bárbara could have lived with her family and married an Indian man:

there ← *here* ← ‖ → *there* → *away* → *(far) away* → *further away*[7]

These oppositions are expressed in abstract terms, but gradually they will become more concrete and specific. That *space* (*espacio*) so vague and indefinite (*here / there, this side / the other side*) will turn into *places* (*lugares*) defined by the human presence. Once again, it is important now to define the terms of this equation. *Space* designates here a geometrical, quantitative, abstract, homogeneous, and mathematically measurable extension; *place*, on the contrary, refers to any site in which social processes "take place," that is, concrete, qualitative, heterogeneous sites which, also in Cureses' play, are sites of appropriation, control, power, and conflict (see Santos, this volume).

The space of the *pampas* becomes populated by human beings in specific sites. To begin with, from Bárbara's *here*, the first thing that she sees is the small fort commanded by Colonel Ordóñez (18). Moreover, Botijo can also see this *fortín* from further south, in Indian lands (*tierra adentro*) where the Christian presence is still non-existent. But they also see, even further away from their *here*, the *posta*, that small civilian settlement close to the frontier separating Indian and Christian domains. When Bárbara insists that Botijo should return to the civilized *North*, according to his father's wishes, she summarizes very succinctly this opposition: "tu lugar dejó de ser a nuestro lado . . . aura está allá . . . pasando la frontera . . . en el fortín y más allá . . ." (60) ["Your place is no longer on our side . . . now it is there . . . crossing the frontier . . . in the small fort and further away"]. Gradually, this space is taking shape now by reference to specific places: Botijo's place, no longer the Indian camp in which he grew up raised by Bárbara, will be that civilized *más allá* from which come not only his father, but also Captain Jasón Ahumada and all the settlers who inhabit those outposts of Christian civilization, the *fortín* and the *posta*. This is also what Botijo sees from further away in Indian lands: lost in the distance, the watchtower from the small fort and even further, at a distance of a league, he could guess the presence of the small settlement in the middle of the "desert" (57–8). We have now a new space configuration:

Bárbara's house ← FRONTIER → *small fort* → *settlement*[8]

There are very few references to other villages or towns in Cureses' play, as if the geography of *La frontera* were focused almost exclusively around that indefinite zone which at the same time brings together and separates both societies. However, there are some scattered indications that expand the cartography of the play toward the extremes of both regions. On the Christian side, for example, Bárbara alludes to a *poblado*, or small village (18) understood as a permanent settlement still in the Province of Buenos Aires. And further away, on the extreme of that continuum, toward the north, is Buenos Aires, capital of the nation into which the "conquista del desierto" (represented by Colonel Ordóñez and Captain Ahumada) wants to incorporate the Indian populations. In the absence of her husband, the Colonel's wife, Mercedes, will travel to her parents' house to give birth there to Botijo. She sets out from Buenos Aires toward an unnamed city in the Province of Buenos Aires' hinterland, but her trip will be cut short by an Indian raid (*malón*) followed by her captivity (19–20). Adding these references to the previous diagrams, the diegetic space of Cureses' play adopts now the following configuration:

Bárbara's house ← FRONTIER → *small fort* → *settlement* → *town(s)* → *city* → *Buenos Aires*[9]

But beyond Bárbara's *rancho* there will be other human settlements, this time, the Indian camps to which she refers when, in addition to the women living in the small fort, the settlements, and towns, on the *other side* of the frontier, she mentions the Indian women living in the *tolderías* (18). Almost nothing is said about their location: Captain Ahumada, for example, places them "in the middle of the pampas" (39), and the Indian

Anambá will situate his *toldería* further South, an area unreachable by the Christian soldiers (49, 50):

> Indian camps ← Bárbara's house ← FRONTIER → small fort → settlement → town(s) → city → Buenos Aires[10]

Thus far, with the exception of the frontier itself, we have human settlements of increasing dimensions: from Bárbara's house—where she lives with Colonel Ordóñez's son and daughter (Aurora-Huinca and Botijo), the two sons she had with Captain Jasón Ahumada, and the Old Woman (*la Vieja*)—to Argentina's capital, Buenos Aires, and in between, human populations such as the Indian camps, to the south, and to the north, the small fort, the small village, the provincial town(s), and the city where Mercedes' parents lived. Everything is visible and tangible, except that wide frontier in the middle, invisible and impassable, as Huinca explains to her brother (15).

Us versus Them

This map of *La frontera*'s world is then much richer than one would expect from those first dichotomies between *this side/the other side, here/there*. There is a *continuum*, but the frontier is still there dividing *rancho* and *tolderías* from *fortín, posta, poblado(s), ciudad*, and *Buenos Aires*. This opposition is in turn subsumed into a cultural one, *us* versus *them*, followed by another even more encompassing, *South* versus *North*, until one reaches the highest level, *civilization* against *barbarism*. The frontiers in Cureses' drama confirm what Border Studies research demonstrates conclusively: that they are multidimensional and multi-layered.

The confrontation between "us" and "them" (the terms are, of course, reversible according to the point of view of Indians and Christians) permeates the whole play. There is almost no scene and even page in which it is not expressed one way or the other by Cureses' characters. At the beginning of *La frontera* Huinca rejects her brother's ideals of equality and confraternity among all humans, defending vehemently a sharp and unequivocal contrast between two worlds that for her are incompatible:

> BOTIJO.—Ricordá también qu'el Jasón es tuito pa ella... qu'él nos enseñó muchito en estos diez años qu'está con la Bárbara...
> HUINCA.—(*Fastidiada*.) Dejate de hablar tanto... la Bárbara es la Bárbara (*Transición*.) y... el Jasón es el Jasón... él es un capitán...
> BOTIJO.—(*Corta, secc*.) La Bárbara te crió y me crió...
> HUINCA.—(*Cortando*.) ¿Y a nosotros qué?... ¿Somos acaso indios por qu'ella nos haiga criado?... Nosotros, Botijo, seguimos siendo de allá... de más allá del Fortín y de la posta... Aquello es lo nuestro, nosotros somos distintos... (14)

> [BOTIJO.—Remember that Jason is everything for her... that he has taught us a lot during these ten years of living together with Barbara...

HUINCA.—(*Annoyed.*) Shut up! . . . Barbara is Barbara . . . (*Transition.*) and . . . Jason is Jason . . . he is a Captain . . .
BOTIJO.—(*Interrupts, brusque.*) Barbara raised you and she raised me . . .
HUINCA.—(*Interrupting.*) So what? Are we Indians because she raised us? We, Botijo, still belong there . . . further away from the small fort and the settlement . . . That is our world, we are different . . .]

Remembering the circumstances in which Jasón was apprehended by the Indians, the Old Woman also opposes both societies: "Los suyos lo habían abandonao, dándolo por muerto, en un encontronazo con los nuestros" (16) ["His men abandoned him, believing that he was dead, in a battle with our men"]. Where do they belong? "This is not his world" ["Lo suyo no es esto"] (28), Colonel Ordóñez tells Bárbara, referring to Jasón and his life spent among the Indians. Huinca thinks the same when she tells her father that "her world" is beyond the *here* in which she lives with Bárbara (22).

But the most contested issue in *La frontera* is where and to whom Bárbara and Jasón's sons belong. Their death, of course, is the most defining feature of Medea's myth, and its causes and motivations have been discussed endlessly from antiquity until today. In Cureses' case, the infanticide is motivated not only by Jasón's repudiation of his wife and his planned wedding with Huinca-Aurora. Like the classical Medeas, Bárbara is also a woman seeking revenge from her estranged husband, but she is also in strong opposition to her sons' assimilation to the Christian civilization if they move to live in the *North* with their father and stepmother. Jasón reminds her that their sons are also his: "pero sabé que pese a tu dolor y rebeldía ellos . . . me pertenecen tanto como a vos" (44–5) ["Despite your pain and rebelliousness, they belong as much to me as to you . . ."]. However, when the Indian Anambá tells her that they are the sons of Christian parents, she replies that they are the sons of an Indian woman (50).

All those previous oppositions seen thus far are subsumed now under a new and more encompassing rubric: *nosotros ‖ ellos, us ‖ them*.

NORTH AND SOUTH

The infanticide, of course, was predictable and it was predetermined by Cureses' fidelity to the Euripidean myth. But, in this play, Bárbara's actions are conditioned not only by her thirst for revenge, but also by her belief in the incompatibility between her own Indian culture and Jasón's (and the state he represents). Again, the distinction between *North* and *South* has more than one dimension and more than one layer. It is not just a geographical opposition, but a real confrontation between civilizations, except for Botijo who advocates the overcoming of all human inequalities. From their side of the frontier, both Bárbara and the Old Woman reaffirm that opposition, and so do, from the other side, Colonel Ordóñez, Captain Ahumada, and Huinca. The two friars, fray Javier and fray Gaudencio, sent by Jasón to retrieve his sons from Bárbara's *rancho*, believe somehow in the abolition of the frontiers, but with the condition that the Indians embrace the Christian faith and be integrated into the Argentine nation-state.

In a play like Cureses' there are scenes or episodes that, arguably, may not contribute decisively to the unfolding of its plot. At first reading, such would be the case of Colonel Ordóñez's narration of the circumstances that led to his wife's captivity in Indian territory. However, it is important to understand how in Cureses' universe *North* and *South* clash without any possibility of reconciliation. Mercedes' trip in a stagecoach, more than a journey from Buenos Aires to that unnamed city in which her parents live, is a voyage to another civilization: "varias leguas más al sur, donde la pampa se torna como el filo de un cuchillo por lo salvaje" (19–20) ["Several leagues towards the South, where the pampa turns itself into the cutting edge of a knife due to its savagery..."], with this image the Colonel remembers the entry of the stagecoach and its occupants into another space dominated now by Indian raids and *malones*, pillage and plundering, killings and captivities.

It is also interesting to note that for the friars, coming from the North, Bárbara's house seems to them the most advanced place toward the South (61). They are now in the vast expanses of the *pampas* where silence and solitude reign, so different from the towns and cities of the north to which they are accustomed. What images of the *North*, then, have the characters living on either side of the boundary? The first mention is made by the Old Woman, at the beginning of the play, when she recalls with nostalgia those times when the Indians were the "owners and lords of the *pampas*" (8). Those were the times of the *malones*, or Indian raids going to the north in search of goods and women, raids that are also documented in several Argentine paintings of the nineteenth century.[11]

From that *North* comes the new commanding officer of the fortress, Colonel Ordóñez, as Botijo announces without knowing that he is his own father (12). To that *North* will go Jasón Ahumada when he abandons his family in the *desierto* leaving them at the mercy of the attacks from that *fortín* (11). And Botijo will lament the same abandonment and hostility from the Christians:

> Sí... ¿te acordás?... al principio nomás, cuando el Jasón se jué pa'l norte... y comenzamos a sentir la soledad y el silencio como si juera parte e nuestro mesmo cuerpo... cuando ia no nos podimos acercar ni a la posta, ni al fortín,... porque éramos como malditos (56)
>
> [Do you remember?... At the beginning, when Jason went to the north... and we started to feel the solitude and the silence as if they were part of our own bodies... when we could not approach the settlement or the small fort... because we were like condemned people]

If for Mercedes her journey to the *South* will end in captivity and death, for Jasón the *North* means not just freedom but also the opportunity to leave in the past his life with the Indians, including his wife, rejecting thus their barbarism and reinserting himself into the Christian civilization. This return to his roots will be reaffirmed by his Christian marriage to Colonel's Ordóñez's daughter, Huinca-Aurora. This is what the Colonel explains to Bárbara in no uncertain terms: "Entendeme bien, india, él partirá hacia el norte . . . partirá con mi hija después de desposarla como la ley de Dios lo manda" (30) ["Understand me well, Indian, he will go to the North . . . with my daughter after marrying her like God's law orders"]. In another long dialogue between both characters, the Colonel insists that he represents the civilizing force from the *North*: "Hacia el Norte, estamos nosotros, la civilización que avanza" ["We are from the North, the advancing civilization"], to which she replies that that civilization corners the Indians until they choke: "Malos pasos trae la civilización que acorrala al indio hasta ahogarlo" (18). ["Civilization surrounds the Indian, entrapping us until we are extinct."] The clash between *nosotros* and *ellos, us* and *them,* can be reformulated by an opposition *North* ‖ *South.*

The Clash of Two Civilizations?

In the preceding paragraphs some of the oppositions between the Indian and the Christian civilizations were described. More could be said about what we could call their "material culture," that is, their weapons, means of transportation, housing, etc., and also about their social mores, economic activities, religious beliefs, etc. But their confrontation goes much deeper, as can be gathered from several dialogues in which this clash of two cultures comes to the fore in dramatic and agonistic ways. Conflicts about concepts of the nation and the fatherland (*patria*), the idea of justice, the rights to conquest and domination, etc. are topics around which the characters clash in strong, indeed irreconcilable, positions. For example, the dialogue between Huinca and Botijo mentioned before shows not just the spatial opposition between the *here* and *there* but also the cultural differences between *us* and *them* as well. If for him it is possible to conceive one nation embracing all its inhabitants without distinctions, for her, on the contrary, those distinctions remain firmly entrenched and if there were one way to overcome them, it would be only by subjugating the Indians and assimilating them to the culture of the *North*. This is also the opposition between Bárbara and Colonel Ordóñez. While he defines himself as a "man of the fatherland" (18) ["hombre de la patria"], she questions this very notion in no uncertain terms:

> ¿Y la patria? . . . ¿Qu'es eso? . . . ¿De qué me habla? . . . Si nos hubieran dejao libres a tuitos loj indios . . . libres como los pájaros en el cielo . . . sin fronteras ni divisiones . . . sin esa justicia e loj hombres y sin ese Dios del que me habló . . . entuavía pudiera ser que conociera la patria. (19)

> [And the fatherland? . . . What is that? . . . What are you talking about? . . . If you had left us free . . . free like the birds in the sky . . . without frontiers or divisions . . . without that human justice and without that God you were telling me about . . . perhaps I could recognize the fatherland.]

Later on they will clash around Jasón, ready to abandon Bárbara and her world, marry Huinca, and return to the *North* to continue in his fight for the "conquest of the desert":

C. ORDOÑEZ.—El tiene sus deberes que cumplir...
BARBARA.—Con sus hijos y conmigo...
C. ORDOÑEZ.—Con su patria... y con los suyos... (26)

[C. ORDOÑEZ.—He has to fulfill his duties.
BARBARA.—With his sons and me...
C. ORDOÑEZ.—With his fatherland... and his people...]

Bárbara also questions the legitimacy of the "conquest" itself (10) and Jasón's duties and obligations toward his family and his fatherland and, above all, his responsibility toward his sons. The conflict between them is, to be sure, the clash between two worlds, but on a more personal level, it is a fight for the possession of their sons:

JASON.—(*Contenido.*) Ellos son mis hijos, y yo tengo mis derechos sobre ellos...
BARBARA.—¡No más que los míos! (44)

[JASON.—(*Containing himself.*) They are my sons, and I have my own rights over them.
BARBARA– No more than mine!]

Jasón insists: "Pero mis hijos sí continúan siendo míos... (43), me pertenecen tanto como a vos..." (45) ["My sons are still mine...," "They belong to me as much as to you..."] and Bárbara says the same: "¡Míos solamente!... ¿Me entendés?... Se avergonzarían de un padre como vos..." (44) ["Only mine!... Do you understand me?... They will be ashamed of a father like you..."]. Moreover, continues Bárbara, by abandoning her for another woman, he has forfeited all his rights over their sons:

BARBARA.—(*Señalándose el vientre.*) Esta jué su cuna... me pertenecen...
(*Continúa sin importarle nada.*) Vos tendrás tus derechos sobre tuito... sobre la tierra... sobre mi cuerpo... y hasta sobre mi honor... pero sobre ellos... ¡no!... (44)

[BARBARA.—(*Pointing to her belly.*) This was their cradle... They belong to me...
(*She continues without caring about what she says.*) You may have your rights over everything... the land... my body... even my honor... but not over them... no!]

Colonel Ordóñez and his son Botijo also clash when the father, invoking his paternal authority, wants to take him back to the *North*, where he was not born or raised, and which he has no interest in knowing. He says to his father:

No quiero estar a su lado... (*Retrocede.*) no quiero que tenga derechos sobre mí... io soy libre como el ñandú en la pampa... a usté ni siquiera le tengo miedo... (*Retrocede más.*) solamente no lo quiero... no lo quiero... no lo quiero... (31)

[I don't want to be with you... (*He steps back.*) I don't want you to have rights over me... I am free like the American ostrich in the pampa... I am not even afraid of you... (*He steps further back...*) I don't love you... I don't love you... I don't love you...]

But he will end up going north with his father. Bárbara herself, although considering Botijo her own son, accepts his father's authority and convinces him that he should leave (60).

At the beginning of the play, in her dialogue with Huinca, the Old Woman recalls a past when the Indians lived in freedom from any external domination (8): against her nostalgic vision of times gone, Jasón describes himself as "Capitán de la conquista del desierto . . . reductor de indios . . . héroe de una empresa, como la de haber vencido al cacique Coliqueo . . ." (42) ["Captain of the conquest of the desert . . . conqueror of Indians . . . hero of a campaign of defeating the chieftain Coliqueo . . ."]. But it is Colonel Ordóñez who will defend even more vigorously those campaigns in the name of the Argentine government. His order to Bárbara to leave the frontier is based on arguments which could hardly have been expressed in more lapidary terms: "El desierto da derechos al hombre que lo conquista . . ." (26) ["The desert gives rights to the man who conquers it . . ."]. And the exercise of such an authority is explained in this way:

> aquí soy como el dueño y señor . . . Dicto las leyes de esta avanzada en el desierto y mis leyes deben respetarse . . . y yo ordeno, me entendés, ordeno . . . que partas a tus tierras antes de que despunte el nuevo día . . . (27)
>
> [Here I am the owner and the master . . . I promulgate the laws in this outpost in the desert and my laws must be obeyed . . . and I order, do you understand me? I order you to go back to your land tomorrow before dawn.]

If Bárbara condemns and rejects four aspects of Christian domination over the Indians (work, justice, fatherland, and religion), the Colonel can express himself also in very precise and terse terms. He does that several times, for instance, when he explains to Bárbara the objectives of his campaigns and the benefits of the civilization that he represents:

> C. ORDOÑEZ.—(*Un poco picado*.) Se resisten a ser gente . . . sólo queremos enseñarles.
> BARBARA.—¿Qué cosa? . . . ¿A ser crestianos? . . .
> C. ORDOÑEZ.—A saber de Dios . . . y de la patria . . . de los deberes y obligaciones del hombre, de la justicia y el trabajo . . . Queremos levantarlos hasta nosotros . . . vernos todos al mismo nivel, ser iguales . . . hermanos como cuadra a los nacidos bajo un mismo cielo . . . sin distingo de raza ni de sangre . . .] (18)
>
> [C. ORDOÑEZ.—(*A little annoyed*) You don't want to be a civilized people . . . We only want to teach you . . .
> BARBARA.—What? . . . to be Christians? . . .
> C. ORDOÑEZ.—To know God . . . the fatherland . . . man's duties and obligations, justice, work . . . We want to lift you towards us . . . see all of us on the same level, be equal, be brothers like people born under the same sky . . . without distinctions of race or blood . . .]

According to Geertz, religions as sets of symbols, myths, rites, and dogmas are "cultural systems" that turn reality into a coherent and intelligible whole as against what may seem at first sight chaotic, absurd, without meaning or explanation (Geertz 2000). On a more fundamental plane, religions situate human existence in what he calls "ultimate contexts." That is, they provide models to explain all aspects of a given culture, from its conception of the divine all the way "down" to the customs and norms of conduct of our daily lives. Even if we reject the notion that the conflict in *La frontera* is above all a clash of two religions, there is no doubt that religious beliefs are an essential component of the ideology of several characters. It is to this idea of "ultimate contexts" that the sorcerer Bárbara refers when she contemplates the future of her sons in the *North*. As is the case of other characters (Huinca, Botijo, Jasón), what is at stake is neither more nor less than the *place* that all of them occupy in the world, more specifically in the Argentina of the 1870s when a new project of nation-building is taking shape. The notion of *place*, of course, is not to be understood only in its geographical sense, although for the Indians it certainly meant a displacement toward the south, pushed by the advancing civilization coming from the *North*. *Place* is also determined by its cultural context, and in this sense Bárbara is, to say the least, sceptical about the future of her sons raised as Christians in the *North*. She says to the Colonel:

> El Dios de ustedes nada nos dio, dende que por primera vez oimos hablar de El, tuito jue pa mal ... (18)
> ['Your God has given us nothing, and since we heard of him for the first time, everything got worse ...']

To which she adds a long list of the pains suffered by the Indians: captivity of the women, hard labor in the fields, a justice imposed by the force of the arms, a fatherland that deprives them of their freedom (18–19). In the new moral and Christian order in which her sons will be raised, Bárbara does not find any virtues; on the contrary, they will fall prey to many vices: they will lie, they will be selfish, they will betray the Indians, they will follow in their father's steps, and finally they will be also soldiers in the "conquest of the desert." They will learn a new language, they will dress like Christians, and they will end up marrying white and Christian women. In sum, Bárbara imagines for her sons a "possible world" in a civilization that she rejects for them, believing that it brings nothing but destruction to the Indians. And this is why, in the last analysis, she decides to kill them (70).

Obviously, the Christians have an opposite view, whether they serve in the army (the Colonel, the Captain), or in the Church (the friars): all of them fight for the incorporation of the Indians into their civilization according to the project of a nation-state advanced by the elites of the generation of 1880. And with this, we have reached the *civilization* || *barbarism* dichotomy that includes all the previous oppositions in their multidimensional and multilayered configurations.

A Borderless Argentina?

Despite all these geographical, ethnic, cultural, and religious oppositions, the frontier that divides Indians and Christians is a porous one. In fact, the conflicts in Cureses' play are due precisely to the crossings of that zone, real or intended, in both directions. Collectively, the Indian *malones* attack the Christian populations, those raids described nostalgically by the

Old Woman, when the Indians armed with spears, bows, and arrows marched toward the *North* to return to their camps with the booty that included "women white like the moon" (8). Or when they attacked the stagecoaches, like the one in which Colonel Ordóñez's wife travelled to her parents' house to give birth there to Botijo (19–20). Attacks like these ones would create an irreconcilable opposition between *North* and *South* and demanded, in the Colonel's view, a fight without any prospects of accommodations, let alone peace. Jasón warns Bárbara that the Colonel's rancor against her race has increased and has a long history (36). For him it is not just plain hostility against the Indians and his desire to fight to advance his civilization beyond the frontier, but also a very personal issue: his wife was made captive of those Indians and she died in their *toldos*, he has not seen his daughter Aurora (Huinca) in many years, and he never knew his son Botijo, born in captivity. And this is why he goes to Bárbara's *rancho*, to reclaim them, Botijo as the son he never met, Aurora to marry Jasón, and all of them to return to their civilization in the *North*.

But there is also the other perspective, from the *other side* of the frontier. From her *here*, Bárbara condemns the Christian attacks against them, in what amounted to nothing more than the Christian version of the Indian *malones* (18–19, 26). The main victims of all these raids were the women, Indian and Christian alike, without distinction, the former abducted from their tribes, the latter, from the villages, fortresses, and small settlements. There is no space here to deal with this topic, but suffice it to note that another frontier takes shape in Cureses' play, one that divides men (Indians, Christians) from women (Indians, Christians), treated without discrimination as objects of conquest, control, and appropriation. The frontiers, as noted above, are multidimensional and multi-layered indeed.

As in the classical Medeas, what sets in motion the tragedy in *La frontera* is Jasón's decision to abandon his family, in this case to marry a Christian woman, take back his sons, and return with them and his new wife to his civilization. Huinca will be killed by Anambá, under Bárbara's instigation, and his sons will die at the hands of their mother. Jasón, Mercedes, and Huinca shared this crossing of the frontier, but only he will go from *North* to *South* and back to the *North*. Mercedes will die in the *toldos*, Huinca, in the frontier, and Botijo will be transplanted to the *North* that he abhors, forced by his father. Both Jasón and his future father-in-law will return to the *North*, no doubt devastated by the deaths of their loved ones: the former's sons and fiancé, the latter's daughter. Huinca's fate is tragic indeed. She crossed the frontier when she was 2 years old as an innocent passenger of that stagecoach that never reached its destination (19), and she lived as a captive of the Indians during 17 years, never completely assimilated to her new life: her *place* is not there, and she longs to return to the world in which she was born and to which also belongs the man whom she loves and plans to marry. In fact, she compares the new life waiting for her with Jasón to a rebirth: "pero sé que va a suceder algo grande . . . ¡grande . . . como nacer de nuevo! . . ." (14) ["I know that something big will take place . . . big . . . like being born again . . ."]. A new birth: it is difficult to conceive a more decisive frontier than this one. And yet, tragically, Huinca will end up crossing a more definitive frontier, between life and death, marked by that distant cry that the friars will hear in the middle of the night (62).

As far as Botijo is concerned, his father's order is irrevocable: "Vos regresarás conmigo, quieras que no ..." (30) ["You will return with me, whether you like it or not ..."]. Botijo will cross that frontier to live in a world that he does not know and with which, unlike his sister, he cannot identify. Jasón crossed that frontier, first in its spatial sense, fighting against the Indians as a soldier of the "conquest of the desert," but he also crossed a cultural barrier, when he lived in the *toldos* with Bárbara. She did the same, but in the opposite direction: she betrayed her people in order to marry that Christian man coming from the despised *North*. He will rule the tribe during ten years, but he finally admits that that was not his destiny (39). His real destiny awaits him on the *other side*, as a military man with a brilliant future in the Argentine army, as Colonel Ordóñez tells Bárbara (27). And Jasón himself is perfectly aware of that future waiting for him, belonging to a history that is also a legend (42).

For her part, Bárbara says to Botijo: "¡estás como marcao!" (61) ["You are marked!"], but so are Jasón and Huinca, with the "mark" of the *North*, as is she "marked" by the *South*. Are those "marks" indelible and unerasable? Cureses' characters offer different answers to this question, but they deserve further analysis and evaluation in another study.

Additional Charts

Based on what the characters themselves say in the play, I have tried to demonstrate the geographical and cultural configuration of *La frontera*'s spaces and places in schematic form:

```
      barbarie    civilización
      sur         norte
      nosotros    ellos
tolderías ← rancho ← FRONTERA → fortín → posta → poblado(s) → ciudad → Buenos Aires
          rancho ← FRONTERA → fortín → posta → poblado(s) → ciudad → Buenos Aires
          rancho ← FRONTERA → fortín → posta
allá ← acá, aquí ← ‖ → allá → más allá → lejos → más lejos
       acá, aquí ← ‖ → allá → más allá → lejos → más lejos
       este lado ← ‖ → el otro lado

      barbarism   civilization
      South       North
      us          them
Indian camps ← Bárbara's house ← FRONTIER → small fort → settlement → town(s) → city
→ Buenos Aires
Bárbara's house ← FRONTIER → small fort → settlement → town(s) → city → Buenos Aires
Bárbara's house ← FRONTIER → small fort → settlement
      there ← here ← ‖ → there → away → (far) away → further away
              here ← ‖ → there → away → (far) away → further away
         this side ← ‖ → the other side
```

Notes

1. I thank Kate Bosher for her tremendous help in giving this chapter its final form. Her thorough, efficient, and meticulous revisions and corrections improved my original version to such an extent that I can truly say that she can be considered as the co-author of this contribution.
2. On Cureses' play see, among others, Bravo de Laguna Romero 2010, Pociña 2007, and Schroeder 1998. On the "conquest of the desert" see Walther 1980, in particular chapters 10, 11, and 12, 367–561, which cover the years 1874 to 1885.
3. On the English terminology see Newman 2001: 150–1, and Newman and Paasi 1998: 189. For the distinction between *frontier* and *boundary* see also Jones 1959: 251. For the several meanings that *frontier* and *frontera* had for Latin Americans and Angloamericans see Weber and Rausch 1994: xiii–xv. For other definitions see Lugo (1997), who registers the following synonyms for the word *border: margin, verge, edge, rim, brim, brink* (43). In Spanish we have also, among other terms, *margen, borde,* and *orilla*.
4. See the definitions of both words in the *British Association Geographical Glossary Committee* in Kristof 1959: 269 n. 5, and note that the frontier is described there as a *belt*, which is what *zōna* means in Greek. In practice it is always a region and not a line.
5. este lado ← ‖ → el otro lado
6. acá, aquí ← ‖ → allá → más allá → lejos → más lejos
7. allá ← acá, aquí ← ‖ → allá → más allá → lejos → más lejos
8. rancho ← FRONTERA→ fortín → posta
9. rancho ← FRONTERA→ fortín → posta → poblado(s) → ciudad → Buenos Aires
10. tolderías ← rancho ← FRONTERA→ fortín → posta → poblado(s) → ciudad → Buenos Aires
11. Among others: Johann Mortiz Rugendas, *Rapto de cristianas por los indios, El malón* and *El rapto de la cautiva* (1845); Otto Grashof, *Cautiva en la Pampa* (1853); Benjamín Franklin Rawson, *La vuelta del malón* (1864) and *Huyendo del malón*; Juan Manuel Blanes, *La cautiva* and *El malón* (1875); Angel Della Valle, *La vuelta del malón* (1892).

References

Bravo De Laguna Romero, F. (2010), "De la Cólquide a la Pampa: una Medea en *La frontera* de David Cureses," *Arrabal* 7–8, 131–7.

Cureses, D. (1964), *La frontera*. Buenos Aires.

Geertz, C. (2000), "Religion as a Cultural System," *The Interpretation of Cultures*. New York, 87–125.

Jones, S. B. (1943), "The Description of International Boundaries," *Annals of the Association of American Geographers* 33, 99–117.

Jones, S. B. (1959), "Boundary Concepts in the Setting of Place and Time," *Annals of the Association of American Geographers* 49, 241–55.

Kristof, L. K. D. (1959), "The Nature of Frontiers and Boundaries," *Annals of the Association of American Geographers* 49, 269–82.

Lugo, A. (1997), "Reflections on Border Theory, Culture, and the Nation," in S. Michaelsen and D. E. Johnson eds., *Border Theory: The Limits of Cultural Politics*. Minneapolis and London, 43–67.

Minghi, J. V. (1963), "Review Article: Boundary Studies in Political Geography," *Annals of the Association of American Geographers* 53, 407–28.

Newman, D. (2001), "Boundaries, Borders, and Barriers: Changing Geographic Perspectives on Territorial Lines," in A. Mathias, D. Jacobson, and Y. Lapid eds., *Identities, Borders, Orders: Rethinking International Relations Theory*. Minneapolis and London, 137–51.

Newman, D. (2003), "Boundaries," in J. Agnew, K. Mitchell, and G. Toal eds., *A Companion to Political Geography*. Malden, MA, 123–37.

Newman, D. (2011), "Contemporary Research Agendas in Border Studies: An Overview," in D. Wastl-Walter ed., *The Ashgate Research Companion to Border Studies*. Farnham, 33–47.

Newman, D. and A. Paasi (1998), "Fences and Neighbours in the Postmodern World: Boundary Narratives in Political Geography," *Progress in Human Geography* 22, 186–207.

Paasi, A. (2011), "A Border Theory: An Unattainable Dream or a Realistic Aim for Border Scholars?," in D. Wastl-Walter ed., *The Ashgate Research Companion to Border Studies*. Farnham, 11–31.

Pociña, A. (2007), "Una Medea argentina: *La frontera* de David Cureses," in A. Pociña and A. López eds., *Otras Medeas: nuevas aportaciones al estudio literario de Medea*. Granada, 51–71.

Schroeder, A. (1998), "*La Frontera* de David Cureses," *Stylos* 7, 63–81.

Walther, J. C. (1980), *La conquista del desierto: síntesis histórica de los principales sucesos ocurridos y operaciones militares realizadas en La Pampa y Patagonia, contra los indios (años 1527–1885)*. Buenos Aires.

Weber, D. J. and J. Rausch (1994), "Introduction," in *Where Cultures Meet: Frontiers in Latin American History*. Wilmington, DE, xiii–xli.

CHAPTER 25

BROTHERS AT WAR

Aeschylus in Cuba, 1968 and 2007

ISABELLE TORRANCE

ELLOS
Un día vendrán a buscarme,
lo aseguro.
Dos hombres vestidos de hombre
subirán la escalera, que la vecina
ha terminado de limpiar.
Los espero sentado en mi sillón
de siempre: donde escribo.
Me llamarán, saben mi nombre.
Después seré expulsado
de los cursos
y de la Historia.

Antón Arrufat, 1964

THE MEN[1]
One day they will come to find me,
of that I am sure.
Two men dressed in suits
will come up the stairs, which the neighbour
has finished cleaning.
I wait for them sitting in my armchair
as always: where I write.
They will call me, they know my name.
After this I will be expelled
from courses[2]
and from History.

(Arrufat 1964: 131)

THIS poem, published in 1964 by Antón Arrufat, Cuban poet, novelist, essayist, and playwright, as part of a collection entitled *Repaso final* ("Final review"), was prophetic (Barquet 2002: 17). Four years later, in 1968, Arrufat's adaptation of Aeschylus' *Seven against Thebes* (*Los siete contra Tebas*) was banned in Cuba, in spite of winning the prestigious drama prize sponsored by the Unión de Escritores y Artistas de Cuba (UNEAC), and Arrufat himself was ostracized for 14 years. Although Arrufat was awarded the prize, the two Cuban judges (from a panel of five Spanish and Latin American judges) were convinced that the play was a criticism of Castro's regime and ideologically opposed to the Cuban Revolution (Barquet 2002: 13–26; Escarpanter 1990: 890; Estévez 1992: 861; Hardwick 2004: 222). They were outvoted, and the play was published according to the procedure for UNEAC prize-winners, but with a preface condemning it as counter-revolutionary. In effect, in spite of its publication and critical acclaim, the play was banned from circulation.[3] The play caused such a furore that Arrufat did not attend the prize-giving ceremony, and it seems that the tragedy was parodied by the Cuban playwright José Ramón Brene (1927–90) in a piece entitled *Tebas contra los siete* "Thebes against the seven." Although the work was never published or staged,[4] the title of the parody and Brene's pro-revolutionary outlook suggest that it was a negative literary response to what was perceived to be a counter-revolutionary work in the late 1960s, when Brene's career as a dramatist was arguably at its height. Brene, a creole whose sympathies lay with workers and those who had suffered discrimination, credited the Revolution for his career. "Without the Revolution, for whom would I have written? For lazy functionaries, affected ladies, americanized wannabes, and dime-a-dozen bourgeoisie? No, thank you."[5] Brene stated that he was interested in the conflicts that men and cities have with their fellow man or with their families (Leal 1984: 14). It is not surprising, then, that Arrufat's *Los siete contra Tebas* struck a chord with him, since themes of internecine conflict and tensions between the interests of the individual and those of the city are central to the play as they are to Aeschylus' original. Arrufat has said that he was aware of the parody's existence, and assumed it to be a humorous response to his drama, although he had no knowledge of its actual content.[6] It is a shame that Brene did not live to see the rehabilitation of Arrufat's reputation and of his *Los siete*.

The official recognition of Arrufat's talent in Cuba was a slow process. He has spoken of and written about the fourteen years, from 1968 to the early 1980s, during which he was forbidden to publish and worked, ironically, shelving books in a library.[7] In 1980, his name got onto the American PEN Club register as one of the writers who was unemployed and persecuted in Cuba. Publicly Arrufat denied these charges in an article entitled "My warning to the PEN Club" published in June of that year in *Granma* (the official newspaper of the Central Committee of the Cuban Communist Party). Indeed Arrufat himself is always very careful in the way he speaks of his ostracism and the controversy surrounding his *Los siete*. He insists that he has never been counter-revolutionary and analysis of the play confirms this, but the play nevertheless presents criticisms of what the Revolution had become by the mid-1960s, or had the potential to become. Arrufat was not the only Cuban artist to be subjected to such accusations, and many artists left Cuba during the late 1960s and early 1970s.[8] Originally, Castro's Revolution was welcomed by intellectuals and artists when it overthrew Batista's dictatorship in 1959. The new regime supported education, literacy, and cultural institutions, and encouraged cultural contacts. But once the regime was established, debate and diversity of thought amongst intellectuals in Cuba became less tolerated (Lievesley 2004: 55–6).

It has been noted, however, in a different context, that "the Cuban Revolution is extraordinary in its ability to admit mistakes and rectify them" although "it is slower to permit a critical discourse that encourages real debate and may prevent such errors from being made."[9] In 1970, for example, Castro recognized in a public speech that Ernesto (Che) Guevara's economic policies, which Cuba had followed in the 1960s, had been disastrous.[10] There is even a hint of this in Arrufat's *Los siete*, when Eteocles (the Castro figure) tells his brother that he has rectified the errors of his brother's government.¹¹ Since the 1990s, in response to the economic collapse following the fall of the U.S.S.R., Cuba has become more tolerant in many areas of society. Tourism has been actively promoted, conditions have improved for gays, and there has been an acceptance of a state of coexistence with the Church.¹² The republication of Arrufat's *Los siete* in 2001 with a new preface underlining the negative response to the play's original publication (Espinosa Mendoza 2001: *passim*), coincided with the world première of the play in a translation by Mike Gonzalez at the Ramshorn Theatre in Scotland, at Glasgow's University of Strathclyde Drama Centre.¹³ These events, just one year after Arrufat won Cuba's National Prize for Literature, were followed by the first performance of *Los siete* in Cuba in 2007 and coincide with this general trend toward a more open society.¹⁴ Nevertheless, there remains, it seems, a tension between literary and political opinion. The official Cuban online encyclopedia EcuRed, launched in December 2010, names Brene as "One of the most important dramatists of Cuban theatre".¹⁵ Meanwhile, Arrufat is described more lukewarmly on the same site as "Cuban writer who won the National Prize for Literature in the year 2000," and there is no mention in the list of prizes and distinctions of the 1968 UNEAC prize for his *Los siete*.¹⁶

How can a play which follows so closely the original on which it is based have caused such controversy? Greek tragedy has been a fruitful medium for political expression throughout the twentieth century. Sophocles' *Antigone*, in particular, has a special place in giving voice to the oppressed. It has been exploited with great influence to express everything from anti-Nazism in the late 1940s, to anti-apartheid views in the South Africa of the 1970s.¹⁷ It is also a play which has been especially pertinent to Latin America, which has experienced several dictators and oppressive regimes over the course of the twentieth century.¹⁸ *Antigone* is one of the best-known and most performed Greek tragedies in modern times, but Aeschylus' *Seven*, which relates mythical events leading up to the situation in *Antigone*, has languished in relative obscurity in terms of modern reception. Arrufat's *Los siete* is a powerful exception. The play caused such outrage in Castro's Cuba because of the easily discernible allegory of the attempted invasion by CIA-sponsored Cuban exiles at the Bay of Pigs in the raw material of the struggle between the two brothers of Aeschylus' play. Just a few years after the 1961 Bay of Pigs/Playa Girón assault on the Cuban regime, the attack on Thebes led by the exile Polinices against his brother Eteocles was easily understandable as a reflection of contemporary Cuba.

In many ways, Arrufat is faithful to the original. He recognizes the influence of Euripides' *Phoenician Women*, particularly in introducing a confrontation between the two brothers (Polynices is an absent character in Aeschylus' *Seven*), and other sources mentioned are Seneca's incomplete *Phoenician Women* and Jean Racine's *La Thébaïde*. But Arrufat has stressed that it was the Aeschylean play which was his primary inspiration.¹⁹ The text of Aeschylus' play as we have it contains an epilogue which is regarded by scholars as spurious. It involves the appearance of a herald and of Antigone and Ismene, sisters of the two dead brothers. The herald announces a decision that Eteocles should be buried with all honors as defender of the city, while Polynices is to be cast out to the dogs. Antigone confronts the herald and insists on burying Polynices also. This final scene is clearly inspired by Sophocles' later play *Antigone*, and it is generally agreed to be an appendage to the original Aeschylean play, added after the Sophoclean version had become popular. Arrufat was aware of scholarly opinion on the spurious ending of *Seven* and omits it from his own version. The play ends with the death of the brothers. No further characters are introduced. Arrufat consulted translations of the play in Spanish, French, and English, and has "translated" passages directly from Aeschylus at some points in the play.[20] But even "translation," as the late Seamus Heaney has remarked, "is not all that different from original composition" (Heaney 2005: 169), and although it may have translated passages, Arrufat's *Los siete* is not a translation. It is a creation closely based on the original, but injected with subtle comments on 1960s Cuba.

In evoking the Bay of Pigs attack, the integral elements of Aeschylus' plot create a natural and striking parallel. Polinice (Arrufat's Polynices), brother of Etéocles (Arrufat's Eteocles), is in exile after Etéocles has taken control of the kingdom of Thebes. The Cuban exiles, largely wealthy Cubans fleeing Castro's communist policies, who have settled in America and have strong links there, are supported by the U.S.A. in their invasion and are clearly represented by Polinice. In his exile, he has created new ties with the powerful state of Argos by marrying the daughter of its king Adrastus, and through this new alliance, he is able to gather an army to march on his native land of Thebes. Etéocles, who leads his men to defend the city under attack, is the Castro figure. Of course, Fidel Castro's real brother Raúl was head of the army and fully supported Castro. Indeed, he is now president of Cuba. But the Cuban exiles are Castro's "brothers" insomuch as they are his fellow Cubans, and the Bay of Pigs can be represented as a kind of fratricidal or civil war for this reason.

The scene which recounts the different characters and motivations of the seven champions who attack Thebes, reflected in the symbol on each man's shield, and which shows Eteocles' careful choices in sending appropriate Theban warriors in each case to defend against attack, is the centerpiece of the Aeschylean play. At the first gate, the Proteid gate, Tydeus is outside the gates beside the river bank, unable to cross the Ismenus River (because of bad omens). He is mad with lust for battle like a snake shrieking at noon. With terrifying cries, he tosses three tall shadowing plumes, his helmet's mane. Bells wrought in bronze send out a terrifying clang from the inside of his shield. The front of his shield is a sky blazing with stars, and in the center shines forth a full moon (*Seven* 377–90).[21] Eteocles prays that the emblem of night on his shield may turn out to be a prophecy against himself, that the night of death may fall upon Tydeus' eyes, and against this arrogant warrior, Eteocles sends Melanippus, who is modest and hates proud speech (*Seven* 400–10). At the Electran gate Capaneus attacks. He is a giant, and a worse boaster still than Tydeus, claiming that he will sack the city even against the will of the gods. On his shield, he has a fire-bearer, torch blazing in his hands, and in golden letters he declares, "I will burn the city" (πρήσω πόλιν) (*Seven* 423–34). Against him, Eteocles sends Polyphontes, fiery in spirit (*Seven* 447–8). Eteoclus attacks the Neïstan gate, his restless mares eager to charge. On his shield, he has a man in armor climbing up by a ladder to the enemy's wall to sack their town. And this man too shouts out in written syllables, saying that not even Ares will repulse him from the walls (*Seven* 458–69). Against him Eteocles sends Megareus whose hands are his boast—i.e., not his words (*Seven* 473–4). The champion assigned to the fourth gate, of Athena Onca, is Hippomedon. He is huge and spins his great round threshing-floor of a shield. The emblem shows Typhon (the mythical hundred-headed serpent), his fire-breathing mouth belching out black smoke, and on the rim of the shield's frame run coils of serpents. He is possessed by Ares (*Seven* 486–98). Against this fearsome attacker, Eteocles sends Hyperbius, whose shield bears Zeus (who had defeated Typhon before coming to power), the fire-bolt flaming in his hand (*Seven* 512–20). The young Parthenopaeus is stationed at the North gate. His eye is grim in spite of his youth. He swears by his spear that he will sack the city. His shield bears an insult to the city: the gleaming embossed figure of the cannibal Sphinx, and in her claws, she carries a man, one of the Thebans (*Seven* 526–44). Against him goes Actor, brother of Hyperbius. He is no boaster, nor will he allow the Sphinx to get inside the city (*Seven* 553–60). At the Homoloïd gate is Amphiaraus, who shouts abuse at his fellow attacker Tydeus. Amphiaraus had not wanted to take part in the expedition, knowing it was doomed. His shield bears no emblem on it, for he cares not to seem the bravest but to be the bravest (*Seven* 568–94). Lasthenes is sent to meet the formidable Amphiaraus. He has an old man's wisdom, a young man's flesh, his eye is alert, and he is swift to act (*Seven* 620–5).

Through these choices, Eteocles has left himself as the city's defender against his own brother at the seventh gate. Polynices has a new shield. On it is a twofold emblem. A fully armed warrior is displayed in hammered gold. A woman leading him goes modestly before. Δίκη (*Dike*) "Justice" is her name, and her words are engraved also: "I will bring this man back from exile and he shall possess the city and go to and fro in his father's halls" (κατάξω δ' ἄνδρα τόνδε καὶ πόλιν| ἕξει πατρῴαν δωμάτων τ' ἐπιστροφάς —647–8) (*Seven* 642–8). Eteocles claims that Polynices, aptly named,[22] has never had justice on his side, and Eteocles' mood is grim as he arms himself to meet his brother (*Seven* 658–76). The chorus of young women appeal to Eteocles in desperation, begging him not to spill kin blood, but to no avail (*Seven* 677–719).

Such is the centerpiece of Aeschylus' play. Arrufat also focuses on this scene, although he reworks certain elements. His defending champions are characters with speaking parts.[23] They are able to demonstrate their attributes in their own words and through their own presence. Arrufat also alters the order of the descriptions of the attackers. In this way, the characteristics of the attackers are presented with a different emphasis, and although the attackers, apart from Polinice, are all technically *xenoi*, "extranjeros," "strangers," the different characters of the attacking champions may be seen to reflect the division amongst the Cuban exiles of the Bay of Pigs invasion and their different motivations. Tideo (Tydeus) remains very close to his Aeschylean counterpart, retaining the same emblem and arrogance, just as Arrufat's Melanipo (Melanippus) counters this. But second in Arrufat comes Hipomedonte, and he is rather different from Aeschylus' Hippomedon. He is clearly a returning landowner intent on getting back his land. This is emphatic in the speech where the spy shouts and screeches in the persona of Hipomedonte,[24] who has "the skilled hands of a landowner":[25]

> I threaten, I threaten to strip
> Thebes of its lands

> and to enslave its men
> to serve my driving need for property.[26]
> The land in front of me,
> mine at last, as far as
> my powerful eye can see.
> ... knowing
> that it is mine, all my own,
> [I wish to] cross over it in my swift chariot
> while all take off
> their helmets and salute me
> and call me "Sir," "Sir,"
> with trembling and submissive voices.[27]

The emotive nature of this speech is partly expressed though the distinctively poetic speech pattern of the spy's report, evident from the short lines, as well as from the poetic language. The overarching selfishness of Hipomedonte's desire to possess the lands of Thebes is negatively portrayed by his obsessive and repeated references to himself—"my," "me," "mine."

Arrufat's Hipomedonte must surely recall prominent landowners whose motive in the expedition was to regain lands nationalized by Castro's 1959 Agrarian Reform Law (Barquet 2002: 91–2). It is then no accident that Arrufat's Hiperbio (Hyperbius), who goes to meet Hipomedonte, had spent some time reflecting on the school he has built before being dispatched on his mission (Arrufat 2001: 39–40). The Agrarian Reform Institute (INRA), designed originally to supervise the reorganization of land, had subsequently become responsible for many projects in rural Cuba, including the building of schools. Arrufat's Hipomedonte is thus met by the very force which had deprived landowners like him of their land. And in this respect, Arrufat's pairing reflects that of Aeschylus. For in Aeschylus also, through the clash of shields, the monster Typhon, symbol of the attacker, is met by Zeus, an opponent who had previously defeated him. The third attacker in Arrufat is Capaneo (Capaneus). Like Tideo, he retains the same shield insignia as his Aeschylean counterpart, complete with the inscription "I will set fire to Thebes,"[28] but Arrufat develops the image of fire in a different way. As one scholar has suggested, Capaneo is presented as a critic of the moral impurities of the Revolution (Barquet 2002: 92–3). This works well with the threat of burning the city to the ground, easily manipulated in Arrufat as a symbol for purification. "Only fire will purify you," claims (the spy in the persona of) Capaneo, addressing the city.[29] But this Capaneo is also hubristic. "Nothing ties him to the land: neither family, nor friends.... Purity is the only thing he loves."[30] Although the concept of purification is not necessarily negative on its own terms, this overbearing obsession with it has negative implications because it excludes everything else.

The next threat comes from Eteoclus whose name Arrufat alters to "Ecleo," presumably to avoid confusion with the main character Eteocles. His Aeschylean shield insignia is also present in Arrufat, again complete with inscription, a very minor adaptation: "No one will throw me off this tower."[31] As in Aeschylus, he is met by Megareo (Megareus).

At Arrufat's fifth gate is stationed Anfiarao (Amphiaraus). His knowledge that the expedition is doomed reflects the sentiment which had apparently been felt by the Cuban exiles during their CIA-run training in Guatemala and Nicaragua. They realized that they were being trained for a conventional military operation and not for the guerrilla warfare which was needed if their brigade of 1,500 men was to defeat Castro's standing army (Leonard 1999: 52). But the CIA, many of whom were themselves Cuban exiles (Leonard 1999: 70), stood firm in their policies and the exiles were fueled against the idea of failure by their anti-Castro passions. Arrufat's Anfiarao, as in Aeschylus, has no insignia. "A man who knows his destiny is fearsome," says the spy.[32] But Etéocles' reaction to Anfiarao is striking, markedly different from that of his Aeschylean counterpart. "I do not admire this man," says Arrufat's Etéocles, "He seems strange to me. He is too caught up with himself."[33] Even in his acknowledgment of failure and death, Anfiarao, as all the invading champions in Arrufat, is intrinsically selfish. A capitalist ideology is pitted against the concept of the common good. Arrufat's Parténopeo (Parthenopaeus) is mentioned briefly, his distinguishing characteristics (as in Aeschylus) are his spear, his oath to destroy the city, and the carnivorous bird of prey with open talons on his shield (a slight variation on the Sphinx) (Arrufat 2001: 50–1). He is met by Háctor (Actor).

Some Cuban exiles involved in the Bay of Pigs invasion "sought a true democracy" for Cuba, others were generally "disenchanted with Castro's policies," and others still "wanted to restore gambling and the vacation paradise of pre-Castro Havana" (Leonard 1999: 52). A reference to this may be seen in Arrufat's introduction of the motif of dice in the play. This is clearly inspired by the assignment by lot in the original play of each of the attacking champions to each of the seven gates. In Arrufat's play, this assignment by lot becomes a game of dice initiated by Polinice. The allocation of each gate becomes a gamble. As the spies relate their report, "the fateful rattle of the dice" is still to be heard.[34] Later, when the spies return for a second time to give Etéocles information as to which champion has been assigned to which gate, the chorus mime the game of dice as the report is related. The remark of the chorus during the report is particularly pointed: "The god of war will play out the victory with dice."[35] This line, in fact, is a direct adaptation of Eteocles' line in the *Seven*: "Ares will decide the matter with his dice."[36] But Arrufat has developed the image of gambling and dice to associate it not only with the god, but also with the invading army.

Of course, of prime importance for the allegory is that the Thebans *win*. The attempted invasion by the Cuban exiles was a complete débacle. In January 1961, the national news in the U.S.A. reported the training of Cuban exiles in Guatemala, giving Castro plenty of time to prepare for the invasion which was attempted in April.[37] This notion of foreknowledge is paralleled in the play by the reports of the spies. Etéocles knows which of the attacking champions is stationed at which gate and is able to choose who should fight there accordingly. Ultimately, however, the invasion failed because the U.S.A. pulled out its air support at a crucial moment (through Kennedy's mistaken belief that he could conceal the U.S.A.'s role in the affair) leaving the Cuban exiles stranded and at the mercy of Castro's army. The Bay of Pigs was a triumph for Castro, allowing him to consolidate his position in Cuba, and to enhance his image in the political world generally (Leonard

1999: 53). Here the direct allegory ends. If Etéocles represents Castro, then his death is not a reflection of reality, but there is nonetheless a subtle political message in Arrufat's choice to follow the ending of the Aeschylean plot: Thebes is victorious, but at a price. At each gate, the Theban champion wins out over his attacker. But at the seventh gate, where Etéocles had seen fit to fight against his own brother, both brothers die, slain by each other's hands. It is clear why Arrufat's play was not well received in Cuba. The message, as in Aeschylus, is that in spite of its victory, Thebes's leader has died because of his own decision, and brother has killed brother in horrific circumstances.[38] The fratricidal war, driven by the two brothers, ends in loss for city and family, *polis* and *oikos*, both strong themes in the Aeschylean play (Sommerstein 2010: 80–4; Thalmann 1978: 31–81; Torrance 2007b: 23–37; Winnington-Ingram 1977). In Arrufat, this emphasis is more on materialism vs. communism, but the overall effect of the play nonetheless entails an emotional conflict for the audience and for the characters in the play. The death of the brothers is a cause for lament, but the salvation of the city demands rejoicing. The two sit uncomfortably together at the drama's close.

In Aeschylus, the fratricide is the awful fulfillment of the ancestral curse of Oedipus on his sons, but Arrufat confines his references to curses reported to have been uttered by Polinice against his brother. Arrufat leaves the relationship with Oedipus out of the equation, but his drama is nonetheless full of archaisms and stylization that create a distance from contemporary reality. Arrufat takes careful measures to compose a play that is full of movement, seemingly inspired by the very choral elements that can make Greek tragedy difficult for a modern audience. He uses the chorus of Theban women along with the characters of the spies to mime events narrated. He also retains the report of the formal ritual of the oath sworn to sack the city or die in the attempt, taken by the seven attackers over the blood of a slaughtered bull. Through such archaisms and the medium of ancient myth, the presentation of a political message is made more palatable. It seems important that Arrufat has kept his play close to the original, at a time which he has described as "absolutely black" for writers in Cuba,[39] when expression was restricted to the confines of the Revolution, and dissidence could mean arrest and prison sentences (Leonard 1999: 93). But in spite of using Aeschylus' play as an indirect means of subtle expression, Arrufat paid the price.

Aeschylus' plot suits Arrufat's purpose and, as we have seen, he also seems to take his cue from Aeschylus in terms of imagery, though often developing it in different ways. The image of the αἰθερία κόνις "air-borne dust" introduced by the Aeschylean chorus at line 81 is developed significantly by Arrufat's chorus in their first choral ode where the word "polvo" "dust" is repeated five times. Everything is unsettled as symbolized by the clouds of dust churned up by the hooves of the attackers' horses. The dust is blinding, and the chorus imagines "the shining blades" of the attackers "rising out through the dust, advancing and seeking out [their] breasts."[40] The wealth of the attackers represented by their shining weapons is exploited by Arrufat to contrast with the poverty of the local Thebans. In fact the image of dust also highlights the poor resources of the Thebans when Etéocles introduces the image expressing his hopes that the houses will not crumble under the enemy's assault or become dust in the wind.[41]

Arrufat's six defending champions, along with Eteocles, are invested with armor in a ceremonious display. It is specified in the stage directions, however, that this is done *without* the physical presence of arms. It is all a mime, reinforcing the vulnerability of the Theban champions. Conversely, much is made of the attackers' new and impressive weapons, but the emphasis is most apparent through the figure of Polinice. Again Arrufat builds on the insignia of the Aeschylean Polynices. The inscription on Polinice's shield is, once again, almost verbatim. The female figure says: "I am Justice. I will give back his fatherland to Polinice as well as his father's inheritance."[42] In fact, the female personification of Justice carved on Polinice's shield could easily be interpreted as a kind of Statue of Liberty, representative of American democracy. His new shield is a sharp contrast to the ancestral shield of their forefathers used by Eteocles, who draws attention to it in his prologue speech.

The confrontation between the two brothers is surprising, particularly because Polinice is a far more sympathetic character than we have been led to expect and, all of a sudden, audience sympathy for Eteocles is challenged. In the opening speech of the play, Eteocles had recalled his relationship with his brother as follows: "My own brother Polinice, who fled our country and forgot the days we shared, forgot the brother's bond of our childhood, our ancestral hearth, our language and our cause, has now equipped an army of foreigners and prepares to lay siege to our city."[43] Later in the same speech Eteocles asserts: "This battle marks us down in history,"[44] perhaps a reference to Castro's speech "History will absolve me," a defence of his attack on the Batista regime of 1953 (Leonard 1999: 92). In any case, the opening picture of Polinice is pretty damning—he has abandoned and betrayed his country, we are told. But when we meet him, we see that things are not so straightforward. Polinice's first words are "I offer you a truce, Eteocles."[45] Eteocles rejects the idea of a truce. Polinice understands this in terms of Eteocles as "the hero who saves the people with powerful gestures,"[46] but he is also patronizing in drawing attention to his superior force of arms in contrast to those of the Thebans, "barefoot people brandishing ancient spears and shabby [lit. 'rotten'] shields."[47] "No one but a madman," says Polinice, "would feel secure when faced with an army like mine."[48] Eteocles is determined that blood will be spilt, in spite of fond memories of time spent with Polinice (Arrufat 2001: 56ff.). But neither brother is entirely sympathetic. Each tries to blame the other. Eteocles blames Polinice for attacking his home and attempting to lay waste to his city. But Polinice reminds Eteocles of a sworn pact they made three years earlier, by which they agreed to govern one year each and share command of the army. Eteocles broke his oath and now refuses a truce.[49] He governs alone and makes decisions alone, and lives in the ancestral house alone.[50] He refuses to share power. This is an emphatic portrayal of absolute rule. Eteocles acknowledges that he broke his oath, and that this was wrong, but he argues it was not unjust.[51] The end justifies the means, so to speak.

We are presented with two conflicting arguments, both of which are partly justified. Eteocles feels justified in that his purpose was to distribute wealth, including his family's wealth, among the poor. He emptied their house, he says, but still there was not enough for everyone, a suggestion that he has failed somehow, that his ideal was not ultimately fulfilled.[52] Polinice is furious that his possessions are in the hands of others.[53] He accuses Eteocles of presuming himself to *be* justice, the fatherland, the good,[54] but of actually representing "absolute power and the iron fist."[55] These are his final words to Eteocles. But ironically, Polinice is guilty of the very charges he makes against Eteocles. Polinice could well be seen as assuming himself to be justice. Polinice's shield, an extension of his character, bears the personification of Justice as its emblem. He refers to the suffering of exile and calls the gods and his native country to witness that he loves his fatherland and did not want the war. Eteocles claims to be no enemy of the human race, but Polinice charges him with being the enemy of his brother, which Eteocles proves by deciding to fight Polinice himself at the seventh gate.[56] The chorus urge him not to spill his brother's blood, but he will not listen. The chorus do not approve of Eteocles' actions, but they profess their affection for him because he sustained the city and organized its defence without worrying about himself.[57] It is also noteworthy that while Polinice dismisses the women as immaterial to the government of the city, Eteocles emphatically defends their importance (Arrufat 2001: 54–5). This is a radical departure from the attitude of the Aeschylean Eteocles who repeatedly tries to silence the chorus and expresses misogynistic sentiments.[58] Such rewriting of Eteocles' beliefs is a further hint at this figure's communist agenda in Arrufat. But, just as Polinice cannot see his own arrogance, the words of the chorus reveal that Eteocles has ultimately become like one of the attackers he vilified—too self-obsessed. "Move that mirror aside. Remember that there are other men in the world," they say.[59] Here are the two faces of rule that Arrufat presents us with: Polinice the traditional aristocrat, and Eteocles the absolute ruler who has the people's interests at heart. And therein lies the paradox, for with absolute rule, the people no longer make decisions for themselves. Eteocles decides what is in the interests of the people.

Arrufat captures in his play the sense of excitement felt at the beginning of the Revolution and how this had subsequently begun to change. Arrufat himself has said of Castro's accession to power:

> It was a moment of great energy, of great happiness, of great vitality. It was like breaking everything that had existed before; just destroying it. We didn't know . . . if what should have been done had actually been done or not, but that didn't matter then, what mattered was the enthusiasm of the moment, the magnitude of the time.[60]

This sense of "the moment" is conveyed by such phrases as "Es nuestra hora," "The time is ours," spoken by Eteocles in his opening speech. But the victory of the moment will be marred by the death of the brothers, and the glory of the time has been undermined throughout by the doubts of the chorus and the poverty of the Thebans. Although Arrufat sticks closely to the original, this poverty represented by the poor arms of the Thebans, along with references to the importance of bread, are ways in which the myth is actualized with twentieth-century resonances for a contemporary Cuban audience.[61] Rusty weapons and the baking of bread are incongruous images in the world of Greek heroes. In his programme notes for the world première of Arrufat's play, Mike Gonzalez sees the Cuban government's choice of awarding Arrufat the National Prize for Literature in 2000 as "odd" (Gonzalez 2001b). Given the original reception of *Los siete* in Cuba, it certainly seems paradoxical. But Arrufat, one of the few writers who has stayed in Cuba through the entire regime, is clearly highly patriotic, and on close inspection, his *Los siete* is not an outright condemnation of either brother or either side. What it *does* condemn is fratricidal war and flawed rule, both capitalist rule, emphasized through the negative portrayal of materialism, and absolute rule.

The battle fought at the Bay of Pigs (Playa Girón) was bloody and lasted four days (Johnson 1964: 101–202). It had a profound effect on Arrufat. Indeed the issue was raised in a revealing discussion on theater in Cuba and Latin America led by Arrufat and published in 1962. At one point, Arrufat says, "If a writer finds things absurd in this society, he ought to reveal them on stage." The respondent comments on the difficulty of writing about present reality, and states as an example that it seems strange that (at that time) no one had yet written about the battle of Playa Girón (Arrufat 1962: 260–1). This discussion may have sown seeds in Arrufat's mind. He had, at any rate, written a poem in 1961 which was published three years later in his *Repaso final* collection. The poem highlights the deep impact that the Bay of Pigs had on the playwright. It reads as follows:

PLAYA GIRÓN
*Con mis manos inútiles
que no saben hacer otra cosa que escribir,
quisiera recoger vuestras cabezas
hermanos míos, compatriotas,
las cabezas de los que murieron viendo
   un sol diferente,
las cabezas voladas y deshechas por los obuses,*

*por el pecho que se llevó la metralla
y dejó las entrañas al aire
—porque allí había un corazón violento—
por la carne hecha trizas
y los pañuelos ensangrentados,
nadie sabe qué pena siento por mi impotencia*

*y cuánto con esta pobre voz quisiera
crearles otra vida distinta y perenne*

*yo que tengo este triste oficio
que espera que los otros vivan por él,
por su sangre.
En mis venas estaría vuestra sangre
y la necesidad de la muerte justa.
Ahora no temo a las palabras:
justicia, libertad, pan.*[64]

GIRÓN BEACH (or BAY OF PIGS)[62]
With my useless hands
which only know how to write,
I would like to gather your heads,
my brothers, compatriots,
the heads of those who died looking towards
   a different sun,
heads blown up and destroyed by mortar
   bombs,

for the breast filled with shrapnel
and left the entrails to the air
—because there was a violent[63] heart—
for the flesh torn to shreds
and for blood-stained neck-scarves,
nobody knows what grief I feel at my
   powerlessness

and how much with this poor voice I wish
to create another life for them, different and
   eternal,

I who have this sad trade
who hope that others might live for him,
through his blood.
In my veins there would be your blood
and the need for just death.
I no longer fear the words:
justice, freedom, bread.

This poem expresses Arrufat's frustration and horror at the gruesome realities of the Bay of Pigs battle. There is no romanticism in the image of collecting heads from among the fragmented and decomposing bodies of the fallen. There is no veiling of the violence of these deaths. Rather we are forced to acknowledge the impact of mortar bombs ripping a human being apart, and the mental disturbance experienced by those who were fighting. But through this pain and grief, the poem concludes with a positive image of blood. The blood of the fallen will live on through the poet's veins; they will live on through his writing. Their passion for the Revolution lives on—justice, freedom, bread. These last three words will be significant themes in Arrufat's later *Los siete*.

But as with any work of literary complexity, the Bay of Pigs allegory is just one strand of interpretation among others. A second, relevant here, is the understanding of the quarrel between brothers as reminiscent of the possible rift that had occurred by the 1960s between the one-time "brothers" Castro and Che Guevara. This was the interpretation of the play when directed by Salvador Flores in Mexico in 1970. Barquet confesses to be mystified by this interpretation (Barquet 2002: 150). It is true that even with the "brothers at war" in Arrufat's play disagreeing on political policy, it is difficult to chart the plot into a comfortable allegory for a falling out between Castro and Guevara. The latter would certainly never have invaded Cuba to wrench control from Castro. Indeed, there is much debate as to whether or not the rift ever occurred between Castro and Guevara. Guevara died in 1967 and Castro is silent on the subject, but there are indications of a growing distance between the two in the years before Guevara left Cuba. Some have gone so far as to argue that Guevara was eventually forced to leave Cuba because Castro viewed him as a rival.[65] Castro's close adviser during the Cuban Revolution, Guevara was made Minister of Industry. But Guevara's policies for the rapid industrialization of Cuba were a failure, and during the 1960s, the country was plunged deep into economic ruin. In 1965, Guevara resigned from his position, though his reasons were not clearly explained (Leonard 1999: 106). Before leaving Cuba, Guevara (an Argentinian national) gave up the Cuban citizenship he had been awarded (Lievesley 2004: 81). After his death, as mentioned above, Castro acknowledged the disastrous effect of Guevara's policies on the Cuban economy, and during the 1970s, economic policies shifted away from Guevara's models (Lievesley 2004: 82). Diverging views on political policy between "brothers" can certainly be read into the play, but perhaps Flores went a bit too far in casting Polinice as a Guevara-figure.

The possibility of interpreting Arrufat's *Los siete* as a quarrel between Guevara and Castro nevertheless highlights the play's complexity, and the focus here on "brothers at war" is but one interpretation. Quite apart from the themes of war and the tragedy of internal conflict within a state or a family, Arrufat's *Los siete* is also a comment on the failure of materialistic society.[66] For all their gleaming blades, the assailants on Thebes cannot penetrate the "escudos podridos" "rotten shields" of the Thebans. As Arrufat himself has said, in an interview published in 1999, those who condemned his *Los siete* had understood the play in black and white terms. In that same interview, he asserts that the play should be compared to the Aeschylean original before it be judged (Chávez 1999: 23). Several people have pointed out in broad strokes where Arrufat deviates from or is faithful to Aeschylus, but, to my knowledge, no one has convincingly studied text and context in *Los siete* with specific reference to the Aeschylean original as I have tried to do here.[67]

The connection between Arrufat's play and its Aeschylean model is something that was stressed in materials discussing the 2007 production in Havana.[68] More important, however, is the great sense of excitement at the Cuban première of this tragedy on October 20, 39 years after its first publication. The production is hailed as a historic moment for Cuban theater (Arcos 2007; Arrufat et al. 2007). Arrufat writes to Ricard Salvat on September 21, 2007, with the news of the upcoming performance, asking him, as one of the judges who awarded him the UNEAC prize for *Los siete* in 1968, to write something for the programme, and mentioning his delight that the play had been chosen for performance by a group of young actors from Havana (Arrufat et al. 2007: 41). This point seems significant. A new generation of Cubans symbolize a potential for change at a moment of transition in Cuban politics in late 2007, when the ailing Fidel Castro had essentially handed over power to his brother Raúl, who officially became president in February 2008. Initially Raúl's new economic policies may have seemed to represent change, but these have been problematic and economic issues continue to dog Cuban politics (Farber 2011: 51–95, 150–2). Potent images of bread and crumbling buildings from Arrufat's play, metonymies for (respectively) the most basic sustenance and state poverty, will still have had a significant resonance in late 2007.

The 2007 production was directed by the Cuban native Alberto Sarraín, and Arrufat is described as "triumphant" on stage at the curtain call by the Cuban news website Cubahora (Oramas 2007). It must, indeed, have been gratifying for Arrufat to see the play produced in Havana. However, there are indications that Arrufat's text was adapted or edited in significant ways. Actors playing Antigone, Ismene, and (rather more surprisingly) Cassandra are mentioned in reviews and in the programme notes (Arrufat et al. 2007: 46; Oramas 2007). The latter case is particularly curious since the author (Salvat) explains in detail how Arrufat followed Greek textual critics in omitting Antigone and Ismene from the end of the play. He then incongruously mentions actors playing these parts in the next paragraph (Arrufat et al. 2007: 46). Two actors are listed for each of the roles of Antigona, Ismene, and Cassandra, while only one actor is listed for each of the male roles (Etéocles, Polionte, Polinice), which suggests that Arrufat's female chorus may have been reconstituted into the identities of Antigone, Ismene, and Cassandra. A thesis on myth in contemporary Cuban theater, published online in 2010 by InterClassica, states, tantalizingly, that Sarraín did not use the original script but produced a structured piece that he had conceived himself in order to stage the play (Pérez Asensio 2010: 317). Unfortunately no further details are given, and my attempts to contact the director have not yielded any responses. One review of the performance states that the director incorporated elements reflective of contemporary Cuba by, for example, giving Afro-Cuban attributes to certain key figures. Again, however, the details are frustratingly sparse and the same review warns that censorship continues in Cuba (Arcos 2007). This may have been an issue for those involved and may account for certain directorial choices. Perhaps Antigone and Ismene were reintroduced to reinforce the classical models which inspired Arrufat's tragedy, thus diffusing the potential political allegory of "brothers at war." The intrusion of Cassandra, who has no place in this mythic cycle, may have been designed to emphasize an aspect of foreknowledge which could be linked to contemporary Cuba, since she is known from mythology for her gift of prophecy (though she is doomed not to be believed). Certainly the immediacy of potential civil war is something that has long left Cuban consciousness, as Arrufat discusses in an interview published in the Spanish newspaper *El País* in March 2007 (Blanco 2007). That aspect of the Seven against Thebes story no longer has a raw resonance in twenty-first-century Cuba.

The way in which a play is received, reinvented, reworked, rewritten, and reinterpreted for a new generation can be important for our appreciation of the original. This approach to the reception of ancient texts is not without its critics, but I am convinced that, in the case of drama at least, it is a valid path of intellectual inquiry. In a new drama which is inspired by an ancient original, certain aspects of the original may become more apparent through the way they have been manipulated in the hypertext. So I would like to conclude by asking: What light, if any, does Arrufat's *Los siete* throw on Aeschylus' play? It seems to me, at least, that Arrufat's play highlights how Aeschylus emphasizes Eteocles' perspective. Although Arrufat follows Aeschylus in reporting an irate Polynices who is continually cursing his brother, Arrufat's Polinice is not so barbaric in the flesh. A contrast is drawn very deftly between reports and reality, something very pertinent in a society subjected to strict censorship laws. Arrufat's interpretation of the play thus confirms the view of scholars who have stressed the responsibility of both brothers in conflict. On the surface, Aeschylus' *Seven* seems to glorify Eteocles and demonize Polynices (Euripides' *Phoenician Women* seems to do the opposite). But the *Seven* is not so straightforward.[69] Indeed there is a certain balance in the madness and impiety of both brothers in Aeschylus, heightened by the emphasis on the dual or double nature of the curse which is fulfilled.[70] In Aeschylus, Eteocles and Polynices are equal agents of Oedipus' curse. In Arrufat, each of the brothers is also a responsible agent, but in this case for a flawed vision of good government which precipitates fratricidal war.[71]

Notes

1. Translations are my own unless otherwise stated.
2. i.e., "expelled from university." I am grateful to Catherine Davies for clarifying this point.
3. The play has subsequently been called "one of the best moments" of Arrufat's career as a dramatist—Escarpanter 1990: 889.
4. It is listed among numerous unpublished and unstaged works gathered after Brene's death in the entry on Brene on the website Cubaliteraria (<http://www.cubaliteraria.cu/autor.php?idautor=1982>) and is mentioned in a few secondary sources (Barquet 2002: 148 reprinted in Arrufat 2007: 258; Cypess 1994: 251; Vasserot 2006: 296 n. 2). Brene was a prolific writer, who suggested in one interview that a writer should write 40 or 50 pages a day, wittily referring doubters to the entry "writer" in the *Dictionary of the Spanish Academy*, where they will find the definition "one who writes"—Leal 1984: 9.
5. Leal 1984: 9: "Sin Revolución, ¿para quién hubiera escrito? ¿Para los manengues, señoronas cursis, pepillitos americanizados y burgueses de a tres por quilo? No, gracias." I am grateful to David Hernandez for clarifying the meaning of the Cuban expressions "manengues," "pepillitos," and "tres por quilo."

6. Barquet 2002: 148 reprinted in Arrufat 2007: 258.
7. See interviews in Chávez 1990: *passim* and esp. 23; Barquet 2002: 137–49, esp. 143; and cf. Estévez 1992: 862.
8. See Escarpanter 1990: *passim* and Barquet 2002: 27–60. There was, as is well known, a mass exodus from Cuba to the United States after the Revolution—some 200,000 people left between January 1959 and October 1962—Lievesley 2004: 68.
9. Randall 1992: 138–9—quoted in Lievesley 2004: 179.
10. Dominguez 1993: 109–10. Castro is also concerned about the economic motivations of those attempting to flee Cuba illegally in Oliver Stone's 2006 documentary *Looking for Fidel*.
11. Arrufat 2001: "Rectifiqué los errors de tu gobierno." All quotations of *Los siete* are taken from the new 2001 edition.
12. Lievesley 2004: 176–9, cf. Farber 2011: 212–15.
13. For information on this production, see Hardwick 2004: 223–4, and details supplied by the Open University project "Reception of the Texts and Images of Ancient Greece in Modern Poetry and Drama" (<www2.open.ac.uk/ClassicalStudies/GreekPlays>) and by the Archive of Performances of Greek and Roman Drama at Oxford University (<http://www.apgrd.ox.ac.uk/research-collections/performance-database/productions>).
14. Even when Martin's "Cuban Theatre" was published in 1990, already "the parameters of artistic expression [were] being challenged"—Martin 1990: 39. The momentous première of Arrufat's *Los siete* in Havana in late 2007 occurred after the publication of both Torrance 2007a and Torrance 2007b in which I claimed (correctly at the time both pieces went to press) that the play had never been performed in Cuba. I am grateful indeed to the editors of this volume for the chance to revise Torrance 2007a in light of this important development, and I take the opportunity to discuss the 2007 Cuban production at the end of this chapter.
15. <http://www.ecured.cu/index.php/José_Ramón_Brene>, "Uno de los más importantes dramaturges del teatro cubano."
16. <http://www.ecured.cu/index.php/Antón_Arrufat>, "Escritor cubano que en el año 2000 obtuvo el Premio Nacional de Literatura."
17. I refer here to Bertolt Brecht's *Antigonemodell* of 1948 and Athol Fugard's *The Island* of 1973 but the number of political adaptations of *Antigone* is vast. See further Steiner 1984, several relevant essays in Hardwick and Gillespie 2007, collected essays in Wilmer and Žukauskaitė 2010 and in Mee and Foley 2011, and Foley 2012: 125–37. The Spanish philosopher Maria Zambrano wrote on Antigone in the 1940s to explore the subject of women's oppression. I owe this last point to Catherine Davies.
18. See, e.g., Pianacci 2004, Nelli 2010, and Chapter 35, this volume. One of Arrufat's fellow Cubans, whose work was also controversial, José Triana, wrote a version of *Antigone* entitled *Detrás queda el polvo* ("The dust is left behind"), significantly in 1968, the same year as Arrufat's *Los siete*. Arrufat himself also wrote a piece inspired by *Antigone* published in 1955. For a brief discussion of several Cuban dramas inspired by Greek tragedy see Vasserot 1998.
19. See interview in Barquet 2002: 137–49, esp. 145–48.
20. Arrufat discusses this in his interview with Barquet (2002: 137–49, esp. 145–8). Cf. Álvarez Morán and Iglesias Montiel (2001) who note various correspondences between ancient sources (especially Aeschylus) and Arrufat's play.
21. All line numbers are taken from Hutchinson 1985.

22. His name in Greek means "Much-strife."
23. The defending champions in Aeschylus certainly have no speaking parts, and moreover it is doubted whether they were even on stage as silent characters. Taplin (1977: 146–56) maintains that the six defending champions were silent characters, but see the convincing arguments against this summarized in Sommerstein (2010: 72–6).
24. Arrufat 2001: 44: "Grito como él, chillo."
25. Arrufat 2001: 44: "hábiles manos de dueño de tierras."
26. The phrase "to serve my driving need for property" is taken from Gonzalez 2001a: 17.
27. Arrufat 2001: 44–5: "amenazo, amenazo despojar | a Tebas de sus tierras | y esclavizar sus hombres a mis ansias de posesión. | La tierra delante de mí, | mía al fin, hasta donde | mi vista poderosa abarca . . . sabiendo | que es la mía, mía tan solo, | [deseo] cruzarla en mi carro veloz | mientras todos se quitan | los cascos y me saludan | y me llaman: 'Señor', 'Señor',| con voces trémulas y sumisas."
28. Arrufat 2001: 45: "Yo incendiaré a Tebas."
29. Arrufat 2001: 45: "Sólo el fuego te purificará."
30. Arrufat 2001: 46: "Nada le ata a la tierra: ni familia, ni amigos . . . Ama tan sólo la pureza."
31. Arrufat 2001: 47: "'Nadie me arrojará de esta torre.'"
32. Arrufat 2001: 48: "Es temible el que conoce su destino."
33. Arrufat 2001: 48: "No admiro a ese hombre. Me es extraño. Se ocupa demasiado de sí mismo." Compare the Aeschylean Eteocles for whom Amphiaraus is σώφρων δίκαιος ἀγαθὸς εὐσεβής ἀνήρ| μέγας προφήτης "a prudent, just, honourable and pious man, a great prophet" (610–11).
34. Arrufat 2001: 29–30: "Escuchamos aún el chasquido fatídico de los dados."
35. Arrufat 2001: 43: "El dios de la guerra jugará a los dados la victoria."
36. *Seven* 414: ἔργον δ' ἐν κύβοις Ἄρης κρινεῖ.
37. Leonard 1999: 52. Cf. Johnson 1964: 93.
38. Barquet (2002: 124) argues that those who analyze the play as a reference to the Bay of Pigs (which, unless it is a typographical error, he misdates to 1965) are guilty of extreme and imprecise contextualization, because there are two elements of the text which do not reflect reality: the two brothers die (and Castro does not), and this leads to a revision of the mechanics of power (again absent from the Bay of Pigs episode). But the allegory is not made redundant simply because it cannot be applied to the final outcome. In fact, the allegory throughout *highlights* the difference in outcome, and the play's messages are emphasized as a result. An analysis of the play in light of the Bay of Pigs does not exclude other readings of the play, as Barquet seems to be suggesting.
39. Quoted in Minaya 2002.
40. Arrufat 2001: 31–2; 32: "Veo sus armas lucientes salir de entre el polvo, avanzar buscando nuestros pechos."
41. Arrufat 2001: 30: "May the dust of the stones [from our houses] not disperse on the wind" ("Que el polvo de sus piedras no se disperse en el viento"). Gonzalez (2001a) 5 translates: "I only hope these houses will not . . . turn to dust on the wind."
42. Arrufat 2001: 52: "'Soy el Derecho. Devolveré su patria a Polinice, y la herencia de su padre.'" The term "el Derecho" as opposed to "justicia" really means "legal right," but the phrase is clumsy in English here, and I have translated it as "Justice," as does Gonzalez (2001a; 25).
43. Arrufat 2001: 27: "Mi propio hermano Polinice, huyendo de nuestra tierra, olvidando los días compartidos, la hermandad de la infancia, el hogar paterno, nuestra lengua y nuestra causa, ha armado un ejército de extranjeros y se acerca a sitiar nuestra ciudad."

44. Arrufat 2001: 28: "... esta batalla ... traza nuestro rostro en la historia."
45. Arrufat 2001: 53: "Te ofrezco una truega, Etéocles."
46. Arrufat 2001: 54: "Eres el héroe que al pueblo salva gesticulando con firmeza."
47. Arrufat 2001 54: "pueblo descalzo que empuña viejas lanzas y escudos podridos." The phrase "shabby shields" is that of Gonzales (2001a: 26). The term "podrido" ("rotten") continues to be used to describe Cuban poverty. See, e.g., Blanco 2007: paragraph 6, and cf. Gorney 2012: 39.
48. Arrufat 2001: 54: "Nadie, sólo un loco, se sentiría seguro frente a un ejército como el mío."
49. This is a departure from the Aeschylean original where the focus is Oedipus' curse on his sons, and the cause of the quarrel between the two brothers is not clearly defined. This may be due to the fact that the play was last in a connected trilogy whose first two plays, in which the origins of the quarrel may have been explained, do not survive. Arrufat here takes inspiration from the Euripidean version of the quarrel as dramatized in his *Phoenician Women*, though in that play the boys' mother Jocasta is the prime force behind the idea of conciliation.
50. Arrufat 2001: 57: "Solo gobiernas, solo decides, solo habitas la casa de mi padre."
51. Arrufat 2001: 58: "Sí, es cierto, profané un juramento. Pero no me importa. Acepto esa impureza, pero no la injusticia."
52. Arrufat 2001: 58: "Repartí nuestros bienes, repartí nuestra herencia, hasta los últimos objetos... Está vacia nuestra casa, y no alcanzó sin embargo para todos."
53. Arrufat 2001: 58: "Mis cosas están en manos ajenas."
54. Arrufat 2001: 58: "Para ti la justicia se llama Etéocles. Etéocles la patria y el bien."
55. Arrufat 2001: 60: "tú representas: el poder infalible y la mano de hierro." My translation is the same as Gonzales 2001a: 32.
56. Cf. Arrufat 2001: 60 for Etéocles' exclamation "¡Morirás!" "You will die!"
57. Arrufat 2001: 62: "Has sostenido la ciudad, organizando la defensa ... sin ocuparte de ti."
58. On Eteocles' misogyny in Aeschylus, see Caldwell 1973 and Torrance 2007b: 94–101.
59. Arrufat 2001: 61: "Aparta ese espejo. Recuerda que hay otros hombres en el mundo."
60. Quoted in Minaya 2002.
61. For references to bread, cf. Arrufat 2001: 38; 42; 58.
62. I am grateful to Catherine Davies for help in translating several difficult passages of this poem.
63. "un corazón violento" could also be translated as "an awkward/embarrassed heart." This double entendre highlights the complexity of the poem's message—emphasizing both the psychological and the physical aspects of war—and perhaps hints at the uncomfortable nature of struggle against one's countrymen.
64. Arrufat 1964: 89–90.
65. See Lievesley 2004: 81; cf. Anderson 1997: 425; 438; 626–8; 638–9; 682; 750–1 on rumors of division between Castro and Guevara.
66. Cf. Chávez 1999: 23, where Arrufat explains that what is religion to Aeschylus is materialism in his play.
67. Among the more detailed discussions of the relationship between *Los siete* and Aeschylus' *Seven* are Álvarez Morán and Iglesias Montiel 2001 and Bejel 1978. The former dutifully note some correspondences between the Aeschylean text and Arrufat's *Los siete*, but there is no real contextual analysis and they even see fit to consider mythographical sources whether or not they were known by Arrufat (17). This approach seems fundamentally flawed given that Arrufat has stated which sources he was aware of and influenced by.

Bejel (1978) looks at the myth of the house of Laius in Arrufat's *Los siete* and the absence of Oedipus' curse from Arrufat's version, but he gives an overly Christian interpretation of the curse of Oedipus in the Aeschylean original, presenting its fulfillment as an "exorcism" which he claims is paralleled by the "exorcism" of the evil of war in the fratricide of Arrufat's play.

68. e.g., Salvat in Arrufat et al. 2007: 46; Hernández 2007; Oramas 2007.
69. Although Eteocles seems to have the moral high ground at the beginning of Aeschylus' play, it is clear that he also bears responsibility for his choice to fight his brother. See Hutchinson 1985: *ad* 631–52 on the brothers becoming morally equal, and Sommerstein 2010: 76–80 on Eteocles' actions.
70. See Torrance 2007b: 31–4 on the language of duality in Aeschylus' play which casts the brothers as a unit.
71. This is a revised version of Isabelle Torrance, "Brothers at War: Aeschylus in Cuba," published in John Hilton and Anne Gosling eds., *Alma Parens Originalis? The Receptions of Classical Literature and Thought in Africa, Europe, the United States and Cuba* (Oxford: Peter Lang, 2007), 291–315. The author and the editors of this volume are grateful to Peter Lang for the permission to reproduce this article in revised form. I am especially grateful to Catherine Davies for comments on an earlier draft of this chapter. Several individuals have provided me with invaluable information about Arrufat's *Los siete* and each of them has my heartfelt thanks. Catherine Davies and Conrad James kindly assisted me in locating a copy of Arrufat's *Los siete* in the early stages of research for this chapter, Mike Gonzalez generously sent a copy of his unpublished translation of the play, Chris Weaver at the Archive of Performances of Greek and Roman Drama (APGRD) at Oxford University was extremely helpful by putting me in touch with Mike Gonzalez and sending me a copy of the program for the 2001 performance in Scotland, and Alexis Torrance photocopied and sent some important material which I had been unable to obtain through inter-library loans.

References

Álvarez Morán, M. C. and R. M. Iglesias Montiel (2001), "Fidelidad y libertad mitográficas en *Los siete contra Tebas* de Antón Arrufat", *Unión* 42, 16–21.
Anderson, J. L. (1997), *Che Guevara: A Revolutionary Life*. London.
Arcos, F. D. (2007), "Siete contra Tebas," *CubaNet* October 25.
Arrufat, A. (1955), "Antígona," *Ciclón* 1.6, 37–45.
Arrufat, A. (1962), "An Interview on the Theatre in Cuba and in Latin America, trans. D. McInnes," *Odyssey Review* 2.4, 248–63.
Arrufat, A. (1964), *Repaso final*. Havana.
Arrufat, A. (1980), "My Warning to the PEN Club," *Granma (Weekly Review)* June 29, 7.
Arrufat, A. (2001), *Los siete contra Tebas*. Havana.
Arrufat, A. (2007), *La manzana y la flecha*. Havana.
Arrufat, A., R. Salvat, A. Gutkin, and H. Padilla (2007), "Monogràfic II. Cuba, data històrica," *Assaig de teatre: revista de l'Associació d'Investigació i Experimentació Teatral* 60–1, 41–50.
Barquet, J. J. (2002), *Teatro y revolución cubana: subversión y utopia en* Los siete contra Tebas *de Antón Arrufat*. New York.
Bejel, E. (1978), "El mito de la casa de Layos en 'Los siete contra Tebas,' de Antón Arrufat," *Hispamérica* 7.20, 110–14.

Blanco, M. L. (2007), "La azotea de los escritores," *El País* (March 3) <http://elpais.com/m/diario/2007/03/03/babelia/1172882350_850215.html>.
Caldwell, R. S. (1973), "The Misogyny of Eteocles," *Arethusa* 6, 197–231.
Chávez, A. (1999), "Mirada y palabra de Antón Arrufat," *Opus Habana* 3.1, 16–24.
Cypess, S. M. (1994), "The Theater," in A. J. Arnold ed., *A History of Literature in the Caribbean*, i: *Hispanic and Francophone Regions*. Amsterdam and Philadelphia, 239–61.
Dominguez, J. (1993), "Cuba since 1959," in L. Bethel ed., *Cuba: A Short History*. Cambridge, 95–148.
Escarpanter, J. A. (1990), "Tres dramaturgos del incio revolucionario: Aberlardo Estorino, Antón Arrufat y José Triana," *Revista Iberoamericana* 56.152–3, 881–96.
Espinosa Mendoza, N. (2001), "Meditación en la séptima puerta: alrededor de *Los siete contra Tebas*," in A. Arrufat, *Los siete contra Tebas*. Havana, v–xxi.
Estévez, A. (1992), "El Golpe de Dados de Arrufat," in Centro de Documentación Teatral ed., *Teatro cubano contemporáneo: antología*. Madrid, 861–7.
Farber, S. (2011), *Cuba Since the Revolution of 1959: A Critical Assessment*. Chicago.
Foley, H. P. (2012), *Reimagining Greek Tragedy on the American Stage*. Berkeley, Los Angeles, and London.
Gonzalez, M. (2001a), *The Seven Against Thebes by Antón Arrufat* (unpublished translation for the 2001 performance at the Ramshorn Theatre, University of Strathclyde, Glasgow).
Gonzalez, M. (2001b), "The Seven Against Thebes: Notes" for the program accompanying the performance of Gonzalez 2001a.
Gorney, C. (2012), "Cuba's New Now," *National Geographic* (November), 28–59.
Hardwick, L. (2004), "Greek Drama and Anti-Colonialism: Decolonizing Classics," in E. Hall, F. Macintosh, and A. Wrigley eds., *Dionysus Since 69: Greek Tragedy at the Dawn of the Third Millenium*. Oxford, 219–42.
Hardwick, L. and C. Gillespie (eds. 2007), *Classics in Post-Colonial Worlds*. Oxford.
Heaney, S. (2005), "'Me' as in 'Metre': On Translating *Antigone*," in J. Dillon and S. E. Wilmer eds., *Rebel Women: Staging Ancient Greek Drama Today*. London, 169–73.
Hernández, Y. (2007), "Las siete puertas de una Tebas que renace," *La Jiribilla: revista de cultura cubana* <http://www.lajiribilla.cu/2007/n337_10/337_13.html>.
Hutchinson, G. O. (1985), *Aeschylus: Seven Against Thebes*. Oxford.
Johnson, H. (1964), *The Bay of Pigs: The Invasion of Cuba by Brigade 2506*. London.
Leal, R. (1984), "Prólogo," in J. R. Brene, *Pasado a la criollo y otras obras*. Havana, 7–21.
Leonard, T. M. (1999), *Castro and the Cuban Revolution*. London.
Lievesley, G. (2004), *The Cuban Revolution: Past, Present and Future Perspectives*. New York.
Martin, R. (1990), "Cuban Theatre under Rectification: The Revolution after the Revolution," *Drama Review* 34.1, 38–59.
Mee, E. B. and H. Foley (eds. 2011), *Antigone on the Contemporary World Stage*. Oxford.
Minaya, E. (2002), "Four Writers" <http://journalism.berkeley.edu/projects/cubans2001/story-fourwriters.html>.
Nelli, M. F. (2010), "From Ancient Greek Drama to Argentina's 'Dirty War'; *Antígona furiosa*: On Bodies and the State," in S. Wilmer and A. Žukauskaitė eds., *Interrogating Antigone in Postmodern Philosophy and Criticism*. Oxford: 353–65.
Oramas, A. (2007), "Los siete contra Tebas: Épica de un tiempo no vivido," *CubAhora* (November 11).
Pérez Asensio, M. (2010), *El mito en el teatro cubano contemporáneo* (diss.). InterClassica <http://interclassica.um.es/investigacion/tesis/el_mito_en_el_teatro_cubano_contemporaneo>.

Pianacci, R. (2004), "Antígona, una tragedia Latinamericana," in F. De Martino and C. Morenilla eds., *El Caliu de l'Oikos*. Bari, 459–86.
Randall, M. (1992), *Gathering Rage: The Failure of Twentieth Century Revolution to Develop a Feminist Agenda*. New York.
Sommerstein, A. H. (2010), *Aeschlyean Tragedy*. London.
Steiner, G. (1984), *Antigones*. Oxford.
Taplin, O. (1977), *The Stagecraft of Aeschylus*. Oxford.
Thalmann, W. G. (1978), *Dramatic Art in Aeschylus' Seven Against Thebes*. New Haven and London.
Torrance, I. (2007a), "Brothers at War: Aeschylus in Cuba," in J. Hilton and A. Gosling eds., *Alma parens originalis? The Receptions of Classical Literature and Thought in Africa, Europe, the United States and Cuba*. Oxford, 291–315.
Torrance, I. (2007b), *Aeschylus: Seven against Thebes*. London.
Vasserot, C. (1998), "Avatares de la tragedia griega en el teatro cubano contemporáneo (1941–1968)," in D. Meyran et al. eds., *Théâtre, public et société = Teatro, público, sociedad*. Perpignan, 342–50.
Vasserot, C. (2006), "La Référence aux modèles européens dans l'approche critique de la dramaturgie cubaine," *CRICCAL* 34 (*Les modèles et leur circulation en Amérique Latine*), 295–303.
Wilmer, S. and A. Žukauskaitė (eds. 2010), *Interrogating Antigone in Postmodern Philosophy and Criticism*. Oxford.
Winnington-Ingram R. P. (1977), "*Septem contra Thebas*," *Yale Classical Studies* 25, 1–45.

PART VI

THE SEARCH FOR THE OMNI-AMERICANS (1970s–2013)

CHAPTER 26

METAPHOR AND MODERNITY

American Themes in Herakles *and* Dionysus in 69

THOMAS E. JENKINS

In a review of Marc Camoletti's silly French farce *Boeing-Boeing*, the *New York Times* reviewer Ben Brantley ruminated on the reasons for the 2008 revival's unlikely success, attributing much of its effectiveness to its director Matthew Warchus: "[Mr. Warchus] has X-ray vision that zeroes in on the bone structure of a play. *Boeing Boeing*, it turns out, has great bones" (Brantley 2008). The same might be said, in radically altered circumstances, of the general success of Greek tragedies, which, sundered from their original social context, still somehow manage to move American audiences, from colonial days to the present. Structurally, it seems, these plays have *fabulous* bones. And as long as the skeleton remains in place, artists have generally allowed themselves great license in fleshing out possible "modern" *metaphors* within the text, even as the structure remains recognizably classical. This chapter therefore examines how two prominent subjects of American political discourse in the 1960s—American military expansion and domestic sexual liberation—display surprising metaphors and interconnections in adaptations of Euripides, including Archibald MacLeish's *Herakles* (1965/7) and the Performance Group's *Dionysus in 69* (1968). Each adaptation explores homosexuality and American imperialism simultaneously, even as the individual adaptors bring Euripidean notions of *sthenos* ("might") and *eros* ("desire") to the stage. These two pieces thus look forward to a "post-'69" era in classical adaptation, which includes explicitly gay versions of the *Bacchae* and transparently apocalyptic versions of Euripides' war plays.[1] Though the Euripidean classical structure—the "bones"—remains the same, the metaphorsc.

Compared to texts such as *Trojan Women* and *Iphigenia in Aulis*, Euripides' *Herakles the Mad* has had at best a checkered production history, and MacLeish's choice of source material might seem, at first, something of a puzzle.[2] The play falls into two distinct parts: the first—longer and more talky—focuses on the tribulations of Herakles' father, Amphitryon; his wife, Megara; and his three sons, all of whom Herakles seems to have abandoned when performing his labors. (The hero is in fact presumed dead—with at least one labor lost.) In the meantime, a usurping and wicked tyrant, Lycus, has taken control of Thebes and the lives of Herakles' family appear forfeit. But lo! Herakles returns; he slaughters the tyrant with panache and justice, and appears to re-establish order through "the annihilation of the bad by the good."[3] This is, however, a tragedy; at the height of Herakles' success, the goddess Hera inflicts Madness on this hero, who seems to be, in her eyes, both ontologically and religiously irritating.[4] Herakles subsequently kills his wife and children—a massacre narrated through a spectacular messenger speech—and at last recognizes the enormity of his crime; only the counsel and friendship of Theseus, King of Athens, enables Herakles to continue living, in the hopes someday of atonement. Herakles' godlike might is first made right—and then wrong.

In MacLeish's version of *Herakles*, the playwright takes the literal might—*sthenos*—of Herakles and transforms it into a peculiarly modern metaphor: *scientific* might, particularly of the American, military variety. After all, MacLeish's *Herakles*, like all classical adaptations, was a product of its social context as well as its author's individual genius; the years preceding *Herakles* witnessed—more or less back to back—the Cold War of the late 1950s; the Cuban Missile Crisis of 1962; and America's entrance into the Vietnam War after the Gulf of Tonkin resolution (1965). In fact, the first draft of *Herakles* dates from that fateful year, with a poorly received production in Wisconsin;[5] an expanded version was published in 1967. As MacLeish later explained in an interview concerning the première of *Herakles*:

> I felt very strongly then [in the early 1960s] that the myth of Herakles was the great modern myth . . . because the labors of Herakles were all of them labors of delivering the world from its fears, from its monsters, delivering it from evil, creating a world in which people would live simply and humanly, which is very much what the modern myth of science has been. Science fights against cancer. It cures infantile paralysis. It puts an end to yellow fever. It accomplishes miracles in regard to the decency of living. The myth of Herakles ends with his return from the labors and the discovery that in his wars against the monsters he has destroyed his own sons. This is also the myth of science for us. Science has produced the bombs; science has produced the destruction of the young.[6]

Thus MacLeish's modern metaphor for a lauded Greek hero is not, surprisingly, a wrestler, or an athlete, or even a soldier, but a Nobel-winning scientist, Professor Hoadley. As the play begins, Professor Hoadley stops over in Athens on his way back from Stockholm, where he has delivered a stupendously well-received acceptance speech concerning the possibilities of (scientific) progress in an era of general hopelessness. Hoadley's wife and daughter, Little Hodd, and governess, Miss Parfit, accompany him. After the departure of Parfit and Hodd, Hoadley launches into a grand peroration on the glories of Herakles, who rails "against the universe" and who "won't despair | or hope or trust or anything—who struggles— | dares to struggle— | dares to overcome" (19).[7] From his own point of view, Hoadley places himself at the end of a long line of valorizing interpretations of Herakles as a "pioneer of civilization," whose spirit of inquiry and statesmanship may find its ultimate origin in the mighty Pericles himself (Bond 1981: xxvii). In disgust, Mrs. Hoadley (a sort of Albee-esque alcoholic shrew) dismisses Herakles as mere myth, which infuriates the professor. Gradually, the evening devolves into a shouting match between Hoadley and his wife, including veiled (and, again, Albee-esque) references to their absent, homosexual son.[8] As part of his defense of Herakles, Professor Hoadley insists that Herakles, having conquered the world, went to the Delphic oracle to find out "what happens to him now"; when the oracle refuses to answer, "[Herakles] gives the oracle himself. That ends it" (21). Mrs. Hoadley, skeptical of this story, vows to travel to Delphi to discover the truth of the myth.

In this first, politically charged act, we see already MacLeish's concerns for drawing a provocative equivalence between American scientific know-how and Heraklean might; Hoadley, "the great | the world-renowned professor," is transparently the Heraklean "hero" of the play (1), a figure of superhuman powers and fame.[9] Indeed, the manager of Hoadley's hotel has already memorized part of the scientist's acceptance speech: "But when in human history before have | triumph and despair, he said, been mated" (3)? (The answer—as we will discover in the second act—is in ancient, mythical Greece.) As Hoadley and his wife continue to spar over their marital difficulties, Professor Hoadley expands on the failures of their (absent) son to understand the special properties of their modern era:

> How would he [the son] know an age like this one,
> years of inconceivable fortitude,
> boundless daring, unknown deeds
> never before attempted, arduous
> undertakings in a room alone,
> impossible discoveries, dreadful weapons
> capable of holocaust, of extermination,
> fire as hot as God's . . . a fabulous century
> worthy of the Greeks
> the great
> imagination of the Greeks, the greatest
> myth of that supreme imagination . . . (17)

It is striking that the greatest imaginative analogue to this modern, atomic age—an age capable of holocaust and calculated human extermination—is ancient Greece, the age "Of Herakles! Against the Universe"![10] And it's striking too that Professor Hoadley, though adverting to the holocausts (literal and metaphorical) in Germany and Japan, refrains from the necessary *moral* judgement: for Professor Hoadley, power is evaluated only for its magnitude, not its means or ends.

The second act features MacLeish at his most verbally dexterous, as he superimposes modernity on top of antiquity, thus ironizing Hoadley's own analogy: Hoadley is indeed like Herakles in his appreciation of power, but not quite for the reasons that Hoadley asserts. As the second act begins, Mrs. Hoadley, with daughter and governess in tow, follows a guide to the oracle at (modern) Delphi. As the guide points to the great bronze doors of the oracle, a woman "appears among the stones, a fine woman in the full of life, shawl fallen back from golden hair" (41). This is Megara, Herakles' wife, and from this point on, antiquity and modernity are inseparable, just as Hoadley argued in Act I. In fact, it's hard to tell whether the modern characters have interloped into ancient Greece, or vice versa: the epochs are indistinguishable. Megara waits (while sewing) for her errant husband to come home: she never believed that he would leave on his foolish quest to become a god, and certainly doesn't believe it's "true" that he's become one:

> If truth were only true because it
> happened to have happened what would
> truth be? Anything can happen. (51)

Next, a triumphant Herakles—played by the same actor as Professor Hoadley—bursts upon the stage; he enacts an awkward recognition scene with Megara, whom he hasn't seen since his departure for his labors. His last triumph was, he boasts, the slaughter of his "enemies [who] were round me, leaping, laughing | big as bullocks in the blundering light.... I killed them at the gate of Thebes!" (58).

The "enemies" were, of course, Herakles' own sons: as Megara sadly remarks, Herakles is "like a dog come back from the wolves who's done | what dogs don't" (59). The remainder of the play limns the Euripidean original, as a painful exchange between the Pythian priestess and Herakles mirrors the Euripidean exchange between Herakles' father, Amphitryon, and his confused son (*Herakles* 1109–52). At first the modern characters interrupt and chastise the ancient ones (Miss Parfit to the hero: "Be patient, Herakles! | Everything is told in time") or interrogate them: (Little Hodd: "That's twice [Megara] has said it. What does she mean?") (65). Gradually, however, the ancient characters take over the drama: as a speaking character, Mrs. Hoadley disappears for dozens of pages, as a sad spectator of a still sadder play. By the time Herakles screams in horror at the recognition of his sons' corpses—"Take them away!" (87)—the drama has morphed from the entirely modern to the quintessentially "classical": just the unhappy trio of Herakles, Megara, and the Pythia, examining the somber aftermath of a godlike rampage.

In adapting the figure of Herakles into an atomic-age hero, MacLeish is telescoping, through metaphor, the ambiguities and tensions built into the original text. In the first instance, MacLeish expands on the Greek text in his evocation of Herakles as a liminal figure, forever pushing the boundaries of the known world. Indeed, in Euripides' play, the chorus not only eulogizes Herakles' famous victories—over the Nemean lion (360), the Centaurs (366), the man-eating horses of Diomedes (381), and the rest—but also stresses these labors' far-flung spatiality; the passage is chockablock with verbs and participles of travel, penetration, and passage ("he crossed the boundary," 386–8; "he arrived at," 395; "he entered," 401; "he went to," 410; "he sailed," 427).[11] In fact, the chorus' expectation that Herakles has met a spatial limit—"he never came back" (429)—turns out to be frustrated when Herakles actually manages a return from Hades, the place from which the chorus asserts there is never a *nostos*, a "return" (431). In the figure of Hoadley-as-Herakles, MacLeish has transformed Herakles' *physical* journey into an *epistemological* one, just as MacLeish (elsewhere) rhapsodizes about the 1960s:

> [Our time] is a great and tragic time which is also heroic as few ages have been heroic—an age which has produced, here and elsewhere, some of the most remarkable figures—remarkable for good and evil—the world has ever seen ... [It is an epoch] in which man has gone farther toward the unknown, even the unknowable, than he had gone in all the centuries and millennia before. (MacLeish 1967a: 7)

In the 1960s, then, mankind's journey to the furthest limits isn't spatial (there is no more Earth to conquer) but cognitive: a modern Herakles leaves the body and journeys to the limit of human understanding.

As in Herakles' labors, Hoadley's journey is both enabled by and enabling of power: the further he travels, the more he is defined by—and, like Herakles, lauded for—his superhuman capacity. And while the unbridled application of *biē*, "might," defines Herakles in Euripides' play, it is striking that the weapons in question—the ones that Hoadley analogizes to weapons capable of holocaust—are not Herakles' club or even the hero's mighty hands, but his bow and arrows, weapons of ambiguous moral worth in Greek thought (Chalk 1962). Indeed the bow tends to be associated with heroes or peoples of few scruples, including the Homeric tricksters Odysseus and Paris; the Aeschylean Persians (*Pers.* 146–9); and the Aristophanic and Herodotean Scythians (*Acharnians* 707; *Histories* 4.54). As Francis Dunn elucidates, the archer is "an outsider, a devious and suspect figure who does not subscribe to the heroic values of the Homeric warrior."[12] Indeed, the bow and arrow is emblematic of a particularly disquieting military relationship: of a potent, remote archer and the distant but nevertheless vulnerable prey. Within *Herakles the Mad*, the bow's inherent moral ambiguity is magnified into twin scenes of stunning theatricality: Herakles' praiseworthy assassination of Lycus (a power-mad villain) and the senseless slaughter of Herakles' family through the catalyst of the goddess Madness.[13]

Herakles' soliloquy over his omnipotent bow thus possesses clear resonances with modern debates over the place, function, and utility of nuclear weapons; as Lycus puts it, the bow is the most cowardly of weapons (161), unlike the manly spear. After the slaughter, Herakles admits that such weapons are indeed "sad company," and debates whether or not to voluntarily disarm (1379); indeed, the weapons hanging at his side practically squeal to him: "with us, you slew your wife and children; you carry your child-killers at your side" (1380–1). The bow and arrows embody the destruction of everything Herakles holds dear and should be destroyed. Herakles reasons, however, that this is an impractical solution:

> Am I still to carry these weapons at my side? Yet, stripped of my weapons—with which I accomplished the most beautiful deeds in Greece—shall I die basely, submitting to my enemies? I cannot leave these weapons behind: they must be preserved, however painful that deed. (1381–5)

If we read this passage *through* MacLeish's metaphor, we see in Euripides' text the language of nuclear science and the nuclear arms race. These are discoveries capable of "holocaust" and "extermination" and yet capable, too, of "beautiful" deeds: the possibilities as well as perils of science. Though Herakles would like to disavow these weapons, he stresses the impossibility, in modern jargon, of bilateral disarmament: he will *always* have enemies, and cannot be caught "naked" of defenses. He is thus stuck in the predicament of the modern arms race, expressed in the Greek with parallel imperatives: he cannot safely abandon his weapons, and cannot safely keep them. Like America the Nuclear, Herakles is caught betwixt and between.

It is striking that another modern metaphor makes its entrance into the text at precisely the point that MacLeish's Hoadley waxes grandiloquent about the possibilities of this new atomic age; and we return to the soliloquy in which Hoadley complains that "he"—meaning his son—will never "know an age like this one, | years of inconceivable fortitude . . . | a fabulous century | worthy of the Greeks . . ." (17). In fact, in his Nobel prize acceptance speech Hoadley berates, seemingly, a whole generation for its intellectual apathy—but particularly indicts his son, one of the "boys with girls' tresses" (14) who engages in "sodomy for something bold to do" (15). So instead of the boldness of science, his son—age 17—engages in the boldness of gay sex: an inquiry of quite a different sort. Moreover, the (anonymous) son is not even an integral part of the family—he only traveled to Stockholm in the speech of his father, as an absent signified. Mrs. Hoadley, desperate to keep the "family" whole, asserts that, in a sense, the son has metaphorically traveled to Athens as part of that same speech; but Professor Hoadley disabuses her of her folly: "Oh, no! Not here! The one place | secrecy, self-pity, and despair | can never come is here [to Athens] . . ." (16). He further argues that his son entirely misses the point of the greatness of Greece and the modern era, only remembering the "afterward when Greece was over | when the endless war that never/ ended, ended, and it all came down" (17). Mrs. Hoadley argues in her turn:

MRS. HOADLEY: Your son would tell you that's where *we* are— | afterward.
HOADLEY: Because my son's a . . .
MRS. HOADLEY: *Don't*. (17)

If the first and second acts of MacLeish's play implicitly equate Professor Hoadley with Herakles, then the first and second acts, by analogizing Herakles' sons with Hoadley's son, implicitly equate homosexuality with death. In each case, the sons are present *only* in their absence, and in the case of Hoadley's argument above, homosexuality, as an *identity*, can't even be named: it's *literally* elided—in an ellipsis. (The text thus forces the audience to supply the missing monosyllable: "fag" works nicely, though "queer" works too.) The play's treatment of homosexuality is therefore both central and slippery: central in that a discussion of the son's homosexuality leads directly to Hoadley's most impassioned defense of the current "age of Herakles"; but slippery in that this homosexuality is entirely constructed, in its absence, by three quarrelling entities—Professor Hoadley, Mrs. Hoadley, and (in a larger architectural sense) by the author Archibald MacLeish. Within the specific context of Act I, homosexuality is damned by Professor Hoadley as effeminate, illegal, insouciant, and despairing: a virtual litany of pre-Stonewall-era prejudices about homosexuality in America.[14] Within the larger argument of the play, however, this enigmatic, homosexual son emerges as someone sympathetic (just as Herakles' dead sons are sympathetic) and, ironically, prescient: he is far more clear-eyed than his famous father about the possibilities—and risks—of power in 1967.

Indeed, this dissolute, sodomizing, morose, effeminate son sees what nobody else can: the end of the play.[15] At first Herakles/Hoadley can't understand his own carnage: the Pythia must persuade him to take another look at the bodies: "Look at them, Herakles . . . Lift their heads! Lift their heads! Lift their bloody heads!" (87). Herakles, unbelieving, recognizes his own dead sons while Megara, his wife, sadly points out to Herakles in his despair:

> You wanted to be a god. You are. . . .
> What's horrible is the will of god—
> The pure, indifferent, effortless, cold will
> that kills because it can . . .
> Nothing, neither love nor trust
> Nor happiness matters to the will of god:
> it *can* and down the city crumbles . . .
> Nothing is terrible as the will of god
> that can and can and can . . . (88–9)

This is an amazing speech, the best in the play. Here, MacLeish even strains against the syntax of English, as Megara employs the verb *can* not as an auxiliary but as an absolute: to *can* is to exercise power without complement, without effort, and without morals. This is godlike, yes, but godlike in the sense of Hera's power in Euripides' original play: arbitrary. MacLeish, who agitated against the Vietnam War, here implicitly indicts the American arms race and America's predilection for dabbling in international affairs: just because America *can*, doesn't mean it *should*: we have lost our moral compass.[16] America's *sthenos*, its might, is thus as indifferent, and dangerous, as Herakles', or any other god's. The introduction of a homosexual character complicates MacLeish's metaphorical scheme: the son is oracular in his indictment of his father (and America), but consistently queered as sliding between categories: male/female, present/absent, natural/unnatural, resistant/submissive. But in that queerness inheres *knowledge*: he is able to see what his father can, or will, not: technology's potential for tragedy. As Anne Carson puts it: "Herakles is a creature whose relation to virtue is a mess: human virtue derives from human limitation and he seems to have none" (Carson 2006: 13). By this definition, the practically obliterated gay son is, paradoxically, the most virtuous creature in the play, even as America lurches toward a radical realignment of its sexual mores.

It is perhaps more than coincidence that another, roughly coeval adaptation of Greek tragedy—that of the *Bacchae*—also features homosexuality as a central metaphorical conceit, and one that is again tied to an adaptation's *political* theme: Dionysus' campaign for the American presidency in 1968, as the god hopes to become (a Heraklean?)

Commander-in-Chief in 1969. (See Sides, this volume.) Performed by the "Performance Group" as a free-form meditation on the ancient text, *Dionysus in 69* takes Classicist William Arrowsmith's popular dramatic translation of *The Bacchae* and transforms it into a performance piece with elements of ritual, peep show, exorcism, political tract, and coming-out story. The evening famously opens with a chorus of scantily clad women re-enacting the birth of the god Dionysus, largely by lining up in a row and then forming a replica of a birth canal with their legs. They then push through this canal the infant Dionysus—played by William Finley—and the play's psychosexual subtext is off to a roaring start. As the *mise-en-scène* switches to Thebes, the elder statesman Cadmus and his adviser Teiresias express their disappointment in the reception given to Dionysus in the *polis*—not a good omen—while the young Pentheus, King of Thebes, makes his entrance, disturbed at reports that a priest of Dionysus is on the way. Pentheus is here played by William (Bill) Shephard, bare chested and clad only in shorts; as for many members of the cast, Shephard's costume is designed to emphasize the character's—and the actor's—access to sexuality.

The orgiastic aspects of the evening blurred the line between actor and character, and between character and audience.[17] Contemporary accounts of the event emphasize that *every* aspect of the evening was a performance—including the audience's act of simply watching. Reactions to this hypersexualized and viscerally physical *Bacchae* differ. Admits one disappointed spectator: "This time I joined in the dancing, but the fondling pile was so far away I could not easily join it" (Kostelanetz 1989: 149). Moreover, given the improvisational nature of the performance, misapprehensions were bound to occur: "[W]hen I saw *Dionysus in 69*, one young woman began slugging a performer to stop him from continuing what she had allowed to begin" (Isaac 1970: 434; Performance Group 1970). Amidst all of the groping and nudity, a certain amount of interpretative nuance seems to have been lost. As one critic laments: "I still cannot follow the Euripides lines or understand their contribution to the evening" (Kostelanetz 1989: 150). This was all, in a sense, part of director Richard Schechner's plan. In his theoretical writings, which emphasize the anthropological bases of performance, Schechner aims for an experience that blends elements of ritual, play, and music. Text is merely one part of the equation (see McConnell and Rankine, this volume).[18]

But in the case of the *Bacchae*, that text is hardly inconsequential; for all its liberties, *Dionysus in 69* is still a version of Euripides' play. Though to some extent *all* of *Dionysus in 69* engages in transgressive re-enactments of Euripidean moments, it is striking that the most "metaphorically-charged" moment arrives precisely at the point of (traditionally) greatest interpretative difficulty by scholars and readers. Having imprisoned Dionysus—whom he thinks is merely an effeminate *dévoté* of the god—Pentheus soon finds Thebes in catastrophe: an earthquake hits the palace, and the city's women are now raving Bacchants. A second interview between Pentheus and Dionysus discloses that Pentheus would happily spy on the Bacchants—presumably for military reconnaissance—but the king is at a loss how to proceed. In one of the most magical, yet curious, scenes in ancient drama, Dionysus convinces Pentheus to cross-dress as a woman.

This famous scene has invited famously conflicting interpretations. For Dodds, it represents "a psychic invasion" of Pentheus by Dionysus; Pentheus' reactions are thus "if not [those] of a maniac, at least of a man whose reactions are ceasing to be normal." His subsequent transformation, by way of a wig, miter, and linen robe, marks him as a "giggling, leering creature, more helpless than a child, nastier than an idiot" (Dodds 1960: 172, 175, 192). In other words, Pentheus has gone wonderfully, theatrically insane. Or it might be that the scene symbolizes, on a more expansively psychosexual level, "the defeat of male phallic power by the female," a defeat which, metatheatrically, "effac[es] the distance between spectator and actor" and thus constitutes "a sinister mirror-image of the play's effect upon its audience, its *theatai*" (Segal 1997: 205, 225). Put another way: the embarrassing transvestitism of Pentheus creates a play-within-a play that makes problematic the real-life experiences of Athenian males dressing as Bacchants in the "real," outer play; the *Bacchae*'s (dis)robing scene thus deconstructs the entire notion of theater. A more ritually oriented analysis of the scene stresses the possible "transvestitism of 'mystic initiation', though a transvestitism that could, if made public, expose the initiand to mockery" (Seaford 1996: 216). Richard Seaford here stresses the *ritual* dimension of the cross-dressing scene: that Pentheus' humiliation lies not in the cross-dressing, per se, but doing so in a public forum.

A closer reading of the scene, in its late 1960s context, reveals why Schechner sought a radical, self-consciously *American* substitution for his adaptation:

D. Now throw linen robes around your skin.
P. What is this? Shall I turn into a woman, from a man?
D. So the Bacchants do not kill you there—if you seem a man.
P. Again, you have spoken well. How clever you are, and have been!
D. Dionysus trained me in all these things.
P. How best to go about the things that you advise me?
D. I shall take you into the house and dress you.
P. In a dress? A female dress? But shame possesses me. (821–8)

Whether the scene is analyzed in terms of performance theory (metatheater), psychology (madness), or ritual (initiatory garb), the Greek text neatly leads up to Pentheus' horrified gasp at the thought of donning female (*thelun*) garb: though it would be desirable to glimpse the women (812) and affecting to see them drunk (814), the key emotion here is *aidôs*, "shame." The entire dialogue builds to this crucial psychological moment: though Pentheus recognizes the potential for shame, he further inquires about the robe, his hair, and the thyrsus, the sacred (and gender-marked) implement of Bacchants. At this moment, his fate is sealed: as he exits the stage, Dionysus notes sardonically that this hunter of women has fallen into his net, where he will pay the penalty with his life (847–8). Dionysus also predicts that Pentheus will endure the necessary concomitant to shame: ridicule. ("I desire for him to be an object of mockery to Thebans as he is led through the streets in the guise of a woman..." 854–5).

As Schechner relates in his diary/script of *Dionysus in 69*, the Performance Group struggled to find an American "equivalent" for this particular scene of shame; it is telling that this scene, as performed by the Group, has the most variations, both "written" (for the four combinations of actors and actresses playing Pentheus and Dionysus) and improvised (because particularly energetic members of the audience occasionally tried to help out Pentheus, "offering comfort or routes of escape"). It is remarkable too that the actors Bill Shephard (Pentheus) and Bill Finley (Dionysus) felt compelled to seek a contemporary equivalent for Euripides' original text. Sensing that mere cross-dressing lacked the necessary mortification, they searched for an American cultural equivalent to original Greek context. The solution? Same-sex sex.

Since the scene features two men kissing, it may be tempting to assume an intention to titillate or provoke, particularly in pre-Stonewall-era Manhattan. This is a misapprehension.[19] As Schechner describes, a homosexual seduction seemed an effective way not to celebrate alternative sexualities, but to mortify this oh-so-American Pentheus:

> In Euripides, Pentheus is possessed and humiliated, rewarded and destroyed. [The actor Bill] Shephard suggested homosexuality as the counterpart. It was the most difficult thing he could think of doing in public. The homosexual kiss is supreme revealment and concealment at the same time. Dionysus's purpose works through Pentheus's submission. And both performers taste something that attracts and repels them. Neither is homosexual. To many homosexuals in the audience the scene is titillating. Sometimes, as much from anxiety as from amusement, spectators shout encouragement to Pentheus. Unwittingly, they mortify him as Euripides intended: "I want him made the laughingstock of Thebes". (n.p.)

There is much to note here. First, the idea for the kiss came from the *actor*, not from the director (or fellow actors). Thus, it is not just that a homosexual kiss is mortifying to Pentheus, but to the actor *playing* Pentheus: Shephard is relying on his cultural experiences as an American to posit the single most mortifying thing that could happen to him in Manhattan in 1968. (Apparently: public, gay sex.) Secondly, the audience for this kiss is explicitly bifurcated; (male) homosexuals experience one emotion (i.e., titillation) while the rest of the (presumably heterosexual) audience experiences amusement, anxiety, or disgust. If the original, Euripidean scene treats the audience as a corporate body of fearful or pitying spectators, Schechner's adaptation aims instead to *divide* his audience into gay and non-gay readers, and thus into sympathetic or mortifying citizens. Lastly, Dionysus' intention to make Pentheus a public laughingstock is brought to fruition by this "unwitting" audience of jeering New Yorkers, who, in shouting out to Pentheus, play their parts just as Dionysus/Schechner intended.

Though Schechner is obviously proud of the theatrical effect of the kiss, the real shock of the scene is not in the kiss per se, but in that kiss's distressing aftermath: the fulfillment of Pentheus' contract with Dionysus. In the Euripidean original, the arrangement was to don women's clothing, an exchange rendered in *Dionysus in 69* like so:

> DIONYSUS: First I want you to relax. To be open. To be open to me. I want you to be vulnerable. To be very loving and very relaxed. Bill, I want you to be a woman for me.

That last line could very well be a translation for γυναικόμορφος, "in a woman's guise," Euripides' term for Pentheus' transformation after the scene (*Bacchae* 855). But *Dionysus in 69* substitutes a strikingly modern parallel for the ancient situation:

> PENTHEUS: What specifically do you want me to do?
> DIONYSUS: Specifically, I want you to take off my shirt and my pants and my underwear. Then I want you to caress my body all over. I want you to caress it very slowly and carefully. And then I want you to caress my cock until it gets hard. And then I want you to take my cock in your mouth and caress it with your lips and your tongue and your teeth. I want you to suck my cock. Bill, I want you to suck my cock.

An alternate text, with the actor Patrick McDermott as Dionysus, is even more explicit (perhaps even a bit purple):

> And then I want you to lick my legs. And eat my hair. And then I want you to bite my ass. And then I you to put your tongue in my crotch and lick my crotch and hold my balls up in your hands and make me feel good and send me up, man, send me up! And put my cock in your mouth! Bill, put my cock in your mouth!

In each case, in order to make the mortification sharper, Pentheus is addressed by the name of the actor ("Bill"), and not as Pentheus: this maneuver strips away any comforting pretense of fictionality, and instead exposes the audience to a cruising scene straight out of the seediest of gay dives. Though Schechner describes the kiss as the moment of revelation/concealment, it is actually the subsequent, offstage fellatio that consummates—so to speak—the humiliation of the actor. The on-stage kiss might be shocking, but notionally, it is the fellatio—under a trapdoor—that makes the scene so wildly, crudely "gay."

As Pentheus disappears into the trap (both literally and figuratively), Finley-as-Dionysus crows:

> Friends, skeptics, fellow Bacchae. That man is ours. To be more precise, he's mine. To quote Euripides: "For sane of mind, that man would never wear a woman's dress, but obsess his soul and he cannot refuse."

Here Finley make explicit the cultural equivalency between Euripides' cross-dressing and the previous scene's focus on homosexuality; it is also problematic in that it draws potentially damaging parallels between insanity and same-sex desire. Finley attempts a sort of interpretative damage control, then, by focusing less on the *object* of desire and more on the *process* of desire: "Now what this means is this: Bill Shephard has to know me. He has to submit to me." Finley here stresses that the mortification of the previous scene did not necessarily concern homosexuality, but of sexual repression and submission more generally. Perhaps this is so; there are other versions of the scene in which Dionysus, played by a woman, orders Pentheus to "put your mouth inside my cunt and bite it gently with your tongue" (etc.), after which the scene proceeds along generally heterosexual lines. But the heterosexual scene has less bite, so to speak: Shephard's original impulse was for a homosexual scene, and a gesture toward cunnilingus does not quite capture the cultural taboo of same-sex fellatio.[20]

Subsequent to the fellatio scene, the chorus begins a group "caress," intended to "liberate the energies Euripides describes in this play". When Pentheus re-emerges, he is the sartorial *opposite* of Euripides' cross-dressed Pentheus: he is naked, vulnerably so. Dionysus next goes through some Euripidean motions—for instance, teaching Pentheus how to dance: "Then you raise up the other foot and the other arm . . . And you go like this. And like this, Bill." As indicated in the stage directions, Dionysus' last tender moment with Pentheus is again figured as a homosexual one, but with ominous overtones: *Dionysus caresses, perhaps kisses, Pentheus, marking him with blood*. This is an unlovely image, this homosexual kiss of death, one that nevertheless signals Pentheus' ineluctable progression from *social* death and mortification to *actual* death and mortification. (And here we see parallels with the alternately gay and dead sons in MacLeish's *Herakles*.) At the moment of Pentheus' greatest peril, his mother Agave, unaware of her own insanity, calls for her son's head with the cheery exhortation: "We must kill this animal. Remember, violence is as American as apple pie." This "Americanization" of the Bacchae has not only updated Pentheus' mortification from effeminization to homosexuality, but has made a cliché of his death.

As in MacLeish's version of *Herakles*, homosexuality plays a central epistemological role in the apprehension of tragedy; Hoadley's uncannily prescient son seems to intuit tragedy *solely* because of his homosexual identity, while Pentheus can only embark on his quest for knowledge—a tragic knowledge, as it happens—after his first same-sex encounter. Similarly, both adaptations juxtapose a wise(r) yet powerless homosexual (Hoadley's son and Pentheus) with an arrogant megalomaniac (Hoadley/Herakles, Dionysus); in each play, this figure is a statesman who ostensibly seeks to further American political interests, but whose selfishness blinkers him to a larger understanding of the consequences of power. In *Dionysus in 69*, the initially charming and sympathetic Dionysus seduces and then slaughters the mortified Pentheus only to reveal himself as a ruthless politician and Washington powerbroker.

Indeed, the Dionysus of *Dionysus in 69* is as much a manifestation of raw, senseless power as the Herakles of either MacLeish or Euripides. Having been punished for his impiety—as in the Euripidean original—Schechner's Cadmus protests the harshness of his penalty: "But gods should be exempt from human passions." The response from Finley-as-Dionysus? "Gods are exempt from anything. They just have more power." Thus, the end of *Dionysus in 69* features Finley-as-Dionysus-as-Raw-Power, inciting wave after wave of unmitigated violence:

> My wrath is militant. I ask you to mobilize yourselves! Get down! . . . Grab a thyrsus! Pack a .45! Arm yourself! Napalm the decay! Burn the slums! Shit bricks on The Man! Power to the Bacchae! . . . I ask only that you follow me. Only that you indulge your fantasies of violence and sensuality.

For Dionysus, the distinction between sensuality and violence is more-than-blurred: as we saw in Dionysus' virtual rape of Pentheus, his will-to-dominate includes the compulsion of fellatio, a sign of (sexual) power. So Dionysus' concluding malediction in

Euripides' play (1330–43) is morphed into a political rally, as Dionysus runs not for god, but—worse—for President:

> Yes, I am running for President. Who else have you got? Remember me and write in my name. William Finley. W-I-L-L-I-A-M F-I-N-L-E-Y. A vote for Finley in 68 brings Dionysus in 69. (*He climbs down the tower as the performers sing the melody of The Stars and Stripes forever.*)

The inclusion of a John Philip Sousa march lends an unmistakable air of jingoism to Dionysus' political exhortation. Patrick McDermott (as Dionysus) even more bluntly equates Dionysus' energies with America's (capitalistic, imperialistic) power:

> God is an unrealistic base for the currency of this nation. I'm going to put the currency on a solid base. I'm going to put our currency where it's really at. Power. Power is where it's at . . . Now what is power? Dig this. Power is power. Do you get it? Let it sink in. Meditate on this. Power is power. Do you see what that means? Power Power.

McDermott-as-Dionysus is the natural culmination of the play's emphasis on liberation—a liberation that might (as Professor Hoadley would argue) perform miracles, but which could also end in profoundest tragedy.

To sum up: this volume, as a collection, examines the ways in which American productions of Greek tragedy speak to (and are informed by) their specific social context, even while advertising the putatively timeless nature of the source material. Both MacLeish and Schechner buttress their highly politicized adaptations of Euripides by invoking as well the complex and contradictory mid-century discourses of homosexuality: America the Mighty is mighty, in part, because of its successful containment of the subversive male homosexual, variously figured as submissive, risible, and dead. At the same time, this submissive homosexual—ostracized from power—is a creature marked by a preternatural knowledge of tragedy, a knowledge useless, however, without any accompanying means of escape. Thus both playwrights interrogate the American discourses of power (*sthenos/biê*) through one particularly striking manifestation of powerlessness: the homosexual. If, as Aeschylus' chorus opined, "wisdom comes through suffering" (*Ag.* 177), the American homosexual of 1967 is (perversely) ontologically wise.

In terms of the later reception of Euripides, these twin interrogations—of American power and sexual mores—can instead function separately, producing adaptations less complicated ideologically, but more focused in their social agitation. For instance, Robert Meagher's adaptation *Herakles Gone Mad. Rethinking Heroism in an Age of Endless War* (2006) is an out-and-out broadside against American imperialism in the wake of the Iraq war; as Meagher explains in his translation of Herakles' civilizing mission ("to tame the world," 20), his *Herakles* directly confronts (and criticizes) contemporary American foreign policy:

> "He will tame the earth, make it a kinder, gentler place". This rendering here is reminiscent as well of George H. W. Bush's promise of a "kinder gentler America", a promise reiterated by his son eight years later and extended to foreign policy. In

none of these cases ... was the promise kept; nor was it ever meant to be. (Meagher 2006: 134–5)

Meagher thus implicitly equates both Bushes—American presidents—with Herakles: ostensibly a force for civilization, but in reality, a force of destruction. Likewise, productions of the *Bacchae* have been able to free the central scene of transvestitism from its purely negative connotations; in fact, as a press release demonstrates, the Celebration Theatre's recent production (2007) flips the central conceit on its head:

> In this radical re-imagining of the ancient Greek Euripides' tragedy, Celebration Theatre replaces the women of the original drama with gay male "West Hollywood-style" clubgoers ... [T]he play explores modern images of gay sexuality, examining the consequences of a marginalization of what it means to be gay outside of a sexual context, using the mythology of the *Bacchae* to represent this marginalization as stemming from a societal and governmental denial of the homosexual as a whole person.[21]

Whereas *Dionysus in 69* attacked the government through the mortification of the homosexual—a mortification with which the audience was largely complicit—the Celebration's *Bacchae* asserts exactly the opposite: that the (presumably gay) audience will sympathize with the plight of the sexually ostracized, degraded, and denied. Thus Euripides' journey from the 1960s to the twenty-first century continues to engage with contemporary discourses of homosexuality and politics, proving again—as if proof were needed—that the plays of Euripides possess, as Ben Brantley might say, the loveliest of bones.

Notes

1. On the idea of *Dionysus in 69* as a turning point in the history of performances of Greek drama, see Hall, Macintosh, and Wrigley 2005.
2. See Riley 2008: 358–65 for a helpful catalog of modern performances or adaptations of this play.
3. Papadopoulou (2005: 24), who argues that Euripides constructs Herakles and Lycus as ostensibly "opposite poles" of virtue and vice, but who share thematic and symbolic parallels. This builds on the analysis of Chalk 1962: 15–17 on the fraught relationship between Herakles' *bie* "might" and *arete* "excellence," and who likewise detects troubling resonances between Lycus and Herakles.
4. See Foley 1985: 157–8 on the overdetermination of Hera's anger toward Herakles, at least partly inspired by the argument that "Herakles has overstepped the limits that separate the divine from human." The hero thus endangers the honor due to gods, expressed through ritual. (Herakles' slaughter of his children is thus a perversion of the ritual of sacrifice, a sort of negative *exemplum*.)
5. Riley 2008: 290–2. Donaldson (1992: 482) notes that *Herakles* lost the backing of prospective Broadway producer T. Edward Hambleton after its disappointing try-out, which scuttled any hope of future professional productions.
6. Draback and Ellis 1986: 213–14. MacLeish's *Herakles* in a sense takes up the mantle from the American-centric productions of Greek tragedy enabled by Edith Hamilton's *The*

Greek Way and subsequent writings. As Hallett puts it, Hamilton "performed her own, idiosyncratic, version of Athenian citizenship in twentieth century America" (Hallett, this volume)—and MacLeish's *Herakles* continues that exploration of the price, and responsibilities, of American citizenship.

7. All page numbers refer to MacLeish 1967b, the published version of the two-act play.
8. On mid-century domestic drama (including Albee) and MacLeish's *Herakles*, see Riley 2008: 296.
9. See also Galinsky 1972: 248: "Sophocles had shown what happens when Herakles used all his powers and labours for his own good. By adapting this theme for dramatizing the uses and abuses of modern technology and science and their destructive and dehumanizing potential, MacLeish has given it a dimension that is both relevant to our time and timeless." Colakis (1993: 31) argues that Professor Hoadley can also claim Theseus as a mythical prototype: "Hoadley presents Theseus as a venturer into the unknown, whose victory nonetheless had devastating consequences for someone close to him. In this respect he resembles Herakles . . . and Hoadley."
10. For a fuller examination of MacLeish's sense of temporality—and its relationship to earlier experiments in Euripidean adaptation, including those of H.D.—see Jenkins 2007.
11. All line numbers in this section refer to the standard edition of Euripides' *Herakles* by Gilbert Murray: Euripides, *Euripidis Fabulae*, vol. ii (Oxford: Clarendon Press, 1913).
12. Dunn 1996: 124. Wolff and Sleigh 2001: 9, "Focus on the bow . . . also evokes for a moment a facet of Herakles' traditional and archaic character as a heroic hunter, a role played at the margins of human communities, among threatening, often monstrous animals . . ."
13. This is senseless slaughter on the level of plot, perhaps, but not on the level of theme; Burnett (1971: 163ff.) argues that Megara's "arrogant agnosticism" prefigures the divine intrusion of madness in the second half of the play: even Herakles' murder of Lycus is an unhealthily private, not public, bloodshed (165). Griffiths (2002) locates the murder of the children within a broader contemporary discourse concerning the structure and "meaning" of the Greek *oikos* "house."
14. It is intriguing that the conference at which this paper was first delivered—"Greek Drama in America, 1900–1970" (part of the Northwestern Sawyer Seminar series from which this volume emerged)—takes as its terminus what is also considered the turning point in the history of gay rights in America: the Stonewall Riots of June 28, 1969, in which the gay patrons of the Stonewall bar in Manhattan protested against police harassment and general oppression. This event is generally credited with spawning the modern gay civil rights movement; the first Gay Pride parade was held the next year in commemoration. Certainly, the absent, sodomizing son of MacLeish's *Herakles* seems a product of mid-century stereotypes about homosexuals and homosexuality.
15. As Riley (2008: 296) points out, the Sibyl also intuits past and present; but only *after* the point of no return, as an agent of catharsis.
16. See Izzo 2009: 139–40 for the political views of MacLeish and in particular the anti-Nixonian slant of MacLeish's next play, *Scratch* (1971). For the interconnections between MacLeish's progressivism and high Modernism, see Newcomb 1990.
17. For Eugene O'Neill's *Bacchae*-inspired doubling of actors and audience in *The Great God Brown*, see Lambropoulos, this volume.
18. For an anthology of Schechner's cross-cultural theories of performance, see Schechner 1988.

19. In 2009, Austin's performance group *The Rude Mechanicals* re-enacted *Dionysus in 69* in Austin, TX; for an illuminating account of that production—including its effect on Austin's gay community—see Shawn Sides's chapter in this volume. See also my autobiographical review in the *San Antonio Current*: "Groping Greatness: Austin's Rude Mechs Cop a Feel in 'Dionysus in 69,'" <http://www2.sacurrent.com/arts/story.asp?id=70740>.
20. For an illuminating discussion of the differences between ancient and modern perceptions of oral sex, including cunnilingus, see Parker 1997: 62–3.
21. <http://www.goldstar.com/events/west-hollywood-ca/the-bacchae.html#event_description> accessed August 4, 2010.

References

Bond, G. (1981), *Herakles*. Oxford.
Brantley, B. (2008), "Up, Up and Away (and Watch Those Swinging Doors)," *New York Times* May 5 <http://theater.nytimes.com/2008/05/05/theater/reviews/05boei.html>.
Burnett, A. P. (1971), *Catastrophe Survived: Euripides' Plays of Mixed Reversal*. Oxford.
Carson, A. (2006), *Grief Lessons: Four Plays by Euripides*. New York.
Chalk, H. H. O. (1962), "Arete and Bia in Euripides' Herakles," *Journal of Hellenic Studies* 82, 7–18.
Colakis, M. (1993), *The Classics in the American Theater of the 1960s and Early 1970s*. Lanham, MD.
Dodds, E. R. (1960), *Euripides: Bacchae*, 2nd edn. Oxford.
Donaldson, S. (1992), *Archibald MacLeish: An American Life*. Boston.
Draback, B. A. and H. Ellis (1986), *Archibald MacLeish: Reflections*. Amherst, MA.
Dunn, F. (1996), *Tragedy's End: Closure and Innovation in Euripidean Drama*. Oxford.
Foley, H. P. (1985), *Ritual Irony: Poetry and Sacrifice in Euripides*. Ithaca, NY.
Galinsky, K. (1972), *The Herakles Theme: Adaptations of the Hero in Literature from Homer to the Twentieth Century*. Oxford.
Griffiths, E. M. (2002), "Euripides' 'Herakles' and the Pursuit of Immortality," *Mnemosyne* 55.6, 641–56.
Hall, E., F. Macintosh, and A. Wrigley (2005), *Dionysus since 69: Greek Tragedy at the Dawn of the Millennium*. Oxford.
Halleran, M. R. (1988), *The Heracles of Euripides*. Newburyport, MA.
Hartigan, K. V. (1995), *Greek Tragedy on the American Stage: Ancient Drama in the Commercial Theater, 1882–1994*. Westport, CT, and London.
Isaac, D. (1970), "Review of Performance Group," *Educational Theatre Journal* 22.4, 432–6.
Izzo, D. G. (2009), *The Influence of Mysticism on 20th Century British and American Literature*. Jefferson, NC.
Jenkins, T. E. (2007), "The 'Ultra-Modern' Euripides of Verrall, H.D., and MacLeish," *Classical and Modern Literature* 27, 121–45.
Kostelanetz, R. (1989), "The Discovery of Alternative Theater: Notes on Art Performances in New York City in the 1960s and 1970s," *Perspectives of New Music* 27.1, Winter, 128–72.
Macleish, A. (1967a), "Who Precisely Do You Think You Are?," in *A Continuing Journey*. Boston.
Macleish, A. (1967b), *Herakles*. Boston.
Meagher, R. E. (2006), *Herakles Gone Mad: Rethinking Heroism in an Age of Endless War*. Northhampton, MA.

Newcomb, J. T. (1990), "Archibald MacLeish and the Poetics of Public Speech: A Critique of High Modernism," *Journal of the Midwest Modern Language Association* 23.1, 9–26.
Papadopoulou, T. (2005), Herakles *and Euripidean Tragedy*. Cambridge.
Parker, H. (1997), "The Teratogenic Grid," in J. Hallett and M. Skinner eds., *Roman Sexualities*. Princeton, 47–65.
Performance Group (1970), *Dionysus in 69*. Ed. R. Schechner. New York.
Riley, K. (2008), *The Reception and Performance of Euripides'* Herakles: *Reasoning Madness*. Oxford.
Schechner, R. (1988), *Performance Theory*. 2nd edn. New York.
Seaford, R. (1996), *Euripides: Bacchae*. Warminster.
Segal, C. (1997), *Dionysiac Poetics and Euripides'* Bacchae. Expanded edn. Princeton.
Walton, J. M. (2009), *Euripides: Our Contemporary*. Berkeley.
Wolff, C. and T. Sleigh (2001), *Euripides: Herakles*. Oxford.

CHAPTER 27

LEE BREUER'S NEW AMERICAN CLASSICISM

The Gospel at Colonus' *"Integration Statement"*

JUSTINE McCONNELL

> What I am interested in doing is to put Europe in its place in American culture.[1]

So says Lee Breuer, the experimental writer and director, whose theatrical career stretches back to the early 1960s. His *The Gospel at Colonus*, which premièred at the Brooklyn Academy of Music's "Next Wave Festival" in 1983, has received exemplary attention from classical reception scholars in recent years;[2] I am indebted to these, but wish here to consider the play from a slightly different perspective. At the heart of this chapter is an analysis of the "American Classicism" that Breuer aimed to contribute to with this play.[3] This is bound in with a consideration of the intricate racial dynamics, which warrant careful explication in order to prevent what could otherwise come close to an "accidental imperialism" (as I term it) on Breuer's part. The political resonances and racial dynamics of the play are, therefore, at the heart of my analysis.

Lee Breuer is a co-founder of Mabou Mines, the theater collective that has, since its inception in 1970, exulted in its artist-driven, avant-garde approach, "dedicated to the development of a new theatrical language."[4] Proudly proclaiming their decision to entitle all members of the company as "Co-Artistic Directors" in the early days, Mabou Mines' inclusive and equalizing ethos was clear from the start.[5] Such an ideology is fundamental to Breuer's "American Classicism," of which *The Gospel at Colonus* is a part. The formation of this new canon of American Classicism is, for Breuer, intricately tied in with a need to escape from the overbearing shadow of Europe; to contain and absorb Europe's influence on American culture, but not be dominated by it. Breuer's mission is driven by concerns that have much in common with those of postcolonial theorists;

however, as we shall see, this is highly problematic in his hands, not least because, in the eyes of some critics, he enacted a colonialist appropriation when he chose to cast his version of Sophocles' *Oedipus at Colonus* as a "gospel musical" from the African-American tradition. This chapter considers the extent to which the United States can itself be considered as a "postcolonial" entity, and goes on to explore the political nuances of Breuer's merging of the genres of ancient Greek drama with "gospel musical." The performative effect of this amalgamation is considered, with the critical reception of *Gospel* contributing to the analysis, and finally, an evaluation of Breuer's new "American Classicism" is offered.

An "American Classicism"

Lee Breuer's play might best be read in the context of postcolonial discourse. When he speaks of America's need to break free from the burden of the "Western canon" and of British English, Breuer's arguments are more reminiscent of mid-twentieth-century artists from nations brutally oppressed and dislocated by Europe than one might immediately expect from a citizen of the United States. However, as the postcolonial theorists Ashcroft, Griffiths, and Tiffin have observed, the United States was in fact the first postcolonial society to develop their own "national" literature (Ashcroft, Griffiths, and Tiffin 2002: 15). As for literature, so for theater: for Breuer, American theater must break free from the European model, just as American literature did toward the end of the eighteenth century. However, Breuer's rhetoric jars somewhat by the end of the twentieth century when he is voicing it, because the United States itself had already become a neo-colonial power not so very different from the imperialist European powers of earlier ages. In other words, the United States can no longer be regarded as a previously colonized nation without its contemporary imperializing missions being simultaneously taken into account; the United States has become more colonizer than colonized (also see Goff and Simpson, this volume). As Sangeeta Ray and Henry Schwarz have remarked, and as quoted in the introduction to this handbook, "Post-colonies are obviously capable of becoming oppressor states, but none has been quite so 'successful' as the US" (Ray and Schwarz 1995: 165 n. 3). Indeed, the United States was inextricably implicated in Britain's colonization of Africa and the Caribbean by being a driving force in the transatlantic slave trade, yet it is a nation that was also oppressed by the British until the revolution, and is thus entitled to a "postcolonial" identity, in some senses, after 1783. While the field of postcolonial studies has tended to focus on former colonies of Europe, the possibility of including America within such a framework has been largely neglected. Furthermore, Paul Gilroy's important argument in "Race and the Right to be Human" must not be overlooked: articulating the case for the connection between colonial violence and modern racism, and the ways in which the international behavior of the United States echoes that of Great Britain in preceding centuries, he demonstrates the aptness of designating modern-day America as "postcolonial" (Gilroy 2004: 31–64).

The United States must be considered in these lights if constructions of American national identity are to be understood, and race relations within the country to be illuminated; both have been crucially informed by America's decolonizing fight for independence, and by its own imperialistic modes of interaction (King 2000: 2–5; Stratton 2000).

Lee Breuer recalls that when he returned to the U.S.A. in 1970 he was "angry and disturbed at the critical establishment's unquestioned purchasing of British culture as American culture" (Cody and Breuer 1989: 62). In response, he determined to establish a new, specifically American theater. *The Gospel at Colonus* was one part of this mission: together with the composer Bob Telson, they worked to create a "canonical counter-discourse" (to use Helen Tiffin's term) in *Gospel*. While they successfully achieve an American recasting of Sophocles' play in a way which brings to the fore specifically American concerns and culture, the production is problematic. Breuer's adoption of the gospel musical form comes dangerously close to an appropriation that obliterates the specifically African-American stories of resistance from which the genre sprang. He identifies with an African-American experience of oppression because he feels himself and the United States as a whole to have been artistically oppressed by Europe, and by Great Britain in particular. Yet to equate non-violent artistic oppression with forcible enslavement and continuing racial discrimination is surely to underestimate and downplay the horror of historical African-American experiences. *The Gospel at Colonus* becomes a politically problematic piece of theater, compounded more by the naive statements of its director than by the performance of the play itself.

After all, Breuer's instinct is unarguably right: any "American Classicism" must include African-American culture. As Ralph Ellison argued so eloquently in his essay, "What America Would Be Like Without Blacks," American society without African-Americans cannot exist (Ellison 1970). But the inference that Breuer appropriates the painful history of others clearly problematizes *The Gospel at Colonus*; it is a play written and directed by a white man, but nearly always staged with an exclusively black cast, and adopting much from the African-American genre of the gospel musical. To some extent it might be argued that Breuer leverages the emotional landscape of other people's experiences to craft his play and his inclusive, experimental theater. One reviewer even remarked that, amidst a glut of recent gospel musicals, "*The Gospel at Colonus* is the first gospel show with a truly innovative idea at its core" (Gussow 1988). In other words, as Goff and Simpson have discussed, the reviewer is dangerously close to saying that a white man has rescued a traditionally black genre, namely gospel theater, which had fallen into a rut of imitation and uninventiveness (Goff and Simpson 2007: 211).

Although black musicals date back to before the start of the twentieth century, and gospel musicals originally grew out of spirituals that were first performed commercially in 1871 (Hatch 2003: 381), Warren Burdine has shown that until the 1960s, the primary target audience of such productions was white, and the black characters were a white-imagined stereotype of poor education and poverty, deployed to intended comic effect (Burdine 1991: 74). However, as the civil rights movement took hold, Langston Hughes, who had already been so influential in the Harlem Renaissance and had had a deep impact on the négritude movement, wrote three musical dramas which helped start the trend of the "gospel musical," whose heyday was in the 1960s and 1970s (Burdine 1991: 74). Ironically, Hughes was a renowned agnostic; indeed the religious conviction underlying gospel musicals could be tenuous. Some of the more militant African-American activists at this time were decrying Christianity as a tool of oppression used by slave-masters to keep slaves in more acquiescent subjugation; while this is undoubtedly a valid point, it fails to take into account the subversive element that has always been an important part of gospel music. Just like the African-American folklore stories of Brer Rabbit outwitting the slower, stupider Brer Bear, which (in keeping with some of the tales in Aesop's fables, also—by tradition at least—written by a slave) are commonly seen to represent the black slaves' efforts to outwit their white slave-owners, gospel music could also carry messages that were hidden from the uncomprehending slave-owners.[6] Famously, for example, "Swing Low, Sweet Chariot" speaks of the Underground Railway, the network that helped slaves escape their bondage. In *The Life and Times of Frederick Douglass* (1881), Douglass asserts that the song "O Canaan, sweet Canaan, | I am bound for the life of Canaan" symbolized "More than a hope of reaching heaven. We meant to reach the *North*, and the North was our Canaan" (Douglass 1962: 159).

As it pertains to the Greek dimension of the play, Breuer's choice of translation is likely to have been determined by its performability—for which Robert Fitzgerald's 1941 translation had been particularly praised.[7] Yet, as Fitzgerald's wife, Penelope, highlighted when she wrote the preface to the published text of *Gospel*, Breuer's play must be considered in its own right, as well as in connection to Sophocles:

> *The Gospel at Colonus* uses the idea of reimagining in a striking and original way. The play is not meant to be Sophocles' *Oedipus*, but to be a new play, derived from the original, different from it and yet true to its essential spirit. (Fitzgerald 1989: xii)

Goff and Simpson have already offered an insightful reading of the play itself, including textual analysis of its engagement with Sophocles, which stretches beyond *Oedipus at Colonus* to incorporate sections from Sophocles' other Theban plays (Goff and Simpson 2007: 178–218; 185–91; 206). My aim here is to focus on the larger political reverberations of Breuer's appropriation both of the ancient drama and of the gospel musical. Certainly he felt free to adapt the ancient text as he saw fit, and to do likewise with the generic norms of the gospel musical; but whether Breuer was as sensitive to the political, especially racial, aspects of this as he thought he was, warrants consideration.

The play opens with "Preacher Oedipus" (played by Morgan Freeman in the 1985 filmed production of the play) announcing that rather than narrating a Bible story as was the tradition in gospel musicals,

> I take as my text this evening the Book of Oedipus. (Breuer 1989: 4)

Thus, the classical myth takes the place of the biblical story. In keeping with the production's gospel musical style, Breuer splices passages from *Antigone* and *Oedipus*

Tyrannus into his adaptation of *Oedipus at Colonus*, in a way not dissimilar to a church preacher's juxtaposition of different biblical texts within one service. Although the published script of Breuer's play never veers far from Fitzgerald's translation, the gospel setting lends a different tone to Sophocles' text, and in performance Freeman adapts his lines to fit the tenor of a Pentecostal service by rhythm and repetition (Fig. 27.1).

Indeed, Breuer's foray into a new "American Classicism" in *Gospel* is made via a model that is highly reminiscent of jazz and the blues. Breuer and Telson saw in jazz and blues music another set of contributions that were uniquely American. Integrally improvisational, the actors diverged from the script at will in order to capture the sense of the evangelical church service more completely. Similarly, the chorus responds to the Preacher Oedipus' words in a form of call and response that is richly evocative of the gospel church service, but that is not reflected in the published play text. The filmed version frequently diverges from the text, missing out sections and ad-libbing around the general theme of the written script, thereby underlining the crucial importance both of watching this production (rather than just reading the text), and of acknowledging the creative input of the actors.

Despite Breuer's rhetoric of wanting to free himself from the European canon, he will accept a European influence so long as it is only one part of the new American theater.

FIG. 27.1 Morgan Freeman as Preacher Oedipus in the 1985 production of *The Gospel at Colonus* at the American Musical Festival in Philadelphia. ©PBS.

As he demonstrates in *Gospel*, African-American and European traditions can be mutually complementary and illuminating:

> American culture today is becoming triangular. The influx of African, Caribbean, and Asian cultural ideas, along with European ideas are creating a new culture—no longer a strictly European one. This is the ultimate melting pot. A country's classicism is its statement. (Cody and Breuer 1989: 62)

If his terminology of a "melting pot" is a little hackneyed, his sentiment is nevertheless clear and important. Although Iris Smith suggests that Breuer's over-reliance on metaphors such as these can result in a blurring of cultural differences (Smith 1997: 46), this is a cousin of the argument that criticizes writers from previously colonized nations for using or admiring the literature which had been part of the apparatus of their oppression.[8] Breuer is repeatedly accused of casting a veil over differences, eliding them even as he hopes to capture them; but much of that impression comes from what he says about his work in interviews and magazine articles, rather than from an analysis of the productions themselves. What he says is certainly interesting, but most crucial of all is the performance piece that he produces.

All of this—African-American folklore, the Greek play, jazz, and blues—combine to form a uniquely American reception of Greek drama that is part of a "hybrid," postcolonial reality. Breuer's assertion of an "American English" language that has broken free from the strictures of British English is also best understood through the prism of postcolonial theory. Within language itself, Breuer endeavors to enact the same kind of synthesis as he does in his staging of *The Gospel at Colonus*.

> I don't feel that I'm very interested in the English language. I prefer to think that I work in the American language. I'm much more interested in a way into an American classicism that's separate from an English classicism. Now the American language is 20% African, unlike the English classical rhythmic dynamic which of course comes from the Church of England. (Rabkin 1984: 49)

Leaving aside his inaccurate dismissal of British English as monolithic and unevolving, it is in a kind of syncretic language that Breuer is expressing his interest. The development of a syncretic language, usually in nations still striving to assert independence both political and cultural from their former imperial oppressors, is closely related to "hybridity," which has been extensively theorized by Homi Bhabha among others.[9]

Hybridity becomes a means by which the authority of the colonial power is shaken by the recognition of a part of themselves in that which they had designated "Other." As Bhabha explains,

> The display of hybridity—its peculiar "replication"—terrorizes authority with the *ruse* of recognition, its mimicry, its mockery. (Bhabha 1985: 157)

Among the audiences of *Gospel*, those more familiar with ancient Greek tragedy suddenly see connections with a Pentecostal church service, while those more familiar with the latter, recognize a connection with the non-Christian forms of the Sophoclean tragedy. This hybrid reaction—what we might even go so far as to call "cross-viewing," to use Susan Manning's phrase—is certainly the play's strength.[10]

While Breuer is clearly attracted by the idea of a syncretic language, it is scarcely in evidence in *Gospel*. Where Breuer does enact his own syncretization is in the production as a whole. As Christopher Balme has identified, syncretic theater is one of the most effective ways of "decolonizing the stage" (Balme 1999). Combining performance techniques from a range of cultures, Breuer works toward achieving the liberation from any one tradition that is necessary in order to "decolonize" drama and break free from the restrictions of conventional monocultural theater.[11]

Nevertheless, there are problems with reading *Gospel* in terms of hybridity, not least related once more to the issue of how dangerously close Breuer and Telson's production comes to enacting a "colonization" of the very gospel medium with which it intends to work in partnership. This assessment is itself fraught with difficulties: is it only because Breuer and Telson are white that critics have suggested they are "colonizing" the gospel medium? Had they been black, this might have been termed an "appropriation" of a work of the classical canon and praised as such. Breuer himself certainly intended it to be a positive process, an "integration statement," as he terms it:

> I wanted to make a statement that a white man can work not with a bunch of black intellectuals who have gone to Yale, but with the real performers—that I could respect their art and they could respect mine and that we would not rip each other off, thus disproving the idea that never the twain shall meet. In other words that I could make an integration statement in terms of this country by making it happen on stage.[12]

What Breuer achieves, therefore, is not his aim of making a political statement within the play, but of making a political statement *by* the play itself: the canonical European, and the African-American religion can interact seamlessly, just as the white and black theater practitioners can work together on a basis of equality and mutual respect.

To transmute Sophocles into a form that contributes toward the American Classicism that Breuer seeks, the classical Greek metaphysics is transformed into a Christian one of redemption, with the chorus at its heart. Breuer sees *Oedipus at Colonus* and the medium of a gospel musical fitting together so well because

> Basically, [*Oedipus at Colonus*] is a sermon on a happy death, a sermon on being blessed after being cursed in life, finally being blessed before one dies. (Rabkin 1984: 48)

The powerful, programmatic opening of Breuer's play[13] announces the production's fusion of ancient Greek drama with modern, African-American Pentecostalism. For Breuer,

> The black church experience here is a wonderful new idea about tragic rhythms and, who knows, maybe closer to what the original Greek performances were like. (Rabkin 1984: 49)

Appealing as this may be, it is undermined to some extent by Breuer's confession that

> I wasn't trying to say anything about gospel, because I don't want to presume that I know anything about it. (Smith 1988)

He is torn between an awareness that he is venturing into cultural territory without adequate knowledge, and a passion to do so because of the connections that he has glimpsed there.

To simply look for one-to-one symmetries and asymmetries between the gospel church and ancient Greek religion as many of the Broadway-production critics attempted to do (eliciting more negative responses from them) is misleading, but to approach it more flexibly, thinking of the "spirit" of each, rather than the letter, is revealing. Breuer deliberately introduces apparently incompatible elements into the production, making a case for the close links between the seemingly incongruous and the familiar. For many of the theater critics, it was the classical norms (with which they were more familiar) that they saw as being disrupted; but for other parts of the audience, the gospel church structure was the familiar form, the Greek the incongruous. Staging *The Gospel at Colonus* at an event like BAM's Next Wave Festival limited their audience to the more elite who usually attend such events (Wetmore 2003: 105); but the play did, nevertheless, draw a more ethnically diverse audience than most performances at similar events.

Critical Reception

While the responses of critics should never be taken as objective assessments of a performance, the rich and varied reactions that *The Gospel at Colonus* provoked shed light both on the cultural milieu of 1980s New York theater and on the play itself.[14] *Gospel* first emerged in embryonic form in 1980 as a half-hour performance with just one actor, five singers, and only two of Bob Telson's songs—staged at Performance Space 122 in New York (Smith 1988). In this format, it was intended as a companion piece to Breuer and Telson's "doo-wop opera" *Sister Suzie Cinema* (1980); perhaps in a nod to the ancient Greek theater's balancing of the tragedies with a satyr play, *Gospel* was here intended to add gravitas to the more light-hearted *Sister Suzie Cinema*. Three years later, greatly expanded and developed into the broad shape that it has retained ever since, *Gospel* was performed at BAM to great critical acclaim. In 1988 it ran for several months on Broadway, though there was a sense that in this larger, more commercial setting the production lost some of its energy and a little of its charm (Gussow 1988). Nevertheless, it brought the play to a wider audience, with reviewers proclaiming it as "unique and stirring" (Beaufort 1988: 19) and expressing wonder at the fusion of Greek tragedy with Pentecostalism.

The critics' reaction to this synthesis of the classical and evangelical was, on the whole, one of admiration. Jack Kroll, writing in *Newsweek*, gushed with an enthusiasm that echoed the ecstatic jubilation of the production itself:

> A triumph of reconciliation, bringing together black and white, pagan and Christian, ancient and modern in a sunburst of joy that seems to touch the secret heart of civilization itself. (Kroll 1988)

There were detractors, of course: two influential critics, Frank Rich and John Simon, both detect the insidious imperialistic appropriation in the work that I have mentioned:

> Instead of liberating its singers, *The Gospel at Colonus* seems to hem them in—gratuitously requiring that Afro-American artists worship at a shrine of Western culture before they can let loose with their own, equally valid art (Rich 1988)

and "those two white boys, Telson and Breuer, coloniz[ing] the gospel" (Simon 1988). These reviewers' concerns are important, but must be tempered by consideration of the New York theater scene at the time: the antagonism between Rich and Breuer is well known;[15] and the flavor of Simon's review suggests that he prefers his classical plays to be as traditional as possible. Simon berates the production for

> Chop[ping] up this text, coarsen[ing] its language, drop[ping] in bits from the other Theban plays, rearrang[ing] the snippets so as to omit or truncate the great choric songs and *agons*, and giv[ing] it all a faux-naïf, gospel-service veneer. [This] is vulgarization of the crassest kind. (Simon 1988: 96)

His objection seems to be that he feels that *The Gospel at Colonus* detracts from Greek tragedy by its other (African-American, and modern-day) influences. Simon has watched the play primarily for its *faithfulness* to Sophocles and to the performance norms of fifth-century Athenian drama; yet to do so is surely to inhabit dangerously the dominating mindset of a traditional imperialistic West.

Throwing off the European Shackles

Lee Breuer seems more interested in an artistic reconciliation between Europe and America than he is in a deeper, racial reconciliation within the United States. He is seeking to escape the shackles of the European canon, appropriating that which appeals to his purpose and discarding that which does not:

> What I am interested in doing is to put Europe in its place in American culture, because it is only about one third of the whole story. I am trying to work against measuring everything by European rules. But right now, in funding circles and throughout the critical establishment, all Third World aesthetics are still being viewed through European aesthetics. Third World art is defined as good, depending on how it approximates European standards. (Cody and Breuer 1989: 61)

This echoes Chinua Achebe's pronouncement on the perniciousness of the term "universalism":

> I should like to see the word *universalism* banned altogether from discussions of African literature until such a time as people cease to use it as a synonym for the narrow, self-serving parochialism of Europe, until their horizon extends to include all the world. (Achebe 1975: 9)

Likewise, it recalls Wole Soyinka's warning to "beware of the neo-colonial wolf, dressed in the sheep's clothing of 'universality'" (Gates 1986: 408); Breuer's motivations in this respect are thus in keeping with those of two of the most renowned postcolonial writers of the twentieth century.

However, coupled with his lack of self-consciousness regarding the derogatory nature of the term "Third World" (which was in more common parlance in the 1980s when Breuer was speaking), Breuer opens himself up to a charge of appropriating the misfortunes of others: aligning himself, who is merely artistically oppressed, with those who are physically, politically, and culturally oppressed. His intention, as we gather from his comments, is benign and even idealistic: he sees the United States as a country that is still new, and therefore still developing. As he puts it,

> [America] is a young country. The Japanese have 800 years going into defining their classicism, while we've got a 250 year old country here. 500 years from now maybe some of these ideas will gel enough that some genius—an American Dante or Shakespeare—will come along and write it out and form our classicism. (Rabkin 1984: 51)

Breuer views the 1776 Declaration of Independence as being the birth of the new nation of America, and the youth of the country to be explanation enough for what he suggests is a lack of American theatrical geniuses. His conceptualization of America as a very young country compels him to view it as *not yet* attaining to the levels of European theater. This perspective is scarcely likely to be credited by many in the twenty-first century, particularly in the United States but also around the world, and it entirely neglects the important work done by postcolonial thinkers to un-privilege history.[16] So while his intention is to "put Europe in its place in American culture," his emphasis on the power of history fails to see that stripping history of its potency is one of the most effective modes of decolonization and liberation. At the same time, for Breuer the experimental nature of his theatrical endeavors is fitting for an inchoate American identity; he does not see himself as exploiting black expressive forms; rather, they are part of the local material from which he draws to stage a broader American drama.

By emphasizing the youth of the American nation, ignoring the Native American performance tradition entirely,[17] by pleading for more time in order to reach maturation, that "500 years from now maybe...," Breuer demonstrates his own lack of urgency in the task he is undertaking, and his own lack of outrage. To contrast his effectively mild-mannered approach to that of the St. Lucian poet and dramatist Derek Walcott is illuminating. Far from suggesting that "the Caribbean will get there in the end" as Breuer seems to suggest of the United States, Walcott makes the case for having "got there" (so to speak) at exactly the same time as those founding, canonical works of literature because the crucial factor is to see the simultaneity of these artistic works. Walcott's "The Muse of History" (1974) articulates a position adopted by a number of Caribbean writers, whereby time is condensed onto the same axis as space, with eras happening simultaneously:[18] "if you think of art as a simultaneity that is inevitable in terms of certain people, then Joyce is a contemporary of Homer."[19] Such an argument prevents the over-privileging of canonical texts by denying that they have primacy over later works. Just as Joyce (and Walcott, presumably) can become contemporaries of Homer, so too Sophocles' *Oedipus at Colonus* and Breuer's *Gospel* can be considered as contemporaneous, and criticisms such as Simon's regarding the "vulgarization" of the ancient text become void.

What is crucial in this assertion of simultaneity is that the power of history is stripped away, so that it can no longer oppress those who have historically been marginalized, disregarded, or subjugated. Perhaps because he has not had to struggle against the kind of inequality and oppression that black artists have faced, Breuer seems unaware of the paralysing grip of traditional notions of historical time. This raises the question of whether something beyond individual personalities lies behind the very different perspectives of Lee Breuer and Derek Walcott. It may be that the most important distinction here is between a United States "postcolonial" perspective, and a Caribbean one. After all, the more contested the postcolonial status of the United States is, the more problematic its positioning within such a framework becomes.

Indeed, although Breuer's amalgamation of Greek drama and African-American gospel may be intended to reflect a racial reconciliation of blacks with whites, as Goff and Simpson suggest is at the heart of the play (Goff and Simpson 2007: 184 and *passim*), this motivation does not seem to me to be sustained within *Gospel*. Certainly the play can be seen as equating the Sophoclean focus on exile and integration with the experience of Africans exiled from their homeland by slavery and seeking acceptance in a new place, and D'Aponte is surely right to say that *Gospel* offers "a stunning metaphor for the easing of Black–White relations around the world."[20] Yet it is nearly always performed by an all-black cast, thereby denying the possibility of visually representing this racial reconciliation which would be offered by a color-blind casting or one that included both black and white actors.[21] Instead, Breuer's identification with an African-American history of oppression (on the grounds of his own artistic oppression by British culture) drives his use of the gospel medium, and it is this that is so problematic: while doing away with racial divisions is clearly appealing and desirable, to elide artistic, self-imposed oppression with forcible physical and social oppression is clearly to underestimate the enormity of the latter.

The Accidental Imperialism of Breuer's Stance

If we accept the United States as a "postcolonial" nation, Lee Breuer's charmingly idealistic vision of a new "American theater" that has abandoned the subdivisions of, for example, "African-American theater," also has dangerous echoes of imperialistic appropriation. Idealism blinds Breuer to the fact that, as the proponents of the Black Arts Movement made clear in the 1960s and 1970s, African-American theater has an important role to play in forwarding cultural and political concerns. Indeed, this period between Lorraine Hansberry's *A Raisin in the Sun* (1959) and Ntozake Shange's *for colored girls who have considered suicide/when the rainbow is enuf* (1976) could be seen as "a second Renaissance of African American poetry, dance, music, and theatre" (Hatch 2003: 376). Specifically, black theater at this time often confronted audiences with their own contemporary racial prejudices (as in Hansberry's *Raisin*) and their historical racial oppression and discrimination (as in Ossie Davis's satirical *Purlie Victorious* (1961), which was later adapted into the musical *Purlie* (1970) and employed many modes of the gospel musical) (Hatch 2003: 381). Breuer's vision of a racially inclusive "American" theater fails to appreciate that, as Harry Elam has articulated, "the black figure on the American stage is always and already fraught with political, cultural, and social significance."[22] Racism has not disappeared, and "representing race and performing blackness remain politically and culturally charged" (Elam and Krasner 2001: 6); Breuer, in his enthusiasm to abandon racial divisions, overlooks this.

Kevin Wetmore has highlighted the difficulties with *The Gospel at Colonus* as being threefold: whether it is accurate to represent Sophocles' play in the form of a gospel musical; whether Greek tragedy and African-American Pentecostalism are really as compatible as Breuer claims; and whether two white American men should be using African-American religion to recreate Greek tragedy (Wetmore 2003: 106). The latter is fraught with cultural as well as politically correct concerns, but if we believe in an ideal world where cultural differences are not used to discriminate but rather to contribute different elements and introduce people to other aspects of culture, then surely a white man has as much right to use the medium of a Pentecostal church service for his play, as a black man or woman has to stage Shakespeare. The manner in which it is used, however, is crucial and sensitive: if Breuer really makes gospel music "worship at the shrine of Western culture"[23] then something has gone awry. Again, his historicizing of the issue belies the deeper historical atrocities that his experiment effaces. Such criticisms were not only made against the white playwright and composer: the Five Blind Boys of Alabama, who collectively, together with Morgan Freeman, play Oedipus in *Gospel*, were denigrated in some quarters for "selling out" to white commercial interests.[24] As a consequence, the Blind Boys' particular form of gospel has been seen by some as having moved too far from the genre that gave rise to the blues. Here again, to "cross-over" from one culturally specific genre to another evidently alarms some critics. However, this is to over-privilege history (as Walcott has urged us not to do) and to close off modes of interaction and dialogue.[25] Breuer's work urges the opposite approach and his arguments remain interesting because they lobby for an American sense of self that is no longer subdivided into disparate ethnic groups. His approach to theater as an experimental space reinforces this egalitarian social approach too, where people of different races coexist and cooperate.

CATHARSIS ON THE AMERICAN STAGE

A primary attraction of the Pentecostal church service for Lee Breuer was the centrality of *catharsis*; he sees *Gospel* as "a true attempt to redefine the cathartic experience in American theatre" (Rabkin 1984: 48). As Aristotle famously discussed, *catharsis* is crucial to tragedy;[26] as a writer and director very conscious of the mechanisms of his own artistry and focused on his ambition to contribute to the formation of a new American Classicism, Breuer returns to one of the fundamental treatises on drama: Aristotle's *Poetics*. Yet the Aristotelian *catharsis* is only one element; with the crucial support of Bob Telson's music, *The Gospel at Colonus* attempts to free itself from the bindings of Europe and its canonical literature, while also utilizing it: Aristotle's educational *catharsis* is transmuted into the redemptive *catharsis* offered by the Pentecostal church and viscerally expressed in *Gospel*. As Wetmore points out, the renowned gospel singer Mahalia Jackson views the Aristotelian term as prefiguring the postclassical, Christian notion of redemption through expression of suffering:

> Gospel songs are songs of hope. When you sing them you are delivered of your burden. (Wetmore 2003: 109)

That the production had the intended effect on at least some of its audience members is evidenced by the review from *The Nation*. With echoes of the problematic identification of black culture as emotive rather than rational, as Dionysiac rather than Apollonian,[27] Thomas Disch writes that, having seen the play on a number of occasions,

> Each time my heart has swelled, my throat has lumped, and I've cried a steady flow of wedding-march tears, feeling foolish and elevated and swept away. (Disch 1988: 690)

As Aristotle expounds, the pity and fear aroused in the audience effect a positive transformation of those very emotions;[28] the *catharsis*, then, is usually confined to the audience. However, when Breuer responds to Sophocles through the prism of an African-American gospel church service, his actors and singers are all both audience (of Sophocles' *Oedipus at Colonus*) and actors (in Breuer and Telson's *Gospel*) at one and the same time. Underlining this fact and proclaiming the work as a "reception" of Sophocles, the cast enact their elation both as outward joy at the miraculous apotheosis of Oedipus, and also pleasure at having just "watched" and responded to Sophocles' tragedy.

Breuer's work not only responds to Sophocles', and thus, in one sense, goes a step beyond the ancient tragedy, but it also attempts to extend the boundaries of what we may expect from tragic drama:

> I really feel that if you go one step further with cathartic theatre you might find pity and terror turning into joy and ecstasy. We have a jubilee in this, an expression of pure ecstatic joy. It may not seem typically tragic in the way we've come to understand what the tragic experience should be, but I have a feeling that catharsis can go right on through pity and terror into joy. And that's what this is about. This is a true attempt to redefine the cathartic experience in American theatre. (Rabkin 1984: 48)

GREEK TRAGEDY MEETS CHRISTIANITY

Breuer's inclusion of a choral ode from *Antigone* and passages from *Oedipus Tyrannus* serve to strengthen the parallels with the evangelical setting by emphasizing the Judaeo-Christian themes of needing to make peace with oneself, with those around one, and with God, before death (Green 1994: 62). Such themes are a far cry from Sophocles' *Oedipus at Colonus*, where an angry patriarch curses his sons; indeed, passages that problematize the play's message of reconciliation, such as Oedipus' criticism of Athens' reluctance to help him (*Oedipus at Colonus*, 258–92), are omitted. This avoids drawing attention to the United States' more reprehensible history, as Goff and Simpson have discussed:

> A speech on the betrayal of ideals by the host country might have been too close to the bone . . . *Gospel* does not want to draw attention to the American republic's great betrayal of its ideals at the beginning of its history. (Goff and Simpson 2007: 207)

In other words, while Breuer and Telson's black Oedipus had the potential to be the Oedipus of postcolonial reckoning, he is, instead, rather anodyne.

Nonetheless, in Breuer's version, Oedipus is a kind of katabatic Christ-figure: first descending to the Underworld and then arising once more from it (Fig. 27.2). Breuer's Oedipus arises from his grave as the singing Oedipuses are raised back up onto the stage, but in a nod to Jesus's time on earth after his crucifixion, we also see the Morgan Freeman Oedipus come down to earth once more, to impart a final message: that of the Messenger speech from Sophocles' play. As Oliver Taplin has remarked, *The Gospel at Colonus* is also deeply subversive of Sophocles' play: not only does Sophocles' Oedipus not rise up to heaven as we see in Breuer's version (instead becoming a powerful spirit of Colonus), but far from the whole drama taking place in the jubilant and celebratory church of the modern adaptation, Sophocles sets his tragedy in the grove of the fearful Furies, who hover between frightening Furies and kindly Eumenides (Taplin 1989: 60).

FIG. 27.2 Clarence Fountain as Oedipus arising from his grave, in the 1985 production of *The Gospel at Colonus* at the American Musical Festival in Philadelphia. ©PBS.

Not needing, narratively, to tie in to the "sequel" of Sophocles' *Antigone*, the grief of the two daughters/sisters is treated in a more concise fashion, with their return to Thebes unmentioned, and the long messenger speech placed at the very end, followed only by the final hymn entitled "Let the Weeping Cease." The effect of this rearrangement is to focus all the attention on Oedipus himself—a move made more emphatic by his "messenger speech"; this doubling up of Preacher and Messenger provides a further structural link between the archetypes of the world of the gospel church and of Greek tragedy (D'Aponte 1991: 107). At the same time, it gives Morgan Freeman's character even more authority: not just as Preacher Oedipus, but also as the Messenger, the speaker of truth. There is no space in the modern envisioning to consider the personal impact of his death on his family: Oedipus has already moved beyond mere personal ties to embody an entity that has power for the wider society. Even his terrible anger against his sons and against the Thebans becomes something broader in this production, chiming in with the Pentecostal ethos of divine rage and punishment that the preacher persistently conveys to his congregation. Moreover, the rearrangement enables the play to end on a jubilant note, having reached that joy that Breuer sees as following the catharsis of the emotions.

Breuer's other interest in the church is less in its religious doctrines than in its mode of presentation: in the fact that the presentation *is* a performance. Many religious ceremonies have fixed patterns, with set roles for the participants to play, and even particular "costumes" for them to wear; as the work of performance theorists such as Richard Schechner has shown, ritual and religion are important areas of study in that discipline. Breuer has described how, for him,

> The narrative experience in church was the right esthetic for the narrative experience in the Greek theater. (Smith 1988)

He reaches this conclusion by a comparison of the structures of *Oedipus at Colonus* and a gospel church service: Breuer sees both as having narrative episodes interspersed with moralizing odes and songs. He can incorporate those odes from *Antigone*, for example, because they do not have to contribute directly to the narrative, yet the inclusion of the choral ode "Numberless are the world's wonders" at the midpoint of *Gospel* is apt for Oedipus' impending death, and for the Christian idea of reconciling oneself to death (Green 1994: 63).

Most importantly of all, the music of Bob Telson and the songs that the vast choir sing (with lyrics written by Breuer) reimagine the play in a twentieth-century American setting that, far from seeming incongruous, celebrates Oedipus' apotheosis in a way that Sophocles' text does not, but which seems a natural culmination of Breuer's vision. Peculiarly however, Breuer seems unaware of the political aspects of gospel music:

> The music [of *Gospel*] essentially is non-political even though the event was highly political. (Cody and Breuer 1989: 65)

More precisely, he should have said that while his lyrics are "essentially non-political," the music itself is not necessarily so. Bob Telson, a frequent collaborator of Breuer's, received great praise for his work on *Gospel*, and having previously been the organist for the Five Blind Boys of Alabama, the accolades for the veracity of his gospel sound seem deserved, even if the play employed the music in a commercial form. Even Rich, in the midst of his damning review of the play as a whole,[29] nevertheless comments that

> This pretentiousness is not to be found either in Mr. Telson's music, which seems at one with the gospel performers rather than an attempt to colonize them, or in Mr. Breuer's lyrics, to the extent that they survive the amplification. (Rich 1988)

The music in *The Gospel at Colonus* is important not only because of its cultural resonances of resistance to slavery and racial oppression, but also because, via the music, Breuer and Telson achieved the rare feat of a successful, engaging, and integrated chorus.[30] This is one of the great contributions that the problematic task of turning classical Greek metaphysics into Christian redemptive metaphysics can offer. Breuer and Telson's play testifies to the fact that an authentic North American Classicism is going to have to be a Christianized classicism, especially if it is going to integrate any portion of the broader historical experiences and artistic expression of African-American people. While that means drastic metaphysical contortions of Sophocles, it offers a very effective synergy in terms of medium: the chorus and the antiphony.

Simon Goldhill has discussed how the choir of *Gospel* fulfill that mediatory role between characters on stage and the audience which the ancient Greek chorus held. Not only were they placed physically in the same position as the audience (the stage was encircled with banks of seating, one of which was filled with the choir), but also their responses to the story unfolding before them directed the audience's reaction (Goldhill 2007: 18). The collective nature of a gospel choir is instantly recognizable, and the odes of Sophocles' play are particularly well suited to this religious framework because the chorus not only praise the holiness of Colonus, but also pray to Zeus that Theseus will successfully rescue Antigone and Ismene, and sing to the gods of the Underworld as Oedipus disappears off to his death (Goldhill 2007: 56–7). This spiritual dimension is a feature of many Greek tragic choruses, who often voiced prayers, hymns, or religious invocations, and thereby underlined the role of the gods in human affairs and the religious implications of the play (Foley 2007: 355). Furthermore, the chorus of *Oedipus at Colonus* are more closely involved in the action than in many tragedies, engaging in stichomythia and repeatedly attempting to participate in the action, as well as singing four choral odes and five lyric dialogues with the actors (Foley 2007: 370). *Gospel*'s choir reflect this centrality, even while they simultaneously reflect the role of the audience.

To conclude we could turn once more to the words of Lee Breuer:

> I wanted to translate Greek tragedy into an American language for American viewers. I wanted to show them: this is the cathartic experience, this is what Aristotle was talking about, this is what Greek tragedy is, this is what our entire dramatic culture is based on. You begin to understand catharsis by experiencing it. (Beaufort 1988: 19)

He is working to create the American Classicism that he so longs for, employing diverse elements that make up contemporary America: the European canon and the black church not only have equal currency, but are seen to interact in ways that are mutually illuminating. The terminology and the model that Breuer uses for the formation of this new American Classicism is heavily dependent on the discourse of postcolonial studies. Yet, as we have seen, he seems unaware of how important arguments regarding the simultaneity of creation can help to overthrow the oppression of colonial history, and likewise seems oblivious to the political power of the spiritual and blues traditions. Oedipus as the man facing and accepting his own inevitable death resounds through the experience of modern men and women's reconciliation to the struggles of life in America,[31] even though the play has ultimately elided the experiences of black and white Americans to such an extent that the pernicious historical racial oppression of African Americans is eclipsed. Nevertheless, Oedipus' integration at the end of the play can still recall that of African-American people into the United States, even if this is a "utopian vision" (Goff and Simpson 2007: 184). Oedipus' final apotheosis is greeted with the joy that would erupt at the easing of that difficult life in contemporary America, and a joy that does erupt at this sign both of hope and of obstacles overcome.

As a contribution to a new Classicism for the United States, Lee Breuer and Bob Telson's play is a rich start. Ending with no reference to Antigone and Ismene's return to Thebes, the play signals the permanent move from the old world of Thebes (for which we may, perhaps, read Europe?) to the new world of Athens (for which we must, surely, read the U.S.A.?). Breuer is staking America's claim to a new form of Classicism.

Notes

1. Cody and Breuer 1989: 60. The "integration statement" of the title is Breuer's term for what he was aiming to achieve in *The Gospel at Colonus*—see p. 480.
2. See, in particular, Wetmore 2003: 102–18; Goff and Simpson 2007: 178–218; and Rankine 2013: 91–6. On the 2010 Edinburgh production, see Hardwick, this volume.
3. Rabkin 1984: 49: "I'm much more interested in a way into an American classicism that's separate from an English classicism."
4. Mabou Mines' Mission Statement—<http://www.maboumines.org/mission> accessed January 18, 2013. On the nature of avant-garde theater at the time, and on Breuer's short 1991 article on the topic, "The Two-Handed Gun: Reflections on Power, Culture, Lambs, Hyenas, and Government Support for the Arts," see Fischer 2011: 8–17.
5. <http://www.maboumines.org/history>.
6. The oral tales of Brer Rabbit and Brer Bear were collected by Joel Chandler Harris and first published as *Uncle Remus: His Songs and his Sayings* in 1880.
7. Lind 1943: 155: "I have no hesitation in saying that this is the best translation yet made of the *Oedipus at Colonus*... It is written in a simple, at times hauntingly beautiful, English which preserves the noble pathos of the Greek as well as humanly possible. It is especially adapted for use as an acting version which no actor would feel foolish at uttering; and in the choruses—the highest test of a translation of Greek drama—Fitzgerald has surpassed himself."
8. McConnell 2013: 76: Ralph Ellison, for example, was frequently castigated in the 1950s and 1960s for his often-expressed admiration for white American writers such as Mark Twain, Herman Melville, and Ernest Hemingway.
9. Bhabha (1985: 162) has explained the power of hybridity thus: "When the words of the master become the site of hybridity—the warlike sign of the native—then we may not only read between the lines but even seek to change the often coercive reality that they so lucidly contain."
10. Manning 2004. As Manning explains (224 n. 10), she borrows the term from Tirza True Latimer, who in turn borrowed it from Patricia Simons. But it is Manning's particular adaptation of the term that resonates here.
11. This has echoes of the mid-twentieth-century Indian "theater of roots" movement—see Mee 2008.
12. Breuer, quoted in quoted in William Harris, "Mabou Mines Sets *Lear* on a Hot Tin Roof," *New York Times* (January 21, 1990), H5.
13. Breuer 1989: 4: "Welcome, brothers and sisters. I take as my text this evening the Book of Oedipus."
14. See Hardwick 1999 on the benefits and potential pitfalls of using theatrical reviews in classical reception studies.

15. Goldberg 1996: reviewing Breuer's *A Prelude to Death in Venice* (1981), Rich called on the National Endowment to cut off Mabou Mines' funding. Breuer responded by writing to Rich, telling him that he "was either stupid or evil, but [Breuer's] guess was, he was both."
16. See section "Throwing off the European Shackles"; Walcott 1998: 37: "their [Caribbean writers] philosophy, based on a contempt for historic time, is revolutionary, for what they repeat to the New World is its simultaneity with the Old."
17. On Native American performance, see (for example) Geiogamah and Darby 2000 and Wilmer 2009.
18. See n. 17.
19. Walcott 1997: 241. See Greenwood 2007: 196 for discussion of Walcott's classic articulation of this position in "The Muse of History."
20. D'Aponte 1991: 106, and quoted in Goff and Simpson 2007: 184.
21. Goff and Simpson (2007: 204) would disagree, seeing the all-black cast as a signifier of reconciliation and integration: "A slippage ... arises if we agree that *Gospel* concerns itself with a model of racial integration; when Oedipus enters the community of the chorus, that chorus must at some level be acting the part of the United States. When the sleight of hand makes a black church chorus represent the predominantly white United States, the notions of inside and outside are clearly important to the play, and the blurring of their boundaries even more so." This idea is appealing, but may well have been lost on audience members less familiar with the ancient play.
22. Elam, in Elam and Krasner 2001: 3–18; 6.
23. Rich 1988; section "Critical Reception."
24. They have covered Bob Dylan and Tom Waits songs, one of the latter of which was adopted as the theme tune for the first season of *The Wire*, which has itself proved of interest to Classicists—see Potter and Marshall 2009; Love 2010. Waits has also collaborated with the renowned avant-garde theater director Robert Wilson, who has adapted a number of classical works for the stage, such as *BYRD woMAN*, which engages with the myth of Medea (1968), *Medea* itself (1981), *Alcestis* (1986), and *The Odyssey* (2012).
25. Indeed it is to fail to take up Ngũgĩ wa Thiong'o's thesis of the "globalectic"—on which, see Hardwick, this volume.
26. Aristotle, *Poetics* 1449b.
27. The Senegalese writer, politician, and co-founder of the négritude movement, Léopold Sédar Senghor contentiously condoned this stereotype when he declared, "Emotion is black as much as reason is Greek"—Senghor 1964: 24.
28. Aristotle, *Poetics* 1449b 24–8.
29. See section "Critical Reception."
30. See Foley 2007 and Billings, Budelmann, and Macintosh 2013 for more on modern choruses.
31. Corliss (1984), instead, considers it to be specifically African-American men and women's reconciliation to the difficulties of life in the United States.

References

Achebe, C. (1975), *Morning Yet on Creation Day*. London.
Ashcroft, B., G. Griffiths, and H. Tiffin (2002 [1989]), *The Empire Writes Back: Theory and Practice in Post-colonial Literatures*, 2nd edn. London and New York.

Balme, C. B. (1999), *Decolonizing the Stage: Theatrical Syncretism and Post-Colonial Drama*. Oxford.
Beaufort, J. (1988), "Greek Tragedy Blended with Afro-American Pentacostalism," *Christian Science Monitor* (March 28), 19.
Bhabha, H. K. (1985), "Signs Taken for Wonders: Questions of Ambivalence and Authority under a Tree outside Delhi, May 181," *Critical Inquiry* 12.1 (Autumn), 122–65.
Billings, J., F. Budelmann, and F. Macintosh (eds. 2013), *Choruses, Ancient and Modern*. Oxford.
Breuer, L. (1989), *The Gospel at Colonus*. New York.
Burdine, W. (1991), "Let the Theatre say 'Amen,'" *Black American Literature Forum* 25.1 (Spring), 73–82.
Cody, G. and L. Breuer (1989), "Lee Breuer on Interculturalism," *Performing Arts Journal* 11.3, 59–66.
Corliss, R. (1984), "Digging for the Roots," *Time* (January 2).
D'Aponte, M. G. (1991), "The Gospel at Colonus (and Other Black Morality Plays)," *Black American Literature Forum* 25.1 (Spring), 101–11.
Disch, T. (1988), "Theater," *The Nation* (May 14), 690.
Douglass, F. (1962 [1892]), *The Life and Times of Frederick Douglass*. New York.
Elam, H. J., Jr., and D. Krasner (eds. 2001), *African-American Performance and Theater History: A Critical Reader*. Oxford and New York.
Ellison, R. (1970), "What Would America Be Like Without Blacks," *Time* (April 6).
Fischer, I. S. (2011), *Mabou Mines: Making Avant-Garde Theater in the 1970s*. Ann Arbor.
Fitzgerald, P. (1989), Preface to *The Gospel at Colonus*. New York, xi—xii.
Foley, H. P. (2007), "Envisioning the Tragic Chorus on the Modern Stage," in C. Kraus, S. Goldhill, H. P. Foley, and J. Elsner eds., *Visualizing the Tragic: Drama, Myth, and Ritual in Greek Art and Literature*. Oxford, 353–80.
Gates, H. L., Jr., (1986), "Talkin' That Talk," in *"Race", Writing, and Difference*. Chicago and London, 402–9.
Geiogamah, H. and J. T. Darby (eds. 2000), *American Indian Theater in Performance: A Reader*. Los Angeles.
Gilroy, P. (2004), *After Empire: Melancholia or Convivial Culture?* Abingdon.
Goff, B. and M. Simpson (2007), *Crossroads in the Black Aegean: Oedipus, Antigone, and Dramas of the African Diaspora*. Oxford.
Goldberg, M. (1996), "Lee Breuer," *Bomb* 56 (Summer).
Goldhill, S. (2007), *How to Stage Greek Tragedy Today*. Chicago.
Green, A. S. (1994), *The Revisionist Stage: American Directors Reinvent the Classics*. Cambridge.
Greenwood, E. (2007), "Arriving Backwards: The Return of The *Odyssey* in the English-Speaking Caribbean," in L. Hardwick and C. Gillespie eds., *Classics in Post-Colonial Worlds*. Oxford, 192–210.
Gussow, M. (1988), "A Gospel Show Marches to a Different Beat," *New York Times* (April 3), Section 2, page 5, column 1.
Hardwick, L. (1999), "The Theatrical Review as a Primary Source for the Modern Reception of Greek Drama—A Preliminary Evaluation" <http://www2.open.ac.uk/ClassicalStudies/GreekPlays/essays/Reviews.html>.
Hatch, J. V. (2003), "From Hansberry to Shange," in E. Hill and J. V. Hatch eds., *A History of African American Theatre*. Cambridge, 375–429.
King, C. R. (ed. 2000), *Post-Colonial America*. Champaign, IL.
Kroll, J. (1988), "An Oedipal Jamboree," *Newsweek* (April 4), 75.

Lind, L. R. (1943), "Review of *Sophocles, Oedipus at Colonus: An English Version* by Robert Fitzgerald," *Classical Philology* 38.2 (April), 155.

Love, C. (2010), "Greek Gods in Baltimore: Greek Tragedy and *The Wire*," *Criticism* 52.3–4 (Summer/Fall), 487–507.

McConnell, J. (2013), *Black Odysseys: The Homeric Odyssey in the African Diaspora since 1939*. Oxford.

McDonald, M. (2001), *Sing Sorrow: Classics, History, and Heroines in Opera*. Westport, CT, and London.

Manning, S. (2004), *Modern Dance, Negro Dance: Race in Motion*. Minneapolis.

Mee, E. B. (2008), *Theatre of Roots: Redirecting the Modern Indian Stage*. London, New York, and Calcutta.

Potter, T. and C. W. Marshall (2009), "'I am the American Dream': Modern Urban Tragedy and the Borders of Fiction," in T. Potter and C. W. Marshall eds., *The Wire: Urban Decay and American Television*. New York and London, 1–14.

Rabkin, G. (1984), "Lee Breuer on *The Gospel of Colonus*," *Performing Arts Journal* 8.1, 48–51.

Rankine, P. D. (2013), *Aristotle and Black Drama: A Theater of Civil Disobedience*. Waco, TX.

Ray, S. and H. Schwarz (1995), "Postcolonial Discourse: The Raw and the Cooked," *Ariel: A Review of International English Literature* 26.1, 147–66.

Rich, F. (1988), "A Musical of Sophocles and Pentecostalism," *The New York Times* (March 25), C5.

Senghor, L. S. (1964), *Liberté 1: Négritude et humanism*. Paris.

Simon, J. (1988), "The Gospel Untruth," *New York Magazine* (April 18), 96.

Smith, I. L. (1997), "The Intercultural Work of Lee Breuer," *Theatre Topics* 7.1, 37–58.

Smith, W. (1988), "Sophocles With a Chorus of Gospel," *New York Times* (March 20), Section 2, page 5, column 1.

Stratton, J. (2000), "The Beast of the Apocalypse: The Postcolonial Experience of the United States", in C. R. King ed., *Post-Colonial America*. Champaign, IL, 21–64.

Taplin, O. (1989), *Greek Fire*. London.

Tiffin, H. (1987), "Post-colonial Literatures and Counter-discourse," *Kunapipi* 9, 17–34.

Walcott, D. (1997), "Reflections on *Omeros*," *South Atlantic Quarterly* 96.2 (Spring), 229–46.

Walcott, D. (1998), *What the Twilight Says: Essays*. New York.

Wetmore, K. J. (2003), *Black Dionysus: Greek Tragedy and African American Theatre*. Jefferson, NC.

Wilmer, S. E. (ed. 2009), *Native American Performance and Representation*. Tucson, AZ.

CHAPTER 28

GREEK TRAGEDY, ENSLAVING OR LIBERATING?

The Example of Rita Dove's The Darker Face of the Earth

NANCY SORKIN RABINOWITZ

Postcoloniality and Classics

The conference that led to this chapter has encouraged me to look more deeply into the question of the place of the ancient Greek Classics in African-American theater.[1] On the one hand "the classical tradition" might be simplistically called racist, since it has been used to validate the dominant culture and to denigrate the culture of colonized peoples (see Powers, this volume); the return to the "great books," on the other hand, has mostly been put forward by a group of conservative colleagues, at my institution and others. Undoubtedly, one of the functions of Classics is or at least was, to cite Seth Schein, a Classicist who has written on the subject, "to legitimate a social order and a set of institutions, beliefs, and values that are commonly associated with western civilization and 'our' western cultural heritage" (Schein 2008: 75). Because of this perception of the field, the official organization of Classicists, the American Philological Association, has entitled its fundraising campaign "From Gatekeeper to Gateway," an acknowledgment of the public relations problem that the field may face in attracting money.

Postcolonial theory can be helpful here because the U.S.A. is in an interestingly dual postcolonial situation. (See Macintosh, McConnell, Rankine, this volume; also Goff and Simpson, this volume.) The United States not only used to be a colony but also was (and still is) an empire with colonies of its own (Gilroy 2005). Moreover, the U.S.A. created an internalized colony of people of color—Native Americans and slaves. Not only did black nationalists like Malcolm X (at times) make comparisons between American and the postcolonial struggles of the 1960s (Malcolm X 1963: 824–5), but twentieth-century black authors from Richard Wright to Toni Morrison called American exceptionalism into question. In the U.S.A. as elsewhere, anti-colonization struggles have gone beyond fighting direct economic and political oppression to recognizing and opposing cultural domination particularly in education. Calls for changes in the curriculum were accompanied to a great extent by challenges to the canonical dominance of the "dead white males."

Why then do postcolonial African writers or writers of color in the U.S.A. go back to the Greeks? When giving a talk at Hamilton College, Mary-Kay Gamel was asked why Luis Alfaro, author of *Oedipus el rey*, didn't write a new play instead of "messing with" the old one (see Banks and Rankine, this volume). (Theater critic Michael Billington raised the same question of Rita Dove's *The Darker Face of the Earth*.) The immediate answer that Gamel gave in the case of *Oedipus el rey* was "the status." If it is true that the Classics convey status (class, but also artistic status), then how resistant can a new African-American version of Greek tragedy be? For instance, can a theater based on tragedy be a theater of the oppressed in Augusto Boal's sense?[2] (See Lodewyck and Monoson, this volume.) Boal was writing in the context of Latin American popular movements, and he takes Aristotle to task, and by extension tragedy. He calls Aristotle's view

> A powerful purgative system, the objective of which is to eliminate all that is not commonly accepted. His system appears in disguised form on television, in the movies, in the circus, in the theaters. . . . It is designed to bridle the individual, to adjust him to what pre-exists. If this is what we want, the Aristotelian system serves the purpose better than any other; if, on the contrary, we want to stimulate the spectator to transform his society, to engage in revolutionary action, in that case we will have to seek another poetics. (Boal 1979: 47; cf. Brecht 1964)

This Boalian view of radical theater challenges any European theater, and especially adaptations of Sophocles' *Oedipus the King*, given Aristotle's endorsement of it, as inherently oppressive. In the face of Boal's call for activist theater that engages with the poor directly, I would ask whether returning to the works of antiquity is necessarily a part of a lingering colonialism or racism, or whether such a turn can be part of the solution to modern problems of colonialism.

As others have argued (even throughout this volume), the ancient material is not so clearly colonizing and oppressive. It is not merely the gatekeeper of the dominant culture. Edith Hall, for instance, has argued that after 1968 productions of ancient drama have been quite radical politically and aesthetically (Hall 2004: 1). Hall's approach is that of reception studies, which is interested in the way that groups can appropriate cultural currency to their own advantage.[3] In point of fact, Greek drama has been used to challenge the U.S. empire, as productions of Auletta's *Persians* (in 1993 and 2005) and Euripides' *Trojan Women* (Rabinowitz 2013), the Lysistrata project, the Medea Project, and many other examples show.[4] Thus, it is possible to argue that classical texts have been a tool for postcolonial agendas.[5]

Nonetheless, I remain suspicious of the trend toward the self-proclaimedly radical performance of ancient texts, and indeed of my pleasure at it. If the canon is, as the authors of *The Empire Writes Back* claim, "the enactment of innumerable individual and community assumptions . . . resident in institutional structures, such as education curricula and publishing networks" (Ashcroft et al. 1989: 189), how successfully can it be redeployed against dominant institutions? Others have wrestled with this question to be sure. For instance, Lorna Hardwick notes the postcolonial uses of tragedy, but warns of the need to "avoid an uncritical sense of relief that classical texts have in recent years been recognized as a source of resistance and liberation as well as, or even rather than, suppression" (Hardwick 2007: 2; cf. Hardwick 2000). In their recent volume on postcolonial Oedipus plays, Barbara Goff and Michael Simpson articulate a potential contradiction:

> By dramatizing . . . the icons of Oedipus and Antigone . . . these adaptations hold colonial culture to account. . . . To make this culture responsible to its own authority, however, exacts a price: in aggressively turning this authority against its culture, these plays enact their own subjection to it.[6]

Goff and Simpson also point out that the adaptations they consider "possess characteristics of Greek plays and of more indigenous drama" (Goff and Simpson 2007: 5), arguing that such complexity or divisions can have the salutary effect of making the author self-conscious. I would agree and add that the mixedness of these plays can have the same or a similar effect on the audience. Like Goff and Simpson, in *Black Dionysus*, Kevin Wetmore argues that "Afro-Greek tragedy can be subversive and resistant, or it can support the hegemony of European culture" (Wetmore 2003: 4; also 7). All these critics acknowledge the ambiguity of the use of Classics in postcolonial texts and contexts.

RACE POLITICS

In the U.S. context the postcolonial is most often seen in references to race, which leads to pedagogical and theoretical questions. What is race, and how important is it? Who gets to speak about it? How do you have to approach the topic? Who gets to teach, direct, or act which plays and texts? And a current question, which I loathe: Are we really post-racial? My answer is a resounding "no," but 100 years after the publication of Du Bois's *Souls of Black Folk*, we can at least say that the color line has moved and shifted its shape. Times have changed, and forms of racism are changing—certain legal rights have apparently been won, though one must be vigilant to retain those rights and make them meaningful (for example, the vote and educational integration can be eroded through the increased imprisonment of black men and the inadequacy of urban education); there is a growing black middle class. And as people are wont to point out, we have a black President as of the time of this writing (early in the election year of 2012).

Nonetheless, during the 2008 election, one of the many challenges posed about Barack Obama was, "Is he black enough?" (See Powers, this volume.) That is the ghost of identity politics, and it still haunts our classrooms and, as I will show, discussions of Rita Dove.

In this essay, I take Rita Dove's *The Darker Face of the Earth*, an African-American version of the Oedipus story, as a way to address the problems with which I am wrestling. Dove presents a particularly good way into these issues because she is an African-American poet, the first black Poet Laureate (1993–5), and one of two black poets to receive a Pulitzer Prize (1987).[7] Clearly Dove has won endorsement from the mainstream (white) establishment.

As is often the case for me, teaching as I do at a liberal arts college, I discovered this text while preparing a course. I have been involved in many campus initiatives developing new courses dealing with race, gender, sexuality, and social class. My research has been integrally related to curriculum—for instance, after teaching a first-year seminar entitled "Coming of Age in America," I was moved to study the prison industrial complex. At about the same time, I was teaching a course on tragedy. Feeling pressure to open up my canonical (and white/male) course, I was self-consciously looking for works on ancient themes by writers of color and by women. I came across the work of Rhodessa Jones's Medea Project, Theater for Incarcerated Women. After teaching Jones's play on the Medea theme, I wrote two essays about the Medea Project itself (Rabinowitz 2008, 2013). At the same time, the activist component remains important in my development; I now participate in a prison education project in upstate New York. When teaching the same course on tragedy, I also found Dove's work. That context most definitely shaped the way I look at the play and grounds my perspective in this chapter. To be blunt, I was looking for a progressive representation of racial politics. I certainly did not want to teach a black author who did not offer a critique of power and oppression.

In a special journal issue on theater, Harvey Young addresses the paranoia that can afflict those presuming to teach (or speak about) black plays (see also Powers, this volume):

> The act of talking publicly about race and/as performance can create anxiety: a respondent may worry that others will misconstrue her motivations and personal politics when her expressed beliefs do not resemble those of others. . . . It is this anxiety, what cultural anthropologist John Jackson Jr. would describe as a manifestation of "racial paranoia," that confronts most people who have to declare their vision of race and/as performance within a public setting in the post-segregationist, post–civil rights present. Teaching is a form of public disclosure. (Young 2009: xiv)

In the same volume, a teacher further remarks that students too may "approach African-American drama with trepidation, afraid that studying 'black' stuff will prove dangerous or alienating" (Gonzalez 2009: 59). I was certainly aware of those anxieties both when I taught the play and when I presented the paper at the Sawyer conference at Northwestern in 2010 with distinguished African-American scholars in the room.

Basically, I was asking myself, "Who am I to speak on the subject?" (McKay 1998). In making this choice to teach and write on Rita Dove as a black writer, I find myself then in the middle of identity politics.

I am also facing the complex question of what is a black play. In the days of Jim Crow and segregation, W. E. B. Du Bois published this definition:

> The plays of a real Negro theatre must be: 1. About us. That is, they must have plots which reveal real Negro life as it is. 2. By us. That is, they must be written by Negro authors who understand from birth and continual association just what it means to be a Negro today. 3. For us. That is, the theatre must cater primarily to Negro audiences and be supported and sustained by their entertainment and approval. 4. Near us. The theatre must be in a Negro neighborhood near the mass of ordinary Negro people.[8]

The later black power movement of the 1960s had a corollary Black Arts movement that similarly insisted on the need for a Black Theater, for black critics who would understand their work, and for the cultivation of black audiences (Clarke 2005: 1–21; Smethurst 2005; Williams 1985: 3–31). According to Amiri Baraka and others, theater was to be an agent for revolution; black writers should focus on black themes (Baraka 1994 [1971]: 84–5; Jeyifous 1987: 329; Neal 1968: 29 and *passim*; Williams 1985: 17, 19). Though short-lived, this movement left a big legacy (Smethurst speaks of it as "haunting" and "something more than haunting") (Smethurst 2005: 2–4). For instance, in 1996 August Wilson reiterated the need for a black theater, basing his claims on the ground of the Black Power movement (see Rankine, this volume); he rejects color-blind casting as a substitute arguing that

> To mount an all black production of *Death of a Salesman* or any other play conceived for white actors as an investigation of the human condition through the specific of white culture is to deny us our own humanity, our own histeory, and the need to make our own investigations from the cultural ground on which we stand as black Americans. (Wilson 1998: 499)

More recently, that aesthetic has been explicitly rejected by writers like Rita Dove and Suzan-Lori Parks, who says, "*The Iceman Cometh* is a black play. *Angels in America* is a black play and Kushner knows he's a brother. Its all black" (Parks 2005: 580). Of course, Parks here is ironic—what does it mean to say that Kushner, white Jewish radical gay writer, is "a brother"? She is saying that blackness is not about color; is she also saying that there is no such thing as blackness? That strikes me as the possible effect of this statement, and that would be a problem given the racialized nature of our contemporary U.S. society, where prisons and the economic downturn, to name only two examples, clearly represent the racial divide as live and well in the U.S.A.

The earlier Black Arts movement created opportunities but also problems for writers like Dove. Indeed, Dove began by publishing in white rather than black periodicals (Keller 1997: 106). In an interview with Therese Steffen, she says:

> I tried to keep out of the political fray. I was young enough to be able to do that. I shied away from publishing early poems like "Agosta the Winged Man" and "Rasha the Black Dove" because I didn't think I was strong enough to withstand the political fall-out. I didn't want to have to answer questions from Black Arts people like, "Why

are you writing about a white *German* artist?" I waited; I stepped out as a writer later, when things had become more tolerant.[9]

Dove wanted to move away from the context of identity politics, but the earlier generation still had considerable power. In a famous incident, Alice Walker once refused to appear with Dove on a panel because of a poem she had published ("Nigger Song: An Odyssey"), and when Dove wrote to her to explain her attempt to reclaim the word, Walker responded politely but said she should not use "nigger" in front of white people (Ingersoll 2003: xiv–xv). Dove's

> Immediate reaction was: "No one's going to put me in that kind of cage—not whites, not blacks, not even myself. I am trying to make the best poem I possibly can, a poem that will defy whatever nefarious purposes people may want to use it for." (Steffen 2001: 170)

The echo here of art for art's sake is of course what was troubling for any politically driven aesthetic, including that of the Black Arts Movement. The claim of art for art's sake has to face the retort of Du Bois: "All art is propaganda." Which is it?

Not surprisingly, Dove has often been discussed in terms that seem to amount to "not black enough"—she is not angry, or is too interested in the craft of writing.[10] While August Wilson called himself a "race man," Houston Baker says that "Rita Dove is not a 'Race Poet'. It is virtually impossible to imagine her saying in unison with W. E. B. Du Bois: 'I don't give a damn for any art that is not propaganda'" (Baker 1990: 574). Speaking with Dove, Steven Ratiner remarked:

> I heard one poet say, "Of course Dove's poetry can be accepted comfortably by white academic society because she doesn't have the edge, the raw angry passion of a poet like Ai. So her work doesn't threaten the safety of that intellectual distance . . ." (Ratiner 2003: 116)

Dove replied:

> Most of the poems are not easy answers. My feeling, my mission if you will—though I don't usually think of it in those global terms—is to restore individual human fates to the oeuvre. Literary portrayals of women and African Americans have been flat, and since the 60s they've been predictably angry. This stock characterization allows the reader to fall into certain categorical thinking. I want to resist that. I don't want you to think of a particular character simply as "this Black angry person"; I want you to think of him as Joe or Mary or Martin. . . . Now—if you can see this man as an individual, then he cannot be lumped into a group and dismissed.[11]

Dove's aesthetic is her form of politics. She explicitly relates the forms of writing to leaders of the civil rights movement: "We needed a Martin Luther King and we needed a Malcolm X" (Ratiner 2003: 117). A culture of resistance can sustain the thinker who works for reconciliation and the one who adamantly opposes the culture itself. Moreover, as Dove acknowledges, all of these heroes, like Emmett Till, ended up dead. It would seem that Dove's awareness of the failure of heroics affects her writing too, leading her to emphasize ordinary people (Ratiner 2003: 103).

Early race-based analyses assumed the singularity of "the" black community. Reading Toni Morrison was important for Dove; she, like Toni Morrison, had to find a way to write from her experience, which was not urban, low income, or Southern (Cavalieri 2003 [1995]: 146–7; Pereira 2003 [1999]: 160; Taleb-Khyar 2003 [1991]: 86). Morrison and Dove each has a Midwestern heritage, and this cultural orientation is suggestive of non-stereotypical perspectives. Dove has spoken often about resisting cages or single identifications as black or female.[12] She studied in Germany, married a German writer, and learned about race and gender in part through her encounters as a black woman in Germany (Taleb-Khyar 2003: 76). Dove's affiliation with things European has made her suspect to some, as she feared it would. As a result, however, she might have added insight into other identifiers outside of blackness, such as geography and class.

As Dove is aware, class was and is a powerful factor and signifier; indeed she said "partisans of the Black Arts Movement are more class-based than racial. Yet no one dares to say so. Class has to be the next battleground" (Steffen 1997: 112). As others have noted, her class is definitely an important part of her identity and her writing. Dove has often spoken about her upwardly mobile, middle-class upbringing in Akron, Ohio; her father was the first black chemist at Goodyear Rubber, having worked there for years as a janitor; her mother was a homemaker. According to Ratiner: ". . . your family background . . . seems to have given you a very stable base from which to speak, and if your voice is not going to be the one putting the torch to certain old ways, perhaps it is implicating a new ground on which to build something new." Dove agreed on the need for "fire, but . . . more than fire, too" (Ratiner 2003: 117). Being bourgeois does not seem to go with being revolutionary but it can go with rebuilding.

Helen Vendler praised Dove for going beyond blackness, for "knowing that blackness need not be one's central subject, but equally need not be omitted" (Vendler 1994b: 393), and further commented approvingly that the poet refrained from earnestness, a characteristic that Vendler identifies with first-generation black American poets (Vendler 1994b: 394, also in 1994a); Dove's avoidance of earnestness (meaning that Dove does not preach or teach a simple lesson), while praised by Vendler, might also be interpreted as an avoidance of race. Arnold Rampersad gets around that possible problem in this way:

> Instead of an obsession with the theme of race, one finds an eagerness, perhaps even an anxiety, to transcend—if not actually to repudiate—black cultural nationalism in the name of a more inclusive sensibility. (Rampersad 1986: 53)

Given the political, social, and economic problems still facing many African-Americans, it is not, however, necessarily "an obsession" to emphasize blackness.

Dove continues to be irritated by the quantifying of gender and race in her work asserting that she is both a feminist woman and black (Gates 1988: 488; Vendler 1994b). Indeed, Dove is well aware of the need for the militant stance, as we can see from the interview with Malin Pereira (Pereira 2003 [1999]: 160), but she sees it as limited. Is the strategy of avoiding current politics in favor of history or a more discreet form of critique in poetry complacent? Or is Dove just trying to move forward and welcome a new day?

Du Bois hypothesized both an advantage and a disadvantage to "double consciousness," and Dove may represent both aspects with her background. Agreeing with Du Bois, Dove notes that as a black writer

> You must learn to fit into the main culture even while you are not of it. Even if you come from an upwardly mobile middle-class background, you grow up with an awareness of *difference* and a set of cultural values rooted in the Black tradition, so in a certain way you are already bilingual. (Taleb-Khyar 2003: 77)

In her book on Dove, Malin Pereira argues that "Dove indeed writes her way back home, but it is to a home and neighborhood far more cosmopolitan—and an identity far less unified or monolithic—than critics and other readers might have wished" (Pereira 2003: 5). It seems that Rita Dove attempts to present the "racialized subject as a figure with whom all readers identify."[13] Her black middle-class background and European connections give her first-hand experience of and insight into cultural mixing and hybridity.

Oedipus as Model for Dove

Dove's use of Greek tragedy and history in *Darker Face of the Earth* has the same potentially conservative effect as her class and European background do, I would argue.[14] Dove acknowledges many creative influences (Johnsen and Peabody 2003: 24; Taleb-Khyar 2003: 84–5; Vendler 1994b: 491); she resists limitation here as elsewhere. In particular, she refuses to give up the European tradition, laying claim to it as part of her heritage. In fact, she asserts that tragedy specifically is familiar to African-Americans.[15] She refuses to make this claim on the basis of Martin Bernal's argument in *Black Athena* that the Greeks borrowed their myths from Africa (Steffen 1997: 117–18). To her mind, it is unnecessary to go the long way around. The Greek stories are the ones people have heard and lived with. Moreover, Dove claims that the Greek heritage is as much hers as the African—she has never been to Africa, and if she went, it would be as a stranger not as a native (Taleb-Khyar 2003: 80). Of course, Dove is right: she has access to the masterpieces of the humanist tradition. Nonetheless, for many immigrants and upwardly mobile students of color or first-generation college students there remains this troublesome question: How much do we leave behind as we "get educated" and act on aspirations to upward mobility? Does Dove manage to avoid both dogmatism and complicity with racism, or does taking on slavery via Greek myth implicate Dove in the colonizing aspect of the canon?

The Darker Face of the Earth (first published in 1994, revised in 1996 and 2000) takes place in the south from 1820 to 1840; it is based on the Oedipus myth. In the play's prologue, Amalia Jennings, the plantation mistress, is giving birth to a son, the fruit of her liaison with a slave named Hector. She reluctantly agrees to sell the child to save his life. Simultaneously and significantly, a slave named Scylla (the play's Tiresias character) gains prophetic powers. Twenty years later, Amalia buys a new slave named Augustus, who has been highly educated by his former owner and has a reputation for rebelliousness. Of course, he turns out to be Amalia's son, though unrecognized through most of the play. Amalia and Augustus soon enter into a sexual relationship. At the same time, Augustus becomes involved in a slave uprising on the Jennings plantation, and for the cause of freedom, he kills both his biological father and the man he presumes is his father, Amalia's emasculated and star-gazing husband, Louis. Though he has been given the task of killing Amalia as a test of loyalty to the movement, he has difficulty doing so. In the first published version of the play, the revolutionaries kill her and him; in the later edition, she kills herself while a seemingly delirious Augustus is carried out on the shoulders of the revolutionaries. Dove was satisfied with both endings—indeed she says that there is not much difference between them. If he lives, it is a living death, and the audience would be aware in any case that the revolutionaries have misunderstood what has taken place.

It would be possible for a reader or audience member to miss the Oedipus references depending on their classical background (Carlisle 2000: 140–1). Many people, after all, don't have any training in Greek tragedy; the names and plots are quite different. But the playbill at the performance I saw (New York 2006, American Theatre of Actors) made the connection explicit, and other playbills have done so as well (Fig. 28.1). Though Dove disclaims the direct connection (Carlisle 2000: 141), she also made it explicit; in her note on the 2006 playbill, she said this:

> What makes Oedipus a creature to be pitied—what awakens our admiration and finally our awe—comes partly from recognizing, in his unraveling, our own blighted dreams. How would we react if caught in the web of a fate so horrendous, so hurtful in its omnipresent cruelty, that we feel shrouded in eternal damnation? What happens to those with genius and talent and compassion when they are enmeshed in a system of forced labour, forced separations, forced breeding? How can they right themselves, in such a crazed universe, how shall they attempt to prevail against it? (Dove 2006)

Thus, if the audience member read the notes before the play begins, he or she would experience the play in its Sophoclean context.

Whether the audience would get the point or not, Dove has repeatedly said she was drawn to Oedipus because his story addresses those questions "posed by great literature: unanswerable, yet forever asked" (Bellin 2003: 135). She was in Jerusalem rereading Sophocles, she says, and she wondered "why is it so compelling when you know everything that's going to happen at the beginning? You see Oedipus struggling against the bonds of fate that you know he can't overcome" (Dove 2006; Berson 1996). Interested primarily in fate, then, Dove made the leap to slavery:

> I saw the institution of slavery as an allegory for the Greek pantheon, the gods who control everything from the beginning. There was an overriding sense that a slave in this system could not possibly emerge from it whole. (Berson 1996; Wetmore 2003: 129)

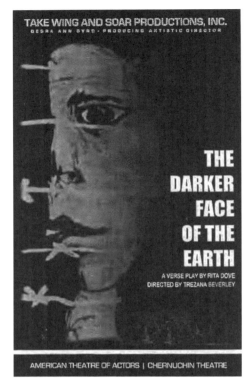

FIG. 28.1 Playbill (cover), from Take Wing And Soar Productions presents Poet Laureate Rita Dove's New American Classic, *The Darker Face of the Earth,* directed by Trezana Beverley.

As is often the case in these modern versions of ancient dramas, however, the very existence of the "original" acts as a form of fate—we know what has to happen because we are aware that it is "an Oedipus" play. Yet authors and directors revise and adapt; thus, in Dove's original version, Augustus died; it was only in production and at the urging of her daughter, that she changed the ending (Pereira 2003: 149).

I fundamentally disagree with Dove about the importance of fate in Sophocles' *Oedipus Tyrannus*; the play rather emphasizes the role of choice within a fated existence. That is, the myth depends on the fatedness of Oedipus' life, but the play shows him as the architect of what happens as a result of the oracle. If there is something compelling about this myth and the play, it is not so much the incest but the question of free will. That might be true with regard to slavery as well (Wetmore 2003: 130–1). Does slavery leave a person any sphere for action?

Dove insists that she was not in any case trying to write a remake of the original, but she takes on other elements from it, using them to address questions she believes are important today. Dove works through the issues of language and knowledge, central to postcoloniality and hybridity (Gilroy 2005; Carlisle 2000). For instance, in a note to the first edition, Dove states that slave language has been standardized for the comprehension of the reader (Dove 1994); she cut that statement in later editions, but it is a useful reminder of the gap in time and the fact that her readers (like herself) are outsiders to the world depicted. She also explicitly represents both European and African knowledge traditions. First of all, it is significant for the plot that Augustus has had an education, which makes him nothing but trouble from the slave owner's point of view.[16] The introduction of his education sparks a conversation between Amalia and the overseer that emphasizes the power dynamic. She says, "I own Augustus Newcastle, and I'll make him serve up" (44).

That education is classical and gives him some status in the slave community, as well. Dove follows the practice of giving slaves mythic names as well as their owners' surnames. Of the slaves, only Augustus knows what the names mean; thus he is distinguished from his peers from the beginning by his knowledge. He seems to have the Adamic power of naming since he explains the classical allusions in their names (Diana, Phebe, etc.). When he says that his name is a king's name, it causes an "uneasy silence" at his arrogance (47–8). He is to some extent westernized. On the basis of his European learning, he is taken to be superior to the other slaves and perhaps even to the mistress. Specifically, Amalia hands him a book she is reading, and says, "Too difficult? No doubt you'd do better with the Greek original—but we are not that cultured a household" (83). His learning makes him an interesting conversationalist and brings him close to his white mistress and mother. In that same scene, however, she circles around him and scrutinizes him—talking about his brains, but looking at his body; she then reminds him that she could have had him flogged and asserts her authority, telling him he can't have an opinion (84). While in Sophocles, Jocasta is the prize that goes with solving the riddle of the sphinx, and while the throne goes along with her, in Dove, the forbidden topic of desire is raised. Though some may find this unconvincing, Dove has made a point of Amalia's dissatisfaction with the white men in her life, specifically her father and her husband Louis (18–20); the attraction she feels is also reminiscent of Strindberg's *Miss Julie*, a rebellious white upper-class woman who seeks out the attentions of her father's servant.

Amalia is insightful enough to know what she can't know—in particular, a slave might hide just how smart he is (83). But as important, Augustus' education itself was not a form of liberation since it was given to him by his owner, who also named him. Nor does it advance him far in the insurgency: he offers to help by reading and writing passes because he knows how to read, but he is told, "that is all for now" (74)—the rebels have other ways of communicating (drums in Haiti, 78, fires in Carolina, 74) (Carlisle 2000). The revolutionaries want him, but they don't perceive themselves as needing his help. They are not dependent on print media. Here we have evidence of the distinction between indigenous and the European modes of communication. There is actually a certain amount of contempt expressed for Augustus; and the leaders of the insurrection rightfully continue to distrust him because of his close relationship to the "big house."

He has another kind of education, as well, also related to his slave status; his former owner took him to distant places. That travel is ethically complicated: as Teiresias/Scylla is quick to point out, his "grand tour" was part of the slave trade. In those travels he learned about the successful Haitian revolution (77–9, cf. Amalia 87–8), which he offers as a model of what the slaves might do. He is overheard by Amalia, who orders that they all work an extra hour, thus showing her power over them and their lack of revolutionary capacity. At the same time, she invites Augustus to the house that evening, showing the contradictory attraction between them. In short, these constructions of canonical gentlemanly knowledge(s) are ambiguous; they implicate him in the structure of domination and win him respect, but they do not necessarily gain him power. I am left questioning what this says about Dove's own position. Does her knowledge of European traditions do the same to and for her? It is quite possible that Dove is identifying across gender with her character, as Goff and Simpson suggest.

Augustus' knowledge is part of the strong African dimension to the play. It opens with a split scene. The slaves are outside, among them Hector, Augustus' father, and Scylla, who gains her prophetic powers at that time (36). She experiences the birth of Augustus in her own body, clutching her stomach when he first cries, then saying, "It's out in the world" (16). As Scylla understands it that is the curse (36–9)—the child of mixed race parentage is out in the world, and the lie about his life and his parentage is also out in the world. Later Scylla recounts the story of that night; she has become a conjure woman, speaks Yoruba, and calls on the deity Eshu Elewa (a form of Eshu Elegba, 54–5) (Carlisle 2000: 139). She expands on what happened:

> The veil was snatched from my eyes—
> And over the hill I saw
> Bad times a-coming. Bad times
> Coming over the hill on mighty horses,
> Horses snorting as they galloped
> Through slave cabin and pillared mansion...
> Like a thin black net
> The curse settled over the land.

The slaves echo her, apparently agreeing; they sing a refrain indicating that the curse has affected "black woman, black man, white woman, white man" (36) (Fig. 28.2).

What is the curse? The opening scene inside "the big house" explains the problem: it is not acceptable for the mistress to sleep with a slave. Though this was known to have happened, historically, it could not be talked about, thus could not be out in the world (Hodes 1997: 1–3). Literature on the subject was censored (Sollors 1997: 4–5), as here Augustus is to be given away and raised as a slave elsewhere, whereas the children of the master were kept, since they were valuable property. The doctor convinces Amalia that she cannot keep her son by pointing out the consequences: "Slaves will begin to speak back, to botch the work and fall ill with mysterious ailments." She won't have any help from "an overseer who knows his mistress is tainted with slave funk," and she won't have any white company: "who will you invite to tea, Amalia—your dashing blackamoor" (23–4). Thus the events, the true story, would have been too subversive of the hegemonic worldview of the ruling power. The only story that can be narrated constructs Amalia as a vengeful wife, not someone who fell in love with a slave who, as she says, played with her as a girl and brought her a single red rose at her wedding (25–6). The love between her and Augustus (if we may call it love) is similarly elided on the narrative level; it is only recognizable on the authorial level.

FIG. 28.2 Scene of the slaves on the Southern plantation, in prayer. Take Wing And Soar Productions presents Poet Laureate Rita Dove's New American Classic, *The Darker Face of the Earth*, directed by Trezana Beverley. ©2006 Hubert Williams.

Dove does not wholeheartedly celebrate the African any more than the European. Scylla's conjuring, though accurate, is not represented as a wonderful sign of a woman's community of healers. Instead her power is morally ambiguous; it terrifies a young slave and seems to urge compliance with authority. Scylla's sayings make Phebe afraid to act and participate in the insurrection ("Guard your footsteps"; "guard your breath" [56]). Augustus mocks the seer (60–1), as Phebe does later, calling Scylla herself the curse (109). In this scene, Augustus is very much the rationalist like his model Oedipus; he depends on science and opposes Scylla in much the same way that Oedipus vilifies Tiresias. Augustus like Oedipus has to learn that the seer does indeed have knowledge. She has intuited the curse of miscegenation that forbids this life to flourish; but the prophecy will be fulfilled by a combination of white power and the force of the insurrection. There is nothing without contradiction here, no easy answer.

African knowledge and Africa are also represented by Hector, Augustus' biological father. Hector was not born in slavery; he came from Africa and is the only character in addition to Scylla to speak an African language. The loss of that heritage is part of the slaves' necessary and oppressive acculturation into the new world they inhabit. Hector has gone from being a slave, to being the chosen partner of the mistress, to being a creature of the margins. The theft (social death) of his child has driven him from the human community into the swamp, where he catches snakes to kill them. The stage directions indicate that in the present he is both more African than he was before, and wilder (52).

When Augustus kills Hector to prevent him from discovering the insurrection, he is not only killing the father, but he seems to be disavowing that paternal lineage and its Afrocentrism. This echoes his treatment of Scylla. Augustus is somewhat successful, since we are told that Hector's words are scattered to the wind (136). This image can suggest power, however, if in being scattered they will have spawned other words as seed does when scattered abroad.

At the end of the play, however, Augusts speaks the same African words that Hector and Scylla have spoken (160); he thus seems to have learned that he is neither European nor free, and that Scylla was right. In terms of race categories, he also does not learn definitively that he *is* African pure and simple. There is no single state of being for him. Neither the African nor the European is a satisfactory solution. He and Amalia are both crushed, as Dove said in one set of program notes (Dove 2006).

The play defies a straightforward postcolonial or anti-colonial, black-centered antiwhite reading. Dove does not build unqualified sympathy for the insurrection; her presentation of them makes them a coercive force. Like other revolutionary groups, they operate on the basis of threats not of trust. When one man questions the need for murder, he is intimidated. People are not free to leave the group (70–1). What keeps Augustus trapped is not only slavery but also the hatred required by the violence of the liberation movement that responds to the violence of the slave system. The uprising appears to be successful; the house is in flames, and the masters are dead. And what of Augustus? The ending seems ironic no matter which version we follow. Sometimes he is dead, as in the first edition (1994). In the published second edition, he is lionized by his confreres when, seeing Amalia dead by suicide, they mistakenly assume he has killed her. In the production I saw in New York (2006), he was carried out in a pose reminiscent of Christ on the cross; that seems ironic as well, since Augustus is the savior of nothing. And indeed we know that the insurrection will fail in the long run because this is only 1840.

Clearly then, Dove refuses to exclude European or the African knowledge; she problematizes both. Similarly she refuses to give up one part of her identity in favor of another. She rejects the dichotomy between being black and being a feminist woman; she creates many important female characters in the play and renders gender norms almost as much of a problem as racial norms. Most obvious and most important is the case of Amalia, the barely recognizable Jocasta character. In this version, unlike Sophocles', the woman's desire is very much at stake. While Jocasta is merely the prize awarded to Oedipus for his solving the riddle of the sphinx, Amalia is attracted first to Hector (21–2), and then to her son (see above). In addition, Dove strives to make Amalia sympathetic at first; she is represented as being affectionate to her infant son and resists giving him up. She is forced to comply with the power structure by the doctor. Moreover, from the beginning of the play, her gender role is at issue. She is more like her father, the slaves say, so she won't have her mother's problems in childbirth (15); she complains to the doctor about her inconsistent upbringing—her father brought her up to "calculate inventory, but he expected his slippers darned come evening! And when I refused, off I went—to finishing school and the Charleston society balls" (20, cf. *Miss Julie* again).

These references in the prologue are designed to make her at least an understandable owning-class white woman, unusual in a play about slavery written by an African-American woman, to say the least. But the slave chorus also tells us that Amalia has changed; by the time Augustus arrives as a 20-year-old, she has become masculine, replete with riding habit and whip, and the slaves say she is a worse master than her father. The slave Alexander believes it is the loss of her baby that changed her; the others dispute that interpretation (34). In killing or abandoning her child, like Medea, she destroyed something soft in her (and continues Louis's downward spiral into effeminacy and/or incompetence). That change reverses when she welcomes Augustus into her life. In an early scene, she wants the Overseer to be harder on the slaves, while toward the end, she does not want the slaves to work late to harvest the crop, which is in danger, because she wants to see Augustus. Thus love has a political/economic effect; to give another turn to the screw, Augustus then replies that they have to get the crop in.

The play makes it clear that Amalia too is trapped in her gender-race role (Wetmore 2003); she plays at being Augustus' equal and would like to deny that he is a "nigger" or that she is "missy" (127), but Augustus refuses her that daydream and reminds her that that is her role. As the final scene between them unfolds, he stays with her, not answering the call from the revolutionaries. Thus, he picks the personal over the political. She fantasizes that they can create a little time and space for themselves, but that is a fairy tale like the one she has been reading. There is no happy ending possible for them because of the institution of slavery and miscegenation laws—the incest seems almost immaterial in comparison (Fig. 28.3). In Dove's reworking of the myth, the sexual and racial, the individual and the collective are interwoven in the wake of slavery. Dove does not make the whites the villains, and the slaves all virtuous; the big "bad guy" is the system of slave labor and racist divisions, which cripple Amalia as well as Augustus (Dove 2006; Pereira 2003: 151). Is she then failing her race, as some would say, or is she bravely preparing the ground for the future?

I want to go back to Du Bois once more: he famously said that the color line was the problem of the twentieth century; in the twenty-first century, with Barack Obama as President, the color line is still here but has different manifestations. In this play Dove shows the roots of our racial present where mixture, shades of brown not simply black and white, must be accounted for. Accurately acknowledging those subtleties, however, may make it difficult to be definitive and to take action as a collective. Are we acting as blacks, as browns, as whites, when in fact those categories are slowly being effaced? Because of the emphasis on mixture, Dove does not seem to take a strong stand—she uses history and offers only critique. Postmodernism and hybridity may not make good platforms for activism, but it is necessary to recognize that all of us can have conflicted loyalties that make for ethical complexity.

To bring this back to my opening questions, and the many questions that I have posed throughout this chapter, I would say that Dove lays claim to Classics, asserting her right to membership in this intellectual western community, but that she is not a slave to the tradition. Indeed, the play addresses history and makes us take seriously the impact of

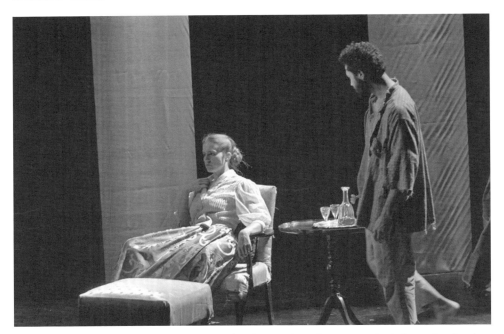

FIG. 28.3 Augustus (Oedipus) and Amalia (Jocasta), Take Wing And Soar Productions presents Poet Laureate Rita Dove's New American Classic, *The Darker Face of the Earth*, directed by Trezana Beverley. ©2006 Hubert Williams.

slavery on *all* by developing the white woman Amalia as a character and asking what losses she sustained. If this makes it seem that Dove is soft on racism, it nonetheless makes her realistic: both black and white have been twisted by the legacy of slavery, indeed by the very categories of black and white. Though the appeal of the Classics to audiences may stem from present-day conservatism, Dove's usage is not reactionary. Dove does not *ignore* race in her desire for transcendence; she rather works through it.

Because Dove has been so often interviewed, we have many statements from her about her goals, and that is part of the problem I have in writing about her work. On the one hand, she says she was initially interested in Oedipus and wanted to address the eternal questions of great literature. In interviews, she simultaneously talks about our difficulty with racial division;[17] she says that she is trying to blur the line and to acknowledge the "others inside" (Pereira 2003: 173). Dove repeatedly rejects the traditional idea of the propagandistic play; she instead offers a new view of political art. She focuses on the individual, but she believes that

> Insisting upon ... individuality is ultimately a political act, and to my mind, this is one of the fundamental principles a writer has to uphold, along with a warning: don't be swallowed up. Don't be swallowed up. (Taleb-Khyar 2003: 83)

Though when I taught the play, I did not find her approach satisfying because she did not take a clear enough position, and racial politics on campus seemed to demand more decisiveness, I now find Dove's plea that we "not be swallowed up" very appealing. It can lead us to think about how to keep one's integrity while acting in a group. Although her references to Greek mythology, like her emphasis on individualism and universalism, may be class based; and although her writing appeals primarily to a select group of educated middle-class whites and African-Americans, that is an important audience, too. In the end, I believe that we still need writers to do political theater that takes a stand while avoiding preachiness before we will be in the place where we can leave our baggage behind. But we don't need all artists to adopt the same style, or to fight colonialism and racism in the way that activists and essayists do. In the end, I would agree with Dove, who said that we need both Malcolms and Martins.

Notes

1. Portions of this chapter have been previously published in *Logeion* 1 (November 2011). The more general problematic of which it is a part also frames other papers, such as "The Expansion of Tragedy as critique" (2013). It began its life at a conference of the Network on Ancient and Modern Imperialisms (November 2007) and was further developed at the Sawyer Seminar Series, Northwestern University. I am indebted to the organizers of both conferences for their interest in and support for this work. Special thanks go to Patrice Rankine for wonderful editorial work.
2. Boal 1979; Bada (2000: 26) argues that in their use of Greek myth "Walcott and Soyinka emphasise the need for individual self-discovery and offer a humanistic, syncretic and crosscultural vision capable of transcending stultifying conventional values and enforced discourses."
3. See also, to cite only a few, Goff 2005; Hardwick 2004; Hardwick and Stray 2008.
4. See essays in Goff 2005, Hardwick and Gillespie 2007, and Goff and Simpson 2007.
5. Paying attention to theater can add significantly to postcolonial theory since in production words are embodied, bringing the abstract issues down to earth, and challenging them. As Helen Gilbert (1999: 2) puts it, "Implicitly and sometimes explicitly, the nature of the theatrical works discussed questions the adequacy of current theoretical concepts to fully account for complex signifying systems and receptions processes."
6. Goff and Simpson 2007: 4; see also Goff 2005: 21.
7. Dove has been extensively interviewed and has eloquently stated her view of her intentions; I will draw on these interviews while at the same time questioning these stated goals.
8. Quoted in Young 2009: xv.
9. Steffen 1997: 108, 112; see also Pereira 2003 [1999]: 159; Ingersoll 2003: 188.
10. See, among others, Van Dyne 1999: esp. 68–9.
11. Ratiner 2003: 116–17; cf. Taleb-Khyar 2003: 83.
12. See, for instance, the interview with Susan Swartwout (2003: 59); also Taleb-Khyar 2003: 81.
13. Keller 1997: 108–9, citing Baker.
14. The main contribution of this chapter is in my perspective from teaching Dove. Analyses of the play that anticipate my own include Wetmore 2003, Goff and Simpson 2007, Cook and Tatum 2010, and Rankine 2013. The depth and breath of these analyses are testimony to the interest that the play creates.
15. On the chorus, see McDowell 2003 [2000]: 175.
16. Dove 1996: 43–4. Future references to the play will be to this edition and made in the text.
17. e.g., Pereira 2003: 172–3.

REFERENCES

Ashcroft, B., G. Griffiths, and H. Tiffin (1989), *The Empire Writes Back: Theory and Practice in Post-Colonial Literatures*. London.
Bada, V. (2000), "Cross-Cultural Dialogues with Greek Classics: Walcot's 'The Odyssey' and Soyinka's The Bacchae of *Euripides*," *Ariel* 31, 7–28.
Baker, H. (1990), "Review of Grace Notes," *Black American Literature Forum* 574–7.
Baraka, A. (1994 [1971]), "What is Black Theater" with M. Coleman, in *Conversations with Amiri Baraka*. Jackson, MS.
Bellin, S. (2003 [1993]), "Tricking the Muse by Taking Out the Trash," in E. G. Ingersoll ed., *Conversations with Rita Dove*. Jackson, MS, 121–35.
Berson, M. (1996), "Bonds of Fate: An Interview with the Playwright," *American Theatre* 9, 34.
Boal, A. (1979), *Theater of the Oppressed*. Trans. C. A. and M.-O. L. McBride. New York.
Brecht, B. (1964), *Brecht on Theatre: The Development of an Aesthetic*. Ed. and trans. J. Willett. London.
Carlisle, T. (2000), "Reading the Scars: Rita Dove's 'The Darker Face of the Earth,'" *African American Review* 34, 135–50.
Cavalieri, G. (2003 [1995]), "Brushed by an Angel's Wings," in E. G. Ingersoll ed., *Conversations with Rita Dove*. Jackson, MS, 136–47.
Clarke, C. (2005), *"After Mecca": Women Poets and the Black Arts Movement*. New Brunswick, NJ.
Cook, W. and J. Tatum (2010), *African American Writers and Classical Tradition*. Chicago.
Dove, R. (1994), *The Darker Face of the Earth: A Verse Play in Fourteen Scenes*. Ashland, OR.
Dove, R. (1996), *The Darker Face of the Earth*, 2nd edn. Ashland, OR.
Dove, R. (2006), "Author Notes," Take Wing and Soar Productions, *The Darker Face of the Earth*.
Du Bois, W. E. B. (1926), "Krigwa Players Little Negro Theatre: The Story of a Little Theatre Movement," *The Crisis*, 134.
Du Bois, W. E. B. (1903 [2007]), *The Souls of Black Folk*. Oxford.
Gates, H. L., Jr. (1988), *The Signifying Monkey: A Theory of Afro-American Literary Criticism*. New York.
Gilbert, H. (ed. 1999), *(Post)Colonial Stages: Critical and Creative Views on Drama, Theatre and Performance*. Hebden Bridge.
Gilroy, P. (2005), *Postcolonial Melancholia*. New York.
Goff, B. (2005), *Classics and Colonialism*. London.
Goff, B. and M. Simpson (2007), *Crossroads in the Black Aegean: Oedipus, Antigone, and Dramas of the African Diaspora*. Oxford.
Gonzalez, A. (2009), "Diversifying African American Drama," *Theatre Topics: Black Plays* 19, 59–66.
Hall, E. (2004), "Introduction," in E. Hall, F. Macintosh, and A. Wrigley eds., *Dionysus since 69: Greek Tragedy at the Dawn of the Third Millennium*. Oxford, 1–41.
Hardwick, L. (2000), *Translating Words, Translating Cultures*. London.
Hardwick, L. (2004), "Shards and Suckers: Modern Receptions of Homer," in R. Fowler ed., *The Cambridge Companion to Homer*. Cambridge, 344–62.
Hardwick, L. (2007), "Introduction," in L. Hardwick and C. Gillespie eds., *Classics in Post-Colonial Worlds*. Oxford, 1–11.
Hardwick, L. and C. Gillespie (eds. 2007), *Classics in Post-Colonial Worlds*. Oxford.
Hardwick, L. and C. Stray (eds. 2008), "Introduction," in *A Companion to Classical Reception*. Oxford, 1–10.
Hodes, M. (1997), *White Women, Black Men: Illicit Sex in the 19th-Century South*. New Haven.
Ingersoll, E. G. (ed. 2003), *Conversations with Rita Dove*. Jackson, MS.

Jeyifous, A. (1987), "Black Critics on Black Theatre in America," in E. Hill ed., *The Theatre of Black Americans*. New York, 327–35.

Johnsen, G. and R. Peabody (2003 [1985]), "A Cage of Sound," in E. G. Ingersoll ed., *Conversations with Rita Dove*. Jackson, MS, 15–37.

Keller, L. (1997), *Forms of Expansion: Recent Long Poems by Women*. Chicago.

McDowell, R. (2003 [2000]), "Language is Not Enough," in E. G. Ingersoll ed., *Conversations with Rita Dove*. Jackson, MS, 174–9.

McKay, N. (1998), "Naming the Problem That Led to the Question," *Who Shall Teach African*, 369.

Malcolm X (1963), "A Summing Up: Louis Lomax Interviews Malcolm X," <teachingamericanhistory.org>.

Neal, L. (1968), "The Black Arts Movement," *TDR: The Drama Review* 12, 28–39.

Parks, S. (2005), "New Black Math," *Theatre Journal* 57, 576–83.

Pereira, M. (1999), "Interview with Rita Dove," *Contemporary Literature* 40, 182–213.

Pereira, M. (2003), *Rita Dove's Cosmopolitanism*. Chicago.

Rabinowitz, N. (2008), "The Medea Project for Incarcerated Women: Liberating Medea," *Syllecta classica* 19, 237–54.

Rabinowitz, N. (2013), "Ancient Myth and Feminist Politics: The Medea Project and San Francisco Women's Prisons," in B. Gold, D. Lateiner, and J. Perkins eds., *Roman Literature, Gender and Reception: Domina illustris*. London, 267–83.

Rampersad, A. (1986), "The Poems of Rita Dove," *Callaloo* 26, 52–60.

Rankine, P. (2013), *Aristotle and Black Drama: A Theater of Civil Disobedience*. Waco, TX.

Ratiner, S. (2003), "A Chorus of Voices," in E. G. Ingersoll ed., *Conversations with Rita Dove*. Jackson, MS, 103–20.

Schein, S. (2008), "'Our Debt to Greece and Rome': Canon, Class and Ideology," in L. Hardwick and C. Stray eds., *A Companion to Classical Reception*. Oxford, 75–85.

Smethurst, J. E. (2005), *The Black Arts Movement: Literary Nationalism in the 1960s and 1970s*. Chapel Hill, NC.

Sollors, W. (1997), *Neither Black nor White Yet Both*. Oxford.

Steffen, T. (1997), "The Darker Face: A Conversation with Rita Dove," *Transition* 74, 104–23.

Steffen, T. (2001), *Crossing Color: Transcultural Space and Place in Rita Dove's Poetry, Fiction, and Drama*. Oxford.

Swartwout, S. (2003 [1989]), "Language Is More Clay Than Stone," in E. G. Ingersoll ed., *Conversations with Rita Dove*. Jackson, MS, 53–61.

Taleb-Khyar, M. (2003 [1991]), "Gifts to Be Earned," in E. G. Ingersoll ed., *Conversations with Rita Dove*. Jackson, MS, 74–87.

Van Dyne, S. (1999), "Siting the Poet: Rita Dove's Refiguring of Traditions," in J. Brogan and C. Candelaria eds., *Women Poets of the Americas: Toward a Pan-American Gathering*. Notre Dame, IN.

Vendler, H. (1994a), "Blackness and Beyond Blackness," *Times Literary Supplement* (February 18), 11–13.

Vendler, H. (1994b), "Rita Dove: Identity Markers," *Callaloo* 17, 381–98.

Wetmore, K. (2003), *Black Dionysus: Greek Tragedy and African American Theatre*. Jefferson, NC.

Williams, M. (1985), *Black Theatre in the 1960s and 1970s*. Westport, CT.

Wilson, A. (1998), "The Ground on which I Stand," *Callaloo* 20, 493–503.

Young, H. (2009), "Introduction," in *Theatre Topics: Teaching African American Plays* 19, xiii–xviii.

CHAPTER 29

THE POWER OF MEDEA'S SISTERHOOD

Democracy on the Margins in Cherríe Moraga's The Hungry Woman: A Mexican Medea

KATIE BILLOTTE

In March 1969 in Denver, Colorado, a group of Mexican-American young people gathered together at an event dubbed the First National Chicano Liberation Youth Conference. The conference had been organized by Denver native and former lightweight boxing champion Rodolfo "Corky" Gonzales in the wake of student walk-outs in East Los Angeles and Denver the previous year. The most enduring product of the gathering would be the adoption of a manifesto whose spirit, if not content, would guide the future of Chicano activism: *El Plan Espiritual de Aztlán*.

While Cherríe Moraga's *The Hungry Woman: A Mexican Medea* would not be performed until 26 years later, March of 1969 and the Chicano Movement inform every aspect of the play. Set in a dystopian early twenty-first century in which the United States has been "balkanized" by an ethnic civil war, *The Hungry Woman* is a theatrical depiction of the movement's promises and failures taken to their *ad absurdum* conclusions. In the play, roughly half of the United States has seceded from the union and formed smaller ethnic states,

> In order to put a halt to its [the United States'] relentless political and economic expansion, as well as the Euro-American cultural domination of all societal fetters including language, religion, family and trial structures, ethics, art, and more. (Moraga 2001: 2)

In the southwestern United States, *Mestizo* and indigenous people have created Aztlán as a real and sovereign state, the highest aspiration of *El Plan* and of mid-twentieth-century activists.

Despite the revolutionary zeal which created these new states in Moraga's play, and the radical ideology upon which they were founded, within a few years these fledgling nations experience counter-revolutions that establish, or rather re-establish, gender hierarchies and heteronormativity, as well as their own rebranded forms of race-based domination. The play begins several years after these counter-revolutions in the ruins of Phoenix, Arizona, now a crumbling city on the border between what remains of the U.S.A. and the Chicano homeland. Importantly, Medea's home is neither part of Aztlán nor of the United States, but rather located in a physical and psychic no man's land reserved for those who have been marginalized by both nations. Medea, who had once served as a leader among Chicano revolutionaries, is exiled there along with Luna her female lover as a consequence of their relationship. Her son Chac-mool has been allowed to come with her, as has her ageing grandmother, Mama Sal. The chorus is comprised of four women warriors—who in accordance with Aztec mythology have died in childbirth and serve also as a convenient reminder of the Euripidean Medea's assertion that she would rather stand before men in battle three times than give birth to a single child (Euripides, *Medea* 250–1). The central action of the play revolves around the arrival of Medea's ex-husband Jasón, who has come to take her son with him to Aztlán since the boy is quickly approaching manhood. Moreover, Jasón (who is, conveniently, Aztlán's Minister of Culture) is about to be remarried to a much younger woman who is of Apache descent (unlike the *mestiza* Medea). Though Chac-mool is initially hesitant to join his father, he ultimately decides to leave Medea for Aztlán. Medea, then, is driven to filicide not principally by her desire to punish Jasón, but by a longing to prevent her son from becoming a masculine enforcer of the patriarchal order. The scenes related to Jasón's return and Chac-mool's murder occur as a flashback, recalled by Medea and her various visitors as she sits in a psychiatric ward following the murder. The device gives the play a dream-like feel and plays with the flexibility of time as the present of an imagined future reflects upon its past.

Beyond being a fascinating dramatic device, Moraga's toying with time is a product of the cultural-historical moment which created the play. *The Hungry Woman: A Mexican Medea*, which was written as a commission of the Berkeley Repertory Theatre in 1995, is a product of a self-reflective time in Chicano intellectual life; the socio-cultural landscape of *The Hungry Woman*'s imagined future is deeply invested in a conversation about the movement in an era when the movement had already largely ended. The extent to which the play is rooted in a historical moment is evidenced by the fact that in subsequent productions of the play (which have been rather frequent), deviations from the published script have often been made to reflect upon current events and social climate. For example, when the Stanford University Drama Department produced the play in May 2005, with Cherríe Moraga co-directing with Adelina Anthony (the director of the play in Los Angeles in 2002), a voiceover describes September 11, 2001 as when "the giant twin *pipis* fell and everyone went to bed with the flag."[1]

Yet even when contemporary adaptations are made, the majority of the attention of the play is centered upon issues of oppression and marginalization within the Chicano Movement. In this, *The Hungry Woman* is part of a large conversation about, and reflection upon, the movement. Perhaps not surprisingly, much of this dialogue on the internal dynamics of power and privilege within the Chicano Movement did not occur until after its zenith and it is only in the early to mid-1990s that we see the appearance of a significant body of artistic and scholarly work concerned specifically with sexism and homophobia within the movement. This same body of literature was also more likely to problematize the question of race within the Chicano Movement.

This conversation was of particular importance to Moraga who, as a lesbian, not to mention the daughter of an Anglo-American father, fell outside many of the parameters of identity set by the Chicano Movement. It is therefore not surprising that these issues were already at play in Moraga's work before *The Hungry Woman*. The most obvious example of these themes in Moraga's prior work is her 1993 essay, "Queer Aztlán: The Re-Formation of the Chicano Tribe." This article will explore the connection between the two pieces and their mutual relationship to self-reflective critiques of the Chicano Movement, with the wider aim of addressing a specific instance of the appropriation of Greek drama as a tool of radical discourse in modern America.

A sense of disappointment with movements dedicated to radical struggles against oppression is most certainly not confined to the Chicano Movement, but the rhetoric of the Chicano Movement might have contributed to a greater acuteness of that disappointment. A prime example of this is the previously mentioned manifesto created at the First National Chicano Liberation Youth Conference, *El Plan Espiritual de Aztlán*. A spiritual plan for Aztlán might in fact be a little redundant as Aztlán is a mythical homeland (the fabled origin point of the Nauha people of Meso-America), but its invocation is a powerful one. The Nauha are regarded as the ancestors of the Aztec and, as such, at least one of the ancestral people of modern Mexicans. Regardless of the finer points of historical accuracy, the appeal to Aztlán in the manifesto was an important symbolic gesture that framed Mexican-Americans as the indigenous inhabitants of the southwestern United States and called upon Chicanos to reclaim this native soil, if not as a geographic reality, then at least as an emotional one that could impact concrete political outcomes. Central to these desired outcomes was the hope that Mexican-Americans would emerge from the margins of mainstream, "Anglo"-American society and achieve self-determination.

The emphasis of the Chicano Movement on self-determination for Chicanos born of the reality of a Chicano nation did not necessarily result in an inclusive and democratic community within the Chicano Movement itself, nor did it always create borders wide enough to encompass all those who might have felt themselves members of *La Raza* (the People). As is often the case within movements seeking radical social change, the rhetoric of democracy and equality did not always result in the materialization of these principles within the movement's practice. Sexism within the civil rights movement and classism within Second Wave feminism are two well-documented cases of this. An exploration of the ways in which oppressed people seek to oppress one another is perhaps one of the most illuminating ways in which to explore the dynamics of oppression at large. Racism, misogyny, homophobia, and classism do not disappear under the activist banner; moreover, that very banner can serve as an authoritative means by which to silence dissent within the ranks of a movement to any kind of oppression within it.

Ultimately, questions about marginalization and oppression are really questions about belonging. This is not just in an anthropological sense of the creation of "in-groups" and "out-groups," rather it is about fundamental issues of what membership cards of identity we all hold and to what exactly that (or those) membership(s) entitle each of us. The question as to whether one belongs to a particular people is clearly central to Moraga with respect to the Chicano Movement; as she openly admits that her membership in the Chicano community was not immediately apparent, even to her. In "Queer Aztlán" Moraga explains that, while she recognized herself in the Chicano Movement, in its heyday she did not feel as though she could participate, and thus her political awakening came through her lesbian identity, not her Chicano one:

> My real politicization began, not through the Chicano Movement, but through the bold recognition of my lesbianism. Coming to terms with that fact meant the radical re-structuring of everything I thought I held sacred ... That was twenty years ago. In those twenty years I traversed territory that extends well beyond the ten-minute trip between East Los Angeles and San Gabriel. In those twenty years, I experienced the racism of the Women's Movement, the elitism of the Gay and Lesbian Movement, the homophobia and sexism of the Chicano Movement, and the benign cultural imperialism of the Latin American Solidarity Movement. (Moraga 2004: 225)

Moraga's early sense of alienation from the Chicano Movement is not surprising given the character of the movement in its early years. While a Mexican-American civil rights movement had been visible since the end of World War II, the more radical Chicano Movement was much more the product of the student revolutions of 1968 than of this earlier struggle for the civil liberties of Mexican-Americans. In 1968, inspired by student protests around the globe, Chicano high school students in East Los Angeles, California, and Denver, Colorado, staged a series of walk-outs to protest the poor quality of education being provided in majority Mexican-American neighborhoods. The next year, as mentioned above, the First National Chicano Liberation Youth Conference convened in Denver, Colorado.

El Plan Espiritual de Aztlán was the most concrete and enduring legacy of the conference and has subsequently served as the manifesto for the Chicano Movement. One of the most obvious differences between the Chicano Movement and prior movements aimed at gaining civil rights for Mexican-Americans was the emphasis which the latter placed on Mexicans' indigenous heritage. The emphasis is clear in the preamble of *El Plan*, which reads:

> In the spirit of a new people that is conscious not only of its proud historical heritage but also of the brutal "gringo" invasion of our territories, *we*, the Chicano inhabitants and civilizers of the northern land of Aztlán from whence came our forefathers, reclaiming the land of their birth and consecrating the determination of our people

of the sun, *declare* that the call of our blood is our power, our responsibility, and our inevitable destiny.

We are free and sovereign to determine those tasks which are justly called for by our house, our land, the sweat of our brows, and by our hearts. Aztlán belongs to those who plant the seeds, water the fields, and gather the crops and not to the foreign Europeans. We do not recognize capricious frontiers on the bronze continent.

Brotherhood unites us, and love for our brothers makes us a people whose time has come and who struggles against the foreigner "gabacho" who exploits our riches and destroys our culture. With our heart in our hands and our hands in the soil, we declare the independence of our mestizo nation. We are a bronze people with a bronze culture. Before the world, before all of North America, before all our brothers in the bronze continent, we are a nation, we are a union of free pueblos, we are Aztlán.[2]

This was radically different from earlier self-constructions of Mexican and Mexican-American identity which stressed the Spanish/European heritage of Mexican people. This shifting position was largely the product of the changing racial climate of the era. The Chicano Movement, after all, owed much to Black Nationalism and to the activities of the American Indian Movement. While once Mexican-Americans had argued for their racial equality by stressing their "whiteness," Chicanos embraced the non-European parts of their heritage and in doing so highlighted the ways in which their racial oppression was linked to other instances of American racism. Furthermore, by claiming an indigenous heritage, Chicanos were able to position themselves as an internally colonized community within the United States and, as such, gain the momentum of anti-colonialist and anti-imperial rhetoric. Finally, by highlighting the indigenous heritage of the Chicano Movement, Chicanos gained access to the image of the Aztec warrior and other images of native strength and independence (Gutiérrez 1993: 46).

There were, of course, less positive consequences of this shift in racial self-construction as well. The most obvious is the fact that by embracing their indigenous heritage and distancing themselves from their European one, the Chicano Movement was also undermining the *mestiza* identity of Mexican people. This had the effect of alienating many people of more recent mixed ancestry, who although they may have had one white parent had suffered the ill effects of racial discrimination, particularly in a United States where ideas about race were pervasively influenced by the "one-drop" principles that had governed the racial identification of African-Americans. This sense of racial alienation certainly held true for Moraga:

At the height of the Chicano Movement in 1968, I was a closeted, lightskinned *(sic)*, mixed-blood Mexican-American, disguised in my father's English last name . . . Although I could not express how at the time, I knew I had a place in that Movement . . . What I didn't know then was that it would take me another ten years to fully traverse that ten-minute drive and to bring all the parts of me—Chicano, lesbiana, halfbreed *(sic)*, and poets—to the revolution, wherever it was. (Moraga 2004: 225)

This distrust of *mestiza* heritage had deep roots in the mythic history of Mexico, which tells of the birth of the Mexican people in a child born from the union of the conqueror Hernán Cortes and the Nahua woman known as Doña Marina or La Malinche. This historical figure has become intermingled with the Aztec goddess Cihuacoatl as well as the very Mexican mythic figure of La Llorona (The Weeping Woman) and has taken on a mythic proportion all her own. Like La Llorona and la Virgen de Guadalupe, La Malinche still looms large in the Mexican imagination and is a significant figure in Mexico's rather large pantheon of mythic mothers. Like her counterparts, La Malinche is an ambiguous figure intimately shaped by ideas about motherhood, virginity, and other aspects of female sexuality. She is at once the mother of the Mexican people and the betrayer of the Aztec. She is in her latter role also *La Chingada*, the Fucked-one, a title that points to how deeply her betrayal of her people is linked to perceived uncontrollability of female sexuality. Perhaps most importantly of all, her continued stigmatization has influenced the lives of Mexican/Chicana women who can be labeled as *malanchista* for any perceived betrayal of "their men." This is particularly true in the context of the Chicano Movement where, as in many contexts, issues of racial oppression and gender were intimately linked:

> Since so much of the ethnic militancy that Chicanos articulated was profoundly influenced by Black Nationalism, it is important to recall one of the truly poignant insights in the *Autobiography of Malcolm X*. Reciting the psychic violence that racism and discrimination had wreaked on African Americans, Malcolm X noted that the most profound had been the emasculation of black men. In the eyes of white America blacks were not deemed men. Thus whatever else the Black Power movement was, it was also about the cultural assertion of masculinity by young radical men. (Gutiérrez 1993: 45)

This reality was particularly evident in glorification of the traditional *familia* as the natural foundation for the Chicano community. This ideology, by extension, justified and even celebrated *machismo* as a central value of Chicano culture and rationalized the relegation of women to subservient roles within the movement itself, where they were "denied leadership roles and were asked to perform only the most traditional stereotypic roles—cleaning up, making coffee, executing the orders men gave, and servicing their needs" (Gutiérrez 1993: 47).

If, by focusing on *la familia* and glorifying *machismo*, the Chicano Movement was an uncomfortable and unwelcoming place for Chicana women, then it was an utterly hostile place for gay men and lesbians, who often found themselves excluded by homophobia from the Chicano community and by racism from the emerging gay community. Proscribed by the Catholic Church, excluded from *la familia*, and inconsistent with the image of the *macho* Chicano man and his loyal *mujer*, gay men and lesbians often found themselves not just ignored by their fellow Chicanos, but actively demonized as "colonized" traitors to *La Raza*, a queer *malanchina*.

It is not insignificant that Cherríe Moraga could be seen as outside of *Chicanidad* at all three major points of contention. Her engagement with Aztlán is therefore a much more complicated one than that of a heterosexual, racially "pure" man. For the dream of Aztlán to have meaning for Moraga and others similarly excluded, it must be reformed. This "reformation" of Aztlán is exactly what she attempts in the "Queer Aztlán" essay, written in the early 1990s during a period when the active Chicano Movement had long since ended, but at the zenith of the Queer Nation Movement as well as ACT-UP AIDS activism. In that historical moment, Moraga was able to recognize freely the shortcomings of the Chicano Movement as well as *el movimento*'s connection to other forms of progressive crusading even if the Chicano Movement had worked actively to exclude those benefiting from these other movements:

> What was right about Chicano Nationalism was its commitment to preserving the integrity of the Chicano people. A generation ago, there were cultural, economic, and political programs to develop Chicano consciousness, autonomy, and self-determination. What was wrong about Chicano Nationalism was its institutionalized heterosexism, its inbred machismo, and its lack of a cohesive national political strategy. Over the years, I have witnessed plenty of progressive nationalisms: Chicano nationalism, Black nationalism, Puerto Rican Independence (still viable as evidenced in the recent mass protest on the Island against the establishment of English as an official language), the "Lesbian Nation" and its lesbian separatist movement, and, of course, the most recent "Queer Nation." What I admired about each was its righteous radicalism, its unabashed anti-assimilationism *(sic)*, and its *rebeldia*. I recognize the dangers of nationalism as a strategy for political change. Its tendency toward separatism can run dangerously close to biological determinism and a kind of fascism. (Moraga 2004: 227)

Moraga's unique position in relationship to both the Queer Movement and the Chicano Movement allow her to articulate the difficulties inherent in each, as well as to rightly honor their efforts to give voice and centrality to positions and people historically silenced and marginalized. In "Queer Aztlán," Moraga envisions an Aztlán, a mythical homeland, where she and others might be free of the twin evils of racism and homophobia, and she calls for a progressive nationalism built on democratic principles which destroy any attempts at marginalizing any group. Additionally she posits that the experience of queer people can bring about this "wiser revolution":

> If women's bodies and those of men and women who transgress their gender roles have been historically regarded as territories to be conquered, they are also territories to be liberated. Feminism has taught us this. The nationalism I seek is one that decolonizes the brown and female body as it decolonizes the brown and female earth. It is a new nationalism in which la Chicana Indigena stands at the center, and heterosexism and homophobia are no longer the cultural order of the day. I cling to the word "nation" because without the specific naming of the nation, the nation will be lost (as when feminism is reduced to humanism, the woman is subsumed). Let us retain our radical naming but expand it to meet a broader and wiser revolution. (Moraga 2004: 227)

It is the consequences of a revolution that is not "broader and wiser" which Moraga explores in *The Hungry Woman*.

The choice of *Medea* as inspiration for *The Hungry Woman* is closely linked to the wider political goals of the play and is absolutely inseparable from the parallels which can be drawn between Medea and La Malinche. Both are "barbarian" women whose lives are defined by their love for a "civilized" man and the ways in which that love leads them each to betray their families and nations. It is a commonality that has been previously explored by other writers, including Jesus Sotelo Inclán in *Malintzin, Medea Americana* (1957) and Sergio Magana in his 1967 play *Los argonautas* which was later renamed *Cortés y la Malinche*.

Of course, the significant difference between Medea and La Malinche lies in the fact that La Malinche, transformed and motivated by Christian love (as we are told), does not betray Cortés and she certainly does not murder her child, even when, like Medea, she is relegated to the status of a concubine and summarily put aside for a proper "civilized" wife. Sandra Messinger Cypess has suggested that by placing La Malinche in the paradigm of Medea, La Malinche becomes the scapegoat for the deaths of all the indigenous people who died in the wake of the European invasion and as such is guilty of a type of infanticide (Cypess 1991). In the context of the Chicano Movement with its glorification of indigenous identity, the branding of La Malinche as a perpetrator of genocide is natural, albeit not entirely logical.

Moraga's lesbian Medea takes this rhetoric a step further still and directly confronts the accusations leveled both at La Malinche and at Chicana lesbians. By forgoing the romantic affections of all men, Moraga's Medea is an extreme version of her forebears. While La Malinche commits her crime by bearing a *mestizo* child, this Medea can do so by simply not bearing any further children. If accusations of being *malanchista* have been an important vehicle by which Chicana women have been kept from speaking out against their experiences of gender-based oppression, then Moraga provides in her Medea a woman who is able to embrace this accusation without ambiguity of sexual desire. This is a Medea who can tell Jasón clearly and without question,

> Don't flatter yourself, Jasón. I wore this dress for myself... the cloths are for me. The feel of silk against my thigh, the caress of satin slip over my breasts, the scent of musk when I bury my own face into the pillow of my arm. (Moraga 2001: 52)

While Euripides' Medea kills her children as a protest against her own treatment at the hands of the patriarchal order and more particularly at the hands of one man, in *The Hungry Woman* Medea murders her son in order to protect him from being turned into the guardian of the patriarchy. The most poignant aspect of this act is its acknowledgment of the destructive effects of patriarchy on both genders, on those who can conform and those who cannot. Moreover, that Medea kills her son not to punish Jasón (although certainly the murder does harm him), but rather to protect her child, is a continuation of Moraga's aim of rehabilitating Medea's image. In essence, by invoking this justification for the filicide, Medea's murder of her child becomes a sacrificial offering to the end of patriarchal domination and to the freedom of women and other marginalized groups.

Furthermore, in sacrificing her son, Medea actually embraces the wishes of Jasón and Aztlán and in doing so forces both to confront consequences of the nation they are creating. This is all evident in an angry exchange between Jasón and Medea in the play's Third Act:

> JASÓN: If you really loved your son, you'd remove him from your tit.
> MEDEA: So his mouth can suck your dick?
> JASÓN: That how your dyke friends talk, Medea? Look at you. You hate men. And boys become men. What good are you for Chac now? He needs a father.
> MEDEA: My son needs no taste of that weakness you call manhood. He is still a boy, not a man and you will not make him one in your likeness! The man I wish my son to be does not exist, must be invented. He will invent himself if he must, but he will not grow up to learn betrayal from your example. (Moraga 2001: 69)

Later Medea continues this line of reasoning when she tells Jasón:

> ... Marry your child-bride. A mi no me importa. No, in that lies no traición. Betrayal occurs when a boy grows into a man and sees his mother as a woman for the first time. A woman. A thing. A creature to be controlled. (Moraga 2001: 70)

It becomes clear later in the same act of the play that it is not mere "man-hating" that is leading Medea to worry for her son's future. As Chac-Mool heads toward his father in Aztlán, he encounters a Border Guard whom he at first tells, "I do not want you to be a man. Men scare me" (78). Yet despite this initial assertion, it is clear as the conversation progresses that Chac-Mool is ever more being perceived as a man, not a boy, and that he is increasingly claiming his male privilege. The Border Guard, who is also Chac-Mool's "revolutionary conscious," tells him:

> ... you are no more than your father's son. The son del Nuevo patron revolucionario, a landowner from whom you will inherit property and a legacy of blood under your fingernails ... I am landless. A woman without country. I am she whom you already know to hate. I wipe your infant ass in another life, sensitive Nazi-boy. (Moraga 2001: 78–9)

Chac-Mool's response betrays the extent to which he is in fact becoming his father's son despite his protestation that he is "not ready to be a man":

> I was always blessed to be a boy. My great-grandmother literally traced my forehead with the cross of her thumb and index finger and my brow was tranquil then. I didn't then have these violent thoughts of a man. At four, my father drilled his fingers into my chest, held me at the gun-point of his glare. You are blessed, he told me. Open your nostrils and flare like a bull. I want you to smell this land. I remember the wings of my nostrils rising up to suck up his breath. It was a birthing of sorts. He penetrated and I was born of him. His land was his mother and mine and I was beholden only to it ... Yes, Aztlán. And then my mother stole me away with the stonemason. (Moraga 2001: 79)

Medea may have taken Chac-Mool from Aztlán but he can return and be a free man there. Even if Medea returns to Aztlán, as Jasón promises her she can if she renounces her lesbianism, she will still be an outsider and a slave. A fact that Jasón too acknowledges even in his attempts to persuade her to return (Moraga 2001: 69). Yet, Jasón too is a servant to the narrow ideology of Aztlán, and his marriage is not merely compelled by the desire for "a tight pussy around (your) dick" (Moraga 2001: 68). Jasón's intended bride is an Apache girl, and Medea, with senses heightened by her own outsider status, recognizes the extent to which Jasón's choice of wife is compelled by his own lackluster racial resumé:

> She'll never call you by your true name, Jasón, so you may fortunately begin to forget it. Forget the U.S. Air Force father, the quarter-breed mestizo-de-mestizo cousins, your mother's coveted Spanish coat-of-arms. That girl can't know you because your lies were sown long before she made root on this earth. Send me your wife. I will teach her of her own embattled and embittered history. I will teach her, as I have learned, to defend women and children against enemies from within. Against fathers and brothers and sons who grow up to be as conquistador as any Cortez. (Moraga 2001: 70)

While the implication of patriarchy in an adaptation of *Medea* is an obvious move, Moraga's critique of the failures of the Chicano Movement's racial ideology is unique. Jasón, as Aztlán's "Minster of Culture," is implicated by his own obvious lack of indigenous roots. His marriage to an Apache girl is an attempt to disguise his own heritage. Yet this action in itself only highlights the difficulty of neglecting any one facet of a heritage that is ultimately characterized by its heterogeneous mixing and not by homogenous purity. It makes it clear that Medea is entirely justified when she accuses Jasón and those who prompt this type of racial construction for Aztlán of being "Traídores de una cultura mas anciana que [Traitors of a culture more ancient than] your pitiful ego'd life can remember" (Moraga 2001: 70). In this accusation, Medea invokes both the imagined matriarchal and matrilineal past of the indigenous people of Meso-America as well as the very real *mestizo* past of Mexico since Cortés. To posit a native identity as the only legitimately Chicano identity and, as such, as the only legitimate identity of a citizen of Aztlán, is to deny the true nature of what it means to be a Chicano and thus to deny the true purpose of Aztlán. Jasón's purposed marriage to an Apache girl is a marriage that, despite whatever pretence Jasón or his allies might have, will ultimately produce even more *mestizo* children whose paternal grandmother will still have had a Spanish coat-of-arms. Jasón's prized bride will follow in the footsteps of her *La Malinche* foremother bearing *mestizo* children to the conqueror even as he exiles other *mestizos* from their rightful homeland.

In the end, Medea is an exile from Aztlán because Aztlán has failed to fulfill its promise of revolution. It has failed to become the homeland for all Chicanos. In *The Hungry Woman*, Moraga places on stage what the failure to create a "Queer Aztlán" would look like and the violent consequences for all that that failure would entail. Ultimately this failure is the failure of democratic rhetoric to become a democratic reality—a failure that not only haunts the Chicano Movement but the mainstream American experience as well. This is why *The Hungry Woman* speaks to an audience that extends beyond the Chicano Movement and its discontents. By invoking the myth of Medea, Moraga invokes traditions of patriarchal oppression, racial domination, and colonial exile that extend beyond the American context and even beyond modernity. This is a way not only to speak to a wider audience, but also to circumvent the modern domestication of democratic rhetoric, calling forward a radical sisterhood both with Medea and beyond her.

NOTES

1. Quoted in Eschen 2006: 103.
2. Movimiento Estudiantil Chicano/a de Aztlan—<http://clubs.asua.arizona.edu/~mecha/pages/ElPlanDeAtzlan.html>.

REFERENCES

Arrizón, A. (2000), "Mythical Performativity: Relocating Aztlán in Chicana Feminist Cultural Productions," *Theatre Journal* 52.1 (March), 23–49.
Arrizón, A. (2006), *Queering Mestizaje: Transculturation and Performance*. Ann Arbor.
Bierhorst, J. (ed. 1984), *The Hungry Woman: Myths and Legends of the Aztecs*. New York.
Camayd-Freixas, E., and J. E. González (2000), *Primitivism and Identity in Latin America*. Tucson, AZ.
Cypess, S. (1991), *La Malinche in Mexican Literature from History to Myth*. Austin, TX.
de Toro, A. (1995), *Borders and Margins*. Madrid.
Eschen, N. (2006), "*The Hungry Woman: A Mexican Medea* (review)," *Theatre Journal* 58.1 (March), 103–6.
Esquibel, C. R. (1998), "Memories of Girlhood: Chicana Lesbian Fictions," *Signs* 23.3, 645–82.
Gutiérrez, R. A. (1993), "Community, Patriarchy and Individualism: The Politics of Chicano History and the Dream of Equality," *American Quarterly* 45.1 (March), 44–72.
Jacobs, E. (2009), "Theatre on the Border in Cherríe Moraga's *The Hungry Woman: A Mexican Medea*," *Journal of Adaptations in Film & Performance* 1.3, 177–89.
Kistenbert, C. J. (1995), *AIDS, Social Change, and the Theater*. New York.
Mar-Molinero, C. (2000), *The Politics of Language in the Spanish-Speaking World*. New York.
Molloy, S. and R. McKee Irwin (1998), *Hispanisms and Homosexualities*. Durham, NC.
Moraga, C. (2001), *The Hungry Woman: A Mexican Medea and Heart of the Earth—A Popul Vuh Story*. Albuquerque, NM.
Moraga, C. (2004), "Queer Azatán: The Re-formation of Chicano Tribe," in D. Carlin and J. Di Grazia eds., *Queer Cultures*. New York, 224–9.
Rodríguez, I. (2001), *The Latin American Subaltern Studies Reader*. Durham, NC.
Tatonetti, L. (2004), "'A Kind of Queer Balance': Cherríe Moraga's Aztlán," *Melus* 29.2, 227–47.
Warner, M. (1993), *Fear of a Queer Planet: Queer Politics and Social Theory*. Minneapolis.
Ybarra, P. (2008), "The Revolution Fails Here: Cherríe Moraga's *The Hungry Woman* as a Mexican Medea," *Aztlán: A Journal of Chicano Studies* 33.1 (Spring), 63–88.

CHAPTER 30

AUGUST WILSON AND GREEK DRAMA

Blackface Minstrelsy, "Spectacle" from Aristotle's Poetics, *and* Radio Golf

PATRICE RANKINE

> The Negro is the symbol of our uninhibited expression, of our uninhibited action. He is our catharsis. He is the disguise behind which we may, for a releasing moment, rejoin that part of ourselves which we have sacrificed to civilization.
>
> Isaac Goldberg, *Tin Pan Alley: A Chronicle of the American Popular Music Racket.* New York: John Day Company, 1930: 32

BLACKFACE minstrelsy is a link in the relationship between Greek drama and African-American performance traditions, as Harry J. Elam suggested in his 2006 lecture "Behind the Minstrel Mask."[1] (See Slater, Hill, this volume.) Blackface minstrelsy, its genealogy in English pantomime, folk drama, and the circus, became popular in earnest within the United States around 1830 and featured white performers with their faces tarred to look as though they were black.[2] Parodying patterns of behavior ostensibly observed on plantations, the white actor in blackface passed for the real thing for their viewers, so much so that "early audiences so often suspected that they were being entertained by actual Negroes that minstrel sheet music began the proto-Brechtian practice of picturing blackface performers out of costume as well as in" (Lott 1995: 20). As it pertains to popular American beliefs and practices in the nineteenth century, blackface performers profited from a view that "blacks were intellectually inferior because in thrall to emotions" (Lott 1995: 32). Blackface was everywhere on the American popular stage, reinforcing stereotypes about black underdevelopment and inferiority in the main (see Hill, this volume).

At the same time, as Susan Curtis emphasizes elsewhere, in her article on black musical performance in the early twentieth century,[3] nothing about race relations in the United States is one-sided or simple. By the end of the nineteenth century, white performers were not the only ones seeking to appropriate and profit from popular images of black people. African-American performers took up the mask of blackness, minstrelsy being coterminous with the phenomena of black dance and musical performance.[4] Black actors' claim to authenticity—as opposed to their fake, white counterparts—brought purchase to their own creative theater pieces (Krasner 1997; Krasner in Brundage 2011). Theater scholar David Krasner affirms Lott's thesis that "for black performers, the real was commodified in order to lead the challenge against minstrel theater" (Brundage 2011: 101). Sisle and Blake's *Shuffle Along* is only one example of an African-American claim to authenticity in blackface minstrelsy, Williams and Walker's *The Two Real Coons* (c.1896–9) being another.[5] The farcical frame of blackface minstrelsy and early black theater made the reception of Greek comedy problematical for African-American theater practitioners, as Lena Hill makes clear in this volume.

Of course, on the surface of things, none of the foregoing summary of blackface minstrelsy sounds even vaguely relatable to Aeschylus, Sophocles, and Euripides, or even Aristophanic comedy, for that matter. Elam's attempt to reconcile blackface minstrelsy to Greek drama, however, is worth further scrutiny. At a visceral and even superficial level, Elam was referring to blackface in terms of the use of masks, ubiquitous in Greek drama.[6] Blackface is a painted-on mask that accomplishes a number of things. As Susan Smith argues (1984), masks are multivalent: they can be satirical, convey a static identity, or they might express heroism and point to deep unconscious tensions and conflicts (see Lambropoulos, this volume). Masks, and the play on masking, whether through blackface or otherwise, are devices of black drama, as they are of modern drama more broadly.[7] As such, masks, and minstrelsy, can be the way that a playwright calls upon Greek drama, even from the standpoint of a basic stage prop. The minstrel mask is a comic device similar to those in Aristophanes' plays, which are aimed at penetrating into deeper recesses of the society—and making social comments—so as to unsettle normative relationships.

At the more profound level, blackface minstrelsy is an indelible phenomenon in American Modernism and the Americanization of Greek drama because it unveils precisely what American identity of the nineteenth and twentieth century was, and to some extent what it continues to be into the twenty-first century. Blackface minstrelsy coexists with American classicism. (See Macintosh, McConnell, Rankine, this volume.) They are not unrelated phenomena, but each is an expression of existential issues about comedy and tragedy as they have been expressed in the American vernacular. Blackface minstrel performances were among the most popular forms of entertainment within the United States in the nineteenth century (Lott 1995; Rogin 1996). It is at the bottom of the archaeology of American vernacular expression. A number of articles in the volume *Beyond Blackface: African Americans and the Creation of American Popular Culture, 1890–1930* point to the emergence from Victorianism at the end of the nineteenth century and into a nexus of primitivism, Modernism, and American popular culture in the twentieth

(Brundage 2011). Within a Modernist context, blackface minstrelsy was North America's very own cultural form, evidence of the primitive within its modern civilization, its local idiom, along with music (in ragtime, jazz, and blues) and dance (in cakewalking, which was created by slaves, and other such dances). As David Krasner puts it, "acting 'primitive'—a catchphrase of the era—by way of cakewalking [an African-American dance made popular by Aida Overton Walker] became one of the cultural artifacts being collected by the West."[8] The "artifact" to which Krasner refers is the remnant out of which Americans created their Modernism; blackface and black music and dance were the "releasing moment" that Americans had abandoned in the name of civilization (to paraphrase the epigraph above).[9] Blackface minstrelsy is a cultural phenomenon that is enmeshed with issues of commerce and artistic creation. In America, it is part of the same market that trades on performances of Greek plays.

In the present volume, Niall Slater argues that Greek drama within the United States of roughly the period with which *Beyond Blackface* is concerned (1890–1930) also looked to native primitivism to dress classical plays in Modernist garb. In America, the rediscovery of the Indian—the "Native" American—repeats the unearthing of foundations of civilization elsewhere. Hiram Bingham's "discovery" of Machu Picchu in 1911 is another parallel. That is, it is important to keep in mind the American coincidences of archaeological digs in Greece (Crete, Mycenae, and Troy, 1870s–1890) during this period because they contribute to Modernist thinking on what "the classical" might be. Each discovery of the ancient regenerated modern culture. By looking to the foundations of their civilization, modern citizens found sources of inspiration for poetry and art, as well as saleable items—songs, dance forms, and even reproductions of artifacts—for commerce. As it pertains to Greek drama, Slater in this volume studies the set design of *Iphigenia among the Taurians* and sees that the play's Modernism was somewhat unprecedented on the American stage, as Greek drama was truly becoming something new within the United States—as opposed to a European import not necessarily from classical Athens, but even from modern London (as the essays in Part II of this volume show).[10]

As a feature of American Modernism, blackface minstrelsy functions in a similar fashion to what Slater describes of the 1903 *Iphigenia*'s primitivism in the modern (or Modernism in the primitive). Not unlike the archaeological and architectural structures that point to the foundations of American civilization, visible on the set of the 1903 *Iphigenia*, the blackface minstrel unveils an archaic idiom at the core of American vernacular culture. Blackface—along with music and dance—is taken to be indicative of the slave's gestures, a set of tropes at the bottom of American life that make their way up to the twentieth century, though "frozen in time" and representing "a link to a 'primitive' past."[11]

Thus because of the superficial (masks, Aristophanic comedy) and deeper (American Modernism, archaeology, commerce) associations, it is worthwhile to discuss blackface minstrelsy in the context of Greek drama in the United States. Though the connection between the phenomena—of blackface minstrelsy, on the one hand, and Greek drama, on the other—might still seem incidental, the events are never far from the minds of many American theater practitioners. Suzan-Lori Parks likens her blackface parody of Abraham Lincoln and John Wilkes Booth, both in *America Play* and *Topdog/Underdog*, to Greek drama, and she names these figures America's "Apollo and Medea and Oedipus" (*New York Times*, April 7, 2002; see Rankine 2013). (See Macintosh, McConnell, Rankine, this volume.)

In the case of August Wilson (1945–2005), undoubtedly the most accomplished and celebrated African-American playwright of the twentieth century, blackface minstrelsy is part of a conversation with "the Greeks" on a particular aspect of classical drama, namely spectacle, Aristotle's *opsis* (Rankine 2013). What Wilson calls his "spectacle character" is *his* reflection of—and riff on—Greek drama. The idea of a riff—a musical one—is appropriate because of Wilson's relationship to jazz and blues. Wilson's theoretical improvisation on Aristotle's *Poetics* makes of the Greek philosopher's *opsis* a Wilsonian rendition, the spectacle character that draws attention away from what seems to be the immediate plot and toward a bigger, overarching concern (Rankine 2013). It is not coincidental that in Wilson's *Radio Golf* (2005) this "spectacle character" is the blackface minstrel Old Joe of nineteenth-century American lore.

August Wilson, Aristotelian *Opsis*, and Blackface Minstrelsy

Within the context of blackface, primitivism, and American Modernism, August Wilson's *Radio Golf* is Americanized Greek drama. Wilson does not stage Greek drama in the sense of adapting Aeschylus, Sophocles, or Euripides. As classical reception, each of the ten major plays that Wilson wrote, each representing a different decade in his "cycle" for the twentieth century, would be on extremely shaky ground—and would in fact be inadmissible.[12] Wilson patterns none of his stories along the lines of the plot of the Oedipus tale, Prometheus' torment, or Medea's dilemma, as three possible examples of what classical reception might look like.[13] His characters resemble the people he encountered growing up in Pittsburgh's Hill District, a Pennsylvania boom-town during the Great Migration of the early twentieth century (Bryer and Hartig 2006). Never do these characters reveal any explicit connections to their Greek forerunners. That is, the relationship between August Wilson's reuse of blackface minstrelsy and Greek drama is not through the Greek playwrights or their stories, but rather through Wilson's theoretical engagement with Aristotle's *Poetics*.

Wilson hoped to encapsulate the Hill District, the setting of most of his plays, onstage, by moving through the twentieth century to represent the evolution of the community and its members.[14] Regarding the "century cycle," Wilson began speaking about his plays as decadal as early as 1984, a year before he won critical acclaim for his play set in the 1950s, *Fences*, which premièred in 1985 and won the Pulitzer Prize for Drama and a Tony

Award. He would go on to win the Pulitzer again in 1990 for *The Piano Lesson*, set in the 1940s. Despite his success, Wilson's relationship to European and American theater and culture was uncomfortable. He emerged as a poet and director during the Black Arts Movement of the 1960s and never wavered—at least ostensibly—from such controversial positions as his opposition to color-blind casting.[15] He claimed, for example, that "the idea of colorblind casting is the same idea of assimilation that black Americans have been rejecting for the past 380 years" (Wilson 1997: 499). Such a claim is not easy to reconcile with Wilson's assertion that the "ground on which I stand has been pioneered by the Greek dramatists, by Euripides, Aeschylus and Sophocles" (1997: 493). Greek drama might easily be robed in black with varying results and meanings (Wetmore 2003, or Powers, this volume), but this was not Wilson's aim.

Wilson's task was to find in the American vernacular, in the black vernacular, something missing from Greek drama, as he argues in a 2003 interview with Sandra Shannon: "If you go to the Greeks or to the white American theater they will have Aristotle's *Poetics*, but they don't have the black nationalism or the blues, or those other things that make black aesthetics unique" (Bryer and Hartig 2006: 241–2).[16] In all aspects of his dramaturgy, Wilson looks to "the Greeks," but not through the Greek dramatists, whether of tragedy or comedy. What Wilson cites is Aristotle's *Poetics*. As I argue elsewhere, Wilson's reading of *opsis*, "spectacle," from *Poetics* is of particular interest.[17] In his 1997 interview with Bonnie Lyons, he calls the interviewer's attention to what he names his spectacle character, and he ultimately turns to the Greek philosopher for his definition. Wilson claims that the spectacle characters are "fully integrated into the other characters' lives, but they are a spectacle for the audience. I think that's my interpretation of Aristotle's spectacle in *Poetics*" (Bryer and Hartig 2006: 213). The spectacle character is "generally a big character." Wilson goes on to explain his interpretation of *Poetics*, and it is clear that, like Aristotle, he juxtaposes plot and story (*mythos*) to spectacle (*opsis*). Plot "becomes very mechanical" (from the 1997 interview, Bryer and Hartig 2006: 241–2). As a result of this, Wilson gives an un-Aristotelian priority to *opsis*. Wilson is looking for aspects of black theater, in the context of American theater, which are "not based on Aristotle," and he endorses the distinction: "I think that [the fact that much of American theater is not based in Aristotle] is good" (from the 2003 interview, Bryer and Hartig 2006: 241–2). Wilson prioritizes *opsis*, and to a lesser extent *mythos*, among the six parts of drama that Aristotle cites; this is not accidental but is deeply tied to the visual expectations that race thinking imposes, and particularly, in this case, blackface minstrelsy (Rankine 2013).

A brief word should be said about *opsis* in Aristotle's *Poetics*. Wilson's prioritization of spectacle leads to a character like Old Joe in *Radio Golf*, a presence that harks back to the minstrel type, itself an element of visual theater. Visual theater is, of course, not necessarily Aristotelian, at least not in terms of the formal characteristics that Aristotle lays out in *Poetics*.[18] In at least two passages from *Poetics*, Aristotle elevates plot above spectacle, to such an extent that he diminishes the significance of stagecraft, for the poet:

> Now what is fearful and pitiable can result from spectacle, but also from the actual structure of events, which is the higher priority and the aim of a superior poet. For

> the plot should be so structured that, even without seeing it performed, the person who hears the event that occur experiences horror and pity at what comes about (as one would feel when hearing the plot of the *Oedipus*). To create this effect through spectacle has little to do with the poet's art (*atechnoteros*), and requires material resources. (1453b1–7)[19]

The idea that creating a drama through spectacle is *atechnos* is a loaded one, philologically and historically. Early twentieth-century translator S. H. Butcher (1907) rendered *atechnos* in such a way as to make Aristotle say that crafting drama by spectacle was "not artful" (or "least artistic," beyond the positive degree). Gerald Else (1967) also renders Aristotle's idea about *opsis* as "least artistic" but also adds that it is "least connected with the poetic art." Stephen Halliwell brings some clarity to this, both in his translations (1987 and 1989) and in an extended analysis in an appendix of his 1995 study of *Poetics*. Spectacle, in the end, is not the job of the poet, with *atechnos* as "ha[ving] little to do with the poet's art." In other words, spectacle is not to be the concern of the poet but that of what might be called in modern times the set designer, costume designer, and so on.

Wilson's appropriation of blackface minstrelsy in *Radio Golf* is an improbable but deft riff on *opsis* in Aristotle's *Poetics*. For Wilson, spectacle *is* to be the concern of the modern playwright, especially—but not exclusively—in such cases where his identity as African-American is first and foremost apprehended by sight (Rankine 2013). From the time of the transatlantic slave trade, and perhaps long before, Europeans and Americans have taken the sight of blackness as a site of difference.[20] Blackface minstrelsy plays on—and plays up—this ostensible dissimilarity, as its popularity in the nineteenth century attests (Lott 1995). Wilson wants to use spectacle, and in *Radio Golf* in particular his appropriation of the blackface minstrel, to undo the damage of racial thinking; herein lies his engagement with Greek drama from a theoretical standpoint. He feels that the difference that race reifies calls for a theater more visually challenging than Oedipus, Antigone, or Electra might allow, even if they were to be set in an African-American cultural context. In other words, through Aristotle's *opsis*, Wilson offers that there is something at stake in African-American receptions of Greek drama that is unique to the particular experience of blacks in modern America.

Of the plays in the "century cycle," *Radio Golf* most clearly displays the link between minstrelsy, spectacle, and the African-American playwright's attempt to craft a modern drama that responds to "the Greeks." Old Joe, Wilson's spectacle character in *Radio Golf*, is the stock minstrel-figure from the foundational times of nineteenth-century popular American theater. From state to state and in various regions of the United States, blackface minstrelsy was a feature of the popular stage and public festivals, and Old Joe was one of the recurring roles. Even in states that were not slaveholding, such as Indiana, the impact of racial identification in such practices as blackface minstrelsy and, later, segregation was widely felt. A few examples should suffice. On June 10, 1868, Robert Gordon, an Indiana veteran of the Grand Army of the Republic, was one of the 200 Civil War survivors to perform at a benefit for the widows and orphans of deceased soldiers.[21] The performance was a tableau, titled *The Drummer Boy, or, The Battle of Shiloh*, no doubt a re-enactment of the 1862 Tennessee confrontation that resulted in a major Union victory. The legendary battle was retold in the Samuel J. Muscroft play *The Drummer Boy of Shiloh*, of which the 1868 Indianapolis performance was a forerunner.[22] The biographical sketch of Robert Gordon recounts that "the most prominent character in the cast was 'Uncle Joe,' portrayed in blackface by Captain Harry McMullen."

The minstrelsy that Joe represents extends into the twentieth century. Photographs from the 1900 Indianapolis Fall Carnival include a group of men in blackface, some wearing women's clothing, a constant trope in minstrelsy.[23] A 1902 pamphlet advertised the Muncie Club's minstrel performance at Wysor's Grand Opera House, which existed from 1892 to 1912.[24] Images as late as 1930 show men in blackface from a Kiwanis Club Show. Characters like "Jim Crow" and "Zip Coon" were popular, and by the later part of the nineteenth century, "Nigger Jim" from Harriet Beecher Stowe's 1851 serial novel *Uncle Tom's Cabin* had made his way to the stage, in performances, as had Old Joe. Thus by the twentieth century, spectacle and the stock motifs of popular American entertainment were mightily in place.[25]

Minstrel performer Frank Brower first popularized the role of Old Joe before playing the (Uncle) "Tom" character (from Stowe's novel) in the nineteenth century (Lott 1995; Mahar 1999). These were not isolated performances, but they are revealing of the American popular stage and, by the early twentieth century, of a widespread sentimentality within the United States. Stephen C. Foster's 1853 song "Old Black Joe" met an ambivalent response from notables like Ralph Waldo Emerson and W. E. B. Du Bois, but it remained an anthem for a certain nostalgia pertaining to the American South. The first stanza and chorus are as follows:

> Gone are the days when my heart was young and gay, Gone are my friends from the cotton fields away, Gone from the earth to a better land I know, I hear their gentle voices calling "Old Black Joe". *Chorus* I'm coming, I'm coming, for my head is bending low: I hear those gentle voices calling, "Old Black Joe."[26]

The song was well known during the middle years of the twentieth century. The young Trapp singers in Wolfgang Liebeneiner's 1956 film *The Trapp Family* perform a rendition of the song, within a scene with American navy officers during World War II. It is ironic that Maria von Trapp, on whose life the film was based, came to the United States from abroad, given that the story of her financial ruin in Europe evoked similar feelings to those that the demise of the American South brought on.[27] The Trapp story as an American one is the case not only in the Liebeneiner film, but her melancholy music inspired *The Sound of Music*, the 1959 Broadway musical, which later became the 1965 film.

"Old Black Joe" itself does not remain a minstrel song, in the sense that it becomes a popular American song extracted from its original context. Its feeling extends to a broader American sentiment within the twentieth century. Its minstrel beginnings, however, are undeniable and, at times, irrepressible. Wilson could not later deploy a character called "Old Joe" onstage in *Radio Golf* without being aware of the extent to which he might to varying degrees evoke his original associations. By appropriating this character, Wilson joins the litany of black writers who sought to wrest the minstrel role from the mainstream of American culture.

Radio Golf

Set in the 1990s, *Radio Golf* premièred on April 22, 2005 at the Yale Repertory Theatre.[28] The play features a number of sophisticated, cosmopolitan characters. The characters are situated in an integrated American context, where they interact with whites in colleges and businesses; they are themselves college educated, owning and being titans of industry. In the play, Harmond Wilks is a real-estate developer on the brink of opening a shopping center in the Hill District, along with his partner and college roommate Roosevelt Hicks. Wilks needs the city to declare the area blighted so that he can cheaply (through government aid) build the development, which features Starbucks, Barnes & Nobles, and a number of other commercial brands. Wilks's wife Mame works in public relations. As such, Mame is of course concerned with image, and she knows that if Wilks is managed correctly, he could easily become the city's mayor. Thus unlike many characters in Wilson's plays, who are placed in the early twentieth century and in some cases have immediate ties to the Southern past and to slavery (such as Solly Two Kings of *Gem of the Ocean*, 2004), the ensemble in *Radio Golf* is future oriented. Slavery and the South are distant memories. At the same time, Wilson commented frequently that for American blacks the South and slavery present inescapable ties (Bryer and Hartig 2006), and in *Radio Golf* these links are made in subtle and explicit ways and are as often to the detriment of characters as to their advantage.

All of the names of Wilson's characters will prove significant, but the moniker Mame is extremely telling, as a black woman linked to image-production and perhaps an audible allusion to "mammy". Mame's name and her career as an image consultant are certainly suggestive of the black women who nurtured America's youth for over two centuries, black and white alike. As it pertains to American popular culture, the mammy character is a well-known feature of twentieth-century film, and black actresses have struggled to put their personal stamp on what would otherwise be a stereotypical, Hollywood role.[29] Black women, however, as Annamarie Beam argues, have always brought a certain distinction to the type of blackface minstrelsy that the mammy would otherwise represent.[30] Beam proffers that, in their roles as both (cross-dressed) men and women, black female performers of the late nineteenth century paved the way for the jazzmen of the twentieth through their refinement of the dandy (Zip Coon) of earlier minstrel shows. In other words, if Wilson *is* playing on the mammy with Mame, he is doing so in a way that is highly self-conscious and consistent with what he will do with Old Joe in the play. Europeans and Americans in the main, more specifically, *white* people, controlled the image of blacks through much of the nineteenth century. Image-producers of the twentieth century who identify as black have a proverbial uphill battle, a Sisyphean task of presenting characters as *they* see them. Mame's job in public relations parallels that of Wilson: to recast blacks as leaders (perhaps mayors), tycoons, and creators of their own fortune, simultaneously having a forward gait while never forgetting their shared past.

Wilson draws upon a number of media in his emphasis on image and spectacle, including literature, radio, and television. In *Radio Golf*'s first scene, Hicks, who is Vice President at Mellon Bank and an avid golfer, hangs a poster of Tiger Woods on the wall of the partners' new storefront office. Here again, the image of a prominent African-American is not coincidental. Woods, who fails to self-identify as black despite his appearance, his mixed heritage, and the American "one-drop" rule, steals the stage, where lesser-known heroes vie for equal time.[31] The business is called Bedford Hills Redevelopment, Inc., but Wilks wants to name it after Sarah Degree, Pittsburgh's first black nurse in the play, in real life a black woman, whom Wilson cites as the reason he attended Catholic church as a child (Bryer and Hartig 2006). Degree rounded up the kids in the neighborhood on Sundays and took them to church, and her benevolence made a lasting impression on Wilson as the kind of silent acts that the grand gestures of a Tiger Woods overshadow. As a parallel to Aristotle's *opsis* and *mythos*, the image factory of the American media threatens to overpower the story that African-Americans want to tell, and in Woods's case, this is even more true than Wilson could have imagined even as late as 2005. As a potential mayoral candidate, Wilks is interested in the "symbolic weight" of the black vote (Wilson 2008: 8). Scholar Margaret Booker refers to Wilks as a "representative of the black middle class" (Bigsby 2007: 185). Tiger Woods and Sarah Degree are synecdochic representations of success, choices individuals make in relation to the group: the former, as individualist, overachiever disconnected from any whole; the latter, modestly successful but ever looking back (to the past) and reaching outward to lend a helping hand to the children. In the play, the various media of radio, posters, and sports are the stage upon which the protagonists act and tell their stories.

At a basic level, the tension between Aristotle's *mythos* and *opsis*, in Wilson's hands, should be clear. Harmond Wilks's story is that of a capitalist Everyman, who wants to advance and make money but is also concerned with being ethical, as his gesture toward Sarah Degree makes clear. He is opening a multimillion-dollar development, but he also wants to be mayor of Pittsburgh because it is good for him and for the community as a whole. Through Mame, he can understand the importance of image in the drama he is creating, and as a result of this he is able to participate in the crafting of his own public image, rather than being the spectacle. His partner, Roosevelt Hicks, will emerge as his foil. Hicks is more self-absorbed than Wilks. He is primarily concerned with his own success; he does not look back to a collective past, nor does he express concern for other individuals in any way similar to what Wilks does.

Into this context of images and narrative walks Old Joe. More than any other character in *Radio Golf*, Old Joe, as Wilson's spectacle character, draws attention to image, through the onstage spectacle of minstrelsy. He interrupts the *mythos* of Wilks's real estate development and his all-but-completed bid for mayor of Pittsburgh.

Old Joe is the only thing that stands in the way of Bedford Hills Redevelopment, Inc.—or even Sarah Degree Redevelopment, Inc. During this first scene, we learn that "someone is actually painting an abandoned house" (Wilson 2008: 17), one of the buildings to be torn down to make way for the development. Old Joe is the "someone," a vexing character so out of place in a modern city as to inevitably draw attention to himself. Although the scene is never shown on stage, the juxtaposition of modern businesses with a red, dilapidated structure in the midst is jarring. The contrast is a visual—even if mental—reminder of what is at stake for Wilson. Old Joe's deed is, on the surface of things, a comic contrast to Wilks's heroic enterprise. In fact, Old Joe threatens to undo Wilks's Herculean labor. When he appears onstage, Joe's speech is as riddling as his actions. He introduces himself, as do Wilson's other spectacle characters, in double: "My name is Elder Joseph Barlow, but people call me Old Joe" (Wilson 2008: 25). Old Joe speaks in the staccato, enigmatic style of a minstrel:

> They say they was gonna charge me with vandalism for painting my own house. They gave me this (*Hands Harmond a complaint summons*). That's why I come by here to get me a lawyer. Is you a Christian? If you was a Christian I figure you would see that I was falsely accused like Jesus Christ and maybe wouldn't charge me as much. (Wilson 2008: 25)

Joe's speech moves from the sensible to the seemingly ridiculous. He needs a lawyer, but what one's religion has to do with the price of a lawyer might seem to be beside the point. Joe's reference to false accusations and Jesus Christ might conjure images of the martyr hung from a tree (whether lynched or crucified), but it is equally likely to be simply comic and off-beat. Joe is the proverbial fly in the ointment, an unexpected presence not easy to ignore.

As the spectacle character, Old Joe is Wilson's answer to Greek drama, as he interprets it. While we have seen that for Aristotle *opsis* is to be a consideration outside of the playwright's craft, the reversal of Wilson's *Radio Golf* itself comes through *opsis*. Laughs abound with Joe's very presence onstage, and what he says throughout the play continues to baffle and vex his interlocutors. If, for Wilson, plot—which is to say Aristotle's *mythos*—can be "very mechanical," the spectacle character brings an unexpected, primarily visual shift in events. But Old Joe is no minstrel character in the old mode, his comedy is not expressly physical. A number of events surrounding Old Joe move the drama toward its unexpected reversal. The house that Old Joe is painting and that he claims belongs to his family is to be torn down for Wilks and Roosevelt's development, and Old Joe is standing in the way. As might be expected, given his individualistic approach, Roosevelt is merciless; Old Joe simply has no claim to the property. Wilks, on the other hand, who as we have seen has a deeper conception of citizenship and responsibility, tries to reason with Old Joe, and in doing so he learns some critical things, even if straightforward logic fails for the jive-talking Joe.

The surprising turn of the drama enmeshes Wilks in everything having to do with Old Joe. In the first place, Wilks discovers that his father was paying taxes on Old Joe's house while he was alive. Secondly, toward the end (in scene 4) of Act 1, the house address is revealed to be 1839 Wylie, the very same location where Aunt Ester lived. If many of Wilson's characters have ties to the nineteenth-century past of blacks in the South during slavery, Aunt Ester is the chief example. Born into slavery, Ester is a character in many of Wilson's plays, and she is even referred to when not present, as is the case in *Radio Golf*. Aunt Ester dies in *King Hedley II*, the last play Wilson wrote before *Gem* and *Radio Golf*. (*King Hedley II* is set in 1985.) She would have been 366 years old at the time of her death! Similar to Aunt Ester, who lived in the house that is being painted, Old Joe is a link to this past. In expected, folkloric fashion, Old Joe says that trying to stop Harmond and Roosevelt from tearing down this house is "like wrestling a bear."[32] Nevertheless, by early (the second scene) in Act 2, Harmond has visited the house and has a change of heart. He explains to Roosevelt what he has seen:

> It's a Federalist brick house with a good double-base foundation. I couldn't believe it. It has beveled glass on every floor. There's a huge stained-glass window leading up to the landing. And the staircase is made of Brazilian wood with a hand-carved balustrade. You don't see that too often. (Wilson 2008: 61)

The description of the interior of Aunt Ester's house is ecphrastic. The Federalist brick is indicative of the mid-1850s, when Aunt Ester's enslavement would have been coming to a close. The firm, double-base foundation makes the house a physical parallel to Aunt Ester herself and the traditions for which she stood. And the Brazilian wood roots these traditions in deeper American soil, pointing at once to the conquest and exploitation of the New World and its resources, and to the Diaspora heritage and values so strong even today in places like Brazil. Touched by what he has seen, and also aware that Old Joe's taxes are in fact paid, so that he does indeed own the house, Harmond decides that he should preserve it and build his development around it.

By this juncture, Roosevelt is already emerging as Harmond's nemesis. Old Joe the blackface minstrel is the catalyst that brings their relationship to a critical point. While Harmond somewhat enjoys Old Joe and treats him humanely, he unsettles Roosevelt, who sees him as a buffoon. From early on, Roosevelt complains that "he don't know how to answer a simple question like, 'What's your name'? He'll make that complicated" (Wilson 2008: 17). Similar to the Christ allusion, the fact that "What's your name"? does actually engender complicated responses again evokes the more serious implications of Old Joe's presence. That is, Joe is pivotal to African-American selfhood and to the identity of characters in *Radio Golf*. He is part of the answer to "what's your name?," or "who are you?," for blacks in America.[33] As a personality that causes dramatic shifts, Old Joe the minstrel to some extent morphs into Joe the trickster, in Wilson's hands. He effects the change in Wilks and Roosevelt's relationship; he is the play's *peripeteia*. Roosevelt was already beginning to show a different face from early in Act 1, when the audience learned that he has been invited to play golf with Bernie Smith, a beleaguered businessman who is being sued by seventeen people (Wilson 2008: 28). Late in the first act (scene 3), Roosevelt returns from his golf outing and announces that Bernie Smith wants to buy WBTZ (perhaps a riff on the role of BET, "Black Entertainment Television," and its sometimes pernicious influence) radio through a Minority Tax Certificate. Wilks's challenge to Harmond suggests the broader context within which blacks interact with whites within American society: "So, you're the black face? You're just the front" (Wilson 2008: 36).

That is, blackface minstrelsy, the way in which whites might understand the behavior of blacks, and the response of blacks as a result of stereotyped expectations, is very much on the writer's mind. Old Joe, whom the audience expects is the comic relief, if not expressly the minstrel, is a deeper personality than this. Roosevelt, on the other hand, with his allegiance to corporate interests over his peers, is potentially the real buffoon. As it becomes increasingly clear that Roosevelt's only allegiance is to money, Wilks's commitment to Old Joe deepens when he discovers that they are related by blood. Black Mary, the woman who helps Aunt Ester in the house in *Gem of the Ocean*, is Joe's mother: Black Mary, sister of Caesar Wilks, Harmond Wilks's grandfather. The entire family is connected through a common ancestor, Henry Samuels, who was a slave. Roosevelt will of course hear none of this upon his re-entry onstage in the next scene (Act 2, scene 3). He claims that Joe is a fraud, and in the last scene of the play (Act 2, scene 4), Harmond learns that Roosevelt has bought him out of his share of the development: "If one of the partners jeopardizes the business by straying from the company's initial charter the other partner can force the sale to protect the company's financing structure" (Wilson 2008: 79). The contrast between Wilks and Hicks is one of conflicting values and behaviors of blacks in relation to American modernity, manifested primarily in capitalism and commerce.[34]

Radio Golf reads like a classically structured play, with sharply drawn characters facing their doubles onstage, Aristotelian *peripeteia*, and discovery, blackface minstrelsy being the mask that does not fit the form, or the spectacle with which Wilson distinguishes himself. Regarding traditional reversal, Harmond Wilks moves from individual identity to a broader consciousness, rooted in his ancestral past, while Roosevelt, the strident, bourgeois individual, assumes the minstrel mask, in the end, even more so than Old Joe. Roosevelt feels empowered by the prospects of financial gain, a motive similar to that of the performers of the nineteenth century and beyond. Bernie Smith's money allows Roosevelt to buy Harmond out. Presumably, Harmond did not recognize Roosevelt's ruthlessness before, perhaps because he himself was behaving in a similar fashion. His better angel prevails, as it were:

> Oh, I see! Bernie Smith ... Bernie's calling in his chips. He used you for the radio station. Now he's using you to get half a stake in a prime redevelopment site that's being funded by the federal government. But he still needs minority involvement. He still needs a black face on the enterprise. Like he needed minority involvement to buy the radio station. Enter Roosevelt Hicks. The shuffling, grinning nigger in the woodpile. How much he pay for something like that? After he rolls over and puts his pants back on, what you got? A hundred dollars? Three hundred dollars? Or are you one of them high-classed thousand dollar whores? (Wilson 2008: 80)

Harmond ("harmony") makes an analysis that resonates with Eric Lott's *Love and Theft*. Roosevelt Hicks ("a hick") is the new blackface minstrel, and Harmond undermines his sense of independence through the metaphor of prostitution. Certainly charges of "sellout" or "Uncle Tom" are easily mounted in a post-racial environment, a notorious twenty-first-century public example being Harry Belafonte's charge against Colin Powell of Uncle Tomming for George W. Bush.[35] Wilson's implicitly Aristotelian terms, however, deepen the treatment. Three statements of "I see" drive Harmond's movement toward recognition ("I see! Bernie Smith . . . ," "I see now," and "I see who you are") (Wilson 2008: 80). Thus the spectacle character unmasks the lies of the others, who seem to be modern sophisticates to his country bumpkin. By the end, the audience sees that Old Joe is not the blackface minstrel but a fount of an ancient wisdom, whereas the modern moneymaker is the actual buffoon.

It is clear that Wilson is not satisfied with simple Aristotelian analogy, and he ends *Radio Golf* with masks that reify, distort, and disrupt our conscious understanding of the scene that audience members have, to varying degrees, recognized. Here again, at a superficial level, it might seem that Wilson is only concerned with masks. Just before Harmond's recognition, a man named Sterling Johnson has undergone similar abuse to that of Old Joe at Roosevelt's hands. Sterling was a pivotal character in Wilson's *Two Trains Running*, written in 1991 but set on the cusp of black power in 1969. He returns in *Radio Golf* as a handyman; he seeks work from Harmond earlier in the play but ends up (re)painting Aunt Ester's red door for Old Joe: "I changed the color to tone down the red a little bit. I mixed some white in there but not enough to make it pink" (Wilson 2008: 57). Earlier in the play, when Sterling entered the office to talk to Harmond, Roosevelt accused him of loitering. Later, Sterling retorts that Roosevelt (still) suffers from "blindyitis": "A dog knows it's a dog. A cat knows it's a cat. But a Negro don't know he's a Negro. He thinks he's a white man" (Wilson 2008: 76). After homing in on a question of identity fundamental to the Black Arts Movement of the 1960s, here again, "What's your name?," Sterling begins to walk off stage. Stage directions read: "Sterling goes over to the paint can and opens it. He dips his finger in, then marks a line from his forehead to his nose" (Wilson 2008: 77). The paint used on Aunt Ester's red door, a color that Harry Elam argues is central to Yoruba passageways, becomes critical in these last scenes, as markers of a new mask, a bit less red—that is, more integrated with other colors, but not with enough white to make it pink:

> STERLING: Look at that. You know what that is? That's a mark. I'm marking myself 'cause I don't want you to misunderstand this.
> *(He dips his hand in the paint and marks both sides of his cheeks.)*
> See that?
> *(He marks his face again.)*
> I learned that from Cochise. We on the battlefield now
> *(Sterling exits).* (Wilson 2008: 77)

The reference to the Apache leader—"Firewood"—who had a stronghold in the American West in 1861, merges the red mask that symbolizes African practice with a native one. Sterling is transformed on a metaphorical battlefield into a "warrior," a term Wilson often used in relation to his life and his art. As Roosevelt had done with Old Joe, he accused Sterling of insanity earlier in the play, but if Sterling is crazy, Harmond is on the brink of a similar pathology. The last person onstage at the end, stage directions move Harmond closer to Sterling: "*Roosevelt exits. Harmond closes the door. He turns around and discovers the office is empty. He takes the WBTZ poster, looks at it for a moment, then drops it in the trash. He discovers the paintbrush left on the desk. He takes off his coat and rolls up his sleeves. He picks up the paintbrush and exits*" (Wilson 2008: 81).

Blackface in *Radio Golf* is highly self-conscious, with Harmond Wilks returning to the jibe time and again throughout the play: Roosevelt is Bernie Smith's "black face"; Hicks is the "shuffling" darky in the woodpile, a clear reference to the stock in trade of the minstrel character. Yet at the same time, the character with the deepest Southern roots and a traceable performance genealogy to the blackface minstrel, Old Joe, emerges as heroic. He single-handedly stops a corporative enterprise.

It is worthwhile to return here to Susan Smith's general categories for the mask in modern drama. As has been indicated, masks can be satiric, pointing to a diminished humanity; a sign of a frozen persona, like the blackface minstrel or the comic satyr; a threshold leading us into deeper psychological dramas, such as the bloodstained mask signifying Oedipus' paradoxical blindness; or heroic, as characters, through the course of the play, takes on a more profound identity. Old Joe is not literally wearing a blackface mask in *Radio Golf*, but the contours of his character can be traced in nineteenth-century minstrel shows. Some of these characteristics include his riddling speech, the rural presence he brings to an urban environment, and the physicality of his humor. The minstrel shows of the nineteenth-century American popular stage that feature blackface masks (tar) on white actors influence literature. Literary figures such as Uncle Tom from *Uncle Tom's Cabin* and Jim from *Huckleberry Finn* give definitive shape to general stock minstrelsy. Black comic writers of the early twentieth century appropriate the character, and this is the tradition into which Wilson steps. Rather than a frozen mask of the minstrel, Wilson's Old Joe in fact dons a heroic, metaphysical mask. Old Joe creates a spectacle because he is so out of place in the twenty-first century. The true blackface minstrel, however, is Roosevelt Hicks, who wears a mask of assimilation, behind which there is nothing but an empty shell. Realizing this, Wilks ends the drama with his own transformation. Already an everyman with whom the audience might easily identify, Wilks puts on the mask of a warrior, the red paint that merges his intent with that of Aunt Ester and Uncle Joe, owners of the little red house that threatens to topple a modern American enterprise.

More than a superficial connection, namely the reality that Greek drama uses masks, and so does Wilson, the blackface minstrel mask is at the core of Wilson's deeper engagement with "the Greeks." The spectacle character, Old Joe in the case of *Radio Golf* and present in other August Wilson plays (Rankine 2013), is the site of Wilson's reception of Aristotle, "my interpretation of spectacle in the *Poetics*," in his words. The spectacle of blackface minstrelsy, moreover, is an indelibly American feature of popular performance. It is linked to American primitivism and local attempts to construct a twentieth-century response to antiquity. African-American playwrights by and large recognize the importance of confronting the stereotype of black primitivism head on, as it were. In the case of Wilson, such an effort precluded staging Greek drama for its own sake. There was too much else at stake for the black playwright of the twentieth century. Fittingly, Alain Locke referred to blacks as "an easily discriminable minority" (Locke 1928: 234), by which he meant, notwithstanding the exception of passing that proves the rule, you know a Negro when you *see* one. (Remember Sterling's diagnosis of blindyitis.) Through spectacle, the visual field of what can be known through sight, Wilson seeks to re-examine the history of the experience of blacks in America and to fashion a heroic black face. In order to do this, he covertly absorbs Aristotle's *Poetics* while never overtly staging a Greek play.

Notes

1. The lecture, "Behind the Minstrel Mask: Noble Sisle and Eubie Blake's *Shuffle Along* and its Image of Blackness," was on September 12, 2006, at Purdue University, and was part of the Classics Lecture Series for that year, which I hosted with Venetria Patton, Director of the African American Studies and Research Center. The series was focused on the relationship between the Classics and African-American literature.
2. For a history and overview, see Lott 1995. See also Rogin (1996) and Mahar (1999). Brundage (2011) is an important theoretical examination of blackface in a broader cultural context, with cultural and economic perspectives.
3. Curtis's article appears in Brundage 2011, titled "Black Creativity and Black Stereotype: Rethinking Twentieth-Century Popular Music in America," 124–46.
4. On black performers' parody of white traditions and blackface, see Krasner 1997; and for a general overview of black performance through the early twentieth century, see Krasner 2002. From as early as the mid-nineteenth century, such appropriation included the work of such black artists as Aida Overton Walker, on which see Elam and Krasner 2001, and Krasner in Brundage 2011, "The Real Thing," 99–123.
5. Krasner 1997, 2002; Krasner in Brundage 2011.
6. Citation here would be innumerable, but for recent material overview of the physical remains of Greek tragedy, including masks, see Hart 2010. For modern performance as a mode of reliving and interpreting Greek masks in theater, see Hall and Harrop 2010.
7. On black performance and parody, see Krasner 1997.
8. Krasner in Brundage 2011: 109.
9. On the interrogation of this notional "civilization," see Goff and Simpson 2007, who examine the work of African authors and black authors in America in dislodging the ties between Greek drama and "civilization."
10. For a study of Greek drama on the British stage, see Hall and Macintosh 2005.
11. Krasner in Brundage 2011: 114.
12. For general studies of August Wilson's plays, see Shannon 1996; Elam 2006. Important essay collections include Nadel 1993 and Bigsby 2007.
13. The plays that Wetmore (2003) covers are certainly more in keeping with classical reception.

14. Wilson's reflections on these plays and his process toward them can be found in Bryer and Hartig 2006.
15. On the Black Arts Movement, the "literary nationalism" of black artists during the 1960s and 1970s, see Smethurst 2005.
16. I explore this quote and the issues raised here more fully in Rankine 2013.
17. The following overview of Wilson's reading of Aristotle repeats material from Rankine 2013, but summary is necessary here.
18. Here again, see Krasner (2002), who also points to a heightened visual priority in black drama, and specifically pageantry, in the early twentieth century.
19. The translation is Halliwell 1987, which he tweaked in 1995. See Rankine 2013.
20. Mudimbe 1994 is the most theoretically sophisticated and philosophical approach to the view of blacks and the idea of Africa in Greek and Roman antiquity. Snowden 1991 is less complex, arguing that there was no "color prejudice" in Rome, and Thompson 1989 gives an overview of blacks specifically in Rome.
21. The information is from the Indiana Historical Society, collection #P 0474, in Robert Gordon's album.
22. It was also the topic of a Melville poem and a song by Will S. Hays.
23. See Indiana Historical Society file, collection #P 0323.
24. The club's programs through 1951 are housed at the Ball State University Archives and Special Collections.
25. In addition to Lott 1995, see Curtis in Brundage 2011 for the commercial and economic aspects of blackface.
26. On Foster, see Milligan 2010.
27. See Peter Kerr's *New York Times* obituary from July 21, 2007.
28. For the production history, see Wilson 2008. The play continues to be performed. The Raven Theatre in Chicago, Illinois, had a run in 2011, under the direction of Aaron Todd Douglas. In 2012, the Indianapolis Repertory Theatre ran it from January 10 to 29. Lou Bellamy founded the Penumbra Theatre Company in Saint Paul, Minnesota, in 1976, a black theater company closely tied to Wilson's career as a playwright. Wilson made his start directing plays at Penumbra.
29. On the struggle of black women to break free from Hollywood stereotypes, see Anderson 1997.
30. See Bean in Elam and Krasner 2001: 171–91.
31. For a terrific history of ties of blood and the American one-drop rule, see Malcolmson 2000. On the relationship between blackness, athletic performance, and the media, see Patterson 1999.
32. Wilson 2008: 44. It seems to me that the simile is not accidental but links Joe to fables from the Old South, the Uncle Remus stories, though this might be a stretch. See Harris 2002 for the tales.
33. Wilson often cited novelist Ralph Ellison as a literary model, and his riff on *Invisible Man* here, which in turn riffs on Homer's *Odyssey*, is striking. See Rankine 2006 on the theme of naming—the Ulysses theme—in Ellison's novel.
34. Lott (1995) again points up the relationship between commerce and blackface minstrelsy.
35. Several sources carried the 2002 story. See, for example, the transcript of Belafonte's October 15, 2002 interview with Larry King on CNN, reprinted at <http://www.blackcommentator.com/14_belafonte.html.> accessed July 30, 2012.

References

Anderson, L. M. (1997), *Mammies No More: The Changing Image of Black Women on Stage and Screen*. New York.
Bigsby, C. W. E. (2007), *The Cambridge Companion to August Wilson*. Cambridge.
Brundage, W. F. (2011), *Beyond Blackface: African Americans and the Creation of American Popular Culture, 1890–1930*. Chapel Hill, NC.
Bryer, J. R. and M. C. Hartig (2006), *Conversations with August Wilson*. Jackson, MS.
Butcher, S. H. [1907] (1932), *Aristotle's Theory of Poetry and Fine Art, with a Critical Text and Translation of the Poetics*. London.
Elam, H. J. (2006), *The Past as Present in the Drama of August Wilson*. Ann Arbor.
Elam, H. J. and D. Krasner (2001), *African American Performance and Theater History: A Critical Reader*. Oxford.
Else, G. (1967), *Aristotle, Poetics*. Ann Arbor.
Goff, B. and M. Simpson (2007), *Crossroads in the Black Aegean: Oedipus, Antigone, and Dramas of the African Diaspora*. Oxford.
Hall, E. and S. Harrop (2010), *Theorising Performance: Greek Drama, Cultural History, and Critical Practice*. London.
Hall, E. and F. Macintosh (2005), *Greek Tragedy and the British Theatre, 1660–1914*. Oxford.
Halliwell, S. (1987), *The Poetics of Aristotle*. Chapel Hill, NC.
Halliwell, S. [1989] (1998), *Aristotle Poetics*. Chicago.
Halliwell, S. (1995), *Aristotle Poetics; Longinus On the Sublime; Demetrius: On Style*. Cambridge, MA.
Harris, J. C. (2002), *The Complete Tales of Uncle Remus*. New York.
Hart, M. L. (2010), *The Art of Greek Theater*. Los Angeles.
Krasner, D. (1997), *Resistance, Parody and Double Consciousness in African American Theatre, 1895–1910*. New York.
Krasner, D. (2002), *A Beautiful Pageant: African American Theatre, Drama, and Performance in the Harlem Renaissance, 1910–1927*. New York.
Locke, A. (1928), "The Negro's Contribution to American Art and Literature," *Annals of the American Academy of Political and Social Science* 140: 234–47.
Lott, E. (1995), *Love and Theft: Blackface Minstrelsy and the American Working Class*. Oxford.
Mahar, W. J. (1999), *Behind the Burnt Cork Mask: Early Blackface Minstrelsy and Antebellum American Popular Culture*. Urbana, IL.
Malcolmson, S. L. (2000), *One Drop of Blood: The American Misadventure of Race*. New York.
Milligan, H. V. (2010), *Stephen Collins Foster: A Biography of America's Folk-Song Composer (1920)*. Whitefish, MT.
Mudimbe, V. Y. (1994), *The Idea of Africa*. Bloomington, IN.
Nadel, A. (1993), *May All Your Fences Have Gates: Essays on the Drama of August Wilson*. Iowa City.
Patterson, O. (1999), *Rituals of Blood: The Consequences of Slavery in Two American Centuries*. New York.
Rankine, P. D. (2006), *Ulysses in Black: Ralph Ellison, Classicism, and African American Literature*. Madison.
Rankine, P. D. (2013), *Aristotle and Black Drama: A Theater of Civil Disobedience*. Waco, TX.
Rogin, M. (1996), *Blackface, White Noise: Jewish Immigrants in the Hollywood Melting Pot*. Berkeley and Los Angeles.

Shannon, S. D. (1996), *The Dramatic Vision of August Wilson*. Washington, DC.
Smethurst, J. E. (2005), *Black Arts Movement: Literary Nationalism in the 1960s and 1970s*. Chapel Hill, NC.
Smith, S. V. H. (1984), *Masks in Modern Drama*. Berkeley.
Snowden, F. (1991), *Before Color Prejudice: The Ancient View of Blacks*. Cambridge, MA.
Thompson, L. A. (1989), *Romans and Blacks*. Norman, OK.
Wetmore, K., Jr. (2003), *Black Dionysus: Greek Tragedy and African American Theatre*. Jefferson, NC.
Wilson, A. (1997), "The Ground on Which I Stand," *Callaloo* 20.3 (Summer), 493–503.
Wilson, A. (2008), *Radio Golf*. New York.

CHAPTER 31

"AESCHYLUS GOT FLOW!"

Afrosporic Greek Tragedy and Will Power's The Seven

KEVIN J. WETMORE, JR.

Since I am the last storyteller of my crew
I know just what I have to do
I wanna teach you the old stories
And then you go make 'em new.

Will Power, *Flow*

HIP HOP DITHRYMBS

THE SEVEN began life through a workshop production with the Thick Description Theatre Company in San Francisco, and was performed in August and September of 2001 at the Thick House, Thick Description's home space (de la Viña 2001: F1). Ironically, Thick Description's production only had six performers. Subsequently, Power revised and remounted the play in New York in January, February, and March of 2006.[1] This *Seven* was produced with a larger budget and higher production values than the San Francisco production. The show was produced again in San Diego at the La Jolla Playhouse in February and March 2008. Power's play maintains many similarities with other African-American adaptations of Greek tragedy, but there is one key element of transculturation which separates Power's play from the others.[2]

Unlike other Afro-Greek or Afrosporic adaptations such as Adrienne Kennedy's *Oedipus the King*, Breuer and Telson's *The Gospel at Colonus*, Rita Dove's *Darker Face of the Earth*, or Eldris Cooper's *The Tragedy of Medea Jackson*, all of which to varying degrees transculturate Athenian narrative into African-American socio-cultural context, *The Seven* does so through hip-hop, and as a result functions in a different manner than these other adaptations.[3] In order to understand *The Seven* in context, I shall use hip-hop theory as a lens by which to consider it as a hip-hop adaptation. (See Banks and Rankine, this volume.) I would like to propose the hip-hop model of the sample and the mashup in order to understand *The Seven*. "Samples" and "sampling" refers to the practice in hip-hop music of taking a small portion of a song and either looping it (playing the same sequence repeatedly) or integrating it within a larger tapestry, adding new lyrics over the song. Power's play is not just an adaptation, it is an intertextual dialogue with fluid and multiple meanings that samples Aeschylus in the same vein as Eminem's "Stan," which samples Dido's "Thank You," or P. Diddy's "Come with Me," which samples Led Zeppelin's "Kashmir," or Ice-T's "The Tower," which samples the theme from the film *Halloween*, or even Third Base's "Pop Goes the Weasel," which blends The Who's "Eminence Front" and Peter Gabriel's "Sledgehammer" into a multi-sample new work. Each sample builds upon the listener's knowledge (or lack thereof) of the original. The artist assumes no a priori knowledge of the original on the part of the listener, but if one knows the source, then further meaning is generated within the song. Meaning is not simply generated by narrative itself, or in the space between audience and performer, but also by reference and mashup—the blending of two texts that talk to each other. What is understood depends on whether or not one gets the reference.

A mashup is a song or composition created by blending two or more songs, usually by overlaying the vocal track of one song seamlessly over the music track of another. They can be done via software to produce a new song or it can be mixed (mashed?) live by a DJ. One of the most famous mashup albums is Danger Mouse's 2004 *The Gray Album*, a mixing of Jay-Z's *The Black Album* with The Beatles' *White Album*. I propose, since Power has created his work using hip-hop, that we analyze the work not as a Greek play but rather that we consider *The Seven* as a mashup that samples Aeschylus. In other words, let us not analyze *The Seven* on Aeschylus' terms, or how well it conforms to an idea of the original, but through hip-hop culture in order to see how Greek tragedy as filtered through hip-hop generates meaning for contemporary American audiences.

Rustom Bharucha has argued that all theater, like all politics, is local anyway, being spatially and temporally located and limited by nature (Bharucha 1993: 240). Will Power's *The Seven* is much more about twenty-first-century America than fifth-century Athens. Hip-hop culture makes this transhistoricity into new historicity even more fast-paced. In a world where the Black-Eyed Peas are already being referred to as "back in the day," and when I tell my students about Run-DMC, whom they only know from reality television, De La Soul, or Grandmaster Flash I may as well be discussing John Adams or Marcus Garvey. Hip-hop moves quickly, and five years is a long time, let alone the 25 centuries since Aeschylus. It is this cultural speed of hip-hop, which also indicates that each iteration of *The Seven* transformed the one before, even as it built on it. The La Jolla *Seven* is not only adapted from Aeschylus, it is adapted from the San Francisco *Seven*.

In that sense, I would like to consider *The Seven* as a fluid text that changed as it continually changed its locality as it was performed in different years in different cities, although not always for the better, and while looking at the larger implications for studying Greek tragedy in the African diaspora. I would also like to frame it in context of Power's earlier work, which also plays with sevens and flows and narrative.

In the critical response to *The Seven*, we see a larger assumption that Power has adapted a classical European text to an African-American context, reducing the act of adaptation to a simple ethnic binary: what was European is now Afrosporic. I would like to argue for a much more complex understanding of *The Seven*, especially considering that Power himself does not see the Aeschylean original, *The Seven against Thebes*, as being solely a European text. He argues for a more complex understanding of Greek culture and I, for one, will accommodate him here in trying to understand what *The Seven* is and how it functions.[4] I ultimately want to consider the different audiences for Power's work and the above-mentioned competing claims on it by audiences, critics, and scholars.[5] Any discussion of *The Seven* as an example of hip-hop culture, however, is further problematized by Power's own identity as a major figure in hip-hop theater, a multiple-grant recipient, whose work appears in major theaters and is reviewed and considered by major media and further problematized by the very locales mentioned above, in which *The Seven* has been performed.[6] Who are the intended and actual audiences for *The Seven*?

Previews and reviews of *The Seven* in newsprint and online have frequently been concerned with some sense of competing claims of authenticity, depending on the individual critic's own concerns and what he or she privileges: "Is it Greek enough?" "Is it street enough?" "Is it really Aeschylus?" "Is it really hip-hop?," and "Is it really hip-hop theater?" One might note the *New York Times*' critics' historic distrust of anything hip-hop near a "legit" theater building. A single example, the title of Bruce Weber's 1999 review of *The Bomb-itty of Errors*: "Rap is to Shakespeare as Bomb is to Comedy," should suffice to demonstrate where the mainstream (read: older Euro-American) critics fall, although things have improved slightly in the past decade. The critical response has been an understanding that Power takes a Greek tragedy (albeit one not very well known) and transculturates it into a "black thing." But is that *The Seven*'s teleology: white to black? The answer is more complex than a simple "yes" or "no."

I argued in *Shakespeare and Youth Culture* that hip-hop expropriations of Shakespeare (and for that matter Shakespearian appropriations of hip-hop) are rooted in what Henry Louis Gates, Jr. refers to in *The Signifying Monkey* as "signifyin(g)."[7] (See Powers, this volume.) The trope of signifyin(g) is the trope of the talking book—the "double voiced text that talks to other texts" (Gates, Jr. 1988: xxv). *Seven* is certainly a talking book in Gates's sense. "The impetus of African-American signifying," states James R. Andreas, Sr., "is the search for the 'black voice' in the 'white written text'" (Andreas, Sr. 1999: 105). And certainly critics on both coasts saw in *The Seven* an African-American appropriation of a "white" text. Yet, I would like to argue here that such a simple binary may work for Shakespeare, who is uncontestedly a European playwright linked to a colonizing/imperialist culture, but does not necessarily apply to Greek tragedy, which bears a more complex relationship to Africa and African-America. I argued in *Athenian Sun in an African Sky* that Shakespeare is perceived in Africa as colonial culture, but Greek culture is perceived as not having "the taint of imperialist Europe and the national literatures of the colonial powers," and, following Bernal, many Africans perceive Greek culture as African in origin.[8] Is African-American Greek tragedy simply, *pace* Gates and Andreas, looking for a black voice in a white text?

In *Black Dionysus: Greek Tragedy and African American Theatre*, I argued for three models of understanding Afrosporic Greek tragedy: black Orpheus, which works as a simile ("this African thing is like this Greek thing"), black Athena, which claims Greek culture is actually derived from African culture and therefore Afrocentric Greek tragedy reclaims a stolen legacy, and black Dionysus, which sees Afrosporic Greek tragedy as "a form of self-aware intertextuality" and "a means by which diverse communities might be encountered in public space and the historical forces that have shaped them might be exposed" (Wetmore 2003: 44, 45). In other words, it is not just black and white.

Will Power, appearing on *The Colbert Report* on September 18, 2006, argues for a modified "Black Athena" approach to understanding the relationship between Athenian cultural material and Afrosporic history, specifically as it related to *The Seven*:

> It's really interesting because the ancient Greeks were not black, but a lot of the ancient Greek myths—we don't know what they were. But they were actually before Greeks...
>
> You're talking about Aeschylus, Sophocles—they were what you call "Greek" but Oedipus and a lot of the myths are from a time when they weren't even considered to be Greek. They were like a different people; they were the Greek's ancestors, so to speak. And they did have connections to Phoenicia and Egypt and other places. I don't know if they would be considered "black" because there were no "African-Americans" a thousand years ago, but there were Egyptians, you know? So I think they had these kind of connections, y'dig?

In other words, Power sees Greek tragedy as already a white voice in an African text. Athenian drama is a European appropriation of older narratives that are at least partially North African in origin.[9] One may agree or disagree with Power's thesis, as the responses to Bernal's *Black Athena* show, but we ought to evaluate Power's project based on his suppositions. In other words, it does not matter for the purposes of this chapter if the dictates of Afrocentric Classicism are true, what matters is that Power believes them to be true. And for Power, it's not a reappropriation but a more complex mashup of a narrative that was already a mashup. Not "is Greek tragedy African" but rather "what does the fact that Will Power lays claim to Greek tragedy as connected to Africa mean for his work" is the question we must ask. Power uses hip-hop music and culture to create a new version of narrative that Aeschylus had already sampled from the prehistoric Greek culture which was connected to or possibly even originated in North Africa.

In other words, Power would argue he is not signifyin(g) in Gates's sense—he is not looking for a black voice in a white text. He is adding a black voice to a white voice speaking an originally brown text (if you will pardon the color analogy being taken to a ridiculous level). Again, let us not reduce this down to a simple binary. In Power's own words, Aeschylus' play is "different" and "connected." Space does not permit a deep discussion of Greek and Egyptian notions of identity and ethnicity, but suffice to say when we engage in the study of classical texts we must be very careful of imposing modern notions of ethnicity, nationality, color, and race on older cultures, as Power himself wisely notes.

Audience and Identity—What Set You Claimin'?

The central concern voiced by both Power and his critics was the audience, their identity, and how their understanding of Greek tragedy and hip-hop would shape their understanding and experience of *The Seven*. Audiences are strange things: groups comprised of individuals who neither have a uniform response nor a uniform background. Even from night to night in the same theater the audiences change and thus the production and its received meaning changes, particularly since plays don't mean but rather generate meaning (Wetmore 2003). The change of locale and hence the change of audiences for a particular show thus further changes the meaning of the show and, for the most recent incarnation of *The Seven*, "The shores of San Diego County are a far cry from downtown Manhattan," as David Ng reports (Ng 2008: F4). While several critics and even Power himself acknowledged that part of the problem in New York was sustaining a youthful, urban (read: young, hip, mostly African-American) audience, and that the New York theater audience is, in Meineck's delightful turn of phrase, "geeky, nit picky and increasingly elderly," with a mixture of hip Brooklyn kids on some nights, if the production was lucky (Meineck 2006: 146).

The La Jolla Playhouse, on the other hand, has a mostly older, suburban audience. Power was quoted as saying he thought there would be an audience for the show in Southern California: "granola bohemian cats" who "might really dig it."[10] Anecdotally the audiences with which I saw the production were mixtures of older, Euro-American audience members, older African-American audience members, and younger audience members of many ethnicities. I suspect that the last were there first and foremost as theater aficionados and tangentially or not at all as "hip-hop heads"—this was not the same crowd as the rapper Nas' concert a week later.

Which brings me to the question, who is the audience for *The Seven*, particularly in San Diego? The short answer is that a hybrid form creates a hybrid audience. Some folks know hip-hop, more know theater, and many know both. But *The Seven* functions less as a traditional African-American adaptation of Greek tragedy (if there is such a thing) than what I would call a meta-mashup of hip-hop and Greek tragedy, functioning simultaneously as both.

On the one hand, the narrative comes from Aeschylus, and the Greeks are responsible for drama-based theatrical performance. And some critics even saw in *The Seven* the closest approximation an audience can come to original Greek performance in a relevant social context. Michael Peter Bolus correctly observed that "*The Seven* dramatizes the idea that modern practitioners must adopt the totality of the Greek tragedian's conception of the theatre—an understanding issuing from a comprehensive employment of drama, music, and dance as integral to achieving the desired emotional, intellectual and aesthetic effects" (Bolus 2007: 123). Will Power's conception of *The Seven* matches Bolus's conjectured Greek tragedian's conception: rhythm, ritual, dance, music, drama, narrative enacted in front of a civic audience. So Greek theater fans can find much to appreciate in *The Seven*. Before we tackle the issue of hip-hop, however, I wish us to examine our ideas about audience once more.

Charles Isherwood, for example, also cannily admits that the "white, middle-aged, still figuring out the iPod-thing" average New York City theater-goer "probably isn't all that conversant with the conventions of classical Greek theater, either" (Isherwood 2006: B4). As an avid theater-goer myself, I do not think I have ever remarked, "Wow! What a great use of the ekkeklema"! What audiences may be experiencing with *The Seven* is not the performance of a specific Greek tragedy but the performance of the idea of Greek tragedy.

Peter Meineck has remarked that to do any kind of adaptation of *Seven against Thebes* is in itself "almost unbelievable" (Meineck 2006: 145). I would agree, but with a caveat. The beauty of Aeschylus' play is that the backstory is known, the idea of Greek tragedy is known, but the play itself is not. A hip-hop *Antigone* or a hip-hop *Medea* is a tricky thing. Knowledgeable audience members know the play well, have most likely seen previous productions of the original and perhaps even other adaptations, and most likely have strong ideas about those plays. But even those average theater-goers well versed in classical texts are not likely to know *Seven against Thebes*, and many Classicists I suspect would be so delighted to see the play mentioned anywhere that a popular adaptation might even be seen as a good thing—a doorway into Aeschylus rather than a desecration of a beloved text. Additionally, theory must give way to economic reality: after Shakespeare, Greek tragedy is the most multicultural bankable adaptation material. Adapting a lesser-known Greek tragedy gives one all the cachet of adapting a Greek tragedy with the freedom to rework a story known only by its bare bones at best. And what Power has done is not so much adapt a specific text (although, admittedly he has done that), as present the audience with the idea of Greek tragedy in hip-hop form. He has mashed up Greek tragic text and practice with hip-hop culture and practice.

Music is one of the places where the play most evidently moves from Aeschylus' Greek theater to a modern, hip-hop theater, although music is also a mark of the choral role in Greek drama. The music changed from production to production of *The Seven*, as the sound of hip-hop changed from 2001 to 2006. Even the two year transition between 2006 and 2008 required that the music be rewritten/remixed to keep up with current hip-hop sounds. What worked in 2001 and 2006 sounded dated or "wack" in 2008. Thus, in order to maintain freshness, Power and his collaborators insisted that the music sound contemporary to hip-hop ears. I politely suggest that the vast majority of average La Jolla subscribers could not tell the difference between 2006 beats and 2008 beats, but they were not the only intended audience. In order to maintain authenticity for hip-hop theater– not the authenticity of the Greeks but the authenticity of the beats—the music had to be contemporary. Greek tragedy has become "universal," but at its origins was highly temporal. Hip-hop, still in its cultural infancy, in a sense, has no sense of transhistoricity yet. Thus the need, for authenticity's sake, to update the sound of the show for San Diego.

Mashups and References

I think it might also be useful to consider *The Seven* as expanding on specific themes in Power's earlier work, especially his solo show called *Flow*, which brought him to national attention as it toured the United States and received much critical attention. It began with the idea of seven individuals joining together as well: "Seven | There were only seven, y'all | only seven storytellers in the neighborhood | I said/there were only seven storytellers in the neighborhood, y'all" is how *Flow* began. Power then embodied seven different individuals, all of whom told their own individual stories in their own individual ways. Concluding with the epigram to this lecture: "Since I am the last storyteller of my crew | I know just what I have to do | I wanna teach you the old stories | And then you go make 'em new," I would argue this might be construed as the central theme both of *Flow* and of Power's work overall: the power of storytelling and the need for both artist and community to make the story one's own. Hip-hop and Greek theater have storytelling in common.

In fact, the Aeschylean original does not dramatize the story that Power's does. Instead, it tells the story through narration. The original play was first performed in Athens in 467 BCE, the third of a trilogy about the Labdacids (*Laius, Oedipus*, being the first two). The play shows Eteocles waiting for his brother Polynices to attack, interacting with the chorus. There is no Oedipus, no Polynices, and the eponymous seven are offstage for the main event. Much of the stage action of Aeschylus' play is simply monologues and dialogues about how Eteocles and the chorus feel about the approaching army and Polynices, lengthy descriptions of the seven champions and their shields, and the Thebans who will face those champions. The battle between brothers takes place offstage and the results are reported, as almost always in Aeschylean tragedy, by messenger.

Power dramatizes everything Aeschylus simply narrates. In *The Seven*, we are introduced to all seven champions. Polynices is present, as is Oedipus. It is this reintroduction of the mythic characters as dramatic presences in the play that transforms Aeschylus' narrative into a mashup of Aeschylus' text, the original myth, and hip-hop popular culture. Suzan-Lori Park's theory of "rev & rep"—revision and repetition—is relevant here. Repeat with variation, and meaning is found in difference. To this pair of dramatization of narrative and repetition we might add the third aspect from hip-hop: reference. A key aspect of hip-hop rhyme is popular culture and historical reference. Whether Will Smith's "Mohammed Ali told me I'm the greatest," Kanye talking about a guy you can see "any given Sunday" (in a song in which Jaime Foxx is referencing and covering

Ray Charles, as well, where Oliver Stone's movie by the same title—starring Foxx—is expected knowledge), or the Fugees, remarking that they are "running through Crown Heights screaming out 'Mazel Tov,'" a reference to the Crown Heights riots of August 1991.[11] We may read the line on the surface level, but the reference reframes the lyric and hence the meaning into a much larger context. Will Power reframes Aeschylus' story using the techniques of rev, rep, and ref.

I wish to briefly illustrate rev, rep, and ref through three characters from *The Seven* not present in Aeschylus' original that demonstrate how Power's mashup works: the DJ, Oedipus, and Polynices. In the first place, the DJ is one of the original four elements[12] and the person who not only provides the beats but who also shapes the story to be told. In the case of the seven, the story begins with the DJ. She frames the entire narrative with the notion of a mashup: "Let me tell ya who I be | The one who makes Shakespeare jam with James Brown . . . There are no two worlds I cannot mix | I am the DJ." She then proceeds to play a record of a sonorous voice reciting lines from the Aeschylus original: "O house of endless tears | O hopeless end | It is the curse of your father that bears fruit in you | And the harvest is no blessing." This "sample" reminds us of the original. But like all good DJs, Power and his onstage alter ego, the DJ, loop it, flip it, and reframe it: "Yo, kinda pessimistic, right? But his voice sound tight. Kinda like Freddy Kruger if he went to Harvard or somethin'." *The Seven* is as much comment on Greek tragedy and the popular idea of how it is performed as it is actual adaptation of Greek tragedy. Power offers this mocking recording to demonstrate a reverence for the Classics in direct contrast to his own, playful, hip-hop approach. The dirge on the record contrasts with the hip-hop beats of the other record on the turntable in self-referential celebration of the power of hip-hip to make Greek tragedy seem more alive.

Hip-hop allows for self-referential criticism and self-conscious reference. The record was pessimistic, but the voice is tight. The play then reframes Aeschylus: Freddy Kruger at Harvard. With this construction of the original as a "pessimistic" voice, Power/the DJ have done more to shape the reception of Aeschylus than any scholarly introduction to the play. The reference only works if you know who Freddy Kruger is and what Harvard is, but, to be honest, writing for a twenty-first-century American audience, Power uses very recognizable references to ground Aeschylus in an American (and specifically African-American) context.

The DJ, working with the chorus, who will also play the seven champions as well, tells the story of the house of Oedipus. Here Power as DJ again brings in the myth rather than the text. In a very controversial and problematic (considering the audience) appearance, Oedipus himself enters, pimped out with sunglasses and cane. Peter Meineck rightly sees the character as transcending stereotype, becoming "a compelling physical manifestation of a visceral and destructive curse" (Meineck 2006: 154). Others see a predominantly white audience seeing a stereotype of urban African-Americans confirmed by the character. Yet I would note, Oedipus also works because the character as represented in the play also fully embodies the double-coded referential world of hip-hop.

Seemingly dressed as a 1970s Blaxploitation pimp, Oedipus (compared by critics to Rudy Ray Moore and his character Dolemite, Superfly, or Huggie Bear, among others), tells the crowd, "Y'all don't know who you fuckin' with," and that he was "the one and only motha fucka," both of which received a laugh from the audience as lines that work on multiple levels as the aforementioned hip-hop references. On the one hand, Classicists can appreciate that Oedipus literally did not know "with whom he was fucking" and he may be the only figure in both literature and history for whom the epithet "motherfucker" is not an insult but an accurate description. It is playful both in its referentiality and in its obscenity. Thus, on the other hand, it is funny because someone just employed lewd and vulgar language in the La Jolla Theatre, and the pleasure of saying and hearing dirty words is one that never quite leaves us, no matter our level of sophistication (right, David Mamet?). In addition to the dramatic irony it provides and its sample of the Oedipus myth, obscenity also gives Oedipus street-cred and links him to a long line of blaxploitation heroes and rap artists. Some examples include Oedipus' line "I hear this cat Shaft is a bad mother... Shut your mouth." Here Oedipus samples famous lyrics from Richard Roundtree's "Theme from *Shaft*," which has a good deal of influence in the rap world. Like the critics, I also saw Superfly and Dolemite in Oedipus, but I also saw rappers DMX and ODB. Power plays on stereotypes of black rappers and cinematic pimps. By doing so, Power not only signifies and double codes through this character, but he is also relying upon multiple references and referents. In the end, Power encourages a proliferation—rather than a limiting—of such cross-references.

Oedipus' own use of multiple names for himself was very much in keeping with hip-hop culture, in which an individual has multiple identities and multiple names: Christopher Wallace is "Notorious B.I.G." and "Biggie Smalls"; Marshall Mathers is "Eminem" who is also "Slim Shady." Oedipus is all of the references the audience conjures: the Greek Oedipus, the rapper, the pimp, the bad motherfucker. The hip-hop artist exists in the past, present, and future simultaneously by speaking of the past in the present while making future promises. The DJ also calls Oedipus "The original ODB," a reference to Ol' Dirty Bastard, the stage name of Russell Tyrone Jones, a member of the Wu Tang Clan. ODB's name itself came from a 1980 Taiwanese martial arts film, *Guai zhao ruan pi she*, released in the United States as *Ol' Dirty & The Bastard*, which Method Man asserted was specific to Jones as there was "no father" to his style which was playful, profane, and free-associative. The line goes under the radar of the individual who does not know the reference, but it creates a whole new world of meaning for one who does (and again, tangentially, bore out my initial feeling that Oedipus was not just a 1970s pimp but also a contemporary rapper posing as a 1970s pimp). Hip-hop culture is nothing if not aware of African-American cultural history and more than happy to play with and against, embracing stereotypes, sometimes to subvert them, sometimes reinforcing them, often in a way that the "granola bohemian cats" audience members most likely would not understand.

In addition to the DJ and Oedipus, Polynices is a character in Power's play. Polynices is also not present in the original except as a corpse and by report, yet Power makes him a central figure in his version. The play begins with Polynices and Eteocles promising to transcend the family curse and rule together peacefully. It ends with brothers killing each other. One reviewer of the San Francisco production read the play as "a forceful contemporary look at the cycle of violence among blacks" (de la Viña 2001: F1). This reading remains present and viable through New York and San Diego. In his review of the production for the *Los Angeles Times*, theater critic Charles McNulty wrote: "The question here is, can a man transcend a miserable and mind-colonizing father? Of course the answer is already decided. The interest is in how the catastrophic psychology plays out" (McNulty 2008: E3). The play and Polynices' role would continue to develop and evolve, however.

Will Power remarked of the difference between the two productions, "It went really well in New York, but we ran out of time and money. We didn't get to do everything we wanted to do. So coming here [to LaJolla] has been great."[13] The 2008 production featured substantial revision, especially of the second act. The final fight between Eteocles and Polynices, in New York a complex dance-combat routine choreographed by Bill T. Jones, received an additional opening ritual "designed to convey a sense of recognition, physical hostility and emotional ambiguity all at once":

> "I have this really ritualistic chant, kind of like the Wu-Tang Clan," [Power] says. When the brothers meet, they begin to exhale rhythmically using heavy, audible breathes, getting louder and faster as they circle each other. The breathing gradually escalates to a kind of chanting that segues into the full-on fight sequence. (Ng 2008: F4)

Polynices thus moves from offstage presence in Aeschylus to equal stage time in Power. What was a quick dance denouement in New York was expanded into a full ritual before battle for San Diego. By adding this sequence to the mythic struggle between brothers, Power moved the piece from comment on black-on-black crime to a full series of references to everything from Cain and Abel to Biggie and Tupac to Iraq. While adding these elements to the narrative of *Seven against Thebes*, Power does not merely recreate the Aeschylean original with a hip-hop soundtrack, he also creates a perspective on violence in society.

Conclusion

So, what does it all mean?[14]

I have argued before that African-American Greek tragedy is a blending of the local (African-American culture and history), the original Greek text (whatever that means), and the "African"—a cultural connection to the motherland (at least for those who profess Afrocentric Classicism) that imbues the appropriation with a link not just to ancient Athens but to ancient and contemporary Africa. *The Seven*, I believe, while embodying this definition of African-American Greek tragedy, also transcends it and leads us to a new way of thinking about African-American Greek tragedy. Will Power's meta-mashup lives in a new cultural and critical space. It is as much comment on Greek tragedy and its production and reception as it is adaptation of Greek tragedy.

As Sabrina Brancato wrote in a recent issue of *Research in African Literatures*, new terminology and new theories are emerging to deal with the complex reality of Afrosporic authors, particularly given the complexities of ethnic and national identity in a multiracial world (Brancato 2008: 1). She terms this literature "Afro-European" and uses this term to identify the fluid nature and multiple sources for emerging literatures, not just dramatic, not to mention the varied locales in which Afro-European literature may be produced (Brancato 2008: 1). For example, Ngũgĩ wa Thiong'o and Wole Soyinka now both live and teach in Southern California, the former at the University of California, Irvine, and the latter at my own school, Loyola Marymount University. Athol Fugard, that most South African of authors, splits his time between Ireland and Southern California as well. His three most recent works have all premièred in Los Angeles. Cornell West refers to the locale in which such works are being created and disseminated as "shared cultural space" and refuses to reduce that space to simple black/white binaries. I would like to make a plea, in conclusion, to consider *The Seven* as both the product of that shared cultural space and a work that itself creates shared cultural space. This model, therefore, offers a new way to think about Greek tragedy in the Americas while also constantly reframing itself. By using sampling and by mashing up Aeschylus' text with African-American cultural history and social concerns, Power has created an adaptation that speaks to contemporary American audiences, even if the individual audience members hear and understand different aspects of that text. The self-referential aspect of hip-hop allows for commentary on both Greek adaptation and on the resulting text itself. Moving beyond a simple African-American/Euro-American binary and recognizing the shared cultural space of both hip-hop and Greek culture allows us to understand texts such as *The Seven* as *American* texts with multiple points of origins and multiple constituent audiences.

Notes

1. See Mee 2006, Dunning 2006, Bolus 2007, and especially Meineck 2006 for descriptions and analyses of the New York production of *The Seven*.
2. For additional information on African-American adaptation of Greek tragedy and the similarities between the many different texts, see Wetmore 2003, especially chapters two and three.
3. Carl Weber defines "transculturation" as "a transfer of culture" from one society to another in which the appropriated text is initially deconstructed and then the "findings" are rearranged according to the codes of the target culture, and the disappearance of the original forms from the adapted text (1991: 34). The above mentioned texts all transculturate Athenian dramatic text into African-American cultural contexts. *The Seven*, as this chapter argues, has hip-hop culture as its target culture of transculturation.
4. See Wetmore 2003, as Power advocates a "Black Athena" model, verging on "Black Dionysus"—see below for a summation of these models.
5. I am, following Adam Krims, forced to note that my own identity, as both a theater scholar and a Euro-American hip-hop fan, "exacerbates the tangle of objective situational impossibility," and I am concerned that when we consider Power's blend of hip-hop culture and

American understanding of ancient Athenian culture, we are in danger of increasing the distance "of commodified forms from the underprivileged creators of these forms"—Krims 2000: 6.
6. "Hip-Hop theater" it should be noted, is a contested term, with Danny Hoch arguing that it is not theater with hip-hop music in it but rather theater that speaks to the hip-hop generation using its own language and tropes—Hoch 1998. See the introductions to Banks 2011 and Hoch 1998 for analyses of what constitutes hip-hop theater in opposition to more mainstream theater or theater that employs hip-hop music without being hip-hop theater in and of itself. See also those texts for exemplary hip-hop dramas.
7. Wetmore 2006, referencing Gates, Jr., 1988: 148.
8. Wetmore 2002: 21. Martin Bernal's *Black Athena* (1987) began the scholarly Afrocentric Classicism movement which argues that Greek culture is derived from North African culture and thus all western classical culture is African in origin. Appropriating Greek texts, therefore, is perceived as a use of African, not western, cultural material.
9. See Bernal 1987 for the arguments behind Power's assertions. For a full summary of the Afrocentric Classicism debate, see Wetmore 2002: 15–20.
10. Quoted in Ng 2008: F4.
11. The respective songs and their references are Will Smith, "Getting' Jiggy with It" (1998) in which Smith, while singing his own praises, cites Muhammad Ali's famous line, "I'm the Greatest"; Kanye West, "Gold Digger" (2005), referencing the Oliver Stone film *Any Given Sunday* about a football team (and thus implying he is rapping about a well-known football player); and The Fugees, "How Many Mics?" (1996), which references the ethnic makeup of Crown Heights, Brooklyn, in which Caribbean-Americans and Orthodox Jews live in the same neighborhood (although it might also be referencing the Crown Heights crisis of 1991, in which a rabbi's car struck and killed an African-American child and in retaliation a young rabbinical student was stabbed. The neighborhood erupted in racial tensions and thus for a young rapper to say he can "run through Crown Heights screaming out 'MazelTov,'" indicates his fearlessness and bravado.).
12. The "four elements," as they are known, are the DJ, who spins the records, the MC, who raps, break dancing, and graffiti. Hip-hop heads consider them the pillars of hip-hop culture.
13. Quoted in Ng 2008: F4.
14. This line is in and of itself a hip-hop reference, as it is repeated numerous times during "The Magic Number," one of De La Soul's hits off of *3 Feet High and Rising* (1989), one of the seminal alternative hip-hop records, now considered a masterpiece (a "classic"?) by hip-hop heads.

References

Andreas, J. R., Sr. (1999), "Signifyin' on *The Tempest* in *Mama Day*," in C. Desmet and R. Sawyer eds., *Shakespeare and Appropriation*. London.
Banks, D. (2011), *Say Word! Voices from Hip Hop Theater*. Ann Arbor.
Bernal, M. (1987), *Black Athena*, i: *The Fabrication of Ancient Greece 1785–1985*. London.
Bharucha, R. (1993), *Theatre and the World*. London.
Bolus, M. P. (2007), "Review: *Hecuba/The Seven*," *Theatre Journal* 59: 121–3.

Brancato, S. (2008), "Afro-European Literature(s): A New Discursive Category?," *Research in African Literatures* 39: 1–13.
de la Viña, M. (2001), "Tragedy of 'Seven' Transcends Years," *San Jose Mercury News* August 23, 1F; 4F.
Dunning, J. (2006), "He's Taking Aeschylus Hip-Hop," *New York Times* February 10, E1.
Gates, H. L., Jr. (1988), *The Signifying Monkey: A Theory of African-American Literary Criticism*. Oxford.
Hoch, D. (1998), *Jails, Hospitals & Hip-Hop/Some People*. New York.
Isherwood, C. (2006), "Hip Hop of the Gods," *New York Times* February 26, B4.
Krims, A. (2000), *Rap Music and the Poetics of Identity*. Cambridge.
McNulty, C. (2008), "Aeschylus Gets Remixed," *Los Angeles Times* February 20, E3.
Mee, C. (2006), "Hip-Hop Visions of an Ancient World," *American Theatre* 23, 28–32, 70.
Meineck, P. (2006), "Live from New York: Hip Hop Aeschylus and Operatic Aristophanes," *Arion* 14, 145–68.
Ng, P. (2008), "Toward a More Magnificent 'Seven,'" *Los Angeles Times* February 17, F4.
Weber, C. (1991), "AC/TC: Currents of Theatrical Exchange," in B. Marranca and G. Dasgupta eds., *Interculturalism and Performance*. New York.
Wetmore, K. J., Jr. (2002), *The Athenian Sun in an African Sky*. Jefferson, NC.
Wetmore, K. J., Jr. (2003), *Black Dionysus: Greek Tragedy and African American Theatre*. Jefferson, NC.
Wetmore, K. J., Jr. (2006), "Big Willie Style: Staging Hip-Hop Shakespeare and Being Down with the Bard," in J. Hulbert, K. J. Wetmore, Jr. and R. York, *Shakespeare and Youth Culture*. New York, 147–70.

CHAPTER 32

MAKING WOMEN VISIBLE

Multiple Antigones on the Colombian Twenty-First-Century Stage

MOIRA FRADINGER

EXTENDING the Latin American theatrical tradition that has brought the Greek tragedy *Antigone* onto the stage since the early nineteenth century, some twenty-first-century plays have featured new scenic strategies such as repetitions and multiplications, whether of the Antigone character or of specific lines, fragments, or scenes. In this chapter I turn my attention to Colombia and look at two such cases: Colombian playwrights Carlos Satizábal's *Antígona y actriz* (2005) and Patricia Ariza's *Antígona* (2006).[1] Written within a single year by two politically committed artists who share a history of collaboration, both plays were inspired by the same historical context: the armed conflict that has ravaged Colombia for the last six decades. This conflict has left, and continues to leave, hundreds of thousands dead with no burial, especially in rural areas: in the telling expression of Colombian writer Arturo Alape, these lands constitute the "immense corpse that continues to be unburied ... and that continues to grow" (Alape 2003: 24–5). Antigone's ancient act of burial serves as a framework for articulating a real-life drama that is all too familiar for the Colombian audience.[2]

The two Colombian plays were part of the theater festival Magdalena-Antígona, which was held from November 3 to 10, 2006 under the motto "Mujeres arte y parte en la paz de Colombia,"[3] and took place both in Colombia and Peru. Ariza's play was staged in the theater *La Candelaria* in downtown Bogotá, also commemorating 40 years (1966–2006) of that legendary theater collective. The festival produced four other plays that have "Antigone" in the title, among them Satizábal's, which had premièred in 2005, produced by *Rapsoda Teatro* and *Tramaluna Teatro*. The other Antigones were Augusto Cubillán's *Antígona factotum* (Venezuela), Cesar Castaño's *Antígona incorpórea* (Colombia), and lastly, *Antigonías* by the collective Grupo Generaciones (Colombia).[4]

Ariza's and Satizábal's versions of *Antigone* share a striking pattern: female characters are doubled or multiplied, narrative segments are twice or thrice told, performance elements such as costumes or hairdos are replicated. As I suggest in the pages that follow, rather than just staging the ancient plot of the tragedy concerning the fate of the unburied, these plays foreground the mode of representation of the story by drawing our attention to a performance of repetition and multiplication. Multiplicity operates as an echo-like scenic strategy enhancing "the return" of the story "over and over again" up to the present Colombian time. In Ariza's play this cyclical return is actually thematized in the lines of the Erinyes, who say that the "offspring" (258) that Antígona will produce is her story told "one and one thousand times" ("una y mil veces," 258).[5]

The performance of repetition and multiplication in these plays does not rehearse the same lines, gestures, and characters on stage: rather each repetition, or multiplication, stresses the need for the same story to be heard in different voices, with different tonalities, gestures, bodies, and colors. In most modern restagings of *Antigone* we see articulations of the ancient frame and its difference from modernity, of the possibilities opened not only by the singular instance of each performance but also by the staging of the ancient plot out of its time and place. The new, modern times and places necessarily impose new interpretations of the ancient text, unlocked from its original temporal and spatial constraints. But a performance of repetition and multiplication does not just give us a new version of the ancient story: it announces that the story told once is not enough. On the one hand, these plays suggest that the real-life situation inspiring them returns and repeats through millennia. On the other hand, their mode of representation counters the invisibility of the subject matter in the context of the Colombian conflict. Herein lies a sense of the tragic in these plays: each repeated and multiplied sentence, fragment, and character points to the insufficiency or failure of its preceding representation. This does not stage an illusory shortening of the distance between antiquity and modernity—between Antigone and the peasant women in Colombia trying to bury their dead. Rather, it points to the fragments of the Colombian modern experience that need to be seen and named. It would seem that the playwrights aim at uncovering the audience's deafness and blindness with respect to the country's conflict and to the fate of rural women within it—by using theatrical repetition beyond any mimetic realism of modern drama.

The effect of repetition and multiplication is to displace, to a certain extent, the centrality of the classic dramatic opposition between Antigone and Creon. Instead, another conflict is highlighted: that which occurs within the storytelling itself, contrasting different ways of making the story visible. In view of the frequency with which Antigone's tragedy has been put on stage throughout modernity in the West, one could say that something concerning the rites of burial resists modern signification, and needs to be made present constantly. But in Satizábal's and Ariza's plays, there is more that resists signification. If *Antigone* helps the playwrights name the experience of peasant women in the midst of political violence, one Antigone proves nonetheless insufficient to capture the experience of rural peasants that inspired both playwrights. In staging the character of Antigone via repetition and multiplication, both productions highlight the telling itself as a problematic site of representation. They honor the struggle that real-life peasant women lead not only to bury their dead, but also to tell their story to an urban audience. In the Colombian context, this form of rewriting *Antigone* speaks to the translation of rural experience into urban experience: to the need to bring visibility to those social agents that remain invisible because they are women in war-torn rural areas, far removed from the urban experience of the audience.

We could say these Colombian plays are about the specific fate of women in "war"-torn lands. A pause is due here to reflect on this armed conflict, which exhibits some unique features in the region. In the last two decades of the twentieth century there were many rewritings of *Antigone* (and of *Medea*) in the region, framed in what may be called "post-dictatorial" narratives, written during long political processes attempting to return to democracy after military rule. In some cases, a collectivity of women was present on stage, but in all cases, the character of Antigone was embodied by one actress. Contrary to previous regional *Antigones*, the two Colombian plays were written amidst ongoing and increasing armed conflict, especially in rural areas, as the agents participating in it proliferate. It may be the case that the proliferation of Antigones on the Colombian stage speaks to the proliferation of social agents involved in Colombia's particular case. Its myriad of agents blur any of the dichotomic frames with which other armed conflicts in the region have been seen—the often quoted opposition between "the military" and "the insurgent guerrillas," for example, or the common understanding of "state terrorism" as the category that explains the specific nature of crimes against humanity in the region. It is true that Colombia's conflict can be seen under the larger frame of "state terrorism," but the extent to which the state has managed to involve the civilian population complicates analytic categories. Colombia's conflict is dispersed into a tri-partite structure, at the very least: the left-wing guerrillas, the military, and the paramilitary militias and their "self-defense groups" ("Autodefensas Unidas de Colombia"/ United Self-defense of Colombia). In turn, drug-trafficking cartels and gangs have been involved with both guerrilla groups and military/paramilitary groups since their emergence. The paramilitary could hardly be said to be autonomous from the military—as many have argued, they are the likely result of the way the military "evolved" to strategically involve civilians in areas where guerrilla forces are still present. But the splintering of armed forces, working with the same aim, generates a dissemination of weapons that is probably unique in the region.[6]

For Ariza and Satizábal, the root cause of the conflict is the economic exclusion of large sectors of the population from any form of participation in public life, the labor force, health, or education. Colombia, unlike other countries in the region, never carried out an agrarian reform. The poverty of indigenous peasants tied to the land has worsened, and the massacres aimed at this population have evolved into what some have started to call a new ethnocide. The conflict appears at times as an excuse to exterminate indigenous peasants and in the most gruesome way "expropriate" their land: if peasants are not killed they are forcibly displaced and, consequently, lose their land. A horrific aspect of forced displacements is that the corpses of peasant casualties of the armed clashes are thrown outside of their native territory, or in rivers, and thus rural women are forced to migrate in search of them. Peasant families leave their towns and lands, and once de-populated, these lands are sold to multinational companies for industrial exploitation.[7]

When I interviewed Ariza and Satizábal in Bogotá in 2010, Ariza estimated that 4 million displaced people lived in Colombia, 70 percent of whom, she calculated, were women. Ariza herself is one of the millions of displaced people in the country, as she came to Bogotá to escape violence when she was a child. Both Ariza and Satizábal have accumulated lifelong experience of working with victims of violence and displaced communities through theater and artistic expression. Ariza recollected that she started thinking of the young girl Antigone during her trips to the devastated areas of the northern Colombian province of Urabá, bordering Panama, where violence against peasant and Afro-Colombian communities is pervasive. There she would consistently meet rural women in search of their missing dead. In February 1997, Urabá was the site of one of the largest forced displacements in the history of the armed conflict, a result of a military operation named "Genesis," along with a paramilitary one named "Cacarica." The "operations" caught thousands of indigenous inhabitants in the cross-fire, and paved the way for capitalist mega-investments in plantations of African palm, banana, and coca, by "clearing" the land. That same year, in July and October 1997 respectively, paramilitary forces carried out two other infamous peasant massacres in Mapiripán-Meta and El Aro-Ituango. This period also saw the emergence of armed private "cooperatives for security and vigilance" known by the name of "Convivir" ("Co-habit"), which have also been linked to paramilitary forces.[8] In turn, the organizations of peasants in "Comunidades de Paz" (Peace Communities) are famous in the area.

Herself a victim of displacement, Ariza recalled Antigone as she saw displaced women roaming about the territory: this was also, for her, the story of Antigone's errant youth, displaced from her home, accompanying her father on a forced journey whose life lessons transformed her into a woman. She had been thinking about the play for eight years before she sat down to write, rescuing from antiquity what she thought was relevant to her context: not only the errant but also the fighter Antigone.[9]

Perhaps the peculiarly long duration of the conflict accounts for noteworthy strategies of resistance—or perhaps one should say resistance *tout court*—in the northern areas of the country.[10] And it is perhaps not so surprising that the massive number of unburied bodies has recently inspired historian Roland Anrup to write two historical accounts that start with a reference to *Antigone*. In 2011, he wrote *Antígona y Creonte: rebeldía y estado en Colombia* (*Antigone and Creon: Rebellion and State in Colombia*) documenting not only military and paramilitary brutal repression and forced displacements, but also innumerable resistance strategies by peasant and rural communities, guerrilla fighters, students, workers, and displaced peoples. Anrup's previous book on this subject starts with a reference to Antigone: it is titled *Una tragedia a la colombiana* (*A Tragedy Colombian Style*) and the first page has an epigraph of Creon's order to leave the corpse unburied.[11] Among the striking resistance strategies that have developed concerning the fate of disappeared corpses in particular, the practice of "adopting" corpses that "re-appear" insistently floating in rivers, or on the land, deserves to be mentioned. Along the River Magdalena, the inhabitants of Puerto Berrío have, for the last three decades, "fished" for corpses drifting downstream, as the 2013 film *Réquiem: NN*, by Colombian artist Juan Manuel Echavarría, explores:

Ordinarily, these unidentified corpses, known as NNs (No Names), would be destined for a mass grave. However, for decades, local townspeople have adopted these bodies and given them names; they decorate their tombs and bring them water, gifts and flowers. In exchange, it is believed that the living are awarded protection and special favors. Some people who adopt the lost souls even baptize them with names from their own family, thereby finding comfort for losses of their own.[12]

The political manipulations of corpses, consisting in their "appearance" and/or "disappearance," are indeed thematized by Ariza, who has her Antigones perform a curious move on stage: instead of sprinkling earth on the body, Ariza's Antigone "drags" the body out of sight, and, as one of the Guards puts it, the corpse has thus been "disappeared." In real life, as unknown corpses are "adopted" by new peasant families who give them names, the military, who are responsible for the "disappearing" of the corpses, also perform their own (per)version of "re-appearing" of the corpses. Consider a single detail, such as the scandal of "false positives" ("falsos positivos"). The military (or paramilitary) "produce" corpses ("positives") that "appear", presented to the public as casualties of armed confrontation. In reality these corpses turn out to be civilians presented as guerrilla fighters, delinquents, or drug traffickers.[13]

Both plays are tightly connected and share their inspirational sources in real life. As corpses disappear, the victims' stories giving an account of their search for the corpses also disappear. A theater of presence, repetition, and multiplication asks how to render these stories visible. Or at least, it renders visible the insufficiency of staging *Antigone* in the realist tradition for the specific case of the current political conjuncture in Colombia.

Satizábal's Double Antígonas

Satizábal's play is a short work made up of ten scenes.[14] It follows a circular movement in space and time: it ends where it began. The curtain opens and we see on stage two female travelers: their initial traveling will be repeated at the end when the curtain falls. The women are almost doubles of each other. They carry two chairs and a trunk that contains rocks, photos of their brothers, and two male dolls made of cloth and with a rope around their necks. These constitute the props on stage, while the two women wear similar white ample dresses in a peasant style, similar hairdos, and paint on their faces. They walk covered by a black net and sing a ballad. In scene 2 the women arrive at a site where they narrate another story, not their own: the story of "the Greek girl" (65). This narration includes enacting Antigone's story: we see the ritual of burial and the capture of Antigone between scenes 2 and 7. In scene 7 the two women talk about themselves: they comment on the photos of their brothers that they carry with them, on their brothers' disappearances, and on their own displacement. But as they agree, it is the "night of the Greek girl" (67) and they quickly proceed with the ancient story: Antigone's rebellion before Creon and her death. The final scene repeats the women's comments about their brothers in scene 7; then they resume their walk singing "the same song as the beginning. The image is almost the same as the beginning" (70, stage directions).

The women travel in space, but they travel in time too, as the play suggests that the rural women of modernity and the tragic characters of antiquity may share the same story. The phrase that Woman One repeats summarizes it all: "I tell you, now you have to do more turns to get to the same place" (64). The "same place" is the site of the unburied, no doubt, and the "more turns" are the details that differentiate them from antiquity. These differentiating details are not clarified by the women, with the exception of one hint provided by Woman Two: they are the turns and travels of global capitalism. As she says, "were it not for the fact that the rich get richer with this slaughter, one would say that we are equal to this race, to Antigone and Polynices, Oedipus and Yocasta, cursed" (67).

It is indeed the night of the "Greek girl," but it is their night too: neither the story of Antigone nor the story of the women is self-sufficient. Much as the two women do, the two stories also depend upon each other. The tragedy of Antigone is reflected back upon the women's story in a doubling, or folding, of time and space. The actresses' doubling appears already in the paradoxical figure of a "monologue" for "two actresses," as the subtitle of the play reads (63). The "monologue"—not the "dialogue"—for "two actresses" forces the question: are the actresses one and the same? Are the two women two aspects of a divided identity? Will the monologue be divided in two parts, or will it be repeated by the two actresses verbatim? The subtitle's repetition foreshadows the structure of repetition that frames the play, text-wise and performance-wise.

As they walk, Woman One and Woman Two sing an old, but well-known, Mexican folk ballad in Spanish in the opening scene. The lyrics express solitude, yet the women sing together: they are not alone on stage. They suffer from a different kind of solitude: they are nostalgic for their land. As they sing, the lyrics bring to mind a familiar context for the Colombian audience, which is all too aware of forced displacements: "how far I am from my native land, an immense nostalgia invades my thought, and at seeing myself so lonely and sad . . ." (63). The stage directions indicate this song is "yucateca" (from the Mexican Yucatán area). I take this reference to signify Mexico, a country whose population has been in migration for a century—including the massive exodus across the northern frontier and into the United States. For many regional spectators the song will be recognizable: it is "Canción Mixteca." This melody was composed in 1912 by Oaxacan José López Alavez. The musician added the lyrics in 1915, expressing nostalgia for his native land. The song is an icon for the nostalgia that migrating Mexican farm workers feel when they leave the country, and it is widely played by indigenous and *mestizo* inhabitants all over Oaxaca, with the lyrics in Mixteco and Spanish. Outside of Mexico, and for those who might recognize it, it conjures up "Mexicanity."[15] The audience hears the lyrics in Spanish and knows that the women are migrants, possibly forcibly displaced. But for Satizábal, Spanish is not enough. The audience soon knows that the women are indigenous: the melody is repeated, but this time in the indigenous language Mixteco, spoken by indigenous communities in López Alavez's native region, Oaxaca. Sung in Mixteco, the literal meaning of the fragment is lost for the Hispanic audience: it serves as a musical gesture to convey repetition and multiplication, which make visible not only Spanish-speaking peasants, but also the fate of indigenous peoples in Central and South America.

Two Women. Two languages: Spanish, Mixteco. Two countries: Mexico, Colombia. Two temporal frames: modernity and antiquity. The latter are already hinted at with the presence of an indigenous, pre-Columbian, language: colonial Spanish indicates the first modernity, that of the conquest of America. To the temporality of pre-and post Spanish conquest, the play adds the layer of Greek antiquity. The two actresses play the roles of the peasant women and they both enter and leave the role of Antígona One and Antígona Two. Double language, country, woman, Antigone, and twice doubled time; but only one story—the "monologue." The story's sameness is expressed by the two Antígonas in scene 3. After Antígona One has explained who she is, both Antígonas say the same line: "this is my story"; both Woman One and Woman Two follow with: "this is our story" (65).

The two migrant women speaking in Mixteco, thereby alluding to indigenous Colombian peasants, have heard, albeit mysteriously, the story of the "Greek girl" (65), a story that foretells the women's own story. It is a cyclical return. But contrary to the audience's traditional reception of the Greek girl's story, nobody wants to hear the women's story. Before starting to narrate in scene 2, Woman One asks the audience:

> Here I am, as always, I bring my verses *(she opens one of her hands and offers us a stone)*, and my tobacco, to open roads for those who want to ask. Is there anyone who wants to ask what will happen to us, anyone who wants to know? Nobody? Well, while the moment for questions arrives, I bring you the tales of a Greek story: Antígona, Creonte, Etéocles and Polinices. (64)

The rocks offered to the audience as "stories" and "tobacco" will later be placed in the shape of a "U" to signal a tomb. The women insist on their story: "as always" indicates both a sense of patience and a sense of despair. The urban audience, the play suggests, may listen to Antigone, but "nobody" at the theater wants the peasant women's stories, which are made of memories of rocks, lands, tombs. The peasant women repeat the story: they tell the ancient story, they embody Antigone's fate acting out the character of the ancient sister, and they expect that the audience will want to hear their own story. Will the story of the modern Mexican women or ancient Greek tragic characters convey the fate of the Colombian peasant women? These are the "many turns" that the playwright takes to "get to the same place" (64).

The play's strategy of repetition and multiplication surely builds on the aspect of "legitimation" granted by the lofty theme of classical theater, the type of theater that the middle classes, educated in this culture, are used to seeing. But legitimation, as everything in this play, also needs to be doubled with the appeal to the historical memory, popularized in songs and films, of the peasants who fought and still fight for their land in Mexico. Classical theater is not enough: on the modern stage, twice told, classical tragedy might end up as a comedy or just an enlightening evening of "universal" theater. But the play's uses of doubles secure instead a sense of the tragic: the story is

FIG. 32.1 Carlos Satizábal's *Antígona y actriz*. © Tramaluna Teatro. Reproduced with permission.

not ancient, it is Mixtecan, it is Colombian, it returns to the present. Rather than the fate of the "Greek girl," it is this return that the peasant women convey to the audience (Fig. 32.1).

Ariza's Triple Antígonas

Ariza triples the stakes.[16] In her production, Satizábal's double Antigone becomes triple, and though there are no peasant women to tell her story, three Erinyes arrive on stage to fulfill the task. Though Ariza's Antigone does not thematize directly errant migration and displacement, we may see this in the proliferation of characters on stage.[17] This proliferation prompts the question whether Ariza's tri-partite Antigone corresponds to the vaguely identifiable tri-partite forces involved in the Colombian armed conflict.[18] Are Ariza's two Ismenes, in turn, made to defend the status quo represented in real life by two of these forces (the military and the far-right paramilitary)? For, onstage and soon after Tiresias has introduced the basics of the ancient story, not one but three Antigones appear together and not one but two Ismenes immediately follow. Within the "Antigone set," Antigone Three tells us that her/their strength comes from the experience of exile, migration, displacement:

> After having to quiet down my breathing in order to steal water and food, I do not fear in the least either suffering or punishment. (221)

While in the first scene we have five women on stage, later on we will have eight: three Erinyes complete the female sets for the main roles (Fig. 32.2).

The play follows the ancient sequence of events with minor changes. The biggest change is no doubt performative: the multiplication of characters. Apart from the eight women, there is a drunkard, two small choruses, and the three Erinyes bring on three more characters: the three ghosts of the dead men of the family who briefly appear to tell their story. They are Oedipus, Eteocles, and Polynices. The stage is almost bare, with the production's theatricality most visible in the very elaborate costumes, and in musical and lighting effects.

FIG. 32.2 The three Antigones and two Ismenes of Patricia Ariza's *Antígona*. Photograph by Carlos Mario Lema. Reproduced with the kind permission of Patricia Ariza.

Central to the performance is the time devoted to staging the relations among all the female character-sets. Interestingly, the classical Sophoclean dialogue between the two sisters, which in Ariza's play develops among five women, takes up 45 minutes in the play's total of 70. It is only interrupted by the arrival of the Erinyes and of other spirits. In scene 9, we finally see Creon fully embodied by an actor as he decrees that Polynices be left unburied. The content of the elaborate and long first dialogue between the sisters follows Sophoclean themes. As with Satizábal's two women, the plurality within each character-set could be interpreted as either fragmentation or collectivity. But whereas Satizábal's play clearly and immediately presents us with two women articulating sameness, in Ariza's play it is difficult, at first sight, to distinguish whether the three Antigones are one and the same, with three interchangeable versions, or different, or fragments of the character. In Ariza's text, the women are numbered: Antígona One, Two, Three. On Ariza's stage, Antigone and Ismene can be perceived as either more fragmented or more multiple by an audience that is habituated to associate a character's lines with one actress/actor on stage.

Consider how the text has each Antigone and each Ismene say distinct lines, while on stage sometimes two Antigones or two Ismenes speak the same line in unison. Sometimes the same line is repeated by one of the Antigones addressing two different Ismenes; sometimes one line that belongs to Antigone in the text is split in two, the first half spoken by one Antigone and the second half by another one. Sometimes one Antigone addresses one Ismene, but the Ismene that responds is situated behind Antigone; or Ismene addresses one Antigone but the one who responds is not in Ismene's line of vision. Sometimes Ismene's three consecutive lines are not addressed to the same Antigone but to three different ones. The effect "watching the performance" is somewhat kaleidoscopic: at times it risks disorienting the spectator.

But we can leave the kaleidoscope of postmodern disorientation to Mac Wellman's 2001 rewriting of *Antigone* and his version of three characters on stage: the three Fates who play all the parts and who make sure the spectator cannot find any point of anchorage. Consider phrases such as: "Creon as Antigone arrests Antigone who is Creon. A confusion arises . . . All change hats. Nothing feels right" (5).[19] In Ariza's play all seems to feel right in its place. Whereas Wellman's play is at times comic, or at least hard to label as "tragic," Ariza's play preserves both the tragic feeling and the political activism proper to the independent theater tradition that Ariza's *La Candelaria* has honored for decades. No sense of comedy: rather, a sense of urgency. The tragic story of Antigone is repeating itself, in the here and now. And in spite of the initial disorientation, several features point to a notion of collectivity and not to fragmentation. Each character-set seems to articulate sameness and difference from the start.

Consider the way in which Tiresias opens and closes the play, articulating a notion of collectivity that immediately emerges as the play's frame. Tiresias opens with the call to the people: "People of Thebes, I know you are there behind doors and half closed windows" (217). He ends the play as he began: "People of Thebes: get out of your shelter, unveil your blinded eyes: Your silence has been the great accomplice of this tragedy.

Go out, I know you are there, hiding" (262). The call to action increases in intensity throughout the play. Antigone in her first conversation with Ismene asks, "what does the city think of all this?" (223). Ismene replies that the city obeys in silence. In the following scene Antigone speaks to Tiresias and she directly addresses the collective: "women of Thebes! I feel your gazes behind the doors and windows and I know many of you approve of my action in silence" (226).

Gender is enlisted also to establish a frame that divides the characters into those conveying a notion of the collective and those conveying what we may see as fragmentation. Women characters are multiplied and male characters are added: but the male characters are not numbered. It could be said that they are "split" (not multiplied) between mind and body. Consider how in scene 1, behind the white transparent screen-plastic cloth dividing the stage from the backstage, we see Creon's shady image appearing almost as a ghost, as some of his garbled words are heard; only later does he fully "materialize" as the actor on stage. The two-man chorus also appears behind the translucent cloth. And, when the Erinyes summon the spirits of the dead men Eteocles, Polynices, and Oedipus, they are all presented on stage as ghosts. With the Erinyes and the spirits, the stage is inhabited by "apparitions." But gender plays a role: the female Erinyes are fully embodied and not staged as ghosts, which again points toward the multiplication of female characters contrasted with the fragmentation of male ghost-characters. In the text, we have hints of that difference: whereas the Erinyes are not introduced with any stage directions, the entrance of Eteocles is prefaced by "[he appears] in the sort of frenetic dance of an 'appeared'" (228). The entrance of Oedipus is prefaced by the stage direction "[he] enters as a ghost" (231) and that of Polynices is prefaced by "Polynices from the shadows" (238).

While a notion of a collectivity frames the play, and does so along gender lines on stage, each female character-set presents yet another sense of collectivity. This is allowed by some anchoring of meaning as to their function, articulated in diverse textual and performative strategies. This anchoring of meaning is perhaps clearer in the text, as it is signaled with the textual strategy of *not* numbering Antigone and Ismene at times. They are simply "Antigone" and "Ismene." The lines spoken by the un-numbered Antigone (or Ismene) stand for an un-shifting meaning granted to the character. In the first scene in the text, the un-numbered Antigone says: "I must return him to the dark earth" (219) and "Polynices is my brother and yours too even if you don't like it" (220). These are the traits of Antígona, much like those of her ancient namesake: she is concerned about her brother, about an address to the sister, and the performance of burial. On stage these phrases are pronounced by Antigone Three, the one who explains she has no more tears to shed after the experience of her exile. In scene 6 in the text, Ismene appears un-numbered three times and says to the Erinyes: "Oh spirits of justice and destiny return to your dwelling. Stop now the thirst for vengeance that is eating you" (233). Ismene's function is to forget and obey, like her ancient pair. The Erinyes and the female chorus in the last scene lose all numbers and become simply "the Erinyes" and "the women," all yelling in unison warnings of vengeance. Their theme could be summarized as "justice" or "punishment." We have, then, three fixed themes as the scaffold of the building—burial, justice, and forgetting—each of them attached to one character-set. With the exception of the Erinyes' addition, these themes follow closely the ancient tragedy: burial-disobedience is attached to the three Antigones, forgetting and obeying to the two Ismenes.

This kind of thematic unity for the female character-sets is particularly highlighted on stage by costumes and performance: colors, movements, gestures. The two Ismenes are dressed in the same yellowish pink and violet; the three Antigones are dressed in red and black—the three Erinyes in white and black. We might even say that each character-set is a variation of a color and dress theme articulating different forms with the same colors. Each Antigone in the Antigone-set demands burial but in different forms, just as each of them wears red and black but combines them in differently shaped skirts and tops. Each actress is almost a musical variation of a theme in the "musical score" that each character-set composes: the character-sets can be seen as "orchestrating" the ancient plot (indeed, there is not only a chorus but also a lot of music in the performance). Thus, on stage each group of actresses articulates difference and sameness, collectivity and individuality (Fig. 32.3).

Ariza, like Satizábal, inserts repetition into the story with textual strategies too. A closer look at the text illuminates the articulation of sameness and difference we have seen in the multiplication of female characters. Whereas Satizábal included a foreign language whose frame of reference immediately conjures up a neighboring country, Ariza chose a similar strategy but with the literary repetition of the text in ancient Greek.

FIG. 32.3 The two Ismenes of Patricia Ariza's *Antígona*. Photograph by Carlos Mario Lema. Reproduced with the kind permission of Patricia Ariza.

Satizábal's inclusion of Mixteco hints at the fate of indigenous peoples throughout the continent, but ancient Greek does not convey any specificity other than antiquity: in urban settings it may convey erudition, or higher education. On stage, scattered lines in Greek are sung by the actresses, who accompany their singing with elaborate gestures lifting their arms in the manner of religious invocations. As a literary repetition, one could even say "revivification" of antiquity, the content of these lines remains meaningless for the intended Hispanic audience, who may even not be able to recognize that they are in ancient Greek. Contrary to Mixteco, Greek transfers onto the present time fragments of a bygone era, inserted as if returning intact and brought back by the tide of millennia, without transformation, or translation, into modernity. Their performative function can be seen as akin to music: non-linguistic meaning, whose import is the emotional effect of incantation. In the printed text I use for this article, only the Erinyes pronounce phrases in Greek, but both in a previous version of the text (given to me by Ariza herself) and in the performance stored in the online video archive, Greek phrases appear pronounced by all female actresses of the three character-sets: the Antigones, the Ismenes, and the Erinyes. These phrases circulate among characters as extracts that resist signification: they signify repetition. This is to say, they stand for a kind of sameness with antiquity that articulates its own difference: these lines connect with the past, but displaced from their time and place, they cannot be understood. They multiply the Spanish text: they are and they are not the text of ancient tragedy.

Whereas the ancient Greek acts as an echo of lines spoken in Spanish, certain Spanish fragments are either repeated or multiplied insistently throughout the play. Interestingly, the text is divided into 18 scenes but Creon does not appear until scene 9 and the entire first half of the play is devoted to performing a repetition of Antigone's preliminary decision. The first scene, which is the conversation between the Antigones and the Ismenes without the interruptions of the Erinyes, lasts 20 minutes in the performance and is considerably longer than any of the other scenes due to its repetitions. The first 45 minutes of the play are thus a repetition, many times over, of the story, told in a variety of ways.

Consider the following examples from the text. After the three Antígonas have informed the two Ismenes about what is happening, they speak thus:

> ANTIGONE ONE: Creon buried Eteocles with all honors because he was a loyal soldier, and has ordered Polynices to be left unburied at the side of the walk, forbidding us all from mourning in his memory.
> ANTIGONE TWO: Eteocles will have funerals as a hero, we will not be able to cry for Polynices nor give him burial.
> ANTIGONE THREE: Creon has given the order to abandon him so that he be devoured by beasts. He does not want laments or burial.
> ANTIGONE TWO: He says that it will be a feast for the birds that prey. That is his will.
> ANTIGONE TWO: We are denied the right to mourning, we, his Erinyes sisters!
> ANTIGONE: I must return him to the dark earth!
> ANTIGONE THREE: Ismene, we must return him to the dark earth!
> ANTIGONE TWO: Creon has come out to shout his new laws, if you had listened to him, you would tremble. He comes towards us yelling out of himself. (218–19)

In this sequence, the first sentence when Antigone One speaks of Creon's decree is expanded by the subsequent sentences by Antigone Two and Three, who either multiply the same information or add a detail that is already implied in the first sentence. The first sentence does not mention the birds of prey, but soon enough Antigone Three summons up the image of beasts and Antigone Two that of birds. Likewise, Antigone One says they have been forbidden from mourning, Antigone Two expands by lamenting that they will not be able to cry, Antigone Three finishes the idea with the impossibility of lament. Midway into the sequence, the theme changes only when the un-numbered Antigone speaks of burial. This theme is taken up by the subsequent sentences pronounced by Antigone Two and Three; the sequence ends exactly where it began, with Antigone Three referring to Creon as Antigone One had done.

Another example in the same scene can be found when, after Ismene tells Antigone (repeatedly too) that she wants to stop the series of affronts, the Antigones reply:

> ANTIGONE ONE: Affront. Affront is to leave a brother with no burial. I will bury him. If no-one helps I will do it alone and will run the risk, even if it implies death.
> ANTIGONE TWO: I will confront Creon and, if it is necessary, everyone who governs the city.
> ANTIGONE THREE: Apollo, let death come. If this is the price I must pay for primordial affects. (224)

These three sentences draw attention to the repetitive variations of "the affront", the "price" and the "proviso": they are all framed by the same type of conditional clause—"if no-one helps me, if it is necessary, if this is the price"—and refer to the same "price to pay". And in scene 12, Creon asks Antigone if she is guilty, and the three Antigones reply with the same affirmation, varying the clarification of lineage and feeling. Antigone-the father's-daughter feels guiltless, Antigone-the mother's-daughter is fearless, and Antigone-the granddaughter and sister urges Creon to act.

> ANTIGONE THREE: I am Antigone, Oedipus's daughter, Polynices' sister. I did it. I do not feel guilt.
> ANTIGONE TWO: I am Antigone, Jocasta's daughter, your own sister's daughter. I did it. I do not feel fear.
> ANTIGONE ONE: I am Antigone, Laius' grand-daughter, Ismene's sister. I did it. Do what you have to do once and for all. (247)

In turn, several phrases migrate from mouth to mouth through different characters in different moments. I have chosen the one announced by Tiresias in the prologue: "People of Thebes, I know you are there behind the doors and windows" (217). This phrase is slightly altered by Antigone Two in scene 2 and becomes: "Women of Thebes! I feel your gazes behind the doors and windows and I know many of you approve of my action" (226). In scene 6, the chorus offers its version: "we will be here listening through our windows, behind the doors, in silence" (234). In scene 17, Antigone Two returns to it with the following variation: "Women of Thebes, I know you are there behind the doors and windows. Look at me. I do not have tears. I know that fear paralyzes you. Erinyes of vengeance, sisters of pain, get out of your shelters" (257). And in scene 18 it is Tiresias again, who recapitulates and closes the play with: "Citizens of Thebes, get out of your homes and your shelters. I know you are there hiding. Get out and come see once and for all the ruins of this war" (262).

The Erinyes grant us the clearest interpretation of repetition and multiplication in this play, as they are the ones who express the hope that the *multiplied retelling* of catastrophe may have an effect. Theirs is a telling of the story as a form of vengeance. In Greek mythology, the Erinyes were goddesses of vengeance; in the play they are thus announced in scene 3. Eriny One says twice that they have come to "punish the crimes" (227). But the sentence that she speaks in between that repetition adds a striking detail: she has come *to narrate* the story, as if this very narration was part of the vengeance: "I will be in charge of spreading the news of their ignoble deeds" (227). Tiresias interjects with a striking remark also: "Oh Thebes! speak now about your evils before the Spartans return" (227). In scene 6 when both Ismene and Tiresias ask them to return to their homes, the Erinyes respond: "we will be here, waiting for misfortune, so that it can be recounted time and again to the survivors" (234). In scene 17 the Erinyes address the chorus's belief that Antigone will die without having children. They do not see Antigone's offspring as coming out of her womb as children. They see it rather as coming out through their mouths as language: "her own story narrated by us, one and one thousand times" (258).

An image of sisterhood is conjured up in the last sentence: the Erinyes, as her sisters, are in charge of Antigone's legacy. It is this legacy—the retelling of the story one and one thousand times—that Ariza's multiplication of characters stages. Tiresias gives the basics of the plot, the sisters insist on its sheer recounting, in as many ways as possible. Attention to the medium is stressed: the text of the tragedy is foregrounded as a resource from which all characters can extract their sentence and perform it regardless of whether it has already been performed by the originally designated character. What matters is to disseminate the news, to bring about visibility and punishment of the culprits. The sheer retelling of the story is in itself a form of punishment: to speak about it until it really has been heard.

Perhaps when Satizábal's and Ariza's Antigones, Ismenes, Mixteca Women, and the Erinyes have been heard, the ancient story can be remembered, instead of repeated. If I am allowed to follow the Freudian insight that to repeat an action means not to be able to remember it with words, and to symbolize traumatic pasts carries with it at least the hope that they will cease to be traumatic,[20] perhaps the Erinyes' insistence on the remembrance is meant to symbolize the violent traumatic events in the story as a legend about fratricide and thus prevent their repetition in the action of fratricide itself. At least that hope is implied in the performative strategies of multiplication that work toward notions of collectivity rather than fragmentation, in order to make visible the invisible real-life peasant women who inspired the Colombian playwrights.

We may thus relate the performance of repetition and multiplication to a theatrical call for *the end* of repetition. The plays' multiplied Antigones are not so much part of a theatrical language that we can call "postdramatic," as new theaters of repetition and fragmentation that go against realist representation have been called (Lehmann 2006). Rather, these plays repeat and multiply the story on stage in response to the urgency of the times. I see them as partaking of a larger cultural narrative, now well established in the region after the last three decades of intense human rights activism. By staging the "yet-again-the-same-story" several times over, they become one more "symbolic vehicle" to convey the meaning of the fruitful political slogan "never again" crimes against humanity.[21] Colombian Antigones, as Ariza's Antígona One says, have "only known the time of errancy" (237): while they roam the territory wandering errantly they will make a stop at the urban sites they find, and as Satizábal's Women say, they will retell the story of the "Greek girl" while they wait for real questions about the fate of real-life peasant women. They will tell the story "one and one thousand times" until Ariza's Antigone Three's plea that "we do not have any more time for laments" (220) conveys the urgency that it may be time to let go of the tears and fears and "get out of our homes and shelters." Antigone's Colombian story becomes a furious echo, almost a terrible musical refrain, caught by the sounding board of the performance of repetition and multiplication: maybe this way her audience will hear their present differently.

Notes

1. I have commented on another such play, Jorge Huertas's 2001 *AntígoneS: Female Lineage*, in Fradinger 2011: 84–8. Huertas's play features a chorus of six women on stage; they are all dressed similarly and they all play different roles when they leave the chorus, but they all return to the chorus.
2. For information about Ariza's career see the one-hour long interview with Ariza, filmed in 1999, in the online archive at the Hemispheric Institute at New York University: <http://hidvl.nyu.edu/video/000508855.html>.
3. The translation for this title cannot convey the original meaning which plays on using the word "art" in the colloquial expression "arte y parte": it thus combines a colloquialism in Spanish with the artistic content of the festival announced by its title. "Arte y parte" is roughly translated as "having to do with": thus the title could be translated as "Women as doing peace for Colombia" though the English misses the word "art" (arte) in the Spanish colloquialism and thus the word play too.
4. For information about the Magdalena-Antígona festival, see: <http://www.themagdalenaproject.org/en/content/magdalena-antigona-2006>. Unfortunately I have no current access to these other plays and have only mentioned here those that directly refer to the ancient tragedy in their titles.
5. I here use the printed versions: Satizábal 2008 and Ariza 2008. All translations from the plays, and from Spanish sources, are mine. I have found Satizábal's name spelled both with a Z and an S in different documents. In my interview with him in Bogotá (November 2010), he spelled it with an S, which is why I have opted for that spelling.
6. For an introduction to the six-decade-long armed conflict in the country, see Molano 2003, Pécaut 2001, and Gonzalo Sánchez 2003. For details about the example of the military Batallón Bárbula and their support of paramilitary forces, see, for instance, the report <http://www.derechos.org/nizkor/colombia/libros/nm/z14I/cap1.html>. For

a comprehensive study of guerrilla forces, see Gallego 2010; for a study on paramilitary forces, see Gallego 2008.

7. In 2012, Colombia was the country with the most displaced peoples in the world, according to the report coming from the IDMC—<http://www.bbc.co.uk/news/world-latin-america-22341119>. See the reports on forced displacements published online by Dejusticia.org and by Universidad de los Andes, such as Garavito et al. 2010; see also <http://www.defensoria.org.co/red/anexos/pdf/11/desplazados/persistDesplaColombia.pdf> and Moncada 2012, which accuses 143 politicians of involvement with what the authors call "criminal structures behind land abandonments" and resulted from research funded by the FF and the IPC in Bogotá.

8. On the infamous Operation Genesis, see Giraldo, Abab, and Guzmán 1997, as well as online accounts in: <http://colombiasupport.net/2010/04/thirteen-years-since-operation-genesis/>; <http://www.cpt.org/cptnet/2006/04/17/uraba-colombia-right-not-have-land-bathed-our-blood>. On the case of the Mapiripán massacre, see the report of the Inter-American Court of Human Rights: <http://www.corteidh.or.cr/docs/casos/articulos/seriec_134_ing.pdf>. See also the history of another emblematic massacre in this region in 2002: the bombing of Bojayá, causing massive displacements. Thanks to Andrés Fabián Henao Castro for this historical summary.

9. Pinzón 2006. See also the statement about the festival Magdalena-Antígona, website information cited above.

10. Today there are only two armed conflicts that are longer in duration than Colombia's: that over the territory of Kashmir dates back to 1947, and over the territory of Palestine back to 1948. The Colombian conflict started around 1948, when peasants armed themselves in protest against the assassination of Gaitán, and the violence between two political parties inaugurated a period known in Colombia as "La Violencia," which many situate as precedent for what came next: the escalation of violence leading to the definite formation of the largest left-wing guerrilla group in the territory, and in South America, in 1964: the FARC (Fuerzas Armadas Revolucionarias de Colombia).

11. The epigraph is taken from the epigraph that Colombian Nobel Laureate Gabriel García Márquez used to start his novella *La hojarasca* (*The Leaf Storm*, 1955). It is a translation into Spanish of Creon's edict, as voiced by, we assume, Antigone: "and with respect to Polynices' corpse . . . they say that he has proclaimed an edict so that no citizen buries him or cries for him, so that as the corpse remains unburied and without the honors of mourning, they leave it as delicious prey for birds to leap on it and devour it"—Anrup 2009: 13; my translation. Anrup cites the epigraph from the 2003 Colombian edition of García Márquez's novella, 9.

12. <http://www.requiemnnfilm.com/about.html>.

13. The strategy has been seen in Colombia as an expression of the political will to increase the number of the dead in the armed conflict in order to show the military as "efficient" in their war. There are even military officers who admit having received pressure to produce dead bodies, a "production" which in turn granted promotions and benefits to those involved in the killings. For introductory information about the "false positives" see <http://www.centrodememoriahistorica.gov.co/>. For an interview on this subject, see <http://www.lasillavacia.com/historia/los-falsos-positivos-segun-sus-protagonistas-33714>.

14. My analysis is based on my interview with Carlos Satizábal and on the text, since there is no archival video of the performance. The play was directed by Satizábal when staged both by Rapsoda Teatro and Tramaluna Teatro, It premièred in 2005 with Carolina Torres and

Sindy Garzón. It is frequently staged for peasant communities, women's organizations, and students. In 2010 the author produced it once more, this time with Patricia Ariza, for the Festival of Women on Stage.
15. The song has traveled out of Mexico in film, and popular culture. Consider too that it was arranged by Ry Cooder for the soundtrack of Wim Wenders's 1984 acclaimed film *Paris, Texas*.
16. The performance is archived online at the Hemispheric Institute at New York University: <http://hidvl.nyu.edu/video/000512472.html>.
17. I have only found one scholarly article about this play: Billotte 2010. This is a nine-page article, but only two pages are devoted to the play. The author compares the ancient source and Ariza's play, following one of the standard critical gestures in reception studies, that takes for granted the possibility of (or usefulness of) a straightforward comparison with antiquity. This comparison serves the author to state that the play is a meditation "on mourning"; the rest of the paper engages not with Colombia, but with Judith Butler's meditations on mourning, and with interpretations of the ancient Greek tragedy. Ariza's strategy of a repetition of the characters is only mentioned in one sentence, bearing no analysis. Unfortunately, the author's generalizing assertions about Colombia, at best unscholarly, do not take into account the historical conjunctures that make of Colombia an exceptional case in Latin America.
18. I share this question with Castro 2013.
19. Mac Wellman's Antigone was put on stage in New York in 2002. A copy of the text can be found online: <http://www.macwellman.com/images/antigone.pdf>. See the reviews: <http://www.nytimes.com/2002/12/16/theater/theater-review-in-the-beginning-maybe-there-was-antigone.html?ref=macwellman>; and: <http://www.berkeleydailyplanet.com/issue/2007-10-19/article/28271>.
20. I am referring to Freud's famous 1914 article, "Remembering, Repeating and Working Through." The discussion whether the remembrance of the past prevents its repetition or not exceeds the scope of this chapter. I should note, nonetheless, that theater's remembrance is of a specific nature that complicates that debate: it is *embodied* memory, not intellectual memory, and thus embedded in everyday community practices and bonds.
21. The slogan "never again," it may be noted, signifies a return itself: it was chosen in 1983 in Argentina by the rabbi Marshall Meyer in honor of the slogan that had been used in 1943 during the uprising of the Warsaw Ghetto in Poland.

References

Alape, A. (2003), "La tierra: objeto de disputa," in *Desde el Jardín de Freud* 3, 24–30.
Anrup, R. (2009), *Una tragedia a la colombiana*. Bogotá.
Anrup, R. (2011), *Antígona y Creonte: rebeldía y estado en Colombia*. Bogotá.
Ariza, P. (2008), "Antígona," in *4 obras del Teatro La Candelaria*. Bogotá, 213–62.
Billotte, K. (2010), "Mourning with Antigone: Civil War and Public Mourning in Patricia Ariza's *Antígona*," *Skepsi* 3.2 (Winter), 1–10.
Castro, A. F. H. (2013), "Antígona y los falsos positivos," *Palabras al margen* (February 14) <http://www.palabrasalmargen.com/index.php/articulos/item/antigona-y-los-falsos-positivos?category_id=70>.
Fradinger, M. (2011), "An Argentine Tradition," in E. B. Mee and H. P. Foley eds., *Antigone on the Contemporary World Stage*. Oxford, 67–89.

Freud, S. (1914), "Remembering, Repeating and Working Through," in *Standard Edition of the Complete Works*. Trans. J. Strachey. London, xii. 145–57.

Gallego, C. M. (2008), "Narco-paramilitarismo: lógicas y procesos en el desarrollo de un capitalismo criminal," in *Capitalismo criminal: ensayos críticos*. Colombia, v. 103–41.

Gallego, C. M. (2010), 'FARC-EP Y ELN: una historia política comparada, 1958–2006, Bogotá <http://www.bdigital.unal.edu.co/3556/1/469029.2010.pdf>.

Garavito, C. R. et al. (2010), "Justicia Global 3: pueblos indígenas y desplazamiento forzado" <http://www.justiciaglobal.info/docs/fa2.pdf>.

Giraldo, C., J. Abab, and P. Guzmán (1997), *Relatos e imágenes: el desplazamiento forzado en Colombia* [Narratives and Images: Forced Internal Displacement in Colombia]. Bogotá.

Gonzalo Sánchez, G. (2003), *Guerras, memoria e historia*. Bogotá.

Lehmann, H.-T. (2006), *Postdramatic Theatre*. Translated and with an introduction by K. Jürs-Munby. London.

Molano, A. (2003), *La segunda expedición por el éxodo*. Bogotá.

Moncada, J. J. (ed. 2012), *Restitución colectiva de tierras en Colombia*. Medellin.

Pécaut, D. (2001), *Guerra contra la sociedad*. Bogotá.

Pinzón, W. C. (2006), "Ariza: Repetirnos es morir," *El tiempo* (June 14) <http://www.eltiempo.com/archivo/documento/MAM-2064718>.

Satizábal, C. (2008), "*Antígona y actriz*", in *Revista Colombiana de las artes escénicas* 2.2 (July–December), 63–70.

CHAPTER 33

DEMOCRATIC APPROPRIATIONS

Lysistrata *and Political Activism*

DOROTA DUTSCH

Democracy, Reception, and the Lysistrata Project

CLASSICAL drama has, in the recent past, become increasingly often used for political advocacy of ideologies of liberation and emancipation, that is, "democratic" ideologies in the modern sense of the word.[1] Such politicized modern reinventions of ancient drama invite questions about the mechanisms of cross-cultural adaptations.[2] Lorna Hardwick (2006) created a useful model for analyzing this new democratic turn in the reception of classical drama, proposing the notion of reception in "diaspora," in which play texts, reconstituted in the new contexts, become the medium of a dialogic relationship between the present and the past. The subject of the present chapter, the Lysistrata Project, a U.S.-based, worldwide protest action against the war in Iraq (2003–11), unfortunately resists such a holistic, dialogic interpretation.[3] The Project's large scale, its radical investment in contemporary political discourse, and its organizers' professed lack of interest in the original context of the play seem to call for a modified approach that would, *faute de mieux*, foreground the situation at the point of reception, leaving the relationship between the present and the past in the background. Consequently, this chapter is both a case study of the Project and an attempt to answer the question of how students of reception might approach such intentionally presentist uses of the classical tradition.

Before turning to the evidence under consideration, it will be useful to comment on the nature of the Project's commitment to current political discourse. The Lysistrata

Project was conceived as an extension of the modern democratic process, a response to the perceived failure of the modern democratic institutions to give a strong enough voice to the views of those U.S. citizens who were opposed to the intervention in Iraq. Two New York actors, Kathryn Blume and Sharron Bower, decided to convey their disagreement—and enable as many other people as possible to express theirs—through multiple readings of Aristophanes' *Lysistrata*, planned for March 3, 2003—03.03.03. The organizers' gesture was arguably "democratic" in the sense reflected in the modern English usage of the word "democracy" as "a form of government in which the supreme power is vested in the people," not institutions.[4] However, the *demos* in the word democracy, as Jean Luc Nancy observed (Nancy 2011 [2009]: 67), contains an instant tension: whether we speak of the power of "the people," "community," or "society," some people are left outside of the empowered in-group.[5] A true democratic society (*demos*) only starts, Nancy posits, "where *interiority* stops, where in-group bonding through kinship and totemic figures or myth ceases" (Nancy 2011 [2009]: 67). This desire to reach beyond the boundaries of the American *demos* and its institutions and open a dialogue that would stretch beyond those limits was essential to Blume and Bower, who began by creating a website and inviting everyone to join in a "healthy community dialogue."[6] In the light of Nancy's comments, the two women's choice of *Lysistrata* appears both very pertinent and somewhat ironic. It is pertinent because Lysistrata's myth dramatizes the desire to transcend the boundaries of *polis* and *demos*, implying at the same time that women should lead this democratic outreach initiative. But it is also ironic because Lysistrata is a "totemic" or "mythical" heroine of Western culture.[7] Thus the organizers' attempt to open a dialogue was formulated in terms of an explicitly Western framework of cultural references. We will later return to the question of whether or not this choice should make their effort invalid; for the moment, it is important to stress two facts. First, that to Blume and Bower, who were looking at Aristophanes' play from the twenty-first-century perspective, the notion that women stand a better chance to negotiate peace than men do appeared inevitably pro-feminist as well as democratic.[8] Second, that this assumption was anachronistic: according to specialist readers, Aristophanes' comedy qualifies neither as a pro-democratic manifesto nor as a call for women's empowerment.[9] The organizers' efforts can consequently be described in terms of deterritorialization of the *Lysistrata*—turning away from the play's topical ancient Greek implications—and its subsequent reterritorialization, recasting the *Lysistrata* in terms of modern ideologies.[10] The *Lysistrata* is thus firmly embedded in a modern framework of references.

The kind of material that we need to examine, in order to observe the Project's results, is another important consideration. The staged readings of Aristophanes' play might fall within the purview of performance reception.[11] However, since the meaning of the modern performances was shaped by contemporary political discourse, it will be crucial to consider these in the context of a whole range of diverse social practices and genres of cultural performance: demonstrations, documentary films, town-hall meetings, journal articles, TV shows, websites, performance scripts, and private letters.[12] Some of these multimodal forms of reception (such as TV reports on the staged readings) would, moreover, have engaged with one another, further inflecting the play's meaning in ways that have little to do with the original and its primary context. The project thus invites us to explore a territory at the limits, or, according to some theorists, even outside the bounds, of classical reception.[13]

I propose to envision the shift of focus necessary to consider political discourse as mode of reception in terms of Deleuze and Guattari's juxtaposition of horizontal ("rhizomatic") versus vertical ("arboreal") models of thought.[14] Using Deleuzian imagery, one can think of the project as an assemblage (*agencement*) or a "machine" whose various parts, the website, the stagings, the comments in the media, are in apposition to one another. In my account of the project, these assembled uses of the *Lysistrata* will receive more attention than the vertical link that (ultimately) ties all of them to the Greek original. This is not to deny the vital importance of this link, but to propose a model of looking at classical reception congenial to the analysis of social discourse, which itself is multimodal, and multifocal, and thus rhizomatic.

In order to map this web of connections and contiguities, we will begin with one day—03.03.03—and outline its backstory as recorded in digital archives. Two sample scripts, Ellen Anderson's *Liz Estrada*, which I watched in Santa Barbara, and Drue Robinson Hagan's translation, staged by several hundred groups in the U.S.A., will then receive special consideration. Beginning from this incision into the rhizome, we will explore some contiguous sections: the reception of the Lysistrata Project in the media, the points of contiguity between the Lysistrata Project and the protests against the Vietnam War, and, finally, Kathryn Blume's one-actor play, as well as *The Accidental Activist*, a reflection on the Lysistrata Project's complex relationship with the sex strikes organized by women peace activists in Africa. This discussion will draw on Kathryn Blume's and Ellen Anderson's unpublished scripts, on my interviews with both playwrights, and on a conversation with the Liberian Nobel Peace Prize Laureate, Leymah Gbowee.[15]

Lysistrata Project: Internet Archives (May 2011)

In December 2002 in New York's Performance Space 122, a group of artists formed Theaters Against War (THAW), in order to organize a protest against the looming Iraq war;[16] it was in response to this call that Kathryn Blume and Sharron Bower put together the Lysistrata Project.[17] The Lysistrata-assemblage was thus embedded in a yet larger initiative. In January 2003, Blume and Bower began planning several theatrical events that were to take place in New York City on March 3, 2003.[18] Since Blume had earlier contemplated writing a screenplay adaptation of Aristophanes' *Lysistrata*, this play was the obvious choice.[19] Bower, who also worked as a graphic designer, created a website,[20] where Bower and Blume posted a message inviting volunteers to organize readings of the *Lysistrata*.[21] They offered practical advice to non-professionals on how to stage a play, provided downloadable posters, and a link to the recommended (but not required) translation of the play by Drue Robinson Hagan, as well as several other ones.[22] The instructions were very simple and designed to include anyone willing to take part: any kind of reading of any version of the text could be considered as part of the project. Blume and Bower posted a list of planned readings on their site to serve as an indicator of the force of opposition against the war.[23] The numbers of volunteers grew exponentially. Two weeks after the website was activated, Blume told Michele Norris of the National Public Radio that 40 readings were scheduled. On March 3, nearly 1,039 readings took place in 59 countries on six continents. Ultimately, the Lysistrata Project reached an estimated 200,000 people and received widespread press coverage (Fig. 33.1).[24]

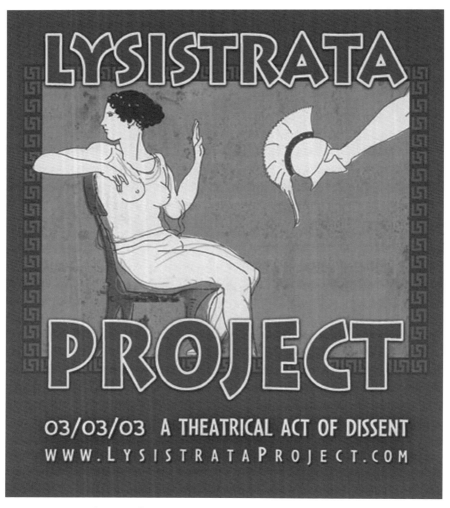

FIG. 33.1 Promotional poster for the Lysistrata Project. Design by Mark Greene. © Lysistrata Project. Reproduced with permission.

Needless to say, the project had no impact whatsoever on political decision-making in the United States or in the allied countries. However, as a civic effort to mobilize global public opinion, the Lysistrata Project was a spectacular success: within days, two private individuals organized a very public act of dissent reaching hundreds of thousands of people. It had also raised over $100,000 for peace-oriented charities (as a fundraising initiative, the project operated within yet another kind of rhizome or assemblage).[25] In the process, an ancient Greek play and its activist reading "went viral": Mark Kelly's documentary *Operation Lysistrata* bears witness to the huge variety of readings that the project inspired, from the professional, such as the one in the Brooklyn Academy of Music,[26] to one that a father and son team staged in their own living room, using plastic dinosaurs. Such a plethora of readings does not allow for easy generalizations. My strategy will be to discuss two appropriations of Aristophanes' play, both as scripts and as performance events staged on March 3, 2003. For the first, Ellen Anderson's play, I will draw on an entry in my personal journal that refers to the staged reading in Santa Barbara. For the second, Robinson Hagan's script, most popular among the project's participants, I will turn to Mark Kelly's documentary.

Lysistrata Project: Santa Barbara

March 3, 2003: It is my first year teaching at the University of California, Santa Barbara. A colleague from the Drama Department, Cathryn Cole, invites me to attend a staged reading of a modern adaptation of Aristophanes' play, *Liz Estrada*, written by Ellen K. Anderson and directed by Peter Lackner at the Center Stage Theater.[27] A revised version of the similarly named *Liz Istrata*, which Ellen wrote in 1991 in connection with the first Gulf War, *Liz Estrada* premièred a year earlier in New York's Fringe Festival and is now performed by Santa Barbara's Dramatic Women production company.[28] The actors, seven men and seven women, all dressed in black, are holding scripts, yet their movements are efficiently choreographed. The play is a vigorous and bawdy reinvention of the ancient text. Anderson projects Aristophanes into the future, which she imagines as a time of relentless global conflict between Our Side and Other Side, with updates constantly broadcast from the media fortress of the Happy News Network (HNN), situated "high atop an unspecified mountain in an unspecified country, unspecified as we all know due to military specifications."[29] The title character is a rock star; she and her band "The Daughters of the Dead" use an unmonitored five minutes of global broadcast to send their message "Peace | or no piece for you | no piece of me." They occupy the fortress/studio, an apt modern equivalent of the Acropolis, and call for a global sex strike (a perky representative of the Other Side, Lamb Pito, lends her support). The script reproduces the basic structure of Aristophanes' play—women go on a sex strike to put an end to war and succeed—but Anderson deftly avoids pitfalls that can make the ancient script unappealing to her audience. For example, she sensibly compensates for the *Lysistrata*'s heterosexual focus by allowing the striking women to tease and flirt with one another and by dramatizing the strike's effects on gay male couples:

> [JOURNALIST] MURINE: Couples of all inklings have been caught up in the effects of this mass movement.
> GAY MAN #1: I said no to him first.
> GAY MAN #2: The hell you did. I said it first.
> GAY MAN #1: We're saying no to each other. We're saying no together.
> GAY MAN #2: Stop the wars, you patriarchal peewees!

Likewise, the problematic finale in which the male representatives of the Greek city-states divide among themselves the female body of Reconciliation is replaced with an environmental crisis. Liz Estrada's act of "sexual terrorism" causes the oceans of the world to swell and the polar ice caps to melt (due to excessive human body heat). The speech offering peace is uttered by Liz's old flame, Dr. Ken Kinesias:

> KEN: You must end this strike! I've just been online to the Global Academy of Science. They've declared an environmental emergency. (*He looks down at the data sheets without moving the printouts towards him*) There's endemic priapism on all five continents. As may be obvious.
> (*Looking at the soldiers*)
>
> There's a cosmic storm brewing. The sex strike has spilled over into the animal kingdom and even the rabbits and guppies aren't doing it anymore. Unreleased sexual energy has dangerously increased the earth's rotational rate and we are all going to either fly off the planet or be crushed into puddles by an exponential increase in the gravitational pull. It is their educated opinion that if something is not done to vent this pent-up energy immediately we are doomed.

Under such pressure Liz and the Daughters relent. Lamb Pito becomes the President. This energetic modern-day Lysistrata is performed to a full house and donations benefit the "Not in Our Name" foundation.[30]

Liz Estrada is a modern anti-war play steeped in contemporary concerns (such as the environment) and reflecting modern views on gender relations. Ellen Anderson's voice is heard clearly over the underlying Aristophanic canvas; she recycles his plot, his characters, and names, but puts them to her own use. When I asked her about her relationship to Aristophanes and why she needed his script at all, Ellen wrote back:

> *Liz Estrada* would not exist without *Lysistrata* because *Lysistrata* possesses what they call in Hollywood a "high concept" . . . Do I think I would have ever imagined withholding sex from the warmongers in order to halt war? Never in a million years! It's a brilliant idea, and it was Aristophanes'.[31]

Ellen's reference to the marketing term of "high concept" is particularly perceptive in that it draws attention to the process of reduction and abstraction that *Lysistrata* underwent as a part of the project. High concept is, as Justin Wyatt put it in his study of the phenomenon, a "striking, easily reducible narrative, which also offers high degree of marketability" that can be reduced to one sentence (Wyatt 1994: 13). This attitude toward Aristophanes' script permeated many interviews featured in Mark Kelly's documentary.

LYSISTRATA PROJECT: PLAYING DRESS-UP WITH ARISTOPHANES

Mark Kelly's film *Operation Lysistrata*, released in 2006, was pieced together from recordings made by the project's participants. While Kelly grants a special place to Blume and Bower and the reading in the Brooklyn Academy of Music performed by well-known actors, his film bears witness to an effort to reflect the multi-focal nature of the project. It is therefore remarkable that some features of the participants' and organizers' reflections are clearly recurrent. Most striking is the interviewees' insistence on the aspect of Aristophanes' play that Ellen Alexander described as its "high concept": that lovemaking and war are mutually exclusive. One woman who directed a performance of *Lysistrata* in Tromsø (Norway) expressed this attitude most candidly: "Because it has an antiwar message, [what we are trying to communicate] is a little simple, a little banal: as long as we drink and make-love we will have peace on earth." That love is good and war is evil is a brilliantly simple message: one need not study ancient Greek syntax to understand it. The speaker claims ownership of this message and reduces Aristophanes' script to an invitation to enjoy life, which she characterizes in words strongly reminiscent of the anti-Vietnam War make-love-not-war slogan. From this perspective *Lysistrata*'s Greekness becomes almost incidental; indeed, this view of Aristophanes was not particular to this staging: Blume and Bower neither consulted any Classicists nor did any research.[32] In the same spirit, the playwright Ellen McLaughlin stated that the *Lysistrata* "is really about erections and how funny they are."[33] "Once you have accepted this fundamental premise," she proposed, "it liberates you enormously in terms of not feeling that you have to do some sort of a scholarly approach to the work." This consistent rejection of scholarly investigation into the original context of the play also informed the approach to the text professed by Robinson Hagan. Like McLaughlin, Hagan stressed that she was "not an Aristophanes scholar," but simply "fell in love with his comedy," and this attitude permeates her adaptation.

Hagan's script is light and irreverent; its humor relies on the contrast between the superficially ancient setting and references to popular culture. Consider, for example, these lines spoken by Lysistrata when negotiating with the Magistrate:

> LYSISTRATA. Very well. I'll try to speak the language of the penis. Although we know you men are from Mars and we're, of course, from Venus.
>
> (*Changing into the cadence of the limerick.*) For decades and centuries on end | we women have had to defend our longing for peace: | that the battles might cease and brother should call brother: friend. (p. 34)

Here Hagan inserts phraseology of modern popular culture, the title of John Grey's immensely popular book, into her plot; elsewhere she deftly blends references to Aphrodite and the Peloponnesian War with terrorism, feminism (p. 35), "axis of evil" (p. 37), Neanderthals (p. 38), healthy hormonal equilibrium, and women's liberation:

> [WOMEN'S LEADER] My woman's ways, my female form, is something I'd not planned. But just because I have two breasts and less testosterone, it doesn't mean that you can oppress and shackle me at home. (p. 38)

While audiences quickly realize that the Greekness of Hagan's Lysistrata is only skin deep, this discourse alluding to women's liberation is quite confusing. The Leader's reference to oppression creates a jarring dissonance with other elements of the plot, especially the scene in which Reconciliation ("*a beautiful female nude perched high for all to see*") is portioned out to satisfy the desires and ambitions of the men of Athens and Sparta. Hagan, unlike Anderson in her free adaptation, retains Aristophanes' troubling finale. As though to compensate for it, however, she adds her own final scene. In this new happy ending, the drunken Magistrate admits that women were right all along and Old Man and Woman "go off to screw."

In attributing modern awareness and values to women of ancient Greece, Hagan collapsed a feminist agenda with the gender patterns built into Aristophanes' script. By modernizing Aristophanes' message as a universal and feminist call for peace, she inadvertently condones some of the misogyny of the Reconciliation scene, in which the female body is a cipher of property (which is precisely the kind of danger that Anderson's futuristic *Liz Estrada* successfully avoids by replacing it with an entirely new finale). As a result, the groups who used Hagan's script combined their modern and democratic anti-war message with the notion that a woman's body is an object to be owned and used.[34] The popularity of Hagan's script confirms that protesters were distinctly unconcerned about the nuances of the play's portrayal of gender roles, but instead hoped that Aristophanes' "high concept" would be effective in garnering support for the cause. This pronounced indifference toward the original context, the desire to sever all links with the past except those perceived as intuitive and visceral, makes the Lysistrata Project an unsuitable subject for an analysis of a conscious engagement with the past. The project instead seems to feature several loci of what one may call reception gone awry, in which the classical tradition becomes radically deterritorialized, its nominal connection with Greece yielding place to more recent and more productive points of reference (feminism, democracy, and sexual freedom). Indeed, the reception of the Lysistrata Project in the media points back to one point of reference particularly vital in the U.S.A.: the American counterculture of the 1960s.

Love, Peace, and the *Lysistrata* in the American Counterculture

To modern U.S. audiences, *Lysistrata*'s juxtaposition of war and love was strongly reminiscent of the famous slogan "Make Love Not War," launched by the opposition against the Vietnam War. Sexual freedom, democratic protests, and anti-war sentiments have been closely intertwined in the American popular imagination since the 1960s.[35] The iconic poster from 1968, featuring the activist and singer Joan Baez and her sisters, invited girls to say "yes" to boys who say "no" to conscription, implying that boys who say "yes" should get the opposite answer.[36] Although the poster itself shows no direct connection with Aristophanes' play, numerous musical versions of the *Lysistrata* were produced in 1960–3 in connection with the Cold War.[37] Most relevant to our inquiry is Robert Fink's Marxist adaptation *Lysistrata Against the War* (published 1979), subtitled "Ancient drama in music for the modern stage." *Lysistrata Against the War* playfully reconfigures the plot of the *Lysistrata* as a model for American peace activism. Composed between 1963 and 1967, it was to be performed by the Wayne State University (Detroit) opera workshop in 1968 as a protest against the Vietnam War, but its première never took place.[38] The libretto features caricatures of politicians: Richard Stillhouse Noxious (Richard Nixon), Democratea Diarrhea (Lyndon B. Johnson), and General Wantsmorewar (General William C. Westmoreland), as well as a generic figure of the good Proletarius. The Russian equivalent of Lampito is named Sexpotchki; an illustration (by Fink himself) printed on the libretto (3–8) shows her as a slim woman in a fur hat. The inscription under the drawing reads: "Make Love not War." Fink follows the Aristophanic plot up to the point where both men and women begin to waver. The women gain courage as Lysistrata reads them the oracle that promises that if doves fly away from the hawks, the end of strife and misery will follow. Men, however, led by senator Diarrhea and General Wantsmorewar, only pretend to enter peace negotiations. As soon as their devious plan to insult the Spartans is uncovered Lysistrata realizes that she has misread the prophecy:

> The Oracle is now clear, and he was surely wise: For both our women and our men must | now quickly organize.... For in social classes and not sex causes of this foul war rest.

With the help of Proletarius, Lysistrata now conducts genuine peace negotiations that overthrow the rule of the corrupt politicians and give power to the people. Fink's emphasis on social issues, including racism, and his knack for political caricature transform the *Lysistrata* into a call for a communist revolution.

However, at the same time, the *Lysistrata* (or perhaps Lysistrata as a "high concept") was also associated with less radical programs. The word "strike" figured in fact in the name of the "Women Strike for Peace," an organization whose official agenda was infinitely more conservative than that of Fink's opera. Despite this, WSP's program was frequently compared to the plot of Aristophanes' *Lysistrata* in the press. The founders of the group expressed ambivalent views on this conflation of their program with the "war of the sexes" represented allegedly in Aristophanes' play. Thus when, in a private letter, one of the co-founders, the deeply Catholic Valerie Delacorte, congratulated Dagmar Wilson, the emerging leader of the WSP, on the speech that Wilson gave at the founding meeting, she chose to call her "the Mother Superior of [their] Lysistrata Convent."[39] While this suggests that comparisons with the Aristophanic plot were welcome in private, Wilson herself, just weeks earlier, had told *The Baltimore Sun*: "our organization has no resemblance to the Lysistrata theme or even the suffragettes . . . [W]e are not striking against our husbands."[40] The leaders, as Amy Swerdlow (herself an active participant of the events) pointed out later, were aware that a traditional, respectable, middle-class image was key to obtaining a positive or at least benign media response (Swerdlow 1989: 230 and n. 14). It was during and after the Vietnam War that *Lysistrata* acquired the status of a mythical paradigm for women's peace making, its protagonist cast both as a communist heroine and a Catholic role model. This unique position made her into the perfect totemic figure for early twenty-first-century peace initiatives.[41] In fact, when Blume and Bower created their website, another Lysistrata Project,[42] which had been put forward in the aftermath of 9/11, was already active and present in cyberspace.

Make-Love-Not-War and the tradition of Women Strike for Peace converge most strikingly with the Lysistrata Project in the promotional photo for the reading used by the Mostly Harmless Theatre in St. Louis, Missouri. The picture is of a female nude stretched on a bed; her breasts and pubis are covered by black rectangles with the inscription in white letters MAKE LOVE | NOT WAR.[43] Another striking example of a reaction colored by memories of the Vietnam era is Debra West's *New York Times* article (March 9, 2003) on the *Lysistrata* Project entitled "No Sex as Antiwar Protest? What Sex?" West wryly contrasts Aristophanes' assumption that married couples engage in

FIG. 33.2 Publicity photo for (Mostly) Harmless Theatre's staged reading of The Lysistrata Project in St. Louis, MO, March 2003. (Photo Credit: John Lamb.) Reproduced with permission.

sex with numerous recent publications deploring the gloomy state of the American bedrooms. While she insists that "none of this de-sexing of [American] culture weakened the impact of the Lysistrata Project," she jokingly concludes that "this era, calls . . . for another idea. It's not very resourceful or creative. It's not even original, but it worked once, so why not try it again: 'Make Love. Not War'" (Fig. 33.2).

LYSISTRATA PROJECT AND SEX STRIKES IN THE MEDIA

West's (playful) misinterpretation of the Lysistrata Project as a call for a sex strike is by no means an exception. In fact, the question of whether Blume and Bower were themselves calling for a sex strike was frequently asked by journalists, although both women repeatedly responded to this question: "absolutely not—unless your husband's name is George or Saddam."[44] This misconstrual is a logical consequence of the activist setting: both *Lysistrata*'s plot and the Project's performance context featured anti-war initiatives; if the war is both fictional and real, shouldn't the fictional solution be put into practice? But yet another reason for this conflation needs to be considered: reports by contemporary media on the use of sex boycotts as a form of political activism. I am not suggesting that the Lysistrata Project was directly inspired by such strikes, nor (which would be particularly absurd) that the strikes were influenced by Blume's and Bower's initiative. Rather I am proposing that both the project and the media discussions of sex strikes belong to the global discourse about peace and the role women might play in promoting it. In this discourse, which I propose to envision as an assemblage of utterances and practices, the strikes and the project occupy contiguous positions without being qualitatively similar. While the scope of this chapter does not call for a detailed discussion of the use of sex strikes as a form of political action, a few highlights will be useful in revealing yet another way in which the Lysistrata Project was embedded in a global context. While some of these boycotts discussed in the media, such as the one in Turkey (2001),[45] were called to alter unbearable living conditions, the strikes in Sudan (2002) and later in Liberia (2003) encompassed entire countries and aimed to put an end to civil wars. Because of its timing, the Sudan strike is particularly relevant to us; in December 2002, just before the inception of the Lysistrata Project, Samira Ahmed (a former lecturer at the University of Cairo) and Sudanese Mothers for Peace called for a sex boycott in order to help put a stop to the civil war that had been ravaging Sudan for 19 years. Journalists covering the events in Sudan immediately compared Ahmed's initiative to the *Lysistrata*. Thus Vivien Morgan, reporting from Cairo for the *Daily Telegraph*, wrote,[46]

> There are direct parallels with Aristophanes's play, in which Lysistrata's disgust with war brings about a scheme to force the men of Greece to the peace table by denying them sex.[47]

Morgan also made efforts to point to local paradigms for such actions, but her use of *Lysistrata* as a byword for sex strikes as anti-war initiatives is symptomatic of

Western perceptions of such actions. This attitude became particularly striking in the media coverage of the Women In Peace-building Network in Liberia (led by Leymah Gbowee), a movement that in summer 2003 resorted to a sex strike—among other actions—in a sustained and successful effort to end 14 years of civil war. When the events in Liberia were later represented in the (award-winning) 2008 documentary *Pray the Devil Back to Hell*, the media compared Gbowee's work with the *Lysistrata*.[48] As my colleague Helen Morales points out, the use of Lysistrata to characterize the Liberian resistance was distinctly unhelpful.[49] Not only did Aristophanes' plot play no part in organizing and implementing political action, but "the prurient humor invoked by the idea of the 'sex strike', for example, is inappropriate in the context of the wide-spread sexual abuse of the women in Liberia by the warlords and their troops." During a visit to Santa Barbara in October 2011, Ms. Gbowee assured Helen and myself, in an interview, that she had never heard about Aristophanes before someone offered her the *Lysistrata* after the release of *Pray the Devil*, and she had so far had no time to read it. When pressed to name antecedents for the WiPNL's call for a sex strike, Ms. Gwobee named a traditional Kpele practice. The comparison with Lysistrata is thus not only unwarranted, but it also threatens to reduce the Sudanese and Liberian women's resistance to a "sex strike," when the reality was in fact far more complex (Morales 2013). And yet—radically different and disconnected though they are—the *Lysistrata* and the strikes function side by side in the global discourse about women and peace.

It is particularly important to clarify the appositive relationship between media coverage of sex strikes and the Lysistrata Project, because Kathryn Blume tells me that she knew about Samira Ahmed's call to strike while working on her project.[50] However, Blume did not consider the Sudanese initiative to be a direct impulse behind her own project, which, she says, she had conceived much earlier. In our e-mail communications, Blume sensibly resisted any comparisons between her use of Aristophanes' *Lysistrata* and the direct actions of women in war-ridden impoverished countries. And yet, this does not mean that the Lysistrata Project could not have been connected to the 2002 action in Sudan in a less structured, less dialogic fashion. Blume's respect for women like Samira Ahmed or Leymah Gbowee, and her thoughts on the role that the strikes played in her own work, are dramatized in her one-actor script *The Accidental Activist* (2006).

Lysistrata Project: *Accidental Activist*

The Accidental Activist is a fictionalized but clearly autobiographical piece, in which Blume gives a first-hand account of her work on the Lysistrata Project. She presents herself as an actor temporarily working as a typist, transcribing interviews with pundits: "middle-aged Harvard-educated experts" who take themselves too seriously; Kathryn paraphrases: "Bush unforeseen danger incalculable danger catastrophic danger read my book." A passionate participant of electronic discussion forums, Kathryn has already been working for some time on a screenplay adaptation of Aristophanes' *Lysistrata*, "the original anti-war sex farce. Plucky Greek women deny sex to their husbands until they lay down their swords." This summary of the play conveys both Kathryn's awareness of the play's "high concept" value and her desire to assimilate Aristophanes' script to something more familiar than Greek comedy ("sex farce").[51]

The idea of using the *Lysistrata* comes to Kathryn as she attends a fundraiser for the (fictional) Right Living Awards. The keynote speaker is this year's winner, the fictional Amira Bakkan, from the (non-fictional) Sudanese Mothers For Peace. Amira's name is a permutation of Samira's and the similarity, Kathryn tells me, is by no means accidental. In the script, the fictional event acts as a catalyst for Kathryn's work and a mouthpiece for her own response to journalists comparing her work with direct actions undertaken by women living under oppressive conditions. This is how she imagines Amira's speech:

> AMIRA: On behalf of Sudanese Mothers for Peace, I am grateful for this recognition of our work in Sudan. Though, I must tell you, if it had not been for the financial gift, which will care for so many children orphaned by these years of war, I might have been disinclined to accept. We have not stopped the fighting altogether, and it hardly seems time for awards.

Amira's story is that of a goddess epiphany that is a response to a sermon on honor and duty that she hears in her church. Listening to the sermon pronounced in the name of the Father, Amira reflects on the death of her own father and the fate of the child she now bears. On her way home, by a river, she hears the mournful song of Mother Earth herself who suffers from endless war. As soon as she arrives home, she goes into labor and gives birth:

> When my husband came in, so handsome, such pride and joy on his face, I melted. I opened my mouth to speak my love, but what came out was: 'I will bear you no more children until you stop this ridiculous war!

It is the midwife who recognizes the potential of Amira's earth-inspired idea and initiates a sex strike for peace. The episode ends with notes of triumph colored with New Age spirituality:

> We felt nothing but freedom and power. The naked me here, naked her there— were nothing. Didn't matter at all. Because we were filled with Her. And as we walked from town to town, I taught them the song the Earth taught me on that first day by the river.

Kathryn reflects on the differences between herself and Amira; unlike the fictional Sudanese mother, Kathryn feels that her problems are global rather than local. Her actions need therefore to be symbolic and far ranging rather than practical and immediate. But her purpose and Samira's are the same. She tries to send e-mails and letters to President Bush, has conversations with her husband and mother-in-law, and contemplates fundraising before she finally decides to stage *Lysistrata* in response to THAW's call. In Kathryn's fictional script at least, her work is a form of response to both the Iraq war and the work of women activists in Africa. Despite the fundamental differences between Kathryn's kind of activism and that of Samira/Amira, the media discourse consistently fails to keep them apart, as this imaginary version of an interview for *The Connection* on NPR illustrates:

> HOST: Excuse me, Kathryn, let me ask you this.
> KATHRYN: Yes?
> HOST: Following the success of the Lysistrata Project, will you continue to advocate withholding sex as a tool for political change?
> KATHRYN: Well, no. We never did advocate—
> HOST: Kathryn, thank you so much for joining us today.

The fictional NPR journalist conflates, just as so many non-fictional interviewers have done, Kathryn's work with political sex strikes in Africa. However, any conflation of staged readings from ancient comedy with political actions of women in war-ridden countries is both naive and harmful. And yet, Kathryn Blume clearly thinks of her work as contiguous to such movements, even if distinct in nature. Such appositive relationships, even when skewed, may need to be taken into consideration if we wish to understand how the classical tradition actually functions in contemporary global discourse.[52]

Conclusion

What, then, can we learn from this case study about democratic appropriation as a mode of reception? Let us begin by confirming the democratic credentials of the Lysistrata Project, credentials problematized in our introduction. Critics have pointed out many limitations of the Project as a democratic initiative. Sue-Ellen Case, for example, argued that because of its method of dissemination via cyberspace and the format of staged readings, the performances within the Project did not focus emphatically enough on the female body (Case 2007). Referring to the project's poster which featured a Greek style drawing of a seated woman in a transparent dress, Case complains: "The classical Greek female body was uploaded into cyberspace, where it served to hail anti-war protestors" (Case 2007: 127). And yet, without the Internet the project would have remained strictly local and Blume and Bower would have been unable to appeal to the wide range of performers and audiences that the project eventually reached. Bodies both male and female did feature prominently in the performances presented by Kelly in his documentary.

The totemic status of the *Lysistrata* was also brought against the Lysistrata Project: both Case and Marina Kotzamani have argued that the assumption that a Western text should serve as a universal paradigm is blatantly Eurocentric.[53] In the aftermath of the Lysistrata Project, Kotzamani sent an open invitation to Arab playwrights and directors asking them whether Aristophanes' play could be relevant in contemporary Arab contexts (Kotzamani 2006b). Most respondents were extremely skeptical, pointing out that the Peloponnesian War could not possibly stand for the complexities of modern war, especially the religious conflicts in which so many Arab countries are involved (Kotzamani 2006b: 13–14). Admittedly, Blume's and Bower's plan to offer the entire world a chance to gather under the aegis of a Western heroine had its inherent limitations.[54] It is worthwhile to remember, however, that the organizers' initial plan was to hold only a few readings of the play in New York and their decision to open the project to all was a gesture of inclusion, not an imposition of a Eurocentric paradigm. In *The Accidental Activist* Kathryn Blume made the vital point that while she, herself and of her own accord, turned to the *Lysistrata* to articulate her support for peaceful conversation, she also undertook this action in concert with and as an expression of her respect and caring for women elsewhere, women like Samira Ahmed or Leimah Gbowee. Far from looking to impose a Western paradigm on other cultures, Blume seems to think of her actions as a response, determined by her own background, to the actions of women in Sudan.

The openness inherent in Blume's and Bower's inclusive democratic agenda generated a response of formidable diversity. The level of the readings varied from professional to playful (from BAM to plastic dinosaurs), the scripts ranged from traditional translations (Sommerstein) through thinly disguised travesties (Robinson Hagan) to futuristic reinventions (Anderson). Moreover, the project activated a multiplicity of connections and associations, both past and contemporaneous, involving a wild variety of contexts. In the U.S.A., *Lysistrata* as the gospel of American peace movements carried a wealth of associations from conservative (WSP) to communist (Fink's libretto). Some of the readings that took place in Greece—especially the one staged at the foot of the Acropolis—were connected directly, almost physically, one might say, to the tradition of Greek theater. Others, such as the one in Tokyo, were staged in places where Greek drama would function as an exotic import. The media reception, in turn, reflected the vast diversity of the staged readings but also contextualized the project within wildly diverse peace initiatives whose programs contrasted war and lovemaking, both past and very recent.[55] All these instances of reception, the website, the staged readings, TV shows, articles, Kelly's documentary, Ellen's script, my journal, and Kathryn's play, as the de- and re-territorializations of the *Lysistrata*, formed an assemblage or machine (to retain the Deleuzian imagery) intersecting with other structures: the media machine, the fundraising network, the activist rhizome, the World Wide Web, and academia. The Lysistrata assemblage initiated by Blume and Bower still remains productive and open today: the new website now sends the visitor both back, to the archives, and forward, to current peace initiatives.[56]

Democratic openness in the case of the Lysistrata Project brought about a multifocal phenomenon with modern frameworks of reference, which lent itself to the presentist, horizontal reading that this chapter has attempted. This of course does not render the relationship between the project and the original Greek *Lysistrata* void. The presence of Aristophanes' script, however transformed, placed every reading in an apposite relationship to the Greek past. A dialogic relationship between the two would need to be plotted on an abstract ontological level, beyond the professed preoccupations and concerns of the project's participants.

Notes

1. See Hardwick 2006 for an excellent discussion of such uses of Greek drama. See also Hardwick and Stray 2008: 3–4. An earlier version of this chapter was delivered at the "Democratic Turn" Conference in June 2010 at the Open University; see <http://www2.open.ac.uk/ClassicalStudies/GreekPlays/Conf2010/confpage2010.htm> for the organizers' description of the scope of the democratic turn. This paper benefited greatly from the discussion that followed. I am also grateful to Helen Morales for her helpful comments on an earlier version of this chapter, to Justine McConnell for encouraging me to engage with theory, and to Donna Williams for her timely advice on the final draft.
2. On efforts to use classical texts in the service of other modern political agendas, see for example Lacoue-Labarthe, Nancy, and Holmes (1990) discussing the role of Greece in the creation of Nazi myths or Mackenzie (2003) on Riefenstahl's appropriation of the Olympic aesthetics.
3. <http://www.npr.org/templates/story/story.php?storyId=923078> accessed May 11, 2011.
4. So *Merriam-Webster*; cf. *OED* "a form of government in which power resides in the people."
5. See Nancy 2011 [2009]: 66–72 for his reflections on the consequences of the notion of power of society.
6. <http://lysistrataprojectarchive.com/lys/play.html> accessed May 1, 2011. Blume and Bower presented themselves as women who were using their democratic freedom to speak and take political action on behalf of women who did not have those freedoms. While such desire to speak on behalf of people who did not ask to be represented might be criticized by some as arrogance, one might also see it, in the spirit of Nancy's definition of democracy, as an attempt to extend democracy beyond the limits of the *demos* of citizens.
7. On *Lysistrata*'s status in the U.S.A. see below.
8. Kelly's interviews with both Bower and Blume reveal this to be a shared assumption of both actors.
9. On Aristophanes' complex attitude toward the democratic institution of the court, see Konstan 1985; on his satire of ardent democratic rhetoric, see Scholtz 2004. On Aristophanes and gender see, for example, Taaffe 1993 and Zeitlin 1996.
10. More than deracination, deterritorialization is understood as the process of disrupting connections and transforming concrete and rooted qualities into abstract entities; see Deleuze and Guattari 1977: 33–5; cf. 301–63.
11. Even so, from the point of view of performance reception theory as outlined in Hall and Harrop 2010, which centers on professional theater, many of our amateurish readings would be considered peripheral (2010: 11). Martindale (2006: 3) states that reception should deal with the "text," in an expanded poststructuralist meaning, which might be "a painting or a marriage ceremony, or a person, or a historical event," but the volume itself does not stray far beyond the traditional subjects of literary works and art.
12. I am employing this term in the sense used by theorists of communication, such as van Dijk 1985 and Fairclough 1992, and not in its poststructuralist sense—see Foucault 1972.

13. For example, Martindale (2006: 11) argues against the study of reception material that is not "high quality." As Hardwick and Stray (2008: 3) note, studies of popular culture are increasingly frequent. Hall (2008: *passim*) advocates a nine-step inquiry into the ramifications of social class in the study of classical reception.
14. On the rhizome, see, for example, Deleuze and Guattari 1986: 2–3).
15. I would like to thank all of them for their generosity. All misinterpretations and mistakes remain, of course, mine.
16. <http://www.thawaction.org/about/index.html> accessed May 1, 2011.
17. <http://www.lysistrataproject.org/aboutus.htm> accessed May 1, 2011; the name of the host website is that of another venture "inspired by the iconoclastic heroine of the ancient Greek comedy *Lysistrata*."
18. <http://rudeguerrilla.org/2003Season/lysistrata/masterlysistrata.html> accessed May 1, 2011.
19. Personal communication (June 6, 2010).
20. The website was originally hosted in the domain "lysistrataproject.com"; this site now features a cursory description of the project and some haphazard links; <http://www.lysistrataproject.com/> accessed May 11, 2011. Both the "rudeguerrilla" site (see above n. 18) and <http://www.lysistrataproject.org/aboutus.html> preserve some of the original information. There is also a new, authorized website created by Mark Greene, Kathryn Blume's husband, at <http://pecosdesign.com/lys/>, which now has a link to the Project's archives: <http://lysistrataprojectarchive.com/lys/> accessed January 20, 2013.
21. <http://lysistrataprojectarchive.com/lys/spearhead.html> accessed May 11, 2011. The original content is available at a new website <http://lysistrataprojectarchive.com/lys/>.
22. <http://lysistrataprojectarchive.com/lys/script.html>; the scripts are no longer posted, but see for information on Hagan's script: <http://www.commondreams.org/headlines03/0301-02.htm> accessed May 11, 2011.
23. <http://lysistrataprojectarchive.com/lys/archive.html> accessed May 11, 2011.
24. <http://www.npr.org/templates/story/story.php?storyId=923078> accessed May 11, 2011.
25. The official charities were "Madre" and the "Education for Peace in Iraq Center." Kathryn Blume, personal communication (June 6, 2010).
26. <http://www.brooklynpaper.com/stories/26/10/26_10lysisbam.html>.
27. *Liz Istrata* was freely adapted from Aristophanes' *Lysistrata* (1991), commissioned by the University of California; it was performed in the Hatlen Theatre and directed by Peter Lackner. A revised version of the play, *Liz Estrada*, premièred in New York as part of the NYC International Fringe Festival (2002); the play was subsequently produced in a reading for the Lysistrata Project (2003) both at the Brecht Project in NYC and at the Center Stage in Santa Barbara.
28. <http://www.dramaticwomen.org/> accessed January 25, 2014.
29. I am most grateful to Ellen Anderson for lending me her script.
30. <http://www.notinourname.net>.
31. Personal communication (May 11, 2011).
32. Personal communication with Blume (June 6, 2010).
33. McLaughlin is the author of several other "Greek" plays, including *Iphigenia and Other Daughters, Helen, Persians, Trojan Women, Oedipus*.
34. *Lysistrata: A Woman's Translation* is available from Playscripts.com. The booklet states that 360 theater groups around the world adopted the play. The description on the website,

however, refers to 420 performances; see <http://www.playscripts.com/play/198> accessed January 25, 2014.
35. The slogan was apparently popularized by Penelope and Franklin Rosemont; cf. Rosemont 2008: 40–1. Gershon Legman claimed to have introduced it; cf. Dudar 1984: 41–3. Cf. also Allyn 2000: 50; 101.
36. On feminist artists' reconfiguration of the "war on terror" in the aftermath of 9/11, see Wilson 2009. In 2008 a group of girls in Brooklyn created a revival of this famous poster to promote the election of Barack Obama for president, creating quite a controversy in the blogosphere; see, for example, <http://www.amptoons.com/blog/2008/10/23/jeff-says-fail-to-girls-say-yes-to-boys-who-say-obama/> accessed January 25, 2014.
37. For a survey of musical versions of the *Lysistrata*, see Beta 2010: 255. Among the best-known scripts were Tony Harrison's *The Common Chorus* and James Simmons's *Aikin Mata*; the latter was staged in Nigeria, at the Ahmadu Bello University at Zaria, and (presciently, as Helen Morales has argued) imagines the *Lysistrata* played out in an African context.
38. Based on Benjamin B. Rogers's translation altered to suit the considerations of a vocal score. Four days before it was to be performed the tenor was drafted and the director, concerned by the text's anti-Vietnam War sentiment, used this as an excuse to move the performance to a smaller studio. With a new, unrehearsed tenor and without room for a regular size audience, Fink withdrew his opera. It has since been revised and published in only 60 copies.
39. December 10, 1961, quoted in Swerdlow 1993: 53 and n. 14.
40. October 29, 1961, quoted in Swerdlow 1993: 22 and n. 25.
41. Putney and Middleton conclude their 1962 study of 1,200 students' attitude to war, stating that a future anti-war operation in America would operate largely as "a feminine responsibility . . . today as in the time of Lysistrata" (1962: 655); cf. Boulding 1962: 1.
42. <http://www.lysistrataproject.org/index.htm> accessed January 25, 2014.
43. Robert Neblett, Founding Artistic Director, St. Louis, Missouri. Photo: John Lamb; see <http://www.playscripts.com/play.php3?playid=198> accessed January 25, 2014.
44. Cf., for example, <http://sm4peace.org/home.html http://news.bbc.co.uk/2/hi/entertainment/2814295.stm>.
45. <http://archives.cnn.com/2001/WORLD/europe/08/16/turkey.women/index.html>. Sex workers' strikes, such as the one in London's Soho district in 2000 or in Bolivia in 2007, are sex strikes by default. <http://news.bbc.co.uk/2/hi/5341574.stm>.
46. <http://www.telegraph.co.uk/news/worldnews/africaandindianocean/sudan/1417009/Sudanese-women-ban-sex-in-effort-to-halt-war.html> accessed May 16, 2011.
47. Morgan mentions that such an action is called "alHair" in Arabic, meaning "sexual abandoning." The Qur'an recommends that a husband not have intercourse with a wife who has displeased him; as a punishment, "abandonment" ranks midway between reprimand and beating; see al-Hibri 2000–1: 61–2.
48. Swan (2009) in *Los Angeles Examiner* wrote: "Not since Aristophanes' . . . *Lysistrata*, has anyone captured quite so poignantly the power of women to take a stand for peace." As models for the strike one might take into consideration the Igbo tradition of women's village councils—and especially their power of strike action; see Amadiume 1987: 67; cf. Moran 1989: 444; see also Fuest 2009: 120–3 and her comments on the "dual sex system" of many West African societies, in which men are considered unable to represent women's interests.
49. I am most grateful to Helen for lending me the texts of her talk to be delivered at the Cambridge Triennial Conference, in July 2011; now published—see Morales 2013.

50. Personal communication (June 6, 2010).
51. On sex farce, see Wainscott 1997: 53–74.
52. I refer here, again, to Martindale's use of text (2006: 3).
53. Case 2007; Kotzamani 2006a. On feminist appropriations of the classics, see Liveley 2006.
54. Cf. Kotzamani (2006a: 105–6) and her emphasis on the project's inclusiveness.
55. On this kind of pseudo-mimicry in which completely distinct phenomena show a superficial yet compelling similarity, see Deleuze and Guattari 1987 and their famous discussion of the wasp and the orchid.
56. <http://lysistrataprojectarchive.com/>.

References

Al-Hibri, A. Y. (2000–1), "Muslim Women's Rights in the Global Village: Challenges and Opportunities," *Journal of Law and Religion* 15.1/2, 37–66.
Allyn, D. (2000), *Make Love Not War. The Sexual Revolution: An Unfettered History*. Boston and New York.
Amadiume, I. (1987), *Male Daughters, Female Husbands*. London.
Bendetti, C. D. and C. Chatfield (1990), *An American Ordeal: The Antiwar Movement in the Vietnam War Era*. Syracuse, NY.
Beta, S. (2010), "The Metamorphosis of a Greek Comedy and its Protagonist: Some Musical Versions of Aristophanes' Lysistrata," in P. Brown and S. Ograjensek eds., *Ancient Drama in Music for the Modern Stage*. Oxford.
Boulding, E. (1962), "What Every Woman Knows", *Women's Peace Movement Bulletin* (May 19, 1965).
Case, S.-E. (2007), "The Masked Activist: Greek Strategies for the Streets," *Theatre Research International* 32.2, 119–29.
Deleuze, G. and F. Guattari (1977 [1972]), *Anti-Oedipous: Capitalism and Schizophrenia*. Preface by M. Foucault. Trans. R. Hurely, M. Seem, and H. R. Lane. New York; repr. Minneapolis, 1983.
Deleuze, G. and F. Guattari (1986), *Kafka: Toward a Minor Literature*. Trans. Dana Polan. Minneapolis.
Deleuze, G. and F. Guattari (1987), *A Thousand Plateaus: Capitalism and Schizophrenia*. Trans. Brian Massumi. Minneapolis.
Dudar, H. (1984), "Love and Death (and Schmutz): G. Legman's Second Thoughts," *Village Voice* May 1, 41–3.
Fairclough, N. (1992), *Discourse and Social Change*. Cambridge.
Fink, B. (1978), *Lysistrata and the War: A Comic Opera*. Saskatoon.
Foucault, M. (1972), *The Archaeology of Knowledge*. Trans. A. M. Sheridan Smith. London.
Fuest, V. (2009), "Liberia's Women Acting for Peace: Collective Action in War Affected Country," in S. Ellis and I. van Kessel eds., *Movers and Shakers: Social Movements in Africa*, 114–37.
Grey, J. (1992), *Men are from Mars; Women are from Venus*. New York.
Hall, E. (2010), "Towards A Theory of Performance Reception," in E. Hall and S. Harrop eds., *Theorizing Performance: Greek Drama Cultural History and Critical Practice*. London, 10–28.
Hall, E. and S. Harrop (eds. 2010), *Theorising Performance Reception: Greek Drama, Cultural History and Critical Practice*. London.
Hardwick, L. (2006), "Remodeling Reception: Greek Drama as Diaspora in Performance," in C. Martindale and R. F. Thomas eds., *Classics and the Uses of Reception*. Malden, MA, and Oxford, 204–15.

Hardwick, L. and C. Stray (2008). "Introduction: Making Connections," in L. Harwick and C. Stray eds., *A Companion to Classical Receptions*. Malden, MA, and Oxford, 1–9.

Konstan, D. (1985), "The Politics of Aristophanes' *Wasps*," *TAPA* 115, 27–46.

Kotzamani, M. (2006a), "Artist Citizens in the Age of the Web," *Theater* 103–10.

Kotzamani, M. (2006b), "*Lysistrata* on the Arabic Stage," *A Journal of Performance and Art* 83.2, 13–40.

Lacoue-Labarthe, P., J.-L. Nancy, and B. Holmes (1990), "The Nazi Myth," *Critical Inquiry* 16. 2, 291–312.

Liveley, G. (2006), "Surfing the Third Wave? Postfeminism and the Hermeneutics of Reception," in C. Martindale and R. F. Thomas eds., *Classics and the Uses of Reception*. Oxford, 55–66.

Mackenzie, M. (2003), "From Athens to Berlin: The 1936 Olympics and Leni Riefenstahl's *Olympia*," *Critical Inquiry* 29.2, 302–36.

Martindale, C. (2006), "Introduction: Thinking through Reception," in C. Martindale and R. F. Thomas eds., *Classics and the Uses of Reception*. Malden, MA, and Oxford, 1–13.

Morales, H. (2013), "Aristophanes' *Lysistrata*, the Liberian 'sex strike', and the Politics of Reception," *Greece and Rome* 60.2, 281–95.

Moran, M. H. (1989), "Collective Action and the Representation of African Women: A Liberian Case Study," *Feminist Studies* 15.3, 443–60.

Nancy, J.-L. (2011 [2009]), "Finite and Infinite Democracy," in G. Agamben et al. eds., *Democracy in What State?* Trans. W. McCuaig. New York, 58–75.

Putney, S. and R. Middleton (1962), "Some Factors Associated with Student Acceptance or Rejection of War," *American Sociological Review* 27.5, 655–67.

Rosemont, P. (2008), *Dreams and Everyday Life: A Sixties Notebook*. Chicago.

Rylance, R. (1997), "Doomsongs: Tony Harrison and War," in S. Byrne ed., *Tony Harrison: Loiner*. Oxford, 137–60.

Scholtz, A. (2004), "Friends, Lovers, Flatterers: Demophilic Courtship in Aristophanes' *Knights*," *TAPA* 134.2, 263–93.

Swan, S. Z. (2009), "Academy Vet's Day Showing of Pray the Devil Back to Hell Highlights Women's World Peace Building," *Los Angeles Examiner* (November 5).

Swerdlow, A. (1989), "Pure Milk not Poison: Women Strike for Peace and the Test Ban Treaty 1963," in A. Harris and Y. King eds., *Rocking the Ship of State: Towards a Feminist Peace Politics*. Boulder, CO, San Francisco, and London, 225–37.

Swerdlow, A. (1993), *Women Strike for Peace: Traditional Motherhood and Radical Politics in the 1960s*. Chicago and London.

Taaffe, L. K. (1993), *Aristophanes and Women*. London.

van Dijk, T. A. (1985), *Handbook of Discourse Analysis*. 4 vols. London.

Wainscott, R. H. (1997), *The Emergence of the Modern American Theater: 1914–1929*. New Haven.

West, D. (2003), "No Sex as Antiwar Protest? What Sex?," *New York Times* (March 9).

Wilson, S. (2009), "Girls Say Yes to Boys who Say No: Four Artists Refigure the Sex War on Terror," *Oxford Art Journal* 32.1, 121–42.

Wyatt, J. (1994), *High Concept: Movies and Marketing in Hollywood*. Austin, TX.

Zeitlin, F. I. (1996), "Travesties of Gender and Genre in Aristophanes' *Thesmophoriazusae*," in F. Zeitlin ed., *Playing the Other: Gender and Society in Classical Greek Literature*. Chicago, 375–416.

CHAPTER 34

RECLAIMING EURIPIDES IN HARLEM

MELINDA POWERS

ALTHOUGH the relationship between Greek drama and Harlem dates back at least to Countee Cullen's 1935 translation of Euripides' *Medea* (see Curtis, and Hill, both this volume),[1] the popular view of classical drama's association with an elite, white, Eurocentric vision that privileges ancient Greece as the "cradle of Western civilization" has influenced the subject's reception by African-American communities both in Cullen's time and subsequently. For example, while ancient Greek theater was often staged at black colleges prior to the 1960s (see Banks and Rankine, this volume),[2] the Black Arts Movement of the late 1960s criticized the performance of the Greek and Roman Classics, as black writers such as Lorraine Hansberry were increasing racial awareness and producing African-American alternatives to the so-called white classical plays. At the same time, for those individuals who still wished to perform ancient drama, the association of the Classics with whiteness has had an impact upon the possibilities for black artists to perform in classical theater, especially on the commercial circuit.

A comparative study of classical drama and African-American theater thus raises questions about the politics of identity, for the historical association of a singular identity with ancient drama has had clear consequences for minority communities. This chapter considers two Harlem-based classical theater companies that foreground the problematic history between artists of color and the Classics, as their 2008 performances work to "reclaim" ancient Greek theater for diverse artists and audiences.[3]

In February 2008, Take Wing and Soar Productions and the Classical Theatre of Harlem staged Euripides' *Medea* and *Trojan Women*, respectively. Representing a plurality of perspectives within the space of 30 blocks, both of these companies embrace classical theater and yet have distinct approaches and philosophies. Take Wing and Soar was founded by Debra Ann Byrd, an African-American woman who aimed to provide opportunities for artists of color in classical theater by supporting "emerging and professional classical artists of color, by fostering their artistic achievement and personal growth, by providing opportunities for career development, and by developing creative programming that fosters diversity in classical theatre."[4] The company has a limited budget, charges 18 dollars per ticket, and primarily attracts a local audience from Harlem. Since their inception, they have been hosted by the National Black Theatre,[5] which is the first black theater arts, revenue-generating institution in the country. From 2002 to 2010,TWAS was the company in residence. Since 2003, the company has primarily produced a variety of works by Shakespeare, and Euripides' *Medea* is the only full production of an ancient Greek play. However, TWAS has also produced two adaptations of ancient Greek drama including Stephen Carter's *Pecong*, an adaptation of *Medea*, and Rita Dove's *The Darker Face of the Earth*, an adaption of Sophocles' *Oedipus Tyrannus*. Through staging such works, TWAS "has served over 400 classically trained artists, directors, designers, technicians and young entrepreneurial artists," and the company has been consistently nominated for fourteen AUDELCO awards for Excellence in Black Theater and won several.[6]

In 1999, Alfred Preisser together with Christopher McElroen founded The Classical Theatre of Harlem (CTH) in order to return Harlem theater to the days of its renaissance.[7] The company enjoys a high production quality, the historic landmark of the Harlem Gatehouse Theatre, which used to be an old pumping station, reviews in the major newspapers, and audiences who pay 40 dollars per ticket (although the company has recently announced a plan to offer free tickets to the housing community being served under their Project Classics mission). According to its website, CTH's mission is: "To maintain a professional theatre company dedicated to presenting the 'classics' in Harlem . . . [and] to create the next great American theatre company . . . that is engaged in producing theatre that has the capacity to change lives and truly reflects the diversity of ideas and racial tapestry that is America."[8] Since its founding, the company has provided opportunities for artists in over 40 productions by authors such as Anton Chekhov, Samuel Beckett, Jean Genet, Langston Hughes, Adrienne Kennedy, William Shakespeare, Derek Walcott, and August Wilson, as well as Euripides. These two companies, from their multiracial casts and audiences to their intercultural scripts, address issues of American identity through their presentations of Greek drama in terms of the diverse, multiracial identity of a partially gentrified Harlem.

During a cultural moment in which the U.S. media was fixated on questions of racial identity, precisely when presidential candidate Barack Obama began the campaign that led to his presidential election, both TWAS's and CTH's productions challenged the traditional connection between Greek drama and mainstream culture as they presented race not as an essentialist, fixed, or immutable entity but instead as a socially constructed category.[9] With the media at times questioning whether Obama was "black enough,"[10] the performances' hybrid aesthetics challenged the media's cultural idea or stereotype of blackness, which Theater/Performance scholar Harvey Young has referred to as the idea of the "black body," i.e., when "when popular connotations of blackness are mapped across or internalized within black people" (Young 2010: 7). According to Young, "it is the black body and not a particular flesh-and-blood body that is the target of a racializing projection" (Young 2010: 7). In the following I will argue that as the mission statements of TWAS and CTH present challenges to the "black body" and the ways in which it prevents opportunities for artists of color, these companies' respective productions of *Medea* and *Trojan Women* also work to reclaim the Classics for a diverse audience. For as Patrick Johnson has stated, "*re*-claiming does not require that we erase the past and script a new one . . . It is to remain aware of its previous 'claims' even as you articulate your own. It is to know the past in the present as you work toward creating a future" (Johnson 2003: 135). In this spirit of "reclaiming," TWAS's *Medea* and CTH's *Trojan Women* re-signify Greek drama in social constructivist terms, as each company simultaneously acknowledges the past and present practices of racial stereotyping that limit black artists and their potential.[11]

TWAS's *Medea*

Debra Ann Byrd,[12] a classically trained African-American artist with a passion for performing Shakespeare and the Greeks, attended acting school with the intention of pursuing a career in classical theater, but in her final year, two professors suggested that she focus on something other than classical acting because she was not "traditional." "Traditional," she explained, was not referring to the style of her acting but rather to the color of her skin. The euphemism, while offensive, nevertheless reflects the reality of the scarcity of roles that have existed for artists of color in commercial theater. In response to these so-called "traditional" casting practices, Ms. Byrd founded Take Wing and Soar to create a venue for artists of color to play classical roles at the professional level. Although some new playwrights searching for the same opportunities as TWAS's performers might criticize their exclusion from the theater and its success, Ms. Byrd believes that other venues exist for playwrights. Her venue exists for performers and audiences, many of whom are experiencing classical works for the first time.

Because opportunities for people of color to perform in classical theater are limited, many of the artists that TWAS has provided with opportunities are award-winning, professional artists who continue to return to the small Off-Off-Broadway venue for the opportunity to perform in the Classics. One such artist is Trezana Beverley who in 1976 won the Tony award for her role in *for colored girls who have considered suicide when the rainbow is enuf*. Ms. Beverley led the *Medea* cast, which was primarily composed of actors of color with the exception of the role of Aegeus, played by Ian Stewart. Beverley's nuanced performance captured the anger, sadness, and confusion of Medea but also offered comic relief through her interpretation of Medea's gripes about the limitations imposed on her gender. However, despite her reputation and the brilliance of her performance, the production still did not attract reviewers nor has it been remounted.

Despite the company's lack of mainstream critical attention, it has a reliable audience, which, according to Ms. Byrd, primarily consists of African-Americans, Africans, as well as some Asians and a few Euro-Americans. Many are not familiar with classical theater and are seeing classically trained artists of color for the first time. Before staging the 2008 *Medea*, Ms. Byrd said that she sometimes found herself explaining that she was staging Euripides' play not Tyler Perry's *Madea* (the popular and sometimes controversial comedies featuring Perry in drag and trading on racial stock), and at the end of some performances her audience would say to her, "Wow! I didn't know we [people of color] could do that [i.e., classical theater]" (Byrd 2009). These remarks suggest not only the unfamiliarity of TWAS's audience with classical theater but also the audience's own stereotypes about classical theater and who can perform it.

Before discussing the means by which the performance of *Medea* has worked to resignify some of these stereotypes, a description of the production is first necessary. While TWAS's *Medea* was primarily performed by artists of color for an audience of color, the performance made no overt attempt to resituate the play in any specific African-American context or any context for that matter. Instead, the director Petronia Paley used Nicholas Rudall's translation of the text to present the fifth-century tragedy about the foreign woman from Colchis who murders her children to avenge herself on her Greek husband Jason who left her to marry a young, Greek princess (see McConnell and Rankine, this volume).

Produced on a very limited budget, the production design evoked a "time out of time" aesthetic through its minimalist costumes and set. For example, the set (Pavlo Bosyy) of the approximately 150-seat theater was simple and sparse, consisting of two benches and two pillars, made of sculpted fabric on wires, which functioned as the *skene* door. Apart from the 1950s inflection of Medea's travelling suit, which she wore for the final scene of the play, and the Nursemaid's uniform, which consisted of a black dress with white apron and white lace collar, the costume design (Ali Turns) was also not specific to any historical time period. Instead, the majority of the male characters wore black suits or tuxedos, which had different styles of ties or trimmings (vests, boutonnières, amulets, watch chains, suspenders, and handerchiefs). Such details helped to differentiate each character from the others (Fig. 34.1). Jason (Dathan B. Williams), for example, arrived in a crisp tuxedo and bow tie with a watch chain accenting his pocket. His booming voice, cigar, and gelled back hair further characterized him.[13]

The children wore school uniforms with crisp white shirts, and Aegeus wore a Panama hat as well as the performance's only white suit, which may have indicated that he was from Athens not Corinth. The chorus wore long, flowing black dresses with tight-fitting bodices. Some donned colorful headscarves or long necklaces. One carried a drum, and another carried a baby wrapped up in a cloth.

In contrast to the chorus's and principal characters' appearance, Medea's costume designated her "otherness." She wore a long, black flowing dress with a tight bustier and a long, black cape with gold sparkles, which highlighted her gold choker, bracelet, and earrings. Her short, loosely curled hair with a reddish tint gave it a snake-like quality, which perhaps alluded to Medusa or Medea's witch-like powers (Fig. 34.2).

FIG. 34.1 Creon, in Take Wing And Soar Productions' *MEDEA*, directed by Petronia Paley, starring Trezana Beverley. Photo ©2008 Renaldo Davidson.

This costume designated Medea as Medea, but later when she appeared *dea ex machina*, with a chauffeur in lieu of the Euripidean chariot, she wore not any goddess-like apparel but what Paley calls her red travelling suit: a fur stole, clutch, and high heels. The overall effect of the production design suggested a setting in the not-too-distant past, and according to Paley, the aim was to give the characters as much style as possible despite the production's limited budget.

In this way, the principal actors' modern costumes, the African inflections of the chorus, the time-out-of-time setting, and the identities of the performers and audience worked symbiotically with the text to create an aesthetic that challenged essentialist notions of a "black" or "white" style of American theater. TWAS's *Medea* instead presented a hybrid performance that underscored the Africanist[14] presence in Greek drama. In other words, the identities of the actors and audience helped to highlight the aesthetic characteristics in Greek drama that are typically associated with Africa as opposed to Europe, such as the mask, choral performance, the call and response between actors and chorus (*amoibaion*), and the repetition and revision of song, such as that between strophe and antistrophe. The performance suggested neither an African contribution to Greek drama, nor an African-American contribution to the American reception of Greek drama, but rather that Greek drama and its reception

FIG. 34.2 Medea, in Take Wing And Soar Productions' *MEDEA*, directed by Petronia Paley, starring Trezana Beverley. Photo ©2008 Renaldo Davidson.

is a hybrid of Africa and Europe, black and white. The relationship between Greek drama and the black community was thus demonstrated as natural as any other.

Brenda Dixon Gottschild has discussed the "Africanist presence" throughout American cultural forms and stated:

> When we are able to see the African reflection as the image of our culture, then finally we will behold ourselves fully—as Americans—in the mirror. At that point it will be silly to talk about Africanist presences as "the Africanist contribution." That is the outdated language of disenfranchisement, the mindset that implies that European is something bigger or better into which the African—the Other—is subsumed. But there is no Other, *we are it*. (Gottschild 1996: 78)

Recognizing the Africanist presence is recognizing the African *in* the American not seeing it as something adjacent to it. Recognizing the Africanist presence runs contrary to essentialism and makes defining America and its theater in terms of "black" and "white" an especially difficult if not futile task. For according to Gottschild, "In spite of the politics of exclusion, Africanisms are inextricably dreadlocked into the weave of the American fabric and, like that hairdo, cannot be undone without cutting off both black and white strands at the root and diminishing the potential quality of life for us all" (Gottschild 1996: 9–10). The hybrid characteristics of TWAS's *Medea* reflect these dreadlocked Africanisms in both American theater and ancient Greek theater itself.

However, despite the inextricable dreadlocking of Africanisms into the American fabric, contemporary productions of *Medea* often perform notions of race and identity. Several contemporary productions have cast Medea as a woman of color opposite a white Jason, and directors often adapt the play into African or African-American contexts.[15] These performances aim to challenge the marginalization of black women, but in the process they may nevertheless reinforce the paradigm of black women as "other." Sensitive to this issue, George C. Wolfe has even parodied such productions in his play *The Colored Museum* in its "Last Mama on the Couch Scene":

> MEDEA: I beseech thee, forgo thine anger and leave wrath to the gods!
> SON: Girl, what has gotten into you.
> MEDEA: Juilliard, good brother. For I am no longer bound by rhythms of race or region. Oh, no. My speech, like my pain and suffering, have become classical and therefore universal.
> LADY: I didn't understand a damn thing she said, but girl you usin' them words.
> (*Lady in Plaid crosses and gives Medea the award and everyone applauds.*) (Wolfe 1988: 28)

Kevin Wetmore has discussed this scene in terms of Wolfe's satire of several theater conventions: "First," he explains, " . . . the scene is a parody of black Medeas, Medea being the tragic figure most identified with women of color. Second, the scene is a parody of 'Black Orpheus' productions that dismiss difference by universalizing—black suffering as the suffering of all. Medea Jones is a self aware stereotype of sorts who mocks that which she praises" (Wetmore 2003: 149). Although TWAS's *Medea* avoided the traps of universalizing black suffering, the essentialist notions of suffering, parodied by Wolfe, were not entirely absent either.

For example, Trezana Beverley, who played Medea, has suggested to Debra Ann Byrd that perhaps as an African-American woman her connection to suffering (e.g., the wounds of slavery, rape, and racism) has allowed her greater access to the depths of Medea's character.[16] These comments could point to an essentialist viewpoint, for Beverley suggests that she has connected to her role through an innate emotional state predetermined by her race rather than through her personal experience as a woman of color. However, her observations may also suggest the actor's use of history to inspire her performance. She may channel the memory of a specific ancestor and perform the history of a past abuse across her present body.[17] Harvey Young has discussed this idea of "touching history" in relation to his concept of the "black body." According to Young:

> the black body, whether on the auction block, the American plantation, hanged from a lightpole as part of a lynching ritual, attacked by police dogs within the Civil Rights era, or staged as a "criminal body" by contemporary law enforcement and judiciary systems, is a body that has been forced into the public spotlight and given a compulsory visibility. *It has been made to be given to be seen.* (Young 2010: 12)

This compulsory visibility of black bodies contributes to the idea of the black body that "materially affects actual bodies."[18] Beverley's comments indicate her use of the image of the black body to express Medea's suffering, so in this respect, she suggests that her body could have served as a "screen on which the drama of racism and abuse get (re) played" even though she is not specifically playing an African-American character. Thus, Beverley's comments, on the one hand, may imply an essentialist view, which links innate emotional states to racial identity and reinforces the idea of the "black body" without regard to specific actual bodies. Yet, on the other hand, her comments also suggest the ways in which her performance may draw on the memory of a specific ancestor to operate as an empowering tool in the present that reconfigures the stereotype of the black body.

Regardless of the literal or implied meaning behind Beverley's words, the performance of TWAS's diverse artists created a production that evaded essentialism and allowed artists of color the opportunity to perform as artists. This company of artists for whom race is always an issue did not reinforce the paradigm of black women as "other." They avoided the reinforcement of *Medea*'s self/other paradigm through the anachronistic paradigm of race. Instead, they were conscious of identity without necessarily performing it. In this way, TWAS's *Medea* presented a powerful cultural critique, which paradoxically rested in the absence of one. The production was not an Afro-centric revision, nor was its content a counter-hegemonic critique in any recognizable sense; nor did it use Greek drama as a metaphor for Africa.[19] Unlike productions such as Lee Breuer and Bob Telson's *The Gospel at Colonus* (see McConnell, this volume), Paley did not perform the identity of her artists. She did not perform or play up any distinct features of African-American culture or identity. Neither did she situate her actors in a distinctly African-American context nor offer any overt cultural or political critique. Perhaps because of the primarily middle-class African-American audience, the artists had a better chance at being "ordinary," so to speak, for as Kobena Mercer has argued, "Black artists are never allowed to be ordinary ... but have to visibly embody a prescribed difference."[20] Thus, while acutely aware that race matters, Paley instead created a space where, as far as possible, race was not a signifier in the performance. Perhaps by making race *the* factor in the production, she succeeded in taking race out of the equation and thereby re-signifying the image of the black body, for as Young has commented, while the black body is socially constructed, it is also continually constructing its own self (Young 2010: 20). TWAS's *Medea* participates in this continual reconstruction by posing a challenge to the idea of ancient Greek theater and its American reception as essentially black or white, yet far from suggesting a post-racial America, the company's mission statement underscores the history of division that has prevented opportunities for artists of color.

CTH's *Trojan Women*

Adapted and directed by Alfred Preisser, the Classical Theatre of Harlem's *Trojan Women* was performed in January of 2008 and received mixed reviews.[21] Although it follows the Euripidean plot rather closely, the production, unlike TWAS's *Medea*, does not rely on a translation but rather adapts the *Trojan Women* to tell the story of the civil war in Sierra Leone, which began in 1991. Preisser asks, "if there is truth in the Greek concept of tragedy, in which cycles of order are governed by fate, then doesn't it stand to reason that the catastrophic disaster always happening somewhere else will someday happen here?"[22] The performance thus uses Greek tragedy as a framework to explore the violence of war and its repercussions for the global community (see further Lodewyck and Monoson, this volume).

Performed before a racially diverse audience at the Harlem Gatehouse Theatre, the play focuses on the Greek army's victimization of the women of Troy after their defeat to Greece in the Trojan War. Preisser intertwines Euripides with eyewitness accounts of women survivors of the recent civil wars in western Africa. Set in the imagined wreckage of Penn Station (one of the major train stations of New York City), the play opens with a multiracial chorus of barefoot women dressed in evening gowns (costumes by Kimberley Glennon). The women stand behind a six-foot-high cyclone fence. An approximately 20-foot-high scaffolding frames the top of the fence, and large metal doors positioned downstage open and shut (set by Troy Hourie). Helen (Zainab Jah), the woman who began the war by betraying her Greek husband Menelaus (Ty Jones) and running away with the Trojan prince Paris, is perched high above the stage on a deconstructed Greek column, which serves as her prison. The chorus stands opposite Helen, as one chorus member begins to sing her harrowing account of the war (original music by Kelvyn Bell).

With Tracy Jack's choreography punctuating the poignancy of their speech, the other chorus members join in the song. They remember stories of torture, violence, and death. "Men walk through church, sprinkle gasoline on us . . .," they recall. "The men ran out of ammunition and they turned to axes and machetes. They came and sprinkled gas on the house. Now you know us. Now you know the bitterness of the war." To which Helen later adds, "Our bodies are currencies in this war and always will be." The horrors they recount and their battered faces are juxtaposed to the beauty of their halter evening gowns, one short, some beaded, others sparkling, with long gloves emphasizing their elegance. They were wearing these dresses when the soldiers took them as they were celebrating the victory they thought they had just won.

The men provide an aggressive contrast. Amidst the women's screaming, the Greek herald Talthybius (Michael Early) arrives costumed in a suit with two soldiers at his side. He informs the women of Odysseus' orders concerning Hecuba (Lizan Mitchell), Cassandra (Tryphena Wade), and Astyanax the child of Andromache and the Trojan warrior Hector. One reviewer describes the character as follows: "Like a CEO whose lot it is to fire half his staff after a bad year, Talthybius lets the women know that he does not want to pain them, but is determined to carry out his orders."[23] When the women ask, "Are we to be slaves?," Talthybius responds, "Let's say wives."[24] He finally delivers the news that Cassandra and Astyanax must die, and from this point on, the battle between the sexes escalates.

However, in this battle, Helen, not the warring men, serves as the scapegoat. The men loathe but adore her. The women curse her. Menelaus, who plans to kill his wife Helen, exclaims, "I'd have to care about you to hate you . . . I came here to kill you." But Helen pleads with him to spare her. She claims that the gods put her in these circumstances, and she blames Hecuba for the war because she gave birth to Paris. Despite the Trojan women's protests, Helen succeeds in seducing Menelaus, and he concedes: "All right, so maybe I don't have to kill you, right now." This moment of comic relief is short-lived before the Greeks' murder of Astyanax leads to chaos. In the rebellion that follows, the Greek soldiers shoot several women and put others behind bars on a ship positioned upstage. Talthybius arrives with the child's body, which Hecuba receives as she warns the herald, "Your death ship is coming too." As the chorus earlier sang, what has happened to these women can happen anywhere. The havoc that the Greeks wreaked on the Trojan women will be requited in turn, yet despite the men's violence, Helen remains to blame.

As the woman who is the "mirror that reflects a man's desire, contempt, indifference, or self-doubt," Helen serves in the production as a scapegoat for the vanity, greed, and corruption that leads to war and violence against women. While Preisser's adaptation does not overtly link the beauty of Helen to the wealth of natural resources in Africa, the work does present Helen as a metaphor. Desire for Helen is compared to the desire for profit aroused by diamonds in the African blood diamond trade, for attempts to explain Sierra Leone's civil war "have varied from 'bad governance' to 'the history of the postcolonial period' to the 'urge to acquire the country's diamond wealth . . .'"[25] Thus, desire for the beauty, wealth, status, and power associated with diamonds, like the desire for Helen, erupted into the violence initiated in Sierra Leone by the violent Revolutionary United Front (Brittain 2000). According to a 2000 article in the *Guardian*, "The PAC [Partnership Africa Canada] report into Sierra Leone concludes that the seven year war there, in which 75,000 civilians were killed, 2 million people displaced and tens of thousands mutilated, opened the country to a gangster economy based on the diamond trade. Neighboring Liberia has, at an official level, been deeply implicated in the trade," the report concludes. Yet the cause of this devastation is not only the diamonds, just as the cause of the Trojan War is not simply Helen herself. Rather the men's behavior over diamonds and over Helen resulted in the waste and destruction of war.

Thus, what is striking about CTH's *Trojan Women* is that, despite the reference to Helen as a "mirror that reflects men's desire," the production still chooses to echo its ancient Greek precursor by having the Trojan women blame Helen for the war. As one reviewer noted,

> Though the women speak with individual voices, they move as a unit. At first their combined force is brute and animal-like; they gang up on Helen, screaming at her and calling her names. Their hatred echoes that of the men who terrorize them; a parallel they realize too late. (O'Brian 2008)

In this production, the women still blame another woman and not any man for their city's ruin.

However, while CTH's production may not include a feminist revision to the plot,[26] it does include an explicit postcolonial critique. By incorporating accounts from the civil wars in Sierra Leone and weaving these events into the plot of an ancient Greek play, the adaptation connects the contemporary African conflict to its British colonial past; for Classics was the hallmark of a curriculum during the age of imperialism.[27] In this way, the plot of the ancient Greek *Trojan Women* functions metonymically in the production. It is a reminder of the colonial antecedents to Sierra Leone's conflict, such as the former British colonial government's division of Sierra Leone into two nations, known as the "Colony" and the "Protectorate," which had "far-reaching implications for issues such as citizenship, land tenure rights and conflict of laws."[28]

In addition to assigning responsibility to the colonial past, the production also implicates western consumerism and the diamond markets that fueled the blood diamond trade. The accusation is subtle and politically charged, for one reviewer, missing the allusion, asked: "what did American G.I.s or CEOs have to do with those crimes [in Sierra Leone]? What's more, the play never explains how those wars are related to a destroyed Penn Station."[29] However, while not exactly explaining these points, the production's setting in a post-apocalyptic New York suggests not only that the U.S.A.'s consumer-driven economy is implicitly contributing to the violence but also that it may not be immune from it. For the imagery of the wreckage of Penn Station connects the wars in foreign lands to American soil, and through this image, Preisser explores his idea of the Greek concept of tragedy and the cycles of order by suggesting the violence in the present and the violence of the colonial past not only has repercussions for Africa but for the U.S.A. as well. (The relative recentness of 9/11/01 and the destruction of the Twin Towers is also relevant.)

In this way, the production engages with the *Trojan Women* through the double-conscious lens of the "Black Atlantic," a term that Paul Gilroy has used to refer to a black identity that is not distinctly African, American, Caribbean, or British, but a conglomeration of these cultures. In his *Black Atlantic: Modernity and Double Consciousness*, Gilroy expands on W. E. B. Dubois's notion of double consciousness, which refers to "a world which yields him [an African-American] no true self-consciousness, but only lets him see himself through the revelation of another world. It is a peculiar sensation this double-consciousness, this sense of always looking at one's self through the eyes of another" (Du Bois [1903] 2008: 3). Gilroy draws on the concept of double consciousness to extend his "implicit argument that the cultures of diaspora blacks can be profitably interpreted as expressions of and commentaries upon ambivalences generated by modernity and their locations within it" (Gilroy 1993: 117). Thus, "however modern they appear to be, the artistic practices of slaves and their descendants are also grounded outside modernity. The invocation of anteriority as anti-modernity is more than a consistent rhetorical flourish linking contemporary Africalogy and its nineteenth-century precursors" (Gilroy 1993: 57–8).

By using an ancient Greek play and gesturing toward its implicit associations with the colonial past, Preisser engages with such a double-conscious perspective. His *Trojan Women* operates as a tool to dismantle the ideas and effects of colonialism, for the production's "gestures [of anteriority as anti-modernity] articulate a memory of pre-slave history that can, in turn, operate as a mechanism to distil and focus the counter-power of those held in bondage and their descendants" (Gilroy 1993: 57–8). Through a double-conscious lens, the performance reimagines a classical Greek drama and its traditional associations with the colonial past to suggest the implication of the West in the suffering of the Black Atlantic.[30] Accordingly, the production uses the Greek metaphor not only to reflect on the impact of colonialism on Africa but also colonialism's repercussions in the network of all global nations.[31]

Conclusion

TWAS's and CTH's distinct founders, members, audiences, and styles defy any singular definition of black theater or the performance of Greek drama within that tradition. Instead, they represent the multiplicity of approaches to Greek drama and African-American theater within the diverse, multicultural, multiracial space of 30 blocks in Harlem. Paley's *Medea* counters the prejudices that prevent opportunities for artists of color in classical theater, and CTH's *Trojan Women* adapts its precursor to comment on the threats posed by the aftermath of British colonialism to global peace and security. (See Goff and Simpson, this volume.) While stereotypical casting practices and the persistence of the "black body" continue to be an obstacle, TWAS's and CTH's performances pursue a diversified trajectory of performance that challenge such stereotypes by presenting Greek drama through the hybridized characteristics of American language, culture, and identity.

Notes

1. The work, published as *Medea and Some Poems*, was the first major attempt by a nineteenth-century black American poet to translate Greek drama. Since the early 1900s, the population in Harlem was developing, and by the 1920s a cultural renaissance blossomed of which Cullen, together with writers such as Langston Hughes, Claude McCay, and Zora Neale Hurston, was a leading figure.
2. Artists such as Glenda E. Gill, while recognizing that many of these performances took place through a lack of racial awareness and access to plays by African-American playwrights, still reflect positively on the learning that took place in spite of the racial consequences.
3. For a discussion of the terms "classic," "classical," see Macintosh, McConnell, and Rankine, this volume.
4. TWAS website <http://www.twasinc.xbuild.com>.
5. For more information on the National Black Theater, see <http://www.nationalblacktheatre.org/about.htm>. The website states that: "Dr. Barbara Ann Teer's National Black Theatre Institute of Action Arts operates from an African context of a spirit culture. The National Black Theatre (NBT) began in 1968 as a non-profit organization and center for research & development known as the National Black Theatre Workshop Incorporated. NBT has

since grown into an institution providing an alternative learning environment offering organizations and individuals, specifically those of African descent born in America, a space to discover, explore, nurture, articulate, address and heal the negative attitudes and emotions blocking freedom of expression."

6. <http://twasinc.xbuild.com/#/company-history/4527929172> accessed January 31, 2010.
7. Preisser and McElroen have since left the company. On this issue, see Propst 2009.
8. <http://www.classicaltheatreofharlem.org/about.html> accessed November 19, 2012.
9. The question of "essentialist" versus "constructivist" paradigms of racial identity is relevant to the study of black theater. Harvey Young, for example, begins his introduction to the December 2009 *Theater Topics*, an issue devoted to the subject of teaching of African-American theater, with the questions, "What is black theater? What is a black play?" In the December 2005 special issue on Black Theater in *Theater Journal*, several artists and scholars addressed the question, "What is a black play and what is playing black?" Harry Elam and David Krasner's 2001 *African American Performance and Theater History* includes a transcript of a roundtable discussion with Elam, Krasner, James Hatch, Sandra Richards, and Margaret Wilkerson titled "African American Theater: The State of the Profession, Past, Present, and Future." In all of these publications, the dynamic relationship between race and theater plays a critical role in the discussions surrounding the field's identity and the performances that shape it.
10. Ta-Nehisi Paul Coates's 2007 *Time* magazine article titled "Is Obama Black Enough?," for example, argued that "Ever since Barack Obama first ascended the national stage at the 2004 Democratic convention, pundits have been tripping over themselves to point out the difference between him and the average Joe from the South Side." In his speech on race in Philadelphia, Obama himself has stated, "At various stages in the campaign, some commentators have deemed me as either 'too black' or 'not black enough.'"
11. "Signifying" refers to one view of African-American, self-conscious relationship to tradition, in literature, specifically, drawn from Gates 1989. See Wetmore, this volume.
12. Byrd 2009, personal interview. I am most grateful to Deborah Ann Byrd and Petronia Paley for their generosity in their interview with me about their work and for providing me with images from their production.
13. My grateful thanks to Debra Ann Byrd for generously providing images of this production.
14. On the contrast between Africanist and European aesthetics, see Gottschild 1996: 9–10.
15. See Wetmore 2003: 144–9 for a discussion of Medeas played by women of color.
16. Byrd interview (2009). Kevin Wetmore (2003: 142) has explained that this view is common, for *Medea* is "a strong candidate for transculturation into African American contexts. She has left her home and family, far away, and was taken to a land across the sea where she was expected to live by their laws, abide by their customs, and was feared for her different appearance, abilities, and manners."
17. In regard to McCauley's performance, Young (2010: 166) states that the actor "channels the memory of an ancestor alongside dreams about her encounters on the plantation grounds and performs them across her body."
18. Young 2010: 11. Young later explains, 14, that "although black bodies vary, thus preventing them from having exactly the same experience, the similarities in how they are seen and see themselves constitute a relatable experience of the body."
19. See Wetmore 2003: 13–14, for his discussion of Black Orpheus, Black Athena, and Black Dionysus style productions. See also note 31.

20. Mercer 1997: 33, 37, quoted in Wetmore 2003: 43.
21. See for example Claudia La Rocco (2008) who found the chorus to be melodramatic and the artistry of the production lacking. Paulanne Simmons (2008), on the other hand, commented, "There are many inspired moments, but the attempt to marry the ancient tragedy with modern wars is not always successful. The chorus, especially in the beginning, sounds much more whiney than tragic. The crimes committed during the wars in Sierra Leone and Liberia have been well documented, and their enumeration serves little dramatic purpose . . ." Kat Chamberlain (2008) thought the production suffered from "emotional overdrive." Maura O'Brian (2008) commented: "There is a lot that Preisser is trying to do with *Trojan Women*, and the production suffers from its grand, but undefined ambitions . . . the production's message is too hazy to inspire critical self-assessment, or change." Alexis Soloski (2008) commented: "Preisser follows the example of Sartre, who thrust the ravages of colonialism into his version, and Charles L. Mee, who added the testimony of holocaust survivors to his *Trojan Women 2.0*. . . . He stages the action behind a chain-link fence, which prevents the audience from really seeing the faces of the women, rendering their performances more generic or anonymous than they ought to be . . . Preisser seems to want us to feel culpable—some lines clearly indict the U.S.—but the action plays out as if at a distance."
22. <http://www.classicaltheatreofharlem.org/trojanwomen_07-08.html> accessed December 11, 2012.
23. Simmons 2008. See n. 22 for quotation.
24. Quotation taken from Margo Jefferson's theater review of an earlier version of this *Trojan Women* produced in 2004.
25. *Witness to Truth: Report of the Sierra Leone Truth and Reconciliation Commission* (2004), 3.
26. An example of such a feminist revision to the plot of the *Trojan Women* appears in Jocelyn Clarke's adaptation, performed by Ann Bogart's SITI Company in 2011 at the J. Paul Getty Museum and in 2012 at the Brooklyn Academy of Music. This production replaced the chorus of Trojan women, who blame Helen, with a single Trojan eunuch priest. Moreover, Clarke gives the bereft Andromache agency in killing her child, whereas Euripides assigns the murder to the Greeks.
27. For further discussion on the Classics and imperialism in the British Empire, see Bradley 2010.
28. *Witness to Truth: Report of the Sierra Leone Truth and Reconciliation Commission*, vol. 3A, Accra, Ghana, <http://www.sierra-leone.org/Other-Conflict/TRCVolume3A.pdf> accessed December 11, 2012, (2004), 5.
29. Simmons 2008; see n. 22.
30. Wetmore (2003: 44) has used the term "Black Dionysos" to describe this style of production. He argues that such productions offer a "Post-Afrocentric formulation of drama that is counter-hegemonic, self-aware, refuses to enforce dominant notions of ethnicity and culture, and uses ancient Greek material to inscribe a new discourse that empowers and critiques all cultures, even as it identifies the colonizer's power and colonized's powerlessness." In addition, Wetmore's *Black Dionysus* proposes two other models for theorizing the relationship between Greek Drama and African-American theater: Black Orpheus (or the Eurocentric use of Greek Tragedy, Myth, and Epic as Metaphor for Africa) and Black Athena (an Afrocentric reclaiming of the Stolen Legacy).
31. For further reading on revisions of Greek drama that comment on colonialism, see Bradley, Barbara Goff, Goff and Michael Simpson, and Lorna Hardwick.

REFERENCES

Bradley, M. (ed. 2010), *Classics and Imperialism in the British Empire*. Oxford.
Brittain, V. (2000), "Criminal Diamond Trade Fuels African War, UN is Told," *The Guardian*, January 13, <http://www.guardian.co.uk/world/2000/jan/13/sierraleone.unitednations> accessed December 11, 2012.
Byrd, D. A. (2009), Telephone Interview by Melinda Powers, November 8.
Chamberlain, K. (2008), "Trojan Women," *New York Theatre*, January <http://www.nytheatre.com/nytheatre/showpage.php?t=troj6227> accessed December 11, 2012.
Coates, T. P. (2007), "Is Obama Black Enough," *Time*, February 1, <http://www.time.com/time/nation/article/> accessed April 7, 2013.
Du Bois, W. E. B. ([1903] 2008), *The Souls of Black Folk*. New York.
Elam, H. and David K. (eds. 2001), *African American Performance and Theater History: A Critical Reader*. Oxford.
Gates, H. L., Jr. (1989), *The Signifying Monkey: A Theory of African-American Literary Criticism*. Oxford.
Gill, G. E. (2005), "The Transforming Power of Performing the Classics in Chocolate, 1949–1954," *Theater Journal* 57.4, 592–6.
Gilroy, P. (1993), *The Black Atlantic: Modernity and Double Consciousness*. Cambridge, MA.
Goff, B. E. (ed. 2005), *Classics and Colonialism*. London.
Goff, B. E. and M. Simpson (2008), *Crossroads in the Black Aegean: Oedipus, Antigone, and Dramas of the African Diaspora*. Oxford.
Gottschild, B. D. (1996), *Digging the Africanist Presence in American Performance*. Santa Barbara, CA.
Hardwick, L. (2010), *Classics in Post-Colonial Worlds*. Oxford.
Jefferson, M. (2004), "After Defeat, Before Slavery, Steeping in Civilization's Tatters," *New York Times*, April 7, <http://www.nytimes.com/2004/04/07/theater/theater-review-after-defeat-before-slavery-steeping-civilization-s-tatters.html> accessed December 11, 2012.
Johnson, E. P. (2003), *Appropriating Blackness: Performance and the Politics of Authenticity*. Durham, NC.
La Rocco, C. (2008), "Bridging Civilizations to Make Sense of Slaughter," *New York Times*, January 23, <http://theater.nytimes.com/2008/01/23/theater/reviews/23troj.html> accessed December 11, 2012.
Mercer, K. (1997), "Interculturality is Ordinary," in R. Lavrijsen ed., *Intercultural Arts Education and Municipal Policy*. Amsterdam.
Obama, B. (2008), "A More Perfect Union" (Campaign Speech in Philadelphia), Transcript from National Public Radio, March 18, <http://www.npr.org/templates/story/story.php?storyId=88478467> accessed April 9, 2013.
O'Brian, M. (2008), "The Tragedy of the Issue Play," *Off Off Online: What's on Off Off Broadway*, January 12, <http://offoffonline.com/?p=3323> accessed April 7, 2013.
Paley, P. (2009), telephone interview by Melinda Powers, December 3.
Propst, A. (2009), "Classical Theatre of Harlem Founders Alfred Preisser, Christopher McElroen to Depart Company," *TheatreMania*, November 2, <http://www.theatermania.com/new-york/news/11-2009/classical-theatre-of-harlem-founders-alfred-preiss_22528.html> accessed December 11, 2012.
Simmons, P. (2008), "Trojan Women," *Curtain Up: The Internet Theatre Magazine of Reviews, Features, Annotated Listings*, January 12, <http://www.curtainup.com/trojanwomencth08.html> accessed December 11, 2012.

Soloski, A. (2008), "Trojan Harlem: A Child Thirsts for Blood in an Uptown Euripides," *Village Voice*, January 22, <http://www.villagevoice.com/2008-01-22/theater/trojan-harlem/http> accessed December 11, 2012.

Wetmore, K. J., Jr. (2003), *Black Dionysus: Greek Tragedy and African American Theatre*. Jefferson, NC.

Wolfe, G. C. (1988), *The Colored Museum*. New York.

Young, H. (2009), "Introduction," *Theater Topics* 19.1 (December), xiii–xviii.

Young, H. (2010), *Embodying Black Experience: Stillness, Critical Memory, and the Black Body*. Ann Arbor.

CHAPTER 35

OEDIPUS TYRANNUS IN SOUTH AMERICA

MARÍA FLORENCIA NELLI

Since its original performance around 429 BCE, Sophocles' *Oedipus Tyrannus* has seen countless enactments, versions, rewritings and rereadings, not only onstage but also on the big screen.[1] From classical performances to modern adaptations, from radio broadcasts to musical satires and operas, *Oedipus Tyrannus* has enticed worldwide audiences for generations. The power of truth, the truth of power, politics, the inability of mankind to comprehend fate, chance, causality, nature, divine intentions, gods, and humans alike, are some of the topics that make *Oedipus Tyrannus* such an attractive and ever relevant play, source and raw material for a multitude of eager playwrights, actors, and directors, each with something different to say, each with their mind focused on a particular aspect of the play. And there is, of course, the subject of taboo. Oedipus' incest, ever so succulent, has nourished our morbid curiosity for centuries.

Even though not as popular as *Antigone*,[2] *Oedipus Tyrannus* has also seen a wealth of Latin American adaptations, particularly in recent times. They fall roughly into two groups: humorous approaches to the myth—comedies, farces, radio sketches, and musical satires—and serious treatments of it—operas, dramas, radio theater, and film adaptations. Whereas serious versions touch upon incest as a tragic development, using it as a means to explore other issues such as gender, politics, and power, humorous adaptations tend to exploit the topics of incest and sexuality for comical purposes. Humorous versions have been increasingly popular and highly successful in the last few decades in Latin America. They seem to be part of a broader post-Freudian move where the burlesque tone has taken over and Oedipus' character has been drastically transformed and displaced, either portrayed as an anti-hero, or dethroned and upstaged by Jocasta's character.[3] Latin American versions, however, have their own distinct interest. The most remarkable humorous adaptations are intrinsically political, making use of their comical approach to the myth to pass harsh judgement on the recent history of their countries or to criticize severely their current socio-political reality.

In this chapter I would like to discuss some comic treatments of *OT* in South America, while mentioning briefly some serious adaptations, focusing not only on stage but also on film, radio, and musical versions, and concentrating particularly on Argentina, Ecuador, Chile, and Colombia.

FROM GUERRILLAS TO *DESAPARECIDOS*: WOMEN, POLITICS, AND POWER IN TRAGIC *OEDIPUSES*

It is clearly impossible to provide a full account of the serious South American adaptations of *Oedipus Tyrannus* and so here I focus on only a few of the experimental versions. A notable example is *Edipo rey*, staged by Teatro de Escritorio and directed by Alejandro Buenaventura, brother to the celebrated Enrique Buenaventura and founding member of TEC (Teatro Experimental de Cali), Colombia.[4] The play was staged using the "teatro escritorio" format (desktop theater), an old theater technique where there is neither action nor scenery. The events and conflicts of the play have to be expressed through the inflection of the actors' voices, demanding significant effort on the part of the actor. The play premièred at Biblioteca Departamental, Cali, in November 2009. In September 2012 Buenaventura staged *Edipo rey* once more, this time with Compañía Municipal de Teatro de Cali at the Teatro Municipal Enrique Buenaventura.

Another interesting Colombian version of the tragedy is the live radio theater broadcast staged by Radio Televisión Nacional de Colombia (RTVC) and the Fonoteca of Radio Nacional de Colombia on the occasion of the 13th Ibero-American Theatre Festival of Bogotá in 2012. The broadcast, an adaptation of a 1954 production, paid tribute to Colombian actor and director Bernardo Romero Lozano, who since 1943 had directed countless radio theater broadcasts on Radio Nacional. Directed by Romero Lozano's granddaughter and starring some of its original actors, this radio theater revival featured original music, a choir providing an eerie musical background to the tragic dialogues, and live sound effects performed in the style of early radio.[5]

A remarkable retelling of the myth is *Yocasta* by Argentinian intellectual, playwright, and director Héctor Levy-Daniel (see further the interview with Levy-Daniel, this volume). It is one of the few adaptations narrating the events of the myth from Jocasta's perspective.[6] As with other post-Freudian rewritings of the tragedy, in this version Jocasta comes completely center stage.[7] She appears not only as the omniscient narrator, but also as a character involved in the action. She is a Brechtian actor in dialogue with the audience, a voice from the future coming back to relive events from the past, the true victim of the tragedy, a woman, a wife, a mother. Motherhood and the role of women in society are key themes in the play. But Levy-Daniel's Yocasta is so much more than a loving wife and a protective mother sitting in the background, waiting for men to play their game of power. Yocasta is a key political player. Power and pragmatism define her role in the play, as do power and truth. Power filters through the play as water, and water is used as the symbolic representation of power.[8]

Power and politics also feature prominently in two noteworthy South American film adaptations: Colombian *Edipo alcalde* (Oedipus Mayor, 1996) directed by Jorge Alí Triana from a screenplay by Gabriel García Márquez, and Argentinian *El recuento de los daños* (The Account of the Damages, 2010) written and directed by Inés de Oliveira Cézar.[9] Both films dealt with difficult issues connected to Colombian and Argentinian recent histories. *Edipo alcalde* is set against the background of the violence and civil strife that engulfed Colombia—guerrillas, drug trafficking, kidnapping; *El recuento* is set in the aftermath of Argentina's last military dictatorship. The differing treatment of the subject of Oedipus' identity in each film is in line with each film's take on the story. In the Colombian version Oedipus is the product of both armed and sexual violence: young Jocasta is raped by a violent and much older Laius, an important landowner usurper to the lands of Jocasta's father on the Andes mountain range. In the Argentine version, Oedipus is a child born in captivity, a *desaparecido*, son of a politically engaged young woman taken and tortured by the military during the dictatorship. The aesthetics of both films is also a reflection of their main thread. Triana's film has the color and sensuality of the Colombian forest; it is noisy and boastful, its scenes full of images, symbols, and metaphors drawing on magical realism through a mixture of oneiric and fantastic elements. De Oliveira's version is mostly silent, dry, grey, distorted like a grimace, toying with strange out-of-focus shots and a fixed camera that does not really show what happens in the scene, turning the spectator into a bystander unsuccessfully craning their neck to get a better view.[10]

MUSICAL SATIRES: CLASSICAL MUSIC, POPULAR LYRICS, FOOTBALL, AND PSYCHOANALYSIS

Amongst the adaptations and rewritings that take a lightly humorous approach to *Oedipus Tyrannus*, there are two fantastic musical versions that deserve a special mention. They are both Argentinian and date from the 1970s: *Epopeya de Edipo de Tebas (Cantar bastante de gesta)*[11] by internationally famous Les Luthiers, a short piece of the most refined humor; and *Edipo rey o ¡Qué luna de miel mamita!*[12] by Cantoría Ars Nova, a musical satire with a highly accomplished musical score.

The first version of *Epopeya de Edipo de Tebas* premièred in 1969. A second—shorter and more polished—version was performed as part of the show *Sonamos pese a todo* (1971),[13] and the final version—under five minutes long—appeared in the show *Viejos fracasos* of 1976.[14] Most pieces in the Les Luthiers' repertoire are attributed to a fictitious composer, Johan Sebastian Mastropiero. In the humorous introduction to the song, the narrator—and writer of the lyrics—Marcos Mundstock explains why Mastropiero decided to compose a song about Oedipus. While staying in Vienna, he had an affair with archduchess "Ursula von Zaubergeige," who reminded him of his mother. Worried about it, he felt the need to research the subject more deeply, and so Mastropiero learnt about Oedipus and the Oedipus complex. After quoting some hilarious made-up bibliography, such as Arnulfo Pérez Campos's *Sin complejos, mamacita* ("Without complexes, mummy"), all of it recited in the most serious of tones, the narrator introduces the song. The beautiful musical score, composed in a medieval style, matches the description of the piece as a *chanson de geste*. The seriousness of the music, the precision of performance on the original and exquisitely crafted instruments, and the skilled and professionally directed voices, contrast comically with the irreverent secular lyrics: "Le dijo el oráculo: | Edipo, tu vida | se pone movida, | serás parricida, | le dijo el oráculo. || Seguía diciendo, | si bien yo detesto | hablarte de esto, | se viene, se viene un incesto, | seguía diciendo."[15]

Cheeky references to Oedipus' incest, to sexual intercourse, and to Laius' death are sung using the most hilarious of rhymes in an old Spanish style. One stanza uses very old fashioned post-verbal clitics—"salvóse," "matólo," "envíolo," instead of the modern and grammatically correct "se salvó," "lo mató," "lo envió," generating an amusing assonance; the stanza is practically a tongue twister: "Edipo salvóse | y a Layo matólo, | peleándolo él sólo | al cielo envíolo."[16]

The final stanza before the "moraleja" (moral of the story) makes fun of Argentinian middle-class obsession with therapy, while making an ironic reference to the Oedipus complex and its crucial role in psychotherapy.[17] At the end, the moral of the story points once more to the incestuous relationship between Oedipus and his mother, alluding to the fundamental figure of the loving mother in Argentinian society,[18] and alerting them to the dangers of their sons' amorous excesses: "Madres amantes, | tomad precauciones | por las efusiones | de hijos varones, | madres amantes."[19]

Whereas Les Luthiers' version of *OT* is a short piece within a bigger show, *Edipo rey o ¡Qué luna de miel mamita!* by Cantoría Ars Nova is a show in its own right. According to scriptwriters Enrique Bugallo and Mario Carpinetti,[20] the idea to write a satirical opera inspired by the myth of Oedipus was born in the 1960s during a National University Choir Festival. They proposed renowned composer and choirmaster Raúl Carpinetti, to compose the music for the opera. Although they wanted to be true to the tragic version of the myth, their main interest was to create a humorous version, and so this musical satire mixes grandiloquent expressions and tragic verses with vulgar elements, *lunfardo* (Argentinian slang), jokes, sarcasm, absurd situations, anachronisms, and mockery of opera's commonplaces. This unlikely combination was skilfully transferred onto the rich musical score, a mixture of arias, recitatives, football chants, traditional Argentinian songs and dances such as the *malambo* and *pericón*, tangos, bits from the National Flag anthem, concertatos, choral songs, and operatic duets, amongst others. The piece became part of the repertoire of Cantoría Ars Nova and has been performed periodically ever since its première in 1971 in La Plata, Argentina. It has always been performed by an ensemble of professional singers directed by Raúl Carpinetti, mainly in La Plata and Buenos Aires, with slightly different versions in 1974 and 2003.

This satirical opera is divided into three acts: "La sangre de Layo" (Laius' blood), "La sangre de la esfinge" (The sphinx's blood), and "La sangre en el ojo" (The blood in the eye). While the titles for the first two acts may indicate a serious approach to the myth, the third is a very colloquial expression meaning "seeing red," used here in a double sense to refer ironically to Oedipus' self-blinding. The first act opens with Oedipus at the crossroads, singing a moving aria and recitative where he introduces himself and the myth, and talks about the oracle and his reasons for leaving Corinth. What could otherwise be seen as the opening of a standard opera is abruptly subverted by voices off singing "Go Thebes go!" in the style of a football chant. Apparently the Olympic Games were held at Thebes. When Laius exits the stadium he has an argument with Oedipus in the manner of a football fanatic's fight, but absurdly mixed with *malambo*—a traditional Argentinian dance where gauchos challenge each other through rhythmical tapping of their feet on the ground—and a sword fight.

In the second act Oedipus confronts the Sphinx in an operatic duet that contrasts with the colloquial tone of the lyrics. Oedipus defeats the Sphinx and Jocasta and the choir enter the stage. There is a comical love scene between Oedipus and his mother sung to a romantic tango. In the end, the script goes back to the events in the myth and the third act sees the arrival of the messenger, Jocasta poisoning herself explaining that unfortunately due to the limitations of the scenery she can't hang herself as in the myth; and Oedipus blinds himself shouting "¡Mamá!" in a parody of "Mimí!" from Puccini's *La Bohème*. The priest sings, in the final verses, the absurd moral of the story: "No mates nunca a tu padre | ni te cases con tu madre | pues los Dioses se calientan | y te tiran a matar."[21] The whole stanza produces a comical contrasting effect: whereas the banal lyrics are a reminder of the urban popular flavor of tango, the melody is linked to the more elitist and cultured sound of the opera.

Radio: In Defence of Language Change

One of the funniest retellings of the myth of Oedipus I have had the fortune to come across is the script "Edipo" by Niní Marshall,[22] one of the most creative and revered Argentinian comedians of all time. Working in radio stations during the 1930s and 1940s—at a time when women were not allowed to write comedy—she became Argentina's first female comedy writer. Born in Buenos Aires at the beginning of the twentieth century, Marina Esther Traveso, a.k.a. Niní Marshall, was the daughter of two immigrants from Asturias, Spain. The city was, at the time, a fantastic melting pot of people from different cultures and ways of life, and Niní Marshall was a perceptive witness. She based her characters on people she met in the streets, on the girls waiting outside the radio station to get autographs, on people living in "conventillos."[23] She captured their cultural and social essence with great attention to detail, portraying them with astonishing linguistic precision.

Since the 1850s, Argentine Spanish had been mutating, incorporating elements from the many different coexisting languages, from various social and cultural strata, including the *lunfardo*.[24] Niní Marshall's linguistic awareness did not go unnoticed. In 1956 the Faculty of Philology of Universidad Nacional de La Plata wrote her a letter inviting her to assist them in their study of the incipient "language of the Argentines"[25] by retelling the story of Oedipus from the point of view of one of her characters, Catita.[26] Catalina Pizzafrola Langanuzzo, Catita (first aired in 1937), was a descendant of Italian immigrants. She represented the aspiring lower middle class born after immigration became established. Her version of the Oedipus myth was recorded for the "Archivo Sincrónico de la Lengua Actual Argentina," but unfortunately all the material, including the results of the research, was lost in a fire. The text resurfaced later and was published in a compilation of Marshall's best scripts, and became one of her most celebrated creations together with her composition on "La madre" ("The mother").

The action is set in a broadcasting studio as a dialogue between Catita and the radio show host. Catita is an opinionated gossipy girl who pretends to know everything while knowing nothing at all. In the script the host asks her why she looks sad, and she explains that it is due to a "novel" that she borrowed that has affected her very much. She refers to it as a "television drama," comparing it to a Latin American "telenovela" (soap opera).[27] Drama is used here almost as an equivalent of melodrama owing to the intrigues and complicated relationships between the characters of the myth, which render it comparable to the over-emotional and sensational plots of the *telenovelas*, where there is always some unknown—and normally absurd—kinship and/or forbidden love revealed to the audience in the most shocking way. Her use of "drama," however, is also acknowledging that the "novel" she read was not a novel at all but a play, a subtle wink to the educated audience.[28] Marshall was not just a witty comedian making fun of ordinary people. She was a highly educated and accomplished writer. In many of her scripts she parodies difficult literary styles, demonstrating her excellent command of the language and her use of scholarly sources.[29]

Catita's account of the myth reveals both her ignorance and her love of gossip, as she particularly gloats over the scandalous details of the story. According to her, the oracle foretold to Oedipus' parents that the child they were expecting "was a degenerate, because when he grew up, he was going to suicide his father and marry his mother." "A case for a psychologist," she adds (Marshall 1994: 33). Trying to sound cultured, Catita wrongly uses "suicidar" for "matar" (to kill). Later she explains that "Edipo agarra por esposa a la viuda del rey anterior, que se casa en segundas náuseas con su propio hijo."[30] The use of the vulgarism "agarra," to grab, instead of "toma," to take, amidst what she intends to be a refined account of the story, reveals once again her lack of education. Similarly, when she tries to explain that the queen remarried her own son, attempting to use the more cultured "segundas nupcias" (remarriage), she mixes it up with "segundas náuseas" (second nauseas), producing a comical effect, while at the same time alluding ironically to the incestuous relationship as a cause of disgust and revulsion.

There is a reason why Catita makes such an incredible effort to sound educated, and a reason why she inevitably makes mistakes and mixes things up.[31] While the language of the Argentinians was mutating and evolving, merging different voices together evidencing linguistic and social conflicts, the government and the educational system were going in the opposite direction. In 1943, the offices of de facto President Pedro Ramírez issued an official statement censoring Marshall's characters and banning her from working on the radio.[32] According to the statement, her characters distorted "correct language" and influenced people "who do not have the ability to discern."[33] The Paternalist State—in Marshall's own words (Narvaez and Abregó 2003: 184)—had initiated a campaign to preserve the "purity" of language, and her accurate depiction of the real language of the Argentinians was contravening the prescriptive crusade. Trying to normalize the language, the educational system was forcing students to speak using vocabulary and pronunciation that was unnatural to them. In turn, they would take these standards home. This resulted in people trying to integrate into society by incorporating these prescribed elements into their everyday language. In failing to do so, they sounded absurd and even uneducated, an easy target for mockery and marginalization.[34] Catita's description of the Sphinx episode is one of Marshall's most insightful portraits in this respect.

After leaving Corinth, Oedipus arrives in Thebes, and Catita explains that "a la entrada de la suidá se topa con la Efinge, una bestia feroz de una especie destinguida, porque ya no hay más, y culio cuerpo pertenece, mitá al seso femenino y mitá al seso animal. Esta bestia dicho sea sin ilusión personal, tiene a su cargo un programa de preguntas y respuestas, liamadas enimas, o prenunciado con firulete, egnimas" (p. 35).[35] The effect of the whole paragraph is hilarious. Her mistakes pile up one after the other. She defines the Sphinx as a "distinguished" instead of an "extinct" species ("extinguida" and "distinguida" sound very similar in Spanish) and classifies it as being part of both the feminine and the animal "gender" (but she pronounces it "seso," which means brains, instead of "sexo," gender).[36] Her description of the Sphinx has the tone of a school lesson gone wrong, as if Catita was standing in front of the class reciting words she had learned by heart but that had little meaning to her. Her vocabulary and definition of terms is a parody of many biology textbooks of the time. One of the most remarkable features of her speech is perhaps the affected pronunciation of "cuyo" as "culio" and of "llamadas" as "liamadas."[37] At school, teachers would force children to pronounce "ll" and "y" using the standard Spanish phoneme /j/ instead of Rioplatense /ʃ/. Trying to reproduce a sound alien to their language, speakers would exaggerate the articulation and pronounce it as /li/, resulting in an artificial-sounding speech.

Marshall was a keen observer of Argentinian society. Through her characters she succeeded in reflecting not only the social and political reality of her time, but also its ethnic and linguistic diversity. She managed to portray a living, changing, evolving language, and to give voice to its real speakers. Her retelling of Oedipus' myth is more than just a mockery of Oedipus' story. It goes beyond comedy to become a political statement against arbitrary language regularization and control, a statement in defence of language change.

From Socio-political Satire to Guilt and Gender in Postmodern Latin America

Edipo y su señora mamacita (presidente que casose con su madre) (1998)[38] by Ecuadorian playwright Peky Andino Moscoso is one of the most noteworthy comedic approaches to the myth.[39] Although the play is presented as a satire and has indeed many laughable moments, its painfully acid humor, bitter sarcasm, grotesque caricatures, and ruthless analysis of Ecuadorian politics set it apart from the rest. Andino Moscoso—considered one of the most influential Latin American dramatists of the present era—was awarded the "Otto Rene Castillo Award for Political Theatre" in 2008 in New York. His irreverent plays, *Kito con K, Ceremonia con sangre, Medea llama por cobrar, Ulises y la máquina de perdices*, amongst others, are inherently political and openly critical; his repeated use of Greek myths, an attempt to understand—from a pretended distance—Ecuador's history and contemporary socio-political crisis.[40] As Andino Moscoso himself defines it, his theater is "una mueca dolorosa. Es catártico, intuitivo, premonitorio, brutal, desgarrador, hiriente, y sacrificial, lo más parecido a una puñalada." But it is at the same time "alegórico, desbordado, excesivo, borracho, estruendoso, como las comparsas ecuatorianas que danzan en las calles para que la vida no se acabe."[41] His *Edipo* is a blunt dissection of Latin American politics, and in particular of Ecuador's political circus (Espinosa Andrade 2010: 498).

The play is set in 1997 in Thebes, alternating between hospital rooms, television talk shows, a plane, the circus, a chess board. It opens with a dedication to "el loco incomprendido de Panamá" (the misunderstood madman of Panama), a reference retrieved later in the Prologue with the mention of Dionysus and his "band of jesters" taking power in 1996. Both references point to Abdalá Bucaram, President of Ecuador between 1996 and 1997, an extravagant politician nicknamed "Loco" who was declared mentally unfit to rule and later exiled to Panama. The topics of insanity, irrationality, and medicalization, added to drugs and drug dealing, television and circus imagery, run through the play and pervade its scenes and characters. The author uses them to challenge Ecuador's social, political, and historical symbols, to call into question its ruling class, government officials, politicians, unions, and political parties, demystifying Ecuadorian politics and democratic institutions.

After a Prologue, in the chorus's voice and using images taken from Greek myths in which the recent history of Ecuador is metaphorically summarized,[42] the first scene introduces the audience to "Clown TV," a news section where the newsreaders are three clowns. The clowns describe the country's current situation and explain that the President and his mother have been locked up in Thebes' Hospital, while outside chaos strikes: natural disasters, tax deficit, protests, doctors on strike, Ecuador eliminated from 1998's Football World Cup,[43] officials running away with state money ("Los funcionarios del reino escapan a Corinto con los maletines de Pandora: la burocracia ha cumplido," 501).[44] All the "prophecies" have come to pass except the last one, and so the clowns urge Oedipus and Jocasta to fulfill their tragic destiny so that Thebes can return to normality. The play is a constant push and pull game between the protagonists who want to challenge their tragic destiny and the rest of the characters who want them to fulfill it.

Television is a permanent presence in the play. Andino Moscoso explains that in his *Edipo*, Oedipus and Jocasta are faced with the worst of tragedies: public humiliation and ridicule by means of a talk show. He is a harsh critic of television and the role that television plays in modern societies. According to him, television in his country is linked to lying, public lynching, theft, and political mafias (Andino Moscoso 2008: 92). In the scene "The Gorgon's show" (505–8), the Gorgon interviews Oedipus and Jocasta who have been invited to a special on "Sons who married their mothers." The talk show features questions by members of the "idiotic public," cynically tackling controversial issues such as incest, power, sex, and gender. Television stars again in the next scene, "Un matrimonio corriente" (An ordinary marriage, 508–10), where Oedipus and Jocasta are shown in a daily life scene: Jocasta is watching football on TV while Oedipus is cooking some pasta. The scene is set in an "American living room," and has the structure and rhythm of popular 1950s–1960s American sitcoms such as "I love Lucy": funny situations, quick, witty dialogues ending in a punch line followed by outbursts of laugher from the audience. The scene pictures the confusion of roles and identities resulting from "destroying the difference" by means of an incestuous relationship that leads to the disintegration of normal family bonds.[45] Oedipus' mother is at the same time his wife, and Jocasta is at the same time Oedipus' mother, wife, and her own mother-in-law. At one point in the marital fight Oedipus tells Jocasta that he is going back to his mum's house, so he exits the stage and enters it again, highlighting the dead-end situation. Oedipus' incest is a metaphor for Ecuador's political incest and the transvestism of social and political relationships. As Jocasta says, "A esta isla siempre la hemos gobernado entre familia" ("We have always ruled this island between family," 505), alluding cynically to the 1970s–1980s idea of Ecuador being an "island of peace" in a zone of conflict (Roldós 2010: 492).

The political game and the political circus are addressed once more in a chess game that Oedipus and Jocasta play against Zeus—the State, Power, Ecuador, the System—before the final scene. Zeus explains to Oedipus and Jocasta why they have to fulfill their tragic destiny: "When kings hurt themselves, the system goes on; when the people hurt them, the system is over. I don't want a revolution, but a change of pieces to keep the game going" (513–14). Finally the characters assume their tragic fates and the results are broadcast on national television. Jocasta gives a speech wearing the presidential sash with which she will eventually hang herself while Oedipus, now blind, ironically translates it into sign language. In the end Oedipus leaves the stage by a plane ladder, suitcase in hand, to begin his travels seeking political asylum. The bitter last words, in the voice of the chorus, draw attention to the allegory that has been playing in the background throughout the whole piece: "Que Zeus te recoja confesada el día en que ya no seas, Tebas querida, Ecuador del alma."[46]

A dark political comedy, *Edipo asesor* ("Oedipus Adviser"), by Chilean dramatist Benjamín Galemiri, is another provocative interpretation of Oedipus' myth, but this time set against the background of the post-dictatorship in Chile. The comedy, written in 2000 and premièred in 2001, a decade after Chile's return to democracy, was presented as a "neo-biblical play set in the corridors of the neo-power."[47] The prefix "neo-," persistently throughout the play, is attached to the most unlikely words, resulting in absurd coinages such as "neo-espada" (neo-sword), "neo-batalla" (neo-battle), "neo-presumido" (neo-smug), "neo-sofisticados" (neo-sophisticated), "neo-enfervorizados" (neo-ecstatic), "neo-real" (neo-royal), "neo-bulimia," "neo-manos" (neo-hands), "neo-angustioso" (neo-distressing), "neo-entertainment." Even the introduction to the play ends with a "manos a la neo-obra,"[48] drawing on the twofold meaning of *obra* as both "work" and "play/drama": Galemiri defines the play itself as a "neo" piece of work. This abuse of the "neo-" prefix makes reference to the novelty of the politics of the time. The dictatorship was over and had given way to a much awaited democratic government. Everything was new. New government, new politics, new faces, new economy, new language, new topics, new characters, new attitudes, new play. *Edipo asesor* offered a critical analysis of the "neo" revolution, and in particular of the "neo-language" of the "neo-politics," a language embellished by the attachment of meaningless adornments; nonsensical, empty, false, incapable of fostering political dialogue in a period of transition that desperately sought political consensus.[49]

The play explores not only the vacuity and ineptitude of political rhetoric but also its relationship with sex and sexuality.[50] Language and sex are two instruments used for the institutionalization of power (Rizk 2008: 5–6). This relationship is staged in the play through five sex scenes between Judith (Jocasta) and Oziel (Oedipus). The scenes occur in emblematic sites connected to politics and power, such as the presidential palace's courtroom, different areas of the presidential house (the kitchen, the shower, the car park), and the inside of the presidential (armoured) car. The scenes are full of wordy dialogues symbolizing the sensuality of political rhetoric. Every time, the Chorus would summarize the scene by identifying the characters' climax with a specific political ideology: "Orgasmos propios de la neo-transición," "Orgasmos radicales," "Orgasmo neo-conservador," "Orgasmo neo-liberal," "Orgasmo neo-autoritario" (Typical neo-transition orgasms, radical, neo-conservative, neo-liberal, neo-authoritarian).

Edipo asesor is a play of rich intertextuality and cultural dialogue. Even though the title of the play alludes to Greek myths and Greek culture, and draws on the Sophoclean text, the characters in the play—biblical King Saúl, Judith, advisers Oziel and Jeremías— belong to a different intertext, the Bible, and a different, specifically Jewish, culture.[51] There is also a dialogue with restaurant menus and culinary books—food and gluttony are major players in the comedy—with the language of globalization, technology, and television, and especially with the world of cinema.[52] The 33 scenes that make up the play provide extremely detailed stage directions (always in capital letters), many of the scenes being only stage directions with no dialogue at all.[53] Galemiri's instructions design the scene by directing the precise use of spaces and describing shots and close-ups in the manner of a film script (Oyarzún 2002: 97). The play ends with a rather poetic stage direction: "Henchidos de un amor neo-bíblico, Oziel y Judith se toman las neo-manos dominados por las luces ultravioletas del aplastante y neo-angustioso neo-entertainment televisión."[54]

Epilogue

Latin American countries share an unfortunate history of violent colonialism and imperialism, repression, totalitarianism, and chronic military rule; civil war, abuse and violation of human rights; shaky returns to democracy, economic crisis; dissipation, corruption, and impunity leading to political disillusionment, anger, and disbelief in socio-political institutions. Latin American theater is an unforgiving reflection of its countries' turbulent history. It is—to put it in Diana Taylor's words—a "theater of crisis." Taylor precisely identifies *Oedipus Tyrannus* as "the prototypical model of the theater of crisis, a play *of* and *about* crisis" exhibiting two features normally connected to it, namely "the loss of identity and the collapse of boundaries" (Taylor 1991: 54). It is not a coincidence that in moments of social, economic, and political catastrophe, Latin American dramatists have chosen to revisit this play.

Notes

1. For a detailed study on the reception of *OT* since its inception, see Macintosh 2009; also McDonald 2009.
2. For Latin American adaptations of *Antigone*, see Nelli 2009, 2010.
3. See Macintosh 2009 "Oedipus dethroned": 159–88, particularly 161–2. I am grateful to Fiona Macintosh for pointing out this connection to me, and for her insightful comments and suggestions when reading my chapter.
4. An earlier version of *Edipo rey*, written and directed by Enrique Buenaventura, had been staged by TEC in 1959, with a second version in 1965.
5. I want to thank the Fonoteca for providing me with a copy of the audio and sending me information on the production. C. Alvarez Baron (personal communication, May 30, 2012). The Fonoteca's catalogue is available online at <http://www.fonoteca.gov.co>. *Edipo rey* was originally broadcast as part of "Teatro Dominical" on February 10, 1954. The 2012 version was staged at Ciudad Teatro de Corferias, Bogotá, on April 4.
6. I am indebted to Héctor Levy-Daniel for his time and generosity not only in agreeing to be interviewed but also in providing me with the script, a video recording of the play, and the play's reviews. *Yocasta* premièred at Teatro Anfitrión, Buenos Aires, on July 29, 2011. The play was performed during 2011 and 2012 in different locations in Buenos Aires.
7. See, e.g., Macintosh 2009: 181ff.
8. Due to limits of space, these topics are only summarized here. For a thorough analysis of the play see Nelli forthcoming. For a discussion of the play with its author and director, see Nelli with Héctor Levy-Daniel, this volume.
9. I want to thank producer Alejandro Israel for generously providing me with a copy of the film.

10. For a detailed analysis of *Edipo alcalde* see Camacho Delgado 2006: 41–50; also Ramírez Aíssa and Muñoz Fernández 2007: 139–50. For *El recuento*, see Quintana 2012.
11. "Epic poem of Oedipus of Thebes (*chanson* quite *de geste*)." Translations from Spanish into English are mine unless otherwise stated. The text is a transcription of the CD version of the piece. Mundstock and Núñez 2006.
12. "Oedipus tyrannus, or What a honeymoon mummy!" "Mamita," "mummy," is also used in Argentina as a cheeky way to refer to a lady. "Mamacita" in Mexico and other Latin American countries.
13. "We sound, despite everything." "Sonamos" in Argentinian Spanish is also slang for failing or being in trouble.
14. "Old failures." In the original version the composer (Carlos Núñez) and writer (Marcos Mundstock) of the piece were acknowledged individually, unlike in later versions where lyrics and music were credited to "Les Luthiers" as a group. The show premièred on July 22, 1976 at Teatro Odeón, Buenos Aires. There were 191 performances in total with the show touring Argentina, Mexico, Chile, and Uruguay. The last show was performed on May 15, 1977 at Teatro Coliseo, Buenos Aires. Information on Les Luthiers and their repertoire is available at <http://www.lesluthiers.org>. Most of their shows have been recorded or filmed. A recording of one of the 1977 performances of *Edipo* is available at <http://youtu.be/GfHrrQyaKpM>.
15. "The oracle told him | Oedipus your life | is going to get busy | you will become parricide | the oracle told him. || He kept saying, | although I detest talking to you about this | an incest, an incest is coming | he kept saying."
16. "Oedipus escaped | and he killed Laius | fighting him on his own | he sent him to heaven."
17. "Oedipus, knowing this, | during an appointment | with his psychologist, | blinds, blinds himself, | Oedipus knowing this."
18. The powerful figure of the mother is a mixture of the all-giving mother of the indigenous peoples ("pueblos originarios"), also related to mother Earth, "la Pacha mama," and the Mediterranean mother, both the Italian "mamma" and the Spanish "madre," embedded in Argentinian culture thanks to centuries of Italian and Spanish immigration. However, the figure of the mother will be completely resignified after the dictatorial period initiated in 1976, and the emergence of the "Mothers of May Square" ('Madres de Plaza de Mayo). See Nelli 2009: 70–1.
19. "Loving mothers | take precautions | against the amorous excesses | of 'male sons,' | loving mothers."
20. From a description of the origins of the opera "Edipo Rey o ¡Qué luna de miel, mamita!" by Enrique Bugallo and Mario Carpinetti, 2013. I am most grateful to Cecilia González, widow to Raúl Carpinetti, for sending me this and other materials, including the opera's script. C. González (personal communication, March 24, 2013).
21. "Don't ever kill your father | or marry your mother | as the Gods get mad | and shoot to kill." "Calentarse" and "Tirar a matar" are popular expressions used in many tango lyrics; e.g., "Rebelde" (1931, F. Loiácono), "Tirando a matar" (1942, P. Castellanos), "Consejos reos" (registered 1971, C. Flores), "El tango se viene con todo" (1970, V. De Marco).
22. Marshall 1994. I am thankful to Silvina Marsimian, an Argentinian researcher at Universidad de Buenos Aires working on Niní Marshall's scripts, for her help and generosity in sending me some of her unpublished work and providing me with details on the story of the script.
23. Tenement houses. During the second half of the nineteenth century Argentina suffered a massive wave of immigration from Europe. Most immigrants stayed in Buenos Aires in the

hope of finding a job, but had little money to spare. Overpopulation and unemployment were at the basis of the popularity of the "conventillos," overcrowded homes with cheap shared rooms. See Carretero 1999: 29–32, 34–6.

24. *Lunfardo* is an Argentinian slang born in Buenos Aires in the second half of the nineteenth century. Many words in the vocabulary of *lunfardo* derive from words from other languages and dialects brought about by immigration. See Teruggi 1974: 21–6. For a classification of borrowings 47–102. For a discussion on linguistic contact in the evolution of Argentine Spanish, see Di Tullio 2011: 123–66.

25. Argentine Spanish—its characteristics, origins, and systematization—had been a subject of great interest since the dawn of the twentieth century, as the language was a determining factor in the construction—and understanding—of national identity. Borges' renowned essay "El idioma de los argentinos" was intended to provide a definition of what was meant by "Argentine Spanish," and addressed the issue of linguistic change (Borges 1994). See Di Tullio 2011: 191–4. For an analysis of Borges' essay, 201–4.

26. According to Prof. Roberto de Souza: "El archivo sincrónico del habla argentina actual deberá registrar dicción, entonación y vocabulario representativos de los estratos culturales del país en todas sus zonas y, como usted sabe, juzgamos de mayor interés para la confección de ese archivo los tipos que usted ha compuesto, reveladores de una fina y penetrante observación lingüística práctica." For the full content of the letters see Narvaez and Abregó 2003: 214–15.

27. Marshall 1994: 33. Catita is quite illiterate, but pretends to be very sophisticated. She usually speaks in a presumptuous way but making many phonetic, syntactic, and semantic mistakes. She also mixes words from Italian. Meaning to use a fancy term, she transforms it into another word that sounds similar but has a completely different meaning, rendering her speech hilarious. The words that she mixes up are cleverly chosen to give the sentence a double meaning or to make a point by the use of irony.

28. At the end of the dialogue, Catita refers back to the play as a "novela." The radio host tries to sum up saying, "Usted me contó que leyó esta historia . . ." ("You said that you read this story . . ."), but Catita stops him, scandalized, repeating that this was not just a story: "¡No! ¡Esta novela! . . . que la escribió un tal Sófocle; pero yo le digo una cosa que si es verídica, Sófocle hace muy mal en publicarla, ¡porque tantos crímenes son un mal enjemplo pa la humanidá!" ("No! This novel! . . . written by some *Sophocle*; but I'll tell you something; if this is a true story, *Sophocle* is wrong to publish it, because so many crimes are a bad example to humanity!," p. 36).

29. According to researcher Paola Pereira, interviewed by Blanc (2012), Niní Marshall was an intellectual. The language of her characters was not exaggerated; she was more interested in working with the tone of the language. She did not aim to parody a marginal language but to appropriate the socially undervalued language in order to parody other discourses.

30. "Oedipus *grabs* as a wife the widow of the former king, who gets married for the second time ('marries in second nauseas') to his own son." Marshall 1994: 35.

31. In her thesis, Marsimian (2010) studies in detail the language of Niní Marshall's scripts. Chapter two, "El discurso de Catita: humor, estereotipo y diferencia," focuses on this particular character. As Marsimian explains, "Muchos libretos construyen, entonces, una *escena cultural* que el personaje protagoniza; en estas circunstancias, Catita parece querer asimilarse a la sociedad de arribo, utilizando los estereotipos verbales que expresan su adhesión a la *doxa* dominante; pero, paradójicamente, su discurso corroe compulsivamente las ideas generalizadas que los sustentan," chapter 2: 16.

32. On Marshall being censored and her exile to Mexico, see Ulanovsky 2003. On broadcasting laws in Argentina from 1934 and their repercussion on Marshall's work, see Marsimian 2011: 11–12. For the 1943 censorship episode, see Marsimian 2011: 13.
33. See Narvaez and Abregó 2003: 207. Also Santos, Petruccelli, and Russo 1993: 51–3.
34. According to Marsimian (2011: 25–6), Marshall's censorship arose from the fact that her linguistic parody was unveiling a social conflict that the government sought to hide, as it could lead to political instability. It was testimony to both the heterogeneity and the intolerance and inflexibility of a society where the immigrant appeared as a hybrid character lacking the necessary command of the national language.
35. "At the entrance to the city he bumps into the Sphinx, a ferocious beast from a *distinguished* species, because there aren't any more, and whose body belongs, half to the feminine gender and half to the animal gender. This beast, said with no personal *illusion*, is in charge of a quiz show, called *enimas*, or *prenounced* with adornment, *egnimas*." I have tried to recreate—in the words in italics—the mistakes that Catita makes, although it is very difficult to render transformations such as "suidá," "culio," "liamadas," and "seso" in English.
36. The humorous mistakes also point to the fact that Catita's Spanish is filtered through her Italian roots.
37. For other examples see Marsimian 2010: chapter 2: 23, 4d. See also 4c for erratic use of the meaning of some words, confusion of meanings due to phonetic similarity, and confusion of words, e.g., "seso" for "sexo."
38. "Oedipus and his lady mummy (President who married his mother)."
39. The play premièred at the Association Humboldt's Theatre in Quito, Ecuador, in September 1998. It was directed by Andino Moscoso and staged by the group Zero no Zero, starring Alfredo Espinosa, María Beatriz Vergara, and José Morán.
40. The survival of Greek myths in Latin American theater and their use as a way of searching for a Latin American cultural identity after the violent obliteration of pre-Columbian drama by the Spanish conquest have been studied by Obregón 2000: see particularly 39–51.
41. "My theater is a painful grimace. It's cathartic, insightful, prophetic, brutal, heartbreaking, hurtful, and sacrificial, the closest thing to a stabbing. My theater is of a 21st baroque, allegorical, overwhelmed, excessive, drunk, loud, like Ecuadorian troupes dancing in the streets so that life does not end." Andino Moscoso 2008: 91.
42. e.g., "Año 79, las siete furias armadas se retiran de Tebas y se restauran los oráculos. La profecía se ha cumplido" (501), referring to the end of the military government ("the seven armed furies") and the restoration of democracy in 1979.
43. Ecuador's obsession with football is harshly criticized in the play. As in most Latin American countries football is the national sport, and its massive popularity has recurrently been used by the ruling power to attempt to avert people's eyes from more pressing matters. A paradigmatic case is the 1978 Football World Cup held in Argentina during a military government that claimed 30,000 *desaparecidos*.
44. "Kingdom officials escape to Corinth with Pandora's briefcases: the bureaucracy has come to pass." The officials' briefcase is another recurring image in Latin American—and probably worldwide—politics. It is featured repeatedly in the news whenever there is a case of corruption and money laundering.
45. On the subject of destroying the difference, Taylor quotes Girard's *The Scapegoat* (15) and *Violence and the Sacred* (74–5): *non vidi*. Taylor 1991: 231 n. 27.
46. "Zeus helps you, the day that you are no longer, dear Thebes, darling Ecuador" (515). "Que Dios nos coja confesados" is an idiom meaning "God helps us," but it implies the fact

that the person wants to die having confessed their sins first; final nudge to the audience. According to Espinosa Andrade (2010) the play refers to a "guilty and abusive Ecuador, of transvestite rulers and children fed with blood" (497, in Spanish in the original).
47. Galemiri 2007: 187. The play, premièred in August 2001, was staged by Grupo La Puerta and directed by Luis Ureta. Details of the staging and some pictures are available at <http://www.teatrolapuerta.cl/noticias/edipo-asesor/> and at <http://www.galemiri.cl/Edipo.html>.
48. "Manos a la obra" can be translated as "back to work," or "put the shoulder to the wheel."
49. On the role of Galemiri as a dramatist of Chile's transitional period, see Rizk 2008. The repeated use of "neo" makes also reference to "neo-liberalism" and its historical role in Chilean politics, particularly the aggressive neoliberal policies in which Chile was immersed at the time. On political language and the prefix "neo", see Urdician 2012: 547.
50. It is not a coincidence that the play is called "Edipo asesor". Oziel is the new adviser, full of new ("neo") ideas and bringing in new policies. His advisory skills depend on his ability to seduce with words. He is the face of the new legislative process. The sensuality of this discourse had to be unparalleled.
51. According to Rizk (2001: 7–8), by drawing on the figure of Jewish King Saúl, Galemiri addresses Chile's transitional period. Whereas the Greek hero is constrained by the past and by his tragic fate, the Jewish figure is linked to a different kind of memory and vision; a vision focused on the future.
52. Rizk (2001: 146) defines Galimiri's plays as *pastiche*. "Sus obras siempre funcionan en varios niveles y traen al ruedo reminiscencias e intromisiones intertextuales de un sin número de fuentes y momentos históricos, a las que se adhiere su experiencia como judío y como habitante urbano posmodernista de fines del siglo XX."
53. Galemiri breaks with traditional dramatic writing. His stage directions are a hybrid between film directions and the voice of the narrator in narrative writing. Oyarzún 2007: 25.
54. "Swollen with neo-biblical love, Oziel and Judith hold hands, dominated by the ultra-violet lights of the overwhelming and neo-distressing neo-entertainment television." Galemiri 2007: 227. The epilogue to the play shows Oziel (blind) and Judith (crowned queen) bingeing on an enormous amount of food, numb in front of the flat TV: the "neo-bulimia." For other humorous *Oedipus*es, see the Mexican plays *Edipo Güey* by Mario Cantú Toscano (2005), and *El Edipo imaginario* by Alberto Castillo (1992). Two further Argentinian examples are *Edipo en Ezeiza* by actor and director Pompeyo Audibert (2013) and *Edipo y Yocasta* by Mariano Moro (2010).

References

Andino Moscoso, P. (2008), "Peky Andino Moscoso (Ecuador, 1962)," K. Pörtl coord., "II. Entrevistas con los dramaturgos latinoamericanos", in S. Hartwig and K. Pörtl eds., *La voz de los dramaturgos: el teatro español y latinoamericano actual*. Tübingen, 91–4.

Andino Moscoso, P. (2010), "Edipo y su señora mamacita (presidente que casose con su madre)," in L. Proaño Gómez and G. Geirola eds., *Antología de teatro latinoamericano*, ii: *1950–2007*. Buenos Aires, INTeatro, Editorial Instituto Nacional del Teatro, 501–15.

Blanc, N. (2012), "Niní va a la Universidad," ADN Cultura, *La Nación* (August 31)—<http://www.lanacion.com.ar/1503587-nini-va-a-la-universidad> accessed December 16, 2012.

Borges, J. L. (1994, 1st edn. 1928), "El idioma de los argentinos," in *El idioma de los argentinos*. Buenos Aires, 135–50.

Camacho Delgado, J. M. (2006), *Magia y desencanto en la narrativa colombiana, Cuadernos de América sin Nombre*, issue 16, Alicante, Universidad de Alicante.

Cantú Toscano, M (2005), "Edipo güey," in "Estreno de Papel," *Paso de Gato. Revista Mexicana de Teatro*, México, 20, año 3, I–XII.

Carretero, A. M. (1999), *Tango, testigo social*. Buenos Aires.

Castillo, A. (1992) "El Edipo imaginario," in H. Arguelles, L. Padrón, et al., *Teatro jóven de México: Antología*, vol. i. Mexico, Consejo Nacional para la Cultura y las Artes.

Di Tullio, A. (2011), "Borges y Arlt. Dos definiciones del *Idioma de los argentinos*," in A. Di Tullio, and R. Kailuweit eds., *El español rioplatense: lengua, literatura, expresiones culturales*. Madrid, 191–208.

Espinosa Andrade, A. (2010), "Peky Andino Moscoso," in L. Proaño Gómez and G. Geirola, *Antología de teatro latinoamericano*, ii: *1950–2007*. Buenos Aires, 495–9.

Galemiri, B. (2007), "Edipo asesor," in *Obras completas*, i. Santiago de Chile, 185–227.

Macintosh, F. (2009), *Sophocles: Oedipus Tyrannus*. Cambridge.

McDonald, M. (2009), "The Dramatic Legacy of Myth: Oedipus in Opera, Radio, Television and Film," *Cambridge Companion to Greek and Roman Theatre*. Cambridge, 303–26.

Marshall, N. (1994), "Edipo," in *Las travesuras de Niní: los mejores libretos de Catita, Cándida, Niña Jovita, y otras criaturas*. Buenos Aires, 33–6.

Marsimian, S. (2010), *Ideas comunes y estereotipos verbales en libretos humorísticos de Niní Marshall*. Tesis de Maestría en Análisis del Discurso, Facultad de Filosofía y Letras, UBA, Argentina. Unpublished.

Marsimian, S. (2011), "Lengua, radio, humor y censura: el caso Niní Marshall," in *Revista páginas de guarda: revista de lenguaje, edición y cultura escrita* 11, otoño, 9–28.

Moro, M. (2010), "Edipo y Yocasta: tragedia grecoide con humor ad hoc," in *Seis obras*. Buenos Aires, 11–40.

Mundstock, M. and C. Núñez (2006), "Epopeya de Edipo de Tebas," in *Les Luthiers: lo mejor de lo mejor*, vol. ii. Buenos Aires, Laida Editora. CD, Track 2

Narvaez, P. and A. Abregó (2003), *Niní está viva!* Buenos Aires.

Nelli, M. F. (2009), "Identity, Dignity and Memory: Performing/Re-writing *Antigone* in Post-1976 Argentina," *New Voices in Classical Reception Studies* 4 (Spring), 70–81.

Nelli, M. F. (2010), "*Antígona furiosa*: From Ancient Greek Drama to Argentina's Dirty War," in S. Wilmer and A. Zukauskaite eds., *Interrogating Antigone in Postmodern Philosophy and Criticism*. Oxford, 353–65.

Nelli, M. F. (forthcoming), "Of Motherly Love, Truth, Politics and the Power of Water: Héctor Levy-Daniel's *Yocasta*."

Obregón, O. (2000), *Teatro Latinoamericano: un caleidoscopio cultural (1930–1990)*. Perpignan.

Oyarzún, C. (2002), "Benjamín Globalización: *Edipo asesor* y los espacios delirantes," *Conjunto* 124, 96–9.

Oyarzún, C. (2007), "Benjamín Galemiri: *Obras completas*," in *Obras completas*, i. Santiago de Chile, 23–7.

Quintana, M. (2012), "Edipo y el recuento de los daños: un análisis (transpositivo) de la apropiación en clave trágica," *Revista afuera* 7.2 (June) <http://www.revistaafuera.com> accessed April 29, 2013.

Ramírez Aíssa, C. and R. Muñoz Fernández (2007), *Forma, estilo e ideología en diez películas colombianas*. Bogotá.

Rizk, B. J. (2001), *Posmodernismo y teatro en América Latina: teorías y prácticas en el umbral del siglo XXI*. Madrid.

Rizk, B. J. (2008), "*Edipo asesor* de Benjamín Galemiri: hacia una dramaturgia de la transición," *Latin American Theatre Review* 41.2 (Spring), 5–16.

Roldós, S. (2010), "Escenarios múltiples de un país falsamente en perpetua des-constitución," in L. Proaño Gómez and G. Geirola, *Antología de teatro latinoamericano*, ii: *1950–2007*. Buenos Aires, 491–4.

Santos, L., A. Petruccelli, and D. Russo (1993), *Niní Marshall: artesana de la risa*. Buenos Aires.

Taylor, D. (1991), *Theatre of Crisis: Drama and Politics in Latin America*. Lexington, KY.

Teruggi, M. E. (1974), *Panorama del lunfardo: génesis y esencia de las hablas coloquiales urbanas*. Buenos Aires.

Ulanovsky, C. (2003), "Niní Marshall: genia y figura," Revista, La Nación, May 25 [Online]. Available at <http://www.lanacion.com.ar/497579-nini-marshall-genia-y-figura> accessed August 25, 2012.

Urdician, S. (2012), "Rebeliones filiales míticas en el teatro hispanoamericano contemporáneo," in A. López, A. Pociña, and M. Silva eds., *De ayer a hoy: influencias clásicas en la literatura*. Coimbra, 543–50.

CHAPTER 36

GREEK DRAMA ON THE U.S. WEST COAST, 1970–2013

MARY-KAY GAMEL

Geography and History

COASTS are inherently dramatic. Edges where the different elements of land, water, and air meet have special visual and emotional power. The west coast of the United States, stretching 7,500 miles from the rocky tip of Olympic State Park in Washington to sandy beaches close to Mexico, is especially vivid. The coastal cities—Seattle, Portland, San Francisco, Los Angeles, and San Diego—are enhanced by their gorgeous natural settings.

This area is considered "newer" than eastern parts of the United States. Not by its indigenous populations, of course, but in the American drama—as usually written—the central characters are white Europeans who landed on the east coast. Native Americans have mostly been ignored in American history and myth, except as impediments. In the mid-nineteenth century Horace Greeley supposedly urged, "Go west, young man, and grow up with the country!," and in 1921 Frederick Jackson Turner argued that the idea of the frontier, which always offered a new start, was crucial to Americans' self-image. Once the land and gold rushes were over, twentieth-century films kept this myth alive by depicting heroic settlers and armies battling natural and human obstacles in order to find riches and create new communities. During the 1930s many thousands fled west from the "dust bowl," and World War II brought GIs and defense workers to California and Washington. The population of the Pacific states (including Oregon, Alaska, and Hawaii) tripled 1930–70.

Today California is the most populous state, with the ninth largest economy in the world. West coast ports host a thriving import–export trade, and contacts with Asia-Pacific nations have increased steadily since 1945. Los Angeles, the home of motion pictures, the great art form of the twentieth century, remains the second largest city in the entire country. In the San Francisco Bay and Seattle areas momentous developments in computer technology have taken place, and the whole coastal region is home to major universities and colleges. The twentieth-century saying goes: "Everything starts in California, and then spreads east."

The decade of the 1960s was tumultuous. The civil rights movement (1955–68) challenged and defeated—at least in terms of law—discrimination against African-Americans. U.S. participation in World War II had widespread support, but many citizens opposed the war in Vietnam (1965–75). One of the first big anti-war protests took place in Berkeley in 1965. The same year saw an uprising in the primarily black Watts district of Los Angeles and the first farm labor strikes, which led to the Chicano Movement (on which see Billotte, this volume).

Between 1970 and 2013 significant events, and the reaction to them, were especially intense in the west: the identification of the AIDS virus in the early 1980s; the U.S. defense industry collapse following the end of the Cold War; increases in race-based urban gangs, and gang-related violence; the U.S. attack on Iraq 1991; in Los Angeles, riots in 1991 (Rodney King) and 1995 (O. J. Simpson); the dot-com industry boom and bust 1997–2000; the Enron scandal, the 9/11 attacks, and wars in Iraq and Afghanistan 2001; the deepest recession since the 1930s; and the election of the first African-American president 2008.

Between 1970 and 2013 two major and contradictory shifts in American society—politics, economics, culture—were taking place. On the one hand, ethnic minorities—in the west, especially Hispanics and Asians—were increasing in numbers and influence. LGBT people too became more visible and vocal; in San Francisco, openly gay Supervisor Harvey Milk campaigned vigorously for gay rights until he was assassinated in 1978. Awareness of environmental concerns and support for maintaining natural resources grew.

On the other hand, the political pendulum swung right. Conservative Republican Ronald Reagan was elected governor of California in 1971, and in 1978 California passed Proposition 13, which drastically reduced taxes and benefited corporations. Since then wages have stagnated, union membership declined, corporate power and income inequality increased. Public support for institutions including universities has shrunk drastically. By 2010 the whole country was deeply divided politically and economically, and the re-election of President Obama intensified the divisions. As I write this the prospect of a government shutdown seems not only possible but likely.

Greek Drama on the West Coast

1970–2013 was an important period for U.S. theater. New York City is unquestionably the drama queen of the U.S.A., followed by "second city" Chicago, but starting in the 1960s a number of professional theaters opened around the country: these included Mark Taper Forum/Ahmanson Theatre, Los Angeles, 1964; American Conservatory Theatre,

San Francisco, 1965; South Coast Repertory, Costa Mesa, CA, 1967; Berkeley Repertory Theatre, Berkeley, CA, 1968; Intiman Theatre, Seattle, 1972; Old Globe Theatre, San Diego, CA, 1981.

Theater is only tangential, however, to U.S. culture overall. Cultural histories of California such as Starr 2004 and Talbot 2012 mention music, visual art, architecture, books, film, food, clubs, fashion—but not theater. The golden age of the 1960s through 1990s, when theater companies received generous grants from the National Endowment for the Arts and private foundations, is over. The number of non-profit theaters doubled from 1990 to 2005, but the percentage of the U.S. adult population attending non-musical theater declined from 13.5 percent to 9.4 percent (All America's a Stage 2008).

In spite of this decline, Hall's declaration that "More Greek tragedy has been performed in the last thirty years than at any point in history since Greco-Roman antiquity" holds true for the west coast during this period.[1] In what follows, I discuss productions I consider significant for various reasons (for reasons of space, omitting opera and dance productions). I pay some attention to the historical and political context, styles and themes, but primarily recognize particular artists and companies (including semi-professional companies and academic institutions) who have a clear record of involvement with and strong ideas about staging Greek drama effectively,

Greek Structures

The idea of constructing outdoor theaters was popular at the beginning of the twentieth century, especially in California where the weather permits open-air performances seven months of the year. The first "Greek" theater in the United States was the small Point Loma theater in San Diego, built in 1901 against the backdrop of the Pacific Ocean (Foley 2012: 38, 42–7). The 6,000-seat Greek Theatre in Griffith Park, Los Angeles, completed in 1939, hosts large music events but not drama. The 8,900-seat Hearst Greek Theatre on the University of California, Berkeley, campus is modeled on the ancient theater at Epidaurus. Aristophanes' *Birds,* performed in Greek, inaugurated it in September 1903 and other Greek dramas were performed there in the early twentieth century (Foley 2012: 38, 47–61). Now it hosts mostly rock concerts and graduation ceremonies, but to celebrate its centennial year the National Theatre of Greece was invited to give two performances of Euripides' *Medea*. A chorus of 23, with the women members wearing white wedding dresses like Medea's, sang, danced, and cavorted in a large onstage pool, offering an interesting mix of traditional and contemporary elements.

The most important Greek theater on the west coast now is the newest one, the Barbara and Lawrence Fleischman Theater at the Getty Villa museum in Los Angeles. In 1974 J. Paul Getty, one of the richest men in the world, built the Getty Villa near his home in a canyon overlooking the ocean, its design inspired by the Villa of the Papyri at Herculaneum. After

Getty died, a much larger museum was built in downtown L.A. to house European art from the Middle Ages to the present, while Greek, Roman, and Etruscan artifacts remained at the Villa. During renovations from 1997 to 2006 a 450-seat semicircular stone theater was added facing the main entrance to the Villa. Productions of ancient drama are now staged there every September: *Hippolytus* translated by Anne Carson, directed by Stephen Sachs, in 2006; *Tug of War,* based on Plautus' *Rudens,* translated by Amy Richlin, directed by Meryl Friedman, in 2007; *Agamemnon* translated by Robert Fagles, directed by Stephen Wadsworth, in 2008; *Peace* adapted by Culture Clash with John Glore, directed by Bill Rauch, in 2009; Sophocles' *Elektra* translated by Timberlake Wertenbaker, directed by Carey Perloff, in 2010; *Trojan Women* adapted by Jocelyn Clarke, directed by Anne Bogart, in 2011; *Helen* adapted by Nick Salamone, directed by Jon Lawrence Rivera, in 2012, and *Prometheus Bound* translated by Joel Agee, directed by Travis Preston, in 2013 (Fig. 36.1).[2]

This theater is elegant, functional, and a much more useful size than the huge L.A. and Berkeley Greek Theatres. There is one odd feature, however. Although the Villa structure with its central door seems appropriate to serve as the *skene*, complete with a balcony above as potential *theologeion*, there is a great deal of space on the sides between the seating area and beyond the circular *orchestra* towards the building; see photos at "The Barbara and Lawrence Fleischman Theater." Some directors use this large space effectively, others not. For the 2008 *Agamemnon* a terracotta-colored pueblo-like *skene* was constructed, but the elegant Villa looming behind it looked strange. In *Elektra* chain-link fencing between the *orchestra* and the museum door suggested that those

FIG. 36.1 The Chorus and Prometheus. *Prometheus Bound* at the Getty Villa 2013. Photo by Craig Schwartz, used by kind permission of The J. Paul Getty Trust.

who had usurped the kingdom needed security, but given the distance there had to be several fences.

The choice of translations/adaptations, directors, and performance styles is often bold. In 2009 *Peace* was a timely script, and Culture Clash made it specific to Angelenos, just as the original script referred to Athens. *Trojan Women* was done in modern dress (very elegant—no rags in sight), with the captured women onstage throughout. Andromache killed her baby son herself—gently, mercifully, to save him from being thrown from the walls—and Odysseus arrived toward the end to offer a philosophical perspective.

Why only one outdoor production per year? Some of the Villa's neighbors sued to stop the theater's construction. The Getty won the lawsuit, but use permits initially enforced a maximum of 35 performances per year and strong limitations on vocal and instrumental sound; fortunately these controls are gradually being relaxed. *Elektra* and *Trojan Women* each had a chorus of one, perhaps because of worries about sound. But a single performer—even, in *Elektra,* Olympia Dukakis—cannot provide the sense of a community responding to a protagonist's situation, a crucial element of Athenian drama. Happily, the 2013 production of *Prometheus Bound* featured a chorus of 12 singing females.

The Villa offers other programs dedicated to ancient theater. The Villa Theater Lab stages new translations of ancient plays, as well as of contemporary works inspired by ancient texts ("Villa Theater Lab"), while the Villa Play-Reading Series offers readings by actors of lesser-known ancient plays. Both programs develop plays with an eye to the outdoor production. The museum's superb art collection has a special focus on art connected to ancient theater, and in fall 2010 hosted an exhibition with materials lent by collections around the world (Hart 2010). The Villa also has an excellent library and bookstore and offers scholarly symposia, research fellowships, concerts and films, courses, lectures, tours, and talks.

In 1994, before the Villa built the theater, Menander's *Samia* and Plautus' *Casina* were staged together in the courtyard. In my own review of the production, I commented that

> The artistic and popular success of the October 1994 productions could be just the beginning of a monumental contribution to both scholarly understanding and public appreciation of ancient drama. (Gamel 1995)

Nineteen years later, that monumental contribution is well under way.

Passing Through

Professional productions of drama frequently tour the west coast, and a few involve Greek-inspired scripts. The U.S. tour of Deborah Warner's *Medea*, created for the Abbey Theatre in Dublin 2000 with Fiona Shaw as the protagonist, came to Berkeley in 2002. The chance for west coast audiences to see a much-reviewed show was very valuable; as it did for the National Theatre of Greece *Medea*, UC Berkeley organized a symposium to allow in-depth discussion of the production.

Asian audiences in California, Oregon, and Washington are very interested in Asian dramatic forms, and this period has seen local productions such as Carol Sorgenfrei's *Medea: A Noh Cycle Based on the Greek Myth* (Theatre of Yugen, San Francisco, 1984) and *Kabuki Medea* (Berkeley Repertory Theatre, 1985) (Foley 2012: 217–20). A prominent Japanese theater practitioner is Tadashi Suzuki, a playwright and director with his own company and training school. He is steeped in Japanese theatrical traditions, but also works on European and American dramas. In Japan western-oriented modern theater is called Shigeki ("New Drama"), and some practitioners have imitated western ideas. Suzuki, however, works in a radically critical, indeed subversive way, revising Noh and Kabuki techniques and combining them with western concepts to create a whole new form of drama (Carruthers and Takahashi 2004: 1–5).

In 1974 Suzuki staged his highly praised version of *Trojan Women* (Carruthers and Takahashi 2004: 124–53). Japanese actors are accustomed to working in a single performance genre, but for this production Suzuki used for the first time major Noh and Shingeki performers along with an actress known for her neo-Kabuki style. Suzuki included an old woman in post-war Japan thinking about the Greek characters, and modern notes, such as a Japanese rock song.

Suzuki frequently revises his productions. He first staged *The Bacchae* in 1978, then created in 1981 a bilingual production with Japanese and American actors, none of whom spoke the others' language, and in 1990 the production, now called *Dionysus*, changed again (Carruthers and Takahashi 2004: 154–79). In 1983 Suzuki produced *Clytemnestra*, based on *Oresteia*, Sophocles' and Euripides' *Elektra*, and *Orestes*. As in *Trojan Women* and *Bacchae/Dionysus*, the action is presented as an internal fantasy.

The script is included in Suzuki's *The Way of Acting*, where he states, "By examining closely the destruction of the family as a fundamental and basic unit, I hope to suggest something of the solitary state in which modern man now finds himself" (Suzuki 1986: 121). Suzuki's bilingual version of *Clytemnestra* was performed 1987 in Los Angeles and Berkeley. The scenes move abruptly and non-chronologically between various moments and versions of the mythic story; in the final scene, based on Euripides' *Orestes*, the siblings, now condemned to death for matricide, incestuously embrace; Clytemnestra appears and silently stabs her children to death with a single blow.

Understanding the meaning of Suzuki's versions of Greek drama to Japanese audiences requires deep understanding of that culture. McDonald thinks Clytemnestra replaces a female ghost taking revenge on her lover.[3] The bilingual *Clytemnestra* featured an American actor speaking English as Orestes, perhaps suggesting a connection with the U.S. treatment of Japan during and after World War II. It is clear that Suzuki has drawn on Greek theater in forming his ideas about performance space and audience discussions (Suzuki 1986: 79–83). He has toured his productions to Greece, and in 1982 built a Greek-style open-air theater in Toga, where he holds an annual international theater festival. Suzuki's combination of traditional and modern elements in both subject matter and theatrical techniques, his deeply thought-provoking topics and themes, his use of poetic language, music, extraordinary physicality, and ritualized action, strongly connect his theater with Greek drama. Suzuki's vision is very dark, yet the open-endedness and the exhilarating physical performances of his actors make his productions thrilling rather than grim.

Why Greek Drama?

Companies, directors, and playwrights get involved with ancient Greek theater for many different reasons.

It's Important—or is it?

Some prominent professional companies on the west coast have staged very few Greek dramas. The Intiman in Seattle has done only three since 1976, Artists Repertory in Portland only one since 1982. Incidental productions such as these, mixed in with predictable modern drama, are not serious efforts to engage audiences in Greek drama, especially since the scripts chosen are usually well known.

Some companies show more sustained involvement. Berkeley Repertory Theatre staged Euripides' *Elektra* in their opening season 1968–9; Anouilh's *Antigone* 1971; Sato's *Kabuki Medea* in summer 1984; Suzuki's *Clytemnestra* 1987; Culture Clash's *Birds* 1998; and *Big Love*, Charles Mee's version of Aeschylus' *Suppliants*, 2001. In that year, to celebrate the opening of the company's second theater they chose the complete *Oresteia* of Aeschylus. Two experienced directors with ample funding assembled a strong cast, and filled the house many times, but unfortunately, they chose Fagles's translation, which was not written to be staged. No music or choreography were included, and most important, the directors seemed to lack a clear vision of what the plays meant or what they wanted their production to convey. In his detailed review, Griffith declared this staging inferior to a University of New Mexico production (Griffith 2001: 578). Respect for the value or prestige of Greek drama is not enough; there needs to be a personal connection and commitment to the issues and meaning of a particular script at a particular moment.

It's Timely

In 1968 the Polish director Jan Kott, then teaching drama at UC Berkeley, staged Euripides' *Orestes* in Arrowsmith's translation with student actors in the small Durham Theatre. First produced in 408 BCE, this play's plot and characters contradict the *Oresteia*'s vision of progress towards law, reflecting contemporary tensions and violence in Athens toward the end of the Peloponnesian War. Although ancient evidence suggests that *Orestes* was the most popular tragedy in antiquity, it is infrequently staged now. Kott made explicit references to current events: a photograph of the U.S. Capitol in Washington, DC, was the backdrop, scenes from the Vietnam War and anti-war demonstrations were shown, the actors wore contemporary dress and sang familiar songs. Said Kott: "I see America driven mad in the same way [as Athens] . . . The violence is at the same time pernicious—and necessary."[4]

Not all productions that address contemporary events arouse such positive responses; two based on Aeschylus' *Persians* demonstrate this clearly. The original script is unique in depicting an historical rather than mythic event: in 480–479 BCE the powerful Persian Empire, after being defeated in an attempt ten years earlier, sent a second invading force against the Greeks; despite facing an enemy with far superior numbers and wealth, the Greeks again defeated the Persians. What is remarkable about this script is that its subject could easily have been depicted in a triumphalist manner—especially since it was staged only seven years after the event. Instead the primary effect is to underline Persian suffering. Darius, the former king and father of the present king Xerxes, who has led the invasion, appears as a ghost, criticizes his son, and says that Persian *hubris* brought about their defeat. But when he urges listeners to remember and avoid such arrogance, the Athenian audience might have heard a warning against the kind of imperial ambitions that would get them into the Peloponnesian War.

In 1993 Peter Sellars directed a "modern version" by Robert Auletta at the Mark Taper Forum in Los Angeles, inspired by the 1991 attack on Iraq by the U.S.A. and allies. Sellars calls theater an "alternative public information system" to the highly censored American news coverage of the war (Auletta 1993: 7), and the adaptation contains explicit references to the invasion: Xerxes is depicted as a still-defiant Saddam Hussein (Auletta 1993: 83); the chorus call the enemy "terrorists" who are "experts at applying sanctions," who want to grab Iraq's oil, and they "curse the name of America" (Auletta 1993: 33–4, 37).

Such rewriting is valid—but the results must be evaluated. Auletta's *Persians* reverses the power differential between the enemies in the conflict by depicting the *weaker* side raging at their more powerful opponents who have won an easy victory. Edith Hall and Helene Foley both offer good discussions of this production, yet neither points out the difference the Auletta/Sellars change makes to the meaning and effect of the play.[5] Auletta/Sellars is not really a response to Aeschylus' play; as Marowitz says,

> There is a play, and a devastating one, to be written about the hypocritical American initiative to "take out" Saddam Hussein . . . but to etch that onto the Persians' invasion of Greece blurs rather than delineates them. (Marowitz 1993: 37)

Audiences in Los Angeles were outraged; at the performance I attended fully half of the audience, infuriated by the critique of the United States, left before the end.

Ellen McLaughlin's *Persians* was also directly inspired by U.S. military action, the invasion of Iraq in 2003 (McLaughlin 2005: 254). But she writes in such a way that the American audience could identify the actors playing Persian characters as either Americans or Iraqis. Above all she wanted the audience to understand "the truth of war . . . the magnitude of its terror" (McLaughlin 2005: 254). Her version was performed in Berkeley in 2007, by which time almost 4,000 U.S. soldiers had been killed in Iraq, in the intimate, 150-seat Aurora Theatre in Berkeley, where the audience sits on three sides of a deep-thrust stage with no one further than 15 feet from the performance. The set was not a royal palace but the interior of a large tent with an upstage opening out to a bright desert, with the audience inside the tent along with the actors. This powerful production provoked both emotion and thought.

Euripides' *Iphigenia in Aulis* (both translations and adaptations) has been staged many times in the U.S.A. starting in 1991 (Foley 2012: 296–300). Western productions included *Iphigenia at the Bay of Aulis* (a musical) by Thick Description, San Francisco, 1991; *IA* in Don Taylor's translation, directed by Paul Graf, University of California, Santa Cruz, 1991; *IA* adapted and directed by Keith Scales, Classic Greek Theatre of Oregon, Portland, 1993; *Furious Blood*, an adaptation of *IA* and the *Oresteia* by Kelly Stuart, directed by Kirsten Brandt, Sledgehammer Theatre, San Diego, 2000; *IA* in Philip Vellacott's translation, directed by Patrick Dooley, Shotgun Players, Berkeley, 2001; *Iphigenia* (*IA* and *Iphigenia among the Taurians*) directed by M. J. Sieber, Poet's Theatre, Seattle, 2003; *IA* in my translation, directed by Jac Royce, University of Puget Sound, Tacoma, 2003; *Iphigenia Crash Land Falls on the Neon Shell That Was Once Her Heart (A Rave Fable)* by Caridad Svich (Svich 2005), directed by Matthew McCray, Son of Semele Ensemble, Los Angeles, 2004; *IA* in Don Taylor's translation, directed by Timothy Near, San Jose Repertory Company, 2006; *Iphigenia 2.0* by Charles Mee, directed by Frédérique Michel, City Garage, Los Angeles, 2006; *Iphigenia and Other Daughters*, an adaptation of *IA*, Sophocles' *Electra*, and *Iphigenia among the Taurians* by Ellen McLaughlin (McLaughlin 2005: 3–76), Chamber Theatre and Washington Ensemble Theatre, Seattle, 2007; *Iph . . .* by Colin Teevan, Brava Theatre and African-American Shakespeare Company, San Francisco, 2010; *Aulis: An Act of Nihilism in One Long Act* by Christopher Chen, Cutting Ball Theatre, San Francisco, 2012. These and other productions around the country, which continue right to this moment, show that Greek drama is a powerful means for asking whether "our" wars in Iraq and Afghanistan were/are really worth the huge sacrifices involved.

It's Mine

Playwrights, directors, and artistic directors sometimes make a personal connection with Greek theater. A company founded in 2010, San Francisco Olympians Festival, produces an annual event staging contemporary plays based on Greek myth. The Bay Area playwrights "show how these gods and myths remain relevant today" by reinterpreting the stories according to their own perspectives (Bousel 2011: vii). Mark Jackson, San Francisco playwright, adaptor, and director, focuses primarily on German drama, but has staged two excellent adaptations of Greek drama: *Messenger #1*, based on *Oresteia*, for Art Street Theatre in 2000 (Foley 2005: 335–7; Jackson 2010: 384–422), and a cabaret-style production called *Io—Princess of Argos!*, loosely based on *Prometheus Bound*, complete with 13 songs, for Encore Theatre in 2001–2. In 2012 Carey Perloff, artistic director of American Conservatory Theatre in San Francisco, published a polemic which asked, "Why do we assume classics are impenetrable and obsolete?" (Perloff 2012). Jackson responded:

> Writers who know well what came before them are indeed more likely to leap off that foundation with a purposeful recklessness. Same goes for directors, actors, and designers. So, yes, let's all collide the old with the new!

The Classic Greek Theatre of Oregon, organized in 1986 in Portland, has staged annual productions of Greek drama from 1993 to the present. London-born Keith Scales, artistic director from 1993 to 2008, developed English versions of each of the 16 scripts he directed: *IA* 1993, *Agamemnon* 1994, *Libation Bearers* 1995, *The Furies* 1996, *Iphigenia among the Taurians* 1997, *Oedipus Tyrannus* 1998, *Antigone* 1999 and 2008, *Oedipus at Colonus* 2000, *Bacchae* 2001, *Birds* 2002, *Medea* 2003, *Prometheus Bound* 2004, *Alcestis* 2005, *Orestes* 2006, and *Peace* 2007. I have seen several of these productions in different locations, of which the most interesting was the outdoor Cerf Amphitheatre at Reed College, where a large lake lies behind the playing space. Scales's versions are definitely written for the stage, but otherwise the productions are quite conservative, probably because the company's major support comes from the Greek community in Portland:

> Classic Greek Theatre of Oregon was created to present the works of the ancient playwrights in style and setting as close to the original as possible... Costume design is based on ancient Greek vase-paintings to allow the plays to be truly authentic. Performances are given outdoors by daylight.[6]

Since Scales's departure CGTO has been in some disarray—there is currently no functioning company website—but they staged a Japanese-influenced *Oedipus Tyrannus* 2010 directed by Elizabeth Huffman, and *IT* 2011 and *Helen* 2012 directed by Leonidas Loizides. One thing is certain: thanks to CGTO, audiences in Portland have had the opportunity to see a sustained body of Greek drama.

Another west coast company with a special interest in Greek drama is Shotgun Players in Berkeley, founded by Patrick Dooley in 1992. Their productions have included *The Bacchae* in Cacoyannis's translation 1999 and *Iphigenia in Aulis* in Vellacott's translation 2001, both directed by Dooley; *Medea* in Robinson Jeffers's adaptation 2002, directed by Russell Blackwood; *Oedipus the King* 2003 in Rudall's translation, directed by Dooley, and *Phaedra*, adapted from Euripides and Racine by Adam Bock, directed by Rose Riordan, 2011. When I asked why Greek plays interest him, Dooley said,

> We avoided doing a Greek play until 1999, mostly out of sheer intimidation. Strong acting, strong writing, no bells and whistles—break it down. ["Break It Down" is the company motto.] We had built a reputation on choosing high-stakes, viscerally compelling stories that required only spartan production values. I wanted my actors to show up every night knowing they were going to HAVE to bring their entire experience to the stage. It should have been no surprise that the Greeks would be a perfect fit for our company.

Shotgun's productions vary (of course) in substance, style, and effect. *Medea* (called "a revenge potboiler") was staged melodramatically in a large abandoned Greek Revival movie theater, complete with a macabre organ score played live on stage. *Iphigenia in Aulis* was performed in John Hinkel Park's semicircular amphitheater constructed in 1934 with 350 stone seats and a circular playing space (another "Greek" theater, though not so called). As in Shotgun's *Oedipus*, only three actors performed all the central roles. *Bacchae*, performed in a tiny room with the audience on bleachers on three sides, was the best production of this difficult play I have ever seen. Adam Bock's Dionysos was captivating, naked except for a short black rubber skirt, gilded hair and nipples, and a totemic staff used with great effect. His Dionysos was fair, giving the uptight Pentheus (dressed in a rubber suit which suggested his connection with his cousin) every chance to save himself, but when that attempt failed delighted and inexorable in his revenge. The chorus of Bacchae, Pentheus, Cadmus, Tiresias, and Agave were far more effective so close up than in large, spectacular *Bacchae* productions. This was a stunning example of limited resources used for maximum theatrical effect.

Epic Productions

Several recent west coast productions have been inspired not by ancient dramatic scripts but by the Homeric poems. In 2010 Shotgun presented *The Salt Plays*, two original works based on the *Iliad* and the *Odyssey* written and staged by Bay Area playwright and director Jon Tracy. *In the Wound* was performed in summer at Hinkel Park with a cast of 31, a set of moveable screens capable of representing many different locations, music and tremendous physicality from the actors, and outstanding battle scenes accompanied by taiko drumming. *Of the Earth* was done in fall in Shotgun's own 100-seat theater, the Ashby Stage, with eight actors and a smaller, quieter, more contemplative production which made fine use of film (Fig. 36.2). These scripts are tremendously ambitious—encompassing the whole Trojan War, the sacrifice of Iphigenia, gods and goddesses, Odysseus' journey—with shifting perspectives and changes of pace which constantly provoke questions. Scenes don't occur in chronological order, but in terms of characters' thoughts and impulses. These are complex, expressionistic scripts, with strong changes of mood and tone, and some plot surprises, yet the central character (Odysseus), his various motives, and the themes are clear. The involvement of the gods is especially powerful, and shows how wrongheaded are adaptations (like the film *Troy*) which omit them. Not least, these scripts offer directors and actors wonderful opportunities for their own creativity.

Tracy says,

> We still have a great need for mythos as we have not truly solved any of the old mysteries of our existence. . . . I believe it is my duty to propagate these ancient stories through my very particular perspective that pays homage to (but potentially

disrespects) these original stories because what I write is what they mean to me now and what you watch is another book in an ever growing library. (Tracy 2010c)

Another Berkeley company which has produced outstanding work based on classical sources is Central Works, founded in 1991. Company co-director Gary Graves, who considers himself a "neo-classicist," comments that "In general, we take an existing story and create a new play."[7] Central Works has staged *Andromache* (based on Racine) 1994, 2006; *Achilles and Patroklos* 2005, *Penelope's Odyssey* 2010, and *The Medea Hypothesis* 2013; the second and third of these, like *The Salt Plays*, are based on the *Iliad* and the *Odyssey*. All of Central Works' productions are performed at the Berkeley City Club, a 1929 Moorish-Romanesque building designed by Julia Morgan. The rectangular, high-ceilinged room is not large—c.20′ × 30′, seating 50–60, with a playing space 8′ × 25′—with two doors into the hallway and one out into a small courtyard. Sets are necessarily minimal. "We're *always* thinking about the space," says Graves, and the small number of characters and their proximity to the audience creates great intimacy and increases the power of the restrained light and sound effects, and above all of the language and acting.

Achilles and Patroklos also includes Briseis, Kassandra, and Agamemnon. The scene is Lyrnessos, the palace of King Mynes, to which the warrior lovers have gone after abandoning the war out of disgust with Agamemnon's leadership. Here again are connections

FIG. 36.2 Telemachus (Daniel Petzold) and Odysseus (Daniel Bruno) confront the Scylla monster. *The Salt Plays 2: Of the Earth* at Ashby Stage 2010. Photo by Pak Han, used by kind permission of Shotgun Players.

between ancient and contemporary wars (Fig. 36.3). Agamemnon: "This is about honor. These people have insulted us in the deepest, darkest, most personal way they possibly could." Achilles: "It's about money. And power. You want to control the straits. And you want to plunder Troy" (Graves 2005a: 36–7). He meets Briseis, here a bastard daughter of Priam unhappily married to Mynes, kills her husband, and they fall in love. For a utopian moment the three live happily in a *ménage à trois*, though Agamemnon tries to get Achilles to return and Kassandra constantly warns of coming disaster. Unlike *In the Wound*, here the characters' inner demons (Kassandra's prescience, Achilles' selfishness and bloodlust, Patroklos' sense of duty, Agamemnon's arrogance) are the gods which drive them. What these characters have to lose, and do lose, is so much more vivid than Achilles' statement in the *Iliad* that he will go home and marry some Greek woman or other (*Il.* 9.409–14) that the tragic potential in the epic poem is fully realized. There are plot twists: when Agamemnon restores Briseis to Achilles, they "look at each other and Achilles looks away," never to see her again; he is killed by friendly fire (Graves 2005a: 67). "It is, I hope, a tragedy, like all tragedies, of what might have been" (Graves 2005b: 7). This play gives its audiences some sense of how Greek dramatists, such as Aeschylus in his lost *Myrmidons*, created dramas from the epic poems and what the effect of those dramas might have been.

FIG. 36.3 Cole Smith as Achilles in *Achilles and Patroklos* 2005. Photo by Daniel David, used by kind permission of Central Works.

Still another Bay Area production based on Homer was formally even bolder. In summer 2012 We Players, a company which specializes in site-specific productions, created *The Odyssey on Angel Island*, directed by Ava Roy (Fig. 36.4). The various buildings on this picturesque island in San Francisco Bay reflect its history as a military outpost, quarantine station, and immigration facility; it is now a state park. Audiences arrived via ferry and congregated at Odysseus' house at Ithaka, welcomed by jolly suitors offering snacks, songs, and dance while Penelope and Telemachus yearned for Odysseus. Prompted by Athena, Telemachus rallied the audience to join him in searching for his father, and we set off. During the next four hours we visited various locations—Aiolia, the Lotus Eaters, Mount Olympus, the Cyclops' cave, Scylla and Charybdis, Circe's and Calypso's domains—always arriving after Odysseus had already departed. Each scene had its own character and the settings were brilliantly chosen; the intervening journeys were rigorous and offered gorgeous views of the island and the bay. Perhaps most striking was the ending: we returned to Ithaka to find the suitors and maids slaughtered, Odysseus gone again, and Penelope furious, glad to be rid of him.[8] As my companion on the journey Al Duncan observed,

> It was as if the drama was performed in the "perfect tense": Odysseus' spectacular exploits had always already occurred, leaving traces for our leader and detective, Telemachus, to discover through inquiry and exploration. Is Odysseus truly a mythic hero—in our imagination, whose reality only exists in the impressions left on others?[9]

FIG. 36.4 Actors and audience at Aiolia in *The Odyssey on Angel Island* 2010. Photo by Mark Kitaoka, used by kind permission of We Players.

RAISING ISSUES

Artists who in the United States context identify themselves as Others in terms of gender, ethnicity, and sexuality are sometimes drawn to Greek drama as a way to frame issues important to them. In the West Latinos are often suspected of being illegal immigrants, and Hispanic artists have focused on this issue. Culture Clash, the troupe who performed *Peace* at the Getty Villa (see above), performed their adaptation of Aristophanes' *Birds* directed by Mark Rucker at South Coast Rep and Berkeley Rep in 1998. Here also the trio change the topical allusions of the Athenian script to fit the U.S. social and historical context; as I have argued elsewhere (Gamel 2010a: 160), such revision is *more* authentic than keeping the ancient allusions—and of course funnier. This version's use of verbal and musical styles—rap, gospel, jazz, and salsa—echoes the variety of the ancient script, and the dramatic illusion is frequently broken. Latino Gato explains why he and African-American Foxx are leaving Southern California: "We're just looking for a place where there's no cops, no cripps, no bloods, no 187, no 209, no 90210, no Governor Pete puto Wilson," until Foxx interrupts, "Gato, I think they get the point" (Culture Clash 1998). Foxx is a good American restlessly searching for a better life; he finds it, but abandons his former loyalties. Birds who dare oppose him become barbecue, and when Gato returns to confront him ("You forgot where you came from, ese! You sold out! Now you gotta pay, homes!") Foxx coolly shoots his pal and ascends into the stratosphere. Such darkness, though very Aristophanic, is rarely included in productions of his comedies.

Luis Alfaro (from the working-class Pico/Union district in Los Angeles) has produced three versions of Greek tragedy in California settings, gaining in skill and power with each one. Having first encountered Greek drama when he bought ten plays for a dollar each, Alfaro has since become obsessed with finding connections with the Greeks. His *Electricidad*, based on Sophocles' *Elektra*, was staged at Mark Taper Forum (Los Angeles) in 2005, directed by Lisa Peterson. The protagonist mourns for her father, the former "king" of the East Side Locos, killed by his wife Clemencia. Agamenón has not killed Ifigenia (who here plays Chrysothemis' role); Clemencia's rage arises from his having raped and abused and robbed her of her dreams for a better life: "I am going to change this neighborhood. And I am going to make it better than he ever did." Electricidad rejects her mother's hopes; she wants to be a traditional *chola*, a girl gang-member devoted to the old ways, and she longs for her brother Orestes' return from Las Vegas. Other women—Ifigenia, her paternal grandmother Abuela, a chorus of three neighbors—try to convince Electricidad to give up her matricidal rage. Orestes returns; Clemencia welcomes him joyfully ("Now, we can be a family!") but Electricidad hounds him into killing his mother (as in Euripides' *Electra*), and he goes mad.

This script is powerful—the use of Spanglish, in particular, makes the setting and characters both familiar and exotic—but structurally flawed. Clemencia is not sufficiently sympathetic and the presence of Ifigenia, Abuela, and the *vecinas* blurs the conflicts. A flirtation between Abuelo and Nino (Orestes' tutor) rings especially false. It is never clear who sent Orestes away to save him. Electricidad shows no sign of understanding how terrible her choices are for all involved. Nothing is learned, nothing changed; the only result is despair.

In 2010 the Magic Theatre in San Francisco staged Alfaro's *Oedipus el Rey*, directed by Loretta Greco. The script, developed during a residency at the Getty Villa, starts with Oedipus' birth and Laius' decision to kill the baby. Here it is Tiresias who decides to save the boy, even following him to prison and educating him every day in the prison library; Oedipus believes him to be his father. Released from prison, Oedipus heads south to Pico-Union, a "weak territory" which needs *un rey*. Having encountered and killed Laius en route, he continues to Los Angeles and meets newly widowed Jocasta. The intense connection between these two damaged characters is deeply moving.

This script is a huge improvement over *Electricidad*. The chorus of four, who play all the characters except Oedipus and Jocasta, also provide rhythmic sounds and movements which frame the more naturalistic action. The combination of Christian and pagan (including Aztec) religious references, and of the ancient story and the modern setting, work very effectively. Only the rushed ending seems false: once their kinship is revealed Oedipus asks Jocasta to blind him—inexplicably, since there is none of Sophocles' vision imagery—and he stabs her, with her consent. Given the power and beauty of their relationship, why accept the traditional conclusion? Steven Berkoff's *Greek* offers a paradigm when it ends with Eddy proclaiming,

> I'll love you even if I am your son
> ... Why should I tear my eyes out Greek style, why should you hang yourself
> ... it's love I feel it's love, what matter what form it takes. (Berkoff 1982b: 52)

In 2012 the Magic staged Alfaro's *Bruja*, based on *Medea*, again directed by Greco (Fig. 36.5). Medea and Jason have come to San Francisco from Mexico "without papers"—no visas, no marriage license. Jason works for Creon (an earlier, successful immigrant) in the construction industry; Medea is a *curandera*, "healer," but in the States is called *bruja*, "witch." She prefers the old ways, the old gods, and says prayers in Nahuatl. The domestic and political issues deftly mesh: Jason loves Medea and his children but, eager to escape outsider status, agrees to marry Creon's daughter in order to inherit the business. As in Euripides, he is unaware of Medea's real powers: that the dress she creates from snakeskin will bite Glauce and Creon to death; that she will kill her sons (here, not to punish Jason but as sacrifice to her ancient gods); and that, in an unforgettable final image, picking up the palm fronds she uses in her rituals, she will be transformed into a *guaco*, a "laughing falcon," and fly away not to another land but to a different realm of existence.

Not only were *Oedipus el Rey* and *Bruja* tighter scripts than *Electricidad*, the more intimate Magic Theatre space proved more effective than the much larger Mark Taper Forum. Many plays based on Greek scripts are large and public, but not Alfaro's; *Bruja* even eliminates the chorus (though Vieja, the nurse figure, stands in for them). The audience, on three sides of the playing space (the yard of Jason and Medea's house), became part of the action.

FIG. 36.5 Sabina Zuniga Varela as Medea in *Bruja* 2012. Photo by Jennifer Reiley, used by kind permission of Magic Theatre.

Scholar-Practitioners

Some west coast residents involved in Greek drama combine scholarship and practice. Starting in 2009 Stanford Classics in Translation (SCIT), a graduate student group, has staged a play each year—versions of Aristophanes (*Acharnians, Clouds, Wasps,* and *Ekklesiazousai*) and Euripides' *Cyclops*. These were lively, pointed, hilarious adaptations, connected to the local surroundings (*Clouds*' in-jokes are specific to Stanford) and time frame: *Ekklesiazousai*, a.k.a. *Women on Top*, involves Wall Street call-girls who, fed up with the ruinous economic practices of their businessman clients, infiltrate the Board of

Directors of "Oldman Sachs." Each script had "parodies" of popular songs with new lyrics. Such parodies are not only effective but legally free from copyright issues and much cheaper than original music.

Marianne McDonald, Professor of Theatre and Classics at the University of California, San Diego, has had an astonishingly prolific career as translator, adaptor, and scholar; her work alone deserves an entire chapter. She has written significant books on Greek drama, cinema, and opera (McDonald 1983, 1992, 2001, and 2003), many articles and reviews, and translations of almost all the extant Greek tragedies, sometimes working with J. Michael Walton. Her translations and adaptations have been staged around the world, many in San Diego. McDonald involves herself in every production as it develops and attends many performances, often leading a talkback after the show. Like the Classic Greek Theatre of Oregon, Marianne McDonald has provided a whole community with the chance to see frequent, lively performances of a broad range of Greek dramas by an accomplished translator.

And finally, a few words about my own work. My formal training is in Greek, Latin, and comparative literature, but in 1985 I got a call I could not resist—from Dionysos. His emissary was Christopher Grabowski, a talented UCSC undergraduate who wanted to direct an outdoor production of *Medea* set in 1953 Hollywood. I provided a translation, stuck around for rehearsals, in the process understood that performing Greek drama offers insights available in no other way, and my life was changed. Chris directed *Ajax* 1986 in another outdoor space; this time, only 11 years after the fall of Saigon, the setting was Vietnam and the production dedicated to the local Veterans of Foreign Wars chapter. Not a word of the Banks translation was changed, but the chorus carried M-16s rather than swords and Ajax's victims were human, recalling the My Lai massacre.

Then I worked on a Greek drama each year as assistant director and/or dramaturge. Chris went on to Yale School of Drama, and undergraduate Timothy Earle gave *Hippolytus* 1987 in Rudkin's version a performance-art staging with all the characters onstage watching the action until needed. In Tim's 1988 *Alcestis* (my translation) three actors played all the individual roles, and the resulting resonances between the characters were fascinating. In *Frogs* in 1989, my colleague Audrey Stanley substituted Eugene O'Neill and Tennessee Williams for Aeschylus and Euripides. To demonstrate how differently Greek playwrights could depict similar events, the 1990 Elektra Project paired Harrison's *Choephori* in the Barn Theatre (in March) with Euripides' *Elektra* in my translation outdoors (in May), with Chris directing and the same cast members repeating their roles. By then I had met Philip Collins, a Santa Cruz composer who can write in any style; he provided neo-primitivist music for *Choephori*, hillbilly tunes for *Elektra*. In 1992 two undergraduate feminists wanted to critique the masculinist politics of *Oresteia*, so we set *The Furies* in the 1950s U.S.A., with proto-beatnik Furies domesticated by Athena's offer of household goodies. *Lysistrata* (in Parker's translation), cross-dressed every which way, followed in 1993. Many of these productions were free; some of the outdoor shows had performances starting at dawn.

Meanwhile I had been honing my skills by observing my co-workers, taking directing and acting classes, assistant directing Shakespeare, and directing modern plays.

Now I took the plunge into adapting and directing: *Effie and the Barbarians*, based on *Iphigenia in Tauris* (1995), and *Eye on Apollo*, my version of *Ion* (1996). In 1998 *Prometheus 1.1* (my version of *Prometheus Bound*; the title shows Mee's influence) was directed by colleague Greg Fritsch, with a wonderful score by Ralph Denzer. From then on I was committed to staging Greek drama with original music. In 2000, inspired by a brilliant suggestion by undergraduate Ali El-Gasseir, I ventured into comedy, transforming Aristophanes' *Thesmophoriazousai* into *The Julie Thesmo Show*, a women-only daytime TV talk show in which the host and guests put Euripides on trial; Ali and I co-directed. I then made a foray into Plautus, Terence, and Hrotsvit before reuniting in 2006 with Chris Grabowski and Phil Collins to do *The Buzzzz!!!! (Wasps*, set at UCSC). Then back to Euripides, with *Helen of Egypt* (2008) directed by colleague Mike Ryan, and *Orestes Terrorist* (2011), directed by colleague Danny Scheie, both with original scores by Phil (Fig. 36.6).

Orestes is an incredible play, but productions sometimes flatten the hard edges and bizarre swings of mood and tone.[10] My fearless director and cast embraced the weirdness but kept the emotional stakes high. Orestes and Elektra are unstable, damaged teenagers, privileged but with a family history of violence and neglect, uncertain what and whom to believe. As the large chorus, eager for spectacle, egg them on, the siblings discover that neither Helen nor Menelaus will help them. In our staging Apollo appeared frequently but was easily distracted, and a Fox News reporter blatantly manipulated the already corrupt trial. Orestes, his lover Pylades, and Elektra share the only real emotional bond in the play. After Orestes and Elektra are condemned to death, they have a poignant farewell scene; I turned this into a song that became erotic, with Pylades joining in.

As the siblings leave to commit suicide, Pylades desperately spins the plot to win over or punish Menelaus by threatening Helen, and Elektra suggests holding Hermione hostage and possibly destroying the palace and themselves with it. As the trio threatened to burn down the whole theater, Apollo's appearance as *deus ex machina* to Wagnerian strains epitomized the power relations of 408 and 2011 and the indifference of the .01 percent to the fate of the masses. In our version the mortals defiantly sang:

> Why should those deadbeats be in charge?
> Why should events down here be steered up there?
> Why don't we protest this crooked system,
> eject these amoral bums from their easy chair?

But Apollo was unmoved:

> Ah, revolution! That eternal dream!
> Go ahead, morons, waste time, let off steam!
> Nothing you can do, no threat, no plea
> will change the way things are and will always be!

In her 2011 review Macintosh suggests that, as with Kott's production, once again a very strange Greek play embodied the chaos going on around the U.S.A. at a particular moment in history (Macintosh 2011).

FIG. 36.6 Annie Ritschel as Elektra and Keith Burgelin as Orestes. *Orestes Terrorist* 2011. Photo by Steve DiBartolomeo, used by kind permission of the University of California, Santa Cruz.

CONCLUSIONS?

This necessarily limited survey suggests that Greek theater is thriving on the U.S. west coast, and the coming years will surely see many more exciting productions. One obvious reason is the combative political climate, which provokes lively debate. Political issues such as California's status as a "majority minority" state (where whites are outnumbered by other ethnicities), same-sex marriage, the treatment of immigrants and transgender people, resistance to increasing inequality of income, excessive education costs, lack of jobs, and continuing questions about U.S. "exceptionalism" will continue to simmer. Another reason is the strong sense of community engendered by proximity, ethnicity, gender, and politics. Still another is a desire to respond to the increasing corporate domination of public life, including the mass media such as film and television.

Some of those issues will set fire to artists and productions which, as in Athens, use strong characters, vivid plots, articulate language, and music to look at issues from a variety of perspectives. Many of these stagings will be produced not by professional theaters dependent on subscribers but by smaller companies and universities, whose productions are worthy of note both because they are often bolder, and also because their conditions of production and artistic aims more closely resemble those at Athens (Gamel forthcoming). The increased availability of electronic media makes publicity cheaper and easier for smaller companies, and the increasing availability of video recordings is likely to encourage understanding and enthusiasm for Greek drama—especially if a digital archive of ancient drama productions can be established in the U.S.A. But recordings will never supplant live production. In an era in which communal gatherings are few, live theater offers one place where the collaboration between actors and audience can provoke thought, arouse indignation, give pleasure, and offer consolation to all present.[11]

Notes

1. Hall 2004a: 2. See Schiffman 2012 for a report on recent Greek drama in the San Francisco Bay Area.
2. The scripts of *Tug of War, Peace, Elektra, Trojan Women*, and *Helen* were commissioned by the Getty. On Perloff and Wertenbaker, see Williamson, this volume.
3. McDonald 1992: 51. See McDonald 1992: 21–73 for discussion of all three of these Suzuki plays, with photos.
4. Stone 1968; see also Colakis 1993: 63–4, and Hartigan 1995: 124–5.
5. Hall 2004b; Foley 2012: 139–41. Cf. Favorini 2003.
6. <http://www.thecommunityfund.com/funding/story/classic_greek_theatre_of_oregon>.
7. See <http://www.centralworks.org/pages/about_method.php>.
8. For alternative endings to the *Odyssey*, see Hall 2008: 36–43, 179–87.
9. See also Duncan 2013.
10. See Gamel 2010b for my review of two stagings.
11. Thanks to Kirsten Brandt, Patrick Dooley, Al Duncan, John Glore, Gary Graves, Mary Louise Hart, Mark Jackson, Dori Jacob, Joanie McBrien, Marianne McDonald, Ava Roy, and Jon Tracy. Many thanks to Justine McConnell for her helpful suggestions and patience (which I severely tested); to Eric Dugdale for helpful suggestions; and to Tom Vogler, *sine qua non*. This chapter is dedicated with love and sorrow to the memory of Kate Bosher, extraordinary scholar, director, teacher, and dear friend.

    I will gladly provide scripts and DVDs of the UCSC productions mentioned: mkgamel@ucsc.edu.

References

Alfaro, L. (2006), "*Electricidad:* A Chicano Take on the Tragedy of Electra," *American Theatre* 23.2, 63–85.
Alfaro, L. (2010), *Oedipus el Rey*. Unpublished script.
Alfaro, L. (2012), *Bruja*. Unpublished script.
"All America's a Stage: Growth and Challenges in Nonprofit Theater." 2008. Report from the National Endowment for the Arts <http://arts.gov/sites/default/files/TheaterBrochure12-08.pdf> accessed July 2013.

Auletta, R. (1993), *The Persians: A Modern Version*. Los Angeles.
Berkoff, S. (1982a), *Decadence*. London.
Berkoff, S. (1982b), *Greek*. London.
Bousel, S. E. (ed. 2011), *Songs of Hestia: Five Plays from the San Francisco Olympians Festival*. San Francisco.
Carruthers, I. and Y. Takahashi (2004), *The Theatre of Suzuki Tadashi*. Cambridge.
Colakis, M. (1993), *The Classics in the American Theater of the 1960s and Early 1970s*. Lanham, NY, and London.
Culture Clash, with John Glore (1998), *The Birds*. Unpublished script.
Duncan, A. (2013), "We Players: The *Odyssey* on Angel Island," *Didaskalia* 10.7, <http://www.didaskalia.net/issues/10/7/>.
Favorini, A. (2003), "History, Collective Memory, and Aeschylus' *The Persians*," *Theatre Journal* 55, 99–111.
Foley, H. P. (2004), "Bad Women: Gender in Modern Performance and Adaptation of Greek Tragedy," in E. Hall, F. Macintosh, and A. Wrigley eds., *Dionysus Since 69: Greek Tragedy at the Dawn of the Third Millennium*. Oxford, 77–111.
Foley, H. P. (2005), "The Millennium Project: *Agamemnon* in the United States," in F. Macintosh, P. Michelakis, E. Hall, and O. Taplin eds., *Agamemnon in Performance 458 BCE to AD 2004*. Oxford and New York, 307–42.
Foley, H. P. (2012), *Reimagining Greek Tragedy on the American Stage*. Berkeley, Los Angeles, and London.
Gamel, M.-K. (1995), "*Casina* and *Samia* in Malibu, California, USA," *Didaskalia* 2.1 <http://www.didaskalia.net/issues/vol2no1/gamel.html>.
Gamel, M.-K. (2010a), "Revising 'Authenticity' in Staging Ancient Mediterranean Drama," in E. Hall and S. Harrop eds., *Theorising Performance: Greek Drama, Cultural History and Critical Practice*. London, 153–70.
Gamel, M.-K. (2010b), "A Tragic Romp?," *Arion* 18.1, 119–33.
Gamel, M.-K. (forthcoming), "The Festival of Dionysos: A Community Theatre," in J. Griffiths, P. Monaghan, and F. Sear eds., *Close Relations: The Spaces of Greek and Roman Theatre*. Newcastle upon Tyne.
Graves, G. (2005a), *Achilles and Patroklos*. Unpublished script.
Graves, G. (2005b), *Achilles and Patroklos* program.
Griffith, M. (2001), "Greek Tragedy Goes West: The *Oresteia* in Berkeley and Albuquerque," *American Journal of Philology* 122.4, 567–78.
Hall, E. (2004a), "Introduction: Why Greek Tragedy in the Late Twentieth Century?," in E. Hall, F. Macintosh, and A. Wrigley eds., *Dionysus Since 69: Greek Tragedy at the Dawn of the Third Millenium*. Oxford, 1–46.
Hall, E. (2004b), "Aeschylus, Race, Class, and War in the 1990s," in E. Hall, F. Macintosh, and A. Wrigley eds., *Dionysus Since 69: Greek Tragedy at the Dawn of the Third Millenium*. Oxford, 169–97.
Hall, E. (2008), *The Return of Ulysses: A Cultural History of Homer's Odyssey*. London.
Hart, M. L. (2010), *The Art of Ancient Greek Theater*. Los Angeles.
Hartigan, K. V. (1995), *Greek Tragedy on the American Stage: Ancient Drama in the Commercial Theater, 1882–1994*. Westport, CT, and London.
Jackson, M. (2010), *Ten Plays*. San Francisco, 384–422.
Jackson, M. (2012), "Not Lost: Visceral Histories" <http://www.theatrebayarea.org/editorial/Chatterbox/Not-Lost-Visceral-Histories.cfm>.

Macintosh, F. (2011), "Review: *Orestes Terrorist* at the University of California, Santa Cruz," *Didaskalia* 8.14 <http://www.didaskalia.net/issues/8/14/>.

McDonald, M. (1983), *Euripides in Cinema: The Heart Made Visible*. Philadelphia.

McDonald, M. (1992), *Ancient Sun, Modern Light: Greek Drama on the Modern Stage*. New York.

McDonald, M. (2001), *Sing Sorrow: Classics, History, and Heroines in Opera*. Westport, CT, and London.

McDonald, M. (2003), *The Living Art of Greek Tragedy*. Bloomington and Indianapolis.

McLaughlin, E. (2005), *The Persians: The Greek Plays*. New York, 253–309.

Marowitz, C. (1993), "L.A. in Review," *TheaterWeek* (October 25–31), 36–7.

"Odyssey on Angel Island Images," <http://www.weplayers.org/tag/odyssey-on-angel-island-photos>.

Perloff, C. (2012), "The Loss of the Old" <http://www.huffingtonpost.com/carey-perloff/theater-classics_b_1469727.html>.

"Point Loma Nazarene University Greek Theatre," <www.youtube.com/watch?v=WgBNlFLwTY8> accessed July 2013.

Schiffman, J. (2012), "It's All Greek to Me," *Theatre Bay Area* (September/October), 24–6.

Starr, K. (2004), *Coast of Dreams: California on the Edge, 1990–2003*. New York.

Stone, J. (1968), "A Greek—or American Tragedy?" <http://www.criticjudystone.com/orestes.html> accessed July 2013.

Suzuki, T. (1986), *The Way of Acting: The Theatre Writings of Tadashi Suzuki*. Trans. J. T. Rimer. New York.

Suzuki, T., "Suzuki's Philosophy of Theatre" <http://www.scot-suzukicompany.com/en/philosophy.php> accessed July 2013.

Svich, C. (2005), *Iphigenia Crash Land Falls on the Neon Shell That Was Once Her Heart (A Rave Fable)*, in C. Svich ed., *Divine Fire: Eight Contemporary Plays Inspired by the Greeks*. New York, 329–73.

Talbot, D. (2012), *Season of the Witch: Enchantment, Terror, and Deliverance in the City of Love*. New York and London.

"The Barbara and Lawrence Fleischman Theater" <http://www.fdaonline.com/project_detail.php?id=50> accessed July 2013.

Tracy, J. (2010a), *In the Wound. The Salt Plays: Part 1*. Unpublished script.

Tracy, J. (2010b), *Of the Earth. The Salt Plays: Part 2*. Unpublished script.

Tracy, J. (2010c), "The Importance of Adaptation," Of the Earth program.

"Villa Theater Lab" <http://www.getty.edu/museum/programs/performances/theater_lab.html> accessed July 2013.

CHAPTER 37

PERFORMING FOR SOLDIERS

Twenty-First-Century Experiments in Greek Theater in the U.S.A.

LAURA LODEWYCK AND S. SARA MONOSON

Stage productions of Greek tragedy in the U.S.A. have addressed thoroughly contemporary experiences of war at least since Michael Cacoyannis's production of Euripides' *Trojan Women* at New York's Circle in the Square in 1963 and Judith Malina's production of Brecht's *Antigone* for The Living Theatre in 1968–9 delivered searing attacks on the Vietnam War. More recently, Aeschylus' *Persians* by Robert Auletta and Peter Sellars (1993, 2003, 2004, 2005, and 2006) offered a stirring, some thought jolting, statement about the use of American military power in Iraq. All these productions were innovative theatrically as well as provocative politically. However, they reached only a "limited, educated, primarily urban audience that might be expected to respond . . . favorably to them."[1] On the other hand, two American actors organized The Lysistrata Project, simultaneous public readings and performances of Aristophanes' *Lysistrata* in 1,029 locations on March 3, 2003 as a "peace action" in protest of the impending U.S.–led invasion of Iraq. (See Dutsch, this volume.) An estimated 225,000 people in 59 countries and all 50 U.S. states participated.[2]

In this chapter, we report on new ways in which theater professionals working in the U.S.A. have turned to Greek drama specifically to be part of urgent public discourse about war. In particular, we observe the emergence of sustained theatrical work with Greek tragedy that does not make a partisan statement about American foreign policy but rather engages American servicemen and women's experiences of deployment, battle, and homecoming. These new projects aspire to facilitate compassionate understanding of the experiences of and related to military service, including the challenges facing active duty troops and veterans as the result of war-related trauma and the widening gap between military and civilian society. As we will detail, this work involves theater professionals conversant with the ancient sources experimenting with new formats and creating events for non-traditional venues and diverse audiences.

Two projects have national profiles: Outside the Wire's ongoing commercial enterprise called "Theater of War" and the non-profit Ancient Greeks/Modern Lives' project called "Homecoming: The Return of the Warrior," which draws on the members of the Aquila Theatre company of New York. Theater of War presents dramatic readings from Sophocles' *Ajax* and *Philoctetes* followed by guided town-hall style discussions with audience members. Theater of War has performed all over the country and overseas on military bases for active duty personnel as well as in civilian settings for mixed audiences of medical personnel, active and veteran military, and the general public. Aquila Theatre's Homecoming presents scenes adapted from Sophocles' *Ajax*, Homer's *Odyssey*, Euripides' *Heracles*, and Aeschylus' *Agamemnon* accompanied by workshops and town-hall style discussions. They perform in spaces such as public libraries across urban and rural America for audiences of veterans and the general public. As their three-year project comes to a close, Aquila is now experimenting with using video of contemporary veterans speaking about their own experiences to voice the chorus in a full-length production of Euripides' *Heracles*.[3]

Theater and performance artists have addressed military personnel in other extended projects,[4] and veterans and official military sources have embraced the usefulness of theater.[5] Outside the Wire's Theater of War and Ancient Greeks/Modern Lives' Homecoming programs are distinct for their insistence that ancient Greek sources can anchor projects with such ambitions. Helene Foley has written compellingly on twentieth- and twenty-first-century attempts to address current social or political issues through performances of Greek tragedy, pointing out that

> The evolving relation between the plays and the U.S. stage . . . reflects and illuminates important changes in the country's sense of itself. Greek tragedy has generally served progressive aesthetic, cultural, and political agendas, from transforming outmoded theatrical conventions to serving identity politics or promoting peace. (Foley 2012: 3)

As Foley describes, such trends are illustrative of the multiplicity evident in the reception of classical work and our understanding of the sources themselves. Our aim in this essay is to turn to theoretical work on theater as social practice to examine each project's uses of ancient sources to create deeply affecting theater experiences about utterly contemporary matters for new kinds of audiences. We explore the nature of these artistic interventions and their intended audiences, including methods of theatrical engagement. We will argue that these projects "democratize" Greek drama in multiple senses. They presume a primary audience other than a theater-going elite, mobilize interpretations of texts to address unseen or neglected public interests, disrupt the format of traditional full-length performances of Greek texts, amplify certain voices in the sources, and occasion public discourse and moments of commonality.[6]

THE PERSPECTIVE OF "SOCIAL THEATER"

Outside the Wire's Theater of War and Ancient Greeks/Modern Lives' Homecoming programs do not necessarily self-identify as "social theater" and we do not intend to label these activities as representative of a movement.[7] But we do suggest that a theory of social practice provides a lens through which to examine these projects' distinguishing characteristics. "Taken as a whole," leading theorists have explained, "social theatre stands alongside of, and sometimes in place of, 'aesthetic theatre' (including art theatres, experimental theatres, university theatres, regional theatres, and commercial theatres)."[8] Drawing this distinction is not meant to deny "either the social aspects of aesthetic theatre or the aesthetic aspects of social theatre but rather point out differences of purpose, audiences, venues, and production values" (Thompson and Schechner 2004: 11). The scholarly literature on this development in theater practice also employs terms such as "applied theatre" (Blatner 2007), "engaged theatre,"[9] and "civic practice" (Rohd 2012). There is no clear consensus in the literature regarding the terminology. None of these terms are restrictive definitions. They all point to an effort to examine theoretically "socially related" theater practices that depart from traditional theatrical productions in both intent and process (Cohen-Cruz 2010).[10]

Social theater refers to events that may forge partnerships among artistic and civic groups and address specific issues of importance to these communities (Prendergast and Saxton 2009; Prentki and Preston 2009; Taylor 2003; Thompson 2009). Social theater "combines aesthetics and politics" and is "inter-relational, embodied, and durational" (Jackson 2011: 11–12). For example, Sojourn Theater's Michael Rohd views social practice as a term "which covers a tremendously varied and large body of work" all of which is in some way marked by the inclusion of non-arts partners and focused attention to felt community needs (Rohd 2012). The particulars of the social practices may vary according to the extent of the emphasis placed on the role of non-arts partners in the collaboration and the specific nature of individual projects: for example, The Living Stage Theatre Company's Program for Teen Mothers (Haedicke and Nellhaus 2001), the Prison Creative Arts Project (Alexander 2010), and Cornerstone Theater's traveling residencies performing *Winter's Tale: An Interstate Adventure* (Kuftinec 2003). But in all cases of social practice, Rohd stresses, "the leading impulse and guiding origin energy is from the artist" (Rohd 2012).

The idea of social theater also calls attention to the character of the public discourse that the theater events prompt. It is informed by a tradition of inquiry in political theory inaugurated by Jürgen Habermas and developed by many others on the "public sphere."[11] In social theater performers and audiences at times form temporary communities that "model new investments in and interactions with variously constituted public spheres" (Dolan 2005: 10). Philosopher Nancy Fraser explains,

> The idea of the public sphere designates a theatre in modern societies in which political participation is enacted through the medium of talk. It is the space in which

> citizens deliberate about their common affairs, hence, an institutionalized arena of discursive interaction. This arena is conceptually distinct from state; it is a site for the production and circulation of discourses that can in principle be critical of the state. (Fraser 1990: 287)

Fraser refers to "theater" metaphorically. The viewpoint of social theater theory explores this connection. It stresses the possibility that theater arts events can occasion and help sustain alternative deliberative spaces or "public spheres" and it directs us to observe precisely how theater professionals can leverage their technical skills to advance this goal when crafting their projects.

We will also propose that Victor Turner's idea of *communitas* can illuminate a key feature of Theater of War and Homecoming programs understood as social theater, specifically, the riveting moments of storytelling by audience members during the town-hall sessions. In explanation of *communitas*, Turner asks:

> Is there any of us who has not known this moment when compatible people—friends, congeners—obtain a flash of lucid mutual understanding on the existential level, when they feel that all problems, not just their problems, could be resolved, whether emotional or cognitive, if only the group which is felt (in the first person) as "essentially us" could sustain its inter-subjective illumination. (Turner 1982: 48)

Turner proposes that this shared realization, a fleeting moment of understanding another's very different experience, ideally generates concrete action. We suspect that Turner's view can help us understand the significance of features of these projects, such as when a civilian physician openly wept during a Theater of War session, confessing that she would never again deliberately dismiss patients who complained of PTSD symptoms because of a misguided desire to avoid complicity in the war.[12]

Theater of War and Homecoming Viewed as Social Theater

Social theater projects frequently utilize nonconventional venues instead of traditional theaters and performance spaces. The projects we detail here indeed follow this practice. But the venue is not what defines them. Instead, the key factors are their partnerships and collaborations, attention to social goals and arts-driven processes. In these programs, theatrical and aesthetic choices are made to advance the social goal and sustain the partnerships.

Similar sets of concerns seem to have motivated the artistic directors of both projects. Bryan Doerries (Outside the Wire's Theater of War) and Peter Meineck (Ancient Greeks/ Modern Lives' Homecoming program) are both advocates of broad public awareness of the contemporary relevance of ancient Greek literature to today's civic discourse and artistic practice. Both start from the premise that elements of Greek literature, especially certain stories, figures, and scenes from particular tragedies, could be part of the arsenal available to active and veteran military personnel as they tackle the medical, personal, and civic challenges posed by the high incidence of war-related post-traumatic stress among the troops. Both Doerries and Meineck have noted that their own knowledge of the fact that great ancient dramatists like Aeschylus and Sophocles were themselves generals and that the audience for ancient theater was full of experienced soldiers prompted them to seek to experiment and take up their respective projects. Both have indicated that they suspected that this material could be used to bridge the widening gap between the experiences of military personnel and the general public (Doerries 2010; Green 2010; Meineck 2009, 2012). And both directors designed programs that aim to use contact with ancient plays to spark conversations among active duty and veteran military personnel and their families as well as among military people and the general theater-going public specifically conceived of as individuals lacking first-hand experience of the struggles of active duty troops and injured veterans. Their projects have different emphases but similar overarching social goals.

These directors were also working at a time when the path-breaking books by Jonathan Shay were garnering considerable public attention for suggesting that Greek literature and the record of Greek theatrical practice address what clinicians today call "combat trauma" and related forms of psychological injury and suffering (e.g., PTSD) endured by military personnel and their families.[13] A psychiatrist at Boston's Department of Veteran Affairs Outpatient Clinic, Shay wrote studies of the Homeric epics that show that they reflect the psychological realities of war as American clinicians had come to understand them from decades of therapeutic work with combat veterans (especially of the Vietnam era). Shay also observed that Greek drama reflects similar themes and was intrigued by contemporary scholarship on Greek tragedy in its civic context that stressed that ancient Greek theater was written and performed by Athenian citizen-soldiers for an audience of Athenian citizen-soldiers on the occasion of a grand public ritual event. As a psychiatrist, he considered that "the process of healing from combat trauma lies fundamentally in communalizing it"; he therefore speculated that Greek tragedy served a particular purpose in keeping with the democratic work of Athenian society, arguing that "the ancient Athenians re-integrated their returning warriors through recurring participation in the rituals of theatre" (Shay 1995: n.p.). Shay suggested that the example of ancient Athenian theater could supply advocates of improved military policies and veterans' services a useful model. The Homecoming unit of Ancient Greeks/Modern Lives and Theater of War both work from the same assumption.

Theatrical Format

The format of Theater of War and Homecoming are similar in many respects. Both programs conceive of their events as having two integrated parts, staged readings of selected scenes from Greek texts and open-ended town-hall style meetings in which audience members participate actively, not a performance event followed by a traditional post-show "talkback." Both programs employ professional performers to conduct the staged readings. Both programs select scenes in which heroic figures from Greek myth struggle personally with the stresses of military service, including suffering wounds ranging from festering physical gashes to psychological injuries that spark "berserk" events and suicide, homecomings full of uncertainty. Both rely on the expertise of professional actors as readers so that the specific words in the passages can he heard and understood and so that the readings provide compelling portrayals of emotions. Both use facilitators to manage the open discussion. Judging from reviews, news coverage, and our own attendance at a number of these events, it is not uncommon for the town-hall sessions to include spontaneous personal storytelling by veterans or their family members. The aesthetics of the programs are quite different, as we shall see below. For example, the Ancient Greeks/Modern Lives program relies on ensemble members of Aquila Theatre to perform the selected scenes in various venues across the country. Theater of War, in contrast, contracts with individual actors for specific events, often employing familiar faces from television or film, to deliver largely unrehearsed readings, script in hand.

The format advances the social goal by employing an unbilled host and panelists during the discussion session. A skillful host/moderator can troubleshoot some potential pitfalls. For example, he can acknowledge audience members' uncertainties about the contemporary interest of the ancient material at the outset as well as the difficulties that attend public expression of wrenching and heavily stigmatized matters. He can also offer some intriguing historical context to draw in the audience (for example, the playwright was a general, the ancient audience members were soldiers, the Greek cities were at war for decades), answer questions in a respectful (not patronizing) way, and direct the conversation with brief on point comments or points of information. Both Doerries and Meineck perform this role often and provide detailed guides to the others they employ on occasion. Using panelists to introduce the town-hall sessions gets the discussions started and can model the diversity of voices and viewpoints welcomed (spouses, clinicians, veterans). Theater of War panels feature individuals with a range of perspectives: for instance, an active duty service member, a previously deployed veteran, a military spouse, and a mental health worker or military chaplain who has a background in the treatment of combat stress. Theater of War promotional materials specify that "the panelists are not expected to be experts in ancient Greek drama, philosophy or psychology. In fact, exactly the opposite is true: their comments are the most powerful when they share unprepared thoughts about how the plays resonate with their personal and professional experience."[14] Ancient Greeks/Modern Lives' Homecoming programs are hosted by a local academic expert (usually a Classicist but not always) who moderates the open discussion following the readings. At times their programs use panelists and for these parts Homecoming turns to veterans (not clinicians), including Classics scholars who are themselves veterans (Paul Woodruff, Lawrence Tritle) and Aquila ensemble members who are veterans.

Both Theater of War and Homecoming projects focus on the presentation of a set of distinctive scenes. This is of course to some extent in service of practicality. Scene selections concentrate the attention on particular themes, reserve time for group discussion, and are less costly to produce. But this format is also absolutely integral to the success of the audience participation part of their projects. The scenes are chosen for their depiction of dilemmas and situations that are familiar to military personal but may be stigmatized today. Theater of War employs three possible performance formats that they can stage in any setting: The Ajax and Philoctetes Program, the Ajax Program, and the Female Warrior Program (featuring a female Ajax and a male Tecmessa). The Ancient Greeks/Modern Lives' Homecoming unit focuses on the stories surrounding specific characters—Philoctetes, Herakles, Ajax and Tecmessa, Penelope and Odysseus. The stories are entry points for discussion of "irresolvable, extreme situations without being crudely topical" (Foley 1999: 2). For instance, the Messenger's speech from *Herakles* reveals the horror and violence of the warrior's madness, while Agamemnon's sacrifice of Iphigenia is used to illustrate devastating decisions that must be made in the course of war.

Doing discrete scenes is consistent with the tradition of Augusto Boal's stance against Aristotle's "coercive" dramatic arc, a foundational idea in theater for social change. In *Theatre of the Oppressed*, Boal proposed a system that rebels against "Aristotle's coercive system of tragedy," which he believed purges the spectator of characteristics undesirable to society, through one's vicarious experiences of the protagonist. Through a play's dramatic arc,

> The spectator experience[s] three changes of a rigorous nature: *peripeteia, anagnorisis,* and *catharsis*;[15] he *suffers a blow* with regard to his fate (the action of the play), *recognizes the error* vicariously committed and *is purified of the antisocial characteristic* which he sees in himself. (Boal 1979: 40, emphasis in the original)

Boal theorized that theater of this nature upholds oppressive institutional forces and persuades the individual not to act against them. By disrupting the dramatic arc and preventing a fluid conclusion to a central narrative, selective scenes heighten Greek drama's applicability to contemporary concerns and encourage responses to the unresolved situations presented in the tragic text. In the Theater and War and Homecoming projects, audiences are expected to connect with the power of the language of the texts and the intensity of the immediate situation being performed. They are also expected to express that connection through their own storytelling, comments, and attentive listening during the discussion sessions. Meineck has invoked Boal to discuss the connections between the staged readings and town-hall style meetings. He suggests that Boal's "invisible theatre" technique stirs dialogue and debate:

> In this kind of theater the audience member becomes a witness to and participant in an *event*, not just a passive receiver of somebody else's art. (Meineck 2009: 175)

We suggest likening this connection between audience and readers to Turner's *communitas*. When Aquila actors perform chilling scenes from *Herakles* in which an honorable returning warrior violently attacks his own family, they do so only a few feet from their audience, not separated from them by an elevated stage or theatrical lighting. The format encourages the room to unite in recognition of the reality of these situations (Meineck 2009).

Staged readings are not typically considered finished theatrical products, or rather, products with their own intentional aesthetic; instead, the staged reading is often used in service of the development or promotion of a full-scale production. In these cases, in contrast, the attributes of the staged reading as a theatrical form contribute substantially to the needs of the projects, consistent with the traditions of social and civic practice. But these performances differ from projects that similarly use scene work in the service of other social goals. For example, Boal's Theater of the Oppressed uses performers to stage scenes based on issues or problems prevalent to that community and welcomes audience participants to step onstage to change how the scene plays out. In Theater of War and Homecoming professional actors focus the audience's attention on the words and the situations that they describe. Theater of War and Homecoming are also unlike other politically engaged productions that encourage audiences to talk among themselves only after dispersing and leaving the event. Their format is designed to facilitate lively face-to-face town-hall sessions. These programs seek to turn the theater event into a new, albeit temporary, space for open talk and attentive listening regarding acute problems facing military men and women today. When they succeed we might say they contribute to the production of a plurality of "public spheres" in the American polity, a condition that political philosopher Fraser argues is necessary if public deliberation in our expansive and diverse nation is to bend in the direction of more inclusion (Fraser 1990).

Candid post-performance reactions to the readings can also create moments of shared vulnerability, making space for open talk by the less powerful and demanding active listening by all present. But it is a fragile moment. It can easily be disrupted, Doerries has observed, once normative interactions resume. He explains:

> ... everyone's been very *activated*. And then all inhibitions, and boundaries, and culture, and hierarchy—just for a small, fleeing moment—have been dissolved. And these things can be said. And expressed. And then it goes away. And then the hierarchy returns.[16]

Doerries recalls one stunning example. In this instance the organizers of an Outside the Wire event being held at a nursing school chose to alter the usual format, preferring to disperse into small breakout sessions right after the performance and prior to coming together for the town-hall style discussion. When they all gathered back together, Doerries reported, in contrast to other group discussions he has facilitated, the most powerful individuals in the room dominated the conversation:

> Normally, what we see when we do the play in a medical setting is that mostly the nurses speak first—the women, mostly. And the women are the ones who can't speak in the normal context. They are the ones who are disempowered. But also because they are the ones who are in front of suffering, who know suffering, who are in the presence of it, who know what it means—what the power of presence mean ... but all these groups went away, and there was only one or two male doctors in every group,

and the rest were nurses, and they all came back . . . and [the respondents] were *all* men, and it was like the hierarchy—just by leaving the room after the performance—had reified itself.[17]

The format of actor readings thus does not only encourage engagement with the text, but a particular *kind* of engagement with these stories. The stories come from the stage, but they also come from the audience. In this immediate and charged moment, the audience considers and comments on complicated, potentially divisive issues. Ideally, these comments generate dialogue that culminates in empathy and understanding across diverse individuals, and perhaps even initiates action that will continue outside the room.

The importance of the scene-based format to the social goal is in evidence in the following examples. Both programs perform scenes that they think invite women affected by war to speak out during the discussion. The Ancient Greeks/Modern Lives program tries to engage issues of importance specifically to women by choosing scenes that focus not only on Ajax's suffering but also on the reality of his wife Tecmessa's vulnerable situation as well as her personal strengths. Meineck reports that these scenes prompt discussion of the specific challenges facing military wives and civilians impacted by war both in war zones and back at home, but also by active duty female service members. He recounted one instance in which a woman Air Force veteran spoke out about a male colleague's violation of trust. She explained that a fellow soldier whom she had always respected told her, during a mock attack, that he would kill her rather than let her fall into the hands of the enemy because *he* could not endure what might happen to *her* (Meineck 2012: 16). Theater of War has tried a different approach. They developed a program that adapts scenes from *Ajax* for performance by a female actor in the lead role. The project's aim seems to be to present a jolting image of a forceful female warrior from Greek mythology—a female Ajax—to unsettle conventional views of women's distance from combat situations in the American military and to highlight the particularities of their experiences of upending psychological trauma. We attended two performances of this program and observed something striking. In contrast to other programs in which veterans in the audience identified with the struggles of the mythic characters and found these portrayals validating, female veterans who spoke out during the discussion after the female Ajax program expressed *both* amazement at how honestly the words and emotions in the texts read by the female actor captured soldiering *and* great irritation with what they perceived to be the text's utter lack of attention to any of the kinds of difficulties that are specific to female soldiers. Since they were unfamiliar with the Greek play or myth and were not prompted at the outset to recognize that this was an imagined rewrite of an ancient source, a number of these speakers expressed delight in learning that venerable Greek mythology included a female warrior and felt validated to that modest extent. But, their stinging disappointment in the scene's shortcomings really stood out. They were struck by the absence of any mention of sex-related belittling and other tensions, including sexual violence, inflicted on female soldiers by their fellow troops, as well as the particular kind of stigmas female veterans suffer in civilian life. Their perception of this gap and eagerness to name it and to bear witness to things not said in the staged readings created powerful moments in which those present—female and male veterans and civilians alike—had to listen to female soldiers' accounts of sexual harassment, sexual assault, and forms of psychological wounds psychiatrist Jonathan Shay has called "moral injuries."[18] Some in the audience who knew the plays found the rewrite nearly impossible to enjoy as theater (present authors included). Knowledge of the play interfered with our ability to see some important details in these scenes. We were caught up in trying to figure out how a specific change would play out in the rest of the drama. However, it is beyond question that these adapted scenes elicited strong reactions from the veterans in the audience and a spirited public airing of normally hidden and overlooked facts of life for women in the military.

Aesthetics

As theatrical events, the performances of Ancient Greeks/Modern Lives and Theater of War are intentionally scaled down. As staged readings, these performances do not employ a set, costumes, or props; they feature actors who appear in regular street clothes, scripts in hand. The staging is limited, with actors usually seated when they are not performing, or acting the entirety of the piece seated from behind a table or standing at a podium. Theater of War, in fact, outlines a brief list of basic technical requirements for all performances: a long table and five chairs, with five microphones; two wireless handheld microphones for the audience; and house lights up for the entire event, with no theatrical lighting necessary.[19] These practices challenge the divide between performer and audience, and between the ancient and the modern.

The two programs' performance styles are distinct, even though they follow similar formats. Theater of War takes the attributes of the staged reading to the extreme by investing in the aural power of the text and pursuing an intentionally "raw" performance. Theater of War's staged readings involve little to no rehearsal among the temporary cast assembled for each particular event. Doerries comments:

> So there is the economic reality, but there is also—as I learned—extreme value in it being rough and raw and under-rehearsed and . . . auditory . . . the note that I give to all actors who work on all of our projects, before they go onstage—and there have been about 120 who have passed through in the last three years, is: "make them wish they'd never come". Now that may not be a genuine feeling—I don't want people to actually walk out, but I want people to *almost* walk out.[20]

This engagement with the text is a direct reflection of the text's status as catalyst, rather than a product intended purely for aesthetic consumption. Theater of War directly confronts traditional expectations about theater and aggressively alerts the audience that the performance is not staged for their pleasure or entertainment. This is especially apparent when the audience is not primarily veterans. Commenting on the expectations of the audience of a performance staged at an academic conference attended by scholars familiar with the sources Doerries said:

> A lot of people came up to me and said, "Oh that was too loud, that was too fast, it was too...."—and that's fine, you know, that's true—if we were doing it for *them*. But when I've got a thousand marines in front of me, it has to be an assault... it's an aural assault. It's loud—what we do is loud—it's fast, it's not what people typically think of as reading. And no stage directions, obviously—so you know, it's a radio play on speed.[21]

In accentuating these qualities of the staged reading—little rehearsal, the focus on the auditory, no movement or stage directions—Theater of War embraces an aesthetic that employs performance and skilled professional actors without submitting to contemporary expectations about how Greek drama should be performed. Further, he objects to the idea that these performances are even "for" a traditional theater-going audience. Instead, the project invests fully in the needs of the communities for which the event is designed. Civilians, if present, are there to listen and to be challenged.

Though Theater of War verbally "assaults" the audience in order to gain their attention, the performers do not physically enact the trauma vocalized. Though their bodies and voices are engaged with the emotion of the text, the performance lacks the specificity that a designer or director's vision would lend a production. With no stage lights or sets, the focus of the performance is not on spectacle or an attempt at a measure of verisimilitude. There is no intention of illusion, or effort to present a fully realized representation of an ancient Greek warrior. As a "radio play on speed," Theater of War audiences of veterans relate the text more fully to their own experiences, undistracted by the details of a full-scale production. For some, this may also serve to instigate but not overwhelm, as military audiences may already viscerally relate to the horrors of the text.

Leaving the house lights on also empowers audience members to publicly share their personal reactions within the context of the communal event (Meineck 2009: 173–4). At one early Theater of War event that employed Aquila members as readers (it predated the Ancient Greeks/Modern Lives project), the audience included numerous military veterans of wars in Iraq, Afghanistan, Vietnam, and Korea. Recalling this event, Meineck observes the "confessional, poignant" nature of the commentary that followed the readings from *Ajax* and *Philoctetes*. He offers that "[t]he acts of watching and being watched became essential to the shared experience that unfolded, and were an important factor in facilitating the remarkably free expression that followed" (Meineck 2009: 174). The connections between audience and performers and among audience members recalls, Meineck suggests, what Josiah Ober refers to as the "inward facing circles" character of fifth-century Athenian theater spaces; they facilitate an exchange of knowledge among the spectators based on the ability to observe and react to others' responses. The Greeks' "seeing-place" is literally in the daylight of the open theater. The act of performance is also a metaphoric "watching," in sense of bearing witness to, and sharing in, another human's story.[22]

The Ancient Greek/Modern Lives' performances are rehearsed and prepared by a touring ensemble affiliated with Aquila Theatre of New York. While still utilizing distinguishing aspects of the staged reading (e.g., script-in-hand, little to no blocking, street clothes, minimal physical distance from the audience), the Homecoming project does offer something more akin to a snippet of a traditional performance. This is crucial for their project because they do not rely on a captive audience on a military base or the professional interests of clinicians and other veterans' advocates to people their audience. Homecoming seeks out the general public, both usual theater-goers and others who might not be inclined to travel to or pay the ticket price for a full-scale performance of a Greek play in a traditional venue. They specifically seek out audiences who might not be aware of the challenges facing active duty and veteran military personnel and to alert the civic community to the concerns of these fellow citizens.

Though lacking the trappings of a full-scale production, staged readings are quality work. As Jan Cohen-Cruz has advocated, we should not presume an automatic aesthetic/utilitarian divide in socially engaged practice.[23] She disavows the connotation that productions that partner with communities in non-traditional ways may be presumed to be "amateurish." Aesthetics and intent are intertwined in social practice (or as Cohen-Cruz terms it, "engaged performance"):

> Aesthetics generally refers to a way of judging the qualities of an art experience, traditionally in such terms as beauty and good taste. Engaged artists do not seek to lower aesthetic standards, but rather to attain qualities of art appropriate to its goals . . . in contrast, some art-making systems call for the art object to be devoid of content, and instead focus rather on a general idea of beauty. Such criteria would be unproductive measures of an art form focused on local meaning and identity . . . singularity about aesthetics is another drawback of some mainstream arts training. (Cohen-Cruz 2010: 168–9)

Likewise, as socially and civically focused practitioners have argued, process- or community-oriented work is still "good theater." However, differing processes that serve the meaning of the project may mark this kind of theatrical work.

Target Audience and Partnerships

Outside the Wire and Ancient Greeks/Modern Lives cultivate different kinds of partnerships between arts and non-arts groups. Their funding models reflect this. Ancient Greeks/Modern Lives performs in venues that welcome civilians and veterans and tries to use its performances to foster new connections among the various members of its own audiences, including with the managers of the venues (chiefly public libraries and community centers), the local community, and scholars at area institutions. Ancient Greeks/Modern Lives' stated objectives include: disseminating quality humanities programming; building new audiences for such events; fostering a public interest in classical literature; and providing opportunity for veterans and families to discuss and examine their experiences, facilitated by the context of classical work. By partnering with libraries, they also aim to invigorate community interest in library resources as well as public and cultural programing, and provide an example of successful partnerships between libraries and arts centers.[24] They leverage Aquila Theatre's "bold reinterpretations of classical plays for contemporary audiences" that "free the spirit of the original work and recreate the excitement of the live performance."[25] The Ancient Greeks/Modern Lives project received support from the National Endowment for the Humanities and the attention of the National Endowment for the Arts and Onassis Public Benefit Foundation.

Outside the Wire defines its mission as "social impact entertainment"[26] and their various programs address public health goals. The project's stated "mission" is to create safe spaces for dialogue, foster candid communication among audiences, elicit understanding across individuals with divergent backgrounds, enable individuals to respond directly to issues within their own community, and circulate knowledge of resources on social or public health topics.[27] It is from this perspective that Theater of War engages active duty military and veterans' communities (Mason 2014). Their funding history, for example, includes support from the Defense Centers of Excellence for Psychological Health and Traumatic Brain Injury (a U.S. Department of Defense organization) and the National Institutes of Health. For years Theater of War collaborated directly only with formal military organizations and performed exclusively for military population. With a grant from the Stavros Niarchos Foundation, Theater of War began training regional theater companies across the country to present Theater of War to mixed civilian and military audiences. They aimed to teach the theater partners "how to leverage the resources regionally and nationally so that everyone new walked away with something, whether it was psychological help or how to get involved as a civilian."[28]

The composition of audiences affects the shape and meaning of the events. Compare, for example, Doerries's reflections on events staged for mixed groups with a large civilian component and those staged on military bases. Regarding the former, Doerries stresses that the exact proportion of military to civilians in the audience can make a big difference. He explains:

> Sometimes when you're performing for a large group of civilians and only a small number of veterans are there, it feels like the project goes back in the direction of what most theater does, which is makes us feel good about our own values and makes us feel more intelligent than we actually are, and sort of pats us on the back for wanting to have this experience. And I'm more interested in people coming into an experience where their presumptions, their judgments, their—the story they tell themselves about who they are and what they believe is confronted and sometimes upended, some by the performance, but mostly by what they hear, by the people sitting right next to them in the audience, and that can only happen when we have a critical mix of people in the audience.... Just coming together in a room and sitting together for two hours is *something*. I'd say ten percent of the audience being the "other," so to speak, for the civilians, is enough ... but when there is a critical enough mass on both sides and both sides open up, it's really powerful.[29]

Regarding events that are closed to the public and staged at sites such as the U.S. Naval Academy, Camp Pendleton, Schreiver Air Force Base, and Guantánamo Bay,[30] Doerries stresses that different kinds of breakthroughs occur. In particular, he asserts that these events temporarily break down hierarchies and grant the troops the freedom to publicly share what are often "tremendously disturbing" personal stories. In Doerries's estimation, this is reflective of ancient theater in that the General is required to "sit up front, and hear the perspective of the hoplite in some way."[31] For instance, on one occasion a service member who had been openly resistant to the entire exercise of attending the performance broke down during the town-hall discussion and confessed that he had been planning violence against members of his own unit because he felt they had betrayed him. Doerries explains, "It's creating that contained safe place where there are also the mental health professionals there to respond."[32] At another event where there were numerous spouses in attendance, a panel composed entirely of military wives matter-of-factly recounted stories of their husbands returning from war, often with traumatic brain injury and post-traumatic stress, and fearing for their family and spouse's safety. One of the men's lives had already ended in suicide. The final panelist stated that she was only able to attend the event because she had someone at home watching her husband. She could not leave him alone, and she could not trust him with their children. One woman in the audience raised her hand and said that while she was moved by the play, she most connected with the panelist who spoke of her husband's mental disintegration and suicide. The same thing happened to her husband, she reported: "he killed himself, and it was just like him, and it was just like Ajax." Women throughout the audience began raising their hands and commenting on the overwhelming similarity of their own experiences, as the General present watched, "his face . . . just ashen." Doerries was convinced that Theater of War would never be invited back. A few weeks later, he received a call from Walter Reed Army Medical Center reporting that the General had arranged a meeting there, and related that after hearing from his community at the Theater of War event, he realized he needed more resources for the families and spouses of his service members. Doerries recounts that though there was substantial risk in uncovering these realities within that community, it was the first time he was aware of Theater of War affecting a change of such magnitude.

The role of the audience in creating the meaning of the event is also evident in a comparison of two Theatre of War events staged within a week of one another in the same city: the first at Chicago's Goodman Theater[33] and the second at the National Veterans Art Museum in downtown Chicago.[34] Both events featured staged readings by members of Chicago's Rivendell Ensemble, the same moderator, and nearly identical panel members. However, the difference in audience composition was striking. At the Goodman, subscribers and theater-goers composed the majority of the audience, many of whom just stood up and left immediately following the performance. They seemed unaware that the town-hall discussion was part of the event even though that format was clearly highlighted in the literature and in the opening remarks of the host. Perhaps they expected a traditional, optional "post-show talkback" and were just not interested. The sparsely attended town-hall meeting nevertheless occasioned some powerful stories. A male veteran stood up and spoke of being angry when he first came home at the fact that people would say that they wanted to hear about his experiences then "switch off" when he started to talk about these. A female veteran raised her voice to vehemently deny that Ajax's bloodlust was an accurate depiction of the female warrior's experience. A mother calmly recalled that her son was forever changed by his deployment and how the betrayal he felt led to his suicide. The rest of the Goodman audience who remained for the session accepted these stories with polite reserve and quietly filed out to return to their own lives. No lively discussion followed. Doerries considers even this modest reaction a success.

> My feeling, some days, is I just want the civilians to listen. Or, I just want those in power to listen to those who have no power—for just 45 minutes. That's all I want. I just want them to actually actively listen with their hearts open, and their minds open.[35]

While the event did not elicit a sense of something akin to *communitas*, where the burden of these realities began to be shared across the audience, we cannot assume that individuals were unmoved by these stories.

A few days later many service members attended Theater of War's performance at the National Veterans Art Museum. The town-hall session was lively; many spoke plainly about the obstacles to dealing with post-war stress, in everything from negotiating the bureaucracy of the Department of Veterans Affairs and the jarringly swift timeline in transitioning from deployment to homecoming, to the reality of military sexual assault and the open hostility that Vietnam veterans encountered. On this occasion the small number of civilians in attendance performed a different role. They largely observed the testimony of military personnel themselves and helped create a temporary community—a "safe" space for critical discussion—by being present and alert. Afterwards, many of the veterans, therapists, and civilians came together to interact and continue to talk for more than an hour, acknowledging one another's experience of the event that had just concluded. Shoulder to shoulder in the National Veterans Art Museum's intimate space, a plurality of individuals formed a public sphere where deeply complicated and sensitive topics could be directly and honestly discussed.

The program also leverages some small details of ancient history to bridge the gap between ancient texts and contemporary issues. Both projects highlight the fact that the ancient playwrights were themselves combat veterans. Doerries typically recalls specific details for Theater of War audiences. For example:

> Sophocles himself was a general. At the time Aeschylus wrote and produced his famous *Oresteia*, Athens was at war on six fronts. The audiences for whom these plays were performed were undoubtedly comprised of citizen-soldiers. Also, the performers themselves were most likely veterans or cadets . . . Given this context, it seemed natural that military audiences today might have something to teach us about the impulses behind these ancient stories. It also seemed like these ancient stories would have something important and relevant to say to military audiences.[36]

When Doerries serves as moderator at Theater of War events, he prompts the audience to reflect on these connections. For instance, after one performance of *Ajax* he reminded the audience that this play was written by a general in a city that had seen 80 years of war, and that it would have been performed for thousands of citizen-soldiers in ancient Greece. He typically opens the town-hall discussion with the query: "What do you think this guy Sophocles was up to? What was his objective?"[37] Pointedly speculating on Sophocles' intentions, Doerries guides the audience to consider and engage with the social objectives of Theater of War for themselves. Sometimes, the proposition is flatly rejected, such as when a Vietnam veteran commented that he was not good with poetry and therefore, "I think there might be something there that actually confuses us, and it's actually *not* helpful . . . [I'd need a] semester's worth of information to figure it out."[38] But this reaction creates meaning as well. Consider an incident at a military base where a service member jumped up to comment on how much he hated the performance. He said it was incredibly boring and that he found it to be one of the worst, most ridiculous things he had ever had to sit through. Doerries reports that this response was highly significant.

> I found myself just like grinning ear to ear, because I believed him. I actually think he didn't like it. I don't think there was anything underlying it. He just hated it. But there was no other context within the military structure where you could go to an event that was mandatory and get up and say, "I thought this was fuckin' bullshit."[39]

As long as this is not the overwhelming majority's reaction, in Doerries's view, this kind of feedback actually "validates the dialogue." We can see this once we recall that at the same event a different service member held up a copy of *Achilles in Vietnam* that he had brought along to the event and related how much both the performance and the Greek example in general spoke to him. Occasioning these two reactions side by side is key to building community spaces—however temporary—where multiple views may be spoken openly and publicly acknowledged.

Concluding Remarks

Viewed as social theater we can see that these projects perform for soldiers in multiple senses. They bring performances of ancient sources to audiences of active duty and veteran military personnel as well as the public. They also mine the material for stories that explicitly engage their experiences of deployment, combat, and homecoming, expecting to facilitate both compassionate self-understanding among these military men and women and generous consideration of their struggles among the full audiences which include veterans' advocates and caregivers as well as the general public. These events have successfully worked to form temporary "public spheres" in which both speaking about and listening to theatrical and first-hand accounts of highly emotional experiences tied to military service have great political import. Sometimes they even spark experiences of what we have referred to as *communitas*, thus helping to bridge the ever-widening gap between military and civilian society. In doing so these projects have a democratizing effect on Greek theater in America by enacting new answers to the question, "Whose stories do these sources address?"

Notes

1. Foley 2012: 159. Auletta and Sellars addressed American militarism more broadly in their staging of Sophocles' *Ajax* (1986) and Sellars took on international refugee crises with his Euripides' *Children of Heracles* (2005). See Foley 2012: 139–58, 259–62 for a detailed account of the performance history.
2. In addition to Dutsch, this volume, also see <http://lysistrataprojectarchive.com/>.
3. Performed at Brooklyn Academy of Music, May 2013. Mendelsohn 2013.
4. See, for example, K. J. Sanchez and Emily Ackerman's *ReEntry* (<http://www.amrec.us/reentry/>); Jonathan Wei's *The Telling Project* (<http://thetellingproject.org/>); and internationally, James Thompson, Michael Balfour, and Jenny Hughes's *In Place of War* Project (<http://www.inplaceofwar.net/>).
5. The Department of Veteran Affairs recognizes drama, along with visual art, creative writing, dance, and music, as "one form of rehabilitative treatment to help Veterans recover from and cope with physical and emotional disabilities," sponsoring an annual National Veterans Creative Arts Competition (<http://www.va.gov/opa/speceven/caf/index.asp>). In the past decade alone, veterans have created theatrical works that engage their experiences as service members and formed companies. For example: Baltimore-based Veteran Artist Program (VAP), Minneapolis' Veterans in the Arts, Los Angeles' United States Veterans' Artists Alliance (USVAA) and Veterans Center for Performing Arts (VCPA), San Francisco's Veteran Artists, and Ohio-based Vet Art Project.
6. Cf. Hardwick and Harrison 2013 on the "democratic turn" in classical receptions work by artists and scholars.
7. "Social practice" is used across a variety of fields in the context of exploring what has been termed a "social turn" in contemporary art. See Jackson 2011.
8. On a possible genealogy of community theater, see Warstat 2005.
9. Cohen-Cruz 2010. See Adamitis and Gamel 2013 on "engaged performance" and contemporary productions of Greek plays.
10. Many note the influence of Brazilian theater practitioner Augusto Boal's "Theatre of the Oppressed." See Cohen-Cruz and Schutzman 1993, and Emert and Friedland 2011.
11. This literature is large. Key contributions include Habermas 1989, Fraser 1990, and Calhoun 1992.
12. Bryan Doerries (Artistic Director, Outside the Wire LLC) in discussion with Laura Lodewyck (June 9, 2012).
13. *Achilles in Vietnam: Combat Trauma and the Undoing of Charac*ter (1994) and *Odysseus in America: Combat Trauma and the Trials of Homecoming* (2002). Consider the following from 1994 (pp. xx–xxi): "[H]aving honored the boundaries of meaning that scholars have pointed out, I can confidently tell you that my reading of the *Iliad* as an account of men in war is not a 'meditation' that is only tenuously rooted in the text . . . This *is* the story of Achilles in the *Iliad*, not some metaphoric translation of it. This was also the story of many combat veterans, both from Vietnam and from other long wars. The reader will find some

of the veterans' narratives disturbing. I have brought them together with the *Iliad* not to tame, appropriate, or co-opt them but to promote a deeper understanding of both, increasing the reader's capacity to be disturbed by the *Iliad* rather than softening the blow of the veterans' stories."
14. "Identifying and Preparing the Panelists," in Theater of War Presentation Package <http://www.outsidethewirellc.com/about/presentation-package>.
15. This interpretation of catharsis, as a structured tension and release that manipulates the audience, differs from his view of catharsis in 1995's *Rainbow of Desire*, in which he uses his theatrical techniques as a therapeutic method intended to help individuals. The catharsis suggested later in Boal's career is "a removal of blocks, not a voiding of desires" (Jackson 1995: xxi).
16. Bryan Doerries (Artistic Director, Outside the Wire LLC) in discussion with Laura Lodewyck (June 9, 2012).
17. Bryan Doerries (Artistic Director, Outside the Wire LLC) in discussion with Laura Lodewyck (June 9, 2012).
18. In Shay's experience counseling veterans, the greatest devastation is inflicted when soldiers feel that they have been neglected or betrayed by their superiors. Shay (1994: 20) argues that "moral injury is an essential part of any combat trauma that leads to lifelong psychological injury. Veterans can usually recover from horror, fear, and grief once they return to civilian life, so long as 'what's right' has not also been violated."
19. "Theater of War Technical Rider," in Theater of War Presentation Package <http://www.outsidethewirellc.com/about/presentation-package>.
20. Bryan Doerries (Artistic Director, Outside the Wire LLC) in discussion with Laura Lodewyck (June 9, 2012).
21. Bryan Doerries (Artistic Director, Outside the Wire LLC) in discussion with Laura Lodewyck (June 9, 2012).
22. Meineck 2009: 174; see also Woodruff 2008: 18, 22–4, 141–3.
23. Cohen-Cruz 2010. See also Thompson 2009.
24. "Ancient Greeks/Modern Lives Press Release", Aquila Theatre Company <http://aquilatheatre.com/home/ancient-greeksmodern-lives-press/>.
25. <http://aquilatheatre.com/about/history/>.
26. This phrase is from their promotional literature. Doerries works together with a producer, Phyllis Kaufman.
27. "Mission," Outside the Wire LLC <http://www.outsidethewirellc.com/about/mission>.
28. Bryan Doerries (Artistic Director, Outside the Wire LLC) in discussion with Laura Lodewyck (June 9, 2012).
29. Bryan Doerries (Artistic Director, Outside the Wire LLC) in discussion with Laura Lodewyck (June 9, 2012).
30. "Past Dates," Theater of War, Outside the Wire, LLC <http://www.outsidethewirellc.com/performances?format=past&month=07&yr=2013>.
31. Bryan Doerries (Artistic Director, Outside the Wire LLC) in discussion with Laura Lodewyck (June 9, 2012).
32. Bryan Doerries (Artistic Director, Outside the Wire LLC) in discussion with Laura Lodewyck (June 9, 2012).
33. Theater of War. "A Dramatic Reading of Scenes from Sophocles' *Ajax*: The Female Warrior Program," Goodman Theater, Chicago (January 18, 2012).

34. Theater of War. "A Dramatic Reading of Scenes from Sophocles' *Ajax*: The Female Warrior Program," National Veterans Art Museum [former location at 1801 S. Indiana Avenue], Chicago (January 25, 2012).
35. Bryan Doerries (Artistic Director, Outside the Wire LLC) in discussion with Laura Lodewyck (June 9, 2012).
36. "Theater of War Overview," Outside the Wire, LLC <http://www.outsidethewirellc.com/projects/theater-of-war/overview>.
37. Doerries, *Theater of War* ("A Pathway Home," annual meeting of The Soldiers Project, University of Southern California, Los Angeles, June 10, 2012).
38. Theater of War ("A Pathway Home," annual meeting of The Soldiers Project, University of Southern California, Los Angeles, June 10, 2012).
39. Bryan Doerries (Artistic Director, Outside the Wire LLC) in discussion with Laura Lodewyck (June 9, 2012).

REFERENCES

Adamitis, J. and M.-K. Gamel (2013), "Theaters of War," in D. Lateiner, B. K. Gold, and J. Perkins eds., *Roman Literature, Gender, and Reception: Domina illustris. Essays in Honor of Judith Peller Hallett*. Routledge monographs in classical studies 13. London.

Alexander, W. (2010), *Is William Martinez Not our Brother? Twenty Years of the Prison Creative Arts Project*. Ann Arbor.

Blatner, A. (ed. 2007), *Interactive and Improvisation Drama: Varieties of Applied Theatre and Performance*. New York.

Boal, A. (1979), *Theatre of the Oppressed*. Trans. C. A. and M.-O. L. McBride. New York. Originally published in Spanish as *Teatro de oprimido* in 1974.

Boal, A. (1995), *The Rainbow of Desire: The Boal Method of Theatre and Therapy*. Trans. A. Jackson. London.

Calhourn, C. (ed. 1992), *Habermas and the Public Sphere*. Cambridge.

Cohen-Cruz, J. (2010), *Engaging Performance: Theatre as Call and Response*. London.

Cohen-Cruz, J. and M. Schutzman (eds. 1993), *Playing Boal: Theater, Therapy, Activism*. New York.

Doerries, B. (2010), "Answering the Call to Help our Soldiers Heal," *Washington Post* (May 31).

Dolan, J. (2005), *Utopia in Performance: Finding Hope at the Theater*. Ann Arbor.

Emert, T. and E. Friedland (eds. 2011), *"Come Closer": Critical Perspectives on Theatre of the Oppressed*. New York.

Foley, H. P. (1999), "Modern Performance and Adaptation of Greek Tragedy," *Transactions of the American Philological Association* 129, 1–12.

Foley, H. P. (2012), *Reimagining Greek Tragedy on the American Stage*. Berkeley, Los Angeles, and London.

Fraser, N. (1990), "Rethinking the Public Sphere: A Contribution to the Critique of Actually Existing Democracy," *Social Text* 24/26, 56–80.

Green, A. (2010), "Theater of War: The Q & A," Art Works: The Official Blog of the National Endowment for the Arts (July 6) <http://artworks.arts.gov/?p=3042>.

Habermas, J. (1989), *The Structural Transformation of the Public Sphere*. Trans. T. Burger with F. Lawrence. Cambridge.

Haedicke, S. C. and T. Nellhaus (eds. 2001), *Performing Democracy: International Perspectives on Urban Community-Based Performance*. Ann Arbor.

Hardwick, L. and S. Harrison (eds. 2013), *Classics in the Modern World: A Democratic Turn?* Oxford.

Jackson, A. (1995), "Translator's Introduction," in A. Boal, *The Rainbow of Desire: The Boal Method of Theatre and Therapy*. London.

Jackson, S. (2011), *Social Works: Performing Art, Supporting Publics*. New York.

Kuftinec, S. (2003), *Staging America: Cornerstone and Community-Based Theater*. Carbondale, IL.

Mason, W. (2014), "You Are Not Alone Across Time: Using Sophocles to Treat PTSD," *Harper's Magazine* (October).

Meineck, P. (2009), "'These Are Men Whose Minds the Dead Have Ravished': Theater of War/ The Philoctetes Project," *Arion* 17, 173–91.

Meineck, P. (2012), "Combat Trauma and the Tragic Stage: 'Restoration' by Cultural Catharsis," *Intertexts* 16.1 (Spring), 7–24.

Mendelsohn, D. (2013), "Herakles: Punished Again," *New York Review of Books* (May 23).

Pinkham, B. (2011), "*Ajax* in Guantanamo," *American Theatre* (July/August), 52–4.

Prendergast, M. and J. Saxton (eds. 2009), *Applied Theatre: International Case Studies and Challenges for Practice*. Bristol.

Prentki, T. and S. Preston (eds. 2009), *The Applied Theatre Reader*. London.

Rohd, M. (2012), "Translations: The Distinction between Social and Civic Practice and Why I Find it Useful," *HowlRound.com* (September 1).

Shay, J. (1994), *Achilles in Vietnam: Combat Trauma and the Undoing of Character*. New York.

Shay, J. (1995), "The Birth of Tragedy—Out of the Needs of Democracy," *Didaskalia* 2.2.

Shay, J. (2002), *Odysseus in America: Combat Trauma and the Trials of Homecoming*. New York.

Taylor, P. (2003), *Applied Theatre: Creating Transformative Encounters in the Community*. Portsmouth.

Thompson, J. (2009), *Performance Affects: Applied Theatre and the End of Effect*. Basingstoke.

Thompson, J. and R. Schechner (2004), "Why 'Social Theatre'?," *TDR: The Drama Review* 48.3 (Fall), 11–16.

Tritle, L. (2000), *From Melos to My Lai: A Study in Violence, Culture and Social Survival*. London.

Tritle, L. (2009), *A New History of the Peloponnesian War*. Chichester.

Turner, V. (1982), *From Ritual to Theatre: The Human Seriousness of Play*. New York.

Warstat, M. (2005), "Community Building within a Festival Frame: Class Celebrations in Germany, 1918–1933," *Theatre Research International* 30, 262–73.

Woodruff, P. (2008), *The Necessity of Theater: The Art of Watching and Being Watched*. Oxford.

CHAPTER 38

GREEK DRAMA IN CANADA

Women's Voices and Minority Views

HALLIE REBECCA MARSHALL

GREEK drama does not hold a significant place in the landscape of Canadian theater, but I hope to demonstrate that there are a number of places where, in various forms, classical plays have found fertile ground. The most significant single production of an ancient Greek play in Canada was the 1954/5 Stratford Festival production of *Oedipus Rex*, using W. B. Yeats's adaptation, directed by Tyrone Guthrie (see Introduction, this volume). Guthrie remounted the production in Australia in the 1970s, and Douglas Campbell, who played Oedipus in the original Stratford production and in the film, directed a remount of Guthrie's production for the Stratford Festival in 1997.[1] The production was an important moment in the reception of Greek drama, for both its approach to staging and its impact, even though it was engaged far more with British theater traditions than Canadian ones. Guthrie wrote in his autobiography of the importance to his early seasons of critics coming from New York to see the productions and writing enthusiastically about what they had seen:

> This was just what we needed. Canadians, very understandably and through the modesty of inexperience, lack self-confidence in artistic judgment. They are apt to wait to be told what to like, and why. (Guthrie 1959: 334–5)

Guthrie would likely be affirmed in his opinion of his Canadian audiences if he were to learn that for Canadians who know of his *Oedipus*, the production is most notable for the fact that actors Bruno Gerussi and William Shatner performed in the chorus.[2]

The university productions of Greek plays in Canada in the first part of the twentieth century have begun to receive critical attention (see Day, this volume). The more recent performances, however, although unlauded internationally, are equally significant because of their regular stagings of Greek drama in Canada. Both the Classics Drama Group at Trent University and the United Players of Vancouver are especially worthy of note because they could both be broadly classified as community theater. This categorization reflects more the intended audience than the participants, at least some of whom are professionals in their fields, be it Theater or Classics. Both groups have an established tradition of performing Greek drama, dating back to the mid-1990s. The Classics Drama Group (CDG), also known as the Desmond Conacher Players, has been producing classical Greek plays for 20 years at Trent University in Peterborough, Ontario.[3] Founded by Martin Boyne, an instructor in the Department of Ancient History and Classics, the intent of the group was to "provide an extra-curricular activity for students within the Department, to allow the students in the course on ancient drama (Classical Literature 100) the opportunity to watch (and evaluate) a Greek play in action, and to explore how an ancient play would respond to production in modern circumstances."[4] The CDG have produced 20 Greek plays, the majority of which have been tragedies.[5] United Players, the resident company at the Jericho Arts Centre in Vancouver, British Columbia, has also had a longstanding commitment to the performance of classical drama, including a classical Greek play regularly in their season, beginning with a production of Euripides' *Trojan Women* in 1995.[6] The impact of both companies lies not in the legacy of any single production, but rather in their commitment to the performance of ancient Greek drama in English translations which have made these plays accessible to community audiences. While the total audience numbers for these productions ranged from a few hundred to at most 2,000, over the course of the past 20 years they have provided access to Greek drama in performance to large numbers of people who would otherwise be likely to have had little to no engagement with ancient plays.

A more international dimension for Greek drama in Canada has been provided by the work of famous poets and playwrights. The translations and adaptations by important figures in Canadian literature, particularly poets Anne Carson and Gwendolyn MacEwen, have been most influential here (see further Carson and Prins, this volume).[7] Both Carson and MacEwen have written translations and adaptations of Greek plays, but neither was particularly involved in production. Gwendolyn MacEwen (1941–87) came to take an interest in Greek drama through Leon Major, then artistic director of the St. Lawrence Centre, who in 1977 invited her to provide a new translation of a Greek tragedy. Together they decided on Euripides' *Trojan Women* (published 1979). While the world of the theater was new to MacEwen, the world of Greece was not. In the fall of 1971 she had traveled to Greece with her fiancé Nikos Tsingos for their wedding. The journal which she kept during her time there, completed after a second trip to Greece in 1976 and published as the travelogue *Mermaids and Ikons*, reveals how enraptured she was by the country and its customs. For a brief time she and Nikos ran a Canadian version of a Greek taverna, decorating it in terracotta, black, and ochre to evoke ancient Greek pottery, with images drawing inspiration from antiquity painted on the walls. But while MacEwen brought an enthusiasm for the classical Greek past, she was not well versed in the classical tradition. She had no post-secondary education and in fact did not finish high school, having quit a few months prior to graduation (Sullivan 1995: 66). Her knowledge of modern Greek came from teaching herself the language with the help of her then husband, who collaborated with her on her translations of works from ancient and modern Greek into English. It is not clear what texts she worked from in producing her adaptation of *Trojan Women*. Her primary concerns seem to have been that her language would work onstage—she had never written for theater before—and what she saw to be the theme of the play. In a letter to the play's director, quoted in a biography of MacEwen, she wrote of her view that the play was about Hecuba's discovery and breakdown in the face of the slow dawning realization that women are as much responsible for the war as men and that perhaps the play had something to say about "the misdirected forces of both male and female sexuality" (Sullivan 1995: 288). Shelagh Wilkinson described MacEwen's *Trojan Women* as a "rare thing—a creative—rather than critical response to a classical text. MacEwen captures in her drama what feminist critics seek to achieve theoretically as the revision of the androcentric canon" (Wilkinson 1987: 81).

The St. Lawrence Centre production of MacEwen's version of *Trojan Women* opened on November 20, 1978 and was well received.[8] MacEwen's adaptation has been staged a number of times since then, primarily in Canada.[9] *Trojan Women* was not MacEwen's only venture into ancient Greek theater, though it seems to have been the only one to reach the stage. Her published works also include a posthumously published adaptation of Aristophanes' *Birds*, the first draft of which, according to the catalogue of her papers held at The Thomas Fisher Rare Book Library at the University of Toronto, dates to 1972. According to the same catalogue records, she also seems to have done a substantial amount of work on "Andromache" (presumably Euripides' play of that name, though possibly Andromache's scenes in *Trojan Women*) beginning in 1974, though this has never been published. She also published translations of Greek poet Yannis Ritsos's poems "Helen" and "Orestes" (published with *Trojan Women* in 1981).

The translations of Anne Carson (b. 1950) represent a very different path of reception from those of MacEwen. Carson completed a Ph.D. in Classics at the University of Toronto in 1981. She has been described variously as Professor of Classics, poet, translator, and essayist. Much of her work is explicitly rooted in the classical world. While there is little in common between the translations and adaptations of Carson and MacEwen, they share a tendency toward feminist readings of Greek tragedy—perhaps a trait of female Canadian poets, given Margaret Atwood's similarly feminist reading of Greek myth in her novella *Penelopiad* (2005, adapted for the stage in 2007). Carson noted in her essay "The Gender of Sound" that women in the stories of the ancient Greeks often "make themselves objectionable by the way they use their voice," and there is a strong commitment in her translations and adaptations to express meaningfully these females voices.[10]

Her first translation of a Greek play was Sophocles' *Electra*, published in 2001. The translation was commissioned not for performance, but for a new Oxford University Press series which was motivated by

> the conviction that poets like Aeschylus, Sophocles, and Euripides can only be properly rendered by translators who are themselves poets. Scholars may, it is true, produce useful and perceptive versions. But our most urgent present need is for a

re-creation of these plays—as though they had been written, freshly and greatly, by masters fully at home in the English of our own times. (Carson 2001: v)

Carson went on to publish *Grief Lessons: Four Plays by Euripides* (2006) and *An Oresteia* (2009), which included Aeschylus' *Agamemnon*, Sophocles' *Elektra*, and Euripides' *Orestes*. Most recently she has done an adaptation of Sophocles' *Antigone*, called *Antigonick* (2012), which received a staged reading at the NYU Gallatin School in the spring of 2013.[11] Judith Butler, who played Creon at the NYU reading, describes the published text in a review, saying,

> Every line of *Antigonick* is printed in boldface handwriting, emphatic, as if something urgent and excessive has to be loudly said. The title and the format suggest that this is a translation of Sophocles' *Antigone* with illustrations. . . . Carson does not "rewrite" *Antigone*. Her text becomes the verbal visual scanning of a prolonged scream or cry. Emphatic, elliptical, *Antigonick* is more transference that translation, a relay of tragedy into a contemporary vernacular that mixes with archaic phrasing, sometimes lacking commas and periods, a halting and then a rushing of words structured by the syntax of grief and rage, spanning centuries . . . at other moments, the text becomes downright discursive. For instance, the sisters Antigone and Ismene self-conciously incorporate bits of Hegel, Beckett, and Freud into their famous standoff, knitting the reception of Antigone into the play itself. (Butler 2012)

While Carson's translations of Greek tragedy have often been performed, her translations, as is the case with all of her poetry, have become increasingly difficult and, for some, inaccessible. Given the poetic uniqueness of Carson's language, it is not surprising that most reviews of the productions of her texts devote more attention to the translation than is typical of most reviews of performances of ancient Greek drama. Both Carson's and MacEwen's translations and adaptations are selected for production because of their poetic language, which is perhaps why they are the most commonly produced Canadian versions of Greek plays.

The most interesting stagings of Greek drama in Canada, however, are two relatively recent productions that use adaptations of Greek tragedy to address aboriginal issues.[12] The first one, unusually for a production of Greek drama, made the national news when an attempt was made to ban it.[13] Its significance, however, is not simply that it made headlines, but rather that it points to the more interesting uses of classical drama in Canada and the cultural spaces where it has been employed for political purposes. Cree lawyer and playwright Deanne Kasokeo, a member of the Saskatchewan Poundmaker Cree Nation, rewrote Sophocles' *Antigone*, setting it on a modern reserve, and used the narrative to explore issues of aboriginal governance, a difficult issue in Canada both on and off reserves.[14] Canadian First Nations reserves are typically governed by a band council headed by a chief, with some councils and chiefs being selected through traditional customs and social structures, while others are elected. Kasokeo's play is set on a reserve with a corrupt band Chief. In her version of the story, Antigone wants to bury her brother, who had been banished from the reserve by the Chief for threatening to make public the fact that the Chief was misspending band money (Hodgson 2002: 107).

As Floyd Favel, director of Kasokeo's *Antigone*, has noted, "On a First Nations Reserve, the Chief has the power to banish people or to prevent burial" (Favel 2012: 1). The plot follows that of Sophocles' play closely, with the illicit burial of Polynices and the deaths of Haemon and Antigone, though the language is adapted to the situation and characters added, such as RCMP officers. The play was first performed as a staged reading by the Red Tattoo Ensemble in 1998 at the Globe Theatre in Regina, Saskatchewan, and premièred as a workshop production in 2001.[15] It was subsequently performed in a number of aboriginal communities in the province, supported in part by a grant from the Saskatchewan Arts Board.

Kasokeo's *Antigone* made national headlines in the spring of 2011 when the Chief and some band council members tried to stop a performance of the play on the Poundmaker reserve. Band Chief Duane Antoine took the play to be specifically about his leadership of the reserve, despite the fact that Kasokeo had written the play before he became Chief. Apparently it had been suggested to him that Antigone was meant to be read as "Antoine gone" (Favel 2012: 2). A closed band meeting was held and a resolution was passed forbidding any public performance of *Antigone* on the reserve. Supported by a band councillor who had voted against banning the performance, they were let into the local school where the performance went ahead.[16] Kasokeo has been clear that the play was not intended to be about one specific band, stating,

> There's a lot of universal issues and contemporary issues with our own governance systems and we need to stop and take a good look and see what we have become because of the imposition of the Indian Act on our governance structure. Our values as First Nations people have gone by the wayside. We need to bring them back and we need to use them in our lives and in our governance.[17]

Yet while the play was not specifically about the Poundmaker reserve, the Chief's response to the play seems to have motivated Kasokeo and Favel, both Poundmaker band members, and others to seek to remove him and other council members from the leadership roles they held. Through their traditional band electoral system Chief Antoine and others were voted out of office in 2012. However, in the words of Favel, "The results of this legal tradition were ignored by the unaccountable leadership and by the Department of Indian Affairs, and unaccountable business continued as usual in my community."[18]

Kasokeo's version of Sophocles' *Antigone* ended up speaking not only to the universal experience of indigenous communities across Canada who are struggling with governance and maintaining traditional values under the influence of colonization and the strictures of the Indian Act, but also, inadvertently, most loudly to the particular situation in her ancestral community. In addition to the direct and immediate impact that the production had on the Poundmaker reserve, and in other communities where it was performed, the play was important on a national scale for opening a space for dialogue about issues of native governance that could be conducted with a more neutral framework than is often the case. Native issues in Canada are often fraught on both a political and community level, with widespread racism often making it difficult to address meaningfully the issues facing aboriginals in Canada. As Jesse Barber noted of Kasokeo's play:

> These aren't just Indian problems. What happens in Saskatchewan in the media often is that it gets turned into as if these are problems that are always plaguing Indian politics. But this play shows that the issues we are facing today are really universal. They're issues that the ancient Greeks faced. That helps to break some of the stereotypes that get put on Indian politics.[19]

Marie Clements's 1994 play *Age of Iron* also uses a classical Greek tragedy to explore the indigenous experience in Canada, though in more complex ways than Kasokeo's *Antigone*. Clements is a Métis artist whose work is increasingly multimedia and insistently intercultural. From *Age of Iron*, her first play, onward, Clements has worked to create theater that not only addresses the experiences of Canadian aboriginal communities, but especially the experience of aboriginal women, who are more often than not deprived of any voice in any forum in Canada. Sheila Rabillard has described what Clements does in *Age of Iron* as indigenizing, "drawing on the ancient play selectively and localizing it. Her localization is unusual in that she creates a double setting and a palimpsest of Trojan and Indigenous referents" (Rabillard 2010: 118).

The intent behind Clements's play was not to produce a version of Euripides' *Trojan Women*, but rather "a serious desire to understand and integrate the elemental connections between Greek mythology and Native thought" (Gilbert 2007: 148). There is an explicit self-awareness within *Age of Iron* that it is rewriting the Greek narrative, at times echoing Euripides' words yet also radically departing to create its own narrative, but never mapping easily on to the original. The Trojans become aboriginal people, with the Greeks being portrayed as what might best be described in this context as colonial agents, such as police officers and social workers. This transference of the narrative and its characters from a mainstream western perspective to an indigenous one skews and changes how the story and characters are read. While professions such as police officer and social worker would be seen by most Canadians as noble professions, the good guys so to speak, Clements reframes them to be seen from an indigenous point of view, through which they become threatening agents of colonial power structures which destroy indigenous communities by many means, including the forcible removal of children from their homes to be educated at residential schools where they often suffered horrific abuse.

Where Kasokeo's *Antigone* is an adaptation, Clements's *Age of Iron* is something else entirely—more a cultural negotiation. The action of the play is extraordinarily difficult to summarize, in part because the narrative is non-linear, with fluidity in the time and space it occupies. Severini valiantly tries to encapsulate the play in a brief description, but has to describe the characters separately from the action of the play:

> The four central characters of *Age of Iron*, dubbed the Trojan Street Warriors, are street people of downtown Vancouver, or "Urban Troy", who are depicted as imprisoned by the victorious Greeks after the Trojan War. The priestess Cassandra is cast as a First Nations prostitute who has been sexually abused at the hands of a priest . . .

> The queen of Troy, Hecuba, is a black bag lady who mourns the daughter that had been taken from her. The other two original Trojan women, Andromache and the Spartan Helen, are not used. In their place Clements places two First Nations men—Wiseguy, an older alcoholic man who functions as a First Nations Elder, and Raven, a younger man in the role of the Trickster. Raven also represents First Nations children who grew up in foster homes, detached from their culture and family heritage.
> (Severini 2010: 183)

There are additionally two choruses: the Sister Chorus, a group of murdered First Nations women, and the System Chorus, who represent "the voices of social, law and governmental bodies which govern the urban Troy."[20] The action of the play departs radically from Euripides' *Trojan Women*. The play begins with Wiseguy and the Walls of Troy speaking not so much to each other as to the audience. Wiseguy uncovers Mother Earth from beneath the pavement. Others seek to remember what has happened to them in the past, but Raven refuses. Raven rapes Cassandra resulting in the arrival of the System Chorus. The System Chorus prompts Hecuba to remember the child that they once took from her. The second act is primarily focused on Cassandra reliving the past, when she was taken to a residential school as a child, returning to the present where she seeks justice from Apollo but realizes that there will be no justice for her, or validation of her experiences, within the world represented by the System Chorus.

The ending of the play is about survival in the face of such suffering and injustice, but there is also a plea from Cassandra to Raven for a new song: "Sing it, so others might hear and know they are not alone, that we are all there in voices ancient and new, too many to be silenced" (Daniels, Clements, and Kane 2001: 270). The use of a Greek tragedy as the underlying model in this play functions both to create a space for dialogue about the native experience in Canada, but it also simultaneously problematizes the use of that model. The inclusion of figures such as Raven points to the fact that Canada has its own rich mythological tradition and performance tradition within aboriginal communities. There are ancient voices, such as Mother Earth, in the existing mythology. To reach a mainstream Canadian audience, however, even if the primary intent is to discuss the experiences of aboriginal communities, the narratives need to be framed in terms familiar to theater audiences from the western tradition, with the inclusion of voices deemed to hold authority for them. Clements is insistent that there needs to be an aboriginal voice in the narrative as well, though, and creates a new kind of story that blends the canonical western tradition with aboriginal tradition and experience. In doing so, she points to the cultural imbalance in storytelling, in which certain kinds of stories are privileged while others are either ignored or silenced. Clements points to a question that should be uncomfortable for any audience—why are we more moved by the plight of Hecuba than by that of aboriginal women in our own communities, destroyed not by war but by decades of racist policies that have wrought havoc on aboriginal communities with intergenerational legacies of poverty, alcoholism, and broken families. Clements's *Age of Iron* is not an easy play in any sense, but it is perhaps the most important reception of Greek drama in Canada to date.

Notes

1. For a review of the 1997 remount, see Bowman 1997.
2. William Shatner is well known internationally, particularly for his role as Captain Kirk in the original *Star Trek* series. Bruno Gerussi starred as Nick Adonidas in CBC's *The Beachcombers*, the longest running weekly dramatic series in Canadian television history (1972–90).
3. Desmond Conacher was for many years Canada's leading scholar of Greek drama, teaching at the University of Toronto 1958–84. Conacher was involved in the founding of the Classics department at Trent University in the mid-1960s. Following his death in October 2000, the CDG decided to add "The Conacher Players" to their name as a memorial to Conacher, who, along with his wife Mary, had been a loyal supporter of their productions over the years.
4. For the history of the Classics Drama Group at Trent University, see Boyne 1998 and <http://www.trentu.ca/ahc/drama_history.php>.
5. In addition to the 20 regular productions in the CDG seasons, there were also affiliated productions at Trent University of Sophocles' *Philoctetes* in 2010 and Plautus' *Curculio* in 1996. *Curculio* was produced by Modern Actors Staging Classics (MASC) directed by C. W. Marshall. With MASC and other groups Marshall has staged a number of ancient plays, including Greek tragedies and comedies. For a list of productions, see <http://www2.cnrs.ubc.ca/masc/>. The company has been inactive since its production of *Rhesus* in 2001 and so has not been included in the discussion above.
6. The company has produced 13 ancient plays between 1995 and 2013. A complete list of plays can be found on the company website at <http://www.unitedplayers.com/Pages/History.html>.
7. For a more extensive survey of translations of Greek drama in Canada, including some French translations, see Marshall 1998.
8. See the review/interview by Adachi 1978.
9. On the Inner Stage production, see Humphrey 1994. For a review of the 2012 Alumnae Theatre production, see D'Amico 2012, which also makes reference to a previous production of the play by the same company in their 1992/3 season. There were also productions by the Durham ShoeString Performers in 1980, at St. Thomas University in November 1996, Georgia College and State University in 2005, The University of Calgary in February 2012, Aurora University in November 2013.
10. Carson 1995: 120. See also the essay "Screaming in Translation" in Carson 2001: 41–8.
11. For a review of the reading, see Maxwell 2013: 175–92.
12. There are a number of terms used in Canada to describe its original people, but there is not a single universally agreed upon term. I have used a variety of terms in what follows, all intended to be respectful. First Nations is used only in the discussion of the *Antigone*, which is associated with a particular kind of native community and system of governance, as it is a term that excludes Inuit and Métis peoples. Indian is used only in reference to the Indian Act, which is a statute of the Canadian government, and consequently the term Indian is irrevocably tied to colonial governance of the native population.
13. For stories on the banning of the play from Canadian media, see <http://www.cbc.ca/news/canada/saskatchewan/adapted-greek-tragedy-banned-on-sask-reserve-1.1120211>.
14. In her acknowledgments following the published text of the play in Hodgson 2002: 132, Kasokeo writes, "This adaptation is set on a contemporary Indian reserve. To properly understand the plot, one must understand the context. In the late 19th century, Indian

people agreed to share their land with the arriving European settlers. These arrangements were formalized and legalized through treaty. More than a century of colonial politics has led to the situation portrayed in this play."

15. On the early production history, see Hodgson 2002: 132. The play was filmed in the summer of 2013, produced by Miyawata Films in partnership with Kunuk Cohn Productions.
16. While the performance went ahead, it would be wrong to suggest that the issues raised by the attempted banning were resolved. In addition to attempting to ban the play, Favel and Kasokeo were fired from their jobs on a literacy project at the reserve school, which involved recording and transcribing the oral history of their community. Allegedly the Chief had also threatened band members, proclaiming that anyone who went to see *Antigone* "would be fired from their jobs and any benefits to them or their family members would be suspended." See Favel 2012: 3.
17. See Kasokeo's comments in an article published by The Aboriginal Multi-Media Society (AMMSA) <http://www.ammsa.com/publications/saskatchewan-sage/play-banned-poundmaker-chief-and-council>.
18. Favel 2012: 1. In 2012 Chief Antoine and others were charged with various crimes and in 2013 were found guilty of stealing land entitlement money from their own band. Despite the charges and convictions, they remained in power on the reserve. See <http://www.huffingtonpost.ca/2013/03/08/poundmaker-first-nation-theft-case_n_2839416.html>.
19. <http://www.carillonregina.com/a-first-nations-twist-on-a-greek-classic/>.
20. Daniels, Clements, and Kane 2001: 195. According to government statistics, native women in Canada are far more likely to die violent deaths than other Canadian women. The abuse of native women is a pervasive problem in Canadian society, often implicitly supported by government policies and practices.

References

Adachi, K. (1978), "Poet Trying her Luck With Euripides Classics and Smattering of Jazz," *Toronto Star*, November 21.

Bowman, L. (1997), "Sophocles' *Oedipus Rex*," *Didaskalia* 4.01. <http://www.didaskalia.net/issues/vol4no1/bowmana.html> accessed January 31, 2014.

Boyne, M. R. (1998), "Old and New Directions: 'Translating' Euripides on a Modern Stage", in J. P. Bews et al. eds., *Celebratio: Thirtieth Anniversary Essays at Trent University*. Peterborough, 22–33.

Butler, J. (2012), "Can't Stop Screaming," *Public Books* September 5. <http://www.publicbooks.org/fiction/cant-stop-screaming> accessed January 31, 2014.

Carson, A. (1995), *Glass, Irony and God*. New York.

Carson, A. (2001), *Sophocles: Electra*. Introduction and notes by M. Shaw. Oxford.

Carson, A. (2006), *Grief Lessons: Four Plays by Euripides*. New York.

Carson, A. (2010), *An Oresteia: Agamemnon by Aiskhylos; Elektra by Sophokles; Orestes by Euripides*. London.

Carson, A. (2012), *Antogonick*. Illustrated by B. Stone. New York.

D'Amico, C. (2012), "'It's a Man's World': Alumnae Theatre Company Presents MacEwen's Masterful Adaptation of *The Trojan Women*," *Toronto Review of Books* January 31. <http://www.torontoreviewofbooks.com/2012/01/its-a-mans-world-alumnae-theatre-company-presents-macewans-masterful-adaptation-of-the-trojan-women/> accessed January 31, 2014.

Daniels, G., M. Clements, and M. Kane (2001), *DraMétis: Three Métis Plays*. Penticton.
Favel, F. (2012), "Antigone: Anatomy of a Drama in a First Nations Community," *IPAA Journal: Claiming Space*, 1–3.
Gilbert, R. (2007), "Profile: Marie Clements," *Baylor Journal of Theatre and Performance* 4.1, 147–51.
Gilbert, R. (2010), "Introduction: Marie Clements," *TRiC/RTaC* 31.2, v–xxvii.
Guthrie, T. (1959), *A Life in the Theatre*. New York.
Hodgson, H. (ed. 2002), *The Great Gift of Tears*. Regina.
Humphrey, C. (1994), "Use of the Chorus in the Inner Stage Production of MacEwen's *Trojan Women*," *Didaskalia* 1.5. <http://www.didaskalia.net/issues/vol1no5/chorus.html> accessed January 31, 2014.
MacEwen, G. (1978), *Mermaids and Ikons: A Greek Summer*. Toronto.
MacEwen, G. (1979). *Trojan Women*. Toronto.
MacEwen, G. and N. Tsingos (1981), *Trojan Women: The Trojan Women by Euripides and Helen and Orestes by Ritsos*. Toronto.
Macintosh, F. (2009), *Sophocles: Oedipus Tyrannus*. Cambridge.
Marshall, C. W. (1998), "Beyond Canadian Translations of Greek Drama," in H. Patrikou ed., Ἡ Μετάφραση τοῦ Ἀρχαίου Ἑλληνικοῦ Δράματος σὲ ὅλες τὶς γλῶσσες τοῦ κόσμου. Athens.
Maxwell, M. (2013), "Questions & Comments from the Audience," *Arion* 21.1, 175–92.
Rabillard, S. (2010), "*Age of Iron*: Adaptation and the Matter of Troy in Clement's Indigenous Urban Drama," *TRiC/RTaC* 31.2, 118–42.
Rossi, A. (1977), *Astonish Us in the Morning: Tyrone Guthrie Remembered*. London.
Severini, G. (2010), "'You Do Not Understand ME': Hybridity and Third Space in *Age of Iron*," *TRiC/RTaC* 31.2, 182–92.
Sullivan, R. (1995), *Shadowmaker: The Life of Gwendolyn MacEwen*. Toronto.
Wilkinson, S. (1987), "Gwendolyn MacEwen's Trojan Women: Old Myth into New Life," *Canadian Woman Studies/Les Cahiers de la femme* 8.3, 81–3.

PART VII
PRACTITIONER PERSPECTIVES

CHAPTER 39

ON REMIXING THE CLASSICS AND DIRECTING COUNTEE CULLEN'S *MEDEA* AND LAW CHAVEZ'S *SEÑORA DE LA PINTA*

An Interview with Theater Director Daniel Banks

PATRICE RANKINE AND DANIEL BANKS

As I walk down seemingly endless flights of stairs and through labyrinthine corridors to the University of New Mexico's Experimental Theatre, which clearly keeps to the tradition of Black Box theater, its very entryway dark and curtained, I am greeted by a poster-sized chart that looks like a mythological family tree. The diagram is, in fact, an outline of the important details of how the New Mexico Penitentiary riot of February 2–3, 1980 unfolded.[1] The death toll numbered 33, with over 200 people injured, including guards and inmates. The scenario is typical: overcrowding, poor diet and treatment, and the general sense of vertigo that must come from living in such conditions led to one of the most violent prison riots in American history. The riots started when two prisoners overpowered an officer and began taking hostages. By the end of the riot, guards had been raped or severely beaten; family members lost loved ones. As becomes clear in Law Chavez's *Señora de la pinta* (2012), the play for which I have come to New Mexico and to which this chart is relevant, what happened in that prison during those days is unspeakable, perhaps as unspeakable as, say, a plague, the plague with which Sophocles' *Oedipus the King* opens. Daniel Banks is directing this play, and from what I know of Daniel, I am in for an experience. The descent into the Black Box was just a prelude.

Along with dancer Adam McKinney, Banks founded the arts and service organization DNAWORKS in 2006. Heritage, healing, and identity: these are central concerns for Banks. He sees that "clearly over the last twenty-five years or so, there's been more and more conversation about people of color, different marginalized groups—lesbian, gay, bisexual, and transgender (LGBT) theater; a theater by women, Black theater, Latino theater, Asian theater; and much less so, but still equally significant, theater by, with, and for people of multiple abilities."[2] DNAWORKS is the outgrowth of Banks's lifelong desire to fill the void, namely the underrepresentation of certain groups that existed in theater. The company has produced such works as McKinney's solo performance, *HaMapah/ The Map*, a "multimedia, genealogical, dance journey," which Banks directed. Through photography, speech, dance, and music, under Banks's direction McKinney expresses the complexity of his own background, as a man of mixed heritage: African-American, Native American, and Ashkenazi and Sephardic Jewish. "I am . . . whole, and full, and all, and not half anything," McKinney declares, as his body stretches to recall all that he is that might not be visible; we see what we think we see: a black man, a man of mixed heritage—it all depends on our experiences. For Banks, identity itself emerges out of body, movement, and expression. Identity includes not only gender and ethnicity, but also the sorts of experiences one has in life, even unexpected and traumatic ones. As one of many examples he shared, Banks cherishes the work he and McKinney did at a hospital in Tel Aviv in 2009 with two teenagers, ages 15 and 19, who were maimed in the attack on the LGBT center earlier that year:

> Their social worker, who is a friend of ours, said that they had been saying that they would never dance again and, without missing a beat, Adam and I just in unison, without even looking at each other, said, "Of course they will." So we went in, and we did a weekly dance workshop with them. Because their upper bodies were mobile, and their wheelchairs were mobile. And there was all kinds of movement and dance happening there.

Banks's early influences include the intense physicality of Romanian émigré Andrei Serban's work, especially *Fragments of a Greek Trilogy*; the composition and socio-political critique of Ping Chong's theatrical landscapes; and the explosive aesthetic of celebration and ritual of Urban Bush Women. "Environmental" rolls off of Daniel's tongue, but it is his own, inflected iteration of the term, inclusive of multiple geographic and cultural heritages, Black American writers of the 1970s and 1980s, and, by 1992, hip-hop. He studied physical theater in Paris, France, in the early 1990s, influenced by meeting, while in college, "master movement teachers from the UK, who were approaching theater from a place of some sort of more physical honesty and emotional honesty." In Paris he was part of an international studio, with some 45 countries represented. While not working with him directly, the "godfather of this movement" was Peter Brook, whose theater also deeply impacted Banks.

The freedom and openness of the Paris experience, however, contrasts with the closed doors Daniel and others faced in New York in the mid-1990s when they tried to advance their projects. "It was literally knock on doors, and hope that they might shout something at you from the other side. I mean, the number of people that actually opened the door to say 'hello' was slim." Artists such as Daniel created their own theater movement: "We just started making work." Thus began his interaction with hip-hop theater. (See Wetmore, this volume.) And here again, evident in Daniel's perspective on hip-hop theater, is how his notions of multiple abilities, marginality, language, and the body meet. He began workshopping a piece that would bring together the writings of such authors as Nikki Giovanni, Audre Lorde, and Sonia Sanchez, whose *Sister Son/Ji* (1969) Banks calls "a quintessential American play," which was little known or performed by that time. Banks made it his business to start "digging into" their writing with other artists: "And again, none of us thought of it as Hip Hop. I mean, really, at that point, Hip Hop to the general public sort of meant Tupac and Biggie." Banks cites Ntozake Shange's *for colored girls who have considered suicide/when the rainbow is enuf* (1975), Stevie Wonder, Parliament, and plays like Abiola Abrams's and Antoy Grant's *Goddess City* (1998) and Anthony Sparks's *Ghetto Punch* (1999) all in the same breath: "So what happened was, and I just think this is a really important moment, because it's easy to put a label on something after the fact, but the process of how it's defined was a group of artists committed—a community of artists committed—to a particular representation of self."[3]

Banks brought his particular sensibility to two of the major classical plays he has staged: Countee Cullen's *Medea*, at Williams College, in 2002; and Law Chavez's *Señora de la pinta*, in April 2012, at the University of New Mexico, in Albuquerque. Cullen (1903–46), who was one of the most important poets of the Harlem Renaissance, wrote his *Medea* in 1935 but never staged it, the story goes, in part because of the untimely death in 1936 of Rose McClendon, whom he intended for the lead role.[4] The fact is that Cullen's star was already somewhat in decline, and it would not have been easy to integrate the aesthetics of the Harlem Renaissance with a strident (European) classicism, even with the breadth of perspectives that Alain Locke advocated in his 1925 volume, *The New Negro* (Locke 1999). By 1938, Cullen had written a prologue and epilogue for the play, evidence that Euripides' masterpiece still occupied his thoughts. Despite the evidence of his homosexuality, Cullen married twice, once to the daughter of W. E. B. Du Bois, Yolande, from 1928 to 1930, and then to Ida Mae Robertson in 1940.

Law Chavez's *Señora de la pinta* was part of the Words Afire! Festival of new plays, an occasion when emerging playwrights showcase their work, produced by then Chair of Dramatic Writing and festival Artistic Director Elaine Avila. The play "is based on Sophocles' *Oedipus the King* with the Chicano emphasis of loyalty and honor as well as cultural complexities of sexual identity and gender expression."[5] "Gringo", or Vicente, the Oedipus figure, has returned from *la pinta*, the penitentiary, and he is ready to take his place as a masculine leader of the New Mexico *barrio*, the neighborhood where his family and friends live. But there is the plague: the darkness of prison experience, his participation in the riot, and the secret of his struggle with his sexuality inside *la pinta*. Gringo comes to love a woman, Yvonne, or "Bon," whose son Tito was in the prison at the same time as Gringo. This is where Chavez departs dramatically from Sophocles: in this narrative, Gringo is not Yvonne's son. Tito, who went by the name "Tattoo" in prison, is. Gringo, her lover at the play's opening, does not realize that Yvonne's son,

Tito, is the same "Tattoo" who was his lover in prison. This homosexual relationship with the son of his lover is the taboo that makes Gringo Oedipus-like. Chavez's is neither a one to one adaptation of the classical play nor an easy case of classical reception.

After a lengthy discussion of DNAWORKS and Daniel's many projects throughout his two decades on the scene, we delve into the matter at hand: Why do these modern playwrights so frequently return to the classical plays?

> PATRICE RANKINE: You speak fairly lovingly [about Countee Cullen]. What about his aesthetics and politics can you share?
>
> DANIEL BANKS: [The Theatre department at] Williams College approached me about directing a play that was written in the Harlem Renaissance. . . . [they] wanted to create an initiative to bring curriculum and mainstage performance together. So that there should be a mainstage performance that would connect with curriculum, and this was a course that they recognized that they needed to do something, they needed to mix it up a little bit on the Williams campus, and do a show that would give a different kind of opportunity to the acting pool, and create some . . .
>
> P.R.: . . . Diversity . . .
>
> D.B.: Yeah, I like to think of it as integration.
>
> [Although Banks does not cite a specific incident, similar to many colleges in the northeast, Williams has a long history of flashpoints in racial tensions, which flare up from time to time. A written racial slur was discovered in February 1993, and was later found to have been posted by a Black student as part of his approach to a class project.[6]]
>
> P.R.: You used the word before. People with multiple heritages, mixed-heritages, and multiple abilities . . .
>
> D.B.: So they called me and, as I began looking at it [the period], I mean really looking at it—I knew it from an academic perspective, but had never really looked at plays of the Harlem Renaissance as a director. I just hadn't . . . So I started reading the plays as a director, and I saw some fundamental challenges. One, I would say, is that most Harlem Renaissance plays written by Black folk in Harlem either were lynching dramas or an attempt to draw class distinctions between the sort of talented tenth and "the folk."[7] I didn't think that either of those would play very well on the Williams campus and, I didn't think that, as progressive as this initiative was to link curriculum with performance, without a huge amount of framing for the widespread audience, I didn't think that these texts were really going to be successful and create some critical commentary about Blackness, racism, etcetera. I feared it would only reinforce certain stereotypes without a huge initiative around it, which just was not what was possible within that time frame. So I was sort of despairing, about this gig, and thinking, maybe this isn't the gig for me . . .
>
> And I encountered, somewhere along the lines in my research, a reference to Countee Cullen's *Medea*, which Owen Dodson called *The African Medea* and also *Medea in Africa* when he produced it numerous times during his career. And it was out of print. I had to track down the book through inter-library loan and found not only the central text, which is published in one edition, but then a prologue and an epilogue, under the title "Byword for Evil," which were later published in a separate book with *Medea*.[8] The other thing that was really amazing, when taking into consideration Dodson's titles, is that when reading it closely—when reading *Medea*, the central

play closely to the original, [Cullen] actually hasn't amplified the "strangeness" or the "outsiderness" at all (Rankine 2006). I remember thinking that he didn't use significantly different language than most other translators. And he hasn't actually done a radical adaptation, with the exception of the songs. And that's what's so interesting, and I think this is going to be a really interesting question for scholars moving forward. And hopefully this will bring it back into the center of some discourses, as we look at the intersection of the Classics with African American Studies, with postcolonial theory, which his versioning of it definitely touches on: Why is it that an African American writer doing a "translation" of *Medea*, or a versioning of Medea, is immediately thought to be doing an full-on adaptation [Fig. 39.1]?

P.R.: Right, and this is part of what I liked about watching Chavez's play last night. I had some questions and ideas about adaptations versus translations (see McConnell and Rankine, this volume), and it seems to me that, in the first instance, Countee Cullen was being extremely conservative in that play, and then went back later and wrote the prologue and epilogue, and that's what I like the most, right? Because those are the portions where he [Cullen] is really kind of putting his stamp on the play.

D.B.: So the interesting thing is, and going back to your original question about what is your motivation? My motivation originally was: What is a play that I can do on this campus [Williams College], that is going to create some productive conversation, and not be retro? I have to say that, although I had heard the name Countee Cullen, I really wasn't as familiar with his writing as other writers of the time. And for me to discover somebody who had been involved in the worlds of poetry and theater, for me to discover that he was considered the Poet Laureate of the Harlem Renaissance, and

FIG. 39.1 Medea and Jason, from *Medea*, which Daniel Banks directed at Williams College, in 2002. Photo by Miguel Romero.

that I had never heard that, was also a big comeuppance for me. And so I then started really from researching the play, and because of my own sense of obligation, I started researching him. And he's a complicated person. His first anthology of poetry, I believe it was his first, was called *Color*, yet he's also the poet who says, "I don't want to be known as a Black poet, I want to be known as a poet." So there's an inherent... there's a kind of bifurcation. There's a split. It's very [W. E. B.] Du Boisian in the sense of the first 50 pages of *The Souls of Black Folk* [the notion of "double consciousness," that there are two selves in the Black body, a soul with its own sensibilities, and the face one presents to society at large]. It's all right there. That sense of "two-ness." I agree with you that the prologue and epilogue, which I believe were written later...

P.R.: They were published about three years after.

D.B.: I agree that those push the envelope more. But I want to also say that I find *Medea* just gorgeous. I find his adaptation—his "adaptation," I also keep using that word—it gets ingrained. But his, I'm going to call it a versioning, because he doesn't radically alter the play, but there's something about the way... I do believe that he humanized the translation. We all know, those of us who deal with classic texts, that there are some translations into English that are more literal and there are some translations that actually flow off the tongue better. The incredible attribute of his *Medea*... is that I think it is the most playable "translation" or versioning of *Medea* that I have ever read.[9]

P.R.: Not to sound like the 1935 critics, but it's "folksy," it's very down to earth, and the language is very down to earth and very accessible.[10]

D.B.: I don't know what "down to earth" means, if it's... *clear*?

P.R.: It's *clear*. Thank you.

D.B.: It's clear, but again you're looking at it from a scholarly perspective, and I'm looking at it from an acting perspective. You are able to play actions and objectives on that text... See, one of the difficulties that I find with a lot of translations of classic texts—and again, maybe it's just an accurate translation, I don't know, I don't read Latin or Greek. I used to read Latin, but I don't anymore—how I wish now I had studied Greek when I had the opportunity. I think I was just rebelling against my high school's classical curriculum!—which is ok for reading, but not ok for production, is all the voices sound alike. (See McConnell and Rankine, this volume.)

P.R.: In translation.

D.B.: Yes, in translation. The characters don't sound like they are different characters, like they have different voices, right? And that may in fact just be a product of how Greek playwrights wrote.

P.R.: It's not. It absolutely isn't. That's a brilliant observation that it absolutely isn't [and yet translations can seem to read that way].

D.B.: I actually think that what he does is that he gives you clearly delineated characters. And that the language that Medea uses—the way that she speaks, the cadence that she speaks in, where Cullen breaks lines, the word choices that he uses—they are all connected to her. They are not connected to some kind of faithfulness to however someone translates a Greek word. It's a version of that word; I mean, he doesn't stray and create a different meaning. But he has a writer's sensibility. And so that, to me, is the great gift of Cullen's *Medea*.

P.R.: The delineation of characters in classical plays depends on the playwright because we see Euripides, who wrote *Medea*—we see him using language that would be specific to a certain class or a certain level of speaker. So he is definitely trying to make those distinctions, and maybe it's something that the academic translator might sometimes miss. Not the poet. So that's a great contribution on the part of Cullen for this text.

D.B.: So I think that this is the most eminently playable version of the text that I've encountered, other than a strict adaptation where somebody has taken it and changed it, and made it be something entirely different. There's something about the sentence construction that allows her otherness to come out more, without changing the language, without changing the adjectives, without adding anything at all to, as it were, pump up her "otherness" or her "Africanness." Which obviously by [Dodson] calling it *The African Medea* is an attempt to do. But there is something about the way that [Cullen] lays bare the conversation of her "otherness," and where she comes from, and the class perceptions of that "otherness." (See Santos, this volume.) There's a way that he just takes all of the shrubbery away and really lays it bare that, for me, hits much harder home. I mean I actually had to go back to some of the other translations and say, "Ok, is he specifically making her seem more 'other' than in the original story?" Because obviously I've studied it and I've seen productions of it, and it never seemed . . . And I went back and, at least my memory ten years later is that, no, he's not necessarily using different words, but the dramatic build is different. The syntax of the sentence is different [Fig. 39.2].

P.R.: That's a wonderful view of the play from the inside, in terms of language. And it sounds as though the frame of a classical play gave you a certain purchase at the college, at Williams, that, let's say Langston Hughes' *Mulatto*, would not have. [Banks directed a deconstruction of *Mulatto* several years earlier at New York University,

FIG. 39.2 From Banks's staging of Countee Cullen's *Medea* at Williams College. Photo by Miguel Romero.

titled *Mixtries*.] In terms of, for lack of a better word, the "packaging" of the dialogues, conversations, and ideas that were at play, that you wanted to work with for this play.

D.B.: Given the kind of the remit of this project, the goal or the reason that I was brought in to do this project, and given the environment and the student body and the issues on that campus, it allowed us to have—I just think it was the right artistic and political choice, for moving a discourse forward on the campus, instead of moving it backwards. Because consider also, if we had done a lynching play, unless I was going to do some radical casting, which I also don't think would have worked, there would have been a reinscription of certain roles. If we had done a play that had an all-Black cast, where there was in-fighting within that community, there really were not a lot of good options [of those scripts], but there are a couple out there. First of all, there probably would not have been enough African heritage actors on campus who would have come out for something like that, to do that kind of a play with an all-Black cast; and also that campus was needing, from my perspective, a particular kind of healing, and doing an all-Black play was not necessarily going to add to the healing, it was going to add to more bifurcation. What *Medea* allowed us to do, in addition to the educational project of looking at Cullen ... [was] to have an integrated cast; it allowed actors who were labeled "too this," or "too that," or "not this," or "not that enough," to be *there*. It's the same thing as with *Señora de la pinta*—I tend to always have the room of people who are extremely talented, extremely heartfelt, extremely politically and socially conscious, who never really get to strut their stuff fully.[11]

P.R.: So let's come to that. I like this word "purchase," for what the—

D.B.: (Smiling) I don't know that I like the word "purchase." Tell me about that.

P.R.: When I say "purchase," I am trying to find a language to talk about why a playwright, director or even a poet would want to continue to return to this material. So, for example in last night's play, to me the best bits of Chavez's play are not necessarily, I'm not saying not ever, but not necessarily the *Oedipus*. It's his own language, in his own poetry. I can see where *Oedipus*, as a kind of point of departure, allows a certain framing and certain "in" for the audience. But there comes a point where too close adherence to the original play, in a way, maybe limits the playwright. In some reviews of Rita Dove's *Darker Face of the Earth*, for example, it was often said that she could have made her point without *Oedipus*.[12] (See Rabinowitz, this volume.) The same thing with this play *MoLoRa* [by Yael Farber] that looks at truth and reconciliation in South African through the frame of Aeschylus' *Oresteia*. The same thing was said in that review: that more mileage could have been gotten if the person had just concentrated on the truth and reconciliation issues.[13] Why use this stuff? When I say "purchase," I mean the people coming to that play—let's say your *Medea*—there's a value-added. There's a kind of coin. There's an exchange. They are in fact buying this as a product in a way. They are coming to the theater. They are filling it because it's *Medea*. And maybe the person reading the description of *Señora de la pinta* is seeing in the description that there's something here of *Oedipus the King*, and that's going to trigger an interest. So it has a certain currency, but how much, why, and what the limits of that currency might be are kind of the things I'm interested in here. And I wonder what you think about this in terms of *Señora*. What does he gain from the *Oedipus* frame?

D.B.: The interesting thing is that I think it's looking at things from two different perspectives, because from a directorial perspective, a good story is a good story. And a good story needs to be told. And certain stories need to be told at certain moments for certain reasons. I think the fact that he remixes *Oedipus* and isn't letter-faithful to it shows that things have changed and they are—it is historical, social, cultural, movement, and so it needs to be reworked, adapted, remixed. (See Wetmore, this volume.)

P.R.: But why? Why not write the play about Vicente [the Oedipus character, also called "Gringo"] and have that be the story.

D.B.: But he did. That's actually what he did.

P.R.: But he also sat down he says with David Grene's *Oedipus the King*, so it is very much at the forefront of this, and he is remixing.

D.B.: But this play could actually have been written by somebody who had never read *Oedipus*.

P.R.: Yes, exactly!

D.B.: And it would have been written exactly the same way. And someone could say to him, "Hey, have you ever read *Oedipus*?" I think that he gave himself such freedom here that it doesn't read like an overworked...

P.R.: Except he doesn't, right? Because at the end for example, he goes through the need to kill the Jocasta character Bon [Yvonne]. He goes through the blinding of Oedipus, which comes out of, in a way, nowhere, although to some extent the owls—

D.B.: But it doesn't come out of nowhere; we talk about the eyes from the beginning of the play.

[Chavez's chorus is made up of three owls, *lechuzas*, who speak as human but are fabled characters in local lore, which is a mix of Mexican and indigenous stories. One is not to look into the eyes of the *lechuzas* directly, or one will be blinded. Given the symbolism of owls and knowledge, even in Greek mythology as Athena's avatar, a theme in the *lechuza* tale is the blindness of ignorance and even of too much knowledge—issues pertinent to *Oedipus the King*.]

P.R.: We talk about it... we do... we do.

D.B.: ... to get to the soul.

P.R.: So you think that play itself could have been written just as is without ever—

D.B.: I think it could have been ... I think if you're looking at a history of Chicano literature, or if you are looking at a history of, sort of, almost melodrama or tragi-comedy, there's a lot... I think her killing herself—sure it's the Jocasta character. But it's also—you should read the newspaper around here... (Long pause.) I'm trying to think of a way to answer this question, because honestly, as the director, I'm not [his] academic advisor, so I didn't start with those questions for him. I started with, "How do we make this work?" So I'm, in a way, so deeply invested—as I would have to be—in the play as it is, that I'm not considering alternatives. Now he did, for instance... originally have *Oedipus* blinding himself, I mean Gringo blinding himself. And I said to Law, "That feels like it comes out of nowhere and you're being overly faithful to the story." I said, "You've set up this world of Chicano mythology."

P.R.: The *lechuzas* blinding him is perfect and, again that's the bit that's his own... Or one of the many bits, you know, a departure from the original text.

D.B.: So I said to him, "Is there something else that can happen at the end, where he is blinded but he doesn't blind himself?" And I didn't give him the answer. And he came back and said, "Oh, you know, there is this mythology in Chicano culture, in Chicano lore, that if you look at an owl in the eye, that will blind you." So I was pushing him to stray from the faithfulness to the original there at the end, but then he came up with his own idea. But I did push him to find something that was more from the Chicano world of the play than from the Greek world of the play. And I thought he came up with a brilliant, brilliant idea. It's just amazing [Fig. 39.3].

P.R.: I think that works great, exactly. That approach works.

D.B.: So let me think about your question about why do it. The funny thing is . . . I think if you're going to apply this pressure to a Law Chavez or a Countee Cullen, then apply the same pressure to Euripides and Sophocles.

P.R.: They are "biting" each other's work, right, so you've got Euripides in his *Electra* biting Aeschylus' character.

FIG. 39.3 Gringo and Josefina mourn the death of Yvonne, "Bon," at the crossroads, with the *lechuzas*, the folkloric owl figures from Chicano stories, in the background. From Law Chavez's *Señora de la pinta*, which Daniel Banks directed at the Words Afire! Festival, University of New Mexico, in 2012. Photo by Pat Berrett.

[In hip-hop culture, when one stylist—as rapper, fashion stylist, or even simply in everyday gestures and gait—copies the manner or technique of another, he or she is said to be "biting" the style of the originator.]

D.B.: I mean, did these myths originate with these playwrights?

P.R.: No, no, no, they are all biting [shared scripts]. They are [tales and stories and] myths first, the playwrights evolve them, and then they are biting each other's work.

D.B.: Then come for Shakespeare for biting Plutarch. I think in a way you're looking at contemporary writers doing something that writers have always been compelled to do, which is to take stories that resonate in different ways through time, and put a time stamp on them.

P.R.: I like that.
It's a mashup, right, it's "Graeco-Roman."

D.B.: But I do think I would rather ask the question philosophically, "why are writers drawn to what they are drawn to?," rather than "why are contemporary writers updating the so-called 'Classics'?" Because "classical" writers were updating something even more ancient. And frankly, I'm sure that some of these myths go back to African lore and Africa.[14] If [we] really wanted to go back to "real" Classics, let's look for the source of the material. I have read that there is source material for some of the Greek dramas predated in Edo civilization. I think it's more a question of why do writers do what they do, rather than why are these writers doing what they are doing, because they are just doing what writers have always done throughout time and history. Why so many adaptations of the Jesus story in so many different contexts? There's something that touches us, that moves us, that helps us make sense of something, and we need that . . . that kernel. We need the DNA—it's in the DNA of the story. So let's talk about that. Also, if we want for a second to really go Greek classical, purging of pity and fear!

P.R.: Yes, absolutely.

D.B.: So, why do certain stories allow for catharsis in certain environments? The Oedipus story has such violence in it, and so Law is finding this connection of just totally brutal and devastating violence. He is finding that connection between that story and what's happened in his own backyard, in his community. Well, literally his backyard and the prison, you know two backyards. And for him it's important to say, "This doesn't just happen in New Mexico. This didn't just happen with the prison riots here. This isn't just a racialized local story reduced to a bunch of criminals, of New Mexican Hispanos. This is a time, age-old issue, problem, journey, situation. And we need to see ourselves as part of that world history, not just part of this colonial history for the past five hundred years . . ."

P.R.: Tell me what your experience was reading this play for the first time. Because you mentioned the catharsis of fear and pity, and one thing that strikes me as the value of the Classics is this mix of strangeness and familiarity all at once. So the minute that I know that this is the Oedipus story, I'm thinking about the structure of the play, I'm looking for the *peripety*, the turning point, and I want to know—I know what is familiar, I know this Oedipus is going to fall. But my question is, how is it going to happen? *That* I don't know. And that to me is the titillation, that to me is the kind of perking up, the moment where I begin to think—

D.B.: But you're also not the average audience member for this play. (Laughs.)

P.R.: You're right. A lot of people in the audience aren't necessarily going to know—

D.B.: I don't think he is writing for the academy, I think he is writing for his community—
P.R.: But to be fair, Daniel, *he* describes it as an *Oedipus the King*.
D.B.: He does. But when I say he is writing for . . . what I mean is that I don't think he is writing for an audience who will necessarily have as vivid a memory of the structure of *Oedipus Rex*.
P.R.: What was your experience reading this play for the first time, do you remember?
D.B.: I was totally taken by his language, and by his use of language. I found it moving. It cut straight. I love his sense of humor, I think his sense of humor is exquisite but not cheap, and not at anyone's expense. Which a lot of ethnic humor often is . . . I personally was struck by the courage of telling this tale of men who in prison love other men, or have sex with other men, and then come back into their communities, because obviously in the past ten or fifteen years, popular culture has exploded with the conversation about the D.L. ["downlow" or sex among men, some of whom who have wives or girlfriends]. Prison is a different situation, but nonetheless, an equally powerful one. I think the love scenes between BonBon and Gringo and between Gringo and Tito [as flashbacks] are some of the most—the juiciest, sexiest, love scenes I've ever seen. And as they played, they are equally convincing and I think you can really believe how this one man can love both people fully. And I didn't really get hung up on the *Oedipus* stuff. Like I said earlier, the only thing that really concerned me was him blinding himself at the end. And that's where I said, "You've created this mashup of Chicano culture and the Oedipus myth. Why finish with Greek?"[15] (See Wetmore, this volume.) If his whole project, which I think a lot of his project was, was to write a New Mexican play, set in his barrio, about challenges that this region has culturally, economically, etcetera, I said to him, "Why fall into the trap of ending on the Greek?" End with something of your world, that you are wanting to put on the stage.
P.R.: And that's the part of it for me. I'm not saying that Bon *shouldn't* kill herself—but the putting of it on the stage, it's kind of a Shakespearian and Greek tragic kind of mashup.
D.B.: Well, we actually talked about the *ekkyklema* and we talked about . . .
TOGETHER: . . . why not have it off-stage . . .
D.B.: And we talked about that and we looked at it and it would have . . . That I feel would have been . . .
TOGETHER: . . . more Greek . . .
D.B.: . . . and being tied to, being shackled to the Greek . . . I'm just saying that if you have that experience of the violence of living here, how you foreground and background elements in the play would be very different, because I think you would see things in different relief. And I think in the same way we can apply that to *Medea* and Countee Cullen's *Medea*, is I think that someone reading it—and this is probably a lot of his project too—somebody reading it, who has the experience of being marginalized because of color, of status, of class, etcetera, is going to read that play with a very different sense of what's going to pop out, than somebody who's coming from a majoritarian perspective, who has never really considered her motivation for doing what she does; her pain, her mental health, is going to be read very differently by people from different—
P.R.: It comes back to your word "ethics"—a word that you use a lot: for me, classical reception isn't about these works per se alone, because I come from that kind of marginal background as well. But it's a question of pushing back against the classical

reception framework, to ask ethically what's on this other side, whether we call it hip-hop theater, whether we call it Chicano, whether we call it Black theater. What ethically does this frame have for us? What ethically do we want to express of our experience that resonates somehow with this frame? I mean, broadly what are the ethics of reception? . . . This is the thing . . . This is part of the reason why I wanted to frame this whole interview around you as an artist. Because my concern is that—and I've used the words atomization and fragmentation—that there's a kind of dissecting of an artist, like, let's say, Rita Dove, where *The Darker Face of the Earth* becomes the main interest of the scholarship, right?, without any sense of what Rita Dove's body of poetry is about, what she claims the body of poetry is about, and how it plays out in a broader context of African-American poetry, American poetry writ large . . .

D.B.: And frankly I would say, honestly, from being inside of this process and working closely with Law and living here, I would say anybody who wants to really do a proper gloss of *Señora de la pinta*—even though the tag line is *Oedipus Rex*—they would also want to go back to Nahuatl and all of the indigenous literatures and tales, oral histories, oral stories, orature of this region. Because somebody from this region, a product of this region, is going to be just as influenced by those. And so I think, probably with very little digging, we could find Bon's suicide being just as connected to one of those as to *Oedipus*, and the only reason we are calling it *Oedipus* is because that's the dominant western cultural frame of reference. So again, I feel that, sure *Oedipus* is an integral part of the mashup, but I don't think it's the only thing that he's . . . it's not the only sample that he's included—he's sampling a lot of things.

[A 'sample' is also a hip-hop reference. Kanye West samples a second or two of Michael Jackson's "Pretty Young Thing" for his song "The Good Life," and the discriminating ear hears the hook. This is only one example of a practice that goes back to the origins of rap music in New York City (Rose 1994).]

P.R.: Let's wrap up with words on performance, then, because on the one hand, the words . . . if I look at the description of the play, what's foregrounded in language is *Oedipus the King*, in terms of description and tagline and all this. Tell me a little bit about what you where doing in terms of staging, costuming, and sort of these phenomena, to highlight—because I think it does highlight in the end, another line of influence—the local lines of influence—

D.B.: For the staging, my impulse was to have a much more intimate setting. This was also the way that we staged *Medea*—we blocked off the first third of the audience and had the stage come out in, so that, instead of a kind of standard traditional auditorium, college auditorium type thing, we completely repurposed the space.[16] With *Señora*, we made it environmental, so the audience felt like they were in the "cul-de-sac," as Law calls it, where he used to live, in that space between the backyards. And I don't know if you noticed—it was meant to be subtle but it was present—for most of the first act, and a little bit of the second, there was ambient sound. So that you never felt like you were in a blackbox theater. You heard the cars and the dogs barking, just what you would hear in a neighborhood in the backyard, different sounds for day, different sounds for night.

P.R.: Different sounds for the crossroad.

D.B.: Well, the crossroad had no sound and the *lechuza* scenes had no sound. The moments that were "out of time" had no sound, but the things that were clearly situated in a particular time of day had ambient sound. And so that was number one, just how to really have it be environmental and have the audience not voyeur, but be there in the scene, witness, a member of the community. That kind of immersion. That was the first choice. I felt that doing it in a proscenium or head-on would have somehow objectified this world rather than had people in the audience be implicated in it. So costumes, we really just did historical research. I mean, it sounds funny to say now that 1980 was period, but it very much was . . .

P.R.: Well at times I thought I was watching *Boyz in the Hood*. Plaid and the pockets, leather jackets . . .

D.B.: That was the style of the period. So we very much went for historical realism there. And the *lechuzas*, it was to find the intersection of human form and animal form. We didn't want to go with feathers and things like that, because they were clearly this sort of integrated form and they needed something that they could move in that would suggest that they were owls, and you could get that sense of flight, but at the same time, that they weren't in a Halloween costume. The lighting, very conscious of trying to get that delicate balance—you have this really amazing balance here of blues and reds—you have this blue sky, red earth, and then at sunset, you get this blue and red mixing, and these incredible purples. I've never seen sunsets anywhere like the ones here. And just really getting that sense of cool and warm that happens simultaneously.

P.R.: The music?

D.B.: You know again, I really wanted the music to be evocative and put us in that world.

P.R.: You know, as we wrap up, I still have a lingering in my mind, this notion of you as an educator. Do you want to say something about the connection; again we've not been able to dig into your notion of the ethical, but is there a connection for you?

D.B.: I think that if we take the Latin root of "educate"—it's about leading. But it's about inspiring people to lead as well. I don't think of myself as an educator who's an artist, or an artist who's an activist, or an activist who's an artist. I don't think in those terms.

P.R.: And so, you also don't divvy out space; it's not the university versus the theater, versus—

D.B.: Oh no, it's actually, at this point in my life . . . This is what I'm committed to as a human being and my spiritual practice—which, of course, I always fall down, but I get back up because it's my practice—is to bring a level of awareness and integratedness to everything that I do. Everything. Every moment of every day, in the grocery store, in the classroom, in the rehearsal room, with my family, with my dog, with whatever. And again, I'm not at all saying that I'm in any way successful at it, but it's the thing that keeps me going, it's the thing that keeps me present. And then I become un-present, and then I notice that I'm not being present, and then I remind myself to be present. And I really think—I heard a great teacher once say that the human being has basically two choices in life, "expand" or "contract." And I've been on the receiving end of a lot of people's contraction, and recognized that that was not something that resonated with my DNA. It was out of harmony. And that for me it's about expansion. It's about creating a welcoming space for everybody, or at least the attempt at it, the belief that it is possible for us all to belong. And that we can all belong equally, and that we can all have . . . going back to my favorite trope, a place at "the welcome table." There's an equal space at the welcome table for all of us, and attempting to gently push against places where exclusion is the ethic, or hierarchy is the ethic, or that kind of unctuous inclusion is the ethic, and really just say, "Breath. Breath. Connect to the Breath." That's what we do in *Señora de la pinta*. We do as a cast, before we start the show, we do "conscious breathing" together, inspired by Thich Nhat Hanh, just as a company, standing shoulder by shoulder, and everybody breathing silently, awareness. That to me is the core and then it manifests itself within—look at this (picking up a ceramic tea bowl he made) . . . Something that you can use, something that I can give you that you can walk away with and can touch, but it's practical, it has a use. It's beautiful, but it's practical. That's just where I am right now in life. And it could change. I doubt it will, I think it's a good place to be. But it is definitely . . . it is my inheritance. This is the legacy that the people that have come before me, the ones who I know are connected by blood and the others who are perhaps connected by something else or maybe by blood . . .

P.R.: At some point they are.

D.B.: Exactly, I'm really just convinced that ultimately we are all connected. And the blessing and the joy is finding those places of connectedness, noticing that we're connected, discovering the ways we are connected.

Notes

1. On the riot, see Morris 1988, which I am told Chavez studied.
2. The quotes are from the longer transcript of my interview, which space here does not allow for me to print. Special thanks go to Denise Paddock for transcription.
3. *Goddess City* appears in Banks 2011, a critical anthology of hip-hop theater. Banks directed the premiers of both *Goddess City* and *Ghetto Punch* in New York City.
4. For background, see Early 1990; for a treatment of the play, see Rankine 2006.
5. The description appears at <http://eventful.com/albuquerque/events/seora-la-pinta-law-chavez-directed-daniel-banks-/E0-001-047203536-5> accessed July 7, 2012.
6. See "A Test of Racism Produces an Uproar," *New York Times* (February 16, 1993). See, most recently, "Violent Hate Speech Incident at Williams College," in *Huffington Post* (November 11, 2011).
7. Krasner 2002 is relevant here.
8. Early 1990 brought Cullen's collected writing together, including all three parts of his *Medea*.
9. Regarding his Classics credentials, Cullen certainly took Latin at DeWitt High School in New York, and there is evidence that he studied Greek at New York University, though how much Greek he had is uncertain. See Rankine 2006.
10. On the reviews, see Rankine 2006.
11. It is worth noting that, as I discovered in conversations with Daniel, the Words Afire! Festival puts out an open call in the Albuquerque community, so that many of the actors in the productions are not professionally trained, and in some cases they are not students at the university.
12. On Dove, see Goff and Simpson 2007.
13. Dan Orrells's 2012 lecture at the American Philological Association raised the issue in depth of *MoLoRa* and the usefulness of the classical frame. It becomes clear that this is a perennial issue for critics.
14. The idea that these stories originate in Africa has, of course, come into the broader culture as the Black Athena approach, but the essentially Afrocentric nature of the idea predates Martin Bernal's studies. See Bernal 1987. On Afrocentrism, see Howe 1999. For the relationship between the Afrocentric idea and contemporary black drama, see Wetmore 2003.

15. Wetmore discusses the idea of mashup, a kind of indiscriminate mixing, in this volume, in his article on *The Seven*, Will Power's hip-hop versioning of Aeschylus' *Seven Against Thebes*.
16. On the role of staging in reshaping a classical play for a different context from what might have been intended, see Hall and Harrop 2010.

References

Banks, D. (2011), *Say Word! Voices from Hip Hop Theater*. Ann Arbor.

Bernal, M. (1987), *Black Athena: The Afroasiatic Roots of Classical Civilization (The Fabrication of Ancient Greece 1785–1985*, volume i). New Brunswick, NJ.

Early, G. (1990), *My Soul's High Song: Countee Cullen*. New York.

Goff, B. and M. Simpson (2007), *Crossroads in the Black Aegean: Oedipus, Antigone, and Dramas of the African Diaspora*. Oxford.

Hall, E. and S. Harrop (2010), *Theorising Performance: Greek Drama, Cultural History, and Critical Practice*. London.

Howe, S. (1999), *Afrocentrism: Mythical Pasts and Imagined Homes*. London.

Krasner, D. (2002), *A Beautiful Pageant: African American Theatre, Drama, and Performance in the Harlem Renaissance, 1910–1927*. New York.

Locke, A. (1999), *The New Negro: Voices of the Harlem Renaissance*. New York.

Morris, R. (1988), *The Devil's Butcher Shop: The New Mexico Prison Uprising*. Albuquerque, NM.

Rankine, P. D. (2006), *Ulysses in Black: Ralph Ellison, Classicism, and African American Literature*. Madison.

Rose, T. (1994), *Black Noise: Rap Music and Black Culture in Contemporary America*. Middletown, CT.

Wetmore, K., Jr. (2003), *Black Dionysus: Greek Tragedy and African American Theatre*. Jefferson, NC.

CHAPTER 40

THIS BIRD THAT NEVER SETTLES

A Virtual Conversation with Anne Carson about Greek Tragedy

YOPIE PRINS

ANNE Carson—Canadian poet, Classicist, essayist, and translator, always blurring the boundaries between—has been working her way through Greek tragedy for several decades. Her translations create a wide spectrum of literary possibilities. Some are published in classical series (like Oxford's Greek Tragedy in New Translations or Chicago's Complete Greek Tragedies), and some have been selected for performance on stage (for example An Oresteia directed by Brian Kulick for The Classic Stage Company in New York, and a new production of The Bacchae directed by James McDonald). More often, Carson's translations are productions for the page, published along with her own meditations on Greek tragedy in a preface or conclusion (including one postscript written "by Euripides" to explain "Why I Wrote Two Plays About Phaedra"). Other translations are radical transformations: a poetic elaboration of a choral ode or dialogue, or a reduction of a tragedy into a few lines, or the dramatic recasting of a whole play. Our virtual interview was conducted by email to create an intermediate space for thinking, somewhere between talking in real time and posting letters, about Carson's ongoing creative process in translating Greek tragedy.

Y.P.: When did you begin reading Greek tragedy?
A.C.: The first play I read, with Professor Michael O'Brien at University of Toronto in 1968, was Aiskhylos' *Agamemnon*. Prof. O'Brien was a sober, punctilious, restrained man and I recall his slow careful way of analyzing the text—there was a physical sensation of sinking down into words—especially his analysis of the argument of the parodos of that difficult play. When he suggested at one point (Agamemnon's "yoke of necessity" was the issue, I believe) that choral reasoning might proceed from a "both ... and" premise rather than an "either ... or" premise, a door dropped open in my mind.
Y.P.: What was the first tragedy you translated for publication?

A.C.: The first play I translated, while living in New York City, was Sophokles' *Elektra*. I had a grant with the grand title Playwright in Residence at the 92nd Street Y, which entitled me to a year off from teaching and a tiny green room on the 8th floor of the Y with a bed, bathroom and hotplate. The Lexington Avenue bus stopped below the window every 12 minutes. I worked on the play all day and dreamed of it at night. One of these dreams (I have recounted this elsewhere) involved my struggle to render the Sophoklean word *lupē* ("grief, pain," etc) in a consistent way through its various iterations in the play. The word seemed to me to render a pattern of associations that might be important to capture. I never did. The dream featured me flying above the gigantic glass house of the *Elektra* with a black-wrapped object in my hands. This object of course was the perfect English translation of *lupē*, which I had only to fly down and place into the play. I began to descend. I awoke.

Y.P.: I remember seeing your translation of *Elektra* performed at Northwestern University in 1993. And when the translation was published in 2001, you wrote a preface called "Screaming in Translation." Instead of translating Electra's cries of pain, you presented them as transliterations: PHEU, AIAI, OIMOI MOI, IO MOI MOI, and so on. Do you think this worked better on the stage or on the page?

A.C.: It seemed a brilliant solution to me on the page (and I had great fun writing that preface to justify it) but I have never heard anyone make it work on stage: even a trained actor's voice has trouble shifting from the register of screaming to that of speech within the same line or sentence. The result is usually both too loud and too precious. Several times, when I was involved with productions, I asked the director to try casting a "screamer" who would pronounce only these sounds and could stand beside the relevant actor as a sort of transparent hyper-voice. A shadow-scream. No one's tried it yet.

Y.P.: In your introduction to *Grief Lessons: Four Plays by Euripides*, you called Greek tragedy "a curious art form." You wrote: "Why does tragedy exist? Because you are full of rage. Why are you full of rage? Because you are full of grief." Turning from Sophoclean to Euripidean tragedy, did you work out a different approach to translation?

A.C.: I've pondered at different times over the years Aristotle's judgment of Euripides as "the most tragic" of the tragic poets. And it gradually came to me, during the time I was working on the four Euripidean plays in *Grief Lessons*, that Euripides is not much interested in language itself (as Sophokles most definitely is) but mainly engaged with making a lot of exciting things happen fast: *praxis* in other words. Since Aristotle seems to be a big fan of *praxis* too, it makes sense he would find Euripides dramaturgically satisfying. I find him less so and much prefer the task of translating Sophoklean sentences, which are deep and wild and travel down into language in a way that makes me wonderfully restless—"they follow, follow, follow . . . this bird that never settles," as Wallace Stevens says of somnambulism. With Euripidean sentences there is more the sense of snapping the lid on and moving to the next: urgent, planed smooth, unforgiving.

Y.P.: Your translations of the Euripidean choral odes are beautifully scattered on the page, where the words seem to take flight. You made a broadside poem out of the fourth stasimon from the *Hippolytos*, translating the power of Aphrodite and Eros. And then holes were burned into the broadsides, each one singed and signed by you.

A.C.: While finishing the translation of *Hippolytos* (as a Visiting Scholar at the Getty Research Institute in Los Angeles), I was also working on a performance piece called *Cassandra Float Can* with my collaborator/friend Currie, who shared the residency with me. *Cassandra Float Can* is a lecture on translation with visual and choreographic layers rotating in and out of the text. At the end of our time at the Getty, Currie and I performed this piece for our fellow scholars and also made a broadside to give to each of them as a memento—it was a choral ode of the *Hippolytos* printed on fine paper with different holes burned into each to personalize it. Our work study student at the Getty, Genevieve Yue, did the printing (she has a letter press) and helped us burn the sheets with a butane torch in the parking garage of the Getty residence. All this to say that Currie adds elements of spatiality, action and chance to any project. Officially we call him the Randomizer.

Y.P.: Later your complete translation of *Hippolytos* was performed at the new amphitheater of the Getty Villa. What was it like to see this in open air?

A.C.: The Getty production of *Hippolytos* was robustly conventional and highly melodramatic—lots of screaming. Too much screaming. You know what I'd like to see some day is a production in which everyone whispers, or at least talks in a quiet voice, all through the play. It would be terrifying.

Y.P.: Have you seen unconventional productions that made you look at Greek drama in a new way?

A.C.: Paradoxically, the productions I've seen that made me think again were non-verbal, e.g., Dimitris Papaioannou's *Medea*, a dance in which Medea wears her two children as big ceramic puppet-bracelets, one on each wrist: at the moment of murder she simply pauses, looks out at the audience and smashes her two arms together. How much language can I lose and still have a sentence, a play, a meaning? is a question I continually ask myself. It is not a question which you should now ask me.

Y.P.: In the preface to your *Hekabe* translation, you describe your reaction to Euripides as "the same response I have to Beckett—that sinking feeling of *oh no here we go again* as the bleakness closes in." And you taught a course called "Euripides and Beckett: Experiments in Drama and Depression."

A.C.: Euripides & Beckett: the larger stereotypes happily coincide—alleged misanthropy, exilic imagination, dramatic brashness, names that are now adjectives of theatrical method (Euripidean, Beckettian). They also share features of tragic strategy: unkempt people on stage, joyless ineradicable gods, dialogue moved ahead by lame jokes and sophistry. But most notably, an overall withholding of redemption, although the tone of this is hard to pin down. Is he winking or weeping, this playwright? Beckett once wrote that his aim as a writer was "to bore hole after hole in [language] until what cowers behind it seeps through." There is for me a feeling of holes in Euripides too—some meaning or help is glimpsed just as it falls away.

Y.P.: Euripides and Beckett are both masters of dialogue. You too seem to like stichomythia.

A.C:. Stichomythia: always a joy, the Myrna Loy part of the translation, as I think of it.

Y.P.: Can you give an example?

A.C.: A bit of stichomythia between Kreon and the Guard from *Antigonick*:
[enter Guard]
GUARD: well
KREON: well what
GUARD: well we
KREON: well we what
GUARD: well we saw someone

KREON: saw someone what
GUARD: or actually no one
KREON: was it someone or no one
GUARD: well hypothetically
KREON: *you goat's anus*, tell me who buried that body I said was unlawful to touch
GUARD: don't know
KREON: so find out
[exit Kreon and Guard]

Y.P.: *Antigonick* also starts with an interesting dialogue:
ANTIGONE: We begin in the dark and birth is the death of us
ISMENE: Who said that
ANTIGONE: Hegel
ISMENE: Sounds more like Beckett
ANTIGONE: He was paraphrasing Hegel
ISMENE: I don't think so

In just six lines you manage to recapitulate a long history of thinking about *Antigone*, and open up new ways to think through the Greek text of Sophocles. You have presented *Antigonick* in different forms: it was published with illustrations by Bianca Stone, a former student, and you have invited various friends to participate in public readings, with yourself in the role of the chorus. At the 2012 book launch of *Antigonick* in Ann Arbor, I relished reading the role of the tyrant: "Here are Kreon's verbs for today," and "Here are Kreon's nouns."

A.C.: *Antigonick* has been staged as a reading in bookstores, university libraries, the Athenaeum Club (London), the 92nd St Y (NYC) and by Skype (from NYC to Kansas during a national blizzard). Readers are usually volunteers conscripted locally. Memorable readers: Judith Butler, who was able to leaven Kreon's tyrannic persona with stand-up-comedian nuance (at NYU); Eleni Sikelianos who read Antigone with a deep innocence tinged in ferocity; Anne Waldman and William Bolcom who each (independently) chose to wear sunglasses in the role of Teiresias. As far as Nick is concerned, I am never fully aware of what he is doing on stage because I'm embedded in the action myself and concentrating on my script. I do know that every time Currie plays Nick he buys a new kind of tape-measure. The retractable ones with a snappy sound are best.

Y.P.: The cast of characters for *Antigonick* includes Nick as "a mute part [always on stage, he measures things]"? Why did you introduce this silent role?

A.C.: I put Nick in as a free space of imaginal adventure for the reader, actor, director, whoever, so I'd rather not paraphrase him.

Y.P.: You just finished translating *The Bakkhai*, where the stichomythia is deeply ironic and terrifying, especially when Dionysus delivers an extra-metrical syllable (ahhhh . . . in line 810 of the Greek text). It seems this is another one of those non-verbal moments that makes Greek tragedy so powerful: a dramatic turning point where Pentheus suddenly falls under the spell of the god. How do you imagine Pentheus and Dionysus in this scene?

A.C.: Marilyn Monroe succumbing gradually to Nabokov.

Y.P.: What about the scene at the end, when Agave awakens from the spell?

A.C.: I really *don't* imagine my way into the visual/aural/plastic theatrics of a play, that's not my task. It's the director's task. I'm trying to make language work within the little theatre of the mind; sentences are the only stage I know. My imagination is severely limited in every direction beyond that. If the play is to go past my limits, past the page, someone else has to take it.

Y.P.: You imagined another version of *The Bakkhai* for an art installation. It is called "Pinplay of Euripides translated by Anne Carson," and published in *Elliott Hundley: The Bacchae* (Wexner Center for the Arts, Ohio State University, 2011). What and how were you "translating" here?

A.C.: Elliott Hundley is a Los Angeles painter and installation artist who likes to stage tableaux from Greek tragedy by posing his friends in exotic costume in his studio. He photographs these and constructs large-scale paintings, sculptures and installations based on the same imagery. The paintings use paint and all sorts of debris affixed to the canvas with tiny pins—thousands of pins, a forest of pins, I was impressed by the pins. So when he asked me to write something for the catalogue of his *Bacchae* installation at the Wexner, I made a 12-minute reduction of Euripides' play featuring as many pins as I could work in. E.g:

BACCHAE ACT IV CHORAL INTERLUDE:
How many pins can dance on the head of a king?
How many kings can you pin to the dance in my head?
How many dances left stains on the woman he was?
How many stains kept him quiet, O Agave!
[enter Agave exultant and covered in blood, carrying the head of Pentheus impaled on a lacuna]

Y.P.: I am curious about "reduction" as a mode of translation. After translating *Prometheus Bound*, you also "reduced" the Greek text in "Quicktime Prometheus." How do you approach Aeschylus, in comparison to Sophocles and Euripides?

A.C.: Aeschylus remains a very dark woods to me, his language so thick with image and metaphor, twining and intercomplicated, it's hard to know where to cut in. (Euripides by comparison more of a LEGO construct). I translated *Prometheus Bound*, which incidentally I don't believe is by Aeschylus, with a view to matching the *strength* of it—there is a driving strength like a freight train to Prometheus himself especially—but also the musicality of the chorus, who are after all made of water. I did the chorus in hip-hop.

Y.P.: Translating the chorus into hip-hop rhymes is one way to 'reduce' the dense language of Aeschylus (or whoever wrote *Prometheus Bound*). You found another way in "Quicktime Prometheus." Can you describe the effect of this reduction?

A.C.: Rather than describe it, here it is.

QUICKTIME PROMETHEUS

Cast

Prometheus: god of Foresight
Govt (formerly Zeus): mute part
Flare and Stench: two henchman of Govt

Ocean: god of oceans
Io: woman turned into a cow by jealous wife of Govt
Hermes: messenger of Govt
Chorus: 50 daughters of Ocean

PROMETHEUS	How it begins. A rock wall. Enter Flare and Stench sent by Govt, to writhe me (Flare does the work). Sounds of sawing, hammering, harvesting, slaughtering, scrubbing. See my pelt sewn to the wall see me still in it.
FLARE	Are you radioactive, pal?
STENCH	Lurch in there. Use your microphone. He's the enemy.
FLARE	Not my enemy.
STENCH	Then close your eyes.
FLARE	Poor little forcemeat.
PROM	Stench laughs from side to side in freezing wind, signals for a cab. Exit Flare and Stench. I'm too alone, the sun is hot, it's a bad position. [pause] Air! Wind! World! Collate my bones! I am what most people talk about, a power spot. I stole fire, I knew what I was doing, that was last week. I'm bored again. Enter Chorus. Hah, I smell you! Talk!
CHORUS	How strangely beautiful your driveway in the dawn. But why so blue? And why you?
PROM	Govt wanted to enforce an analogy between improvisation and catastrophe.
CHORUS	We shudder as a free skin.
PROM	Bit your whip did I.
CH	Tell us about the boy and the night and the tree at your window.
PROM	No it was later I lost my breath. To humans!
CH	Oh yes Louis Armstrong.
PROM	Him too.
CH	What now?
PROM	I stroll not. Neither do I sail.
CH	Till when?

PROM	Ten thousand years
	is the current estimate.
CH	And then?
PROM	Here comes Ocean!
	Enter Ocean.
OCEAN	Here I am Ocean
	I feel your pain.
PROM	Only simple words,
	as Beckett says,
	give trouble.
OCEAN	I have an "in" with Govt you know.
PROM	Just go home.
OCEAN	Who prefers (by the way) to be called
	Head Boy.
PROM	I don't care if you call him Laurie Anderson
	just
	leave it alone.
OCEAN	Dare to dream.
PROM	Zip and go.
	Exit Ocean.
CH	Here's an Ode:
	O tears!
	We shed our tears for you!
	O tears!
	All shed their tears for you!
PROM	Thanks. Nice ode.
CH	So what exactly did you do?
	Your crime
	this time.
PROM	I took one look at wretched human beings
	living without chairs or reason,
	my heart broke.
	What is it to be locked in a bleeding kind?
	I said to them.
	They could not answer.
	Plus, I like inventing stuff.
	Alphabets.
	Simple stops.
CH	Speaking of which, how about
	a way out.
PROM	Oh I have to bruise a while yet.
CH	Why?
PROM	Here's Io!
IO	Enter Io in cow clothes.
	Am I a cow or a clever dessert?
PROM	You're Io and I can soothe you with words
IO	Dear fellow.

PROM	But your pain will go on.
IO	How long?
PROM	Til the thirteenth generation.
IO	Heck. Get this,
	I didn't even bonk the guy.
PROM	Didn't bonk Govt?
IO	Called a cab, was home by ten.
CH	His wife thought otherwise.
PROM	That's enough detail.
	Point is, you'll eventually
	bear a son
	whose son's son's son's son's son's son's son's son
	will release me from this rock.
	Okay cupcake,
	off you go.
	Ticktock.
IO	Exit Io.
CH	A woman like that shouldn't wave her ass
	at the top brass.
	Act Five.
PROM	He won't be top much longer.
	Our dear Govt's 15 minutes
	are just about up.
CH	You silly pup.
PROM	Yes foresight is silly but that's who I am.
	Look it's all written here on the palm of my hand.
CH	Foresight? You?
	Why didn't you use some?
PROM	Lots of little reasons.
	A painter will tell you,
	it's hard to learn
	to paint an open door.
CH	Say more.
PROM	Here's someone coming,
	who is it running?
	Oh good it's Hermes! Darling!
	Enter Hermes all a-tremble.
HERM	Govt demands
	to know what you know.
	Show us your palms.
PROM	I never noticed before you have a dimple.
HERM	Talk or you'll suffer.
PROM	[laughs]
HERM	Talk or you'll pay.
PROM	Thing is,
	I've watched you gods day after day
	dip your toothbrushes

| | in the abyss
| | where you also piss.
| | I don't need you.
| | I don't like you.
| | Go away.
| HERM | Then put on your goggles.
| | He's going to blast you flat.
| PROM | I might enjoy that.
| HERM | If you could start over—
| PROM | I'd do it all again.
| HERM | Well, hit the road, girls.
| PROM | Exit Hermes.
| CH | Hit the road? Is he serious?
| | What kind of friend—
| PROM | Dolls, this is the end,
| | Tsunamis of fire engulf the stage!
| | Turn the page,
| | that's it for us
| | (and most of the audience has
| | already gone to the bus).
| | Now you may have heard
| | this play is part I of a trilogy:
| | that's true,
| | but as parts III and II
| | are lost, I'd say
| | we're through!
| | Gents and dames,
| | *exeunt omnes*
| | in flames.

CHAPTER 41

MEDEA IN BRAZIL

Interview with Director Heron Coelho

CESAR GEMELLI

HERON Coelho was born in 1977. He has a Bachelor's degree in Letters from the Universidade de São Paulo (USP) and a Master's degree in Brazilian Literature. He began his artistic career in 1997 working with Hermínio Bello de Carvalho[1] as a producer. Heron Coelho is a director, producer, author, playwright, and composer. In the year 2000 he directed, produced, and wrote the musical *Rainha de Quelé* (Queen of Quelé), a tribute to the Brazilian singer Clementina de Jesus.[2] Together with Marcus Vinícius de Andrade,[3] he produced and directed the album *Dona Inah—Divino Samba Meu* ("Lady Inah—My Divine Samba"), which won the TIM Award in 2005 in the category new artist. In the same year, he began his work at SESC[4] São Paulo, where he developed the project *Em Cena: Ações* ("On Stage; Actions!"). In this project, he worked with such renowned actors, actresses, and musicians as Gianfrancesco Guarnieri,[5] Ferreira Gullar,[6] Maria Alice Vergueiro,[7] Zezé Motta,[8] José Wisnik,[9] Hermínio Bello de Carvalho, Paula Picarelli,[10] Alessandro Penezzi,[11] and Georgette Fadel,[12] to bring back classical texts from the Brazilian theatrical tradition, such as *Opinião*,[13] *Arena Conta Zumbi*,[14] *Arena Conta Tiradentes*,[15] *Roda viva*,[16] *O Rei da Vela*,[17] among others. In 2006 he directed the play *Gota d'água—Breviário* ("Water Drop—Breviary"), which is a theater-in-the-round adaptation of the play *Gota d'água* ("Water Drop") by Chico Buarque,[18] and Paulo Pontes.[19] The play deals with the tragic life of Joana and Jasão, an adaptation of Euripides' *Medea* set in the suburbs of Rio de Janeiro. Heron Coelho adapted Chico Buarque and Paulo Pontes's text to theater-in-the-round, shifting the focus to the social issues which could not be directly dealt with by the authors during the 1970s. His staging won the 2006 Shell Award for best actress for Georgette Fadel and was nominated for best soundtrack as well for Alessandro Penezzi. Heron Coelho's theater-in-the-round adaptation of *Gota d'aágua* is an important example of how theater nowadays relies on a long tradition in order to engage with socio-political matters. In this case, Medea serves as a model through which Brazilian social context is discussed and criticized. By interviewing the director of *Gota d'água—Breviário*, it is possible to gain greater insight into his understanding and his positioning in face of these matters. Heron

Coelho has also been working as a music producer. He kindly gave this interview through video-conference in the months of September and October of 2013.

Why is Medea still relevant in Brazil? How did *Medea* become *Gota d'água—Breviário*? What is the process of adaptation?

It was the circumstance. Plays like *Gota d'água* and *Medea* cannot be transposed *ipsis litteris* to a different context. There is always some kind of adaptation. A play cannot be completely sold out for eight years straight without a reference to its context. It is like what Ruy Guerra[20] told me about *Calabar*.[21] The first time it was attempted, it was censored. A decade later, Fernando Peixoto,[22] who introduced Brecht in Brazil, was not successful because he was using the exact same text from years ago, while we were already experiencing an opening in the military dictatorship. It was strange to criticize something when its overthrow was already highly expected and anticipated. I do not mean to say it is unnecessary. The adaptation seems to rely on something other than the text. There was no urgency to the matter; hence the proposition of the *Breviário*. The main idea behind the *Breviário* is to bring the text to a new context, to adapt it. To show a play like [Gianfrancesco] Guarnieri did in the 1970s but within the theater-in-the-round. When people say that Guarnieri's *Eles não usam Black-tie*[23] ("They do not wear black tie") is outdated, which it is not, they mean some of the lines that make reference to objects specific to that period become dated. It is our job to update them. For instance a reference to a car that is no longer being produced, that is just silly. We change that. Because there is absolutely no way that the first play to focus on Brazilian proletarians can be outdated. I did that with *Breviário*.

What is your trajectory with this staging of *Gota d'água—Breviário* ("Water Drop—Breviary")? In what context did this idea come to life and how does it fit with the theatrical context in Brazil nowadays?

What happened was actually very interesting. I personally was not expecting what happened with the play *Gota d'água—Breviário*, because out of 17 or 19 stagings of the original *Gota d'água* that were produced in Brazil, Chico [Buarque] only recognized three as significant. The first one was with Gianni Ratto[24] and Bibi Ferreira[25] in the 1970s, the second one with Gabriel Villela[26] in the early 2000s, which was very hard to produce, and mine. The *Gota d'água—Breviário* came out of a project called *Em Cena: Ações!* in 2004 supported by SESC Ipiranga, at a time when SESC São Paulo gave special attention to Brazilian theater. This period lasted for six years and it was greatly beneficial to us. By us, I mean a group of people that worked with theater, a very underground group, outside of the commercial circuit. I do not mean underground in any aesthetic dimension. It was a time before the Roosevelt Square in São Paulo had established itself. I do not consider what is being done nowadays at Roosevelt Square underground. I consider that to be completely commercial. Whenever there is financial support from companies like Petrobrás, it becomes commercial. Back then, it was still marginal. At least until 2003 and 2004, there was a movement headed by Maria Alice Vergueiro and even more so by Myriam Muniz,[27] which I was able to take part in. Myriam Muniz worked until the end of her life. She died working and creating. She was one of the greatest Brazilian actresses of all time and practically did not work on television. They both headed this movement of marginal theater, in which there was no need for financial subsidies, nor sceneries. I can remember Myriam saying that the text and its delivery come first and that the scenery lies on the face of the actor. That is why you should always hire good actors and those actors usually stay out of television in Brazil. Today I can understand why an actress like Georgette Fadel cannot achieve a complete integration with television, unlike, for instance, Leona Cavalli,[28] who was a great theater actress. It is a brutal transition which is hard to achieve. Myriam Muniz was a genius. She used to say that people in theater have to hold hands with god and the devil and must not let themselves be pulled either way. It is similar to what is happening now during the riots with Mídia Ninja[29] here in São Paulo. Reporters that were fired from Abril, which is one of the biggest publishers in the country, want to create an independent reporting community, but they want their financial support to come from the government through the Rouanet[30] law and other federal grants. It is in part on account of this kind of contradiction that I withdrew a bit from theater. The last play I did was *Breviário Calabar*, which was rewritten together with Ruy Guerra. Chico Buarque is the author, but Ruy was willing to rework the text precisely because it had to become a Breviário, and it had to fit the theater-in-the-round. I was planning to produce and direct *Roda viva*,[31] but there were some impediments. It was not Chico. Some people say that he has forbidden the production, but that was not it. He would never do something like that. Sometimes he forbids some songs. There are some of his songs from before 1965 that he disregards. He does not like the play *Roda viva* because the text actually has some problems. The main idea of the *Breviário* is the system, the machine devouring and deforming the artist so it can fit the latest artistic fashion and imposed aesthetic movements. Things are still complicated since the coup of 1964. By the way, this is a project of mine. Next year, it will be 50 years since the military dictatorship took power. It is going to be 50 years of an anesthetized passion. These protests and riots are not arbitrary, nor propagandistic, nor demagogic. I am in favor of the people that were vandalizing banks. Brecht says, "What is the burgling of a bank to the founding of a bank?"

So this theatrical group was kind of underground. Later some of them surrendered to the economic system, but many remained in the avant-garde movement which will always be outside the center, even if it is on account of the precariousness of its budget. This is so ironic. You do it any way you can, even at your own expenses. You have a good text, a good cast, and good music and musicians. You gather together all this energy and suddenly Georgette receives a Shell Award, which gave a strong push to a work that actually began in Ilo Krugli's backyard,[32] in the backyard of Ventoforte.[33] *Gota d'água— Breviário* came out of an idea during the project *Em Cena: Ações!* that lasted from 2003 to 2006, but in 2004 I had to choose an author to develop the project at SESC Ipiranga. The first one was Vianinha,[34] then I chose Cláudia Pacheco to do *Opinião*.[35] Later Ferreira Gullar gave a talk there. Guarnieri was still alive. We did *Arena Conta Zumbi* and he watched it. When the chosen author of the series was Chico Buarque, they wanted a famous name, but I said no and I insisted on Georgette Fadel to play Joana, since she had already worked with that text in her classes with her students. She is an important art-educator. No one was known at the time in the *Em Cena: Ações!* project. To every author that we chose, there was a plan to invite a famous actor or actress, a heavy name that would attract more people. They did not want Georgette at that time, but I insisted, I told them that she had already worked on a soap opera, and they believed me. It was as hard as it was to stage *Calabar*.

Did you have any access to Paulo Pontes or Chico Buarque in your staging of the play?

This is a usual confusion, this was the first conflict, the first neuralgia that I faced during the production of the play. Paulo Pontes had already passed away in 2005, when it all began, and Chico is not very accessible. He likes to keep a certain distance.

Considering the changes that happen between the text of Euripides, Chico Buarque and Paulo Pontes, and yours, what would you say is the most significant difference?

What is the main idea in Euripides' *Medea*? There is a pact between a barbarian and Jason. But he is trying to complete his social ascension by marrying the daughter of the king. Medea would be relegated to an intermediate stage in his trajectory. There is a rupture of the previous pact between them. The only way they can both carry on with their lives is to bring closure to the previous agreement, a sort of asepsis or hygienization of their stories. So what does she do? She kills her children, Creusa, and Creon. She does not kill herself. After that, she needs a *deus ex machina* to carry on. Chico Buarque and Paulo Pontes kill Joana. Instead of carrying on, she dies with her children after her plot fails. There is no way out for her.

And how this transition developed from their play to yours, *Gota d'água—Breviário*?

I did not have much to do except to find a way of, at first, reducing the text, since the original is almost six hours long, with a huge scenery, lights, cast, dancers . . . It was a huge staging with Bibi Ferreira. It is scary to transpose this to a misery, an absence, a structure lacking absolutely everything, maliciously lacking resources. Furthermore, there was no need for it. I had already staged *Arena Conta Zumbi* and *Arena Conta Tiradentes* by Guarnieri when he was alive. He was present during the staging of it. I also wrote a play with him, which has not been staged yet. I intend to produce it next year, in the 50-year anniversary of the military coup. It is *Arena Conta Guevara*.[36] Francis Hime[37] and I were responsible for the music. I have not touched it since, because I miss him so much. There was no other way except to get the backbone of Chico and Paulo Pontes's text, filter it, and apply my Brechtian approach to the text with its distancings and ruptures. So, instead of Georgette acting that Joana, the character, she actually did not stop being the actress on stage. It was the actress herself on the stage. It was what I wanted, a way to bring forth to the stage the irritation that sometimes would come up on rehearsals. It was absolutely organic and spontaneous.

How does the theater-in-the-round setting mold your staging of the play? It is different from the traditional proscenium format. How did you do it?

Live music is very important. It is part of the items of this Breviário's aesthetic: live music, Brechtian approach, the theater-in-the-round format. It allows for innovation, but it also imposes different limits. It is very difficult to work in a theater-in-the-round.

When you work on a traditional stage you know that there is a pre-established range of possibilities. On a theater-in-the-round stage you have to be very careful. If you are not, you will end up giving your back to the audience at a certain point.

And how would you describe the audience's reaction to it?

It worked out. It worked very well and it was very fulfilling, especially in the beginning, when there was the goal of exposing young people to Brazilian texts. It was incredible. The audience was composed mostly of young people, around 15 and 20 years old. When I was 20 years old, I could watch Vianninha, Paulo Pontes, Chico Buarque, texts by Ferreira Gullar, etc. Even with the fame of Chico Buarque nowadays, if he launches a new record, all newspapers and magazines praise it, everyone talks about it. But if you ask someone to talk about a song they like, they cannot do it, they do not know what to say. Sometimes it feels that his celebrity status overshadows his work. His dramaturgy is like that. It is unknown. These youngsters know about Chico Buarque, he is a celebrity, but his dramaturgy is not well known. I feel very honored when I realize that I helped people to get to know these plays. I frequently have to allow images of my staging to be used in pedagogical books about art by the government. One of the images that they use is the one with Georgette cutting the bread, which I used instead of the meatloaf that Chico and Paulo Pontes use. There was no way I could use any kind of meat on a theater-in-the-round staging, unless I could buy pounds and pounds of Kibbe every night. Besides that, the bread adds the notion of the eucharist, the poison in the bread, sharing the bread. A companion is one who shares the bread. Theater needs that, this complicity, this camaraderie of sharing the bread, even if it is the bread that has been to hell and back, the bread that the devil kneaded himself, even if it is poisoned, that is the bread that Georgette shares with her children and with the audience. I did not expect it to become a success. It was not profitable, however. I actually spent a lot of money doing it, because of the copyrights. Not on account of Chico Buarque. He did not charge anything and gave the green light. His only request was that 2 percent of the ticketing went towards Vianninha's family, since it was Vianninha's idea. It was the first time that Medea appeared in Brazilian television. It was an episode of *Caso especial* ("Special Case") made by Globo with Fernanda Montenegro in 1973.[38] There was some trouble with the family of Paulo Pontes, which is kind of ironic, since he was one of the most generous people in the Brazilian theater. It was thanks to an intervention by Bibi Ferreira, who called Tereza Rachel, that I was able to produce the play.[39] The pantheon of Brazilian theater had to come together to make it happen. This is something important. This was something that Chico avoids, this vanity of awards. Awards are only good as paper weights when it is windy. This is a matter of formation. I got it from Myriam Muniz.

Why did you decide to stop after eight years of staging the *Gota d'água—Breviário*?

It was a crazy thing. Myriam had already passed away. But Maria Alice told me that it had been going on for too long. It should have lasted three years at the most, but it went on for eight. And this year was the last one. I bought the rights of the *Breviário* and I do not want them to stage it anymore, at least not in the theater-in-the-round style. There comes a time when you cannot take it anymore. I was not even present in the last staging. There were 600 people in a theater with a capacity for 400. It was incredible, I could barely understand it. The same thing happened with *Breviário Calabar*. We were sold out for three months, with bad press and still sold out, because people wanted to know what was going on.

How does the context of your staging of *Gota d'água* relate to the context of the 1970s when Paulo Pontes and Chico Buarque were composing it?

The dictatorship in Brazil killed workers, subversive students, middle- or low-class people, artists and their children, like Stuart Angel.[40] Chico went to exile because he could not take it.[41] The dictatorship in Brazil was not like Pinochet's, who used to cut the hands of composers on the street, on the squares. Ours was more cowardly. They killed workers, students, poor people. It was imposed by cowards, traitors. They destroyed the big dream, the big plan; they destroyed a project that existed before 1964, when they took down Jango.[42] It has been 50 years now and I think these protests will become more intense. This is an awakening after 50 years of numbness, 50 years of being anesthetized by the military rule that established unprecedented levels of corruption in Brazil, which later spread to all sectors of society, even more so in the cultural sector, mainly through Globo Network, which supported the regime and received many benefits from the military rule. There is a whole system that is mobilized to control information and spread a hegemonic perspective of entertainment, conformity, and alienation approved by the military. Authors like Dias Gomes had to accept these circumstances and attempt to utilize a cryptic language.[43] I mention this because *Gota d'água*, due to its circumstance, crosses this gap, because it can be easily commercialized, just because it is by Chico Buarque. Everything that has his name nowadays receives a lot of attention. Still, his most staged play is *Ópera do Malandro*,[44] which I consider his least interesting play.

Do you think that elements of Greek theater are still present nowadays? What is the importance of the plays of Euripides in Brazilian theater?

Euripides breaks with an archetype that prevails up to today, of a psychoanalytical, philosophical, sociological, and anthropological order, which Marsha Norman later picks up with *'night, Mother*. Euripides is groundbreaking. Besides being the cradle of classical theater, Euripides is in Edward Albee, he is in O'Neill, he is in that suicidal maniac Sarah Kane. Euripides deals with the archetypes of the human soul, he deals with pre-existing knowledge before culture establishes itself as a pivotal element of the construction of human thought. I do not want to dismiss Aeschylus or Sophocles, but Euripides works with archetypes and deconstructs totems which were paradigmatic, such as the mother figure for instance. Consider it in contrast to our Christian tradition, that scene with King Solomon in which he threatens to cut a baby in two and the real mother offers to give up the child just to assure its integrity. There are many other examples that establish the mother as a capable being, a provider, a bringer, a maker or generator, a giver of life, which slowly becomes the Mater Dolorosa in the tradition. A mother that is capable of saving everything and holds the power of life which she can bestow upon the son. There is a succession of images that culminate in the Pietà. There are many similar examples in Brazilian literature as well. Euripides provides us with a way to deconstruct this notion, to challenge it. An example of Euripides' continuity is that, for Medea, there is something more important than the filial relationship. However, in the cultural context which Euripides is dealing with, there is something else which allows a *deus ex machina*. In that tradition, there is a possible transcendence. It is destiny, it is a predestinated trajectory, fate. Jason, for instance, already has a complex history when he meets Medea. He is already dealing with power disputes within his family, whereas Medea is a barbarian whom he can use as a tool in his political struggles. There is a similarity to Brecht's *Pirate Jenny*. Jason is the supposed hero and Medea is just a barbarian. What is surprising is that this pact can be broken, the pact between them, but for that to happen there is a central condition, which is the *deus ex machina*, which essentially means that the barbarian is not only a lesser woman. She has divine blood. This is present in the tragedy, there is this brutal shift. In this play, the only way out is to kill both of her children. She crushes any possibility of construction of supreme power, of paternal love. This desire for a clean slate will later appear in Freud. The desire to kill the mother is like a need for hygienization, like a rupture with a historical continuity that allows for the birth of a kind of freer being that can decide their own future without being attached to their own history. It is through cultural elements from her barbarism that he can become a hero. Without it, Jason cannot reach that position of power through marriage with Creusa. Medea refuses to become part of this scheme. She does not let herself be coopted by Creon. The fact that she kills her children is the result of the broken pact between Jason and her. She kills Creusa and Creonte and cleans everything up so they can go on, so they can move on with their lives. There is a possibility of life after that. She does not kill herself.

How would you describe your representation of Medea in the character of Joana? How is the female role represented under your direction?

My Medea cuts a slice of bread, she shares it and then eats this poisoned bread (Fig, 41.1).

She tells her children that they are going to a place where people do not cry, where the movie theater is free, the bunk beds are made of clouds. And Georgette is very cynical. As she eats the bread and poisons herself she says it smells like ether. Her last line is that childhood is perpetuated in formol. She cringes, they put some green light on her, and in the *Breviário* the samba "Gota d'água" is never sung until the end, someone always interrupts it. Then she dies. So the light changes, Georgette, the actress, gets up and starts to move. She gets a guitar and starts singing it. It is so beautiful, it is chilling. Some people cry, and I am proud of having done something that touched someone. But just to finish my comment regarding *'night, Mother*, I would like to say that they both live together, mother and daughter. The daughter tells the mother that she found her father's gun and that she will kill herself. From that point onwards, the mother tries to convince her not to do it. The mother employs all the cognitive and pscyhoclogical resources she has. That is an example of a Mater Dolorosa, another Pietà, Our Lady, or the mother from the Solomon tale, but not Medea. What does Medea do? She legitimizes the suicide [Fig. 41.2].

FIG. 41.1 Joana (Georgette Fadel) preparing the poisoned bread. © Heron Coelho.

FIG. 41.2 Joana (Georgette Fadel) lying dead next to the poisoned bread. © Heron Coelho.

She accepts this rupture. Try to conceive a similar situation where Medea is the mother. What would she do? Ask for a reason? Would she try to stop the daughter? Euripides is Brecht's father. The circumstance makes the man. Brecht's Mother Courage fails to understand her circumstance. And in the face of despair she utters the mute scream. The mother does not have this awe character. Isabel Allende creates another Pietà in the character of the tortured daughter in *La casa de los espíritus*, which is beautiful and has a whole other bunch of references. It is the circumstance which matters the most. The group of decisions, obligations, agreements, and connections, which, if broken, necessarily result in tragic action, but only within that circumstance. There are all these resonances: Euripides, Brecht, Chico Buarque. And it does not mean that one thing is better than the other. Some stay closer to others, as Vinicius de Moraes's[45] reworking of Orpheus. He stays closer to the myth with *Orfeu da Conceição*.[46] Chico is faithful to Euripides' work, he said so himself. In their version, Joana is carried away by Master Aegeus. Lars von Trier and Brecht have a more violent female character, whereas Chico in his *Geni e o Zeppelim*[47] has a more passive reading. There is a whole trajectory and plot to reveal the corruption. This is what I call a compassion for the feminine. A lot of Brazilian artists seem to work with this idea somehow, like Paulo Vanzolini,[48] Caetano Veloso,[49] Gilberto Gil.[50] My understanding is that Chico Buarque and Paulo Pontes depart a little bit from the most didactic concept of tragedy, but without betraying Euripides' Greek ideal. Tragedy is tragedy, there is no way out of it. This transposition requires this passional context, which has resonance with criminality of its context. Think of passion crimes. It is not an arbitrary adaptation; they use Brazilian references to make it. It is common in Brazilian literature. You can also see it in Manuel Bandeira's poem *Tragédia Brasileira* ("Brazilian Tragedy").[51] Misael attempts to save Maria Elvira from prostitution and ends up killing her because of jealousy. It is almost as a news piece. Chico and Paulo Pontes are dealing with a Brazilian context and Brazilian cultural references. There is a samba of the 1940s which deals with a very similar situation. It talks about a Joana who commits suicide on account of someone called João. It is called *Notícia de jornal* ("News Piece"). Chico recorded this song later. Nelson Rodrigues also explores this thematic in his tragedies.[52] The changes they make to the play are to contextualize it to the Brazilian reality. At that time, until 1940, there were lawyers and experts who argued that it was a lesser crime to kill a wife caught cheating. There are historical factors in this. What moves Joana into action is passion and she kills herself because she cannot live without her children. And what moves Medea into action are the circumstances. That is why she kills Creusa. Medea kills Creon, Creusa, and her two children and does not kill herself. She is cold. She is aware that life is just a game and that we will lose this game because we are doomed to death. For Joana, it is passion. Mestre Egeu (Master Aegeus), the godfather of her children, is fighting for the remodeling of their housing complex. He complains and tries to find a way to solve their problem, to make their struggle about the people and their living conditions, but Joana insists in personalizing it, she wants to pick a fight; she creates a political struggle because her husband was co-opted. She wants the scandal. I believe this is the only pro-active female character in Chico's work besides the voice singing in the song *Anos dourados* ("Golden Years"), who does not passively wait for her lover to come back. She does something. She calls and leaves messages on the answering machine trying to seduce him again. Unlike his other female characters, this one has the foresight to consider the hypothesis that there might already be another woman there listening to this message with him. She uses her happiness to try to win him over. José Wisnik discusses this really well. This representation of women as a passive and submissive creature is not a unique characteristic of his work. There are many other instances in Brazilian literature and music as well. Brazil is the country of tragedy. The country is a tragedy.

You already mentioned it when you talked about the recent protests, but how does politics appear in the *Gota d'água—Breviário*?

Politics was always present; the idea that man is the result of his surroundings, as Brecht says. To deflagrate the characters in this aspect is very interesting. Mestre Egeu in *Gota d'água—Breviário* is a union leader. He reads a text by Brecht from his book of poems which I freely translated. It is a poem without a title in which he asks Hitler a question. I had to adapt it drastically to keep it in conformity with the context of the characters of the play. So Brecht asks "In dark times, will there also be singing? Yes, there will also be singing. About the dark times." Then he sings *Levantados do chão* ("Risen from the Ground"), which is a song by Chico Buarque and Milton Nascimento.[53] This song also appears in *Terra*, a book by Sebastião Salgado. This use of the song was completely authorized. And it even calls Chico's attention because then he realized that I was dealing more with the social issue than with the personal drama of Joana, which was not possible to do in the time of Bibi Ferreira and her staging of the play. He sings it precisely when Creonte is able to convince the people to back down. Creonte promises things, he says he will fix and remodel the buildings when the people complain to him about the village and the exploitation of labor. This appears in the preface of the play by Chico and Paulo Pontes, that the structure of Brazil, the formation of this contemporary Brazil, as Caio Prado Junior says,[54] is made up of social layers which explore other layers beneath them. And it is a contemporary Brazil after 1964. I remember discussing this context a lot with Myriam Muniz, Gianfrancesco, Valkyria Britto, a little bit with Gianni Ratto, but he passed away soon after. I talked to them about what happened at that time, after 1964, because there was a project before the coup and this is the great wound. Before they got rid of João Goulart, before the military took the power, there was a project. And you can see traces of this project in the changes Juscelino [Kubitschek][55] makes to the automotive industry in Brazil. Music became more assertive. We used to have sad boleros, Nora Ney's[56] samba-canção, and suddenly you see songs like *Eu sei que vou te amar* ("I know that I will love you"), *Eu não existo sem você* ("I cannot exist without you"), *Brigas nunca mais* ("Fighting nevermore"), all this movement, all this happiness. That project, from which we got people like Paulo Freire[57] and Sérgio Buarque,[58] where there was a whole conjecture of Brazil, was thrown down by the military coup. There is a very interesting moment in this new movie about Elizabeth Bishop directed by Bruno Barreto,[59] *Flores raras* ("Rare Flowers"). And, at the same time, I understand this lack of memory of North American cinema. It took a Brazilian to make a movie about the greatest contemporary North American poet, Elizabeth Bishop. I mention her because she lives through this exact transition. When Carlos Lacerda[60] becomes Governor of Rio de Janeiro and allies himself with Castelo Branco,[61] a period when the coup was being praised, she expressed her incapacity to understand the approval of the coup. There was a project before 1964 and I tried to understand it, to understand this pain, so I could begin the production process of these plays that are considered to be outdated by a lot of people. This is absurd! People actually say that *Eles não usam black-tie* by Gianfrancesco Guarnieri is outdated. That is to say that the first Brazilian play that brings a proletarian as a protagonist is considered outdated at the same time that plays by Sarah Kane or stagings of Shakespeare's texts with Globo Network actors are being staged. Another person to whom I got closer was Ferreira Gullar. They went through the hardest period of the dictatorship. They were creating in a moment when Brazil was being destroyed. They persisted in creating while the military were trying to undo it. This still goes on nowadays. Our passion was anesthetized, when Paulo Freire's ideas about education were forbidden, for instance. His method was not alienating. His method was against the political alienation that favored to the regime. It was necessary to take away from the people any possibility of thinking. In the recent riots, the scene of a young man, who is actually a student of architecture, attacking a bank is a symbol of a waking up from 50 years of numbness, that voice is a wake-up call from 50 years of being anesthetized.

You mentioned before that you spent a lot of your own money to stage your plays. Could you talk a little bit about the present financial situations in Brazilian theater? Is there some kind of institutional support?

This is an interesting and tragic phenomenon. I do not believe in commercializing that which is underground, in turning into a product that which would be marginal and which has a marginal origin. I do not need the system, I need space, and that can be the streets; street theater is wonderful. There are some people who are just struggling for attention and publicity. You cannot turn something into merchandise, because it becomes crooked. That is what happens at Roosevelt Square. But it does not work. And Joana talks about this.[62] She says that since Jasão broke up with her, he will try to make samba, but it will be crooked, not good. It will never be as good as *Gota d'água*. This samba is the reflection of Joana's soul, of the soul of the woman he once had and no longer has access to. Joana puts a curse on him, saying he will not be able to create good samba anymore. She has this oracular side to her, and Chico and Paulo Pontes take advantage of that. These are the distortions that we have here.

I am distorted as well. If you live too close to the masters too early, you end up getting old faster, you take their pain as your own. At the same time that this is an education, it is also a deformation, but it is necessary. It is one of the many contradictions of the country. José Sarney wrote a book called *20 Anos de Democracia* ("20 Years of Democracy").[63] It is like Netinho de Paula[64] writing about Maria da Penha law.[65] Myriam Muniz now is the name of an award, but no one knows who she is. I have this idea that it is possible to communicate and inform at the same time, to spread information that was kept under the carpet during the military dictatorship and is still left unknown by inertia, by a system that still keeps its deformations from that time.

Where did your interest for theater come from? Considering all the difficulties to make and produce plays in Brazil as well as the aftermath of more than 20 years of military dictatorship, how did you decide to get into this field?

My interest in theater came from Mário de Andrade.[66] He had a sentence that said it was necessary to "Brazilianize" the Brazilian, and I realized that people did not know about Brazilian culture, they only knew what they saw on television. Hermínio told me that. He used to repeat it a lot. It is from a book called *Vida do cantador* ("Life of the Singer") by Mário de Andrade. This put me in touch with the song by Aldir Blanc,[67] *Querelas do Brasil* ("Laments of Brazil"). Then I realized that this was real, that people did not know the voice of Clementina, the work of Lygia Clark,[68] they only knew what they would watch on TV. There was no Internet then. I am talking about 1996. Nana Caymmi only became known as the singer that she has always been after a TV mini-series had one of her songs as its opening theme.[69] I do believe, though, that Brazil has begun to reassess itself since the turn of the millennium and it is beginning to move forward. It has been 50 years since the coup. Now people are beginning to question what they missed. We talk about Medea, *deus ex machina*, Quarteto em Cy (a Brazilian musical group), Clementina de Jesus, Mário de Andrade, and we think this is common knowledge. It is not. I thought everyone knew about this, that Brazilians knew about Brazilian culture, but they do not. I recently saw, on a bookstore window that the complete poetry of Paulo Leminski was among the national bestsellers.[70] This is a sign that there is something happening. At the same time that there is an interdiction or even a manipulation by the mass communication media, which takes advantage of a Macunaimic laziness of its audiences,[71] Paulo Leminksi is receiving attention. There are actresses that make an enormous effort to put together an adaptation of Virginia Woolf, which had already been staged recently, and set aside Brazilian authors such as Vianinha, Ruy Guerra, Paulo Pontes, Tite de Lemos,[72] Armando Costa,[73] and many others. That really upset me. At that time, I really believed I could do something about it. Nowadays I do not believe in anything anymore. Just as Myriam used to say: "Life is a horror. That is why we have to make theater. So we do not die." And I was also interested in American theater of the 1950s and 1960s, such as O'Neill's *Mourning Becomes Electra*, Edward Albee's *Who's Afraid of Virginia Woolf*, Tennessee Williams's *A Streetcar Named Desire*, Miller's *The Death of a Salesman*. I thought this kind of theater was directly connected to the Brazilian aesthetic. Fernando Peixoto was the one who called my attention to this connection between the American theater of the 1950s and 1960s and Brazilian theater. It did not deal with only the stream of consciousness and psychologism, but also with the social aspect of it. It is impossible to think about theater or any artistic work without a social or political aspect. It is just impossible; especially nowadays. There was some peace during Juscelino's time with Bossa Nova and the New Cinema.[74] After that it became hell. We have an epidemic of violence. There are groups of police officers who come together to create hit squads. They stage the whole crime scene if necessary. This has always been the intention; to bring Brazilian culture to the Brazilian people, to give continuity to the ideas of Mário de Andrade, a commitment with information. What happened during the military dictatorship was a fracture in education. They managed to break completely away education, culture, and social engagement. Education was isolated in schools as subjects that must be learned and which do not have any social use. Culture became a product and there was just no space for social and political engagement. These things were never meant to be apart. They all stand together, they are parts of the same thing. It is impossible to conceive any artistic endeavor without political and social concerns. Besides the commercialization of cultural products, academia is also part of this alienating process. Professors decide which texts should be read based on the previous generation of professors and perpetuate the exclusion of several important texts. Brecht fought his whole life for the democratization of knowledge. It is a little bit utopic, of course, but I just cannot allow myself to become more market-oriented and give up on staging these plays. If I did so, I would not have staged *Calabar* with my own money, I would not have worked with Célia Gouvêa,[75] I would not have done a lot of things. It is a constant struggle against a cultural imperialism. And by this I mean for example what happened when we were staging *Um grito parado no ar* ("A Scream Frozen in the Air") in 2010. I was directing Georgette Fadel on a text written by Gianfrancesco Guarnieri. It was one of the texts that managed to escape censorship when it was first staged in the 1970s. On the day of the opening of the play, the Supreme Court voted to keep the Amnesty law, that is to say that there could be no alterations in the law from 1979, meaning that torturers in the military dictatorship who were still alive could not be prosecuted in any way. So we changed the play in the last minute. It was at SESC Pompéia. During the play, we spoke the name of around 50 torturers. Drauzio Varella[76] and his wife gave a standing ovation. Later the directors of SESC Pompeia called us to tell us to stop that, because some of the torturers we had mentioned were directors of SESCs in other states. These are the conditions we face. It is not a democracy. It is a kleptocracy. It is like Professor Antônio [Cândido][77] said on an interview for *Brasil de Fato* that socialism is an eternal struggle,[78] a battle that cannot be won, but that must be fought. Otherwise, it is a direct fall into hell.

Do the political issues become financial issues? Is it possible to bypass one without the other?

It is this kind of thing that I do not want to get involved with. I would rather go for a crowd funding scheme than to accept dirty money from Petrobrás or some other company like that. And this is not a kind of sectarianism or proselytism, it is respect for an idea similar to what [Sábato] Magaldi mentions,[79] Décio [de Almeida Prado] too,[80] that there is the need for something similar to what happened in the 1980s, especially in New York, when a government would fund theater. Here we have what is called promotion,[81] but it does not work, and it is dirty money. I have some experience with that, with governmental project in which money from the budget is taken by politicians. Magaldi is right on this aspect. It is a Brechtian perspective that there is a need for some kind of state funding to all the kinds of artistic expressions. In a country such as Brazil, there must be a mechanism to create some balance between the two spheres, between the state thinking and artistic posture. Some artists resort to private funding. I went through this. While asking for support from one of the biggest banks in Brazil, the person who was responsible for the projects admitted that he did not go to watch the plays. It was a pure marketing strategy. Heavyweight names being associated with their brand. And that is it. That is one of the reasons why Ana de Holanda,[82] Chico's sister, had so many problems in her term as Minister of Culture. She was interested in creating a mechanism that would provide a follow up of these private sponsorships for which the companies can get huge tax discounts. She was unwilling to be corrupted by the system.

Notes

1. Hermínio Bello de Carvalho (Rio de Janeiro, RJ 1935) is one of the great names in Brazilian music. Born in 1935, he began his career in the early 1950s working as a radio-journalist. Later he was responsible for several cultural programs focusing on Brazilian music and culture. He lost his position at public radio during the military dictatorship. He is a composer, poet, author, and music producer.
2. Clementina de Jesus (Valença, RJ 1901–87 Rio de Janeiro, RJ) is a Brazilian singer and composer who was discovered by Hermínio Bello de Carvalho. Before being recognized as a singer, she worked as a maid for many years. She is often described as a link to old traditional slave songs from Brazil due to the work songs which she learned with her mother.
3. Marcus Vinícius de Andrade (Recife, PE 1949) is a singer, composer, producer, playwright, and author. He was part of the group that began the Tropicalist movement.
4. SESC (Serviço Social do Comércio) is a non-profit private institution created by the Confederação Nacional do Comércio (National Comerce Confederation) in 1946 with the goal of improving the lives of people that work in commerce by offering services in Education and Health.
5. Gianfrancesco Guarnieri (Milan, Italy 1934–2006 São Paulo, SP) is one of the greatest actors in Brazilian history. He is also a playwright, director, and poet. His play *Eles não usam black-tie* ("They do not wear black tie") is acclaimed as the play that marks the beginning of the focus on Brazilian themes in the theater-in-the-round and one of the most important plays in Brazilian literature.
6. Ferreira Gullar is the pseudonym of José Ribamar Ferreira (São Luís, MA 1930). He is a poet, art critic, translator, playwright, biographer, author, essayist, and poet. He is part of Concrete poetical movement. During his exile on account of the military dictatorship, he wrote the famous *Poema sujo* ("Dirty Poem").
7. Maria Alice Vergueiro was born Maria Alice Monteiro de Campos Vergueiro (São Paulo, SP 1935). She is a famous underground actress, director, and professor. Her career spans more than 40 years.
8. Maria José Motta de Oliveira (Campos de Goytacazes, RJ 1948) is a singer and actress. She began her career with *Roda viva*, a play by Chico Buarque.
9. José Miguel Wisnik (São Vicente, SP 1948) is a Professor of Brazilian Literature at Universidade de São Paulo (USP). His research focuses mainly on Brazilian Modernism and Music. He received his degree in Letters from Universidade de São Paulo as well as his Master's and Ph.D. degree in Literary Theory and Comparative Literature from the same university under Professor Antônio Cândido Mello e Souza. He was a visiting professor in UCLA Berkeley in 2006. He is also an accomplished musician, composer, and essayist.

10. Paula Picarelli Ribeiro Porto (São Paulo, SP 1978) is an actress and TV host. In 2003 she was acclaimed for her role as Rafaela who made a romantic homosexual pair with Clara in the prime time soap opera *Mulheres apaixonadas* ("Women in Love").
11. Alessandro Penezzi (Piracicaba, SP 1974) is a musician, composer, and arranger. He has a Bachelor's degree in Popular Music from Universidade de Campinas (UNICAMP). He won several music awards.
12. Georgette Fadel (Laranjal Paulista, SP 1973) is an actress and director. She received a Shell Award for her role as Joana in the play *Gota d'água—Breviário* ("Water Drop—Breviary") directed by Heron Coelho.
13. *Opinião* ("Opinion") was a musical show directed by Augusto Boal in the theater-in-the-round. The show was an important collaboration among Paulo Pontes, Augusto Boal, Oduvaldo Vianna Filho, and Armando Costa. The play was central in a censorship dispute before the establishment of the AI-5 (Institutional Act 5) which was the final blow to civil rights in Brazil during the military rule.
14. *Arena conta Zumbi* ("Theater-in-the-round tells Zumbi") is an important play whose authors are Gianfrancesco Guarnieri and Augusto Boal. The play is a first experiment with the Joker System, in which one actor plays more than one role in a play. *Arena conta Zumbi* focuses on the history of the resistance of the Quilombo of Palmares against the Portuguese forces in the seventeenth century.
15. *Arena conta Tiradentes* ("Theater-in-the-round tells Tiradentes") is part of the same series in this collaboration. It focuses on the history of the Inconfidência Mineira, a failed revolutionary movement of the end of the eighteenth century in the state of Minas Gerais which was inspired by the independence of the 13 Colonies in North America. Tiradentes was the alias of Joaquim José da Silva Xavier who was the only rebel who did not have his death sentence commuted. He is considered a national hero in Brazil and the day of his hanging (April 21) is a national holiday.
16. *Roda viva* ("Live Wheel") is a play directed by José Celso Martinez Corrêa. The play deals with a political division between people who support the military dictatorship and those who oppose it. The play was written by Chico Buarque and tells the story of a musician who accepts to change his name in an attempt to achieve greater commercial success.
17. *O rei da vela* ("The King of the Candles") is a play written by Oswald de Andrade in 1933. It was only published four years later and staged for the first time in 1967 under the direction of José Celso Martinez Corrêa. The play deals with the ascent of bourgeoisie values in Brazil where the old rural elite needs to adjust to a new setting in which financial speculation holds the power.
18. Francisco Buarque de Holanda (Rio de Janeiro, RJ 1944), best known as Chico Buarque, is a singer, composer, playwright, poet, and author. He is widely acclaimed for his music. He wrote the play *Gota d'água* with Paulo Pontes.
19. Vicente de Paula Holanda Pontes (Campina Grande, PB 1940–76 Rio de Janeiro, RJ) was an acclaimed playwright. He focuses on the common people and culture of Brazil.
20. Ruy Alexandre Guerra Coelho Pereira (Lourenço Marques, Moçambique 1931) is an actor, film director, producer, and editor. He is an important name in Brazil's Cinema Novo (New Cinema) movement.
21. *Calabar, o elogio da traição* ("Calabar, in Praise of Betrayal") is a play from 1973 that deals with the life of Domingos Fernandes Calabar (c.1600–1635) who sided with the Dutch

invaders against the Portuguese rulers in the Brazilian northeast. The play offers a veiled critique of the military dictatorship in Brazil.
22. Fernando Amaral dos Guimarães Peixoto (Porto Alegre, RS 1937–2012 São Paulo, SP) was an actor, translator, director. He directed a famous staging of *Um grito parado no ar* ("A Scream Frozen in the Air") by Gianfrancesco Guarnieri.
23. See n. 7 above.
24. Gianni Ratto (Milan 1916–2005 São Paulo, SP) was an actor, director, scenographer, and author.
25. Abigail Izquierdo Ferreira (Rio de Janeiro, RJ 1922) is a Brazilian actress, singer, director, and composer.
26. Antônio Gabriel Santana Villela (Carmo do Rio Claro, 1958) is a Brazilian theater director, scenographer, and costume designer.
27. Myriam Muniz de Melo (São Paulo, SP 1931–2004) is an important actress, director, and art-educator.
28. Alleyona Canedo da Silva (Rosário do Sul, RS 1969) is a Brazilian actress.
29. Mídia Ninja is a collaborative group of journalists that gained attention for their live coverage of the protests and riots of 2013 in Brazil.
30. Rouanet law allows companies to fund cultural events in exchange for tax deductions.
31. *Roda viva* is the first play written by Chico Buarque at the end of the 1960s.
32. Ilo Krugli (Buenos Aires, Argentina 1930) is an award winning actor, director, author, and artist. He moved to Brazil in the 1960s. He is the founder of Ventoforte.
33. Ventoforte is an important theatrical group created by Ilo Krugli in 1974.
34. Oduvaldo Vianna Filho (Rio de Janeiro, RJ 1936–74) was an actor and author. He was acclaimed by his colleagues and co-workers as one of the greatest playwrights of this period. The original concept of the play *Gota d'água* by Paulo Pontes and Chico Buarque is his.
35. Cláudia Pacheco is a Brazilian actress and TV hostess.
36. *Arena conta Guevara* ("Theater-in-the-round tells Guevara") is a play still unstaged.
37. Francis Hime (Rio de Janeiro, RJ 1939) is an accomplished Brazilian pianist, singer, and composer.
38. Fernanda Montenegro (Rio de Janeiro, RJ 1929) is a famous Brazilian actress who was nominated for the Academy Award for Best Actress.
39. Tereza Rachel (Nilópolis, RJ 1935) is a Brazilian actress and producer.
40. Stuart Edgart Angel Jones (Salvador, BA 1946–71 Rio de Janeiro, RJ) was a member of the guerrilla group MR-8 (Revolutionary Movement October 8). He is the son of Zuleika Angel Jones, best known as Zuzu Angel. She was an internationally recognized stylist who searched for many years for official evidence about the disappearance of her son. Stuart Angel went missing in 1971. He was arrested by the Brazilian Air Force, tortured, and killed while being dragged by a vehicle in the backyard of a military base while his mouth was glued to the tail pipe of the car.
41. Chico Buarque went to Italy in 1970 and returned to Brazil in 1972. He had already lived in Italy during his childhood.
42. João Belchior Marques Goulart (São Borja, RS 1918/9–76 Mercedes, Argentina), best known as João Goulart or by the nickname Jango, was a Brazilian politician. He was Vice-President of Brazil from 1956 to 1961 when Juscelino Kubitschek was the President. Jango assumed the office of President in 1961 and was deposed by the military coup in 1964.

43. Alfredo de Freitas Dias Gomes (Salvador, BA 1922–99 São Paulo, SP) was a prolific author, playwright, and screenwriter.
44. *Ópera do malandro* ("Opera of the Hustler") is a 1978 Brazilian musical play written by Chico Buarque. It is based on John Gay's *The Beggar's Opera* and Brecht's *Threepenny Opera*.
45. Marcus Vinícius de Moraes (Rio de Janeiro, RJ 1913–80) was a Brazilian poet, composer, diplomat, and playwright. He worked with great names from music such as Chico Buarque, Tom Jobim, João Gilberto, Baden Powell, among others. He achieved a great success with the Bossa Nova movement.
46. *Orfeu da Conceição* is a musical play written by Vinicius de Moraes. The songs were composed by Tom Jobim. The sceneries were developed by the famous architect Oscar Niemeyer. It is an adaptation of the myth of Orpheus and Eurydice to the shanty towns of Rio de Janeiro.
47. A song by Chico Buarque based on Brecht's *Pirate Jenny*.
48. Paulo Emílio Vanzolini (São Paulo, SP 1924–2013) was a zoologist and composer. He obtained a Bachelor's degree in Medicine from Universidade de São Paulo (USP) and a Ph.D. in Zoology from Harvard University.
49. Caetano Emanuel Vianna Telles Velloso (Santo Amaro da Purificação, BA 1942), best known as Caetano Veloso, is a famous singer, composer, and writer. He was part of the Tropicália movement in the late 1960s. He lived in exile in London from 1969 to 1972 when he then returned to Brazil.
50. Gilberto Passos Gil Moreira (Salvador, BA 1942) is best known as Gilberto Gil. He is an internationally acclaimed singer, composer, and writer.
51. Manuel Carneiro de Sousa Bandeira Filho (Recife, PE 1886–1968 Rio de Janeiro, RJ) was an important poet, translator, and professor.
52. Nélson Falcão Rodrigues (Recife, PE 1912–80 Rio de Janeiro, RJ) was a Brazilian playwright, journalist, and author.
53. Milton Nascimento (Rio de Janeiro, RJ 1942) is an internationally acclaimed musician, singer, composer, and guitarist.
54. Caio da Silva Prado Junior (São Paulo, SP 1907–90) was a geographer, historian, editor, writer, and politician. He published the acclaimed book *Formação do Brasil contemporâneo* ("Formation of Contemporary Brazil—Colony").
55. Juscelino Kubitschek de Oliveira (Diamantina, MG 1902–76 Resende, RJ) was a Brazilian politician. He was President of Brazil from 1956 to 1961. He founded Brasília.
56. Iracema de Sousa Ferreira (Rio de Janeiro, RJ 1922–2003) was a Brazilian singer best known as Nora Ney. She achieved great success singing samba-canção (samba-song).
57. Paulo Reglus Neves Freire (Recife, PE 1921–97 São Paulo, SP) was a Brazilian philosopher and historian. He is best known for his book *Pedagogy of the Oppressed*.
58. Sérgio Buarque de Holanda (São Paulo, SP 1902–82) was a journalist, literary critic, and historian. His best-known book is *Roots of Brazil*. He is the father of Ana de Holanda and Chico Buarque.
59. Bruno Barreto (Rio de Janeiro, RJ 1955) is a Brazilian movie director.
60. Carlos Frederico Werneck de Lacerda (Vassouras, RJ 1914–77 Rio de Janeiro, RJ) was a politician and journalist.
61. Marshal Humberto de Alencar Castelo Branco (Fortaleza, CE 1897–1967) was a Brazilian marshal and politician. He was one of the leaders of the military coup from 1964 which overthrew President João Goulart.
62. Joana is the main character in the play *Gota d'água* and *Gota d'água—Breviário*.

63. José Sarney de Araújo Costa (Pinheiro, MA 1930) is a Brazilian politician and author, He was the President of Brazil from 1985 to 1990 after the death of Tancredo Neves. As President, José Sarney was succeeded by Fernando Collor de Mello, the first president elected by direct vote after the military dictatorship. José Sarney has been re-elected to the Brazilian Senate three times.
64. José de Paula Neto (São Paulo, SP 1970) is best known as Netinho de Paula. He is a singer, TV host, actor, and politician. He was accused of domestic violence by his wife in 2005.
65. A law created to reduce domestic violence. It establishes harsher sentences for the perpetrators.
66. Mário Raul de Morais Andrade (São Paulo, SP 1893–1945) is an important author, poet, researcher, musicologist, ethnomusicologist, and historian.
67. Aldir Blanc Mendes (Rio de Janeiro, RJ 1946) is a composer and writer.
68. Lygia Clark (Belo Horizonte, MG 1920–88 Rio de Janeiro, RJ) is a Brazilian artist.
69. Dinair Tostes Caymmi (Rio de Janeiro, RJ 1941) is a Brazilian singer.
70. Paulo Leminski Filho (Curitiba, PR 1944–89) was a writer, author, translator, poet, literary critic, composer, and professor.
71. The word refers to the Modernist novel *Macunaíma* by Mário de Andrade.
72. Tite de Lemos (Rio de Janeiro, RJ 1942–89) was a poet, playwright, and journalist.
73. Armando Costa (Rio de Janeiro, RJ 1933–84) was a playwright and director. He took part in the theatrical group Opinião (Opinion).
74. Cinema Novo (New Cinema) was a Brazilian movement that focused on a more socially engaged production.
75. Célia Regina Gouvêa Vaneau is a choreographer and a ballet dancer.
76. Drauzio Varella (São Paulo, SP 1943) is a Brazilian medical doctor, writer, and TV host.
77. Antônio Cândido de Mello e Souza (Rio de Janeiro, RJ 1918) is a prominent Brazilian sociologist, literary critic, professor, and researcher.
78. *Brasil de Fato* is a weekly Brazilian newspaper which focuses on politics.
79. Sábato Antônio Magaldi (Belo Horizonte, MG 1927) is a Brazilian theater critic, journalist, professor, historian, and researcher.
80. Décio de Almeida Prado (São Paulo, SP 1917–2000) is a Brazilian theater critic, historian, professor, and researcher. He and Sábato Magaldi specialize in Brazilian theater.
81. Fomento, in Portuguese.
82. Anna Maria Buarque de Hollanda (São Paulo, SP 1948) is a singer and composer. She was Minister of Culture from 2011 to 2012.

CHAPTER 42

AN INTERVIEW WITH HÉCTOR LEVY-DANIEL

MARÍA FLORENCIA NELLI

HÉCTOR Levy-Daniel is an Argentine playwright, director, teacher, researcher, and scriptwriter.[1] As well as having a B.A. in Philosophy from the University of Buenos Aires, he studied film with Rodolfo Hermida and screenwriting with Ricardo Piglia. He trained as a director with Laura Yusem and as an actor with Ricardo Halak. Some of his most noteworthy works include: *Memorias de Praga* (*Memories of Prague*; Faiga Award 1997), *La noche del impostor* (*The Night of the Impostor*, 1997), *La postergación* (*The Postponement*, 1999), *El archivista* (*The Archivist*, in *Teatro por la identidad*, 2009, Buenos Aires, Colihue), *Destiempos* (*Untimely*, in *Exilios: 18 obras de teatro de autores argentinos, españoles y mexicanos*, 2003, Buenos Aires, Biblos), *Serena danza del olvido* (*Serene Dance of Oblivion*, 2000, Argentores Award 2005; Honorary Mention in the 2000 International Competition "Tramoya" at Universidad Veracruzana, Mexico), *Lo que esconde el Kaiser* (*What the Kaiser Hides*; feature film screenplay, Honorary Mention Award Fondo Nacional de las Artes 2003), *Las mujeres de los nazis. Trilogía* (*Nazis' Women. Trilogy*: "Mrs. Goebbels' restlessness," "The Conviction of Irma Grese," and "Geli Raubal's dilemma," 2013, Buenos Aires, Losada. Florencio Sánchez Award for best author 2008), *El mal de la colina* (*Hill's Evil*, in *Exilio*, 2012, Mexico), and *Yocasta* (2011). His works have been the subject of numerous studies in Latin America, Europe and the United States. He currently teaches Drama at Universidad del Salvador, Instituto Universitario Nacional del Arte (IUNA) and Escuela Municipal de Arte Dramático (EMAD), Buenos Aires.

F.N.: Why stage a classic in Argentina today? Moreover, why *rewrite* a classic? I am referring to your recent staging of *Yocasta* in Buenos Aires [in 2011].[2]

H.L.-D.: I will always want to stage a classic. Staging a classic implies a challenge. Any classic for me means an opportunity to undertake a series of reflections on theatricality. Staging a classic represents the possibility of posing problems: how to tell the story, how to avoid the pressure of a "culture" that leads us down the path of solemnity, how to account for that particular classic concentrating above all on the dramatic action, and subordinating all elements of the performance to it, first and foremost the acting: the actor performing a classical text has to endure the temptation of solemnity most of all. And here there is something essential to me: staging a classic means working every little piece of text as a dramatic action, avoiding the unproductive reverence for the written text that often leads to declamation and to forgetting that we are onstage and that something is happening worth noting, even in the smallest of details. However, this does not mean neglecting the text, but subordinating its beauty to its function as action. Having said that, in Argentina, which has a vast theatrical production, Greek and Elizabethan Classics are constantly performed. In fact, at the same time that *Yocasta* premièred, there were at least three other Greek tragedies on show, each performed from a completely different perspective and with a very distinct meaning. Evidently, artists find in these texts multiple resonances. For me, Sophocles made sense because I have been fascinated by the figure of Oedipus since I was a child and I have read the play many times throughout my life, but I could not really begin to think about this character until I read Foucault's lecture on *Oedipus Tyrannus* in his *Lectures on the Will to Know*.

Reading Foucault awoke in me the desire to rewrite *Oedipus* avoiding the weight of the psychoanalytic tradition and concentrating on this character obsessed with politics and with exercising power. In my version, Oedipus believes that the most important thing is to stay in power. Moreover, knowing the truth about what happened is nothing but a means to prevent him from losing power, allowing him to continue to rule unhindered. Embarking on this re-writing gave me true satisfaction. It was for me a stimulating research project.

F.N.: Why did you choose the figure of Jocasta to come center stage? What attracted you to this character and how was it transformed in your rewriting?

H.L.-D.: Women fascinate me: their depth, intelligence, complexity. In my works I guess there is a prevalence of female characters. Consequently, I could not begin to think about this version until I realized that Jocasta had to be the bearer of the narrative, the person not only narrating the events of the story, but also—thanks to her telling—giving them a meaning that is not present in the original piece or is there only in an embryonic state. In *Oedipus Tyrannus*, Jocasta is a minor character, who has virtually no relevance. However, in my version Jocasta comes out as the character who is always one step ahead of the others. She has a thorough understanding of the power relationships in place and intervenes to prevent conflicts between the members of the political circle. At the same time, she is aware of the priorities that need to be respected: from the beginning she warns Oedipus about the implications of the research he is carrying forward, and advises him—with no success—to live forever in doubt rather than with the truth. In my version, Jocasta's character is absolutely pragmatic. She is also a character who, interestingly (and this is already suggested in the original), represents, in a tragic-deterministic context, the affirmation of chance: she proposes to disbelieve the prophecies and the prophets, and this to me seems extraordinary.

F.N.: You said that you felt Jocasta had to be the bearer of the narrative. Why did you feel that you had to narrate the events of the myth from her perspective in particular?

H.L.-D.: For several reasons. First of all, Jocasta is, in my opinion, the main victim of the tragedy. And it has always been attractive to me to give voice to the victims, at least in some of my plays. Therefore, in the version I wrote Jocasta has the voice as the main victim, and she presents the events that have happened as a way of trying to understand them. The complexity of the sequence of events is such that it is necessary to retell them over and over again to get to a place where they can be explained.

The second reason is that as she moves from being a secondary character to a major character, her role in the action's development becomes crucial: she tries to mitigate Oedipus' obsession; she acts as mediator between him and her brother Creon when their relationship is in conflict; by pragmatic means she tries to convince Oedipus to abandon his inquiry, as she senses that if he continues searching for truth, the result will be disastrous. Whereupon her influence as a wife and as a queen, namely as a politician, becomes clear.

The third reason, as important as the other two, is that unlike in the original text, here Jocasta makes clear that she has not been an accomplice of her husband Laius, who had decided to put his son to death when he learnt about the oracle. On the contrary, Jocasta begged the king for Oedipus' life, but without success. This highlights the importance that motherhood has had for her. Jocasta is a mother who loves her newborn son. She is also a woman who is deeply in love with the person who has become the new king and who is ultimately her own son, even though she is not able to recognize him as such.

F.N.: What is the relationship between power and women in the play? And between women and politics? Do they have any connection with, or reflect in any way, the Argentine reality?

H.L.-D.: As already suggested, in my version Jocasta is a woman with power. And that is the way we approached her character with the actress during rehearsals. Jocasta is fully aware of the realities of politics and is able to sail through the field of tensions and stress created by power with absolute competence. Thanks to her power and influence over Oedipus, she prevents Creon, her brother, from being sentenced to death. She also tries to keep away the shepherd whose evidence, she forebodes, will eventually ruin them. Although I do not think that the play directly reflects Argentine reality today (Cristina Fernández de Kirchner was twice elected President by an overwhelming number of votes, for instance) and has not been developed in that sense in particular, one cannot help but make some connections. However, these connections should not be restricted solely to Argentina. It is necessary to recognize that the role of women in politics has been revalued worldwide (Cristina Fernández de Kirchner in Argentina, Michelle Bachelet in Chile, Dilma Rousseff in Brazil, Angela Merkel in Germany, Hillary Clinton in the U.S.A., etc.). Jocasta is linked directly to the current role of women in society and in politics.

F.N.: Are there any parallels between your play and Argentina's recent history? I'm thinking, in particular, of the figure of the mother, which has been resignified since 1973's military dictatorship. Has this particular mother influenced your composition of Jocasta's character? What kind of mother is your Jocasta?

H.L.-D.: If there is indeed a parallel, it is not at all straightforward. Jocasta is a mother in her own right, who puts up a fight to prevent Laius killing their own son, as guided by the oracles. Deep down Jocasta was never able to forgive him for his criminal choice. I think that if we were to establish some kind of connection between the play *Yocasta* and Argentine reality, it would have to do mainly with Jocasta's intention of returning to the past to try to understand what happened. And above all, with the idea of giving voice to the victims (in this case, Jocasta herself).

F.N.: Was the audience physically involved in the staging? Were you looking for a different participation of or relationship with the audience?

H.L.-D.: The staging did not include any intention to incorporate the public physically in the performance, and therefore the classic separation between stage and audience remained. However, as Jocasta's monologues, which served to disrupt the action or call attention to a particular point in the story, were addressed directly to the public, they functioned as a privileged channel of communication: the audience gets the story directly from the source, the main victim of the tragedy.

F.N.: Why use water as a symbol of power? Is it in any way related to the fact that water is starting to be considered as the "oil" of the future?

H.L.-D.: *Yocasta*'s staging originated from a sensory image: dryness, the lack of water, thirst as an expression of the threat to Oedipus' power that is cast when the plague begins to spread throughout Thebes. While this sensory image was developing, water started to appear, by contrast and in general terms, as the expression of the threatened power. This general image started to get more specific in the staging process and during rehearsals. For instance, Jocasta offers water to Creon in the scene in which he has just come back from consulting the oracles; and Oedipus is the person who gives water to Teiresias when he arrives after being summoned by Creon. As the staging process progressed, water started to take on an increasingly important narrative role: the water fountain to which Oedipus goes over and over again, to wash his hands or to refresh himself, gradually started to become a fundamental element during rehearsals, and at one stage it became such an essential object for the performance that it turned into the very heart of the stage, a center around which the characters revolve throughout the performance. Creon dares to touch the water of the fountain during the intense argument that he has with Oedipus—when Oedipus wants to sentence him to death, and also in the final scene between the two. When Oedipus lies blind and vanquished, Creon listens to him smugly while wetting his head with the fountain's water. This action has great significance. The course of events has placed power on this new figure, and this action tells us that Creon has now become fully aware of his new powers. He is the new king. In answer to your question, no, there was no intention of interpreting water as the "oil" of the new century in the play; it is only a coincidence.

F.N.: In your *Yocasta*, not only the text, but also the scenery, the costumes, and the sound, have been extremely well thought out. They reflect the plot's conflicts, but they are also conveyors of meaning, giving the audience clues to understanding what is happening onstage. How did you work on these aspects of the staging and what did you want to achieve with them?

H.L.-D.: As already mentioned, water was an essential element for both the narrative and the scenery. The water fountain in the centre and the dry arid floor around it became the perfect expression of this tension. The topic of water was also addressed through the music: in some scenes it becomes easily recognizable. The key musical theme, which is directly linked to the story of Jocasta and is repeated with variations throughout the play, follows the essential movements of the dramatic curve of her story. At the same time, we worked on the costumes with a criterion that followed Jocasta's opening words in the play: if she comes every so often to reveal her story to mortals, then the characters should dress in a way that can be recognized as practically contemporary to those who attend the performance. Therefore, we completely disregarded period costumes and looked instead, for each character, for pieces of clothing that could be identified by the public as current. Even Jocasta's dress, with strong Greek reminiscences, is nevertheless eminently modern.

Notes

1. Translated from Spanish by M. F. Nelli.
2. *Yocasta* premièred at Teatro Anfitrión, Buenos Aires on July 29, 2011, and was performed throughout 2011 and 2012 in different locations around Buenos Aires. It was nominated for the María Guerrero Awards for Best Argentine Author and Best Supporting Actor (2011), and for the Florencio Sánchez Awards for Best Director, Best Supporting Actor, Sets, Costumes, and Music (2011).

CHAPTER 43

CHARLES MEE'S "(RE)MAKING" OF GREEK DRAMA

ERIN B. MEE

The playwright Charles Mee has "(re)made" numerous Greek plays from the 1990s onwards: Orestes 2.0 (1992), The Bacchae 2.1 (1993), Trojan Women: A Love Story (1994), Agamemnon 2.0 (1994), Iphigenia 2.0 (2007). Here he explains his collage-playwriting technique and his reasons for turning to the Greeks in an interview with his daughter, the theater director and theater historian Erin Mee.

EMEE: Why do you think so many playwrights and directors turned to Greek tragedy for inspiration and material in the 1970s, and why does that trend continue today?

CMEE: I'm sure other people understand better than I do why there was this intense revival of interest in Greek theater in the 1970s. But for me, it came out of the Vietnam War. In the 1960s (I think it was the 1960s) Arthur Schlesinger wrote a book called *The Imperial Presidency*. There was a lot of conversation in the United States about the beginning and end of the American empire. The Greeks offered a great example of an empire that began and ended at the very beginnings of western civilization. That's one of the reasons I looked at the Greeks, and I think it might have been a reason for other people too, whether they articulated it that way or not. The beginning and end of American Empire was in the air, and we were all looking for other examples to study.

Iphigenia 2.0 and *The Trojan Women*, and *Orestes 2.0* and *Agamemnon* come directly out of my involvement with anti-Vietnam War activities. And with the beginning of my obsessive-compulsive preoccupation with the end of the American Empire. And with my thinking about empires in general: what brings empires to an end, what brings them down. I think the Greek plays have a lot to say about that because the Greek playwrights who thought about it understood a lot about what brings an empire down.

This is a *non sequitur*, but once you begin to think about the Greeks, you begin to think of Greek tragedy as one of the earliest examples of western dramaturgy. I looked at the Greeks and thought: "Right, the basic structure of a Greek play is: the principals advance the plot, the chorus riffs; the principals advance the plot, the chorus riffs." And then you look at Shakespeare, and you see what he did with this structure. It's almost as though he woke up one morning and thought, "Oh I get it. The principals advance the plot and then the chorus is not fifteen people all saying the same thing at the same time, it's fifteen individuals." It's like an NBC reporter goes out on the street and says to a guy passing by, "What do you think of the war in Iraq?" And then she says to the next woman who comes along, "What do you think of the war in Iraq?" And then she says to a cabdriver, "What do you think of the war in Iraq?" And together they are the voice of the community, but they speak as individuals. Those are Shakespeare's subplots. You can see western dramaturgy evolve over the next centuries, and by the time you get to Ibsen you see its structure is: principals advance the plot, principals advance the plot, principals advance the plot. There's no chorus. In the 1970s people went back to the Greeks to go back to the roots of how to write a good play that included the voice of the people.

These two powerful forces come together, then, in the 1970s: a radical questioning of America's political and economic role as an empire, and people in the theater looking for a different way of making theater that would reflect how they live in the world. Both of those take you to the Greeks. Theatrically the Greeks gave us a bigger notion of how to write a good play than the realism of Ibsen and O'Neill.

EMEE: Wasn't this also connected to the disillusionment of people who had grown up in 1950s post-war suburbs believing in equal rights and the American dream, and then they got to college and found that not everyone's rights were equal, and that not everyone had access to the American dream? So the desire to rebel against the well-made three-act play set in a nice living room is connected to the political rebellion against the social structures in society as a whole, and the family structure at home?

CMEE: I think that's a big part of it. The other part of it connected to the art historian Janson's theory that you can read the history of western art as the history of increased democratization. So the earliest art is about the gods, and then it becomes about the ruling class. And then as you get to the Renaissance, it's about merchant bankers. By the time you get to the nineteenth century, it's farmers in the fields. Ibsen, though I think of him as this terrific conservative, was part of that great move towards increasing democratization. In Ibsen's plays, middle-class families in their living room, and their topics of conversation, are worthy subjects for art. And we go from Ibsen to Williams and O'Neill and Arthur Miller, and then to Beckett where bums are appropriate subjects for art.

EMEE: Of course this is connected to linear notions of progress...

CMEE: Right. And in the late 1960s and early 1970s it became clear that this notion that we were somehow progressing socially and politically was false. It became clear we weren't progressing.

EMEE: So the notions of progress and linearity began to be questioned.

CMEE: Right.

EMEE: Would you also say that there was an increased interest in multi-vocality as opposed to a single authorial (often patriarchal) voice?

CMEE: Yes.

EMEE: So in questioning the 1950s lifestyle you also begin to question who has the right to speak, who has the right to be heard, whose stories we can and should tell, who has the right to take center stage, etc.

CMEE: Absolutely. Part of that came out of the Marshall Plan of 1945, with the United States moving into Europe and not being so isolationist. And then, as the NATO alliance begins to disintegrate, understanding that there are actually other countries in the world, too. Other hemispheres and other voices and other values and other visions and other ways of thinking and feeling and living that deserve respect. That no one is inherently entitled to complete dominion of the earth or the stage.

EMEE: So then you get multiple ways of looking and seeing and being and experiencing on stage.

CMEE: Right. And then the theater is not just a place to sit and listen to a text being spoken by actors who are seated on a couch, it's a place where you have a dance and choral singing.

EMEE: And you move off the proscenium stage, which puts the viewer at the center of the viewing/viewed world. So then the spectator isn't (at) the center of the world.

CMEE: Right.

EMEE: So you are saying that all the things that were being called into question artistically were reflective of the things that were being called into question socially and politically?

CMEE: Yes, that's what I think.

EMEE: Can I tie this back to something you said earlier, which is that the Greeks offer a good example of how to write a good play. Are you saying the Greeks provided a model for multidisciplinary, multivocal, multispacial theater?

CMEE: Yes.

EMEE: So is this why you think so many people returned to Greek theater?

CMEE: I can't speak for everybody else, but that's why I did. And I think I am a typical person.

EMEE: When Richard Schechner did *Dionysus in 69* he put an entire ritual into his production that was part of a questioning what theater is, of asking: why can't ritual be theater?

CMEE: Yes. But I also think, to come back to American realism for a minute, that when you have thousands and thousands of plays with a couch and an easy chair, that's a private space. There's no public space there. Greek plays all have public space as well as private space. If not with the lead characters, at least with the chorus. The chorus is always "the rest of society." In Arthur Miller's plays the individuals were meant to represent the larger society, but still, the larger society was not there. They were offstage.

EMEE: So their multiple points of view are not heard.

CMEE: No. And then you are inevitably focusing on personal relationships between the family or whatever. You are dealing with a Freudian world in which the assumption is that every piece of human behavior can ultimately be explained by the psycho-dynamics of a person's early childhood home, and they live out that destiny. Whereas the Greeks believed, no, that was certainly part of an explanation, but people were also shaped by history, culture, gender, genetics, civilization, historical experience. So the Greeks had a larger and more complex understanding of what makes human beings human than was had by American Realism. So then in the 1970s JoAnne Akalaitis, Mabou Mines, Richard Foreman, the Wooster Group, Pina Bausch, want to escape from this narrow vision, this single explanation of human beings that existed in American realism. They step out into this larger, more complex world that the Greeks had been dealing with.

EMEE: I want to shift focus for a minute and talk about why you write the way you do. In some of your adaptations of Greek plays (such as *Iphigenia 2.0*) you stick very closely to the original story and structure, but you use chunks of text from different sources: soldiers' blogs, Generals' speeches, diaries, etc. Why do you write that way?

CMEE: When I got out of college I was writing plays, and then I drifted out of that into anti-Vietnam War activities which I did for 20, 25 years. And then as part of that I began writing books about American foreign relations. I only returned to writing plays 25 years later, and I came back as somebody who had written history books in which, if you have a thesis and you are laying out your thesis, you go to original sources and you quote them. You appropriate those quotes as pieces of evidence, and you're not allowed to edit them. You're not allowed to make them fit your argument. You have to take them verbatim, and you have to deal with that even if it makes your thesis difficult. That's part of the evidence. You have to take the evidence that both seems to contrast and seems to undermine your argument and put it into the book you're writing. And so, when I came back to writing plays, I thought of appropriating pieces of the world I live in as evidence of who and how we are. And then I had to deal with that. I couldn't make it up. I couldn't re-write it. I couldn't change it. I couldn't make it fit what I was trying to do. If it was an obstacle, I had to work around it or see what I could do with it.

EMEE: Like archaeological evidence of the civilization we are currently living in.

CMEE: Yeah. I had to put it there and see: does that wreck the play, does that destroy the argument? Or do you see how that fits in? Or do you see how that makes the world indeed a more complicated place that we're trying to negotiate? This linear storyline you're trying to follow through the world keeps getting derailed and undone by stuff. So that's what all those quotations are doing: they are evidence of who we are today. I've taken a classical structure because we are not people without a history, a past, a genetics, and all the rest of it. There is no such thing as an original play because you start with what you were born into, and you take that. And then you do the stuff in your own lifetime, and the stuff in your own lifetime fits into or destroys the pattern of streets and architecture state borderlines that you were born into. So I think that taking a Greek play and putting chunks of the modern world into that foundation is simply a statement about how life is in the world. For everyone, for every generation. You are taking the story of Iphigenia, which was a classical Greek story about how human beings behave with each other, and then you're saying: "Right, now I throw in this stuff from the year 2000, 2006, whatever it is, and does that structure get destroyed?" Does it hold? Or does it get shattered here and there? So it gets re-made. And that's what we do with everything: with the lives we live, the books we write, the buses we manufacture, the airplanes we fly...

EMEE: Do you use collage differently in your remakings of Greek plays than you do in your own plays?

CMEE: Yes and no. If you take Greek plays and compare them to Ibsen and Pina Bausch there is a range of relationships between the chorus and the principals. And I get to choose where I want to be on that continuum. With a collage approach to the Greek plays, I'm usually keeping their narrative story and throwing things into it. And then you think about the structure of a piece of theater. When you look at a painting you can see the whole painting and any detail of it at the same time. With a work of art that occurs in time, you don't see the whole of it until you get to the end. With a play, it's usually 2 hours, 2.5 hours. With a movie, it's 90 minutes. With a novel, it's 300, 600, 2,000 pages, whatever. But only when you get to the end do you see the whole. But human beings are like cockroaches, they don't like it if they get disoriented. They like some method of orientation so their principal feeling is not one of anxiety, because that's not the most interesting thing to feel. So for most works of art that occur in time, you're given a method of orientation. One of the easy ways of orienting people is a plot. Boy meets girl, got it. Boy wants to be Chairman of a major Fortune 500 corporation. Right, okay. Now we're on the ride. We know what the ride is. We can settle in and watch the details. But if you're doing a collage, the pieces are often tied together by a theme. You announce the theme, and then the audience says: "Right, I get it, this is life in Sicily today." In a jazz piece you play the tune at the top, then you riff for 20 minutes, then you play the tune at the end. So these pure collage pieces often have other dramaturgical structures so you are oriented.

EMEE: *Big Love* has been performed on almost every college campus in the country, and in numerous regional theaters. It is, in fact, one of the most-performed plays of the past ten years. Why do you think that is?

CMEE: I can only guess why, but I would guess that colleges do it for some of the same reasons I wrote it. I wrote it because Actor's Theater of Louisville said they wanted to do a millennial festival, and asked me to write a play for the festival. I decided to go back to one of the oldest plays in the western world and see if it still speaks to us today. And amazingly, it does. And I think it speaks to college students who are grappling with a lot of the questions raised in the play particularly intensely: namely, the relationships between men and women; how a country ought to behave in the world; what our feelings are about immigrants and refugees and whether we take them in or not. The original play contains a lot of talk about war and going to war and our place in the world. And I think these issue that are still very much on people's minds and particularly on the minds of college students who are thinking: "When I graduate, I'm going to step into the world. What world am I stepping into? And how should I behave in that world? Who should I be, and what can I change?"

CHAPTER 44

AN INTERVIEW WITH CAREY PERLOFF

MARGARET WILLIAMSON

THEATER director Carey Perloff has directed numerous Greek plays in the United States, regularly collaborating with playwright Timberlake Wertenbaker. Here she discusses her work with Classicist Margaret Williamson, who has herself enjoyed a 20-year collaboration as academic consultant with Wertenbaker for her versions of Greek tragedy.

M.W.: You're obviously very committed to Greek tragedy, because you've done several productions now: Pound's version of Sophocles' *Electra* in the late 1980s, for the Classic Stage Company, then *Antigone* and *Hecuba* in the 1990s, and then another *Electra*. So I wanted to start by asking you what's special about the Greeks?

C.P.: My love of the Greeks preceded my love of theater. I started working on the Greeks when I was in second grade. I had an incredible teacher who introduced us to the ancient world, and it completely captured my imagination. We didn't have Greek at my high school, but I did a lot of Latin, and went to Greece a lot, and I wanted to be an archaeologist, so my summers in high school I spent excavating. And I went to Stanford to do Classics to be an archaeologist; the first class I had was first-year Greek, and my teacher was Helene Foley.

I always say to my children, you have three teachers in your life that change your life, and the second one was Helene. She introduced me to Greek tragedy in this very visceral and theatrical way: it wasn't just literary, it was really about the nature of that kind of dramaturgy. And when I look back I think the fact that it was this enormous civic event made a big impression on me: the craziness of spending an entire year rehearsing something that was not only spoken but danced and sung, and then performed one time. And it was a drama that actually mattered, that was part of the cultural discourse, and that I think more than anything was metaphoric. I've never been interested in realism; I don't know why, everyone has their own native aesthetic. There's something about the fact that Greek tragedy was absolutely trenchant to its own period, a period of war, a place about justice and gender and all of those things, but done in a metaphoric way. That really appealed to me.

I majored in Greek at Stanford, and we read a lot of plays in Greek, and staged a lot of Greek plays. And even though we were quite scholarly—Helene certainly was very rigorous about the Greek text—they were always looked at as drama. Helene had started to do her work on women in tragedies, and I was really fascinated by these extremely powerful women in Greek tragedy and why it was that in this patriarchal culture there was a dramaturgy of all great female roles. With Shakespeare you always end up in a room with 22 men and two women because that's how the plays were written, whereas when you do Racine or Euripides you're in a room with a lot of unbelievable women and two men. It's very rare for women to take center stage that way.

It was a very fertile, wonderful time, but it never occurred to me that because of that I would end up in the theater: I was really doing it as a Classicist. I migrated my junior year of college to the drama department, and that's when I started reading Beckett and Pinter and all of that in drama, but I think the Greeks somehow got imprinted on me.

When I graduated I had a Fulbright, and I went to Oxford, and the first thing I did was a theatrical version of the *Satyricon* as a sort of homage to Jack Winkler, who was the other huge influence on my life. And then the first production I did when I became Artistic Director of the Classic Stage Company was, oddly, Ezra Pound's version of Sophocles' *Electra*.

M.W.: I really wanted to ask you about that because Sophocles' *Electra* does not have a good reputation: only recently a professor at Oxford said to me "It's such an awful play." And certainly I think if you're used to reading tragedies through Aristotle, and *Oedipus Tyrannus* is the perfect play according to him, but *Medea* is not so good because it has an arbitrary, inorganic ending, then *Electra* does look like an awful play. But clearly it doesn't look like that to you because you did the Pound then, and more recently you've commissioned and directed another version by Timberlake Wertenbaker.

C.P.: Well, it was sort of accidental that I found Pound's version. I went with my mother, who's a literary critic, to visit James Laughlin, who had been very close to Pound. And he knew that I was a Classicist and pulled a manuscript out of his desk drawer and said, "You know when Ezra was in St. Elizabeth's, he did an *Electra*. Would you like to have a look?" And I was absolutely captivated by it.

Now, it's very much Ezra Pound. And I guess the first thing about it that interested me—and this is true of the Sophocles, but Pound went much further with it—is that it is a study in madness. He was incarcerated in a hospital for the mad after his really violent war broadcasts during World War II: very anti-American, very anti-Semitic. So here's this brilliant American poet, in a hospital for the mad in Washington, wondering whether he really was mad or not and writing about that.

And so *Electra* was deeply personal to him, and I thought his version of it, while obviously not a literal translation, was astonishing. And the reason I think it's such a fascinating play is that to me it asks the question: what happens to someone who cannot forget? And is forgetting ultimately a crime or a salvation?

Electra obviously thinks it's a crime to forget, and that a huge injustice was done which must be rectified and that the culture has gone on and washed it away, and that she is the only one who tells the truth and who remembers. And indeed she wills the vendetta to happen, but you can say in doing that she has absolutely destroyed herself. She's one of those bizarre heroines that has been completely hollowed out from the inside, which I found incredibly moving. You know when you have one motor in your life, and that is the only thing that matters, when the deed finally happens, she is an absolute shell: there's nothing left there.

And that seemed to me a great parable about women. So I think the other thing for me is that over the centuries women have constantly been robbed of agency and of speech. Here is a woman who has nothing but speech at the beginning of the play, never shuts up, stands outside the gates, screams and yells and demands attention, demands that the courts pay attention, demands that her mother pay attention, and calls forth her brother. And the moment her brother comes, he says, "And now could you please be quiet? I'm going to go in and do the deed." And she is literally silenced. And I always wondered what Sophocles meant about the very end of the play. And I don't know that I did it "right," but the more I worked on it, the more I realized that at the end of the play Aegisthus is tied up or whatever and dragged into the house by the men, and she is not invited in. The doors slam, and she is left, the daughter, alone onstage with the corpse of her dead mother. Now what does *that* mean? That is such an unbelievable image; and you cannot say it's a victory. Killing one's mother, no matter how just the cause, in the end can never be a victory.

M.W.: And the other thing is the way the relationship between Electra and Clytemnestra is staged, and how Electra, who's been abused, turns into the abuser.

C.P.: That's right. I think the scene between Clytemnestra and Electra is truly one of the great scenes in any drama, and one of the greatest trial scenes ever. And you actually are as compelled by Clytemnestra's argument, if it's done right, as you are by Electra's. And in fact Electra blows the argument and crosses the line and because she makes it so vicious and personal she ends up losing the high ground.

And the argument that Clytemnestra makes about the death of Iphigenia is so poignant and compelling that as an audience member you have to go back and ask, "Where does justice lie? And where does vendetta finally stop?" And with many, many Greek tragedies that seemed to be such a prevailing theme, that question of the revenge always coming back around. What finally, if not democracy or justice, or the court of law, what finally stops the cycle of vendetta? And of course with Sophocles' *Electra* we don't know because we don't know what other plays went with it or in what order that trilogy went, and whether the Furies are going to come at the end. Those are all open questions: that's what makes it so fascinating.

I found it endlessly compelling, but also incredibly challenging to do until I sat and worked on it with Helene, and she said something that I've used forever after. She wrote this amazing essay called "The Politics of Tragic Lamentation," in which she so clearly demonstrated that lamentation is not complaining, and it's not tears; it is a really targeted political assertion of will that rallies a culture that has forgotten justice to take justice. And that it was the role of women to do that. It is true that for a modern audience *Electra* seems like a lot of complaining, and it's a very hard thing for an actress to motor, to give action to. And so you have to try to figure out what it is that Electra is trying to do to her mother, and do most particularly to the chorus and by association to us as the jury to make us change our mind. And then it's active; it's not a character who's up there weeping and complaining, but a character who actually has the agency to make something happen.

When you do it in an open-air theater like the Getty Theater, you realize that the whole play is about the audience and about the chorus—because you can see them.

And the chorus at every moment turns to the audience and says, "Did you just see what happened? Where are the thunderbolts of justice? Are we going to do nothing about this?" And you feel that much more when you do it outdoors.

M.W.: And yet you had a very small chorus—just Olympia Dukakis and one other actress—in the Getty production. Is that in any sense because you had the audience in the physical space?

C.P.: Yes, I think maybe so. When we took the production to ACT [American Conservatory Theater, San Francisco] it was only her, I didn't even have the second woman, only a cellist and Olympia. Very early on when you and Timberlake were working on the play, she rang me and said, "You know this chorus is really different. This chorus has a personal relationship to Electra; it often speaks in the first person, and it changes a lot during the play." So Timberlake was worried about it being difficult to actually hear their arguments if it were a chorus of a lot of women. And embodying it in one woman of such power as Olympia would allow you to see the way in which Electra was persuading the chorus or failing to persuade the chorus. Whereas when we did Euripides' *Hecuba* the chorus were not there for us to watch how they navigated an argument, they were there as a kind of force of lamentation.

M.W.: Yes, well I guess in Hecuba the persuasion is all directed somewhere else, to Odysseus, to Agamemnon...

C.P.: That's right. So we're tracking them and seeing whether their minds get changed, or Polymestor's mind gets changed. So we set all those choruses to music, we left a lot of it in Greek and they were sung. In *Electra* it's really directed at the chorus. In *Antigone* I used a group, so my *Antigone* was somewhat in between. The conflict there is between Antigone and Creon, and the chorus is fearful to get too involved.

You have to really look at each chorus in each play, depending on what you're doing, and say: is this a chorus as in *Electra*, which has agency? Or is it for instance like the Deborah Warner/Fiona Shaw *Medea*, where they made the chorus just paparazzi, which was sort of fun and ultimately a little bit annoying, but interesting. Because that chorus are just observers of this horror: they're there to photograph it and report on it, but they're not going to change the action. Whereas Euripides' Trojan Women *are* the action, and they're sort of deeply engrained in it.

It's sometimes hard for the other actors to realize that the chorus is the centerpiece. American actors tend to want to play two-character scenes; they are trained in psychological realism. So when we did *Electra* in LA, but particularly when we did it in San Francisco, René as Electra would get on the stage with her sister Chrysothemis or with her mother Clytemnestra, and she would want to play the scene across from her as if it were a two-character scene. And Olympia, as the chorus, would be onstage waving her arms, saying, "Excuse me, I'm here, too." And it drove René crazy, but it wasn't about Olympia. It was saying: this is a three-character scene, and the third character is a crowd of women, so pay attention.

What you realize in *Electra* is, she's never going to change Clytemnestra's mind. This argument has gone on for fifteen years: so why are they having it again? For the benefit of the chorus, and by extension the audience. We are the jury. We have to decide whether the murder of Iphigenia was so egregious that it justified the murder of Agamemnon. So I kept saying to René, "If you don't use the attacks on your mother to persuade the chorus, you haven't actually done the scene."

But even Olympia got very stuck when we did *Hecuba*. Helene was the dramaturge, and she was with us for most of the rehearsal. We got to the end, after Hecuba goes into the tent and kills Polymestor's children and puts out his eyes, and comes back out. And here comes Agamemnon, and she says to him, "I did the deed." And then she proceeds to justify it. Well, to Olympia this was completely incomprehensible. And she just stopped the rehearsal, and said, "Why do I have to do this? I've done it, I've gotten my revenge. Why am I telling him this? What do I care?" And Helene said, "You are writing history. This is your opportunity to write history so that your story will be the story told." And Olympia is very aware of the fact that women never get to write history, and that our stories are usually relegated, and she understood why that was important. And it was a thrilling moment, when she turned right to the audience, and told them "This is how I want you to remember this story, and tell this story."

I think because I grew up with this material it never felt foreign to me. When you get in a room with actors, very often the actors really resist. And they will say, "Well, we don't like the Greeks." And you say, "Why?" And they say, "Because it's all declamation. They're not real characters; it's all rhetoric." So then you have to invite them to understand a culture in which rhetoric was part of life. And if you deny that, if you try to denude the plays of rhetoric or make it naturalistic, you've lost something. But if you understand that the Greeks were the first and foremost political culture, that everything was political, and that rhetoric was your way of persuading somebody to your side of an argument, then they understand that actually, as in *Julius Caesar*, let's say, it's both deeply character-based and very polemical. That doesn't mean it's without feeling: it's a real emotional journey, but the emotional journey has a purpose. And I've never found audiences had a problem with that.

This isn't American dramaturgy, it's not naturalism; and you have to accept that if you're going to get what is the joy of these plays. For me the closest is Brecht, who also works in a kind of choral form, though not quite like the Greeks. And there is a lot of direct address in Brecht too, and he asks you to consider the moral implications of something. But I think it's more exciting in the Greeks because they love trial by jury, and they let the audience be the jury. Brecht tends to heckle the audience and they have to respond. But I always feel, particularly with Sophocles, a bit less so with Euripides, that we are the ones asked to make the judgment.

It's funny that people think *Electra* is a terrible play, because lots of people always thought *Hecuba* was a terrible play. And when we decided to do it, people thought we were crazy and said "This is a terrible play. It's just a melodrama." And one of the things I was curious about is if that were the case, why was it the most popular play in Elizabethan England, which it was?

M.W.: Revenge!

C.P.: Yes, and there is something unbelievably gratifying about that kind of really symmetrical revenge. But it's also horrifying, and I think the thing that the Greeks understood about revenge is that it makes you an animal. Hecuba becomes a dog at the end of the play; so you can say she's gotten her revenge, she's persuaded us of her point of view, but in the end she is reduced to a kind of bestiality. The Greeks were obviously really aware that they had created a rule of law that was always going to be vulnerable to people's sense of vendetta, and that you don't really end it that easily.

And maybe the plays center around women because for women getting justice is always that much harder. We're not good at arguing for ourselves; we've been silenced for so long; we aren't the centerpiece of our own stories. And so when injustices are done to us, it's really hard for us to argue in our favor. It's very gratifying material to work on, for me: it always yields up more.

These plays are still so trenchant, particularly right now. The first time we did *Hecuba* was during the Rodney King riots. And so the question we as Americans were asking ourselves was, "What happens when a whole group of people thinks they can't get justice?" And those blacks in South-Central LA knew that by having that trial in a white suburb in California they were never going to get justice. And they didn't. And so they did the only thing that they knew how to do which was take to the streets. If you feel like it's rigged and that no matter what your voice isn't going to be there, then you do something really violent.

The second time we did it was during Clinton's Monica Lewinsky scandal. And so it became a whole other kind of play, about the hypocrisy of male leadership. When Agamemnon comes out at the end of *Hecuba*, and you know what a weak leader he is, and there he is sleeping with Cassandra and talking about justice, it's just horrifying. So in a way the plays are a Rorschach test because at whatever political moment they happen they seem to ring our bell still.

M.W.: This theater does seem to be very close to the heart of the difference between tribalism and some kind of civic society: it's on that cusp. I guess that's partly because it was a small society, and people had to come face to face. But there must be other theatrical traditions that deal with something similar. And we haven't always been realists, have we?

C.P.: No, not at all. And I wouldn't call Shakespeare realism, or Molière, or Racine. But it is the most public drama. Shakespeare was a very public drama, absolutely, but coming out of a very different political and judicial system. I think for the Greeks drama was so near justice, and they were the first people, I think, to think up trial by jury: that hadn't existed before the Greeks, right, in any culture that we know? And it didn't exist in common-law England. Drama becomes a kind of civic argument in Greece. I don't know that there is another dramaturgy quite like that, where we really are the jury.

And then by the time you get to, let's say, French classical drama, it's a very private drama because it's a drama of the court. It's very hard for a contemporary audience because it's so repressed, and so Catholic, and so private. Whereas I don't think the Greeks are hard for anybody: I think that there's something about the muscle of those plays that still feels really immediate. And the fact that it was outdoor drama, that the audience was so visible, and important, and asked to participate.

And here's another thing that the Greeks wrestled with that I think we're still wrestling with: the collision between a kind of natural and positive law. Is there a native sense of justice, and how does that sit with a codified state sense of justice? And what happens when the justice that the state propagates does not seem to jive with our private sense of justice? So for instance right now in India, we're watching the systematic repeated raping of women. It's not a medieval culture, it's a twenty-first-century culture that permits that. And I cannot wrap my head around it, except to realize that so-called positive law, the Indian political system, is completely at odds with the sense of natural law or tribal behavior which dictates that women are second-class citizens and that when they tempt or transgress or whatever, they deserve to be destroyed.

And that collision I think really lies at the heart of *Antigone*, her sense of natural law tells her that her brother must be buried because it's her brother. And state law says the brother's a traitor, and so he should be cast aside. And I don't think that quandary's ever going to go away in any culture. We fabricate what we think are the right laws of justice, but then our instincts tell us other things, which is why we take to the streets. Greek drama is so richly interpretable, probably because it was dance drama. You can do it in so many different ways depending on your bent. You can do it all male; you can do it all female. You can do it indoors; you can do it as a big public thing. You can do it with music; you can update it . . . it's very malleable that way.

M.W.: But isn't it also a huge challenge to make it accessible here and now for an American audience, who have a very different sense of the state and feel very much alienated from it? The state now is seen as a distant thing, and we all have lives that are much more privatized. We don't in a sense have a choral experience of living. That must make it really hard when it comes to the actual staging of it.

C.P.: Well, it does. And that's why if you can figure out how to break the fourth wall, it makes a big difference. When we did *Electra* outdoors, at the Getty, it was easy: all we had to do was turn and talk to the audience, and they realized that they were implicated, because they were right there. When we went indoors with that production in San Francisco, we kept the house lights up for a lot of the choral odes and for the Clytemnestra scene, and for the tutor's speech giving the fake story of Orestes' death. And at first the actor playing the tutor in San Francisco, a different guy from LA, didn't understand the speech at all: he said, "I don't understand. It's horrible—he's telling Orestes' mother that Orestes is dead; what's with all this endless fabrication and lies? He gets so excited about the race; what's the point?"

And I said, "First of all, every mother wants to think her son is a hero. So you have to remind her of what a great hero Orestes was, and *then* tell her that he died. But also, the Greeks were native storytellers, and they loved meta-theatricality. So when he comes onstage his task as an actor is to tell a story that is so convincing that even though we know he's making it up we'll believe it." And that is a fantastic, ridiculous acting challenge. So we left the house lights up and we let him go right to the audience and tell the story. And it's so dramatic: they're coming around the bend, and the axle breaks and he's thrown off and so on. And the audience gets so caught up in it that they believe it. And then they get to the end and think, "Oh, my God, wait a minute, that was all false." And it makes the audience really think about the way in which language can be either a purveyor of truth or a complete smokescreen. And the Greeks were so suspicious of the way in which language could manipulate. So the action *is* the audience, it isn't just for the audience. And I think if you do that, then the audience experiences exactly what Clytemnestra's experienced when she says, "Zeus, can I say this is lucky? Or terrible, but to my advantage?"

You have to really invest in your audience when you're doing a Greek play, and find some way to bridge the worlds. And it doesn't mean you have to update it. One of the great, great productions I've ever seen of Greek tragedy was Peter Stein's *Oresteia* in Berlin. The chorus were these very, very, very old men. This was shortly after the Wall fell, and I think he was thinking about all the elderly in East Germany who'd lived through the war and the incredible privation, and at the very ends of their lives were seeing the world change again, and what were they going to make of it? So for the audiences there to see these blind old men as the chorus was very personal. It wasn't that it was literal. I don't know that that helps; it's nice to keep the metaphor as wide as possible.

In different eras different Greek tragedies seem to pop up and ask to be revisited. The *Persians* came back, and that's a great play that had kind of disappeared. And *Ajax* is very trenchant right now, because finally we're beginning to understand the collateral damage of war and PTSD and the broken mind of a great general. So I think because they are metaphoric and they are templates, they sit well in different moments in our own cultural history.

M.W.: That goes back to what you said at the beginning: even in their time they were at one remove from the contemporary world.

C.P.: I suppose Shakespeare's like that as well, because he was really writing about Elizabeth when he wrote about Richard the Third. And when that happens, there's so much more room for them to survive and travel because they're not literal, and you don't actually have to know the politics of their time to make sense of it. Whereas when you look at plays that are absolutely tied to the politics of their own time—Ben Jonson, for example—they don't travel as well. I think that's why the Greeks don't date: although they were writing about the Peloponnesian War and the horrors of Athenian territorialism and expansionism, and so on, they weren't set in that moment. And there's room for it to apply in lots of different ways to other cultural moments depending on what it is that we're obsessed with at the time. And those themes are never going to go away. War, gender, vendetta, justice, memory...

To go back to *Electra*: I was reading a lot about the role of memory in human life. And that forgetting is curative, that when you have a traumatic event the sign of damaged mental health is the inability to forget—and this is the horror of PTSD, it keeps coming back to you in your dreams, you can't let go of it. And somehow you have to cure yourself by putting that memory somewhere where it is not constantly disrupting your life. We actually naturally forget most of what happens during the course of the day; your brain makes you do that because you'd never survive if you remembered everything.

And Electra is an emotionally damaged person because she can't forget. She wills herself to remember this deed 15 years later. And whether she's right or wrong about the nature of the act, it's done: the culture is moving on. And yet it can't, in her mind, and she is destroyed by her own inability to forget. People who've gone through terrible trauma or war and can't move past it destroy themselves. And I'm sure that's why at the end of the play she's absolutely silent. It's why I like the Sophocles *Electra* much better than the Euripides version, because I think he really gets at that.

M.W.: I think that question of whether you can move on from trauma also depends on what's going on around you: it depends on whether there is some public recognition. You can see that in *Antigone*, where her burial of Polyneices isn't complete because there's no public mourning.

C.P.: Yes, and is it a good thing for a culture to revisit war crimes, and to have a war tribunal, or to somehow move on? And what happens when a culture moves on and doesn't deal with horror like South Africa did?

So in a way they were on to everything, and I guess that's what is always so humbling and thrilling about the Greeks. Everything we wrestle with today about governance, and the way our political systems work, and is our government there to protect us from ourselves or to free us from ourselves, and who gets to speak, and who represents themselves, and what happens when language becomes demagoguery—they thought of all of it. They knew the minute they invented democracy that they had invented its own demise.

I remember the first time I read the *Frogs,* and I thought it was so hilarious that Dionysus is in such despair about the state of his own culture that he goes back to the underworld to bring a playwright back to solve the problem. And here we are: to be in theater in America is to feel completely marginalized no matter what you do—drama never matters to anybody, it's not going to change anybody's life. But to go back and realize that that is the role drama had—it's just thrilling, and very moving.

M.W.: I wanted to ask you about translations, and why you commission translations from Greek. Because you could perfectly well do them yourself: you have a Classics degree, and you're a playwright as well.

C.P.: What I love about the theater is the collaboration. I don't direct my own plays, and people find that equally puzzling because I am a director, and I must know how I see the plays. But there is something that happens to a piece of theater that is really clarifying when two people come at it from slightly different angles and work it together. It's been like that in all my time with Timberlake: I love collaborating with her, and I think she has an incredibly strong intuitive sense of the Greeks. And I love the simplicity of her language and the almost dryness of it—that she doesn't go for the melodrama, she's incredibly spare. It means I can come in and infuse it with all of this feeling and muscle and heat because the text has such a strong envelope itself.

And partly I do really revere translation. In this country we give very little credit to it because we're not interested in foreign languages and we think that's the purview of old Aunt Millie who comes from Russia and can do the translation. But actually translation's a great art form in and of itself, and not many people are really that good at it. I think the Greeks are particularly difficult, because the language functions in such a different way. You can never do anything in English that you can do in Greek, and so it is like creating a new play. I'm really fascinated by translation and why translation needs to keep happening, that there isn't a definitive translation.

I know for Timberlake to have you is also part of the collaboration. It's that thing where you sit and look at one word and say, "What is that really about? If you dropped that penny in a well, what are the ripples?" Not just what it literally means. And you never know where that moment is going to come, when you think, "Oh, *that's* what that is."

And even now having spent years on the *Electra,* when we did this version, many things we came back to, and we'd say to Timberlake, "Why did you make that a question?" Or "What is the real implication of...?" There was a choral ode that started, "Pity the cry." As if pity were a verb. And in the Greek it is more "piteous the cry." But I could tell that Timberlake wanted the action of the verb.

I've commissioned lots of translations of other languages from lots of different people. Sometimes they've been really happy experiences, but I've also had really unhappy experiences with translators who don't go the distance—who are too protective of the literal meaning of the text even when it doesn't come through in any way in the English. One of the happiest translation collaborations I've had is with a guy called Paul Walsh who does Scandinavian languages. And I worked with the late, great Paul Schmidt on the Russians. I find it a really humbling experience, and I think carrying the impulse of one language to another is the most challenging thing you can do. So I've always wanted to do it with a collaborator.

M.W.: One final question. I was very interested when I sat in on your *Electra* workshop by the fact that Timberlake was in a sense in the position of a playwright. It didn't look very different to me from the way it would have been if the playwright had been there.

C.P.: You're exactly right. I can't have Sophocles in the room, I can't have Gorky or Strindberg or Racine. So I can have their best advocate. And if you have someone as brilliant as Timberlake who really understands that native culture but also is a theater person of our own time, that is absolute gold, it's fantastic.

I'll tell you one really funny story. We were doing Chekhov's *The Seagull,* and there's this embarrassing moment where someone runs after Arkadina to say, "Don't forget the plums for the train." And she turns around, horrified, and says, "Leave me alone!" And I said to Paul Schmidt, the translator, what is that moment? And he said, "Well, it's really prunes. And the message is: you might be irregular on the train, it's a long journey." And how embarrassing that was in front of everybody; she's the lady of the house, all dressed up, and somebody says, "Don't forget the prunes." And how precarious her sense of status really is. And it was just a tiny note, but it formed the entire scene.

And that's the kind of thing you just never get otherwise, but what you look for as a director are those behavioral moments that ring absolutely true. And that's what Paul gave me, and what Timberlake gives me all the time in the Greeks. And that's why it's great to have her.

CHAPTER 45

ECLECTIC ENCOUNTERS
Staging Greek Tragedy in America, 1973–2009

RUSH REHM

I offer this account of my theatrical engagements with Greek tragedy out of an abiding respect for the original material—its impulses, subject matter, and dramatic form. I believe that modern audiences have more to gain from productions of tragedy that maintain such respect than from those which treat ancient tragedies as if they were written yesterday and so conform, willy-nilly, to contemporary theatrical assumptions and conditions. That approach, unfortunately, informs many contemporary productions of Greek tragedy, including a fair few that have proven popular and influential.

My regard for form of tragedy, however, has not translated into a historicist recreation of fifth-century theatrical conventions.[1]

I have never directed tragedy with an all-male cast or done a production in ancient Greek. I rarely have used masks, convinced that this ancient convention alienates a modern audience more than it captures the objectivity and "otherness" basic to the genre. Only occasionally have I staged tragedies out of doors. Nonetheless, I believe that the ancient focus on poetic language, rhetorical argument, relatively simple plots, archetypal characters, and a communal Chorus—as opposed to our current preference for conversation, character psychology, personal idiosyncrasy, and realistic situations—offers transformative potential for the contemporary stage.

Tragedy depends on, and celebrates, the power of language and dramatic structure to release the imagination of the audience. In doing so, tragedy offers a powerful alternative to much contemporary theater, which tends to imitate television with its generic crime dramas, situation comedies, soap operas, game shows, and reality TV. Theater based on these models usually reduces speech to the conversational and the world to a room with chairs, laptops, and cell phones. Similarly, Greek tragedy provides a welcome antidote to the influence of Hollywood on live performance, where spectacle and graphic visualization find their way into the mega-musical and theatrical blockbuster. Finally the elite world of performance art shows little interest in the close observation, verbal subtlety, lyric complexity, and tragic conflict that characterizes ancient Greek drama.

The productions I discuss span four decades, and their manifold differences justify the title "eclectic encounters." Each represents a specific response to the original, reflecting the personal concerns of the artists involved (particularly my own political convictions), the material conditions available to them, and the cultural and political environment that shape their, and their audiences', perceptions. The productions include Euripides' *Electra* (1973), *Cyclops* (1983, adapted as a musical, *Cyclops—Nobody's Musical*), and *Suppliant Women* (1993); Sophocles' *Oedipus Tyrannus* (1981), *Women of Trachis* (2006, adapted for solo performance as *Deianeira*), and *Electra* (2009); and Aeschylus' *Persians* (1990), along with a brief account of my work on the *Oresteia* (translator, actor, assistant director) in Australia in 1974.

Euripides' *Electra* (1973)

I first read *Electra* in Greek at university, and I found myself so puzzled by its anti-tragic flavor that I began to translate it for the stage. The strange shifts in tone, the anomalous rural setting, the atypical characterization of the principals, the apparently disconnected choruses, the unpleasant thrust of the action (the murders of Aegisthus and Clytemnestra seem more slaughter than revenge), the double-talk of the Dioscuri at the play's close—Euripides seemed to be describing the world of the late 1960s and early 1970s.

I attended university on an army scholarship, which I gave up when I became active in the anti-war movement. Like many others, I was horrified at the secret bombing campaigns in Laos; our undeclared war against Vietnamese national liberation, packaged as a Cold War struggle against Soviet and/or Chinese expansion; the U.S. "incursion" into Cambodia, overthrowing the government of Prince Sihanouk; the massive U.S. bombing that followed, leading to the rise of the genocidal Khmer Rouge (whom the U.S.A. later supported after Vietnam's invasion of Cambodia in 1979–80); and the campaign at home against civil rights, free expression, and alternative politics. *Mutatis mutandis*, Euripides seemed to grasp the violence, absurdity, pathos, and horror of this madness. His undermining of heroic tragedy, and his exposé of the ideals on which it was based, mirrored my own disillusionment with the myth of U.S. exceptionalism. The moral and psychic distance I felt from my earlier beliefs took comfort in Euripides' reworking of the myth of the house of Atreus—*Iphigenia in Aulis, Orestes* (I played the title role in a college production), and most prominently *Electra*.

Given this background, it may seem strange that our production of *Electra* bore no resemblance to Richard Schechner's influential *Dionysus in 69*, a version of Euripides' *Bacchae* as an orgy of nudity and blood that failed to speak to me (on Schechner's play, see Jenkins, Sides, this volume). I preferred that the parallels between Euripides' play and contemporary America emerge *through* the performance, rather than overwhelm it from the start. I invited electronic composer John Selleck to write a score using computer-generated sounds, frequently with a strong lyric feeling. A graduate student in Composition at Princeton, John found an effective musical analogue for the tension between Euripides' sources and his treatment of them. For example, we chose a fanfare for Clytemnestra's luxurious arrival at Electra's sooty cottage. But the electronic sounds lacked the full confidence and clarity of normal trumpet-blasts, suggesting something at odds with itself, in this case the bizarre nature of the scene between a regal (but apologetic) Clytemnestra and her disheveled (but deadly deceptive) daughter.

For the Chorus of young women, choreographer Lucy Graves combined passages of ballet-like fluidity with Duncanesque shapes and poses, in contrast with Electra's determined, earth-bound movement. Her labored physicality gave the impression that she sustained her hatred with every deliberate step (*El.* 112–39). *Electra* belongs to the actor playing the title role, and Roxanne Hart fully captured her unsettling mix of bitter fixation and disturbed vulnerability, nowhere more so than in her speech to the head of Aegisthus:

> There's so much to say. Do I start with the worst,
> or save that for last? What should I fit in between? . . .
> As for your other women, it's not proper for a virgin
> to speak of such things. I'll keep quiet, only hint at all I know.
> You let it go to your head—you held the royal palace
> and knew you were so damned handsome. I don't want a husband
> with your delicate features, but a real man to father men
> who cling to war, not pretty-boys only fit for dancing.
> To hell with you! . . . (Eur. *El.* 907–8, 945–52)

My translation gives a sense of Electra's rhetorical self-awareness and vituperative excess, and the stage image (Fig. 45.1) catches the essential Euripidean *gestus*: rhetoric and *logos* undermined by the passion of the speaker and the futility of her outburst.

Standing over the corpse of their mother, blood-spattered and full of remorse, neither Electra nor Orestes drew comfort from the future, no matter how hard Castor, the upbeat *deus ex machina*, encouraged them to do so. In our *Electra*, the sense of horror and loss not only accompanied Electra, Orestes, and Chorus when they left the stage, but also remained all-too-visibly on it. The lights faded on the corpses of Clytemnestra and Aegisthus—ghastly slaughter polluting a peasant's cottage.

Aeschylus' *Oresteia* Trilogy (1974)

I joined Melbourne's Greek Theatre Project in 1973, translating and acting in Aeschylus' *Oresteia* and working closely with the Australian director James McCaughey. The translation and rehearsals took the better part of a year, and we presented the trilogy 20 times, from 6 p.m. to 11 p.m. (with a dinner break), changing the seating between plays to suggest the different relationship each forges with the audience.[2] McCaughey's approach to

FIG. 45.1 Electra (Roxanne Hart) with the head of Aegisthus, Euripides' *Electra* (1973). Photograph by John Coventry.

choral lyric aimed at generating compelling choral events rather than a consistent choral "character." In *Agamemnon*, for example, the creation of the evocation of the eagles and pregnant hare (*Ag.* 109–21), the sacrifice of Iphigenia (184–249), the celebration at the fall of Troy (355–66), the grief when a family welcomes home "an urn of ashes instead of a man" (427–36), the pet lion cub that reveals its nature when it grows (717–36) took precedence over the depiction of weak old men. The Chorus in *Agamemnon* were effete elders only when described as such; at other times, they were a physical ensemble committed to bringing Aeschylus' complex lyric to life. I brought these lessons with me when I returned to the United States, translating and directing Sophocles' *Oedipus Tyrannus*.

Oedipus Tyrannus (1981)

On a bare stage and with simple rehearsal costumes, this taut production focused on the text and actors. The ensemble formed the Chorus, out of which individual characters emerged and into which they returned after their scene, all save Oedipus, who remained apart from the group. This relationship helped convey the irony inherent in the situation—an apparent outsider who proves to embody the group's identity in horrifying ways.

In the translation of *Oedipus*, I selectively followed the inflected word order of the Greek, trying to catch Sophocles' strange emphases—for example the Priest's account of the plague:

> Wasting away the seeds of grain across the earth,
> wasting away the flocks of the field, wasted are the stillborn
> cries of women in their childless labor... (*OT* 25–7)

Sometimes the choice took the form of an unexpected apostrophe, as if the word itself were being addressed, as in Oedipus' plea to Teiresias: "Our city, although you cannot see, still you know | the plague that lives inside her" (302–3). I kept the key term *deina* untranslated, and its repetition gained significance for the audience over the course of the play.

The highly physical Chorus featured bodies *in extremis*, appropriate for lyric dealing with plague (*OT* 167–202), comparing Laius' killer to a bull fleeing sacrifice (477–82), and celebrating the wild possibility that Oedipus' parents might have been divine (1086–109). In that short lyric passage (following Jocasta's despairing exit and before Oedipus' own recognition), the Chorus spun together arm in arm, whirling with such speed that some left the ground (Fig. 45.2). Their "taking flight" suggested that Oedipus' pinned ankles might not root him to the earth of Thebes—dead wrong, as events will prove.

The Chorus' physical freedom contrasted with the stillness of the Messenger from the palace, who delivered her account on her knees, barely moving. Only when she described Oedipus' blinding did one clenched fist twist hard against the other. The Messenger's posture recalled Oedipus' supplication of Teiresias earlier in the play, when he too went down on his knees (*OT* 326–7). The prophet's brusque rejection of the king's appeal on behalf of his city helped to justify Oedipus' angry reaction. After his blinding, the audience saw a man struggling to find reasons to live and not follow his wife's suicidal example (as the Chorus urge him to do, 1367–8). Carefully orchestrated over the last 350 lines, Oedipus' return to the stage culminates in his embrace of his incestuous daughters. That the girls came from the ensemble reminded us that they had always been present, but only in Oedipus' blindness were they seen, and accepted, for who they were. The revelation of what is before our eyes but goes unrecognized lies at the heart of the play and informed our version of it.

Euripides *Cyclops*, or *Cyclops—Nobody's Musical* (1983)

I directed an adaptation of Euripides' satyr-play *Cyclops* in the form of a rock musical, writing the book and lyrics, with music composed by Francis James Brown. Scored for percussion, guitars, and keyboard, *Cyclops—Nobody's Musical* featured original

FIG. 45.2 Chorus (Andre Braugher standing), Sophocles' *Oedipus Tyrannus* (1981). Photograph by James Carmody.

songs using the bass register for Cyclops and a high tessitura (in the mode of Andrew Lloyd Webber's *Jesus Christ Superstar*) for Odysseus. We followed the basic form of Euripides' original, translating lyric passages into songs for the satyr Chorus and occasionally converting speeches into songs for the principals (Silenus, Odysseus, Cyclops).

In Homer's *Odyssey*, Odysseus visits the island for provisions and guest-gifts, but he also adopts the "colonial gaze," imagining what civilized men like himself could make of the land (*Od.* 9. 116–41, echoed somewhat at *Cyc.* 113–62). In both Homer and Euripides, Odysseus boasts of his role in the Trojan War (*Od.* 9.259–66, *Cyc.* 177–8, 198–202, 290–8), an expedition that Euripides' Cyclops finds shameful—a war waged for a single woman (*Cyc.* 280–4). Exhibiting his antinomian instincts and suspicion of Homeric heroics (316–40), the title character of our version resembled Rousseau's "natural man," unmoved by civilization with its religion, collective violence, and expansionist instincts.

Cyclops—Nobody's Musical did not minimize the monster's cannibalism, but presented it as a natural (albeit grisly) response to foreign intervention. Cyclops's rejection of social convention and accepted ideology struck me as a humorous response to the patriotic rhetoric and militarism of the Reagan administration, most absurdly manifest in the invasion of the tiny island of Grenada in 1983. At the same time, the U.S.A. built up its nuclear arsenal, embarked on the Strategic Defense Initiative (SDI, or "Star Wars"), introduced cruise missiles into Europe (in spite of tremendous protest there), and so on. Simultaneously, the U.S.A. offered virtually unqualified support for dictators across the Caribbean, Central America, and South America, all in the name of "national security."[3]

For all these political resonances, *Cyclops* did not stint on bawdy sexual humor. Designer William Eddelman equipped the satyrs with humongous phalloi with ithyphallic potential (via a hidden drawstring) (Fig. 45.3). A secondary female Chorus played Cyclops's ovine herd, moving with delightful suggestiveness in Stacey Greenberg's choreography. In a drunken dream sequence following Odysseus' gift of wine, the sheep slipped out of their sheepskins to reveal gorgeous women unleashed by the power of Dionysus. The dream of the satyrs coincided with Polyphemus' nightmare, culminating in his blinding by Odysseus with the olive stake (*Cyc.* 455–63, 593–5, 656–62). As in Euripides' *Bacchae*, Dionysiac abandon leads to gruesome violence, a destructive possibility suggested earlier when the satyrs fantasize about raping Helen after the fall of Troy (*Cyc.* 179–87).

The sexual atmosphere of Euripides' original includes strong homoerotic elements, indicated in the set design by the phallic-like Aetna rising above the anatomically suggestive cave mouth. When the drunken Cyclops retires with Silenus as his reluctant

FIG. 45.3 Satyrs (Frank Murray, Michael Ramsey-Perez, Graham Winton, Sam Barker) with Odysseus (Marc Accornero), *Cyclops—Nobody's Musical* (1983), adapted from Euripides' *Cyclops*. Photograph by Connie Strayer.

Ganymede, Euripides has the monster say, "Anyway, I take more pleasure | in boys than in women" (*Cyc.* 582–9; see also 266–7). In our *Cyclops,* Silenus lost his initial disgust following his offstage intimacies with Polyphemus, and he seemed distraught at the blinding. Being Silenus, however, his distress was short-lived, and he ran off with the other satyrs to join Odysseus and his crew in pursuit of further Dionysiac adventures. The final scene showed the blind Cyclops alone, cradling the master ram whose throat Odysseus had slit (paralleled at *Od.* 9.431–5, 548–53). For all its fun and games, *Nobody's Musical* left the audience commiserating with another victim of the "march of civilization."

AESCHYLUS' *PERSIANS* (1990)

Any serious production of Aeschylus' *Persians* must deal with the devastation of imperial expansion. Our production, however, avoided the topical (and confusing) choices that some directors foist on the play. Consider, for example, Peter Sellars's much-discussed 1993 version set in Iraq after the first Gulf War, which lamented the destruction wreaked on the Iraqi people by the U.S. "Operation Desert Storm."[4] I joined many in protesting that war, and consider U.S. leaders guilty of war crimes (100,000 dead Iraqis, and another 500,000 to a million civilian deaths from sanctions).[5] However, using Aeschylus' drama to do so skews the power relationships that ground the play. *Persians* describes the defeat of a great empire by a small and relatively minor country, *not* the reduction of a weak nation by the world's superpower.

We staged Aeschylus' *Persians* in the soaring-roofed Canon Chapel at Emory University in Atlanta. Not unlike the theater of Dionysus in Athens, the audience sat on three sides of a bare stage (the chapel altar was removed), most of them looking down on the action. The high roof gave a sense of scale lacking in many indoor venues, and the balconied back wall allowed for the appearance of the Ghost of Darius "on high."[6] The bare stage included an elevated platform at one end for the tomb of Darius, covered with a large purple cloth to suggest the wealth of the royal family.

We approached the choral lyric much like a staged oratorio. Atlanta composer Don Rechtman arranged a layered vocal score reflecting the prominence of lament and mourning in the play. Rechtman accompanied the lyric voices with a lyre tuned to a nine-tone scale and run through a synthesizer, avoiding any quaint or ethnic associations. The vocal music featured patterns of overlapping words, with various leitmotifs (for royalty, battle, drowning, yoking, etc.). Rhythmic chanting alternated with song, choral unison gave way to solo descant, leading to the final *kommos* between the Chorus and Xerxes.

Costumes also reflected the play's mournful tone, the Chorus of seven men in black pants and turtlenecks, the Queen in a modest black evening dress, with a single decorative element—a large metallic necklace hanging over the bodice. Her hair was tied with a ribbon of purple and red, the color motif we adopted for the house of Darius. When the Queen returned to the stage with libations for her husband's tomb, she used a metal vessel of the same color and material of the necklace she no longer wore. Her ritual for the dead had replaced the ostentations of wealth. The ghost of Darius also appeared in black, but with a red and purple shoulder sash; their son Xerxes wore a similar outfit, but in tatters. The basic black suggested the commonality of grief, with the red and purple accents indicating the despotic royal family.

In *Persians*, images of yoking—of forced, constrained, or unnatural union—point to imperial excess, particularly Xerxes' "yoking" of the Hellespont.[7] We brought these elements together by using a swath of red fabric to represent the yoked chariot in which the Queen first enters. Drawing it tight across the Queen's back and then crossing it in front of her, two attendants stretched the red cloth to its full length (some 20 feet) and drew her onstage. The Queen dismounted by lifting the cloth over her head, and the attendants laid the red fabric over the pre-set purple cloth, fully displaying the royal colors. After learning of the Persian defeat in the great Messenger speech, the Queen "remounted" the chariot and was led offstage, the sense of loss suggested by the color draining away from the set. When the Queen returned with offerings for her husband's tomb, she arrived not in a red-cloth "chariot" but on foot, unattended, and without the genuflections of the Chorus that marked her first entrance (*P.* 150–60 vs. 607–9).

As the Queen made her offerings, the Chorus took hold of the edges of the pre-set purple cloth, which they rippled and shook. The invocation of Darius intensified; the cloth rose and fell, until it billowed to its full extent. In a rapid cross-fade, the cloth fell to the earth, and a pin-spot revealed the ghost of Darius on high, caught in an eerie shadow. His prediction of the cost of Xerxes' *hubris* anticipated the appearance of his son in rags, lamenting with the Chorus the countless Persians who were "gone, dead and gone."[8] Resisting the popular view that Aeschylus laid the foundation for western orientalism by "inventing the barbarian," our production did not mock the fallen "other" or their manner of mourning. In my view, *Persians* focuses on the catastrophe that awaits *any* empire, a case made more powerfully through shared grief than partisan derision.

Two months after the fall of the Berlin Wall, and three months before our production of *Persians*, the U.S.A. invaded Panama, an impoverished country with a legacy of U.S. continental yoking. U.S. policy makers needed new justifications for our giant military, and the narco-trafficking Manuel Noriega (formerly a CIA asset) provided the excuse. "Operation Just Cause" left thousands of Panamanians homeless and some 3,000 civilians dead. I could think of no play of any period more relevant to the United States, consumed then (as it is now) with Persian-like *hubris*. Our work on *Persians* represented a plea for future compassion, not compassion for others, but that which others might extend to us when our time of grief comes.[9]

Euripides' *Suppliant Women* (1993)

I directed a production of this neglected tragedy in 1993, part of the Democracy 2500 project, which celebrated the 2500th anniversary of the Cleisthenic reforms that instituted Athenian democracy.[10] The reasons for the play's relative neglect involve precisely those qualities that attracted me to it: the debate about politics and political systems; the argument for a "just war"; the exposé of ideological manipulation and its transmission to the young; the differing responses to war by men and women, old and young, parents and children; and the perpetuation of the cycle of violence.

Using a large (1,700-seat) proscenium theater, we reversed the standard seating arrangement by erecting bleacher seats on the stage and constructing a circular orchestra that extended over the normal seating area. This inversion gave the audience the sensation that they were watching a floating world, but one with the visual expanse of an outdoor theater. The stage-circle was backed by a large T-shaped platform, creating two staging areas, useful for highlighting the tensions between age, gender, and civic loyalties. Suspended behind the platform was a large (24 × 24 feet square) projection screen—actually a scrim, opaque when lit from the front, but translucent when backlit. This arrangement allowed for the unexpected appearance of Evadne from behind the projections, high above the pyre of her husband Capaneus, followed by her suicidal leap into the flames.

On the scrim we projected a sequence of images that helped with the shifting focus of the text (temple façade, battle ground, expansive terrain, corpses, the sun, public demagogues, death rituals), while fleshing out the mythic background that might be lost on a modern audience (Fig. 45.4). These images reached their climax with Athena's

FIG. 45.4 Chorus (with Adrastos in background), Euripides' *Suppliant Women* (1993). Photograph by John B. Wilson.

appearance *ex machina*, beginning with a series of still images of Athena that then were overlaid with a film sequence (the only time we used moving, rather than still or morphing pictures). A larger-than-life figure on the screen, the goddess counseled the sons of the Seven to initiate *another* invasion of Thebes once they had grown to manhood (*Supp.* 1213–26), undermining the tentative peace that followed Theseus' recovery of the bodies. The fact that the actress playing Athena was not present but "in the can" suited Euripides' disturbing ending. By failing to be literally present and open to the challenges of live performance, Athena's appearance emphasized how deeply embedded the ideology of war was in late fifth-century Athens, and in late twentieth-century America. The film of "patriotic war" (manipulative, persuasive, and hard to challenge) keeps playing in our heads, internalized by repetition in popular culture and the mass media. Even a good leader like Theseus (721–39, 1165–75) cannot stop the outbreak of a new conflict when forces like Athena insist that it occur.

The floating stage included a small circle covered with plexiglass located dead center. This area was lit from below to represent the altar at Eleusis (where Aethra makes her sacrifice at the start of the play), but it disappeared when the play "forgets" its Eleusinian setting and shifts toward Athens.[11] Designer John Wilson painted the stage floor terracotta-orange, suggesting both the sun-baked earth and the body of a fifth-century Attic vase. The Chorus wore heavily draped black linen with orange and purple accents, favorite colors of Attic black-figure artists like the Amassis Painter. The costumes of the principals maintained the earth-tone palette, appropriate for a play connected to the land, fertility, burial, and the prospect of new life associated with the sanctuary of Demeter at Eleusis.

The production featured the contributions of choreographer Ze'eva Cohen and composer Michael Keck. The choreography combined ritual-like movement (drawn from Yemenite dance) with freer expressive gestures, usually performed by the Chorus in unison. The suppliant women moved to a richly textured score featuring driving percussion and the haunting sounds of shofar and oud. From the outset, Keck conveyed the high stakes of the drama by introducing a searing, long-descending tone swelling in volume, like the sound of a bomb falling from thousands of feet. The climax, however, was not a Hollywood explosion but a deep reverberation, like an earthquake moving a massive volume of air (sub-woofers were located under the seats). During this sequence, the women arrived at Eleusis and supplicated Aethra who stood at the altar, bathed in light from below. Keck used softer eastern flute motifs for the appearance of Evadne above the pyre of her husband, for the procession of the recovered corpses onstage, and for the return of the ashes to the mothers of the Seven after their sons' cremation.

The Chorus of suppliant women and the secondary Chorus of their grandsons wore half-masks, giving them a certain anonymity. As victims—and, for the sons of the Seven, as future perpetrators—of violence, the Chorus members have a deeply personal connection to their dead sons/fathers, but the half-masks suggested an objectivity beyond individual grief. The women represented any parents in anguish over their children, and the boys stood for archetypal young males who dream of heroic exploits without considering the consequences. We played public speeches out to the audience, striving to maintain the immediacy of Euripides' argument. In the debate on monarchy versus democracy, for example, the Theban Herald (*Supp*. 412–25, 479–85) makes a strong case against democracy as practiced, anticipating later Athenian critics. Sleazy politicians simplify confusing issues for their own gain; money and influence dominate decision-making; the myth of popular rule camouflages powerful interests that determine the agenda, propagating an ideology that sounds democratic but is not.

Euripides offers a clear-cut instance of ideological manipulation in Adrastos' funeral oration (*Supp*. 857–917), echoing the Athenian institution of the *patrios nomos*. Adrastos rewrites the story of the Argive invaders of Thebes, converting them into paragons of self-control, civic virtue, and rational deliberation, qualities clearly absent in their invasion of Thebes. Contemporary examples of political and corporate powerbrokers misleading the public are legion, and I dedicated the production to the people of Nicaragua. The program described how the U.S.A. considered this impoverished country of 3 million a direct threat to our national security ("only a three-day drive to Harlingen, Texas," President Reagan insisted). Instead of ridicule, the corporate media adopted the Reagan administration's euphemistic term "freedom fighters" for the U.S.-backed Contra who butchered some 20,000 civilians in their rampage against grass-roots Nicaraguan democracy (Sklar 1988; Walker 1987). No "just war" here—just ideological manipulation and its deadly consequences. *Suppliant Women* proved timely, and it continues to.

Sophocles' *Women of Trachis*— Deianeira (2006)

I translated and adapted Sophocles' *Women of Trachis* as a 45-minute solo piece for the dancer, choreographer, and performance artist Aleta Hayes. Focusing on the protagonist Deianeira, we exploited the fact that she and Heracles were played by the same actor in the fifth century. I used a taped voice for the Messenger who reports Heracles' sack of Oechalia, his mad passion for Iole, and her fate as an uprooted war bride (a situation not unlike Deianeira's). We solved other dramaturgical problems via projections (still and moving) on the two screens that formed the ends of our alley staging, with audience facing each other on opposite sides.

The performance opened with the swirling leaves of Dodona, the source of the prophecy so crucial to Heracles' fate (*Trach*. 166–74, 1164–74). As in *Suppliant Women*, the scrim enabled Deianeira to emerge as if out of the projected leaves when the backlight slowly took over. In this way her story seemed as ephemeral and as cyclical as the leaves, their bright colors and dance-like movements setting the tone for the other projections—oak trees at Dodona, the meadows and crags of Mt. Oeta, the cliffs of Euboea, the rivers Achelous and Evenus, the bright sun, and the night canopy where "the big bear wheels forever | deep in the star bright sky" (129–30). These images usually began as photographs, but video artist Ethan Hoerneman hand-painted many of them, making the visuals at either end of the stage magical and otherworldly. These "book ends" conjured a mythic cosmos, while the performance within told of a particular woman's love, fear, and jealousy, and the passion that drove her husband to wreak havoc, and her (unwittingly) to do the same.

As with the Sophoclean original, *Deianeira* depends for its impact on the actress playing Deianeira. Hayes gave a *tour de force* performance, her movement vocabulary expressing a range of emotions from Deianeira's childlike freedom to her horror at Achelous' pursuit, from the excitement of a young bride to the anxiety of a wife who has lost her husband's love. After her transformation into Heracles (particularly moving when he cries in pain like a girl, *Trach.* 1070–5), the projections shifted from erotic flames to a wildfire and then to the sack of Oechalia suggested by images of contemporary war.[12] Against this background of burnt-out trees and urban conflagration, *Deianeira* ended with a horrific sense of the destruction that arises when reason loses its grip, overwhelmed by the passions of the moment (*Trach.* 438–48, 660–2, 765–71, 851–61, 1082–4). As my version puts it, "Desire is a curse, passion breeds grief, | and love—if that's its name—flames the world to ash."

Sophocles' *Electra* (2009)

As part of the Stanford Repertory Theater (SRT) Electra Festival, I directed Sophocles' version of the story in Anne Carson's translation (Carson 2001). The festival also included productions of Aeschylus' *Choephori* and Euripides' *Electra*, using the Greek myth to explore the interrelationship of memory, resistance, revenge, and justice. SRT had mounted an African festival in 2007, including a play on the 1994 Rwandan genocide that dealt with the contradictory demands of justice and reconciliation. The 2008 SRT festival had focused on the work of Brian Friel and Field Day, a group of Northern Irish writers trying to find a cultural path through "the Troubles," focusing on the links between memory and violence, and between forgetting and injustice. Prior to that, I had traveled to the West Bank, experiencing first hand (albeit briefly) what life under Israeli occupation was like, challenging my confidence that non-violent resistance offered the path to Palestinian liberation. Although none of these influences directly affected the staging of Sophocles' *Electra*, they influenced my decision to produce the play and inform my sense of why the play matters now.

Designer Eric Flatmo configured the palace at Mycenae as a dark red manor-like structure sitting high on a platform walled below with trellises of ivy, its double-doors opening and closing invisibly.[13] The porch had a steep stairway leading down to the main playing area. Covered with highly reflective, bright white laminate panels, the stage floor moved the play beyond realism into a world of extremity and excess. At the back stood a copse of thin trees, painted red, their wiry, leafless branches resembling the lines of a CAT-scan. Near the edge of the stage stood the altar of Apollo, the site of the antithetical prayers to the god offered by Clytemnestra (S. *El.* 636–59) and Electra (1376–83).

As with *Suppliant Women*, we set up scaffold seating on the cavernous stage, but in this case the audience faced the closed fire curtain, which sealed the auditorium seats from view. Constructed of thick fireproof fabric, the curtain resembled a wall of concrete on which the shadows of the trees fell. Above the audience, the ceiling (designed nearly a century ago to fly scenic elements) rose 100 feet; on the sides, the walls of the theater—including the rigging rails with their mass of ropes and counterweights—remained visible. The contrast between the rough theater space and the polished scenic elements mirrored the play's complex shift between truth (often incredible) and deception (all-too-credible), exemplified in the offerings at Agamemnon's tomb (*El.* 871–933), the elaborate death of Orestes (673–763), the empty urn that Electra cannot abandon (1113–223), and the corpse of Orestes which is actually that of Clytemnestra (1466–75).

Friends and confidantes of Electra, the Chorus invoke mythic archetypes against which the story unfolds (*El.* 482–515, 1075–80). Occasionally speaking in unison, they more often delivered the lines individually, the text moving rapidly among the seven Chorus members, supported by the seamless choreography of Aleta Hayes (the actor-choreographer of *Deianeira*). For the first strophe of the second stasimon (1058–69), the Chorus leader sang a powerful solo (how birds sustain life and family, unlike people),

FIG. 45.5 Chorus leader (Kay Kostopoulos) with Chorus, Sophocles' *Electra* (2009). Photograph by Sefanie Okuda.

accompanied by an intense dance from the group (Fig. 45.5). When not performing lyric, the women provided a sculptural-like background that changed subtly with the action—a rapid movement of the head or lifting of the arms, a sharp contraction, a small impulse moving from one member through the group. These accents highlighted an argument, or suggested the women's attitude toward a character, or indicated a change in the dynamic between speakers. Here, the Chorus embodied Schlegel's "ideal spectator," always focused on the dramatic event, their attention evident in their gaze, attitude, posture, and gesture.

As with Euripides' *Electra*, Sophocles' tragedy demands an extraordinary performance from the actor playing the title role. Colombian-born Valentina Condé rehearsed with me for several months until Electra's raw intensity became second nature. Only then did the rest of the company join the rehearsals. Time and again Electra manifests a desperate willfulness and uncompromising resilience, especially in her exchange with her mother Clytemnestra (played formidably by Courtney Walsh).

We chose dramatic means rather than program notes to bring the audience to the passionate intensity on which Electra's confrontations depend. We began the play with a prologue going back ten years, showing a young Electra gathering flowers to give to her father on his homecoming from Troy. Hidden beneath the stairs, she watches her mother's welcome of Agamemnon, the spreading of the red tapestries, his entry into the palace, Clytemnestra's ecstatic outburst over the corpse, and her embrace of Aegisthus (Fig. 45.6), using speeches from Aeschylus' *Agamemnon* (*Ag.* 855–913, 958–74, 1372–94, 1431–6).[14] After Clytemnestra's exit, the young Electra climbed the stairs to embrace her dead father and then stood by the corpse, resolved to fight back. The prologue helped establish the background of murder, desecration, trauma, and the compulsions to revenge that lie at the heart of Sophocles' *Electra*.

Over the course of the production, those compulsions were revealed to be more problematic than restorative. Sophocles' "sword of Damocles" ending means that Aegisthus always awaits Orestes' torture and murder (*El.* 1491–507), and Electra never regains her youthful integrity, insisting that Orestes deny burial rites to Aegisthus (1483–90). Our production closed with Electra once again embracing a corpse, this time her mother's. Instead of the bouquet of flowers, she tore off ivy leaves from the dark red trellis, placing them on the body of Clytemnestra as she lay down beside her. In spite of her triumph, and in part because of it, Electra cannot rise above the bloodshed of the past.

Greek tragedy offers a daunting challenge to anyone working in the American theater, a call to artistic engagement that respects and learns from the past, even as it finds a way to speak to a modern audience. I am reminded of Seamus Heaney's noble wish at the end of his version of *Philoctetes* that—somehow—hope and history align. As this summary of my work suggests, we may find that it is not hope with which our history rhymes, but tragedy.[15]

FIG. 45.6 Clytemnestra (Courtney Walsh) and Aegisthus (Donnell Hill) over the corpse of Agamemnon (James Kierstead), with the young Electra (Davia Schendel) watching, Sophocles' *Electra* (2009). Photograph by Sefanie Okuda.

Notes

1. See Rehm 1988; 1992: 43–74; 2002: 35–75. For very different perspectives, see Wiles 2000 and Goldhill 2007.
2. See Rehm forthcoming. *Agamemnon* featured alley staging that focused on the linearity of arrival; *Choephori* was played against a back wall, with the audience on three sides, emphasizing the claustrophobic nature of the murder plot; *Eumenides* opened the playing space up in a V-shaped arrangement, suggesting the possibility of a less constricted, more "democratic" future. Playing the trilogy on one evening was not a problem, given that the trilogy comprises fewer lines than Shakespeare's *Hamlet* and roughly the same number as

Richard III. And yet I have seen productions of *Agamemnon* by itself that have included an intermission!

3. The list of U.S.-backed regimes included the colonels in Argentina, the Stronato regime of General Stroessner in Paraguay, the Bonzer dictatorship in Bolivia (its death squads trained at the School of the Americas in Ft. Benning, Georgia), military regimes in Brazil, Ecuador, Colombia, Dominican Republic, Haiti, Guatemala, El Salvador, and Nicaragua. After the fall of the Somoza regime in Nicaragua in 1979, the U.S.A. then backed the "Contras," who waged a savage counter-revolution against the freely elected (1984) Sandinista government, using U.S. bases in Honduras and Costa Rica.
4. On Sellars's production, see Hall 2007: 191–2.
5. On first Gulf War casualties, see Ali and Shah 2000; also Daponte 2007. For the second Gulf War, see Brecher, Cutler, and Smith 2005.
6. In Rehm 2002: 239–40 I have argued that the roof of the *skênê* façade was available in the theater of Dionysus for *Persians*, and provided the platform for the ghost of Darius' appearance; see also Seaford 2012.
7. A. *Pers.* 67–72, 128–31, 722–3, 734, 736, 745–50; also used for the yoke of slavery at 49–50 and 585–93.
8. Aeschylus' *Persians* 1981.
9. A lesson clearly *not* learned after 9/11, when the Bush (2) administration used world sympathy as an umbrella to mount a disastrous war against Afghanistan, followed by the invasion and occupation of Iraq. See Rehm 2003: 76–7; 88–90, and above n. 5.
10. For critical response to the production, see Hartigan 1995: 144–6. Using the translation by R. Warren and S. Scully (New York 1995), the production was staged at Memorial Theatre, Stanford University, and the Folger Library, Washington, DC.
11. On the shifting locales, the lack of any entrances through the *skênê* façade, and other staging issues in the play, see Rehm 1988: 283–90.
12. The war images included photographs of the U.S. assault on Falujah in 2004—Operation Phantom Fury, which used white phosphorus bombs on human targets. The rates of cancer, infant mortality, and leukemia in the survivors exceed those reported in Hiroshima and Nagasaki. See Monbiot 2005; Busby, Hamdan, and Ariabi 2010; Cockburn 2010.
13. Worked by stagehands positioned underneath the platform, the doors seemed to respond to the commands of Clytemnestra in the prologue, and then increasingly to Electra and Orestes as the play progressed.
14. In this prologue, Agamemnon and the young Electra remained silent; we integrated Clytemnestra's speeches from *Agamemnon* to provide relevant background.
15. Heaney 1990. For the fear that modern history and ancient tragedy are reflecting mirrors, see Schmidt 2001: 6–19; 271–84.

References

Aeschylus (1981), *Persians*. Trans. C. J. Herington and J. Lembke. New York.
Ali, M. M. and I. H. Shah (2000), "Sanctions and Childhood Mortality in Iraq," *The Lancet* (May), 1851–8.
Brecher, J., J. Cutler, and B. Smith (eds. 2005), *In the Name of Democracy: American War Crimes in Iraq and Beyond*. New York.

Busby, C., M. Hamdan, and E. Ariabi (2010), "Cancer, Infant Mortality and Birth Sex-Ratio in Fallujah, Iraq 2005–2009," *International Journal of Environmental Research and Public Health* 7.7, 2828–37.

Carson, A. (2001), *Sophocles' Electra*. Introduction and notes by M. Shaw. New York.

Cockburn, P. (2010), "Toxic Legacy of U.S. Assault on Fallujah 'Worse than Hiroshima,'" *The Independent* (July 24).

Daponte, B. O. (2007), "Wartime Estimates of Iraqi Civilian Casualties," *International Review of the Red Cross* 89, 943–57.

Goldhill, S. (2007), *How to Stage Greek Tragedy Today*. Chicago.

Hall, E. (2007), "Aeschylus' Persians via the Ottoman Empire to Saddam Hussein," in E. Bridges, E. Hall, and P. J. Rhodes eds., *Cultural Responses to the Persian Wars: Antiquity to the Third Millenium*. Oxford, 167–200.

Hartigan, K. V. (1995), *Greek Tragedy on the American Stage: Ancient Drama in the Commercial Theater, 1882–1994*. Westport, CT, and London.

Heaney, S. (1990), *The Cure at Troy: A Version of Sophocles' Philoctetes*. London.

Monbiot, G. (2005), "Behind the Phosphorus Clouds Are War Crimes within War Crimes," *The Guardian* (November 22).

Rehm, R. (1988), "The Staging of Suppliant Plays," *Greek, Roman, and Byzantine Studies* 29, 263–307.

Rehm, R. (1992), *Greek Tragic Theatre*. London.

Rehm, R. (2002), *The Play of Space*. Princeton.

Rehm, R. (2003), *Radical Theatre: Greek Tragedy and the Modern* World. London.

Rehm, R. (forthcoming), "Translating Space: The Pram Factory *Oresteia*," in J. M. Griffiths, P. Monaghan, and F. Sear eds., *Close Relations: The Spaces of Greek and Roman Theatre*. Newcastle upon Tyne.

Schmidt, D. J. (2001), *On Germans and Other Greeks: Tragedy and Ethical Life*. Bloomington, IN.

Seaford, R. (2012), *Cosmology and the Polis: The Social Construction of Space and Time in the Tragedies of Aeschylus*. Cambridge.

Sklar, H. (1988), *Washington's War on Nicaragua*. Boston.

Walker, T. (ed. 1987), *Reagan vs. the Sandinistas*. Boulder, CO.

Wiles, D. (2000), *Greek Theatre Performance: An Introduction*. Cambridge.

CHAPTER 46

THE SHOCK OF RECOGNITION

Nicholas Rudall's Translation of Greek Drama for the Chicago Stage at Court Theatre

JUSTINE McCONNELL AND PATRICE RANKINE

THERE are moments in life when time melts away.[1] Beyond the pressures of getting to work, picking the children up from school, grocery shopping, and all the obligations that mark our busy, modern lives, there is the stillness of an instant. The photographs that Nick Rudall is perusing in this particular moment to some extent unmask time in the *longue durée*. Nick is enthused. He has traveled to such places as Costa Rica and the Galápagos Islands with his family, and he enjoys capturing the passage of time through the stillness of photography, finding a kind of theater in these images. He talks excitedly about the creatures that learned to swim over millennia because they had to find food, seeing these places through Charles Darwin's eyes. There is drama in the vibrant colors and the stories of these diverse species. We are viewing time, the evolutionary changes that come with conflict and harmony, what Albert Murray called "antagonistic cooperation," *in medias res*. In this volume, we have now gained two central concepts from the late, great Murray: this second concept of antagonistic cooperation—between old and new, Greek and American, past and present—and then the first one, of Omni-Americans, which we discussed in the Introduction. As we shall see, the Welsh-born Rudall has himself become an Omni-American. He brings a distinctly American idiom to bear on Greek drama.

Nick Rudall: Translator, actor, dramaturge, director, and skilled photographer. To use an Americanism, when he discusses these photographs, like when he turns to drama, or later to the Chicago Bears, Nick is "all in." "All in" is certainly the way Rudall approaches theater and the translation of classical drama; after all, as he says, "I'm 73 years old, and I've been doing it since I was 11." From such a paragon of old-world traditions—learning ancient Greek as an adolescent; valuing the slowness and stillness of poetry, a medium not unlike photography; the love of alliteration that he learned from his Welsh forebears—one might expect disdain for the new, or at least suspicion of Richard Schechner's modern shamanism, to cite another approach to classical theater (see Jenkins, Sides, this volume). Rudall's thick Welsh accent, however, belies a lifetime lived in the United States, as an American—or, more precisely, a Chicagoan. Regarding Schechner's self-avowed destruction of classical scripts, Rudall says he objects to none of it, which is surprising given that he is such a careful craftsperson of scripts and has been translating for a lifetime. He's all in. It's the same way he approaches the impending preseason opener for the Chicago Bears tonight, so—as generous as he is—I know not to tamper with an American's football time. (There is a viral YouTube video in which a priest hurries through his entire Sunday morning service in a handful of minutes so that he and his congregation can watch a playoff game. Some things are sacred.)

Nick was waiting outside as I approached his apartment in Chicago's Hyde Park, around the corner from Court Theatre, of which he became founding director in 1971 before spearheading its development into a professional theater in 1975. A generous, enthusiastic, warm spirit, he wanted to make certain that I didn't get lost. (Nick couldn't know it, but it's my tendency to get lost.) It is an absolutely gorgeous, sunny, late summer afternoon. Life is good for me because I am about to commune with a living legend. And like a man who has found his life's loves, life is good for Nick, whether he is reminiscing about time spent with his family, talking about his love of theater and poetry, or watching the Chicago Bears in only a couple of hours. Justine McConnell is not with me in person, but she has sent some questions by video, and we later craft this essay together, recalling the various plays we have seen together over the years at Court Theatre.

The interview ranges broadly and generously. Before the first question is even formally voiced, Nick has gone right to the heart of the issues involved for someone so engaged with ancient drama on such a multiplicity of levels. It is, he tells us, important to make the distinction between translation and adaptation of a text, and to be entirely self-aware of what you are doing:

> Let me start by saying that one of the most interesting questions about all of this is whether you're doing an adaptation or a translation. And actually, I don't do adaptations because with adaptations, inherent in the word, is change. Whereas what I have tried to do with the dozen or so Greek plays that I have translated—I have tried not to adapt, meaning to change—but to make a kind of translation that is as accurate as I can possibly make it, in terms of the original Greek; but with a different slant on what "accuracy" means.

Rudall goes on to explain that David Grene, of the important Grene and Lattimore series, was a mentor of his and someone with whom he worked over many decades at the University of Chicago. But their aims, and the "accuracy" to which they were aspiring, was different in each case: for Grene, translation was for academic, instructional purposes. Similar to Edith Hamilton's work in making Greek mythology accessible for the American classroom (on Hamilton, see Hallett, this volume), Grene intended his translations of Greek drama to bring American students as close to the Greek originals as possible. Students might later learn Greek, but they would have a sense of the aims of the ancient poet even before they did so. For Rudall, the performability of the translation and its aptness for the stage has always been at the heart of his motivation. Making a distinction between the educational translations of someone like Grene, the literary translations intended for silent and solitary reading, and his own translations for the stage, Rudall concludes that "Each one of those has its place, but they can't be fused."

The tension which Rudall has identified between an adaptation and a translation lies in the inevitable change that comes with time and context on the one hand, and accuracy on the other. Rudall sees the enterprise as an imperfect art, but it is one in which he is fully invested. So, while Schechner's *Dionysus in 69* is certainly not a translation of Euripides' *Bacchae*, it is recognizably an adaptation. The success or failure of a play, whether this example or one of Rudall's translations, depends on the "slant," as he puts it.

While the literary translator might try to disregard the inevitability of change, it is a different matter when it comes to theater and the staging of ancient Greek drama for a modern audience. Recalling Grene once again, Rudall laughingly remembers his colleague's repeated refrain, "Don't let them wear bloody bed-sheets for costumes!" Even a translator most accustomed to remain as close as possible to the ancient Greek—for the sake of the students for whom he was writing—found it anathema to see a production staged in such a way, with no attention paid to contemporary circumstances or to performance *per se*, and no attempt made to adapt the drama into one that resonated with both the ancient and the modern worlds. This, of course, underlines the importance of "performance reception" that is at the heart of so many of the essays collected in this handbook: analysis of a text or a translation tells a different story to the consideration of a performance as a whole. The latter will frequently pay attention to the translation used, but an array of performative elements including acting, diction, staging, costumes, lighting, music, location, and contemporary circumstances, will all also inform the discussion (Hall and Harrop 2010).

It should not be surprising that Rudall, upon whom the Galápagos Islands made such a visual impression, often talks about translation in visual terms, as *opsis*, as images for the stage. One must translate "with an awareness of what the original had architecturally." He compares the audience in the Greek theater to an audience in Wrigley Field, looking down on the Chicago Cubs playing below. The translator for the modern stage has to keep *opsis* in mind, always thinking of how the linguistic register is borne out visually. Seen from above, at the top of a Greek theater, or in the bleachers at Wrigley, patterns pop and appeal to the eye in ways that the director must imagine. The translator, a poet, works with this visual field in mind. For Rudall, the linguistic seems to be always linked to the visual, and vice versa. Even his discussion of the Greek playwrights' reception of mythological material is visual:

> The Greek notion of myth, especially in Euripides, is prismatic. Meaning that, the Greeks did not have dogma, and orthodoxy, and statement; every playwright could make changes, in order to look at the intellectual or political question posed.

Rudall understands much of the process of Greek drama visually and poetically, and it is worth noting the extent to which he sees that the Greek playwrights were already doing "reception," so to speak, in the ways they relate to one another.

So how do we translate for modern audiences in a way that conveys what we see in the Greek? The question is central to any discussion of classical reception. One must "burrow into the text," an image that Nick uses more than once in the course of our hour-and-a-half discussion. And then, along with his visual sensibilities, he speaks of the music of language: "I think in text . . . I think in rhythm." The translator must be interested in "what an actor can get his tongue around in the English language." For Nick, the process of translation, in which he has spent so much of his life, is a solitary one: "When I translate, I'm alone." My mind immediately goes to an image of Euripides writing his plays in a cave in Salamina. Once again, time stands still, and the Americanness of this enterprise no longer seems to matter.

At the same time, when Nick puts pen to paper, the images that flood his mind and the streams of which he craftily directs are from modern American experiences. Not only anticipating a theater audience, but anticipating a specifically North American theater audience, has been an important factor in Rudall's approach. Notwithstanding his upbringing in Wales and the way that Welsh poetry has informed his work, particularly the rhythms and alliterations of Dylan Thomas and Rudall's own poet-grandfather, nevertheless at a more instantaneous, visceral level, he seeks to connect with an American audience. He has made his entire career in the United States. As he explains,

> I consciously try to make my plays more American, in terms of American speech. There's one other bug-bear which gets to me: one of the hardest things to do when you're translating is to have an internal judgmental clock about anachronistic words. That is, you have a sense of what a Greek would have said.

To "translate" the contemporary nature of the plays into modern-day America, Rudall not only employs American turns of phrase, but he goes as far as to bathe the drama in an American idiom. His *Iphigenia Cycle*, directed by JoAnne Akalaitis at the Court Theatre in 1997 and starring Anne Dudek, is an excellent example of his method and its outcomes. For the play, he united Euripides' *Iphigenia in Aulis* and *Iphigenia in Tauris* into one, and was determined to be linguistically accessible and immediately recognizable and comprehensible for a modern audience. (On November 6 through December 7, 2014, Rudall revisited *Iphigenia in Aulis* with a critically acclaimed update, directed by Charles Newell. The visual vocabulary was in full display, male actors in monochrome matching the set, the chorus of women in vibrant colors reminiscent of a Seurat painting.)

For Rudall, the story of Iphigenia in and of itself has motifs and themes that resonate with American experience. In Aeschylus' *Agamemnon*, which he has also translated and staged, Iphigenia is a victim, in the purest sense of that word; she is a sacrifice. She replaces the animal victim, her blood its blood, so that Agamemnon can appease Artemis and wage his war against Troy. Iphigenia is still victim in Euripides' *Iphigenia in Aulis*, but at least a right order of things is restored, to the extent that the animal sacrifice replaces the human one in the end. In *Iphigenia in Tauris*, Euripides flips the paradigm, as Rudall explains:

> In *Iphigenia in Aulis*, Iphigenia is a victim; in the *Taurians*, she is in fact put in the position of making her brother a victim. The victim is turned into killer. Which is an

incredibly complicated political question in Greece, in Athens in particular; just as it is—let's say—in Israel and Palestine. Victims become the oppressors.

Does this transition not parallel the conversion whereby some of the colonized of North America (the envoys of Great Britain) become the colonizer? The victim, if we think of the American revolutionaries dumping tea at Boston harbor, becomes the killer in time, whether in that particular revolutionary war, or in more recent wars in Korea and Vietnam (in the twentieth century), or Iraq and Afghanistan (in the twenty-first). Paul Gilroy's *Postcolonial Melancholia* (2005) discusses this process well, and the topic of American (post)coloniality is one that we have taken up at various stages in this book, notably Goff and Simpson's and McConnell's contributions, because it has been fundamental to New World engagements with classical antiquity. As Rudall has hinted, Iphigenia is America; America is Iphigenia.

For his *Iphigenia Cycle* with Akalaitis, Rudall brought out the everyday natures of the characters involved, in part through these very American concerns. Translating Euripides' *Iphigenia in Aulis* for his own American version, Rudall saw a "suburban" Clytemnestra, a woman who immediately asks about Achilles' family background and financial status when she hears that her daughter is to be married to him. Rudall thus translates Iphigenia and Clytemnestra into recognizable, modern American characters:

> You try to find an American equivalent. That this is a middle-class drama, and then to stress the enormous difference it makes to then go from poignant victim to calculating, comparatively cold, enforced oppressor.

Given how Rudall sees these plays, it is clear why bringing them together in a cycle worked extremely well and helped to focalize the tropes we find throughout this particular mythological motif, through Euripides—and then Rudall's—prisms.

Two years after this production of his *Iphigenia Cycle*, Akalaitis directed *Trojan Women* at The Shakespeare Theatre in Washington, DC (March 23–May 8, 1999), working from Rudall's translation once again. For Rudall, this production exemplified the importance of feeling free to adapt a play to the modern era.

> A production that sets the play in a different environment is *completely* right.... I'll give you an example: JoAnne Akalaitis did a production—an adaptation... whatever you want to call it—of the *Trojan Women*. It was at the same time as Kosovo. She'd been planning the production for six months, but the news just came out about the slaughter of the men, and the enslavement (virtually) of the women and children. And when this production started on the stage in Washington, she had used shaven heads for the women; a rape—which is inherent in the story of Cassandra; and it was set in a concrete block at the quayside where the women were going to be deported. And everyone in the audience thought she had done it that day. The news had just broken... But she had been doing it forever, in terms of design and costumes and shaven heads—that was just in her mind.

The modern context is thus inextricable from the quality of Rudall's translation. In many cases, North America is the specific cultural framework into which he invests his time, seeing modern analogs for the Greek characters and settings. As another example, in speaking about Sophocles' *Oedipus at Colonus*, he says that setting the play in this hamlet is "sort of like setting the play in Peoria." Colonus is to Athens as Peoria is to Chicago, population just over 100,000, to Chicago's 2.7 million, with all of the attendant differences that the comparison conveys. These analogies help us to map an American landscape for a local theater. Here again, we start with language. Importantly for Rudall, translations for the American stage cannot be achieved by archaisms or what he repeatedly describes as "Victoriana," thereby evoking the period in which such translations were perhaps most prevalent. It is this tendency to archaize that makes many translations problematic, at least for the stage, and less engaging in performance than non-literary ones:

> The tradition started a century or so ago by Gilbert Murray and others, that felt that because this was ancient you should use archaisms and say "thee" and "thou" is completely false, because it was contemporary Greek. It may be elevated in tone but it was contemporary Greek.

Like an Aristotle warning young playwrights about certain pitfalls, Rudall asks the American poet/translator to avoid archaizing in an ill-fated attempt to elevate the language of the play. The quality of the drama is in the language, its characters, and its setting.

America, Chicago, Peoria. We have gone quite local by this point in the conversation, and judging from all that Rudall says about Greek drama within the United States, this is precisely the right movement: from universal to particular. That is, American theater *is* regional theater, and therefore Greek drama in the United States, if successful, is local, perhaps like all politics. As Nick rightly points out, there is no national theater in the United States, whereas there is such a phenomenon in England. Even the Kennedy Center's efforts at something that looks like a national theater in the United States is, at the end of the day, local theater; their American College Theater Festival breaks down regionally. Thus, to say that Rudall has been translating for the American stage is to say that he is a Chicagoan. He inhabits the United States locally. This is not to say that as a whole America (here specifically the United States) lacks a theatrical idiom. In addition to the "middle-class" drama that makes out of Clytemnestra an American suburbanite, Rudall cites *The Gospel at Colonus* as one of the most successful adaptations of *Oedipus at Colonus* within the context of the United States. (See McConnell, this volume.) Albert Murray points to the African-American as the original Omni-American, and thus it follows that the gospel idiom, along with the blues and other art forms that emerge out of the *Weltschmerz* of the slave, is in origin an American sound. That sound is the same as the sounds of liberty for which Aaron Copland's "Fanfare for the Common Man" reaches. Nick has been doing the same thing for the American stage when he translates Greek drama. So the American idiom in theater can be regional, middle class, and often has the inflections of the struggles for liberty among particular groups, such as blacks, Jews, women, Latinos, Asians, and other groups in the minority. We also discuss the success of high school theatrical productions in terms of American regionalism. Through no fault of Rudall, *Glee*, the highly successful television show about high school musical productions, enters the conversation as an example of the tension within the United States of small-town regionalism coupled with a quest for national identity.

The quest for a national theater within the United States calls to mind the quest for a national literature, particularly in the nineteenth and twentieth centuries. Twain, Faulkner, Ellison, and Roth each sought to write the Great American Novel. This is a significant parallel because of Rudall's efforts through Court Theatre to create what he calls a "literary theater." The national literatures brought to bear at Court reflect a number of regionalisms, not just in the United States. Through Court, Rudall wanted to stage everything from Aeschylus to Harold Pinter, from Chekhov to Ibsen. The conversation at times sounds like interviews I have read of August Wilson, the black playwright himself so eager for a national conversation about American identity. Similar to Rudall, Wilson saw himself in a longstanding, classical conversation. On the one hand, there is a regionalism in Wilson's attempt to hone in on "the most important issues confronting black Americans" in each decade of the twentieth century. On the other hand, the poet crafts a classic literature: "I approach playwriting as literature, as opposed to a craft—though craft is important. It occurred to me one day that when I sit down to write, I am sitting in the same chair as Ibsen, Shaw, Miller, Beckett—every playwright" (Bryer and Hartig 2006: 5; 24). The ongoing appeal of Greek drama is in this interplay between the regional (the local) and the larger human conversation. In Ibsen, Rudall sees similar themes about the small-town life—the *polis*—as that found in the fifth-century playwrights in Athens; the local becomes the universal, the classic emerging from the familiar.

Rudall's "literary theater" has brought classic literature to the stage, while retaining an emphasis on the contemporary context. The "classic" of such a notion refers not only to ancient Greek and Roman drama, but to canonical literature from all times and places. From Aeschylus to Euripides, Shakespeare to Oscar Wilde, George Bernard Shaw to Caryl Churchill, Tennessee Williams to Eugene O'Neill, Anton Chekhov to Samuel Beckett—at Court Theatre, Rudall has directed plays by all of them, as well as by many others. This mission has remained central to Court Theatre, even since Rudall retired, as their 2011–12 staging of both Ralph Ellison's landmark 1952 novel *Invisible Man*, and Lisa Petersen and Denis O'Hare's one-man *An Iliad*, typify. In the coming years, Court Theatre will stage Rudall's translations of *Iphigenia in Aulis*, produce a new, commissioned *Agammenon* by Rudall, and stage his *Electra* of Sophocles.

Ralph Ellison, so attuned to American idiom, once wrote of the genre of the novel as the world in a jug.[2] For this interview, we seem to have captured the world on a stage. We revel in the stillness of a moment in time, captured in language. That moment was the Athenian stage in the fifth century BCE, from which we look prismatically onto the American stage. We are in Hyde Park, Chicago, at a given moment in time, where particular language and images prevail, but we have also glanced at images from the Galápagos Islands and Costa Rica, photographs taken by Nick, which give some impression of prehistory, the drama of evolution through the snapshot of a single moment. For us—a black American born in Brooklyn to Caribbean parents, a South

FIG. 46.1 Anne Dudek as Iphigenia in Court Theatre's 1997 production of Nicholas Rudall's *Iphigenia Cycle*, directed by JoAnne Akalaitis. Photograph by Dan Rest.

African Brit with Scottish and Dutch lineage—to connect as we have, we must recognize something in these photographs and in the conversation that is our own. Perhaps it is Nick's love of his family that draws us, making us think of our own. Perhaps it is his love of nature, the childlike wonder with which we admire these photographs. In fact, Aristotle himself spoke of this very feeling of connection and similarity that we have on hearing, reading, or watching the lives of others, as his discussion of our fear and pity at hearing, reading about, or watching Oedipus exemplifies (*Poetics* 53b1). Just as the characters onstage come to recognize themselves through the narrative process, we in the audience recognize ourselves in the characters onstage. Theater orders the narratives of our lives in much the same way as these photographs have. Or as Nick puts it,

> Theater when it is at its best is what I used to call the shock of recognition: that is, the moment when you see Agamemnon talking to Menelaus and you immediately think "I know those two guys. I can't believe that they talked to each other that way 2500 years ago."

That's it: the shock of recognition. He has expressed so clearly what we have experienced so many times at Court Theatre and elsewhere. We're all in. Nick reminds us of our own fathers, in the same way that Iphigenia reminds us of the experience of Americans, or how Ellison's character onstage called back memories of experiences we might have had. "It is that thing that when you are in the audience . . . it is recognizing something intensely from other cultures." Who knows, but that on some frequencies, Greek drama in these Americas speaks for you, too.[3]

Notes

1. With many thanks to Nicholas Rudall, this interview was conducted on August 9, 2013.
2. Ellison 1995: 107–43: "The World and the Jug" (first published in 1964).
3. This is a paraphrase of the very last line of Ellison's *Invisible Man* (2002), 439: "Who knows, but that on the lower frequencies, I speak for you?"

References

Bryer, J. R. and M. C. Hartig (2006), *Conversations with August Wilson*. Jackson, MS.
Ellison, R. (1995), *Shadow and Act*. New York.
Ellison, R. (2002 [1952]), *Invisible Man*. New York.
Gilroy, Paul (2005), *Postcolonial Melancholia*. New York.
Hall, E. and S. Harrop (eds. 2010), *Theorising Performance: Greek Drama, Cultural Theory, and Critical Practice*. London.
Murray, A. (1990), *The Omni-Americans: Black Experience and American Culture*. Cambridge, MA.
Rudall, N. (1997), *Iphigenia among the Taurians*. Lanham, MD.
Rudall, N. (1999), *Iphigenia in Aulis*. New York.
Rudall, N. (1999), *Trojan Women*. Lanham, MD.

CHAPTER 47

IN CONVERSATION WITH PETER SELLARS

What Does Greek Tragedy Mean to You?

AVERY WILLIS HOFFMAN

It is a cool spring day when we sit down to lunch at the Lincoln Center Le Pain Quotidien. Among his many talents, Peter boasts precision radar for ideal spots for post-show/rehearsal rejuvenation, the right combination of delicious food, accommodating staff, and ambience. Whether a tucked-away Japanese fusion restaurant in Vienna, an after-hours gelateria in Aix-en-Provence, a Käsekuchen café in Bochum, or a chefs' collective in Chicago, Peter knows the staff on a first-name basis, greeting each with a generous hug. No matter the location, each menu is committed to memory and selections are made carefully, predicting the tenor of the conversation to come. It is a ritual that is essential to the assessment of the day's progress—"edible education" as Peter (under the influence of his dear friend Alice Waters) calls it. Today, we are faced with a long roughly hewn farm table bustling with New York's Upper West side elite, bowls of Lapsang Souchong tea, and café latte.

I begin with the question to hand, "Why the Classics, Peter?" He returns, with characteristic generosity, "Why did *you* turn to the Classics, Avery?" I know, and am not surprised, that the conversation will veer into unexpected directions, and, undoubtedly along the way, open a window onto his particular approach to theater-making. The question hits the mark with me: a Classicist by training and a theater-artist by trade. But I am momentarily stumped because I realize that no one has ever asked me this question: why I became fascinated by the Classics in the first place? "Why would an African-American woman find a home in the Classics, in Greek Tragedy?," Peter clarifies. The refined question hits a different mark because for the past two years, through two different projects (Shakespeare's *Othello* and *Desdemona*, a literary and musical collaboration with Nobel Prize winner Toni Morrison and Malian singer Rokia Traore), we have been wrestling with the question of race. A question which has plagued American politics and society for nearly 400 years and a question that no doubt needs to be addressed when your approach to making theater is as politically attuned as Peter's is.

When the salmon and avocado tartine (Quotidien's signature open-faced Belgian sandwich) arrives, I offer the beginning of an answer to Peter's question and the conversation veers off in a new direction. "I think," I propose to Peter, "that I was drawn to the Classics because so many works focused on those who were marginalized in the culture—women, foreigners, prisoners, slaves. The plays that gave voice and agency to Medea, Iphigenia, Antigone, Electra, etc, most ignited my imagination, their complexity, and the poetic voice of those plays inspired me in my own writing. I'm not sure that my race had much to do with it; I'm not sure I was as racially aware then as I am now."

"But," says Peter, "did you not have a response to Mary Lefkowitz who challenged the new wave of scholarship forged by Martin Bernal's Black Athena? Remember how she couldn't fathom the idea that there was scholarship out there that proposed that Africa and Africans, especially Egyptians and Phoenicians, had more of an influence on (God forbid the genesis of) Greek ideals and philosophy and literature than had ever been proposed before?" I confess to Peter that I was too young when that explosive debate tangled up the academic community. But later, in my studies, when I became acutely aware of the intricacies of both sides of debate, the Black Athena volumes still remained firmly planted on my book shelf simply because the vehement assertion of the "whiteness" of the Classics did not sit well with me. However irked I may have been by the (white and black) racist tones of the debate, I did not set out to prove Professor Lefkowitz and others (or Professor Bernal) wrong, at least not through scholarship.

Putting aside the scholarly and evidentiary dispute, what I did take away from the debate was that in America, after a divisive and deadly civil rights movement, the right to discover an accurate and clear picture of the past, the right to question your roots, and the right to discover your true identity should never be denied. The debate also highlighted something that I came to believe very strongly and to pursue in my own creative work, what Peter (and many scholars) has always asserted, that the Classics, especially Greek Tragedy, survive because each generation is able (and should be permitted) to interpret the texts for their own time. The minute that is not allowed or these texts are no longer relevant to a new generation it will be the death of the field. And, in a multicultural, globalized society, finding relevancy in productions that maintain the status quo—I evade defining what that is—is harder and harder.

Over the years, Peter has sometimes been praised, often heavily criticized and broadly misunderstood by the press for his unique ways of reinterpreting the "classics." From Greek tragedy to Mozart operas, he remains steadfastly rooted in his idea of art as social action and art as moral action (indeed the name of his popular course at UCLA). His productions strive to reflect the times in which they are performed, intending, as Peter says often, to be a mirror to our society. This might have been the moment in the conversation to launch into a discussion of his interpretations of *Ajax* (1986), *The Persians* (1993), *The Children of Herakles* (2003) (see Figs. 48.1, 48.2, and 48.3), or even the recent *Hercules* (2011), but Peter has just returned from Paris, Berlin, and Brussels where

FIG. 47.1 Program for *Ajax*, Cover image, La Jolla Playhouse (1986).

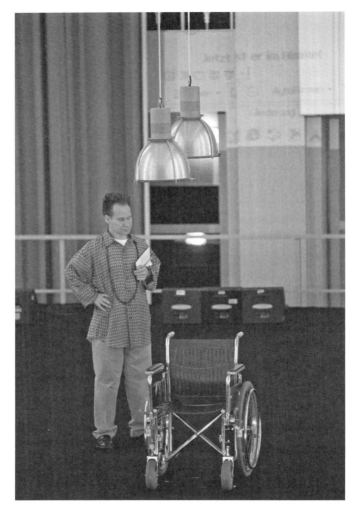

FIG. 47.2 Peter Sellars in rehearsal, *Children of Herakles* by Euripides (directed by Peter Sellars, Ruhr Triennale, Bottrop, Germany, 2002). Courtesy of Ruth Walz.

Desdemona was last performed, so the topic of how to reinterpret a Shakespearian classic is fresher and dominates. So we divert from the question at hand to catch up on *Desdemona*'s progress (you will see the relevance, I promise).

A little background for you: the *Othello* and *Desdemona* projects grew out of a lunch in Princeton long ago during which Peter asserted to Toni Morrison that *Othello* was a play he'd always disliked and would never direct, because Desdemona was too simplistically good and the racial politics were hopelessly archaic. The play, he said, was like a supermarket product that had been on the shelf too long: it had passed its "use by" date. Toni surprised him by disagreeing and challenged him to direct a production of *Othello* that would tackle those gender and racial questions for a new generation; and she agreed to

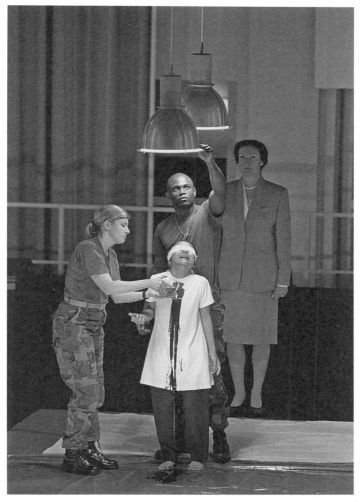

FIG. 47.3 Julie Baldauff (attendant), Julyana Soelysto (Macaria), Albert S. (attendant), Brenda Wehle (Demophon). *Children of Herakles* by Euripides (directed by Peter Sellars, Ruhr Triennale, Bottrop, Germany, 2002). Courtesy of Ruth Walz.

write a response to Shakespeare and call it *Desdemona*. After many months of preparation, the result of that lunch long ago was the 2009 touring production starring Puerto Rican American John Ortiz as Othello, Academy Award winner Philip Seymour Hoffman as Iago, and the soon-to-be celebrated Hollywood starlet Jessica Chastain as Desdemona.

As Assistant Director and Dramaturge on this production (my third project with Peter since 2006), I was struck by the daily debate in the rehearsal room about the play's merits and demerits, but what actually dominated conversation was that an African-American was seeking the White House, with a real chance of winning, and that his winning could change everything. I kept a rehearsal diary during that intense time. If you would allow, I propose suspending the tale of this interview for a moment to share a few of my observances.[1] They, I believe, shed some light on how the "path to performance," as Peter defines it, in this case had less to do with *Othello* in its 1603 context and everything to do with how it illuminated the question of race in America, in 2008. (Then, I promise to get back to the topic at hand.)

OTHELLO REHEARSAL DIARY

September 22, 2008
In medias res

Our first day digesting this play called Othello. As we navigate the text together during this two-week workshop, we begin to create a collective reimagining of this highly fraught, deeply feared, and misunderstood text. As each actor begins to absorb the text with Peter's probing guidance, there is a palpable sense that this particular group at this particular time has the skills and the endurance to actually reclaim Othello from those who still fear black sexuality and still feel that blackness is "other." A new vision of the world of the play emerges, based on a democratic ideal, like the LABynth company itself, in which every voice is counted, and every soul, as Cassio says, is in line to be saved.

September 27, 2008
Odi et amo
Odi et amo. quare id faciam, fortasse requiris?

nescio, sed fieri sentio et excrucior.

I hate and I love. Why do I do this, perhaps you might ask? I don't know, but I feel it happening to me and I'm burning up.—Catullus (84–54 bce), no. 85

Working around the table, Peter and this magnificent ensemble of actors, I am beginning to comprehend that the tender unearthing of these characters is not concerned at all with whether to color in Othello as a "blackamoor" or a "tawny North African" or an Arab (as our dear Arden editor insists is the most important point for actors to ponder) or whether Othello has a foreign accent to identify him as "not-Venetian" or how to navigate the shock of a black man kissing a white woman. The fact that this cast is so diverse—comprised of Puerto-Ricans: Othello, Emilia, and Roderigo; African-Americans: Duke, Cassio, and Montano; and Caucasians: Desdemona and Iago—defies the usual racial profiling of the play, and I think refreshingly sharpens the issue of race and introduces a new set of stereotypes to confront within the scope of the play: military men, military wives, African-Americans and Latinos in the military, women in the military. With even deeper diving, the depths reveal that Othello and each person in the world of this play if asked to check a box on the census form for race—Black (Caribbean, African, Negro, 10% Black, a drop of Black), Hispanic (South American, Central American, Mexican, Spanish, Cuban), White?—in the blank space after the last category entitled "some other race," they will all write in bold handwriting: human. In honor of the great Ira Aldridge, Paul Robeson, and James Earl Jones and all the other black actors who boldly steered through a climate prejudiced against them to present Othello as a real human being (not just a white man smeared with black boot polish), this cast presents painfully and clearly that it is that human emotion, love, that truly is the central obsession of this play. Love inspires, love burns you up, love "turns you almost the wrong side out," love has "carnal stings," love breeds jealousy and envy and offence and violence, love complicates.

November 4, 2008
"Is it possible?"

The extraordinary discoveries made in last month's workshop are now permeated with multiple, new and inspiring meanings. Today Barack Hussein Obama II was elected the 44th President of the United States of America, a country that declared 232 years ago that "all men are created equal," and yet only just, just today answered one of the central recurring questions in Othello: "Is it possible?" Is it possible that the youngest man in the room—the Duke must now, of course, be a mirror of the new President—holds the highest office in the land, a son of Kenya, a son of Kansas? Is it possible that Othello now has a new set of relevancies? Is it possible, as Peter says on our victory call, that in the Age of Obama strangulation doesn't have to be the only conclusion for an interracial marriage?

May 19, 2009
"Kill Racists"

As I rush down Theresianumgasse to the Theatre Akzent on my way to the first day of Othello rehearsals in Vienna, a man glares at me from across the street as if to say what are you doing walking in my street? As I try to recover by the chills I feel, I am stung further as I pass by "Kill Racists" graffiti on the wall of Argentinierstrasse. These messages linger in my consciousness as we struggle with Brabantio's disembodied racist assumptions and foul rants against Othello in Act I. Brabantio seems to screech like Senator Jesse Helms laying a sentence on every black man in America, declaring the 1964 Civil Rights Act "the single most dangerous piece of legislation ever introduced in the Congress." And wasn't it Helms who raged in a public letter railing against native peoples: "Your tax dollars are being used to pay for grade school classes that teach our children that cannibalism, wife-swapping, and the murder of infants and the elderly are acceptable behavior." In deep contrast, over 400 years ago, Shakespeare elevated his hero Othello, calling him "noble" and "valiant" and instilling in him the precious gifts of the West African griots. John reaches deep to spice these stories with lyrical richness, humor and terrifying power, his tales of cannibals and "Anthropophagi" and "men whose heads do grow beneath their shoulders" are the very reasons Desdemona falls so deeply and genuinely in love with him. And during each iteration, Jessica is able to respond more and more profoundly to John's evermore richly layered personality with her pure love and affection, visually defying before us her father's indictments and false reading of her own character as "a maiden never bold" who "falls in love with what she feared to look upon." John and Jessica slowly shape their love, working to transform their bed into a honeymoon suite, while still trying to protect their already fragile love from intruding outside influences. I feel privileged to witness such a beautiful, organic process. May 30, 2009 *"Farewell the plumed troop, and the big wars"* "Well, loyalty is a trait that I value, and yes, I am loyal and there are some who said, 'Well, you shouldn't have supported it, you should have resigned,'" replied General Colin Powell the first (and so far the only) African-American to serve on the Joint Chiefs of Staff.

Peter suggests that Othello's "Farewell" speech might just reflect the internal workings of a certain four star General in his hotel room the night after his 2003 speech to the UN, the one where he gave a detailed description of Iraqi "weapons of mass destruction" programs that turned out not to exist. Feeling the shock of lost love and banishing everything that makes Othello a lifetime soldier—"neighing steed," "shrill trump," etc—is totally devastating to him, and to us. With the bed teeming with images of the Navy ship "Intrepid," John transforms himself into a terrifying *deus-ex-machina* rising out of the bed. But instead of throwing out the usual bombastic Shakespearian tone, he summons the marrow out of his bones, low guttural murmurings, and like Phil has done in previous scenes, really batters himself. His explosive lyricism is so beautiful and shocking—reclaiming Shakespeare as a poet of the vernacular, pulsing with the rhythm of the street—ending in a overwhelming, hollow "Othello's occupation's gone." We know too that Othello's heart has finally turned to stone.

June 4, 2009
Camp Victory

On May 11 at 14:00 hours a U.S. soldier shot dead five of his colleagues at a clinic at the Camp Victory base where troops receive help for combat stress, in the Iraqi capital of Baghdad. The single deadliest episode of soldier-on-soldier violence among American forces since the United States-led invasion of Iraq six years ago, the Pentagon reports.

The destruction of this dysfunctional family is at hand. Today, especially today, Act V distills itself into and out of Desdemona's dream/nightmare. It's raining and dark outside and the gloom of nature pervades the company as they collectively wrestle with this final reckoning. Iago and Othello's freshly engendered "blood, blood, blood" ritual has united them and catapulted them into a non-rational zone allowing for murder to be possible. "It is the cause, it is the cause" billows out of Othello's ceremonial perambulation, taking on a foreboding eeriness that everyone feels. As chaos ensues and Iago starts to unravel, acutely feeling—as Roderigo leaves behind his broken life—for the first time the real presence of death, it is clear that all trust has been broken and never can be recovered. The company rallies through. Desdemona attempts, with the clairvoyance of her own death, to deflect the portents and jealousies which burden Othello's heart, but it is not possible. She keeps trying to encourage him to look more deeply, to see his true self (his own "visage in his mind"), his goodly, heavenly, best self. Neither her fervent prayers nor her unmitigated love can compete with the monster that consumes him, that pulses dangerously out of the bed. Jessica and John capture a transcendent moment suddenly: a suffocating carnal embrace stops her breath, breath which lingers within her just long enough to allow her a final act of kindness, exculpating Othello. "It is too late." "Lord, Lord, Lord" echoes heartbreakingly around the theater, but no one can move. The Act barrels on with a life of its own, there is no break today. Othello crawls up into his lair, surveying his kill. Emilia is substituted for Desdemona for a few minutes longer. The final stand. The President is left alone to salvage the remnants of this devil's work. Othello descends into his own personally prepared nightmare of "sulphur" and "liquid fire," wounding Iago but deliberately leaving him to marinate in his own living hell. Othello's final fantastic story propels him to suicide. Iago recuses himself with that devastating final line: "You know what you know." Silence. Cassio, like a ghost recovered, rolls in to lay on the final judgment of Othello's character. More breathless silence on this side of the stage. The play recycles itself back to the beginning, the deepest part of night, the birds are strangely awake, but this time,

Peter proclaims, the President (Gaius embodies him so perfectly) ensures that the CIA torture program will indeed continue on into the next era.

June 14, 2009
Opening

Every cast and crew cultivates its own spiritual journey of a production, a journey of discovery, a journey filled with roadblocks and sometimes insurmountable obstacles, but a journey nonetheless peopled with noble companions of serious mettle. There can be no better yogi on this journey than Peter with his own long-honed sense of the cosmos, his penetrating unearthing of the text, his ability to help actors emerge through the heights of their talents, his generosity and patience and willingness to be wrong and to try, try, try again. It is a journey along which each traveler is willing to humiliate and castigate themselves, willing to conjure up and wrestle their own demons, willing to comfort each other, willing to regenerate along the way, and ultimately, willing to communicate in a way that only theater can. Special conditions are created in this sacred space where actors can offer a pearl (like the one in Othello's final tall-tale), something really meaningful.

Thank you for permitting this diversion which I hope gives you a bit of an insider's view of the intimate relationship in Peter's world between the political climate and the careful interpretation of a work, in this case Shakespeare, to provide a fresh perspective on some pressing topics of the time.

While the issue of race in an "Obama world" may have been the hot topic in 2008–9, there were different issues at play when Peter first turned to Greek tragedy. In 1986, Peter was creating his version of Sophocles' *Ajax*, set at the Pentagon, at a time when some of the great avant-garde theater directors, including Andrei Serban, Robert Wilson, Lee Breuer, Tadashi Suzuki, and Yukio Ninagawa, were also tackling Greek tragedy. It was a time when there was a seemingly growing public appetite for reinvented Classics, as Arthur Holmberg wrote in the New York Times:

> Today's audiences respond to these plays with a new sensitivity, because the 80's are a tragic decade. A tragic sense of life has seeped, perhaps for the first time, into the American consciousness. AIDS has cast its pall everywhere, and the facile optimism of both enlightened liberalism and the early Reagan years has vanished, baffled by the realities of a shrinking middle class and the failure to achieve racial parity. The Greeks knew and dramatized how elusive, fragile and important the ideal of justice was. Tragedies, written for public festivals, celebrated the state and, at the same time, called into question its official rhetoric. (Holmberg 1987)

Holmberg went on to observe that "Greek tragedy has attracted so many experimental directors . . . because it liberates the imagination from the straitjacket of social realism." While Andrei Serban revived his 1970s production of "Fragments of a Greek Trilogy" at La Mama—featuring a rare combination of arresting visuals, a guttural soundscape of different languages, ancient, modern, primitive, and a ritualistic approach which brought the audience almost into a trance-like state—and Tadashi Suzuki placed *Trojan Women* into the context of a city destroyed by an atomic blast and featured an old woman stumbling through a graveyard, haunted by the terror of war, Peter used *Ajax* to expose the limits of a nation consumed by war. He says, in his interview with Holmberg:

> I return to the Greeks because it was a civic-minded theater that discussed unflinchingly serious public issues. Sophocles is not anti-military. He himself was a general. But he asks hard questions like, "Given a military engine, how can one contain it within moral limits? At what point does justified self-defense become a lust for power?"

Peter envisioned the play as a case of martial law with Athena as the judge and jury, Odysseus as an investigative agent, and Menelaus and Agamemnon as a prosecuting team. In an interview by Dan Sullivan of the *Los Angeles Times*, he calls the play "a terrifying image of death in the 20th Century... you have to lie there gasping as everybody's debating your reputation" (Sullivan 1986). He goes on to say why he chose that play, at that particular time:

> I read it a few years ago and was stunned by its dangerous modernity, its trick edges and odd shapes. Then something happened this spring—I think it was Libya—that was so outrageous that I felt an imperative to respond to that sort of militarism in theatrical terms. It was a civic gesture.

Peter wants to add that his commitment to what the critics like to call "non-traditional casting" (the cause of much media and audience consternation in *Othello*) was also a defining feature of *Ajax*. Tecmessa, the "spear-won bride," was Vietnamese. The chorus consisted of five actors—three black, one Asian, one white—dressed in military camouflage who also double as Odysseus, Agamemnon, Menelaus, Teucer, and the Messenger. Even more startling to many, Ajax was played by Howie Seago, a leading actor with the National Theater for the Deaf, whose signing was translated by various members of the cast. The chorus music was inspired by African-American spirituals and work songs. But, just as Peter says now about *Othello*, the casting of his plays is not simply to shake things up for the sake of doing so or to keep the critics in business, but to reflect America, and the world, as the diverse place it really is. The lasting image of Ajax attended in death by a black goddess, a black angel, and an Asian musician inspired one critic—who clearly understood one of Peter's many messages in the play—to describe it as a "tableau which, intentionally or not, suggested the symbolic death of the white man, the end of white hegemony in world power, the recognition that colored peoples make up most of the earth's population" (Shewey 1991). No matter the critical perspective, Peter genuinely believed then and believes now that theater and art is meant to provoke thought and debate, and ultimately, to encourage the audience to think differently about their own time and place.

Just a few years later, in 1991, as the first Gulf War was being played out on CNN, Peter responded with an interpretation of Aeschylus's *Persians* (472 BCE), the earliest play in the western canon to highlight a conflict in the very recent past, and boldly from the point of view of the enemy just conquered by the playwright's compatriots.

Peter's production once again starred Howie Seago as the ghost of Darius and John Ortiz (who would later play Bassanio in Peter's 1994 *Merchant of Venice* and, as mentioned above, the title role in *Othello*) as Xerxes. Peter recalls that the idea of using the Persians to highlight Gulf War misfires came to him during the 1991 rehearsals of his *Death of Klinghoffer*, one of his many collaborations with American opera composer John Adams featuring the treatment of the tragic 1985 Achille Lauro hijacking. In an interview with Mark Pappenheim of the *Independent*, he remembered:

> ... the pain of watching the news on CNN "and then walking into the rehearsal room to see very similar events taking place". Even more painful was the knowledge of what wasn't being shown—thanks to the censors. "I have come to think of theatre now as almost an alternative information system—what can't be shown on television can be said on stage. In America the war in Iraq was shown with no Iraqis at all—dead or alive. So, in this evening, we're saying come and meet a few." (Pappenheim 1993)

Unpublished photographs of the "highway of death" when the American army used lethal and experimental weapons to force Iraq's retreat from Kuwait informed some of Peter's lengthy research into the circumstances of the Gulf War. In an attempt to find meaning and catharsis in the brutality of these scenes in the theater of war, Peter collaborated with Martinus Miroto, one of Java's most esteemed traditional dancers and a specialist in the art of spirit possession. Peter recollects how Miroto, in mask, dressed in a military uniform, with bare feet, hosted the spirits of the 150,000 Iraqi soldiers who died in agony. To bring the action of the war into the theater itself, they placed speakers beneath a strategic set of seats out of which arose the whizzing of shrapnel mixed with the sounds of New York City traffic, thereby putting the audience into the middle of the violence of everyday culture. This sound effect was juxtaposed with the haunting ancient music of Nubian oud player Hamza El Din.

The multiracial casting and incorporation of a globalized, cultural perspective once again tripped up reviewers. John's portrayal of Xerxes as a cross between Saddam Hussein and an LA gang leader did not sit well with audiences and critics who couldn't stand the sympathetic portrayal of the enemy. European critics and audiences offered mixed reviews of Peter's presentation of the play (the production toured to Salzburg, Edinburgh, and Bobigny festivals in 1993). Mark Pappenheim, in his interview of Peter for the *Independent*, points out the irony that the Iraqis "substituted for the Persians whose descendants are the very Iranians who are today Iraq's deadliest foes," sharing Peter's insight that "we're all suffering this century from the effects of borderlines drawn by bloody victors in earlier wars. So what, really, is a victory? What is the victory of the Gulf war, for example?" (Pappenheim 1993). Scholar Edith Hall's assessment (published nearly 15 years later) also astutely aligned with Peter's intentions:

> That the "message" of this production was addressed to advanced global citizens, aware of the need to abandon militarism and transcend ethnic and national loyalties, was fully demonstrated by Sellars's insistence on a fully international team of actors,

and the use of traditions of performance and gesture extending from Javanese dancing to North African music and western deaf signing. (Hall 2007)

Much of the American media seemed to miss Peter's point that the production was fundamentally shining a light on the brutality and senselessness of American militarism and ultimately challenging the American image of ordinary people who were deemed enemies in the Gulf War.[2] Furthermore, the essence of his approach is expressed in his introduction to Robert Auletta's published translation of the play: "By humanizing the enemy, Aeschylus begins to suggest that we have much to learn about ourselves through the eyes of others, and that what we think we know about others should be questioned and expanded" (Sellars 1993).

It took nearly a decade for Peter to return to Greek tragedy. Peter's version of Euripides' *The Children of Herakles* (430 bce), much like Ariane Mnouchkine's "total theater" approach, consisted of a four-part evening: (1) Discussion and Testimony (approximately 45 minutes), (2) Performance (110 minutes), (3) Half-hour break for food and conversation with cast members and panelists, and (4) a film—one of a series of films made in countries that are generating large numbers of refugees. Peter says this is one of the few times he was able to achieve "total immersion" with a theater production, using art to convene a public forum on matters of social importance. Theater, as Peter writes in the program for the show, is one of the "last remaining public spaces" in society; "art is creating space for people to meet." In an interview with the *Boston Phoenix*, Peter makes a direct connection between his approach to presenting this play and practices in ancient Greece:

> The production is intended to be an occasion in each community for discussions that should take place to take place. The great thing is that the people who invented Western theater also invented Western democracy—at the same time. The idea is that the theater, the arts, are this [de-militarized zone] where people can put down their weapons. You can come in here and we can say things that are difficult to say in a way that nobody has to be hurt. (Clay 2003a)

The dialogue prior to the performance at the Ruhr-Triennale Festival in Bottrop highlighted many pertinent issues facing the host town, a re-settlement center for Kurdish refugees in Germany. During the American Repertory Theatre run (the longest on tour), the first part of the program began with a panel discussion hosted by Boston broadcast journalist Christopher Lydon, former host of *The Connection* (a public radio talk show dedicated to in-depth discussion of current events, the arts, and culture; produced by WBUR/NPR), and featuring policy makers, lawyers, law enforcement, relief workers, scholars, and refugees living in Boston. Stephen Kinzer, writing for the *New York Times*, reported one particularly "lively discussion" between an immigration lawyer, Michael Posner, and Bo Cooper, the general counsel of the Immigration and Naturalization Service.

> "After Sept. 11 the reaction of this administration, this government, has been to say 'Refugees are now part of the security problem,'" Mr. Posner said. "Again and again we see people who are clearly eligible for asylum who are left in detention for a year, two years, three years."

Mr. Cooper acknowledged that there now was "an increased focus on security" in deciding which refugees qualify for entry into the United States. He said detentions were part of "an immigration policy that is generous on one side, but also has rules." (Kinzer 2003)

The lobby featured an exhibit curated by the Harvard Program in Refugee Trauma. On tour in Vienna in 2004, Peter recalls, "it was the first time the Austrian Minister of the Interior spoke to or broke bread with African refugees living in his streets." He remembers how those public dialogues across Europe (including Rome and Paris) and in Boston began to shift people's perceptions of immigrants and refugees: "people got beyond who they thought they were and saw the world in a different way."

Peter still believes that the one of the most effective ways to guide an audience to a fresh perspective on their world is to combine a public forum—in which the people on both sides of topical issues are brought together in dialogue—with a theater presentation. Several years after *Children of Herakles*, on a smaller scale, I witnessed the powerful effect of this approach when I worked with Peter, and others in each community on the tour, to organize a forum on modern slavery for our opera production of Mozart's *Zaide* (Vienna, Aix-en-Provence, London, New York; 2006–8–see Figs. 48.4, 48.5, and 48.6).

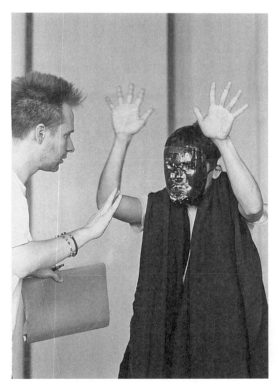

FIG. 47.4 Peter Sellars in rehearsal with Martinus Miroto (Chorus/dancer), *The Persians* by Aeschylus (directed by Peter Sellars, Salzburg, 1993). Courtesy of Ruth Walz.

FIG. 47.5 Hyunah Yu (Zaide), Norman Shankle (Gomatz), Terry Cook (Osmin), Russell Thomas (Sultan Soliman). *Zaide* by Wolfgang Amadeus Mozart (directed by Peter Sellars, Vienna, 2006). Courtesy of Ruth Walz.

FIG. 47.6 Hyunah Yu (Zaide), Norman Shankle (Gomatz), Alfred Walker (Allazim), Russell Thomas (Sultan Soliman). *Zaide* by Wolfgang Amadeus Mozart (directed by Peter Sellars, Vienna, 2006). Courtesy of Ruth Walz.

There was a particularly eye-opening (and deeply uncomfortable) evening when UN and UNESCO representatives were present in the audience en masse and the pre-show discussion centered a Viennese social worker and former slave talking about the rise of domestic slavery in diplomatic households.

But I digress—we return to *Children of Herakles*. Part One of the evening was created not only to put the theater production into a particular context, but also to focus the audience in on a few key themes, even if those themes provoked debate or disagreement. In terms of the production itself, the ART's online tagline perfectly captured the essence of Peter's approach: "After their father's death, the children of Herakles are exiled from their home by a hostile regime. They flee from country to country in search of sanctuary, finding every border closed to them. Euripides' twenty-four-hundred-year-old investigation of the plight of refugees could have been written this morning."[3] Some critics chided Peter for choosing a play that could easily exploit post-9/11 themes of immigrant or refugee issues ("It's not much of a stretch to find contemporary resonance in Euripides' play")[4] while also noting that this was the first time the play had ever been professionally produced in America (it had only ever been produced seven other times worldwide in 200 years—many scholars deemed it "a thoroughly bad play").[5] This kind of disconnect has been typical fare in reviews of Peter's productions over the years, often revealing a critic's pre-conceived notion of what a Peter Sellars play is going to be instead of going a little deeper, attempting to understand the reasons behind his directorial choices or even acknowledging the value of debating the issues his productions raise. For this reason, we hardly ever talk about reviews, so let us return instead to Peter's vision for the production.

As in *Ajax* and the *Persians*, Peter's use of a multiracial cast and unexpected musical accompaniment was deliberate in order to highlight the global nature of the issues. In each location, the children of Herakles are portrayed on stage by a chorus of young refugees currently living in that community (in Germany, for example, they were Kurds). Dressed in their own clothes, mostly jeans and t-shirts, they sit within the confines of a florescent box drawn on the stage until the Athenians finally win the battle that determines the children's fate, and the lighted cage lifts like a spaceship, hung on cables. They are voiceless (as in Euripides' play), silent witnesses to the course of events, drawing attention through their stoic faces and enticing the audience to wonder about who they are and what their story could be. Carolyn Clay, for the *Boston Phoenix* describes the image of the refugee children juxtaposed with Ulzhan Baibussynova's music:

> The choral odes are replaced by the remarkable contribution of Ulzhan Baibussynova. An epic singer from Kazakhstan, garbed in lush native costume and perched three steps above the bejeaned children like a goddess on an altar, she plays a two-stringed instrument called a dombra and offers up the guttural, then full-throated, vocals that are the soul of the production. (Clay 2003b)

The rest of the cast is deliberately multicultural/racial (from the U.S.A., Europe, Eastern Europe, Kazakhstan, and Indonesia) with personal vocal patterns and ethnic features left untouched. The cast is also gender-bending—Peter's tribute both to Euripides who reimagined the mythical story to assign the two most significant actions in the story to women (he invents a daughter for Herakles called Macaria who sacrifices herself to ensure that her fellow refugees are given a home and he also makes Alcmene a larger and more sinister presence who has Eurystheus killed) and to today's increasingly feminized power-structure: Copreus, the envoy, is played by Elaine Tse and Brenda Wehle plays Demophon. There are other surprising portrayals, such as Iolaus (Jan Triska, one of the Czech Republic's leading actors) who is trapped in a wheelchair.

The staging is intentionally stark and spare, "played against a blank backdrop on which shadows of the action loom, dance, and disperse to form" (Clay 2003b). There are references to Serbian Slobodan Milošević's war crimes tribunal in the Hague: dressed in an orange prison jumpsuit, Eurystheus is brought in chains behind clear plexi-glass; as Alcmene accused him of atrocities against her grandchildren (the refugees), he looks past her with a smile, justifying his actions as necessary defense against feuds waged long before he was born . . .

We pause here—time has slipped away from us and the evening's engagement calls. We could go on, but Peter once again turns the conversation back to me. "We've talked too much about my productions, I am more interested in what Greek tragedy offers you and your generation?" I am still stumped for a personal response but I promise to think about it knowing there is so much more we said we'd talk about—Peter's 2011 staging of Handel's oratorio, *Hercules*, my current project, a new version of Aeschylus' *Prometheus* (inspired by our work on modern slavery for *Zaide*), and the possibility of a new production of Euripides' *Ion* on the horizon—but, we agree to leave it there and continue the thread in next conversation.

Notes

1. The full rehearsal diary was published in the performance playbill for the Vienna, Bochum (Germany), and New York productions.
2. For example, Drake 1993 writes that the production "borrows from too many styles that never come together—from intimations of Kathakali and Kabuki in the movement of Martinus Miroto to the beautiful oud music composed and performed by Hamza El Din . . . from an American perspective, it's a misfired exercise in misplaced activism."
3. <www.americanrepertorytheater.org/events/show/children-herakles>.
4. For example, Shewey 2003: "More than a night out at the theater, the show is designed like a graduate seminar . . . It's not much of a stretch to find contemporary resonance in Euripides' play . . . The production's topicality is theoretically supportable as a way of enlivening an ancient text (although Deborah Warner and Fiona Shaw's *Medea* currently on Broadway hardly needs to be prefaced by a panel on 'Mothers Who Kill') . . . These interludes were meant to resemble the we-are-all-one moment in church services where you turn and greet the people around you, but they came off as sanctimonious and exploitative."
5. For example, Aristotle scholar John Jones.

REFERENCES

Clay, C. (2003a), "Modern Greek Peter Sellars Adopts Herakles's Children," *Boston Phoenix*, January 2–9.

Clay, C. (2003b), "Political Theater: Peter Sellars Surrounds *The Children of Herakles*," *Boston Phoenix*, January 16–23.

Drake, S. (1993), "Peter Sellars' 'Persians': Muddled East vs. West: Gulf War," *Los Angeles Times*, October 2.

Hall, E. (2007), "Aeschylus' *Persians* via the Ottoman Empire to Saddam Hussein," in E. Bridges, E. Hall, and P. J. Rhodes eds., *Cultural Responses to the Persian Wars*. Oxford.

Holmberg, A. (1987), "Greek Tragedy in a New Mask Speaks to Today's Audiences," *New York Times*, March 1.

Kinzer, S. (2003), "A Provocateur's Homecoming; Peter Sellars Returns With an Urgent, and Ancient, Message," *New York Times*, January 14.

Pappenheim, M. (1993), "Edinburgh Festival Day 1: The Greeks have a Word for it: Read the Signs in the Work of Peter Sellars and you'll See Actions Speak Louder than Words," *The Independent*, August 16.

Sellars, P. (1993), "Introduction," *The Persians*. Trans. R. Auletta. New York.

Shewey, D. (1991), "Not Either/Or but and: Fragmentation and Consolidation in the Postmodern Theatre of Peter Sellars," in B. King ed., *Contemporary American Theatre*. London.

Shewey, D. (2003), "Peter Sellars's CNN Euripides: Some People do have to Live like a Refugee," *Village Voice*, January 28.

Sullivan, D. (1986), "Peter Sellars: Boy Wonder Grows Up," *Los Angeles Times*, August 24.

CHAPTER 48

THE WOMEN AND WAR PROJECT

PEGGY SHANNON

WAR. Women.

Two words that find themselves conjoined a great deal in the twenty-first century. As a theater director, I have been hired to direct plays in theaters all over the world. Shortly after 9/11, I began to notice productions of ancient Greek tragedies being staged everywhere from schools to community centers to fringe venues and mainstream theaters. These productions offered contemporary settings such as Bosnia, Croatia, Columbia, Darfur, Iraq, Ireland, and Vietnam as backdrops for modern adaptations of familiar ancient plays. I began to wonder if the plays of Aeschylus, Sophocles, and Euripides could offer a lens to view and consider the contemporary *female* and her engagement with war.

Ancient Greek tragedy, with its themes of war-related suffering, served to animate a narrative of pain, offering audiences of men who had fought or were shipping off to war the ability to collectively mourn and heal from psychological wounds associated with war. The theater became the place for processing emotional pain and for communal healing to occur. Curiously, many of the ancient tragedies featured traumatized female characters carrying central themes and plotlines although females were not seen in combat, were not leaders, and were rarely visible in the public sphere (Hall 2010: 104–155). Classicists have argued that the prominence of female characters in the tragedies of Aeschylus, Sophocles, and Euripides provided symbolic representation of certain trauma-inducing events (loss of a loved one; a fallen leader; prisoner of war; self sacrifice) enabling a male audience to view war experiences with a requisite emotional distance (Foley 2003; Zeitlin 1996). This "aesthetic distancing" necessitated the use of female characters as emotional surrogates carrying male war experience. With twenty-first-century women involved directly or indirectly with war, I began to question whether these same ancient tragedies and war themes could yield recognition and catharsis for women. Might *male* characters carrying themes of war trauma become surrogates for modern women? Might *female* characters serve to animate war trauma and war-related roles for women?

As a mother of two children, a daughter of a U.S. Women's Auxiliary Corps member, a niece of an Air Force Senior Master Sergeant, and a friend to many who lost their lives or their minds in Vietnam, I have always been opposed to war. I have longed to see people use words, reasoning, and logic to deal with conflict instead of guns and bombs. I have often questioned whether contemporary theater performance was capable of inciting global dialogue—specifically regarding women's role(s) in war. I asked friends and colleagues if they felt theater could be used effectively as a tool to reduce stigmatization of trauma-related symptoms for women, girls, and returning troops; if theater performance could indeed shine a light on certain atrocities and perhaps incite social change with respect to women. Across geography, across gender, across conflict, and across discipline, came the same answer: Yes. Theater could make a difference. Theater performance could become "the words" instead of the bombs. Make something bold.

Theater as an agent for social development and change evolved throughout the twentieth century from Augusto Boal's "Theatre of the Oppressed" (Boal 1985) to "Bond Street Theatre for Social Development"[1] to David Diamond's "Theatre for Living"[2] to new forms of theatrical performance found in Bryan Doerries's "Theater of War," which uses theater to explore war trauma with veterans and active duty personnel in the U.S.A. (see further Lodewyck and Monoson, this volume).[3] Now, in the twenty-first century, poetry as a form of gender expression and political resistance is occurring today in Kabul, Afghanistan, in "Mirman Baheer," a secret women's literary society whose female members risk death to hear their poems read aloud to the other female members (Grizwold 2012). Knowing this, and encouraged by friends and colleagues, I conceived of *The Women and War Project* in 2010 and began to think about how to fund such an endeavor.

As I prepared to start a new job in Toronto, Ontario, I was encouraged to articulate my research agenda. I decided to apply for a Social Sciences and Humanities Research Council of Canada Partnership Development Grant. Four months to the day that I began my new job as Chair of the Theatre School at Ryerson University, I received word that my application had been funded. *The Women and War Project* (WWP) was formally launched. I was a theater director with a large grant and an even larger desire to use theater to shine a bright light on the issue of women and war.

I designed the WWP to build on the insights and approaches provided by prior scholarship and theatrical practice in matters relating to arts and social change, war-related drama therapy, and catharsis research. WWP was and is distinguished by its concern to understand, and formally assess, theatrical performances that may contribute to community healing and gender empowerment through catharsis in the face of war-induced mental health problems caused by decades of war.

One of the most significant influences on my decision to form *The Women and War Project* was American psychiatrist Jonathan Shay who, in the 1990s, articulated a connection between the veterans of the fifth century BCE and the deployed and returning veterans of the twentieth and twenty-first centuries. He argued that the poetry of Homer provided a therapeutic vocabulary and offered medical value in treating soldiers suffering war-induced psychic trauma. By 2011, and inspired by Shay's seminal works *Achilles in Vietnam* and *Odysseus in America* (Shay 1995, 2003), researchers, therapists, counsellors, clergy, and former veterans were drawing on the ancient Greek plays and poems, and personal narratives, to treat war-induced trauma. One such researcher, Stéphanie A. H. Bélanger, examined catharsis, and the impact of the discourses used in ancient Greek theater, on modern soldiers' communication of war experiences. In 2011, Bélanger embarked upon a new study in which she interviewed 100 soldiers, both female and male, who served in either Afghanistan or Iraq, for first-person accounts of their experience in war. She has told me that she hopes to add to the field of knowledge about a soldier's actual experience in and of war by documenting a verbatim account of what each one has encountered.[4]

I assembled an international and interdisciplinary team of one theater director (myself), a choreographer, three playwrights, three composers, seven professional actors from four countries, 23 undergraduate actors/dancers/technicians, master's and doctoral research assistants, Ryerson University professors (theater and psychology), University of Athens professors (literature and theater), a University of Southern California professor (playwright), professional Greek artists (producer, mask designer, sound and light technicians), and international mental health researchers, scholars, and military personnel to design and test new and innovative approaches to creative performance regarding women and war. The international WWP team was and remains interested in seeing the female point of view and the female experience understood globally.

The WWP Trilogy

The three original theater plays commissioned for this project were adaptations of ancient Greek plays chosen to provoke ethical and moral questions regarding women and war. The objective of the performances was to enhance knowledge and inform a country's thinking about critical social and cultural issues such as the notion of sacrifice, and the roles of women in war as both active and passive participants, as victims and victimizers.

Judith Thompson (representing Canada) wrote *Elektra in Bosnia*, a bold adaptation of Sophocles' *Electra*, set in the Bosnian War of the 1990s (Fig. 48.1). Thompson is one of Canada's premier female playwrights, often writing about pressing social, political, sexual, and class issues facing women and girls. The focus of her interpretation in this play is on the psychology of the family dynamic as a microcosm of the theater of war. Elektra, Cassandra, and Clytemnestra are the principal characters driving this version of the story. Thompson examines the way these women's lives are catastrophically intertwined. Composing original music for this production was Canadian actor and musician Jacob Vanderham, a theater student in the Ryerson Theatre School.

FIG. 48.1 Animals in the Forest. From left to right: Kaleigh Gorka, Sierra Chin Sawdy, Rhanda Jones. Photographer: Richard Burdett. Reproduced with kind permission.

Velina Hasu Houston (representing the United States and Japan) is an award-winning playwright and scholar whose work often addresses the ravages of war. Houston created *The Intuition of Iphigenia*, a dance/theater adaptation of Euripides' *Iphigenia in Aulis* that looks at the act of female sacrifice. Houston's text is written in a traditional Haiku and Tanka structure and given theatrical life through narrative, dance, singing, and Bunraku puppetry (Fig. 48.2). Fascinated with the pivotal decision Iphigenia makes concerning her own self-sacrifice, Houston questions what drives a girl, a woman, to change her mind—to be willing to sacrifice herself for her country. Does Iphigenia believe she cannot stand in the way of national honor when so many men have come to fight for it? Composing original music for Houston's piece was Chinese-American composer Nathan Wang.

Timberlake Wertenbaker is a leading prize-winning British playwright, with a history of translating and adapting the ancient Greek plays into modern versions (see further Williamson, this volume). She offered us *Ajax in Afghanistan*, a play based on Sophocles' *Ajax*, in which she examines the issue of post-traumatic stress disorder (PTSD) resulting from engagement in the war in Afghanistan (Fig. 48.3). Wertenbaker's contemporary version of the play follows the original the most faithfully of the three writers and, although the central character of Ajax carries the theme of a leader suffering with PTSD, Wertenbaker's play offers female characters affected by his mental state (Athena and Tecmessa). Composing original music for this production was Greek composer Stavros Gasparatos.

FIG. 48.2 Cassandra and Agamemnon in a brothel. Kaleigh Gorka and Stathis Grapsas. Photographer: Richard Burdett. Reproduced with kind permission.

Rehearsing in Toronto, Ontario for five weeks in May and June 2012, and for two weeks in Greece in June–July 2012, the WWP Trilogy had its world première on the island of Hydra, Greece, at Hydrama Theatre and Arts Centre in conjunction with *The First Annual Women & War Conference* and The Women & War Photo Exhibition, before touring to Athens, Delphi, and Elefsina, Greece, for additional performances and installation of the photo exhibition (in Athens at the Athens University History Museum). Since the initial tour in 2012, Thompson's play has been further developed and is slated to receive its Canadian première in December 2014; Houston's play has become an opera and was workshopped in May 2014 at the Los Angeles Opera, and will be further developed in Toronto in January 2015; and Wertenbaker's play (now titled *Our Ajax*) received its English première in London's Southwark Theatre in November 2013.

As the artistic director of *The Women and War Project*, I imagined a trilogy capable of providing various cultural, thematic, and artistic modes of examining the female experience in and around war. The three writers, the three composers, and the multinational professional actors were selected to represent their respective countries and cultural experiences. My social science partner was Candice Monson, a leading expert in the treatment of PTSD.[5]

FIG. 48.3 Agamemnon and his men restless for war. From left to right: Felix Beauchamp, Andrew Pimento, Andrew Lawrie, Jordan Campbell, Tal Shulman. Photographer: Richard Burdett. Reproduced with kind permission.

As a theater director and project leader, I remain interested in how the original female characters found within the ancient Greek tragedies might serve to elucidate patterns of modern female activity (suicide bombers, prisoners of war, victims of rape, abused and abusers, wives, mothers, daughters, children, and so on). I have posed the following questions throughout all aspects of this project:

- Can the recovery process for war-related post traumatic stress disorder (PTSD) be assisted by the transformative power of theater?
- Does interaction with classical Greek drama and specifically, with the female characters found within this canon of work, serve as an effective medium to interrogate gender, war, and conflict-related trauma?
- Will the consequences of trauma, loss, incapacity, shock, and grief yield to the healing power of poetry, story, and dramatic text—all intended to enlarge an understanding of the human condition?

It is important to mention something about the methodology adopted by the project. The trilogy of world première plays and a dance piece was at the centre of the WWP. Audience members attended one or more of these separate and fully produced dramas. Prior to a performance, they were handed questionnaires and asked to fill them out before seeing the performance. Immediately following a show's performance, audience members were asked if they were willing to fill out a second paper-based questionnaire to determine their views on women and war, their knowledge regarding trauma-related sequelae, and the extent to which they believed trauma-related symptoms are stigmatized. This questionnaire was used to assess intentionality to change any specific behaviors related to themes of war, remembrance, or trauma, changes in knowledge, and changes in attitude. The research findings were encouraging. A total of 99 participants completed the English-language survey questionnaire before and after a performance of one of the plays in Greece. The specific performances surveyed took place in July 2012, and all audience members were invited to participate. Participants' questionnaires were de-identified and linked only through a participant ID. Written consent from each participant was obtained. This study was approved by Ryerson University's Research Ethics Board.

Nearly 70 % of participants were female (N = 68), and the mean age of the sample was 41.70 (SD = 16.65). Participants were from a wide range of countries, capturing the diverse demographic attending the performances. Nearly half the sample reported that they resided in Greece (N = 45), while over 30% reported that they lived in North America (Canada, N = 23, U.S.A., N = 8). The rest of the participants identified themselves as residing in other European countries, South Africa, or Australia. The majority of participants reported that they had had a family member serve in a military (65.7%), and 12.1% of the sample reported that they had served in a military themselves. The mean number of years of education of the sample was 15.22 (SD = 6.39), and participants reported a range of occupations (27.3% in academia, 15.2% in the arts and students, respectively, 9.1% in business and healthcare, respectively, 1% in trade, and 22.2% in other occupations).

While participants did not indicate that the performances changed their beliefs regarding war or their mood, their response to the performances in terms of increased awareness and education regarding the effects of war was positive. The vast majority of participants (77.8%) had reported prior to the performances that they would have encouraged a loved one affected by war to seek treatment if they believed they had suffered negative consequence, and this percentage remained relatively stable post-performance. Notably, 58.6% of participants reported that the performance had helped increase their understanding of military problems and 65.6% of the sample reported that it had increased their understanding of who is affected by war. Additionally, 67.7% of the sample reported that the performance had increased their understanding of how people are affected by war.

With *The Women and War Project*, theater performance is bringing together art and science in a bold and transformational partnership. Artistic, academic, public, and private sectors using theater to investigate women, war, gender, and mental health offer new and meaningful interdisciplinary work. The first three plays that I commissioned for the WWP have now been performed before more than 4,000 people. I intend to write more grants and commission more creative work. With *The Women and War Project* I hope to continue to provoke attention, incite dialogue, and develop necessary assessment tools for theatrical performance in this multinational and multidisciplinary creative research focused on the effects of war on gender. The ancient Greek tragedies of the fifth century BCE and the epic poems of Homer have served—and continue to serve—as a potent tool for investigating new insights into trauma's effects on women, children, active duty personnel and their loved ones, and on veterans. The challenge of examining moral and ethical issues pertaining to war and gender continues to confront all of us whether we are theater directors, social scientists, humanities scholars, or policy makers in local and global communities. I sincerely hope that through *The Women and War Project*, war-induced trauma, the plight of women, public policy, and social engagement will receive a global platform.

Theater *can* and *does* make a difference. Live performance *will* provide "the words"—I only hope that people in power will listen.

Notes

1. For an overview of the work of the Bond Street Theatre Company, see: <http://www.bondst.org>.
2. David Diamond, *Theatre For Living*. See: <http://www.headlinestheatre.com/tflbook/tfl-book.htm>.
3. Bryan Doerries, *Theatre of War*. See: <http://www.outsidethewirellc.com/projects/theater-of-war/overview>.
4. This information comes from meetings between the author and Bélanger. See also Bélanger and Davis 2010.
5. Candice Monson is Professor of Psychology and Director of Clinical Training at Ryerson University. She is also an affiliate of the Women's Health Sciences Division of the VA National Center for PTSD. Her primary research focus is on the development and testing of treatments for PTSD. She recently completed a grant-funded trial of Cognitive Processing Therapy for military-related PTSD, and is currently conducting a funded project to further develop Cognitive-Behavioral Conjoint Therapy for PTSD. In addition to her treatment outcome efforts, Dr. Monson investigates gender differences in the perpetration of interpersonal violence and its consequences.

References

Bélanger, S. and K. D. Davis (2010), *Transforming Traditions: Women, Leadership and the Canadian Navy, 1942–2010*. Kingston, Ontario.
Boal, A. (1985), *Theatre of the Oppressed*. New York.
Foley, H. P. (2003), *Female Acts in Greek Tragedy*. Princeton.
Grizwold, E. (2012), "Why Afghan Women Risk Death to Write Poetry," *New York Times*, April 27.
Hall, E. (2010), *Greek Tragedy: Suffering Under the Sun*. Oxford.
Shay, J. (1995), *Achilles in Vietnam: Combat Trauma and the Undoing of Character*. New York.
Shay, J. (2003), *Odysseus in America: Combat Training and the Trials of Homecoming*. New York.
Zeitlin, F. (1996), *Playing the Other: Gender and Society in Classical Greek Literature*. Chicago.

CHAPTER 49

DIONYSUS IN 69 IN 2009

SHAWN SIDES

IN 2009, my small, Austin-based, ensemble theater company, Rude Mechs, attempted to "re-enact" The Performance Group's groundbreaking adaptation of *The Bacchae*, *Dionysus in 69*. We were stunned by the results. The following discussion attempts to locate *Dionysus in 69*'s effectiveness in its ritual aspects and to recount my company's odyssey through the re-creation process.

Experimental theater artists can't keep their hands off the Classics. Exploiting a narrative from antiquity to cook up something hip or innovative has become standard practice for those in the theatrical vanguard. In just the current century, a quick and incomplete checklist includes: Italian company MOTUS' "Antigone Contest" series; Elevator Repair Service's 2000 riff on *The Bacchae*, *Highway to Tomorrow*; Big Dance Theater's *Supernatural Wife* (based on *Alkestis*); and Societas Raffaello Sanzio's *Tragedia Endogonidia*. Apparently, ancient dramatic texts make excellent playgrounds for artists to mess around with new techniques or drill down into their latest aesthetic preoccupations.

In the downtown New York art scene of the late 1960s and early 1970s, that aesthetic preoccupation was Dionysian ritual.[1] In 1967, when The Performance Group (hereafter, "The Group") was still pondering which production to do, there was a brief moment when they toyed with *Peer Gynt*. But director Richard Schechner insisted, instead, upon *The Bacchae*. He writes that he ". . . felt strongly that Euripides was more in our way: obstacle, challenge, evocation, and initiation."[2] "Evocation" and "initiation" are key words here, since much of Schechner's work, both scholarly and practical, focuses on the relationship between—the continuum of—ritual and theater, and their "efficacy."[3] Schechner defines both as "restored behavior" (Schechner 1985: 35–8). He explains,

> Restored behavior is living behavior treated as a film director treats a strip of film. These strips of behavior can be rearranged or reconstructed; they are independent of the causal systems . . . that brought them into existence. They have a life of their own . . .[R]estored behavior is used in all kinds of performances from . . . ritual to aesthetic dance and theater. (Schechner 1985: 35)

FIG. 49.1 Preparing for the birth of Dionysus. Photograph by Bret Brookshire. Reproduced with kind permission of Rude Mechs.

Schechner was drawn to *The Bacchae* by the many ritual actions and opportunities inherent in it: the ritual within the play itself; the ritual roots of all Greek drama; the ritual action that is performing ancient drama—the retracing of those paths; and the possibility the script offered to incorporate original ritual gesture, whether invented whole-cloth, like the mortification of Pentheus in the "Dionysus Game",[4] or appropriated, like the birth ritual, from another culture (Fig. 49.1) (Schechner 1988: 131). *Dionysus in 69* fairly teems with little rites and ceremonies from the initiation of the audience upon entrance,[5] to the procession through the city's streets at the end (on *Dionysus in 69*, see also Jenkins, this volume).[6] Though the play is both politically and aesthetically dated, I believe that the performers' earnest attempt to invoke the sacred through ritual action allows *Dionysus in 69* still to resonate powerfully with contemporary audiences.

Dionysus in 69 in 09—Process

Workshops

Normally, my theater company, Rude Mechs, only devises original work. But we'd long been planning a series of "re-enactments" of significant, experimental performances from the 1960s, 1970s, and 1980s. Driven by a desire to celebrate and learn about our own aesthetic ancestry, and to share it with our audience, our idea was to recreate, as faithfully as possible, performances from the mid-to-late twentieth century that have been more influential as events than as texts, *per se*. The goal was to remount these productions as closely as possible to the originals, recreating, as best we could, the original circumstances, rehearsal processes, and performance context and vocabulary.

For us Rudes, then, re-enacting *Dionysus in 69* was itself a kind of ceremonial rite. Twice removed from the Greek drama—the behavior we were "restoring" was mid–late twentieth-century "downtown" performance culture, engaged in a complex conversation with Euripides. We "restored" the behavior of The Group as exactly as possible in an effort to evoke, not ancient Greece, but the thriving NYC art scene of 1968. It's a testament to the power and flexibility of Euripides' ancient text—and to the canniness of The Group's adaptation—that our production of *Dionysus in 69 in 09* succeeded far beyond our hopes. The Austin performances verged on orgies of Dionysian ecstasy (Fig. 49.2).

We began by immersing ourselves in The Group's original process. We experimented with games and ritual exercises as The Group had done in 1967, following a rehearsal template we pieced together from conversations with Schechner, The Group's 1970 book (edited by Schechner), *Dionysus in 69*, Schechner's *Environmental Theater* (in which he describes rehearsal exercises in meticulous detail), Jerzy Grotowski's *Towards a Poor Theatre* (which was the basis of much of The Group's work and Schechner's inspiration), and a revelatory memoir of the process called *The Dionysus Group*, written by Bill Shephard, the actor who played Pentheus. A typical rehearsal started with Grotowski-inspired head, hip, and spine rolls, Yoga, slow-motion running, and somersaults. Warm-ups were performed in silence and with as few clothes as each individual cast member found comfortable. Rehearsals then advanced to more complicated exercises from Schechner's book, many of which The Group had inserted in their entirety into the production.

The Total Caress was one such exercise. My co-director (and fellow Co-Producing Artistic Director of Rude Mechs) Madge or I chose an actor (no volunteers). This actor picked a partner with whom to perform the exercise. Already, the exercise was difficult and emotionally precarious. To openly choose another cast member demands a vulnerable kind of confession: an admission of desire/curiosity. Then these two (clothed) actors silently and slowly took turns gathering information about each other's bodies. One actor lay, sat, or stood passively, while the other used all the senses in discovering as much as possible about the other's body, as though she or he were an alien making discoveries about an unfamiliar life form. As the first couple moved to a safe place in the room to perform the exercise, Madge or I picked the next actor, who, subsequently, chose a partner, and so on, until all cast members were participating in the Total Caress in pairs. After approximately an hour, Madge and I asked the couples to move into groups of four and continue. Finally, the entire group came together as one to "gently massage, kiss, stroke, push, pull and caress one another."[7] While the description sounds overtly sexual, in practice it's more sensual than passionate.

We transferred this exercise directly into the performance as The Group had originally done. Here's how Schechner describes the Total Caress in The Group's book:

Performers moved slowly into the audience... usually in groups of two, three, or four. Members of the audience were selected at random within the framework of simple rules: no one anyone knew; someone who seemed responsive... [S]oon resistances fall away, a basic animal-comfort trust arises, and one flows with the touching... We brought this exercise into the performance because it suited Pentheus's fantasies of his "reward" and Euripides's description of what the first or second phase of the Dionysian revels was like.[8]

Other rehearsal exercises included ritual stalking and combat, initiation (including the birth ritual that The Group used in the final performance), and a ritual/exercise to facilitate our first full, group nakedness. In this, the group formed a circle and a volunteer

FIG. 49.2 The death of Pentheus. Photograph by Bret Brookshire. Reproduced with kind permission of Rude Mechs.

began. She or he made a statement to the group that "cost something" and, optionally, removed one piece of clothing. Our circle continued until all were naked. (In an unheated warehouse in December, I might add.)

I'm compelled to point out here how radically different this kind of rehearsal is from Rudes' typical process. While we don't have a codified way of going about making plays, we have consciously, definitively rejected anything that smacks of emotional manipulation of the actors by the director(s). And since part of a director's job is to create a safe environment within which actors can take risks, Madge and I often felt we were jeopardizing our reputations as responsible stewards of the process. Plus, many of the exercises felt embarrassingly naive to us—based on the presumption that one might be able (or want) to strip away cultural "hang ups" and reveal a pure, expressive self. But, these were the presumptions and techniques of The Group and of the time. Stronger than our feelings of resistance and doubt were our desires to temporarily set aside our skepticism and immerse ourselves as deeply as we could into the world of The Group.

Staging

After eight workshops over the course of a month, we transitioned to a month-long, very technical staging process: one completely different than The Group's, but familiar to our company. Each of the actors was assigned a particular Performance Group member. We watched the De Palma film to precisely recreate each actor's floor pattern, gesture, and vocal inflection. We played particular moments in slow motion, and over and over, to scrupulously re-embody the rhythm and tempo, vocal pitch and quality, shape, gesture, and location in space. This "karaoke," as we call it, is a technique we've applied to several past productions. It's a common contemporary strategy (see any number of works by The Wooster Group, Nature Theatre of Oklahoma, Radiohole, or Elevator Repair Service, for example) and different artists use it for different reasons at different times. For *Dionysus in 69 in 09*, we used the "karaoke" to build a kind of mask of the original performers.

Our production necessarily diverged from the film at times; slavish loyalty to each and every gesture and glance would have been not only impossible (we couldn't prescribe audience placement and response) but, also, unfaithful to the spirit of the original production. The Group built fluidity and improvisation into their work, and their shows would change drastically from night to night. They valued—above all—truth to the "present moment," however that "truth" might manifest itself. In 1968, the actors improvised, changed roles, and once audience members even "rescued" Pentheus before the end of the play. So we tried to strike a balance. We left sections of the play open to improvisation and spontaneity, rooting the performance in "the now," to honor *Dionysus in 69*'s intrinsic values and intentions. Then we very precisely set particularly idiosyncratic gesture sequences, sounds, or lines ("strips of behavior") to fold the original Group performers in between Euripides' characters and the "Rude Mechs." Selecting bits of behavior from the film to "restore" tied us to "the then" (1968) and trained our focus on re-enactment rather than reinterpretation.

Schechner's visit

This familiar territory gave way once again to the thrilling and strange when Schechner himself came to check on our work, lead some rehearsals, and impart precious knowledge about the original production unavailable from any other source.[9] We couldn't believe our luck. Soon enough, though, our excitement surrendered to awkwardness when he requested alterations to those original gestures and floor patterns, the "strips of behavior," we'd chosen to function as character masks. In part, he said, he wanted to correct his "mistakes" (his word) from 40 years ago. For instance, William Finley and Bill Shephard, The Group's Dionysus and Pentheus respectively, did a lot of random and complicated pointing here and there, with no apparent indicative purpose. These quirky gesture sequences were pure character gold for us and "quoting" them gave us no end of delight. But Schechner importuned us to change these sequences. He said "pointing is weak" and he wanted us to adapt the movement to reflect contemporary ideas of what powerful acting looks like. For us Rudes, the whole point of the project had always been to recreate the original production—not to adapt or try to improve upon it or create our own new interpretation. Though we were giddy with this opportunity to work with the maestro on his opus, we found ourselves in the uncomfortable position of refusing his suggestions. He took our refusals to "improve upon" the original in good-natured stride. In the end, I believe, we were vindicated in our choice.

Occasional differences of opinion notwithstanding, Schechner imparted treasure-troves of information, inspiration, and councel. For instance, he cautioned us to adapt our set in order to accomplish more intimacy and warmth. In our compulsion for accuracy, we had recreated the platforms and towers exactly as they had been in the original production. But The Performing Garage had seated between 200 and 300 people for each performance. For safety reasons we could only seat 100. So Schechner advised us to cut a few of the platforms and close everything in to keep the main playing space—the 12' × 8' rectangle of mats in the middle of wooden platforms and "towers"—as close as possible to everyone in the audience. This reconfiguration was vital to the success of the piece. *Dionysus in 69*'s environmental setting has everything to do with the audience's capacity to participate in the action. The actors are in among the audience from the beginning—sometimes sitting right next to a spectator, sometimes asking another to move. There are no chairs. Sometimes the chorus is above the audience, or behind, or below. But primary action takes place on the central mats. Cutting platforms brought each audience member closer to the main action and made them more visible to one another. It was clear from the beginning that the audience was an integral part of the show. They could lie down, sprawl out, or get up and walk around and change their seat or view. We encouraged our audience to experience the room this way, inviting them in the playbill to "feel free to wander throughout the room, change your view, climb one of the towers, or descend to the floor level, disappear and reappear, fall asleep, participate in the fun or fade into the background."

We hoped this invitation to optional participation would pry open a space for the audience to access the show on a ritual level if they wanted. Madge and I hoped to allow individual audience members to experience "themselves" as an audience from 1968—to play that role, and to become possessed by the spirit of the time. They could be as shy or courageous as the '68 audiences had been. They could be "from the past"—not just their contemporary selves—and hopefully, therefore, feel freer to surrender into the ecstasy of the dance or risk physical touch in the Total Caress.

But my hopes aside, my actual expectations were that the audience would receive the work as a museum piece. I wasn't going to be upset with that—I still believed we would be offering a more visceral encounter with this important piece of American theater history than audiences could access by watching the movie or reading The Group's book version. I won't argue here that the live experience of a drama is the most important experience of it, but it is certainly *an* important experience, and the more access points one has into a work, the deeper the potential understanding. A deeper understanding seemed good enough reason to do the piece, even if the audience maintained a distanced reserve. Audience participation wasn't mandatory in the Performing Garage back in 1968 and it wasn't in our version either, and while I naturally hoped audiences would come away thrilled with the experience, I still anticipated that most wouldn't allow themselves to jump in to the dance. As it turned out, my fears were entirely misplaced: judging from our experience with *Dionysus in 69 in 09*, audiences have become *more*, not less, participatory.

Performances

Ecstatic ritual is mostly missing from our contemporary culture, but it's not missing entirely and we know how to do it when we see it. Audiences joined in the dance every night: clothes were shed, whoops whooped, wine drunk, and Dionysus must have been pleased. One night an audience member brought a statue of the god and a small faction of audience performed an only slightly ironic version of cultic worship.

It's hard to articulate how deeply involved and how enthusiastically participatory they were. Certainly, there were those who maintained self-consciousness, or timidity, or (worst of all) a sort of resigned acquiescence about the participation. And, of course, there were those who didn't participate at all. But so many of our audiences exhibited such eagerness and seeming *earnestness* that I can only describe their actions as ecstatic.

These audience/participants sometimes arrived in self-formed groups. One particular group, representing themselves as "the witches," were especially enthralled by the blood ritual at the end and began to sway and moan together as the women dipped their hands into the font (Fig. 49.3). The Hill Country Nudists came as a group, took their clothes off at the very beginning of the birth ritual, and watched the whole performance naked from the west "tower."

Couples split off into the darker corners of the room and had sex on more than one occasion. Our favorite anecdote involves the couple that "found" one another during the

FIG. 49.3 From Rude Mechs' *Dionysus in 69*. Photograph by Bret Brookshire. Reproduced with kind permission of Rude Mechs.

Total Caress (one of them came with another date) and, though they remained clothed, they wouldn't stop rolling around and grunting and humping in the middle of the very well-lit stage area for the whole rest of the play. The actors had to step around them to finish the death ritual. They're still together. This is true.

As it turned out, we didn't need our audience to be other than themselves in order to experience ritual ecstasy, which should have been obvious to us all along. Since *Dionysus in 69* originally opened in June of '68, our culture has birthed Woodstock (and its evil twin Altamont), disco, designer drugs, raves, Burning Man: ecstasy is accessible in contemporary America, though perhaps our experience of it is slightly more self-conscious than it was at mid-century.

Once we opened *Dionysus in 69 in 09* we didn't have an empty "seat" in the house for the rest of the run. We were thrilled, shocked, and deeply humbled. And, okay, it would be naive or disingenuous to allege that this had nothing to do with ten naked bodies on stage. But it was the carefully structured invitation to ritual within The Performance Group's work that freed the audience to participate with such abandon. And that invitation, once you dig past the strata of Rude Mechs and Performance Group, is founded on the premise of ancient drama as ritual, regardless of whether that premise truly inheres in the work or is merely a culturally projected illusion. The very classic-ness of

The Bacchae is what made *Dionysus in 69* and *Dionysus in 69 in 09* work as avant-garde experiences.

Contemporary artists from the revolutionary to the commercial use vintage stuff as stem cells to generate new work. And as vintage stuff goes, the Classics run deep in our collective DNA. For the experimental artist, the attraction of classic works lies less in their (illusion of) "timelessness" than in the freedom they lend theater-makers to touch the mythic and archetypal and springboard from there.

Regardless of how "truthful" any access to the sacred actually is, no matter how "authentic" or "inauthentic" the ritual action, the *promise* of efficacious ritual was the siren song that drew The Performance Group to Euripides in the first place. And it is the gesture toward the sacred—immanent and possible in the ancient text, magnified and multiplied by Schechner and The Group, then "restored" by Rude Mechs—that made *Dionysus in 69* a provocative, participatory event, even, again, in '09.

Notes

1. Or at least one of the preoccupations. See Innes 1981.
2. The Performance Group (1970), unpaginated.
3. See, for instance, his table, "The Efficacy-Entertainment Braid," in Schechner 1988: 120.
4. For a complete description of the "The Dionysus Game," see The Performance Group 1970: unpaginated.
5. As Vicki May Strang, The Group's stage manager, writes in The Performance Group 1970: unpaginated: "We let the public in one at a time. People on the queue outside the theater ask me why. I explain that this is a rite of initiation, a chance for each person to confront the environment alone, without comparing notes with friends."
6. Schechner would maintain that *all* performances contain/enact these rituals (see "Points of Contact" in Schechner 1985: 3–34). I argue here that as an adaptation of a classical drama, *Dionysus in 69*'s rites are clearly more conspicuous and overtly ritualistic.
7. The Performance Group 1970: unpaginated.
8. The Performance Group 1970: unpaginated.
9. Rude Mechs is deeply grateful to the Humanities Institute at the University of Texas who made Schechner's work with us possible.

References

Innes, C. (1981), *Holy Theatre: Ritual and the Avant Garde*. Cambridge.
Schechner, R. (ed. 1970), *Dionysus in 69: The Performance Group*. New York.
Schechner, R. (1985), *Between Theater and Anthropology*. Philadelphia.
Schechner, R. (1988), *Performance Theory*. New York.

CHAPTER 50
....

TALKING GREEKS WITH DEREK WALCOTT

....

HELEN EASTMAN

A picturesque cottage in the quintessentially English village of Wivenhoe, on a drizzly Saturday afternoon, seems an unlikely place to be meeting Caribbean Nobel Laureate Derek Walcott to discuss the impact of the Greek world on his work.[1]

He is staying here while spending two weeks at the University of Essex, in his capacity as Professor of Poetry, fitting in teaching students and directing a show at the campus theater. A week earlier I listened to him "in dialogue" with friend, colleague and former student, poet Glyn Maxwell. They read, generously, from each other's work and talked about the business of poetry, the octogenarian declaring, "the older I get in the profession, the more I love it." It was an afternoon packed with gnomic pronouncements from Walcott: "if you don't enjoy form, write prose"; "writing poetry should be taught in every school, in every culture"; "a poet is a sacred vessel and carries the conscience of the race."

It's a rare treat to hear a poet talk with such conviction and confidence about the wider importance of their craft. I also noticed how hard his great friend, Maxwell, was working to interview him. Walcott simply doesn't answer questions that don't engage him. It was, therefore, with some trepidation I approached interviewing him about his complex relationship with classical literature and the European canon. I started with asking about his early poem, "Roots":

H.E.: You speak in your poem "Roots" of "our Homer." Who is your Homer and when did you first encounter him?
D.W.: Like every school boy, you got to know Homer. You don't know all of Homer, you just know the fables. Odysseus. Polyphemus. The lotus eaters. Either you got it through some simpler poetry, or you got it from reading parts, not the whole work. I never read the *Iliad* or the *Odyssey* completely.[2] But naturally I knew all the fables.
   I think the thing which made me appreciate the strength in Homer, was the presence of the sea. The changes of the sea. The reality of living off the sea—fishing villages, storms. So the Caribbean for me was similar to the Aegean. We are an

archipelago and each island in the archipelago has its own rumours and superstitions, so the succession of chapters of differing islands in the *Odyssey*, when you came to read the book, became even more real and close.

H.E.: Is it that shared relationship between land and sea which brings the Caribbean and the Aegean together in *Omeros* and allows the poem to draw on both?

D.W.: When I say the sea, I hope I'm not just over-gesturing. But the islands and the fact that if you see a single sailor out in the ocean, out in the *sea* (you don't say "the ocean"), then that represents Odysseus, that's a great iconic symbol of expedition and return.

H.E.: Did *Omeros* come to you gradually, or was there a decision "I'm going to write an epic for the Caribbean." To be "our Homer"?

D.W.: No. I didn't begin with a plan to duplicate Homer. I think it's quite desultory to do that. What I remember about the beginning was that I wrote a poem which seemed to be about Philoctetes, the wounded guy, but also seemed to connect to a friend of mine who had just died. I remember writing this elegy about my friend, and also about Philoctetes, himself, on the island. Why it began to take shape and break into that particular design, I don't quite know. I know that it broke away from a pentametrical pattern, into something that had a design plaited in homage to Homer and to Dante, so that the line, the individual verse line, was not pentametrical but hexametrical.

Hexametrical, because generally in the hexameter, there's a kind of a caesura in the middle, even if it's just a breath resting, which is a kind of prose feel in a verse form. The hexametrical design was a longer line. And that longer line for me represented the horizon. The horizon is not pentrametrical. It's certainly at least hexametrical.

So I had that as a Homeric homage in a way, and the Dantesque homage was the design of the *terza rima* and the space in between. If I did a quatrain like Gray's Elegy[3] it would be a different kind of design; it would be an almost predictable adaptation of a classic to do it that way. Whereas the width that exists between stanzas in the three line design, the space that is there for the missing fourth line ... that is the equivalent of space, air ... right? ...

H.E.: ... And the combination of the hexameter and the *terza rima* gives it an incredible forward flow; we are always expecting, looking towards the next stanza for the echo of the rhyme.

D.W.: There's no rhyme in Homer. And I don't read Greek. But there was something very challenging and exciting about *terza rima*, to have to come back up with the rhyme. It's very challenging.

H.E.: And it's an exciting way to play with expectation and counter-expectation ...

D.W.: It homages to the form I'm working in, which is English verse. Even if I'm a West Indian. The language is English. The debt then to Homer and to Dante is a debt to the origin, *origins* in a way, of literature as we know it now.

H.E.: And is there a tension between working in English and being a Caribbean poet? Or to you does it feel organic, complete?

D.W.: It's very strong and it's strong in the sense that the material that you have ... it's very much like painting. Painting in the Caribbean. There are certain colors that are there, that are very fixed. The sky is always very blue. The sea is always the same color. All that vocabulary is the equivalent of a palette which you reach for and use. But it's new because you are describing territory that has not really been made part of literature ever, so the sense of doing something for the first time, in terms of describing the landscape or the sea is a very, very strong thing, you know?

H.E.: But the names you choose for your characters in *Omeros*. They are derivations of Greek names... Not Caribbean names. Achille?

D.W.: Ah, Achille [*he corrects my pronunciation*]. French pronunciation. I met him. Achille—I met him on the beach in Choiseul in St Lucia, and he had a cousin whose name was Hector. Genuinely.

H.E.: Really?

D.W.: Yes, I thought "this is incredible." They didn't know anything about Homer or why they were given those names. But that's a fact. That these people were given these names—it's just the history of American slavery. There's a lot of those epic classical names that were given to slaves, often the names of Emperors—Caesar, Pompey and so on.

H.E.: How does a classical education sit beside that history of slavery? Is giving Caribbean children a European classical education a vestige of that colonial imposition?

D.W.: I didn't have a classical education. I just had an education. I'm certainly not a Homeric scholar or a Dantesque scholar. So I don't consider myself to be educated classically.

H.E.: What should the relationship be in education between indigenous literatures and dominant literary traditions?

D.W.: The Caribbean culture is old. Older than American culture. But reading in the Caribbean is much more exciting than reading in Europe, because it's new. And you claim it more. And you don't have to claim it, but you do. And it becomes yours much more than the average school boy in Italy or anywhere: how you relate to what you've read.

Writing *Omeros*, it was easy for me. Because of the background my version comes from. It comes from a totally fresh and new, exciting background—the Caribbean ocean, the Caribbean sea, Caribbean land, the people too.

A European poet would have been assuming a responsibility of hundreds of years and would have done a faithful account of it—for me it was very exciting for me to do something that was a totally new world. I used to get up very excited to have to go to work. Everyday to have that job to do.

The great thing about writing a poem like that, which has a structure laid out, is that it's like going to work each day. The structure is there—you know what you have to do.

You have to put three lines there. You have to rhyme them. Tomorrow is Thursday, you are going to do the same thing. So on, so forth. You are given a job to do. It's easy to understand how poems can become very long. When I began the book—I knew I couldn't do "Oh Muse etc." so I was thinking, "How am I going to begin?" There's a joke about Dylan Thomas. He gets up in the morning, writes a big "O" then he goes to the pub...

H.E.: ... I've started work...

D.W.: ... I'll come back to it later...

Anyway, the first line is, "this is how we something-or-other them canoes"—right?

So I thought, grammatically, it's not good English. "We build *them* canoes." Not good. And I thought, am I going to have some guy in Oxford teaching "*This is how we build them canoes*. Bad English."

So I said, "You have to make up your mind, you are either going to change it to good English—but then it will be bullshit. Or you have to write how he talks." I thought to myself: "This is a long work. And a very ambitious thing. Don't deny it. So are you going to say that from now on the first line of your poem is going to be bad grammar," and I thought, "Yes, I have no choice."

Sometimes what is bad grammar is correct in a way. Even when a singular is there for a plural, or a plural for a singular. What may be the bad grammar of a dialect can be stronger than grammatical correctness. And I think you can see it in poets. Not just dialect poets. But poets who have that acceptance of the language that they come from.

Walcott then asked me about a particular passage in Homer, a description of a storm he remembered reading in translation. He remembered thinking that it must have been written originally in prose, it was "too fluent," "pure Hemingway in continuity."

He asked me about Homer's verse, having never had the opportunity to read the original. I gave a rather cumbersome account of the history of Homeric scholarship, theories of monumental composition, evidence of orality in the poetry . . . but he kept asking me how the verse *feels* and whether it feels prosaic. I recited a little bit of the *Odyssey*, and we talked about the difference between a language metered by stress and a language metered by length of vowels. We agreed that Homeric verse has an ebb and flow like the sea, which must be part of its hexameter nature—rising and falling in a way that a pentameter, with an odd number of feet, cannot.

We started to discuss translations of Homer. Walcott asked me whether the early formal verse translations or some of the later prose translations feel more authentically like the Greek. We discussed how poets like Seamus Heaney have returned to Anglo-Saxon verse forms to translate Greek lyric to escape the Shakespearian pentameter. We both admired Christopher Logue's *War Music* and Walcott told me he had just read Alice Oswald's *Memorial* and thought it terrific. We talked about "place" in her work and the relationship between her Devon landscape and Troy, the relationship between femininity and war.

Finally we returned, full circle, to "Achille" and names, in particular to the *katabasis* in *Omeros* where Achille goes back to find his father, asks him his name, and he doesn't know. I ask about this theme of namelessness in the poem, and whether it reflects a cultural journey of restoring indigenous names, or a search for Caribbean identity.

Walcott described how French Creole, like Anglo-Saxon, often places two nouns together to create a name. It's a strong choice for a poet, because it carries implicit metaphor. He explained how the French Creole for scissor bird is a juxtaposition of the words "scissors" and "sea." You can't call it "scissors sea" in English, because it's meaningless. In French "de la" is added: "scissors of the sea." This makes the metaphor too conspicuous, more like a simile, too emblematic. Thus, in renaming things the inherent poetry of their name is lost or becomes unusable.

  H.E.: Do you then feel you have multiple palettes of language to work with? Is there a kind of joy when you blend them and get different metaphorical releases from them?

D.W.: I began to work on translating some lyric poems into French Creole and I got very scared. A lot of translations in French Creole read like bad French, but I was really trying to rhyme in that language and head for a certain kind of elegance, a certain kind of compression, another level—well, I got a tremendous kick, it made me very happy, out of the fact that a section I was describing rhymed in French Creole and it didn't rhyme like a grunt, it rhymed elegantly. That is a whole language that is not explored there...

But I cannot explore it because I don't really think in that language.

I wanted to ask Walcott about his plays; as a prolific playwright (he has written over 20 plays) and theater director, he has spent a large amount of his career working in that genre, but his theater work is little known internationally. We talked about how his current production of *Pantomime*, at the University of Essex, was going.

H.E.: When you write drama, do you think in prose?
D.W.: No, I think in verse. Verse structure.
H.E.: But some of your drama is prose. *Pantomime* is prose?
D.W.: But it's not a problem because the background I am coming from is continuous rhythm. I come from that "calypso," whatever it is. Even in the rhythm of speech it's very percussive.
H.E.: But do you ever, when you are writing drama, have a desire to end the line, to give it a stronger verse structure, use line break? Or do you trust your actors to find the rhythm in there.
D.W.: There's a difficulty of doing English verse for the theater. What you have to see if you can achieve is a conversational quality. Eliot didn't use the pentameter because it was too dated, everything would become heroic, in a sense. So he tried to do something by making a flatter, more conversational scansion, in which the pitch of the voice is not heroic, but descriptive. It is like people talking. But it doesn't have the grandeur of the pentameter. Right? So what you get is a great poet flattening his diction because he wants the verse to work. But it's very dull, drab. The guy who wrote *The Wasteland* should not have written *The Cocktail Party*. Not that way, anyway.
H.E.: What do you think of his attempts at translating Greek tragedy? And Pound's?
D.W.: Do you know what Pound said about Eliot. "Instead of the goddamn crooning, put me down for the *temporis acti*."

The actions of the time. Pound is saying that, with the recordings of *The Cocktail Party*, the crooning, he betrayed them both, by turning into a kind of numb, crooning bitch that had none of the vigour of his poetry. Tough criticism. But it was an achievement because he did achieve a verse that was conversational—which was what he wanted. So in a way it worked.
H.E.: Will there be a resurgence of verse drama? Or is that form lost to us?
D.W.: *Sweeney Agonistes* works because it's not the long line—it's the short line. The scansion works, the staccato rhythm. Maybe that's the answer...

We discuss some contemporary verse plays and translations, and their various approaches to metre and scansion. We digress to pondering why the Royal Shakespeare Company's contemporary productions all currently seem to be prose. They have commissioned a number of major poets to write plays, but none of them are actually using verse. Which brings me to asking...

H.E.: How did your RSC *Odyssey* come about?

D.W.: Greg[4] wanted to do the *Odyssey*, and he wanted someone to adapt it, so he asked me to do it.

H.E.: Had he read *Omeros*?

D.W.: Ah, yes, maybe.

H.E.: Did he have a vision of what an RSC *Odyssey* might be like, or was it a completely open brief?

D.W.: He didn't ask for anything in particular. He wanted an adaptation which worked.

H.E.: Obviously, you directed Seamus Heaney's *Antigone*, his *Burial at Thebes*, in opera form at the Globe, but have you ever been attracted to Greek tragedy as a writer? To stage it, translate it, respond to it? There's a strong response to epic in your work, but not so much a response to tragedy. Is that true? (Fig. 50.1)

D.W.: Greek tragedy has become so academic. That's the territory it seems to belong to. So you do another play about some unmentionable character doing something... When it works of course, if you get involved in it, it's terrifying and terrible and great to do. But it has such an aura of the school room and the class room and the lectern that I'm not instantly attracted to it.

H.E.: Could you reclaim it? From the classroom? It was popular theater when it was written. Could you wrestle it back?

D.W.: I have never been attracted to adapting or translating Greek theater directly from the original. I feel as if I'd just be another poet translating another Greek drama—the *Antigone*... the *Bacchae*...

H.E.: How was directing *The Burial at Thebes*—was it more exciting because it was an opera? What grabbed you about that? The fusion of Heaney's verse and Dominique le Gendre's score?

D.W.: No, I am very interested in theater. Poetry and theater. Poetry as theater. Theater as poetry. I have repeatedly asked American poets to try to write plays—some of them had some brilliant ideas.

One guy, Charlie Simic, I said: "how would you like to stage a play?"

I think Charlie said, "I'd like to get America and Russia in a wrestling ring"—terrific! Different poets said different things, which immediately, because they were poets, immediately, were attractive as ideas. And they each thought of something which was a great beginning but worried about writing a play. I said "just write the thing and put *enters, exits*." Everyone was concerned about what to do with people coming in and going out. "Just put *enter somebody, exit somebody*; that's what Shakespeare did! Don't describe people coming in..."

I think the prose reality of theater made them...

That's it... that's the betrayal that's happened. The theater becoming prosaic reality. How you get inside the door and get outside the fucking door—you know, *that* inhibited the poets I think, because they feel they can't write a play because they don't know the action. But the action is in the poetry.

I did a thing once. I took a class and I said, take Blanche Dubois's "I have always depended on the kindness of strangers," which if you look at it is a pentametric line; also Arthur Miller's "Attention, attention must finally be paid to such a person"—that's

FIG. 50.1 A Derek Walcott illustration in the rehearsal notebook of his 2008 production of *Burial at Thebes*. Held at the APGRD, and reproduced with kind permission of Derek Walcott.

pentametrical.⁵ So there you have two emblematic lines from American theater, which are already pentametrical. And I said, instead of that, instead of prose, instead of Blanche saying "I have always depended on the kindness of strangers," instead, take this passage of verse from James Wright. Imagine Blanche saying in a southern accent, "I want to be lifted up. By some great white bird unknown to the police." Unknown to the fucking police!

You know what I mean?

That's the end of a poem by James Wright.

That's what American poetry has. That parenthesis sometimes. You know?

Now that would be great poetry on the stage. That's *Duchess of Malfi* time.

And I said instead of doing "attention should be paid" etc. which is like hyperbole in scansion, how about

"A salesman is an it that stinks Excuse
Me..."

From ee cummings.

When I made the actors change the texts, the theater reverberated with what that contained.

Imagine Linda saying that over Willy's grave. Over the dead salesman. "A salesman is an it that stinks Excuse | Me." "It" is "shit," of course.

Oh fuck, really, oh fuck.

FIG. 50.2 A Derek Walcott illustration in the rehearsal notebook of his 2008 production of *Burial at Thebes*. Held at the APGRD, and reproduced with kind permission of Derek Walcott.

Because, he spends his whole life saying "excuse me—can I?" So, what an epitaph.
So what I'm arguing is that American poetry has already done the equivalent of Elizabethan or Jacobean poetry in lyric writing (Fig. 50.2).

We chat about this for some time and broader questions about the relationship of theater and poetry. The conversation veers for a while to my ensemble, Live Canon. Walcott makes me promise to never give it up. I notice the time, and am aware that Glyn Maxwell and Derek's wife, who have both tactfully left the cottage while we talk, will soon be returning. We have a series of plans that evening, including dinner with Walcott's neighbor in Wivenhoe, seeing the performance of Walcott's play, and an impromptu gathering at the house of another Visiting Lecturer. I come back to this ultimate fusion of the Greek and the Caribbean.

H.E.: I'd like to end by asking you about the phrase in your poem "Homecoming: Anse La Raye": "the solemn Afrogreeks eager for grades." It's such a potent name "Afrogreeks," bringing together two cultures, juxtaposing two words to make a compound (I guess like the Anglo-Saxon and French Creole compounds we discussed earlier). Did you create that label in that poem?

D.W.: It's not a common expression. "Afrosaxon," that's a common expression—but "Afrogreeks"—I think the Greek thing is the geography—the sea, the islands.

No one in the Caribbean knows Greek or thinks in Greek terms, but, particularly if you paint, you see references there continually. If you see a black fisherman against a blue sea and a brilliant sky, he's a silhouette, he could be on a Greek vase easily. Now, for you to think of a Greek vase—it's a little esoteric I mean by yourself to do that—but the emblematic thing that you see in front of you, that can make the reference happen.

For me, when I did read the *Odyssey* (and I still haven't read the full *Iliad*), I recognized things. I recognized the taste of surf, I recognized a wave, as it was described in Homer . . . and it was in a language without adjectives too; it was a language of nouns . . .

H.E.: . . . and that recognition was fresh to you. Perhaps unlike modern Greek poets—I'm thinking of Seferis—where there's a struggle to write freshly about Greece, to own its landscape. In his poem "Mycenae" he struggles to write about the rocks beneath him, without the literary baggage of his heritage.

D.W.: The translations of Seferis are so unsatisfactory—I used to look at Seferis and think "yeah, very nice."

But when a Greek friend started to translate it for me, Jesus, I was blown away. By the solidity of the language, not the waspy translation, you know what I mean . . .

I think you are right, though. The same is true of Italian poetry.

H.E.: You spoke in the platform last week with Glyn, about having finally gone to Italy and arrived at a love of it for yourself, not out of tradition or literature. Have you been to Greece?

D.W.: Very briefly.

H.E.: Do you have a desire to explore it?

D.W.: Literature . . . Poetry has a way of playing tricks on you. You mustn't screw around with it, because it's going to catch you.

I mean, look at me. Montale. What am I doing with Montale?

It's hard to describe what is going on in this particular context. You are in Umbria. You look out and you see a terrific landscape. What are you looking at? Are you looking at "Italy"—in inverted commas—or are you looking at a landscape that is really a knockout thing that has nothing to do with association.

Sometimes I play the trick of looking at the wrong landscape and giving it the wrong name; in other words, if I looked out there now and I said "we are in Tuscany" everything changes. It gets very important. History is attached to it. And it becomes a farmhouse in Tuscany. And I'm looking at a farmhouse in Tuscany and I'm a traveler, and all that. It's difficult to know what you are looking at and how you are looking at it. That's why names matter.

H.E.: So do I need to travel in Greece? As a lover of Greek literature. Or is the reality of the landscape utterly unrelated to its literary realization?

D.W.: There's a whole book in that. Names. Associations. The validity of a name for a place.

The other day I was taken to Constable country. If someone hadn't said to me "Constable country," would I have been very impressed?

It was really beautiful.

But you can have a whole culture based on visiting a name. All of Europe went south to Lombardie... (or somewhere else). Then you put it in a poem. And you get an Award. You have to be very judicious where you place the names you refer to in your career.

Put it at the bottom of a poem. Lombardie 1949...

H.E.: ...I was there. I wrote...something...

D.W.: ...and I suffered...

We laughed. And Derek declared it time for tea. And for a bit we sat and drank English tea, looking out through the windows at an English cottage garden, and calling it "Tuscany."

Notes

1. Walcott widely references the ancient world in his poems, particularly using characters from the Homeric cycles, culminating in his epic poem *Omeros* (1990). He wrote a stage adaptation of *The Odyssey* for the Royal Shakespeare Company (1992/3) and, as a director, directed the world première of Seamus Heaney and Dominique le Gendre's opera version of *Antigone, The Burial at Thebes*, at Shakespeare's Globe (2008). Walcott received the Nobel Prize for Literature in 1992.
2. Cf. Derek Walcott, *Omeros*. New York, 1990: 283 where the narrator-figure declares to Omeros (in reference to the *Odyssey*), "I never read it... Not all the way through."
3. Thomas Gray's poem "Elegy in a Country Churchyard" is written in four line quatrains with an ABAB rhyme scheme.
4. Gregory Doran, who directed *The Odyssey*, who has gone on to become the Artistic Director of the Royal Shakespeare Company.
5. The references are, of course, to Tennessee Williams's *A Streetcar Named Desire* (1947) and Arthur Miller's *Death of a Salesman* (1949).

AFTERWORD

CHAPTER 51

AUDIENCES ACROSS THE POND

Oceans Apart or Shared Experiences?

LORNA HARDWICK

> Oceans apart—these words ... conjure images of the harsh physical journeys across huge expanses of sea. They also suggest the often brutal suppression wrought by colonial invasion. But most of all they suggest an expansive imaginative territory between places of extraordinary cultural diversity.
>
> (Jonathan Mills, in "Welcome to Festival," Edinburgh 2010)

THIS chapter discusses cultural traffic, focusing on theater productions that have crossed the Atlantic. I have chosen examples that raise questions, sometimes contentious, about how performance is shaped by overt and covert assumptions concerning the cultural horizons and socio-political perspectives of audiences. These in turn raise issues about the distinctive agendas of writers and producers (including commercial considerations). I hope that these examples also contribute to wider debates about the relationship between aesthetic and contextual aspects of performance and its histories. The role of the spectators (actual and imagined) is crucial in negotiating this interface. I use the term "spectator" to include theater critics as well as the bulk of the audience and in analysing performance I draw on the categories set out by Erika Fischer-Lichte: co-presence of actors and spectators; ephemerality and intensity; production of meaning in performance and performance as event (Fischer-Lichte 2010). Equally important is the way in which theater poetry both energizes and is contained by the formal elements of Greek theater and its texts.

Setting the Scene: Tents in the Camp

In 2005 Tony Harrison's version of Euripides' *Hecuba* was staged in the United States. It crossed the Atlantic after a poorly received run at the Albery Theatre in London (Fig. 51.1). The reasons for the theater critics' dislike of the London production mingled the aesthetic and the political. The critics (variously) thought that Vanessa Redgrave's long awaited return to performing with the Royal Shakespeare Company was disappointing, her Hecuba insufficiently "feral," and that Harrison's performance text was too bulky and full of epithets and alliterations. Critics objected to the use of neologisms like "coalition," to the description of Talthybius as "Agamemnon's ADC," and to the "pseudo American accent" of Darrell D'Silva's Odysseus. Some commented that there was "tragedy fatigue" after the plethora of adaptations that had addressed political conflicts in Ireland and the Balkans, as well as Iraq. Paradoxically, critics were determined to read the production as simplistically equating the Chorus of Trojan Women with Muslims (in defiance of the set and costumes used in the London production). They also pointed to ideological weariness—"there is something rather smug and pointless about the theatricals declaring how anti-war they

FIG. 51.1 The RSC's *Hecuba* at the Albery Theatre, London (2005). Written by Tony Harrison, directed by Laurence Boswell, with stage design by Es Devlin. Photograph reproduced with kind permission of Es Devlin.

are to audiences who are probably equally convinced of the same position" (Lawson 2005). In contrast, few critics commented on how close Harrison's text was to the Greek, notably in its presentation of the parody of democracy in Euripides' play, for example in the army's debate about whether to sacrifice Polyxena. In that sense, their reaction could be seen as a denial of the most radical of the ancient play's relationships to the present.[1]

The rehearsals had been beset by difficulties, ranging from Redgrave's illness to problems in the working relationships between cast, director, and writer. When the production toured to the United States, the director (Laurence Boswell) did not, and Tony Harrison in effect took over—the play was described in the press materials as "written by and developed for its US engagements by British poet Tony Harrison." In the States the play was staged at the John F. Kennedy Center for the Performing Arts (May/June 2005, with Accenture as the Global High Performance Business Partner of the Royal Shakespeare Company) and in the Brooklyn Academy of Music Spring Season (June 2005, with Calyon Corporate Investment Bank as the presenting sponsor) (Fig. 51.2). The synopsis given to spectators, as in the London program, contextualized the play by proclaiming that "the first Great War between the East and the West is over." In his *New York Times* review of the BAM performance, Charles Isherwood commented on the unhappy history of the production and added, "the most reliable way to tap into the power of Greek tragedy is not by larding it with topical allusions but by giving full expression to the range of emotion its formal structure so elegantly contains" (Isherwood 2005).

In fact, the most striking change from the London performances was not to allusions made in the performance text but in the set. In place of the London design, which was neutral in terms of modern place and suggested the shape and texture of ancient pottery, Harrison substituted a series of tents representing the Greek army camp, with the initials US or UK painted on their roofs. These visually dominated the audience's view and intensified the resonances with the present. Harrison also subsequently recalled that the second-hand materials had come impregnated with insecticide, giving off an overpowering stench that nearly overcame the stagehands. It is unlikely that Harrison thought that U.S. audiences would be less quick than British to spot the contemporary allusions in the text so the set surely represented a defiant gesture toward the critics, as well as a reaffirmation of the passionate closing paragraph of Harrison's introduction to the published text: "We may still be weeping for Hecuba, but we allow our politicians to flood the streets of Iraq with more and more Hecubas in the name of freedom and democracy. The audience might weep for Hecuba in Washington when the tragedy plays there, but will they squirm with regret for Iraq, or for the re-election of George Bush or pause a moment before going for the gullet of Iran?" (Harrison 2005: x).

Cure and Reconciliation

I turn now to a play in which, after the initial performances, the author toned down rather than intensified the direct political references, claiming that there were aesthetic reasons for doing so. Seamus Heaney's *The Cure at Troy* was first performed in 1990. Subtitled "A

FIG. 51.2 *Hecuba* at Brooklyn Academy of Music, New York (2005). As the stage designer, Es Devlin, remarked, "We had a design that suddenly found new resonance in the light of the events of 2003. I sourced the tents from the army surplus shops around Washington DC—some of them had sand in them—presumably from the gulf states." Photograph reproduced with kind permission of Es Devlin.

Version of Sophocles's *Philoctetes*," it was created for the performance program of Field Day. Field Day was founded in Derry in the north of Ireland in 1980 by the actor Stephen Rea and the playwright Brian Friel, whose play *Translations* (1981) was the first Field Day production. Derry/Londonderry is a city near the border between the north of Ireland and the Republic of Ireland. The way in which it is referred to usually indicates political affiliations (desire for even-handedness has been satirized in the term "Stroke City"). Field Day's activities came to be cultural, political, and literary as well as theatrical and it subsequently published a three-volume anthology of Irish writing and a series of pamphlets and monographs.[2] There has been considerable controversy about whether and how Field Day's idealistic aims for cultural, social, and political life in Ireland could in practice be achieved in ways that reflected the plural and sometimes overlapping identities of Irish people from north and south, whether from Catholic or Protestant traditions (Howe 2000: 107–45).

Heaney joined the editorial board of Field Day in 1981, along with Tom Paulin, David Hammond, and Seamus Deane (O'Driscoll 2008: 414–16). *The Cure at Troy* toured in Ireland as part of Field Day's aim of taking theater into the community. Venues included Andersonstown, a working-class area in Belfast, where the performance continued a tradition of staging Sophocles' play in areas of unemployment and deprivation that had a precedent in the economic depression of 1933. *Cure* was subsequently staged at the Lyric Theatre, Belfast, and in England and Scotland by a number of companies (Hardwick 2007b: 319, fig. 21.2). It was performed at the Tricycle Theatre Kilburn (an area of London noted for its Irish diaspora) and at several arts festivals, including the Edinburgh Fringe. In 1995 it crossed the Atlantic and was staged at the Berkeley Repertory Theatre and the Oregon Shakespeare Festival (directed by Tony Taccone) (Heaney 2002a). It was also produced in New York in 1997 (Jean Cocteau Repertory).

Two factors make the play of particular significance for this volume. First, the performance history ranges from community halls and student companies to major theaters and festivals so its actual and assumed audiences cross a wider than usual spectrum for an adaptation of a Greek play. Secondly, Heaney has recorded in a number of interviews and essays his observations on the creation of the play and on changes in his views about it, including comparisons with what he wanted to achieve in his later work with another Sophocles play, *Antigone* (which became the basis for his 2004 version *The Burial at Thebes*). This material offers a map of his perspectives through time as well as the opportunity to cross-check different sources. The extensive evidence from interviews provides important insights into the relationship between creativity, aesthetics, and cultural politics, both in the genesis of the play and in the judgements and decisions that Heaney subsequently made about it (and which influenced his future work with Greek plays).

THE GENESIS OF *THE CURE AT TROY*

In response to a question about why *Philoctetes* was chosen, Heaney has described how the play was part of "the theater of your own conscience and consciousness" and also indissolubly linked with the audiences for which it was intended:[3]

Well, undoubtedly, it was the conditions we were living in, or have lived in, in Northern Ireland. They were intensified and made romantic and extreme from about 1968 to 1996 but anyone who grew up in the north of Ireland from their moment of consciousness was aware of, if you like, a public dimension to their lives. They were bonded into a group, one side or the other side. And they were also living in *the theater of your own conscience and consciousness* [italics added]. So, the demand for solidarity was there from the start with your group, and if you were growing into some kind of authentic individual life, the imperative for solitude or self-respect or integrity or self-definition was there also. So there was always . . . an ill-fit between the group line, the party line if you like, and the personal condition. And that is precisely what drew me to the *Philoctetes*, where . . . the young fellow, Neoptolemus is caught between the demands of loyalty and solidarity. He is a soldier on the Greek expedition and so he has to help the cause but in order to help the cause, he has to do something which infringes his own sense of truth and justice and self-respect, he has to tell a lie to this wounded man. So it's that friction between the demands of the group and the demands of the individual integrity. . . . I changed the title of *Philoctetes* or *Philoctetes*—because I wasn't quite sure how you pronounced it among other things—but mainly because it was being toured in Ireland, to certainly non-classical people. It was being brought into all kinds of parish halls and arts centres and, as my mother would call them, *the common five-eighths were coming in to see it* [italics added]. So, there is a miraculous cure at the end of the play; Philoctetes, the wounded man is cured. So, I thought in that phrase, the Cure at Troy, [the senses] the word "cure" has for both sides in Ireland, north and south, there can be, if you like, faith healing cures or they can be miraculous cures at Lourdes and holy wells and so on. So it gave it that kind of, if you like, anthropological dimension.[4]

Heaney's Idiom and Audiences: Local, American, Global

A major aspect of Heaney's approach to the Sophocles was his use of existing translations. In many respects his play stuck closely to the theatrical conventions of the Greek but he did make major additions to the Choral Odes, and these are included in the published text (Heaney 1990). Heaney commented that he wrote the play in verse "in order to preserve something of the formal ritualistic quality of the Greek theatrical experience" but had nevertheless "felt free to compose a number of new lines for the Chorus" (Program Notes, Tricycle Theatre production, 1991). The extra Odes for the Chorus are at the very beginning and near the end. In Sophocles the Chorus first enters at line 135, after the prologue between Odysseus and Neoptolemus. In Heaney, the Chorus opens the play, introducing Philoctetes, Hercules, and Odysseus to the audience ("Heroes. Victims") (Heaney 1990: 1). The opening Chorus controversially implies in idiom and image the connections between the story of Philoctetes and the Irish context of the time ("Licking their wounds | And flashing them round like decorations") (Heaney

1990: 2) and reflects on the role of poetry in crossing the borderlines between reality and aspiration. This poetic agency is picked up in the additional Chorus material at the end of Heaney's play, when an Ode is added following Neoptolemus' exchange with Philoctetes (Sophocles, line 1484).

Two interpolations in the new Ode that have been widely discussed:

> But then, once in a lifetime
> The longed-for tidal wave
> Of justice can rise up,
> And *hope and history rhyme.* (italics added) (Heaney 1990: 77)

The phrase proved rhetorically memorable and was taken up as a "sound-bite" by public figures, including: Mary Robinson the President of the Irish Republic (1990–7), in her inauguration speech; U.S. President Bill Clinton in a speech given on the steps of the Bank of Ireland (December 1, 1995) (Denard 2000); the address by the President of the European Commission Jacques Santer to the Forum for Peace and Reconciliation in Dublin Castle, 1995; newspaper headlines at the time of the Good Friday peace agreement (Belfast 1998). Subsequently, Martin McGuinness, the Sinn Fein Deputy First Minister under the power-sharing agreement, gave a framed copy of the lines, written on parchment by Heaney himself, to the Democratic Unionist First Minister Ian Paisley to mark the latter's retirement and Paisley hung this on the wall of his room in the Stormont Parliament (see interview with McGuinness, *Observer* (September 1, 2013), News, 23). The second interpolation was, in contrast, specifically related to the time and place of Heaney's original intended audiences. It was widely criticized as anachronistic, intrusively overt, and even as "an attempt to create a new mythology" (Meir 1991). It occurs earlier in the same Ode, when the Chorus meditate on suffering:

> A hunger striker's father
> Stands in the graveyard dumb
> The police widow in veils
> Faints at the funeral home.

I asked Seamus Heaney about those images of the suffering that was endured by both communities, loyalist and nationalist, during the Troubles in the north of Ireland and he commented on the lived experience that underlay them:

> During the [IRA] hunger strikes in 1981, the second hunger striker to die was a guy called Francis Hughes whose parents lived very close, I knew his father, I knew his brothers and sister, I didn't know him. But he died in the Maze Prison and of course, it was highly emotional time . . . after he died, he died in the prison, they [the security forces] took control of the body and . . . they delivered the body to Toombridge which was a few miles away from his birthplace so there was kind of outrage at that. (Note: Heaney subsequently reflected on that experience in his poem "The Wood Road") (Heaney 2010: 22–3)

In 1995 in the production notes that he compiled for the director of the U.S. performances, Heaney justified the Choral interpolations that "were meant to contextualise the action, and not just within a discourse that could apply to Northern Ireland politics. These two speeches also (I see it even more clearly in retrospect) defend the right of poetry/poetic drama to be something other than "protest"" (Heaney 2002a). In those notes Heaney also refers the director to a sequence in his essay *The Government of the Tongue* (1988), in which he wrote,

> In one sense the efficacy of poetry is nil—no lyric has ever stopped a tank. In another sense it is unlimited. It is like the writing in the sand in the face of which accusers and accused are left speechless and renewed. (Heaney 2002a: 173)

Yet subsequently Heaney changed his views about the aesthetic impact of these particular images of suffering and especially about their shortcomings in making the links between the local and the global:

> I thought that I made a mistake, actually, in *Cure at Troy*, introducing the pointed up relevant information, the kind of hook and eye to the present moment relationship. *The Cure at Troy* had a touch of, if you like, the adult education broadcast about it. I mean, I offended the conventions of Greek theater by having a Chorus come on at the beginning and, you know, lay down the law about what you're going to see. I actually felt that the audiences wouldn't know who the blazes Heracles or Hercules was and that all this was necessary. Like a BBC Third Programme introduction to the first act of an opera, you tell them what's going to happen. So, I did that, that was the first thing I had ever done for the stage and I think it was an error, definitely. And then when I saw the thing and heard the thing on the stage, police widows, hunger strikers, I thought it was altogether too pious towards the audience and towards the situation so when I reprinted that chorus in *Selected Poems*, I left out that stanza.[5]

However, Heaney did include in his play northern Irish idiom and intonation that was part of his "subliminal orientation" for his non-metropolitan audiences in Ireland (Heaney 2002a: 172). He emphasized that although he "meant to make the play at home in the ear of its [first] audience," he had not been aiming for a dialect drama and suggested that intonation (though not idiom) should be changed for U.S. performances (Heaney 2002a: 174). This is partly a practical matter of actors' voices and audiences' ears but nevertheless, there is no doubt that in his 1995 notes for the director of the U.S. productions, Heaney was already drawing back from his radical emphasis on the suffering of both sides in the Irish context. Also in 1995, in a lecture at Trinity College Dublin, Heaney commented, "I think if I were doing that again I would leave out the local colour stanza . . . I remember feeling it was like a puncture . . . Nowhere else is there Northern local reference."[6] It has also been suggested that these lines were deleted in a U.S. performance in the same year,[7] and they were omitted from the recitation by the actor Liam Neeson for *Across the Bridge of Hope* (1998), a compilation album produced in aid of the Omagh Bomb Memorial Fund.

Heaney's Multiple Identities in Tension: Northerner, Irishman, Catholic, Nationalist, Writer

The question then becomes whether Heaney had the pragmatic aim of avoiding specific Irish cultural referents that would puzzle or even alienate U.S. audiences that were not part of that particular "interpretative community"—a community that might not appreciate that suffering in the Troubles crossed all sections of both the Catholic and Protestant communities, whatever their attitude to British presence in the North—or whether he was changing his poetic and social stance on the relationship between the local and the universal, a relationship that he had imbibed from the poetry of Patrick Kavanagh (Hardwick 2011; Heaney 2002c; Stafford 2010: 1–30).

The risk of alienating Irish-American audiences, who might have had a standpoint originating in experiences earlier than the late twentieth-century Troubles, should not be underestimated. The importance of generational distance in the different phases involved in the formulation of cultural memory has been extensively studied. Subjective and experiential memories are collectively assimilated into social memories and then mediated into political and cultural memories, which can then mutate into a mythology of the past (Assmann 2006). In his memoir *Just Garret: Tales from the Political Frontline* (2010), the former Irish Taoiseach and Minister for External Affairs Garret Fitzgerald recounts in some detail the perceptions of the Irish situation and especially of the role of the IRA held by Irish-Americans and others in the United States in the last part of the twentieth century. IRA supporters disrupted meetings he was addressing in visits to the U.S.A. (for instance in 1974 in New York) and he recounts the comments of a New York policeman: "I t'ought de IRA was de good guys. Aint dey fighting de British? But when I went to the old country last summer everyone told me dey were [expletive deleted]. I don't understand it all anymore" (Fitzgerald 2010: 231 (*sic*)). Fitzgerald also documents similar attitudes that he encountered in various U.S. Congressmen and committee organizers (Fitzgerald 2010: 293).

Fitzgerald formed the view that second or third generation Irish-Americans had inherited parental or grandparental memories of "what they saw as a colonial war, and with their curious frozen-in-aspic concepts of Irish nationalism, saw democratically elected Irish governments, whatever their composition, as quislings" (Fitzgerald 2010: 231). He writes at some length of the difficult process of "challenging the IRA myth in the US" (a process started by his predecessor Jack Lynch in 1972) and so reducing "the flow of funds from Noraid to the IRA." Fitzgerald uses strong language when describing the aim of successive Irish governments in cooperation with the nationalist party in the North, the SDLP, to "win as much as we could of Irish America back from its tendency to sympathise with the IRA as an atavistic expression of inherited anti-British feeling" (Fitzgerald 2010: 293).

In evaluating Fitzgerald's analysis as evidence about the issues discussed in this essay, it should be noted that he was a member and then leader of Fine Gael, which was the party known as the descendent of the Treaty Party in Ireland, i.e., the groups that had been in favor of coming to an agreement with the British after the war of independence (dispute on this question between political groups in Ireland led to civil war in 1922–3; Fine Gael was formally established in 1938). However, both Fitzgerald's parents were strongly involved in the Easter Rising in Dublin (1916). His father (Desmond Fitzgerald) was imprisoned by the British before he eventually became Minister for External Affairs in Cosgrove's Irish government in 1923 (Lyons 1971: 455), and Garret Fitzgerald records that although his father supported the Treaty his mother did not (Foster 2014: 284). Fitzgerald was to be the lead negotiator for the government of the Irish Republic in the Anglo-Irish Agreement of 1985, which marked a step in the progress toward the Good Friday peace agreement made in 1998. His records of his experiences of political negotiations in the U.S.A. in the 1970s and 1980s draw both on governmental and political contacts and on demotic accounts of the kind quoted above. Taken together, these provide some evidence that in the 1970s and 1980s attitudes to the [Provisional] IRA and to militant republicanism among Irish-Americans had been shaped by a cultural memory that was into its second and third generation of development, and necessarily included "post-memory," i.e., perceptions that were not based on direct experience but which resulted from the oral testimony of those who had experienced the situation of Ireland when it was under British rule but had generally not experienced life in Ireland at the time that Heaney and his fellow writers were growing up and publishing their work. Post-memory in particular has been widely investigated as a major feature in ongoing trauma and its literature.[8]

In addition, I think the generalization "Irish-American" is also problematic in the context of Heaney's play in that Irish immigrants to the U.S.A. had also included substantial numbers of Ulster-Scots, who continued to have close affinities with Protestant loyalists in the north of Ireland and who were equally likely to have "post-memory" (although of a different hue) as the basis for their attitudes to Irish politics. Taken together, these factors suggest that U.S. audiences were unlikely to have the nuanced immediacy of understanding of the reality of the sufferings of both communities. It was this element that allowed Heaney's choral odes a radical resonance with audiences across the sectarian divide in Belfast, when the Chorus accepted the "policeman's widow" and the "hunger striker's father" as of equal significance in the suffering of the communities. W. B. Stanford suggested in his study *Ireland and the Classical Tradition* that the classical strand in Irish culture (which he called the "fourth cultural root of Ireland," alongside the Gaelic, the Christian, and the British) provided common ground between polarized elements in the population, providing "an intellectual and emotional link" between those in conflict (Stanford 1984: viii; ix; 245). Heaney seems to have aligned with this view in his creation of *The Cure at Troy* for Field Day and his play can be seen as an attempt to bring together different strands in cultural memory and to shape a new kind of consciousness. However, the complex temporal, cultural, and spatial disjunctions between Irish-Americans and Irish people in Ireland, north and south, provide a political as well as an aesthetic rationale for the changes made in the choral odes when the play crossed the Atlantic in the late twentieth century. Cultural horizons in the U.S.A., and the experiences that shaped memory and post-memory, were simply different from those in Ireland (or indeed in Kilburn).

Further problematic relationships between the local and the universal/international are intertwined with the stresses sometimes imposed by Heaney's own multiple consciousness. There is evidence from his lyric poetry of his continuing concern with the tensions between conflicting aspects of identity. For example, in the Antaeus poems in *Death of a Naturalist*, 1966, and in *North*, 1975, the struggle is between Antaeus and Hercules, who lifts Antaeus from his roots in the earth and leaves him as "pap for the dispossessed." The struggle for balance between dual burdens comes out in "Terminus" (*The Haw Lantern*, 1987) in which "Two buckets were easier carried than one | I grew up in between." Poems such as "Requiem for the Croppies" (1969) and "Orange Drums, Tyrone 1966" (1975) mark Heaney's engagement with the continuing history of Irish nationalism and the present emblems associated with its repression, while the sequence "Whatever You Say Say Nothing" (1975) reflects on the fear of being misrepresented that underlay reticence.

However, in the case of Heaney's renouncement of the Choral interpolation in *Cure*, I think the decisive factor in a complex web was probably not the cultural weight of reticence but the impulse for poetic freshness, in terms of aesthetics and "public" context. This rested on his conception of his own status as a writer. Already in his 1995 Notes to the U.S. director, Heaney had referred to the burden of "dutiful commentary-type drama ('Troubles art')" (Heaney 2002a: 178). The desire to break free of this became apparent in his 2007 reflections when, in response to a question about why his 2004 play *The Burial at Thebes*, commissioned to mark the centenary of the Abbey Theatre in Dublin, had not exploited the civil war theme of Sophocles' *Antigone* in order to address the history of early twentieth-century Ireland, Heaney commented:

> by 2004, 2003 when I started this thing [sc. *Burial*], you do a thing once in literature, the second time you do it, it's cliché, you know? So, you do a thing once in life, you do it a thousand times . . . But, you know, you're gonna get fed up with it. So, the Irish question was imaginatively exhausted in a way, as far as I was concerned.

It is significant, too (especially in terms of this discussion), that, rather than revisiting Irish political history, Heaney seemed by 2007 more interested in writing a version of Sophocles' *Oedipus at Colonus*, notably in order to follow the path of W. B. Yeats but also because of the *OC*'s force as a play of religious resolution and closure. Perhaps that will come. However, so far as Heaney's overtly "political" plays are concerned, it seems that it was his understanding and experience of flexible and plural identities and his aesthetic practice of "two-mindedness" that initially drew him to *Philoctetes*, and which also induced him to first to implement and then to change the didactic approach to the audiences ("spelling things out like that is almost patronizing to the audience"; and, more generally—"To transmogrify Wilfred Owen's famous line, I'd say that the politics are there in the poetry").[9]

Lee Breuer's *The Gospel at Colonus*

My third example is of a production that crossed the Atlantic in the opposite direction in 2010. Although Lee Breuer's *The Gospel at Colonus* had been workshopped three decades previously (including in the Assembly Rooms at the Edinburgh Fringe festival in 1982) and had toured internationally, its development into a substantial theater event had been on the U.S. stage and its contexts of performance and interpretation were American. Justine McConnell (this volume) discusses its migration from the iconic performances at the Brooklyn Academy of Music in 1983 to Broadway (1988). The full performance history of *Gospel* requires comparison of productions through time as well as place but here I shall focus entirely on the production context and audience expectations and responses in the situation of its further migration to the Edinburgh International Festival of 2010.

Gospel was staged at the Edinburgh Playhouse over three days, August 21–3, 2010, as a centerpiece in the Festival's International Program. There were four performances in all, two matinees and two evenings. The Playhouse is a nineteenth-century proscenium arch theater that can seat approximately 3,000 people and a total of over 9,000 spectators saw the production. The theme of the 2010 International Festival was "Oceans Apart" and in a TV interview the Festival Director, Jonathan Mills, cited *Gospel* as an example of international enterprise, a meeting of "new" Classics and liveliness.[10] The context of this interview was a debate about criticisms that the International Festival had become "flat" and was being overtaken by other festivals (not least the Edinburgh "Fringe"); there was also concern about the demographic of the audiences at the international festival (audiences were thought to be predominantly white, middle class, and middle aged). Mills's broadcast comments and his foreword to the program for the production sought to present an alternative view. His program note thanked the sponsor Standard Life (described as a corporate partner and "an iconic Scottish financial institution") and characterized *Gospel* as "extraordinary" and "exuberant," bracketing it with a companion production at the Playhouse, the world première of the Paco Pena Flamenco Dance Company's *Quimeras*. The sponsor's note in the same program took up the tone, describing the performance of *The Gospel at Colonus* as "unique and pioneering" and the festival as "a vibrant and innovative gathering from the performing arts," with *Gospel* contributing "40 powerhouse voices." Another TV program, *The Culture Show*, broadcast to the whole of the U.K. at a more popular time slot, also promoted the production as evidence of the vibrancy of the Edinburgh International Festival but added that, at a time when many people were suffering from the uncertainties of the depressed economic situation (following the global banking crisis of 2008), the production "promoted the feel-good factor" (*sic*).[11] This claim was accompanied by clips of Oedipus, with the Blind Boys of Alabama and Antigone, taken from the later part of the performance.

What the Audience Saw: What the Audience Read

The festival director's promotion of the production was clearly intended to appeal to a modern, international, and perhaps "younger" audience, attracted by spectacle. *The Culture Show* was explicitly linking this to the capacity of the arts to "cheer things up" at times of economic crisis. The extended Notes in the program to the performance displayed a different set of assumptions about the likely audience. The program, which was extensively illustrated with photographs, included information about the Brooklyn Academy of Music and Broadway productions, a detailed breakdown of "Musical Numbers and Settings" for each of the two acts, and three informative articles. The first and longest, "From Ancient Greece to North America," was contributed by the Classicist and ancient theater scholar Edith Hall. Hall summarized the ancient context of composition and production, explaining that the three surviving Sophoclean plays on the family of Oedipus were not designed to be performed as a trilogy. Her article included detailed discussion of the differences between ancient and modern theatrical contexts and of the differences between the worldviews of ancient pagan and modern largely monotheistic audiences, with special attention to the problems of adapting the metaphysics of ancient tragic theater to its Christian framework of performance and understanding represented by *Gospel*. Hall also pointed to the increasing engagement in modern adaptations of Greek tragedy with "the counterpoint between the collective and the individual perspectives on painful and momentous events," linking this to musical modality and especially the ways in which the ancient tragic chorus shifts "between moods and in and out of a marked group identity" (remarks which could equally well apply to the Chorus in *Cure*).

Hall quoted Lee Breuer's argument that making links between apparently disparate traditions is a necessary part of liberation from the culturally imperialistic associations with European theater. She also identified the major changes from the Sophocles' *Oedipus at Colonus*, commenting on the inclusion in *Gospel* of passages from *Oedipus Tyrannus* and *Antigone*. Pointing out that there are losses as well as gains in cultural translocation, she acknowledged that "any authentic North American classicism must inevitably be Christianized, especially if it is going to integrate (as it must in order to be authentically American) a Black sensibility."[12] Yet she also acknowledged that the response of the religiously sensitive singing collective in *Gospel* would lose "the harsh grandeur of ancient Greek ethics and metaphysics" as the oratorio moved to "a proto-Christian redemptive metaphysics wholly alien to the ancient Athenian hero cult which the original drama explained."

The inclusion of an essay of this kind in a theater program assumes that at least some members of the audience are not only interested in performance that goes further than spectacle but are also able and willing to reflect after the performance on the cultural significance of the production and the traditions on which it draws. This assumption about the audiences was reinforced by the second essay in the program—"Music of the Soul," contributed by another academic, Jerry Zolten. His essay summarized the genesis and history of African-American gospel music, characterizing it as "music that evolved as a *balm* against the pain of slavery and, later, institutionalised segregation" (italics added). Zolten asserted that "gospel" developed from late eighteenth-century "spirituals" that were derived from a blend of English hymns (introduced by slave owners wishing to convert slaves to Christianity) and African performance style. He pointed out the importance of improvisation as a characteristic of spiritual performance and charted the changes in spirituals after the American Civil War, describing how they were sometimes used in concert tours in the nineteenth century to raise money for the education of freed slaves and young people. Zolten also discussed ways in which the gospel tradition became infused with other musical styles popular with African-Americans, including rhythm and blues. This resulted in the creation of new songs and the introduction of a larger range of modern instruments, including electric guitar, as well as innovation in performance styles that combined "roots" music with sensitivity to contemporary oppressions, war, and poverty. Zolten described the histories of the singing groups associated with gospel, such as the Blind Boys of Alabama, and commented on how they popularized gospel music to international audiences. However, effects were not to be confined to popularization and he emphasized the exploitation of every nuance and range of the human voice in order to communicate emotion and "move audiences to spiritual nirvana." Unlike Hall, Zolten did not point up potential conflicts, either within gospel music or in its interactions with other traditions. In particular, he did not draw out the contrasts between gospel and the spiritual. Spirituals originated in the brutality and alienation of slavery whereas gospel involves a joyous affirmation of liberation from bondage in which instrumental and vocal music expresses jubilation.

The information given to the audience members in Zolten's essay paved the way for the third in the program series, a short discussion of Breuer's career by Mark Fisher (freelance writer). Fisher's essay brought out another aspect of the tensions and multiplicities in *Gospel* by giving examples of the many strands in Breuer's artistic development. Breuer was shown as auteur (rather than director) and Fisher drew attention especially to his positive approach to changes, both from the ante-text (whether Ibsen or Sophocles) and in the performances of a particular work:

> There are two reasons for making changes: first, I feel I have better ideas about the production, that I understand things more . . . the second is the idea of keeping the performance alive. I put in changes to the *Gospel at Colonus*, for example, 28 years after we opened.

Two questions then become paramount. First, to what extent is creative tension between the specificities of cultural genesis and the multiple different performance contexts possible, and secondly, to what extent were the strands in the religious aesthetics and performance histories evident to the Edinburgh spectators, most of whom were unlikely to study the program essays in detail until after the performance (if at all)?

I use the word "spectators" advisedly. In contrast with the performances in Brooklyn and Harlem discussed by Patrick Pacheo in the *National Theatre Magazine* (1988), the audience in Edinburgh 2010 was clearly not regarded as a "congregation." The performers connected with the audience by waving as they entered (performance documented, Monday August 23, 2010, 2.30 p.m.). This promised a closer relationship to come and compensated for the fairly slow start in which the music was subservient to the impact of the Messenger/Preacher's announcement that his text would be from "the Book of Oedipus" (which prompted delighted laughter from the audience). The limitations of the proscenium arch theater as a performance space contrasted with the scaffolding that had allowed to the congregation to sit on three sides in the 1985 performance at the American Music Theatre Festival in Philadelphia.[13] The effects of the playing space in Edinburgh meant that staging had to be a more self-conscious process. The ushers used the blind Oedipus' white stick to prod the singers into their places on the stage, recalling the rod-bearers who kept order in ancient Greek theater (see the *scholion* at Aristophanes *Peace* 724). Direct address was used, not just in the Messenger/Preacher's welcome and invocations but also in comments on the performance ("shall I go for this note?") and in the way in which the references to specific lines in Sophocles' text were directed outward to the audience. The visual impact of the costumes was intended to be stunning (and was), especially the brightly colored African robes and head-dresses worn by female singers. Equally striking was the architecture of the set, which set the arches and columns of the palace at Thebes as a backdrop to the steps that spread across the whole stage and provided places for the singers and the stage congregation that were visually accessible to the audience and yet enabled a stream of movement and color as the smaller musical groups came and went.

The lighting and sound design, especially in the storm scene, fulfilled the claims for the "spectacular" impact made by the publicity. A new feature (so far as I have been able to ascertain) was the multimedia design in which graphics projected onto the buildings showed the dead Oedipus and the falling figures of Jack and Jill in the vicissitudes of the storm. Other than showing a "nursery-rhyme" projection of the effects of a fall, it was hard to see what this somewhat pantomime effect added to the production. Because of the stepped stage there was a contrast between the musical physicality of the large singing groups and the somewhat contrived movement when the smaller groups were in place; at one point the blue-suited guitarists even seemed to be replicating the stereotypical gestures that older members of the audience might have remembered from the Black and White Minstrel Show, a popular TV program in Britain in the 1960s in which white performers "blacked up," played banjos, and sang songs associated with the deep south of America.[14] Since the Edinburgh International Festival audiences are usually drawn from many different countries, including the U.S.A., it is impossible to tell how many made that connection or what construction they placed on it.

The performance that I attended was rapturously received by many but a noticeable number remained firmly sitting in their seats during the standing ovation at the end. The most positive response that I had in discussions with fellow theater-goers was from music aficionados. As the Festival Newssheet put it in a top rating 4* review (September 2010):

> *Gospel at Colonus* juxtaposes Greek classical theater and black American religious music and those highbrow allusions may have offered it a place on the official festival programme. But forget Greece, abandon your intellect. With a cast including the Blind Boys of Alabama, the legendary Soul Stirrers and the Steeles, it's an inspirational celebration. Yes, there's a bit of theatrical jiggery-pokery, and it's surprising and a little worrying, to see frail leader of the blind Boys, Jimmy Carter, leaving the stage strapped to a piano, but this is all about the music.

An emphasis on spectacle and the exotic as well as music was evident in the responses of theater critics. For example Susanna Clapp in the *Observer Review* commented that "Oedipus jumps, Antigone swings and the chorus wear turbans so saffronly, crimsonly gorgeous that you begin to wonder why anyone bothers with hair" (Clapp 2010: 32–3). She judged that "This is probably the most popular theatrical event of the festival—with the 3,000-seater Playhouse packed to the gills even on a sleepy matinee. The swaying, shoulder-rolling, tambourine-shaking chorus doesn't quite get the audience into the aisles—it remains, just about, not a concert but a drama" (Clapp 2010: 32–3). For Clapp, as for many spectators, the ritual and congregational ambience had been lost in the translocation to a multimedia theatrical space. However, Clapp did experience a sense of disjunction: "The idea is that the story of 'evil Oedipus,' followed on his last day on Earth, can be taken as a text at a Pentecostal meeting, and rendered as a tale of Christian redemption. But that is to sugar over Sophocles, in whom rage and resignation are more present that the hope of reward" (Clapp 2010: 32–3). Clapp's emphasis suggests that awareness of Breuer's manipulative double consciousness in embedding the communal experiences of oppression and slavery (see McConnell, this volume) was lost somewhere during the migration of the work to Edinburgh. Broadway spectacle had taken over from Brooklyn rawness and the interwoven strands of African-American history had been further eroded in the Edinburgh desire for a production that could be marketed as exotic. Even the exotic can, however, be mocked in the parochialism of a blinkered interpretative community—one of Clapp's jibes was that "Sophocles' cast has undergone a sea change in the vowels of the American south. Our hero is Edda Puss. His mother becomes a little-known relative of a former *Observer* editor, Joke Astor." Clapp's comparative framework, and probably that of most of the audience if they had one at all, was taken as Sophocles/Breuer and no attempt was made to extend to comparison between the cultural and political subtlety of Breuer's concept as staged in its early performance history in the U.S.A. and its dilution and refocusing in the performance created for Edinburgh audiences.

What then might be the most illuminating points of comparison to be made about the three productions that crossed the Atlantic? Two closely related aspects seem to me to be crucial. The first is the smoothing out of the jagged experiences that are part of the interaction between performance and cultural memory. Both *Cure* and *Gospel* were generated by the rawness of oppression and suffering. Both saw those aspects progressively eroded by distance, both chronological (in terms of the length of performance history) and spatial (in terms of performance locations). Both these aspects intensify issues of cultural distance. Cultural distance between ancient and modern was complicated by the differences in cultural provenance and expectations in the audiences on either side of the Atlantic (even allowing that in both cases there would be an international diversity). This marked a repression of experiences that were not easily assimilated into the consciousness of international audiences and involved at least a partial sanitization of suffering. Both perhaps also marked a desire to move toward a new conception of societies, Irish and American. In contrast, Tony Harrison's resistance to blandness (within a much shorter chronological span of performance history that preserved the urgency for audiences of the "present" impact in his work) provided an example of the "auteur writing back."

The second aspect of comparison is partly derived from the first and concerns the nature and direction of the catharsis/resolution focus. This is again shared by *Cure* and *Gospel*, both of which are religious works, the second more overtly so. Although all three productions started as radical and "edgy," Harrison's *Hecuba* has a different tone (Fig. 51.3). Here, the driving vision of the modern writer was secular (and the timescale for assessment of the impact of the production is much shorter). Harrison was raging against "denial," not just of the effects of war but also of the deficiencies in the workings of the democracies that instigated or colluded with it. His audiences, on both sides of the Atlantic, had been very recently immersed in the public controversies that accompanied the U.S./U.K.-led invasion of Iraq. There was an immediate and shared basis of public

FIG. 51.3 Vanessa Redgrave as Hecuba in Tony Harrison's *Hecuba* at BAM, New York (2005), with stage design by Es Devlin. Photograph reproduced with kind permission of Es Devlin.

experience and contextual understanding. Perhaps that is one reason why Harrison felt that he could and should be more aggressive in order to provoke further response.

In contrast, the performative dynamics in both *Cure* and *Gospel* had a religious tone—strong in *Gospel*, but nevertheless present in Heaney's language of healing and resolution in *Cure*. Both were rooted in suffering and violence but in some ways aimed to transcend the traumatic histories that had generated them. This process was complicated by the conditions of the travelling revivals, which had to appeal to audiences who had not directly experienced the visceral pain of the contexts from which they arose. Both had to aim at a transformative effect on their audience's understanding; to enrol the audiences in the "post-memory" community. The migrations of both *Cure* and *Gospel* offer insights into the aesthetic implications and the interpretative variations that occur when actual or imagined audiences are less attuned to the cultural histories and nuances of "imported" productions. The prospect of resolution, whether in the rhyming of "hope and history" in *Cure* or in the singing of "Now Let the Weeping Cease" (the Closing Hymn in *Gospel*), is problematic. It can be interpreted (and exploited) as a means of smoothing over the pain of vicious oppression and struggle, of reimagining the cultural memory and repressing historical energies. It can be appropriated as part of a drive toward the creation of a "feel good" factor in a troubled society. Or it can be seen as a basis for "moving-on," of emancipation from the constraints of victimhood and the gateway to development of an autonomous future, artistically and politically.[15] Heaney's impatience with the Irish Troubles *topos* can be seen as an aspect of this.

Trends in the global adaptation and performance of Greek tragedy are already shedding a good deal of light on this "past slavery" and "past colonial" watershed, which is closely linked with the role of the construction and transmission of post-memory. *Cure* and *Gospel* in their different ways provide insights into what can happen when a work generated by a sense of political urgency is "exported" and the initial energy and hermeneutic framework of the spectating communities transformed. They provide a window into the successive and multiple refractions involved in re-performance across temporal and spatial boundaries. The challenges to the original jaggedness and urgency of both works also enable a nuanced focus on some of the claims that have been made about globalization of culture. For example, Irene De Jong has written that the association of the "spatial turn" with globalization has accentuated the significance of locations (De Jong 2012: 2). In the case of the performances discussed here, analysis shows that the accentuation was on the location to which the work was transferred, rather than on the one in which it was created. There may well be other examples, especially in the case of iconic productions such as *Gospel*. For example, *The Island* was a radical work of protest in its initial performances in apartheid South Africa but its metamorphosis over time into a staple of the international stage complicated the transformative function of interventionist drama.

The migration of productions in both directions across the Atlantic provides a microcosm of global traffic and suggests some ways of approaching larger questions about whether and in what respects long-lived iconic modern productions can still offer their extensive audiences an experience that is "good to think with" and even transformative. Ngũgĩ wa Thiong'o has expressed this global potential aspirationally as:

> Reading globalectically is a way of approaching any text from whatever times and places to allow its content and themes to form a free conversation with other texts of one's time and place, the better to make it yield its maximum to the human. It is to allow it to speak to our own cultural present even as we speak to it from our own cultural present. It is to read a text with the eyes of the world; it is to see the world with the eyes of the text. (Ngũgĩ 2012: 60)

Reading performance globalectically is complicated because no two performances are the same, even if they are part of the same production sequence (Fischer-Lichte 2010). Productions that travel encounter a new set of circumstances, not the least of which is the positioning of the successive audiences, both to one another and to the communities represented through and in the performance. Ngũgĩ saw the hierarchies of language as an impediment to globalectics because of the way they carry markers of power and prestige (Ngũgĩ 2012: 61). The examples analyzed in this discussion suggest that temporalities and spaces of experience and the construction of memory are equally important in allowing, shaping, and redirecting audience response; furthermore, commercial and artistic power and prestige are certainly not absent. The Harrison example was the least complicated, partly because it had the smallest time-lag between première and revival and partly because it was directed at audiences with a high degree of commonality in their experiences and attitudes. It did, however, raise crucial questions about the complacency of liberal audiences and their possible denial of the most radical elements of Euripides' treatment of democracy. The Heaney play *The Cure at Troy* occupied a midway point between this position and that of *The Gospel at Colonus* and provides a window into different possible interpretations of the changes that were involved. The test for *Gospel* lies still in the future—whether its translocation to an international festival marks a contribution to what Ngũgĩ (following Auerbach's assertion that "our philological home is the earth") characterizes as "a global consciousness of our common humanity" (Ngũgĩ 2012: 61). In his meditation on the situation of poets in Russia and Eastern Europe, Seamus Heaney used the metaphor of "amphibious survival" to describe the tension between the pull of "the time" and that of the creative moral and artistic self-respect of the writer (Heaney 1988). The image resonates with the crossings of the Atlantic that I have discussed, but it demands extension from its poetic context to include the role of the spectators, theater practitioners, and sponsors. Intrinsic to their moral and artistic status is their awareness that the pull of their own "time," temporally and spatially, is only one strand in the dynamics between the histories and the presentness of performance.[16]

Notes

1. For detailed discussion, see Hardwick 2007a.
2. Deane 1991; for a brief account of Field Day, see Welch 1996 ad loc., and for extended treatment, Richtarik 1995.
3. Interview with Lorna Hardwick (September 2007).

4. Interview with Lorna Hardwick (September 2007).
5. Interview with Lorna Hardwick (September 2007).
6. Quoted in Wilmer 1999: 224.
7. Mentioned in Wilmer 1999: 225, unreferenced.
8. For example in civil war as in ancient Rome, see Walde 2011; Holst-Warhaft 2011; and, in holocaust literature, see Kuhiwczak 2011. For "Memory Beyond Historiography," see Grethlein 2010: 1–5.
9. Heaney in O'Driscoll 2008: 421; 382.
10. Broadcast interview on BBC2 *Newsnight Scotland* (Wednesday August 25, 2010, 11 p.m.).
11. *The Culture Show*, BBC2 (Thursday August 26, 7 p.m.).
12. See also Golder 1996.
13. See the video from the "Great Performances Series," Educational Broadcasting Centre, 1985.
14. On minstrelsy and "black face" in the U.S. context of the nineteenth and twentieth centuries, see Rankine 2013: 9, with bibliography on self-parody as a response to stereotypes and pseudo-scientific racist literature; also Rankine, this volume.
15. On these debates in postcolonial contexts, see further Ramazani 1997; Hardwick 2002, 2007b.
16. Special thanks to Carol Gillespie (Project Officer at the Reception of Classical Texts research project at the Open University) and Naomi Setchell (Archivist at the Archive of Performances of Greek and Roman Drama, Oxford) for their help in researching material for this essay. An earlier version of this chapter was presented at the Classics seminar at the University of Nottingham and I thank the participants for their comments and questions. I am also very grateful to Justine McConnell for her comments and editorial guidance.

REFERENCES

Assmann, A. (2006), "Memory, Individual and Collective," in R. E. Goody and C. Tilly eds., *The Oxford Handbook of Contextual Political Analysis*. Oxford, 210–24.
Breuer, L. (1989), *The Gospel at Colonus*. New York.
Clapp, S. (2010), "Review of *Gospel at Colonus*," *Observer Review* (August 29), 32–3.
Deane, S. (ed. 1991), *The Field Day Anthology of Irish Writing*. Introd. by S. Deane. Derry.
De Jong, I. (ed. 2012), *Space in Ancient Greek Literature: Studies in Ancient Greek Narrative*. Introduced by I. De Jong. Leiden and Boston.
Denard, H. (2000), "Seamus Heaney, Colonialism and the Cure," *PAJ: A Journal of Performance and Art* 22.3, 1–18.
Easterling, P. and E. Hall (eds. 2002), *Greek and Roman Actors: Aspects of an Ancient Profession*. Cambridge.
Fischer-Lichte, E. (2010), "Performance as Event—Reception as Transformation," in E. Hall and S. Harrop eds., *Theorising Performance: Greek Drama, Cultural History and Critical Practice*. London, 29–42.
Fitzgerald, G. (2010), *Just Garret: Tales from the Political Frontline*. Dublin.
Foster, R. F. (2014), *Vivid Faces: The Revolutionary Generation in Ireland 1890–1923*. London.
Goff, B. and M. Simpson (2007), *Crossroads in the Black Aegean*. Oxford.
Golder, H. (1996), 'Geek Tragedy? Why I'd rather go to the Movies', *Arion*, 3rd series 4.1, 174–209.
Grethlein, J. (2010), *The Greeks and their Past: Poetry, Oratory and History in the Fifth Century BCE*. Cambridge.

Hall, E. (2011), "Antigone and the Internationalisation of Theatre in Antiquity," in E. Mee and H. Foley eds., *Antigone on the Contemporary World Stage.* Oxford, 51–63.

Hall, E. and S. Harrop (eds. 2010), *Theorising Performance: Greek Drama, Cultural History and Critical Practice.* London.

Hall, E. and R. Wyles (eds. 2008), *New Directions in Ancient Pantomime.* Oxford.

Hardwick, L. (2000), *Translating Words, Translating Cultures.* London.

Hardwick, L. (2002), "Classical Texts in Post-Colonial Literatures: Consolation, Redress and New Beginnings in the Work of Derek Walcott and Seamus Heaney," *International Journal of the Classical Tradition* 9.2, 236–56.

Hardwick, L. (2003), *New Surveys in the Classics: Reception Studies.* Oxford.

Hardwick, L. (2006), "Remodelling Receptions: Greek Drama as Diaspora in Performance," in C. Martindale and R. Thomas eds., *Classics and the Uses of Reception.* Oxford, 204–15.

Hardwick, L. (2007a), "Decolonising the Mind? Controversial Productions of Greek Drama in Post-Colonial England, Scotland and Ireland," in C. A. Stray ed., *Remaking the Classics: Literature, Genre and Media in Britain 1800–2000.* London, 89–105.

Hardwick, L. (2007b), "Postcolonial Studies," in C. Kallendorf ed., *A Companion to the Classical Tradition.* Oxford, 312–27.

Hardwick, L. (2011), "Fuzzy Connections: Classical Texts and Modern Poetry in English," in J. Parker and T. Mathews eds., *Translation, Trauma and Tradition.* Oxford, 39–60.

Hardwick, L. (2013), "The Problem of the Spectators, Ancient and Modern," in A. Bakogianni ed., *Dialogues with the Past 1: Classical Reception Theory and Practice*, BICS Suppl. 126.1, London, 11–26.

Harrison, T. (2005), *Hecuba by Euripides.* London.

Heaney, S. (1975), *North.* London.

Heaney, S. (1988), *The Government of the Tongue: The 1986 T. S. Eliot Memorial Lectures and Other Critical Writings.* London and New York.

Heaney, S. (1990), *The Cure at Troy: A Version of Sophocles' Philoctetes.* London.

Heaney, S. (1995), *The Redress of Poetry: Oxford Lectures.* London.

Heaney, S. (1998), *Opened Ground: Poems 1966–1996.* London.

Heaney, S. (2002a), "The Cure at Troy: Production Notes in No Particular Order," in M. McDonald and J. M. Walton eds., *Amid our Troubles: Irish Versions of Greek Tragedy.* London, 171–80.

Heaney, S. (2002b), *Finders Keepers: Selected Prose 1971–2001.* London.

Heaney, S. (2002c), "The Placeless Heaven: Another Look at Kavanagh," Opening Address, Kavanagh's Yearly, Carrickmacross, November 1985, in S. Heaney ed., *Finders Keepers: Selected Prose 1971–2001.* London, 134–44.

Heaney, S. (2010), *Human Chain.* London.

Holst-Warhaft, G. (2011), "No Consolation: The Lamenting Voice and Public Memory," in J. Parker and T. Mathews eds., *Translation, Trauma and Tradition.* Part III: *The Time of Memory, the Time of Trauma.* Oxford, 211–28.

Howe, S. (2000), *Ireland and Empire: Colonial Histories in Irish History and Culture.* Oxford.

Isherwood, C. (2005), "Review of Hecuba at BAM," *New York Times* (June 20).

Kuhiwczak, P. (2011), "Mediating Trauma: How do we Read the Holocaust Memoirs?," in J. Parker and T. Mathews eds., *Translation, Trauma and Tradition.* Oxford, 283–98.

Lawson, M. (2005), "Review of *Hecuba* at the Albery Theatre," *The Tablet* (April 16).

Lyons, F. S. L. (1971), *Ireland Since the Famine.* London.

McDonald, M. and J. M. Walton (eds. 2002), *Amid our Troubles: Irish Versions of Greek Tragedy.* London.

Meir, C. (1991), "Irish Poetic Drama: Seamus Heaney's The Cure at Troy," in J. Genet and E. Hellegouarc'h eds., *Studies on the Contemporary Irish Theatre*. Caen, 67–8.

Ngũgĩ wa Thiong'o (2012), *Globalectics: Theory and the Politics of Knowing* (The Welleck Library Lectures in Critical Theory). New York.

O'Driscoll, D. (2008), *Stepping Stones: Interviews with Seamus Heaney*. London.

Ramazani, J. (1997), "The Wound of History: Walcott's *Omeros* and the Post-Colonial Poetics of Afflication," *Publications of the Modern Literature Association* 112.3, 405–15.

Rankine, P. D. (2013), *Aristotle and Black Drama: A Theater of Civil Disobedience*. Waco, TX.

Rehm, R. (2005), *Radical Theatre*. London.

Richtarik, M. (1995), *Between the Lines*. Oxford.

Stafford, F. (2010), *Local Attachments: The Province of Poetry*. Oxford.

Stanford, W. B. (1984), *Ireland and the Classical Tradition*. Dublin. (Revised edition, first published 1976.)

Walde, C. (2011), "Lucan's Bellum Civile: A Specimen of a Roman 'Literature of Trauma,'" in P. Asso ed., *Brill's Companion to Lucan*. Leiden and Boston, 283–302.

Welch, R. (1996), *The Oxford Companion to Irish Literature*. Oxford.

Wilmer, S. E. (1999), "Seamus Heaney and the Tragedy of Stasis," in S. Patsalidis and E. Sakellaridou eds., *(Dis)Placing Classical Greek Theatre*. Thessaloniki.

Index

Note: Page numbers in italics refer to illustrations; those followed by 'n' to information in a note. Works appear in the author's entry.

Aannestad, Elling 274, 279
abolitionist movement 63, 65, 85
aboriginal people *see* indigenous people and cultures
Abrams, Abiola: *Goddess City* (with Grant) 685
Achebe, Chinua 483
Acocella, Joan 247
Acosta, Mercedes de 237
activist movements and internal oppression 516–17
actors and acting
  opportunities for African-American artists 595–6, 597, 602
  see also actresses; casting issues
actresses
  black actresses and essentialist notions of race 601–2
  Canadian actresses and need to move to New York 193–4
  and Canadian post-WWI university drama 189–91, 196–9
  Medea as female part viii–ix, *viii–ix*
    actresses in nineteenth-century Philadelphia 58–60, 65
    interpretations of Heron and Ristori 119–25
    reception in Mexico 256–8
  in nineteenth century
    Antigone in New York 70–1
    Heron and Ristori as Medea 119–25
    Medea in Philadelphia 58–60, 65
    and Phaedra in Howe's *Hippolytus* 85, 87, 89, 90, 91, 93
    rival Cleopatras in New York 126, 127–8
  see also Cushman; female characters; Ristori

adaptations of Greek drama
  "Black Dionysus" and African-American adaptations 39, 546, 608n.31
  Canadian women poets as translators and adaptors 672–3
  challenges of Menander's work 303–4
  Chavez's *Señora de la pinta* and constraints of original story 690–2, 694
  in Cuba
    Piñera's *Electra Garrigó* 335, 336–7, 339, 361–74
    Triana's *Medea in the Mirror* 334–6, 339–50, 401
  Cullen's version of *Medea* 685, 686–90, 694, 695
  doubling and repetition in Colombian Antigones 556–71
  Dove's retelling of Oedipus in slavery context 502–11, *507*, *510*
  in Latin America 333, 400–2
  MacLeish's 1960s *Herakles* 457–63, 468, 469
  Mee on interest in Greek subject matter 731–5
  musical theater adaptations of Aristophanic comedy 301–26
  in nineteenth century
    Chicago theaters 98
    in Mexican theaters 253, 254, 262
    for moral acceptability 135
    New York theaters 71–2
    Philadelphia theaters 56–61, 79
  Oedipus Tyrannus in Latin America 611–25
  postcolonial context 497
  psychoanalysis and Electra adaptations 366
  Rudall on distinction between adaptation and translation 765

Addams, Jane 97–8, 103, 281
Aeschylus viii, 56, 264
  Edith Hamilton's writing on and
      translations of 273–4, 275–6, 280
  military background 655, 665
  Oresteia trilogy x–xi
    Edith Hamilton's translation of
        Agamemnon 274, 276, 278, 279
    Rehm and Australian production
        (1974) 748–9
    Rudall's *Agamemnon* 767
    Stein's production in Berlin 742–3
  The Persians 143, 214–15, 215, 743
    Rehm's production 753–4
    Sellars's production 635, 651, 753,
        782–4, 785
    West Coast productions 635–6, 651
  Prometheus Bound (attrib.)
    Carson's "Quicktime Prometheus" 703–7
    Hamilton's translation 271, 274, 276–7
    production at Delphi 204–5, 209–12, 213,
        275, 275, 277–8
  The Seven against Thebes
    and Arrufat's adaption in Cuba 434–51
    as hip hop mashup in Power's *The
        Seven* 544, 546, 547–8, 549–52, 553
  The Suppliant Women 208–9, 210
aesthetic sensibilities of Athenians 258
aesthetic theater 653
Afghanistan *see* Iraq War (2003–11)
Africa
  and origins of Greek drama 39, 502, 545–6,
      599–601, 774
  races and racial theories 113, 114, 115, 297
  women's activism against war 585–6,
      587–8, 589
African Americans
  adaptations of *Lysistrata* 286–99
  African heritage in Dove's *The Darker Face
      of the Earth* 507–8
  archival material on stage productions 6
  archive of American life 26–7
  archive of Negro life 17, 20
  and Breuer's *The Gospel at Colonus* 476,
      480, 482, 483, 484, 485–6, 602,
      769, 832
  cast of Papp's *Electra* (1969) x

classical tradition and western
    hegemony 495, 502, 595
and Greek drama in twenty-first
    century xi, 545–6, 773–4
  Harlem productions of
      Euripides 595–609
as omni-Americans 14, 769
and postcolonial experience and theory 31,
    34, 35–6
classical tradition and reception of Greek
    drama 36–40, 495–6, 502, 595–7
identity politics and black
    theater 498–502
representing race on the American
    stage 485
"subterranean" presence of Classics 11
Wilson's *Radio Golf* 528–39
see also blackface theater; Frogs society;
    racial issues and discrimination;
    slavery
Afro-Brazilian culture
  "Baiana" women in 412, 413
  Black Experimental Theater 403–4
  candomblé religion 384, 386–7, 405
  capoeira 391–2, 398
Afro-Cubans
  place in Castro's Cuba 349
  racial protocols for marriage 346–7
  religious beliefs and ritual 344–5, 370
  visibility in Triana's *Medea* 350, 401
Afrocentric Classicism movement 554n.8
Ahmed, Samira 585, 586, 589
Ailey, Alvin 247
Akalaitis, JoAnne 733
  production of *Iphigenia Cycle* 767, 768
  production of *Trojan Women* 768–9
Alape, Arturo 556
Albee, Edward 229
Albright, A. Cooper 217n.6, 237
Aldington, Richard 152
Aldrich, Thomas Bailey 142
Aldridge, Ira 286
Alfaro, Luis
  Bruja 643, 644
  Electricidad 642–3
  Oedipus el rey 496, 643
Alfieri, Vittorio: *Oreste* 253, 255

Allan, Maud 142, 234
Allen, Scott Joseph 413–14
Allen, T. W. 8
Allende, Isabel 716
Altamirano, Ignacio Manuel 253, 256–8, 263
American Classicism
   and blackface minstrelsy 526
   and Breuer's *The Gospel at Colonus* 474–92, 602, 769
American Conservatory Theater, San Francisco 629–30, 636–7, 739
"American exceptionalism" 31, 33, 36, 495–6, 647
American West and national identity 628
Americanization of Greek tragedy and Edith Hamilton 272, 274, 275–6, 279–80
amphitheater stage 214–15
ancient Egypt 53
   see also Cleopatra
ancient Greece
   culture and civilization 113, 115, 116–17
      absence of Greek drama on nineteenth-century stage 133–6, 144
      adoption in America 134
      attitudes in nineteenth-century America 22, 133, 134
   see also dance: modern dance and recreation of Greek poses and dance; Greek language and productions
Ancient Greeks/Modern Lives program
   Homecoming: The Return of the Warrior project 652, 654–67
ancient Rome
   America's identification with 23, 53, 112
   and feminine resistance to slavery 63, 65
   in nineteenth-century theater 133, 136–41
   see also Latin
ancient world and nineteenth-century American theater 133–44
Anderson, Benedict 27
Anderson, Ellen: *Liz Estrada* 577, 579–81, 582, 589
Anderson, Judith ix
Andino Moscoso, Peky: *Edipo y su señora mamacita* 618–19
Andrade, Jorge: *Pedreira das Almas* 375n.8, 402

Andrade, Mário de 719
Andreas, James R., Sr. 545
Angel, Marina 160
Angel Island, San Francisco: *Odyssey* production 641, *641*
Anglin, Margaret *viii*, ix, 192, 194
   as Phaedra in Howe's *Hippolytus* 85, *86*, *87*, 93
Anouilh, Jean 341
Anrup, Ronald 559
anti-war message of Greek drama vii–viii, x, xi, 97, 167, 316–17, 747
   critics and "tragedy fatigue" 820–1
   Harrison's *Hecuba* 821, 835–6
   Kott's 1960s *Orestes* 635
   Lysistrata Project and political activism 575–93, 651
   and "Make Love Not War" slogan 581, 582–4, *585*, 589
   women's activism and media sex strikes 584–6, 588, 589
Antoine, Chief Duane 675, 679n.18
Apollo Belvedere and racial theory 113, *114*
Après-midi d'un faune, L' (ballet) 240–2, *241*, 245
Aquila Theatre company 652, 656, 661, 662
   see also Ancient Greeks/Modern Lives program
Arch Street Theatre, Philadelphia 54, 55, 62, 79
archaeology
   Greek architecture and modern dance 207–8
   and Modernist view of "the classical" 527
   and revelations of recreated dance 204–5, 216
architecture
   neoclassical architecture 34, 55, 134
   Philadelphia theaters 54–5
"archival turn" in scholarship 26
Archive of Performances of Greek and Roman Drama (APGRD), Oxford 6, 28n.3
archives on Greek drama and performance in Americas 6–7, 17–28
   belated appearance and reasons for 20, 26–7
   Frogs society archive on Negro life 17–18, 26

archives on Greek drama and performance in Americas *(Cont.)*
    limited literature on 18–19
    on *Peace* musical 313–14
    theory and meaning of archives 19–20
Ardura, Ernesto 371
Argentina 375n.8
    Border Studies and Cureses' *La frontera* 417–32
    Levy-Daniel's *Yocasta* 612–13, 726–30
    Oedipus Tyrannus films and musicals 613–17
    political readings of *Antigone* 400–1
Aristophanes 56
    Acharnians production (1886) 302
    Assemblywomen 158
    Birds 302, 303
        Culture Clash's West Coast production 642
    Ecclesiazusae 303
    The Frogs 17–18, 134, 302, 303, 744
    Lysistrata x, 158, 160
        African-American adaptations 287, 289–98
        The Happiest Girl in the World musical version 302, 304, 309–12, 315, 318, 319
        Lysistrata Project and political activism 575–93, 651
        Moscow Art Theatre musical adaptation 302, 303, 304–9, 312, 318, 319
        productions in north America 302–3
    masks in plays 526
    musical versions of comedies 301–26
    Peace as musical 302, 312–19, 317
    Thesmophoriazusae 303
Aristotle 227–8, 496, 657, 700, 737
    Poetics 13
        on catharsis 486, 490
        opsis and Wilson's *Radio Golf* 528–31, 533–4, 538–9
Ariza, Patricia: *Antígona* 556–8, 559, 560, 563–71, 564, 567
Arnold, Matthew 71
Arrowsmith, William 464
Arrufat, Antón 362, 375n.5
    "Girón Beach (Bay of Pigs)" (poem) 444–5
    "The Men" (poem) 434
    ostracism in Cuba and rehabilitation 434–6
    Seven against Thebes (Los siete contra Tebas) 434–51
        premiere in Cuba (2007) and changes 436, 446–7
Artists Repertory, Portland 634
Arts and Letters Club (Toronto) 191, 193, 194
Ashby Stage, Berkeley 638, 639
Ashcroft, B. 33, 475, 497
Asian productions in California 633–4
Asquith, Herbert 178n.3
Athenian playwrights
    absence from nineteenth-century stage 133–4, 135
    comparison with *Ben-Hur* 140
Athenian Touch, The (musical) 303
Athens
    aesthetic sensibilities of citizens 258
    Edith Hamilton as honorary citizen 271–2, 282
Atkinson, B. 320n.18
atomic war and MacLeish's *Herakles* 461–2, 463
Atwood, Margaret: *Penelopiad* (novella) 673
audiences
    aesthetics of Theater of War readings 660–1
    for African-American classical performance 598, 602
    ballet and sexual dissidence 240, 240–1, 244, 248
    Breuer's *The Gospel at Colonus*
        and catharsis 486–7, 490
        in Edinburgh 831–5, 836
        and hybridity 479–80
    for British and American performances 819–38
    changes in behavior in nineteenth century 105–6
    and chorus 490, 738–9, 742–3
    decline in numbers in recent history 630
    efforts to attract women 101–2
    gay audience and Celebration Theater's *The Bacchae* 470
    and hip hop and Power's *The Seven* 545, 547–9, 553
    Irish-American audiences and Heaney's *The Cure at Troy* 827–9, 834–5, 836

and knowledge of Classics 548, 693–4
moral sensibilities and absence of Greek
  drama 135–6, 144
participation
  Alfaro's *Bruja* 643
  involvement in outdoor performances of
    Electra 738–9, 742
  Performance Group's *Dionysus in 69* and
    re-enactment 464, 801, 803–6
  public venues and engagement with
    military personnel 652, 655–6, 662–7
  social theater and public
    engagement 653–4, 658–9, 662–7
  Women and War Project
    questionnaires 795–6
  racial stereotypes and expectations 286,
    292, 532–3, 536, 550–1, 598, 606
  reaction to homosexual kiss in *Dionysus in
    69* 466–7
  soldiers in ancient and modern
    contexts 655, 656, 665
  see also classical performance reception
Auletta, Robert: *The Persians* adaptation 635,
  651, 784
Auric, Georges 322n.45
Aurora Theatre, Berkeley 636
Aztec history and Mexican national
  tragedy 263–5

Babylonian empire in American
  theater 133, 143–4
Badeau, Adam 122
"Baiana" women in Afro-Brazilian
  culture 412, *413*
Baibussynova, Ulzhan 787
Baker, Houston 500
Bakst, Léon 240
Balanchine, George 234
  Apollon Musagète/Apollo 242–4, *243*, 247
ballet
  Duncan's rejection of 235
  male dancer and sexual dissidence 239–42,
    242–3, 247–8
Ballets Russes 239, 240, 242, 243, 244
Balme, Christopher 480
Bandeira, Manuel: *Tragédia Brasileira*
  (poem) 716

Banim, John: *Damon and Pythias* (with
  Sheil) 55, 98, 106, 107, 108, 136–7
Banks, Daniel 683–98
Baraka, Amiri 499
Baralt, Alejandro 338
Barbara and Lawrence Fleischman
  Theater, Getty Villa Museum, Los
  Angeles 630–2, *631*, 701, 738–9
barbarians
  barbarian women and attitudes to
    antiquity 112–30
    Barker's production of *Iphigenia in
      Tauris* 167, 169
    Medea as barbarian Other 342, 403, 408,
      411, 521
    sculptures of Medea and
      Cleopatra 116–19
  clash of civilizations in Cureses' *La
    frontera* 417–32
Barber, Jesse 676
Barker, Harley Granville vii, 166–76, 184,
  191, 192
Barney, Natalie 237
Barnum, P. T. 143
Barquet, J. J. 445
Barreto, Bruno 717–18
Barrett, Wilson: *The Sign of the
  Cross* 139, 140
Barrows, Mabel Hay 192
Bartholomew, William: *Antigone*
  translation 70, 73, 75, 80
Barton, John *The Greeks* (with Kenneth
  Cavander) xi
Barton, Melissa 291
Bates, Herbert 154
Batista, General Fulgencio 335–6, 340–1, 349,
  367–8, 372–3
Bauer, R. 31
Bausch, Pina 234, 733
Bay of Pigs invasion 436, 437, 438–41, 444–5
Beam, Annamarie 532
Beard, George Miller 125
Beckett, Samuel 701, 732
Bel Geddes, Norman 322n.45
Bélanger, Stéphanie A. H. 792
Bell, James 63
Ben-Zvi, Linda 159

Bennett, Robert Russell 323n.55
Berkeley City Club 639
Berkeley Repertory Theatre 515, 630, 634, 823
Bernal, Martin 38, 39, 502, 546, 554n.8, 774
Bernhardt, Sarah 93, 126, 127, 128
Bernstein, Leonard 302
Bérubé, Alan 244
Beverly, Trezana 597, 600, 601–2
Bhabha, Homi 45, 479
Bharucha, Rustom 544
Biblical subjects in nineteenth-century theater 133, 141–3
Billington, Michael 496
Billotte, K. 573n.18
"Billy the Kid" (William Bonney) 141
Bird, Robert Montgomery *see* Montgomery Bird
Birth of a Nation (film) 137, 170, 176
Bischoff, Henry 21
Bishop, Elizabeth 717–18
Black Arts movement and racial politics 485, 499–502, 529, 595
"Black Athena" 39, 546, 608n.31, 774
Black Atlantic 8, 14, 605–6
"black body" and visibility of race 596–7, 601–2, 606
"Black Dionysus" 39, 546, 608n.31
Black Experimental Theater (TEN) 403–4
"Black Orpheus" 39, 546, 601, 608n.31
blackface theater
  African-American performance and Greek drama 525–8
  appropriation in Wilson's *Radio Golf* 528, 530–9
  and Breuer's *The Gospel at Colonus* in Edinburgh 833
  knowing use in *Peace* musical 313, 314, 315–16, 317–18, 324–5n.66
  and Modernism 526–7
  in nineteenth century 12, 62–3, 65, 77, 525, 526, 530–1
  stereotypes and portrayal of African Americans 286–7, 292, 525, 536
Blanc, Aldir 719
Blanco, Luis Amado 372
Blauner, R. 35

Blind Boys of Alabama 485–6, 489, 832, 834
Blondell, Ruby 346
Blume, Kathryn
  and Lysistrata Project 576, 577–8, 581
  The Accidental Activist 577, 586–8, 589
Boal, Augusto 13, 398, 496, 657, 658, 791
body
  "black body" and visibility of race 596–7, 601–2, 606
  female body and Lysistrata Project 588
  and modern dance 213
  and liberation of women 236
Boeckh, August 74
Bolus, Michael Peter 548
Bond Street Theatre for Social Development 791
Bonney, William ("Billy the Kid") 141
Booker, Margaret 533
Booth, Edwin 85, 87, 90–1
Boothenian Dramatic Society 57
Border Studies and Cureses' *La frontera* 417–32
border theory 46
Borges, Jorge Luis 623n.25
Bosnian conflict: Thompson's *Elektra in Bosnia* 792, 793, 794
Boucicault, Ruth Holt 93
Bourlos, Mr (Greek actor) 271, 277, 283n.9
Bower, Sharron and Lysistrata Project 576, 577–8, 581, 589
Bowers, Mrs. David P. (*née* Elizabeth Crocker) 58
Bowery Theatre, New York 73
  Oedipus in 1834 71–2, 134
Boyne, Mark 672
Bracho, Julio 262
Braham, Lionel 171–2
Brancato, Sabrina 553
Brazil 375n.8
  Antigone retellings
    Andrade's *Pedreira das Almas* 402
    Dias Gomes's *O pagador de promessas* 380–99
  Coelho's production of *Gota d'água—Breviário* and theater in 708–21, 715
  marginalization of education and culture 719–20

Olavo's *Além do Rio (Medea)* 402, 403–5, 408–15
   slave societies and syncretic religion 413–14
Brecht, Bertolt 714, 716, 717, 720, 740
Brene, José Ramón 435, 436
Brennan, T. 45
Breuer, Lee 781
   The Gospel at Colonus
      at Edinburgh Festival 830–5, 836, 837
      and new American Classicism 13, 474–92, 543, 602, 769
Briggs, Charles 25, 26
Briggs, Ward 34
Britain
   political parallels with ancient Rome 136, 137
   transfer of productions to Americas 71–2, 819–38
Britto, Valkyria 717
Brock, H. I. 309
Brooklyn Academy of Music 474, 579, 581, 830
Brough, Robert 72
Brower, Frank 531
Brown, James Francis 750
Brown, John Mason 273, 276, 279
Browne, Maurice 97–8, 103, 178n.8, 184
Browne, Theodore: *Lysistrata* 287, 289, 291–8, 293
Brownson, Orestes 25–6
Bryn Mawr School, Baltimore 272, 273
Buarque de Hollanda, Anna Maria (Ana de Holanda) 721
Buarque de Hollanda, Chico (Francisco)
   Breviário Calabar 710
   Gota d'água (with Pontes) 333, 402–3
      Coelho's *Breviário* version in Brazil 708–21, 715
   Ópera do Malandro 713
   popularity as musician 712
   Roda viva 710
Budelmann, F. 39
Buenaventura, Alejandro 612
bufo theater in Cuba 350, 361–2
Bugallo, Enrique 614
Bulfinch, Thomas: *Age of Fable* 60, 134
Bulwer-Lytton, Edward 137
Burdine, Warren 476

Burgess, Ernest W. 296
burial repression and displaced people in Colombia 558–60, 561
burlesques
   humorous adaptations of *Oedipus Tyrannus* in Latin America 611
   London *Medea* 125, 134
   in nineteenth-century America
      Antigone productions 72, 74, 77, 79
      English imports in Chicago 98–9
      in Philadelphia theaters 12, 61, 62
   see also blackface theater
Burnett, Anne Pippin 471n.13
Burnham, Agnes 189
Burt, A. L. 185, 199
Burt, Ramsay 239
Buschor, Ernst 204–5, 207, 209, 216
Bush, George H. W. 469–70
Butcher, S. H. 530
Butler, Judith 674
Butsch, Richard 105–6
Bynner, Witter 151
Byrd, Debra Ann 595–6, 597, 598, 601
Byzantine music and Greek chorus 208–9, 210, 212, 214, 282n.8

Cabaret (musical) 301
Cacoyannis, Michael 276, 303
Calame, Claude 224–5
Calderón, Fernando: *Ifigenia* 252, 257
Calderón de la Barca, Pedro 254, 255
California *see* West Coast productions
Callas, Maria 353n.32
Calvino, I. 7
camp aesthetic of *Peace* (musical) 312–13, 316
Campbell, Douglas x–xi, 3, 4, 671
Campbell, Wilfred 186
Canada
   American dominance of theater world 193–4
   Greek drama and women's and minorities' perspectives 671–9
   national identity and classical associations 185–6, 190, 198
   participation in World War I 184–5, 190
   postcoloniality 9

Canada *(Cont.)*
    university productions of Greek
        drama 186–200, 671–2
    see also Carson, Anne; Stratford, Ontario
Canadian National Arts Centre, Ottawa 303
Cândido, Antônio 720
candomblé religion in Brazil 384, 386–7, 405
canonical counter-discourse 38
Cantoría Ars Nova: *Edipo rey* 613, 614–15
capoeira chorus in Dias Gomes's *O pagador de
    promessas* 391–2, 398
Carballido, Emilio 266
Caribbean
    classical names and history of slavery 809
    literature of 809
    and postcolonial experience and
        discourse 8, 31, 35
        equivalence with European literary
            tradition 484
        and reception of Greek drama 40, 41–4
    writers and classical spirit 39
    see also Cuba; Walcott, Derek
Carmines, Al: *Peace* (with Reynolds) 302,
    312–19, *317*
Carpinetti, Mario 614
Carpinetti, Raúl 614
Carrillo, Fernão 414
Carson, Anne 463
    Antigonick 674, 701–2
    Cassandra Float Can (with Currie) 700–1
    "Quicktime Prometheus" 703–7
    translations 672, 673–4
    thoughts on 699–707
Carter, Stephen: *Pecong* 596
Case, Sue-Ellen 588
Casey, Edward 406
Castaño, Cesar: *Antígona incorporéa* 556
casting issues
    African-American cast for Papp's *Electra* x
    Banks's integrated cast at Williams
        College 690
    color-blind casting 484, 499, 529
    Sellars' non-traditional casting 782,
        787–788
    see also actors and acting; actresses
Castro, Fidel 343, 347–50, 362, 372, 373, 374,
    434, 435–6, 445

Castro, Raúl 437, 446
catharsis
    Breuer's *The Gospel at Colonus* 486–7,
        488, 490
    and soldiers' experiences 792
Cather, Willa 150, 163
    The Professor's House (novel) 153–7
Catholicism in Brazil 382–91, 410, 411
    slave societies and syncretic religion 414
Cavalli, Leona 710
Cavander, Kenneth: *The Greeks* (with John
    Barton) xi
Cayer, Jennifer 298n.5
Caymmi, Nana 719
Celebration Theater: *The Bacchae* 470
censorship 382
    and corruption in Brazil 713, 720
    Cree chief and Kasokeo's
        Antigone 674, 675
    in Cuba 446
    Marshall's work in Argentina 617
Centennial International Exhibition,
    Philadelphia (1876) 115–19
    "Centennial City" and "primitive"
        sideshows 115–16
Central Works: *Achilles and
    Patroklos* 639–40, *640*
Chamberlain, Kat 608n.22
Chanter, Tina 392
Chastain, Jessica 777, 779, 780
Chavero, Alfredo: *Quetzalcóatl* 263
Chavez, Law: *Señora de la pinta* 683, 685–6,
    690–7, 692
Chestnut Street Theatre, Philadelphia 53–4,
    54–5, 58, 59, 62
Chicago
    Court Theatre and Rudall's
        translations 764–72
    Federal Theatre Project Negro unit 292
    nineteenth-century Greek drama and
        adaptations 97–110
        Legouvé's *Medea* 98, 99–106
    Theater of War events and audience
        responses 664–5
Chicago Little Theatre 97, 106, 178n.8, 184
Chicano folklore and Chavez's *Señora de la
    pinta* 691–2

Chicano Movement and Moraga's *The Hungry Woman* 514-24
   El Plan Espiritual de Aztlán manifesto 514, 516, 517-18
Child, Lydia Maria 24
Chile: Galemiri's *Edipo asesor* 620-1
Choate, E. Teresa 18
chorus
   Africanist elements in Greek drama 599
   in Arrufat's *Seven against Thebes* 438, 440, 441, 443, 446
   and audience 490, 738-9, 742-3
   in Breuer's *The Gospel at Colonus* 489-90
   capoeira chorus in Dias Gomes's *O pagador de promessas* 391-2, 398
   in Classical Theater of Harlem's *Trojan Women* 603, 604
   Edith Hamilton on size of 275, 277-8
   Heaney's use of idiom in *The Cure at Troy* 824-6
   hip-hop chorus in Power's *The Seven* 550
   and Howe's *Hippolytus* 89-90
   limits on numbers in Getty Museum outdoor productions 632, 739
   in Mendelssohn's *Antigone* 72, 73, 75, 78-9, 89
   and modern dance
      Duncan's inspiration and interpretation 207, 208-9, 212, 235
      Palmer Sikelianos's productions 204-5, 210, 211, 214
   and Modernist poetry 152
   in Perloff's productions 738-9, 742
   in Piñera's Cuban *Electra Garrigó* 362, 366, 368, 372
   in Rehm's dramaturgy 749-50, 756-7, 759-60, 759
   in Toronto University productions 188, 196-7
choteo in Piñera's Cuban *Electra Garrigó* 362, 369-70
Christianity
   Border Studies and clash of civilizations in Cureses' *La frontera* 418, 420-1, 424-31
   and conflict with Romans in toga plays 139-41
   and gender inequality 25-6
   Pentecostalism in Breuer's *The Gospel at Colonus* 478, 479, 480-1, 485, 486, 487-90
   see also Catholicism in Brazil
CIA *see* Bay of Pigs invasion
City College stadium, New York 172-3
civil rights movement and West Coast 629
civilization
   and American identity 112, 125
      discovery of pre-Columbian civilizations 156-7
   on display at Centennial Exhibition (1876) 115-19
   pre-Columbian myth and Mexican tragedy 264
   and racial theory 113, 115, 297
Clapp, Susanna 834
Clarendon, Miss (actress) 73, 78, 80
Clark, Lygia 719
Clark, Michael 234, 247
Clark, William J. 118
Clarke, Jocelyn: *Trojan Women* adaptation 608n.27
Classic Greek Theatre of Oregon, Portland 637
"classical" drama: use of term 7
classical education
   and African-American students and scholars 22, 37, 63, 290-1, 502
   Dove's slave setting 505
   and Canadian identity 186
   of colonizers 9, 10, 605
   and cultural equality 37, 38, 502, 505
   Edith Hamilton's education 272-3
   and history of slavery 809
   marginalization of Latin American oeuvre 333-4
   in Mexico 258, 265
   Modernist move away from 149-50
   in nineteenth-century America
      absence of Greek drama in curriculum 134
      college students 56-7
      women 22-3, 60-1, 154
   and Perloff's love of ancient world 736-7

classical education *(Cont.)*
    see also school curriculum and Classics in Americas
classical performance reception 766
    academic study 6, 26
    African-American reception issues 36–40, 495–6, 502, 595
    and dance studies 233–4
    and ethics 694–5
    Lysistrata Project readings and contexts 576–7
    in nineteenth-century Philadelphia 53–67, 79
    and postcolonial theory 30–48
    see also audiences
Classical Theater of Harlem, The (CTH): *Trojan Women* production (2008) 595, 596–7, 602–6
Classics Drama Group, Trent University, Canada 671–2
Clay, Carolyn 787
Clements, Marie: *Age of Iron* 676–7
Cleopatra and attitudes to antiquity 112, 125–8
    sculpture at Centennial Exhibition (1876) 116, 117–19, *118*
Club Atenas, Havana 355n.61
Coburn Players 177–8n.2
Cocteau, Jean: Mexican *Antigone* 262
Coelho, Heron 708–25
    and theater-in-the-round *Gota d'água—Breviário* 708–21, 715
Coelho, Maria Cecília de Miranda Nogueira 402–3
Cohen, Nathan 199
Cohen, Ze'eva 756
Cohen-Cruz, Jan 662
Colakis, Marianthe 18, 19, 471n.9
Cole, Bob 17
Coliseo Nuevo, Mexico City 254
colleges *see* education; universities and colleges
Collins, Philip 645, 646
Colman, George, the Elder: *Medea and Jason* 57
Colombia
    Antigone and women in war-torn country 556–73
    productions of *Edipo rey* 612–13
colonialism
    Border Studies and Argentina 417–32
    classical education of colonizers 9, 10, 605
    and Classical Theater of Harlem's *Trojan Women* 605–6
    disparate histories in Americas 32–6
    dual position of United States 475–6, 495–6, 768
    experience of indigenous people in North America 32, 33, 35
    Homer's *The Odyssey* and colonial gaze 751
    "internal colonization" in the Americas 35–6, 45, 475, 495–6
    legacy of Spanish drama in Cuban theater 336–7, 339
    mediation of reception of Greek drama in Latin America 341–2, 350
    and Mexican reconfiguration of Greek drama 153
    neo-colonialism of United States 31, 46–7, 768
    and Breuer's American Classicism 475–6, 485–6
    and science in adaptations of Euripides 457, 458–62, 463, 469–70
    and "subterranean" presence of Classics 10
    see also postcolonialism; slavery
color-blind casting 484, 499, 529
comedy *see* humor
communitas and social theater 654, 657–8, 667
community
    British and Irish audiences for Heaney's *The Cure at Troy* 823, 824, 827–9
    community theater in Canada 671–2
    and independent theater in Chicago 97
    see also public venues and discussion; social theater
Condé, Valentina 760
Constructivism and Nemirovich-Danchenko's *Lysistrata* 305–6, *306*, 308, 318
Cook, George Cram "Jig" 150, 157–8, 221
    The Athenian Women (with Glaspell) 158–9, 163
Cook, W. 37, 39–40
Cooke, Richard P. 310

Coolidge, Calvin 149–50
Cooper, Bo 784–5
Cooper, Eldris: *The Tragedy of Medea Jackson* 543
Cooper, James Fenimore 129n.1
Corneille, Pierre 341
Coronil, Fernando 32–3
cosmic forces and Greek tragedy in Mexico 259
costume design
 and authentic Grecian dance 205
 Breuer's *The Gospel at Colonus* in Edinburgh 833
 color in Ariza's *Antígona* 567
 Duncan's Grecian tunic 207, 208, 213, 235–6
 Hoffman's costume for Salomé's dance 142
 Levy-Daniel's *Yocasta* 730
 Piñera's "Cubanizing" *Electra Garrigó* 368
 Rehm's *The Persians* 753–4
 timelessness of Harlem *Medea* 598–9, 599–600
 Wilkinson's work for Barker's *Iphigenia in Tauris* 168–9, 169–70, 171–2, 173–4, 177, 527
counterculture and Lysistrata Project 582–4
Court Theatre, Chicago and Rudall's translations 764–72
Craig, Edith 161
Cree Nation version of *Antigone* 674–6
cross-dressing in Euripides' *Bacchae* 464–6, 466–7, 470
Cuauhtémoc and Mexican tragedy 264–5
Cuba
 Bay of Pigs invasion 436, 437, 438–41, 444–5
 Castro regime and Arrufat's *Seven against Thebes* 434–51
 modernization of theater 336–42
  first performances of Greek tragedies 337–8, 337–8
  Piñera's *Electra Garrigó* 335, 336–7, 339, 361–77
 Triana's *Medea in the Mirror* 334–50, 401
Cubillán, Augusto: *Antígona factotum* 556
Cullen, Countee 595
 Medea 685, 686–90, 687, 689, 694, 695
cultural distance and transfer of productions 835

cultural space: "shared cultural space" 553
Culture Clash
 Birds production 642
 Peace production 632
Culture Show, The (BBC TV program) 830, 831
cummings, ee 814
Cunningham, Merce 247
Cureses, David 375n.8
 La frontera 417–32
curriculum *see* school curriculum and Classics in Americas; universities and colleges: classical curriculum
Currie, Robert and *Cassandra Float Can* 700–1
Curtis, Susan 11, 525–6
Cushman, Charlotte 73, 78, 116, 124
 as Ion 5, 5
 as Phaedra in Howe's *Hippolytus* 85, 87, 89, 90, 91
Cypess, Sandra Messinger 521
"Dahomey Village" at expositions 172
Dalzell, Andrew: *Graeca Majora* 56–7
dance
 capoeira chorus in Dias Gomes's *O pagador de promessas* 391–2
 classical themes and sexual dissidence 13, 234–48
 dance studies and classical performance reception 233–4
 modern dance and recreation of Greek poses and dance 204–19, 233
  Duncan's interpretations 142–3, 151–2, 205–9, 235–7
  Palmer Sikelianos's study and work 204–5, 209–16
 in Power's hip-hop *The Seven* 552
 and racial attitudes 143, 236
  "Nubian style" dances in *Cleopatra* 126
 in Rehm's productions
  Electra 748, 759
  Women of Trachis—Deianeira 757–8
 Salomé's dances on nineteenth-century stage 142
 in Sellars' *The Persians* 783
 see also ballet
D'Aponte, M. G. 484

Darwin, Charles 65, 113
Davenport, E. L. 85
Davenport, Fanny 126, 127–8
Davenport, Jean Margaret 58, 99
Davies, Carole Boyce 15n.5
Davis, Ossie: *Purlie Victorious* 485
Davis, Robert 134
de Beauvoir, Simone 336, 373
De Cecco, Sergio 375n.8
de Certeau, Michel 406
De Jong, Irene 836
de la Campa, Román 46
de la Fuente, Alejandro 342–3
de Oliveira Cézar, Inés 613
de Quincey, Thomas 71
Debussy, Claude 228, 240
Degree, Sarah 533
del Carlo, Omar 375n.8
Delacorte Theatre, Central Park, New York: Papp's *Electra* x
Delacorte, Valerie 583
Deleuze, Gilles 577, 589
Delphi: *Prometheus Bound* performance 204–5, 209–12, 213, 275, 275, 277–8
Delsarte, François 143, 206–7, 235–6
democracy
    and American identification with ancient world 112
    ancient Rome on nineteenth-century stage 136
    and Roman democracy 23, 53, 63, 65, 112, 136–7
    Iraq war and Lysistrata Project 575–6, 588–9
Democracy 2500 project 754–5
Demos, John 27
Denishawn dance company 209, 213
Derrida, Jacques 19, 20, 225
Derwent, Clarence 277
Descalzi del Castillo, Ricardo 375n.8
Desmond Conacher Players 672
Devlin, Es 822
Diaghilev, Serge 228, 239, 240, 242, 243, 244
Diamond, David 791
Dias Gomes, Alfredo de Freitas 13, 713
    O pagador de promessas (Payment as Pledged) 11, 380–99
    O santo inquérito (The Holy Inquisition) 393

Díaz de la Vega, Silvestre 254
Dickens, Charles 73
Dinneford, William: *Antigone* production 70–1, 75–6, 77, 79
Dionysus
    cult in ancient Greece 222
    Duncan and Dionysian dance 208
    in O'Neill's *The Great God Brown* 221–9
    as subject of Greek tragedy 222, 227
    see also Performance Group: *Dionysus in 69* production
Disch, Thomas 486
discrimination *see* gender equality issues; racial issues and discrimination
displaced people and Antigone in Colombia 558–63
dissident sexualities and modern dance 13, 234–48
Dixon, John 407
DNAWORKS 684
Dodds, E. R. 465
Dodson, Owen 686, 689
Doerries, Bryan 654–5, 656, 658–9, 660–1, 663–6, 791
Donnelly, Lucy 278
Donner, Johann Jakob Christian: *Antigone* translation 70, 74
Dooley, Patrick 637
Doolittle, Hilda (H.D.) 150, 152–3, 163
    Sea Garden (poems) 152
    The Sword Went Out to Sea (novel) 152
    translations of Euripides 152
Doran, Greg 812
Dorf, Samuel 237
Dorizas, Mike 175–6, *175*
double consciousness and black identity 605–6, 688
doubling
    and duality and O'Neill's *The Great God Brown* 221, 223, 226–7, 228
    and repetition in Colombian Antigones 556–71
Douglass, Frederick 17, 37, 297–8, 477
Doussis, Georgios 348
Dove, Rita
    The Darker Face of the Earth 496, 502–11, 507, 510, 543, 596, 690, 695
    racial politics and writing 497–502, 508–11

Dowling, Joe 4
Dreiser, Theodore: *An American Tragedy* (novel) 272, 281
Duarte, Anselmo 381
Dublin: Mendelssohn *Antigone* production 70–1, 72–3, 80–1
DuBois, W.E.B. 297, 497, 499, 500, 502, 509, 531, 605, 688
Dukakis, Olympia 632, 739, 740
Dumas, Alexandre, père 124
Duncan, Al 641
Duncan, Isadora 14, 150, 163, 234, *238*, 239
  and chorus 207, 208–9, 212, 235
  in Greece 205–9, 216
  interpretations of Greek poses and dances 142–3, 151–2, 205–9, 235–7
  and Palmer Sikelianos's work 210–12, 278
  production of *The Suppliant Women* 208–9
Duncan, Penelope (*née* Sikelianos) 208–9, 210, 235, 278
Duncan, Raymond 205–6, 207, 208–9, 210, 235
Dunn, Francis 461
Dunnock, Mildred 276
Duprez and Benedict's Minstrels 59, 62–3, 65
Durand, Evelyn 189
Durrheim, Kevin 407
Dussel, E. 8

Earle, Timothy 645
early white settler societies 31, 32, 33, 35
Eastman, Helen and Live Canon 815
Eby, Clare 281
Echavarría, Juan Manuel: *Réquiem: NN* (film) 559–60
Echeverría, Esteban: *La cautiva* 418, 419
Ecuador 375n.8
  Andino Moscoso's *Edipo* as satire 618–19
Eddelman, William 752
Edinburgh International Festival and Breuer's *The Gospel at Colonus* 830–5, 836, 837
Edipo alcalde (film) 613
education
  challenges of teaching black theater 498
  racial discrimination and African-American scholars 22, 37, 297–8

see also classical education; scholarship; school curriculum and Classics in Americas; universities and colleges
Egypt *see* ancient Egypt
Ehrlich, Ida 320n.18
El Din, Hamza 783
Elam, Harry J. 485, 525, 526, 537, 607n.9
Elektra Project 645
Eliot, T. S. 811
Elliott, James S. 276, 277
Ellison, Ralph 11, 291, 476, 491n.8, 540n.33, 770
Else, Gerald 530
Em Cena:Ações ("On Stage; Actions!") project in Brazil 708, 709, 710
Emerson, Ralph Waldo 23, 531
Emmanuel, Maurice 215, 234, 235
  La Danse grecque antique 207, 208, 215
empire
  ancient empires on nineteenth-century stage 133, 143–4
  depiction in toga plays 139–41
  see also ancient Rome; colonialism
epic poem genre 150, 151
Escalante, Ximena 266
Espinosa, Eugenio Hernández: *María Antonia* 350
Espinosa Domínguez, C. 368, 375n.5
essentialist notions of race 601–2
Esteban Ríos Rey, Juan 333
ethics and reception 694–5
Ethiopian Burlesques Opera Company 77
Euripides 56, 743
  Bacchae x, 222, 223, 224, 225, 226–7, 229
    Carson's translation 702–3
    Performance Group's *Dionysus in 69* 457, 463–9, 470, 733, 747, 798–806
    West Coast production 638
  Barker's touring outdoor productions 166–77, 184
  Carson on 700–1, 703
  in Cather's *The Professor's House* 154
  The Children of Heracles 58
    Sellars' production 776–7, 784–5, 787–788
  Cyclops as Rehm's *Cyclops—Nobody's Musical* 750–3, *752*
  Electra and Rehm's production 747–8, *749*

Euripides *(Cont.)*
  feminization of tragedies 151
  Edith Hamilton's writing on and translation of 275–6
  in Harlem 595–609
  H.D.'s translations 152
  Hecuba
    Harrison's adaptation 820–1, *820*, 822, 835–6, *835*, 837
    Perloff's production 739, 740–1
  Hippolytus 56, 85, 86–7, 88–9
    Carson on translation 700–1
  Ion 57
  Iphigenia in Aulis xi, 151, 767
    Houston's *The Intuition of Iphigenia* 793, *794*, 794
    and Rudall's *Iphigenia Cycle* 767, 768
    West Coast productions 636, 638
  Iphigenia in Tauris 151, 152–3
    outdoor productions 166–73, *173–5*, 174–6, *177*, 527
    and Reyes's *Ifigenia cruel* 259
    Rudall on 767–8
    and Rudall's *Iphigenia Cycle* 767, 768
  The Madness of Herakles
    and MacLeish's 1960s adaptation 457–63, 468, 469
    social theater and combat veterans 657–8
  Medea viii–ix, *viii–ix*
    Alfaro's *Bruja* 643, *644*
    and attitudes to antiquity 112, 119–25, 350
    Border Studies and Cureses' *La frontera* 417–32
    and Brazilian theater 713–14
    Buarque de Hollanda and Pontes's *Gota d'água* 333, 402–3, 708–21, *715*
    Cullen's *Medea* 685, 686–90, 694, *695*
    and female resistance to slavery 63, *64*, 65
    first performance in Cuba 338, *338*
    and gender equality 100
    in Latin American literature 333, 401–2, 403–5
    as legendary figure 256–7
    Moraga's *The Hungry Woman* 401–2, 514–15, 521–4
    in nineteenth-century Philadelphia theaters 56–61, 63, 65
    outdoor performance at Berkeley 630
    relevance to "the woman question" 59–60
    sculpture at Centennial Exhibition (1876) 116–17, *117*, 119, 124, 125
    Take Wing and Soar production in Harlem 595–602, *599–600*, 606
    Triana's *Medea in the Mirror* and Cuban theater 334–50, 401
  Orestes
    Gamel's *Orestes Terrorist* 646, *647*
    Kott's UC Berkeley 1960s production 634–5, 646
    popularity in 1960s and 1970s x
  Phoenician Women 58, 436
  Suppliant Women 58
    Rehm's production 754–7, *755*
  Trojan Women 184, 266
    anti-war message vii, x, xi, 97, 103, 167
    Classical Theater of Harlem production 595–7, 602–6
    Clements's *Age of Iron* adaptation 676–7
    Edith Hamilton's translation 276, 280
    Fleischman Theater production at Getty Villa Museum 632
    MacEwen's translation and adaptation 672, 673
    outdoor productions vii, x, 166–7, 173–4, 191, 632
    Rudall's translation 768–9
    Suzuki's Japanese production in California 633, 781–2
    University of Toronto production 191, 192, 194–200, *197*
Europe and European culture
  and *Antigone* in New York (1845) 73–5
  hegemony and influence 545–6, 595
  and colonial Americas 33–4, 37, 38
  Dove's affinity with European tradition 502, 506, 508
  Eurocentrism of Lysistrata Project 588–9
  and literary canon 474, 475, 476, 478–9, 482–4, 497
  "shared cultural space" and Afro-European literature 553
  see also colonialism
evolution *see* Darwin; social evolution theory
Ewans, Michael 289

exercises and re-enactment of *Dionysus in 69* 800–2, 804–5
Experimental Theatre, The 221
extravaganzas *see* spectacle: extravaganzas in nineteenth century

Fadel, Georgette 708, 710–11, 712, 714, *715*, 720
Farber, Yael: *MoLoRa* 690
Farmer, Lydia Hoyt 126
fate: Oedipus story and Dove's retelling 503–4
Faucit, Helen 70–1, 73, 80, 81
Faucit, John Savill: *Oedipus: A Musical Drama in Three Acts* 71–2
Favel, Floyd 675
Federal Theatre Project (FTP) Negro units 288–9, 292, 293
female characters viii–ix, *viii–ix*
 doubling in *Antigone* productions in Colombia 556–71
 as examples to women in Fuller's treatise 23–4, 25–6
 in Modernist productions 150–1
 moral unacceptability to nineteenth-century audiences 135–6
 strong roles and Phaedra in Howe's *Hippolytus* 90
 see also actresses; barbarians: barbarian women *and individual plays*
feminism
 African-American writing and classical tradition 40
 Canadian women poets' adaptations and translations 673
 Modernist reconfiguration of Greek drama 149, 157–63
 Robinson Hagan's translation of *Lysistrata* 581–2
 see also Fuller, Margaret; women's rights movement
Fernández de Córdova, Ignacio: *Hermione* 267n.12
Ferreira, Bibi 709, 711, 712, 717
Field Day (Irish writers group) 758, 823
film adaptations of *Oedipus Tyrannus* in Latin America 613
film and video recordings of performances 6–7

Fineman, Frances 321–2n.40
Fink, Robert: *Lysistrata Against the War* 583, 589
Finley, William (Bill) 464, 466, 467–9, 803
First Nations in Canada and Greek drama 674–7
Fischer-Lichte, Erika 819
Fisher, Mark 832
Fiske, Shannyn 59
Fitts, Donald Cummings 168, 176
Fitzball, Edward: *The Greek Slave* 107
Fitzgerald, F. Scott: *The Great Gatsby* (novel) 281
Fitzgerald, Garret 827–8
Fitzgerald, Penelope 477
Fitzgerald, Robert 477, 478, 480
Five Blind Boys of Alabama 485–6, 489, 832, 834
Flanagan, Hallie 288, 289
Flatmo, Eric 758
Flores raras (*Rare Flowers*) (film) 717–18
Flores, Salvador 445
Fokine, Michel 240
Foley, Helene P. 18, 194, 223, 226, 403, 635, 652, 736–7, 738, 740
folk Catholicism in Brazil 382–91
folk culture and African-American playwrights 290, 293–4
Foote, Horton 276
foreign-language productions
 Nemirovich-Danchenko's *Lysistrata* in Russian 304
 in nineteenth century 133
  Grillparzer's *Medea* in German 59
  Legouvé's *Medea* in Italian 103–4, 123
  opera and theater in German in New York 72–3, 79
 Suzuki's Japanese-American productions 633–4, 781–2
 see also Greek language and productions
Foreman, Richard 733
Forrest, Edwin 91, 98, 105, 119, 136
Forsythe, William 234, 247
Foster, Stephen C. 531
Foucault, Michel 727
Fradinger, Moira 41
Fraser, Nancy 653–4, 658

Frazer, James 143
Freeman, Morgan 477, 478, *478*, 485, 487
Freire, Paulo 717, 718
Freud, Sigmund 366
Freyre, Gilberto 412
Friedrich Wilhelm IV, king of Prussia 73–4
Friel, Brian 758, 823
Fritsch, Greg 646
Frogs society 10, 11, 17–18, 20–1, 22, 26
frontiers *see* Border Studies
Fugard, Athol 553
Fuller, Loie 207
Fuller, Margaret 73, 78, 79–80
  *Woman in the Nineteenth
    Century* 10, 22–6
Fuller, Timothy 22–3
funding theater in Brazil 718–19, 720–1
*Funny Thing Happened on the Way to the
    Forum, A* (Plautus adaptation) 304

Galemiri, Benjamín: *Edipo asesor* (*Oedipus
    Adviser*) 620–1
Galinsky, K. 471n.9
Gambaro, Griselda: *Antígona
    furiosa* 375n.8, 400–1
Gamel, Mary-Kay 496
  The Julie Thesmo Show 646
  Orestes Terrorist 646, *647*
  and West Coast productions 645–6
Garafola, Lynn 240
García Márquez, Gabriel 572n.12, 613
Gardiner, J. 193
Garibay K., Ángel María 265, 266
Garner, Margaret 63, *64*, 65
Garrettson, M. Augusta 58
Garry, Charles 93
Gasparatos, Stavros 793
El-Gasseir, Ali 646
Gates, Henry Louis, Jr. 545, 546
Gavila, Fernando 255
Gbowee, Leymah 577, 586, 589
gender divisions
  conflict
    in character of Triana's *Medea* 345
    Graham's ballets as psychodrama 245
    and Howe's *Hippolytus* 93–4
  confusion and reversal

    cross-dressing in Euripides'
      Bacchae 464–6, 466–7, 470
    dissident sexualities in dance 234, 237,
      239–42, 244, 247–8
    Heron as *Medea* 119, 121–3, 124
    Howe's *Hippolytus* 87, 91
    Ixion, or the Man at the Wheel 99
  gendered space in Moscow Art Theatre's
    Lysistrata 306
  racism and emasculation of black men 519
  sexism and homophobia in Chicano
    culture 519, 520
  and space 406–7
  and women's role in university drama in
    Canada 189–90, 196–9
gender equality issues
  audience participation in Theater of War
    project 658–9
  Legouvé's *Medea* and French society 99,
    100–1, 102, 104–5
  Modernism and moves to equality 150
  press reports on ill-treated women in
    Chicago 102–3
  references to Greek drama in Fuller's
    treatise 22–6
Genet, Jean 335
geographical space
  Border Studies and Cureses' *La
    frontera* 417–32
  Olavo's *Além do Rio* and construction of
    racial Other 408–15
German opera and theater in
  New York 72–3, 79
Getty Villa Museum, Los Angeles: outdoor
  productions 630–2, *631*, 701, 738–9
Ghosh, Amitav 7
Giacometti, Paul: *Giuditta* 141–2
Gil, Gilberto 716
Gilbert, Helen 38–9, 511n.5
Gilbert, W. S.: *Pygmalion and Galatea* 108
Gilder, Rosamond 273, 274, 279
Gilpin, Charles 286
Gilroy, Paul 8, 14, 47, 475–6, 605–6, 768
Giovanni, Nikki 685
Glaspell, Susan 12, 150, 157–63
  The Athenian Women (with
    Cook) 158–9, 163

Fugitive's Return (novel) 157
The Inheritors 157, 161–3
The Outside 160–1
The Road to the Temple (biography) 158
Trifles 159–60
The Verge 161
Glee (TV series) 770
Gliddon, George: *Types of Mankind* 113, 114, 127
Glière, Reinhold 307
globalization
   Ngũgĩ's globalectical texts 836–7
   as successor to postcolonialism 45–7
   and transfer of productions 836–7
Gluck, Christoph Willibald: Iphigénie operas 151
Goff, Barbara 8–9, 39, 476, 477, 484, 487, 492n.21, 497, 506
Goff, John W. 21, 22
Goings, Kenneth 37
Goldhill, Simon 490
Gomes, Alfredo Dias *see* Dias Gomes, Alfredo
Gonsioroski, Gisa: *Antígona: o nordeste quer falar* 402
Gonzalez, Mike 436, 443
González, Roberto 375n.8
González Mello, Flavio 264, 266
Goodrich, Wallace 93
Gordon, Robert 530–1
Gorney, Jay 323n.54
Gorostiza, Celestino 262
gospel and Breuer's *The Gospel at Colonus* 475, 476–7, 478, 480–1, 482, 484, 485–6, 488, 769
   and catharsis 486–7, 488, 490
   and Edinburgh production 831–2, 834, 836
   music and chorus 489–90
Gottfried, M. 325n.74
Gottschild, Brenda Dixon 600–1
Gouvêa, Célia 720
Grabowski, Christopher 645, 646
Graham, Martha 13, 215–16, 234, 244–5
   Errand into the Maze (dance) 245, 246, 247–8
   Hellenic Journey (dance series) 209
   Night Journey (dance) 233
Graham, Shirley 292
Granger, Maude 86

Grant, Antoy: *Goddess City* (with Abrams) 685
Granville-Barker *see* Barker, Harley Granville
Grau, Jacob 123
Graves, Gary 639–40
Graves, Lucy 748
Greco, Loretta 643
Greece
   performance of Greek tragedies in 274–5
   performance of modern dance in 204–5, 207–8
   touring companies in America ix–x, 98
   Women and War Project trilogy in 794
   see also ancient Greece; Athens; Delphi
Greek language and productions
   in Ariza's *Antígona* 568
   early productions in Americas 56, 186–8, 302
   Prometheus Bound at Delphi 277, 282–3n.8
Greek Revival architecture 55, 134
Greek Theater, Griffin Park, Los Angeles 630
Greeley, Horace 24, 26
Green, Paul 286
Greenberg, Stacey 752
Greenwich Village Theatre, New York 192
Greenwood, E. 39
Greet, Ben 178n.2
   Ben Greet Players in Toronto 192
Grene, David 765–6
Griffith, D. W. 137, 170
Griffiths, E. M. 471n.13
Griffiths, G. 33, 475, 497
Grillparzer, Franz: *Medea* 59, 60
Grotowski, Jerzy 800
Group of Seven Canadian artists 196
Grupo Generaciones: *Antígonas* 556
Guarnieri, Gianfrancesco 710, 711, 717, 720
   Eles não usam black-tie 709, 718
Guattari, Félix 577
Guerra, Ruy 709, 710
Guevara, Ernesto (Che) 336, 349, 374, 435–6, 445
Gulf War *see* Iraq War (1990-91)
Gullar, Ferreira 710, 718
Guthrie, Sir Tyrone x–xi
   as director of *Oedipus Rex* in Stratford, Ontario 3–4, 671

Guthrie Theatre, Minneapolis 4
    Atreus trilogy (1967–8) xi

Habermas, Jürgen 653
Habimah Theatre Company, Tel Aviv 3
Hagan, Drue Robinson *see* Robinson Hagan, Drue
Hairston, Eric 290
Hall, Edith 9–10, 12, 57, 58, 247, 496, 630, 635, 783–4, 831
Hall, Stuart 36
Halliwell, Stephen 530
Halm, Frederick: *Ingomar the Barbarian* 105, 107, 108
Hamilton, Alice 273, 281
Hamilton, Edith 271–83, 765
    ceremony to honour as Athenian citizen 271–2, 282
    classical education and writings 272–4
    and Eva Palmer Sikelianos 272, 274–9
    The Greek Way and Americanization of Greek drama 272, 274, 275–6, 279–80, 471n.6
    The Roman Way 274
    translations of Greek tragedies and performance 271–2, 274–9
Hamilton, Emma 233
Hammerstein, Oscar, II 308–9
    see also Rodgers and Hammerstein musicals
Hampden, William 85, 93
Hansberry, Lorraine 595
    A Raisin in the Sun 485
Happiest Girl in the World, The (musical) 302, 304, 309–12, 315, 318, 319
Harburg, E. Y. (Yip): *The Happiest Girl in the World* 302, 304, 309–12, 315, 318, 319
Hardwick, Lorna 39, 341–2, 497, 575
Harlem
    Euripides' productions in 2000s 595–609
    Federal Theatre Project Negro unit in 288
Harlem Renaissance 286, 287, 288, 290, 296
    Countee Cullen as writer of 685, 686, 687–8
Harper, E. W. 297
Harper, Frances Ellen Watkins: "The Slave Mother: A Tale of Ohio" 63
Harris, Lawren 196
Harrison, Jane Ellen 143, 152, 234, 235

Harrison, Tony: *Hecuba* in Britain and America 820–1, *820*, 822, 835–6, *835*, 837
Hart, Roxanne 748, *749*
Hartigan, Karelisa 18, 276–7
Harvard University 177n.2
    Oedipus Tyrannus (1881) 34, 56, 188
    outdoor productions 174, 178n.2
Haviland, John 55
Hawkins, Erick 244–5, 247
Hawthorne, Nathaniel 92
Hayes, Aleta 757–8, 759
H.D. *see* Doolittle, Hilda
Heaney, Seamus 760, 810, 812
    "amphibious survival" 837
    Burial at Thebes (opera) 812, 823, 829
    The Cure at Troy 821, 823–9, 834–5, 836, 837
    multiple consciousnesses in poems 829
Hearst Greek Theater, UC Berkeley 630, 632–3
Hegel, Georg Wilhelm Friedrich 13, 74, 380, 389
Helms, Jesse 779
Hemispheric Institute of Performance and Politics, New York University 6
Henríquez Ureña, Pedro 258
Hepburn, Katharine 276
Hercules and Omphale (theatrical spectacle) 62
Herman, Henry: *Claudian* (with Wills) 108
Hernández, José: *Martín Fierro* 418, 419
Herodotus 143, 342
Heron, Matilda 90
    as actress 99, 119–23, 124
    Medea translations and adaptations 56, 58, 99, 119
Herrera, Gustavo 374
Hickey, Margarita 255
Hinkel Park amphitheater, Berkeley 638
hip hop and theater
    Banks's experimental theater 685
    Power's *The Seven* 543–54
Hiriart, Hugo 266
Hoerneman, Ethan 758
Hoffman, Avery Willis 773–4, 777–81
Hoffman, Gertrude 142
Hoffman, Philip Seymour 777, 780
Holanda, Ana de 721

Holm, Hanya 246
Holmberg, Arthur 781
Holst-Warhaft, G. 217n.7
Holzer, Hans: *All's Fair* 322n.45
Homecoming: The Return of the Warrior project 652, 654–67
Homer
 The Odyssey and postcolonial responses 40, 41–4, 751
 and psychological reality of war 655, 791–2
 Walcott's affinity with 807–8, 810, 815
 West Coast productions of epic poems 638–41
homophobia in Chicano culture 519, 520
homosexuality *see* same-sex desire
Horst, Louis 244
Horton, Lester 246–7
Hossack, Margaret 159–60
Houseman, John 288, 289–90, 291
Houston, Velina Hasu: *The Intuition of Iphigenia* 793, 794: 794
Howe, Julia Ward
 The Hermaphrodite (novel) 87, 92–3
 Hippolytus 85–95, 86
 Passion Flowers (poems) 87, 91–2
 Words for the Hour (poems) 87
 The World's Own 87, 90
Howe, Samuel Gridley 87, 91
Howells, William Dean 119
Huertas, Jorge: *AntígonaS: Female Lineage* 571n.1
Hughes, Francis 825
Hughes, Langston 476–7
 Mulatto 689–90
Hull-House settlement and theater, Chicago 97, 106, 281
Hulme, Peter 31
humor
 African Americans and humorous Greek drama 286–99, 526
 choteo in Piñera's Cuban *Electra Garrigó* 362, 369–70
 Latin American adaptations of *Oedipus Tyrannus* 611, 613–21
 musical theater and Aristophanic comedy 301–26
 see also Aristophanes; burlesques

Humphrey, Doris 246
Hundley, Elliott 703
Hunter, Charlotte 189, *189*
Huntington, Dan 25
Huntington, Helen 176
Hurston, Zora Neale 286–7
 Lysistrata 289–91, 298
 Mules and Men (novel) 287, 291
 Their Eyes Were Watching God (novel) 286–7, 290
Hutton, Maurice 186, *187*, 188, 198
hybridity
 Africanist elements in Greek drama 599–601, 774
 and postcolonial theory 479–80

Ibargüengoitia, Jorge 265
Ibsen, Henrik 732, 770
identity
 classical influences on early American writers 19
 double consciousness and black identity 605–6, 688
 identity politics and black theater 498–502
 lesbian identity and Moraga's work and Chicano Movement 516, 517, 521–4
 see also Black Atlantic; national identity
Imbert, Julio 375n.8
immigration: *see also* migration
immigration and Sellars' *Children of Herakles* 784–5, 787
imperialism *see* colonialism; neo-colonialism
improvisation
 and gospel music 832
 and Rude Mechs' re-enactment of *Dionysus in 69* 802
incest and Oedipus in Latin America 611, 614, 616, 619, 620–1
Inclán, Jesus Sotelo: *Malintzin, Medea Americana* 521
independent theater movement in Chicago 97
indigenous people and cultures
 Cather's Modernism and "indigenous Muse" 155–6
 and colonial experience 32, 33, 35
 Cureses' *La frontera* and Argentina 417–32
 and Greek drama in Canada 674–7

indigenous people and cultures *(Cont.)*
    postcolonial experience and lack of
        engagement with Greek drama 30–1
    and postcolonial theory 31, 34
    primitivism and Modernism 12–13, 527
    see also African Americans; Chicano
        Movement and Moraga's *The
        Hungry Woman*
Ingram, J. S. 118–19
integration *see* structural integration
"internal colonization" 35–6, 45, 475, 495–6
internet
    and Lysistrata Project 577–8, 584, 588
    recordings of productions 6–7
Intiman Theater, Seattle 630, 634
Iraq War (1990-91) and Sellars' *Persians* 635,
        651, 753, 782–4
Iraq War (2003–11)
    and Harrison's *Hecuba* 821, 835–6
    and Lysistrata Project 575, 576, 577,
        587–8, 651
    and McLaughlin's *Persians* 635–6
    and Sellars' *Othello* 779–81
    and Wertenbaker's *Ajax in
        Afghanistan* 793, 794
Ireland
    Heaney's *The Cure at Troy* 823–9, 836
        Irish-American audiences 827–9, 834–5
    Irish nationalism and Dublin
        Antigone 80–1
Ireland, Joseph 78
Isherwood, Charles 548, 821
Ixion, or the Man at the Wheel (burlesque) 98,
        99, 107

Jack, Tracy 603
Jackson, A. Y. 196
Jackson, Mahalia 486
Jackson, Mark 636–7
    Io–Princess of Argos! 636
    Messenger #1 636
Jacobs, Harriet 10, 11
Jacob's Pillow school, Massachusetts 214
Janauschek, Francesca 58, 59, 60, 65, 121
Janin, Jules 124
Japan
    popularity of *Medea* x
    Suzuki's *Trojan Women* 633, 781–2

Jáuregui, C. A. 8
Jebb, Richard 70
Jefferson, Thomas 37
Jesus, Clementina de 708, 719
John Hinkel Park amphitheater, Berkeley 638
Johnson, Patrick 597
Johnson, Rosamund 17
Jones, Avonia 58, 121
Jones, Rhodessa: Medea Project 498
Jones, Robert Edmond 221
Jones, S. B. 418
Jones, Susan 244
Josephus 141
Judith and Holofernes on Victorian
    stage 141–2
Judson Poets' Theatre, New York: *Peace*
    production 312, 313, 314, 325n.74
justice in Greek drama
    and revenge 740–1
    and women 741–2

Kane, Sarah 713, 718
Kasokeo, Deanne: *Antigone* adaptation 674–6
Kasson, Joy 125
Kay, Hershy 323n.55
Keck, Michael 756
Keene, Laura 129n.12
Keita, M. 38
Kellard, John 192
Kelly, Mark: *Operation Lysistrata* (film) 579,
    581–2, 589
Kennedy, Adrienne: *Oedipus the King* 543
Kennedy, Robert F. 272, 279, 280
Kerr, Walter 276, 302, 310
King, R. C. 36
King and I, The (musical) 311
Kipnis, Leonid (Lola) 3
Kiralfy, Imre
    The Fall of Babylon 143–4
    Nero or the Destruction of Rome 108
Kirchner, Cristina Fernández de 728
Klor de Alva, Jorge 31
Knowles, Caroline 408
Knowles, James Sheridan *see* Sheridan
    Knowles
Kornfeld, Lawrence 316
Kott, Jan: UC Berkeley 1960s *Orestes*
    production 634–5, 646

Kotzamani, Marina 588–9
Krasner, David 526, 527, 607n.9
Kristof, L.K.D. 419–20
Kroll, Jack 482
Krutch, Joseph Wood 221, 229
Ku Klux Klan 13, 170
Kushner, Tony: *Angels in America* 499
Kutzinski, Vera 347

La Bute, Neil 12
La Rocco, Claudia 608n.22
Lacan, Jacques and mirror stage 345–6
Lackner, Peter 579
Lahr, Bert 303
Landor, Walter Savage: *Pericles and Aspasia* 23–4
language
  Afro-Brazilian dialect 392
  Anglophone focus and neglect of Latin American literature 334
  archaisms in translations 769
  Border Studies and frontiers in Cureses' *La frontera* 419–20, 421
  Breuer and American Classicism 479, 480
  and Canadian identity and nationhood 186
  changing language in Argentina 615–17
  in Dove's *The Darker Face of the Earth* 504–5
  and globalectics 837
  idiom in Heaney's *The Cure at Troy* 824–6
  and migrants' song of nostalgia in Satizábal's *Antígona* 561–2, 567–8
  multiple voices and Ariza's *Antígona* 568–70
  obscene language in Power's *The Seven* 551
  offensive language in *Peace* 314
  rhetoric in Greek culture and drama 740
  and sex in Galemiri's *Edipo asesor* 620
  slave dialect in *Peace* 315–16
  translations and capturing original 688–9
  Walcott and local language 809–10, 810–1
  see also foreign-language productions; Greek language and productions; translation
Last Days of Pompeii, The (pyrodrama) 119, 137, *138*, 139

Latin
  and colonizers and colonized in Mexico 33–4
  Edith Hamilton's early education 272–3
Latin America
  adaptation of Greek drama in 333, 400–2
  humor and *Oedipus Tyrannus* productions 613–25
  marginalization of literature 333–4
  Mexico and European colonialism 153
  and postcolonial experience and discourse 8, 31, 35
  migration and global relations 46
  and reception of Greek drama 40–1, 341–2, 350
  timing of colonialism in 32–3
  see also Argentina; Brazil; Colombia; Cuba; Mexico
Laughlin, James 737
Lauten, Flora 374
Lawler, Lillian 234
le Gendre, Dominique: *Burial at Thebes* opera 812
Leal, Rine 339, 375nn.3&5
Lears, Jackson 281
Lecuona, Ernesto: *María la O* 343
Lee, Hermione 154
Lefkowitz, Mary 774
Legouvé, Ernest
  Médée (*Medea*) 5, 56, 58–9, 60, 72
  Heron's translation 119–23
  reception in Chicago 98, 99–106, 107
  Ristori as Medea 99, 101–2, 103, 104, 121, 123–5, 256–8
Lemercier, Némopucène: *Agamemnon* 253, 255
Leminski, Paulo 719
Leontis, Artemis 14
lesbian identity: Moraga's work and Chicano Movement 516, 517, 521–4
Lescarbot, Marc: *The Theatre of Neptune in the New World* 185–6
Levy-Daniel, Héctor: *Yocasta* 612–13, 726–30
Lewin, John: *Atreus* trilogy x–xi
Lewis, Mary Edmonia: *Death of Cleopatra* (sculpture) 116, 117–19, *118*
Lezama Lima, José 372

Liberia: Women In Peace-building
    Network 586
libraries as venues 652, 662, 663
Lifar, Serge 242, 243
Lima, Radeúnda 372
liminality
    Herakles in MacLeish's adaptation 460
    Triana's *Medea* and Castro's Cuba 340,
        347–8, 350
Limon, Jose 247
Lincoln, Abraham 9
Lismer, Arthur 196, 197–8
literature in Americas
    classical influences 19
        African-American writers and classical
            tradition 37, 38–40, 502–11
        and colonial cultural superiority 33, 34
        European influence on literary canon 474,
            475, 476, 478–9, 482–4, 497
        Hamilton's Americanization of Greek
            tragedy and Dreiser's *An American
            Tragedy* 272, 281
        Modernist reconfigurations of Greek
            drama 153–7
        postcolonial search for national identity 33
        Rudall and literary theater 770
        see also poetry
Little Theatre movement
    in Canada 193, 194
    see also Chicago Little Theatre
Live Canon ensemble 815
local/locality *see* place
Locke, Alain 539
Loder, George 79
Logue, Christopher: *War Music* (poem) 810
Longfellow, Henry Wadsworth 92
Lorde, Audre 685
Lott, E. 525, 526
Luthiers, Les: production of *Epopeya de Edipo
    de Tebas* 613–14
Lysistrata Jones (musical) 303
Lysistrata Project and political
    activism 575–93, 651
    and anti-Vietnam War activism 577,
        581, 582–4
    poster 578, 588
    women's activism and media conflation
        with sex strikes 584–6, 588, 589

Mabou Mines (theater collective) 474, 733
McCarthy, Lillah 166, 167, 168–71, *169*, 176,*177*
McCaughey, James 748–9
McClendon, Rose 288
McConachie, Bruce 136
McConnell, Fannie 291
McConnell, Justine 40
McDermott, Patrick 467, 469
MacDonald, J.E.H. 196
McDonald, Marianne 633, 645
McElroen, Christopher 596
MacEwen, Gwendolyn 672–3, 674
Macfarren, George 75
Macfarren, John 75
Macgowan, Kenneth 221
McGuinness, Martin 825
machismo in Chicano culture 519, 520
Macintosh, Fiona 9–10, 28n.3, 233–4, 236, 646
Mackaye, Steele 206
McKinney, Adam 684
McLaughlin, Ellen 581
    Persians 635–6
MacLeish, Archibald: *Herakles*
    adaptation 457–63, 468, 469
McNulty, Charles 552
Macready, Charles 5
Magaldi, Sábato 720
Magaña, Sergio
    Los argonautas (*Cortés y la
        Malinche*) 333, 521
    Moctezuma II 263
Magic Theatre, San Francisco 643
magical powers *see* witchcraft
Magoon, Elias 112, 113
"Make Love Not War" slogan and Lysistrata
    Project 581, 582–4, *585*, 589
Malamud, Margaret 34, 37, 136
"malandro" figure in Brazilian theater 393, 395
Malcolm X 495–6, 519
male ballet dancer and sexual dissidence 239–
    42, 242–3, 247–8
Mallarmé, Stéphane 228, 240
Manning, Susan 13, 480
Mansilla, Lucio V.: *Una excursión a los indios
    ranqueles* 418
Marchand, S. 217n.8
Marechal, Leopoldo: *Antígona Vélez* 375n.8,
    401, 418

marginalized communities
    Greek drama and women's and minorities' perspectives in Canada 671–9
    Medea and racialized space in Olavo's *Além do Rio* 408–15
    representation in Greek drama 774
    and theater in Chicago 97
    see also gender equality issues; indigenous people and cultures; racial issues and discrimination; slavery
Mark Taper Forum/Ahmanson Theatre, Los Angeles 629–30
    Elecricidad production (2005) 642–3
    Persians production (1993) 635
maroon societies in Brazil and resistance 413–14
Marowitz, C. 635
Márquez, Gabriel García *see* García Márquez
Marshall, C. W. 678n.5
Marshall, Niní (Marina Esther Traveso): *Edipo* 615–17
Marsimian, S. 623n.31, 634n.34
Martin-Harvey, John 192
Martindale, Charles 341
Martinez-Alier, Verena 347
Martinez de la Rosa, Francisco: *Edipo* 6, 253
Martins, Leda M. 414
masculine norms and male dancers 239–42, 242–3
mashups and Power's *The Seven* 544, 546, 547–8, 549–52, 553
masks xi, 3
    Africanist elements in Greek drama 599
    O'Neill's *The Great God Brown* 221, 223–5
    Wilson's *Radio Golf* 526, 537–8
Massey, Doreen 406–7
Massey, Vincent 192, 195
Maxwell, Glyn 815
Mazzotti, J. A. 31
Meagher, Robert: *Herakles Gone Mad* 469–70
Medea and Jason (New York pantomime, 1798) 57
Medea Project 498
media
    and Lysistrata Project 578, 582
        women's activism and sex strikes 584–6, 588, 589
    see also press

Medina, Louisa 139
    The Last Days of Pompeii 119, 137, *138*, 139
Mee, Charles L. xi, 608n.22, 731–5
    Agamemnon 731
    Big Love 735
    collage approach 734–5
    Iphigenia 2.0 731, 734
    Orestes 2.0 731
    The Trojan Women 731
Meineck, Peter 547, 548, 550, 654–5, 656, 657, 659, 661
Meisner, Nadine 247
melodramas 98, 105
    ancient Rome and nineteenth-century plays 136–41
    Parisian production of *Antigone* 74–5
memory
    and British and American productions 834–5, 836
    and *Electra* 743
    Irish-American perceptions of Irish nationalism 827–8
Men Dancers (Shawn's company) 209, 213, 214
Menander and challenges of performance 303–4
Mendelssohn Bartholdy, Felix: *Antigone* productions in Europe and New York 70–82
Mendoza, Héctor 266
Mercer, Kobena 602
Meurice, Paul 74
Mexico
    contemporary engagement with Greek drama 265–6
    and European colonialism 153, 264
    Latin and colonizers and colonized 33–4
    migrants' song of nostalgia in Colombian *Antigone* 561–2, 567–8
    nineteenth-century productions in 5–6
    overview of Greek tragedy and national theater 252–68
    pre-Hispanic myth and formation of national tragedy 263–5
    see also Chicano Movement and Moraga's *The Hungry Woman*
Meyerhold, Vsevolod 305, 306–7
Michelakis, Pantelis 213

migration
    and global relations 46
    Mexican migrants' song of
        nostalgia 561–2, 567–8
    see also immigration
military see soldiers' experiences; war
Milk, Harvey 629
Miller, Arthur 12, 732, 733, 812, 814
Mills, Jonathan 830
minstrel shows see blackface theater
"Mirman Baheer" (Kabul women's literary
        society) 791
Miroto, Martinus 783
Mitchell, Charity 197
Mitchell, Roy 191–2, 194–200, 197
Mitchell, William 79, 80
Mnouchkine, Ariane 784
    Les Atrides xi
Mobile Theatre: Electra production (1969) x
Modern Actors Staging Classics
        (MASC) 678n.5
Modern Language Association 22
Modernism and Greek drama 12–13, 149–63
    and blackface theater 526–7
    feminist reconfiguration 149, 157–63
    move away from classicism 149–50
    and regeneration of Cuban theater 336–42
    use of masks 224
    see also Cuba: modernization of theater in;
        dance: modern dance and recreation
        of Greek poses and dance
Moiseiwitsch, Tanya 3
Monk, Isabell ix
Monreal, Arenas 260
Monson, Candice 794
Montemayor, Carlos 260
Montero, Reinaldo: Medea 333, 401
Montgomery Bird, Robert
    The Gladiator 98, 105, 106, 107, 108, 119, 136
    Spartacus 108
Monti, Ricardo 375n.8
Montoya, María Tereza 265
Moraga, Cherríe
    and Chicano Movement 514–24
    The Hungry Woman: A Mexican
        Medea 401–2, 514–15, 521–4
    "Queer Aztlán: The Re-Formation of the
        Chicano Tribe" (essay) 516, 517, 520

Morales, Helen 586
morality: unacceptability of Greek
        drama 135–6, 144
Moraña, M. 8
Morgan, Vivien 585–6
Morín, Francisco 334, 335, 369, 370, 372
Morris, Mark 234
    Dido and Aeneas (ballet) 247–8, 248
Morrison, Clara 193
Morrison, Toni 12, 496, 501
Moscow Art Theatre (MAT) Musical
        Studio: Lysistrata musical tour in
        US 302, 303, 304–9, 312, 318, 319
Mostly Harmless Theatre, St Louis and
        Lysistrata Project 584, 585
Mounet-Sully, Jean 81
Mozart, Wolfgang Amadeus: Sellars'
        Zaide 785, 786, 787
multiple versions of characters in Ariza's
        Antígona 563–71, 564
Munich, Adrienne 135
Muniz, Myriam 709–10, 712, 717, 718, 719
Murray, Albert
    "antagonistic cooperation" 764
    The Omni-Americans 14, 764, 769
Murray, Gilbert 143, 166, 213, 769
Muscroft, Samuel J.: The Drummer Boy of
        Shiloh 531
music
    Baibussynova's music for Sellars' Children of
        Herakles 787
    capoeira chorus in Dias Gomes's O pagador
        de promessas 391–2, 398
    chorus in Piñera's Electra Garrigó 366, 368
    discontinuity of Carmines's Peace 315
    Harburg's use of Offenbach in The Happiest
        Girl 310, 315
    hip hop and Power's The Seven 543–54
    live music and Coelho's theater-in-the-
        round format 711–12
    Palmer Sikelianos's approach 212
    Rechtman's score for The Persians 753
    response to Breuer's The Gospel at Colonus
        in Edinburgh 834
    Selleck's electronic score for Electra 748
    song of nostalgia of Mexican migrants
        in Colombian Antigone 561–2,
        567–8

synthetic theater and Nemirovich-
Danchenko's *Lysistrata* 307, 309, 318
see also Byzantine music and Greek chorus;
chorus; musical theater
musical theater
and Aristophanic comedy 301–26
characters and "discontinuity" 302, 313,
314–16
Fink's *Lysistrata Against the War*
opera 583, 589
structural integration 301, 304, 308–9,
310, 318
gospel musicals and Breuer's *The Gospel at
Colonus* 475, 476–7, 478, 480–1, 482,
484, 485–6, 488, 489–90, 769, 832, 834
humorous versions of *Oedipus Tyrannus* in
Latin America 613–17
Rehm's *Cyclops—Nobody's
Musical* 750–3, 752
zarzuela tradition in Cuba 343
Myers, Henry 310, 318

names: classical names in Caribbean 809
Nancy, Jean Luc 576
Nascimento, Abdias do 403–4
Nascimento, Milton 717
Nash, Ogden 322n.45
Nathan, George Jean 178n.9, 221
National Black Theater, Harlem 596
national identity
and American West 628
America's identification with ancient
world 34
as heirs to classical civilization 112
incompatibility with Greeks 22
Modernist reconfigurations of Greek
drama 149–63
and Roman democracy 23, 53, 63, 65,
112, 136–7
Canadian identity and classical
associations 185–6, 190, 198
Chicano Movement and Moraga's *The
Hungry Woman* 514–24
Greek tragedy and Mexican national
theater 252–68
and Heaney's *The Cure at Troy* 823,
827–9, 836
imagined communities 27

Irish nationalism and Dublin
Antigone 80–1
lack of national theater in US 769–70
Mexican identity and Chicano Movement
manifesto 517–18
politics and national theater in
Mexico 252–3, 253–5, 257–8, 260–2
and pre-Columbian myth as
tragedy 263–5
scholarship and narrative of multicultural
America 26–7
National Theatre of Greece: *Medea* production
at Berkeley 630, 633
National Veterans Art Museum,
Chicago: Theater of War event 665
Neelands, Florence 189
Neely, Brooke 412
Negro Repertory Company 289
Negro units of Federal Theatre Project 288–9,
292, 293
Nemirovich-Danchenko, Vladimir: staging of
Lysistrata musical 304–9
neo-colonialism of United States 31, 46–7, 768
and Breuer's American
Classicism 475–6, 485–6
Europe and literary canon 482–4
imperialism and adaptations of
Euripides 457, 458–62, 463, 469–70
neoclassicism
architecture 34, 55, 134
Balanchine's *Apollo* 244
Canadian productions of Greek
drama 185–8
drama and reception in Philadelphia 53–67
in Mexican theater 254, 257
sculpture and barbarian women 116–19
Nerval, Gérard de 74
Nervo, Amado 258
neurasthenia and modernity 125
New Comedy and adaptation 304
New Mexico
Lincoln County range-war (1878–81) 141
penitentiary riot (1980) 683, 693
University of New Mexico Experimental
Theatre productions 683, 685, 692
New York
Antigone production in 1845 and
context 70–82

866 INDEX

New York *(Cont.)*
    early adaptations of Greek drama in 71–2
    Edith Hamilton's translations on Broadway 276–7
    reception of German-language productions 72–3, 79
New York Age (newspaper) 18, 20–1
New York City Ballet 243, 244
Newman, D. 418, 420, 421
Ng, David 547, 552
Ngũgĩ wa Thiong'o 553, 836–7
Nietzsche, Friedrich Wilhelm 13, 143, 151, 208, 234, 235
    and O'Neill 221–2, 223, 227
Nijinsky, Vaslav 13, 228, 234, 239–42
    L'Après-midi d'un faune 240–2, *241*, 245, 247–8
Nikoloutsos, K. P. 333–4
Ninagawa, Yukio 781
NNs (unidentified corpses in Colombia) 559–60
Noble, Thomas Satterwhite: *Margaret Garner* 63, 64
normativity
    masculine norms and male dancers 239–42, 242–3
    and subterranean realities 13
North and South and Cureses' *La frontera* 421–31
Northern Ireland and Heaney's *The Cure at Troy* 823–9, 836
Notícia de jornal ("News Piece") (samba song) 716
Nott, Josiah: *Types of Mankind* 113, *114*, 127
Noverre, Jean-Georges 233
Novo, Salvador 265
nuclear science and war in *Herakles* 461–2, 463
Nuñes, Carlinda Fragale Pate 400

O pagador de promessas (film) 381, *381*
Obama, Barack 497–8, 509, 596, 777, 779
O'Brian, Maura 608n.22
O'Brien, Fitz-James: "Mother of Pearl" (short story) 122
O'Brien, Michael 699
O'Connor, Eugene 37

Odets, Clifford: *Waiting for Lefty* 296
Off-Off-Broadway theaters 312, 313–14, 318
Offenbach, Jacques 309, 310, 315
Oklahoma! (musical) 309, 310, 311
Olavo, Agostinho 13
    Além do rio (Medea) 333, 402, 403–5, 408–15
Old Globe Theatre, San Diego 630
Oliveira, Joci de: *Kseni – A Estrangeira* (opera) 403
Oliveira Cézar, Inés de 613
Oliver, E. H. 185
Olivier, Laurence 3
Olympic Theatre, New York: *Antigone* burlesque 79
"omni-Americans" 9–14, 764, 769
O'Neil, Nance 142
O'Neill, Eugene 12, 157, 159, 286, 732
    The Emperor Jones 403, 409
    and Glaspell 157, 159
    The Iceman Cometh 499
    Mourning Becomes Electra 363, 366, 368
    tragedy and *The Great God Brown* 221–9
Opera House, Chicago 101, 105
Operation Lysistrata (film) 579, 581–2, 589
opsis
    and Rudall's approach to translation 766
    and Wilson's *Radio Golf* 528–31, 533–4, 538–9
Orientación *see* Teatro de Orientación
Orrells, D. L. 37, 38, 39, 697n.13
Ortiz, Fernando 344
Ortiz, John 777, 779, 780, 783
Ortiz Bullé Goyri, A. 262
Oswald, Alice: *Memorial* (poem) 810
Other
    barbarian women and American imagination 112–13, 167
    Medea as Other 342, 403, 408, 411, 521, 601
    mixed-race exoticism of Cleopatra 125–8
    and Cullen's *Medea* 687, 689
    space and construction of racial Other 407, 408–15
outdoor performances
    audience involvement in *Electra* 738–9, 742

Euripides vii, x, 166–81, 632
outdoor theaters in California 630–2
Outside the Wire
   Theater of War project 652, 791
   as social theater 654–67
Oxford University Press: *Iphigenia in Tauris* 168

Paasi, A. 418, 420, 421
Pacheo, Patrick 833
Pain's Firework Company: *Last Days of Pompeii* 137, 138, 139
Paisley, Ian 825
Paley, Petronia 598, 602, 606
Palmares maroon society in Brazil 413–14
Palmer Sikelianos, Eva 14, 209–16, 215–16, 234, 236, 237
   building on Duncan's work 210–12
   collaboration with Shawn 212–15
   and Edith Hamilton 272, 274–9
   and gender 278–9
   political sympathies and marginalization 279
   Prometheus Bound production at Delphi 204–5, 209–12, 213, 275, 275, 277–8
Palmo, Ferdinand 76–7
Palmo's Opera House, New York 70, 71, 76–8, 76, 79, 81
pampas and Argentinian nation-building 417, 422–3, 425
Pan and O'Neill's *The Great God Brown* 227–8
Papaioannou, Dimitris: *Medea* (dance piece) 701
Papp, Joseph: *Electra* production (1969) x
Pappenheim, Mark 783
Paris: *Antigone* at Odéon (1844) 74–5, 81
Park, Robert E. 296
Parker, Theodore 25
Parkhurst, E. R. 198
Parks, Suzan-Lori 499, 528, 549
   Topdog/Underdog 9, 14
parody in Piñero's *Electra Garrigó* 369–70
Parthenon, Athens: modern dance at 205, 207–8
Parthenon, Nashville: Shawn at 134, 205, 206, 215

Patagonia and Argentinian nation-building 417
Payne, John Howard: *Brutus or the Fall of Tarquin* 61, 107
Peace (musical) 302, 312–19, *317*
   camp aesthetic 312–13, 316
peace activism *see* anti-war message of Greek drama
Peixoto, Fernando 709, 719
PEN Club and writers' rights 435
Penelope (burlesque) 98, 108
Penezzi, Alessandro 708
Pennsylvania *see* University of Pennsylvania
Pentecostal Christianity in Breuer's *The Gospel at Colonus* 478, 479, 480–1, 485, 486, 487–90
Pereira, Malin 502
Performance Group
   Dionysus in 69 production 457, 463–9, 470, 733, 747
   Rude Mechs' re-enactment (2009) 798–806, *799, 801, 805*
performance reception *see* classical performance reception
Perloff, Carey 636–7, 736–45
   Electra production 632, 736, 737–9, 742, 743
   Hecuba production 739, 740–1
Perry, Tyler: *Madea* 598
Persian empire in American theater 133, 143–4
Peru: political readings of *Antigone* 401
Peterson, Lisa 642
Philadelphia
   Acharnians production (1886) 302
   theaters and Greek drama 1800–1870 53–67, 79
   see also Centennial International Exhibition
Phillips, Ambrose: *The Distress'd Mother* 136
Pindar 342
Piñera, Virgilio
   Electra Garrigó 335, 336–7, 339, 361–77
   "Cubanization" of story 361, 362, 367–71
   unsettling of classical story 362, 363–7
Piñero, Carlos 374

place
    idiom and Heaney's *The Cure at Troy* 824–6
    issues with international transfer of productions 836–7
    locality and performance and evolution of Power's *The Seven* 544–5, 547, 548–9, 552
    regional theatrical cultures in United States 54, 769–70
    and space and social relationships 405–8
Planché, James Robinson
    The Deep, Deep Sea 62
    extravaganzas in Philadelphia 62
Plautus 304
Players' Club (University of Toronto) 190, 191, 192, 194, 196
Plum, Jay 288, 299n.7
Poe, Edgar Allan 24–5, 75, 78, 79
poetry
    Cullen as Harlem Renaissance poet 687–8
    Heaney's multiple consciousnesses in poems 829
    Heaney's use of idiom in *The Cure at Troy* 824–6
    Modernist poetry and Greek drama 149, 150, 152–3
    Walcott on Greek drama 807–16
    poets as playwrights 812–4
    West Coast productions of epic poems 638–41
    women poets and political resistance 791
    women poets as translators in Canada 672–3
Point Loma theater, San Diego 630
political readings of classical drama
    Akalaitis's production of *Trojan Women* 768
    ancient and contemporary commentary of *Lysistrata* 289–90, 291, 294–8, 304
    Antigone in Latin America 400–1, 402, 556
    story of rural women in war-torn Colombia 557–61
    Antigone in New York and Dublin 73, 80–1
    Arrufat's *Seven against Thebes* and Castro regime 434–47
    in Chicago 97, 103
    Cook's *The Athenian Women* and American politics 158–9
    Dias Gomes's *O pagador de promessas* 395–7
    gender equality and Legouvé's *Medea* 100–1, 103–4, 104–5
    Gota d'água—Breviário in Brazil 717–18
    humorous adaptations of *Oedipus Tyrannus* in Latin America 611, 613–21
    Lysistrata Project and political activism 575–93, 651
    Mee on Greek tragedy and state of America 731–3
    Oedipus Tyrannus adaptations in Latin America 611–21
    parallels in Roman dramas on American stage 136–41
    Performance Group's *Dionysus in 69* 463–9
    Perloff's production of *Hecuba* 741
    Piñera's *Electra Garrigó* as post-Revolutionary drama 362, 367–8, 372–3
    Rehm's productions 751–2, 754, 757
    Sellars' work 781–788
    Triana's *Medea* as commentary on contemporary Cuba 335–6, 340–1, 347–50, 401
    and West Coast productions 635, 645, 646, 647
    see also anti-war message of Greek drama; national identity; war
Pontes, Paulo
    Gota d'água (with Buarque de Hollanda) 333, 402–3
    Coelho's *Breviário* version in Brazil 708–21, 715
popular entertainment
    "bad taste" and "good taste" in Mexican theater 254–5
    bufo theater in Cuba 361–2
    "Centennial City" sideshows in Philadelphia 115–16
    Denishawn dances in vaudeville theaters 209, 213
    portrayal of African Americans and racial stereotypes 286–7, 292, 532–3, 536, 598, 606

see also blackface theater; burlesques; musical theater; spectacle
Posner, Michael 784–5
post-memory and Irish-Americans 828, 836
post-traumatic stress disorder (PTSD) 654, 655, 743, 795–6
postcolonialism 7–8, 9
  caution on use of term 7, 32
  critiques and dimensions of globalization 45–7
  dual position of United States 475–6, 495–6, 768
  European culture and colonial Americas 33–4, 37, 38
  European influence on literary canon 474, 475, 476, 478–9, 482–4, 497
  postcolonial theory and classical reception 8–9, 30–48, 495–7, 768
    African-American classical tradition 36–40, 495–6, 595–609
    and "American exceptionalism" argument 31, 33, 36, 495–6, 647
    and Breuer's *The Gospel at Colonus* 474–5, 475–81, 482–4, 490, 602
    Classical Theater of Harlem's *Trojan Women* 605–6
    hybridity and Breuer's *The Gospel at Colonus* 479–80
    Latin American and Caribbean classical traditions 40–4
    mediation of reception of Greek drama in Latin America 341–2, 350
    varieties of postcolonial in Americas 30–2, 33, 47
    variety of American societies and colonial histories 32–6
    racial politics and Dove in context of black writing 497–502, 508–11
Pound, Ezra 152, 811
  version of *Electra* 736, 737
Power, Will
  Flow (performance piece) 543, 549
  The Seven 543–54
power
  in 1960s adaptations of Euripides 468–9
  activist movements and internal oppression 516–17

African-American appropriation of classical tradition 38–9
ambivalence in Dove's *The Darker Face of the Earth* 505–6
of women in Levy-Daniel's *Yocasta* 612–13, 728
see also colonialism
Powers, Hiram: *The Greek Slave* (sculpture) 134
Preisser, Alfred 596, 602–3, 604, 605–6
press
  "fighting editors" during Civil War 99
  support for *Frogs* 20–1
  sympathy for ill-treated women in Chicago 102–3
  see also media
"primitive" types and racial theory 113, *114*, 115, 297
primitivism and Modernism 12–13, 527
Prins, Yopi 278
private sphere *see* separate spheres
production requirements
  Banks's productions of Cullen's *Medea* and Chavez's *Señora de la pinta* 695–6
  communal approach to *Peace* 314
  demands of Greek tragedy 193, 275, 277
  minimal for Theater of War staged readings 660
  see also costume design; set design
proscenium stage 214–15
Provincetown Players 191, 221
  and Glaspell's and Cook's plays 157, 158–9, 161
Prussia: *Antigone* production in Potsdam 73–5
psychoanalysis and Electra adaptations 366
psychological disorders and injury
  Greek drama and relevance for soldiers 655, 660, 791–2, 795
  see also post-traumatic stress disorder
psycho-sexual drama of *Bacchae/Dionysus in 69* 464–9, 470
psychotherapy in Argentinian Oedipus satire 614
public sphere *see* separate spheres
public venues and discussion
  and Heaney's *The Cure at Troy* 823, 824

public venues and discussion *(Cont.)*
    and projects with military services 651, 652
        social theater and public discourse 653–4, 655–6, 662–7
    public library venues 652, 662, 663
    and Sellars' *Children of Herakles* 784–5, 787–788
    and understanding of post-traumatic stress disorder 795–6
    see also community
pyrodrama of *Last Days of Pompeii* 137, *138*, 139

Quetzalcóatl 263, 265
Quincey, Thomas de 71
Quinn, Arthur Hobson 89

Rabillard, Sheila 676
Rabinovich, Isaak 305, *306*, 308
Rachel (Rachel Félix) 89, 93, 123, 124
racial issues and discrimination 10–11, 773–4
    and African-American classical tradition 37–8, 502, 595–7, 601
    and African-American scholars 22, 37, 297–8
    archives and inclusion of African-American experience 20, 26–7
    barbarian women and attitudes to antiquity 112–30, 167
        Medea as barbarian Other 342, 403, 408, 411, 521
        sensuality of Cleopatra 126, 127
    and Breuer's appropriation of gospel 475, 476–7, 480–1, 482, 483, 484, 485–6, 602
    and Canadian aboriginal people 675–6, 677
    Chicano Movement and Moraga's *The Hungry Woman* 514–24
    color-blind casting problems 484, 499, 529
    Cullen's *Medea* in twenty-first century context 686–7, 694
    dance and racial attitudes 143, 236
    Frogs society and Justice Goff 20–1, 22
    and globalization 46–7
    and imperialism of United States 475–6
    "internal colonization" and postcolonial in Americas 35–6, 45, 475, 495–6
    and Modernism 150
    in Olavo's *Além do rio (Medea)* 403–5, 408–15
    Philadelphia theatre prices 63
    portrayal of African Americans and racial stereotypes 286–7, 292, 532–3, 536, 598, 606
        hip-hop referencing 550–1
    in post-Revolutionary Cuba 348–9
    protocols of marriage and relationships in Cuba 346–7
    racial politics and Dove as writer 497–502, 508–11
    "scientific" theories on race 113, *114*, 115, 296, 297–8
    and Sellars' *Desdemona* and *Othello* projects 776–81
    and sociology in early twentieth century 296
    and space 407, 408–15
    in Triana's *Medea in the Mirror* 343–4, 401
    see also African Americans; blackface theater; Other; slavery
Racine, Jean
    Andromaque 136, 254
    Phèdre 85, 86–7, 88–9, 90, 93, 254
    La Thébaïde 436
Radio Televisión Nacional de Colombia (RTVC): *Edipo rey* production 612
Radrigán, Juan 333
Raff, Emma Scott *see* Scott Raff, Emma
Raftopoulou, Bella: drawings 211, *211*
Rains, Claude 175, *175*
Ralm: *Der Fechter von Ravenna (The Gladiator of Ravenna)* 108
Rampersad, Arnold 501
Rankine, Patrice 18, 39
Ratiner, Steven 500, 501
Ratto, Gianni 709, 717
Rau, E. J. 101, 103
Rausch, J. 420
Ray, Sangeeta 9, 475
Rea, Stephen 823
Read, Harriette Fanning 93
readings *see* Homecoming: The Return of the Warrior project; Lysistrata Project; Theater of War project
reception *see* classical performance reception

Rechtman, Don 753
recuento de los daños, El (film) 613
Red Tattoo Ensemble: Kasokeo's *Antigone* 675
Redd, Tina 292
Redgrave, Vanessa 820, 821, 835
re-enactments *see* Rude Mechs theater company
referencing
    Hagan Robinson's *Lysistrata* 581–2
    hip hop and Power's *The Seven* 549–51, 552, 553
    regional theatrical cultures in United States 54, 769–70
    rehearsal exercises and Rude Mechs' re-enactment 800–2
Rehm, Rush 746–62
    Cyclops—Nobody's Musical 750–3, 752
    Euripides' *Electra* 747–8, 749
    Oedipus Tyrannus 749–50, 751
    Oresteia in Australia 748–9
    The Persians 753–4
    Sophocles' *Electra* 758–60, 759, 761
    Suppliant Women 754–7, 755
    Women of Trachis—Deianeira 757–8
Reid, Dorian Fielding 273
Reid, Doris Fielding 271, 272–4, 276, 277, 278, 279
Reinagle, Alexander 53
Reinhold, Meyer 19, 26
religion
    in Cuba 343, 344–5, 370
    "low" and "high" religion in Dias Gomes's work 382–98
    and Modernism 150
    slave societies and syncretic religion in Brazil 414
    and toga plays 139–41
    see also Catholicism in Brazil; Christianity
repetition in Colombian Antigone plays 556–71
Republican Rome and nineteenth-century plays 136–7
Resto, Guillermo 247, 248
Retes, Ignacio 265
Rettig, John 143
revenge and justice in Greek drama 740–1
Reyes, Alfonso

Ifigenia cruel 41, 153, 258–61, 262
"Las tres *Electras*" 259, 260
Reyes, General Bernardo 260–1
Reynolds, Tim: *Peace* (with Carmines) 302, 312–19, 317
rhetoric in Greek culture and drama 740
Rich, Frank 482, 489
Richard, Carl J. 19, 26, 73, 112
Richards, Jeffrey 135
Ripstein, Arturo 333
Ristori, Adelaide 5, 58–9, 60, 65, 72, 141
    in Legouvé's *Medea* 121, 123–5
    in Chicago 99, 101–2, 103, 104
    reception in Mexico 256–8
Ritchard, Cyril 310, 311, 325n.76
ritual
    and Afro-Cuban religious beliefs 344–5, 370
    and Modernism and Greek drama 151–2
    "ritual theater" in Cuba 350
    and Schechner's work 798–9
    audience and Rude Mechs' re-enactment 804–6
Rizk, B. J. 625nn.51–2
Robbins, Jerome 247
Robeson, Paul 286
Robinson Hagan, Drue: *Lysistrata* translation 577, 578, 579, 581–2, 589
Robson, Frederick 72
Roca, General Julio A. 417
Rodgers and Hammerstein musicals
    The King and I 311
    Oklahoma! 309, 310, 311
Rodrigues, Nelson 375n.8, 716
Rodríguez, Asenneh 334, *334*
Rohd, Michael 653
Rome *see* ancient Rome
Romero Lozano, Bernardo 612
Ronnick, Michele V. 22, 26, 37
Roosevelt, Theodore 125
Rosa, Edvanda Bonavina de 413
Ross, Ronald 289
Rourke, Constance 11
Roy, Ava 641
Royal Shakespeare Company (RSC) 811–2, 820
Rucker, Mark 642

Rudall, Nicholas 598, 764–72
 Iphigenia Cycle 767, 768, 771
 Trojan Women 768–9
Rude Mechs theater company: re-enactment of *Dionysus in 69* 798–806, *799, 801, 805*
Rule, Janice 310
Russell, Henrietta 206
Rusticatio Mexicana (Latin poem) 34
Ryan, Mike 646

Said, Edward 47, 412
Saidy, Fred 310, 318
St Barbara and Brazilian folk Catholicism 382–7, 390–1
St Denis, Ruth 209
St Jean, Shawn 281
St Lawrence Centre production of *Trojan Women* (1978) 672, 673
St Luke, John 79
salitas in Havana 351n.3
Sallé, Marie 233
Salomé and John the Baptist on nineteenth-century stage 141, 142–3
Salter, Susan 151
Salvaneschi, Luis María: *Medea de Moquehua* 333, 401
same-sex desire
 in Anderson's *Liz Estrada* 579–80
 homophobia in Chicano culture 519, 520
 homosexual relations in prisons 694
 homosexuality and 1960s adaptations 457, 462–3, 466–70
 in Rehm's *Cyclops—Nobody's Musical* 752–3
 sexual dissidence and modern dance 237, 239–40, 242, 244, 247–8
 see also lesbian identity
sampling and hip-hop culture 544, 550, 553, 695
Samura, Michelle 412
San Francisco Olympians Festival 636
Sánchez, Luis Rafael 375n.8
Sanchez, Sonia: *Sister Son/ji* 685
Sandwell, Bernard K. 193–4
Santaliz, Pedro: *El castillo interior de Medea Camuñas* 333, 401
Sardou, Victorien: *Cleopatra* 108, 126–8

Sarmiento, Domingo Faustino: *Facundo* 417, 418
Sarney, José 718
Sarraín, Alberto 446
Sartre, Jean-Paul 336, 373–4
Saskatchewan Poundmaker reserve and Kasokeo's *Antigone* 674, 675
Satizábal, Carlos: *Antígona y actriz* 556–8, 559, 560–3, 563, 565, 567–8, 570–1
Saumet, A.: *Galba, The Gladiator* 108
Sawyer, Mark 349
Scales, Keith 637
Scarborough, William S. 22
Schajowicz, Ludwig 338, 369
Schechner, Richard 489, 765
 Dionysus in 69 production 464–9, 733, 747, 766
 on restored behavior and ritual 798–9
 and Rude Mechs' re-enactment of *Dionysus in 69* 800–2, 803–4
 see also Performance Group: *Dionysus in 69* production
Scheie, Danny 646
Schein, Seth 495
Schlesinger, Arthur 731
Schliemann, Heinrich 10
Schmidt, P. 36
Schmidt, Paul 745
scholarship 26–7
 and racial discrimination 22, 37, 297–8
 and West Coast productions of Greek drama 644–6
 see also education
school curriculum and Classics in Americas 26
 and African-American students 17, 39, 496
 Mexico 258, 265
 and national identity in Canada 186
Schueller, M. J. 33, 34, 36, 45, 46–7
Schwarz, Henry 9, 475
science
 at Centennial Exhibition (1876) 115
 in MacLeish's *Herakles* production 458–62, 463, 469
Scott, Robert 189, 193
Scott Raff, Emma 189, 193
sea
 and journeys and Greek drama 13–14
 Walcott's affinity with Homer 807–8, 815

Seaford, Richard 465
Seago, Howie 782, 783
Seattle Federal Theatre Project Negro unit 292
Seferis, Giorgos: "Mycenae" (poem) 815
Seldes, Gilbert 303, 322n.45
Sellars, Peter 773–788
  Ajax production (1986) 775, 782
  The Children of Herakles production (2003) 776–7, 784–5, 787–788
  Desdemona and *Othello* projects 776–81
  Mozart's *Zaide* production 785, 786, 787
  Persians production (1993) 635, 651, 753, 782–4, 785
Selleck, John 748
Seneca, Lucius Annaeus 341
  Medea 100, 354n.41
  Phaedra 86–7, 88–9
  Phoenician Women 436
Seneca Falls Convention (1848) 24
Senghor, Léopold Sédar 492n.27
separate spheres
  public spheres and social theater 653, 655–6, 658, 662–7
  and sexual dissidence in ballet 239–40
Serban, Andrei: *Fragments of a Greek Trilogy* 684, 781
set design
  Breuer's *The Gospel at Colonus* in Edinburgh 833
  Rabinovich's Constructivist set for *Lysistrata* 305–6, 306, 308, 318
  Rehm's *Electra* at Stanford Summer Theater 758–9
  Rehm's *Women of Trachis—Deianeira* 757–8
  timelessness of Harlem *Medea* 598
  and water in Levy-Daniel's *Yocasta* 730
setting and lack of integration in *Peace* 315–16
settlers 31, 32, 33, 35
Severini, G. 676–7
sex and sexuality
  Biblical women on nineteenth-century stage 141–2
  "Make Love Not War" slogan and Lysistrata Project 581, 582–4, 585, 589
  modern dance and sexual dissidence 13, 234–48

Moraga's lesbian identity and work 516, 517, 521–4
and Performance Group's *Dionysus in 69* 464
and Rude Mechs' re-enactment 800–2, 804
shock value of homosexual sex 466–9
in Rehm's *Cyclops—Nobody's Musical* 752–3
sensuality of *Cleopatra* 126, 127, 128
sex strikes as activism and Lysistrata Project 584–6, 588
women of modern dance 210
see also Aristophanes: *Lysistrata*; same-sex desire
Seymour, Thomas Day 273
Shakespeare, William 264, 731–2, 741, 743
  Antony and Cleopatra 126, 127
  Canadian identity and popularity in 192, 195
  and European colonialism 545–6
  Sellars' *Desdemona* and *Othello* projects 776–81
  Welles's *Voodoo Macbeth* production 293
Shange, Ntozake: *for colored girls who have considered suicide / when the rainbow is enuf* 485, 597
Shannon, Peggy *see* Women and War Project
"shared cultural space" and Afro-European literature 553
Sharpe, Jenny 33, 35, 45
Shaw, Fiona 632–3, 739
Shawn, Ted 205, 206, 209, 216, 234
  collaboration with Palmer Sikelianos 212–15
  Death of Adonis (dance) 213
  Kinetic Molpai 213
Shay, Jonathan 655, 660, 791–2
Sheil, John *see* Banim: *Damon and Pythias*
Shephard, William (Bill) 464, 466, 467–8, 800, 803
Sheppard, Si 99
Sheridan Knowles, James 139
  Caius Gracchus 119, 136
  Virginius, or the Roman Father 63, 98, 106, 107, 108, 136
Sherman, Robert 99
Shields, John C. 19, 26
Shohat, Ella 31, 33, 35

Shotgun Players, Berkeley 637–8
  The Salt Plays 638–9, 639
Showalter, Elaine 159
Sides, Shawn *see* Rude Mechs theater company
Siege of Oxydrache, The (spectacle) 61–2
Sienkiewicz, Henryk: *Quo Vadis?* 139
Sierra Leone: *Trojan Women*
  production 603–6
Sikelianos, Angelos 210, 277, 282–3n.8
Sikelianos, Eva Palmer *see* Palmer
  Sikelianos, Eva
Sikelianos, Penelope *see* Duncan, Penelope
Silva y Sarmiento, Pedro de: *Al amor de madre
  no hay afecto que le iguale* (*There's no
  love like a mother's love*) 254–5
Simic, Charlie 812
Simmons, Paulanne 608n.22
Simon, John 482, 484
Simpson, Michael 39, 476, 477, 484, 487,
  492n.21, 497, 506
Sinfield, Alan 234
Singh, A. 36, 40
Slater, Niall 527
slavery
  African Americans and classical
    reception 37
  "Baiana" women in Afro-Brazilian
    culture 412, 413
  Brazilian history and Olavo's *Além do
    Rio* 404–5, 409–10, 412–13
  Brazilian maroon societies and
    resistance 413–14
  and *candomblé* religion in Brazil 384, 405
  and *capoeira* in Brazil 391–2, 398
  classical names in Caribbean 809
  in Dove's *The Darker Face of the Earth* 502–
    11, 507, 510
  gospel musicals and heritage of 477, 480,
    484, 769, 832
  resistance and comparisons with Greek
    drama 63, 64, 65
  slave characters in *Peace* 315, 318
  slave trade and American
    postcolonialism 9
  and social hierarchies in Sophocles'
    Antigone 392

Smith, Bonnie 216
Smith, Iris 479
Smith, Susan 225–6, 526, 538
social change and attitudes to sexual
  dissidence 234–5, 244, 247, 248
social class
  and Cullen's *Medea* 688–9
  and marriage in Cuba 346–7
  racial politics and Dove as writer 501,
    502, 508–9
social evolution theory and
  women 113–15, 297
social theater 653–4
  Theater of War and Homecoming
    projects 654–67
sociology and theories on race 296
soldiers' experiences
  and catharsis 792
  psychological trauma and relevance
    of Greek drama 655, 660, 791–2,
    793, 795–6
  and social theater 651–69
    aesthetics of staged readings 660–2
    target audiences and engagement
      662–6
  Women and War Project 790–7
Solé, José 266
Solomon, Jon 136
Soloski, Alexis 608n.22
Sondheim, Stephen 309
Sontag, Susan 312–13
Sophocles 56
  Ajax vii–viii, 743
    Sellars' production 782
    and soldiers' experiences 652, 657, 659,
      661, 664–5, 666
    Wertenbaker's *Ajax in Afghanistan* 793,
      794, 795
  Antigone ix, 11, 41, 57–8, 436, 437
    Carson's *Antigonick* 674, 701–2
    Cocteau's version in Mexico 262
    Cree Nation adaptation 674–6
    and Dias Gomes's *O pagador de
      promessas* 380–99
    doubling of female characters in Latin
      America 556–71

first performance in Latin
America 337–8, *337*
and Glaspell's *The Inheritors* 157,
161–2, 163
and Heaney's *Burial at Thebes*
opera 823, 829
"high" and "low" readings 380–1
in Latin American political
contexts 400–1
New York and European productions
in 1840s 70–82
Perloff on 742, 743
slavery and social hierarchy in 392
University of Toronto production in
Greek 186–8, *187*
Electra viii–ix, x
Alfaro's *Electricidad* 642–3
Carson's translation 673–4, 700
Perloff's production 632, 736, 737–9,
742, 743
Piñera's *Electra Garrigó* 335, 336–7, 339,
361–74
psychoanalysis and adaptations 366
Rehm's production 758–60, *759, 761*
Thompson's *Elektra in Bosnia* 792,
793, 794
Edith Hamilton's writing on and translation
of 275–6
military background 655, 665, 666
Oedipus at Colonus
and Breuer's *The Gospel at Colonus* 475,
476, 477, 482, 484, 485, 486–7, 487–8,
490, 602, 834, 837
Heaney's plans for 829
Levy-Daniel's *Yocasta* 612–13, 726–30
Rudall on 769
Oedipus Rex (*Oedipus Tyrannus/Oedipus
the King*) 42, 57, 496
Alfaro's *Oedipus el rey* 496, 643
Bowery Theatre production 71–2, 134
Chavez's *Señora de la pinta* 685–6, 690–7
dance and reception of 233
Dove's *The Darker Face of the Earth* 498,
502–11, 690
first performance of Greek drama at
Harvard (1881) 34, 56, 188

Latin American productions 611–25
Rehm's production 749–50, *751*
Stratford, Ontario production (1954) 3–4,
4, 671
Philoctetes
Heaney's *The Cure at Troy* 821, 823–9,
836, 837
and soldiers' experiences 652, 657, 661
Trachiniae 56
Women of Trachis and Rehm's
Deianeira 757–8
Sorgenfrei, Carol: *Medea* production 633
Sotelo Inclán, Jesús 333
Soumet, M.: *Gladiator* 108
Sound of Music (musical and film) 531
South *see* North and South
South America *see* Latin America
South Coast Repertory, Costa Mesa 630
Southwark Theatre, Philadelphia 54
Soyinka, Wole 483, 553
space
Border Studies and Cureses' *La
frontera* 417–32
gendered space in Moscow Art Theatre's
Lysistrata 306
and place and social relationships 405–8
Olavo's *Além do Rio* and construction of
racial Other 408–15
"shared cultural space" and Afro-European
literature 553
use of space in Barbara and Lawrence
Fleischman Theater 631–2, *631*
see also geographical space; place; set design
Sparks, Anthony: *Ghetto Punch* 685
spectacle
Breuer's *The Gospel at Colonus* in
Edinburgh 831–4, 836
extravaganzas in nineteenth century
Fall of Babylon 143–4
Philadelphia theaters 61–2, 63
see also burlesques; pyrodrama of *Last
Days of Pompeii*
Greek drama and spectacle in Wilson's
Radio Golf 528–31, 533–4, 538–9
spheres *see* separate spheres
spirituals and gospel music 832

stage for Greek drama 214–15
Stam, Robert 31, 33, 35
Stanford, W. B. 828
Stanford Classics in Translation
   productions 644–5
Stanford Summer Theater (SST) Electra
   Festival 758
Stanger, Arabella 244, 247
Stanislavsky, Konstantin 304–5, 306
Stebbins, Genevieve 206
Steedman, Carolyn 19
Steen, Christine 189
Steichen, Edward: photogravure of Isadora
   Duncan 205, 208
Stein, Peter: *Oresteia* production 742–3
stereotype African-American characters 286–
   7, 292, 532–3, 536, 598, 606
   and hip-hop referencing 550–1
   see also blackface theater
Sterling, Elizabeth 190, 197, *197*, 198, 199
sthenos and MacLeish's *Herakles* 457, 458,
   463, 469
Stoesser, P.J.M. 194, 196, 197
Stoklos, Denise: *Des-Medeia* 403
Stoler, Ann 36
Stoneley, Peter 244
Stonewall Riots (1969) 471n.14
Story, William Wetmore
   Cleopatra (sculpture) 118
   Medea (sculpture) 116–17, *117*, 119, 124, 125
Stratford, Ontario: *Oedipus Rex* (1954) 3–4,
   4, 671
Strindberg, August: *Miss Julie* 505
structural integration in musicals 301, 304,
   308–9, 310, 318
   lack of integration of *Peace* 312–19
"subterranean" presence of Classics in modern
   life 9–10, 11–12, 14
Sudanese Mothers for Peace 585–6, 587, 589
suffrage for women 102, 151
Sugg, Katherine 45–6
Sumner, Charles 91
Sundstrom, Ronald R. 407
Suzuki, Tadashi: *Trojan Women*
   production 633–4, 781–2
Swedenborg, Emmanuel 92–3
Swedish Theatre, Helsinki 3

Swerdlow, Amy 583–4
syncretism
   and Breuer's *The Gospel at
      Colonus* 479, 480
   of classical and local traditions 38
   slave societies and syncretic religion in
      Brazil 413–14
synthetic theater and Nemirovich-
   Danchenko 305, 306–8, 309, 318

Tairov, Alexander 306–7, 308
Takaki, Ronald 27
Take Wing and Soar Productions: *Medea*
   in Harlem (2008) 595–602,
   599–600, 606
Talfourd, Thomas: *Ion, or The Foundling of
   Argos* 5, *5*, 55, 57–8, 72, 75
Taplin, Oliver 487
Tatum, J. 37, 39–40
Taubman, Howard 310
Taxidou, Olga 228–9
Taylor, Diana 621
Teatro de Escritorio: *Edipo rey* production 612
Teatro de Orientación and national theater in
   Mexico 261–2, 265
"teatro escritorio" (desktop theater) 612
Teatro Experimental Negro *see* Black
   Experimental Theater (TEN)
telenovela in Latin America 382, 616
Telson, Bob: *The Gospel at Colonus* (with
   Breuer) 476, 478, 480, 482, 486, 489,
   543, 602, 769
theater companies
   unsuitability of Victorian companies for
      Greek drama 134–5
   see also actresses; touring actors and
      companies
theater-in-the-round *see* Coelho, Heron
Theater of War project 652, 654–67, 791
Theaters Against War (THAW) 577
Théâtre du Soleil, Paris: Mnouchkine's *Les
   Atrides* xi
theosophical movement and Canadian
   drama 194–5
Theseus and Ariadna (melodrama) 57
Thick Description Theatre Company, San
   Francisco 543

Thomas, Evan 280
Thompson, Judith: *Elektra in Bosnia* 792, 793, 794
Thompson, Lydia and the Blondes 98–9
Tieck, Johann Ludwig 74
Tiffin, H. 33, 475, 497
timeless themes of Greek drama 743–4, 774
Tingley, D. 97
Tingley, Katharine 194
toga plays 139–41
Tompkins, J. 38–9
Toronto *see* University of Toronto
Toronto Theosophical Society 194
Total Caress exercise and *Dionysus in 69* re-enactment 800–1, 804–5
touring actors and companies 58, 98, 184–5
    Barker's outdoor productions of Euripides 166–77, 184
    in Mexico 252–3, 257
    Moscow Art Theatre's *Lysistrata* musical in US 302, 303, 304–9, 312, 318, 319
    overseas productions in California 632–4
town-hall sessions and Greek drama for veterans 652, 654, 655–6, 664–5
Tracy, Jon: *The Salt Plays* 638–9
tragedy
    Aztec history and Mexican national tragedy 263–5
    Boal's resistance to Aristotle 657
    collision of "high" and "low" faith in Dias Gomes's work 389–98
    feminine and tragedy in Brazil 716–17
    O'Neill's exploration and *The Great God Brown* 221–9
    postcolonial perspective 496, 497
    production demands 193, 275, 277
transatlantic productions 71–2, 819–38
    global transferability of performances 836–7
Transcendentalism 23, 25
transculturation 607n.17
    hip hop and Power's *The Seven* 543–4
translation 699–707
    Canadian women poets as translators 672–3
    Perloff on collaborative working 744–5

problem of capturing original 688–9
Rudall's approach to work 764–72
use of archaisms 769
transvestitism in Euripides' *Bacchae* 464–6, 466–7, 470
Trapp family singers 531
Tremont Theatre, Boston: one-day production of Howe's *Hippolytus* 85, 93
Trent University, Ontario 671–2
Triana, Jorge Alí 613
Triana, José
    The dust is left behind (Detrás queda el polvo) 448n.18
    The Major General Will Speak of Theogony 335–6
    Medea in the Mirror (Medea en el espejo) 334–6, 334, 339–50, 348, 362, 401
    The Night of the Assassins 336
Trigger, Bruce 216
Tsingos, Nikos 672
Tuan, Yu-Fu 405–6
Turner, Victor 654, 657
Twain, Mark 109n.13
Tylor, Edward 113

Ugarte, Rafael 338
Unamuno, Miguel de 341
unburied corpses in Colombia 558–60, 561
United Players of Vancouver 671–2
United States
    absence of national theater 769–70
    attitudes to barbarian women figures 112–30, 167
    CIA and Bay of Pigs invasion 436, 437, 438–41, 444–5
    and postcolonial discourse 7–8, 9, 33, 36
        dual position as colonized and colonizer 475–6, 495–6, 768
        imperialism and adaptations of Euripides 457, 458–62, 463, 469–70
        neo-colonial label 31, 46–7, 475–6
    regional theatrical cultures 54, 769–70
    Rehm's work and foreign policy 751–2, 754, 757
universities and colleges
    Aristophanes productions 302–3

universities and colleges (Cont.)
  Barker's touring outdoor
     productions 166–76
  students as extras 175–6, *175*
  Canadian productions of Greek
     drama 186–200, 671–2
  classical curriculum 56–7
  productions in Greek 56, 186–9, 302
  UPenn production of *Iphigenia in
     Tauris* 152, *173–5*, 175–6
University of New Mexico Experimental
  Theatre: Chavez's *Señora de la pinta*
  production 683, 685, 690–7, 692
University of Pennsylvania (UPenn)
  Greek-language production of *Acharnians*
     (1886) 302
  outdoor production of *Iphigenia in
     Tauris* 152, *173–5*, 175–6
University of Toronto
  Greek-language productions of
     Antigone 186–9, *187*, *189*
  Hart House Theatre 192, 194, 196, 199
  Mitchell's production of *Trojan Women* 191,
     192, 194–200, *197*
University Women's Dramatic Club
  (Toronto) 189, 190, 196
Urueta, Jesús 258
Usigli, Rodolfo 252, 262
  Corono de fuego (Crown of Fire) 263–5

Vacquerie, Auguste 74
Valero, José 5–6, 252–3, 256
Valldaura, Sala 255
Vandenhoff, Charlotte 71, 75, 77–8
Vandenhoff, George 75, 77–8, 80, 89
Vandenhoff, John 75, 77
Vanderham, Jacob 792
Vanderlyn, John 57
Vanzolini, Paulo 716
Varella, Drauzio 720
Vasconcelos, José 259, 265
Vaughan, David 325n.76
Vázquez Gallo, Antonio 338
Veloso, Caetano 716
Vendler, Helen 501
Vergueiro, Maria Alice 708, 709, 712
Vestris, Gaetano: *Medea and Jason* 57

Vianninha (Oduvaldo Vianna Filho) 712
Victoria College Women's Dramatic Club
  (Toronto) 190, 196–7
Videla, Lieutenant Jorge Rafaél 400–1
video recordings of performances 6–7
Vietnam War
  and Lysistrata Project 577
  "Make Love Not War" slogan and peace
     activism 581, 582–4, *585*, 589
  and staging of Greek drama x, 316–17,
     635, 645
  Euripides' *Trojan Women* vii, x, xi
  practitioners' anti-war sentiments 731,
     734, 747
Villaurrutia, Xavier 265
Villaverde, Cirilo: *Cecilia Valdés* (novel and
     zarzuela) 353n.36
Villela, Gabriel 709
Vinicius de Moraes, Marcus: *Orfeu da
     Conceição* 716
von Trapp family singers 531

Waits, Tom 492n.24
Walcott, Derek 484, 807–16
  as director of Heaney's *Burial at Thebes*
     opera 812, *813–4*
  The Odyssey: A Stage Version 41–4, 812,
     816n.1
  Omeros (poem) 44, 808–10, 816n.1
  Pantomime (verse drama) 811
Wald, Priscilla 27
Walker, Aida Overton 143, 527, 539n.4
Walker, Alice 500
Walker, George W. 17
Wall, C. 298n.6
Wallace, Horace Binney 91
Wallace, Lew: *Ben-Hur* (novel) 140, 141
Walnut Street Theatre, Philadelphia 54, 55, 58,
     59, 60, 62
Walsh, Paul 745
Walters, T. 39
Walton, J. Michael 645
Walton, Lester A. 17, 20–1
Wang, Nathan 793
war 13
  imperialism and adaptations of
     Euripides 461–2, 463, 469–70

and Sellars' work 781–788
Sierra Leone civil war and *Trojan Women* 603–6
soldiers' experiences and discourse on war 651–69
West Coast *Persians* productions and Iraq wars 635–6, 651, 753, 782–4
women's experiences
  Antigone and rural women in war-torn Colombia 557–61
  and social theater 658–60
  Women and War Project 790–7
  see also anti-war message of Greek drama; Iraq Wars; political readings of classical drama; Vietnam War
Ward, Theodore: *Big White Fog* 292
Warner, Deborah: *Medea* production 632–3, 739
Washington, Booker T. 296
Washington, George: theatrical commemoration 53–4, 115
Watanabe, José: *Antígona* 375n.8, 401
Watkins, Mel 287
We Players: *The Odyssey on Angel Island* 641, 641
Weber, D. J. 420
Welles, Orson: *Voodoo Macbeth* production 293
Wellman, Mac: *Antigone* 565
Wertenbaker, Timberlake 736, 737, 739, 744, 745
  Ajax in Afghanistan (*Our Ajax*) 793, 794, 795
West Coast productions of Greek drama 628–48
  epic poems as theater 638–41
  issue-driven productions 642–3
  outdoor theaters and productions 630–2
  overseas productions 632–4
  reasons for staging Greek drama 634–8
  and scholarship 644–6
West, Cornell 553
West, Debra 584
West, Ron 289, 298
Wetmore, Kevin, Jr 18, 299n.8, 485, 486, 497, 601, 607n.17
  "Black Dionysus" 39, 546, 608n.31

Wheatley, Phillis 10, 37
white settlers 31, 32, 33, 35
Whitehead, William: *The Roman Father* 53
Whitman, Walt 149, 150, 151, 214
Wignell, Thomas 53
Wilde, Oscar: *Salomé* 142
Wilder, Thornton 176
Wiles, D. 224
Wilkinson, Norman 168–9, 170, 171–2, 173
Wilkinson, Shelagh 673
Willan, Healey 198
Williams, Bert 17, 286
Williams, Eunice 27
Williams, Tennessee 732, 812–3
Williams, William 152
Williams College: Cullen's *Medea* production 685, 686–90, *687*, *689*, 695
Williamson, Margaret 736
Wills, W. G.: *Claudian* (with Herman) 108
Wilson, A. H. 55
Wilson, August 499, 770
  Fences 528–9
  The Piano Lesson 529
  Radio Golf 13, 528–40
Wilson, Dagmar 583
Wilson, Emily 364
Wilson, John 756
Wilson, Robert 492n.24, 781
Winant, Howard 36, 46
Winkler, Jack 737
Winter, William 121, 122, 128
Winterer, Caroline 26, 60, 65, 73, 81, 112
Wisnik, José 708, 717
witchcraft
  in Olavo's *Além do Rio* 410, 411
  in Triana's *Medea* 344–5
Wolfe, George C.: *The Colored Museum* 601
women
  aboriginal women in Canada and Clements's *Age of Iron* 676–7
  African-American stereotype characters 532
  and anti-war message of Lysistrata Project 576
  women's activism and media sex strikes 584–6, 588, 589

women (Cont.)
  Antigone and rural women in war-torn Colombia 557–61
  attitudes to women artists in nineteenth century 116, 117
  feminine and tragedy in Brazil 716–17
  Fuller's use of Greek drama in feminist petition 22–6
  Howe's expression of personal life in work 87, 91–2, 93–4
  Medea and relevance to "the woman question" 59–61
  modern dance and liberation of 236
  Modernism and moves to equality 150
  poets as translators in Canada 672–3
  and post-WWI university drama in Canada 189–91, 196–9
  and postcolonial theory 34
  power and Levy-Daniel's Jocasta 728
  racial protocols and marriage in Cuba 346–7
  racial theories and African Americans 296, 297–8
  resistance to slavery 63, *64*, 65
  social change and attitudes to sexual dissidence 234–5
    responses to Duncan's dancing 237
    and World War II 244
  social theater and participation of military personnel 658–60
  see also actresses; barbarians: barbarian women; female characters; feminism; gender equality issues; sex and sexuality
Women and War Project (WWP) 790–7
Women In Peace-building Network in Liberia 586

Women Strike for Peace (WSP) movement 583–4, 589
women's rights movement 94, 102–3
  influence of Fuller's treatise 24
  and Legouvé's *Medea* 100–1, 102, 103–4, 104–5
  see also feminism; gender equality issues
Woods, Tiger 533
Wooster Group 733
Words Afire festival in New Mexico 685–6, 692, 697n.11
World War I 97, 167, 184–5, 190
World War II: ballet and social change 244–5
Worrall, N. 321n.39
Wright, Garland 4
Wright, James 813
Wright, Richard 286–7, 496
Wyatt, Justin 580–1
Wyke, Maria 136

Xenophon 23

Yale Bowl and Barker's *Iphigenia* 166, 168, 171–2, 174–5
Young, Harvey 498, 596–7, 601, 602, 607nn.9&18
Young, William: *Ben Hur* (toga play) 140–1
Yurka, Blanche 276, 277

Zabaleta, Juan 255
Zanobi, Alessandra 247
zarzuela genre in Cuban theater 337, 343, 350
Zeitlin, Froma 363
Zeno, Apostolo: *Andromaque* 254
Zimmerman, Mary 279
Zolten, Jerry 832